Microsoft

Microsoft
Windows 2000 Server
Deployment Planning Guide

PUBLISHED BY
Microsoft Press
A Division of Microsoft Corporation
One Microsoft Way
Redmond, Washington 98052-6399

Library of Congress Cataloging-in-Publication Data
Microsoft Windows 2000 Server Resource Kit / Microsoft Corporation.
      p. cm.
  Includes index.
  ISBN 1-57231-805-8
  1. Microsoft Windows 2000 Server. 2. Operating systems (Computers) I. Microsoft
Corporation.
  QA76.76.O63 M5241328 2000
  005.4'4769--dc21   99-045616

Printed and bound in the United States of America.

1 2 3 4 5 6 7 8 9   WCWC   4 3 2 1 0 9

Distributed in Canada by Penguin Books Canada Limited.

A CIP catalogue record for this book is available from the British Library.

Microsoft Press books are available through booksellers and distributors worldwide. For further information about international editions, contact your local Microsoft Corporation office or contact Microsoft Press International directly at fax (425) 936-7329. Visit our Web site at mspress.microsoft.com.

Acquisitions Editor: Juliana Aldous
Project Editor: Maureen Williams Zimmerman

Part No. 097-0001946

Thank you to those who contributed to this book:

Department Managers: Paul Goode, Ken Western
Documentation Managers: Peggy Etchevers, Laura Burris, Martin DelRe
Resource Kit Program Managers: Louis Kahn, Ryan Marshall, Martin Holladay, Chris Hallum, Paul Sutton

Deployment Planning Guide

Deployment Planning Guide Program Managers: Todd Hafer, John Gehlsen
Documentation Manager: Louise Rudnicki

Technical Writing Lead: Linda Apsley
Writers: Phyllis Collier, Pat Collins, August Depner, Todd Hafer, Stuart Kwan, Joy Miller, Darryl Mondrow, Susan Stevenson, Marc Strauch, Paul Thomsen, Joel Wingert, Roland Winkler, Ellen Zehr

Editing Leads: Jennifer Hendrix, Deborah Annan, Kate O'Leary
Book Editing Lead: Susan Stevenson
Developmental Editors: Bonnie Birger, Sandra Faucett, Kristen Gill, Thelma Warren
Copy Editors: Scott Somohano, Mary Rose Sliwoski, Kate McLaughlin, Debbie Uyeshiro

Resource Kit Tools Software Developers: Dan Grube, Michael Hawkins, Zeyong Xu, Darryl Wood
Documentation Tools Software Developers: Tom Carey, Ryan Farber, Amy Buck

Production Leads: Keri Grassl, Jason Hershey, Jane Dow, Sandy Dean
Production Specialists: Lori Robinson, Dani McIntyre, Michael Faber

Indexing Leads: Jane Dow, Veronica Maier
Indexer: Diana Rain

Lead Graphic Designer: Flora Goldthwaite
Designers: Chris Blanton, Siamack Sahafi

Art Production: Blaine Dollard, Jenna Kiter, Gabriel Varela

Test Lead and Testers: Jonathan Fricke, Brian Klauber, Jeremy Sullivan

Windows 2000 Resource Kit Lab

Manager: Edward Lafferty
Administrators: Deborah Jay, Grant Mericle, Dave Meyer,
Dean Prince, Robert Thingwold, Luke Walker, Joel Wingert, Frank Zamarron
Lab Partners: Cisco Systems, Inc., Compaq, Inc., Hewlett-Packard Corporation, Intel Corporation

Technical contributors:

Paul Adare, Steven Adler, Brent Albrecht, Zubair Ansari, Michael Armijo, Sandy Arthur, David B. Harding, Bill Bain, Rudolph Balaz, Shelly Ballmer, Mark Bartlett, Peres Bayer, Pat Beacham, Mary Beihl, Sid Benavente, Peter Bergler, Andy Berschauer, Manish Bhatt, Amrik Bhogal, Shelly Bird, Frank Blando, Susan Boher, Richard Bond, Russ Bracewell, Kim Brandenburg, John Brezak, Kevin Briody, Eljin Brown, Peter Brundrett, Kevin Bushnell, David C. Winkler, Gavin Carius, Ty Carlson, Carl Carter-Schwendler, Brian Cates, Charlie Chase, Michael Cherry, Behrooz Chitsaz, Eric Churchill, Olivier Ciesielski, John Claugherty, Larry Cleeton, Arren Conner, Michael Conrad, Ray Cort, Ken Crocker, David Cross, Joseph Dadzie, Lamar Damata, Chris Darling, Joseph Davies, Tony de Freitas, Ann Demirtjis, Michael Dennis, Paul Dix, William Dixon, Sandy Donovan, Bo Downey, Simon Earnshaw, David Eitelbach, Joyce Etheridge, Neil Fairhead, Carl Fischer, Tom Fout, Daniel Fox, Michele Freed, Angie Fultz, Rod Gamache, John Gehlsen, Lee Gibson, Marsha Gladney, Bill Gloyeske, Jim Glynn, Mark Gordon, Mark Graceffa, Brad Graziadio, Douglas Groncki, Ye Gu, Shai Guday, Vic Gupta, Don Hacherl, Scott Harang, Andy Harjanto, Brent Harman, Shaun Hayes, Scott Haynie, Sid Hayutin, Bob Heath, André Heim, David Heuss, Sue Hill Grinius-Hill, Anne Hopkins, Seth Hummel, Steve Hvidsten, John Jackson, Michael Jacquet, Romano Jerez, Margaret Johnson, Nikhil Joshi, Steven Judd, Nitin Kanase, Jan Keller, MaryEllen Kennedy, Anat Kerry, Glenn Kieser, Sachin Kukreja, Scott Kuntz, Stuart Kwan, Edward Lafferty, Demetrios Lambrou, Terry Lanfear, Gerry Lang, Klaas Langhout, Robert Larson, Mark Lawrence, Wook Lee, Eric Leseberg, Darlene Lewis-Chinn, Jason Leznek, Jimin Li, Larry Lieberman, Doug Lindsey, Adele Loessberg, Chris Lowde, Hong Lu, Pankaj Lunia, Andreas Luther, Valerie Lutz, Dave MacDonald, Sharon Maffett, Will Martin, Steve Marzulla, Michael McCartney, Patrick McFarland, Andrew McGehee, Randy McKee, Ed McLees, Lyle Meier, Wayne Melvin, John Miller, Pradyumna Misra, Sharon Montgomery, Brian Moore, Tim Moore, Johann Muller, Elliott Munger, Diana Murray, Mark Myers, Joe Neal, Randy Neal, Gregory Newman, Allen Nieman, Karl Noakes, Noel Nyman, Michael Ohata, Lars Opstad, Derrick Orlando, Chris O'Rourke, Krishnan P. Iyer, Luke Packard, Sivaprasad Padisetty, Ashwin Palekar, Jeff Parham, Rashmi Patankar, Dan Perry, Kurt Phillips, Glenn Pittaway, David Potter, Bohdan Raciborski, Kartik Raghavan, Bjorn Rettig, Michael Rian, Brady Richardson, Allison Robin, Ingrid Robson, Cynda Rochester, Yordan Rouskov, Donald Rule, David S. Loudon, John Sanchez, Benjamin Savage, Angela Schmeil, Craig Schwandt, Hannes Sehestedt, Jim Selders, Mark Sestak, Kyle Shannon, Art Shelest, Ron Sherrell, Karthik Sridharan, Eric Stadter, Jonathan Stephens, Matthew Storer, Tom Stratton, Marc Strauch, Chittur Subbaraman, Ace Swerling, Bogdan Tepordei, Varadarajan Thiruvillamalai, Jeff Thomas, Manoj Thomas, Dan Thompson, Rob Trace, David Trulli, Luis Ulloa, Ron Van Zuylen, Helle Vu, Mike Ware, Peter Waxman, Tammy White, Christer Wikström, Kevin Willems, Jon Wojan, Mark Wood, Valerie Wright, Julie Xu, Zev Yanovich, Glen Zorn

A special thank you to the Joint Development Program partners who contributed to and supported this effort:

Compaq, Credit Suisse First Boston, Merrill Lynch, Nortel Networks, Siemens, Texaco

Contents

Part 3   Active Directory Infrastructure   251

Part 5   Advanced Management   623

Part 6   Windows 2000 Professional/Client Deployment   769

Introduction

Welcome to the *Microsoft® Windows® 2000 Server Resource Kit Deployment Planning Guide*.

The *Microsoft® Windows® 2000 Server Resource Kit* consists of seven volumes and a single compact disc (CD) containing tools, additional reference materials, and an online version of the books. Supplements to the *Windows 2000 Server Resource Kit* will be released as new information becomes available, and updates and information will be available on the Web on an ongoing basis.

About the Deployment Planning Guide

The *Deployment Planning Guide* provides both rollout planning guidelines and strategies for deploying the various technologies that make up Microsoft® Windows® 2000. This guide provides decision points and technical information that help you determine the sequence and processes for your deployment. The guide also provides step-by-step procedures for automating both server and client installations. You can use the other volumes in the *Windows 2000 Server Resource Kit* for more detailed information on all Windows 2000 technologies, including how they work and how to maintain them in your organization.

Goals of This Guide

This guide is designed to assist project planning teams who are tasked with deploying Microsoft® Windows® 2000 Server and Microsoft® Windows® 2000 Professional. There is information for management, network architects, system administrators, and others in your Information Technology (IT) organization who will be involved in planning your Windows 2000 deployment.

The primary goals of this guide are to help you:

- Determine the current state of your network, where you want it to be, and how you can get there by using Windows 2000.

- Determine what you need to consider at all levels of planning, from your business goals to deploying Windows 2000 in stages to lab testing.

- Create planning documents that will pave the way to a smooth rollout of your new network infrastructure.
- Get started installing Windows 2000 to take advantage of many features.

Guide Features

The structure of this guide is designed to help organizations with varying needs easily find and focus on the content that is most relevant to their deployment goals.

Guide Structure

This guide is structured so that you can approach the content in a variety of ways. You can proceed through the chapters in a linear fashion, beginning in Part 1 with a high-level overview of all deployment planning issues and processes. Then you can go on to the next phase, presented in Part 2, to learn about preparing your current network infrastructure to make the transition to Windows 2000 as smooth as possible. You can then proceed to either Active Directory™ planning, or go to Part 4, "Windows 2000 Upgrade and Installation," and learn step-by-step procedures for server installation. Or, you might go directly to Part 6, if client deployment is of initial interest to you. At the beginning of each part you will find an overview of the content.

Chapter Structure

You can gain the most from the chapters by reading them from beginning to end, and focusing on the chapter elements described as follows.

Chapter Goals

At the beginning of each chapter you will see "Chapter Goals." These goals identify the planning documents the chapter help you to create. The chapters present recommendations and guidelines for gathering the information you need to create these planning documents.

Flowcharts

The first part of each chapter also presents a task flowchart. These are the recommended primary tasks you should perform to create a plan or plans for a particular phase of your deployment, such as your plan for deploying the Active Directory directory service, or building a test lab. The content of the chapter is presented in the order of the tasks in the flowchart.

Critical Decision Points

At some stages of your deployment planning, you will make critical decisions that will have significant consequences related to costs or time or both. Decisions made at these points can affect not only your Windows 2000 deployment but also future productivity for your organization and subsequently profitability. These decision points that could affect your "bottom line" are called out in various chapters.

Planning Tasks Lists

Each chapter ends with a table listing the tasks described in the chapter. You can use this as checklist to be sure you have addressed all the important issues.

Planning Worksheets

Many of the chapters also direct you to "Sample Planning Worksheets" in this book. You can use these to help you develop your planning documents, or you can use them as starting points to create your own forms. You will need some formalized way to gather and collate information for planning purposes.

Document Conventions

The following style conventions and terminology are used throughout this guide.

Element	Meaning
bold font	Characters that you type exactly as shown, including commands and switches. User interface elements are also bold.
Italic font	Variables for which you supply a specific value. For example, *Filename.ext* could refer to any valid file name for the case in question.
Monospace font	Code samples.
%SystemRoot%	The folder in which Windows 2000 is installed.

Reader Alert	Meaning
Tip	Alerts you to supplementary information that is not essential to the completion of the task at hand.
Note	Alerts you to supplementary information.
Important	Alerts you to supplementary information that is essential to the completion of a task.
Caution	Alerts you to possible data loss, breaches of security, or other more serious problems.
Warning	Alerts you that failure to take or avoid a specific action might result in physical harm to you or to the hardware.
Critical Decision Point	Alerts you to a decision that is difficult to reverse.

Artwork Symbols

Table I.1 contains the artwork symbols used in this volume. You can use it as a resource as you study the diagrams in this guide.

Table I.1   Artwork Symbols

Symbol	Meaning	Symbol	Meaning	Symbol	Meaning
	Access token. An object that contains user information and is used for security purposes.		*Automated Library.* Tape/disk libraries that contain a collection of media and one or more drives.		*Client.* A computer that accesses shared network resources provided by another computer.
	Cluster. A group of independent computers that works together as a single system.		*Database.* Any collection of data organized for storage and access by computers.		*Document.* Any self-contained piece of work created with an application program and saved on a disk.
	Domain. In Windows 2000, a collection of computers defined by the administrator that share a common directory database.		*E-mail.* The exchange of text messages and computer files over a communications network.		*Failure.* The inability of a computer system or related device to fail gracefully over a period of time.

continued

Table I.1   Artwork Symbols *(continued)*

Symbol	Meaning	Symbol	Meaning	Symbol	Meaning
	File Folder. A directory or subdirectory.		*Firewall.* A piece of a security system used to prevent unauthorized access to a network.		*Generic Server.* A computer running administrative software.
	Hard Disk. A device used for storing data magnetically.		*Host.* The main computer in a system of computers or terminals connected by communications links.		*Host.* The main computer in a system of computers or terminals connected by communications links.
	I/O Filter. A series of definitions that indicate to a router the type of traffic allowed on each interface.		*Internet.* Refers to the worldwide collection of networks that communicate with each other.		*Laptop or Portable Computer.* A small, portable personal computer.
	Macintosh Client. A networked personal computer manufactured by Apple Computer Corporation.		*Mainframe Computer.* A high-level computer designed for the most intensive computational tasks.		*Mainframe Computer.* A high-level computer designed for the most intensive computational tasks.
	Mixed mode domain. A mode in which Windows 2000 and Windows NT domain controllers coexist in a domain.		*Modem.* A communications device that enables a computer to transmit information over a standard telephone line.		*Modem Bank.* A collection of modems connected to a single server.
	Network Adapter. An expansion card or other device for connecting a computer to a local area network.		*Organizational unit.* A structure within a domain.		*Organizational unit.* A logical container holding users, groups, computers, and other organizational units.

continued

Table I.1   Artwork Symbols *(continued)*

Symbol	Meaning	Symbol	Meaning	Symbol	Meaning
	Packets. A network transmission unit of fixed maximum size.		*Printer.* A print device that is directly connected to your network.		*Remote Access connection.* A dial-up connection between servers, domain controllers, and sites.
" . "	*Root.* The highest or uppermost level in a hierarchically organized set of information.		*Router.* An intermediary device that directs and optimizes network traffic.		*Security Key.* A security descriptor that contains the local security policy, such as specific user rights.
	Server Farm. A group of servers that provides services to the network.		*Site.* One or more well-connected TCP/IP subnets.		*Steelhead router.* A computer acting as an intermediary device on a communications network.
	Switch or Gateway. A device connecting two networks that is capable of passing or blocking packets.		*Tape or Tape Backup.* A tape cartridge format used for data backups.		*Tape Drive.* A device for reading and writing tapes.
	Terminal. A device consisting of a video adapter, a monitor, and a keyboard that does little processing on its own and is connected to a computer via a communications link.		*Tunnel.* The logical path by which the encapsulated packets travel through the transit internetwork.		*Windows NT domain.* A networked set of computers that runs Windows NT 4.0, that shares a SAM database, and that can be administered as a group.
	Windows 2000 Server. A server that provides centralized management on the network.		*Uninterruptible power supply.* A device between a power source and a computer that ensures electrical flow is not interrupted.		

Resource Kit Compact Disc

The *Windows 2000 Server Resource Kit* companion CD includes a wide variety of tools and resources to help you work more efficiently with Windows 2000.

Note The tools on the CD are designed and tested for the U.S. version of Windows 2000. Use of these programs on other versions of Windows 2000 or on versions of Microsoft® Windows NT® can cause unpredictable results.

The *Resource Kit* companion CD contains the following:

Windows 2000 Server Resource Kit Online Books An HTML Help version of the print books. Use these books to find the same detailed information about Windows 2000 as is found in the print versions. Search across all of the books to find the most pertinent information to complete the task at hand.

Windows 2000 Server Resource Kit Tools Help Over 200 software tools, tools documentation, and other resources that harness the power of Windows 2000. Use these tools to manage Active Directory™, administer security features, work with the registry, automate recurring jobs, and many other important tasks. Use Tools Help documentation to discover and learn how to use these administrative tools.

Windows 2000 Resource Kit References A set of HTML Help references:

- **Error and Event Messages Help** contains most of the error and event messages generated by Windows 2000. With each message comes a detailed explanation and a suggested user action.

- **Technical Reference to the Registry** provides detailed descriptions of Windows 2000 registry content, such as the subtrees, keys, subkeys, and entries that advanced users want to know about, including many entries that cannot be changed by using Windows 2000 tools or programming interfaces.

- **Performance Counter Reference** describes all performance objects and counters provided for use with tools in the Performance snap-in of Windows 2000. Use this reference to learn how monitoring counter values can assist you in diagnosing problems or detecting bottlenecks in your system.

- **Group Policy Reference** provides detailed descriptions of the Group Policy settings in Windows 2000. These descriptions explain the effect of enabling, disabling, or not configuring each policy, as well as explanations of how related policies interact.

Resource Kit Support Policy

The software supplied in the *Windows 2000 Server Resource Kit* is not supported. Microsoft does not guarantee the performance of the *Windows 2000 Server Resource Kit* tools, response times for answering questions, or bug fixes to the tools. However, we do provide a way for customers who purchase the *Windows 2000 Server Resource Kit* to report bugs and receive possible fixes for their issues. You can do this by sending e-mail to rkinput@microsoft.com. This e-mail address is only for *Windows 2000 Server Resource Kit* related issues. For issues relating to the Windows 2000 operating system, please refer to the support information included with your product.

PART 1

Planning Overview

Determining the best course of action for deploying Microsoft® Windows® 2000 in your organization sets the stage for success. Part 1 provides planning information that will help you determine the Windows 2000 features appropriate for your organization, create a deployment plan, prepare your test lab, and conduct your pilot project.

In This Part

C H A P T E R   1

Introducing Windows 2000 Deployment Planning

The *Microsoft® Windows® 2000 Server Resource Kit Deployment Planning Guide* is a tool for you to use as you design, plan, and develop your deployment of Microsoft® Windows® 2000. As you read through this book, you will gain insight about how to plan your deployment on both a project management and a feature level. This book addresses planning information that will help you get started, such as how to run a test lab and a pilot project, and provides important technical discussions that will assist you in deploying Windows 2000 technologies.

You begin the planning process in this chapter. It includes an introduction to this book, followed by a brief overview of Windows 2000 and its features. Next, you are introduced to case studies that illustrate how four companies started their deployment planning process. Finally, the chapter provides a feature overview from an IT business perspective. You can use this overview to begin your deployment planning process.

In This Chapter

Chapter Goals

This chapter will help you develop the following planning documents:

- Windows 2000 product list for your organization
- A plan for mapping Windows 2000 features to your business needs

Related Information in the Resource Kit

- For more information about how to begin your deployment planning process, see "Creating a Deployment Roadmap" in this book.
- For more information about deployment planning, see "Planning for Deployment" in this book.

Starting Your Plan

Deploying a new operating system such as Windows 2000 in an enterprise environment is a task that requires executive approval and funding as well as a substantial planning effort. As you begin your planning effort, you need to understand the Windows 2000 product family. Then, you need to gain an understanding of the features and how you can take advantage of them to increase productivity and reduce total cost of ownership (TCO) in your organization. The following two sections provide an overview of the planning process described in this chapter and an introduction to using this book.

Effectively Using This Book

This book will help you design, plan, and implement your Microsoft® Windows® 2000 Professional and Microsoft® Windows® 2000 Server deployment. It provides guidelines and caveats for solving critical business needs by deploying the main features of Windows 2000. Also included are step-by-step instructions for automating Windows 2000 Server and Windows 2000 Professional installation by using utilities such as unattended Setup tools, scripting, and Microsoft® Systems Management Server. The information is presented in a logical flow that you can use as you begin your deployment.

To accomplish these goals, this book contains three different types of chapters:

- Planning chapters that provide you with information that will help you be successful as you begin planning your rollout, such as testing and planning chapters.

- Technical design chapters that provide you with information that will assist you in implementing specific features of Windows 2000, such as Active Directory™ directory service, and in designing your Windows 2000 network to meet the needs of your organization.

- Automated installation chapters that provide step-by-step instructions for installing Windows 2000 Server and Windows 2000 Professional by using tools such as Systems Management Server.

Table 1.1 lists the six parts of this book and the chapters that fall under each part.

Table 1.1   Deployment Planning Guide Chapters

No.	Part/Chapter Title	Type
	Part 1: Planning Overview Provides information that will assist you in the planning aspects of your deployment and includes information on testing and piloting.	
1	Introducing Windows 2000 Deployment Planning	Planning
2	Creating a Deployment Roadmap	Planning
3	Planning for Deployment	Planning
4	Building a Windows 2000 Test Lab	Planning
5	Conducting Your Windows 2000 Pilot	Planning
	Part 2: Network Infrastructure Prerequisites Provides information that will assist you in assessing your current network and in planning your network upgrade.	
6	Preparing Your Network Infrastructure for Windows 2000	Technical design
7	Determining Network Connectivity Strategies	Technical design
8	Using Systems Management Server to Analyze Your Network Infrastructure	Technical design
	Part 3: Active Directory Infrastructure Provides information that will assist you in planning your deployment of specific technical features.	
9	Designing the Active Directory Structure	Technical design
10	Determining Domain Migration Strategies	Technical design
11	Planning Distributed Security	Technical design
12	Planning Your Public Key Infrastructure	Technical design
	Part 4: Windows 2000 Upgrade and Installation Provides information on upgrading and installing servers, member servers, and terminal services.	
13	Automating Server Installation and Upgrade	Automated installation
14	Using Systems Management Server to Deploy Windows 2000	Automated installation
15	Upgrading and Installing Member Servers	Automated installation
16	Deploying Terminal Services	Technical design

(continued)

Table 1.1   Deployment Planning Guide Chapters *(continued)*

No.	Part/Chapter Title	Type
	Part 5: Advanced Management Provides information that will help you plan for using more advanced features.	
17	Determining Windows 2000 Network Security Strategies	Technical design
18	Ensuring the Availability of Applications and Services	Technical design
19	Determining Windows 2000 Storage Management Strategies	Technical design
20	Synchronizing Active Directory with Exchange Server Directory Service	Technical design
	Part 6: Windows Professional/Client Deployment Provides information that will help you plan for and deploy Windows 2000 Professional clients.	
21	Testing Applications for Compatibility with Windows 2000	Technical design
22	Defining a Client Connectivity Strategy	Technical design
23	Defining Client Administration and Configuration Standards	Technical design
24	Applying Change and Configuration Management	Technical design
25	Automating Client Installation and Upgrade	Automated installation

How to Begin Planning

Planning for an operating system installation or upgrade requires many steps and in-depth planning. This chapter provides information that will help you get your planning process started. Figure 1.1 illustrates the planning steps presented in this chapter.

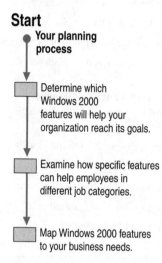

Figure 1.1   How to Begin Planning

Overview of the Windows 2000 Product Family

Staying competitive in the new digital economy requires an advanced computer-based, client/server infrastructure that lowers costs and enables your organization to adapt quickly to change. The Microsoft Windows 2000 platform—the combination of Windows 2000 Professional and Windows 2000 Server—can deliver the following benefits to organizations of all sizes:

- Lower total cost of ownership (TCO).
- A reliable platform for computing 24-hours-a-day, seven-days-a-week.
- A digital infrastructure that can accommodate rapid change.

The entire product family is designed to provide networking, application, communications, and Web services with increased manageability, reliability, availability, interoperability, scalability, and security. To accommodate the computing needs of organizations of all sizes, there are several Windows 2000 products available. The following sections introduce you to specific products that make up the Windows 2000 family.

Windows 2000 Professional

Windows 2000 Professional allows users to be more productive in a variety of work and user situations (such as mobile and remote users), to ensure the highest level of security for user data, and to deliver the performance necessary for a new generation of personal productivity applications. Windows 2000 Professional helps you to lower the total cost of ownership through:

Improved Client Administration Capabilities Windows 2000 allows your administrators to have total control over your client data and application and system settings, thereby helping you to reduce the number of help desk calls. It also ensures that users do not accidentally damage their systems and allows your users to have 24-hour access to the tools they need to get their jobs done, even when they are working from someone else's computer.

Broad Management Tool Support Designed to improve information technology manageability, Windows 2000 Professional includes "client agents" that enable leading management solutions such as Systems Management Server to work effectively.

Ease of Use The user interface has been designed for easier access to information through the use of personalized menus and Most Recently Used lists. (The operating system determines which tasks you use most often and then displays those tasks in the visible portion of each menu.)

Higher Levels of Stability Windows 2000 Professional is designed to be the most reliable client and mobile operating system available. Clients stay running longer, helping you to ensure higher levels of productivity.

Greater Device Support Windows 2000 Professional supports over 7,000 devices, including expanded support for many devices not previously supported by Microsoft® Windows NT® Workstation version 4.0, such as many older printers, scanners, and digital cameras. This represents a 60 percent increase over the number of devices supported in Windows NT 4.0. Windows 2000 Professional also supports Microsoft® DirectX® version 7.0, a group of low-level application programming interfaces (APIs) that give access to high-performance media acceleration on Windows-based computers.

Note For more information about supported devices, see the Microsoft Windows Hardware Compatibility List (HCL) link on the Web Resources page at http://windows.microsoft.com/windows2000/reskit/webresources.

Easier to Configure New wizards take the guesswork out of configuring and setting up Windows 2000 Professional.

More Language Options MultiLanguage technology provides unparalleled multilingual options for end users and administrators.

For more information about Windows 2000 Professional, see the chapters in Part 6 of this book.

Windows 2000 Server Family

The Windows 2000 Server family has two members: Standard and Advanced. The Standard edition offers core functionality for essential services (including file, print, communications, infrastructure, and Web servers) appropriate to small- and medium-sized organizations with numerous workgroups and branch offices. The Advanced edition is designed to meet mission-critical needs, such as large data warehouses, e-commerce, or Web hosting services for medium-sized and large-sized organizations and Internet service providers (ISPs).

Windows 2000 Server Standard Edition

At the core of Windows 2000 Server is a complete set of infrastructure services based on Active Directory directory service. Active Directory simplifies management, strengthens security, and extends interoperability. It provides a centralized method for managing users, groups, security services, and network resources. In addition, Active Directory has a number of standard interfaces allowing interoperability with a variety of applications and devices.

Windows 2000 Server provides a comprehensive set of Internet services that allows organizations to take advantage of the latest Web technologies. This integrated, flexible Web platform has a full range of services you can use to deploy intranets and Web-based business solutions. These services include site hosting, advanced Web applications, and streaming media.

Windows 2000 Server extends the application services established by Microsoft® Windows NT® Server version 4.0. By integrating application services such as Component Services, transaction and message queuing, and Extensible Markup Language (XML) support, Windows 2000 Server is an ideal platform for both independent software vendor solutions and custom line-of-business applications.

Over the last few years, many companies have benefited from the rapid progress manufacturers have made in the speed of microprocessors. To enhance system performance with faster processors, Windows 2000 Server also supports uniprocessor systems and four-way symmetric multiprocessing *(SMP)* systems with up to 4 gigabytes (GB) of physical memory.

A business server running the Windows 2000 operating system has the multipurpose capabilities required for both clients and servers in both a traditional client/server model and workgroups. Your organization might also require additional departmental deployments of file and print servers, application servers, Web servers, and communication servers. Some key features of the operating system that will assist you in installing and configuring servers that perform these various roles include:

- Active Directory
- IntelliMirror and Group Policy
- Kerberos authentication and Public Key Infrastructure (PKI) security
- Terminal Services
- Component Services
- Enhanced Internet and Web services
- Up to four-way SMP support

Windows 2000 Advanced Server

Windows 2000 Advanced Server is the new version of Windows NT Server 4.0, Enterprise Edition. It provides a comprehensive clustering infrastructure for high availability and scalability of applications and services, including main memory support of up to 8 gigabytes (GB) on Page Address Extension (PAE) systems. Designed for demanding enterprise applications, Advanced Server supports new systems by using up to eight-way symmetric multiprocessing (SMP). SMP enables any one of the multiple processors in a computer to run any operating system or application thread simultaneously with other processors in the system. Windows 2000 Advanced Server is well suited to database-intensive work, and provides high-availability server clustering and load balancing for high system and application availability.

Windows 2000 Advanced Server includes the full feature set of Windows 2000 Server and adds the high availability and scalability required for enterprise and larger departmental solutions. Key features of Advanced Server include:

- All Windows 2000 Server features
- Network (TCP/IP) Load Balancing
- Enhanced two-node server clusters based on the Microsoft Windows Cluster Server (MSCS) in the Windows NT Server 4.0 Enterprise Edition
- Up to 8 GB main memory on PAE systems
- Up to eight-way SMP

Terminal Services

The Terminal Services feature of Microsoft Windows 2000 Server delivers Windows 2000 Professional and the latest Windows-based applications to computers that normally cannot run Windows. Terminal Services also offers a remote administration mode that allows administrators to access, manage, and troubleshoot clients. Through terminal emulation, Terminal Services allows the same set of applications to run on diverse types of computer hardware. For organizations wanting to increase flexibility in application deployment and control computer management costs, the Terminal Services architecture offers an important enhancement to the traditional two- or three-tier, client/server architecture based on servers and full-scale personal computers. For more information about Terminal Services, see "Deploying Terminal Services" in this book.

Using Windows 2000 to Improve the Way You Work

As your organization plans to migrate to Windows 2000, one of the first questions many people will ask is, "What's in it for me?" The advantages of migrating to Windows 2000 will be enjoyed by your administrators as well as your users. Your administrators will enjoy being able to provide greater mobile support, easier client installation, and less administrative overhead. The workers in your organization will be able to take advantage of an easier user interface and increased reliability and availability. Additionally, individual users will be able to see specific enhancements based on the type of work they do.

Looking at how the Windows 2000 platform might affect three different job categories— Information Technology (IT) administrator, department manager, and sales representative—can help you answer questions about how Windows 2000 can improve the work accomplished in your organization. The following sections do not provide a comprehensive list of the features that each of these job categories will use. They provide a sample that you can use to begin planning.

IT Administrator

As an IT administrator, Windows 2000 provides you with centralized control over all of the clients in an organization. An administrator will also be able to use applications written specifically to take advantage of the new technologies of Windows 2000. These applications will be easier to deploy, more manageable, and more reliable. As a result, you will be able to provide better service. The following Windows 2000 features are examples of new Windows 2000 Server technologies that can allow you to work more effectively.

IntelliMirror and Active Directory   These features let you use Group Policy to configure clients to meet the varying needs of particular user groups. For example, you can make sure that everyone in the finance department has the spreadsheet, word processing, and presentation applications they need. Likewise, you can assign sales-tracking software to the sales team. And, you can set policies that let users see their preferred arrangements from any computer on the network. To reduce Help desk costs, you can secure users' computers so they cannot change their computer configurations.

Remote Install Technologies   Remote Install (RI) technologies allow you use Group Policy to perform an automated clean installation of the Windows 2000 Professional operating system onto a client. You can use this technology (the RIPrep tool is available on the Windows 2000 Server operating system CD) to install the Windows 2000 Professional operating system from one central location. You can combine RI with Microsoft® IntelliMirror technologies to image a complete system. If you also use roaming profiles, this combination of features can assist greatly in the disaster recovery process.

Windows 2000 Logo Application Certification Program   The Windows 2000 Logo program is a Microsoft specification that helps developers build applications that take advantage of Active Directory, Windows Installer software, and other features of Windows 2000 that make applications easier to manage on a company-wide basis. Using the information in this specification, you can develop applications that use Windows 2000 features to reduce your TCO and that run well with other applications in use in your organization. For more information about the Windows 2000 Logo Application specification, see the MSDN Online link on the Web Resources page at http://windows.microsoft.com/Windows 2000/reskit/webresources.

Terminal Services and Mobile Devices   These features let you manage services from anywhere on the network. For example, if you receive a call about a network bandwidth issue while you are visiting a branch office, you can use a wireless handheld computer to access the network's centralized management tools, diagnose the issue, and work to resolve it.

Department Manager

As a department manager, you are responsible for coordinating a number of projects and employees. As a result of improved information access, you can now gather and analyze information more easily. The following are examples of how some specific Windows 2000 features will make your work as a manager easier.

Terminal Services or Change and Configuration Management Technologies

By using Change and Configuration Management technologies, your administrator can make sure that the software, data, and desktop settings you need are available, regardless of where you are when you log on to the network. If you are visiting the accounting group and you need to look up a report, you can log on to a thin client device by using Terminal Services and work as if you were still in your office.

NetMeeting, Quality of Service, and USB Plug and Play Support
Microsoft® NetMeeting® lets multiple users on a network see each other over a video link and work together on documents in real time. To ensure that the video connection does not degrade, the Quality of Service (QoS) support integrated with Active Directory lets the administrator assign more bandwidth to the users and applications that need it. And, universal serial bus (USB) support lets users quickly install devices that plug in and work right away, such as video cameras. To set up a video conference, for example, all you have to do is plug in a camera and click on the appropriate names in your address book.

Sales Representative

By using the Change and Configuration Management technologies, your administrator can ensure that you always have the software you need, thereby granting you easy access to your specific tools and information. Additional capabilities are designed for users that spend most of their time away from their primary offices. There are several Windows 2000 features that will make your work time more efficient—whether you are on the road or conducting meetings from your office.

Synchronization Manager
Synchronization Manager lets you work with information offline, as if you were working on the network. For example, you can take your customer files with you, work with them in the field, and resynchronize them with the network-based versions the next time you log on. Likewise, you can download Web pages from your company's intranet site and work on them offline. The next time you log on, you can update the intranet information on your laptop and the customer records stored on the network.

Roaming User Profiles
Roaming user profiles allows you to use your customized desktop settings and access all of your documents from any location on the network. As you travel, you can log on to the corporate network from any location and still have access to all of your data. You no longer need to worry about transferring data onto floppy disks or through e-mail to have access to your critical information.

Examples of How Business Needs are Satisfied by Windows 2000

Organizations approach deployment from many different perspectives, depending on how they plan to implement a new operating system into their environment. Most organizations deploy an operating system incrementally (or, in phases) to prevent user downtime and to guarantee success at critical steps along the way.

The following sections provide some case studies and examples of how organizations have approached deployment from a product feature perspective. These examples provide information about how some enterprise-scale organizations resolve pressing business issues. Use the information provided in this section for ideas that will help you promote and more effectively use Windows 2000 in your organization.

Case Study 1: North American Industrial Manufacturer

Manufacturing is the primary business of this organization. Product assembly takes place at numerous locations in North America; however, their business offices are located all over the world, creating a highly distributed global computing environment. There are several primary product divisions with multiple product lines. The numerous internal teams distributed worldwide require diverse levels of access to customer and internal documents. The users in each division require a high level of client-based customization. Additionally, there are numerous vendors and subcontractors, some of whom need network access within the firewall, and others whose needs require only external access. Network administrators need to provide varying levels of security based on the needs of each unique internal and external team.

Existing IT Environment

Currently, this organization supports a mixed Windows NT Server 4.0 Service Pack (SP) 4 and UNIX network operating system environment and a mixed Microsoft® Windows® 95 (85 percent), Windows NT Workstation 4.0 (10 percent), and UNIX (5 percent) client environment. Information technology is centrally managed with control of applications and resources distributed to lower level IT managers. The organization has high bandwidth needs and requires strong client management. Microsoft® Exchange Server is currently a global mission-critical application for communications and scheduling.

Goals for Deploying Windows 2000

This corporation wants to standardize on one network operating system and one client system to reduce support costs. It will also be integrating the Exchange Server directory service with Active Directory to create a common directory and for increased team collaboration. In addition, they plan to expand into a multimedia network for collaboration and information sharing.

Table 1.2 summarizes the IT goals of this organization and includes the reasons why this organization chose Windows 2000 to meet their goals.

Table 1.2   IT Goals for a North American Industrial Manufacturer

Goals	What Windows 2000 Offers
Support and install one standard client operating system for rapid installation and configuration as well as inexpensive deployment.	Provides client management features, such as IntelliMirror and automated client install and upgrade technologies, such as Remote Install Services and Systems Management Server.
Install a network operating system that is secure, but flexible and robust enough to run on a wide variety of hardware.	Provides the security features of Kerberos authentication and Internet Protocol security (IPSec). Provides more hardware choices listed in the HCL. Provides Plug and Play functionality.
Reduce deployment and management costs by deploying only one server image. Support only one common server platform and consolidate smaller servers into larger ones.	Advanced Server functionality provides for the computing needs of the entire organization because it provides clustering, load balancing, and additional processor support capabilities.
Maintain high server uptime for Exchange Server because it is mission-critical to the organization.	Windows 2000 provides a stable operating system platform for Exchange Server.
Create a centralized administrative model that provides the ability for distributed control at lower level domains.	Active Directory provides the ability for higher level administrators to delegate control for specific elements within Active Directory to individuals or groups. This eliminates the need for multiple administrators to have authority over an entire domain. Active Directory allows the company to model its networking environment after its business model.
Provide interoperability with current UNIX servers and use a common security protocol.	Domain Name System (DNS) dynamic update protocol provides interoperability. Kerberos security works on both platforms.

(continued)

Table 1.2   IT Goals for a North American Industrial Manufacturer *(continued)*

Goals	What Windows 2000 Offers
Support other cross-platform security across their enterprise.	Distributed security, including IPSec, Kerberos authentication, and PKI.
Use a network operating system and domain structure that reflect business needs.	Windows 2000 is flexible enough for you to shape the domain and security boundaries to reflect the structure of your business rather than requiring you to organize your business around the limitations of the server operating system.
Create one large corporate computer directory.	Allows you to merge Active Directory data with Exchange Server data for a common directory.
Expand into a multimedia network for collaboration and information sharing.	NetMeeting allows groups in diverse parts of the globe to converse. QoS allows you to allocate bandwidth as appropriate during multimedia network events. Plug and Play makes it easy to connect cameras for multimedia events.

Case Study 2: Large Multinational Manufacturer

With headquarters in Europe, this multinational organization maintains offices in more than 190 countries. Growth takes place through expanded markets, increased product sales, and mergers and acquisitions. The company manufactures a wide range of products, including consumer and industrial electronics, computers, and instrumentation. Each separate manufacturing entity is run as an independent company under the umbrella of the parent corporation. There are over 130 separate operating companies, each with its own reporting structure and chief financial, information, and executive officers. This affects inter- and intra-organizational dynamics because each IT organization has different goals, budgets, objectives, and constraints. The parent company needs to provide support and guidelines for intercompany IT cooperation.

Existing IT Environment

There is no centralized IT operations group and few common IT standards across all operating companies, either for network or client operating systems, or for client productivity applications. The centralized IT office is responsible for cross-company directions and standards.

Goals for Deploying Windows 2000

In 1998, this company's IT office sponsored a project to design a global Windows 2000 Active Directory architecture—a unifying concept across each of the decentralized operating companies. Representative groups from several of the operating companies focused on Windows 2000 Server and Windows 2000 Professional architecture and deployment, and then integrated when necessary and appropriate. The parent company was tasked with developing a common framework that would be adopted as needed by each separate operating company.

Table 1.3 summarizes the IT goals of this organization, and includes the reasons why this organization chose Windows 2000 to meet their goals.

Table 1.3   IT Goals for a Large Multinational Manufacturer

Goals	What Windows 2000 Offers
Establish a common IT reference that all operating company IT groups can use to establish a global multioperator model.	The forest architecture of Active Directory provides a single logon point and Global Catalog capabilities.
Establish one common directory service that can be used by all operating companies.	Active Directory is flexible, extensible, and customizable to accommodate the IT and business needs of separate operating companies.
Establish one common model for migrating from the Windows NT environment to Windows 2000.	Availability of Remote Install technologies and other remote or automatic installation tools such as Systems Management Server.
Conduct a pilot rollout that can be used as an implementation standard for all IT groups in other operating companies.	The capability to clone a security principal from another Windows NT domain, and the security identifier (SID) history features that enable the safe move to a pilot environment with rollback options.
Establish one common client operating system that can be used for all operating companies.	A common security model for desktop and portable computers. Plug and Play capability. Common hardware support. Group Policy, IntelliMirror, and other client management tools administered through Active Directory.

Case Study 3: Multinational Financial Services Corporation

A multinational financial services organization comprised of seven separate operating companies has primary headquarters located in North America, Europe, Asia Minor, and Southeast Asia. Over 50 major regional offices provide a complete range of financial services (investment and personal banking, asset management and insurance). Each operating company is an autonomous business unit; however, at the local level, each company might share offices with one or more operating companies.

This company operates under the strict regulatory scrutiny of many countries and under their respective statutes regarding financial privacy, trading, and IT functionality and security. As a result, maintaining secure and stable systems at both the network operating system level and the desktop operating system level is required.

Existing IT Environment

There is no central IT group for all operating companies, so there are no comprehensive IT standards for the entire organization. Each operating company has created its own standards; therefore, each company has its own IT infrastructure. In some locations, operating companies share one common network. In other locations, the number of networks matches the number of operating companies sharing that office location. Local offices, especially the consumer and retail locations, maintain their own file and print servers, although regional offices usually have domain controllers. Regional offices are otherwise limited in their IT functions.

Some financial services applications require the UNIX operating system. Currently, all infrastructure services such as Dynamic Host Configuration Protocol (DHCP) and DNS are managed in a UNIX environment. Windows 2000 DNS dynamic update protocol will be used while the company researches the possibility of migrating the custom applications running on UNIX servers to Windows 2000.

Their current network operating system environment runs 95 percent on Windows NT Server 4.0 and five percent on Novell NetWare Bindery. The current client operating systems in use at each operating company include 80 percent Windows NT Workstation 4.0, approximately 15 percent Windows NT Workstation 3.51, and about 5 percent Windows 95. Some financial services professionals use both UNIX and Windows NT 4.0 clients.

Goals for Deploying Windows 2000

One of the operating companies is developing its own Active Directory structure with the goal of creating a common global directory design for the entire organization. A parent company IT initiative driven by a group of IT professionals that represent each of the operating companies is also working to develop a company-wide Active Directory structure.

The organization plans to retire NetWare Bindery when they install Windows 2000. The network will use both Windows 2000 and UNIX for the foreseeable future.

Table 1.4 summarizes the IT goals of this organization and includes the reasons why this organization chose Windows 2000 to meet their goals.

Table 1.4   IT Goals for a Multinational Financial Services Corporation

Goals	What Windows 2000 Offers
Common client operating system across the entire environment to enable standardization, improve manageability and administrative capability, and reduce TCO.	Increased hardware support allows for a wider selection of company-standard computers (desktop and portable). Improved power management enables network information to be as accessible on portable computers as it is on desktop computers. Group Policy and other management tools can be enabled across the entire IT environment.
Common network operating systems that offer scalability and availability for IT environments with different needs throughout all operating companies.	Offers clustering, load balancing, and the ability to handle large data stores and complex objects. Single point of administration requires only one set of administrators. Group Policy enables refined management for all clients.
Client security on all desktops and portable computers.	Can secure a portable computer as you can a desktop.
Need for multiple monitors at each desktop to simultaneously track trading and access customer information.	Allows one CPU to support more than one monitor.
Reduce TCO through reduced client management while increasing the level of service.	Improved Group Policy and integration with Systems Management Server.

(continued)

Table 1.4   IT Goals for a Multinational Financial Services Corporation *(continued)*

Goals	What Windows 2000 Offers
Reduce in-house software development and associated costs.	Component Services and other tools, such as Windows Installer, that are included with Windows 2000 Server enable easier tool building and reduce the time invested in developing custom applications.
Common directory for all operating companies.	Active Directory has sufficient flexibility to accommodate all operating companies.
Allow each separate company to have its own child domain or domains.	Active Directory design uses a top-level domain name as a placeholder domain, thereby allowing each separate company to have its own child domain or domains.
Share a common directory between Exchange Server and Windows 2000 Server.	Synchronize Microsoft® Exchange Server version 5.5 directory with Active Directory by using Active Directory Connector.
Remote administration of services.	Terminal Services is configured in the lightweight Administrative mode rather than Application Server mode. This gives administrators another option for remote administration without negatively impacting server performance.

Case Study 4: International Software Development Company

A leading developer of computer-based operating system and applications software for consumer and business use has its main headquarters in the Western United States. The sales, support, and software development offices are located in 180 worldwide locations. The Information Technology (IT) division has two primary areas of responsibility:

- Providing and maintaining IT systems and solutions that help employees work efficiently and effectively.

- Working with product development groups to test and deploy beta products in an enterprise environment.

Existing IT Environment

The company's current IT environment is a homogenous Windows NT Server 4.0 environment with a broad mix of Windows NT 4.0, Windows 95, and Microsoft® Windows® 98 clients, including multiple computers in user offices that often run beta software. IT provides centralized:

- Directory services.

- Mail and collaboration services.

- Management of Windows NT Server 4.0 security services, network accounts, Web services, and networking.

Users are geographically scattered throughout the globe. Eighty to 90 percent of employees troubleshoot their own client desktops. A large number of users access the network remotely, requiring stable remote access services. IT also supports off-site telecommuters and employees who require international access to the corporate network.

Goals for Deploying Windows 2000

The major goal of this company is to upgrade all of the servers and users to Windows 2000 within 12 months. During migration, the IT group must maintain services of critical applications and at the same time collapse resource domains into geographically-based master user domains. Eliminating many of the resource domains should reduce the number of servers on the network and streamline administration, as well as reduce hardware and software support costs.

The IT department must also keep user attribute information synchronized between Active Directory directory service, Exchange Server 5.5 directory service, and additional systems in use across the company. Everything that is brought online that uses Active Directory must work together. Finally, they want to create a common console tree and create a common directory.

Table 1.5 summarizes the IT goals of this organization and includes the reasons why this organization chose Windows 2000 to meet their goals.

Table 1.5   IT Goals for International Software Development Company

Goals	What Windows 2000 Offers
Consolidate global servers to improve manageability and decrease support costs.	Server consolidation is enabled by the high-performance memory management and multiprocessing capability of Advanced Server. These features improve the scalability of the platform making it an appropriate base for server consolidation efforts.
Purchase new state-of-the-art hardware to create a new high-speed corporate network.	New technologies in Windows 2000 Server are designed to integrate with advances in computer architecture and microchip design, including Advanced Power Management, USB devices, FireWire, smart card readers, and infrared support.
Standardize to one client for better administrative control and authority delegation, and more options for remote installation and management.	Achieve improved desktop management through Group Policy and organizational units enabled by Active Directory, IntelliMirror, and other Change and Configuration Management technologies.
Obtain 50% improvement in performance and reliability over Windows NT 4.0 Server on all Advanced servers.	Baseline improvements at the kernel level of the core operating system enable improvement in memory management, caching, and preemptive multitasking.
Move from a moderately complex Windows NT Server 4.0 environment to a highly simplified Windows 2000 environment.	Active Directory provides increased object storage, more granular management of servers and clients, and improvements in simplified domain design through use of Domain Name System and DNS dynamic update protocol.
Change Windows NT Server 4.0 domain structure to Active Directory model with domains and forests.	Active Directory provides a more flexible domain structure to accommodate current and future organizational needs.
Improve security, information sharing, and transaction capability within the company as well as with other businesses and customers.	Enable a virtual private network using the advanced networking and security features of Windows 2000 Advanced Server.
Improve e-mail security.	Use PKI and certificates.
Maintain a fully functioning corporate network throughout the transition period.	Simultaneous administration and auditing of servers running Windows NT Server 4.0 and Windows 2000 Advanced Server, including all corporate printers, file servers, remote access servers, proxy servers, and internal Web servers. Interoperability with Windows 95, Windows 98, and Windows NT 4.0 clients.

Mapping Windows 2000 Features to Your Business Needs

The prior sections have examined the features and benefits of the Windows 2000 platform from a high-level perspective of business needs, sample corporations and users, and product features. In this section, you will review specific technology features with the goal of determining which technologies are most important for your organization. Review these features while keeping in mind your organization's short-term, mid-term, and long-term plans. The chapters in this book that focus on design go into detail about how each technology is integrated with other Windows 2000 technologies and what the design dependencies are.

The following sections contain tables that list many of the Windows 2000 features that you will want to deploy and configure in your organization. Assess the benefits of the listed features and determine their relative priority for your organization. Then, you can develop a deployment plan that is both timely and cost effective.

All of the tables in this section are included in "Sample Planning Worksheets" in this book. The tables in the appendix are formatted so that you can enter your own comments about the potential role of these features within your organization. Use these worksheets to prepare a customized executive summary of the Windows 2000 features your organization requires.

Note The following tables highlight the main benefits of Windows 2000 Server and Windows 2000 Professional, and are not intended to be a complete description of all features. For more information about a particular feature, see the product Help files or the appropriate book and chapter in the *Microsoft® Windows® 2000 Server Resource Kit*.

Management Infrastructure Services

The management infrastructure services in Windows 2000 Server provide IT departments with tools that enable you to provide the highest levels of service available and reduce ownership costs. Table 1.6 describes the Windows 2000 Server management infrastructure services and their benefits.

Table 1.6   Management Infrastructure Services

Feature	Description	Benefits
Directory services	Active Directory stores information about all objects on the network, making this information easy to find. Provides a flexible directory hierarchy, granular security delegation, efficient permissions delegation, integrated DNS, high-level programming interfaces, and an extensible object store.	Provides a single set of interfaces for performing administrative tasks, such as adding users, managing printers, and locating resources by only logging on once. Makes it easy for developers to enable their applications on a particular directory.
Administration services	Microsoft Management Console (MMC) provides administrators with a common console for monitoring network functions and using administrative tools. MMC is completely customizable.	MMC standardizes your management tool set, reducing training time and increasing productivity for new administrators. It also simplifies remote administration and allows for delegation of tasks.
Group Policy	Group Policy allows an administrator to define and control the state of computers and users. Group Policy can be set at any level of the directory service, including sites, domains, and organizational units. Group Policy can also be filtered based on Security Group memberships.	Group Policy gives administrators control over which users have access to specific computers, features, data, and applications.
Instrumentation services	With Windows Management Instrumentation (WMI), administrators can correlate data and events from multiple sources on a local or organization-wide basis.	WMI allows you to create custom applications and snap-ins by giving you access to Windows 2000 objects.
Scripting services	Windows Script Host (WSH) supports direct execution of Microsoft® Visual Basic Script, Java, and other scripts from the user interface or command line.	WSH allows administrators and users to automate actions, including network connection and disconnection.

For more information about designing and deploying Windows 2000 directory services and Group Policy, see "Designing the Active Directory Structure," "Planning Distributed Security," "Defining Client Administration and Configuration Standards," and "Applying Change and Configuration Management" in this book.

Desktop Management Solutions

Desktop management solutions are features that allow you to reduce the TCO in your organization by making it easier for you to install, configure, and manage clients. These features are also designed as tools that make computers easier to use. Table 1.7 highlights Windows 2000 Server and Windows 2000 Professional desktop management features that increase user productivity.

Table 1.7   Desktop Management Solutions

Feature	Description	Benefits
IntelliMirror	IntelliMirror is a group of features that can be used to make users' data, applications, and customized operating system settings follow them as they move to different computers within their organization.	Users have access to all of their information and applications, whether or not they are connected to the network. Reduces the need for administrators to revisit desktops for application or operating system updates.
Windows Installer	Controls the installation, modification, repair, and removal of software. Provides a model for packaging install information and APIs for applications to function with Windows Installer.	Enables remote deployment and maintenance of applications by system administrators. Reduces the number of dynamic-link library (DLL) conflicts. Enables self-repairing applications.
Remote Install	DHCP-based remote start technology installs the operating system on a client's local hard disk from a remote source. A network start can be initiated by either a pre-boot execution (PXE) environment, a PXE-enabled network card, specific function key, or remote boot floppy provided for clients without PXE.	An administrator does not have to visit a computer to install the operating system. Remote OS Installation also provides a solution for propagating and maintaining a common desktop image throughout your enterprise.
Roaming User Profiles	Roaming User Profiles copies registry values and document information to a location on the network so that a user's settings are available wherever the user logs on.	Users have the ability to travel and still have their documents and system information readily available.
Option Component Manager	Windows 2000 Server Setup allows you to bundle and install add-on components during or after any system setup through an installation module.	Reduces the amount of time required for deployment setup and reduces the number of trips to individual computers.
Disk Duplication	You can customize a single Windows 2000 Server or Windows 2000 Professional setup and clone it across similar computers.	Cloning can save you time and money when deploying a large number of servers or clients.

Note You can use Systems Management Server to complement the desktop management technologies in Windows 2000.

For more information about deploying Windows 2000 Server and Windows 2000 Professional management solutions, see "Defining Client Administration and Configuration Standards" and "Applying Change and Configuration Management" in this book.

Security Features

Enterprise-level security needs to be flexible and robust so that administrators can configure rules to address possible security liability without hindering the free flow of needed information. Table 1.8 highlights Windows 2000 security features.

Table 1.8   Security Features

Feature	Description	Benefits
Security Templates	Allows administrators to set various global and local security settings, including security-sensitive registry values; access controls on files and the registry; and security on system services.	Allows administrators to define security configuration templates, then apply these templates to selected computers in one operation.
Kerberos authentication	The primary security protocol for access within or across Windows 2000 domains. Provides mutual authentication of clients and servers, and supports delegation and authorization through proxy mechanisms.	Speeds performance by reducing server loads while connections are being established. You can also use it to access other enterprise computing platforms that support the Kerberos protocol.
Public key infrastructure (PKI)	You can use integrated PKI for strong security in multiple Windows 2000 Internet and enterprise services, including extranet-based communications.	Using PKI, businesses can share information securely without having to create many individual Windows 2000 accounts. Also enables smart cards and secure e-mail.
Smart card infrastructure	Windows 2000 includes a standard model for connecting smart card readers and cards with computers and device-independent APIs to enable applications that are smart card-aware.	Windows 2000 Smart Card technologies can be used to enable security solutions throughout your intranet, extranet, and public Web site.
Internet Protocol security (IPSec) management	IPSec supports network-level authentication, data integrity, and encryption to secure intranet, extranet, and Internet Web communications.	Transparently secures enterprise communications without user interaction. Existing applications can use IPSec for secure communications.
NTFS file system encryption	Public key–based NTFS can be enabled on a per file or per directory basis.	Allows administrators and users to encrypt data using a randomly generated key.

For more information about deploying Windows 2000 security services, see "Planning Distributed Security" and "Determining Windows 2000 Network Security Strategies" in this book.

Information Publishing and Sharing

Windows 2000 information publishing and sharing technologies make it easier to share information over your organization's intranet, extranet, or the Web. Table 1.9 highlights features for information publishing and sharing.

Table 1.9   Information Publishing and Sharing

Feature	Description	Benefits
Integrated Web services	Windows 2000 Server integrated Web services allow you to use a variety of Web publishing protocols.	Flexible opportunities for publishing information on your extranet, intranet, or the Web.
Indexing Services	Integrated index services allow users to perform full text searches on files in different formats and languages.	Improves productivity.
Removable Storage	Consists of server and tool components for delivering audio, video, illustrated audio, and other types of multimedia over networks.	New opportunities in training, collaboration, and information sharing improve productivity.
Printing	Windows 2000 makes all shared printers in your domain available in Active Directory.	Allows users to quickly locate the most convenient printing source.

For more information about deploying Windows 2000 information publishing and sharing services, see "Upgrading and Installing Member Servers" in this book, and the *Microsoft® Windows® 2000 Server Resource Kit Internet Information Services Resource Guide.*

Component Application Services

As a development platform, Windows 2000 offers Component Object Model (COM) and Distributed COM (DCOM) support that extends a development team's capabilities to efficiently create more scalable component-based applications. Table 1.10 highlights Component Application Services features.

Table 1.10   Component Application Services

Feature	Description	Benefits
Queued Components	Developers and administrators can choose the appropriate communications protocol (DCOM or asynchronous) to use at the time of deployment.	Easier for developers to take advantage of the store and forward services offered by the integrated message queuing services in Windows 2000 Server without having to write any code.
Publish and Subscribe	COM Events provide a uniform publish and subscribe mechanism for all Windows 2000 Server applications.	Developers do not have to reinvent and program fundamental services.
Transaction Services	Provides information updates by calling an application on a mainframe, or sending and receiving a message to or from a message queue.	Provides a way for developers to guarantee correctness of their applications when updating multiple data sources
Message Queuing Services	Ensures that a message transaction is either completed or safely rolled back to the enterprise environment.	Provides developers with the facilities to build and deploy applications that run reliably over unreliable networks and operate with other applications running on different platforms.
Web Application Services	Developers can use Active Server Pages to build a Web-based front-end to their existing server-based applications.	Web Application Services allows remote servers to be administrated through a Web browser with minimum connectivity cost.

For more information about deploying Windows 2000 Component Application Services and the Microsoft® Security Support Provider Interface, see "Determining Windows 2000 Network Security Strategies" in this book. For more information for developers, see the MSDN Platform SDK link on the Web Resources page at http://windows.microsoft.com/windows2000/reskit/webresources.

Note   You might want to discuss these features and their potential business value with members of your application development team. Their knowledge can assist you in determining the potential business value of these technologies to your organization.

Scalability and Availability

Faster CPUs and network adapters are the traditional benchmarks of network performance. In the future, more efficient read/write capabilities, improved input/output (I/O) performance, and faster disk access will be equally important characteristics of network architectures. Environments that require mission-critical computers can now use the extended capabilities of Windows 2000. Table 1.11 highlights Windows 2000 features that will assist you in improving network scalability and availability.

Table 1.11   Scalability and Availability

Feature	Description	Benefits
Enterprise Memory Architecture	Windows 2000 Advanced Server allows you to access up to 32 GB of memory on processors.	Allows applications that perform transaction processing or decision support on large data sets to keep more data in memory for improved performance.
Improved symmetric multiprocessing (SMP) scalability	Windows 2000 Advanced Server has been optimized for eight-way SMP servers.	Allows organizations to take full advantage of faster processors.
Cluster service	Allows two or more servers to work together as a single system.	Allows greater availability, reliability, stability, and security with simplified management.
Intelligent Input/Output (I2O) support	I2O relieves the host of interrupt-intensive I/O tasks by offloading processing from main CPUs.	Improves I/O performance in high-bandwidth applications.
Terminal Services	Through terminal emulation, Terminal Services allows the same set of applications to run on diverse types of client hardware, including thin clients, older computers, or clients not running Windows. Can also be used as a remote administration option.	Allows for centralized management of applications and desktops for task-based workers. Provides technology for bridging existing desktops to a full Microsoft® Win32® environment. Gives remote users local network performance over dial-up remote access connections. Also provides for graphical remote administration of any Windows 2000 Server.

(continued)

Table 1.11   Scalability and Availability *(continued)*

Feature	Description	Benefits
Network Load Balancing	Combines up to 32 servers running Windows 2000 Advanced Server into a single load balancing cluster. It is used most often to distribute incoming Web requests among its cluster of Internet server applications.	Enhances the availability and scalability of Web servers, File Transfer Protocol (FTP) servers, streaming media servers, and other mission-critical programs by combining the functionality of two or more host computers (servers that are members of the cluster).
IntelliMirror	IntelliMirror allows users to have their data, applications, and settings follow them when they are not connected to the network.	Data is always available and the user's view of the computing environment is consistent, whether or not the client is connected to the network.

For more information about deploying Windows 2000 Cluster service, see "Ensuring the Availability of Applications and Services" in this book.

For more information about Terminal Services, see "Deploying Terminal Services" in this book.

Networking and Communications

To enhance your networking environment, consider the Windows 2000 technologies listed in Table 1.12, which can give you greater bandwidth control, secure remote network access, and native support for a new generation of communications solutions.

Table 1.12   Networking and Communications

Feature	Description	Benefits
DNS dynamic update protocol	Eliminates the need to manually edit and replicate the DNS database.	Reduces administration and equipment costs by reducing the number of DNS servers needed to support a network.
Quality of Service (QoS)	QoS protocols and services provide a guaranteed, end-to-end express delivery system for IP traffic.	Allows you to prioritize network traffic to ensure that critical processes are completed and data is delivered promptly and accurately.

(continued)

Table 1.12   Networking and Communications *(continued)*

Feature	Description	Benefits
Resource Reservation Protocol (RSVP)	A signaling protocol that allows the sender and receiver to set up a reserved path for data transmission with a specified quality of service.	Improves connection reliability and data transfer.
Asynchronous Transfer Mode (ATM)	An ATM network can simultaneously transport a wide variety of network traffic, including voice, data, images, and video.	Unifying multiple types of traffic on a single network can dramatically reduce costs.
Streaming Media services	Server and tool components for delivering multimedia files over the network.	Streaming Media can dramatically reduce the cost of travel, team collaboration, and training by offering online meeting and information sharing.
Fibre Channel	Fibre Channel provides one gigabit per second data transfer by mapping common transport protocols and merging networking and high-speed input and output in a single connection.	Improved flexibility, scalability, manageability, capacity, and availability over small computer system interface (SCSI) technologies for demanding applications.
IP Telephony	The Telephony API 3.0 (TAPI) unifies IP and traditional telephony.	Developers can use TAPI to create applications that work as well over the Internet or intranet as they do over a traditional telephone network.

For more information about Windows 2000 networking and communications features, see "Preparing Your Network Infrastructure for Windows 2000" and "Determining Network Connectivity Strategies" in this book.

Storage Management

Windows 2000 Server provides storage services designed to improve both reliability and user access. Table 1.13 highlights these services.

Table 1.13   Storage Management

Feature	Description	Benefits
Remote Storage	Monitors the amount of space available on a local hard disk. When free space on the primary hard disk drops below the level necessary for reliable operation, Remote Storage removes local data that has been copied to remote storage.	Allows administrators to manage the amount of free disk space by migrating files to a tape library where the files remain active from the user's perspective.
Removable Storage	Allows administrators to manage removable storage devices and functions. Administrators can create media pools that are owned and used by a particular application.	Allows administrators to optimize network performance by controlling where data is stored. Also makes it possible for multiple applications to share the same storage media resources.
NTFS file system enhancements	Supports performance enhancements such as file encryption, the ability to add disk space to an NTFS volume without restarting, distributed link tracking, and per-user volume quotas to monitor and limit disk space use.	File encryption reduces the risk that confidential data is exposed to unauthorized users. Being able to extend partitions quickly reduces server and network down time and the risk of data loss.
Disk Quotas	Helps administrators plan for and implement disk utilization.	Reduces the need for hardware administration and decreases maintenance costs.
Backup	With Backup, users can back up data to a variety of storage media, including hard drives, and magnetic and optical media.	Helps protect data from accidental loss due to hardware or storage media failure.
Distributed File System (Dfs) Support	Allows administrators to create a single directory tree that includes multiple file servers and file shares, and allows interoperability between Windows 2000 clients and any file server that has a matching protocol.	Dfs makes it easier for administrators and users to find and manage data on the network. Dfs also provides a fault-tolerant share for important network files.

For information about deploying Windows 2000 Server storage management technologies, see "Determining Windows 2000 Storage Management Strategies" in this book.

Planning Task List for Mapping Windows 2000 Features

Use the planning task list contained in Table 1.14 as you begin your Windows 2000 deployment planning process.

Table 1.14   Planning Task List for Mapping Windows 2000 Features

Task	Location in Chapter
Understand how the structure of this book will assist you in your deployment planning process.	Starting Your Plan
Learn about the Windows 2000 product family.	Overview of Windows 2000 Product Family
Analyze how specific features can be used to enhance worker productivity.	Using Windows 2000 to Improve the Way You Work
Review Windows 2000 features in context of your business goals.	Mapping Windows 2000 Features to Your Business Needs

C H A P T E R   2

Creating a Deployment Roadmap

Planning your deployment project is an important step in the logical progression of implementing Microsoft® Windows® 2000. Because Windows 2000 is designed to be deployed incrementally—based upon the specific business needs and information technology (IT) capabilities of any size organization—you need to decide which features are appropriate for your organization. You also need to consider the technical and project management dependencies of the Windows 2000 features you have chosen to deploy. And, finally, you need to consider the interoperability or coexistence requirements of your existing IT environment.

This chapter presents an overall project management process and identifies key deployment phases to help you create a project plan—a roadmap—for your team to follow when deploying Windows 2000 in your organization.

In This Chapter

Chapter Goals

This chapter will help you develop the following planning documents:

- A project plan.

- A project management process appropriate for your organization.

Related Information in the Resource Kit

- For more information about developing your deployment project plan, see "Planning for Deployment" in this book.

- For more information about how to run a successful Windows 2000 pilot project, see "Conducting Your Windows 2000 Pilot" in this book.

- For more information about designing a test lab and evaluating Windows 2000 features, see "Testing Windows 2000 in a Lab Environment" in this book.

Creating a Project Plan

Creating a project plan for deploying Windows 2000 ensures a successful deployment. Although you will create a project plan that will uniquely meet your business and IT requirements, there are common elements that need to be included in your plan for it to be an effective roadmap for your project. This chapter focuses on integrating preliminary technology decisions into a project management plan that you can use to deploy Windows 2000. For more information about specific project management issues to consider when preparing your project plan, see "Planning for Deployment" in this book. Figure 2.1 illustrates some steps you can use to create a project plan.

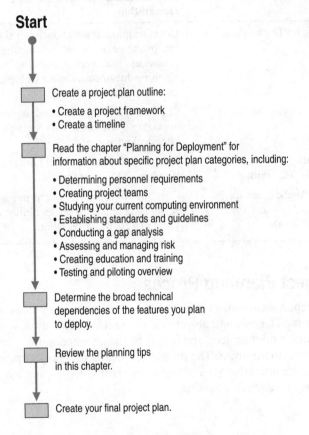

Start

Create a project plan outline:

• Create a project framework
• Create a timeline

Read the chapter "Planning for Deployment" for information about specific project plan categories, including:

• Determining personnel requirements
• Creating project teams
• Studying your current computing environment
• Establishing standards and guidelines
• Conducting a gap analysis
• Assessing and managing risk
• Creating education and training
• Testing and piloting overview

Determine the broad technical dependencies of the features you plan to deploy.

Review the planning tips in this chapter.

Create your final project plan.

Figure 2.1   Creating a Project Plan

Used effectively, a project plan can clearly identify specific phases of your deployment process and provide a clear and functional roadmap. While it is not necessary to follow a deployment process in a prescriptive manner—as you would an installation procedure—an infrastructure deployment process provides a conceptual framework for your Windows 2000 deployment project and makes it easier for your deployment teams to assess progress.

Many organizations already have project management methods and structures in place. To maximize the success of your deployment, follow a project management structure that is appropriate for your organization. The following sections outline a sample project management structure and then describe the project management structures used by two sample companies.

As you read through this chapter, you will find references to your deployment team, project planning documents, creating and using a test lab, and piloting Windows 2000. Table 2.1 is a list of the chapters in this book that contain additional information to assist you in developing your project plan.

Table 2.1   Deploying Planning Information Contained in this Book

Chapter	Description
Planning for Deployment	Contains information about analyzing your current computing environment, conducting a gap analysis, personnel requirements, planning tasks, deployment planning documents, capacity planning, risk assessment, and education and training.
Building a Windows 2000 Test Lab	Contains information about designing, building, and managing a test lab; testing for deployment; and testing after deployment.
Conducting Your Windows 2000 Pilot	Contains information about how to run a successful Windows 2000 pilot project.
Testing Applications for Compatibility with Windows 2000	Contains information about testing applications (both custom and retail) for compatibility with your Windows 2000 configuration.

Preparing Your Project Planning Process

Every deployment project goes through a life cycle—a process that includes determining IT goals and objectives, designing and developing features, conducting a pilot project, and installing the new operating system in your production environment. The principal function of a project planning process is to establish the order that your deployment team specifies, implements, tests, and performs the required activities.

Figure 2.2 illustrates a sample project management process for deploying Windows 2000. Each phase is listed at the top of the figure. The main body of the figure contains tasks you need to accomplish during the various phases of deployment and gives suggestions of Windows 2000 technologies you might consider for deployment.

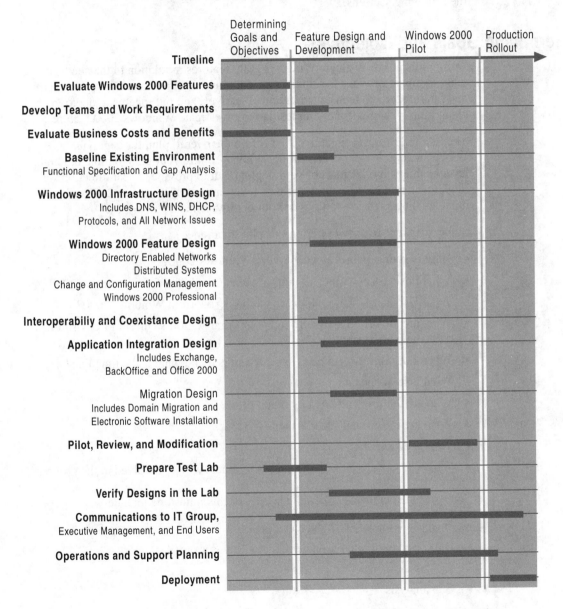

Figure 2.2   Sample Project Management Process for Windows 2000

The two bars near the bottom of the figure refer to a test lab. Testing is an integral part of Windows 2000 deployment that you will use throughout the whole deployment process.

Each of the four project management steps illustrated in Figure 2.2 is described in the following sections.

Determining Goals and Objectives

During this phase, evaluate Windows 2000 features in relation to the needs of your organization. This is also the time for you to secure executive sponsorship and funding, create focused goals and objectives, and put together a deployment team. Finally, begin using your test lab to investigate Windows 2000 features.

The first milestone is executive sign-off on the overall plan for deploying Windows 2000 in your organization. When defining your plan, outline the high-level business and IT goals of your deployment to provide a clear direction for implementation. Also, clearly define which features of Windows 2000 will be included during various phases of your deployment.

Some questions to answer during this phase include:

- Why is your organization deploying Windows 2000?
- What business benefits will your organization derive from Windows 2000?
- What IT benefits will your organization derive from Windows 2000?
- What are the differences between your organization's current IT environment and where you want to be?
- When does this project need to be completed and what is the time line?
- What is in-scope and out-of-scope for this project?
- Who are the users affected by this project?
- What are the critical success factors?
- What are the risks?
- Which groups, organizations, and individuals will be involved in the process?

Some of the documents you might create for this milestone include:

- Goals and objectives document.
- Outline of current environment, including user profiles.
- Risk assessment.
- Gap analysis.

For more information about risk assessment and gap analysis, see "Planning for Deployment" in this book.

This phase is important for creating your deployment roadmap. After defining your goals, it is easier to determine the Windows 2000 features you need, and how these features relate to your existing environment. Your analysis can also help you understand critical technology dependencies. While you need to be thorough in your assessment, this phase can be accomplished in a short amount of time. A goals and objectives phase helps you develop a project vision that is shared by the IT department, end-users, and management, and helps create a successful deployment.

Note Your organization might have already completed this phase, either formally or informally. If management has already made a decision to deploy Windows 2000, you still need to create a goals and objectives document and get formal sign-off before moving to the feature design and development phase.

Feature Design and Development

During the feature design and development phase, you create the actual design—sometimes called the functional specification—for the Windows 2000 features you intend to implement in your organization. This is also the time to determine how the features you have selected will actually work in a production environment.

The technical dependencies of Windows 2000 features become more important during this phase, so it is important that the various deployment teams collaborate and share insight into the capabilities, functionality, and interdependencies of each feature. The technical design chapters in the remainder of this book will help you determine how to deploy specific features in your organization.

The functional design specification is the complete set of designs that you will test and refine. For example, you might have multiple design variations of your Microsoft® Active Directory™ namespace based on different business or IT requirements, each of which will be evaluated against business and IT criteria appropriate to your organization. Eventually, through technical testing and analysis, you will be ready to implement one Active Directory namespace for your organization. It is important to remember that this process and its results are specific to your organization.

The iterative design and testing process starts in this phase as each of your deployment teams creates their own plans and then synchronizes with each other to create a comprehensive design specification. Your test lab is also important during this phase as you test various configurations to determine how to use Windows 2000 features to meet your project objectives.

The functional design specification needs to provide your project teams with enough details about the features and functions your organization will deploy to help them easily identify resource requirements and commitments for implementing your Windows 2000 infrastructure.

During this phase, also create a project plan that contains the functional specification (the combined plans of each team) and a schedule. You will be ready to implement your project plan after you receive management approval to proceed with the deployment. Some primary deliverables you can include in your plan are:

- Functional design specification
- Updated risk management plan
- Master project plan and master project schedule
- Features plan, listing which features are in and out of scope

Windows 2000 Pilot

After you have completed your feature design and development, and thoroughly tested your feature configurations, you are ready to conduct a pilot project. The deployment team needs to set a number of interim delivery milestones, each of which involves solutions development, testing, validating against prespecified performance criteria, and redesign. Tracking deployment issues and efficiently resolving them is vital to reaching your deployment goals while remaining on schedule and within budget.

After your pilot project is running and stable, your sponsor and the deployment team can meet to assess the functionality of the new Windows 2000 infrastructure and verify that production rollout and support plans are in place. During this phase, primary milestones and deployment documents can include:

- Technology validation complete
- Complete and stable functional specification
- Proof-of-concept complete
- Preproduction test complete
- Pilot complete
- Updated risk management plan

Additional deployment documents you might want to develop include:

- Training plan
- Support or helpdesk plan
- Operations transfer plan
- Disaster recovery plan
- Tools list

During this phase, you will adjust your designs based upon pilot testing. You will notice changes that need to be made because you are integrating the designs of each feature you will deploy and then testing those designs to ensure appropriate integration.

For more information about validating and testing your Windows 2000 Server deployment plan through proof-of-concept lab testing and a pilot, see "Building a Windows 2000 Test Lab" and "Conducting Your Windows 2000 Pilot" in this book.

For more information about testing applications compatibility with Windows 2000 Professional, see "Testing Applications for Compatibility with Windows 2000" in this book.

Production Rollout

The final phase of your Windows 2000 project is production rollout. At this point, you have tested all of your designs in the lab and conducted a pilot program to refine your plan and further test your designs. Now you are ready to incrementally deploy Windows 2000 throughout your enterprise. For some companies, the initial pilot project is the first phase of their rollout. Others might remove their pilot project installations and start their production rollout with clean installations.

During the production rollout phase, testing and support activities are still important as iterative cycles of deployment, testing, validation, and support become the primary focus. The new Windows 2000 Server and Windows 2000 Professional infrastructure is formally turned over to the operations and support groups at the deployment complete milestone. Now is the time to conduct a project review. Primary milestones and deployment documents that you might want to consider creating during this phase include:

- Production rollout plan.
- Release plans for Windows 2000 Server, Windows 2000 Professional, or both.
- Operations and support information system (knowledge base, procedures, and processes for performance support, including test results and testing tools).
- Load or image set and installation scripts.
- Documentation repository (hard and electronic copies of all project documents, including deployment notes, are archived).
- Training material for end-users, administrators, helpdesk, and operations staff.
- Project closeout report.
- Disaster recovery plan.

After your deployment is complete and you have prepared your project closeout report for the executive sponsor, you might decide to conduct a project review. You can use a project review to objectively assess the strengths and weaknesses of your entire project and analyze how you could improve on future infrastructure deployments with the knowledge you have gained from hands-on experience.

Deployment Scenarios

Each company will create a unique project plan based on its own business needs and the project management procedures. The following scenarios provide samples of how goals and objectives were translated into milestones and performance criteria for several enterprise-scale organizations. These scenarios are based on the experiences of companies who participated in the Joint Development Program for Windows 2000.

Scenario 1: Multinational Financial Services

This organization has nine distinct operating companies, each with its own IT organization, and no common IT standards. As an organization, they experience problems with security policies, domain structure, and network configurations. Most of their servers are currently running Microsoft® Windows NT® Server 4.0. The key objectives they want to accomplish are to create:

- A new IT environment with Windows 2000 functionality.
- A common directory for all nine operating companies.

The deployment team identified several key issues that define how they stage their deployment, as follows:

- Phase 1: Assessment
- Phase 2: Design and Engineering
- Phase 3: Testing
- Phase 4: Migration (Deployment)

Phase 1: Assessment

During the assessment phase, IT management from each company agrees on the need for a common namespace. Although several Domain Name System (DNS) names are already registered by and for each of the operating companies, the challenge is to find one name to use as the root name for all companies. This single "placeholder" name needs to meet the following criteria:

- Accurately define the root of the tree for all nine operating companies.
- Be new to the organization (never been used by any of the operating companies, either internally or externally).

IT management defines global engineering teams that are split into eight working groups based on plans for a basic configuration that can be tested, modified, and customized for each operating company. Table 2.2 shows the deployment teams and their responsibilities.

Table 2.2   Deployment Planning Teams

Deployment Team	Focus
Server and Infrastructure Design	Responsible for overall design, design iterations, and final engineering.
Active Directory	Domain and tree design below the main domain level and ongoing management of Active Directory in their respective domains, especially as they relate to security and administrative privileges.
Mobile and Desktop Design	Develop Windows 2000 configurations for all desktop and portable computers and determine the appropriate Group Policy and Microsoft® IntelliMirror™ features to use for managing those configurations.
Security	Permissions, group memberships, and administrative delegation (provide input to Active Directory group on organizational unit design).
Migration	Migrating Windows NT Server 4.0 to a Windows 2000 Server environment. Focus on interoperability, migration, and coexistence during the interim period of parallel domains until migration is complete.
Certificate Services	File encryption and PKI.
Free Seating	Develop Windows 2000 configuration for free-seating clients and determine appropriate Group Policy and IntelliMirror features to use for managing those configurations.
Application Management	Ensure that all in-house applications are Windows 2000 Logo–compliant. Determine the best deployment vehicle to use for desktop and portable computers (through an in-house developed push application or Windows 2000 installation tools). Determine shared run-time components. Study system file protection mechanisms. Run existing applications side-by-side for minimal maintenance.

The team determines that the business and IT needs will be principally met through the following:

- Active Directory
- New domain design
- IntelliMirror
- Distributed File System
- Disk Quota Management
- Remote OS Installation
- Synchronization of Active Directory with Exchange directory services

Phase 2: Design and Engineering

The primary issue during this phase is to decide whether the domain root name needs to be visible or accessible through the Internet or available only internally. An Internet presence already exists for the entire group of operating companies, so the intranet name needs to be different. An internal root name is created as a placeholder name so that individual domains can be created for each of the nine operating companies. Each company retains autonomy in areas such as configuration creation, management, and security.

They also use this phase to design and test the configuration for each feature. Then, the teams work together to determine how the selected Windows 2000 features affect each other. They also create training documentation and start developing a support plan.

Primary Goals

As the driving force behind the migration to Windows 2000, Active Directory and domain design need to meet the following business and IT criteria to be acceptable for all operating companies:

- One root domain is necessary so that all operating companies can participate in a common directory.
- Each business unit wants to retain complete administrative control of its entire organization, including all separate Windows NT Server 4.0 domains and structures, and to be totally independent of any other operating company.
- Domain and directory design has to be flexible enough to allow for company acquisitions, divestitures, and reorganization of existing operating companies.
- Each operating company is responsible for its own domain and everything below it based on that operating company's specific needs.

As the Active Directory design is developed, the migration team needs to consider issues of computer cloning versus computer upgrade. Computer cloning is a process in which you create one installation and configuration for new operating system installations and then copy that configuration to all new computers you install.

Because the namespace decisions are so important to meeting the company's goals, a namespace design board is formed with representatives from the IT groups of each operating company. The senior management of the board and the IT organizations of each operating company need to agree on the final namespace design. The namespace design factors they consider include:

- Impact on Windows 2000 domain model
- Impact on existing Windows NT Server 4.0 namespace
- Conflicts with the existing DNS namespace

The company considers both domain design and DNS to be critical decision points when upgrading from Windows NT Server 4.0 to Windows 2000 for two reasons:

- If the proposed Windows 2000 domain structure mirrors the existing Windows NT Server 4.0 domain structure, then they can upgrade directly from their Windows NT domain to their Windows 2000 domain.

- If they decide to use the same Windows 2000 domain structure they used in Windows NT Server 4.0, then they need to have two parallel domain structures. They also need to keep the Windows NT environment until they have stabilized the new Windows 2000 environment.

The team determines that the upgrade or migration decision will be dictated by:

- The existing domain structure
- The existing functionality
- New functionality that they will implement because of Windows 2000

The team then realizes that deciding what will exist in each domain requires analysis of the following items:

- Assessing the problems in their current Windows NT Server 4.0 domain design.

- Deciding which Windows NT Server 4.0 features they want to continue in the Windows 2000 domain design.

- Deciding which new features of Windows 2000 they want to implement based upon their added value to the new domain structure.

- Determining if they have a native Windows NT Server 4.0 environment, or if it has been modified or customized (either by in-house development teams or a third-party solution provider or developer).

   For example, this organization uses an in-house scripting tool that associates users with specific applications. This tool performs application publishing similar to Windows Installer in Windows 2000, so a decision needs to be made whether to continue using the in-house tool or to use Windows Installer. Using Windows Installer would reduce internal development costs and thereby reduce total cost of ownership (TCO). As a result, they decide to use Windows Installer.

For more information about Active Directory domain design, see "Designing the Active Directory Structure" in this book. For more information about domain migration, see "Determining Domain Migration Strategies" in this book.

Secondary Goal

Their secondary goal is to determine other features of Windows 2000 that are beneficial to their environment, but which might not be features of Windows NT Server 4.0. Then, they develop a plan to determine if the new features are appropriate for their environment. For example, this sample organization decides that the following features meet their business and IT needs:

Offline Files   Portable computer users can have access to network data when traveling by having personal and network files on their local computers. For nontraveling end-users, this feature helps ensure continuous end-user productivity if the LAN or WAN has service interruptions, because files are stored on the user's local hard-drive.

Fault-tolerant Distributed File System   With Distributed file system (Dfs), they can create a single directory tree that includes multiple file servers and file shares for a group, division, or enterprise. This allows users to easily find files or folders distributed across the network. Having a fault-tolerant Dfs is linked to roaming user profiles, which are already in use through their Windows NT Server 4.0 infrastructure. Files can be stored on the network, providing improved replication among the company's partners.

Disk Quota Management   Disk quota management allows the company to use volumes formatted with the NTFS file system to monitor and limit the amount of server disk space available to individual users. They can also define the responses that result when users exceed the specified thresholds. In the past, the organization used third-party tools. They are moving to Windows 2000 native tools in an effort to reduce in-house development costs and total cost of ownership (TCO).

Remote OS Installation   An enhanced scripting process for installation already exists in this organization, but scripts must be updated every time the basic client computer configuration changes. They will use Windows 2000 Remote OS Installation to deploy Windows 2000 Professional for first-time installations, and also use Remote OS Installation for rapid updates of malfunctioning computers. They plan to use Remote OS Installation in conjunction with IntelliMirror to accelerate and simplify computer replacement, resulting in reduced TCO.

Exchange directory service with Active Directory integration   This organization plans to synchronize Exchange 5.5 directory using the Active Directory Connector (ADC), and eventually integrate the directory services when the organization upgrades to the next version of Exchange.

Phase 3: Testing

This sample organization set up a test lab for feature and pilot testing. They want to simulate the actual conditions of their production migration. After the lab and pilot tests validate the migration process, the organization will be ready to begin the production rollout. The preliminary design pilots will be rolled out to IT personnel during the design phase so they can test and refine the designs.

The initial design issues they plan to test and evaluate include:

- Active Directory design (placeholder domain and four child domains).
- Standard client configuration.

Their pilot objectives include:

- Evaluate Windows 2000 and the proposed Active Directory model in a real production environment.
- Use new technology that is native to Windows 2000 as much as possible.
- Merge the standard client stationary and mobile configurations.
- Demonstrate the proposed future configuration to business units throughout the organization and collect constructive criticism.
- Consolidate and refocus isolated Windows 2000 projects within the entire organization.

During this phase, the deployment team redesigns and tests until consensus is reached. The new design needs to meet the following acceptance criteria:

- Increases stability
- Provides an improved working environment
- Can be managed with current and new or additional administrative resources
- Meets budget requirements

After the domain design is tested and finalized, each global engineering team within the organization will sign off on the domain design. Then, the design must be approved by higher IT management through all nine operating companies.

Phase 4: Migration

Because the organization finds it necessary to maintain Roaming User Profiles for mobile users, they decide to maintain two parallel environments throughout the transition period. Many roaming users who upgrade to Windows 2000 at home will find that their work environment has not yet upgraded. By maintaining parallel environments, the infrastructure will support all users and allow them to access their files, regardless of which operating system they are using.

However, migration needs to occur as quickly as possible. The organization plans to maintain the dual Windows NT Server 4.0 and Windows 2000 environment for 12 to 24 months. Users will be able to remain in both environments until the IT environment in all nine operating companies is completely transitioned to Windows 2000.

For this organization, collapsing the Windows NT Server 4.0 environment is the most critical decision point for their entire migration. They want to be sure that they perform adequate lab and pilot testing to alleviate any significant problems that can arise as a result of improper design. By performing adequate testing, they hope to avoid causing network downtime. After they complete testing, they will proceed with migrating to Windows 2000 throughout the operating companies and then collapse the Windows NT Server 4.0 environment.

Scenario 2: Multinational Consumer and Industrial Manufacturer

Scenario 2 is based on a highly decentralized business organization with a distributed IT environment comprised of 175 separate operating companies. Manufacturing and assembly take place in 49 countries on six continents. They employ approximately 390,000 employees worldwide who speak approximately 120 different languages. A common interface and implementation process is required to ease transition for all of the operating companies and to reduce deployment support costs. All of the operating companies want to address the following common issues:

- Provide customers with easy access to a common set of knowledge relevant to the company and its business.
- Reduce IT administration costs and improve service by creating one forest.
- Consolidate Windows NT 4.0–based servers for upgrading.
- Provide a common IT environment for all of the operating companies.
- Set guidelines for Windows 2000 deployment throughout the organization that will provide a stable IT environment and prevent individual groups from deploying separate products or features that are not supported by the central IT department.
- Communicate IT issues throughout all operating companies.
- Design Active Directory effectively because it enables many other Windows 2000 features.

Deployment Teams

The organization creates a deployment team consisting of both a server and a client team. Each team has representatives from each of the primary operating companies. Their goal is to develop a model for both server and client operating environments that can be used and applied at all of the operating companies. As such, their goal is to establish and validate a design and deployment process that can be used by all of the operating companies rather than to deploy Windows 2000 in a production environment. They divide their plan into three phases:

- Phase 1: Infrastructure backbone design and development
    - Establish core services for the primary corporate domain
    - Deploy servers in major corporate offices

- Phase 2: Deployment planning at the operating companies
    - Establish pilot domains in all operating companies
    - Configure sites and site-link bridges
    - Create user accounts
    - Establish trusts between Windows NT Server 4.0 and Windows 2000 domains
    - Pilot Windows 2000 Professional in multiple operating companies

- Phase 3: Migrate primary services from Windows NT Server 4.0 to Windows 2000 Server
    - Windows Internet Name Service (WINS)
    - Dynamic Host Configuration Protocol (DHCP)
    - Print
    - Web servers using Windows Internet Information Services (IIS)

One of the first tasks the team accomplishes is creating a list of the primary concerns and risks for the overall project. This list includes:

- Recognize that the coordination required to build a global enterprise is unprecedented. (It takes an average of three years to deploy an operating system for both servers and clients throughout all operating companies.)
- Prepare for coexistence with UNIX and mainframe line-of-business applications, as required. (For example, many operating companies have Sun RISC 6000 Servers containing an accounting program running on the Windows NT Server 4.0 operating system.)
- Provide tools to move and merge parts of the forest, when necessary, based on internal company changes and frequent acquisitions, mergers, and divestitures.
- Fill the position for a first domain administrator who is:
    - Responsive to change requirements and root domain support.
    - Able to effectively delegate child domains and site creation.

- Recognize that a single schema might not meet the configuration requirements for all operating companies; therefore, a directory synchronization tool might be required for interoperation among the companies.
- Recognize corporate Internet Protocol (IP) dependencies, such as:
    - Firewalls
    - Network performance

The Server Deployment Team

The server deployment team is responsible for planning and designing the server deployment process based on the phases defined for the overall deployment team. The server deployment team is further divided into teams focused on technical planning, Active Directory, logistics, and migration. The strategic goals the server team identifies are:

- Define Windows 2000 Active Directory services that can be used by all operating companies.

- Develop a migration plan from the current Windows NT Server 4.0 environment to a Windows 2000 environment.

- Develop short-term preparation steps.

- Implement a corporate backbone pilot.

- Implement guidelines and Windows 2000 models for all operating companies.

Figure 2.3 illustrates the project management framework the server team is using for deploying Windows 2000.

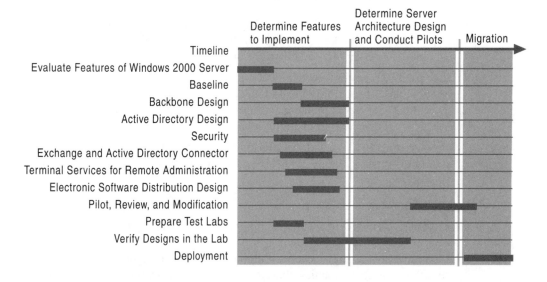

Figure 2.3   Server Deployment Process for a Multinational Manufacturer

Server Phase 1: Determine Features to Implement

The primary goal for the server deployment team is to create deployment standards for a common directory and domain model that all operating companies can use. They also need to establish a global Windows 2000 infrastructure to support all of the operating companies. First, the team focuses its attention on designing an infrastructure backbone using the main corporate IP backbone points of presence worldwide. The backbone is a logical backbone of root namespace and domain controllers, not a physical network backbone. Using the Windows 2000 infrastructure, they need to develop a backbone that all of the operating companies can join. Each operating company needs to interface at the forest root and share a common global catalog.

Then, the team starts to identify specific technologies that the enterprise will require based on business needs. For example, because English is the common language for all system administrators worldwide, MultiLanguage capability at the server level is not required. The specific issues they decide to focus on include:

- Designing domains and sites
- Designing organization units
- Determining use of DNS or WINS name resolution
- Understanding replication and containers of Active Directory
- Synchronizing Exchange directory service with Active Directory
- Designing the Windows 2000 Active Directory
- Developing standards for a common server operating system configuration
- Determining domain controller and Global Catalog placement criteria and where they will be located

Table 2.3 provides a checklist of activities that the company developed to determine when the server team's Phase 1 goals are complete.

Table 2.3   Phase 1 Milestone Completion Checklist

Completed	Item
	Establish pilots of four to six servers in a minimum of three locations.
	Get approval to use *<domainname>*.net/*<domain>*.int for the root domain name.
	Install Windows 2000 Server in a specified number of corporate IT points of presence.
	Define the *<company.XXX>* DNS structure, including:
	Configure integrated DNS dynamic update server for the *<company.XXX>* domain in European location *X*.
	Configure an integrated DNS dynamic update server in US location *A*.
	Update the core IT servers with the new domain information.
	Verify record serialization and zone transfer with the core operating site.
	Start Direct Host at *<company.XXX>* on *mm/dd/yyyy*.
	Define the core operating configuration, including:
	Establish global catalogs at European locations *X* and *Z*.
	Identify subnets.
	Create *X* number of sites.
	Establish site links between European locations *X* and *Z*.
	Enhance management capability by installing Windows 2000 Terminal Services for remote administration.
	Enable electronic software distribution by configuring backbone sites to replicate Windows 2000 builds to European location *Z*.
	Create the directory service in a pilot scenario by:
	Populating the pilot directory service from the corporate directory data (200,000+ names).
	Verifying replication and load on the system.
	Deleting the population after the test.

Server Phase 2: Prepare Final Server Architecture Design and Conduct Pilots

The team is now ready to focus on phase 2 and begin establishing the various operating company domains for the pilot. Some domains are new, while others will be migrated from Windows NT Server 4.0. The specific issues they have decided to focus on include:

- Design the Active Directory structure and validate it in the test lab.
- Develop migration plans for Windows NT Server 4.0 to Windows 2000 Server.
- Develop a standard installation process for server deployment.
- Establish an enterprise integration lab.
- Define specifications for other Windows 2000 features.
- Activate a communications plan to end users, including IT in other operating companies, IT administrators, and desktop users.

Table 2.4 provides a checklist of activities the company developed to determine when the server team's Phase 2 goals are complete.

Table 2.4   Phase 2 Completion Checklist

Completed	Item
	Identify 10 pilot locations, including four in the USA and five in Europe, one of which is the European client lab.
	Deploy 18 to 24 servers in a pilot environment.
	Deploy 30 to 40 workstations in a pilot environment.
	Configure the corporate IP backbone through a virtual private network (VPN) by configuring firewalls for VPN access between operating companies and appropriate corporate backbone locations.
	Define administrative delegation, including:
	Pre-create domains for the operating companies.
	Delegate operating companies into DNS zones.
	Create a domain for the operating companies, including:
	Installing operating company domains in five European and four US locations.
	Identifying participating operating company subnets.
	Creating sites and delegating site management.
	Creating site links between operating company sites and backbone sites.
	Establishing a global catalog at every participating site (not operating company).

(continued)

Table 2.4   Phase 2 Completion Checklist *(continued)*

Completed	Item
	Define delegations for each operating company, including:
	Creating an organizational unit structure within the operating company domain.
	Delegating administration of organizational units.
	Determine user accounts and create accounts for members of the server and client deployment teams.
	Attach client computers belonging to the Windows 2000 deployment team to the operating company domains.
	Establish a Windows NT Server 4.0–style trust as a production resource domain for the operating company.
	Integrate WINS in the operating company backbone as appropriate.
	Integrate Microsoft® Exchange Server by configuring the Active Directory Connector at each operating company and providing one-way synchronization to update Active Directory information.
	Create a certificate authority.
	Create directory service replication.
	Deploy Windows 2000 Professional in coordination with the client deployment team through:
	Developing an unattended setup of a client prototype in different domains.
	Using Group Policy for clients on all domains.
	Installing MultiLanguage packs on a client prototype with three sample languages.
	Enabling international client roaming.
	Installing and using each operating company's standard software on all sites that are Group Policy object–based.
	Ensuring that workstations can access Windows 2000–based resources through existing Windows NT 4.0 Remote Access Services.
	Define users by:
	Using Group Policy for users on all domains.
	Ensuring that user roaming in different domains is operating correctly (default client language needs to be identical).
	Ensuring that user roaming internationally is operating correctly (different default client languages).
	Ensuring that resource access in different worldwide domains is operational.

Server Phase 3: Present Migration Plans to Operating Companies

The focus for phase 3 is on migrating services from Windows NT Server 4.0 to Windows 2000. The services will be migrated following a risk assessment designed to reduce the impact on existing production systems. As the team achieves some success in migrating key components, the level of complexity increases, which in turn increases risk. The deployment team will present the plans to the operating companies for use as prototypes after the team completes thorough testing. The activities during this phase include:

- Present a migration strategy.
- Introduce Windows 2000 concepts and proposed designs to the operating companies.
- Market the proposed design to executive management (IT Review Board).
- Market the project and proposed design to end-users.
- Prepare a disaster recovery plan to ensure business continuum, especially:
    - A backup strategy
    - A rollback (fallback) strategy to Windows NT 4.0 after migration to Windows 2000

Table 2.5 provides a checklist of activities the company developed to determine when the server team's Phase 3 goals are complete.

Table 2.5   Phase 3 Completion Checklist

Completed	Issue
	Determine site migration locations in multiple geographical locations including North America, Europe, and Asia.
	Determine the number of servers to migrate for each domain and each site.
	Determine the number of client computers to be migrated for each domain and each site.
	Conduct WINS migration by incorporating a Windows 2000 WINS server in an existing environment.
	Conduct a DHCP migration by incorporating a Windows DHCP server into an existing environment.
	Conduct a print server migration by selecting a number of print servers that are not Windows NT Server 4.0 domain controllers and upgrade them to Windows 2000.
	Conduct an Internet server migration by implementing a Windows 2000 deployment Web site using IIS 5.0 and creating a pointer from the existing central site. Replicate content from the trial site to the new site. Add DNS records to this server.
	Reduce resource domains by selecting a Windows NT 4.0 resource domain and migrate it to Windows 2000 Server.
	Create new account domains by migrating the Windows NT 4.0 account domain primary domain controller to Windows 2000 Server.

The Client Deployment Team

The greatest challenge for the client deployment team is to work with all of the operating companies to get consensus on one client computer configuration. The existing client operating systems in the organization include Windows 95, Windows 98, and Windows NT 4.0 Workstation. Additional client issues the team considers are:

- Reducing the number of applications in use company-wide. There are currently 1,000 or more applications, making it difficult for the IT team to provide support.

- Changing the IT focus from the traveling computer to the traveling user.

- Studying whether to change from the existing method of deploying software in Windows NT Server 4.0.

- Providing more hardware support for laptop computers.

The team needs to develop a proposal that will help the operating companies decide whether to upgrade their clients or their server infrastructure first. While the team realizes that both options are possible, the members decide that the following issues in favor of upgrading the server infrastructure first are relevant for the organization:

- More centralized control over the client computers.

- Limit users' capability to modify the client computer configuration.

- Use Windows 2000 tools for installation.

- Have a global catalog enabled for all users to access.

The team discovers that most of the operating companies in the organization would like to upgrade their servers first, and then after Active Directory and a global catalog are enabled, implement Group Policy and other change and configuration management tools for more granular client computer administration. They also realize that deciding whether to upgrade the servers first is particularly important if the team plans to recommend the use of Windows 2000 Group Policy for software deployment. The team will need to study how the use of Group Policy will affect Active Directory.

This organization has the following goals for the client architecture team:

- Develop a standard client configuration as a modular product for all of the operating companies.

- Create a reference installation including hardware, software, and operations.

- Design a framework for a global model that allows users to log on anywhere in the world.

- Develop a model for training and helpdesk support.

The client team's work is divided into two phases:

- Phase 1: Client standard configuration issues
- Phase 2: Software logistics

Phase 1: Client Standard Configuration Issues

To meet their worldwide business use goals, the client team decides to use a standardized configuration that includes:

- Windows 2000 Professional clients
- Microsoft® Office 97 or Office 2000
- Virus scanning capability
- Web browser
- E-mail client
- MultiLanguage capability
- Windows Terminal Services capability (ensure that client design is suitable for Terminal Services).
- Enabling international client roaming so that users can connect or dial-up to the corporate IP backbone from anywhere in the world and access:
  - Personal settings for desktops and applications.
  - Personal documents and mail available everywhere.
  - Enterprise-wide standard software.

Phase 2: Software Logistics

During phase 2, the team focuses on developing a strategy for getting the new operating system and client configuration to both stationary and mobile clients in a stable and efficient manner. The team identifies the following issues:

- Creating installation packages for:
  - Enterprise applications.
  - Common applications for all operating companies.
  - Custom applications for each operating company (as necessary).

- Creating a guide for installation packages to include:
    - Standardized package development worldwide for all operating companies.
    - Unique installation package per application worldwide for nonstandard software.

- Application repackaging as necessary for each operating company.
- Assigning installation packages:
    - For all users.
    - For user groups by function or organization.
    - For client specific needs.

- Installing applications based on user demand

The client deployment team has found that management wants to continue the practice of installing new client operating systems and configuration images in conjunction with buying new hardware. The average operating system deployment in this organization takes three years. Internal TCO studies determine that spending more money up front on better hardware and then upgrading the new client configuration image prior to installing the new hardware on users' systems reduces TCO.

Additionally, significant client benefits for system administrators and IT professionals are based on new features and enhanced functionality; whereas, users and executives need to see tangible evidence that productivity is enhanced. Therefore, buy-in by both executive decision-makers and end-users is required before the project can move to the deployment phase in each operating company.

Technology Dependencies

Because Windows 2000 Server is a multipurpose network operating system that is designed with distinct—but integrated—features that can be deployed incrementally, there are numerous technology dependencies that you must consider as you plan your deployment. The following examples illustrate some of these technology dependencies.

Active Directory and Domain Namespace

Your Active Directory structure and Domain Name System (DNS), along with your infrastructure plans for Windows Internet Name Service (WINS), Dynamic Host Configuration Protocol (DHCP), network protocols, files, printing, streaming media, and other bandwidth-intensive applications, must be designed to accommodate business requirements and IT capabilities. If your business needs dictate numerous subsidiaries, and roaming or remote access users, then you need to consider organizational units, Group Policy, security, and IntelliMirror technologies. If you want to offer secure intranet or extranet capabilities, then IP Security (IPSec), and PKI are important components to design.

If you will deploy Windows 2000 Professional as your primary operating system for desktops and laptops, then you might want to consider installation options, MultiLanguage capabilities, security, Active Directory, and other change and configuration management technologies. Finally, if you are in a heterogeneous environment that includes network operating systems other than Windows NT or Windows 2000, you will need to consider interoperability and coexistence options.

Active Directory and Exchange Server

You might be planning to deploy Active Directory in a geographically dispersed environment where centralized IT management is difficult because of low-speed WAN links, and there is great potential for compromising a stable and secure connection. Yet, you also might have a business requirement for a stable, secure, and common e-mail and collaboration system across different operating companies, including geographically remote sites. You need to consider the relationships between Active Directory and Exchange Server 5.5 directory service, with Group Policy, IPSec, and virtual private networks (VPNs). Plan to use the Active Directory Connector (ADC) to keep your data synchronized with your Exchange directory.

You must also consider DNS design, especially if you have multiple organizations, subsidiary operating units each with its own Internet domain name, domain and tree structures, security requirements, and different network operating system or IT standards. DNS design is especially important if groups other than the Windows 2000 team are responsible for the DNS namespace, as with many UNIX-centric IT organizations.

Integrating Exchange Server

If you require a common e-mail standard and a common directory, but your organization does not use Exchange Server 5.5, then you might need to implement Exchange Server 5.5 prior to deploying Windows 2000 so you can synchronize with Active Directory using ADC. Alternately, you could scale back this goal until you have completed your Windows 2000 deployment and then deploy the next version of Exchange.

Remote OS Installation

Another example might take place in a user location with limited support but excellent connectivity where local client installation was maintained manually in the past. Using Remote OS Installation and IntelliMirror technologies, you now have an opportunity for remote installation and troubleshooting without needing on-site support.

You will find more information on technology dependencies in each of the technical planning chapters in this book. Remember, each feature that you want to deploy needs to have its own design so that it can be formally tested in both lab and pilot environments.

Tips for Planning Your Windows 2000 Deployment

Your ultimate goal when creating planning documents and formulating a deployment plan is to successfully deploy Windows 2000 using project management techniques that work in your organization. The following sections provide lists of items to consider as you plan your deployment.

General Best Practices

The following list contains overall best practices as identified by some early adopters of Windows 2000.

- Use your organizational chart and see how the management structure in your organization matches up against both your organizational needs and your network LAN links. Build an Active Directory infrastructure based on these considerations.

- Determine what level of international functionality you want to achieve and what trade-offs you are willing to make to get there.

- Schedule for an additional level of complexity in testing your product.

- Plan your application setup around Windows Installer.

- Decide how you will break down system administration responsibilities for your application and identify who will be given administrative permissions.

- Determine what policies are enforced on a typical user's system.

- Utilize the new components provided by Windows 2000. Integrate them wisely to minimize their impact on the performance of your application.

- Schedule enough time for installing Windows 2000 server—a several-hour process.

- Add international issues to your Windows 2000 issue lists and test tracking systems.

- Develop "working groups" to study task-based architecture decisions.

- Write a good test plan and set up a test lab that exactly mirrors your production environment in terms of types of hardware and software in use.

- Upgrade conservatively at first. You can speed up the process and rate of deployment as you start achieving success.

Deployment Phases

Determine the best overall order to deploy Windows 2000 in your organizations. The following order was used by one company:

- Define your current environment by determining which server and client operating systems are currently in use in your organization. Study their functionality and the purposes they serve.

- Study whether the number of users is likely to change due to mergers, acquisitions, reorganizations, or growth.

- Study the need to scale your server environment (determine your needs for clustering and load balancing as well as Terminal Services).

- Design your Active Directory structure including your DNS namespace.

- Upgrade your network infrastructure and member servers.

- Implement Active Directory and storage management.

- Upgrade or migrate your clients to Windows 2000 Professional.

- Implement desktop management using change and configuration management tools.

Application Installation Issues

Use the following planning tips as you plan for installing applications in your organizations.

- Make an early investment in setup authoring. Take the time to lay out your setup process early in the product development cycle.
- Involve developers in the setup authoring process. This will help uncover dependencies early on.
- Be aware that Windows Installer validations can affect your application's performance.
- Avoid reboots during install wherever possible.
- Do not add to Win.ini, System.ini, Autoexec.bat, or Config.sys.
- Require everyone testing your applications to install them using the Windows Installer.
- Keep in mind that an administrator can advertise your product on the user's Start menu or desktop without fully installing the product. The application will be installed when the user double-clicks on a shortcut or on a document of the type served by your application.
- Understand and plan for "system file protection" issues.

International Issues

The following tips will help you plan for an international installation.

- Avoid assumptions about the language version of the operating system that your application is running.
- Avoid assuming that the locale, code page, and user interface match for a given user or computer.
- Use Windows Installer. It is available in both ANSI and Unicode.
- Determine what fonts are needed. Often all that is needed to support international functionality are the correct fonts.
- Use the latest Windows 2000 printer drivers. They will provide the best support for international features.
- Check both your application and the operating system when tracking down international problems.

Performance Issues

Maintaining high performance is important to meeting the goals of most deployments. The following tips will help you plan for improved performance.

- Delay any startup initialization that you can.
- Simplify startup screens so that fewer graphic bits are being sent across the network.

- Plan for network interruptions and general network performance issues.
- Use the caching layer that Windows 2000 provides for its file systems when a share goes offline.

Roaming Users and Terminal Services

The following tips will help you plan for roaming users and for Terminal Services installations.

- If you plan your roaming user scenario carefully, a substantial part of your Terminal Services implementation will be done as well.
- Support roaming user profiles and state separation.
- Separate per-user settings from per-computer settings.
- Do not require write access to the per-computer settings.
- Keep in mind that regular Windows 2000 users have the ability to modify data only in their user profiles. Your application will not be able to change portions of the HKEY_LOCAL_MACHINE subtree in the registry.
- Run your application while logged on as a user (rather than as an administrator) and test it on computers where users do not have administrative privileges. This will let you catch problems early.

Administration

As you create your plan, use the following administration tips to make it easier for you to administer your Windows 2000 installation.

- Make sure that the administrative features of your application are as simple as possible while still providing full functionality. This will help deployment of the application in small or medium-sized organizations where custom tools are not developed.
- Support scripting in your application. One strategy: If you write a provider for Windows Management Instrumentation (WMI), it will allow you to provide simple scripting support in your application inexpensively.
- Support OnNow/ACPI requirements. Handle sleep and wake notifications and requests.
- Keep in mind that default security settings are substantially more secure for regular users than they were under Windows NT 4.0—what worked under Windows NT 4.0 for regular users might require them to be power users with Windows 2000.

Planning Task List

Table 2.6 summarizes the tasks you need to perform when creating your Windows 2000 deployment roadmap.

Table 2.6   Deployment Roadmap Task List

Task	Location in Chapter
Define a project management process that identifies key milestones and deliverables appropriate to your organization.	Preparing Your Project Planning Process
As you identify specific features you want to deploy, study their technological dependencies on other Windows 2000 features and technologies.	Feature Design and Development
Identify any project management constraints that can affect deployment. For example, financial or human resource constraints, or organizational logistics such as holiday season fulfillment or year-end finance issues.	Determining Goals and Objectives
Develop a process for risk assessment and prepare a thorough risk analysis.	Determining Goals and Objectives
Define the order in which you will stage your deployment.	Deployment Scenarios
Create a project plan for your organization focused on Windows 2000 features, deployment teams, schedules, and associated dependencies.	Deployment Scenarios

For more information about project management, see the Microsoft Solutions Framework link on the Web Resources page at http://windows.microsoft.com/windows2000/reskit/webresources.

CHAPTER 3

Planning for Deployment

After you have determined the project management structure you will use for planning your deployment, it is time to start addressing the details of your plan. This chapter provides information about how to create specific sections of your project plan. For example, project managers need to determine their personnel requirements, deployment teams, the types of deployment documents to create, a gap analysis, and a functional specification.

While Microsoft has found that the methods described in this chapter contribute to a successful deployment, they are recommendations that can be adapted to the needs and structure of your organization.

In This Chapter

Chapter Goals

This chapter will help you develop the following planning documents:

- Project scope and objectives
- Personnel requirements and project teams
- Gap analysis
- Administrative plans
- Communications strategy
- Education and training plan
- Risk assessment matrix

Related Information in the Resource Kit

- For more information about developing your project plan, see "Creating a Deployment Roadmap" in this book.
- For more information about how to run a successful Microsoft® Windows® 2000 pilot project, see "Conducting Your Windows 2000 Pilot" in this book.
- For more information about designing a test lab and evaluating Windows 2000 features, see "Building a Windows 2000 Test Lab" in this book.

Detailing Your Project Plan

To obtain the greatest benefit from Windows 2000, you need to plan your deployment carefully. Your overall project plan will include various aspects of both your business and your technical network infrastructure. As you begin, consider the steps discussed in the following sections.

Project Scope and Objectives

The first step in planning your deployment is defining your project objectives. It is in this step that you identify the specific business goals you want to achieve and how Windows 2000 can help you achieve them. This strategy will also help you choose the most useful Windows 2000 features.

In your project objectives, indicate the specific business concerns that you need to address. Include specific, short-term objectives, for example, "deploy Windows 2000 to 2,500 computers by the end of the business quarter," as well as more general, long-term objectives, such as "reduce ongoing software distribution costs."

Determine your objectives before you proceed with your deployment planning because they affect what you do and how you do it. Clear objectives help you stay on course.

When you document your project scope, indicate the areas, functions, and environments that your Windows 2000 implementation will cover. For example, you might be interested in updating an older file server but not in implementing an infrastructure-wide deployment of Active Directory.

Table 3.1 outlines some common Windows 2000–related business concerns and project objectives. Note that this table is only an example. You need to assess your own business concerns to derive your own objectives. You might find that a single business concern could be addressed by a number of project objectives, or that a single project objective could address a number of business concerns.

Table 3.1   Sample Windows 2000–Related Business Concerns and Project Objectives

Business Concern	Project Objective
Reduce total cost of ownership by extending the life of older systems.	Use Terminal Services to provide a Windows 2000 desktop experience to systems that would otherwise require an upgrade.
Make it easier for users to locate and access resources on the network.	Use Microsoft® Active Directory™ to store information about all objects on the network.
Support roaming users by providing access to their documents and system information from multiple computers.	Use Roaming User Profiles to copy desktop settings and documents to a location on the network so that a user's settings and documents are available wherever the user logs on.

Personnel Requirements

Organize your deployment team and then assign specific roles to team members. Depending on the size of your organization and the complexity of your deployment, you might also want to create subteams.

Assess the core competencies of your information technology (IT) staff. Also, assess their skill sets with regard to Windows 2000 technologies. Then, decide how you are going to manage any shortcomings. The following list provides options you might consider in regard to managing training issues:

- Delay the deployment until the staff is fully trained in the new technologies.

- Outsource portions of the work to cover weak points. Then, have your staff members learn the required skills from the contracted personnel.

- Outsource the deployment, support, and maintenance of your enterprise.

Important Securing an executive sponsor who can speak for the organization's overall needs for the project is usually critical for success. This person can help ensure that the deployment team understands and achieves its goals.

Organizing Your Deployment Teams

Although staffing needs can change as you plan and deploy Windows 2000, operating system deployments usually require several team members. For a large organization, include at least two or three operating system administrators on your centralized team. Also, be sure to include help desk or support personnel. From the beginning of your deployment project, try to involve people with a great extent of corporate knowledge and provide them with an overview of Windows 2000 and its benefits; they can help you meet the broader needs of your organization. If yours is an international organization, it is recommended that you include key people from locations in other countries. Include people who are trained in the Windows 2000 operating system and who thoroughly understand your network environment.

A core team made up of experts in security, networking, interoperability, and applications testing could also serve as leaders of subteams within their areas of expertise. Team members require such skills as detail-oriented project management skills, hands-on technical experience, and the ability to be innovative and master new technologies quickly and independently. Team members also need strong analytical abilities to be able to link the project vision with the details needed to achieve the vision.

Using your project scope and objectives document as a guide, identify which subteams will be responsible for planning and testing the deployment of the features you want to deploy. You might consider dividing your core deployment team into a server team and a client team, and then delegate responsibilities to subteams as in the following list:

- Base Server Team
  - Active Directory
  - Domain Name System (DNS)
  - Networking Design
  - Dynamic Host Configuration Protocol (DHCP) and Windows Internet Name Service (WINS)
  - Security
  - Administration Tools
  - Microsoft Exchange Server and E-mail
- Base Client Team
  - Client and desktop features such as Microsoft® IntelliMirror™, operating system and application installation, and existing applications.
  - Notebook and laptop issues such as power management, docking, remote access, and roaming profiles.

Plan your teams to reflect your internal structure, business needs, the Windows 2000 features and services you want to deploy, and the way you want to deploy them. The organization of your deployment teams will reflect the roles shown above.

One way you can organize a deployment team is shown in Table 3.2.

Table 3.2   Deployment Teams Example

Team	Responsibilities
Steering	Include the leads from all other teams to perform overall coordination and communications. Include strategic planners who know their way around the organization—people who remember that existing systems are in place and why they are needed, for example.
Planning and Coordination	Handles support and training, business planning, premigration planning, mission-critical systems, and third-party consulting.
Server	Test and develop solutions in: clustering, Hierarchical Storage Management (HSM), backup, disaster recovery, Terminal Services, integration, and hardware requirements
Infrastructure Design	Address the domain model, Active Directory, local area network (LAN) issues, telecommunications, Distributed file system (Dfs), global file access, Domain Name System (DNS), and remote access.
Security	Develop standards for Internet, intranet, and extranet services, as well as domain security and policy implementation.
Interoperability	Systems Network Architecture (SNA), Kerberos links with mainframes and UNIX, and UNIX/mainframe integration, NetWare and OS/2 integration/coexistence.
Application Integration	Integrate messaging, database, workgroup applications and suites, Internet tools, and line-of-business and third-party applications.
Networking	Research, test, and develop directory-enabled networking solutions.
Client	Test and resolve application, upgrade/migration, hardware, and laptop issues
Desktop Administration	Test and develop the organization's change and configuration management plans, including Group Policy, software installation, and user data and settings management.
Request for Comment Committee	Comprised of members from the user community. Provide feedback on decisions made by the deployment teams.

Assigning Windows 2000 Team Roles

Windows 2000 deployment activities fall into many categories. In small implementation projects, one person might fill several roles; in large implementation projects, several people might be assigned to each role.

Keep in mind that if you enable directory services, Windows 2000 is very different from environments that do not use directory services. To use a directory service, the IT organization needs to be educated and slowly migrated to a new support and administrative structure. This is a change that affects the entire organization and necessitates an even higher level of management education and involvement than a typical upgrade.

Table 3.3 describes the Windows 2000 personnel roles, responsibilities, requirements, and workload variables to consider when you determine your personnel needs.

Table 3.3   Windows 2000 Management Roles

Roles and Responsibilities	Required skills
IT Management or Executive Sponsor Sets priorities for the Windows 2000 infrastructure. Establishes the business case for the project. Defines deployment vision and secures funding. Acts as an advocate to both the team and the organization. Clears roadblocks, drives features versus schedule tradeoffs, and is responsible for the communications plan.	Understanding of the organization's business problems and the solutions that Windows 2000 will provide. Knowledge of primary features and capabilities of Windows 2000 Server and Windows 2000 Professional.
Project Management Drives the critical decisions necessary to release the Windows 2000 infrastructure. Conceives solutions and defines deployment scope with the deployment team. Creates the functional specification with other team members. Facilitates the day-to-day coordination to deliver the Windows 2000 systems consistent with organizational standards and interoperability goals. Drives overall critical tradeoff decisions.	Knowledge of details of Windows 2000 Server and Windows 2000 Professional functionality. Ability to coordinate executive management goals with project team goals.

(continued)

Table 3.3   Windows 2000 Management Roles *(continued)*

Roles and Responsibilities	Required skills
Development/Design Evaluates technical solutions to be used in designing and developing the Windows 2000 infrastructure. Defines the strategy for each Windows 2000 feature released during the deployment. Plays fundamental role in designing the initial infrastructure. Designs and builds the infrastructure necessary for implementation.	Experience in developing complex operating system services. Understanding of technical requirements for the existing and new network infrastructure.
Subject Matter/Technical Experts Responsible for designing and developing strategy for their subject areas. Provides leadership for subteams.	A high level of technical skill in their areas of expertise and with the Windows 2000 operating system. Detail-oriented project management skills.
Testing Assists in developing the initial solutions design. Ensures that all issues are known to the team and addressed prior to conducting production rollout. Designs and builds test lab and performs all testing and validation procedures prior to production rollout. Performs scalability analysis and performance testing.	Familiarity with Windows 2000 Server and related network hardware, or Windows 2000 Professional connectivity. Experience designing, running, and debugging tests. Experience in testing applications.
Documentation Assists in developing project documentation including planning documents, reports, and white papers. Could include writers, editors, and production personnel.	Familiarity with relevant technologies. Communication, writing, and editing skills as well as technology documentation knowledge.
User Education/Training Acts as the user advocate. Assesses user requirements, determines training objectives, and develops education and training programs to enable users to maximize use of the Windows 2000 infrastructure.	Familiarity with the organization's IT system, network infrastructure, and Windows 2000 features. Knowledge of self-help solutions and presentation software. Communication and training skills.
Logistics Management Ensures smooth rollout, installation, and migration to the operations and support groups, including help desk and training.	Good understanding of Windows 2000 Server and Windows 2000 Professional features and functionality.

As you examine your administrative requirements, you might find that you want to make changes to your current organization. Take this opportunity to look at how the system is administered today, and whether a reorganization would be beneficial. For example, if two separate teams administer Microsoft Exchange and Microsoft® Windows NT®, you might want to create a separate team to administer Windows 2000.

Current Computing Environment

Before you design your Windows 2000 environment, you need to thoroughly understand your current computing environment. Documenting your existing computing environment will help you understand your organization's structure and how it supports your users, and it will help you design your Windows 2000 deployment plan. Diagrams are a useful way to deal with complex concepts such as network layout. Where appropriate, create these diagrams and include them in your project plan documentation.

For more information about network diagrams, see "Preparing Your Network Infrastructure for Windows 2000" and "Determining Network Connectivity Strategies" in this book.

When reviewing your current computing environment, be sure to document the following:

Business Organization and Geographical Requirements   Describe the location and organization of your business units. Are large groups of employees located in widely separated geographic areas or are they all located in close proximity to each other? Are your business units closely related, or do they have significantly different needs and requirements?

Key Business Processes   If you are modifying key business processes, include diagrams that illustrate these processes and how the new IT infrastructure will affect them. For example, in some organizations, a key Windows 2000 Server deployment goal might be to use Active Directory to distribute administration to local administrators. By distributing administration, you allow administrators to provide better responsiveness to local user requirements. If this is the case, create a model that illustrates how the overall plan will achieve that goal.

Information Architecture   When you diagram your key business processes, illustrate how the information needed to make critical decisions will be available at the right place and time. For example, are sales and marketing personnel able to confirm precise delivery dates for customer orders? In your conceptual design, verify that key data stores are well organized and easily accessible.

Application Requirements   Conduct a complete inventory of the applications that are used in your organization. Include all custom (in-house) applications. As you are documenting your computing environment, also note the different tasks for which employees use computers and note how the change to Windows 2000 will affect their work. For example, if employees are using an old line-of-business application that is reliant upon certain Open Database Connectivity (ODBC) driver versions, the line-of-business application needs to be tested to ensure that it will work.

Technology Architecture   When documenting your network architecture, be sure to include topology, size, type, and traffic patterns. Any significant changes you plan to make to your technology architecture, such as hardware, networking, and services, needs to be illustrated in high-level diagrams.

Current and Future IT Standards   Over time, the network and application standards in many organizations become fragmented or obsolete. This is common in organizations that have merged with or acquired other companies. Disparate systems, built over a wide time frame, designed by different people, and often geographically separated, are a potential risk to a successful deployment. An audit of existing systems contributes to the success of the deployment team.

Administrative Model   By examining your existing administrative model you identify the administrative tasks that IT personnel have been performing in all areas of your organization. This helps determine whether you need to change any aspect of the existing administrative operations design to accommodate features of Windows 2000 you want to deploy.

Establishing Standards and Guidelines

Many organizations find that establishing Windows 2000 standards and guidelines can save time and money. This is because a standard environment reduces the potential for too many configuration combinations, making administrative and architectural workloads more efficient. Base these standards on how employees use their computers. For example, an employee doing computer-aided design has higher requirements than an employee using general office applications.

For best results, establish standard configurations for your clients and servers. Include guidelines for minimum and recommended values for CPU, RAM, and hard disks, as well as for accessories such as CD-ROM drives and uninterruptible power supplies.

Establish the standard software configurations that are used in your organization. Include operating systems and other application software and guidelines for how you distribute, support, and restrict the use of this software.

Establish guidelines for the network operating systems and protocols that are used in your organization. Include standard configurations for all network components (such as routers, hubs, and repeaters). Establish guidelines for supporting and maintaining these configurations.

Finally, establish the new standards and guidelines required by Windows 2000, including schema management and tracking, site design, and naming standards.

Conducting a Gap Analysis

Compare your current computing environment to your future environment based on your project objectives. The gap between the existing environment and your goals will help identify which Windows 2000 features you want to deploy. The primary steps for performing a gap analysis are:

- Identify the gap between the way employees work today and how you want them to work when the deployment is complete.

  Computers and operating systems are only of value to your business if they are of value to your employees. A successful deployment closes the gap between the way employees work today and the way the new system will empower employees to work when the deployment is complete. Later, when the team begins to measure the rate of success, the primary measure will be how it has improved the work of those who are using the system.

- Review documents, if any, from previous computer and network upgrades. In addition to providing useful information about the current computing environment, existing documents could provide a template to follow as you move through the decision-making process.

- Review documents obtained from hardware or software vendors. Documents that relate to the current hardware and software in your infrastructure will help you decide whether to upgrade or replace computing resources.

- Identify tasks and determine resource requirements for each task. After you have identified the tasks and determined what resources are required to accomplish those tasks, you can determine which groups within the organization need to be involved and whether you will need additional resources outside the organization.

- Update any documents such as spreadsheets or schedules with planning, work, and resource assignments. Keeping documents up-to-date will make it easier to plan work schedules and to allocate resources.

- Send the gap analysis documents to the appropriate decision makers in your organization for approval. If approval is granted, then the project can begin; if not, you need to make changes to the documents and put them through the approval process again before you begin implementation

Specific planning and design guidelines are provided throughout this book.

Testing and Piloting Windows 2000

Test your Windows 2000 design in a lab before deploying Windows 2000. In the early planning stages, you will need to select testing and piloting sites and assess hardware requirements. As soon as your lab is operational you can use the lab to better understand the product, prove concepts, and validate solutions. Expect the lab to evolve as the project progresses.

In general, provide as much detail as possible in your test plan documents so that your test and deployment teams have all the information they need to be successful. Describe the scope, objectives, methodology, schedule, and resources (hardware, software, personnel, training, and tools) in your test plan. Individual teams and subteams need to create their own test plans for their areas of technical expertise and write test cases. Test cases describe how the testing is to be done. This makes it possible to replicate and compare test results.

In the early phases of the project, testing will focus on components to validate design. Later testing will focus on interoperability of components to ensure that all the pieces work together. You need to test applications for compatibility with Windows 2000. Start by testing features that are mission-critical to your organization and whose design choice would be expensive and time-consuming to change.

Include a plan to escalate any issues that arise to the person most able to resolve the situation. A clear escalation process helps the team focus on the solution and take immediate corrective action.

If you are deploying Active Directory, be sure to provide for application testing with the directory service.

After you verify your Windows 2000 deployment in your lab environment, perform at least one pilot project before beginning your general deployment. The pilot project sets the tone for the final deployment, so it is important to be completely prepared for all aspects of the project. You need to determine the time it takes for installation, the personnel and tools needed to facilitate the process, and the overall schedule. The pilot provides a way to test your deployment plans. The pilot project also provides an opportunity to train your support staff and to gauge user reaction to the product so you can anticipate support needs.

For more information about setting up a test lab, see "Building a Windows 2000 Test Lab " in this book. For more information about pilots, see "Conducting Your Windows 2000 Pilot" in this book.

Note Complete your pilot project before proceeding to full-scale production deployment. As you complete each phase of your pilot project, document your results, verify that you met your project requirements, and rework your plan if necessary. Resolve any major issues before proceeding to the full-scale deployment phase. Be sure to include all aspects of your production environment in the pilot. For example, if you are going to deploy on an international scale that includes various languages, be sure that you successfully address international language issues in your pilot.

Creating Project Planning Documents

Throughout your deployment project, you need to create a variety of documents that define your vision, encourage support, guide, and summarize the deployment process. Whether this information is contained in a few documents or in many, include the information discussed in the following sections.

Administrative Documents

Your administrative documents are part of your project plan. They help you identify your goals and define your objectives. They help you stay organized and on schedule. Include the following information in your administrative documents:

Scope and Objectives As previously discussed, make sure that your plan clearly states the project objectives, defines the scope, and provides methods that measure progress and success.

Phases and Milestones Establish project phases to give your staff time to get oriented and to help you verify the assumptions you made in the planning stage. Expect at least some of the process to be iterative. Establish and monitor milestones to keep the project on track. For more information, see "Creating a Deployment Roadmap" in this book.

Budget Identify and track the expected costs and cost constraints for the project, including development, hardware, facilities, training, personnel, testing, and deployment. Identify backup sources of funding to cover unexpected expenses. Make sure the corporate vision for the project is clear so that the division of funds is clear.

Staffing Plan how you will staff your Windows 2000 sites. A document that outlines the reporting structure, responsibilities, frequency of meetings, communication strategies, and overall task and feature owners is useful. For more information, see "Assigning Windows 2000 Team Roles" earlier in this chapter.

Facilities Identify facilities requirements and communicate with the appropriate groups within your organization. Define your facilities requirements and obtain the necessary space early to minimize the likelihood that these issues will become obstacles to your deployment.

Overall Risk Assessment Identify the project risks that exist outside the deployment. Possible risks can include resource availability, impending mergers, or the loss of key personnel.

Communications Strategy Raise management and user awareness of the deployment project by communicating your plans to other groups in your organization. Start building support and acceptance early in the project by having other managers and key personnel review your plans at agreed-upon intervals. For more information, see "Communications Strategy" later in this chapter.

Deployment Documents

The following are recommended deployment documents that you can create as a part of your project plan.

Overview of the Current Networking Environment Include a high-level description of the current networking environment, including network infrastructure, hardware, policies, number and types of users, and geographic locations.

Deployment Design Detail how the transition to Windows 2000 will take place, including the upgrade and migration strategy for your servers and client computers; where, when, and how these upgrades will take place; and who will be involved. Take existing systems and applications into account, such as the impact an operating system change will have on existing applications, and storage and hardware capabilities.

Gap Analysis Address the specific gaps between your existing environment and the project goal. Then list the specific changes that are required to support the project goals. For more information, see "Conducting a Gap Analysis" earlier in this chapter.

Capacity Plan   Identify the issues and contingencies that you will address to ensure that there is sufficient hardware and network capacity for the Windows 2000 features you will deploy (for example, the replication traffic created by the Active Directory or remote operating system installation). You want to be sure that vital services are not degraded during or after rollout. For more information, see "Capacity Planning" later in this chapter.

Risk Assessment   Identify the risks in your plan and develop contingency plans for dealing with those risks. Reevaluate your deployment plan continually and make a formal evaluation after you complete each phase of the project. For more information, see "Risk Assessment" later in this chapter.

Problem Escalation Plan   Specify an escalation path that people in your organization can use to resolve and escalate issues as needed. Match the types of problems or situations to the people who can best address them. An escalation process enables the team to focus on getting the problem solved.

Pilot Plan   Identify the goals and objectives for the servers and clients that will participate in the first rollout, which features you will deploy, and what mechanisms you will use to gather feedback from pilot participants. For more information about preparing for and conducting a pilot, see, "Conducting Your Windows 2000 Pilot" in this book.

Testing and Deployment Strategies   Plan how you will test and deploy Windows 2000. For more information, see "Testing and Piloting Windows 2000" earlier in this chapter.

Functional Specification

Your functional specification details the operating system features that you will implement, and how they will be configured and deployed. All of these elements need to align with the scope and objectives of the deployment project.

Describe the different types of users, the key tasks they perform, how these tasks are currently performed, and how performance can be improved in the new network environment. If yours is a large organization with multiple sites, or an international organization, you need to detail your geographical issues.

Many features of Windows 2000 are interrelated, particularly if you plan to deploy Active Directory. For this reason, a dependencies matrix is very important and can be considered a primary document.

Deployment teams need to work together to identify the tasks needed to integrate each component and estimate the amount of time it will take to accomplish these tasks. Identify any issues that team members and management needs to be aware of. It is particularly important to identify the dependencies that affect other teams. For example, you might find that the work of a number of teams involves the structure of Domain Name System (DNS) and that their tasks need to be coordinated to avoid duplicating efforts.

Communications Strategy

A detailed communications plan can enhance the effectiveness of your deployment project. With proper communication, your work in planning and deploying Windows 2000 is more likely to complement and integrate with the work of other teams deploying new IT projects. This helps management to assist project teams in overcoming obstacles, and prepares users to take advantage of the new infrastructure.

An effective communications strategy identifies the needs of several types of audiences, such as executive management, project teams, IT organization, and users at all levels. Keeping people informed keeps them involved. Use your communications strategy to build support for your deployment project, the new Windows 2000 technologies, and the business processes that the technologies support.

When you create your communications plan, it is important to address the following questions:

How will deployment information be distributed?   You can use e-mail and intranets to complement more traditional media, such as print. Creating an intranet site that is simple to update with deployment status reports is one of the best means of keeping users informed. User experience is enhanced by sufficient self-help. This reduces confusion and lowers support costs.

What information will be conveyed?   Explain how the new infrastructure will make users' jobs easier and how it will serve the business needs of the organization. The status of the deployment is one of the most important pieces of information you can convey to users and deployment team members. Highlight the successes, but also acknowledge any obstacles.

How frequently will information be distributed?   For end-users, monthly updates might be sufficient. For line-of-business managers, more frequent updates might be appropriate, particularly when you get close to the pilot and production rollouts. For members of the IT department, whether they are directly involved in the deployment or not, weekly updates are recommended. The changes that you are instituting have a direct impact on the way IT personnel do their jobs. They need to keep a close watch on the progress of your deployment project.

What type of feedback mechanism will you implement?   Detail your plans for end-user feedback. Creating a feedback mechanism that your users can use to express their concerns and frustrations is important to your success. A two-way communication channel allows users to be part of the project and act as team members who provide valuable information that can contribute to the success of your project.

Education and Training Plan

Educate your users about Windows 2000 features and functions before you begin deployment. You might also want to provide formal training and develop a feedback mechanism.

Microsoft Official Curriculum (MOC) for Microsoft Windows 2000 Professional and Windows 2000 Server offers computer professionals training to deploy, administer, and support a Windows 2000–based network. This hands-on technical curriculum includes courses that provide participants with the knowledge and skills to:

- Understand the functionality and features of Windows 2000.
- Install, configure, and upgrade to Windows 2000.
- Administer a Windows 2000–based network.
- Update support skills from Microsoft Windows NT version 4.0 to Windows 2000.
- Design a Windows 2000 directory services infrastructure.
- Design a Windows 2000 networking services infrastructure.
- Design a change and configuration management infrastructure.

For more information about MOC for Windows 2000, see the Microsoft Training and Certification - Microsoft Official Curriculum link on the Web resources page at http://windows.microsoft.com/windows2000/reskit/webresources.

Capacity Planning

Capacity planning provides a solid foundation for planning and managing the computing environment. When you determine the computing resources needed to meet your business requirements, you gain the following benefits:

- Service objectives are met.
- Productivity is improved.
- Scalability is developed and maintained.
- Total cost of ownership (TCO) is controlled or reduced.

One of the most important tasks in capacity planning is to construct a representative baseline for the workload and the computing resources. Capacity planners and business planners must work together to identify the components of the business that are dependent on computing resources and to forecast the workload demands. Asset management is key to performing hardware inventory. If you need to replace hardware, look carefully at what needs to be replaced before upgrading.

Some organizations rely on the expertise of managers for capacity planning, others use analytic modeling, simulation, benchmarking, or, in critical situations, actual experimentation in their capacity planning. No matter what techniques you use, successful management of the computing environment requires a proactive approach.

A good starting point is to profile the different activities that take place on your network or subnets per hour, day, and month, like the following:

- Number of password changes.
- Number of times users log on.
- Number of DNS queries.
- Number of machine account password changes.

Then, determine the minimum, maximum, and average for each of the above items. You want to know how many of these events take place, how much bandwidth they take on the net and how much processing power and disk space they use on the server.

Find out how much these same entities exhibit on the new product. You can then use this information to optimize your servers and to plan your domain and site structure.

For more information about capacity planning and Windows 2000 features, see the chapters in this book relevant to the technologies for which you are planning.

Risk Assessment

When you plan to deploy an operating system and network infrastructure, plan for the unexpected. Even the best deployment plans can be affected by changes in business needs, economics, user requirements, or disruptions such as power outages or storms.

A risk management plan helps you identify potential risks before they occur and prepares you for a quick response if they do occur. A well thought-out and proactive risk management plan can help you:

Reduce the likelihood that a risk factor will actually occur. If only one person on your staff fully understands your security infrastructure, losing that person in the middle of the deployment could have serious repercussions. You can reduce the risk by training a backup for each key expert and keeping documentation up-to-date and accessible.

Reduce the magnitude of loss if a risk occurs. If you suspect that your Windows 2000 Server deployment project has been under-budgeted, you might be able to identify several backup sources to cover unexpected expenses.

Change the consequences of a risk. A sudden reorganization, business acquisition, or divestiture in the middle of a deployment can seriously disrupt your plans. If you have established a process for making abrupt changes, you can meet the challenge with little or no impact to the project schedule.

Be prepared to mitigate risk during your deployment. You can do this by strategically planning your installation and rollout. For example, you can start by adding new Windows 2000 domain controllers to an existing Windows NT 4.0 domain. Alternatively, you could build a new Windows 2000 domain, establish a trust relationship with the existing accounts domain, and then clone the user accounts. Or, you could install new Windows NT 4.0 domain controllers into your domain, move them to a private network, and then upgrade them to install the new domain. In each of these examples, you could easily roll back to the previous environment if you needed to.

Risk Management

To manage risk effectively, your risk management plan needs to:

- Identify mission-critical applications.
- Identify and analyze potential risks.
- Quantify the potential impact of the risks.
- Detail escalation processes.
- Identify solutions.
- Be communicated to senior management and project members.
- Become a part of day-to-day project management.
- Be kept up-to-date.

Risk management needs to be a part of your team's regular activities and cover all key people, processes, business, and technology areas of your Windows 2000 deployment. You need to:

Assess risk in all areas that could affect your project. Ask each team to identify and to manage the potential risks associated with its area of responsibility, such as security, networking, facilities, support, or training.

Prioritize your risks. Risks can vary in severity and likelihood. Determine which risks pose the greatest threat to your organization. Address your primary risk factors first.

Meet with those who support line-of-business and existing applications.
Older and line-of-business applications present special risks. Meet early with those who have a broad knowledge of these applications. If a third party is responsible for any of these applications, involve them in the process as early as possible.

Avoid making a viability judgment based solely on the number of risks uncovered.
A project with 20 identified risks is not necessarily more stable than a project with 40 identified risks. A risk assessment that identifies a higher number of risks could simply be more thorough than one with fewer risks. Use this document to pinpoint the risks that could derail a project as well as those that have lesser impact.

Foster an environment where people who identify risks are not judged negatively.
Workers who do the hands-on tasks in an organization often recognize problems before their supervisors do. If they are reluctant to communicate bad news, your risk assessment could be compromised. Consider implementing a reward program for those who identify risks as well as for those who help provide resolutions for those risks.

Risk Assessment Matrix

To fully identify potential risks, develop a solid understanding of the interdependencies between the various elements of the deployment. A risk matrix can help you identify and link these elements.

Table 3.4 contains a sample risk assessment matrix that lists issues, such as probability that the risk will occur, the degree of impact any particular risk might have on your project, and the strategy that is necessary to mitigate the risk.

Table 3.4   Sample Risk Assessment Matrix

Risk	Probability	Impact	Owner	Date resolved	Mitigation strategy
A merger is under consideration.	Medium	High	Deployment Team Manager	*mm/dd/yy*	Create a strategy for a rapid integration with team counterparts in other organizations.
Not all users will have a computer configured to minimum hardware requirements before Windows 2000 is deployed.	Medium	Medium	Program Management, Help Desk, and Logistics teams	*mm/dd/yy*	Make a decision whether to upgrade hardware at the time of installation, or to wait for a hardware upgrade throughout the organization.

Create the matrix early in your planning phase and update it at regularly-scheduled intervals, or when there is a change in schedule, specification, management, team, scope, or rollout strategy.

Risk-Driven Schedule

Few elements of a deployment can do more to create risks than a poorly conceived schedule. For example, if your organization institutes a fourth-quarter freeze on deployments, squeezing in too many key steps at the last minute might diminish the quality of your testing and rollout. If you schedule the simplest components of your deployment first and leave the most complex and riskiest components to the end, you reduce the amount of time available to resolve more complex problems.

A schedule that considers risk assessment can minimize the likelihood of serious problems. The following guidelines can help you create a risk-driven schedule:

Base the schedule on task-level estimates.   Begin with task-level estimates and work up through team schedules, then integrate the schedules of multiple teams. Basing your schedule on bottom-up, task-level estimates forces you to identify and resolve the issues that can delay or even derail a project.

Develop high-risk components first.   Address the high-risk elements of your deployment first. The consequences of delays, design changes, or other problems have less impact on the rest of the deployment when they are addressed early.

Establish major and interim milestones.   Milestones are checkpoints against progress that are verified by testing. Frequent interim milestones let you reevaluate progress against new information early in the process and reduce the risk of missing the major milestones.

Allocate time for unforeseen circumstances. Few major deployments are completed without being affected by events that disrupt schedules, like the illness of key personnel, a hardware back-order, or problems with funding. Cushion your schedule with extra time for those unforeseen circumstances.

Schedule time for project management. It takes time to define the vision, secure funding, and do all the other project management tasks. Schedule the appropriate amount of time to manage the project.

Use a project scheduling tool. Project scheduling tools allow you to link tasks with dependencies and interdependencies, and to identify task owners and task status quickly. They can also be useful in tracking the progress of the different teams and their tasks to ensure your project stays on schedule.

Keep the schedule up-to-date. Update the schedule whenever business or deployment circumstances change, new activities are added, and milestones are reached.

Keep project leads informed when changes to the schedule are needed.
Defining objectives lets people know when to stop deployment. For example, if you rolled out Windows 2000 on ten computers and found that you had a compromised third-party service, you might want to resolve the issue before continuing.

Windows 2000 Deployment

The final stage in deployment planning is to define how to create a smooth transition from pilot to production. Your goal is to deploy Windows 2000 successfully and efficiently, with minimum interruption to your users, the network, and the core business functions of the organization.

Deploying Windows 2000 to the production environment shares many characteristics with deploying Windows 2000 in the pilot phase. Some recommended steps to ensure success include:

Phase your deployment efforts. Incremental deployment allows you to reduce risk and minimize disruption.

Create a deployment backup plan. A reliable and tested backup plan will enable you to recover quickly and easily if you encounter any problems during the deployment.

Create a backup/recovery plan. Because a computer or site disaster can overcome even the best data protection strategies, you need to have a system disaster recovery plan. For more information about creating disaster recovery plans, see "Determining Windows 2000 Storage Management Strategies" in this book.

Provide proper training. Make sure that your support and administrative teams are fully trained and prepared for the deployment.

Keep end-users informed. Inform and educate end-users about Windows 2000 before you deploy it to their computers. Some organizations require end-user training before any new technology can be deployed. If this is a strategy you are considering, allow for additional resources and costs.

Keep teams informed. Make sure the teams are aware of deployment plans as a whole, the scope of their responsibility and involvement, and any changes to the plan or schedule.

Schedule major deployment activities for off-hours. You can minimize the impact to your users and network with thoughtful scheduling of major Windows 2000 activities. For example, wait to deploy Windows 2000 to a specific group until after that group has completed a deadline or other major project.

Deployment Planning Task List

Table 3.5 summarizes the tasks you need to perform when planning your Windows 2000 deployment.

Table 3.5   Deployment Planning Task List

Task	Location in chapter
Define the project scope and both long-term and short-term objectives.	Project Scope and Objectives
Map Windows 2000 features to your project objectives.	Project Scope and Objectives
Document your current computing environment.	Current Computing Environment
Conduct a gap analysis.	Conducting a Gap Analysis
Define personnel roles and the amount of time necessary to accomplish tasks.	Personnel Requirements
Set standards for hardware, software, and network configurations.	Establishing Standards and Guidelines
Create your administrative documents.	Administrative Documents
Create your deployment documents.	Deployment Documents
Develop your deployment design.	Deployment Design
Create your communications strategy.	Communications Strategy
Evaluate capacity requirements.	Capacity Planning
Identify risks.	Risk Assessment
Create and maintain a schedule.	Risk-Driven Schedule
Establish an education and training plan.	Education and Training Plan
Develop a test plan.	Testing and Piloting Windows 2000
Plan a pilot project.	Testing and Piloting Windows 2000
Plan for a smooth transition to Windows 2000.	Windows 2000 Deployment

C H A P T E R   4

Building a Windows 2000 Test Lab

Before you deploy Microsoft® Windows® 2000, even in a pilot, be sure to test your proposed design in an environment that simulates and protects your production environment. You can verify your design by devising and conducting tests that reflect conditions in your target environment.

This chapter provides the test manager, as well as your deployment project teams, with general considerations for designing and running a test lab that meets the particular needs of your organization. Also, chapters throughout this book address testing issues with regard to particular Windows 2000 features.

In This Chapter

Chapter Goals

This chapter will help you develop the following planning documents:

- Lab description
- Lab diagram
- Escalation plan
- Test plan
- Test cases

Related Information in the Resource Kit

- For more information about planning for application testing, see "Testing Applications for Compatibility with Windows 2000" in this book.
- For more information about planning a pilot in your production environment, see "Conducting Your Windows 2000 Pilot" in this book.

Getting Started with Your Test Environment

A key factor in the success of your Windows 2000 project is thorough testing based on realistic scenarios. Realistic scenarios require a test environment that simulates your production environment as much as possible. In this test environment, members of the planning teams can verify their assumptions, uncover deployment problems, and optimize the deployment design, as well as improve their understanding of the technology. Such activities reduce the risk of errors and minimize downtime in the production environment during and after deployment.

Creating a Test Environment

A test environment encompasses all the locations that support testing without risk to your corporate network. Many large organizations distribute their test environments across numerous physical, or even geographical, locations for testing in various technical, business, or political contexts. The following factors influence the decisions you make about your test environment:

- Your testing methodology
- Features and components you will test
- Personnel who will perform the testing

A test environment might include one or more labs, and a lab might include one or more locations. The term lab is used in this chapter to refer to a network that is designed for testing and is isolated from the corporate network.

For your Windows 2000 project, you might decide to have several independent labs for different testing purposes. For example, you could have one lab for network infrastructure and server testing and another lab for client computer and application testing. Conversely, a single lab might consist of multiple locations. For example, you could have a network infrastructure lab with multiple locations connected by a wide area network (WAN) for testing the effects of various link speeds.

If you are deploying Microsoft® Windows® 2000 Server and Microsoft® Windows® 2000 Professional at the same time, many factors influence your decision about whether the two projects should have separate labs or a shared one. Some of these factors are:

- Complexity of your deployment (such as variability in your production environment and the new features you plan to implement).
- Size, location, and structure of your project teams.
- Size of your budget.
- Availability of physical space.

- Location of testers.
- Use of the labs after deployment.

The considerations in this chapter apply to labs you design for testing either Windows 2000 Server or Windows 2000 Professional.

Using the Lab for Risk Management

A well-designed test lab provides a controlled environment for the range of testing throughout the project life cycle —from experimenting with the technology, to comparing design solutions, to fine-tuning the rollout process. A good lab need not be a large resource or capital funding investment; it can range from a few pieces of hardware in a small room to a full-scale network in a data center environment.

The test lab is an investment that can pay for itself many times over in reduced support and redeployment costs that arise from poorly tested solutions. It is an important part of the risk management plan for your Windows 2000 project. You can identify risks in the lab when tests uncover problems such as:

- Hardware or software incompatibilities
- Design flaws
- Performance issues
- Interoperability difficulties
- Limited knowledge of new technologies
- Operational or deployment inefficiencies

When testing uncovers problems such as these, the lab can provide the means for developing and validating alternative solutions. The lab is also the place to:

- Design and validate back-out plans, thus reducing risk to the business during pilot and production rollouts.
- Learn how to optimize the deployment process, thus reducing the time and cost spent on deployment activities.
- Develop efficient administrative procedures, thus reducing the time and personnel required for ongoing maintenance after deployment.
- Verify your progress against the project plan and refine your project schedule.

Lab Development Process

Figure 4.1 is a flowchart illustrating the phases for preparing the lab for testing. In the strategy phase, you establish the goals and general approach for the lab. The decisions you make in this phase influence decisions in the design phase.

In the design phase, you plan and document the logical and physical structure of the lab. The decisions you make in the design phase determine what you create in the build phase.

In the build phase, you set up the lab and test the network components before Windows 2000 testing begins. The design and build phases are iterative: as knowledge increases, requirements evolve, and the focus of testing changes, you need to redesign and rebuild components of the lab. You also need to rebuild components if accumulated changes to hardware, software, or testing methodology start to affect the test results.

Start

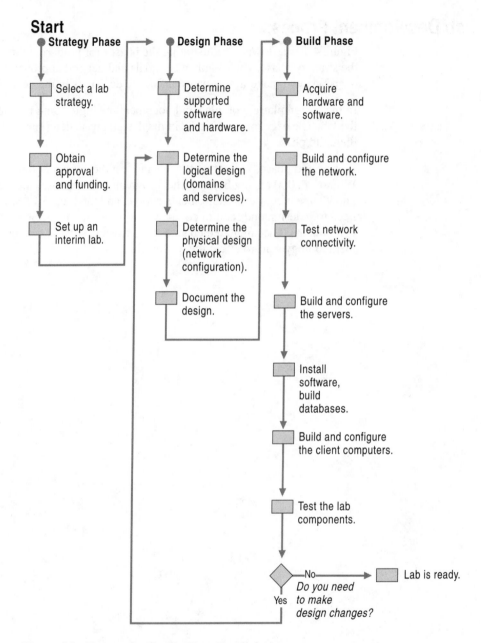

Figure 4.1   Process for Setting Up a Test Lab

Testing Process

Figure 4.2 is a flowchart illustrating the phases for planning and conducting tests in the lab.

The primary activities are:

- Creating a test plan that describes scope, objectives, and methodology.
- Designing test cases that describe how to conduct tests.
- Conducting tests and evaluating results.
- Documenting test results.
- Escalating problems to the proper people for resolution.

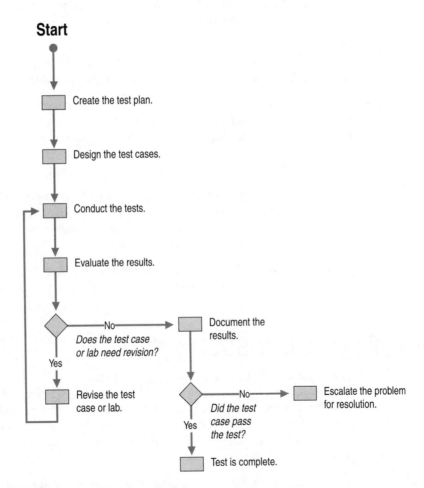

Figure 4.2   Process for Planning and Conducting Tests

Setting Up a Preliminary Lab

If you do not already have a lab, it is important to start working on one as early as possible in your Windows 2000 deployment project. You need the lab early in the planning phase for learning about the product, proving concepts, testing various scenarios against your business model, and validating solutions. Very early in the project you can select the location, start assessing hardware requirements, reconfigure existing lab equipment, and perhaps start purchasing or recycling hardware for the lab.

Your early planning pays off at test time when you have provided adequate space for the necessary equipment and the proper configurations for accurate tests. As you make decisions regarding the hardware, software, and personnel requirements for testing, document them in your test plan. For more information about the test plan, see "Testing" later in this chapter.

If you plan to build a permanent lab, you might need to obtain management approval and funding that is independent of your Windows 2000 deployment project. If so, start the approval process as early as possible.

Early in the planning process your lab can help you establish your basic namespace design and high-level deployment plan, which you can then use as a baseline for further testing and development. When you use the lab as a baseline configuration and then add functionality in stages, you can avoid the problems associated with designs that are developed independently of each other.

To get started on exploratory testing, you can build an interim lab with two or three servers and client computers, use an existing lab, or set up a server/client computer configuration in an office. Then, as you decide on the high-level design, start putting the pieces together for your formal lab.

Although the lab evolves throughout the project to reflect changes in testing focus, make sure it is fully equipped and stable prior to prepilot integration testing.

Determining the Lab Strategy

You might already have a lab that you plan to use for Windows 2000 testing, or maybe you hope to build a new lab for the project. Regardless of your current situation, it is valuable to think through your goals for the lab and its long-term purpose. You might decide that now is the time to upgrade a lab created for another purpose so that you can use it in the future for change management in your Windows 2000 environment.

If you already have a permanent lab that you plan to use for testing your Windows 2000 design, you might want to go directly to "Designing the Lab" later in this chapter.

Considering Return on Investment

If you decide to create a new lab for Windows 2000 deployment testing, you might need to justify the investment to your project sponsors. To help you do this, take a broad view of all the associated costs. The testing performed in the lab leads to cleaner implementations and reduced support costs. By using the lab to develop operational efficiencies, such as automated administrative tools and remote procedures, you can reduce your organization's total cost of ownership. When viewed over time, therefore, the costs of building and maintaining the lab are likely to be dramatically lower than the costs of fixing problems in production, redeploying poorly thought out or poorly tested solutions, or managing the production environment with resource-intensive processes.

Economy of scale is often possible in organizations that build separate labs for different projects. By consolidating labs and formalizing the use and maintenance of the new lab, you can let several projects share in the reduced cost of a single lab. If you decide to share a lab, however, try to choose projects that have compatible scheduling and equipment requirements It is simpler and less expensive to add a few new components to upgrade the lab for a new project than to start from scratch each time.

The more multipurpose you make the lab, the easier it is to justify the capital cost of the space, equipment, and support needed to build and run it. The lab can serve purposes ranging from early hands-on training to post-implementation problem resolution. You might consider the lab as your initial investment in training. You can even use it for educational purposes such as demonstrating functionality or deployment processes to management or other groups.

Using the Lab During the Project Life Cycle

To help you justify the cost of the lab, consider the many ways you can use it throughout the project. This section provides examples of ways you might use your lab.

Planning

During early planning, project team members use the lab for hands-on experience: increasing their understanding of the technology, testing their hypotheses, and uncovering implementation issues and support requirements. This is also a good time to look for ways to optimize existing operational processes, such as identifying tasks that can be automated or performed remotely.

As designing progresses, team members use the lab to try out new technologies, models, and processes while they resolve business requirements. Such prototyping and modeling leads to business decisions about how you will implement Windows 2000 features and functions.

Developing

During development, the lab provides a controlled environment for testing and evaluating a variety of issues, such as the following:

- Windows 2000 features
- Network infrastructure compatibility
- Interoperability with other network operating systems
- Hardware compatibility
- Application compatibility
- Performance and capacity planning
- Installation and configuration documentation
- Administrative procedures and documentation
- Production rollout (processes, scripts, and files; back-out plans)
- Baseline traffic patterns (traffic volumes without user activity)
- Tools (Windows 2000, third-party, or custom)
- Operational efficiencies

Deploying

During the pilot deployment, the lab provides operational teams, such as the help desk and operations staff, with a place to start planning the ongoing support structure. You can also use the lab during the pilot and production deployment to isolate, reproduce, analyze, and correct problems with the deployment process.

Post-deployment

After deployment, the support team can use the lab to reproduce and resolve problems found in the production environment. The lab also provides a secure location for testing changes, such as service packs, patches, new applications, or new desktop configurations, as part of the change management process.

Figure 4.3 illustrates a variety of uses for the lab and the project phase in which some activities might occur. The time frames are estimations and do not represent an actual deployment.

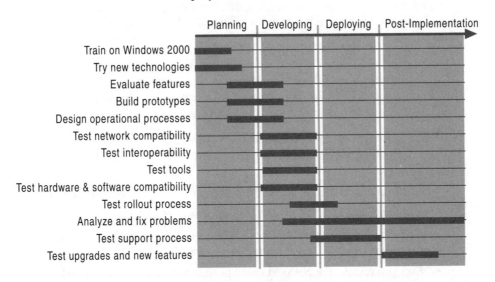

Figure 4.3   Role of the Lab in the Project Life Cycle

The lab is not the only place where testing occurs. Project team members can also test functionality on their individual test computers. However, the test lab is the place to verify that components and features work together in an integrated environment that simulates your target production environment. The simulated environment should reflect both the phase-in period, when you have a mix of functionality, and the end of the project, when you have completely implemented the new functionality.

Evaluating Lab Models

Many organizations build an ad hoc lab each time they need test facilities for a new project. Other organizations build a permanent lab that is scalable for various projects and use it for change management. Both ad hoc labs and change management labs have their advantages and disadvantages.

Ad Hoc Labs

Ad hoc labs are set up for a specific project. When the project is over, the equipment is redeployed for a different use. For example, the equipment might be used in the production environment, become part of inventory, or be returned to the vendor.

The short-term costs of an ad hoc lab might be less than a permanent lab because all the equipment is redeployed for other uses. This view of cost is shortsighted, however, because a new lab must be built for every project that requires one. Ad hoc labs can lead to problems such as the following:

- When a new lab is required for each new project, time becomes a critical factor. Because teams need the lab early in a project, issues such as the following arise:
  - Can you obtain the appropriate hardware and software licenses in time?
  - Will hardware or software substitutions lead to inadequate testing?
  - Can you locate the vendors, models, and versions needed to adequately test the production mix of hardware and software?
  - Can you reserve the physical space needed for building the network configuration and performing the tests?
  - Will the time spent building and debugging the lab reduce the testing time, possibly resulting in incomplete testing?
- When many teams are searching for hardware and software licenses, it becomes difficult to track who is using what and who authorizes purchases. The resulting lack of accountability can lead to excess expenditures and increased costs.

Change Management Labs

The problems mentioned in the preceding section present compelling reasons for building a permanent, formalized lab. After Windows 2000 is implemented, you can use a permanent lab to test changes to your environment, such as:

- Network upgrades
- Service packs and software patches
- Business application compatibility
- Desktop configurations
- New hardware platforms
- Administrative and support processes
- Client computer management tools

A fully equipped, permanent lab that is used for change management has the following advantages:

Saves costs in the long run.

When viewed across projects, the cost of a permanent lab is likely to be more reasonable than ad hoc labs for which purchases are not tracked or financial accountability is diluted.

Reduces risk to your business.

Labs reduce risk to your production environment because solid testing leads to cleaner implementations. For example, it is tempting to forgo comprehensive testing of an apparently insignificant change if a test lab is not readily available. But even a minor change can bring a business process to a halt. Having a permanent lab for change management makes it easier to test even the simplest change. The more the lab reflects the production environment, the more valid the tests can be.

Saves time for the project.

Setup and debugging time are minimized because upgrades to an existing lab are faster than assembling a new lab each time. The time saving is critical if you plan to use lab equipment for ongoing developmental prototyping. If you use the lab for development as well as for testing, you have less time available to assemble it.

Helps equip the lab appropriately.

You might find it easier to justify the purchase of equipment you need for specific testing requirements if you plan to have a change management lab. With ad hoc labs, the equipment is likely to be reallocated from another use or purchased to meet the specifications of its future use and, therefore, might not meet your testing requirements.

You are also more likely to maintain the proper mix of equipment to accurately reflect your production environment. As time passes, you can retain the original equipment and acquire new equipment to reflect the constantly changing, diverse production environment. Maintaining the proper mix of equipment in the lab provides for thorough regression testing during the change management process.

Helps establish consistent methodologies.

When you have a permanent lab, you can assign dedicated personnel to support it. With a permanent lab and continuity in lab management, you can establish consistent testing processes and techniques which produce consistent results that can be compared over time.

Selecting a Lab Model

Many factors contribute to your decision about the type of lab you choose: ad hoc or change management. The following factors can influence your decision:

- Budget
- Time and staff available for building the lab
- Existing labs
- Physical space or environmental limitations
- Corporate culture
- Project or corporate goals

The first step in making this decision is to assess your long-term testing and risk management goals. Then, consider the advantages and disadvantages of each model in relation to your goals.

You might determine that one model fits your goals best, but circumstances seem to dictate another approach. For example, you might see advantages to having a long-term lab that you can use for testing software patches and upgrades, but your organization does not seem to have the budget to build and maintain a permanent lab. Although you need to weigh the possible outcomes of the opposing solutions, you might come up with creative ways to support your ideal solution. Ask yourself questions such as the following:

- How will the decision impact test quality?
- How will the decision impact team training and design support?
- Will the lab also benefit other existing projects?
- Can other projects combine efforts and budgets to share a lab?
- Can you build the lab in stages, starting with the most essential components and then adding to it as the budget allows?
- Will hardware vendors agree to a special arrangement?

  For example, can the vendors provide equipment on loan before it is purchased, or will they give you the equipment in return for using your organization's name for marketing purposes?

Selecting a Lab Location

Your decisions about the lab model and the lab location are likely to be interrelated. The location for a permanent lab to be used by a wide variety of groups requires more consideration than a short-term lab to be used by a few groups. Room for future growth, for example, is an important issue if you plan to use the lab long-term. To help you make these decisions, consider the following questions:

- What lab facilities already exist? How adequate are they? How easily can you modify them to fit test requirements?
- Can you consolidate existing labs?
- What is the scale and complexity of the implementation?
- How do you want to allocate your lab budget? Consider the following:
  - Facility and workspace expenses (space, heating, ventilation, air conditioning, power, cabling, patch panels, server racks, and workbenches).
  - Hardware and software.
  - Support and other lab personnel.
- Does the lab need to connect to the production network or to other labs? If it needs to connect to the production network, how will you regulate the connection and configure routers to protect the production network?

For more information about connecting the lab to the production network, see "Simulating the Proposed Server Environment" later in this chapter.

Additional issues to consider when selecting lab locations are:

Upgrading or Building New

If you decide to use an existing lab, you might be able to do minor upgrades to accommodate Windows 2000 testing. For example, you might want to upgrade the servers to the same amount of memory and hard disk capacity, and to the same processor type and speed as the servers you plan to deploy.

Accessibility

The lab should be accessible to all of the groups using it. If you implement a program in which people from outside the project team come to test their own applications, the lab should have facilities, such as parking, to accommodate visitors.

Security

Ensure that you can physically secure the lab to protect your equipment from unauthorized use.

Space

Whether you build a new lab or upgrade an existing one, space is a major consideration. Windows 2000 in itself does not require sophisticated, expensive equipment to get up and running. Because it is important to simulate the production environment as closely as possible, the complexity of that environment influences the complexity of the lab.

Factors in your current and proposed production environment that can determine the complexity, and therefore the space requirements, of your lab include the following:

- Number and combination of functions and features you plan to implement.

  Do you plan to implement a domain that spans multiple sites? Do you plan to implement a virtual private network (VPN)?

- Amount of variability in your production environment.

  Do you have—and plan to deploy—standard equipment, applications, and configurations in your production environment? Or will you use many vendors, models, versions, and configurations?

- Level of complexity in your network configuration.

  Do you have more than one type of topology in your production network? Do you plan to have interfaces between Windows 2000 Server and mainframe, Macintosh, or UNIX systems?

In addition to factors in your production environment, some test situations can also affect the complexity of your lab. For example, you might want additional servers so that you can isolate certain types of testing, as described later in this chapter.

Space requirements are also influenced by the number of people you think will participate in testing. Consider how many users you need to accommodate at one time.

Environmental Conditions

The lab location should support suitable environmental conditions, such as temperature, humidity, and cleanliness. These requirements are similar to those of your data center. The lab location should also support your power, cabling, and network connectivity requirements.

Number of Locations

In certain cases, you might want your lab to have multiple interconnected locations so that you can test the effect of geographically separated network segments. For example, if you plan to implement Microsoft® Active Directory™ directory service with multiple Active Directory sites, you might want to test replication over a similar WAN or Internet connection. For more information about Active Directory sites and replication, see "Designing the Active Directory Structure" in this book.

In other cases, you might want to have multiple independent labs for different uses. You might want a separate lab for application testing or perhaps separate labs for Windows 2000 Server and Windows 2000 Professional testing.

Testing in a Distributed Lab Environment

A lab environment can be distributed across numerous physical, or even geographical, locations. The case studies presented here describe how two organizations decided to use labs in this way.

Case Study 1: Functional Lab Sites

A large high-technology hardware manufacturer is organized along functional lines. Its regional offices are located at various geographical sites, selected for proximity to the suppliers and vendors who support each region's particular function. This manufacturer developed a lab that spans three of its major United States sites, ranging across Southwestern and Western states. Each lab location is designed to test the functions and configurations used for that site's business. Each one is a permanent lab that is used for change management of the production environment.

Eventually the organization plans to expand the lab to encompass remote international locations, such as cities in the Far East, Middle East, Eastern Europe, and the British Isles. The organization will use these remote sites to design and test solutions for the challenges of a global enterprise, such as:

- Connectivity in controlled countries
- Slow links
- Intermittent links
- Multiple languages
- Multiple time zones
- International currencies
- Variations in computer and networking hardware

Case Study 2: Contingency Lab Sites

Another organization finds it important to be prepared in case of a disaster. This organization wants its geographically separated sites to be ready to function in the role of a centralized Information Technology (IT) department, if required. In this organization, the lab is a permanent change management lab that is also used for disaster-recovery testing.

In the event of a disaster, production machines at the selected location would be used to perform the IT department functions. To be in a state of readiness, the organization performs testing in the lab to ensure that all the needed hardware and software components are available and can function properly at the alternate location. These tests include the following:

- Loading applications and databases
- Setting configurations
- Running applications

Designing the Lab

Before you design the lab, you need to have a high-level deployment plan. You might need to know, for example, the proposed namespace design. You also need to know the domain architecture and how you will configure servers for services such as Domain Name System (DNS), Dynamic Host Configuration Protocol (DHCP), and Windows Internet Name Service (WINS). To ensure that the lab design reflects testing requirements, the project subteams should provide information about the hardware, software, and configurations they need.

If you decide to build a permanent lab that you can use for change management after Windows 2000 is deployed, the design should be flexible enough, both in space and layout, to accommodate the future.

The more planning that goes into designing the lab, the more the tests can accurately reflect the actual implementation.

Prerequisites for Designing the Lab

Because the lab should simulate the environment where you will deploy Windows 2000, you need information about your current and proposed environments before you can design the lab. Microsoft® Systems Management Server (SMS) can help you collect information about your current system. For more information about using SMS to inventory your system, see "Using Systems Management Server To Analyze Your Network Infrastructure" in this book. The information about the proposed environment should be available in the planning documents produced by the project team. In addition to a high-level understanding of Windows 2000 features and functionality, you need the following information:

- The current network design (logical and physical).
- The proposed Windows 2000 design.
- A list of features to evaluate and explore.
- An inventory of existing hardware (servers, client computers, and portable computers).
- A list of hardware proposed for Windows 2000.

  This list might evolve during testing, but you need an initial list to equip the lab.
- A list of administrative tools (Windows 2000, third party, and custom built).
- A list of the upgrades, such as service packs, drivers, and basic input/output system (BIOS), that you need to install to be ready for Windows 2000.

Designing for Test Scenarios

Strive to design your lab for flexibility. In addition, at a minimum, try to meet the following two criteria:

- Simulate the proposed environment—design for what you will test.
- Accommodate the testing process—design for how you will test.

Although you might decide to use one lab for both server and client computer testing, this section presents lab design considerations for each separately.

Simulating the Proposed Server Environment

Plan to test as much of the proposed logical and physical production environment as possible, including computer hardware, network topology, WAN connections, domain architecture, services, databases, business applications, administrative tools, security model, application deployment methodology, and network server storage methods.

This section presents some considerations for designing a lab to test Windows 2000 Server. The issues presented here might not apply to all Windows 2000 Server implementations. Focus on the considerations that apply to your design.

Server Hardware and Drivers

Use the same type of hardware components and drivers that you use, or plan to use, on servers in the production environment. Be sure to obtain an updated BIOS that is compatible with Windows 2000.

Services and Configurations

Use the same services and configurations that you will use in the actual deployment. For example, duplicate the DNS, DHCP, and WINS configurations. If you are not planning on using the DNS and DHCP services built into Windows 2000, include the third-party services you plan to use.

User Accounts

If you are migrating from Microsoft® Windows NT® 4.0, set up your domain controllers as replicas of your production domain controllers, using copies of the production user accounts. You can use the ClonePrincipal tool to copy production users to your test domain. For more information about strategies for migrating user accounts and the tools to use, see "Determining Domain Migration Strategies" in this book. Coordinate with your IT security division whenever you copy production data to lab databases.

Domain Structure

If you are implementing Active Directory, simulate the domain hierarchy. For example, include a forest with multiple trees, a tree with parent and child domains, and transitive and one-way trust relationships, as appropriate. Reflect your IT centralized or decentralized administration in the organizational unit. Include Active Directory sites as appropriate.

Server Strategy

Include file and print servers, application servers, Web servers, database servers, and other utility servers that are, or will be, in your production environment. If you plan to use SMS to deploy Windows 2000 Server, include it in the lab.

Mixed Environments

To accommodate both the mixed environment during a phased rollout and the Windows 2000 environment after the completion of the rollout, plan for some domains of the following types:

- Native mode
- Mixed mode
- Current production operating system

By simulating the interim state, you can determine functional problems that might occur during the phased implementation. The servers with operating systems other than Windows 2000 Server should mirror the services in the current production environment.

Client Computer Configuration

Use the same mix of client computers as in your production environment. If you plan to deploy Windows 2000 Server first and Windows 2000 Professional later, include the client computer operating system that you will use until Windows 2000 Professional is deployed.

If you plan to deploy Windows 2000 Professional first, test for how the extended server functionality will be introduced into your environment as the infrastructure is deployed.

If you plan to have a phased rollout, include the same mix that will occur during rollout. For example, have client computers with Microsoft® Windows® 95 and client computers with Windows 2000 Professional.

Network Topology and Protocols

Mirror the network topology and protocols you use in your production environment as closely as possible. For example, if your production network uses both Ethernet and Token Ring, the lab should include both.

WAN Connections

If you have a WAN, the lab should have routers to test network latency. If you have the facilities and budget, you might want to set up a secondary lab at a remote location to test network latency across the WAN link. For example, you should test domain controller and Global Catalog replication across the link. If you have a multinational organization, it is recommended that the secondary lab be in a different region of the world to test real-world latency problems.

If you do not have a secondary lab location where you can test the WAN link, you can cable two routers together in the same lab and use a link simulator to test the link.

Remote Connectivity

Provide the same types of remote connectivity, such as Routing and Remote Access Service and VPN, to allow you to test Point-to-Point Tunneling Protocol (PPTP), Internet Protocol Security (IPSec), Layer 2 Tunneling Protocol (L2TP), and Demand Dial Routing.

Peripherals

Include a representative sample of the types of peripherals used in your production environment. For example, include the same types of printers and scanners, along with their associated drivers.

Interoperability

If you plan to implement Windows 2000 Server so that it operates with networks or computers using another operating system, mimic the interoperability infrastructure. For example, include connections to mainframe hosts, UNIX systems, or other network operating systems. To keep your lab configuration and test suite manageable, decide which interoperability scenarios are most important to your organization and focus on those.

Administrative Tools

Include the tools (Windows 2000, third party, or custom built) that you currently use or plan to use for server-based administrative tasks. You need to test the tools for compatibility and effectiveness in the new environment.

Fault Tolerance Techniques

Test any fault tolerance techniques you plan to use in your production environment. For example, if you plan to use clustering, include a clustered server in the lab.

Terminal Services

If you plan to implement Terminal Services, install the appropriate mix of applications on the server. You need to understand the impact of running applications in a multi-user environment. You might need to modify the default operating environment for some applications to obtain the desired functionality. For more information about Terminal Services, see "Deploying Terminal Services" in this book.

Note If you are concerned that some of your critical applications might not be compatible with Windows 2000 Professional, consider installing Terminal Services. You can install Terminal Services on a Windows NT 4.0 server and set up your Windows 2000 client computers to access the applications with problems from that server. Think of this approach only as a contingency plan to avoid last minute schedule slips.

Production Network Connectivity

You should isolate the test lab from your corporate network. If you need to provide a connection from the lab to the corporate network, plan for ways to regulate and control the connection and devise a way to quickly terminate the connection.

Design router configurations to protect the production network. For example, consider using a multihomed router with two network adapters to connect the lab to the production network for specific, controlled uses. Configure the router so that the production network can access the test network, but the test network cannot access the production network. This approach protects the production environment from anything going on in the lab but allows a user in production to access resources in the lab. For example, you could use this approach to test logon scripts on a lab server with a small number of users before moving the scripts to a pilot in the production environment.

Simulating the Proposed Client Computer Environment

Design the client computer lab so that you can test the same functions and features you use in your production environment. Include the same types of hardware, applications, and network configurations. This section covers some considerations for designing a lab to test Windows 2000 Professional. The issues presented here might not apply to all Windows 2000 Professional implementations. Focus on the considerations that apply to your design.

Client Computer Hardware

Include at least one client computer for each vendor and model that is to run Windows 2000 in your production environment. If your organization uses laptops, docking stations, or port replicators, be sure to include those vendors and models as well. Be sure to obtain an updated BIOS that is compatible with Windows 2000.

It is recommended that you develop a standard hardware configuration for Windows 2000 Professional as part of your deployment project. Your lab testing can help you define and refine a standard configuration. As you define hardware configurations, verify that the components are compatible with Windows 2000. For example, you might need to verify compatibility for the following components:

- Universal serial bus (USB) adapters
- Compact disc (CD) and digital video disc (DVD) drives
- Sound adapters
- Network adapters
- Video adapters

- Small computer system interface (SCSI) adapters
- Mass storage controllers
- Removable storage devices
- Pointing devices (mice, trackballs, tablets)
- Keyboards

To determine compatibility, look up the components on the Microsoft Hardware Compatibility List (HCL), which you can find at http://www.microsoft.com by searching with the keyword "HCL." The HCL includes all the hardware that Microsoft supports. If your hardware is not on the list, contact the vendor to find out if there is a driver. If your components use 16-bit drivers, you need to obtain a 32-bit driver.

You can also use Windows 2000 Professional Setup to check for hardware compatibility. Run Setup in check-upgrade-only mode to obtain log files that indicate hardware and software incompatibilities and device drivers that need to be updated. The command line format for check-upgrade-only mode is:

```
winnt32 /checkupgradeonly
```

On computers running Windows 9*x*, the log file, called Upgrade.txt, is located in the Windows installation folder. On systems running Windows NT, the log file is called Winnt32.log and is located in the installation folder.

If updated device drivers for your devices are not included with Windows 2000, contact the vendor to obtain an updated driver.

Once you decide on the standard hardware configuration, inventory the computers in your production environment to determine which ones need to be upgraded before you deploy Windows 2000. For information about how to use SMS to perform the inventory, see "Using Systems Management Server To Analyze Your Network Infrastructure" in this book.

For more information about developing client computer standards, see "Defining Client Administration and Configuration Standards" in this book.

Network Connectivity

Provide connectivity to the same types of networks that you use in the production environment, such as a local area network (LAN), a WAN, or the Internet.

If you plan to use Routing and Remote Access or a proxy network service in the production environment, include these types of connections in the lab.

Server-Based Services

Configure servers for the services used in the production environment. For example, include services such as:

- DNS, WINS, and DHCP
- Directory services (such as X.500 and NetWare)
- File sharing
- Network printing
- Server-based line-of-business applications, both centralized and decentralized
- IntelliMirror

Remember to provide for administrative services such as:

- Remote operating system installation
- Server-based application deployment
- Tools for managing client computers (SMS, for example)

Domain Authentication

If your organization uses, or plans to use, domain authentication, simulate your authentication configuration in the lab. If you are migrating from Windows NT 4.0 to Windows 2000 Server, plan for authentication in the mixed environment that will occur during the phased rollout.

Network Management Services

Include network services used in your environment, such as Simple Network Management Protocol (SNMP).

Network Protocols

Use the protocols you plan to use in the production environment. Verify the protocols you use on client computers before connecting them to the production network.

Applications

You need licenses for and access to the software for all applications, stand-alone or server-based, that are to be supported on Windows 2000 Professional client computers. For more information about testing applications in a lab, see "Testing Applications for Compatibility with Windows 2000" in this book.

Peripherals

Include a representative sample of the types of peripherals, such as printers and scanners, used in the production environment.

Server Platform Interoperability

Simulate the server platforms to be accessed by Windows 2000 Professional client computers. If you have a separate server lab, consider connecting the client computer lab to it instead of installing servers in the client computer lab. You might need to establish connectivity to the following systems:

- Windows 2000 Server
- Windows NT
- Mainframes supporting 3270 emulation
- UNIX
- Other network operating systems

If you plan to deploy Windows 2000 Professional at the same time as Windows 2000 Server, include any type of server that a client computer can access during the deployment period, unless these tests are to be performed by the Windows 2000 Server team.

Desktop Configurations

As part of your Windows 2000 Professional project, your organization might decide to evaluate standard client configurations and Group Policy for managing them. Lab tests can provide information for recommending specific configurations and Group Policy objects to management. If you decide to perform this type of evaluative testing, include side-by-side comparisons of different configurations and Group Policy settings.

Plan to have enough computers of the same make and model to allow for the side-by-side evaluations. Evaluate client configurations based on performance, ease of use, stability, hardware and software compatibility, functionality, and security model. Evaluate Group Policy objects by verifying that they produce the desired result, particularly when more than one applies to a configuration, and that the resulting logon time is acceptable.

Performance

Use the lab to start evaluating the impact on your network traffic by testing for changes in baseline traffic patterns without user activity. For more information about performance concepts and monitoring tools, see "Overview of Performance Monitoring" in the *Microsoft® Windows® 2000 Server Resource Kit Server Operations Guide*.

Production Network Connectivity

Your client computer lab, like the server lab, needs to be isolated from the corporate network. If you need to provide a connection from the lab to the corporate network, plan how you will use routers to separate the two networks.

Accommodating Test Processes

Because some tests alter the lab environment, they can inadvertently influence other tests. Care must be taken to isolate, coordinate, and manage these types of tests. For example, server upgrade tests change the state of the servers. Address scenarios such as these in the lab domain design. Other scenarios might need to be addressed in the lab management procedures. For example, schema changes affect the entire forest, so schedule this type of test and communicate it to other lab users.

Remember that the lab needs to change frequently to reflect the current focus of testing. Make backups of baseline configurations so testers can quickly restore a computer to its prior state. Be sure to test the restore process. Document the backup files and store them in a safe, accessible place.

Designing Domains for Testing

Design the lab domain structure to provide consistent setup and configuration so that testers can rely on a known-state infrastructure. For example, allocate a single domain for migration and mixed-mode testing. If you do this, the domain should always be in the mixed-mode state except for scheduled periods when it is rolled back to the prior state to test the migration process. In this way, lab users always know what to expect.

To summarize, design the lab domain hierarchy to segregate tests into separate domains. Examples of the types of tests that might require separate domains are:

- DNS
- Native mode
- Mixed mode
- Migration process
- Replica of production data

Case Study for Designing Test Domains

A large manufacturing company designed its lab with specific testing in mind. Figure 4.4 illustrates the logical domain structure of the lab.

This company created a root domain with four child domains. The domain structure allowed the project team to use a separate domain for each of these types of tests:

- Windows 2000 Server functionality in a native mode domain, including printing.
- Virtual private networks.

- Mixed mode interoperability and the migration process.
- Microsoft® Exchange Server integration with Windows 2000.

An isolated domain allowed the team to test DNS without affecting any other testing.

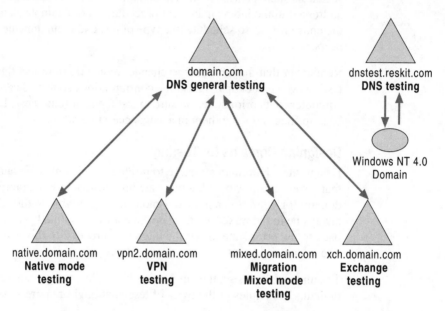

Figure 4.4   Example of Test Lab Logical Domain Design

Documenting the Lab Configuration

As you design the lab, document it with both a text description and a diagram. Post the diagram in the lab to provide easy access to lab information and to keep lab users up-to-date on design changes. Testers can use the lab description and diagram when they design test cases to ensure that the test plan is comprehensive and that tests are reproducible.

Lab Description

Include the following types of information in your lab description:

- Domain structure, including:
  - Forest and tree hierarchy.
  - Group Policy objects (settings and where they apply).
  - Purpose for each domain.
  - Method for populating user account data.
  - Trust relationships (transitive and explicit).
- Domain controllers, including:
  - Primary Domain Controllers (PDCs) and Backup Domain Controllers (BDCs), if migrating from Windows NT 4.0.
  - Servers to be promoted to domain controllers, if migrating from any other operating system.
- Member servers, including the services that will run on them.
- Client computers, including:
  - Computer make and model.
  - Amount of memory.
  - Processor type and speed.
  - Hard disk capacity.
  - Graphics cards (type, resolution, and color depth).
- Use of lab design for specific tests, including:
  - Mixed and native mode testing.
  - Dial-up and other remote testing.
  - Interoperability testing (UNIX, mainframes, and other systems).
  - Replication and Active Directory site testing.
  - WAN link testing.

Lab Diagrams

The lab diagram should show both the logical and the physical structure of the lab. Depending on the complexity of your lab network, the logical and physical views can be combined into one diagram.

Logical Diagram

Include the following information in the logical diagram:

- Domain hierarchy, including forests and trees.
- Domain names.
- Active Directory sites.
- Special service servers (domain controllers, Global Catalog, DNS, DHCP, and WINS), with the following information:
  - Computer name
  - Internet Protocol (IP) address
  - Server function
- Transitive trusts.
- Explicit one-way trusts.

Figure 4.5 is an example of a logical diagram. This lab has one tree, which consists of a root and three child domains. Double-headed arrows indicate transitive trusts between the Windows 2000 domains. The Windows NT 4.0 domain has explicit one-way trust relationships with the Windows 2000 tree. This lab does not have Active Directory sites. At this stage in testing, the lab includes domain controllers, some of which are also DNS servers supporting the dynamic update protocol, DHCP servers, and one global catalog server.

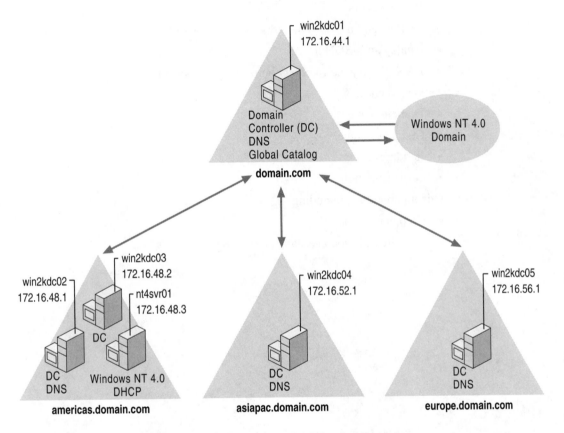

Figure 4.5   Example of a Test Lab Logical Diagram

Physical Diagram

Include the following information in the physical diagram:

- Network components, such as:
  - Routers and bridges.
  - Hubs.
  - Link simulators.
  - Proxy servers.
  - Sniffers and traffic generators.
  - Analog and ISDN lines.
  - LAN, WAN, and Internet connections and speeds.
- Servers, including:
  - Domain name.
  - Computer name.
  - IP address.
  - Server function.
- Client computers, including:
  - Computer name.
  - IP address, if you use static addressing.

Figure 4.6 is an example of a physical diagram. This physical diagram is for the same lab as the logical diagram in Figure 4.5. In this diagram, you see the three subnets for the three child domains. Each subnet has both a Windows 2000 Professional client computer and another type of client computer. The lab uses simulated Frame Relay links and has a UNIX server.

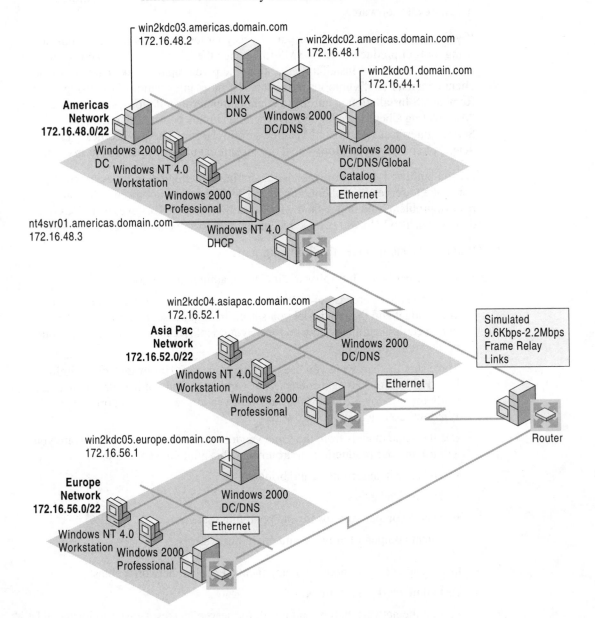

Figure 4.6   Example of a Test Lab Physical Diagram

Building the Lab

Once you have designed and documented your lab, have your project subteams review the plan to ensure that all the necessary conditions have been addressed. When the lab plan has been approved, you can start acquiring and installing the hardware and software.

If you plan to rebuild the lab periodically as your testing focus changes, consider using tools or products such as SMS to manage the lab changes. Also consider using the Remote OS Installation feature to help you rapidly make changes to the client computer configurations in the lab. For more information about using Remote OS Installation to automate client computer installations, see "Automating Client Installation and Upgrade" in this book. Active Directory Service Interfaces (ADSI) and Windows Script Host can help you quickly create, delete, or change users, groups, and organizational units in your lab environment.

As you build and rebuild the lab, document in chronological order every change you make to servers and client computers. This documentation can help you resolve problems and understand why a specific computer behaves as it does over time. It can also help you reverse recent changes to solve a short-term problem.

Building the lab involves the following steps:

- Acquire hardware and software, including administrative tools.

    You can either purchase or redeploy equipment. Which you do depends on your budget and the lab model you select. In either case, it is important to obtain equipment that adequately tests your deployment and that mirrors your production equipment.

    Make sure the hardware you use is on the Microsoft Hardware Compatibility List (HCL). You can also contact your vendors to find out if your products are ready for Windows 2000. Make sure your vendors actively support Windows 2000 with your hardware.

    Use the same models from the same vendors as the hardware and software you will use in your production environment. This guideline applies to:

    - Hubs, switches, routers, and bridges
    - Network adapters
    - Server computer hardware and operating systems
    - Client computer hardware and operating systems

- Install and configure network components. Label all network cables.
- Test all network connections.

    Testing the network before you install the servers makes it easier to locate and solve problems.

- Install and configure all servers.

  If you are redeploying servers, you might need to upgrade them to accommodate Windows 2000 Server. Use the same memory, disk capacity, and CPU speed that you plan to deploy. Be sure to check for viruses and defragment the hard disks.

  Install the appropriate operating system, either Windows 2000 Server or the operating system from which you plan to upgrade. Partition the hard disks in the same way you plan to partition them during deployment.

  If you are upgrading your domain controllers, back up the servers before you upgrade them. Test the backups and store them in a safe place. By making reliable backups, you avoid intruding on your production environment if your upgrade process changes or fails or if you need to restore to the original state.

  If you are purchasing new equipment, burn in the components for two or three days to be sure they are working properly.

- Install application software when you are ready to include it in testing. Install all server-based applications such as Microsoft® BackOffice® and business applications that are in your production environment.

  Build or load copies of the associated databases. Install the administrative tools that you use or plan to use.

- Install tools for testing and administration. If you are planning to verify network traffic or test performance, you might want to include a hardware sniffer or a software sniffer.

- If you are implementing Terminal Services, install a representative set of applications so you can test concurrent users.

- Install and configure all client computers.

- If you plan to create backups for restoring baseline configurations, set up the baseline configurations and make the backups.

  For example, if you plan to upgrade Windows 95 to Windows 2000 Professional instead of performing a clean installation, back up a Windows 95 client computer that is loaded with your standard set of applications.

  The baseline configurations should include all the service packs that are supported in your environment. Be sure to test and document the restore process.

- Test the individual components in the lab to isolate problems that are not related to Windows 2000 Server and deployment.

  When testing starts, you will want to spend your time debugging deployment problems, not fixing problems with the lab.

- If you need to provide connectivity to the production network, configure and test routers to isolate the lab from production.

Managing the Lab

If your lab is to be permanent or used by many groups, you might need to assign someone to manage it. This is particularly the case if the lab is to be used by several groups for testing during the change management process. Smaller labs or labs used by a single team might not need to have an assigned manager. Even if you decide not to assign a full-time manager, select someone to be responsible for the lab.

Regardless of your decision about a lab manager, establish a good communication system to disseminate information about the availability and state of the lab. Lab users need to know when they can perform their own tests, whether their testing will disrupt any other tests, and what state the lab is in. For example, if a domain in the lab is used for testing the migration process as well as mixed mode functionality, lab users need to know if the computers are ready for an upgrade or have already been upgraded.

If you decide to have a lab manager, weigh the tradeoffs and costs of hiring a dedicated lab manager against assigning the role to a project team member. Which decision you make depends on the size and complexity of the lab. The extra duties as lab manager might be too demanding in addition to other project responsibilities.

Lab Management Responsibilities

A lab manager is responsible for the following types of tasks:

- Procuring hardware and software.
- Managing network taps and server capacity and configurations.
- Managing hardware and software configurations and updates.
- Coordinating testing among subteams (who tests what and when).

  If tests require server or client computer configuration changes, the changes need to be scheduled and communicated to the other lab users.

- Developing and monitoring the change control process.

  The change control process defines who is allowed to make changes to the lab environment.

- Maintaining lab documentation (such as lab descriptions, diagrams, and processes).

- Establishing physical security.

  The lab manager takes measures to prevent unauthorized use of lab equipment and manages lab access with keys or electronic locks.

- Setting up an inventory control system.
- Establishing a lab budget for support costs.

- Labeling hardware, including cabling.
- Resolving environmental problems.
- Implementing a preventative maintenance program for equipment.
- Establishing an approval process for removing any equipment (borrowing, for example).
- Making periodic server backups.
- Ensuring the lab is kept clean and orderly.

Ultimately, a lab manager is responsible for making the lab as usable and flexible as possible. All of the processes designed to accomplish these tasks should facilitate, not inhibit, use of the lab.

Developing Lab Guidelines

It is recommended that you develop and implement guidelines for how team members should use the lab. Make the guidelines easy to remember and follow, with the intent to clarify rather than to dictate. Identify and document the following:

Roles and responsibilities. Identify who is responsible for tasks such as scheduling lab use and performing backups.

Facilities and guidelines for special types of tests. For example, identify the domains and configurations team members should use for testing the migration process.

Change control guidelines for the lab. Identify who is allowed to make configuration changes. Define the approval process for change requests. For example, identify who can make schema changes and who should be notified when a change is made. Define the documentation required whenever someone makes a change to the lab.

Initialization procedures for servers. Document the steps for installing, configuring, and populating domain controllers and member servers. Include DNS settings if you do not use the DNS built into Windows 2000.

Lab restore procedures for testing rollout. Document the steps for restoring domain controllers to their original state and for refreshing user account data. Document all server configurations. Test the refresh process before you begin migration testing.

Restore procedures for client computers. If you plan to rebuild client computers frequently to test various configurations, document the tools to be used to quickly restore the computer to a known initial state. For example, you might want to use RIS.

Testing

Good testing reduces the risk to your business when you introduce changes into your production environment. Thorough testing, however, requires careful planning. If you want your tests to accurately reflect how your proposed design will work, you must design them to realistically represent the conditions and variations in your environment. Even a well-designed test lab cannot compensate for a poorly designed test.

As a key component of risk management, testing:

- Validates that your design satisfies the business and technical requirements identified for your Windows 2000 project.
- Uncovers potential risks to your production environment.
- Uncovers potential risks to your project schedule.

When planning your tests, keep in mind that it is not feasible to test everything. Instead of trying to test every combination, focus on limits. For example, test the slowest client computer, the busiest server, or the least reliable network link. In addition, focus on areas having the greatest risk or the greatest probability of occurring. It is important to keep your suite of test cases manageable.

Testing continues throughout the entire project, evolving from component level (or unit) testing to integration testing defined as follows:

Unit Tests

These tests validate that individual features, components, or applications function properly. Unit testing begins when design starts and continues until your design is stable. It is iterative with design—test results validate the proposed design or lead to modifications. Architects and developers typically conduct unit tests.

Integration Tests

These tests validate that features and components work together cohesively. While unit tests address the depth of a component, integration tests address the breadth of a system.

Integration testing occurs after unit testing, when the design is stable. As the design falls into place, tests become increasingly complex and integrated until they encompass full interoperability of features and components. Integration testing requires a fully equipped test lab, where testers can carefully control test configurations and conditions.

It is recommended that integration tests be performed by a group other than the designers. Many organizations have testing teams who plan and conduct integration tests. In addition to verifying that the technology works as proposed, integration testers should look at test results from a business point of view: they should think about how the end user will work with the solution and how the solution performs in that use. They also should verify that the proposed solution meets the business and technical requirements for the Windows 2000 project.

Defining an Escalation Plan

Before you begin testing, define an escalation plan for the project team to use when problems arise. The escalation plan should address these issues:

- Where do team members post test failures and other issues? Do they enter both in the incident tracking system or do they enter issues elsewhere, such as at a Web site?
- What steps do they follow before posting the issue or problem? For example, does the problem need to be reproduced? By whom?
- What information do they include when posting the issue? Examples are:
    - Contact information (phone number, pager number, and e-mail address for subteam lead and external support)
    - Status of the problem (new or ongoing)
    - Priority and business justification of the problem
    - Sequence of events leading to the problem (include relevant information such as IP addresses and domain name)
    - Causes (known or suspected)
    - Troubleshooting information (traces, diagnostics)
- How do they notify the design group of the issue or problem?
- Who reviews and resolves issues?
- What is the notification hierarchy?

Creating the Test Plan

Early in your Windows 2000 planning, each design subteam should write a test plan that describes how they will test their specific technology. For example, the networking team might write a test plan that describes how they will test networking features. All members of the subteam should review and approve the test plan before testing begins. From the test plan, test cases (or scenarios) are developed to describe how to test each feature or function. Test cases are described in more detail in the section "Designing Test Cases" later in this chapter.

The test plan applies to both unit and integration testing. It provides the big picture for the testing effort and should address the topics that follow.

Scope and Objectives

In this section of the test plan, describe what you will and will not cover in your testing. For example, you might limit your testing of client computer hardware to the minimum supported configurations or the standard configurations.

Describe what you want your testing to accomplish. For example, one organization had an objective of migrating the Windows NT 4.0 environment to Windows 2000, component by component, keeping the access control lists (ACLs) and Exchange permissions intact. Another organization had an objective to measure network traffic and observe server performance during specific directory service tasks.

Testing Methodology

Describe the general strategy you will use for your testing. For example, your strategy for testing schema changes might be to configure an isolated domain in the lab where schema changes can be applied without affecting other lab tests. This section of the test plan might include the following descriptions:

- Domain architecture used for the test
- Tools and techniques used to conduct the tests or to measure results
- Automated techniques used for tests

Resources Required

Itemize the following types of resources that you require to support testing:

Hardware For example, identify the standard configurations you plan to support for client computers. Include components such as video cards, modems, and external drives.

Software For example, include Microsoft® BackOffice® or other server-based products that you need to test.

Databases Include databases that you need to set up for testing applications. It is recommended that you include a description of resources, such as personnel and production data, that you need to populate the databases.

Personnel Describe the number of testers you need and the skill level you require. Include consultants and other support personnel.

Training Specify the Windows 2000 training that your testers need to understand the technology they are testing.

Tools For example, include link simulators for testing WAN links if you do not have a second lab you can use for this purpose. Include any tools you need to automate testing and to track test results.

Features and Functions

Include a list of all the features or aspects of features to be tested. This is a list of what to test, not how to test. Some organizations include a list of tests as an appendix to their test plan. Other organizations create a separate document, or test specification, that lists the tests and briefly describes what each test must cover. Still other organizations include the list of tests as tasks in their project schedule.

The following is an example from one organization's test specification:

```
Test 1 – Trust retention

Description: all trusts to and from a domain should be retained when the
domain controllers are upgraded to Windows 2000. Use the Domain Tree
Manager to view the trusts. If the trusts do not appear, then the test
failed.
```

Note that the description does not include instructions on how to perform the test.

Later in the project, team members develop detailed procedures that describe how to perform each test listed in the test plan. The section "Designing Test Cases" later in this chapter provides more information about developing test procedures.

Your test plan should address the following types of tests:

- The functionality of each feature and service you will implement.
- Interoperability with existing components and systems in the production environment, both during and following a phased rollout. These tests include the mixed environment that will occur during your phased rollout and the Windows 2000 environment after the completion of your rollout.
- Hardware and driver compatibility for every type of computer that will run on Windows 2000.
- Application compatibility for every application that will run on Windows 2000.
- Baselines and stress tests for capacity planning.
- Baselines for performance monitoring.
- Optimization of configurations, such as for standardized desktops on client computers.

- Procedures for deployment and post-deployment administration, such as upgrading a client computer and back-out plans.
- Tools and utilities.

For more information about planning for application compatibility testing, see "Testing Applications for Compatibility with Windows 2000" in this book.

Risks

Describe the known risks that could prevent successful testing. For example, the test lab might be behind schedule, hardware or software might be unavailable, or testers might be working on other projects or need additional training.

Schedule

Draft a schedule that includes each test you listed in the test plan. The schedule can help you coordinate lab use with other subteams.

Designing Test Cases

A test case is a detailed procedure that fully tests a feature or an aspect of a feature. Whereas the test plan describes what is to be tested, a test case describes how to perform a particular test. You need to develop a test case for each test listed in the test plan or test specification.

Test cases should be written by someone who understands the function or technology being tested and should go through a peer review.

Test cases include information such as the following:

- Purpose of the test
- Special hardware requirements, such as a modem
- Special software requirements, such as a tool
- Specific setup or configuration requirements
- Description of how to perform the test
- Expected results or success criteria for the test

Designing test cases can be a time-consuming phase in your testing schedule. Although you might be tempted to take shortcuts, the time you spend will pay off in the long run. You can conduct tests faster when they are carefully planned. Otherwise, testers spend time debugging and rerunning tests.

Organizations take a variety of approaches to documenting test cases; these range from developing detailed, recipe-like steps to writing general descriptions. In detailed test cases, the steps describe exactly how to perform the test. In descriptive test cases, the tester decides at the time of the test how to perform the test and what data to use.

Some advantages of detailed test cases are that they are reproducible and they are easier to automate. This approach is particularly important if you plan to compare the results of tests over time, such as when you are optimizing configurations. A disadvantage of detailed test cases is that they are more time-consuming to develop and maintain. On the other hand, test cases that are open to interpretation are not repeatable and can lead to debugging time that pertains more to the test itself than to what is being tested.

It is recommended that you find a compromise between the two extremes, one that tends toward more detail. Balance thoroughness with practicality to reach your goal of test integrity and manageability.

Table 4.1 provides an example of the first few steps of a detailed test case:

Table 4.1   Example Test Case

Step	Procedure	Success Criteria	Outcome
1	Log off the server, and return to the netlogon screen.	None.	
2	Click the domain list to open it.	The local server name does not appear in the list.	
3	Click the domain list to open it.	The root domain appears in the list.	
4	Using an account with administrative privileges, log on to the server.	The account logs on to the server without error.	

Conducting Tests

Before you begin testing, modify the lab setup as necessary to meet the requirements specified in the test case. When performing tests, follow the written test case carefully. You need to know the precise steps that the tester performed before you can accurately assess the results or reproduce the test to compare it over time.

As you perform the tests, analyze the results against the criteria in the test case to determine if the test passed or failed. If a test failed, it might be a problem with the test itself, the lab setup, or the proposed design. For failed tests, consider doing the following:

Test case problem.   Revise the test case, rerun the test, and document all the changes that you made.

Lab setup problem.   Follow the change control process for the lab, reconfigure the lab, and rerun the test.

Design problem.   Follow the escalation procedure for the project to notify the proper people about the problem. Prioritize the outstanding problems and track them until they are resolved and retested. To prioritize problems, consider the potential impact and the probability that they will occur.

Documenting Test Results

Although you might record problems and bugs in your incident tracking system, you also need a tracking system for recording tests results. A tracking system helps you monitor testing progress and the success rate of tests. This information is useful for management reporting, reviewing trends, and validating staffing levels.

Some organizations use a paper-based system, documenting the test results on the test case sheet. Such a paper-based system, however, makes it more difficult to keep track of what has been tested and to create reports.

One alternative is to purchase a commercial product that tracks and reports test cases. Another is to develop a database application to organize and manage them. With these approaches, you can automate reports to monitor test results and progress. Whatever method you choose, it is important that members of the project team can access the test log easily. For more information about setting up a test tracking system, see "Testing Applications for Compatibility with Windows 2000" in this book.

However you decide to track your tests, it is important to document the results of each one. Include information such as:

- Tester's name and department
- Date and time the test was performed
- Windows 2000 product name (Server or Professional)
- Full description of the results
- Resolution of any problem
- Problem numbers entered into the incident tracking system

Testing After Deployment

Your lab can prove valuable long after you deploy Windows 2000 if you use it as part of your change management process. The importance of testing changes to your computing environment—whether you are adding new network infrastructure components, installing new servers, changing vendors for client computers, changing configurations, or implementing service packs and patches—cannot be overemphasized.

Having a lab available—even a well-designed and well-equipped one—is not enough. To maximize the effectiveness of the lab, define how you will use it to implement changes in the production environment. Remember to periodically evaluate your lab components to determine the effects of accumulated changes. For example, a computer that has had many changes applied to it might not behave in the same way as a computer that has been newly installed with the same configuration.

Using the Lab for Change Management

A change management lab is where you test any proposed change to your environment before implementing it in production, even as a pilot. When you use the lab to manage change, it becomes part of a larger process. This process identifies the flow of information and the sequence of activities from the time a change is proposed to the time it is implemented. The process you develop depends on the types of changes you perform, the teams involved, and the corporate culture.

Many resources are available to help you put together a change management process in an IT environment. The first step is to write a change management plan. To begin writing your plan, consider the following issues:

- Who authorizes changes?
- How to document and submit a proposal.
- Who analyzes the proposal to determine its importance and impact?
- What role do methods and procedures play (including the lab)?
- How to document and report the status of a change.

Testing in the lab is one step in the process of making changes to your production environment. Many enterprises test every patch and service pack until it is certified before they set up a pilot or limited rollout. When you test changes in a variety of scenarios and situations, you greatly reduce the risk of encountering problems during implementation.

Defining the Role of the Lab in Change Management

To reiterate, it is important that you use testing in the lab as part of your process for implementing changes. It is also important to define how you use the lab in that process. You can reduce the chance of oversights in the lab by describing the steps and requirements for common changes. For example, it is helpful to identify the following:

- Components required before implementing the change in the lab.
- Steps required to implement the change.
- Documentation to be produced in the lab.
- Action to take if lab tests fail.
- Action to take if lab tests succeed.

Figure 4.7 illustrates how one major organization uses its client computer lab to test changes to the standard desktop configurations.

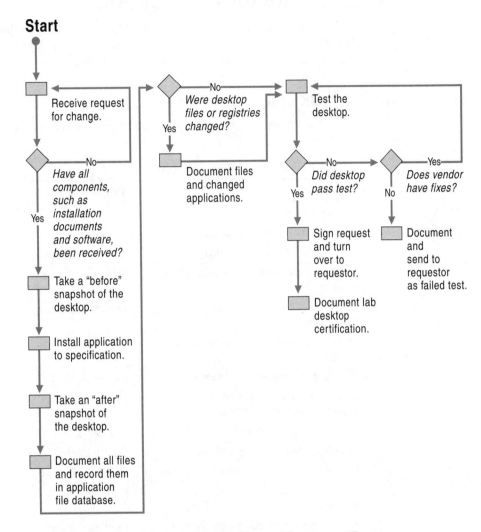

Figure 4.7   Sample Use of a Lab in the Change Management Process

Planning Task Lists for Lab Testing

Use the two task lists that follow as a quick reference for planning how you will test Windows 2000 for deployment. The first checklist helps you prepare your lab; the second helps you create, run, and document your tests.

Lab Preparation Task List

Table 4.2 summarizes the tasks you need to perform when designing and building a test lab.

Table 4.2   Lab Preparation Task List

Task	Location in Chapter
Select a lab model.	Determining the Lab Strategy
Select one or more lab locations.	Determining the Lab Strategy
Set up an interim lab (if needed).	Setting Up a Preliminary Lab
Determine lab space and environmental requirements.	Designing the Lab
Determine power and network connection requirements.	Designing the Lab
Design and document logical and physical configuration for the lab.	Designing the Lab
Determine hardware requirements.	Designing the Lab
Determine software requirements, including business applications and tools.	Designing the Lab
Determine who needs to use the lab.	Designing the Lab
Determine database requirements.	Designing the Lab
Determine wiring and network tap plans.	Designing the Lab
Acquire hardware, including cables and software.	Building the Lab
Acquire workspace equipment, such as desks, chairs, whiteboards, corkboards, lamps, telephones, and shelving.	Building the Lab
Build and configure the network.	Building the Lab
Test network connectivity.	Building the Lab
Build and configure the servers.	Building the Lab
Install applications and build databases on the servers.	Building the Lab

(continued)

Table 4.2   Lab Preparation Task List *(continued)*

Task	Location in Chapter
Install testing and administrative tools.	Building the Lab
Build and configure the client computers.	Building the Lab
Install applications on the client computers.	Building the Lab
Test all the lab components.	Building the Lab
Assign a lab manager.	Managing the Lab
Define a change control process for the lab.	Developing Lab Guidelines
Create, test, and document the lab restore process.	Developing Lab Guidelines

Testing Task List

Table 4.3 summarizes the testing tasks you need to perform.

Table 4.3   Testing Task List

Task	Location in Chapter
Write a test plan.	Creating the Test Plan
Build test cases.	Designing Test Cases
Develop escalation procedure.	Defining an Escalation Plan
Conduct tests and evaluate results.	Conducting Tests
Document test results.	Documenting Test Results

C H A P T E R   5

Conducting Your Windows 2000 Pilot

The pilot is the last major step before your full-scale deployment of Microsoft® Windows® 2000. Prior to the pilot, you must have completed integration testing in your lab environment. During the pilot, you test your design in a controlled real-world environment in which users perform their normal business tasks using the new features.

Well in advance of the pilot, your project manager and system designers need to plan where and how you will perform the pilot. This chapter helps you create a pilot plan, select users and sites, and determine how to set up your pilot environment.

In This Chapter

Chapter Goals

This chapter will help you develop the following planning documents:

- Pilot plan
- Pilot rollout procedure

Related Information in the Resource Kit

- For more information about testing prior to the pilot, see "Building a Windows 2000 Test Lab" in this book.

- For more information about migrating to Windows 2000 from Microsoft® Windows NT® version 3.51 or later, see "Determining Domain Migration Strategies" in this book.

- For more information about automating the Windows 2000 installation for servers, see "Automating Server Installation and Upgrade" in this book.

- For more information about automating the Windows 2000 installation for client computers, see "Automating Client Installation and Upgrade" in this book.

Overview of Conducting a Pilot

After you verify your Windows 2000 design in your test environment, you need to test it in your production environment with a limited number of users. A pilot reduces your risk of encountering problems during your full-scale deployment.

The primary purposes of a pilot are to demonstrate that your design works in the production environment as you expected and that it meets your organization's business requirements. A secondary purpose is that the pilot gives the installation team a chance to practice and refine the deployment process.

The pilot provides an opportunity for users to give you feedback about how features work. Use this feedback to resolve any issues or to create a contingency plan. The feedback can also help you determine the level of support you are likely to need after full deployment. Ultimately, the pilot leads to a decision to proceed with a full deployment or to slow down so you can resolve problems that could jeopardize your deployment.

To minimize your risk during deployment, you might want to have several pilots or pilot phases. For example, you might have one pilot for your namespace design, another one for your standard desktop configurations and security model, and still another one for deploying applications remotely.

Pilot Process

The pilot process is iterative. You deploy a limited number of computers in a controlled environment, evaluate the results, fix problems, and deploy another pilot until you reach the scope and quality that indicate you are ready for a full deployment. Figure 5.1 illustrates the primary steps for planning and conducting a pilot.

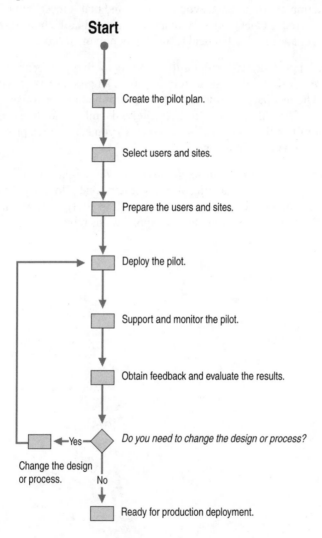

Figure 5.1   Process for Conducting a Pilot

Starting with Information Technology

If you plan to have multiple pilots, start small and gradually increase the scope of the pilots. Many organizations use their information technology (IT) department for the first pilot. They begin by building a system that emulates what they plan to deploy in the production environment; participants use test computers on a test network. Then these organizations gradually add IT staff to the pilot.

You can use an IT pilot such as this to resolve scalability and performance issues as you add more and more users to the system. After you have resolved any problems, you can start your first pilot in the production environment. At this point, you deploy Windows 2000 on production computers in business units for end users.

Prerequisites for a Production Pilot

Before you start your first pilot in production, your test lab must be stable and your testing teams should have finished integration and application testing. Be sure to validate the components of your design before you implement them on your corporate network. For example, validate the protocols you plan to use, the replication traffic across your wide area network (WAN) links, and your backup and restore procedures. You should not introduce any new technologies or procedures into the pilot that have not been tested in the lab. If one of your goals for the pilot is to test the rollout process, the installation team should have thoroughly developed, tested, and documented the process. Resolve any outstanding problems with your design or develop a contingency plan.

You also need to develop and validate a series of tests that the installation team can run after upgrading the computers. These tests ensure that the installation is working properly before you turn it over to the users.

Before you begin deploying the pilot, obtain management approval of your pilot plan. Start working on the pilot plan early so that you have your communication channels in place and the participants prepared by the time you are ready to deploy the pilot.

Creating a Pilot Plan

The pilot sets the tone for the full deployment, so it is important that you plan carefully, communicate well with the participants, and evaluate the results thoroughly. Creating a plan for your pilot helps you think through the issues and set expectations for everyone involved.

If you have multiple pilots, you might have multiple pilot plans. For example, each subteam might have their own pilot and write their own plan. Your pilot plan should include the following:

- Scope and objectives
- Participating users and locations
- Training plan for pilot users
- Support plan for the pilot
- Communication plan for the pilot
- Known risks and contingency plans
- Rollback plan
- Schedule for deploying and conducting the pilot

When you have your pilot plan ready, ask IT management and management from the participating business units to review and approve the plan before you proceed.

Scope and Objectives

The first step in planning your pilot is to define what you plan to include and exclude (scope) and what you want to accomplish (objectives). Define the scope and objectives clearly to help you set expectations and identify your success criteria. If possible, use your objectives to develop metrics for evaluating your pilot. You should also specify a duration for the pilot, either in terms of time or in terms of criteria to be met.

Pilot Scope

A pilot extends testing to involve users working on production tasks. Do not expect to test every piece of functionality during your pilot. Focus on functions that have the greatest risk and events that have the greatest probability of occurring.

Define the scope of your pilot by stating what is included and what is excluded. List the services and features you plan to include in the pilot and what you hope to accomplish with them. Describe the areas of functionality that the pilot implementation will affect, to what extent, and in what situations.

List the service and features you plan to exclude from the pilot. If certain aspects of your design cannot be covered by the pilot, describe them. For example, if you plan to upgrade using your existing domain architecture and restructure later, the first pilot might not include the restructure process.

Describe what you expect to happen after the pilot. If you plan to keep some functions in place and dismantle others, set up expectations about what will stay and what will go. If you think you might want to dismantle the pilot instead of keeping it for your production system, set the expectation for backing it out in your pilot plan. For example, if you are redesigning your namespace, you might want the option of changing it after the pilot. Specifying information such as this in your pilot plan sets expectations in the user community ahead of time.

Pilot Objectives

State explicit objectives that your pilot should meet. Use your objectives to identify criteria for measuring the success of your pilot. Many organizations have primary objectives such as the following:

- Ensure that the system works properly in your environment.
- Ensure that the design meets your business requirements.
- Build user support for your Windows 2000 project.

Many organizations have additional objectives such as the following:

- Test the deployment process.
- Train the installation team.
- Create documentation for the full deployment.
- Train the support and help desk teams.
- Gather information for estimating future support requirements.
- Train the administrative teams.
- Develop and test end-user training materials.

Pilot Users and Sites

Carefully select the users and sites that you want to participate in the pilot. First establish your selection criteria and then choose a method for selecting candidates. Methods you can use include interviews, questionnaires, and requests for volunteers.

If you have multiple pilots, the type of users you select might vary as the pilots progress. Eventually, you should include end users that are typical of your organization. For an early pilot, however, a good group of users has these attributes:

- Able to derive tangible benefit from Windows 2000.
- Plays a noncritical role in day-to-day operations.

    The group should be able to absorb some downtime or performance degradation if problems occur.

- Representative of the target environment.

    Choose groups or sites that do not have unique requirements or operating environments because you want the pilot to predict how your design and rollout will work in your environment at large.

- Performs a variety of activities with a variety of computer hardware.

- Enthusiastic about the Windows 2000 project.

- Comfortable with technology.

    Users who are comfortable with technology tend to be more patient with problems that occur during a pilot and are more likely to push the system. This type of user, however, might accept problems that should be supported. Encourage these users to report every problem they encounter, or you might find that their learning curve will not represent that of the typical user. When you plan subsequent pilots and the full deployment, consider the effect of such differences in user groups.

- Willing to receive training.

Remember that users who are less experienced with technology need more guidance to prepare them for their role and more support during the pilot.

Determine the number of sites and users for the pilot based on these criteria:

- Goals for the pilot
- Number of functions and features you are testing
- Size of your support staff

After you select your participants, choose one of them as your user liaison. Select someone who has good communication skills and a good relationship with both the pilot group and the project team. Work with the user liaison as you plan the pilot. The liaison can provide you with information about the type of work the pilot group performs and can prepare the group for their role. To encourage users to participate and offer feedback, provide an incentive program. For example, you might give away prizes or have managers give recognition to participants who make a special effort to contribute during the pilot.

Pilot Training Plan

Well in advance of the pilot, you need to determine how and when you will train the participants. Identify the resources that you will use for training. For example, consider hiring an external trainer, holding brown-bag seminars, developing a train-the-trainer program, or using media technology to broadcast training.

Many organizations find that it works best to provide training just prior to installation. Determine what the training should cover and estimate how long it will take. Limit training to what the users must know to do their work. Remember to include training in your pilot schedule.

Pilot Support Plan

Be sure to develop your support plan early because you might need to provide training to the support staff. Your support plan should address who will provide support, what level of support they need to provide, and how users can report problems.

Determine who will support the pilot users: will it be the project team, the help desk, or external resources? If the help desk provides the support, how will you train them? What will be the role of the project team? If one of your pilot objectives is to train the help desk, you need resources from both the project team and the help desk.

Determine what service levels you can support during the pilot. For example, must critical problems be resolved within a specified number of hours? During what hours must support be available to the users?

Document the change management and problem management processes for the pilot. Your process should address these issues:

- How are change requests submitted, approved, tested, and implemented?
- Where do users post their problems?

  Can they report problems to an existing system or do you need a new mechanism, such as a Web site, where users can log their problems and questions?

- How will you review, prioritize, and fix problems?
- What escalation process will you use to notify the appropriate personnel?

Communication

In your pilot plan, describe how you will communicate with participants to prepare them prior to the pilot and to exchange status reports during the pilot. Include the type of information you will communicate, to whom, by what means, and how often. For example, describe how and when you will notify users about the pilot rollout. For more information about communication strategies, see "Planning for Deployment" in this book.

As you determine how you will communicate during your pilot, begin creating the mechanisms you will use. For example, set up e-mail distribution lists for the various groups that need to receive specific types of information. You might want to note the types of information you will send to those on each distribution list. Set up mechanisms for communicating information about the pilot, such as Web sites, frequently asked questions, procedures, and status reports.

Pilot Rollback Plan

A critical part of your pilot plan is the rollback procedure you will use should the pilot fail. Develop a detailed procedure that explains when and how to make backups and how to restore them. For example, will you use image copies or incremental backups? Document the backup and restore process, and test it. Choose a safe place to store the backup media and include the location in your rollback plan.

Specify the criteria for when to use the rollback procedure. For example, you might establish a system for classifying the severity of problems and describe which levels warrant backing out of the pilot. You also might decide to have different rollback plans for different types of problems. For example, you might develop one procedure for backing out the entire pilot if the problem is pervasive and another procedure for backing out specific components if the problem is isolated. You might want an additional procedure for recovering from severe data corruption in your directory service.

Schedule

One of the earliest activities in planning a pilot is to start a schedule. Include tasks for planning the pilot, preparing the users and sites, deploying the pilot, and testing during the pilot. Remember to schedule time for training users, support staff, and the installation team. Also allow time to inventory the sites, upgrade hardware, and evaluate the pilot. You might need to include tasks for developing the support and communication mechanisms you identify during planning.

To create the schedule for the deployment phase, you need to know the number of computers to be upgraded and the estimated time it takes for each one. Determine how many machines you plan to upgrade per day and the sequence in which you plan to upgrade them. Think through which hours of the day and which days of the week are best for upgrading servers and client computers. Should you upgrade computers during off-hours to avoid disrupting users? Should you upgrade clients during working hours so that the users can attend training during that time? Do you plan to require that end users receive training before you upgrade or install their computers with Microsoft® Windows® 2000 Professional? If you do, the training schedule is a dependency for your pilot deployment.

As you deploy the pilot, you can refine your schedule with updated estimates based on your installation experience so that it is more accurate for the full deployment.

Preparing for the Pilot

As the start date for your pilot approaches, begin preparing for the rollout. Allow enough time in advance to prepare both the users and the physical sites. As the users test the Windows 2000 design, the installation team needs to develop, test, document, and refine the rollout procedure.

Preparing Pilot Sites

Prepare the pilot sites in advance so that the installation team can begin to upgrade the operating system when the pilot begins. You should already have an inventory of computers and network components. For more information about compiling an inventory of your network equipment, see "Preparing Your Network Infrastructure for Windows 2000" in this book.

Assess the computers and network equipment that are used at the pilot site and then determine what hardware upgrades are required. At the very least, identify the required modifications and acquire the components. If possible, install the new components and test them ahead of time. Check for the following types of upgrades:

- Client computer upgrades to meet your minimum supported hardware configuration (memory, hard disk capacity, processor speed and type, network adapters).
- Server upgrades for optimal hardware configurations.
- Network upgrades to meet design requirements.
- Client and server upgrades for compatibility with Windows 2000 (hardware, applications, drivers).

You also need to determine the following:

- Applications in use at the site.
- Special security requirements.
- Special connectivity requirements.

Ensure that you have tested all the hardware and software for compatibility and that the installation team is prepared for any special requirements.

Preparing Pilot Users

It is important to establish early communication with the pilot group. Your initial contact should open the channel of communication and set expectations. As the start date for the pilot approaches, train the users and inform them of specific deployment plans and target dates.

Establishing Early Communication

Soon after you select the participants, meet with them to do the following:

- Obtain commitment to the pilot.
- Establish a user liaison.
- Clarify responsibilities.
- Discuss support and rollback plans.

Pilot participants need to understand what the pilot will entail. They need to understand how the pilot might affect their work and what responsibilities they will have. Discuss the duration of the pilot, the level of support you will provide, and what testing they are to perform. Although pilot participants continue to perform their daily business tasks, you might want to specify some areas they should focus on. Address any concerns they might have about the pilot or their role.

Keeping Participants Informed

As your pilot plans progress, the user liaison can inform you of the users' concerns and can update the users on new developments. As you develop your support plans, communicate to the users how and when they need to request support and how they should submit problems or issues.

Inform the users about the type of training they will receive and when they can expect it. Some organizations provide one to two hours of training just prior to deployment.

As you begin to deploy the pilot, remind the participants of the following:

- Target dates for training and for upgrading computers.
- Procedures they need to follow before their computers are upgraded.
- Contact names and numbers for support.

Developing the Rollout Process

If one of your pilot goals is to test the rollout process, the installation team must develop, document, and test the procedures during the project testing phase. The test lab is a good place to debug problems, but the pilot provides a real-world test in which the procedures can be fine-tuned for accuracy and efficiency. Make sure the scripts and tools for automating upgrades are appropriate for the computers in the pilot environment.

As you develop procedures for deploying Windows 2000 to various types of computers, create documentation that is helpful to the installers. Your rollout documentation might include the following:

- Lists of tools and supplies the installer needs.
- Lists of scripts and their locations.
- Backups that installers are to make before and during deployment.

    Include backups of user data on client computers.

- Steps for migrating to your new domain structure.

    For more information about strategies for migrating to your new domain structure and the tools to use, see "Determining Domain Migration Strategies" in this book.

- Steps for performing both automated and manual computer upgrades.

    The manual method can be used if the automated method does not work properly. For more information about automating your installations, see "Automating Server Installation and Upgrade" and "Automating Client Installation and Upgrade" in this book.

- Acceptance tests that installers are to perform during and immediately following deployment to verify that the deployment works as expected.
- Operational procedures that installers and administrators are to perform (resetting permissions, changing passwords, restoring user data).
- Steps for backing out if the pilot fails.

Deploying the Pilot

Before you deploy your pilot, perform a dry run of the process. A dry run involves scheduling a time during nonbusiness hours to perform the entire upgrade process, testing the new setup thoroughly, and then backing out everything.

As you deploy the pilot, remember to validate all your backups. Label them clearly and store them in a safe place. Verify each step as you perform it. As you proceed, keep records of how long installation takes so you can refine your schedule. During the deployment, have a system administrator available who has full security privileges, including rights to administer mail and database server passwords.

Remember to keep track of any corrections to the rollout procedures. Make corrections as you go, and test the corrections on the next upgrade. Identify and document any inefficient steps and methods, and use the information to refine the rollout process.

Evaluating the Pilot

Your team needs to monitor progress throughout the pilot, fixing and retesting problems that arise. Have your problem-tracking system in place at the very beginning of the pilot and encourage the pilot users to use it for reporting their problems. Users often neglect to report problems, either because they think a problem is insignificant or because they find a way to work around it. To accurately assess your pilot, however, you need the users to report every problem.

At the end of the pilot, you need to obtain input from a variety of sources to evaluate the success of the pilot. The more information you accumulate during the pilot, the more accurately you can evaluate it at the end.

Monitoring the Pilot

Your team should continually monitor the pilot network, looking for bottlenecks and areas that need to be tuned. Monitor both traffic flow and application performance. Although monitoring tools provide much information, it also helps to visit the pilot site periodically. Talking with users frequently uncovers issues that might otherwise go unnoticed. Be sure to check problem reports frequently and look for trends.

During the pilot, assess risks to the project. For example, look for the following:

- Scope changes
- Cost increases
- Interoperability problems
- Unanticipated downtime

Obtaining Feedback

At the end of the pilot, evaluate its success and make a recommendation to management about the next step. Management then needs to decide whether to continue the project beyond the pilot. To help you with the evaluation and recommendation, analyze information from a variety of sources. For example, obtain information from:

- Web site feedback forms
- Sessions with business managers
- Problem reports
- End-user surveys
- Observations of the IT project team

Try to obtain information about both the design and the deployment process. Review what did and what did not work so that you can revise and refine your plan. Gather information about issues such as:

- Training
- Rollout process
- Support
- Communications
- Problems encountered
- Suggestions for improvements

Use the feedback to validate that the delivered design meets the design specification, as well as the business requirements. Did the pilot meet the success criteria you defined before the pilot began? If you established metrics to measure your success, how did the pilot measure up?

Planning Task List for Conducting a Pilot

Table 5.1 summarizes the tasks you need to perform when planning a pilot.

Table 5.1   Planning Task List for Conducting a Pilot

Task	Location in Chapter
Create a plan for your pilot project that includes:	Creating a Pilot Plan
▪ Pilot scope and objectives.	
▪ Users and sites.	
▪ Training, support, communication, and rollback plans.	
▪ Schedule.	
Prepare your users and sites.	Preparing for the Pilot
Develop the rollout process.	Preparing for the Pilot
Deploy the pilot.	Deploying the Pilot
Support and monitor the pilot.	Evaluating the Pilot
Obtain feedback about the pilot.	Evaluating the Pilot
Evaluate the results of the pilot.	Evaluating the Pilot

P A R T 2

Network Infrastructure Prerequisites

Preparing your network infrastructure is an essential first step toward deployment. Part 2 assists you in documenting your current networking environment and in preparing your network for Microsoft® Windows® 2000.

In This Part

CHAPTER 6

Preparing Your Network Infrastructure for Windows 2000

Before you deploy Microsoft® Windows® 2000 into your organization, you must prepare your network. This chapter will help you, the network administrator, identify the areas of the network infrastructure, such as servers, routers, and network services, that might need to be upgraded or modified before deploying Windows 2000. This chapter also discusses documenting your current network infrastructure.

Before reading this chapter, review the material presented in "Creating a Deployment Roadmap" and "Planning for Deployment" in this book.

In This Chapter

Chapter Goals

This chapter will help you develop the following planning documents:

- Inventories, diagrams, and documentation of your current networking environment.

- An infrastructure preparation plan for Windows 2000 deployment.

Related Information in the Resource Kit

- For more information about Windows 2000 TCP/IP, see the *Microsoft® Windows® 2000 Server Resource Kit TCP/IP Core Networking Guide.*

- For more information about evaluating your existing network, infrastructure, and protocols, see "Determining Network Connectivity Strategies" in this book.

- For more information about creating a domain migration plan, see "Determining Domain Migration Strategies" in this book.

Documenting Your Current Environment

Documenting your existing network's physical and logical topology, and having a complete and accurate inventory of the hardware and software your organization uses are very important preliminary steps before you begin planning for your Windows 2000 network infrastructure.

The areas of your current network environment that you need to document to prepare your network for deploying Windows 2000 are as follows:

- Hardware and software
- Network infrastructure
- File, print, and Web servers
- Line-of-business applications
- Directory services architecture
- Security

Microsoft Windows NT® network diagnostic applications such as Network Monitor are useful for documenting your network. Often, original equipment manufacturers offer troubleshooting or configuration software that is ideal for documenting the configuration of equipment and drivers.

You will be doing a considerable amount of planning while you are preparing your network infrastructure for Windows 2000. In "Creating a Deployment Roadmap" earlier in this book, you defined your deployment project scope and selected the Windows 2000 features you wanted to deploy. You also identified technical dependencies of Windows 2000 that might affect your planning, and created a project plan for deployment.

This chapter focuses on preparing your network infrastructure for Windows 2000, but this preparation cannot stand apart from the planning described in other chapters of this book. Whether you are preparing a new network or migrating Windows 2000 into an existing network structure, your planning in the areas of domain restructuring, server upgrades, and infrastructure requirements will determine the specific tasks you need to do to prepare your infrastructure.

Hardware and Software Inventory

If you have not already done so, conduct hardware and software inventories of all servers and client computers in use on your network. Document all routers, printers, modems, and other hardware, such as redundant array of independent disks (RAID) arrays and Remote Access Service (RAS) server hardware. Be sure that you include such details as basic input/output system (BIOS) settings and the configuration of any peripheral devices such as printers, scanners, and input devices. Record driver versions and other software and firmware information.

Your software inventory should list all applications found on all computers, and include version numbers (or date and time stamp data) of dynamic link libraries associated with the applications on your system. Remember to document any service packs you might have applied to your operating system or applications. You can use scripts and a variety of third-party applications to obtain this information from Windows and Windows NT networks that use Windows Management Instrumentation (WMI).

Systems Management Server is helpful for gathering information about your Windows NT network and can produce detailed reports about the hardware, software, and applications in use in your organization. For more information about analyzing your network using Systems Management Server, see "Using Systems Management Server to Analyze Your Network Infrastructure" in this book.

Document network configurations for servers and client computers. On computers running Windows NT, network settings are easily obtained.

▶ **To obtain network settings in Windows NT**

1. Click **Start**, point to **Settings**, and then click **Control Panel**.

2. Double-click **Network**.

3. Note the information on the **Identification**, **Services**, **Protocols**, **Adapters**, and **Bindings** tabs.

On each computer that is assigned a static Internet Protocol (IP) address, open a command prompt window, run the **ipconfig /all** command, and record the results. Third-party hardware vendors often provide diagnostic and administrative software that gathers detailed information about hardware and configuration settings.

You can use these inventories to:

- Confirm that your current infrastructure, server hardware, computer BIOS, and software configurations are compatible with Windows 2000 Server by comparing your inventory to the Hardware Compatibility List (HCL). For more information about the HCL, see the Microsoft Windows Hardware Compatibility List link on the Web Resources page at http://windows.microsoft.com/windows2000/reskit/webresources.

- Determine the specific upgrade path for each server and client computer and draft specifications for acquiring new equipment.

Network Infrastructure

While you are documenting your current network environment, take special note of areas where you are currently experiencing problems. If you stabilize your network before deploying a new operating system, deployment and troubleshooting will be easier, and you can have increased confidence in the upgraded network. Setting up a test lab to duplicate problems and configurations is a good way to evaluate the impact of deploying Windows 2000 with a given set of protocols, hardware drivers, and client/server configurations. For more information about setting up a test lab, see "Building a Windows 2000 Test Lab" in this book.

When documenting your network infrastructure, you are obtaining both hardware data to document your infrastructure's physical structure and software data to document the existence and configuration of the protocols in use on your network. You also need to document the logical organization of your network, name and address resolution methods, and the existence and configuration of services used. Documenting the location of your network sites and the available bandwidth between them will also assist you in deciding whether to perform push or on-demand installations when you upgrade or migrate to Windows 2000. For more information about installing, upgrading, and migrating to the Windows 2000 operating system, see "Automating Client Installation and Upgrade" and "Automating Server Installation and Upgrade" in this book.

Developing a physical and logical diagram of your network will help you organize the information you gather in an understandable and intuitive manner.

Physical Network Diagram

The physical diagram presents the following information about your existing network:

- Details of physical communication links, such as cable length, grade, and approximation of the physical paths of the wiring, analog, and ISDN lines.

- Servers, with computer name, IP address (if static), server role, and domain membership. A server can operate in many roles, including primary or backup domain controller, Dynamic Host Configuration Protocol (DHCP) service server, Domain Name System (DNS) server, Windows Internet Name Service (WINS) server, print server, router, and application or file server.

- Location of devices such as printers, hubs, switches, modems, routers and bridges, and proxy servers that are on the network.

- Wide area network (WAN) communication links (analog and ISDN) and the available bandwidth between sites. This could be an approximation or the actual measured capacity.

- Number of users at each site, including mobile users.

Figure 6.1 is an example of a physical network diagram.

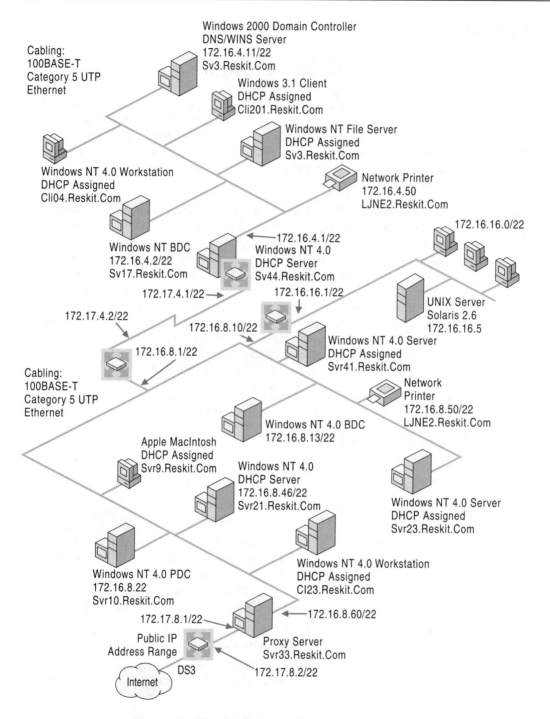

Figure 6.1   Physical Network Diagram

Document firmware version, throughput, and any special configuration requirements for any devices on the network. If you assign static IP addresses to any of these devices, record them. For more information about network connectivity and Windows 2000, see "Determining Network Connectivity Strategies" in this book.

Logical Network Diagram

The logical diagram shows the network architecture, including the following information:

- Domain architecture, including the existing domain hierarchy, names, and addressing scheme.

- Server roles, including primary or backup domain controllers, DHCP service servers, or WINS servers.

- Trust relationships, including representations of transitive, one-way, and two-way trust relationships.

Figure 6.2 is an example of a logical network diagram.

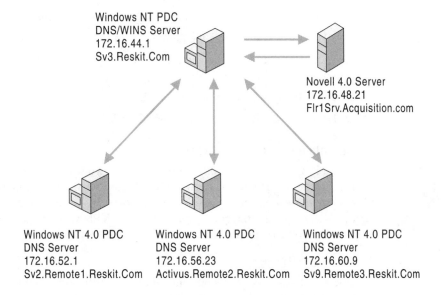

Windows NT PDC
DNS/WINS Server
172.16.44.1
Sv3.Reskit.Com

Novell 4.0 Server
172.16.48.21
Flr1Srv.Acquisition.com

Windows NT 4.0 PDC
DNS Server
172.16.52.1
Sv2.Remote1.Reskit.Com

Windows NT 4.0 PDC
DNS Server
172.16.56.23
Activus.Remote2.Reskit.Com

Windows NT 4.0 PDC
DNS Server
172.16.60.9
Sv9.Remote3.Reskit.Com

Figure 6.2   Logical Network Diagram

Network Configuration

In general, the areas of your network configuration that you need to document are listed in the following sections.

Name Resolution Services

Ensure that you have documented all DNS and WINS servers that are on your network, noting configuration and version information as well as hardware details. Note whether any of the DNS servers not running Windows NT on your network can support dynamic registration and Service (SRV) resource records, and whether upgrades for this capability are available from the software manufacturer.

If you have hosts on your network that are not running Windows NT, document the services they use and provide, such as UNIX BIND. You should also document the version of each service in use. For example, if BIND is used on your network, note that versions earlier than 4.9.4 are not compatible with Windows 2000. Document Service Advertising Protocol (SAP) and Routing Information Protocol (RIP) services, if either are presently in use on your network.

IP Addressing Methods and Service Configurations

Ensure that you have documented all DHCP service servers on your network, including the following:

- Any IP addresses that you have assigned servers or client computers.
- DHCP settings, such as the default gateway.
- Details of your subnets, and relate them to your overall domain structure.
- The number of subnets and hosts on your network, and record the IP addresses and submasks used on your network.
- How long a client can lease an IP address on your network.

Remote and Dial-up Networking

If you have remote or mobile users, document your remote access and dial-up configurations. If you use third-party software for mobile users, review and document the configuration of those products. If you use virtual private networks (VPNs), document the configuration of your VPN with the goal of evaluating whether you can replace it with Windows 2000 VPN.

Bandwidth Issues

Document your network's current bandwidth utilization. Do this to establish a baseline from which changes can be measured. You can use a variety of third-party and Microsoft tools to measure bandwidth metrics such as bytes and packets sent or received, transmit and receive errors, and packets per second. Document the speed of the network links between your organization's network segments and geographical locations.

Look at the logical and geographical dispersion of your organization in terms of bandwidth considerations. Does it have branch offices, or mobile or remote employees? Consider the amount and type of traffic over your organization's communication links. For instance, are your WAN links periodically slowed by domain replication between domain controllers at different sites? Document the net available bandwidth of all WAN links and network segments. Try to record available bandwidth during the course of low, normal, and high network utilization.

File, Print, and Web Servers

Document the configuration details of your member servers, paying particular attention to any unique configurations, such as a server hosting a bank of modems, or a departmental server with multiple network adapters. Note whether the server is an enterprise or a departmental server. Note any special operational requirements of your servers, and identify whether any of these servers rely on special protocols or drivers. For instance, if a product needs to reside on a backup domain controller, the functionality of this product might be impacted when the backup controller is upgraded to Windows 2000. As with any computer, evaluate the hardware and associated drivers on these computers for Windows 2000 compatibility through the HCL.

Locate the printers in your organization and document their configurations. Pay special attention to Web and proxy servers—while planning for your deployment, you need to consider the security implications in this class of server and the bandwidth each can require, particularly for Active Directory™. For more information about planning file, print, and Web servers, see "Upgrading and Installing Member Servers" in this book.

Line-of-Business Applications

Identify all applications that your enterprise must have to perform its core mission. Typically, you might find a core set of applications such as a database application, an e-mail system, and a financial package, each of which must be operating correctly for your business's objectives to be achieved. Check these applications for compatibility with Windows 2000. For instance, if you want your e-mail program to integrate with Active Directory, you need to contact the vendor and ask whether an upgrade path to Windows 2000 and Active Directory compatibility is available or planned. Many software vendors have partnered with Microsoft to ensure that their products run correctly with Windows 2000. The "Certified for Windows" logo is your best assurance of compatibility. For more information about determining whether your applications are Windows 2000–compatible, see "Testing Applications for Compatibility with Windows 2000" in this book. For information about Windows 2000–compatible applications, see the Directory of Windows 2000 Applications link on the Web Resources page at http://windows.microsoft.com/windows2000/reskit/webresources.

Directory Services Architecture

Document your existing domain structure as part of your plan to move to Active Directory. Identify your domain architectures, the users and user groups in your organization and their geographical location, and resource and administrative domains. Document the one- and two-way trust relationships that exist between domains. Document whether you have a noncontiguous namespace, possibly created by acquisitions, mergers, or other actions. This information will assist you when you are planning your Windows 2000 domain forest and determining the type of trust relationship you will establish among these domains.

Identify any directory services that are not Windows NT currently running on your network, such as Microsoft® Exchange Server directory service extensions, or UNIX BIND. Identify all of the user accounts that exist for each user. This information will be useful both during the migration to Active Directory and in maintaining correct functionality between Active Directory and other directory services because you will have all account information for each user.

Domain Administration Model

Identify your main administration model (or standards) for domain administration. Do you have a centralized, hierarchical administrative model, or does your organization permit a distributed model of administration? What can local administrators do compared to enterprise-wide administrators? Is there overlap between administrative models in your organization? This information will help to determine whether administrative duties can be restructured under Windows 2000, making domain administration less expensive and more efficient. Windows 2000 offers significant improvements in your ability to administer both the largest and smallest details of your network.

When examining your existing domain structure, document the following information for your network:

Type of domain structure   Most networks have multiple master account domains with many more resource domains. When migrating or upgrading existing domains to Windows 2000, your existing domain structure will influence your Windows 2000 domain structure design. For more information, see "Determining Domain Migration Strategies" in this book.

Existing trust relationships   Note the existing one- and two-way trust relationships in your network. Identify any domains and trust relationships that you do not want to move into your Windows 2000 domain forest structure. Domains that are upgraded to Windows 2000 domains and designated as part of the same forest will connect to other Windows 2000 domains through transitive trust relationships. After you upgrade your domains to Windows 2000, you need to create explicit trust relationships between Windows 2000 domains and any domains that you do not want to move into the new forest.

The number and location of domain controllers on your network   This will allow you to plan the upgrade for each domain. You should have the primary and backup domain controllers identified on your physical and logical network diagrams. Note their physical locations and configuration details. For more information about determining the sequence and timing of domain controller upgrades, see "Determining Domain Migration Strategies" in this book.

The DNS namespaces that exist in your organization   Knowing what namespaces exist in your organization will help you to create a unique namespace for your Windows 2000 forest. Deciding on a DNS namespace as the root of your Active Directory hierarchy is an important part of your planning, because it is not easy to change the root namespace after designing your hierarchy. For more information about planning your domain structure for Active Directory, see "Designing the Active Directory Structure" in this book.

Security

A review of your organization's security standards and how they are implemented is useful even if you are not moving to a new operating system, but it becomes particularly important when you do. Review your security standards and procedures for mobile and desktop users, internal and external networks, and dial-up and remote access accounts.

Are administrative tasks such as creating users, groups, and file shares, changing passwords, and configuring device and object attributes performed by a centralized group or by several groups? What are the specific rights and membership lists of these groups?

Document the types of relationships that currently exist among office locations, business units, and divisions in your organization. Are the administrative tasks in these units shared or is each unit responsible for its own administration? Do your user groups extend over company divisions or locations, or do you construct them by organizational unit? Document this and any existing user and enterprise security policies. Document what types of information are available to which groups, and any significant restrictions required for certain types of information, such as accounting data.

Document any guidelines that exist regarding appropriate network usage, such as whether staff members can access the Web and for what purposes, and what constitutes prohibited or inappropriate access.

The relationships your company has with outside vendors, customers, and joint venture or business partners affect your security strategy. Answer the following questions about your company's relationships:

- Do you have service-level commitments with your partners or permit them access to your network on a recognized user level?
- What are your policies concerning their access to your network data and resources?
- Can they view data on a read-only basis, or can they change or add to data on your network?
- How do you restrict access to applications?

Document the security and encryption standards currently in place or planned for the future in your organization by including the following information:

- Document security permissions on your network by user and user group.
- List your domains and the existing trust relationships between domain controllers.
- Document your password standards—how long a password must be, approved combinations of characters, how long a user is permitted to retain a password, and so on.
- List the security protocols used in your network.
- Document how you authenticate external users from the Internet, dial-up, and wide-area network (WAN) links to your network.
- Document the details of any multiple accounts that exist for a single user. For instance, do some of your users have an account for Windows NT and another account for UNIX? Document the permissions, user and user group memberships, and other details of these multiple accounts.

For more information about the issues involved in creating a network security plan, see "Planning Distributed Security" in this book. These issues involve recognizing the types of security risks your organization might face and planning ways to meet these risks. As part of this process, you will plan and develop policies concerning public key infrastructure and user authentication, and develop ways to secure e-mail and Web servers.

While you are reviewing your existing security arrangements, review your backup schemes, including whether you might reduce security risks by storing backups offsite, and whether your disaster recovery plan is up-to-date and appropriate to your current network size and demands. For more information about developing a storage configuration policy and disaster recovery plan, see "Determining Windows 2000 Storage Management Strategies" in this book.

For more information about security issues and planning using Windows 2000 features, see "Internet Protocol Security" in the *Microsoft Windows 2000 Server Resource Kit TCP/IP Core Networking Guide*, and "Planning Distributed Security" in this book.

Preparing Your Network Architecture

The following sections address how to prepare your network infrastructure for Windows 2000. While each network is different, and your priorities will be determined by many technical and organizational factors, you can use the general preparation path as shown in Figure 6.3.

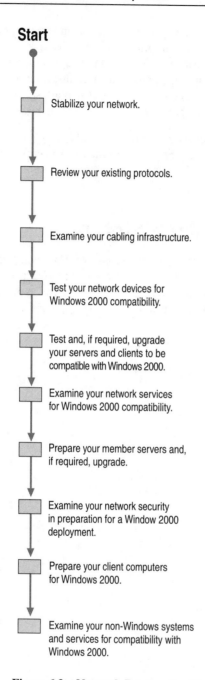

Start

Stabilize your network.

Review your existing protocols.

Examine your cabling infrastructure.

Test your network devices for Windows 2000 compatibility.

Test and, if required, upgrade your servers and clients to be compatible with Windows 2000.

Examine your network services for Windows 2000 compatibility.

Prepare your member servers and, if required, upgrade.

Examine your network security in preparation for a Window 2000 deployment.

Prepare your client computers for Windows 2000.

Examine your non-Windows systems and services for compatibility with Windows 2000.

Figure 6.3   Network Preparation Flowchart

Each of these topics is discussed in detail in chapters later in this book. This chapter explains the issues you should be aware of in each of these areas when preparing your network infrastructure for Windows 2000. It also guides you to the appropriate chapter in this book where you can find more details about these subjects.

Preliminary Steps

As you begin to prepare your network infrastructure for Windows 2000, stabilize your existing network and review your network protocols.

Stabilizing Your Existing Network

Before implementing a network upgrade or migration project, you should identify and correct any network transmission bottlenecks, poorly functioning hardware, unstable or problematic configurations, and other areas of concern. In a migration or upgrade project, marginal bandwidth and unstable network components will make reaching the goals of your project more difficult.

Target unstable computers, peripherals, and network devices as part of your hardware upgrade planning. Work to make your network maintenance schedule current before upgrading. When replacing network devices such as network adapters, replace them with Windows 2000–compatible devices, which are listed in the HCL.

Reviewing Your Network Protocols

Any network uses a variety of protocols as appropriate. Organizations that maintain an Ethernet network might use a combination of TCP/IP, NetBEUI, SPX/IPX, and others, depending on the networking, authentication, and security needs and capabilities of the operating systems in place. Identify the protocols in use on your network. As you do so, consider whether any of these protocols can be replaced by Windows 2000 versions or eliminated because they are no longer needed by upgraded clients. For instance, if you replace all clients that use SPX/IPX with Windows 98 or Windows 2000 Professional clients as part of your migration, you might be able to eliminate the use of IPX/SPX on your network, freeing up bandwidth. Consider simplifying your network by using only protocols in the TCP/IP suite.

Windows 2000 delivers a TCP/IP protocol suite that offers more functionality than previous versions, such as large window support and selective acknowledgment. You need to use the Microsoft TCP/IP protocol stack to obtain specific functionality, such as Active Directory support, and to take advantage of Windows 2000 advanced features. For example, previous versions of Windows NT use Point-to-Point Tunneling Protocol (PPTP) to secure communication links. Windows 2000 supports PPTP but offers increased functionality and communication link security by also supporting the Layer 2 Tunneling Protocol (L2TP). For more information about the features and performance enhancements in the Windows 2000 TCP/IP suite, see "Windows 2000 TCP/IP" in the *Microsoft Windows 2000 Server Resource Kit TCP/IP Core Networking Guide.*

Preparing Your Physical Infrastructure

Consider the quality and bandwidth of your existing network wiring and devices, and whether they will support your upgrade or migration plans. Are the network devices, such as hubs and cabling, fast enough for your purposes? How fast are your links to geographically dispersed sites? How much traffic is generated on your network internally and over links? For example, a remote office that uses a word processor or spreadsheet as its main desktop application does not generate much network traffic to the branch server, so Category 3 network cabling capable of 10-Mbps transmission matched with the same speed hubs might be acceptable. In the main office, shared applications with shared data, such as databases and accounting systems, are the main desktop applications. These applications generate considerably more network traffic, and require faster network devices and cabling.

The growing importance of having Internet access and multimedia available on the corporate desktop adds to the demand for bandwidth. Ethernet networks running shared applications might require Category 5 cable capable of 100-Mbps transmission speeds.

Evaluate bandwidth demand in your test lab for a specific configuration. For instance, if your organization plans to carry voice and video over your data network, your cabling and switches must be capable of handling the bandwidth demand of those services.

Third-party and built-in Windows NT diagnostic tools can help you to determine the bandwidth demand of, for instance, sending a compressed video signal over your network's WAN links. However, in a test lab you can test several possible configurations of your equipment and operating parameters to determine the lowest demand.

Your deployment plan will be affected by configuration requirements for the Windows 2000 features you plan to use. For example, if a Dfs volume in a branch office replicates over a slow link to an alternative Dfs volume, you might decide to either upgrade the link to improve bandwidth or place the alternative volume in the branch office to reduce the amount of network traffic on the slow link.

Some features of Windows 2000 require a specific configuration, such as placing a VPN server at one end of a WAN connection as part of establishing a secure VPN connection. You need to include configuration considerations, such as how you plan to integrate the VPN server with proxy servers, in your plan. Look at the existing infrastructure of your network and the anticipated benefits and features, such as secure WAN links using VPN, that you expect to deploy with Windows 2000. For more information about configuring your Windows 2000 security strategy, see "Determining Windows 2000 Network Security Strategies" in this book. For additional security-related information, see "Planning Distributed Security" in this book.

Review your network devices for compatibility with Windows 2000. Check the Hardware Compatibility List for network cards, modems, and certain kinds of hubs. For instance, Windows 2000 can offload TCP checksum calculations onto network adapters that support this Windows 2000 feature, improving network performance. For more information about the approved systems and devices on the HCL, see the Microsoft Windows Hardware Compatibility List link on the Web Resources page at http://windows.microsoft.com/windows2000/reskit/webresources.

Windows 2000 supports Asynchronous Transfer Mode (ATM), and offers an additional migration pathway from traditional shared-media networks to ATM by offering LAN emulation (LANE) services. Windows 2000 also supports IP over ATM. If you are planning to use Windows 2000 ATM or are currently using Windows NT 4.0 ATM, make sure that your ATM vendor supplies updated drivers for Windows 2000. Make certain that your ATM adapters are listed on the HCL.

Preparing Your Servers

You might be deploying Windows 2000 into a mixed-mode environment, or you might eventually move to a native Windows 2000 network. The planning you do in "Designing the Active Directory Structure" and "Determining Domain Migration Strategies" later in this book, for example, will be helpful when you implement or upgrade your IP addressing plan in conjunction with your Active Directory planning.

You have already identified your infrastructure servers—the primary and backup domain controllers, DNS, DHCP, WINS and other servers that comprise your infrastructure. Verify that your hardware drivers are available for Windows 2000. If the drivers or equipment you use are not on the HCL, check with the manufacturer for updated drivers, or test them yourself to determine compatibility with Windows 2000.

Previous versions of Windows NT and many third-party DNS servers cannot synchronize dynamically with DHCP, and therefore cannot maintain up-to-date associations between names and IP addresses. For this reason, consider upgrading your DNS services to Windows 2000–compatible DNS. Windows 2000 DNS automatically updates DNS record fields, thereby reducing the need for manual updating that was required previously.

When you are considering upgrading your network, consider the placement of your DHCP servers in regard to the number and size of geographical sites on your network and the speed and reliability of its WAN links. DHCP traffic between remote sites requires an improvement in the bandwidth and reliability of the link between sites. For more information about this topic, see "Determining Network Connectivity Strategies" in this book.

If you plan to support clients that resolve IP addressing using NetBIOS requests, you will continue to need WINS to resolve computer names to IP addresses. In general, MS-DOS®, Windows version 3.2x and earlier, Windows 95, Windows 98, and Windows NT systems use NetBIOS to resolve IP addresses. Now is a good time to begin eliminating the use of WINS on your network.

Windows 2000 DHCP offers multimedia support through enhanced monitoring, a management snap-in, and support for multicasting. Windows 2000 DHCP is also dynamically integrated with Windows 2000 DNS in support of Active Directory. Older versions of DNS do not offer this support, and you should consider upgrading if you plan to deploy Active Directory or want to use Network Load Balancing to balance demand on your DHCP servers.

Installing Windows 2000 Routing and Remote Access servers is necessary for LAN-to-LAN and secure VPN links and remote access. Routing and Remote Access is integrated into Windows 2000, and supports a variety of other protocols, such as IPX/SPX and AppleTalk.

If you are deploying Windows 2000 in a mixed environment with UNIX systems, note the version of BIND that exists on your system. While Windows 2000 is fully compatible with earlier versions of BIND, it offers improved DNS functionality with BIND versions 4.9.4 and later.

Preparing Your Domain Controllers

Some companies will plan an incremental deployment of Windows 2000 into their production environment, while others will plan for a complete migration to the new system. By installing Windows 2000 on a few servers in your organization, you can maintain your existing Windows NT 4.0 domain and trust relationships within the Windows 2000 domain framework, and give your company time to become familiar with Windows 2000 operations and concepts. For more information about migration strategies, see "Determining Domain Migration Strategies" in this book.

Windows 2000 is designed to work within a Windows NT 4.0 network. Windows NT 4.0 workstations, using the NTLM protocol, can send network authentication requests to any Windows 2000 domain controller acting as a domain controller in a Windows NT domain. Trust relationships are easily established between Windows 2000 domains and Windows NT 4.0 domains, supporting authentication between domains. When deploying Windows 2000, you do not need to migrate all of your Windows NT 4.0 domains to Windows 2000 at the same time.

When you upgrade a domain to Windows 2000, you need to upgrade the primary domain controller in a given domain first. Then upgrade the backup domain controllers in that domain to Windows 2000 domain controllers at your own pace. Then add the domain to the Active Directory tree. You can upgrade member servers and client computers independently from your domain upgrade strategy, but if no Windows 2000 domain controller is installed, these computers will not have access to Active Directory or other advanced features.

When you upgrade a domain controller, as in most network-related operations, have a plan to roll back your changes if something goes wrong. One of the tasks you should perform to prepare for a domain controller upgrade is to bring current and then isolate a backup domain controller, so it can act as a recovery domain controller. For more information about preparing a recovery domain controller, see "Determining Domain Migration Strategies" in this book.

If a Windows 2000 domain controller is functioning within a domain containing Windows NT backup domain controllers, the total number of objects (users, user groups, and computers) in that domain should not exceed the recommended limit for Windows NT domains of 40,000.

Preparing Your Member Servers

A member server is any server that functions as a member of a Windows NT or Windows 2000 domain, but whose role is not that of domain controller. Member server roles include:

- File, application, and print servers
- Web, proxy, and remote access servers
- Database servers
- Certificate servers

Installing Windows 2000 on your member servers permits improved functionality in each of the member server roles.

Remember, when assessing the hardware compatibility of a computer, to consider its role after the upgrade. There are no rigid specifications for estimating the hardware components required for a particular function. You will need to test the computer in its role (preferably in your test lab rather than in your production network) to determine whether it is adequate in terms of CPU speed, RAM, and hard disk space, and whether it performs adequately while running the drivers, applications, and protocols of its intended role.

For more information about preparing your member servers, see "Upgrading and Installing Member Servers" and "Automating Server Installation and Upgrade" in this book.

Preparing Your Security Infrastructure

Microsoft Windows 2000 has been designed to provide very high levels of data security, while offering administrators the benefits of ease of implementation and administration. New features such as IPSec, Kerberos authentication, and public keys offer a higher level of security than previous versions of Windows NT.

Because Windows 2000 is designed to operate within an existing Windows NT domain structure, you can easily introduce Windows 2000–based servers into your existing network security structure. However, as you migrate or upgrade your existing Windows NT network to Windows 2000, your security strategy will be influenced by the security-specific features of Windows 2000 that you plan to deploy. For instance, if you are currently using Microsoft Proxy Server in your network, you will need to upgrade this product for Windows 2000, and install the proper client software to use the service.

Windows 2000 supports public key infrastructure (PKI), an authentication method employing digital certificates, certification authorities, and certificate management software. You can use certificate authentication to secure e-mail clients and Internet communication, in support of smart card technology, and to secure communication (using IPSec) with non-Kerberos clients. For more information about planning and deploying a PKI, see "Planning Your Public Key Infrastructure" in this book. The details of how you deploy your PKI are determined by the specific certificate services you employ—you can use Microsoft Certificate Services or third-party certificate services.

Define your certificate requirements, practices, and strategies. If you are thinking of implementing a third-party PKI, make sure it is compatible with Windows 2000. In this case, compatibility means support of rooted certification hierarchies as implemented in Windows 2000. Note that the Windows 2000 PKI will not replace existing Windows domain trust and authorization mechanisms, such as the Kerberos protocol. The PKI features of Windows 2000 are integrated with the domain controller and Kerberos authentication services.

You can implement PKI in stages to support particular goals, such as in support of e-mail or to support authentication to existing systems, depending on your priorities.

▶ **To implement PKI in stages**

1. Install root certification authorities in the parent domains for each Windows 2000 tree in your domain forest.

2. Install intermediate certification authorities in the domains of each business unit.

3. Install and configure issuing certificate authorities and services in the domains for each user group, at each site as required.

Preparing Your Clients

Because Windows 2000 is designed for interoperability, client computers running previous versions of Windows are interoperable with Windows 2000 in a mixed-mode environment. However, upgrading your client computers to Windows 2000 Professional offers improved client computer and user security, improved reliability, and increased functionality.

Not all versions of Windows can be upgraded to Windows 2000 Professional. You can upgrade the following versions of Windows and Windows NT to Windows 2000 Professional:

Windows 95 All versions are supported for upgrade, including OSR2.x. However, if your clients are running Windows 95 from a server, you need to install it directly on the computer, or perform a clean installation of Windows 2000 Professional.

Windows 98   All versions are supported for upgrade. See "Windows 2000 Professional Upgrade Considerations" later in this chapter.

Windows NT 4.0 Workstation   All versions are supported for upgrade. See "Windows 2000 Professional Upgrade Considerations" later in this chapter.

Windows NT 3.51 Workstation   All versions are supported for upgrade.

An important requirement for your client computers is hardware and driver compatibility with Windows 2000.

Windows 2000 Professional Upgrade Considerations

Some applications and drivers that worked with the previous operating system will have problems functioning properly in a Windows 2000 Professional environment. The following sections discuss issues that you might encounter when upgrading Windows NT, Windows 95, and Windows 98 clients.

Note   Windows version 3.1 and earlier are not suitable candidates for upgrade.

Upgrading Windows NT Clients

Windows NT clients are, in general, easily upgraded to Windows 2000 Professional, with the following considerations:

- Any client-level applications that depend on file system filters, such as antivirus or disk quota software, will not operate properly because of changes in the Windows 2000 file system model.

- If your clients are running networking protocols that do not have an updated version in the I386\Winntupg folder, found on the Windows 2000 operating system CD, reconsider your use of these protocols or find updated, Windows 2000–compatible versions for the upgrade.

- If your clients are using third-party power management tools, consider using the Windows 2000 Advanced Configuration and Power Interface (ACPI) and Advanced Power Management (APM) to replace these previous solutions.

- Remove third-party Plug and Play drivers before upgrading to Windows 2000.

Upgrading Windows 95 and Windows 98 Clients

The upgrade path for Windows 95 and Windows 98 clients is generally easy. However, keep the following cautions in mind as you consider upgrading these clients:

- As noted previously, any client-level applications that depend on previous file systems will not operate properly. For example, any compressed disk utilities will not work, nor will tools such as disk defragmenters. Antivirus applications must be compatible with Windows 2000 to run properly.

- Applications and tools that use virtual device drivers (VxDs) and .386 drivers will not operate correctly. Contact the manufacturer of these applications to find out if updated drivers exist.

- Many client computers have existing third-party device drivers installed. When these device drivers are installed, sometimes a Control Panel application is also installed to provide additional functionality (such as configuration control). Test these Control Panel applications in a Windows 2000 environment and ask the manufacturer about Windows 2000 compatibility.

- The same cautions given previously concerning network protocols, third-party power management tools, and third-party Plug and Play drivers also apply to your Windows 98 and Windows 95 clients.

Preparing to Operate with Other Systems

Many organizations operate in a heterogeneous environment, with a mix of operating systems. Windows 2000 Server offers gateway services to other operating systems, permitting Windows clients to gain access to other operating systems and resources. For instance, by installing Gateway Services for NetWare, your Windows clients can benefit from being in a Windows 2000 network while also retaining the ability to navigate Novell Directory Services (NDS) hierarchies, use Novell version 4.x or later logon scripts, and authenticate with a Novell server.

Network Infrastructure Preparation Task List

Table 6.1 outlines the recommended tasks you need to complete to prepare your existing network infrastructure for Windows 2000.

Table 6.1   Planning Task List for Infrastructure Preparation

Task	Chapter section
Create a hardware and software inventory.	Hardware and Software Inventory
Confirm that all hardware conforms to the HCL and is appropriate for your deployment plans, and determine a specific hardware upgrade plan for each computer.	Hardware and Software Inventory
Document server and client network configurations. Document your infrastructure servers.	Network Infrastructure
Document the details of your network configuration—your name resolution services, IP addressing, WAN link details, and physical layout.	Network Infrastructure
Create a physical and logical diagram of your network.	Network Infrastructure
Document the configuration of your member servers.	File, Print, and Web Servers
Identify all critical applications and check them for Windows 2000 compatibility.	Line-of-Business Applications
Document your domain structure and administrative model, including trust relationships, primary domain controller and backup domain controller locations, and DNS namespaces.	Domain Services Architecture
Document your network security details.	Security
Stabilize your network.	Preliminary Steps
Review network protocols.	Preliminary Steps
Prepare your physical infrastructure.	Preparing Your Physical Infrastructure
Review network devices for Windows 2000 compatibility.	Preparing Your Physical Infrastructure
Prepare your infrastructure servers.	Preparing Your Infrastructure
Upgrade your domain controllers.	Preparing Your Domain Controllers

C H A P T E R   7

Determining Network Connectivity Strategies

Microsoft® Windows® 2000 Server has several new features that network administrators can use to enhance their new or existing network infrastructures. This chapter includes information about network connectivity issues, address allocation, TCP/IP, and other protocol issues. This information will help you determine the best network connectivity strategy for your organization.

To get the most from reading this chapter, some knowledge of Microsoft® Windows NT® and Windows NT networking is helpful. You also need to be familiar with fundamental and advanced networking concepts, such as TCP/IP addressing, routing protocols, and remote access.

In This Chapter

Chapter Goals

This chapter will help you develop the following planning documents:

- An evaluation of your current network, protocols, and routing infrastructure.
- A network connectivity strategy.
- A physical network design diagram.
- A network protocol and routing infrastructure design.

Related Information in the Resource Kit

- For more information about Windows 2000 TCP/IP, see the *Microsoft® Windows® 2000 Server Resource Kit TCP/IP Core Networking Guide*.
- For more information about Windows 2000 Routing And Remote Access, see the *Microsoft® Windows® 2000 Server Resource Kit Internetworking Guide*.
- For more information about deploying security within a Windows 2000 infrastructure, see "Determining Windows 2000 Network Security Strategies" in this book.

Network Connectivity Overview

There are several things to consider when determining how to implement or upgrade your network to Windows 2000. If a network diagram that relates to your current network exists, then consult that diagram to determine where to strategically implement the new features of Windows 2000. As an example, you need to examine clients, servers, switches, and routers to see whether or not they currently use services such as Quality of Service (QoS), Asynchronous Transfer Mode (ATM), or routing protocols. Also examine and modify TCP/IP addressing schemes, if necessary, to take advantage of the new options in Windows 2000 Dynamic Host Configuration Protocol (DHCP).

If you have not done so already, create physical and logical diagrams that reflect your network needs. This is essential because the diagrams give an overall view of the infrastructure before any steps are taken to physically assemble the network. This allows the designer and administrator to work together to put network systems and devices in place. The following sections describe what you can include in the diagram.

Sites

Show a graphic depiction of where sites are located in the diagram. This helps when you determine wide-area and remote-site connectivity methods. You need to implement sites according to geographical boundaries, administrative boundaries, or both.

Remote Connectivity Methods

Include mediums for connecting remote sites to the central site in your diagram. This can include T1, E1, Frame Relay, Integrated Services Digital Network (ISDN), or plain old telephone service (POTS). You can also use the diagram to show the types of routers used to connect the sites to the wide-area backbone. These routers can be Windows 2000 routers or routers from various third-party vendors. Show methods for connecting remote users to sites, using technologies such as direct dial-up and virtual private networks (VPNs).

Internal Local Area Network Connectivity Within Sites

Create a graphical depiction of the internal networks of the sites in order to utilize the new features of Windows 2000 most efficiently. Include the following information:

Network medium Include the type of infrastructure you plan to use, such as 10 or 100BaseT connectivity, ATM, or gigabit Ethernet. If you plan to use ATM, determine which sections of the network will be directly connected to ATM, using IP over ATM or local area network emulation (LANE).

Routing and switching infrastructure Determine where you plan to place routers and switches. This is important to maintain network bandwidth and minimize bottlenecks. Also make sure that the routing and switching hardware you plan to use can support technologies such as QoS.

Protocols If you plan to use TCP/IP, show the IP addressing scheme for each subnet within the site. If you plan to use other protocols such as IPX, AppleTalk, or NetBIOS Enhanced User Interface (NetBEUI), show them also. Also consider including the routing protocols such as OSPF or RIP that you might use for connecting your networks. For more information about using TCP/IP, see "Windows 2000 TCP/IP" in the *Microsoft Windows 2000 Core Networking Guide.* Also see "Unicast IP Routing," "IPX Routing," and "Services for Macintosh" in the *Microsoft Windows 2000 Server Internetworking Guide.*

DNS and Active Directory structure Design the DNS and Active Directory™ structure for your network. Include a logical domain diagram with your network diagram that shows the domains and forests in your company. For more information about the Active Directory directory service, see "Designing the Active Directory Structure" in this book.

Server infrastructure Show placement of DNS, DHCP, and WINS servers in your diagram.

Remote connectivity methods Show how remote clients and remote networks will connect to the corporate network in your diagram.

The following sections discuss designing a network that best incorporates the features of Windows 2000 Server into your organization and outline steps for determining a network connectivity strategy.

Figure 7.1 illustrates the primary steps for determining your network connectivity strategy.

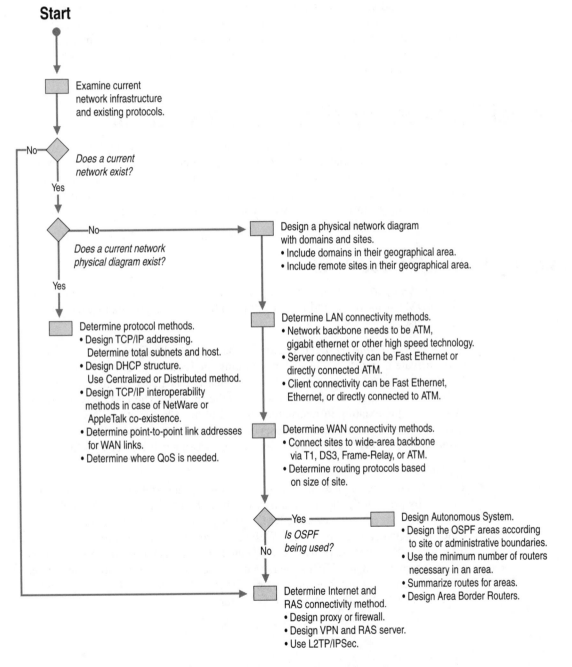

Figure 7.1   Process for Determining Network Connectivity Strategies

Designing a network for Windows 2000 consists of first designing many small parts of a network that form the overall infrastructure. The sections that follow describe the different aspects of a wide area network (WAN), along with some procedures and design considerations for each. The external, wide-area aspects of a corporate network infrastructure are covered, such as demilitarized zones (DMZs), site implementation, and remote access connectivity. The internal aspects of the network, such as protocols, security, and local area network (LAN) connectivity methods, are also examined.

External Connectivity Within an Organization

For remote users to gain access to the central site, you need to deploy a connectivity method that allows site-to-site and remote client connectivity. Your organization's central site needs to have a network that permits these other sites and remote clients to gain access to the central site's internal network structure. The following sections describe what you need to include in an external connectivity strategy.

Designing the Demilitarized Zone

An important part of a large corporate network is the DMZ. This section describes what a DMZ is used for, and later sections in this chapter give examples of how a DMZ is used.

A *demilitarized zone (DMZ)* is a network that permits the egression of the Internet into a private network, while still maintaining the security of that network. The DMZ gives a business the ability to use the Internet as a cost-saving medium, while also allowing it to have a presence on the Internet. The DMZ saves money by utilizing the existing infrastructure of the Internet along with VPNs, thereby saving the wide-area connection costs of leasing communications lines. Essentially, the DMZ is a network that is in between a private network and the Internet.

The DMZ contains devices such as servers, routers, and switches that maintain security by preventing the internal network from being exposed on the Internet. The servers that reside within the DMZ usually consist of proxy server arrays, which the network uses to provide Web access for internal users; external Internet Information Services (IIS), which an organization can use to promote its presence on the Internet; and any VPN servers that are used to provide secure connections for remote clients. For more information about VPNs, see "VPN Security" and "L2TP over IPSec VPNs" later in this chapter.

An example of a DMZ is shown in Figure 7.2. The device on the edge of the DMZ is a router. Preferably, the speed of the connection exposed to the Internet is at least DS3, or 45 megabits per second (Mbps) for a large corporation. The connection between the router and the servers in the DMZ can be any high-speed LAN, but gigabit Ethernet or ATM are recommended if you expect heavy Internet traffic.

You can use a Windows 2000 Routing and Remote Access router on a DMZ interface for small- to medium-sized networks. You can enable packet filtering on the Internet interfaces to protect against unwanted traffic and provide security.

Site Connectivity for an Organization

Many large corporations have offices that are spread out in various geographical locations. These offices need a way to connect and remain connected to the main or central site. Different wide-area connection media are used in different parts of the world. Table 7.1 describes the various wide-area technologies and their uses.

Table 7.1   Wide-Area Technologies

Wide-Area Technology	Definition
T1	Transmits at a speed of 1.544 Mbps, and consists of 23 B channels, which are used for data, and a 1 D channel which is used for clocking. T1 can also be fractionalized into separate 64 kilobytes per second (Kbps) segments.
E1	Used primarily in Europe. Transmits at a speed of 2.048 Mbps.
T3	Transmits DS3 data at 44.736 Mbps.
Frame Relay	Packet-switched technology that is considered the replacement for X.25. Commonly runs at speeds up to T1.
Digital Subscriber Line (DSL)	DSL consists of an asymmetric digital subscriber line (ADSL), a high-data-rate digital subscriber line (HDSL), a single-line digital subscriber line (SDSL), and a very-high-data-rate digital subscriber line (VDSL).

Site connectivity can also rely on the use of dial-up mediums such as Integrated Services Digital Network (ISDN), or analog phone lines (POTS) for low traffic links or backup purposes. For instance, an organization might have a small site to which they normally connect by using a fractional T1 line, but in the event that their wide-area provider fails, they can use the POTS line as a backup.

Multiple sites within an organization are normally connected through routers. Windows 2000 Routing and Remote Access offers routing services that enable an organization to cost-effectively connect remote sites to the central corporate site. Sites can be connected through the Internet using VPNs, saving money for your organization. If you have a site that does not require a full-time connection to the central site, then you can implement a demand-dial router-to-router connection, saving wide-area connection costs.

Remote Client Connectivity

One of the things that makes an organization more effective is the ability of its users to access corporate resources, whether they are at home or traveling. Many corporations are starting to use a work-at-home strategy. This strategy allows employees to save the expense of commuting, while allowing the corporation the ability to cost-effectively manage office space as the number of employees grows. Another benefit of implementing remote client connectivity is the ability to permit traveling sales and technical people to dial in and retrieve files and e-mail.

In either case, users who are away from the office need to be able to connect to their mail and file servers, which are located within the corporate network infrastructure. The Windows 2000 Routing and Remote Access service allows this by being able to receive incoming remote access connections, and then routing the data to its intended destination. The Routing and Remote Access service can also be used to receive incoming VPN connections, providing a secure way to transfer data across the Internet. For more information about VPNs, see "VPN Security" and "L2TP over IPSec VPNs" later in this chapter.

Remote client access to a corporate infrastructure is not limited to just Internet Protocol (IP) clients. Windows 2000 Routing and Remote Access service also permits other clients, such as Macintosh, UNIX, or NetWare clients, to use remote access through its multiprotocol functionality. The VPN protocols supported in Windows 2000 PPTP) and Layer 2 Tunneling Protocol (L2TP) also support multiprotocol connections across the Internet.

Windows 2000 TCP/IP

Networks in today's organizations require a protocol that rates high in performance and scalability, and places a high degree of importance on Internet interoperability. The TCP/IP protocol is an industry-standard suite of protocols that is the foundation for large-scale internetworks that span LAN and WAN networks, and is quickly becoming the leading protocol for both intranets and the Internet.

Windows 2000 TCP/IP is:

- A networking protocol based on industry standards.
- A routable networking protocol that supports connecting Windows-based servers and clients to LANs and WANs.
- A scalable protocol for integrating Windows-based servers and workstations with heterogeneous systems.
- A foundation for gaining access to global Internet services.

Microsoft TCP/IP provides basic and advanced features that enable a computer running Windows 2000 to connect and share information with computers running other operating systems such as UNIX.

New Features in the Windows 2000 TCP/IP Suite

The new Microsoft TCP/IP suite is designed to adjust itself for reliability and performance. The next four sections discuss the new features in the TCP/IP suite.

Automatic Private IP Addressing Configuration

Automatic Private IP Addressing (APIPA) configuration consists of automatically allocating a unique address in the range of 169.254.0.1 through 169.254.255.254, with a subnet mask of 255.255.0.0 when a DHCP server is not present. APIPA is used for single subnet networks such as SOHO networks that are too small to justify running a separate DHCP server.

For example, if you have a home office and need a way to distribute IP addresses to internal Windows 2000 servers and clients, all you need to do is to connect the systems together through a network medium, then each Windows 2000 computer self-assigns an address from the APIPA address range.

Large Window Support

Large receive window support increases the amount of data that can be buffered on a connection at one time, reducing network traffic and speeding up data transfer.

Note Large window support is not enabled by default. The window size defaults to about 16 kilobytes (KB), which is double the window size of Windows NT 4.0.

Selective Acknowledgment

Selective acknowledgments allow the receiver to inform the sender to retransmit only the data it has not received as opposed to entire blocks of data. This enables more efficient use of network bandwidth.

Improved Estimation of Round Trip Time

TCP uses round trip time (RTT) to estimate the amount of time that is needed for roundtrip communication between the sender and receiver. Windows 2000 TCP makes better estimates of RTT for setting transmission timers, which improves overall TCP performance. This improvement in TCP primarily helps in WANs that span very long distances, or over slow links such as satellite communication.

Planning Considerations for Microsoft TCP/IP

If your network does not already use TCP/IP, then you need to develop a comprehensive IP addressing plan for your network. When planning your IP infrastructure, include IP network IDs and subnet masks. Use the information in the following sections to create a workable plan.

IP Address Classes

Choosing which address class to use depends on whether your network is private or connected to the Internet. Network addressing is also determined by the size of your infrastructure, which directly relates to which address range to use. Consider the following when planning IP addresses for your network:

Physical Subnet and Host Inventory Count the subnets and hosts that you have in your current network and then determine how many you need for your new one by subnetting your IP address space. As you do this, plan ahead for at least five years of growth so that you do not run out of addresses or subnets prematurely. If your network is connected directly to the Internet, you will need an IP address range assigned to you from your Internet service provider. For more information about subnetting IP addresses spaces, see "Internet Protocol Security" in the *Windows 2000 Server Resource Kit TCP/IP Core Networking Guide*.

Note It is important to have only a few TCP/IP systems within your network that are directly connected to the Internet, such as the DMZ. The fewer systems that are accessible from the Internet, the safer your network is from attack.

Private Networks with or without Proxy Connection to the Internet

For private TCP/IP networks that are not connected to the Internet, or are connected to the Internet through a proxy server, you can use any range of valid IP addresses from the Class A, B, or C address classes. It is recommended, however, that you use private addresses to prevent a renumbering of your internetwork when you eventually connect to the Internet. The private IP address space is defined as three sets of IP addresses set aside by the Internet Assigned Numbers Authority (IANA). The reserved IP ranges are:

- 10.0.0.1/8 through 10.255.255.254/8
- 172.16.0.1/12 through 172.31.255.254/12
- 192.168.0.1/16 through 192.168.255.254/16

Note For more information about private addressing, see RFC 1918. The private network address range shown here uses network prefix notation, also known as Classless Interdomain Routing (CIDR) notation to define subnet masks.

Subnet Masks and Custom Subnetting

With public IP addresses in short supply, you can use customized subnet masks to implement IP subnetting. Custom subnetting is defined either as subnetting, Classless Interdomain Routing (CIDR), or variable length subnet mask (VLSM). With custom IP subnetting, you can go beyond the limitations of default subnet masks and use your IP address range more efficiently.

By customizing the subnet mask length, you can reduce the number of bits that are used for the actual host ID. In some cases, you can use default subnet masks for standard-size class A, B, and C networks. Default subnet masks are dotted decimal values that separate the network ID from the host ID of an IP address. For example, if you have a network segment and are using the class A IP address range starting at 10.0.0.0, the default subnet mask that you would use is 255.0.0.0. Typically, default values for subnet masks are acceptable for networks with no special requirements where each IP network segment corresponds to a single physical network.

Note To prevent addressing and routing problems, make sure all TCP/IP computers on any network segment use the same subnet mask.

You can also show subnet masks with your IP addresses by using network prefix notation. This option allows you to show a shortened version of the subnet mask while still maintaining its value. Table 7.2 describes this process. The underlined bits in Table 7.2 make up the network prefix.

Table 7.2   Network Prefix Length Subnet Masking

Address Class	Subnet Mask in Binary	Network Prefix with Decimal Equivalent
Class A	11111111 00000000 00000000 00000000	/8 = 255.0.0.0
Class B	11111111 11111111 00000000 00000000	/16 = 255.255.0.0
Class C	11111111 11111111 11111111 00000000	/24 = 255.255.255.0

TCP/IP and Windows Internet Name Service

The Windows Internet Name Service (WINS) is a service that maps network basic input/output system (NetBIOS) names to IP addresses. In versions of Windows earlier than Windows 2000, WINS is used in conjunction with DHCP to register NetBIOS names and dynamically-assigned IP addresses with the WINS database. In this case, a DHCP-enabled host queries a DHCP server for an IP address, the DHCP server then allocates a WINS server to the DHCP client as a DHCP option. After the DHCP lease allocation process is complete, the NetBIOS name and its associated IP address are registered in the WINS database by the DHCP client.

Windows 2000 provides integration between DNS and WINS. If a Windows 2000 DNS server cannot resolve a fully qualified domain name (FQDN), it converts the FQDN to a NetBIOS name and queries a configured WINS server. The IP address returned by the WINS server is forwarded to the DNS client.

In Windows 2000, you do not need WINS and NetBIOS over TCP/IP if you are using only Windows 2000 servers and clients. If you use systems such as Windows NT version 3.5x, Windows NT 4.0, Windows 95, Windows 98, or Windows 3.x, WINS is still required because those operating systems use NetBIOS name resolution and NetBIOS sessions to create file and print sharing connections.

WINS Design Considerations

If NetBIOS name resolution is required, each site within a domain needs to have at least one WINS server. You can install the WINS server on the same system as the DNS server, or you can install it separately. You also need to install a backup WINS server elsewhere in the network. You can install the backup WINS server on the same system as a Windows 2000 domain controller, or you can install it separately.

Routing and Remote Access

Routing is the process of using addressing information present in a network packet to determine the path that packet should take to reach its destination. Routing is required when the source host and destination host are on different logical networks. Routing is required in larger network infrastructures because it is impractical to use one set of addresses for the entire network. This is because as networks increase in size, so does the addressing complexity. In addition, it is impractical to put all systems in a large network on the same logical network. This causes a large amount of network traffic.

You can segment a TCP/IP network by dividing the IP address range into subnets. Once the IP addresses are broken up, the newly formed *subnets* use routers to forward data from one subnet to another. You can also use routing to connect dissimilar networks such as Ethernet, ATM, and Token Ring.

Routing tables are used to keep track of routes from hosts that reside in one subnet to hosts that reside in another. As networks increase in size, so do the number of routers within the infrastructure and the size of routing tables. If administrators had to keep track of these routes, they would have to constantly monitor the network for routers that go offline or links that temporarily fail, then manually enter this information into routing tables. Routers use industry standard routing protocols to dynamically update routing tables as the network changes.

Windows 2000 Server supplies businesses with LAN-to-LAN routing and offers an alternative to purchasing dedicated router hardware, by integrating the Routing and Remote Access service within Windows 2000 Server. This service supports the ability to dynamically route TCP/IP, Internetwork Packet Exchange (IPX), and AppleTalk traffic by utilizing built-in routing protocols. The Routing and Remote Access service can also provide remote office connectivity by supporting wide-area connections.

New Features of Windows 2000 Routing and Remote Access Service

This section discusses the new features of the Windows 2000 Routing and Remote Access service, which allows businesses and their associated remote access clients to send and receive data more securely by utilizing the Internet as a data path. Clients within the Windows 2000 network structure can enjoy the benefit of accessing multicast data from the Internet.

Table 7.3 describes the new features of Windows 2000 Routing and Remote Access.

Table 7.3   New Features of Windows 2000 Routing and Remote Access

Feature	Description
Windows 2000 Active Directory Integration	Permits browsing and managing Remote Access servers by using Active Directory-based tools such as the Routing and Remote Access administrative tool.
Version 2 of Microsoft Challenge Handshake Authentication Protocol (CHAP)	Strong security credential passing and encryption key generation. This protocol is designed specifically for authenticating VPN connections using the PPTP protocol.
Extensible Authentication Protocol (EAP)	Allows third-party authentication methods to plug in to the Windows 2000 point-to-point protocol (PPP) implementation. The built-in EAP/Transport Layer Security (TLS) method supports deployment of smart cards for secure authentication and strong encryption key generation.
Bandwidth Allocation Protocol	Allows a more efficient Multilink PPP connection by dynamically adding and dropping links to accommodate changes in traffic flow. This is useful for networks that carry charges based on bandwidth use. Useful with ISDN channels and similar communications technologies.
Remote access policies	Gives administrators the ability to control connections based on time of day, group membership, type of connection, and other criteria.
Layer 2 Tunneling Protocol (L2TP)	Provides client-to-gateway and gateway-to-gateway VPN connections, secured by Internet Protocol security (IPSec).
IP multicast support	Supports Internet Group Membership Protocol IGMP Version 2 and acts as a multicast forwarding router, which allows the forwarding of IP multicast traffic between connected clients and the Internet or a corporate network.
Network Address Translation (NAT)	Provides a small to medium network with a single interface that connects to the Internet and provides IP address translation services between public and private IP addresses. Also provides IP address assignment and DNS proxy name resolution services to internal network clients.
Internet Connection Sharing (ICS)	Provides a small network with an easy to configure, but limited interface that connects SOHO clients to the Internet. ICS provides DNS name resolution, automatic address allocation, and a single IP address range for IP distribution.

Remote Access Policy

In Windows NT versions 3.5*x* and 4.0, remote access authorization was based on a simple **Grant dial-in permission to user** option in User Manager or the Remote Access Administration tool. Callback options were also configured on a per-user basis. In Windows 2000, authorization is granted based on the dial-up properties of a user account and remote access policies. Remote access policies are a set of conditions and connection settings that give network administrators more flexibility when authorizing connection attempts. Windows 2000 Routing and Remote Access service and Windows 2000 Internet Authentication Service (IAS) both use remote access policies to determine whether to accept or reject connection attempts. In both cases, the remote access policies are stored locally. Policy is now dictated on a per-call basis.

With remote access policies, you can grant or deny authorization by time of day or day of the week, by the Windows 2000 group to which the remote access user belongs, by the type of connection being requested (dial-up networking or VPN connection), and so on. You can configure settings that limit the maximum session time, specify the authentication and encryption strengths, set Bandwidth Allocation Protocol (BAP) policies, and so on.

It is important to remember that with remote access policies, a connection is authorized only if the settings of the connection attempt to match at least one of the remote access policies (subject to the conditions of the dial-up properties of the user account and the profile properties of the remote access policy). If the settings of the connection attempt do not match at least one of the remote access policies, the connection attempt is denied regardless of the dial-up properties of the user account.

Remote Access Design Considerations

The following are some considerations when designing remote access schemes:

- If you have installed a DHCP server, configure the Routing and Remote Access server to use DHCP to obtain IP addresses for remote access clients.

- If you do not have a DHCP server installed, configure the Routing and Remote Access server with a static IP address pool, which is a subset of addresses from the subnet to which the remote access server is attached.

- If configuring IPX, configure the remote access server to automatically allocate the same IPX network ID to all remote access clients.

VPN Security

Network security is a concern for most organizations, and two protocols that Windows 2000 networks use to ensure secure communications across the Internet are the Point-to-Point Tunneling Protocol (PPTP) and the L2TP, which is used in conjunction with Internet Protocol security (IPSec). Microsoft TCP/IP, PPTP, and L2TP/IPSec provide the highest levels of security, protecting paths between hosts and gateways.

Benefits of Virtual Private Networking

The following list contains reasons why it is beneficial to use VPN connections instead of long distance direct-dial connections.

Reduced Cost Overhead One of the major concerns of a large organization is cost overhead, and phone costs are one of the largest expenses a company has. Using the Internet as a connection medium instead of a long distance telephone service saves the company phone expenses and requires less hardware. For example, the client only needs to call the local ISP, then, L2TP and IPSec allow users to obtain secure connections to Internet-attached Windows 2000 VPN servers running Routing and Remote Access service.

Reduced Management Overhead Because the local phone company owns and manages the phone lines that support your VPN connections, there is less management for network administrators.

Added Security Windows 2000 uses standard, interoperable authentication and encryption protocols that allow data to be hidden from the unsecured environment of the Internet, but remain accessible to corporate users through a VPN. Also, if the VPN tunnel is encrypted with IPSec, the Internet only sees the external IP addresses while the internal addresses are protected. In other words, it is extremely difficult for a hacker to interpret the data sent across a VPN tunnel.

Point-to-Point Tunneling Protocol VPNs

PPTP is an excellent solution to the tunneling needs of clients. It is relatively simple to set up when compared to L2TP/IPSec, and it provides good security when used with a user name/strong password method. PPTP is an industry standard protocol that was first supported in Windows NT 4.0. This protocol uses the authentication, compression, and encryption of the PPP. PPTP is still in wide use on networks today. Because L2TP along with IPSec can provide better security, this chapter discusses L2TP and IPSec encryption in more depth.

L2TP over IPSec VPNs

L2TP over IPSec VPNs enable a business to transport data over the Internet, while still maintaining a high level of security to protect data. You can use this type of secure connection for small or remote office clients that need access to the corporate network. You can also use L2TP over IPSec VPNs for routers at remote sites by using the local ISP and creating a demand-dial connection into corporate headquarters.

When you are deciding where and how to design L2TP over IPSec connections, remember that the Internet access point or DMZ of the network is where the VPN server will reside. The VPN server is responsible for enforcing user access policy decisions that might be configured on the user account in the Windows 2000 domain controller, in remote access policy and dial-up user profiles on the VPN server, or in the IAS.

L2TP creates the necessary IPSec security policy to secure tunnel traffic. You do not need to assign or activate your own IPSec policy on either computer. If the computer already has an IPSec policy active, the L2TP will simply add a security rule to protect L2TP tunnel traffic to the existing policy.

L2TP Deployment Considerations

For an L2TP over IPSec connection to occur, you need to install computer certificates on the VPN client and VPN server computers. After a client requests a VPN connection, VPN access is granted through the combination of the dial-up properties on the user account and remote access policies. In Windows NT 4.0, the administrator only needed to select **Grant dial-in permission to user** on the dial-up properties in **User Manager** or **User Manager for Domains** to allow remote access use.

In Windows 2000, the administrator can permit or deny remote access to the corporate network using remote access policies on the VPN server and in IAS, allowing you to better define security settings. With remote access policies, a connection is accepted only if its settings match at least one of the remote access policies. If it does not match, the connection is denied.

For deployment of large remote access VPNs, you can use the Connection Manager and the Connection Manager Administration Kit to provide a custom dialer with preconfigured VPN connections to all remote access clients across your organization. These tools produce a one-click dial-up and VPN connection for users, combining what would normally be two or three steps into one.

L2TP Examples

Following are a few situations where you can use L2TP:

Persistent Connection Router-to-Router VPN   A router-to-router VPN is typically used to connect remote offices when both routers are connected to the Internet through permanent WAN links such as T1, T3, Frame-Relay, and cable modems. In this type of configuration, you only need to configure a single demand-dial interface at each router. Permanent connections can be initiated and left in a connected state 24 hours a day. Figure 7.2 depicts a router-to-router VPN.

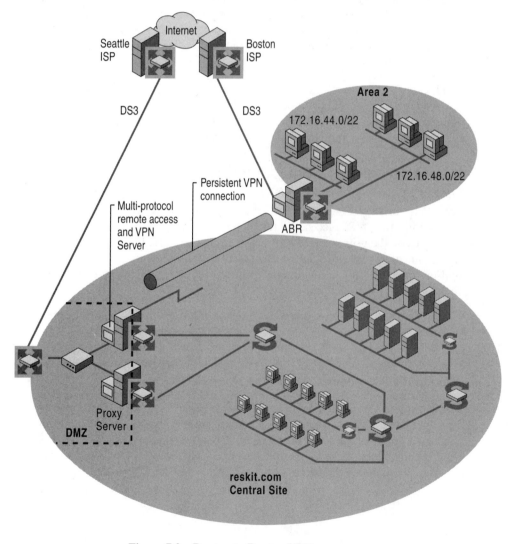

Figure 7.2   Router-to-Router VPN

On-demand Router-to-Router VPN   When a permanent WAN link is not possible or practical because of location or cost, you can configure an on-demand router-to-router VPN connection. This requires you to permanently connect the answering router to the Internet. The calling router connects to the Internet by using a dial-up link such as an analog phone line or ISDN. Then, you only need to configure a single demand-dial interface at the answering router.

VPN Security with IPSec

IPSec needs to be deployed on the VPN server that is located in the corporate DMZ. The design that is shown in Figure 7.3 shows the VPN server being combined with a multiprotocol remote access server. This combination is an effective way to keep the remote access part of the network together for easier manageability and security. Also, when a client dials in to the corporate network using VPN with IPSec, the client determines the type of IPSec security policy to use and the remote access server in which IPSec is installed. Then, it automatically sets up the tunnel, as defined by the client.

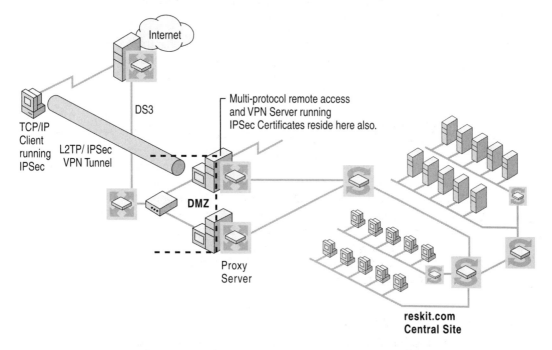

Figure 7.3   Routing and Remote Access Client Connection Through an L2TP/IPSec Tunnel

In this example, the VPN server has three interfaces, one is in the DMZ, the second interface is in the internal network connected to a router, and the third is a remote access interface. The interface that is the least secure is the interface in the DMZ. The DMZ is an area where, as stated earlier, the Internet egresses into the internal, private network, and needs to contain all of the servers that have a presence on the Internet.

The Windows 2000 implementation of IPSec is based on industry standards in development by the Internet Engineering Task Force IPSec working group.

Data encryption allows businesses to use the Internet as a secure, cost-effective way of getting information from a remote site or user to the corporate infrastructure. This strategy is cost effective because you use the already existing medium of the Internet. The security comes from IPSec.

On the Internet, L2TP puts the data into a tunnel, and IPSec provides security for the tunnel itself to keep the data safe, but what about the exposed interface itself?

You can protect the Internet-exposed interface on the VPN server from hackers in the following ways:

- When you initially set up the VPN server, ensure that there is not a routing protocol on the interface that is in the DMZ. Instead, the interface needs to point into the private corporate network through a set of summarized static routes.

- Have a routing protocol running on the interface that is on the private network.

- Use Routing and Remote Access filters (not IPSec filtering) on the Internet interface to set input and output permit filters for L2TP, which uses User Datagram Protocol (UDP) port "Any" and destination port 1701. Also set routing and remote access input and output permit filters for the Internet key exchange (IKE) protocol, which uses UDP source port "Any" and destination port 500, prohibiting everything but L2TP over IPSec traffic. Then, configure packet filtering in the remote access policy profile for user groups, permitting or denying certain types of IP traffic. To make this easier for the user, these filters are configured when you use the Routing and Remote Access setup wizard. No configuration by the user is required.

For L2TP over IPSec connections, the IPSec security negotiation (IKE) uses certificate-based authentication for the computers themselves. L2TP performs user authentication by using either a domain\userid and password, or by using a smart card, certificate, or token card with the Extensible Authentication Protocol (EAP). For more information about overriding this default behavior and using preshared key authentication, see "Virtual Private Networking" in the *Microsoft Windows 2000 Server Internetworking Guide.*

IPSec requires that you establish the trust relationship using certificates issued to each computer. For example, a salesperson from domain.com has regular sales transactions with reskit.com. In order to expedite the process of ordering, the salesperson dials in on a weekly basis to download the product order form from the Reskit supply department.

To ensure that all of the transactions are secure from competitors of domain.com, the salesperson dials in to reskit.com through an ISP using an L2TP over IPSec VPN. Both the remote client and the VPN server need to have a certificate issued to them, and to be able to trust each other's certificate. The salesperson's computer needs to have a computer certificate installed to negotiate a trust relationship with the reskit.com VPN server. Typically, the salesperson's computer received a certificate from a Windows 2000 certificate server when the computer was joined to domain.com. The computer received a Group Policy setting containing instructions for enrolling in the domain.com certificate server, called a certificate auto-enrollment policy. The public key infrastructure (PKI) certificate policy also specified that the client can trust the certificate server that issued the VPN server a certificate, probably the reskit.com certificate server. The VPN server is configured to trust the domain.com certificate server, so it will accept certificates that the client provides.

After the IPSec security association for L2TP is made, the salesperson's remote access policy is checked. This is a property that enables remote access for the user account in the domain. You can control user access in more detail by using Internet Authentication Service (IAS), a server that communicates access policy using the Remote Access Dial-In User Service (RADIUS) protocol.

You can also use IPSec to ensure that only certain computers with the proper certificates and credentials can connect to other computers. Windows 2000 user IDs and groups specified in access control lists (ACLs) control who can access specific shares.

Note You can also use IPSec inside a corporate network to encrypt data from client to client, or from client to server.

For more information about IPSec, see "Internet Protocol Security" in the *TCP/IP Core Networking Guide*.

Internet Authentication Service and Centralized Management

In large corporate networks, managing policies on more than one remote access server can be task intensive. IAS can assist network administrators in managing geographically dispersed remote access servers from a central location.

IAS provides:

Centralized user authentication IAS supports the ability to centrally manage user policy by authenticating users who are in Windows NT 4.0 and Windows 2000 domains. For authenticating users, IAS supports a variety of authentication protocols. They are:

- Password Authentication Protocol (PAP)
- Challenge Handshake Protocol (CHAP)
- Microsoft Challenge Handshake Protocol (MS-CHAP)
- Extensible Authentication Protocol (EAP)

Outsourcing remote access This allows you to use a local ISP's network to allow employees to connect to the corporate network through a VPN tunnel. IAS allows you to track expenses and users who connect to the ISP, which then permits you to pay the ISP for the services used. This approach results in monetary savings for the organization.

Centralized administration of remote access servers IAS enables network administrators to configure remote access policies on just one remote access server, then the rest of the remote access servers can act as RADIUS clients, getting policy from the IAS server.

Scalability Small- and medium-sized networks in large corporations and ISPs can use IAS.

Remote monitoring A network administrator can monitor IAS servers from anywhere on the network by using Event Viewer or Network Monitor, or by installing the Simple Network Management Protocol.

Import/Export IAS configuration A network administrator can important or export IAS configuration by using a command-line utility. For more information about IAS, see "Internet Authentication Service" in the *Microsoft Windows 2000 Server Internetworking Guide*.

Multihoming

A computer that is configured with more than one IP address is referred to as a multihomed system. You can implement a multihomed system in several ways, depending on your needs. You can multihome DHCP servers to provide service to more than one subnet. DNS can also benefit from multihoming because the DNS service can be enabled on individual interfaces and can be bound only to IP addresses that are specified. By default, DNS binds to all individual interfaces configured on the computer.

Multihoming is supported in several different ways:

- Multiple IP addresses for each network adapter
- Multiple network adapters

IP Routing Infrastructure

In order for users and administrators to fully utilize the features of Windows 2000 Server as a router, you need to analyze the network structure and make decisions about what type of routing infrastructure best meets your organization's needs. Table 7.4 describes the various types of routing configurations and their uses.

Table 7.4   Routing Configurations

Routing Configuration	Description
Static Routed Internetwork	Uses manually added routes to route network traffic.
Routing Information Protocol (RIP)-for-IP Internetwork	Uses RIP for IP to dynamically communicate routing information between routers.
Open Shortest Path First (OSPF) Internetwork	Uses the OSPF routing protocol to dynamically communicate routing information between routers.

Static Routed Networks

A static routed IP internetwork does not use routing protocols such as RIP-for-IP or OSPF to communicate routing information between routers. All of the routing information is stored in a routing table on each router. If you decide to implement static routing, ensure that each router has the appropriate routes in its routing table so that traffic can be exchanged between any two endpoints on the IP internetwork.

You can use the network diagram described at the beginning of this chapter to document any static routes in a network infrastructure, and it is an ideal way to keep the routes organized for future reference. Static routes can be entered into the routing table in a Windows 2000 router by using the Routing and Remote Access management console. For more information about adding static routes, see "Unicast IP Routing" in the *Microsoft Windows 2000 Server Internetworking Guide*.

Before you can use this routing service, you need to configure and enable it from within the management console. For more information about starting and configuring the Windows 2000 Routing and Remote Access service, see Windows 2000 Server online Help. For more information about installing and upgrading Windows 2000 member servers, see "Upgrading and Installing Member Servers" in this book.

You can implement static routes in small networks that require little administration and are not subject to a lot of growth over time, such as a small business with fewer than 10 network segments. However, because they require some administration, you might consider them impractical, especially with the ability of the Windows 2000 Routing and Remote Access service to dynamically build routing information tables for small to large networks using Open Shortest Path First (OSPF) or RIP for IP.

RIP-for-IP Network Design

RIP for IP is a distance-vector routing protocol that dynamically communicates routing information between neighboring routers, automatically adding and removing routes as needed. RIP has a hop limitation of 16. All destinations that are 16 hops and greater are considered unreachable. RIP networks are best implemented in small to medium infrastructures such as medium-sized businesses or branch offices.

Other caveats for using RIP for IP in your network include:

- RIP for IP uses hop count as the metric for the best route. For example, if a site has a T1 link and a satellite backup link, and the costs associated with both of the links are identical, then RIP for IP is free to select either link. To prevent this problem, you can configure the slow link (the satellite) with a cost of two, which forces the router to select the T1 link as the primary link.

- Bandwidth consumption is another consideration because RIP routers announce their lists of reachable networks every 30 seconds. Depending on the size of the network, these announcements can use up expensive WAN bandwidth. Also, as network size increases, the possibility of bottlenecks increases. You can use autostatic RIP updates to reduce bandwidth used by the routing protocol.

Windows 2000 Routing and Remote Access service supports versions 1 and 2 of RIP for IP. RIP version 1 is designed for classful environments and does not announce the subnet mask for each route. If there are routers in your network that only support RIP version 1, and you want to use classless interdomain routing (CIDR) or Variable Length Subnet Mask (VLSM), then upgrade the routers to support RIP version 2, or skip RIP altogether and use OSPF.

You can implement RIP for IP using the following steps:

1. Consult your network diagram to find out where the RIP routers are going to be placed. If you do not have a current diagram, consider designing one before you start. Consider putting routers on a high-bandwidth network in order to keep bottlenecks to a minimum.

2. Determine which IP address scheme is going to be used. Write down which addresses will be used for routers, which ones for servers, and which ones for clients. For example, if you use the private address range of 172.16 0.0/22, you can follow the format shown in Table 7.5.

Table 7.5   IP Address Schemes

Router	Address
Interface on Router1 on the 172.16.4.0/22 network	172.16.4.1
Interface on Router2 on the 172.16.8.0/22 network	172.16.8.1
Domain controller on the 172.16.4.0/22 network	172.16.4.10
Domain controller on the 172.16.8.0/22 network	172.16.8.10
Client on the 172.16.4.0/22 network	172.16.4.20
Client on the 172.16.8.0/22 network	172.16.8.20

3. Next, decide which RIP version is going to be used on each interface. If you are setting up a new network, consider using only RIP version 2, because this version supports CIDR and VLSM. If you have an existing network that uses RIP version 1, consider upgrading to RIP version 2.

OSPF Network Design

RIP for IP is an easy way to integrate a routing protocol into your small- to medium-sized network environment. But, if you have a larger network implemented, RIP for IP might not be sufficient. Another routing protocol that is supported by Windows 2000 Routing and Remote Access is called Open Shortest Path First (OSPF). An OSPF network is best suited for a large infrastructure with more than 50 networks.

OSPF is a link-state routing protocol that calculates routing table entries by constructing a shortest-path tree. It is a more efficient protocol than RIP and does not have the restrictive 16 hop-count problem, which causes data to be dropped after the 16th hop. An OSPF network can have an accumulated path cost of 65,535, which enables you to construct very large networks (within the maximum Time-To-Live value of 255) and assign a wide range of costs. OSPF also supports point-to-point dedicated connections, broadcast networks such as Ethernet, and nonbroadcast networks such as frame relay. One disadvantage to using OSPF is that it is more complex to configure than other routing protocols, such as RIP.

You can structure these networks hierarchically. The sections that follow describe OSPF in more detail.

Autonomous Systems

An autonomous system (AS) is a collection of networks that share a common administrative authority. The following guidelines are recommended when designing an OSPF AS:

- Subdivide the AS into OSPF areas.

  Partition an AS into areas so that OSPF can control traffic to maximize its ability to pass only intra-area traffic, keeping communication to other areas within the AS to a minimum.

- Designate the backbone area as a high-bandwidth network.

  Create a backbone that is capable of maintaining high capacity to help keep inter-area bottlenecks to a minimum.

- Ensure that all inter-area traffic transverses the backbone. Avoid creating virtual links that connect new or changing areas to the backbone.

Figure 7.4 depicts an AS.

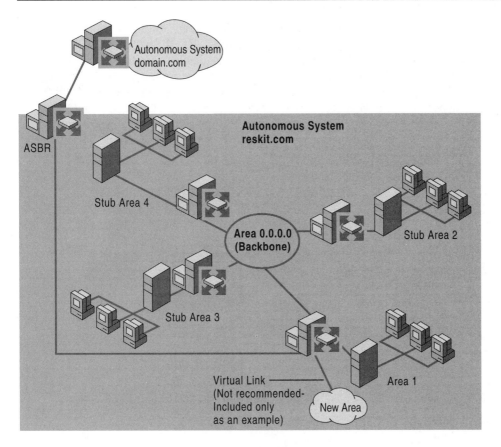

Figure 7.4   An Autonomous System

OSPF Area Design

OSPF areas are subdivisions of an OSPF AS that contain a contiguous collection of subnets. Areas are administrative boundaries that you can use to separate sites, domains, or groups. Within these areas are networks, which, when joined together through a backbone, form an AS.

In an internal network, configure these areas so that inter-area communication is kept to a minimum. This could include DNS name resolution traffic and Active Directory replication traffic.

One way that traffic leaves and enters an OSPF area is through a router called an area border router (ABR). This router is connected to the backbone called Area 0.0.0.0, which then connects OSPF areas together. ABRs typically have an interface on a backbone area network. However, there are situations where the ABR cannot be physically connected to a backbone network segment. If this happens, you can connect the new OSPF areas to the backbone through a virtual link. Even though this method will work, it is not recommended because it can be complicated to set up and inclined to error. Figure 7.5 shows the backbone, the areas, and a virtual link.

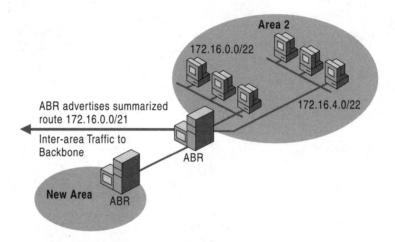

Figure 7.5   An OSPF Area Design

To design an OSPF area, follow these guidelines:

- Assign IP addresses in a contiguous manner, allowing them to be summarized. Route summarization is the act of condensing ranges of IP addresses. Ideally, the ABR for an area would summarize all of its network IP addresses into one. This approach condenses routing information, reducing the workload on the ABRs and the number of OSPF routing table entries.

- Create stub areas whenever possible. Keep the following in mind:
    - Stub areas can be configured so that all external routes and routes for destinations outside the OSPF AS are summarized by a single static default route.
    - Any routes that are external to the AS (external routes) cannot be carried by a stub area, including routes that use other routing protocols. This means that stub areas cannot use AS boundary routers (ASBRs).
- Avoid creating virtual links. Virtual links are used to connect new areas in an AS to the backbone. Virtual links can cause routing and other problems, and can be difficult to configure. Always make an effort to connect new areas in your AS directly to the backbone. Ensure this by planning ahead before your AS is implemented.

IPX Routing Structure

NetWare servers and Windows 2000 systems are made interoperable on the same network by using NWLink, Client Services for NetWare, and Gateway Services for NetWare. Windows 2000 Server provides services that coexist and are interoperable with Novell NetWare networks and servers. The NWLink IPX/SPX/NetBIOS Compatible Transport Protocol (NWLink) is included with Windows 2000. This protocol provides connectivity between Windows 2000 and Novell NetWare systems. Reasons for using IPX/SPX in a mixed environment and enabling IPX routing are:

- Windows 2000 routers might be required to route traffic between NetWare clients and servers.
- Windows 2000 clients might need to access services on NetWare servers.

Windows 2000 routing supports RIP for IPX, which is very similar in function to RIP for IP and Service Advertising Protocol (SAP) for IPX, a protocol that gives nodes such as file servers and print servers the ability to advertise their service names and IPX addresses. Servers that host services send periodic SAP broadcasts, and IPX routers and SAP servers receive the broadcasts and propagate the service information through SAP announcements, which are sent every 60 seconds.

IPX Network Design

The IPX network ID is a 4-byte identifier expressed as an 8-digit hexadecimal number. This network ID has to be unique, or network connection problems can occur for NetWare clients. The 4-byte IPX network ID is an address space that you can use to group IPX networks based on the following:

Internal vs. External Networks   Internal networks are virtual networks inside Novell NetWare servers, Windows 2000 routers, and other IPX routers that are also hosting services. The designation of an internal network ensures proper routing to these services.

Networks for Various Ethernet Frame Types   For IPX environments that need to support multiple Ethernet frame types, you need to configure each Ethernet frame type with its own IPX network ID.

Remote Access Networks   When you use a computer running Windows 2000 as a remote access server, remote access clients are assigned an IPX network ID. By default, the remote access server chooses a unique IPX network ID. You can specify an IPX network ID or range of IPX network IDs so that remote access IPX traffic is identified by its source IPX network address.

Department or Geographic Location   You can allocate portions of the IPX address space based on geography (by building or site) or department (such as sales or research). For example, in a large campus environment, all of the IPX networks in building 5 might use 5 as the first digit of their addresses.

Maximum Diameter   The maximum diameter of RIP and SAP for IPX is 16 hops, the same as for RIP for IP. The diameter is a measure of the size of an internetwork in terms of the number of routers a packet must cross to reach its destination. Networks and services that are more than 16 hops away are considered unreachable.

Confining and Directing NetBIOS-over-IPX Traffic   You can control NetBIOS-over-IPX traffic by disabling the propagation of NetBIOS-over-IPX broadcasts on specific interfaces and by configuring static NetBIOS names. For example, if a specific IPX network does not contain any nodes that use NetBIOS over IPX, then you can disable NetBIOS-over-IPX broadcast propagation on all of the router interfaces connected to that network.

Preventing the Propagation of SAP Broadcasts   The Service Advertising Protocol (SAP) is used on IPX networks to inform network clients of available network resources and services. If there are SAP broadcasts that do not need to propagate throughout the entire internetwork, you can use SAP filtering to prevent the IPX services from being advertised outside of a group of IPX networks. For example, if you want to hide the file servers in the human resources department, configure the routers that are connected to the human resources network to filter SAP broadcasts corresponding to the file and print sharing services of the human resources file servers. Another reason is to reduce traffic sent to subnets that do not require SAP services.

AppleTalk Routing Structure

Networking on the Macintosh platform relies on the AppleTalk suite of protocols. These protocols contain built-in routing capabilities that can be enabled to establish routers in an AppleTalk internetwork.

Multicast Support

Media services are becoming common on the Internet and on private networks. Windows 2000 TCP/IP supports the forwarding of multicast traffic, and Windows 2000 Routing and Remote Access service supports the Internet Group Management Protocol (IGMP) as a router. IGMP is used by hosts to join a multicast group. The Routing and Remote Access Service IGMP–enabled interfaces can operate in one of two modes:

- IGMP proxy mode interfaces forward IGMP reports and multicast traffic from other interfaces that are running in IGMP router mode.

- IGMP router mode interfaces listen for IGMP traffic from hosts and update the TCP/IP multicast forwarding table as appropriate, as well as sending IGMP queries.

The IGMP proxy that is provided with Windows 2000 Server is designed to pass IGMP Membership Report packets from a single network intranet to a multicast-capable portion of the Internet.

You can position the IGMP proxy router in the DMZ of the corporate infrastructure to provide internal network hosts with video and audio traffic from the Internet. Ensure that the IGMP router is on a high-bandwidth network with fast switches to minimize bottlenecking. The VPN server that is in the DMZ can also be used as an IGMP router, but only in smaller network structures where the server will not be overloaded with remote access and multicast traffic.

When you configure the IGMP interfaces, the interface that is in proxy mode faces the multicast-enabled Internet and the interface that is in router mode faces the internal network. An example is shown in Figure 7.6.

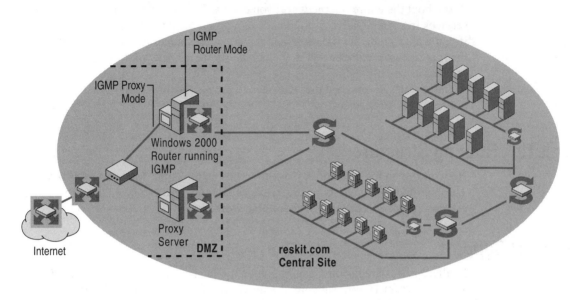

Figure 7.6   IGMP Interface in Proxy Mode

Note   The example in Figure 7.6 will work only if the hardware router connecting the Windows 2000 IGMP router to the Internet is multicast capable, and if the ISP is on the multicast backbone.

Network Address Translation

Windows 2000 network address translation (NAT) allows computers on a small network, such as a small office/home office (SOHO), to share a single Internet connection. The computer on which NAT is installed can act as a network address translator, a simplified DHCP server, a DNS proxy, and a WINS proxy. NAT allows host computers to share one or more publicly registered IP addresses, helping to conserve public address space.

There are two types of connections to the Internet: routed and translated. When planning for a routed connection, you will need a range of IP addresses from your ISP to use on the internal portion of your network, and they will also give you the IP address of the DNS server you need to use. You can either statically configure the IP address configuration of each SOHO computer, or use a DHCP server.

The Windows 2000 router needs to be configured with a network adapter for the internal network (10 or 100BaseT Ethernet, for example). It also needs to be configured with an Internet connection such as an analog or ISDN modem, *x*DSL modem, cable modem, or a fractional T1 line.

The translated method, or NAT, gives you a more secure network because the addresses of your private network are completely hidden from the Internet. The connection shared computer, which uses NAT, does all of the translation of Internet addresses to your private network, and vice versa. However, be aware that the NAT computer does not have the ability to translate all payloads. This is because some applications use IP addresses in other fields besides the standard TCP/IP header fields.

The following protocols do not work with NAT:

- Kerberos
- IPSec

The DHCP allocator functionality in NAT enables all DHCP clients in the SOHO network to automatically obtain an IP address, subnet mask, default gateway, and DNS server address from the NAT computer. If you have any non-DHCP computers on the network, then statically configure their IP address configuration.

To keep resource costs to a minimum with a SOHO network, only one Windows 2000 server is needed. Depending on whether you are running a translated or routed connection, this single server can suffice for NAT, APIPA, Routing and Remote Access, or DHCP.

For more information about NAT and its configuration, see the Windows 2000 Server online Help.

Windows 2000 DHCP

Every computer on a TCP/IP network needs to have a unique name and IP address. The Windows 2000 Dynamic Host Control Protocol (DHCP) offers you a way to simplify and automate this process, providing dynamic assignment of IP addresses to clients on the network no matter where they are or how much they move. This reduces administrator workload.

Benefits of Using DHCP

DHCP allows for reliable assignment of IP addresses in a network by reducing the need to manually assign addresses to each host. This prevents IP conflicts that can disable a network.

Mobile users receive much of the benefit of DHCP, which allows them to travel anywhere on the intranetwork and automatically receive IP addresses when they reconnect to the network.

Interoperability with DNS servers provides name resolution for network resources, allowing DHCP servers and DHCP clients to register with DNS.

New Features of Windows 2000 DHCP

The new features of Windows 2000 DHCP allow for a more flexible and extensible way to assign IP addresses to hosts. These new features are described in the following sections.

Enhanced Server Reporting

The general status of DHCP servers, scopes, and clients, or "member items," can be graphically tracked by the use of icons displayed in the DHCP Manager. For more information about this subject, see the DHCP Manager online Help.

Additional Scope Support

An extension to the Windows 2000 DHCP protocol standard supports the assignment of IP multicast addresses that are distributed in the same manner as unicast addresses. In Multicast DHCP, multicast scopes are configured in the same manner as regular DHCP scopes, but instead of using Class A, B, or C addresses, Class D scope uses a range of 224.0.0.0 to 239.255.255.255.

Typical applications for multicast are video and audio conferencing, which usually require users to specially configure multicast addresses. Unlike IP broadcasts, which need to be readable by all computers on the network, a multicast address is a group of computers that uses group membership to identify who receives the message.

The multicast address allocation feature has two parts: the server side, which hands out multicast addresses; and the client side application programming interface (API), which requests, renews, and releases multicast addresses. To use this feature, you need to first configure the multicast scopes and the corresponding multicast IP ranges on the server through the DHCP snap-in. The multicast addresses are then managed like normal IP addresses, and the client can call the APIs to request a multicast address from a scope.

DHCP and DNS Integration

Domain Name Servers provide name resolution for network resources and are closely related to DHCP services. In Windows 2000, DHCP servers and clients can register with Windows 2000 DNS dynamic update protocol. The integration of DHCP and DNS enables the registration of both type A (name-to-address) and Pointer (PTR) or address-to-name records. This allows the DHCP server to act as a proxy on behalf of Windows 95 and Windows NT 4.0 Workstation clients for the purpose of dynamic update registration within Active Directory.

Design Considerations for DHCP and DNS Integration

When using DHCP and DNS together on your network, consider whether or not you have older, static DNS servers in use. Static DNS servers cannot interact dynamically with DHCP and keep name-to-address mapping information synchronized in cases where DHCP client configurations change, such as with a mobile user who is always moving from subnet to subnet within an intranetwork. In this situation, it is best for you to upgrade all static DNS servers to Windows 2000 DNS.

Unauthorized DHCP Server Detection

The DHCP service for Windows 2000 is designed to prevent unauthorized DHCP servers from creating address assignment conflicts. This solves problems that might otherwise occur if users created unauthorized DHCP servers that could assign invalid IP addresses to clients elsewhere on the network. For example, a user could create what was intended to be a local DHCP server by using addresses that are not unique, which could lease the addresses to unintended clients requesting addresses from elsewhere on the network.

The DHCP server for Windows 2000 has management features to prevent unauthorized deployments and to detect existing unauthorized DHCP servers. In the past, anyone could create a DHCP server on a network, but now an authorization step is required. Authorized personnel usually include the administrator of the domain that the Windows 2000 Server platform belongs to or someone to whom they have delegated the task of managing the DHCP servers.

Dynamic Support for Bootstrap Protocol Clients

DHCP servers respond to both bootstrap protocol (BOOTP) requests and DHCP requests. BOOTP is an established TCP/IP standard [RFC 951] for host configuration that precedes DHCP. BOOTP was originally designed to enable boot configuration for diskless workstations. These workstations have a limited ability to store and locally retrieve IP addresses, and other configurable information that you need during the boot process to join a TCP/IP-based network.

With the new support for dynamic BOOTP, a pool of addresses can be designated for BOOTP clients in the same manner in which a scope is used for DHCP clients. This allows IP addresses to be dynamically managed for distribution to BOOTP clients. This also allows the DHCP service to reclaim IP addresses used in the dynamic BOOTP address pool, after first verifying that a specified lease time has elapsed and that each address is still in use by the BOOTP client.

Read-Only Console Access to the DHCP Manager

This feature provides a special-purpose local users group, the DHCP Users group, that is added when you install the DHCP service. By using the DHCP Manager console to add members to this group, you can provide read-only access to information related to DHCP services on a server computer for nonadministrators. This allows a user who has membership in this local group to view, but not modify, information and properties stored at a specified DHCP server. This feature is useful to Help desks when they need to pull DHCP status reports. Read/write access can only be granted though membership in the DHCP Administrators group.

Designing DHCP Into Your Network

When designing or upgrading your network, you can implement DHCP by using a centralized or distributed approach. (See Figures 7.7 and 7.8.) In a centralized environment, IP addresses are distributed centrally to the DHCP server with one DHCP server responsible for distributing addresses in its associated subnet or site. In a distributed environment, a DHCP server can be responsible for the site that it resides in, and any other site, local or remote, that is included in the given corporate structure.

In order to effectively plan which address distribution scheme you will use, consider the issues discussed in the following sections.

Network Infrastructure Size

How many sites do you have in your domain structure? If you have only a central site and two remote sites, then implementing distributed DHCP is ideal. A domain structure with three or more sites requires a centralized DHCP structure in which DHCP servers assign IP addresses to their given sites.

Figures 7.7 and 7.8 are examples of distributed and centralized DHCP environments. A distributed environment is used to distribute IP addresses to remote sites. A centralized environment is used to distribute IP addresses within the site. Because Windows Clustering works with all clustering-enabled Windows services, other clustering-enabled services can be run on the same server that is running cluster-enabled DHCP services.

In Figure 7.7, there are two sites, one main or central site, and one remote site. Both sites have a DHCP cluster that hands out IP addresses in their respective sites with no DHCP traffic traversing the wide area link.

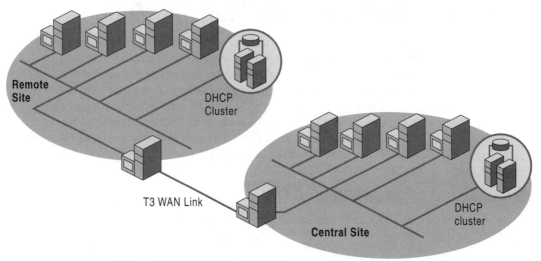

Figure 7.7   Centralized DHCP

In Figure 7.8, there are again two sites, central and remote, but this time the central site is responsible for distributing IP addresses to itself and the remote site. Note that the remote site has a backup DHCP cluster server that handles DHCP traffic in case of a wide area link failure or other problem.

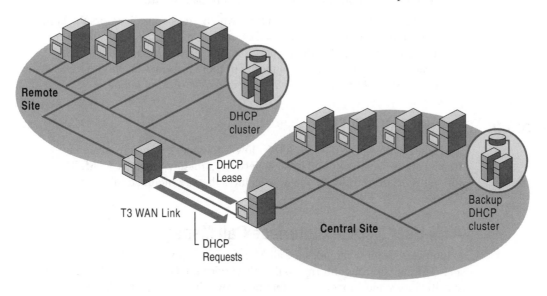

Figure 7.8   Distributed DHCP

For more information about DHCP, see Windows 2000 Help and the *Windows® 2000 Resource Kit TCP/IP core Networking Guide*.

Windows 2000 Asynchronous Transfer Mode

Windows 2000 ATM provides a flexible, scalable, high-speed solution to the increasing need for quality of service in networks where multiple information types, such as data, voice, and real-time video and audio, are supported. With ATM, each of these information types can pass through a single network connection. Windows 2000 ATM services allow seamless migration of existing network backbones to ATM, and interconnecting with traditional LANs using Windows 2000 LAN Emulation (LANE) services. For more information about LANE, see "Features of Windows 2000 ATM" later in this chapter.

Benefits of Using Windows 2000 ATM

Windows 2000 ATM has the following benefits:

- High-speed communication.
- Connection-oriented service, similar to traditional telephony.
- Fast hardware-based switching.
- A single, universal, interoperable network transport.
- A single network connection that can reliably mix voice, video, and data.
- Flexible and efficient allocation of network bandwidth.
- Support for Quality of Service (QoS), which gives administrators the ability to dedicate network bandwidth based on several parameters, including but not limited to who initiated the request, the type of data being sent (such as streaming video), or the destination. For more information about QoS, see the *Windows® 2000 Resource Kit TCP/IP core Networking Guide*.

Features of Windows 2000 ATM

The new features of Windows 2000 allow for a more extensible, scalable framework in which to build diverse network structures such as ATM. The following sections describe the new features that are included in Windows 2000 ATM.

ATM User Network Interface Call Manager

Windows 2000 now includes a Call Manager that supports and manages calls on an ATM network. It conforms to the ATM Forum UNI Version 3.1 signaling specifications and supports the creation of switched virtual circuits (SVCs) and permanent virtual circuits (PVCs).

Updated NDIS and ATM Hardware Support

NDIS version 5 now supports ATM network adapters directly. This permits ATM adapter vendors to more effectively use their hardware by writing ATM miniport device drivers that interface with Windows 2000. Drivers for most vendors of ATM network adapters are now included with Windows 2000.

ATM LAN Emulation

ATM LAN Emulation (LANE) services are needed to provide interoperability between ATM and traditional LAN environments. LANE allows easier migration and integration with traditional networking LAN technologies such as Ethernet or Token Ring by emulating these LANs on ATM networks. Windows 2000 includes support for ATM LAN Emulation, and can participate in an Emulated LAN (ELAN) as a LAN Emulation Client (LEC). The Windows 2000 LAN Emulation Client can use the LAN Emulation Services that ATM vendors supply with their network switches. By default, Windows 2000 will install the LAN Emulation Client if it detects that an ATM network adapter has been installed. The LEC will also, by default, attempt to participate in a default unspecified ELAN. Your LAN emulation services must be configured for this default ELAN.

Figure 7.9 illustrates a LANE network.

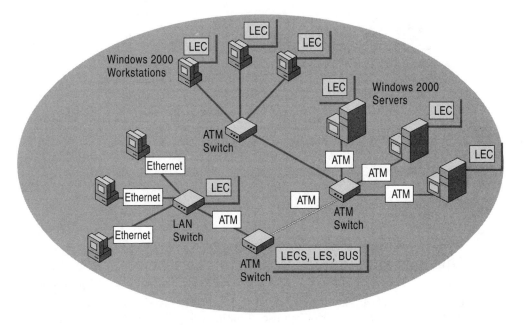

Figure 7.9   LANE Network

IP/ATM

IP/ATM enables TCP/IP to use the features of ATM networks directly.
Windows 2000 now includes IP/ATM support. With this support, applications
written to use TCP/IP can make direct use of ATM networks. Also, applications
written to use Generic Quality of Service (QoS) under Windows Sockets will
benefit directly from the inherent QoS capabilities provided by the ATM network.

IP/ATM is a group of services for communicating over an ATM network that can
be used as an alternative to ATM LAN emulation. IP/ATM is handled by two
main components: the IP/ATM client and the IP/ATM server. The IP/ATM server
includes an ATM ARP server and a multicast address resolution server (MARS).
IP/ATM server components can reside on a Windows 2000 server or an ATM
switch.

The main advantage of using IP/ATM is that it is faster than LANE, because with
IP/ATM, no additional header information is added to packets as they move
through the protocol stack. Once an IP/ATM client has established a connection,
data can be transferred without modification.

With IP/ATM, you can either use a static IP address or configure the TCP/IP
profile to use a DHCP server. Figure 7.10 depicts an IP-over-ATM network.

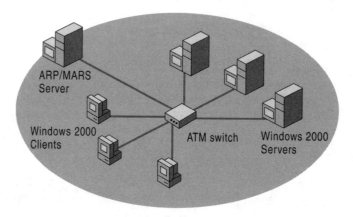

Figure 7.10   IP/ATM

Multicast and Address Resolution Service

Windows 2000 includes a Multicast and Address Resolution Service to support
the use of IP/ATM. This service supports the IP/ATM Address Resolution
Protocol and enables the efficient use of multicasting with ATM networks.

PPP/ATM

With the coming of digital subscriber line (*x*DSL) technologies, high-speed
network access from the home and small office environment is becoming more
common. Several standards exist in these areas, including Asymmetric DSL
(ADSL) and Universal ADSL (UADSL or DSL Lite). These technologies operate
over the local loop (the last run of copper wire between the telephone network and
the home). In most areas in the U.S., this local loop then connects to an ATM core
network.

ATM over the *x*DSL service preserves high-speed characteristics, and QoS
guarantees availability in the core networking layer, without changing protocols.
This creates the potential for an end-to-end ATM network to the residence or
small office. This network model provides several advantages, including:

- Protocol transparency
- Support for multiple classes of QoS with guarantees
- Bandwidth scalability
- An evolution path to newer DSL technologies

Adding Point-to-Point Protocol (PPP) over this end-to-end architecture adds
functionality and usefulness. PPP provides the following additional advantages:

- User-level connection authentication
- Layer 3 address assignment
- Multiple concurrent sessions to different destinations
- Layer 3 protocol transparency
- Encryption and compression

If each virtual circuit (VC) carries only one Point-to-Point Protocol (PPP) session,
each destination will have its own authenticated PPP session, providing
authentication for each VC. This provides an extra measure of security and
guaranteed bandwidth as if you had a dedicated line. Using Null Encapsulation
over AAL5 (because PPP provides the protocol multiplexing) can further reduce
overhead.

ATM Design Considerations

ATM networks are made up of three distinct components: endpoint elements
(users), ATM switches, and interfaces. Consider the guidelines discussed in the
following sections when you design an ATM network.

Use the Default ELAN

Windows 2000 ATM is initially configured with a default unspecified ELAN name. If you plan to implement a small LAN emulation, it is recommended that you use the preconfigured default unspecified ELAN. If you are implementing a large ATM network, multiple ELANs are more manageable and secure.

When purchasing an ATM switch, it is recommended that you check the product specifications to ensure that it is preconfigured with an ELAN that uses the default unspecified ELAN name. Switches that are preconfigured with a default ELAN allow for a more trouble-free setup in a small ATM environment.

Use Supported ATM Adapters

Before you buy an ATM adapter for use with Windows 2000, be certain that it is on the Windows 2000 Hardware Compatibility List. For more information, see the Hardware Compatibility List link on the Web resources page at http://windows.microsoft.com/windows2000/reskit/webresources.

Note Configurations Before You Upgrade

Before upgrading from Windows NT 4.0 to Windows 2000, note the following configuration information for each of the LAN emulation clients you plan to upgrade:

- The ELAN name
- The media type to be emulated on the LAN
- ATM addresses for the LAN Emulation Server (LES) and Broadcast and Unknown Server (BUS) associated with the ELAN

Configure the ELANs

After you note these configuration parameters, use the configuration interface on your ATM switch to configure the LAN Emulation Configuration Service (LECS), the LAN Emulation Service (LES), and the Broadcast and Unknown Service (BUS) to support the ELANs and their associated parameters. Next, install Windows 2000 and configure the ELAN name for each LEC.

Use Only One ATM ARP/MARS for Each Logical IP Subnet

If your network uses IP/ATM, it is recommended that you configure only one ATM ARP/MARS for each logical IP subnet on your network. If you have multiple ARP servers on the same network segment, and your ARP client is configured with the addresses for these servers, the ARP caches could become out of sync. This can render parts of the network unreachable.

Quality of Service

Windows 2000 Quality of Service (QoS) is a set of components and technologies that enable a network administrator to allocate and manage end-to-end network resources. QoS enables consistent bandwidth results for network traffic, such as video and audio applications and ERP applications that normally use large amounts of network bandwidth. QoS is a method that allows networks to control their traffic efficiently, potentially reducing the costs spent on new hardware resources. Management becomes easier with Admission Control Service, an administrative interface of QoS, which allows for the centralized management of QoS policies. These policies, which you can configure to meet the requirements of users, programs, or physical locations, determine how you can reserve and allocate priority bandwidth. In the past, QoS has been incorporated into router and switch hardware. Now that it is available as part of Windows 2000, a new level of control across the entire enterprise can be achieved right down to the desktop.

Windows 2000 QoS offers you these benefits:

- Centralized policy and subnet configuration through the QoS Admission Control Services Manager.

- Uses enterprise, subnet and user identities as criteria for reserving network resources and setting priorities.

- Ensures a priority bandwidth reservation that is transparent to the user and requires no user training.

- Enables a network administrator to allocate network resources to prioritized traffic.

- Safeguards for end-to-end delivery service with low delay guarantees.

- Interoperability with LAN, WAN, ATM, Ethernet, and Token Ring configurations.

- Support for multicast transmission of bandwidth reservation messages.

- Windows 2000 QoS Admission Control simplifies your management of priority bandwidth at a low cost of ownership. In this instance, lower cost of ownership equates to not having to replace network media to gain bandwidth.

For more information about DHCP, see Windows 2000 Help and the *Windows® 2000 Resource Kit TCP/IP core Networking Guide*.

Planning Task List for Networking Strategies

Table 7.6 outlines the tasks you need to perform when determining your network connectivity strategies.

Table 7.6   Planning Task List for Networking Strategies

Task	Chapter Section
Examine your current network diagram for connectivity structure. If none exists, design one.	Network Connectivity Overview
Examine TCP/IP structure.	Windows 2000 TCP/IP
Determine Internet and Routing and Remote Access connectivity methods.	Routing and Remote Access
Determine WINS needs.	TCP/IP and Windows Internet Name Service
Examine Routing and Remote Access considerations.	Routing and Remote Access
Examine data security considerations.	VPN Security and L2TP-over- IPSec VPNs
Examine IP routing structure.	IP Routing Infrastructure
Determine multicast needs.	Multicast Support
Determine DHCP requirements.	Windows 2000 DHCP
Examine any Quality of Service issues.	Quality of Service

CHAPTER 8

Using Systems Management Server to Analyze Your Network Infrastructure

Network administrators can use Microsoft® Systems Management Server (SMS) to perform a variety of Microsoft® Windows® 2000 deployment tasks, including collecting planning details, preparing computers, deploying Windows 2000, and monitoring the deployment process. This chapter focuses on SMS features you can use to analyze your network infrastructure. The results of this analysis will help you determine network infrastructure changes you need to make in preparation for deploying Windows 2000. By using SMS, you can save costs associated with performing an enterprise-level deployment.

You do not need any prior experience with SMS to understand the concepts and processes presented in this chapter. However, the chapter does not include procedures for deploying and using SMS. Refer to the SMS documentation for those details. You will need personnel trained in SMS to properly deploy and use it in a well-planned manner. See the Additional Resources section at the end of the chapter for resources that can help you learn more about SMS.

In This Chapter

Chapter Goals

This chapter will help you develop the following planning documents:

- A network infrastructure analysis process that incorporates SMS
- Reports detailing the existing network infrastructure, including all hardware and software

Related Information in the Resource Kit

- For more information about deploying Windows 2000 with SMS, see "Using Systems Management Server to Deploy Windows 2000" in this book.
- For more information about testing applications for Windows 2000 compatibility, see "Testing Applications for Compatibility with Windows 2000" in this book.

Analyzing Your Network Infrastructure

A critical step in your Windows 2000 deployment is preparing your network infrastructure. In order to have your network ready for deployment, you need to perform a variety of tasks, beginning with an analysis of the current state of your network infrastructure.

Primary tasks you will perform when analyzing and preparing your network for Windows 2000 deployment include the following:

- Identify computers that do not have sufficient or compatible hardware.
- Upgrade hardware.
- Identify computers with software that is not compatible or that will not operate properly with Windows 2000.
- Identify the applications most often used, so that compatibility testing is done on all of the most important applications.
- Analyze network usage to determine network capacity availability, protocols in use, and which computers are being used as servers.
- Upgrade incompatible applications.
- Ensure that incompatible applications are not used.

Systems Management Server (SMS) provides you with the tools you need to perform these tasks most efficiently in an enterprise environment.

Using Systems Management Server

SMS is an extremely scalable system that you can use to perform a variety of computer administration tasks. When deploying Windows 2000, you can use SMS to expedite the performance of many repetitive tasks. The deployment planning tasks for network analysis and preparation are shown in Figure 8.1.

Note For this chapter, network infrastructure is defined to include all of the SMS-compatible computers in your network. This includes computers running Windows 2000, Windows NT Server, Windows NT Workstation, Windows 95, Windows 98, Windows 3.1, and Windows for Workgroups.

Start

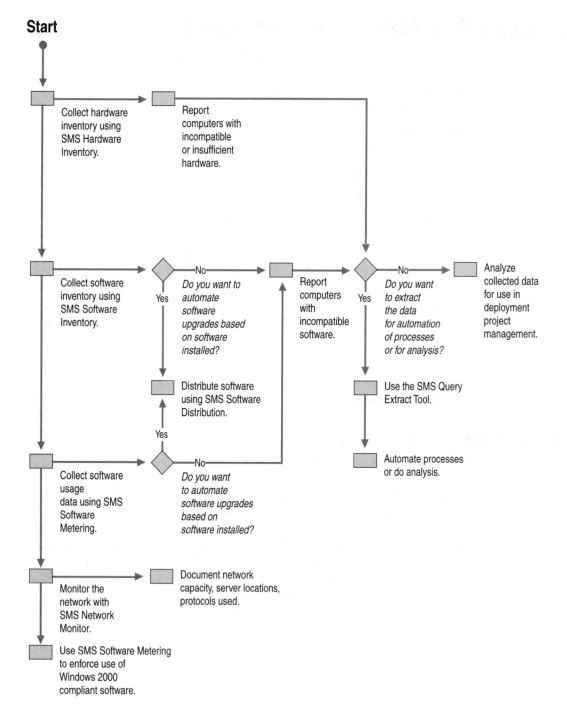

Figure 8.1   Process Flow for Analyzing Your Network Infrastructure with SMS

Using SMS for your Windows 2000 planning and deployment processes requires additional resources. However, the costs you incur to plan for and use SMS are easily recouped through the ability to automate Windows 2000 deployment tasks.

You can use SMS to automate tasks for deploying Windows 2000 to many end-users at once. The tasks, and even the inclusion of computers into SMS in the first place, can all be done without technical staff visiting the computers. The automated tasks provide the following benefits:

- Greatly reduced manual labor and site visits.
- Distribution over a large geographical area.
- Graceful recovery in the event of some errors.
- Flexible scheduling.
- Status updates on a daily (or more frequent) basis.

Note SMS is dependent on software components that run on the client and that (at least occasionally) connect to the SMS infrastructure through a network. Therefore, you cannot use SMS to install Windows 2000 on new computers that do not yet have an operating system and network client. The chapter "Automating Client Installation and Upgrade" in this book suggests methods that you can use to set up new computers with Windows 2000.

How Systems Management Server Can Expedite Windows 2000 Deployment

SMS can help you plan your Windows 2000 deployment by answering a wide variety of important questions. It can help you deploy Windows 2000 by:

- Preparing your computers.
- Distributing the Windows 2000 source files close to user computers.
- Initiating the Windows 2000 upgrades in a controlled, secure manner.
- Reporting the status of the deployment.

SMS can also help you resolve problems related to the deployment, and provide an in-place Windows 2000 infrastructure management structure when deployment is complete.

This chapter focuses on how you can use SMS to collect the details about your network infrastructure that you need for Windows 2000 deployment. You can use a variety of reporting tools to format data in easy-to-use reports. For further analysis, you can extract information to other programs, such as Microsoft® Excel. And, you can use the collected information to automate deployment tasks.

The information you collect allows you to answer a variety of important deployment planning questions, such as:

- How many computers do you have? Where are they? Do they have hardware with sufficient capacity for Windows 2000? Which computers have hardware that is incompatible with Windows 2000?

- What software is installed on your users' computers? What software are they actually using? Which computers have software that is incompatible with Windows 2000?

- How much capacity is available on your network links? Which protocols are used on your network?

You will also learn how SMS can help with application compatibility issues.

Note Another important benefit of using SMS in your deployment of Windows 2000 is its ability to distribute Windows 2000 to computers to be migrated and then to initiate the upgrade and report on its status. These topics are discussed thoroughly in "Using Systems Management Server to Deploy Windows 2000" in this book.

Systems Management Server 1.2 Differences

SMS 2.0 is dramatically different from its predecessor, SMS 1.2. Both versions have similar overall feature sets, but each version accomplishes the features using dramatically different techniques. If you are planning to use SMS 1.2 for network analysis and Windows 2000 deployment, you need to be aware of the following differences between it and SMS 2.0:

- Software inventory is based on predefined application definitions. Therefore, you must research which applications might be found in your organization, and then ensure that those applications are defined for SMS. While SMS includes a large number of predefined applications, most organizations will have to define many more for SMS 1.2 software inventory collection to serve their needs. Such definitions are also available from consultants, the Internet, and independent software vendors.

- Hardware inventory is not as extensive; therefore, it might be difficult to gather all of the hardware details you require. First tier computer manufacturers have Desktop Management Interface (DMI) computer management agents that provide extensive hardware inventory information that SMS 1.2 can collect. However, each manufacturer has a different solution, so these can be difficult to deploy in a mixed environment. Independent software vendors provide solutions that can improve hardware inventory in these ways.

- Software distribution is not as flexible, both in terms of targeting and execution options.

- Hardware inventory is required for all clients. There is no equivalent to SMS 2.0 client discovery processes. Therefore, SMS 1.2 cannot work with clients until they have been reported through hardware inventory.

- There is no software metering facility. Therefore, SMS 1.2 cannot prevent users from running incompatible applications. However, third-party software metering applications are available, and many integrate with SMS 1.2 in various ways.

- There is no product compliance database. However, an equivalent system can be set up by defining a comparable database table.

- There is no Network Monitor Control Tool and no Network Monitor Experts, which are enhancements to Network Monitor (discussed later in this chapter).

- SMS 1.2 relies on Windows NT replication between domain controllers for the propagation of SMS logon scripts and their components, if used.

Collecting Inventory

You begin your network infrastructure analysis by collecting hardware and software inventory. This data will be essential to your Windows 2000 deployment.

Assessing the Current State of Your Hardware

Windows 2000 is designed to run on a wide range of computers. However, there have been so many different models of computers and components manufactured over the years, that it is reasonable to think that not all computers will be ready for Windows 2000. SMS can help to identify those computers.

Hardware Capacity

Recently purchased computers probably have sufficient capacity for Windows 2000, but older computers might lack the required resources. Insufficient resources are typically considered to be a lack of computer memory, lack of disk space, an excessively slow processor, lack of a CD-ROM drive, or a particularly old processor.

You will have to find computers with insufficient resources so that you can upgrade or replace them. Also, your process for upgrading computers will be more efficient if you pre-plan your distribution and know specifically where the computers are that need upgrades. Then when you arrive at a site, you will have the correct components and can go directly to the computers requiring work.

Hardware Compatibility

A wide variety of hardware details can be important to your upgrade planning. In addition to the usual disk space, computer memory, and processor speed issues, you might need to consider the following:

- BIOS
- Video card
- Network card
- Disk controller
- Power management
- Other hardware, such as CPU chipset

It is unusual for these components to be incompatible with Windows 2000, but it is possible. If you have purchased computers that are certified by the vendor as being Windows 2000 compatible, or if they are on the Windows 2000 Hardware Compatibility List, then you should have no problems. The Hardware Compatibility List can be found at http://www.microsoft.com using the keyword "HCL." Otherwise, you should do a pilot test to discover any such issues. Pilot testing involves testing a reasonable number of each model of computer that your company uses prior to upgrading users who rely on them.

When you have identified models or components that are incompatible, you can then use the SMS inventory feature to find all of the other computers in your company that have the same problem.

By examining the SMS hardware inventory details of the components that cause problems with Windows 2000, you can select characteristics that specifically identify those components, and thus computers with those components that will fail. You can then adjust your hardware reports to find other computers with the same problems. It is recommended that further testing be done to verify that all computers identified in this way do indeed have problems and that all problems have been found. As your confidence in testing and test results increases, you can be more confident that upgrades done on the basis of these reports are successful.

Using Systems Management Server Hardware Inventory

When you have SMS deployed in your organization, enabling SMS Hardware Inventory is relatively straightforward. The SMS client software that collects hardware inventory details works with Windows Management Instrumentation (WMI) components to explore the computer for hardware details. WMI is part of SMS, and is also available from other sources. The client computers automatically report the hardware inventory details to the SMS servers, and the data is transferred up the hierarchy. You can then access the data from a central location. By default, the data is updated once a week, but you can change the frequency.

Note SMS finds computers through processes called discovery methods. Discovery does provide some basic information about your computers, including the fact that they exist, their names, their network addresses, and where they are located. This might be sufficient for some hardware inventory types of queries and reports. Discovery has the advantage that less resources are required for it than for hardware inventory. However, the differences in resources are often not significant.

SMS collects a very rich set of hardware inventory details, which includes most of the information you require. SMS hardware inventory can be readily extended if you require additional details. A typical extension is to ask users which floor they are on, which office they are located in, and so forth. Another typical extension is to collect vendor-specific information that might be included in the BIOS, such as serial number or model number. These kinds of data are often difficult to collect electronically, are not available using standardized techniques, or are dependent on subjective preferences; therefore, customer-specific extensions are required. However, such extensions are readily implemented, as described in the SMS documentation.

Table 8.1 provides hypothetical examples of hardware components that might have Windows 2000 capacity or compatibility issues. It includes the SMS class and properties that are used to check them. How the classes and values are used is discussed in the following section on reporting, analyzing, and using the collected data.

Table 8.1   Example Windows 2000 Hardware Requirements

Resource	Professional	Server	SMS Class	SMS Property
Memory	90 Meg	128 Meg	SMS_G_System_X86_PC_MEMORY	TotalPhysicalMemory
Disk Space	1 Gig	1 Gig	SMS_G_System_Logical_Disk	FreeSpace
Processor	Pentium	Pentium II	SMS_G_System_PROCESSOR	Name
Video Card	not identified	not identified	MS_G_System_VIDEO	AdapterChipType

The values listed in the table as requirements are hypothetical values only, as might be used at some companies. Requirements will vary based on different types of users and different upgrade paths, and similar computer configurations will perform differently. Therefore, it is important you make your own judgement as to minimum requirements for Windows 2000. Also, video cards do not generally have compatibility problems with Windows 2000. Selecting systems for upgrade based on whether or not their video cards have been identified by SMS is only used as an example of one hardware compatibility criterion—you might find that you have to exclude computers because of a particular video card chip, or because of any number of other hardware details for which SMS can provide data.

Assessing the Current State of Your Software

Windows 2000 includes the same programming interfaces and features that have been available in previous versions of Windows; however, improved features do not always behave in the same way. Compatibility issues are usually minimized by various programming standards, but not all applications have been developed in strict accordance to those standards. For these and similar reasons, some software that is designed for the various versions of Windows might not be compatible with Windows 2000.

The chapter "Testing Applications for Compatibility with Windows 2000" discusses the software compatibility issues in depth, and provides details on how to determine whether your applications are compatible with Windows 2000. However, you will still have two very large questions facing you: "Which software applications does your company use?" and "Which computers are they installed or used on?" SMS provides the answers to these questions.

You enable and use SMS software inventory much like SMS hardware inventory. The method that SMS uses to collect the information is quite different because it involves scanning each client computer's hard disk for files with a name extension of .exe. These files are then inspected for additional details, if they are available, and this information is reported to the SMS site servers. You can extend SMS software inventory by configuring SMS to find files with extensions other than .exe, such as .dll or .com.

Because SMS software inventory collects details on all executable programs on each computer, you can be confident that you can identify all software that is installed on your organization's computers. SMS software inventory also attempts to extract header data from each program. Header data is information about the software, and is included in the executable files. Header data is available in most recently developed programs, but all computers will include some older programs. From the extracted program header information, descriptive names are available, rather than the often cryptic program file names.

Table 8.2 lists several properties that you will need to work with data from SMS software inventory. The properties for software with header data are from the SMS_G_System_SoftwareProduct class. The properties for software without header data are from the SMS_G_System_UnknownFile class.

Table 8.2   Software Data

Data	Software with Header Data	Software without Header Data
File Name	FileName	FileName
File Size	FileSize	FileSize
Product Name	ProductName	N/A
Product Version	ProductVersion	N/A
Product Language	ProductLanguage	N/A

SMS software inventory can identify all of the software installed on computers, but it does not tell you which software is actually used. When software is no longer used, it is not necessary to incur the cost of upgrading those applications.

SMS software inventory can collect files from client computers. If you have many client computers with large files, this can impose quite a load on your network and on the disk space on your site servers. However, used sparingly, software inventory can be a powerful tool. For instance, you can run the Windows 2000 upgrade on Windows 95 or Windows 98 computers in such a way that only an upgrade report is created (Upgrade.txt in the Windows directory).

To create an upgrade report, you use the command **Winnt32 /checkupgradeonly** or an appropriate answer file, and procedures described in "Using Systems Management Server to Deploy Windows 2000" in this book. SMS software inventory can then collect this file for each computer and store the files centrally for review at your convenience. The upgrade reports might give suggestions for hardware or software issues that need to be resolved before attempting to upgrade the computers.

SMS has a feature, called software metering, that reports on actual software usage. Software metering reports the invocation of every program, and then records this data in the SMS site database. Programs that come with the operating system, such as Notepad, are often excluded from this data collection.

The chapter "Metering Software" in the *Microsoft® Systems Management Server Administrator's Guide* describes how to use SMS software metering, including how to create reports based on its data. Give particular consideration to using offline mode, which collects the same information but reports it on an infrequent basis. This greatly reduces the load on the network, clients, and servers.

Using Inventory to Prepare Your Network Infrastructure

When you have collected all of your data, you can use it to answer questions that arise as you plan your Windows 2000 deployment. You can also use the data to drive the deployment processes.

Reporting the Collected Data

The primary way to use SMS inventory data is to generate reports that answer specific questions. For more information about how to generate SMS reports, see the Microsoft Systems Management Server Technical Details link on the Web Resources page at http://windows.microsoft.com/windows2000/reskit/webresources.

For the purpose of Windows 2000 deployment, you can generate reports such as the following:

- Computers with Capacity For Windows 2000
- Computers Compatible with Windows 2000

  Technical staff who are performing Windows 2000 upgrades can use these two reports to identify which computers might require hardware upgrades.

  You might want to use a combination of these two reports if it is likely that you are going to have both issues.

- Computers Requiring Hardware Upgrades

  This can be used by technical staff who are doing hardware upgrades so that they can order appropriate hardware and identify which computers might need upgrades.

- Computers Requiring Software Upgrades

  This can be used by technical staff who are performing software upgrades, so that they can order appropriate software and identify which computers might need upgrades.

Each of these reports can be broken down by site, or possibly into more detail, depending on how your organization can best use the information.

Sample Systems Management Server Report of Windows 2000 Readiness

The following query uses SMS classes as listed in Table 8.1 to find computers that are ready to be upgraded to Windows 2000. The criteria used in this case are that the C: drive has 1 Gigabyte of free disk space, the computer has at least 90 Megabytes of memory and a Pentium processor, and the video card is not unidentified (that is, not equal to a null string). These criteria presume that the C: drive is the user's system partition. The report generated from this sample query is shown in Figure 8.2

Windows 2000-Ready PCs

Site	Computer	Disk Free	CPU	Memory	Video
ORA					
	ORANGE2	1505	Intel Pentium II processor	97	ATI 3D RAGE PRO AGP (GT
	RED1	2242	Intel Pentium II processor	130	ATI 3D RAGE PRO AGP (GT
	RED2	1504	Intel Pentium II processor	130	ATI 3D RAGE PRO AGP (GT
PUR					
	PURPLE1	1331	Intel Pentium II processor	97	ATI 3D RAGE PRO AGP (GT
RED					
	ORANGE2	1505	Intel Pentium II processor	97	ATI 3D RAGE PRO AGP (GT
	RED1	2242	Intel Pentium II processor	130	ATI 3D RAGE PRO AGP (GT
	RED2	1504	Intel Pentium II processor	130	ATI 3D RAGE PRO AGP (GT

Figure 8.2   Sample SMS Report of Computers with Capacity for Windows 2000

Many organizations might also be comfortable upgrading computers with less than 90 Megabytes of memory or 1 Gigabyte of free disk space. There is no reason to think that a video card which SMS has not identified would be incompatible with Windows 2000 If you have any video cards that you suspect might be incompatible with Windows 2000, you can substitute the null string with their chip type values. Additional criteria could be added if desired.

The sample query is as follows:

```
SELECT DISTINCT SMS_G_System_LOGICAL_DISK.FreeSpace,
SMS_G_System_PROCESSOR.Name,
SMS_G_System_X86_PC_MEMORY.TotalPhysicalMemory,
SMS_G_System_VIDEO.AdapterChipType, SMS_R_System.Name,
SMS_R_System.SMSAssignedSites
FROM (((SMS_R_System LEFT JOIN SMS_G_System_PROCESSOR ON
SMS_R_System.ResourceId = SMS_G_System_PROCESSOR.ResourceID) LEFT JOIN
SMS_G_System_VIDEO ON SMS_R_System.ResourceId =
SMS_G_System_VIDEO.ResourceID) LEFT JOIN SMS_G_System_X86_PC_MEMORY ON
SMS_R_System.ResourceId = SMS_G_System_X86_PC_MEMORY.ResourceID) LEFT
JOIN SMS_G_System_LOGICAL_DISK ON SMS_R_System.ResourceId =
SMS_G_System_LOGICAL_DISK.ResourceID
WHERE (((SMS_G_System_LOGICAL_DISK.FreeSpace)>1000) AND
((SMS_G_System_X86_PC_MEMORY.TotalPhysicalMemory)>90000) AND
((SMS_G_System_VIDEO.AdapterChipType)<>'') AND
((SMS_G_System_LOGICAL_DISK.DeviceID)='C:') AND
((InStr(1,[SMS_G_System_PROCESSOR].[Name],"Pentium"))>0))
ORDER BY SMS_R_System.SMSAssignedSites;
```

You can use this query with Microsoft Access. If you use this query in the SMS Administrator console, it can then be used directly in Microsoft Access through the SMS Query Extract Tool. This tool is in the Support directory of the SMS 2.0 CD-ROM and is included with the *Microsoft® BackOffice® Resource Kit 4.5*. See the Web resources page previously referenced for a detailed discussion of how to generate SMS reports using Microsoft Access with or without the SMS Query Extract Tool.

Using the Product Compliance Subsystem

SMS has a product compliance database that is commonly used to compare the software on each computer, as reported by the SMS software inventory subsystem, to a list of software with known Year 2000 compliance issues. You can also use this subsystem to compare the software with a list of software with known Euro currency compliance issues. The same can be done for Windows 2000 compatibility—you can use the product compliance database in SMS reports to highlight computers with Windows 2000 application compatibility problems.

SMS does not include a list of software products known to have compatibility issues with Windows 2000. The chapter "Testing Applications for Compatibility with Windows 2000" in this book helps you investigate where there are any applications with compatibility issues in your organization.

Extending the Product Compliance Subsystem with Windows 2000 Hardware or Software Compatibility Information

The chapter "Determining Product Compliance" in the *Microsoft® Systems Management Server Administrator's Guide* describes the SMS product compliance subsystem. This includes procedures for adding new products and for reporting based on product compliance class fields.

Briefly, you add a new entry to the product compliance database with the SMS Administrator console. Select **Product Compliance,** and from the **Action** menu, select **New** and then **Product Compliance.** The **Product Compliance Properties** dialog box is displayed. The online help describes each of the fields.

Caution The product compliance fields must exactly match those found by the SMS software inventory process. Using the **Browse** button to find a particular example of the file ensures that the name and size are exactly correct. The product name, version, and language fields provide drop-down list boxes which allow you to select the exact values that SMS software inventory has found.

Pay particular attention to the **Compliance Type** and **Compliance Level** fields. Each field includes a drop-down list box that lists all the values previously used in that field. By default, **Compliance Type** only has a value of "Year 2000 Compliance," but you can type in any value you like. You might want to use "Windows 2000 Compat." (The value is limited to 20 characters).

The **Compliance Level** list will be empty until you select a compliance type. When you select a compliance type, the **Compliance Level** list will include all values that have been previously used for that compliance type. Initially no values will have been previously used, and so the list will be empty. You can type in any value you like, such as "Compatible," "Incompatible," "Compatible with minor issues," or "Compatible with major issues."

Tip If you want to use the same compliance levels for Windows 2000 as are provided for Year 2000 compliance, then temporarily select "Year 2000 Compliance" as the compliance type, select the compliance level you want to use, and copy it to the clipboard. Change the compliance type to Windows 2000 and paste the copied value into the **Compliance Level** field.

Reporting with the Product Compliance Subsystem

You use the SMS site database to report on Windows 2000 compliance. The SMS_G_System_SoftwareProduct class has the properties for all of the software products that the SMS software inventory process has discovered. SoftwareProductCompliance has the properties from the compliance database. Comparing the related properties in the two tables allows you to find whether each software product is known to have compatibility issues. Table 8.3 lists the properties you need.

Table 8.3   Product Compliance Data

Data	SMS Software Inventory Property	SMS Product Compliance Property
File Name	FileName	FileName
File Size	FileSize	FileSize
Product Name	ProductName	ResProdName
Product Version	ProductVersion	ResProdVer
Product Language	ProductLanguage	ResProdLangID
Compliance Type	N/A	Type
Compliance Level	N/A	Category

The easiest way to start using the SMS compliance subsystem for Windows 2000 compatibility reporting is to copy the query statement from one of the currently existing Year 2000 compliance queries. Then, create a new blank query and paste the query statement into the new query. Change the compliance type value and enter the rest of the query details. For instance, the following query is based on the standard "Y2K All Compliant Software by System in This Site and Its Subsites" query. The query has only been changed in two places—where "Year 2000 Compliance" has been replaced with "Windows 2000 Compat."

The sample query is as follows:

```
SELECT DISTINCT sys.Name, compl.Category, compl.ProdName, compl.ProdVer,
compl.ProdCompany, compl.ProdLang, compl.URL, compl.Comment FROM
SMS_SoftwareProductCompliance as compl INNER JOIN
SMS_G_System_UnknownFile as unknownfile ON UPPER(unknownfile.FileName) =
UPPER(compl.FileName) AND unknownfile.FileSize = compl.FileSize AND
unknownfile.ProductId = 0 INNER JOIN SMS_R_System as sys ON
unknownfile.ResourceID = sys.ResourceID WHERE compl.Category !=
"Compliant" AND compl.Type = "Windows 2000 Compat." UNION SELECT
DISTINCT sys.Name, compl.Category, compl.ProdName, compl.ProdVer,
compl.ProdCompany, compl.ProdLang, compl.URL, compl.Comment FROM
SMS_SoftwareProductCompliance as compl INNER JOIN
SMS_G_System_SoftwareProduct as prod ON compl.ResProdName =
prod.ProductName AND compl.ResProdVer = prod.ProductVersion INNER JOIN
SMS_G_System_SoftwareFile as prodfile ON UPPER(prodfile.FileName) =
UPPER(compl.FileName) AND prodfile.FileSize = compl.FileSize INNER JOIN
SMS_R_System as sys ON prod.ResourceID = sys.ResourceID WHERE
compl.Category != "Compliant" AND compl.Type = "Windows 2000 Compat."
AND (compl.ResProdLangID = prod.ProductLanguage OR compl.ResProdLangID =
65535) AND prod.ProductID = prodfile.ProductID
```

This query returns data that lists incompatible software by site. You can create a Microsoft Access report using this data as shown in Figure 8.3.

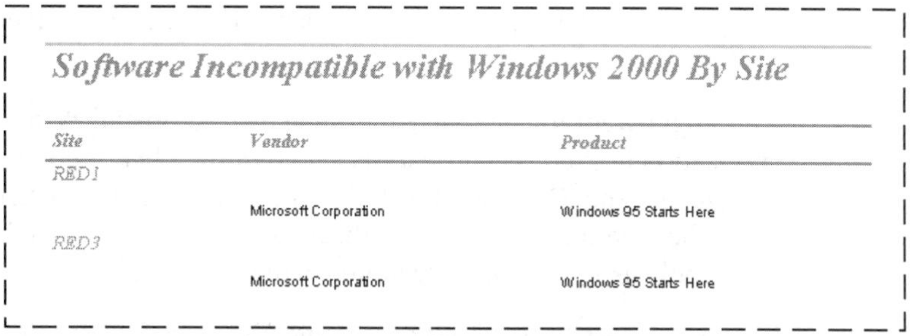
Software Incompatible with Windows 2000 By Site

Site	Vendor	Product
RED1		
	Microsoft Corporation	Windows 95 Starts Here
RED3		
	Microsoft Corporation	Windows 95 Starts Here

Figure 8.3 Sample Software Compatibility Report

The administrators at the appropriate sites can then be alerted that they have to resolve these application compatibility problems at their sites. The computer names or other details could easily be included in the report, if desired. The query results could also be used as the basis of an SMS collection, to which an SMS package could be advertised to upgrade or remove the application.

Analyzing and Using the Collected Data

Often people analyze the data from reports to answer questions such as: "How much will it cost to upgrade client computers for Windows 2000?" or "How much should I bill this cost center?" However, it can be prohibitively labor intensive to do such analysis manually when many sites and computers are involved. Therefore, it might be more appropriate to extract the data to a tool that you would like to use for performing your analysis.

You can use the SMS Query Extract Tool to easily extract SMS data that can be helpful to Windows 2000 deployment to tools such as Microsoft Excel or Microsoft Access. This is described in detail in the chapter "Reporting Options for SMS 2.0" in the *Microsoft® Systems Management Server Resource Guide*, which is part of the *Microsoft® BackOffice® Resource Kit 4.5*.

Your ultimate goal is to deploy Windows 2000, and you can use the data that SMS has collected to automate that process. The same queries that provide data for reports such as "Our Windows 2000–Ready PCs" can also be used as the basis of collections of computers in the SMS database to which Windows 2000 is advertised.

Similarly, as shown with the SMS product compliance subsystem, in order to be ready for Windows 2000 some computers might need to have their software upgraded. The collected software inventory data can also be used to target those computers for the appropriate upgrades, which can be delivered by means of SMS.

You might want to use tools other than SMS to install Windows 2000 or the application upgrades. Those tools also require a list of computers to target, and you can use the SMS data for that purpose as well. The data can be extracted using the techniques previously discussed, and the data can be imported into the other tools using whatever techniques they provide.

For more information about deploying Windows 2000 with SMS, see "Using Systems Management Server to Deploy Windows 2000" in this book. Deploying Windows 2000–compatible applications is done in a very similar manner.

Monitoring Your Network

An important aspect of preparing for Windows 2000 deployment is understanding your network. You need to answer questions such as:

- Which network links and segments have limited capacity?
- Which protocols are used?
- Where are the Dynamic Host Configuration Protocol (DHCP), Windows Internet Name Service (WINS), and similar servers?

Transferring the Windows 2000 source files to remote sites takes considerable network capacity. Installing Windows 2000 from shares requires even more capacity, but it needs to be available on local area networks. Verifying which protocols are used and where all the network servers are located helps to ensure that your plans include all relevant details.

SMS includes Network Monitor and related features to help you analyze your network and answer these and similar questions. You can use Network Monitor to display the activity levels on each network segment, as shown in Figure 8.4. You can also use Network Monitor to capture network packets. You can then review these packets to see which protocols are being used and which computers are providing services. Network Monitor includes a feature, called Network Monitor Experts, that even produces a table of protocols and the percentage of frames and bytes used by each protocol.

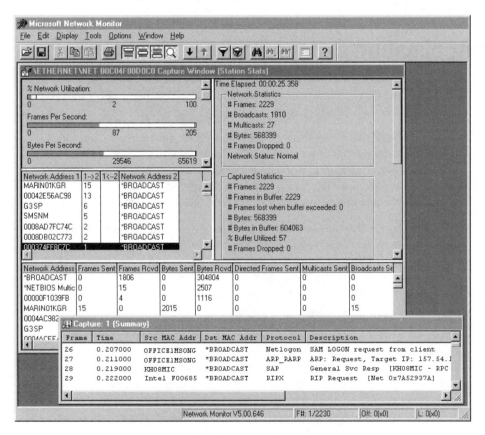

Figure 8.4   SMS Network Monitor

You can configure the Network Monitor Control Tool to continuously monitor network activity for unauthorized DHCP and WINS servers. You supply the tool with the address of the DHCP and WINS servers you are aware of, and it displays the addresses of any other DHCP and WINS servers that it sees packets for.

The chapter "Using SMS for Network Maintenance" in the *Systems Management Server Administrator's Guide* describes the use of Network Monitor in detail.

Note Windows 2000 includes a version of Network Monitor. However, that version of Network Monitor only monitors traffic to and from the computer it is installed on, including broadcasts. The SMS version of Network Monitor monitors all network traffic on the segments that it is configured to monitor. The SMS 2.0 version of Network Monitor also includes other enhancements, such as Network Monitor Experts.

Ensuring Application Compatibility

SMS can help in various ways with your Windows 2000 deployment. One important function of SMS is to enforce the use of Windows 2000 compatible applications.

You can use SMS to target the appropriate computers for software upgrades and deliver the software to the computers. The upgrades can be done automatically or with user input. The timing of the upgrades can be scheduled by the SMS administrator, and the users can adjust the schedule so that the upgrade is done while the users are at meetings or another time that is convenient.

The upgrade can also be done with special security rights that are given to SMS, so that the users do not have to have advanced rights, even temporarily, on the computers they are using. One of the most important benefits of using SMS software distribution is that the upgrades return status messages. Therefore, you can readily report on the progress of the upgrades.

SMS can help to ensure application compatibility with Windows 2000 by disallowing users to run incompatible applications. Users might want to use applications, or versions of those applications, that they are familiar with, despite the benefits of corporate standards or new features available in upgraded applications. Therefore, it might be necessary to enforce compliance with application standards. The techniques presented in "Testing Applications for Compatibility with Windows 2000" in this book are required to determine which applications are incompatible with Windows 2000.

Once compatibility is determined, the applications can be defined for SMS software metering, and the number of licenses available can be set to 0. This disallows users from using the old versions of the software. Of course, such an approach is preferably accompanied with an effective communication and training plan, so that users understand the need to use approved applications, and so that they can easily make the transition.

Note   SMS software metering can operate in two modes: online or offline. In online mode, the clients check with the servers every time a program is invoked. This mode is required for license sharing. In offline mode, the clients record all program invocations, but they upload the data at infrequent intervals. This dramatically reduces the workload on the network, clients, and servers. In offline mode, license sharing cannot be enforced, but programs can be disallowed by setting the number of licenses available to 0, and the unavailable schedule to 24 hours a day. The license enforcement must not be based on Windows NT user group membership.

For more information about software distribution, including the processes for producing, distributing, advertising, and monitoring an SMS software distribution package, see "Using Systems Management Server to Deploy Windows 2000" in this book. Refer to the *Systems Management Server Administrator's Guide* for a general discussion of SMS software distribution and SMS software metering.

Network Analysis Planning Task List

Use Table 8.4 to be sure you are taking all the necessary steps to prepare your network infrastructure.

Table 8.4   Network Analysis Planning Task List

Task	Location in Chapter
Collect hardware inventory	Assessing the Current State of Your Hardware
Collect software inventory	Assessing the Current State of Your Software
Collect software usage data	Assessing the Current State of Your Software
Report on collected data	Reporting the Collected Data
Analyze collected data	Analyzing and Using the Collected Data
Analyze collected data with the compliance database	Reporting the Collected Data
Monitor your network	Monitoring Your Network

Additional Resources

- For more information about planning for and using SMS, see the *Microsoft® Systems Management Server Administrator's Guide*, which is included with SMS.

- For information about the SMS product, see the Microsoft Systems Management Server link on the Web Resources page at http://windows.microsoft.com/windows2000/reskit/webresources

- For information about writing reports based on the data SMS collects, see the Microsoft Systems Management Server Technical Details link on the Web Resources page at http://windows.microsoft.com/windows2000/reskit/webresources.

- For advanced information about SMS, see the *Microsoft® Systems Management Server Resource Guide* in the *Microsoft® BackOffice® Resource Kit 4.5.*

PART 3

Active Directory Infrastructure

Planning for Microsoft® Active Directory™ requires knowledge of many features of Microsoft® Windows® 2000 as well as an understanding of how these features interrelate. Part 3 provides you with information for developing Active Directory, security, and domain migration plans appropriate for your organization.

In This Part

C H A P T E R   9

Designing the Active Directory Structure

Microsoft® Windows® 2000 Server includes a directory service called *Active Directory*™. The Active Directory concepts, architectural elements, and features presented in this chapter will help the IT architect and strategic planner in your organization to produce design documents essential to a successful Microsoft® Windows® 2000 Active Directory deployment.

Prior to reading this chapter, it is important that you obtain detailed knowledge of the IT administration groups, administrative hierarchy, and network topology in your organization. This knowledge will help you apply the planning guidelines in this chapter to your own unique environment.

In This Chapter

Chapter Goals

This chapter will help you develop the following planning documents:

- Forest Plan
- Domain Plan for each forest
- Organizational Unit (OU) Plan for each domain
- Site Topology Plan for each forest

Related Information in the Resource Kit

- For more information about migrating domains to Windows 2000, see "Determining Domain Migration Strategies" in this book.
- For more information about Windows 2000 security standards, such as the Kerberos protocol, see "Planning Distributed Security" in this book.
- For more information about advanced networking, see "Determining Network Connectivity Strategies" in this book.
- For more information about Microsoft® IntelliMirror™ or Group Policy, see "Applying Change and Configuration Management " in this book.
- For more technical information about Active Directory, see the *Microsoft® Windows® 2000 Server Resource Kit Distributed Systems Guide*.
- For more information about Domain Name System (DNS), see "Introduction to DNS" and "Windows 2000 DNS" in the *Microsoft® Windows® 2000 Server Resource Kit TCP/IP Core Networking Guide*.

Overview of Active Directory

Active Directory plays many roles, from being the backbone of distributed security to providing a service publishing framework. Active Directory provides a central service for administrators to organize network resources, to manage users, computers, and applications; and to secure intranet and Internet network access.

As an increasing number of distributed applications take advantage of Active Directory, you can benefit by not having to implement and manage application-specific directory services. The result is that you save administrative and hardware costs.

Note   You can deploy Windows 2000 Server and Microsoft® Windows® 2000 Professional before, in parallel with, or after Active Directory. It is not necessary to deploy Active Directory first. You can take advantage of many of the new features in Windows 2000 by upgrading member servers and client computers right away. For more information about upgrading member servers, see "Upgrading and Installing Member Servers" in this book.

Primary Active Directory Features

Windows 2000 Active Directory features offer many advantages for your network, including the following:

Security

Active Directory provides the infrastructure for a variety of new security capabilities. Using mutual authentication, clients can now verify the identity of a server before transferring sensitive data. Using public key security support, users can log on using smart cards instead of passwords.

Simplified and Flexible Administration

Objects in the Active Directory have per-attribute access control, which allows fine-grained delegation of administration. Delegation of administration allows you to more efficiently distribute administrative responsibility in your organization, and reduce the number of users that must have domain-wide control.

Scalability

Active Directory uses the *Domain Name System (DNS)* as a locator mechanism. DNS is the hierarchical, distributed, highly scalable namespace used on the Internet to resolve computer and service names to Transmission Control Protocol/Internet Protocol (TCP/IP) addresses.

The directory stores information using *domains*, which are partitions that let you distribute the directory over a large network of varying speed and reliability. The directory uses database technology and has been tested to accept millions of *objects* (users, groups, computers, shared file folders, printers, and more). This combination of scalable locator, partitioning, and scalable storage ensures that the directory scales gracefully as your organization grows.

High Availability

Traditional directories with single master replication offer high availability for query operations, but not update operations. With multimaster replication, Active Directory offers high availability of both query and update operations.

Extensibility

The schema, which contains a definition for every object class that can exist in a directory service, is extensible. This allows both administrators and software developers to tailor the directory to their needs.

Open Standards Support

Active Directory is built on standards-based protocols such as:

- DNS, for locating servers running Active Directory.
- *Lightweight Directory Access Protocol (LDAP)* as a query and update protocol.
- The *Kerberos* protocol for logging on and authentication.

This support for open standards makes it possible to use a wide variety of software with Active Directory, such as LDAP-based address book clients.

Simple Programmatic Access

The Active Directory Service Interfaces (ADSI) are accessible from a variety of programming platforms, including script languages such as Visual Basic Script. When using ADSI, administrators and software developers can quickly create powerful directory-aware applications. An example of a directory-aware application is an application that reads the directory for data or configuration information.

Providing a Foundation for New Technologies

In addition to the fundamental advantages previously discussed, Active Directory plays an important role in your Windows 2000 deployment as an enabling infrastructure for other new technologies and capabilities, such as the following:

IntelliMirror

Windows 2000 provides a variety of Change and Configuration Management technologies. IntelliMirror and Remote Operating System Installation Management can help you reduce the amount of work and costs associated with managing and supporting clients. For more information about implementing these technologies, see "Applying Change and Configuration Management" and "Defining Client Administration and Configuration Standards" in this book.

Directory Consolidation

The scalability and extensibility of Active Directory makes it an ideal point of consolidation for applications on your network that use separate, internal directories. For example, you can:

- Have complete directory consolidation, where products like Microsoft® Exchange Server shed the directory components and rely solely on Active Directory for administration and operation.

- Consolidate administration, where you manage directory information in Active Directory and use directory synchronization to keep remote directories up to date.

- Consolidate your existing Microsoft® Windows NT® domains, potentially reducing the total number of objects and hardware to be managed on your network.

Advanced Networking

Internet Protocol security (IPSec), networking Quality of Service features, and new remote access capabilities are examples of advanced networking features that are enabled by Active Directory.

Planning for Active Directory

When you plan for and deploy your enterprise-scale Active Directory, you are defining a significant part of the network infrastructure of your organization. In this plan, you create a set of structures that best reflects your organization. The structures you create will determine:

- The availability and fault tolerance of the directory.

- The network usage characteristics of directory clients and servers.

- How efficiently you can manage the contents of the directory.

- The way users view and interact with the directory.

- The ability of your directory structures to evolve as your organization evolves.

Having a well thought-out Active Directory plan is essential to a cost-effective deployment. Investing time in the planning phase will help you avoid spending time and money in the future reworking structures that you have already put in place.

To create your directory structure plans, follow the sequence of planning steps as presented in this chapter. While you create your plans:

- Learn the key Active Directory concepts that influence structure planning, and adjust the suggested planning steps as necessary to best suit your organization.
- Identify the people in your organization who should participate in structure planning.
- Understand how existing business practices might need to change or evolve to take full advantage of Active Directory.
- Understand the flexibility of the structures you create, and realize which of your choices will be easy to change or hard to change in the future.

Figure 9.1 illustrates the primary steps for designing the Active Directory structure. This chapter will take a close look at each one of these steps.

Start

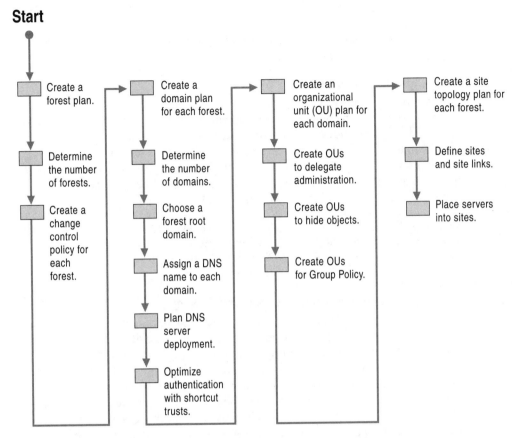

Figure 9.1   Process for Designing an Active Directory Structure

General Design Principles

When working on your Active Directory plan, use the following design principles to guide your decision making:

Simplicity is the best investment.

Simple structures are easier to explain, easier to maintain, and easier to debug. Although some added complexity can add value, be sure to weigh the incremental added value against the potential maintenance costs in the future. For example, the maximum optimization of query and replication traffic might require a complex site topology. However, a complex site topology is harder to maintain than a simple site topology. Always evaluate the tradeoff between added capabilities and added complexity before deciding on a complex structure.

Everything that you create will require some maintenance over its lifetime. When you create a structure without well-defined reasons, it will end up costing you more in the long run than any value that it adds. Justify the existence of any structure you create.

Your business and your organization will always change.

The normal changes that occur within any organization, ranging from employee moves to enterprise-wide reorganizations or acquisitions, will affect your Active Directory structure. When designing your structure, consider how these potential changes will affect end-user and administrator interaction with the directory. For example, consider the impact that your last major business reorganization would have had on the structures you have designed. What changes would be necessary if you add a new location or branch office? Would the changes have required significant and expensive changes to the Active Directory structure? Make sure your design is general enough and flexible enough to accommodate constant and significant change.

Aim for the ideal design.

In your first design pass, design what you consider to be the ideal structure, even if it does not reflect your current domain or directory infrastructure. It is useful and practical to understand what would be ideal, even if it is not currently attainable. For more information about the costs involved in migrating your network to the ideal plan, see "Determining Domain Migration Strategies" in this book. Weigh those costs against the long-term savings of the ideal plan, and refine the design appropriately.

Explore design alternatives.

Make more than one pass at each design. The value of a design becomes more evident when you compare it to other design ideas. Combine the best of all designs into the plan that you will implement.

Composing Your Active Directory Structure Plans

There are four basic components that make up an Active Directory structure: forests, domains, organizational units, and sites. The objective of an Active Directory Structure Plan is to create a planning document for each component of the structure, capturing important decisions and justifications along the way. These planning documents then serve as a starting point for your next planning task, migration. The four planning documents that make up the Active Directory Structure Plan are the following:

- Forest Plan
- Domain Plan for each forest
- Organizational Unit (OU) Plan for each domain
- Site Topology Plan for each forest

Creating a Forest Plan

A forest is a collection of Active Directory domains. Forests serve two main purposes: to simplify user interaction with the directory, and to simplify the management of multiple domains. Forests have the following key characteristics:

Single Schema

The Active Directory schema defines the *object classes* and the attributes of object classes that can be created in the directory. Object classes define the types of objects that can be created in the directory. The schema exists as a naming context that is replicated to every domain controller in the forest. The schema administrators security group has full control over the schema.

Single Configuration Container

The Active Directory *Configuration container* is a naming context that is replicated to every domain controller in the forest. Directory-aware applications store information in the Configuration container that applies forest wide. For example, Active Directory stores information about the physical network in the Configuration container and uses it to guide the creation of replication connections between domain controllers. The enterprise administrators security group has full control over the Configuration container.

Sharing a single, consistent configuration across the domains of a forest eliminates the need to configure domains separately.

Complete Trust

Active Directory automatically creates transitive, two-way trust relationships between the domains in a forest. Users and groups from any domain can be recognized by any member computer in the forest, and included in groups or access control lists (ACLs).

Complete trust makes managing multiple domains simpler in Windows 2000. In previous versions of Windows NT, a popular model for deploying domains was the Multiple Master Domain model. In that model, a domain containing primarily user accounts was called a master user domain, and a domain that contained primarily computer accounts and resources was called a resource domain. A common deployment consisted of a small number of master user domains, each of which was trusted by a large number of resource domains. Adding a new domain to the deployment required several trusts to be created. With Windows 2000 Active Directory, when you add a domain to a forest it is automatically configured with two-way transitive trust. This eliminates the need to create additional trusts with domains in the same forest.

Single Global Catalog

The *global catalog* contains a copy of every object from every domain in the forest but only a select set of the attributes from each object. The global catalog enables fast, efficient searches that span the entire forest.

The global catalog makes directory structures within a forest transparent to end users. Using the global catalog as a search scope makes finding objects in the directory simple. Logging on is made simpler through the global catalog and user principal names, described as follows:

Users Search the Global Catalog   In the directory search user interface, the global catalog is abstracted as the **Entire Directory** when selecting a search scope. Users can search the forest without having any prior knowledge of the forest structure. Having a single, consistent search interface reduces the need to educate users on directory structure, and allows administrators to change the structure within a forest without affecting the way users interact with the directory.

Users Log on Using User Principal Names   A *user principal name (UPN)* is an e-mail-like name that uniquely represents a user. A UPN consists of two parts, a user identification portion and a domain portion. The two parts are separated by an "@" symbol, to form *<user>@<DNS-domain-name>*, for example, liz@noam.reskit.com. Every user is automatically assigned a default UPN, where the *<user>* portion of the name is the same as the user's logon name, and the *<DNS-domain-name>* portion of the name is the DNS name of the Active Directory domain where the user account is located. When logging on using a UPN, users no longer have to choose a domain from a list on the logon dialog box.

You can set UPNs to arbitrary values. For example, even if Liz's account is in the noam.reskit.com domain, her UPN could be set to liz@reskit.com. When the user logs on, the user account to be validated is discovered by searching the global catalog for a user account with a matching UPN value. By making UPN values independent from domain names, administrators can move user accounts between domains, leaving UPN values unchanged and making interdomain moves more transparent to users.

Forest Planning Process

The primary steps for creating a forest plan for your organization are as follows:

- Determine the number of forests for your network.
- Create a forest change control policy.
- Understand the impact of changes to the forest plan after deployment.

When creating the forest plan, you will probably need to consult:

- Your current domain administrators that are responsible for user accounts, groups, and computers.
- Your network security team.

Determining the Number of Forests for Your Network

When you begin to plan your forest model, start with a single forest. A single forest is sufficient in many situations; however, if you decide to create additional forests, ensure that you have valid, technical justification.

Creating a Single Forest Environment

A single forest environment is simple to create and maintain. All users see a single directory through the global catalog, and do not need to be aware of any directory structure. When adding a new domain to the forest, no additional trust configuration is required. Configuration changes only need to be applied once to affect all domains.

Creating a Multiple-Forest Environment

If administration of your network is distributed among many autonomous divisions, it might be necessary to create more than one forest.

Because forests have shared elements, such as schema, it is necessary for all the participants in a forest to agree on the content and administration of those shared elements. Organizations such as partnerships and conglomerates might not have a central body that can drive this process. In short-lived organizations like joint ventures, it might not be realistic to expect administrators from each organization to collaborate on forest administration.

It might be necessary to create more than one forest if individual organizations:

Do not trust each other's administrators. A representation of every object in the forest resides in the global catalog. It is possible for an administrator who has been delegated the ability to create objects to intentionally or unintentionally create a "denial of service" condition. You can create this condition by rapidly creating or deleting objects, thus causing a large amount of replication to the global catalog. Excessive replication can waste network bandwidth and slow down global catalog servers as they spend time to process replication.

Cannot agree on a forest change policy. Schema changes, configuration changes, and the addition of new domains to a forest have forest-wide impact. Each of the organizations in a forest must agree on a process for implementing these changes, and on the membership of the schema administrators and enterprise administrators groups. If organizations cannot agree on a common policy, they cannot share the same forest. Creating a forest change policy is discussed later in this chapter.

Want to limit the scope of a trust relationship. Every domain in a forest trusts every other domain in the forest. Every user in the forest can be included in a group membership or appear on an access control list on any computer in the forest. If you want to prevent certain users from ever being granted permissions to certain resources, then those users must reside in a different forest than the resources. If necessary, you can use explicit trust relationships to allow those users to be granted access to resources in specific domains.

Incremental Costs for an Additional Forest

Each forest you create incurs a fixed management overhead as follows:

- Each additional forest must contain at least one domain. This might require you to have more domains than you had originally planned. There are fixed costs associated with creating and maintaining a domain. These costs are detailed later in this chapter.

- You must manage the forest-wide components of each forest separately (for example, the Schema and Configuration container elements and their associated administration group memberships), even if they are essentially the same.

In order for a user in one forest to use a resource in a different forest, you need to perform additional configuration as follows:

- For users in one forest to access resources in another forest, you must create and maintain an explicit trust relationship between the two domains. An explicit trust relationship between domains in different forests is one-way and not transitive. Without an established trust relationship, users in one forest cannot be granted access to objects in another forest.

- By default, users in one forest are only aware of objects in the global catalog of their own forest. To discover objects in a different forest, users must explicitly query domains that are outside their forest. Alternatively, administrators can import data from other domains into the forest where the user resides. This can add cost because:

  - Users must be trained to understand the directory structure so that they know where to direct queries when global catalog queries fail.

  - When you import data from a domain in a separate forest, you must put a process into place to keep the imported data up-to-date when it changes in the source domain.

Figure 9.2 is an example of an interforest configuration where a user in one forest needs to access a published resource in a different forest. An explicit, one-way trust relationship is created so the user can be granted access to the resource. The representation of the resource in the directory is imported into the user's forest, where it appears in the global catalog.

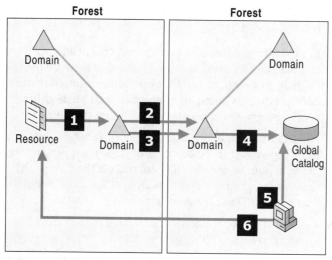

1. Resource published in Directory Service.
2. Administrator configures explicit one-way trust relationship.
3. Administrator imports object into forest.
4. Object replicates to Global Catalog.
5. User finds object by querying Global Catalog.
6. User accesses resource.

Figure 9.2   Additional Configuration for Interforest Resource Access

Some features that are available within a forest are not available between forests, such as the following:

- You can only use default UPNs if a user account is in a different forest than the computer being used for logging on. Default UPNs are required because a domain controller in the computer's forest will not find a user account with a matching UPN in the global catalog. The user account appears in the global catalog of a different forest. The domain controller handling the logon must then use the *<DNS-domain-name>* portion of the UPN to try to find a domain controller to verify the user's identity.

- Logging on using a smart card relies on a user principal name. Default UPNs must be used for a cross-forest logon process that uses smart cards to work.

- You can move security principals between domains in the same forest, but they must be cloned between domains in separate forests. Cloning is not as transparent to an end user as moving a user between domains. For more information about cloning, see "Determining Domain Migration Strategies" in this book.

When deciding on the number of forests that you will need, keep in mind that what is important to users is not necessarily the same as what is important to administrators. However, users stand to lose the most from a multiple forest scenario. For example, some organizations outsource their network administration to several different contractors. Generally, the contractor is paid based on network performance, and the number one responsibility is to maintain a stable network. One contractor might not want another contractor being able to influence computers under their control, and having separate forests can solve that challenge. However, separate forests can be a disadvantage for the users who no longer have a single, consistent view of the directory. In these situations, try not to create separate forests to solve the boundary of administration problem.

In cases where it is not important for all users to have a consistent view of the directory, it might be appropriate to have multiple forests. For example, consider a company such as an Internet service provider (ISP) that hosts Active Directory on behalf of several companies. The users in the different client companies have no reason to share a consistent view of the directory. Additionally, there is no reason to have a transitive trust relationship between the companies. In this case, maintaining separate forests is useful and appropriate.

Creating a Forest Change Control Policy

Each forest you create should have an associated Forest Change Control Policy as part of your Forest Plan document. You will use this policy to guide changes that have forest-wide impact. You do not need to determine the individual processes before continuing, but understanding their ownership is important. The policy should include information about each of the shared elements in a forest.

Schema Change Policy

The schema administrators group has full control over the schema for a forest. The schema change policy should include:

- The name of the team in your organization that controls the schema administrators group.

- The starting membership of the schema administrators group.

- Guidelines and a process for requesting and evaluating schema changes.

For more information about Active Directory schema, see the *Microsoft® Windows® 2000 Server Resource Kit Distributed Systems Guide.*

Configuration Change Policy

The enterprise administrators group has full control over the Configuration container that is replicated throughout the forest. The configuration change policy should include:

- The name of the team in your organization that controls the enterprise administrators group.
- The starting membership of the enterprise administrators group.
- Guidelines and a process for creating new domains in the forest.
- Guidelines and a process for modifying the forest site topology. (Site topology is discussed in "Creating a Site Topology Plan" later in this chapter.)

Changing the Forest Plan After Deployment

When a domain is created, it can be joined to an existing forest. You can create a domain by promoting a Windows 2000–based server to the Active Directory domain controller role, or by upgrading a Microsoft® Windows NT® version 3.51 or Microsoft® Windows NT® version 4.0 primary domain controller to Windows 2000.

 Critical Decision Point   Two forests cannot be merged in a one-step operation, nor can you move a domain between forests as a one-step operation. It is important that you design your forest plan so that it requires a minimum amount of restructuring as your organization evolves.

Individual objects can be moved between forests. The type of object being moved determines the particular tool that you use to move it. Most bulk importing and exporting can be achieved with the LDAP Data Interchange Format (LDIFDE.EXE) command-line tool; security principals can be cloned using the ClonePrincipal tool. For more information about these tools, see Tools Help on the *Windows 2000 Resource Kit* companion CD.

Creating a Domain Plan

The following are some of the key characteristics of a Windows 2000 domain that you will need to consider when you begin creating your domain structure plan:

Partition of the Forest

An Active Directory forest is a distributed database, where the partitions of the database are defined by domains. A *distributed database* is a database that is made up of many partial databases spread across many computers, instead of a single database on a single computer. Splitting a database into smaller parts and placing those parts where the data is most relevant allows a large database to be distributed efficiently over a large network.

Service by Domain Controller Servers

As in Windows NT 4.0, servers running Windows 2000 that host a domain database are called domain controllers. A *domain controller* can host exactly one domain. You can make changes to objects in the domain on any domain controller of that domain. All of the domain controllers in a particular forest also host a copy of the forest Configuration and Schema containers.

Unit of Authentication

Each domain database contains security principal objects, such as users, groups, and computers. Security principal objects are special in that they can be granted or denied access to the resources on a network. Security principal objects must be authenticated by a domain controller for the domain in which the security principal objects are located. Authentication is done to prove the identity of the objects before they access a resource.

Boundary of Administration and Group Policy

Each domain has a domain administrators group. Domain administrators have full control over every object in the domain. These administrative rights are valid within the domain only and do not propagate to other domains.

Group Policy that is associated with one domain does not automatically propagate to other domains in the forest. For a Group Policy from one domain to be associated with another domain, it must be explicitly linked.

Security Policy for Unique Domain User Accounts

A small set of security policies that apply to domain user accounts can only be set on a per-domain basis:

- Password policy. Determines the rules that must be met, such as password length, when a user sets a password.
- Account lockout policy. Defines rules for intruder detection and account deactivation.
- Kerberos ticket policy. Determines the lifetime of a Kerberos ticket. A Kerberos ticket is obtained during the logon process and is used for network authentication. A particular ticket is only valid for the lifetime specified in the policy. When tickets expire, the system automatically tries to obtain a new ticket.

For more information about security policy for domain user accounts, see "Authentication" in the *Microsoft® Windows 2000 Server Resource Kit Distributed Systems Guide*.

DNS Domain Names

A domain is identified by a DNS name. You use DNS to locate the domain controller servers for a given domain. DNS names are hierarchical, and the DNS name of an Active Directory domain indicates its position in the forest hierarchy. For example, reskit.com might be the name of a domain. A domain named eu.reskit.com can be a child domain of reskit.com in the forest hierarchy.

Domain Planning Process

Your domain plan will determine the availability of the directory on the network, the query traffic characteristics of clients, and the replication traffic characteristics of domain controllers.

Each forest that you create will contain one or more domains. The steps to creating a domain plan for a forest are:

- Determine the number of domains in each forest.
- Choose a forest root domain.
- Assign a DNS name to each domain to create a domain hierarchy.
- Plan DNS server deployment.
- Optimize authentication with shortcut trust relationships.
- Understand the impact of changes to the domain plan after deployment.

When creating the Domain Plan for each forest, you will most likely need to consult the following groups:

- Current domain administrators that are responsible for user accounts, groups, and computers
- Teams that manage and monitor your physical network
- Teams that manage the DNS service for your network
- Security teams

Determining the Number of Domains in Each Forest

To determine the number of domains that you will have in each forest, start by considering a single domain only, even if you currently have more than one Windows NT 4.0 domain. Next, provide a detailed justification for each additional domain. Every domain that you create will introduce some incremental cost in terms of additional management overhead. For that reason, be certain that the domains you add to a forest serve a beneficial purpose.

How Creating Domains Has Changed

Some of the factors that lead to the creation of multiple domain environments in previous versions of Windows NT Server no longer apply to Active Directory and Windows 2000. These factors are as follows:

Security Accounts Manager (SAM) Size Limitations   In previous versions of Microsoft® Windows NT® Server, the SAM database had a practical limitation of about 40,000 objects per domain. Active Directory can scale easily to millions of objects per domain. It should never be necessary to create additional domains in order to handle more objects.

Primary Domain Controller (PDC) Availability Requirements   In previous versions of Windows NT Server, only a single domain controller, the PDC, could accept updates to the domain database. In an organization with a large network, this limitation made it difficult to ensure high availability of the PDC, because a network outage could prevent administrators on one part of the network from being able to update the domain. To satisfy the availability requirement, you created additional domains so that PDC servers could be distributed throughout the network. This is no longer necessary in Windows 2000, because all Active Directory domain controllers can accept updates.

Limited Delegation of Administration Within a Domain   In previous versions of Windows NT Server, you delegated administration using built-in local groups such as the Account Operators group, or by creating multiple domains and having distinct sets of domain administrators. For example, to delegate the management of a set of users, you created a new user domain. To delegate management of resource servers like file or print servers, you created resource domains. In Windows 2000, it is possible to delegate administration within a domain using *organizational units (OUs)*. An OU is a container that you use to organize objects within a domain into logical administrative subgroups. OUs are easier to create, delete, move, and modify than domains, and they are better suited to the delegation role.

For more information about using OUs to delegate administration, see "Creating an Organizational Unit Plan" later in this chapter.

When to Create More Than One Domain

Three possible reasons for creating additional domains are:

- Preserving existing Windows NT domains.
- Administrative partitioning.
- Physical partitioning.

Preserving Existing Windows NT Domains

If you already have Windows NT domains in place today, you might prefer to keep them as they are instead of consolidating them into a smaller number of Active Directory domains. If you decide to keep or consolidate a domain, be sure to weigh those costs against the long-term benefits of having fewer domains. The costs associated with domain consolidation are discussed in the chapter "Determining Domain Migration Strategies" in this book. If this is your first time through domain design, it is recommended that you aim for the fewest domains possible, and reevaluate this plan after reading that chapter.

Administrative Partitioning

More domains might be necessary depending on the administrative and policy requirements of your organization, described as follows.

Unique domain user security policy requirements   You might want to have a set of users on your network abide by a domain user security policy that is different from the security policy applied to the rest of the user community. For example, you might want your administrators to have a stronger password policy, such as a shorter password change interval, than the regular users on your network. To do this, you must place those users in a separate domain.

Division requires autonomous domain administration supervision

The members of the domain administrators group in a particular domain have complete control over all objects in that domain. If you have a subdivision in your organization that will not allow outside administrators control over their objects, place those objects in a separate domain. For example, for legal reasons, it might not be prudent for a subdivision of an organization that works on highly sensitive projects to accept domain supervision from a higher level IT group. Remember that all domains in the forest must share the Configuration and Schema containers.

Physical Partitioning

Physical partitioning involves taking the domains you have in a forest and dividing them up into a greater number of smaller domains. Having a greater number of smaller domains allows you to optimize replication traffic by only replicating objects to places where they are most relevant. For example, in a forest containing a single domain, every object in the forest is replicated to every domain controller in the forest. This might lead to objects being replicated to places where they are rarely used, which is an inefficient use of bandwidth. For example, a user that always logs on at a headquarters location does not need their user account replicated to a branch office location. Replication traffic can be avoided by creating a separate domain for the headquarters location and not replicating that domain to the branch office.

Note If you have already deployed Windows NT 4.0 domains, you might be satisfied with your existing physical partitioning. Looking at partitioning again from a clean sheet can help you identify areas for possible domain consolidation. If you have already decided to upgrade your Windows NT 4.0 domains in place and not perform any consolidation, you can skip the partitioning discussion.

To determine if, and how, to partition a forest, you should:

- Draw your network topology.
- Place domain controllers in the network according to availability requirements.
- Partition the forest based on the replication traffic between domain controllers.

Draw Your Network Topology

Begin by drawing a basic network topology diagram. Later in the planning process you will add more detail to this diagram when you plan your site topology. To create the topology diagram:

- Draw collections of sites.

  A site is a network of fast, reliable connectivity. A local area network (LAN) or set of LANs connected by a high-speed backbone can be considered a site. Draw each site on your network diagram and indicate the approximate number of users at the site.

- Connect sites with site links.

  A site link is a slow or unreliable link that connects two sites. A wide area network (WAN) that connects two fast networks is an example of a site link. It is recommended you treat any link that is slower than LAN speed as a slow link. On the topology diagram, show how each site connects to other sites with site links.

  For each site link, record the following:

  - Link speed and current usage levels
  - Whether the link is pay-by-usage
  - Whether the link is historically unreliable
  - Whether the link is only intermittently available

- Mark sites with SMTP connectivity only.

  If you have a site that has no physical connection to the rest of your network but can be reached via Simple Mail Transfer Protocol (SMTP) mail, mark that site as having mail-based connectivity only.

Figure 9.3 shows the network topology for the fictitious Reskit company.

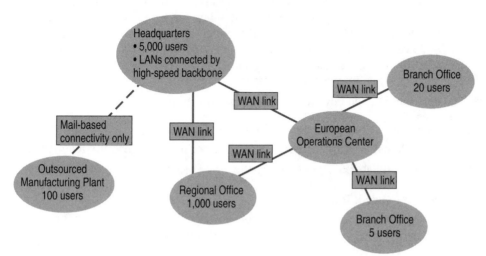

Figure 9.3   Reskit Company Network Topology

Place Domain Controllers

The availability of Active Directory is determined by the availability of domain controllers. Domain controllers must be available so that users can be authenticated. In this step, you will determine where you need to place domain controllers to maintain availability in case of possible network outages.

To place domain controllers, use the following process:

- Select a "home" site and place a domain controller in the site by marking it on the topology diagram.

  You can select the home site arbitrarily. For example, use your headquarters location, the site with the largest number of users, or the site with the best overall connectivity to the rest of your network. All the users in the home site will authenticate with this domain controller. Ignore for now the question of what domain is being serviced by that domain controller, and how many replicas of that domain will be necessary in the site.

- For each site that is directly connected to the home site, determine if you need to place a domain controller into that site.

  Or, instead of placing a domain controller in that site, determine if users in that site can authenticate over the site link back to the domain controller in the home site. If it is acceptable to you that authentication fails when the site link fails, then you do not need to place a domain controller into the site.

For small branch offices that have client computers but no servers, a domain controller is not necessary. If the link back to the central site fails, users in the office will still be able to log on to their computers using cached credentials. Further authentication is unnecessary because there are no other server-based resources to access in the office—all of the resources are back at the central site.

You should put a domain controller into the site if:

- There are a large number of users in the site, and the site link is slow or near capacity. In this case, you do not want Active Directory client traffic to take up capacity on the link. For more information about network capacity planning and the traffic generated by an Active Directory client, see the Microsoft Windows 2000 Server link on the Web Resources page at http://windows.microsoft.com/windows2000/reskit/webresources.

- The link is historically unreliable. You do not want authentication to fail if the link is down.

- The link is intermittently available. You do not want authentication to fail at certain times of the day or to rely on a demand-dial link.

- The site is only accessible using SMTP mail. Users must have a local domain controller for authentication if the site is only accessible via SMTP mail.

- Repeat the previous process to determine where you need to place domain controllers.

    Apply the same process to the next adjacent site, until you have visited every site and determined whether or not a local domain controller is necessary.

Note Domain controllers contain security-sensitive information, such as copies of users' secret keys used for domain authentication. Having fewer copies of this information reduces the opportunities for unauthorized access. Domain controllers must be physically secure from unauthorized access. For example, it is recommended that domain controllers be located in a locked room with limited access. Physical access can allow an intruder to obtain copies of encrypted password data to use for an off-line password attack. Stronger security options are available using the Syskey tool. For more information about Syskey, see "Encrypting File System" in the *Distributed Systems Guide*.

When a user logs on, the domain controller servicing the authentication request must be able to communicate with a global catalog server. When you decide to place a domain controller in a site, you need to also consider that domain controller as a global catalog server. As you proceed, keep in mind that global catalog servers generate more replication traffic than regular domain controllers. They contain both a complete copy of one domain and a read-only partial copy of every other domain in the forest.

Figure 9.4 shows the domain controller placement for the Reskit company.

- The first domain controller is placed in the headquarters home location.
- A domain controller is placed in the European operations center because the transoceanic WAN link is already near capacity.
- A domain controller is placed in the regional office because there are too many users for the WAN to carry the authentication traffic.
- Domain controllers are not placed in the branch offices because there are no local servers in the branch offices.
- A domain controller is placed in the manufacturing plant because it is can be reached by SMTP mail only.

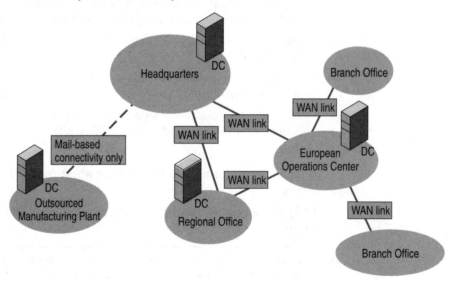

Figure 9.4   Reskit Company Domain Controller Placement

Partition the Forest

Now you will assign a domain to each domain controller, determine if your network can handle the replication traffic, and partition your forest into smaller domains if necessary. While doing this, remember that the objective of partitioning is to put physical copies of directory objects near the users that need those objects. For example, a user's user account object needs to be located on a domain controller that is in the same site as the user.

To partition the forest, perform the following steps for each domain currently in the domain plan:

- For each site that contains a domain controller, decide if the domain is relevant to the users in the site. If appropriate, place a domain controller for the domain into the site.

- Trace the path that replication will follow between domain controllers for the domain. Assume that each domain controller will choose the next nearest domain controller for the same domain as a replication partner, where "nearest" is determined by the most cost-effective path through the network.

- The volume of replication traffic between any two domain controllers for a domain is a factor of how often the objects in the domain change, how many of them change, and how often objects are added and deleted. By splitting a domain into two or more smaller domains, you can decrease the amount of replication traffic that will travel over a particular link. Examine each edge in the replication path and decide if you will permit the replication traffic or split the domain.

Consider these factors when deciding whether or not to replicate a domain between sites, or to split it into two or more smaller domains:

- Consider splitting the domain if a site link in the replication path cannot accommodate the anticipated replication traffic.

    The actual capacity of a site link is a function of link speed, daily usage characteristics, reliability, and availability. Consider the following information about a link when deciding whether to create a domain:

    - A link operating near capacity might not be able to accommodate replication. Keep in mind that Active Directory replication can be scheduled, so if the link has idle periods during the day, there might be enough actual bandwidth for replication to keep up.

    - A link might only be available during certain times of day, lowering its actual bandwidth. Active Directory replication can be scheduled to occur only when the link is available, but the actual bandwidth must be high enough to accommodate replication.

    For more information about network capacity planning and Active Directory replication traffic, see the Microsoft Windows 2000 Server link on the Web Resources page at http://windows.microsoft.com/windows2000/reskit/webresources.

- Consider splitting the domain if you do not want replication traffic to compete with other, more important traffic on a link.

    Interrupting or delaying business-critical traffic might be much more costly than adding an additional domain.

- Consider splitting the domain if replication traffic will cross a pay-by-usage link.

    When a link is pay-by-usage, minimizing usage will minimize your costs.

- Create domains for sites that are connected by SMTP mail only.

  Active Directory mail-based replication can only occur between domains. Mail-based replication cannot be used between domain controllers of the same domain.

If you do decide to split a large domain into several smaller domains, a good strategy for creating the smaller domains is to base them on geography or geo-political boundaries. For example, create domains that map to countries or continents. Geographical mapping for domains is recommended because network topologies tend to map to geographical locations, and geography tends to change less than any other basis for divisions.

You might want to create a greater number of smaller domains simply to optimize replication traffic on your network. Remember, optimization is a tradeoff against other factors, such as:

- Complexity

  As discussed earlier, each additional domain introduces a fixed on-going management overhead.

- Query traffic versus replication traffic

  The fewer the number of objects in a domain, the more likely a user in that domain will want to access objects that are in some other domain. If there is no local domain controller for the other domain, the query will cause traffic to leave the site.

Note A model with a single large domain works best with a large roaming user population because every user account will be available in every site that has a domain controller. In this case, a roaming user will never lose the ability to log on if a network outage occurs between the user's current location and home location.

Figure 9.5 shows the physical partitioning for the Reskit company. The domain assignments are as follows:

- The Noam domain for users in North America is assigned to a domain controller in the home site.

- The Avionics domain, which was created for administrative reasons, is assigned to a domain controller in the home site since there are Avionics users at headquarters.

- A new domain, Eu, is assigned to a domain controller in the European operations center because the transoceanic WAN link is near capacity. The link cannot handle the replication traffic for both the North American and European domains combined.

- The Avionics domain is also represented in the European Operations center, since there are Avionics users in Europe.

- A new domain, Seville, is assigned to a domain controller in the regional office in Seville because the WAN link back to the European operations center is carrying business-critical traffic.

- A new domain, Mfg, is assigned to a domain controller in the manufacturing plant because it can only be accessed by SMTP mail.

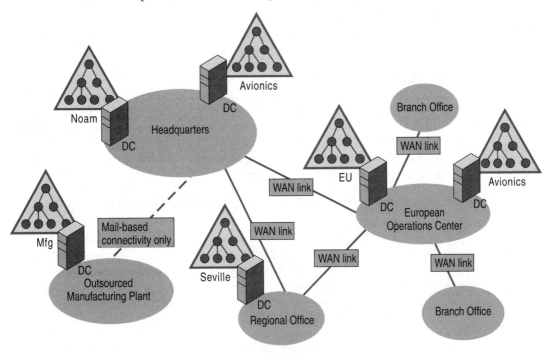

Figure 9.5   Reskit Company Domain Assignment

Incremental Costs for an Additional Domain

Each domain in the forest will introduce some amount of management overhead. When debating whether or not to add a domain to your domain plan, weigh the following costs against the benefits you determined earlier in the chapter.

More Domain Administrators   Because domain administrators have full control over a domain, the membership of the domain administrators group for a domain must be closely monitored. Each added domain in a forest incurs this management overhead.

More Domain Controller Hardware   In Windows 2000, a domain controller can host only a single domain. Each new domain that you create will require at least one computer, and in most cases will require two computers to meet reliability and availability requirements. Because all Windows 2000 domain controllers can accept and originate changes, you must physically guard them more carefully than you did Windows NT 4.0 backup domain controllers (BDCs), which were read-only computers. Note that the administration delegation within Active Directory domains reduces the requirement for resource domains. Some remote locations that currently must host two domain controllers (a master user domain and a local resource domain) will now only require one domain controller if you choose to consolidate to fewer Active Directory domains.

More Trust Links   For a domain controller in one domain to authenticate a user from another domain, it must be able to contact a domain controller within the second domain. This communication represents an added possible point of failure if, for example, the network between the two domain controllers is malfunctioning at the time. The more users and resources located in a single domain, the less an individual domain controller must rely on being able to communicate with other domain controllers to maintain service.

Greater Chance of Having to Move a Security Principal Between Domains

The more domains you have, the greater the chance you have to move security principals, such as users and groups, between two domains. For example, a business reorganization or a job change for a user can create the need to move a user between domains. To end users and administrators, moving a security principal between OUs inside a domain is a trivial and transparent operation. However, moving a security principal between domains is more involved and can impact the end user.

For more information about moving security principals between domains, see "Determining Domain Migration Strategies" in this book.

Group Policy and Access Control Do Not Flow Between Domains   Group Policy and access control applied within a domain do not flow automatically into other domains. If you have policies or delegated administration through access control that is uniform across many domains, they must be applied separately to each domain.

Choosing a Forest Root Domain

After you have determined how many domains you will place in your forest, you need to decide which domain will be the forest root domain. The *forest root domain* is the first domain that you create in a forest. The two forest-wide groups, enterprise administrators and schema administrators, will reside in this domain.

Note If all of the domain controllers for the forest root domain are lost in a catastrophic event, and one or more domain controllers cannot be restored from backup, the enterprise administrators and schema administrators groups will be permanently lost. There is no way to reinstall the forest root domain of a forest.

If your forest contains only one domain, that domain will be the forest root. If your forest contains two or more domains, consider the following two approaches for selecting the forest root domain.

Using an Existing Domain

From the list of domains you have, select a domain that is critical to the operation of your organization and make it the forest root. Because you cannot afford to lose this domain, it will already require the kind of fault tolerance and recoverability that is required for a forest root.

Using a Dedicated Domain

Creating an additional, dedicated domain to serve solely as the forest root carries all the costs of an extra domain, but it has certain benefits that might apply to your organization, such as:

- The domain administrator in the forest root domain will be able to manipulate the membership of the enterprise administrators and schema administrators groups. You might have administrators who require domain administrator privilege for some part of their duties, but you do not want them to manipulate the forest-wide administrators groups. By creating a separate domain, you avoid having to place these administrators into the domain administrators group of the forest root domain.

- Because the domain is small, it can be easily replicated anywhere on your network to provide protection against geographically-centered catastrophes.

- Because the only role the domain has is to serve as the forest root, it never risks becoming obsolete. In the case where you select a domain from your planned list of domains to be the forest root, there is always a chance that particular domain will become obsolete, perhaps due to a change in your organization. However, you will never be able to fully retire such a domain, because it must play the role of forest root.

Assigning DNS Names to Create a Domain Hierarchy

Active Directory domains are named with DNS names. Because DNS is the predominant name system on the Internet, DNS names are globally recognized and have well-known registration authorities. Active Directory clients requesting to log on to the network query DNS to locate domain controllers.

In Windows NT 4.0, the domain locator was based on the network basic input/output system (NetBIOS) Name System (NBNS), and domains were identified with NetBIOS names. The server-based component of NBNS is called the Windows Internet Name Service (WINS) server. NetBIOS names are simple, single-part names, and the NetBIOS namespace cannot be partitioned. In contrast, DNS names are hierarchical, and the DNS namespace can be partitioned along the lines of the hierarchy. As a result, DNS is more scalable than NBNS and can accommodate a larger database spread over a larger network. Internet mail, which leverages DNS in a manner similar to Active Directory, is a good example of how DNS as a locator mechanism can scale to extraordinarily large networks such as the Internet.

Note For interoperability with computers that run earlier versions of Windows, Active Directory domains have NetBIOS names and Active Directory domain controllers register in NBNS and query NBNS when necessary. This allows clients that run earlier versions of Windows to locate Active Directory domain controllers, and allows Active Directory domain controllers and Windows NT 3.51 and Windows NT 4.0 domain controllers to locate each other.

Arranging Domains into Trees

A *tree* is a set of one or more Windows 2000 domains with contiguous names. Figure 9.6 presents a single tree with a contiguous namespace. Because reskit.com does not have a parent domain, it is considered the *tree root domain*. The *child domains* of reskit.com are eu.reskit.com and noam.reskit.com. A grandchild domain of reskit.com is mfg.noam.reskit.com. These domain names are contiguous because each name is only one label different than the name of the domain above it in the domain hierarchy.

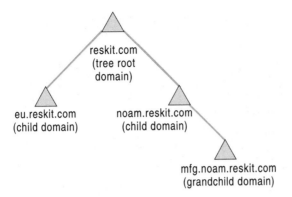

Figure 9.6   Single Tree with Four Domains

A forest can have more than one tree. In a multiple tree forest, the names of the tree root domains are not contiguous, as shown in Figure 9.7. You might have multiple trees in your forest if a division of your organization has its own registered DNS name and runs its own DNS servers.

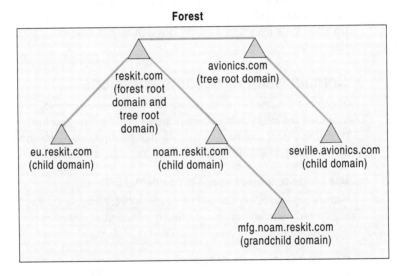

Figure 9.7   Forest with Multiple Trees

The domain hierarchy in a forest determines the transitive trust links that connect each domain. Each domain has a direct trust link with its parent and each of its children. If there are multiple trees in a forest, then the forest root domain is at the top of the trust tree and all other tree roots are children, from a trust perspective. Figure 9.8 depicts a transitive trust relationship between two trees.

Forest

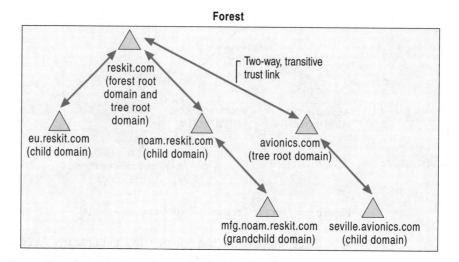

Figure 9.8   Transitive Trust Relationship Between Trees

The parent-child relationship is a naming and trust relationship only.
Administrators in a parent domain are not automatically administrators of a child
domain. Policies set in a parent domain do not automatically apply to child
domains.

Domain Naming Recommendations

To create the domain hierarchy in a forest, assign a DNS name to the first domain,
and then for every subsequent domain decide if it is a child of an existing domain
or if it is a new tree root. Based on that evaluation, assign names accordingly.
Some recommendations for naming domains are as follows:

Use names relative to a registered Internet DNS name.

Names registered on the Internet are globally unique. If you have one or more
registered Internet names, use those names as suffixes in your Active Directory
domain names.

Use Internet standard characters.

Internet standard characters for DNS host names are defined in Request for
Comments (RFC) 1123 as A–Z, a–z, 0–9, and the hyphen (–). Using only Internet
standard characters ensures that your Active Directory will comply with
standards-based software. To support the upgrade of earlier Windows-based
domains to Windows 2000 domains that have nonstandard names, Microsoft
clients and the Windows 2000 DNS service will support almost any Unicode
character in a name.

Never use the same name twice.

Never give the same name to two different domains, even if those domains are on unconnected networks with different DNS namespaces. For example, if the Reskit company decides to name a domain on the intranet reskit.com, it should not also create a domain on the Internet called reskit.com. If a reskit.com client connects to both the intranet and Internet simultaneously, it would select the domain that answered first during the locator search. To the client, this selection would appear random, and there is no guarantee that the client will select the "correct" domain. An example of such a configuration is a client that has established a virtual private network connection to the intranet over the Internet.

Use names that are distinct.

Some proxy client software, such as the proxy client built into Microsoft® Internet Explorer or the Winsock Proxy client, use the name of a host to determine if that host is on the Internet. Most software of this type provides, at minimum, a way of excluding names with certain suffixes as being local names, instead of assuming that they are on the Internet.

If the Reskit company wants to call an Active Directory domain on their intranet reskit.com, they would have to enter reskit.com in the exclusion list of their proxy client software. This would prevent clients on the Reskit intranet from seeing a host on the Internet called www.reskit.com, unless they provide an identical site on the intranet.

To avoid having this problem, the Reskit company could use a registered name that does not have a presence on the Internet, such as reskit-int01.com, or establish a company policy that states names ending in a specific suffix of reskit.com, for example corp.reskit.com, would never appear on the Internet. In both cases, it is easy to configure proxy client exclusion lists so that they can determine which names are on the intranet and which are on the Internet.

There are many different techniques for accessing the Internet from a private intranet. Before using any name, ensure that it can be properly resolved by clients on your intranet within your specific Internet access strategy.

Use the fewest number of trees possible.

There are some advantages to minimizing the number of trees in your forest. The following advantages could apply in your environment:

- After you have been given control over a particular DNS name, you own all names that are subordinate to that name. The smaller the number of trees, the smaller the number of DNS names that you must take ownership of in your organization.

- There are fewer names to enter in the proxy client-excluded suffixes list.

- LDAP client computers that are not Microsoft clients might not use the global catalog when searching the directory. Instead, to perform directory-wide searches, these clients will use deep searches. A deep search covers all of the objects in a particular subtree. The fewer the number of trees in a forest, the fewer deep searches you will have to perform to cover the entire forest.

Make the first part of the DNS name the same as the NetBIOS name.

It is possible to assign a domain a DNS name and NetBIOS name that are entirely unrelated. For example, the DNS name of a domain could be sales.reskit.com, but the NetBIOS name could be "Marketing." Keep in mind that pre-Windows 2000 computers and non–Active Directory–aware software will display and accept NetBIOS names; whereas, Windows 2000 computers and Active Directory–aware software will display and accept DNS names. This can potentially lead to confusion on the part of your end users and administrators.

You should only use unmatched NetBIOS and DNS names if:

- You want to migrate to a new naming convention on your network.

- You are upgrading a NetBIOS name that contains nonstandard characters but you want the DNS name to have all standard characters.

Review names internationally.

Names that have a benign or useful meaning in one language can sometimes be derogatory or offensive in another language. DNS is a global namespace; be sure to review your names globally within your organization.

Note   If you have multiple localized versions of Windows running on your network, all computers, including Windows 2000 Professional and all versions of Windows 2000 Server, must use only Internet-standard characters in both their DNS and NetBIOS names. If you use characters other than those described above, only computers with the same locale setting will be able to communicate with each other.

Use names that are short enough to remember.

Length should not be a significant deciding factor when choosing names. Users typically interact with the global catalog and are not concerned with domain names. Typically, only administrators are exposed to domain names. Administrative tools almost always present a list of domains to choose from, and the number of cases where an administrator has to type a full name will be the exception, not the rule. In general, if you can remember all the components of a name then it is not too long.

Domain Names and Computer Names

Windows 2000 computers that are joined to a domain will, by default, assign themselves a DNS name that is made up of the host name of the computer and the DNS name of the domain the computer has joined. For example, in Figure 9.9 if the computer account for Server 1 is located in eu.reskit.com, the computer will name itself by default server1.eu.reskit.com. However, it is possible to use any arbitrary DNS suffix instead of the Active Directory domain name. For this reason, it is not necessary to name your Active Directory domains to fit a DNS structure that is already deployed in your organization. Your Active Directory domains can use any name, and your computers can retain their existing names.

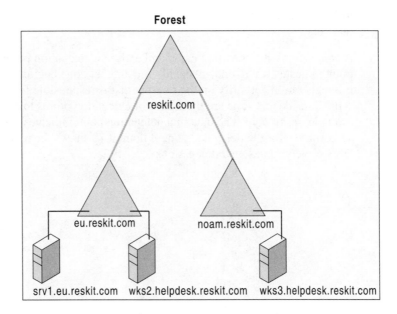

Figure 9.9   **Member Computers with Default and Nondefault Names**

For more information about computer naming, see "Windows 2000 DNS" in the *TCP/IP Core Networking Guide*.

Planning DNS Server Deployment

To plan DNS server deployment for support of your Active Directory domains, you must identify the DNS servers that will be authoritative for your domain names, and ensure that they meet the requirements of the domain controller locator system.

Authority and Delegation in DNS

The Domain Name System is a hierarchical, distributed database. The database itself consists of resource records, which primarily consist of a DNS name, a record type, and data values that are associated with that record type. For example, the most common records in the DNS database are Address (A) records, where the name of an Address record is the name of a computer, and the data in the record is the TCP/IP address of that computer.

Like Active Directory, the DNS database is divided into partitions that enable the database to scale efficiently even on very large networks. A partition of the DNS database is called a zone. A zone contains the records for a contiguous set of DNS names. A DNS server that loads a zone is said to be authoritative for the names in that zone.

A zone begins at a specified name and ends at a delegation point. A delegation point indicates where one zone ends and another zone begins. For example, there is a registration authority on the Internet that is responsible for the zone called "com." Inside this zone are thousands of delegation points to other zones, for example, reskit.com. The data in a delegation point indicates which servers are authoritative for the delegated zone. Figure 9.10 shows the relationship among DNS servers, zones, and delegations.

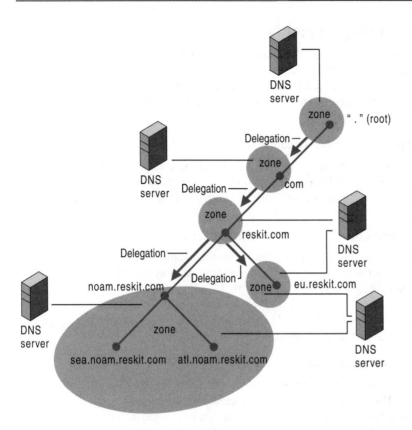

Figure 9.10   Servers, Zones, and Delegations in DNS

Domain Controller Locator System

Domain controllers register a set of records in DNS. These records are collectively called the locator records. When a client requires a particular service from a domain, it sends a query for a specific name and type of record to the nearest DNS server. The answer is a list of domain controllers that can satisfy the request.

The names of the locator records for each domain end in *<DNS-domain-name>* and *<DNS-forest-name>*. The DNS servers that are authoritative for each *<DNS-domain-name>* are authoritative for the locator records.

Note Windows 2000 does not require reverse lookup zones to be configured. Reverse lookup zones might be necessary for other applications, or for administrative convenience.

DNS Server Requirements

If you do not already have DNS servers running on your network, it is recommended that you deploy the DNS service that is provided with Windows 2000 Server. If you have existing DNS servers, then the servers that are authoritative for the locator records must meet the following requirements to support Active Directory:

- Must support the Service Location resource record.

  The DNS servers that are authoritative for the locator records must support the *Service Location (SRV)* resource record type. For more information about the SRV record, see "Introduction to DNS" in the *TCP/IP Core Networking Guide*.

- Should support the DNS dynamic update protocol.

  The DNS servers that are authoritative for the locator records and are the primary master servers for those zones should support the DNS dynamic update protocol as defined in RFC 2136.

The DNS service provided with Windows 2000 Server meets both these requirements and also offers two important additional features:

- Active Directory integration

  Using this feature, the Windows 2000 DNS service stores zone data in the directory. This makes DNS replication create multiple masters, and it allows any DNS server to accept updates for a directory service–integrated zone. Using Active Directory integration also reduces the need to maintain a separate DNS zone transfer replication topology.

- Secure dynamic update

  Secure dynamic update is integrated with Windows security. It allows an administrator to precisely control which computers can update which names, and it prevents unauthorized computers from obtaining existing names from DNS.

The remaining DNS servers on your network that are not authoritative for the locator records do not need to meet these requirements. Servers that are not authoritative are generally able to answer SRV record queries even if they do not explicitly support that record type.

Locate Authoritative Servers

For each DNS name you choose, consult your DNS management team and find out if the DNS server supports the listed requirements. If you find one that does not, there are three basic courses of action that you can take:

Upgrade the server to a version that supports the requirements.

If the authoritative servers are running the Windows NT 4.0 DNS service, simply upgrade those servers to Windows 2000. For other DNS server implementations, consult the vendor's documentation to find out which version supports the features necessary to support Active Directory.

If the authoritative DNS servers are not under your control, and you cannot persuade the owners of those servers to upgrade, you can use one of the other options.

Migrate the zone to Windows 2000 DNS.

You can migrate the zone from the authoritative servers to Windows 2000 DNS instead of upgrading those servers to a version that supports Active Directory requirements. Migrating a zone to Windows 2000 DNS is a straightforward process. Introduce one or more Windows 2000 DNS servers as secondary servers for the zone. After you are comfortable with the performance and manageability of the servers, convert the zone on one of the servers to be the primary copy, and rearrange the DNS zone transfer topology as necessary.

Delegate the name to a DNS server that meets the requirements.

If upgrading and migrating authoritative servers are not suitable options, you can change the authoritative servers by delegating the domain name to Windows 2000 DNS servers. How this is done depends on the relationship of the domain name to the existing zone structure.

- If the domain name is not the same as the name of the root of a zone, the name can be delegated directly to Windows 2000 DNS servers. For example, if the name of the domain is noam.reskit.com and the zone that contains this name is reskit.com, delegate noam.reskit.com to a Windows 2000 DNS server.

- If the domain name is the same as the name of the root of a zone, you cannot delegate the name directly to a Windows 2000 DNS server. Instead, delegate each of the subdomains used by the locator records to a Windows 2000 DNS server. Those subdomains are: _msdcs.<*DNS-domain-name*>, _sites.<*DNS-domain-name*>, _tcp.<*DNS-domain-name*>, and _udp.<*DNS-domain-name*>. If you do this, you will have to register the <*DNS-domain-name*> address (A) records by hand. For more information about this topic, see "Windows 2000 DNS" in the *TCP/IP Core Networking Guide*.

Optimizing Authentication with Shortcut Trust Relationships

When a user requests access to a network resource, a domain controller from the user's domain must communicate with a domain controller from the resource's domain. If the two domains are not in a parent-child relationship, the user's domain controller must also communicate with a domain controller from each domain in the trust tree between the user's domain and the resource's domain. Depending on the network location of the domain controllers for each domain, each extra authentication hop between the two domains can increase the chance of a possible failure, or increase the likelihood of authentication traffic having to cross a slow link. To reduce the amount of communication necessary for such interactions, you can connect any two domains with a *shortcut trust* relationship.

For example, if you have multiple trees in a forest, you might want to connect the group of tree roots in a complete mesh of trust. Remember that in the default arrangement, all tree roots are considered children of the forest root from a trust perspective. That means authentication traffic between any two domains in different trees must pass through the forest root. Creating a complete mesh of trust allows any two tree root domains to communicate with each other directly.

Figure 9.11 shows a complete mesh of trust created between four tree root domains.

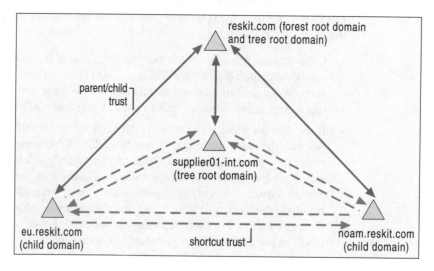

Figure 9.11   Complete Mesh of Trust Between Four Domains

Changing the Domain Plan After Deployment

Domain hierarchies are not easy to restructure after they have been created. For this reason, it is best not to create domains that are based on a temporary or short-lived organizational structure. For example, creating a domain that maps to a particular business unit in your organization might create work for you if that business unit is split up, disbanded, or merged with another unit during a corporate reorganization.

However, there are cases where organization-based partitioning is appropriate. Geopolitical boundaries provide a relatively stable template for partitioning, but only if the organization does not frequently move across those boundaries. Consider a domain plan for an army, where the army has different divisions spread across a number of bases. It might be common for divisions to move between bases. If the forest were partitioned according to geographic location, administrators would have to move large numbers of user accounts between domains when a division moved between bases. If the forest were partitioned according to divisions, administrators would only have to move domain controllers between bases. In this case, organization-based partitioning is more appropriate than geographic partitioning.

Adding New Domains and Removing Existing Domains

It is easy to add new domains to a forest; however you cannot move existing Windows 2000 Active Directory domains between forests.

 Critical Decision Point   After a tree root domain has been established, you cannot add a domain with a higher level name to the forest. You cannot create a parent of an existing domain; you can only create a child. For example, if the first domain in a tree is called eu.reskit.com, you cannot later add a parent domain called reskit.com.

Demoting all of the domain controllers for a domain to the member server or standalone role will remove a domain from a forest and delete all of the information that was stored in the domain. A domain can only be removed from the forest if it has no child domains.

Merging and Splitting Domains

Windows 2000 does not provide the ability to split a domain into two domains or to merge two domains into one domain in a single operation.

 Critical Decision Point   It is important that you design your domain plan to require a minimum amount of partitioning changes as your organization evolves.

It is possible to split a domain by adding an empty domain to a forest and then move objects into that domain from other domains. In the same way, it is possible to merge one domain with another domain by moving all of the objects from the source domain into the target domain. As mentioned previously, moving security principals between domains can impact end users. For more information about moving objects between domains, see "Determining Domain Migration Strategies" in this book.

Renaming Domains

Windows 2000 does not provide the ability to rename a domain in-place. Because the name of a domain is also representative of its position in a tree hierarchy, it is also true that a domain cannot be moved within a forest.

 Critical Decision Point   When selecting names for your domains, choose names that you believe will continue to be meaningful as your organization evolves.

The alternative to in-place renaming is to create a new domain in the forest with the desired new name, and then move all the objects from the old domain into the new domain.

Creating an Organizational Unit Plan

An Organizational Unit (OU) is the container you use to create structure within a domain. The following characteristics of OUs are important to consider when creating structure in a domain.

OUs can be nested. An OU can contain child OUs, enabling you to create a hierarchical tree structure inside a domain.

OUs can be used to delegate administration and control access to directory objects. When you use a combination of OU nesting and access control lists, you can delegate the administration of objects in the directory in a very granular manner. For example, you could grant a group of Help desk technicians the right to reset passwords for a specific set of users, but not the right to create users or modify any other attribute of a user object.

OUs are not security principals. You cannot make OUs members of security groups, nor can you grant users permission to a resource because they reside in a particular OU. Because OUs are used for delegation of administration, the parent OU of a user object indicates who manages the user object, but it does not indicate the resources a user can access.

Group Policy can be associated with an OU. Group Policy enables you to define desktop configurations for users and computers. You can associate Group Policy with sites, domains, and OUs. Defining Group Policy on an OU basis allows you to use different policies within the same domain. For more information about Group Policy, see "Applying Change and Configuration Management" and "Defining Client Administration and Configuration Standards" in this book.

Users will not navigate the OU structure. It is not necessary to design an OU structure that will appeal to end users. Although it is possible for users to navigate the OU structure of a domain, it is not the most efficient way for a user to discover resources. The most efficient way to find resources in the directory is by querying the global catalog.

OU Structure and Business Structure

At first, the phrase "organizational unit structure" might start you thinking about creating a structure that mirrors your business organization and its various divisions, departments, and projects. It is possible to create such a structure, but it might prove difficult and expensive to manage. OUs are for delegating administration, so the structure you create is most likely a reflection of your administrative model. The administrative model of your organization might not map exactly to your business organization.

For example, consider the business-oriented structure shown in Figure 9.12. OUs have been created for the Home Electronics (Electronics OU), Medical Systems (Medical OU), and Automotive (Automotive OU) divisions, where the users on the Automotive teams are in the Automotive OU, and so on.

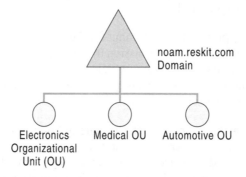

Figure 9.12   OU Structure Aligned with Business Structure

Assume that the company in this example uses a centralized administration model. A single group of administrators manages all of the users across the company, regardless of business division. During the day-to-day operation of the company, many things can happen. If a person transfers between the Home Electronics and Automotive divisions, an administrator has to move that person's user account from the Electronics OU to the Automotive OU. If the number of transfers is high, this could amount to a significant amount of work for the administration group. But what is actually being accomplished?

For the same company, now consider an OU structure that consists of a single OU that contains all user accounts. If a user transfers between divisions, no additional work to move the object is created for an administrator. Whenever you create structure, make sure that it serves a meaningful purpose. Structure without justification will always create unnecessary work.

You might want to mirror your business structure in your OU structure to make it easy to generate lists of users based on business unit. Using OUs is just one way of doing this. Your business structure might more closely reflect the way resource access is granted to your users. For example, users on a particular project might be granted access to a specific set of file servers, or users in a particular division might be granted access to a particular Web site. Because resource access is granted using security groups, you might find that your business organizational structure is best represented in security group structures instead of OUs.

OU Planning Process

The steps to creating an OU structure plan for a domain are:

- Create OUs to delegate administration.
- Create OUs to hide objects.
- Create OUs for Group Policy.
- Understand the impact of changing OU structures after deployment.

It is important to follow the steps in the order presented. You will find that an OU structure designed purely for delegation of administration is shaped differently than an OU structure designed purely for Group Policy. Because there are multiple ways of applying Group Policy, but only one way to delegate administration, you should create OUs for delegation of administration first.

Your OU structure can become complex very quickly. Note the specific reason for creating an OU each time you add one to the plan. This will help you make sure that every OU has a purpose, and it will help the readers of your plan to understand the reasoning behind the structure.

When creating the OU plan for each domain, consult the following groups in your administrative organizations:

- Current domain administrators who are responsible for user accounts, security groups, and computers accounts.
- Current resource domain owners and administrators.

Creating OUs to Delegate Administration

In versions of Windows NT previous to Windows 2000, delegation of administration within a domain was limited to the use of built-in local groups, such as the Account Administrators group. These groups had predefined capabilities, and in some cases the capabilities did not fit the needs of a particular situation. As a result, there were situations where administrators in an organization needed high levels of administrative access, such as Domain Administrators rights.

In Windows 2000, delegation of administration is more powerful and flexible. This flexibility is achieved through a combination of organizational units, per-attribute access control, and access control inheritance. Administration can be delegated arbitrarily by granting a set of users the ability to create specific classes of objects, or modify specific attributes on specific classes of objects.

For example, your human resources department can be granted the ability to create user objects in a particular OU, but nowhere else. Helpdesk technicians can be granted the ability to reset the passwords of users in that OU, but not the ability to create users. Other directory administrators can be granted the ability to modify the address book attributes of a user object, but not be allowed to create users or reset passwords.

Delegating administration in your organization has several benefits. Delegating specific rights enables you to minimize the number of users who must have high levels of access. Accidents or mistakes made by an administrator with restricted capability will only have an impact within their area of responsibility. Previously, in your organization it might have been necessary for groups other than IT to submit change requests to high-level administrators, who would make these changes on their behalf. With delegation of administration, you can push responsibility down to the individual groups in your organization and eliminate the overhead of sending requests to high-level administrative groups.

Modifying Access Control Lists

To delegate administration, grant a group specific rights over an OU. To do this, you need to modify the access control list (ACL) of the OU. The access control entries (ACEs) in the ACL of an object determine who can access that object and what kind of access they have. When an object is created in the directory, a default ACL is applied to it. The default ACL is described in the schema definition of the object class.

ACEs can be inherited by child objects of a container object. If any of the child objects are also containers, the ACEs are applied to the children of those containers as well. With inheritance, you can apply a delegated right to an entire subtree of OUs instead of a single OU. You can also block ACE inheritance on an object to prevent ACEs from a parent container from applying to that object or any child objects. Inheritable ACEs only apply within a domain and do not flow down to child domains.

To delegate control over a set of objects in an OU subtree, you edit the ACL on the OU. The easiest way to do this is by using the Delegation of Control wizard in the Microsoft Management Control (MMC) snap-in for Active Directory Users and Groups. To view the ACL on an object or to perform advanced editing of an ACL, use the **Security** tab on the property page for the object.

Always reference groups in ACLs, not individual users. Managing the membership of a group is simpler than managing an ACL on an OU. When users change roles, it is much easier to discover and change their group memberships than to check the ACLs on every OU. Where possible, delegate to local groups instead of global or universal groups. Unlike global groups, local groups can have members from any trusted domain, making them better suited for granting resource permissions. Unlike universal groups, local group membership is not replicated to the global catalog, making local groups less resource intensive.

Deciding What OUs to Create

The OU structure that you create will depend entirely on how administration is delegated within your organization. Three ways to delegate administration are:

- By physical location. For example, administration for objects in Europe can be handled by an autonomous set of administrators.

- By business unit. For example, administration of objects belonging to the Avionics division can be handled by an autonomous set of administrators.

- By role or task. This division is according to the type of object being managed. For example, a set of administrators might be responsible only for computer account objects.

These three dimensions are frequently combined. For example, as shown in Figure 9.13, there can be an administrative group that is responsible for computer account objects in Atlanta for the Automotive business unit.

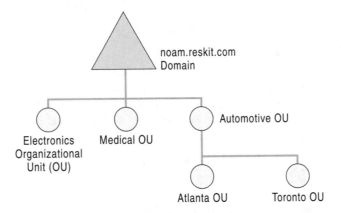

Figure 9.13   Two-Tiered Delegation

Whether or not the Atlanta OU is the child of the Automotive OU depends on whether the Automotive administrators delegate authority to the Atlanta administrators, or vice versa. It is also possible that the Atlanta administrators are completely autonomous from the Automotive administrators; therefore, the two OUs would be peers.

Note Some organizations have geographically distributed administrative groups in order to support 24-hour operation. The combined normal work hours of all administrative groups gives the organization 24-hour coverage. In this situation, the scope of each administrative group is not specific to location, because the administrators must be able to assist users all around the world. Even though this scenario has administrators distributed over many locations, it is not an example of location-based delegation.

Delegation Procedures

Starting with the default structure inside a domain, create an OU structure using the following primary steps:

- Create the top layers of OUs by delegating full control.
- Create the bottom layers of OUs to delegate per-object class control.

Delegating Full Control

To begin, only domain administrators have full control over all objects. Ideally, domain administrators should only be responsible for:

- Creating the initial OU structure.
- Repairing mistakes.

  Domain administrators not only have full control by default, they also have the right to take ownership of any object in the domain. Using this right, domain administrators can gain full control over any object in the domain, regardless of the permissions that have been set on the object.

- Creating additional domain controllers.

  Only members of the domain administrators group can create additional domain controllers for a domain.

Because domain administrators can have limited and specific duties, the membership of the group can be kept small and controlled.

If you have units in your organization that need to be allowed to determine their own OU structure and their own administrative model, use the following steps:

- Create an OU for each unit.

- Create a local group for each unit representing the highest level administrators in that unit.

- Assign the corresponding group full control over its OU.

- If the unit is allowed to set their its membership, place the unit's administrators group into the OU. If the unit is not allowed to set its own administrator membership, leave the group outside of the OU.

Example of Delegating Full Control

The Automotive unit of the Reskit company is the result of a merger of two companies, where the Automotive unit retained a fully autonomous IT group. In this situation, the Automotive unit gets its own OU from the root of the domain. Because they are also allowed to define the membership of their administrators group, the group is placed into the Automotive OU. If the Automotive unit itself had completely autonomous operations in Atlanta and Toronto, the Automotive administrators might again create OUs and delegate full control. As shown in Figure 9.14, the Automotive administrators have retained the ability to set the membership of the Atlanta and Toronto administrators groups.

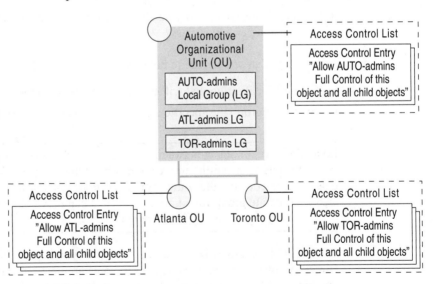

Figure 9.14   Delegating Full Control

If you do not have any units in your organization that need full control, domain administrators will determine the remainder of the OU structure.

Delegating Per-Object Class Control

Groups with full control can decide if additional OUs are necessary to delegate more restrictive control. A simple way to do this is to consider each object class that will be created in the directory, and determine if management of that object class is delegated further in the organization. Although the schema defines many different kinds of object classes, it is only necessary to consider the object classes that your administrators will create in the Active Directory. At minimum, you should consider:

- User account objects
- Computer account objects
- Group objects
- Organizational unit objects

As you examine each object class, separately consider:

- Which groups should be granted full control over objects of a particular class? Groups with full control can create and delete objects of the specified class and modify any attribute on objects of the specified class.
- Which groups should be allowed to create objects of a particular class? By default, users have full control over objects that they create.
- Which groups should only be allowed to modify specific attributes of existing objects of a particular class?

In each case that you decide to delegate control, you will:

- Create a local group that will be allowed to perform the specific function.
- Grant that group the specific right on the highest OU possible.

Note To move an object between two OUs, the administrator performing the move must have the ability to create the object in the destination container and to delete the object from the source container. For these reasons, you might want to create a separate group for administrators that can move objects, and grant them the necessary rights on a common parent OU.

The list of objects to be considered can grow as you deploy more Active Directory–aware applications. However, some applications will create objects in the directory that do not require hands-on management. For example, print servers running Windows 2000 automatically publish print queues in the directory. Because the print server takes care of the management of the print queue object, it is not necessary to delegate management to a special administrators group.

By modifying the ACL on the default Computers container, you can delegate the ability to create computer account objects to all users, with no administrative attention required. Computer accounts would be created when users join a computer to a domain in the default Computers container.

Example of Delegating Per-Object Class Control

The Atlanta location for the Automotive unit of the Reskit company is home to two Windows NT 4.0 resource domains, Powertrain and Chassis. Part of the Windows 2000 migration will involve consolidating those two domains into the noam.reskit.com domain.

The Powertrain and Chassis administrators use the domain today to:

- Create computer accounts for team members.

- Share file system space on Windows NT 4.0 backup domain controllers (BDCs), where access to the file system and shares are controlled by local group membership.

Using delegation of administration, it is simple to replace resource domains with OUs. In this case, groups are created to administer each kind of object, and they are granted full control in a project-specific OU. Project-specific OUs are necessary to prevent Powertrain administrators from being able to manipulate Chassis objects, and vice versa. Figure 9.15 illustrates this concept.

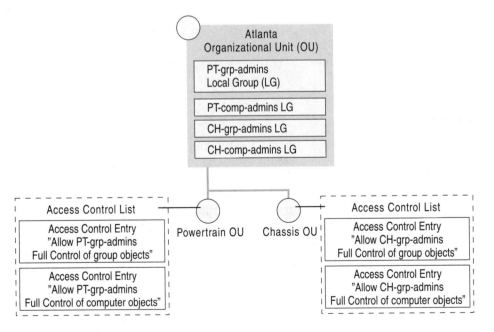

Figure 9.15   Replacing Resource Domains

Creating OUs to Hide Objects

Even if a user does not have the right to read the attributes of an object, that user can still see that the object exists by enumerating the contents of that object's parent container. The easiest and most efficient way to hide an object or set of objects is to create an OU for those objects and limit the set of users who have the List Contents right for that OU.

▶ **To create an OU to hide objects**

1. Create the OU where you will hide objects.

2. Click the **Security** tab on the property sheet on the OU.

3. Remove all existing permissions from the OU.

4. In the **Advanced** dialog box, clear the **Inherit permissions from parent** check box.

5. Identify the groups that you want to have full control on the OU. Using the **Security** tab on the property sheet, grant those groups full control.

6. Identify the groups that should have generic read access on the OU and its contents. Using the **Security** tab on the property sheet, grant those groups read access.

7. Identify any other groups that might need specific access, such as the right to create or delete a particular class of objects, on the OU. Using the **Security** tab on the property sheet, grant those groups the specific access.

8. Move the objects you want to hide into the OU.

Only users who can modify the ACL on an OU will be able to hide objects in this manner.

Creating OUs for Group Policy

In Windows NT 4.0, you can use the System Policy Editor to define user and computer configurations for all of the users and computers in a domain. With Windows 2000, you use Group Policy to define user and computer configurations, and associate those policies with sites, domains or OUs. Whether or not you will need to create additional OUs to support the application of Group Policy depends on the policies you create and the implementation options you select. For more information about Group Policy, see "Applying Change and Configuration Management" and "Defining Client Administration and Configuration Standards" in this book.

Changing the OU Plan After Deployment

Creating new OUs, moving OU subtrees within a domain, moving objects between OUs in the same domain, and deleting OUs are simple tasks.

Moving an object or subtree of objects will change the parent container of those objects. ACEs that were inherited from the old parent will no longer apply, and there might be new inherited ACEs from the new parent. To avoid unexpected changes in access, evaluate in advance what the changes will be and determine whether those changes will have any impact on the users that currently access and manage those objects.

Moving a user object, computer object, or a subtree containing user or computer objects can change the Group Policy that is applied to those objects. To avoid unexpected changes in client configurations, evaluate the changes in Group Policy and ensure that they are acceptable for end users.

Creating a Site Topology Plan

An Active Directory site topology is a logical representation of a physical network. Site topology is defined on a per-forest basis. Active Directory clients and servers use the site topology of a forest to route query and replication traffic efficiently. A site topology also helps you decide where to place domain controllers on your network. Keep the following key concepts in mind when designing your site topology:

A site is a set of networks with fast, reliable connectivity.

A site is defined as a set of IP subnets connected by fast, reliable connectivity. As a rule of thumb, networks with LAN speed or better are considered fast networks.

A site link is a low-bandwidth or unreliable network that connects two or more sites.

Site links are used to model the amount of available bandwidth between two sites. As a general rule, any two networks connected by a link that is slower than LAN speed is considered to be connected by a site link. A fast link that is near capacity has a low effective bandwidth, and can also be considered a site link. Site links have four parameters:

- Cost

  The cost value of a site link helps the replication system determine when to use the link when compared to other links. Cost values will determine the paths that replication will take through your network.

- Replication schedule

  A site link has an associated schedule that indicates at what times of day the link is available to carry replication traffic.

- Replication interval

  The replication interval indicates how often the system polls domain controllers on the other side of the site link for replication changes.

- Transport

  The transport that is used for replication.

Client computers first try to communicate with servers located in the same site as the client.

When a user turns on a client computer, the computer sends a message to a randomly selected domain controller of the domain in which the client is a member. The domain controller determines the site in which the client is located based on its IP address, and returns the name of the site to the client. The client caches this information and uses it the next time it is looking for a replicated server in the site.

Active Directory replication uses the site topology to generate replication connections.

The knowledge consistency checker (KCC) is a built-in process that creates and maintains replication connections between domain controllers. Site topology information is used to guide the creation of these connections. Intra-site replication is tuned to minimize replication latency, and inter-site replication is tuned to minimize bandwidth usage. Table 9.1 shows the differences between intra-site and inter-site replication.

Table 9.1   Intra-site vs. Inter-site Replication

Intra-site replication	Inter-site replication
Replication traffic is not compressed to save processor time.	Replication traffic is compressed to save bandwidth.
Replication partners notify each other when changes need to be replicated, to reduce replication latency.	Replication partners do not notify each other when changes need to be replicated, to save bandwidth.
Replication partners poll each other for changes on a periodic basis.	Replication partners poll each other for changes on a specified polling interval, during scheduled periods only.
Replication uses the remote procedure call (RPC) transport.	Replication uses the TCP/IP or SMTP transport.

(continued)

Table 9.1   Intra-site vs. Inter-site Replication *(continued)*

Intra-site replication	Inter-site replication
Replication connections can be created between any two domain controllers located in the same site.	Replication connections are only created between bridgehead servers.
The KCC creates connections with multiple domain controllers to reduce replication latency.	One domain controller from each domain in a site is designated by the KCC as a bridgehead server. The bridgehead server handles all inter-site replication for that domain.
	The KCC creates connections between bridgehead servers using the lowest cost route, according to site link cost. The KCC will only create connections over a higher cost route if all of the domain controllers in lower cost routes are unreachable.

Site topology information is stored in the Configuration container.

Sites, site links, and subnets are all stored in the configuration container, which is replicated to every domain controller in the forest. Every domain controller in the forest has complete knowledge of the site topology. A change to the site topology causes replication to every domain controller in the forest.

Note Site topology is separate and unrelated to domain hierarchy. A site can contain many domains, and a domain can appear in many sites.

Site Topology Planning Process

To create a site topology for a forest, use the following process:

- Define sites and site links using your physical network topology as a starting point.
- Place servers into sites.
- Understand how changes to your site topology after deployment will impact end users.

When creating the site topology plan, you will most likely need to consult:

- Teams that manage and monitor the TCP/IP implementation on your network.
- Domain administrators for each domain in the forest.

For more information about sites or any of the topics discussed in this section, see the *Distributed Systems Guide.*

Defining Sites and Site Links

To create the site topology for a forest, you will take the physical topology of your network and create a more general topology based on available bandwidth and network reliability.

If you performed the physical partitioning exercise when you created your domain plan, you can use the site topology and domain controller placement plan that you created as a starting point for your site topology. If you skipped the physical partitioning exercise earlier in this chapter, it is recommended that you see "Determining the Number of Domains in Each Forest" and create a basic site topology now.

When creating your site topology, it is useful to have a complete map of the physical topology of your network. That map should include the list of physical subnets on your network, the media type and speed of each network, and the interconnections between each network.

Creating Sites

To begin, create a list of sites on your network.

- Create a site for each LAN, or set of LANs, that are connected by a high speed backbone, and assign the site a name. Connectivity within the site must be reliable and always available.

- Create a site for each location that does not have direct connectivity to the rest of your network and is only reachable via SMTP mail.

- Determine which sites will not have local domain controllers, and merge those sites with other, nearby sites. Sites help route client–to–domain controller and domain controller–to–domain controller traffic efficiently. Without a domain controller in a site, there is no replication traffic into the site to be controlled.

For each site you add to the plan, record the set of IP subnets that comprise the site. You will need this information later when you create the sites in the directory.

Note Site names are used in the records that are registered in DNS by the domain locator, so they must be legal DNS names. It is recommended that you only use the standard characters A–Z, a–z, 0–9, and the hyphen (–) in site names.

Remember, clients will attempt to communicate with domain controllers in the same site as the client before trying to communicate with domain controllers in any other site. Any time bandwidth between a set of networks is plentiful enough that you do not care whether a client on one network communicates with a server on a different network, then consider those networks all to be in one site.

If a client is on a subnet that is not defined in the directory, it is not considered part of a site, and it selects randomly from all domain controllers for a particular domain. You might encounter situations where not all subnets are defined in the directory, such as when new subnets are being added to your network. To associate these clients with a site, create the two default subnets shown in Table 9.2 and then associate them with a site.

Table 9.2   Default Subnets

Subnet ID	Mask	Description
128.0.0.0	192.0.0.0	Captures all clients on class B networks not yet defined in the directory.
192.0.0.0	224.0.0.0	Captures all clients on class C networks not yet defined in the directory.

There is no default subnet for clients on a class A network.

Any time two networks are separated by links that are heavily used during parts of the day and are idle during other parts of the day, put those networks into separate sites. You can use the ability to schedule replication between sites to prevent replication traffic from competing with other traffic during high usage hours.

If your entire network consists of fast, reliable connectivity, the entire network can be considered a single site.

Connecting Sites with Site Links

Next, connect sites with site links to reflect the physical connectivity of your network. Assign each site link a name.

Site links are transitive, so if site A is connected to site B, and site B is connected to site C, then the KCC assumes that domain controllers in site A can communicate with domain controllers in site C. You only need to create a site link between site A and site C if there is in fact a distinct network connection between those two sites.

For each site link you create, record the following information:

- Replication schedule

  Replication polling only occurs during the scheduled period or periods over a seven-day interval. The default schedule on a link allows replication polling to happen throughout the seven-day interval.

- Replication interval

  Replication polling occurs at the specified interval when the schedule allows replication. The default polling interval is three hours.

- Replication transport

  If the site is only reachable via SMTP, select the SMTP transport. Otherwise, select the TCP/IP transport.

- Link cost

  Assign a cost value to each site link to reflect the available bandwidth or cost of bandwidth as compared to other site links.

A backbone network that connects many sites can be represented by a single site link that connects many sites, instead of creating a mesh of links between sites. This is a useful way to reduce the number of site links that need to be created and managed if many links have the same characteristics. Figure 9.16 illustrates how a frame relay network that connects four offices can be represented as a single link, instead of a mesh of six individual links.

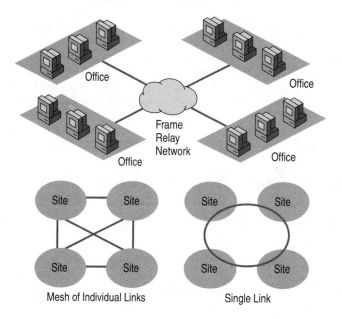

Figure 9.16   Single Link or Mesh of Links

Note   The replication schedule determines when a domain controller polls replication partners for changes. If a replication cycle is underway when the scheduled window closes, replication continues until the current cycle is complete.

Figure 9.17 shows the site topology for the Reskit company. The site naming convention uses a combination of region code, the code of the nearest airport, and an identifying number. Site link names include the names of the connected sites.

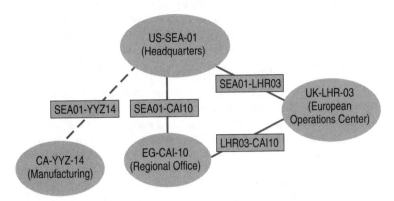

Figure 9.17   Reskit Company Site Topology

Table 9.3 shows the parameters for each site link in the Reskit site topology.

Table 9.3   Site Link Parameters for Reskit Site Topology

Site Link	Transport	Cost	Polling Interval	Schedule
SEA01-YYZ14	SMTP	100	30 mins	0500 to 0900 UTC daily
SEA01-CAI10	IP	100	30 mins	2000 to 0400 UTC daily
SEA01-LHR03	IP	25	1 hr	(always)
LHR03-CAI10	IP	50	15 mins	2000 to 0400 UTC daily

Replication is scheduled to occur only during off-hours for the link between the manufacturing plant and headquarters. Replication is also scheduled for off-hours only between the regional office and other sites. Since the link cost between the regional office and the operations center is lower than the cost between the regional office and headquarters, the KCC attempts to make connections with bridgeheads in the operations center before making connections with bridgeheads in headquarters. The schedule for the link between headquarters and the operations center is wide open, but uses a longer polling interval to reduce traffic.

Placing Servers into Sites

The location of servers on your site topology has a direct effect on the availability of Active Directory. During the physical partitioning exercise of the domain plan, you created a basic plan for domain controller placement. By placing servers onto the site topology, you will complete the details of this plan.

Placing Additional Domain Controllers

During the partitioning exercise, you decided which sites would have domain controllers for each domain, but you did not decide on the number of domain controllers that would be placed in each site for each domain. The number of domain controllers you will create for a particular domain is driven by two factors: fault tolerance requirements and load distribution requirements.

For each domain, use the following guidelines to determine if more domain controllers are necessary:

Always create at least two domain controllers. Even for small domains with small user populations, create at least two domain controllers so that there is no single point of failure for the domain.

For each site that contains a single domain controller, decide if you trust the WAN for failover.

If the single domain controller fails, clients in the site can be serviced by other domain controllers for that domain that are located in other sites. If network connectivity is unreliable or intermittently available, you might not want to trust the network to handle failover. In that case, place a second domain controller for that domain into the site.

Place additional domain controllers for a domain into a site to handle the client workload.

The number of clients that a particular server can handle depends on the workload characteristics and the hardware configuration of the server. Clients randomly select from the available domain controllers in a site to distribute client load evenly.

Placing Global Catalog Servers

The availability of global catalog servers is crucial to the operation of the directory. For example, a global catalog server must be available when processing a user log on request for a native-mode domain, or when a user logs on with a user principal name.

Note When processing a log on request for a user in a native-mode domain, a domain controller sends a query to a global catalog server to determine the user's universal group memberships. Since groups can be explicitly denied access to a resource, complete knowledge of a user's group memberships are necessary to enforce access control correctly. If a domain controller of a native-mode domain cannot contact a global catalog server when a user wants to log on, the domain controller refuses the log on request.

As a general rule, designate at least one domain controller in each site as a global catalog server.

Use the same failover and load distribution rules that you used for individual domain controllers to determine whether additional global catalog servers are necessary in each site.

Note In a single domain environment, global catalog servers are not required to process a user log on request. However, you should still designate global catalog servers using the suggested process. Clients still seek global catalog servers for search operations. Also, having global catalog servers already in place allows the system to adapt gracefully if you add more domains later.

Placing DNS Servers

The availability of DNS directly affects the availability of Active Directory. Clients rely on DNS to be able to find a domain controller, and domain controllers rely on DNS to find other domain controllers. Even if you already have DNS servers deployed on your network today, you might need to adjust the number and placement of servers to meet the needs of your Active Directory clients and domain controllers.

As a general rule, place at least one DNS server in every site. The DNS servers in the site should be authoritative for the locator records of the domains in the site, so that clients do not need to query DNS servers off-site to locate domain controllers that are in a site. Domain controllers will also periodically verify that the entries on the primary master server for each locator record are correct.

A simple configuration that satisfies all requirements is to use Active Directory–integrated DNS, store the locator records for a domain within the domain itself, and run the Windows 2000 DNS service on one or more domain controllers for each site where those domain controllers appear.

Distributing the Forest Wide Locator Records

Each domain controller in the forest registers two sets of locator records: a set of domain-specific records that end in *<DNS-domain-name>*, and a set of forest-wide records that end in *_msdcs.<DNS-forest-name>*. The forest-wide records are interesting to clients and domain controllers from all parts of the forest. For example, the global catalog locator records, and the records used by the replication system to locate replication partners, are included in the forest-wide records.

For any two domain controllers to replicate between each other, including two domain controllers from the same domain, they must be able to look up forest-wide locator records. In order for a newly created domain controller to participate in replication, it must be able to register its forest-wide records in DNS, and other domain controllers must be able to look up these records. For this reason, it is important to make the forest-wide locator records available to every DNS server in every site.

To do this, create a separate zone called *_msdcs.<DNS-forest-name>*, and replicate that zone to every DNS server. If you are using the simple Active Directory-integrated configuration, you can place the primary copy of this zone in the forest root domain along with the *<DNS-forest-name>* zone. You can then replicate the zone to DNS servers outside the domain using standard DNS replication.

Generally, it is not sufficient to replicate the zone to only one DNS server per site. If a DNS server does not have a local copy of the *_msdcs.<DNS-forest-name>* zone, it must use DNS recursion to look up a name in that zone. For a DNS server to perform recursion, it contacts a DNS server that is authoritative for the root of the namespace (a DNS root server) and proceeds down the delegations in DNS until it finds the record in question. If there is no DNS root server in a site, and the links between that site and other sites are down, a DNS server cannot perform recursion. Thus, it will not be able to find any DNS servers that are authoritative for *_msdcs.<DNS-forest-name>*, even if those DNS servers are in the same site.

DNS Client Configuration

Clients and domain controllers should be configured with at least two DNS server IP addresses: a preferred local server, and an alternate server. The alternate server can be in the local site, or it can be remote if you trust your network to handle the failover.

Changing the Site Topology After Deployment

A forest site topology is very flexible and easily changed after your initial deployment. As your physical network evolves, remember to evaluate and tune your site topology. As changes to your network increase or decrease bandwidth or reliability, remember to create or remove sites and site links, and be sure to tune site link parameters to balance replication latency against bandwidth usage.

Before making a change to your site topology, anticipate the impact of the change on availability, replication latency and replication bandwidth, and how that might affect end users. Because site topology is stored in the Configuration container, changes will replicate to every domain controller in the forest. Frequent changes to the site topology will cause a large amount of replication traffic, so changes should be rolled up into fewer, larger changes instead of many, smaller changes. Depending on your replication topology and schedule, site topology changes can take a long time to reach every domain controller in the forest.

Planning Task List for Designing the Active Directory Structure

Use Table 9.4 as a checklist to be sure you have performed all the primary tasks necessary to design your Active Directory structure.

Table 9.4   Active Directory Planning Task List

Task	Location in Chapter
Determine the number of forests.	Creating a Forest Plan
Create a change control policy for each forest.	Creating a Forest Plan
Determine the number of domains in each forest.	Creating a Domain Plan
Choose a forest root domain.	Creating a Domain Plan
Assign a DNS name to each domain.	Creating a Domain Plan
Plan DNS server deployment.	Creating a Domain Plan
Optimize authentication with shortcut trust relationships.	Creating a Domain Plan
Create OUs to delegate administration.	Creating an Organizational Unit Plan
Create OUs to hide objects.	Creating an Organizational Unit Plan
Create OUs for Group Policy.	Creating an Organizational Unit Plan
Define sites and site links.	Creating a Site Topology Plan
Place servers into sites.	Creating a Site Topology Plan

CHAPTER 10

Determining Domain Migration Strategies

Migrating successfully from Microsoft® Windows NT® 3.51 and Microsoft® Windows NT 4.0 to Microsoft® Windows® 2000 requires careful analysis of your current system and in-depth planning. Network engineers involved in the logical design of the upgrade process need to become familiar with the recommended configurations and procedures described in this chapter. Although these recommendations also work for smaller organizations, the emphasis in this chapter is on organizations with at least 2,500 personal computers.

Because the focus of this chapter is on planning for domain upgrade and restructure, and planning your Microsoft® Active Directory™ directory service namespace through an upgrade of Windows NT domains, most of your Active Directory namespace planning needs to be already completed. In addition, as a prerequisite to this chapter, you need to be familiar with the following: the features that can be deployed in Windows 2000, the deployment objectives of your organization, the current domain model of your organization, and the inventory of hardware and software in your current network configuration.

In This Chapter

Chapter Goals

This chapter will help you develop the following planning documents:

- Migration Project Roadmap
- Revised Active Directory Namespace Planning Document
- Domain Migration Plan

Related Information in the Resource Kit

- For more information about Active Directory, Domain Name System (DNS) namespace design, site topology, or groups, see "Designing the Active Directory Structure" in this book.

- For more information about automated installation of Windows 2000 Server, see "Automating Server Installation and Upgrade" in this book.

- For more information about automated installation of Windows 2000 Professional, see "Automating Client Installation and Upgrade" in this book.

Starting the Migration Planning Process

Before proceeding with a domain upgrade or restructure, it is important that you understand the planning process.

Note The procedures and suggestions in this chapter are based on the upgrade of noncloned computers. Upgrading to Windows 2000 Server is supported only on computers running Windows NT Server 3.51 and Windows NT Server 4.0. Older versions cannot be upgraded to Windows 2000 Server. In this chapter, the term "Windows NT" represents both the 3.51 and 4.0 versions of Windows NT Server.

Planning Process Phases

The planning process for migrating domains consists of the following phases:

1. Design the Windows 2000 forest. For information about how to design your Windows 2000 forest, see "Designing the Active Directory Structure" in this book.

2. Plan the migration of Windows NT domains to Windows 2000 native domains and deploy new features of Windows 2000 Server.

3. Plan the restructure of the Windows 2000 domains.

   This phase might not be necessary, or might be appropriate in the future, depending on the requirements of your organization. For more information about how to restructure domains, see "Planning Domain Restructure" later in this chapter.

Figure 10.1 illustrates the primary steps you must take to migrate to Windows 2000 Server. This chapter takes a close look at each of these steps, from the initial planning phase through the specific tasks for domain upgrade and restructure.

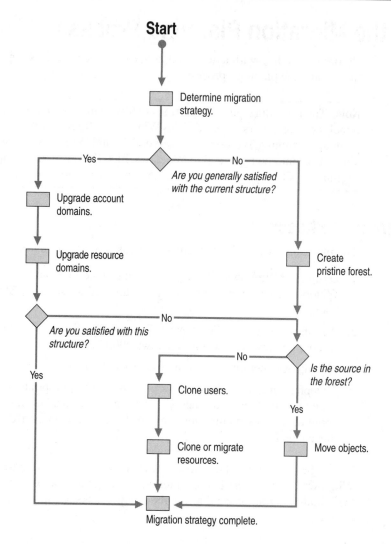

Figure 10.1   Migration Plan Flowchart

Determining Your Migration Roadmap

In any planning process it is normal to make and refine important decisions. The choices you make while planning your migration might cause you to defer deployment of some of the system features until a later date. The first steps in creating your migration roadmap are to identify and prioritize your migration goals and to understand the implications of your choices.

In choosing to migrate to Windows 2000, you no doubt have identified certain features and benefits that you are eager to deploy. The following section lists some typical migration goals and explains key concepts and their implications for these goals. After finishing this section, you should have enough information to complete your Migration Project Roadmap.

Migration Goals

Your migration planning needs to reflect your primary migration goals. These goals might be business related or they might relate to the migration itself.

In most cases, business-related goals drive the initial migration decision. Examples of such goals are greater scalability and improved security. Business-related goals are involved when making implementation choices, and can be used to evaluate possible tradeoffs. Usually some form of compliance table is prepared, which in later stages is used to identify the technologies and product features to be implemented in the final platform. These technologies and features will help you to achieve your business-related goals.

Migration-related goals could include such concerns as the effect of disruption on production systems, final system performance, and ways to increase mean time between failures. These goals can determine how test plans and acceptance criteria are formulated.

Migration-related goals are not driven by the need to implement specific technical features of Windows 2000 Server; but rather are concerned with the migration process itself. Some migration-related goals are listed in Table 10.1.

Table 10.1   Migration-Related Goals

Goals	Implications for Migration Process
Minimize disruption to the production environment	User access to data, resources, and applications needs to be maintained during and after the migration.
	The user's familiar environment needs to be maintained during and after the migration.
Maintain system performance	User access to data, resources, and applications needs to be maintained during and after the migration.
	The user's familiar environment needs to be maintained during and after the migration

(continued)

Table 10.1   Migration-Related Goals *(continued)*

Goals	Implications for Migration Process
Increase mean time between failures	User access to data, resources, and applications needs to be maintained during and after the migration.
	The user's familiar environment needs to be maintained during and after the migration
Minimize administrative overhead	There needs to be seamless migration of user accounts.
	If possible, users need to be able to retain their passwords.
	Administrators should only have to visit the client computer a minimum number of times.
	There needs to be minimal setup of new permissions for resources.
Maximize "quick wins"	The enterprise needs to obtain earliest access to key features of the new platform.
Maintain system security	There needs to be minimal impact on security policy.

To receive maximum benefit from Windows 2000 technologies and fully realize your migration-related goals, it is recommended that you switch your Windows 2000 domains to native mode as soon as possible. However, depending on your existing network configuration, you might not be able to switch to native mode until you have completely eliminated Windows NT backup domain controllers (BDCs) from your domain. For a definition of *native mode*, see "Determining When to Move to Native Mode" later in this chapter.

Note that you can still deploy Windows 2000 clients and member servers before upgrading the domain infrastructure. See "Upgrading Clients and Servers" later in this chapter.

Migration Concepts

There are two ways to arrive at your desired infrastructure:

- *Domain Upgrade* – sometimes referred to as "in-place upgrade" or "upgrade."

  A *domain upgrade* is the process of upgrading the Primary Domain Controller (PDC) and the BDCs of a Windows NT domain from Windows NT Server to Windows 2000 Server.

- *Domain Restructure* – sometimes referred to as "domain consolidation."

  A *domain restructure* is a complete redesign of the domain structure, usually resulting in fewer, larger domains. This choice is for those who are dissatisfied with their current domain structure or who feel that they cannot manage an upgrade without serious impact to their production environment.

Upgrade and restructure are not mutually exclusive; some organizations might upgrade first and then restructure, while others might restructure from the start. Both require careful thought and planning before choices are implemented.

Upgrading Clients and Servers

Though the focus of this chapter is domain upgrade and restructure, do not interpret this to mean that you must postpone deployment of Windows 2000 clients and member servers until you have upgraded the domain infrastructure. You can use Windows 2000 clients and servers in your existing Windows NT environment and still gain a number of benefits from the new technologies. Table 10.2 lists some of the benefits gained simply by upgrading clients and servers to Windows 2000.

Table 10.2   Benefits from Simple Client or Server Upgrade

Benefit	Features
Manageability	Plug and Play
	Hardware wizard with Device Manager
	Support for Universal Serial Bus
	Microsoft Management Console
	New Backup utility
Setup and troubleshooting tools	Automatic application installation allows an administrator to specify a set of applications that are always available to a user or group of users. If a required application is not available when needed, it is automatically installed in the system.
File system support	NTFS 5.0 enhancements include support for disk quotas, the ability to defragment directory structures, and compressed network I/O
	FAT32

(continued)

Table 10.2   Benefits from Simple Client or Server Upgrade *(continued)*

Benefit	Features
Application services	Win32® Driver Model
	DirectX® 5.0
	Windows Script Host
Information sharing and publishing	Microsoft Distributed file system (Dfs) for Windows 2000 Server makes it easier for users to find and manage data on the network.
	Integrated Internet Shell
Print server services	Easier location of printer through Active Directory
	Printing from the Internet
Scalability and availability	Improved Symmetric Multiprocessor support
Security	Encrypting File System

Domain Migration Considerations

This section takes you through the important planning and preparation activities you must undertake for any migration. Your own planning process will determine the exact steps, but the following sections highlight areas you need to consider.

Upgrade Decisions

Consider the following questions when determining how to upgrade your domains:

- Is upgrade appropriate for you?

  You will probably answer "yes" if some or all of the following conditions are true:

  - You are happy with your current domain structure.
  - You are happy with much of your domain structure and can carry out a two-phase migration: upgrade to Windows 2000, then restructure to fix any problems.
  - You feel you can manage the migration without impacting your production environment.

- In what order do you need to upgrade?

  The answer depends on whether you are referring to order of upgrade of domain controllers or order of upgrade of domains:

- In what order do you need to upgrade domain controllers?

  Within a domain, the order of upgrade is straightforward. You need to upgrade the PDC first, but be aware of possible complications, such as the use of LAN Manager Replication Service in the domain to be upgraded, with the PDC hosting the export directory. In this case you need to change the export directory host before upgrading the PDC. For more information on LAN Manager Replication, see "LAN Manager Replication Service Process" later in this chapter.

- In what order do you need to upgrade domains?

  You will experience easier administration and delegation if you upgrade your account domains first. You then need to upgrade your resource domains.

- In what order do you need to upgrade servers and clients?

  You can upgrade servers and clients at any time. This does not depend on a Windows 2000 infrastructure.

- When do you need to switch the domain to native mode?

  You need to switch the domain to native mode as soon as possible to have access to full Windows 2000 functionality, such as better directory scalability, universal and domain local groups, and group nesting.

Note You cannot switch the domain to native mode until all the domain controllers have been upgraded.

Restructure Decisions

Consider the following questions when determining whether and how to restructure your domains:

- Do you need to restructure?

  You will probably answer "yes" if some or all of the following conditions are true:

  - You are happy with much of your domain structure and can carry out a two-phase migration: upgrade to Windows 2000, then restructure to fix any problems.
  - You are unhappy with your current domain structure.
  - You feel you cannot manage the migration without impacting your production environment.

- When do you need to restructure?

    The answer depends on the reason you are restructuring.

    - If you can solve your migration requirements by doing a two-phase migration, then you need to restructure after upgrade.

    - If you feel your domain structure cannot be salvaged (for example, if you decide you need to redesign your directory services infrastructure to take advantage of the enhanced capabilities of Active Directory), you need to restructure at the beginning of the migration process.

    - If you feel you cannot avoid impacting your production environment, you need to restructure at the beginning of the migration process.

Note It is recommended that you restructure after completing the upgrade but before using features such as application deployment or the new Group Policy. If you restructure after some of these features have been used, it can create more difficulties than if the restructure had taken place at the beginning of the migration process.

Application Compatibility

After you have decided how you will perform the overall domain migration, it is important to determine whether your business applications are compatible with Windows 2000. This step is critical to the success of your deployment and must be done before you decide how and when to migrate your application servers. After you have identified your strategic applications, be sure to include them in your test plan. All strategic applications must be tested before beginning the migration process. For more information about migrating application servers, see "Upgrading and Installing Member Servers" in this book.

Some important questions you need to ask about your applications include the following:

- Will the application run on Windows 2000?

    If the answer is "no," this might have implications for your upgrade plans.

- Does the application need to run on a BDC?

    If the answer is "yes," and the application will not run on Windows 2000, it will be difficult to switch the upgraded domain to native mode.

- Do you have contacts with your application software vendors?

    If you experience problems running the application on Windows 2000, you need to be aware of how the application vendor plans to provide support for Windows 2000.

- If the application was internally developed, do you have plans to develop a Windows 2000 version?

  If the application cannot run on Windows 2000, you need to be aware of any plans to provide Windows 2000 support.

- What operating systems do you have deployed on your clients and servers?

  The answer to this has implications for your migration path. Certain software upgrade paths to Windows 2000 are not supported (for example, from Windows NT 3.5).

Note You might not want to maintain Windows NT 3.51 servers in your resource domains, because Windows NT 3.51 does not support universal or domain local group membership. Windows NT 3.51 does *not* recognize the SIDhistory capability for user accounts that move between Windows 2000 domains.

Knowing the answers to these questions will help you formulate a test plan covering the important test cases. It will also help you develop a project risk assessment that spells out the implications of various applications not functioning correctly, including any proposed mitigation.

For more information about testing your business applications, see "Testing Applications for Compatibility with Windows 2000" in this book.

Note Some application services designed for Windows NT, such as Windows NT Routing and Remote Access Service (RRAS), assume unauthenticated access to user account information. The default security permissions of Active Directory do not allow unauthenticated access to account information. The Active Directory Installation Wizard gives you the option of configuring Active Directory security for compatibility by granting additional permissions. If you feel that loosening the security of Active Directory to allow the use of RRAS servers would compromise your security policy, you need to upgrade these servers first.

If you are using LAN Manager Replication Service to replicate scripts within the domain, then you need to upgrade the server hosting the export directory last.

Interoperability Requirements

The next step is to consider the extent to which your Windows 2000 system needs to interoperate with both Windows legacy systems and non-Microsoft operating systems. If you plan to maintain a heterogeneous environment that includes network operating systems other than Windows 2000, you need to determine which legacy applications and services must be retained or upgraded to maintain acceptable functionality across all platforms.

Interoperability considerations have two aspects:

- What are the interoperability requirements with respect to operating in a heterogeneous environment?

  This encompasses the degree to which the migrated environment needs to interoperate with other operating systems and network services.

  Important considerations might include:

  - The need to maintain pre–Windows 2000 clients, which means that you have to plan to maintain services such as Windows Internet Name Service (WINS) to support name resolution.

  - The need to maintain pre–Windows 2000 domains, which means that you need to maintain and manage explicit trusts.

  - The need to interoperate with non-Microsoft operating systems, such as UNIX. This could be a reason for rapid migration to enable widespread use of the Kerberos authentication.

- What are the interoperability requirements with respect to the source environment? (Where you are migrating from?)

  Managing a transitional environment can be a complex task and needs careful planning, as described in the following sections.

Disk Storage Requirements for Active Directory Objects

Early in your migration planning, it is important to consider how much disk space you will need to store the objects required by Active Directory. The total disk space required depends on the size of your Windows 2000 forest. For information about designing this forest, see "Designing the Active Directory Structure" in this book.

Table 10.3 shows the disk space requirement for each type of Active Directory object.

Table 10.3   Disk Space Required for Active Directory Objects

Object	Disk Space Required (bytes)
User object	3.6K
Organizational unit (OU) object	1.1K
Attribute (10 bytes)	100
Public key certificate (X.509 v3 certificate issued by Windows 2000 Certificate Services)	1.7K

Planning Domain Upgrade

After you have considered the issues involving your domain migration and created a plan for resolving any problems that arise, you are ready to begin planning for the actual upgrade process.

Note   You must complete the design of your Windows 2000 forest *before* you plan your upgrade. For information about designing this forest, see "Designing the Active Directory Structure" in this book.

Domain upgrade is the process of upgrading the PDC and the BDCs in a Windows NT domain from Windows NT Server to Windows 2000 Server. Upgrading is the easiest and lowest risk migration route because it retains most of your system settings, preferences, and program installations.

Because Windows 2000 Server is designed to support mixed networks with full interoperability, you do not have to upgrade all servers in a domain to take advantage of Windows 2000 features. Consider the upgrade to your PDC as simply the first stage in the process; you will gain additional, incremental benefits by upgrading your BDCs, and then your member servers.

Because migration involves an operating system upgrade rather than a new installation, the existing domain structure, users, and groups are maintained, though Windows 2000 features are enabled in the process. When you have completed your upgrade and have access to advanced Windows 2000 management tools and features, you might want to consider restructuring your domains. Be aware, however, that domain restructure is not a trivial task. If structural change is one of your goals, consider performing a domain restructure during the initial migration phase rather than after an upgrade. But consider both options carefully before you move forward.

A domain upgrade accomplishes the following:

- Maintains access to Windows NT domains through existing Windows NT trust relationships.
- Maintains access to Windows NT servers and to Windows 95 and Windows 98 clients. This access is transparent to users at client computers.
- Maintains user account passwords so that users log on to the same account domain using the same password.

When planning an upgrade, you need to do the following:

- Determine which upgrade paths are supported.
- Examine your existing domain structure.
- Develop a recovery plan.
- Determine the order for upgrading domains.
- Determine your strategy for upgrading domain controllers.
- Determine when to switch to native mode.

Note You do not need to upgrade your server infrastructure to Windows 2000 Server before upgrading clients. You can even upgrade clients and member servers before upgrading domain controllers, but you will not be able to access the features of Active Directory until you upgrade your domain controllers.

Determining Supported Upgrade Paths

When planning your upgrade, you must determine if your current operating system can be upgraded directly to Windows 2000. Table 10.4 contains a list of currently supported upgrade paths. If you find that a direct upgrade of your operating system is not supported, you must first upgrade to an operating system such as Windows 95 or Windows 98 for clients, or Windows NT for clients and servers. Make sure that this intermediate step is reflected in your upgrade plan.

For more information about upgrading member servers, see "Upgrading and Installing Member Servers" in this book.

Table 10.4   Supported Upgrade Paths

Operating System	Upgrade to Windows 2000 Professional	Upgrade to Windows 2000 Server
Windows 3.x	No	No
Windows NT 3.1	No	No
Windows NT Workstation 3.51	Yes	No
Windows NT Server 3.51	No	Yes
Windows 95 and Windows 98	Yes	No
Windows NT Workstation 4.0	Yes	No
Windows NT Server 4.0	No	Yes

Examining the Existing Domain Structure

After you have made sure that your current operating system can be upgraded to Windows 2000, your next task is to examine your existing domain structure. To help you understand the concepts being discussed, consider the Windows NT domain structure shown in Figure 10.2. This example is based on a domain design found in many organizations: a multiple-master domain model. This example shows an upgrade that begins with an account domain, which is typically the first domain to be upgraded.

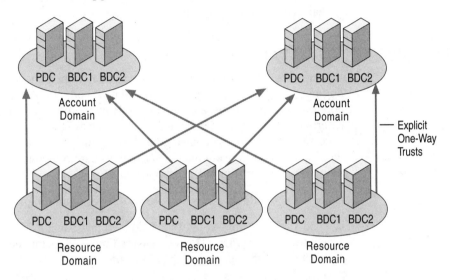

Figure 10.2   Example Multiple-master Domain Model

Consider the following when you examine your existing Windows NT domain structure:

- What type of domain structure do you have?

  Your existing domain structure helps determine how to plan your domain upgrade.

- Are there any existing trust relationships (one- and two-way) and domains that you do not want to include in the forest?

  These Windows NT domains use explicit one-way trusts to connect to the forest. Domains upgraded to Windows 2000 Server and designated as part of the same forest will be connected by transitive two-way trusts. This is why it is important to know which trusts must remain explicit. Note that all trusts existing before the upgrade will be preserved.

- How many domain controllers do you have, and where are they located within each domain?

   This information will help you project how much effort will be required to upgrade a given domain.

- What DNS namespace(s) exist within your organization?

   Because you cannot rename domains in Windows 2000, you need to know the existing namespace(s) in use in your organization and what additional namespaces your organization allows so that you can create a unique namespace for the forest.

Developing a Recovery Plan

It is important that you develop a recovery plan to prevent accidental data loss during upgrade. This plan needs to detail how you will back up your domain controllers, applications, and other data. How thorough your plan is will determine whether you can completely fall back to the original configuration, if necessary, or whether you have gone past a point of no return. When you are developing your recovery plan, determine if there is a point at which incremental migration can stop and full migration can begin.

Complete the following tasks before you perform your migration:

- Add a BDC to any Windows NT domain that contains only a single domain controller—the PDC. This will ensure that the domain does not become orphaned if the upgrade to the PDC fails.

- Determine if services such as file and print services or Dynamic Host Configuration Protocol (DHCP) are running on the PDC and the BDCs.

   Back up these services to tape, and test the backup tapes.

- Fully synchronize all BDCs with the PDC.

   Take one BDC offline before you upgrade the PDC and the other BDCs to Windows 2000 Server. As a test, perform the following steps before you begin the migration:

   1. Promote the offline BDC to a PDC and check the data.

   2. Keep this PDC offline and available after the migration, and make sure the remaining BDCs are backed up regularly.

> **Caution**   Track all changes to the domain (for example, new accounts and password updates) while the offline PDC remains offline. If a disaster occurs with the Windows 2000 domain controllers, it will be necessary to roll back to the offline PDC. If you have not tracked all domain changes made while the offline PDC remains offline, the changes will be lost when the offline PDC replicates its data to the BDCs. Note that recreated accounts have a different security identifier (SID); therefore, they might not have access to some resources.

- For each step in the flowchart in Figure 10.1, answer the following questions:
  - How would you roll back the system to a recovery state?
  - What administrative tools do you need to accomplish both the upgrade and recovery state?

Managing the Transition to the Windows 2000 Forest

As part of your domain upgrade plan, you must carefully manage the transition to the Windows 2000 forest you have designed. Be sure to keep the following in mind:

- Define the forest namespace properly. If not, you will need to restructure the forest to correct the namespace.

- Create the root domain of the forest carefully. After the root domain is created, it cannot be changed.

- Create child domains carefully. If you join a child domain to the wrong part of the forest, you will have to perform a restructure that was not part of your plan.

- Set up policies, such as those concerning the use of groups and Access Control Lists (ACLs), that do not obstruct your future plans.

For more information about designing your Windows 2000 forest, see "Designing the Active Directory Structure" in this book.

Considering the Upgrade of Resource Domains

If you are performing an in-place upgrade, you might consider upgrading your resource domains. Resource domains were used in Windows NT to hold the computer accounts of resources such as servers and client computers. Resource domains existed primarily to:

- Limit the size of the account database.

  In Windows NT, the maximum size recommended for the Security Account Manager (SAM) account database is 40 MB. In a domain containing user accounts, security groups, and Windows NT client and server accounts, this might equal less than 20,000 user accounts. To scale an organization with more than this number, user and computer accounts need to be stored in separate domains, that is, account domains for user accounts, and resource domains for computer accounts. This is the norm for Windows NT, where resource domains are usually created with explicit one-way trusts to either a single account domain (master domain model) or a number of account domains (multiple-master domain model).

- Provide local administrative capability.

  In a decentralized organization with geographically disparate facilities, it is often desirable to have local personnel authorized to administer resources. To allow this kind of decentralized responsibility in Windows NT systems, it was recommended that resource domains be created with their own administrative structure. As with scaling beyond SAM size limits, this resulted in master or multiple-master domain structures with explicit one-way trusts to the account domains in the organization. The one-way nature of these trusts ensured that resource domain administrators only had administrative scope over the resource domain.

Note As part of your upgrade plan, your administrative model must reflect the implications of upgrading a resource domain. If you have already upgraded the account domain, and then you upgrade the resource domain as a child of the account domain, a transitive trust is established between them. For this reason, you need to consider how this transitive trust affects local administration of resources.

If you do not want administrative permissions to extend beyond the resource domain, you might consider other options, which include:

Restructuring resource domains into organizational units

You might rethink your domain structure and consider merging your resource domains as organizational units (OUs) into the upgraded account domain at a later time. This option would obviously influence your thinking on the order of domain upgrade.

Upgrading a resource domain within the existing forest and using Windows 2000 delegation of administration features

You can upgrade your resource domain to be in the same forest as the account domain(s) and use Windows 2000 delegation of administration features to limit the capabilities of the local administrators. Before you do this, check the administrative groups in the resource domain and remove all administrators who are not administrators in the account domains. If there are only local resource domain administrators, add one or more of your account domain administrators. These administrators will be able to administer the domain while it is being upgraded. As a further precaution, make sure that resource domain administrators do not have administrative access to the domain controllers through local computer accounts.

After the PDC is upgraded, you might create a new domain local group to hold your resource administrators, and use Windows 2000 delegated administration to grant them sufficient privilege to carry out their roles.

Upgrading a resource domain as a tree in a new forest

You can upgrade your resource domain and make it a tree in a new forest, linking the tree to the account domain through an explicit one-way trust. This would effectively mirror the structure that existed before the upgrade.

Determining a Strategy for Upgrading Domain Controllers

The first step in the domain upgrade process is to upgrade the PDC to Windows 2000 Server. After you have upgraded the PDC, your next goal is to upgrade all the BDCs in the domain as soon as possible. This step is necessary to minimize the impact of having Windows 2000 features that are not supported on Windows NT BDCs.

Windows 2000 Domain Modes

A domain is considered a Windows NT domain if the PDC has not been upgraded to Windows 2000. During the process of upgrading the PDC and BDCs, the domain is in the intermediate operational state known as mixed mode. You can leave the domain operating in mixed mode indefinitely or move it to the final operational state known as *native mode*.

Mixed Mode

A domain is considered to be in *mixed mode* when one of the following conditions exist:

- The PDC has been upgraded but not all BDCs have been upgraded.
- The PDC and all BDCs have all been upgraded but the native mode switch has not been enabled.

Table 10.5 summarizes the Windows 2000 features available in mixed mode, and those available only by switching to native mode. If you are hesitant about switching the domain to native mode, review your migration goals to determine whether remaining in mixed mode compromises your goals, or if the tradeoffs are acceptable.

Table 10.5   Availability of Windows 2000 Features in Mixed Mode

Feature	Available in Mixed Mode?
Transitive trusts for Kerberos authentication	Yes. Windows 2000 Server and Windows 2000 Professional use Kerberos services available on the Windows 2000 domain controller.
Active Directory organizational units (OUs)	Yes, but only visible using Windows 2000 administration tools. Cannot be administered from Windows NT BDCs or member servers.
Active Directory security groups	No, only Global and Local groups available.
IntelliMirror	Yes, but only for client computers running Windows 2000 Professional in an Active Directory environment.
Windows Installer	Yes.
64-bit memory architecture	Yes, with hardware support.
Active Directory scalability	Yes, but only when all BDCs have been upgraded and are running Active Directory. You need to be cautious of taking advantage of this feature, because new Windows NT BDCs can still be added while the domain is in mixed mode. This feature might be an important part of your fallback planning, so it must not be compromised.
Kerberos authentication	Yes, for Windows 2000 computers running Active Directory.
Microsoft Management Console (MMC)	Yes.
Group Policy	Yes, but only for client computers running Windows 2000 Professional in an Active Directory environment.
Security configuration and analysis	Yes.
Active Directory multiple-master replication	Yes, between the PDC and BDCs that have been upgraded.

Until you decide to switch the domain to native mode, the domain remains in mixed mode even if all the BDCs have been upgraded.

Note that when you set the native mode switch, the domain could still contain member servers running Windows NT Server 4.0 or clients running Windows NT Workstation 4.0 or Windows 95 or Windows 98.

Figure 10.3 shows the transition from a Windows NT domain to a native mode Windows 2000 domain.

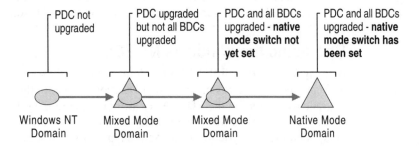

Figure 10.3   Domain Upgrade Modes

Native Mode

Native mode is the final operational state of a Windows 2000 domain, and is enabled by setting a switch on the user interface. It means that the upgraded domain is now considered a Windows 2000 domain and can take advantage of the full range of Windows 2000 features as described in "Reasons for Moving to Native Mode" later in this chapter. After you have upgraded all domain controllers to Windows 2000, you can then choose to move the domain to native mode. During the switch, the following occurs:

- Netlogon synchronization is switched off, and the domain uses only Active Directory multiple-master replication between domain controllers.

- Because Netlogon synchronization is now switched off, you can no longer add Windows NT BDCs to the domain.

- Because multiple-master replication is enabled, the former PDC is no longer the master of the domain, and all domain controllers can now perform directory updates. Despite this, Windows 2000 still designates the role of PDC emulator to the former PDC. Usually the former PDC continues as PDC emulator, which in a native mode environment means that password changes are replicated to the former PDC preferentially by other domain controllers.

All pre–Windows 2000 clients use the PDC emulator to locate the PDC and perform password changes. In addition, Windows NT resource domains use the PDC location information to establish trusts. The PDC emulator is defined later in this chapter.

Group nesting and Windows 2000 group types, such as universal and domain local groups, are available.

 Critical Decision   Until you decide to switch the domain to Windows 2000 native mode, it remains in mixed mode. You can leave the domain operating in mixed mode indefinitely, even if you have upgraded all the BDCs in the domain. However, once you switch the domain to native mode, it cannot be returned to mixed mode or become a Windows NT domain.

Upgrading the Windows NT PDC

After synchronizing all BDCs in the domain so that they are completely updated with any recent changes made at the PDC, you can begin the account domain upgrade by upgrading the PDC. After the core operating system is installed on the PDC, Windows 2000 Setup detects that a domain controller is being upgraded. Setup then prompts you to install Active Directory on the server by automatically running the Active Directory Installation Wizard.

For more information about how to install Windows 2000 Server, see "Automating Server Installation and Upgrade" in this book.

The Active Directory Installation Wizard gives you the following options:

- Creating the first tree in a new forest
- Creating a new tree in an existing forest
- Creating a new replica of an existing domain
- Installing a child domain

The option you choose depends on the outcome of your namespace planning. For more information about planning your namespace, see "Designing the Active Directory Structure" in this book, which is a prerequisite to this chapter.

During the upgrade process, the contents of the Windows NT account database (SAM) are copied into Active Directory. These objects are the security principals (user accounts, local and global groups, and computer accounts). Note that for large account domains, this process can take some time.

Active Directory also incorporates support for Kerberos authentication. After the Active Directory Installation Wizard completes, the Kerberos authentication service is available for Windows 2000 systems. At this time, if you decide to join a domain containing an upgraded PDC to an existing tree, a transitive (two-way) trust relationship is established with the parent domain. Any trust relationships created before the PDC was upgraded still exist, but they remain explicit one-way trusts.

PDC Emulation in Windows 2000

Because Active Directory supports multiple-master updates, a Windows 2000 domain controller is not a PDC in the same manner as a Windows NT 4.0 PDC. When you upgrade a Windows NT PDC to a Windows 2000 domain controller, it then acts as a PDC by holding the role of *PDC emulator.* In Windows 2000, there is one PDC emulator for each domain in the forest.

The PDC emulator supports Windows NT clients, member servers, and domain controllers; and Windows 95 and Windows 98 clients through the following:

- A Windows NT, Windows 95 or Windows 98 client performs directory writes (for example, password changes) at the PDC emulator.
- Password checks.
- Windows NT BDCs replicate from the PDC emulator.
- In a network running the Windows NT browser service, the PDC emulator plays the role of Domain Master browser. It registers the NetBIOS name Domain name<0x1B>.

These functions of the PDC emulator become unnecessary after Windows NT clients, member servers, and domain controllers; and Windows 95 and Windows 98 clients are all upgraded.

Note   Windows 2000 clients—and all Windows 95 and Windows 98 clients that have the ADClient package installed—can use any domain controller in the domain to perform directory writes, such as password changes. These activities are no longer limited to the domain controller that advertised itself as the PDC.

The PDC emulator retains some functions in fully upgraded Windows 2000 domains. Password changes performed by other domain controllers in the domain are replicated preferentially to the PDC emulator. When an authentication request fails due to a bad password at the other domain controllers in the domain, the domain controllers forward the authentication request to the PDC emulator before failing the request. This is done in case the password had been recently changed. Account lockouts are processed on the PDC emulator. Group Policy also defaults to the PDC emulator when you edit Group Policy objects on a server.

For more information about security policies, see the *Microsoft® Windows 2000 Server Resource Kit Distributed Systems Guide.*

PDC Emulator Properties

The PDC emulator provides backward compatibility by exposing the data in Active Directory as a flat store to Windows 95, Windows 98, and Windows NT computers, including BDCs, during replication. This compatibility manifests itself in the following ways:

- The PDC emulator appears as a Windows 2000 domain controller to other Windows 2000 computers, and as a Windows NT PDC to computers that have not been upgraded.

- The PDC emulator can still be used to create new security principals and to replicate these changes to the Windows NT BDCs.

- Windows 95, Windows 98, and Windows NT clients can use the PDC emulator as a possible logon server.

- If the PDC emulator goes offline or becomes unavailable, and another Windows 2000 domain controller exists in the domain, then that domain controller needs to be made the PDC emulator. If no other Windows 2000 domain controllers exist in the domain, then a Windows NT BDC can be promoted to a PDC, then upgraded to Windows 2000 Server.

Conflict Resolution

Multiple-master replication means that you can perform an update at any Windows 2000 domain controller, even if that domain controller is disconnected from the rest of the network. For instance, if you make an update at a disconnected domain controller, and at the same time, someone else makes an update at another domain controller that conflicts with your update, both updates will replicate when network connectivity is restored. In spite of the conflicting updates, all domain controllers eventually converge to the same value. This convergence process is called *conflict resolution*.

However, some conflicts are too difficult to resolve. Suppose that different domain controllers have conflicting versions of the directory schema. Schema conflicts can be resolved using the same rules that Active Directory uses to resolve normal conflicts (the "last writer wins").

Access Control Components

Having moved security principals into Active Directory during the PDC upgrade, one key concern is the effect this move has on access to resources. The following sections describe the components that control resource access.

Security Identifiers

The Windows NT security model (the basis for Windows NT and Windows 2000 security) identifies security principals such as users, groups, computers, and domains by security identifiers (SIDs). SIDs are domain-unique values, built when the user or group is created, or when the computer or trust is registered with the domain.

The components of a SID follow a hierarchical convention. A SID contains parts that identify the revision number, the authority that assigned the SID, the domain, and a variable number of sub-authority or Relative Identifier (RID) values that uniquely identify the security principal relative to the issuing authority.

Important Though there are well-known SIDs that identify generic groups and users across all systems, the security principals discussed are identified in the context of a domain. These security principals cannot be moved between domains without their SIDs changing. If SIDs are altered in any way, resource access is affected. During an upgrade, however, security principals remain in the same domain in which they were created, so the SIDs identifying the security principals remain unchanged. As a result, resource access is unaffected by upgrade.

Authentication and Access Tokens

Authentication is an essential component of the Windows NT security model. *Authentication* is the means by which a user is identified to the domain through the presentation of credentials, usually in the form of a user name and password. Assuming these credentials are acceptable, the security subsystem creates an access token for the user that includes the primary SID (the SID of the user) as well as the SIDs of all the domain and local computer groups of which the user is a member. Every process the user creates, such as running an application, carries the user access token.

The user access token can be thought of as the form of user ID presented to the system. It is used by the system to determine whether the user needs to be granted access to system resources.

Authorization and Security Descriptors

The counterpart of the user access token is the security descriptor attached to resources such as files or printers. A security descriptor contains an access control list (ACL), which consists of access control entries (ACEs). An ACE consists of a SID, together with an indicator that the security principal identified by the SID is granted or denied some sort of access to the resource, such as read, write, and execute permissions. The system performs access check verification by comparing the SIDs in the access token against the SIDs in the ACL to determine whether to grant requested permissions.

Determining the Order for Upgrading Domains

After you have a strategy in place for upgrading domain controllers, your next step is to determine which domain to upgrade first. Your choice depends on your overall upgrade goals. For example, if you plan to restructure certain domains, there might be little point in upgrading those domains first. Also, if an existing domain is to become the forest root, you must upgrade that domain first.

It is recommended that you upgrade your domains in the following order:

1. Account domains
2. Resource domains

Guidelines for Upgrading Account Domains

Generally, you will get the most benefit from upgrading your account domains first because, in many cases, there are more users to administer than computers. Upgrading your account domains to Windows 2000 offers you the following benefits:

- Improved scalability of Active Directory—Many organizations are pushing the upper bounds of the recommended SAM size with their existing numbers of users and groups. Active Directory provides improved scalability to support larger user populations running a wide range of applications.

- Delegated administration—The Windows 2000 infrastructure allows delegation of administrative capability at very fine granularity, without requiring that absolute power be granted to local administrators.

If you have more than one account domain, the following guidelines will help you choose which order to upgrade them:

Mitigate risk and maintain control. Even when you have tested your upgrade strategy in a lab or through a pilot project migration, the first production migration is the riskiest. To mitigate risk, upgrade the account domains in which you have the easiest access to domain controllers.

Minimize disruption. First, upgrade the account domains with fewer users and with local control of domain controllers. This will minimize disruption to the greatest number of users, particularly while you are gaining experience in the deployment process.

Get the job done. After you have gained experience, have confidence in the process, and have reduced the risk factor, move on to upgrading the larger account domains, which most likely will become consolidation points for other domains. As your user base grows, it will experience greater value of Windows 2000 features.

Identify account domains that are targets for restructure. If you are planning to restructure your account domains, initially upgrade the ones that are the likely restructure targets. You cannot consolidate domains into a target domain that does not exist. Identify the account domains to be restructured.

Guidelines for Upgrading Resource Domains

If you have more than one resource domain, use the following guidelines to determine which order to upgrade them:

Choose domains in which new applications will require Windows 2000 platform or features.

Your first step is to upgrade domains where you plan to deploy applications that demand Windows 2000 infrastructure or features, such as Active Directory, which is required by Exchange Platinum (the next major release of Microsoft Exchange).

Choose domains with many clients. Your next step is to upgrade domains that have many Windows NT clients, so that you can take advantage of Windows 2000 infrastructure components such as Microsoft® IntelliMirror™.

Choose domains that are targets for restructure. As with account domains, if you are planning to restructure your resource domains, first upgrade the domains that are the likely restructure targets. Identify the smaller resource domains to be restructured.

Child Domains and Trusts

The domain controller of the parent domain eventually copies all schema and configuration information to the new child domain. After this information is replicated, the upgraded domain is a fully functional member of the Windows 2000 tree. Note that until you decide to switch the domain to native mode, it remains in mixed mode and has limited access to Active Directory features.

Active Directory–aware clients such as computers running
Windows 2000 Professional or Windows 95 or Windows 98 (running Active
Directory client software) can now make use of Active Directory and perform
tasks such as querying global catalogs (GCs) to locate resources and people.
Transitive trusts allow clients existing within the forest to access resources
throughout that forest. How this occurs depends on whether the client is running
Windows 2000 or a pre–Windows 2000 operating system such as Windows NT,
Windows 95, or Windows 98, and also on the upgrade state of the target domain.
Resources are available across the forest through transitive trust when the clients
reside in any of the following:

- Native mode domains.

- Mixed mode domains in which all the domain controllers have been upgraded
  to Windows 2000.

- Mixed mode domains in which the domain controller servicing the Kerberos or
  NTLM authentication request has been upgraded to Windows 2000.

In all other cases, clients have access only to those resources available through
existing one-way explicit trusts, which remain unchanged as a result of the
upgrade. Figure 10.4 illustrates how transitive trusts work between parent and
child domains. The two-way arrows indicate transitive trusts between domains.

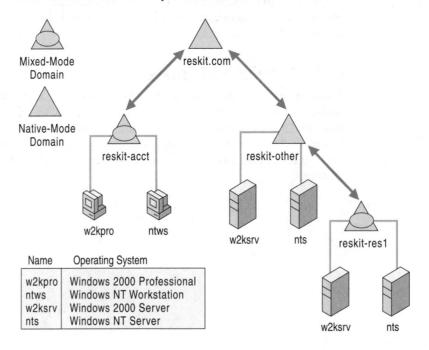

Figure 10.4   Example of Transitive Trusts Between Parent and Child Domains

Using NTLM Authentication

NTLM is an authentication protocol that is the default protocol for network authentication in Windows NT. It is retained in Windows 2000 for compatibility with clients and servers that are running versions of Windows NT.

For example, a user logs onto the domain *reskit-acct.reskit.com,* a mixed mode domain, from the Windows NT workstation *ntws*, which is in the same domain, as shown in Figure 10.5. The user then tries to make a network connection to a Windows NT server, *nts*, in the domain *reskit-other.reskit.com*, a native mode Windows 2000 domain. Because *ntws* is a pre–Windows 2000 client, it uses NTLM.

Nts determines that the domain name specified in the credentials passed to it, *reskit-acct.reskit.com*, does not refer to its own account database. So *Nts* sends the logon request to a domain controller in its own domain for authentication. The domain controller checks the domain name and, because it does not match the domain name of the domain controller, the domain controller checks to see whether the domain is a trusted domain. Domains *reskit-acct.reskit.com* and *reskit-other.reskit.com* are both children of the same root, *reskit.com*, so transitive trust exists between the two domains. Therefore, the domain controller passes the logon request through to a domain controller in the trusted domain. That domain controller authenticates the user name and password against its domain account database and, assuming the credentials match, passes the account identification information and group membership list back to the domain controller that contacted it, which in turn sends it back to the server.

The server then creates an impersonation access token for the user, containing the user SID and the SIDs of any domain groups of which the user is a member. The server handling the client request uses a thread to impersonate the security context of the user, which bears the impersonation token and attempts to access the resource on behalf of the user.

This example demonstrates that a pre–Windows 2000 client in a mixed mode domain can access a pre–Windows 2000 server in a native mode domain through transitive trusts using NTLM. Because all trees in the same forest are linked by transitive trusts, the same would be true even if the two domains were in different trees.

By extension, it follows that if a user attempts to access a resource on the Windows NT server *nts* in the mixed mode domain *reskit-res1.reskit-other.reskit.com*, that resource is accessible across the forest through a transitive trust, as long as the domain controller that receives the logon request from the server is running Windows 2000.

Using Kerberos Authentication

The Kerberos service is the default network authentication protocol for computers running Windows 2000. Secure Sockets Layer (SSL) and NTLM authentication are also available for network authentication within and between Windows 2000 domains. Kerberos authentication is a ticket-based protocol, in which users are issued Ticket Granting Tickets (TGTs) by the Key Distribution Center (KDC) on a Windows 2000 domain controller at initial logon to the domain. TGTs contain authentication information about the user and are encrypted with a key known by the KDC. After the client obtains the TGT, it can be presented back to the domain controller as part of the requests for additional service tickets to connect to other servers in the domain. After the user is granted a TGT, subsequent checks are quick and efficient, since the domain controller only needs to decrypt the TGT to check user credentials. Service tickets are similar to TGTs, but are encrypted using a key shared between the server and the domain controller.

In the example shown in Figure 10.4, the user now logs onto the domain *reskit-acct.reskit.com* as before, but this time from the computer *w2kpro* in the same domain, which is running Windows 2000. The user wants to make a network connection to a Windows 2000 Server, *w2ksrv*, in the *reskit-other.reskit.com* domain. Because *w2kpro* is a Windows 2000 client, the client attempts to use the Kerberos protocol.

The Kerberos protocol, like NTLM, can operate across domain boundaries. A client in one domain can authenticate to a server in another domain if the two domains have established a trust relationship. When domains establish trust, they exchange inter-domain keys. The authentication service for each domain uses its inter-domain key to encrypt tickets to the KDC of the other domain.

When a client wants access to a server in a remote domain, the client contacts the domain controller in its home domain for a TGT. The client then presents the TGT to the KDC on the domain controller of the remote domain if the client has a direct trust relationship with the remote domain, or its parent domain. This process is repeated with all intermediate domains until a trust path has been built between the home domain of the client and the remote domain.

The client presents the referral TGT to the KDC of the remote domain controller, asking for a ticket to a server in the client domain. The remote domain controller uses its inter-domain key to decrypt the TGT of the client. If decryption is successful, the remote domain controller can be sure that the TGT was issued by a trusted authority. The remote domain controller then grants the client a ticket to the requested server.

Figure 10.4 shows that a trust path can be built between the two domains *reskit-acct.reskit.com* and *reskit-other.reskit.com* because they are children of the same root and a transitive trust exists between them. On receiving the referral TGT, the domain controller in the target domain checks to see if it has a shared key for the server in question. If so, the domain controller issues a service ticket to the client. Because *w2ksrv* is a Windows 2000 computer, a shared key exists, so a ticket can be issued to *w2kpro*.

The important factors in this example are the existence of a domain controller in the target domain running the Kerberos KDC, and the existence of a shared key between the domain controller and the server. Windows 2000 domain controllers have the Kerberos service enabled as part of the Active Directory installation process, and adding a member server to a Windows 2000 domain involves the creation of a shared key. From this it follows that *w2kpro* is able to access *w2ksrv.reski-res1.reskit-other.reskit.com* using Kerberos as long as there is a Windows 2000 domain controller available to issue the session ticket.

If *w2kpro* attempts to access a resource on a Windows NT computer such as *nts.reskit-res1.reskit-other.reskit.com*, Kerberos authentication fails, and the client then attempts NTLM authentication, as described earlier in this section under "Using NTLM Authentication."

Determining When to Move to Native Mode

It is easy to switch the domain from mixed to native mode, but the switch cannot be undone. To determine when to make the switch, you need to consider all the factors in this section. You cannot switch the domain to native mode if the domain currently contains or will contain any Windows NT domain controllers.

Reasons for Continuing in Mixed Mode

The primary reasons for keeping your domain in mixed mode are as follows:

Cannot Upgrade Application Servers

You have application servers that cannot be upgraded or demoted to member servers. For example, to achieve high throughput, some applications need to be installed on BDCs to avoid pass-through authentication. BDCs that host such applications are called *application servers*.

Inadequate Physical Security of BDCs

Security is an important consideration in domain planning. A fundamental aspect of security is the physical security of the computer itself; any computer that is physically easy to access is vulnerable to attack. A consideration here could be the difference between single-master updating of the SAM by the PDC alone, and Active Directory multiple-master updating of the account database by all domain controllers.

Because of the single-master nature of Windows NT directory updates, you might be comfortable with comparatively relaxed security on your BDCs. If this is the case, you need to reconsider this when upgrading them to Windows 2000 domain controllers. If you cannot upgrade security of your BDC appropriately, you might consider demoting the BDC to a member server during upgrade, adding a new Windows 2000 domain controller in a different location, or possibly reconsidering your proposed domain structure.

Complete Fallback to Windows NT Remains Necessary

One of the benefits of mixed mode is the degree of backward compatibility. Mixed mode allows new BDCs to be added to the domain if a problem arises. After the new BDC has joined the domain, you can resynchronize the account database. As long as there are no other Windows 2000 domains, you are able to promote the BDC to a PDC.

You need to plan for fallback or recovery, but at some point you will want to switch over to the new environment completely to take full advantage of Windows 2000 features.

One good reason to move to native mode is to be able to use all Windows 2000 groups, including nested groups. At this point, you need to consider which groups you might want to promote to universal groups.

Reasons for Moving to Native Mode

Though you can benefit greatly from upgrading your PDC and BDCs and by keeping your domain in mixed mode, it is recommended that you make the switch to native mode as soon as possible. Native mode can help you increase the overall functionality of your network as follows:

- New Windows 2000 group types are available.

- Native mode domains can use universal groups and group nesting.

As discussed, the switch to native mode is not performed automatically; you must initiate the change through the Active Directory Domains and Trusts snap-in from the Microsoft Management Console (MMC). For details on how to use this snap-in, see the Windows 2000 Server Help files.

Examining Windows 2000 Groups

It is essential that you determine how migration to Windows 2000 will affect security policy and your pre–Windows 2000 group structure. Changes to security policy will most likely require restructuring groups.

Windows 2000 supports four types of security groups:

- Local
- Domain local
- Global
- Universal

Local Groups

Local groups, which existed in Windows NT, can contain members from anywhere in the forest, in other trusted forests, or in a trusted pre–Windows 2000 domain. However, local groups can only grant resource permissions on the computer on which they exist.

A special case for local groups in Windows NT are those created on a PDC. The replication of the domain SAM among the BDCs resulted in these local groups being shared between the PDC and the BDCs. In mixed mode, local groups behave the same in both Windows NT and Windows 2000. In native mode, local groups on a domain controller become domain local groups, which are described in the next section. Typically, local groups are used to grant specific access to resources on a local computer.

Domain Local Groups

Domain local groups are a new feature of Windows 2000, though similar in concept and use to the local groups created on the PDC in a Windows NT domain.

Domain local groups are only available in native mode domains and can contain members from anywhere in the forest, in trusted forests, or in a trusted pre–Windows 2000 domain. Domain local groups can only grant permissions to resources within the domain in which they exist. Typically, domain local groups are used to gather security principals from across the forest to control access to resources within the domain.

Global Groups

Windows 2000 *global groups* are effectively the same as Windows NT global groups. Windows 2000 global groups can only contain members from within the domain in which they exist. These groups can be granted permissions to resources in any domain in the forest or in trusted forests.

Universal Groups

Universal groups can contain members from any Windows 2000 domain in the forest, and can be granted permissions in any domain in the forest or in trusted forests. Though universal groups can have members from mixed mode domains in the same forest, members from such domains do not have the universal group added to their access tokens because universal groups are not available in mixed mode. Though you can add users to a universal group, it is recommended that you restrict membership to global groups. Note that universal groups are only available in native mode domains.

You can use universal groups to build groups that perform a common function within an enterprise. An example of this is virtual teams. The membership of such teams in a large company could be nation-wide, or world-wide, and almost certainly forest-wide, with team resources being similarly distributed. In these circumstances, universal groups could be used as a container to hold global groups from each subsidiary or department, with the team resources being protected by a single ACE for the universal group.

Universal groups and their members are listed in the Global Catalog (GC). Though global and domain local groups are also listed in the GC, their members are not. This has implications for GC replication traffic. It is recommended that you use universal groups with care. If your entire network has high-speed connectivity, you can simply use universal groups for all your groups, and benefit from not having to manage global groups and domain local groups. If, however, your network spans wide area networks (WANs), you can improve performance by using global groups and domain local groups.

If you use global groups and domain local groups, you can also designate as universal groups any widely used groups that are seldom changed.

Table 10.6 lists the properties of Windows 2000 groups.

Table 10.6   Windows 2000 Group Properties

Group Type	Membership from	Scope	Available in Mixed Mode?
Local	The same forest Other trusted forests Trusted pre–Windows 2000 domains	Computer-wide	Yes
Domain Local	The same forest Other trusted forests Trusted pre–Windows 2000 domains	The local domain	No

(continued)

Table 10.6   Windows 2000 Group Properties *(continued)*

Group Type	Membership from	Scope	Available in Mixed Mode?
Global	Local domain	Any trusted domain	Yes
Universal	The same forest	Any trusted native mode domain	No

Nesting Groups

It is recommended that you limit group size to 5,000 members, because the Active Directory store must be able to be updated in a single transaction. Because group memberships are stored in a single multivalue attribute, a change to the membership requires the whole membership list to be replicated between domain controllers and updated within a single transaction. Microsoft has tested and supports group memberships up to 5,000 members.

However, you can nest groups to increase the effective number of members. Doing this will help reduce traffic caused by replication of group membership changes. Your nesting options depend on whether the domain is in native mode or mixed mode. The following list describes what can be contained in a group that exists in a native-mode domain. These rules are determined by the scope of the group.

- Universal groups can contain user accounts, computer accounts, universal groups, and global groups from any domain.
- Global groups can contain user accounts and computer accounts from the same domain, and global groups from the same domain.
- Domain local groups can contain user accounts, computer accounts, universal groups, and global groups from any domain. They can also contain other domain local groups from within the same domain.

Security groups in a mixed-mode domain can contain only the following:

- Local groups that can contain global groups and user accounts from trusted domains.
- Global groups that can contain only user accounts.

Group Membership Expansion

When a user logs on to a client or makes a network connection to a server, the group membership of the user is expanded as part of building the user access token. Group expansion occurs as follows:

- During interactive logon to a client, the client contacts the domain controller to verify user credentials and obtain a Kerberos TGT. The domain controller expands the list of all group memberships for the user for the following group types:
  - Universal groups defined anywhere in the forest
  - Global groups
  - Domain local groups for the same domain as the user account.

  These group lists are included in the TGT as authorization data.

- When the client initiates a network connection to a server, if the server is located in a different domain than the user account, a cross-domain referral is used to get a service ticket from the KDC of the server. When the service ticket is issued, group expansion adds the domain local groups of which the user is a member to the domain of the server. These groups are added to authorization data in the service ticket along with the group list in the TGT. If the server is in the same domain as the user account, the domain local groups are already available in the TGT from the initial interactive logon.

- When the client connects to the server, expansion of the local groups occurs if the user account, or one of the groups of which the user is a member, is also a member of any local groups on the server.

When the user access token is being created, all the group membership information expanded by the domain controller or the resource server is used to identify the user.

Effects of Upgrade on Groups

Upgrading a PDC to Windows 2000 has no immediate effect on groups: Windows NT local groups become Windows 2000 local groups, and Windows NT global groups become Windows 2000 global groups. The real change occurs when you switch the domain to native mode, at which point local groups on the PDC become domain local groups.

Using NetBIOS with Windows 2000

NetBIOS is a high-level network-programming interface that has been used in pre–Windows 2000 networking components. Network resources are identified in the NetBIOS namespace by unique NetBIOS names. WINS is a service that was supplied as part of Windows NT Server 4.0 to support registration of dynamic mappings of NetBIOS names to IP addresses, and to provide NetBIOS name resolution.

With the release of Windows 2000, support for the NetBIOS naming interface is required only for cluster servers. For this reason, coupled with the use of DNS and the advent of Active Directory, the use of NetBIOS will decline over time.

Note that upgrading your domain to Windows 2000 does not necessarily remove the need for NetBIOS support on your network, nor does it affect the degree of support you currently have. For example, if your network is multisegmented, WINS is required to create the NetBIOS browse list. Without WINS the network must rely on Active Directory for browsing resources. This could have a significant impact on pre–Windows clients.

You can discontinue the use of NetBIOS and WINS after upgrade if the following conditions are met:

- There are no clients (such as Windows for Workgroups, Windows 95, Windows 98, or Windows NT) and no servers running Windows NT that use NetBIOS. However, clients running earlier versions of Windows operating systems might still require NetBIOS names to provide file and print services and as support for legacy applications.

  In your testing plan, be sure you assess the impact of legacy applications and services. For more information about testing, see "Building a Windows 2000 Test Lab" in this book.

- You have a pure Windows 2000 network and are certain that all computers and applications on your network can function using another naming service, such as DNS. Network naming is a vital service for locating computers and resources throughout your network, even where NetBIOS names are not required.

The Windows 2000 WINS client caches resolved names locally and uses a component called the Caching Resolver to look in the cache before submitting a query to DNS. The HOST file is cached as soon as the client starts running, and any updates to the HOST file are reflected immediately in the cache. The name resolution sequence is as follows:

1. Client attempts name resolution from the client cache.

2. If resolution from the client cache fails, the client attempts name resolution through DNS.

3. If DNS name resolution fails, the client attempts resolution through WINS.

If these criteria are met, the move away from NETBIOS and WINS is seamless, as long as you have removed all legacy conditions and implemented sufficient change control over your newly upgraded clients.

Transitioning to File Replication Service

Windows NT Server provided a replication facility known as LAN Manager Replication Service. The File Replication service (FRS) in Windows 2000 Server replaces the LAN Manager Replication Service.

Note Windows 2000 Server does not support LAN Manager Replication Service in mixed or native mode, so if you have been using LAN Manager Replication, you need to include a strategy in your upgrade plan for moving to FRS to provide the same functionality.

LAN Manager Replication Service Process

LAN Manager Replication Service uses the concept of import and export directories. You configure LAN Manager Replication Service by selecting a server on which to host an export directory and a number of servers to host import directories. The servers hosting the directories do not need to be domain controllers; they can be ordinary member servers. Figure 10.5 illustrates the LAN Manager Replication Service process.

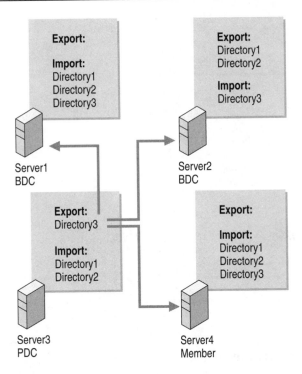

Figure 10.5   The LAN Manager Replication Service Process

The FRS Process

FRS in Windows 2000 Server is automatically configured so that every domain controller has a replicated System Volume (SYSVOL). Any change you make to a logon script stored in the SYSVOL of any domain controller is replicated in multiple-master fashion to other domain controllers. Unlike LAN Manager Replication, where ordinary member servers can host import and export directories, with FRS only domain controllers can host the SYSVOL. Figure 10.6 illustrates the FRS process.

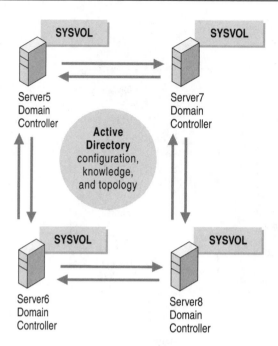

Figure 10.6   The FRS Process

Maintaining LAN Manager Replication Service in a Mixed Environment

During an upgrade, you can maintain a mixed environment of Windows NT BDCs and member servers operating with Windows 2000 domain controllers. Because Windows 2000 Server does not support LAN Manager Replication Service, maintaining in a mixed environment could be an issue. To provide this support, you need to create a bridge between LAN Manager Replication Service and FRS so that both services can operate. You do this by selecting a Windows 2000 domain controller to copy the files that will be replicated to the Windows NT export directory. The copying is done through a regularly scheduled script called *L-bridge.cmd*.

Note Do not confuse the term *mixed environment* with *mixed mode*, which refers to the PDC and zero or more BDCs within a Windows 2000 domain. A *mixed environment* refers to a Windows 2000 domain in mixed or native mode and containing pre–Windows 2000 clients or servers.

Setting up the Bridge Between LAN Manager Replication Service and FRS

Before you set up the bridge between LAN Manager Replication Service and FRS, you must do the following:

- Determine the Windows NT export server for the directory in question.
- Select a Windows 2000 computer that can push files to that directory.

It is recommended that you manually disable the LAN Manager Replication Service from **Services** in Control Panel before each domain controller or member server upgrade. Though not recommended, you can disable the Directory Replicator from MMC after the upgrade.

▶ **To upgrade the export server before upgrading to Windows 2000, perform the following steps:**

1. Run SrvMgr.exe on the current export server and remove the export directory.
2. From the new export server, add the export directory to the export list through SrvMgr.exe.

A batch file provides the link between the Windows NT scripts directory and the Windows 2000 System Volume. The benefit of this approach is that the two replication mechanisms are physically separated from one another, thus no legacy services are being introduced on the Windows 2000 domain controller.

▶ **To set up a batch file for the bridge between LAN Manager Replication Service and FRS, perform the following steps:**

1. Select a Windows 2000 domain controller.
2. Create a batch file named *L-bridge.cmd* that copies the logon scripts to the Windows NT export server, as in the following example.

   ```
   xcopy \\domain.com\Sysvol\domain.com\scripts \\Srv3\Export\scripts /s
   /D
   ```

   Note that the /D command line switch tells xcopy to copy only newer files. The /s command line switch tells xcopy to copy the directory and all subdirectories, provided they are not empty.

3. Using the Windows 2000 Schedule service, set up a reasonable interval for the batch file to be run. An interval of every two hours is more than sufficient, particularly because using the /D option prevents the creation of unnecessary file copies.

A sample version of *L-bridge.cmd* is included on the *Windows 2000 Resource Kit* compact disc.

Keeping LAN Manager Replication Service Available During Upgrade

To keep LAN Manager Replication Service available during upgrade, you need to upgrade the server hosting the export directory only after all the other servers hosting import directories have been upgraded. If the server hosting the export directory is the PDC, you need to select a new export server and reconfigure LAN Manager Replication Service. It is recommended that the new server you select is one that you believe will be the last server to be upgraded to Windows 2000; otherwise, you will need to select another export server and go through the process again, since servers are upgraded sequentially.

Using Routing and Remote Access Service in a Mixed Environment

If you are using Routing and Remote Access Service (RRAS) in a Windows NT environment to provide your users with remote access to the corporate network, consider upgrading your RRAS server early in the process of upgrading member servers. Upgrading early is valuable because of the way the RRAS process works in Windows NT; specifically, the way it checks RRAS properties such as availability of RRAS access or dial-back for a user.

RRAS must run even when there are no users logged onto the system. The service runs as LocalSystem. When a service logs on as LocalSystem, it logs on with NULL credentials, which means the service does not provide a user name or password. This means that the account cannot be used to access network resources relying on NTLM authentication unless the remote computer allows access with NULL credentials (referred to as a NULL session). RRAS in Windows NT uses the LocalSystem account.

By default, Active Directory does not accept querying of object attributes through NULL sessions, so in a mixed environment, a Windows NT RRAS server is not able to retrieve user RRAS properties unless all of the following conditions are met:

- The domain is in mixed mode and the Windows NT RRAS server is also a BDC. In this case, RRAS has local access to the SAM.

- The domain is in mixed mode and the Windows NT RRAS server contacts a Windows NT BDC, which results in behavior identical to current Windows NT behavior. This behavior is based on the location of the secure channel.

- The domain is in mixed or native mode and Active Directory security has been relaxed to grant the built-in user "Everyone" permissions to read any property on any user object. Active Directory Installation Wizard allows the user to select this configuration by means of a "Weaken the permissions" option on certain Active Directory objects.

Use the workaround in the last condition only after understanding its impact on Active Directory security. If this workaround conflicts with your security requirements, it is recommended that you upgrade the Windows NT RRAS server to Windows 2000 and make it a member of a Windows 2000 mixed or native domain. This will prevent inconsistent behavior while the domain is in mixed mode, as described in the second condition.

Planning Domain Restructure

While domain upgrade allows you to maintain as much of your current environment as possible, including your domain structure, domain restructure allows you to redesign the forest according to the needs of your organization. Though domain restructure can have various results, typically your current structure is reorganized into fewer, larger domains.

Windows 2000 provides native functionality to allow domain restructure as follows:

- Security principals can be moved from one domain to another while maintaining access to resources available before the move.

- Domain controllers can be moved from one domain to another without complete reinstallation of the operating system.

Note Domain restructure is not a requirement for deploying Windows 2000 Server. You can restructure over time as needed. It can be an intensive, time-consuming operation to move computers to new domains and update or verify access control.

To assist in your domain migration, Microsoft has created *Domain Migration Basic Utilities*. These utilities are a set of Component Object Model (COM) objects and sample scripts designed to form the basis of customer-adapted administration utilities, and to support a number of domain migration examples that Microsoft has documented and tested. The examples have been developed based on feedback from customers concerning their migration requirements. The basic utility ClonePrincipal is described later in this chapter.

Determining the Reasons to Restructure Domains

The primary focus of this chapter is the initial migration from Windows NT to Windows 2000. Some of the restructuring methods described later in this chapter might prove useful during the post-migration period.

Though you might have a number of reasons for restructuring your domains, a major reason would be to take full advantage of Windows 2000 features. These features allow you to make better use of your domains to reflect the requirements of your organization. Some key benefits you gain by restructuring your domains include:

Greater Scalability.   You might have designed your previous Windows NT domain structure around the size limitations of the SAM accounts database, leading you to implement a master or multiple-master domain model. With the vastly improved scalability of Active Directory, which scales to millions of user accounts or groups, you could restructure your current Windows NT domains into fewer, larger Windows 2000 domains.

Delegation of Administration.   In your current model you might have implemented resource domains to allow administrative responsibility to be delegated. Windows 2000 OUs can contain any type of security principal, and administration can be delegated as you require. In many instances, converting resource domains into OUs is more appropriate for delegating administration.

Finer Granularity of Administration.   To allow finer granularity of administrative responsibility, perhaps as a result of corporate acquisition, your domain structure could be connected by a complex mesh of trusts. You might consider implementing some of these domains as OUs to simplify administration, or you might redesign your domain model to benefit from fewer explicit trusts.

Note that the examples described in the next section do not require you to have completed an upgrade, though some of the restructuring methods might require that you have already upgraded a BDC in the domain you plan to restructure.

Determining When to Restructure Domains

Depending on your migration plan, you might choose to restructure your domains immediately after upgrade, in place of an upgrade, or as a general domain redesign some time in the future. These options are described as follows:

Post Upgrade

The most likely time for domain restructure is after an upgrade, as the second phase of migration to Windows 2000. The upgrade has then addressed the less complex migration situations, such as groups of domains in which the trust structure is essentially correct and in which there are no administrative issues.

When you choose to restructure after upgrade, most likely your goals involve reworking the domain structure to reduce complexity, or to bring resource domains with low rights administrators into the forest in a secure way.

Instead of Upgrade

You might feel that your current domain structure cannot be salvaged (for example, if you need to redesign your directory services infrastructure to take advantage of Active Directory), or that you cannot afford to jeopardize the stability of the current production environment during migration. In either case, the easiest migration path might be to design and build a *pristine forest*: an ideal Windows 2000 forest isolated from the current production environment. This ensures that business can carry on normally during pilot project operation and that the pilot project eventually becomes the production environment.

After you have built the pilot project, you can begin domain restructuring by migrating a small number of users, groups, and resources into the pilot. When this phase has been completed successfully, transition the pilot project into a staged migration to the new environment. Subsequently, make Windows 2000 the production environment, decommission the old domain structure, and redeploy the remaining resources.

Post Migration

At this stage, domain restructure takes place as part of a general domain redesign in a pure Windows 2000 environment. This might occur several years down the line, when, for reasons such as organizational change or a corporate acquisition, the current structure becomes inappropriate.

Examining the Implications of Restructuring Domains

After you have determined why and when you need to restructure domains, you need to examine the implications of such a restructure. The following sections describe:

- Moving security principals, users and global groups, computers, and member servers.
- Establishing trusts.
- Cloning security principals.

Moving Security Principals

What makes domain restructure fundamentally possible is the ability to move security principals and domain controllers between domains in Windows 2000. This has a number of important implications on how security principals are identified by the system, and how access to resources is maintained. Such implications could affect your preferred approach to domain restructure.

Effect on SIDs

The domain-relative nature of SIDs has the following consequence: when you move a security principal such as a user or a group between domains, the security principal must be issued a new SID for the account in the new domain.

In the Windows NT security model, access to resources is affected by the way the operating system looks at the user access token and compares the primary SID of the user—as well as the SIDs of any groups the user is a member of—to the ACL on the resource security descriptor. Because the lists of SIDs contained in the ACL have information that can cause access to be granted or denied to the security principals identified by the SIDs, changing the SID has far-reaching implications.

The implications of changing the SID are illustrated in the following example and in Figure 10.7. Bob is an employee of Reskit Corporation and has an account in the Windows NT account domain Reskit-Acct. Bob is a member of the global group "Finance Analysts" in the same domain.

Reskit Corporation uses a Windows NT financial application that runs on a number of Windows NT servers in a resource domain Reskit-Res1. Because local groups created on the PDC are shared among all domain controllers in the domain, the servers running the application are also set up as BDCs for the domain. A shared local group "Financial Resources" has been created on the PDC and is used on the ACLs of the files used by the application. The global group "Reskit-Acct\Finance Analysts" is a member of "Reskit-Res1\Financial Resources."

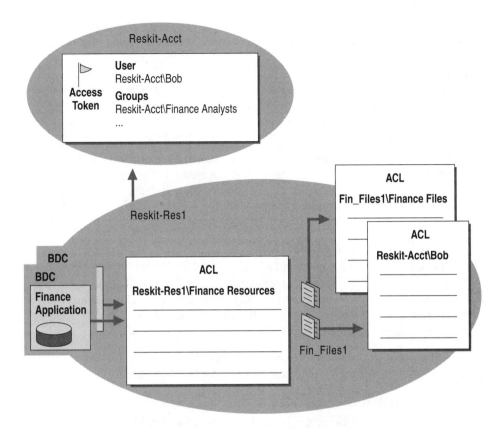

Figure 10.7   Resource Access Example

Bob also has access to a file server, Fin_Files1 in the resource domain. Fin_Files1 is a Windows NT server set up as a member server. Fin_Files1 uses a local group "Finance Files" on the ACLs of files relating to Reskit-Acct\Finance Analysts, which is a member of Fin_Files1\Finance Files. Bob works on some private projects and has a directory on Fin_Files1 that is protected so that only he can access the files in that directory. This directory has an ACL that contains a single entry allowing Bob full control of the directory.

The implications of moving security principals can be seen by tracing what would happen if Reskit-Acct\Bob were moved to another domain as part of a migration involving domain restructure. In this example, Reskit-Acct has been upgraded to Windows 2000, and has joined the Windows 2000 forest as a child of the root domain reskit.com. The domain Reskit-Acct has been switched to native mode, but is restructured and its members moved to a Windows 2000 domain, called Reskit-Acct2, in another part of the forest.

Note This example illustrates what happens when the Windows 2000 feature known as "SIDhistory" is not available. It is important that you understand how to handle such a situation if it arises during your restructure. Note that SIDhistory is discussed later in this chapter.

Effect on Global Group Membership

Reskit-Acct\Bob is a member of the global group Reskit-Acct\Finance Analysts. Because a global group can only contain members from its own domain, moving Bob to the new domain would cause his new account to be excluded from Reskit-Acct\Finance Analysts. Bob would then lose access to valuable resources available to Reskit-Acct\Finance Analysts.

Assuming sufficient trust exists between the new domain and the resource domain, it would seem that this situation could be fixed in a number of ways.

Adding the new SID to resource ACLs

Access to resources could be maintained by adding the new SID for Bob to the ACLs on all the resources he formerly had access to as a member of Reskit-Acct\Finance Analysts. This fix would be time consuming and complicated for the following reasons:

- Many domain restructuring operations are carried out incrementally over a period of time. There is no guarantee that during that time new resources will not be created for Reskit-Acct\Finance Analysts. Because of this, "repermissioning" would have to continue for the duration of the restructure.

- If Bob were to change job function and no longer need to be a member of Reskit-Acct\Finance Analysts, it would be much easier to remove Bob from Reskit-Acct\Finance Analysts than to change the ACLs of the resources referencing him. It is recommended that you set up ACLs using groups rather than individuals, because users and their specific job functions can change over time.

Moving the group

Since security principals can be moved in Windows 2000, Reskit-Acct\Finance Analysts could be moved to the new domain. However, the ACLs referencing the group also reference the group SID, so the resources would have to be repermissioned to refer to the new SID.

Creating a "parallel" group in the target domain

If Reskit-Acct\Finance Analysts is moved to another domain, a problem would occur if all the group members are not moved in one transaction. This would mean that the group would have to be maintained in the old domain, and a new "parallel" group created in the new domain. Resource access would be maintained for the original group and its members, but resources would need to be repermissioned to grant access to the new group. Again, repermissioning would have to continue while the groups existed in both domains.

Note that this is what would occur when SIDhistory is unavailable. SIDhistory is explained later in this chapter.

Effect on ACLs Directly Referencing the User

Reskit-Acct\Bob is also granted direct access to some resources on the member server Fin_Files, because his SID appears on ACLs on that server. It is perfectly legitimate to add users to ACLs on resources, but moving Reskit-Acct\Bob would require repermissioning resources on that server. This would add the new domain SID to Bob's account.

SIDhistory

In many instances, the activities in the Reskit Corporation example have become unnecessary due to a Windows 2000 feature called *SIDhistory*. SIDhistory is an attribute of Active Directory security principals, and is used to store the former SIDs of moved objects such as users and security groups.

When a user is moved using Windows 2000 utilities provided by Microsoft, the SIDhistory attribute of the user object in Active Directory is updated with the former SID. When the user then logs onto the system, the system retrieves the entries in the user SIDhistory and adds them to the user access token. Because groups can be moved, the system also retrieves the SIDhistory attributes of all the groups the user is a member of and adds these to the user access token.

The SIDhistory entries in the token appear to the system like normal group memberships during authorization checks, and can grant appropriate access even on pre–Windows 2000 systems that know nothing about Windows 2000 or Active Directory. Figure 10.8 shows how resource access is granted using SIDhistory.

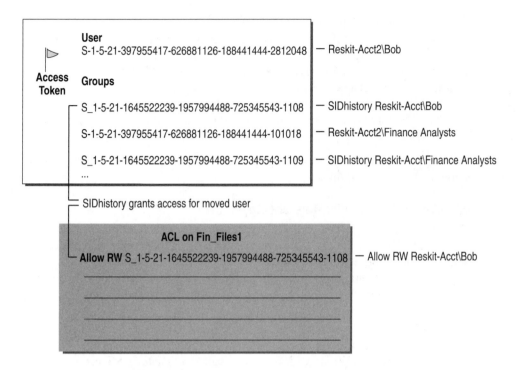

Figure 10.8 Resource Access Granted Through SIDhistory

Windows NT 3.51 and SIDhistory

There is an issue concerning group membership and the use of Windows NT 3.51 systems in Windows 2000 domains. The issue involves the way Windows NT 3.51 receives group membership SIDs from the domain controller and builds a security access token. When a user is authenticated, the Windows NT 3.51 access token is built using only SIDs relative to the user account domain and the local groups from the server or client where authentication takes place. The result is that Windows NT 3.51 systems cannot recognize universal groups from outside the account domain, or domain local groups from the resource domain.

Since entries from the SIDhistory of the user or any universal groups of which the user is a member are from domains other than the account domain, these entries are excluded from the token. The implication is that with Windows NT 3.51, group membership SIDs from domains other than the account domain of the user logging on are ignored when evaluated for access control. In most cases, access is denied, though this might not be the desired result.

Moving Users and Global Groups

Because a global group can only contain members from its own domain, when a user moves between domains, any global groups of which the user is a member must also be moved. This must occur to maintain access to resources protected by ACLs that refer to global groups. A corollary of this is that if a global group is moved, its members must also be moved.

In this instance, a closed set of users and global groups is a set in which the following is true:

- For each user being moved, all the global groups of the set are also being moved.
- For each group being moved, all of its members are also being moved.

If the source domain is a native mode domain, global groups can also contain other global groups. This means all of the members of each nested group and all of the global groups that have members in that nested group must be moved.

Moving Profiles and SIDhistory

When formulating your domain restructure plan, you must be aware that migrated users receive new SIDs and this can affect their profile use. Users logging onto their computers after migration could lose access to their logon profiles, because their primary SIDs will have changed while their old profiles might still be stored under their old primary SIDs. This could occur under the following circumstances:

- A user has been cloned from a Windows NT 4.0 domain.
- A user has been cloned from a Windows 2000 domain.
- A user has been cloned from a Windows 2000 domain, but is still logging on at a Windows NT 4.0 Workstation.

If users lose access to their logon profiles, you have two options for making a profile available to a migrated user: copying profiles or sharing profiles. The preferred method is to copy the profiles.

Copying Profiles

The first option is to copy the original profile from its current location under the key named after the user's original SID to a key named after the user's new SID. Each account is associated with its own separate copy of the profile. Updates to one are not reflected in the other.

The advantage of using this method is that the behavior of Windows 2000 is more predictable. Because data is not shared between the profiles, there is no chance of one profile accessing an account with data appropriate only for another account in another domain or forest.

The disadvantages of using this method include that it:

- Consumes extra disk space because two profiles are stored.

- Creates unpredictable fallback results. You must thoroughly test the impact of installing applications that use Group Policy so that you are prepared for any contingency.

Sharing Profiles

This option make the same profile available to both the user's original account and the new account. Under these circumstances, one copy of the profile is accessed and updated by both accounts. The advantages of using this method include:

- Updates to the profile (for instance, changes to My Documents, shortcuts, and so on) while a user is logged onto one account are accessible when the user subsequently logs onto another account.

- Disk space is conserved because only one copy of the profile is stored.

The disadvantage of using this method is that there are unknown variables that could impact its use. For example, if you create a new Windows 2000 account profile that contains Group Policy references, you will need to test the impact of falling back to a source account where Group Policy is different or has not been used.

Moving Computers

Because shared local groups and domain local groups only have scope within the domain in which they were created, moving such a group would leave unresolvable any references to the group in the source domain ACLs.

In this instance a closed set of computers and shared or domain local groups is a set in which the following exists:

- For each computer being moved, all shared or domain local groups referenced in ACLs on the computer resources are also being moved.

- For each group being moved, all computers in the domain containing ACLs referencing the group are also moved.

Restrictions on moving populated global groups and closed sets are particularly strict. Depopulating and repopulating large global groups can be time consuming. In some cases, the smallest closed set that can be achieved is the entire source domain. Three possible ways to solve this problem include:

1. Creating parallel global groups in the target domain for each group to be moved, then finding all resources in the enterprise containing ACLs referencing the original group and repermissioning them to include reference to the parallel group.

    When moving global groups, this method is likely to be a large undertaking in the following instances:

    - Where the group could be referenced on resources in any trusting domain.

    - With domain local groups from native mode source domains where domain local groups can be used on any computer in the domain.

2. Switching the source domain to native mode, then changing the group type of the groups to be moved to universal. Because universal groups have scope across the entire forest, changing the groups to universal groups means that they can be moved safely while still maintaining access to resources left behind.

    Be careful when using this method, because universal group membership is stored in the GC, which has implications for GC replication traffic. For this reason, you might want to use this method strictly as a transitional strategy while users and groups are being migrated to the new domain. After migration is complete, you can change the groups back to their original types.

3. Cloning groups from the source domain into the target domain while retaining their SIDhistory. This technique has some constraints, and is described in "Cloning Security Principals" later in this chapter.

Moving Member Servers

In the example, Bob has access to some resources on the member server Fin_Files1 through ACLs referencing a computer local group Fin_Files1\Finance Files, and referencing his domain account directly.

The implications of moving domain controllers, including the need to ensure that shared local groups and domain local groups are maintained, have been described earlier in this chapter. However, those implications are different from the ones involved in moving a member server such as Fin_Files or a client.

Assuming the member server is moved to a domain with trust to the new account domain for Bob, SIDhistory would ensure that Bob could access resources with ACLs referencing him directly. ACLs referencing the computer local group would also continue to function because the group exists in the account database of the local computer. This means that the group is unaffected by the move, so its SID would not need to be changed.

Establishing Trusts

During domain upgrade it is assumed that sufficient trust existed from the target domain to any relevant resource domains, so that access to resources is maintained. However, such trusts must first be established in any domain restructure scenario.

Netdom is a tool used to carry out such tasks as enumerating domain trusts and establishing new trusts. This tool is also useful for creating computer accounts and updating the domain membership of a client or server.

Cloning Security Principals

Up to this point, restructure has been involved with moving security principals. Moving security principals creates a new identical account in a destination domain and removes the account from the source domain. The move operation does not allow a return to the old account status if there are problems with the migration.

To ensure that you can recover from problems during the pilot project or production migration, it is recommended that you migrate users incrementally to a Windows 2000 domain while maintaining the old accounts in the source domain. This is possible through *cloning*, which is creating a duplicate user or group through the use of the ClonePrincipal utility, which contains a set of Microsoft® Visual Basic® (VB) scripts that perform tasks such as cloning global groups and cloning users.

Domain Restructure Scenarios

The two scenarios described in this section satisfy most requirements for domain restructure. Both scenarios facilitate the movement of users and computers from Windows NT source domains to Windows 2000 target domains. The examples are as follows:

- Migrating Users Incrementally to Windows 2000 (Inter-Forest)
- Migrating Resources into a Windows 2000 OU (Inter-Forest)

Scenario #1: Migrating Users Incrementally from Windows NT to Windows 2000

In this scenario, you migrate users incrementally to a pristine Windows 2000 environment without impacting the Windows NT production environment. Figure 10.9 illustrates this example. The steps and utilities required for incremental migration are described in this section.

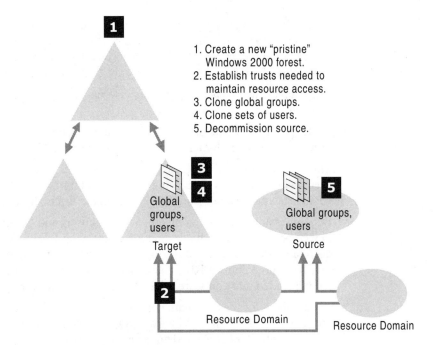

1. Create a new "pristine" Windows 2000 forest.
2. Establish trusts needed to maintain resource access.
3. Clone global groups.
4. Clone sets of users.
5. Decommission source.

Figure 10.9   Migrating Users Incrementally

Note Protecting the current production environment from migration changes ensures that it remains untouched during the process. This will allow you to revert back to the old production environment if the need arises.

After the migration is complete, you can decommission the old account domain and reassign the domain controllers. Then perform the following steps:

1. Create the pristine Windows 2000 forest. Use standard procedure to create a Windows 2000 destination forest that reflects the requirements and structure identified in the namespace planning activities of the organization. The domains you create in the new forest will be native mode Windows 2000 domains.

2. Establish the trusts required for the forest to maintain resource access. This involves using Netdom to query what trusts currently exist from any resource domains to the Windows NT source domain.

   You can then compare the output from Netdom with the list of trusts that are required to allow resource access to users and groups in the target domain. Then use Netdom to establish any trusts that do not already exist.

3. Clone all source global groups in the target domain. Most resources are protected using ACLs that reference global groups, usually indirectly through shared or computer local groups. After you have established trusts, you must ensure that the relevant global groups are available in the target domain.

   The simplest way to accomplish this is to clone all global groups using ClonePrincipal.

4. Identify and clone sets of users. After you have cloned the source global groups to the target domain, you can begin the task of migrating users.

   This is an iterative task, because in most instances you want to move sets of users, which involves identifying user sets to migrate and then using ClonePrincipal to clone the source users in the destination domain.

5. Decommission the source domain. When all users and groups have been moved permanently to the destination forest, your final task is to decommission the source domain. This involves powering off and removing first the source domain BDCs, and then the source domain PDC. It is recommended that you store the PDC for disaster recovery purposes.

   If you intend for these domain controllers to be reassigned in the new forest, you can upgrade them to Windows 2000 and then either promote them to domain controllers or leave them as member servers.

Particularly during the user migration phase, it might be prudent to test logon for certain users during each migration. If an error occurs at any stage before decommissioning, you can suspend the process and work can continue in the source production domain.

Scenario #2: Consolidating a Resource Domain into an OU

In this example, you consolidate a resource domain into an OU within a native mode Windows 2000 domain. You might do this to reduce the costs of administering complex trusts. Figure 10.10 illustrates this example. The steps and basic utilities required for the incremental migration are described in this section.

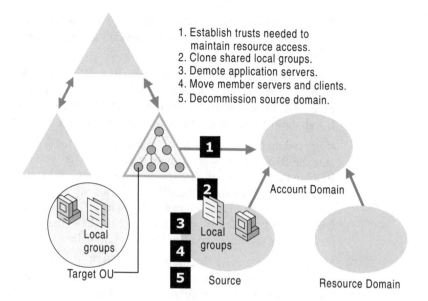

1. Establish trusts needed to
   maintain resource access.
2. Clone shared local groups.
3. Demote application servers.
4. Move member servers and clients.
5. Decommission source domain.

Account Domain

Local groups

Local groups

Target OU

Source

Resource Domain

Figure 10.10   Consolidating a Resource Domain into a Windows 2000 OU

In this example, the application servers become member servers in the target OU.
It is assumed that the application servers in each domain are making use of shared
local groups. It is also assumed that the domains might contain some member
servers and clients.

After the domain restructure is complete, you can decommission the old domains.
The process to consolidate a resource domain into a Windows 2000 OU is as
follows:

1. Establish any trusts required from the target domain to account domains
   outside the forest. This involves using Netdom to query what trusts currently
   exist from the resource domains to the account domains. You can then
   compare the output from Netdom with the trusts that already exist from the
   target domain to the account domains. Then use Netdom to establish any trusts
   that do not already exist.

2. Clone all shared local groups. Shared local groups have scope only within the
   domain in which they were created, and are shared only between domain
   controllers in that domain. It is not necessary for you to move all domain
   controllers to the target domain immediately. To ensure that resource access is
   maintained while domain controllers and resources are split between source
   and target domains, you need to clone shared local groups to the target domain
   using ClonePrincipal.

3. Demote application servers to member servers. After you have cloned all the shared local groups, you can start converting the application servers to member servers in the target OU.

Upgrade the PDC of the resource domain to Windows 2000 and run the domain in mixed mode during the transition period. You can then upgrade each BDC to be demoted. During the BDC upgrade, run Active Directory Installation Wizard and choose to make the BDC a member server.

If upgrading the PDC is not possible or desired, for each upgrade you need to take the BDC offline and promote it to PDC. After you have promoted the BDC to PDC you can then upgrade to Windows 2000, effectively making the offline domain controller the PDC in a "cloned" Windows 2000 mixed mode domain. After you have upgraded the PDC offline, you can run the Active Directory Installation Wizard to demote the PDC to a member server. You then join the member server to the target domain.

4. Move member servers (including former BDCs) and clients. During this step you can use Netdom to create a computer account in a destination domain OU for the member server or client to be moved. Join the computer to the destination domain.

5. Decommission the source domain. When you have permanently moved all groups and computers to the destination forest, your final task is to decommission the source domain. This involves powering off and removing first the source domain BDCs and then the source domain PDC.

If you plan to reassign the source domain controllers in the new forest, you can upgrade them to Windows 2000. You can then either promote them to Windows 2000 domain controllers or leave them as member servers.

Note For this scenario, when demoting BDCs to member servers, you need to move them over to the target domain as quickly as possible. Unless the domain is in native mode and shared local groups have been converted to domain local groups, resources accessible through these groups will not be available on the member servers.

Domain Migration Tools

This section contains general information about the Domain Migration Basic Utilities and the *Windows 2000 Server Resource Kit* tools referred to elsewhere in this chapter. Definitive documentation of features and usage can be found in the sources listed in each section.

ClonePrincipal

ClonePrincipal is a utility that consists of the following COM object and sample scripts. You can customize the scripts using Visual Basic.

- **DSUtils.ClonePrincipal**, a COM object supporting three methods:
  - **AddSidHistory** — copies the SID of a source principal to the SIDhistory of an existing destination principal.
  - **CopyDownlevelUserProperties** — copies the Windows NT properties of the source principal to the destination principal.
  - **Connect** — establishes authenticated connections to the source and destination domain controllers.

ClonePrincipal allows you to migrate users incrementally to a Windows 2000 environment without impacting your existing Windows NT production environment. This is done by creating clones of the Windows NT users and groups in the Windows 2000 environment. The benefits achieved using ClonePrincipal in this manner are as follows:

- Users can log on to the destination account (clone) yet have emergency fallback to the source account during the trial period.
- Several users can be introduced to the destination Windows 2000 environment at the same time.
- The source production environment is not disrupted while users are being migrated to the destination Windows 2000 environment.
- It is not necessary to update ACLs to preserve group memberships and network access for the destination accounts.
- Multiple groups with the same name or purpose from different source domains can be "merged" into the same destination object.

In addition, you can consolidate large numbers of small resource domains into Windows 2000 OUs by using ClonePrincipal to clone local groups.

Note that the AddSidHistory method is a security-sensitive operation with the following constraints:

- AddSidHistory requires you to have or provide Domain Administrator credentials in the source and destination domains. The source and destination domains MUST NOT be in the same forest. Though an external trust *can* exist between the source and destination domains, such a trust is not required for this function.

- AddSidHistory events can be audited, which ensures that both source and destination domain administrators can detect when this function has been run. Auditing in the source domain is recommended, but is not required, whereas auditing MUST be enabled in the destination domain for AddSidHistory to succeed.

- ClonePrincipal sample scripts call the underlying AddSidHistory method; therefore the other ClonePrincipal utilities are subject to the same security sensitivity and constraints as AddSidHistory.

Netdom

Netdom is a tool that allows you to manage Windows 2000 domains and trust relationships from the command line.

Use Netdom to do the following:

- Join a Windows 2000 computer to a Windows NT or Windows 2000 domain, and:
  - Provide an option to specify the OU for the computer account.
  - Generate a random computer password for the initial join.
- Manage computer accounts for domain member clients and member servers:
  - Add, Remove, and Query.
  - Provide an option to specify the OU for the computer account. Provide an option to move an existing computer account for a member client from one domain to another and maintain the security descriptor on the computer account.
- Establish (one- or two-way) trust relationships between domains, including trust for the following domain types:
  - Windows NT domains.
  - Windows 2000 parent and child domains in a domain tree.
  - The Windows 2000 portion of a trust link to a Kerberos realm.
- Verify and reset the secure channel for the following configurations:
  - Member clients and servers.
  - BDCs in a Windows NT domain.
  - Specific Windows 2000 replicas.
- Manage trust relationships between domains
  - View all trust relationships.
  - Enumerate direct trust relationships.
  - Enumerate all (direct and indirect) trust relationships.

Migration Planning Task List

Table 10.7 is a summary of the tasks involved in planning your migration.

Table 10.7   Summary of Migration Planning Tasks

Task	Location in chapter
Determine your migration roadmap.	Starting the Migration Planning Process
Determine supported upgrade paths.	Planning Domain Upgrade
Examine your existing domain structure.	Planning Domain Upgrade
Develop your recovery plan.	Planning Domain Upgrade
Determine your strategy for upgrading domain controllers.	Planning Domain Upgrade
Determine the order for upgrading domains.	Planning Domain Upgrade
Determine when to move to native mode.	Planning Domain Upgrade
Determine the reasons for restructuring domains.	Planning Domain Restructure
Determine when to restructure domains.	Planning Domain Restructure
Move users and groups.	Planning Domain Restructure
Move computers.	Planning Domain Restructure
Move member servers.	Planning Domain Restructure
Establish trusts.	Planning Domain Restructure
Clone security principals.	Planning Domain Restructure
Switch to native mode.	Planning Domain Upgrade
	Planning Domain Restructure

C H A P T E R   1 1

Planning Distributed Security

A security plan is an essential component of your Microsoft® Windows® 2000 deployment plan. Representatives of many of your deployment subteams will be involved in this task. This chapter guides you through a strategy for planning distributed security in your Windows 2000 network. It outlines the primary objectives for a distributed security plan and introduces the security features of Windows 2000.

This chapter puts into context the important factors to consider in order to use Microsoft Windows 2000 security effectively. However, distributed computer security is a fairly complex topic that you will need to research further.

In This Chapter

Chapter Goals

This chapter will help you develop the following planning documents:

- Security Risk Analysis
- Security Strategies
- Security Group Descriptions and Associated Policies
- Network Logon and Authentication Strategies
- Information Security Strategies
- Administrative Policies

Related Information in the Resource Kit

- For more information about distributed security, see the *Microsoft® Windows® 2000 Server Resource Kit Distributed Systems Guide.*

- For more information about security groups, see "Designing the Active Directory Structure" in this book.

- For more information about public key infrastructure, see "Planning Your Public Key Infrastructure" in this book.

Developing a Network Security Plan

Distributed security involves the coordination of many security functions on a computer network to implement an overall security policy. Distributed security enables users to log on to appropriate computer systems, find the information they need, and use it. Much of the information on computer networks is available for anyone to read, but only a small group of people are allowed to update it. If the information is sensitive or private, only authorized individuals or groups are allowed to read the files. Protection and privacy of information transferred over public telephone networks, the Internet, and even segments of internal company networks are also a concern.

Although security technologies are some of the most advanced technologies, security itself combines those technologies with good business and social practices. No matter how advanced and well implemented the technology is, it is only as good as the methods used in employing and managing it.

Your security deployment team develops the network security plan. The network security deployment plan describes how you use the features of Windows 2000 distributed security to deploy distributed security and information security solutions. A typical security plan includes sections like those shown in Table 11.1.

Table 11.1   Sections in a Security Plan

Sections in the Plan	Description
Security risks	Enumerates the types of security hazards that affect your enterprise.
Security strategies	Describes the general security strategies necessary to meet the risks.
Public key infrastructure policies	Includes your plans for deploying certification authorities for internal and external security features.
Security group descriptions	Includes descriptions of security groups and their relationship to one another. This section maps group policies to security groups.
Group Policy	Includes how you configure security Group Policy settings, such as network password policies.
Network logon and authentication strategies	Includes authentication strategies for logging on to the network and for using remote access and smart card to log on.
Information security strategies	Includes how you implement information security solutions, such as secure e-mail and secure Web communications.
Administrative policies	Includes policies for delegation of administrative tasks and monitoring of audit logs to detect suspicious activity.

Your network security deployment plan can contain more sections than these; however, these are suggested as a minimum. Additionally, your organization might need more than one security plan. How many plans you have depends on the scope of your deployment. An international organization might need separate plans for each of its major subdivisions or locations, whereas, a regional organization might need only one plan. Organizations with distinct policies for different user groups might need a network security plan for each group.

Test and revise your network security plans by using test labs that represent the computing environments for your organization. Also, conduct pilot programs to further test and refine your network security plans.

Security Risks

Before this chapter examines the security features of Windows 2000, it is a good idea to review the types of network security problems that an IT manager faces. Table 11.2 describes several types of security risks and provides a common basis for the subsequent discussion of security features, strategies, and technologies. Creating a list similar to this in your security plan demonstrates the complexity of security problems you face and will help you establish a set of standard labels for each category of risk.

Table 11.2   Types of Security Risks in an Organization

Security Risk	Description
Identity interception	The intruder discovers the user name and password of a valid user. This can occur by a variety of methods, both social and technical.
Masquerade	An unauthorized user pretends to be a valid user. For example, a user assumes the IP address of a trusted system and uses it to gain the access rights that are granted to the impersonated device or system.
Replay attack	The intruder records a network exchange between a user and a server and plays it back at a later time to impersonate the user.
Data interception	If data is moved across the network as plaintext, unauthorized persons can monitor and capture the data.
Manipulation	The intruder causes network data to be modified or corrupted. Unencrypted network financial transactions are vulnerable to manipulation. Viruses can corrupt network data.
Repudiation	Network-based business and financial transactions are compromised if the recipient of the transaction cannot be certain who sent the message.
Macro viruses	Application-specific viruses could exploit the macro language of sophisticated documents and spreadsheets.

(continued)

Table 11.3   **Types of Security Risks in an Organization** *(continued)*

Security Risk	Description
Denial of service	The intruder floods a server with requests that consume system resources and either crash the server or prevent useful work from being done. Crashing the server sometimes provides opportunities to penetrate the system.
Malicious mobile code	This term refers to malicious code running as an auto-executed ActiveX® control or Java Applet uploaded from the Internet on a Web server.
Misuse of privileges	An administrator of a computing system knowingly or mistakenly uses full privileges over the operating system to obtain private data.
Trojan horse	This is a general term for a malicious program that masquerades as a desirable and harmless utility.
Social engineering attack	Sometimes breaking into a network is as simple as calling new employees, telling them you are from the IT department, and asking them to verify their password for your records.

Security Concepts

The following concepts are useful in describing distributed security strategies under Windows 2000. You might also find it useful to include them in your security plan to familiarize readers with distributed security.

Security Model

Windows 2000 security is based on a simple model of authentication and authorization that uses Microsoft® Active Directory™ directory service. Authentication identifies the user when the user logs on and when the user makes network connections to services. Once identified, the user is authorized access to a specific set of network resources based on permissions. Authorization takes place through the mechanism of access control, using access control lists (ACLs) that define permissions on file systems, network file and print shares, and entries in Active Directory.

Domain Model

In Windows 2000, a domain is a collection of network objects, such as user accounts, groups, and computers, that share a common directory database with respect to security. A domain identifies a security authority and forms a boundary of security with consistent internal policies and explicit security relationships to other domains.

Trust Management

A trust is a logical relationship established between domains to allow pass-through authentication in which a trusting domain honors the logon authentications of a trusted domain. The term transitive trust refers to authentication across a chain of trust relationships. In Windows 2000, trust relationships support authentication across domains by using Kerberos v5 protocol and NTLM authentication for backward compatibility.

Security Policy

Security policy settings define the security behavior of the system. Through the use of Group Policy objects in Active Directory, administrators can centrally apply explicit security profiles to various classes of computers in the enterprise. For example, Windows 2000 comes with a default Group Policy object called **Default Domain Controllers Policy** that governs the security behavior of domain controllers.

Security Configuration and Analysis

Security Configuration and Analysis, a feature of Windows 2000, offers the ability to compare the security settings of a computer to a standard template, view the results, and resolve any discrepancies revealed by the analysis. You can also import a security template into a Group Policy object and apply that security profile to many computers at once. Windows 2000 contains several predefined security templates appropriate to various levels of security and to different types of clients and servers on the network.

Symmetric Key Encryption

Also called secret key encryption, symmetric key encryption uses the same key to encrypt and decrypt the data. It provides rapid processing of data and is used in many forms of data encryption for networks and file systems.

Public Key Encryption

Public key encryption has two keys, one public and one private. Either key can encrypt data that can only be decrypted by the other key. This technology opens up numerous security strategies and is the basis for several Windows 2000 security features. These features are dependent on a public key infrastructure (PKI). For more information about PKI, see "Planning Your Public Key Infrastructure" in this book.

Authentication

Authentication confirms the identity of any user trying to log on to a domain or to access network resources. Windows 2000 authentication enables single sign-on to all network resources. With single sign-on, a user can log on to the client computer once, using a single password or smart card, and authenticate to any computer in the domain. Authentication in Windows 2000 is implemented by using Kerberos v5 protocol, NTLM authentication, or the Windows NT logon feature to Windows NT 4.0 domains.

Single Sign-On

Users dislike having to authenticate separately to multiple network servers and applications. A user might have to provide separate passwords to log on to the local computer, to access a file or print server, to send an e-mail, to use a database, and so forth. Different servers can demand a change of password at different intervals, often with no reuse permitted; so a typical user might be required to remember half a dozen passwords. Not only is authentication tedious for the user, but at some point, users begin to write down a list of current passwords. In this way, a multiple-authentication network can become vulnerable to identity interception.

The single sign-on strategy makes a user authenticate interactively once and then permits authenticated sign-on to other network applications and devices. These subsequent authentication events are transparent to the user.

Two-Factor Authentication

Two-factor authentication requires users to present a physical object that encodes their identities plus a password. The most common example of two-factor authentication is the automated teller machine (ATM) card that requires a personal identification number (PIN).

Biometric identification is another form of two-factor authentication. A special device scans the user's handprint, thumbprint, iris, retina, or voiceprint in place of an access card. Then the user enters the equivalent of a password. This approach is expensive but it makes identity interception and masquerading very difficult.

For business enterprises, the emerging two-factor technology is the smart card. This card is not much larger than an ATM card and is physically carried by the user. It contains a chip that stores a digital certificate and the user's private key. The user enters a password or PIN after inserting the card into a card reader at the client computer. Because the private key is carried on a chip in the user's pocket, it is very hard for a network intruder to steal. Windows 2000 directly supports smart card authentication.

Access Control

Access control is the model for implementing authorization. After a user has authenticated to a domain and attempts to access a resource, such as a network file, the type of operation permitted is determined by the permissions that are attached to the resource, such as read-only or read/write. Access control in Windows 2000 is implemented by using object-specific ACLs. You can view an ACL on the **Security** tab of the property sheet of a file or folder. The list contains the names of user groups that have access to the object.

Data Integrity

Ensuring data integrity means to protect data against malicious or accidental modification. For stored data, this means that only authorized users can edit, overwrite, or delete the data. On a network, this means that a data packet must contain a digital signature so that tampering with the packet can be detected by the recipient computer.

Data Confidentiality

A strategy of data confidentiality means to encrypt data before it passes through the network and to decrypt it afterward. This strategy prevents data from being read by someone eavesdropping on the network (data interception). A packet of nonencrypted data that is transmitted across a network can be easily viewed from any computer on the network by using a packet-sniffing program downloaded from the Internet.

Nonrepudiation

There are two parts to a nonrepudiation strategy. The first is to establish that a message was sent by a specific user, who cannot disavow it. The second part is to ensure that the message could not have been sent by anyone masquerading as the user.

This is another application for public key infrastructure. The user's private key is used to place a digital signature on the message. If the recipient can read the message using the sender's public key, then the message could have been sent only by that specific user and no one else.

Code Authentication

This strategy requires that code downloaded from the Internet be signed with the digital signature of a trusted software publisher. You can configure Web browsers to avoid running unsigned code. Note that software signing proves that the code is authentic, meaning it has not been tampered with after publication. It does not guarantee that the code is safe to run. You have to decide which software publishers to trust. (The digital signature on the executable file is another example of public key infrastructure.)

Audit Logs

Auditing user account management as well as access to important network resources is an important security policy. Auditing leaves a trail of network operations, showing what was attempted and by whom. Not only does this help to detect intrusion, but the logs become legal evidence if the intruder is caught and prosecuted. Finally, finding and deleting or modifying the audit logs poses an additional time-consuming task for the sophisticated intruder, making detection and intervention easier.

Physical Security

It goes without saying that a critical enterprise network services network needs to reside in locked facilities. If intruders can sit down at the network server console, they might be able to take control of the network server. If critical network servers are not physically secure, a disgruntled employee can damage your hardware by using a simple, old-fashioned tool, such as a hammer. Your data is also open to physical attack: every novice user knows how to press the delete key. Damage from such intrusions can result in just as much loss of data and downtime as you can have from a more sophisticated, external attack to your network. Attacks on the network do not have to be sophisticated to be effective.

User Education

The best defense against a social engineering attack is to educate your users about keeping their passwords confidential and secure. Business policies about distribution of critical information need to be clearly stated. Publish a security policy and require everyone to follow it. One way to educate is by example: make sure that your IT professionals protect their passwords and that they encourage users to protect theirs too.

Distributed Security Strategies

Distributed security refers to the logical security features that operate primarily within the enterprise network. There are seven primary security strategies to pursue in making your network resources secure.

- Authenticate all user access to system resources.
- Apply appropriate access control to all resources.
- Establish appropriate trust relationships between multiple domains.
- Enable data protection for sensitive data.
- Set uniform security policies.

- Deploy secure applications.
- Manage security administration.

Make these seven themes central to your distributed security plan. In the pages that follow, you will find an in-depth discussion of each strategy.

Authenticating All User Access

To provide security for your Windows 2000 network, you must provide access for legitimate users but screen out intruders who are trying to break in. This means you must set up your security features to authenticate all user access to system resources. Authentication strategies set the level of protection against intruders trying to steal identities or impersonate users.

In Windows 2000, authentication for domain users is based on user accounts in Active Directory. Administrators manage these accounts using the Active Directory Users and Computers snap-in to the Microsoft Management Console (MMC). User accounts can be organized into containers called "organization units" that reflect the design of your Active Directory namespace. The default location for user accounts is the **Users** folder of this snap-in.

When a new user joins the organization, the administrator creates only a single account for that user rather than having to create half a dozen or more separate accounts on different servers and application databases. With the domain authentication service integrated with the enterprise directory, the single user account is also a directory entry for global address book information, as well as providing access to all network services. The user can log on at different client computers or laptops in the domain using only one password.

Windows 2000 automatically supports single sign-on for users within a domain forest. Domain trust relationships in the forest are bidirectional by default, so authentication in one domain is sufficient for referral or pass-through authentication to resources in other domains in the forest. The user logs on interactively at the beginning of a session, after which network security protocols (Kerberos v5 protocol, NTLM, and Secure Sockets Layer/Transport Layer Security) transparently prove the user's identity to all requested network services.

Windows 2000 optionally supports logging on with smart cards for strong authentication. The smart card is an identification card carried by the user that is used for interactive logon instead of a password. It can also be used for remote dial-up network connections and as a place to store public key certificates used for Secure Sockets Layer (SSL) client authentication or secure e-mail.

Authentication is not limited to users. Computers and services are also authenticated when they make network connections to other servers. For example, Windows 2000–based servers and client computers connect to their domain's Active Directory for policy information during startup. They authenticate to Active Directory and download computer policy from Active Directory before any user can log on to that computer. Computers and services also prove their identity to clients that request mutual authentication. Mutual authentication prevents an intruder from adding another computer as an imposter between the client and the real network server.

Computers and services can be "trusted for delegation," which means services can make other network connections "on behalf of" a user without knowing the user's password. The user must already have a mutually authenticated network connection to the service before the service can make a new network connection to another computer for that user. This is useful for multitier applications designed to use single sign-on capabilities across multiple computers. This feature is particularly useful in the context of an Encrypting File System (EFS) running on a file server. To use a service to delegate a network connection, use the Active Directory Users and Computers MMC snap-in. Then select the **Trust computer for delegation** check box on the property sheet.

Planning Considerations

Be sure to address these considerations and best practices when planning your authentication policies.

The simplest way to defend against brute force or dictionary password cracking tools is to establish and enforce long, complex passwords. Windows 2000 lets you set policy to govern the complexity, length, lifetime, and reusability of user passwords. A complex password has ten or more characters, including upper and lowercase, punctuation, and numerals. An example of a complex password is: "My,Birthday,Is,623".

Smart cards provide much stronger authentication than passwords, but they also involve extra overhead. Smart cards require configuration of the Microsoft Certificate Services, smart card reader devices, and the smart cards themselves. For more information about deploying smart cards, see "Smart Card Logon" later in this chapter and "Planning Your Public Key Infrastructure" in this book.

Note that third-party vendors offer a variety of security products to provide two-factor authentication, including "security tokens" and biometric accessories. These accessories use extensible features of the Windows 2000 graphical logon user interface to provide alternate methods of user authentication.

"Trust computer for delegation" is a very powerful capability. It is not enabled by default and requires Domain Administrator privileges to enable for specific computers or service accounts. Computers or accounts that are trusted for delegation need to be under restricted access to prevent introduction of Trojan horse programs that would misuse the capability of making network connections on behalf of users.

Some accounts might be too sensitive to permit delegation, even by a trusted server. You can set individual user accounts so that they cannot be delegated, even if the service is trusted for delegation. To use this feature, go to the Active Directory Users and Computers MMC snap-in and open the property sheet for the account. Look for the **Account is sensitive and cannot be delegated** check box on the **Account** tab of the property sheet.

Kerberos Authentication and Trust

The Kerberos authentication protocol is a technology for single sign-on to network resources. Windows 2000 uses the Kerberos v5 protocol to provide fast, single sign-on to network services within a domain, and to services residing in trusted domains. Kerberos protocol verifies both the identity of the user and of the network services, providing mutual authentication.

How Kerberos Authentication Works

When a user enters domain credentials (by user name and password or smart card logon), Windows 2000 locates an Active Directory server and Kerberos authentication service. The Kerberos service issues a "ticket" to the user. This is a temporary certificate containing information that identifies the user to network servers. After the initial interactive logon, the first Kerberos ticket is used to request other Kerberos tickets to log on to subsequent network services. This process is complex and involves mutual authentication of the user and the server to one another, but it is completely transparent to the user. (For more information about Kerberos v5 authentication, see Windows 2000 Server Help.)

Kerberos authentication reduces the number of passwords a user needs to remember, and thereby reduces the risk of identity interception. Trust relationships between domains in a forest extend the scope of Kerberos authentication to a wide range of network resources.

Implementing Kerberos Authentication

There are no prerequisites for implementing Kerberos authentication. The Kerberos protocol is used pervasively in Windows 2000. You do not need to install or initiate it.

Kerberos security policy parameters can be set in the Group Policy snap-in to MMC. Within a Group Policy object, the Kerberos settings are located under Account Policies:

```
Group Policy object
  └ Computer Configuration
  └ Windows Settings
   └ Security Settings
   └ Account Policies
    └ Kerberos Policy
```

These settings must be used only by qualified administrators who are familiar with the Kerberos protocol.

Considerations about Kerberos Security

To reap the full benefits of the enhanced performance and security of Kerberos authentication, consider deploying Kerberos sign in as the only network logon protocol in your enterprise. Windows 2000 implements the IETF standard version of Kerberos v5 authentication protocol for cross-platform interoperability. For example, users on UNIX systems can use Kerberos credentials to log on to UNIX systems and to securely connect to Windows 2000 services for applications that are enabled by Kerberos authentication. Enterprise networks that already use Kerberos authentication based on UNIX realms can create trust relationships with Windows 2000 domains and integrate Windows 2000 authorization for UNIX accounts using Kerberos name mapping.

Note that computers on a Kerberos-authenticated network typically must have their time settings synchronized with a common time service within five minutes, or authentication fails. Windows 2000 computers automatically update the current time using the domain controller as a network time service. Domain controllers use the primary domain controller for the domain as the authoritative time service. Even if the current time is different on computers within a domain, or across domains, Windows 2000 automatically handles clock differences to avoid logon problems.

When using transitive trust between domains in a forest, the Kerberos service searches for a trust path between the domains to create a cross-domain referral. In large trees it might be more efficient to establish cross-links of bidirectional trusts between domains where there is a high degree of cross-domain interaction. This permits faster authentication by giving the Kerberos protocol "shortcuts" to follow when generating the referral message.

Kerberos authentication uses transparent transitive trust among domains in a forest, but it cannot authenticate between domains in separate forests. To use a resource in a separate forest, the user has to provide credentials that are valid for logging on to a domain in that forest. Alternatively, if a one-way trust relationship exists, applications will use NTLM authentication, if the security policy permits.

Windows 2000 still maintains compatibility with the NTLM authentication protocol to support compatibility with previous versions of Microsoft operating systems. You can continue to use NTLM for Microsoft® Windows® 95, Microsoft® Windows® 98, Microsoft® Windows® NT 4.0 Server, and Windows NT 4.0 Workstation clients. NTLM authentication is also used on Windows 2000 by applications designed for previous versions of Windows NT that specifically request NTLM security.

Smart Card Logon

Windows 2000 supports optional smart card authentication. Smart cards provide a very secure means of user authentication, interactive logon, code signing, and secure e-mail. However, deploying and maintaining a smart card program requires additional resources and costs.

How Smart Cards Work

The smart card contains a chip that stores the user's private key, logon information, and public key certificate for various purposes. The user inserts the card into a smart card reader attached to the computer. The user then types in a personal identification number (PIN) when requested.

Smart cards provide tamper-resistant authentication through onboard private key storage. The private key is used in turn to provide other forms of security related to digital signatures and encryption.

Smart cards directly implement a two-factor authentication policy, and indirectly permit data confidentiality, data integrity, and nonrepudiation for multiple applications, including domain logon, secure mail, and secure Web access.

Prerequisites for Implementing Smart Cards

Smart cards rely on the public key infrastructure (PKI) of Windows 2000. For more information about PKI, see "Planning Your Public Key Infrastructure" in this book.

How to Implement Smart Cards

In addition to PKI and the cards themselves, each computer needs a smart-card reader. Set up at least one computer as a smart-card enrollment station, and authorize at least one user to operate it. This does not require special hardware beyond a smart card reader, but the user who operates the enrollment station needs to be issued an Enrollment Agent certificate.

For detailed procedures on implementing smart cards, see Windows 2000 Server Help.

Considerations about Smart Cards

You need an enterprise certification authority rather than a stand-alone or third-party certification authority to support smart card logon to Windows 2000 domains.

Microsoft supports industry standard Personal Computer/Smart Card (PC/SC)–compliant smart cards and readers and provides drivers for commercially available Plug and Play smart card readers. Smart card logon is supported for Windows 2000 Professional, Windows 2000 Server, and Windows 2000 Advanced Server systems. The security benefits of using smart cards are realized as more users of the enterprise become able to use smart cards for domain authentication, remote dial-up network access, and other applications.

Microsoft Windows 2000 does not support non-PC/SC-compliant or non–Plug and Play smart card readers. Some manufacturers might provide drivers for non–Plug and Play smart card readers that work with Windows 2000; nevertheless, it is recommended that you purchase only Plug and Play PC/SC-compliant smart card readers.

Smart cards can be combined with employee card keys and identification badges to support multiple uses per card.

The overall cost of administering the smart card program depends on several factors, including:

- The number of users enrolled in the smart card program and their location.
- Your practices for issuing smart cards to users, including the requirements for verifying user identities. For example, will you require users to simply present a valid personal identification card or will you require a background investigation? Your policies affect the level of security provided as well the actual cost.

- Your practices for users who lose or misplace their smart cards. For example, will you issue temporary smart cards, authorize temporary alternate logon to the network, or make users go home to retrieve their smart cards? Your policies affect how much worker time is lost and how much help desk support is needed.

Your network security deployment plan needs to describe the network logon and authentication methods you use. Include the following information in your security plan:

- Identify network logon and authentication strategies you want to deploy.

- Describe smart card deployment considerations and issues.

- Describe PKI certificate services required to support smart cards.

Remote Access

Routing and Remote Access is the service that lets remote users connect to your local network by phone. This section deals only with the remote access security features of Routing and Remote Access. Remote access by its nature is an invitation to intruders; so Windows 2000 provides multiple security features to permit authorized access while limiting opportunities for mischief.

How Remote Access Works

A client dials a remote access server on your network. The client is granted access to the network if:

- The request matches one of the remote access policies defined for the server.

- The user's account is enabled for remote access.

- Client/server authentication succeeds.

After the client has been identified and authorized, access to the network can be limited to specific servers, subnets, and protocol types, depending on the remote access profile of the client. Otherwise, all services typically available to a user connected to a local area network (including file and print sharing, Web server access, and messaging) are enabled by means of the remote access connection.

Remote Access Policies

Windows 2000–based servers are governed by security policies that determine their remote access behavior. These policies establish whether a server accepts requests for remote access and, if so, during what hours of what days, what protocols are used, and what types of authentication are required.

You define remote access policies by using the Computer Management snap-in to MMC. You define the policy in the Remote Access Policies node:

```
Computer Management (local)
  └ Services and Applications
  └ Routing and Remote Access
    └ Remote Access Policies
```

Right-click a policy in the console tree and select **Properties**. A remote access policy is defined as a rule with conditions and actions. If the conditions are met, the action is taken. For example, if the time of day is appropriate for remote access, if the requested protocol is permitted, and if the requested port type is available, then access is granted. If granted, remote access is limited by the access profile of the policy. Click **Edit Profile** to view the available profile options.

How to Enable Remote Access

To enable remote access for a user, open the Active Directory Users and Computers snap-in to MMC. Right-click a user, and select **Properties**. Select the **Dial-In** tab in the property sheet.

For more information about remote access and installing and configuring the remote access server, see Windows 2000 Server Help. For more information about remote access authentication, see "Remote Access Server" in the *Microsoft® Windows® 2000 Server Resource Kit Internetworking Guide.*

Considerations About Remote Access

Granting remote access permission to a user is ineffective if there is no appropriate remote access policy in place for the remote access server.

Windows 2000 supports the following authentication options for remote access:

- Standard Point-to-Point Protocol (PPP) challenge and response authentication methods based on user name and passwords.

  Standard PPP authentication methods offer limited security.

- Custom Extensible Authentication Protocol (EAP) authentication methods.

  EAP modules can be developed or provided by third parties to extend the authentication capabilities of PPP. For example, you can use EAP to provide stronger authentication using token cards, smart cards, biometric hardware, or one-time password systems.

- EAP Transport Layer Security (EAP-TLS) authentication based on digital certificates and smart cards.

  EAP-TLS provides strong authentication. Users' credentials are stored on tamper-proof smart cards. You can issue each user one smart card to use for all logon needs.

It is recommended that your network security plan include strategies for remote access and authentication, including the following information:

- Logon authentication strategies to be used.

- Remote access strategies by using Routing and Remote Access and virtual private networks.

- Certificate services needed to support user logon authentication by digital certificates.

- Process and strategies to enroll users for logon authentication certificates and remote access.

- Whether to use callback with remote access, to help eliminate impersonation attacks.

Applying Access Control

After a user logs on, the user is authorized to access various network resources, such as file servers and printers that grant permissions to Authenticated Users. Make certain you restrict a user's view of network resources to the devices, services, and directories that are job related. This limits the damage that an intruder can do by impersonating a legitimate user.

Access to network resources is based on permissions. Permissions identify users and groups who are allowed to perform specific actions by using specific resources. For example, the Accounting Group has read/write permission to access files in the Accounting Reports folder. The Auditor Group has read-only access to files in the Accounting Reports folder.

Permissions are enabled by using the ACL associated with each resource. You can find the ACL on the **Security** tab of the property sheet. An ACL is a list of the security groups (and rarely the individuals) who have access to that resource.

Security groups are the most efficient way to manage permissions. You can assign permissions to individuals; but in most cases, it is easier to grant permissions to a group and then add or remove users as members of the group.

Windows 2000 has a security group called "Everyone" which appears on network-share ACLs by default when they are created. To restrict access to network shares, you must remove the Everyone group and substitute a more appropriate group or groups. Do not assume the default permissions for a resource are necessarily appropriate permissions.

File system permissions by default are granted to a security group called Users. Any user authenticated to the domain is in the group called Authenticated Users, which is also a member of Users. Look at what the resource is used for and determine the appropriate policy. Some resources are public while others need to be available to specific sets of people. Sometimes a large group has read-only permission to a file or directory, and a smaller group has read/write permission.

Access Control Lists

ACLs describe the groups and individuals who have access to specific objects in Windows 2000. The individuals and security groups are defined in the Active Directory Users and Computers snap-in to MMC. Many types of Windows 2000 objects have associated ACLs, including all Active Directory objects, local NTFS files and folders, the registry, and printers. The granularity of ACLs is so fine that you can even place security access restrictions on individual fonts.

How ACLs Work

Access control lists implement usage restriction strategies. Windows 2000 offers a very fine degree of security control over access to a wide variety of objects. To give a group access to an object, you add the group to the ACL of the object. Then you can adjust the specific permissions that the group can exercise over the object. In terms of a local file folder, for example, the available permissions for a group begin with **read, write, modify,** and **delete**, but those are only the first four of thirteen available permissions.

Prerequisites for Implementing ACLs

Access control lists are pervasive throughout Windows 2000. The only prerequisite is that ACLs are lists of security groups and users. You must define the groups that describe your organization project teams or business roles before adding them to the ACLs.

How to Implement ACLs

The access control list for an object is generally found in the **Security** tab of the property sheet. This tab shows the list of groups that have access to this object, plus a summary of the permissions enjoyed by each group. There is an **Advanced** button that displays the group permissions in detail so that users can use more advanced features for granting permissions, such as defining access inheritance options.

For example, to view the access control list for a printer, click **Start**, and then point to **Settings**. Point to the folder that contains **Control Panel**, and then click **Printers**. Right-click a printer and select **Properties**. The access control list for that printer is in the **Security** tab.

To see the access control list for a local file folder, open **My Computer** and use Explore to navigate to the folder. Right-click the folder. Point to **Properties**, and click the **Security** tab.

To view the access control list of an organizational unit (folder) in the Active Directory Users and Computers MMC snap-in, you must open the **View** menu and select **Advanced Features**. Otherwise, the **Security** tab is not visible in the **Properties** dialog box.

For additional information about access control and ACLs, open Windows 2000 Server Help and click the **Index** tab. Scroll to **Access Control**. There are many related topics in the index because ACLs are available throughout the product.

Security Groups

Windows 2000 allows you to organize users and other domain objects into groups for easy administration of access permissions. Defining your security groups is a major task for your distributed security plan.

The Windows 2000 security groups let you assign the same security permissions to large numbers of users in one operation. This ensures consistent security permissions across all members of a group. Using security groups to assign permissions means the access control on resources remains fairly static and easy to control and audit. Users who need access are added or removed from the appropriate security groups as needed, and the access control lists change infrequently.

How Security Groups Work

Windows 2000 Active Directory supports security groups and distribution groups. The security groups can have security permissions associated with them and can also function as mailing lists. The distribution groups are used for mailing lists only. They have no security function.

When you create a new user, you can add the user to an existing security group to completely define the user's permissions and access limits. Changing a permission for the group affects all users in the group. Windows 2000 comes with several predefined security groups, and it is easy to create your own.

Security Group Types

Windows 2000 supports four types of security groups, differentiated by scope:

- Domain local groups are best used for granting access rights to resources such as file systems or printers that are located on any computer in the domain where common access permissions are required. The advantage of domain local groups used to protect resources is that members of the domain local groups can come from both inside the same domain and outside the domain. Typically, resource servers are in domains that have trust to one or more Master User Domains, or what are known as account domains. (A domain local group can be used to grant access to resources on any computer only in native mode domains. In mixed mode, domain local groups must be on domain controllers only.)

- Global groups are used for combining users who share a common access profile based on job function or business role. Typically, organizations use global groups for all groups where membership is expected to change frequently. These groups can only have as members user accounts defined in the same domain as the global group. Global groups can be nested to allow for overlapping access needs or to scale for very large group structures. The most convenient way to grant access to global groups is by making the global group a member of a resource group that is granted access permissions to a set of related project resources.

- Universal groups are used in larger, multidomain organizations where there is a need to grant access to similar groups of accounts defined in multiple domains. It is better to use global groups as members of universal groups to reduce overall replication traffic from changes to universal group membership. Users can be added and removed from the corresponding global group within their account domains and a small number of global groups are the direct members of the universal group. Universal groups are easily granted access by making them a member of a domain local group used to grant access permissions to resources.

  Universal groups are used only in multiple domain trees or forests that have a global catalog. A Windows 2000 domain must be in native mode to use universal groups. A domain model that has only a single domain does not need or support universal groups.

- Computer local groups are security groups that are specific to a computer and are not recognized elsewhere in the domain. If a member server is a file server and hosts 100 gigabytes (GB) of data on multiple shares, you can use a local server group for administrative tasks performed directly on that computer or for defining local access permission groups.

Default Permissions of Security Groups

For member servers and client computers, the default Windows 2000 access control permissions provide the following levels of security:

- Members of the Everyone and Users groups (normal users) do not have broad read/write permission as in Windows NT 4.0. These users have read-only permission to most parts of the system and read/write permission only in their own profile folders. Users cannot install applications that require modification to system directories nor can they perform administrative tasks.

- Members of the Power Users group have all the access permissions that Users and Power Users had in Windows NT 4.0. Power Users have read/write permission to other parts of the system in addition to their own profile folders. Power users can install applications and perform many administrative tasks.

- Members of the Administrators group have the same level of rights and permissions as they did for Windows NT 4.0.

For servers configured as domain controllers, the default Windows 2000 security groups provide the following security:

- Members of the Everyone and Users groups do not have broad read/write permission as in Windows NT 4.0. Normal users have read-only permission to most parts of the system and read/write permission in their own profile folders. However, normal users can only access domain controllers over the network — interactive logon to domain controllers is not granted to users as in Windows NT 4.0.

- Members of the Account Operators, Server Operators, and Print Operators groups have the same access permissions as in Windows NT 4.0.

- Members of the Administrators group have total control of the system as in Windows NT 4.0.

Prerequisites for Implementing Security Groups

Security groups are a built-in feature of Active Directory. No special installation or prerequisite is required.

Implementing Security Groups

To create new users and place them in Security groups, use the Active Directory Users and Computers snap-in of MMC. For more information about creating new users, see Windows 2000 Server Help.

Considerations About Security Groups

When designing potential security groups, a good strategy is for project or resource owners to define their own local groups based on required access permissions, and to delegate the ability to manage the group memberships, which itself is a permission of groups. This strategy allows the resource owners or project leads to manage access by updating the appropriate group.

A security group is composed of people who have similar roles in the department or in the enterprise. The group is often named after the role, such as the Windows 2000 built-in groups for Account Operators, Administrators, and Backup Operators. Personnel who naturally belong on the same project or department mailing list probably belong in the same security group in Active Directory. Windows 2000 security groups have a secondary role as mailing lists, so this analogy is not a coincidence.

Using groups that correspond to project teams or responsibilities is an effective way to grant access appropriately. Everyone in a department needs access to the department printers. The engineers on a software project need access to the common source directories. These are natural groups.

Note that the system has to determine all of a user's universal and global group affiliations at logon time. When a user is a member of many groups, this has some impact on performance while the system determines all the group memberships.

There is an upper limit on the number of groups a user can enroll in. For an individual user operating in a single domain, the total sum of universal, global, domain local, and local computer groups cannot exceed 1,000 groups. The user is not strictly limited to 1,000 groups, however, because the limit applies from the point of view of an individual domain. In a multiple domain model, a user could hypothetically be a member of 500 universal and global groups in their account domain, in 400 domain local groups in one resource domain, in 400 domain local groups in another resource domain, in 50 local groups in one server, and 100 local groups on another server. For most practical purposes, the 1,000-group limit is very generous.

Use nested groups to make it easier to manage group membership for large groups. (A large group might have 5,000 members in it.) Do not list every employee individually in your whole-company group. The whole-company group will be easier to administer if defined as the group that contains your department groups. The department groups can be nested within the whole-company group.

This is especially important if your whole-company group is a universal group. An organization with a single local area network (LAN) site can use universal groups with no performance degradation. However, an organization with a wide area network (WAN) needs to consider the impact of frequent changes to universal group membership on replication traffic across links between sites. If a universal group contains only other groups as members, it does not change very often and replication traffic is essentially nothing. A universal group containing thousands of individual users is likely to require frequent updates across multiple WAN links as each change replicates to all Global Catalog servers in the enterprise. Defining universal groups as groups of groups reduces this network activity.

You might find that your Windows 2000 Server does not permit nested groups. Windows 2000 Server initially operates in mixed mode, which means that Windows 2000 and Windows NT 4.0 Servers can interoperate in the same network. Mixed mode places some restrictions on security groups. When all servers have been upgraded to Windows 2000, you can switch to native mode. This is a one-way transition that enables advanced features such as nesting of security groups.

For a specific computer, the users in the local administrator security group have full rights and permissions for that computer. When a Windows 2000 computer is joined to a domain, the Domain Administrators group is added as a member of the local administrator group. Local users of the computer generally do not need to be members of the administrators group. The full-privilege administrator group must be used for local administration activities, such as changing the system configuration.

Your network security deployment plan describes your strategies for security groups. Include the following information in your deployment plan:

- Identify the universal and global security groups you want to create in addition to the built-in groups.
- Identify membership requirements for universal, global, and local security groups, including the built-in groups.

Security Groups and Replication Conflicts

If administrators at two different two domain controllers in different site change group membership simultaneously, one of the changes might be lost. This situation can occur only if you are making group membership changes faster than the system can replicate them. When an administrator adds or removes members from a group, the entire group membership is replicated, not just the changed members. If two administrators change group membership on two different domain controllers and replication takes place on the second domain controller before the first domain controller completes replication, only one of the changes remain after the Active Directory resolves the replication conflict. The other change is lost. As a result, a user might unexpectedly retain access to a resource.

One way to minimize this problem is to use nested groups. Create site-specific groups and make them members of a parent group that will be used to grant or deny access to a resource. Administrators in a site can then change the membership of a site-specific group and not lose changes as long the membership of the site-specific group is not updated on multiple domain controllers faster than intra-site replication can complete. Also, if you delegate responsibility for group membership changes to one administrator per site, all changes will be made on a single domain controller and no replication conflicts will occur.

Note Within a single Active Directory site, the amount of time it takes for a change to reach all of the domain controllers will increase as the number of domain controllers increases with a maximum latency of approximately three times the replicator notify pause interval. Generally, replication will finish quickly within a single site. Replication between two or more Active Directory sites generally takes longer, and is dependent on the replication schedule configured by the administrator as well as whether or not the administrator configures inter-site replicator notifications.

To avoid this situation completely, make all group membership changes on a single domain controller. This will prevent changes from being lost due to replication conflicts. For more information about both the multimaster conflict resolution policy for Active Directory and how to configure Active Directory to minimize replication latency, see "Active Directory Replication" in the *Microsoft Windows Server Resource Kit Distributed Systems Guide*.

Establishing Trust Relationships

Your distributed security plan needs to take into consideration the proposed structure of your domains, trees of domains, forests, and non–Windows 2000 Servers. Although Windows 2000 establishes default trust relationships automatically, your plan needs to address what domains need to be part of the domain forest and what domains might require explicit trusts for your network.

For Windows 2000 computers in the same forest, account authentication between domains is enabled by two-way, transitive trusts. The transitive trust relationship is automatically established when a new domain is joined to a domain tree. A trust relationship is defined by a secret key that is shared by both domains and that gets updated on a regular basis. Trust relationships are used by the Kerberos v5 authentication when clients and servers are in separate domains in the forest. The trust secret key is used by the Kerberos service to create a referral ticket to the trusting domain. NTLM authentication also uses trust relationships for pass-through authentication. Pass-through authentication uses the trust link secret key to establish a secure channel between domains. In Windows 2000, NTLM authentication also supports transitive trust if the domains are in native mode.

Domain Trust

A domain trust is a useful way to allow users from a trusted domain to access services in a trusting domain. If all users and services can be managed in a single enterprise domain, there is no need for trust relationships. However, there are several advantages to creating separate domains. Domains are a useful way to separate the scope of responsibility of the domain administrators. Each administrator is responsible for the users and resources within a domain. Domains are also the scope for security policy settings, such as account policies. Most trust relationships in a Windows 2000 forest are implicit two-way transitive trusts that require no planning. It is the *external* trust relationships to Windows NT 4.0 domains, or other Windows 2000 domains in a separate forest, that need to be mentioned in your plan.

How Trust Relationships Work

All domain trust relationships have only two domains in the relationship: the trusting domain and the trusted domain. A domain trust relationship is characterized by whether it is:

- One-way
- Two-way
- Transitive
- Nontransitive

A one-way trust is a single trust relationship, where domain A trusts domain B. All one-way relationships are nontransitive. Authentication requests can only be passed from the trusting domain to the trusted domain. This means that if domain A has a one-way trust with domain B and domain B has a one-way trust with domain C, domain A does not have a trust relationship with domain C.

A Windows 2000 domain can establish a one-way trust with:

- Windows 2000 domains in a different forest
- Windows NT 4.0 domains
- MIT Kerberos v5 realms

Since all Windows 2000 domains in a forest are automatically linked by transitive trusts, it is generally not necessary to create one-way trusts between all Windows 2000 domains in the same forest.

All domain trusts within a Windows 2000 forest are two-way transitive trusts. Transitive trusts are always two-way: both domains in the relationship trust each other. Each time you create a new child domain, a two-way transitive trust relationship is created between the parent and new child domain. In this way, transitive trust relationships flow upward through the domain tree as it is formed, creating transitive trusts between all domains in the domain tree.

Each time you create a new domain tree in a forest, a two-way transitive trust relationship is created between the forest root domain and the new domain (the root of the new domain tree). In this way, transitive trust relationships flow through all domains in the forest. Authentication requests follow these trust paths, so accounts from any domain in the forest can be authenticated at any other domain in the forest.

You can also explicitly (manually) create transitive trusts between Windows 2000 domains on different branches of the same domain tree or in different trees of a forest. These cross-linked trust relations can be used to shorten the trust path in large and complex domain trees or forests. These explicit trusts need to be provided for in your distributed security plan.

A nontransitive trust is bounded by the two domains in the trust relationship and does not flow to any other domains in the forest. You must explicitly create nontransitive trusts. Nontransitive trusts are one-way by default, although you can also create a two-way relationship by creating two one-way trusts. All trust relationships established between domains that are not in the same forest are nontransitive.

Transitive trusts can only exist between Windows 2000 domains in the same forest.

In summary, nontransitive domain trusts are the only form of trust relationship possible between:

- A Windows 2000 domain and a Windows NT domain.
- A Windows 2000 domain in one forest and a Windows 2000 domain in another forest.
- A Windows 2000 domain and an MIT Kerberos v5 realm.

Prerequisites for Implementing Trusts

There are no specific prerequisites for trusts except to understand that trusts are links between domains. You need to set up at least two domains before you can define a trust relationship.

How to Implement Trusts

To set up explicit trusts among domains in a forest, open MMC snap-in for Active Directory Domains and Trusts. Right-click a domain and open the property sheet. Select the **Trusts** tab. This tab allows you to add, edit, or delete trust relationships between the selected domain and others in the same forest.

Considerations About Trusts

Mixed mode domains (where Windows NT 4.0 backup domain controllers are temporarily combined with a Windows 2000 primary domain controller during network upgrades) implement trust relationships in a manner consistent with Windows NT 4.0 domains for Windows NT 4.0 Workstations and Servers. In other words, all trust relationships required for Windows NT 4.0 Workstations and Servers are still needed for mixed mode domains. Native mode domains (where all servers are running Windows 2000) support transitive trust.

Domain administrators of any domain in the forest have the potential to take ownership and modify any information in the Configuration container of Active Directory. These changes will be available and replicate to all domain controllers in the forest. Therefore, for any domain that is joined to the forest, you must consider that the domain administrator of that domain is trusted as an equal to any other domain administrator.

Domains where the domain administrators are not fully or equally trusted can be handled in two ways. The first is to set up an explicit one-way trust (or external trust) to that domain. In this way, users logging on to the suspect domain do not have automatic access to the rest of the forest.

To control this situation with a finer degree of granularity, consider collapsing the resources of the suspect domain into an organizational unit (Active Directory folder) of a domain under the control of a trusted administrator. Remove the separate domain altogether. The administrator of the suspect domain can be delegated only the appropriate degree of control over the computers and local groups that are the administrator's domain resources.

Enabling Data Protection

Information security strategies protect data on your servers and client computers, and also conceal and protect packets traversing insecure networks. Your distributed security plan needs to identify which information must be protected in the event computer equipment is lost or stolen. Also, types of network traffic that are sensitive or private and need to be protected from network sniffers must be included in the plan.

In terms of users on your enterprise network, access control is the primary mechanism to protect sensitive files from unauthorized access. Access control is discussed earlier in this chapter. However, the computers themselves might be portable and subject to physical theft. Therefore, access control is not sufficient to protect the data stored on these computers. This is a special problem with laptop computers that can be easily stolen while traveling. Windows 2000 provides the Encrypting File System (EFS) to address this problem.

To keep network data packets confidential, you can use Internet Protocol security (IPSec) to encrypt network traffic among some or all of your servers. IPSec provides the ability to set up authenticated and encrypted network connections between two computers. For example, you could configure your e-mail server to require secure communication with clients and thereby prevent a packet sniffer from reading e-mail messages between the clients and the server. IPSec is ideal for protecting data from existing applications that were not designed with security in mind.

Network and Dial-up Connections (remote access) always protect network data transmitted over the Internet or public phone lines. Remote access uses a virtual private network that uses the PPTP or LT2P tunneling protocol over IPSec.

Encrypting File System

The Windows 2000 Encrypting File System (EFS) lets a user encrypt designated files or folders on a local computer for added protection of data stored locally. EFS automatically decrypts the file for use and reencrypts the file when it is saved. No one can read these files except the user who encrypted the file and an administrator with an EFS Recovery certificate. Since the encryption mechanism is built into the file system, its operation is transparent to the user and extremely difficult to attack.

EFS is particularly useful for protecting data on a computer that might be physically stolen, such as a laptop. You can configure EFS on laptops to ensure that all business information is encrypted in users' document folders. Encryption protects information even if someone bypasses EFS and uses low-level disk utilities to try to read information.

EFS is intended primarily for protection of user files on the disk of the local NTFS file system. As you move away from this model (remote drives, multiple users, editing encrypted files) there are numerous exceptions and special conditions to be aware of.

How EFS Works

EFS encrypts a file using a symmetric encryption key unique to each file. Then it encrypts the encryption key as well, using the public key from the file owner's EFS certificate. Since the file owner is the only person with access to the private key, that person is the only one who can decrypt the key, and therefore the file.

There is also provision for the original encryption key to be encrypted using the public key of an administrator's EFS File Recovery certificate. The private key from that certificate can be used to recover the file in an emergency. It is highly recommended that an organization establish a recovery agent.

Even if the file can be stolen, over the network or physically, it cannot be decrypted without first logging on the network as the appropriate user. Since it cannot be read, it cannot be surreptitiously modified. EFS addresses an aspect of a policy of data confidentiality.

Prerequisites for Implementing EFS

To implement EFS, a public key infrastructure must be in place and at least one administrator must have an EFS Data Recovery certificate so the file can be decrypted if anything happens to the original author. The author of the file must have an EFS certificate. The files and folders to be encrypted must be stored on the version of NTFS included with Windows 2000.

How to Implement EFS

Open Windows Explorer and right-click a folder or a file. Select **Properties**. On the **General** tab, click **Advanced**. Then select the **Encrypt Contents to Secure Data** check box. The contents of the file, or of all the files in the selected folder, are now encrypted until you clear the check box.

For more information about best practices for encrypting file systems, see the Windows 2000 Server Help. See also "Encrypting File System" in the *Microsoft® Windows® 2000 Server Resource Kit Distributed Systems Guide.*

Considerations About EFS

EFS is only supported for the version of NTFS used in Windows 2000. It does not work with any other file system, including previous versions of NTFS.

EFS can be used to store sensitive data securely on shared servers to allow for normal data management (backup). The servers must be well protected and must be "Trusted for Delegation." EFS services will "impersonate" the EFS user and make other network connections on their behalf when encrypting and decrypting files.

EFS uses a Data Recovery policy that enables an authorized data recovery agent to decrypt encrypted files. EFS requires at least one recovery agent. Recovery agents can use EFS to recover encrypted files if users leave the organization or lose their encryption credentials. You need to plan to deploy the PKI components and issue one or more certificates for EFS data recovery. These certificates need to be securely stored offline so they cannot be compromised. EFS can generate its own certificates for EFS users and EFS recovery agents. By default, EFS issues EFS Recovery certificates to the Domain Administrator account as the recovery agent for the domain. For stand-alone computers that are not joined to a domain, EFS issues EFS Recovery certificates to the local Administrator user account as the recovery agent for that computer. Many organizations might want to designate other EFS recovery agents to centrally administer the EFS recovery program. For example, you can create organizational units for groups of computers and designate specific recovery agent accounts to manage EFS recovery for specific organizational units.

You can deploy Microsoft Certificate Services to issue certificates to EFS recovery agents and EFS users. When certificate services are available online, EFS uses the certificate services to generate EFS certificates.

Note that because cluster services do not support reparse points on shared storage, EFS cannot be used if the file server is actually a Windows cluster.

Include strategies for EFS and EFS recovery in your network security deployment plan. EFS strategies might include the following information:

- File system strategies for laptops and other computers.
- EFS recovery agents.
- Recommended EFS recovery process.
- Recommended EFS recovery agent private key management and archive process.
- Certificate services needed to support EFS recovery certificates.

IP Security

Windows 2000 incorporates Internet Protocol security (IPSec) for data protection of network traffic. IPSec is a suite of protocols that allow secure, encrypted communication between two computers over an insecure network. The encryption is applied at the IP network layer, which means that it is transparent to most applications that use specific protocols for network communication. IPSec provides end-to-end security, meaning that the IP packets are encrypted by the sending computer, are unreadable en route, and can be decrypted only by the recipient computer. Due to a special algorithm for generating the same shared encryption key at both ends of the connection, the key does not need to be passed over the network.

How IPSec Works

IPSec has many intricate components and options that are worthy of detailed study; but at a high level the process operates in this manner:

1. An application on Computer A generates outbound packets to send to Computer B across the network.

2. Inside TCP/IP, the IPSec driver compares the outbound packets against IPSec filters, checking to see if the packets need to be secured. The filters are associated with a filter action in IPSec security rules. Many IPSec security rules can be inside one IPSec policy that is assigned to a computer.

3. If a matched filter has to a negotiate security action, Computer A begins security negotiations with Computer B, using a protocol called the "Internet Key Exchange" (IKE). The two computers exchange identity credentials according to the authentication method specified in the security rule. Authentication methods could be Kerberos authentication, public key certificates, or a preshared key value (much like a password). The IKE negotiation establishes two types of agreements, called "security associations," between the two computers. One type (called the "phase I IKE SA") specifies how the two computers trust each other and protects their negotiation. The other type is an agreement on how to protect a particular type of application communication. This consists of two SAs (called "phase II IPSec SAs") that specify security methods and keys for each direction of communication. IKE automatically creates and refreshes a shared, secret key for each SA. The secret key is created independently at both ends without being transmitted across the network.

4. The IPSec driver on Computer A signs the outgoing packets for integrity, and optionally encrypts them for confidentially using the methods agreed upon during the negotiation. It transmits the secured packets to Computer B.

Note Firewalls, routers, and servers along the network path from Computer A to Computer B do not require IPSec. They simply pass along the packets in the usual manner.

5. The IPSec driver on Computer B checks the packets for integrity and decrypts their content if necessary. It then transfers the packets to the receiving application.

IPSec provides security against data manipulation, data interception, and replay attacks.

IPSec is important to strategies of data confidentiality, data integrity, and nonrepudiation.

Prerequisites for Implementing IPSec

The computers in your network need to have an IPSec security policy defined that is appropriate for your network security strategy and for the type of network communication that they perform. Computers in the same domain might be organized into groups with IP security policy applied to the groups. Computers in different domains might have complementary IPSec security policies to support secure network communications.

How to Implement IPSec

You can view the default IP security policies in the Group Policy snap-in to MMC. The policies are listed under **IP Security Policies on Active Directory**, or under **IP Security Policies (Local Computer)**:

```
Group Policy object
 └ Computer Configuration
 └ Windows Settings
  └ Security Settings
  └ IP Security Policies on Active Directory
```

You can also view IPSec policies by using the IP Security Policy Management snap-in to MMC. Each IP Security policy contains security rules that determine when and how traffic is protected. Right-click a policy and select **Properties**. The **Rules** tab lists the policy rules. Rules can be further decomposed into filter lists, filter actions, and additional properties.

For more information about Internet Protocol security, see the Windows 2000 Server Help. See also "Internet Protocol Security" in the *Microsoft® Windows® 2000 Server Resource Kit TCP/IP Core Networking Guide*.

Considerations for IPSec

IPSec provides encryption of outgoing and incoming packets, but at a cost of additional CPU utilization when encryption is performed by the operating system. For many deployments, the clients and servers might have considerable CPU resources available, so that IPSec encryption will not have a noticeable impact on performance. For servers supporting many simultaneous network connections or servers that transmit large volumes of data to other servers, the additional cost of encryption is significant. For this reason, you need to test IPSec using simulated network traffic before you deploy it. Testing is also important if you are using a third-party hardware or software product to provide IP security.

Windows 2000 provides device interfaces to allow hardware acceleration of IPSec per-packet encryption by intelligent network cards. Network card vendors might provide several versions of client and server cards, and might not support all combinations of IPSec security methods. Consult the product documentation for each card to be sure that it supports the security methods and the number of connections you expect in your deployment.

You can define Internet Protocol security (IPSec) policies for each domain or organizational unit. You can also define local IPSec policy on computers that do not have domain IPSec policy assigned to them. You can configure IPSec policies to:

- Specify the levels of authentication and confidentiality required between IPSec clients.
- Specify the lowest security level at which communications are allowed to occur between IPSec-aware clients.
- Allow or prevent communications with non-IPSec-aware clients.
- Require all communications to be encrypted for confidentiality or you can allow communications in plaintext.

Consider using IPSec to provide security for the following applications:

- Peer-to-peer communications over your organization's intranet, such as legal department or executive committee communications.
- Client-server communications to protect sensitive (confidential) information stored on servers. For file share points that require user access controls, consider using IPSec to ensure that other network users cannot see the data as it is being communicated.

- Remote access (dial-up or virtual private network) communications. (For virtual private networks using IPSec with L2TP, remember to set up Group Policy to permit autoenrollment for IPSec computer certificates. For detailed information about computer certificates for L2TP over IPSec VPN connections, see Windows 2000 Help.)
- Secure router-to-router WAN communications.

Consider the following strategies for IPSec in your network security deployment plan:

- Identify clients and servers to use IPSec communications.
- Identify whether client authentication is based on Kerberos trust or digital certificates.
- Describe how each computer will initially receive the proper IPSec policy and will continue to receive policy updates.
- Describe the security rules inside each IPSec policy. Consider how certificate services are needed to support client authentication by digital certificates.
- Describe enrollment process and strategies to enroll computers for IPSec certificates.

Setting Uniform Security Policies

Uniform security policies allow consistent security settings to be applied and enforced on classes of computers in the enterprise, such as the domain controller class. This is a simple matter of creating an organizational unit, a folder in Active Directory, collecting appropriate computer account objects into the organizational unit, and then applying a Group Policy object to the organizational unit. The security policies specified in the Group Policy are then enforced automatically and consistently on all the computers represented by the computer accounts in the OU.

Windows 2000 comes with a selection of default Group Policy objects that are automatically applied to new domains and to domain controllers. There is also a selection of security *templates* representing different levels of security for various types of enterprise computers. A template can be used to create a Group Policy for a group of computers or to critique the security settings on a specific computer.

Note that the present discussion is confined to the *security* settings of Group Policy. When you apply a Group Policy to an organizational unit, many policies unrelated to security are also included. For a broader discussion of this mechanism, see Windows 2000 Help and "Defining Client Administration and Configuration Standards" in this book.

Group Policy

A Group Policy object contains an extensive profile of security permissions that apply primarily to the security settings of a domain or a computer (rather than to users). A single Group Policy object can be applied to all of the computers in an organizational unit. Group Policy gets applied when the individual computer starts up, and periodically is refreshed if changes are made without restarting.

How Group Policy Works

Group Policy objects are associated with domains and organizational units (folders) in the Active Directory Users and Computers snap-in to MMC. The permissions granted by the Group Policy are applied to the computers stored in that folder. Group Policy can also be applied to sites using the Active Directory Sites and Services snap-in.

Group Policy settings are inherited from parent folders to child folders, which might in turn have their own Group Policy objects. A single folder could have more than one Group Policy object assigned to it. For more information on Group Policy precedence and how conflicts are resolved among multiple policy objects, see Windows 2000 Help.

Group Policy is the complementary component to security groups. Group Policy lets you apply a single security profile to multiple computers. It enforces consistency and provides easy administration.

Group Policy objects contain permissions and parameters that implement multiple types of security strategies.

Prerequisites for Implementing Group Policy

Group Policy is a feature of the Windows 2000 Active Directory. Active Directory must be installed on a server before you can edit and apply Group Policy objects.

How to Implement Group Policy

To view a sample organizational unit and its associated Group Policy, open the Active Directory Users and Computers MMC snap-in and right-click the **Domain Controllers** OU. Open the property sheet and click the **Group Policy** tab. Select the **Default Domain Controllers Policy** and click **Edit**. This opens the Group Policy snap-in to MMC. In this module, navigate to the **Security Settings** container:

```
Group Policy object
 └ Computer Configuration
  └ Windows Settings
   └ Security Settings
```

Under **Security Settings** there are nine subdirectories of security policy settings. These nine groups are briefly described later in this chapter.

Implementing Group Policy consists of creating a new Group Policy object (or modifying an existing one), enabling appropriate settings within the object, and then linking the Group Policy object to an organizational unit that contains computers in the domain.

Considerations About Group Policy

Create organizational units to contain computers with similar roles in the enterprise. Use one organizational unit for your domain controllers. Create another one for application servers. Another organizational unit could contain all your client computers. Apply a single Group Policy object to each of these groups to implement consistent security settings.

It is recommended that you minimize the number of Group Policy objects that apply to users and computers. Do this first, because each computer and user Group Policy object must be downloaded to a computer during startup and to user profiles at user logon time. Multiple Group Policy objects increase computer startup and user logon time. Second, applying multiple Group Policy objects can create policy conflicts that are difficult to troubleshoot.

In general, Group Policy can be passed down from parent to child sites, domains and organizational units. If you have assigned a specific Group Policy to a high level parent, that Group Policy applies to all organizational units beneath the parent, including the user and computer objects in each container. For more information on inheritance of Group Policy settings, see "Defining Client Administration and Configuration Standards" in this book.

Security templates (described later in this chapter) could be useful to you as models of security settings appropriate to different types of Group Policy.

Your network security deployment plan needs to describe significant policy choices for each policy category and subcategory. You can include the following information in your security plan:

- Identify Group Policy settings you want to change from the default settings.
- Describe all issues related to changing settings for Group Policy.
- Describe special security requirements and how you can configure Group Policy to meet the special requirements.

Group Policy Security Settings

These are the nine types of Group Policy security features mentioned previously in this chapter. They are containers located in the **Security Settings** node of a Group Policy object. They include:

- Account Policies
- Local Policies
- Event Log
- Restricted Groups
- Systems Services
- Registry
- File System
- Public Key Policies
- Internet Protocol Security Policies on Active Directory

Some of the policy areas apply only to the scope of a domain, that is, the policy settings are domain-wide. Account policies, for example, apply uniformly to all user accounts in the domain. You cannot define different account policies for different organizational units in the same domain.

Of the security policy areas, Account policies and Public Key policies have domain-wide scope. All other policy areas can be specified at level of the organizational unit.

Account Policies

Account policies are the first subcategory of Security Settings. The Account policies include the following:

Password Policy   You can modify password policy to meet your organization's security needs. For example, you can specify minimum password length and maximum password age. You can also require complex passwords and prevent users from reusing passwords or simple variations of passwords.

Account Lockout Policy   You can force users to be locked out after a specified number of failed logon attempts. You can also specify the period of time that accounts are frozen.

Kerberos Authentication Policy   You can modify the default Kerberos settings for each domain. For example, you can set the maximum lifetime of a user ticket.

The policies you choose affect the level of help desk support required for users as well as the vulnerability of your network to security breaches and attacks. For example, specifying a restrictive account lockout policy increases the potential for denial of service attacks, and setting a restrictive password policy results in increased help desk calls from users who cannot log on to the network.

In addition, specifying restrictive password policy can actually reduce the security of the network. For example, if you require passwords longer than seven characters, most users have difficulty remembering them. They might write their passwords down and leave them where an intruder can easily find them.

Local Computer Policies

The second subcategory of Security Settings is Local Computer policies. Local Computer policies include the following:

Audit Policy   Windows 2000 can record a range of security event types, from a system-wide event, such as a user logging on, to an attempt by a particular user to read a specific file. Both successful and unsuccessful attempts to perform an action can be recorded.

User Rights Assignment   You can control the rights assigned to user accounts and security groups for local computers. You can specify users and security groups who have rights to perform a variety of tasks affecting security. For example, you can control who can access computers from the network, who can log on locally, or who can shut down the system. You can specify who has rights to perform critical administrative tasks on the computer, such as backing up and restoring files and directories, taking ownership of files and objects, and forcing shutdown from a remote system.

Security Options   You can control a wide variety of security options for local computers. For example, you can specify policies that force users to log off when logon hours expire, disable CTRL+ALT+DEL for logon (to force smart card logon), and force computers to halt if unable to audit.

Event Log Policies

You can use Event Log policies to control the settings of the application, system, and security event logs on local computers. For example, you can specify maximum log sizes, how long logged events are maintained, and log retention methods.

Restricted Groups Policies

You can define Restricted groups policies to manage and enforce the membership of built-in or user-defined groups that have special rights and permissions. Restricted Groups policies contain a list of members of specific groups whose membership are defined centrally as part of the security policy. Enforcement of Restricted Groups automatically sets any computer local group membership to match the membership list settings defined in the policy. Changes to group membership by the local computer administrator are overwritten by the Restricted Groups policy defined in Active Directory.

Restricted Groups can be used to manage membership in the built-in groups. Built-in groups include local groups such as Administrators, Power Users, Print Operators, and Server Operators, as well as global groups such as Domain Administrators. You can add groups that you consider sensitive or privileged to the Restricted Groups list, along with their membership information. This allows you to enforce the membership of these groups by policy and not allow local variations on each computer.

Systems Services Policies

System services offer a mechanism for potential exploitation by intruders, who can take over the service or use the service as an entry point to gain access to computers and network resources. For example, an intruder can try to exploit weaknesses in a running Web server to gain access to a computer's operating system or files. You can use Systems Services policies to:

- Specify the startup mode for Windows 2000 services (manual or automatic) or to disable services.

  For example, you can configure system services to prevent unnecessary services from running. This provides maximum security for special servers such as domain controllers, DNS servers, proxy servers, remote access servers, and certification authority servers.

- Specify rights and permissions granted to system services when they run.

  For example, you can configure system services to operate with minimum rights and permissions to limit the scope of potential damage caused by intruders who try to exploit the service.

- Refine security auditing levels for system services.

  You can specify the type of events to be logged for both failed and successful events. For example, when auditing is enabled, you can refine auditing to monitor for inappropriate actions taken by running services.

Registry Policies

You can use registry policies to configure security and control security auditing for registry keys and their subkeys. For example, to ensure that only administrators can change certain information in the registry, you can use registry policies to grant administrators full control over registry keys and their subkeys and to grant read-only permission to other users. You can also use registry policies to prevent certain users from viewing portions of the registry.

You can use registry policies to audit user activity in the registry of the computer when auditing is enabled. You can specify which users and which user events are logged for both failed and successful events.

File System Policies

You can use File System policies to configure security for files and folders and control security auditing of files and folders. For example, to ensure that only administrators can modify system files and folders, you can use File System policies to grant administrators full control over system files and folders and to grant read-only permission to other users. You can also use File System policies to prevent certain users from viewing files and folders.

You can use File System policies to audit user activity affecting files and folders when auditing is enabled. You can specify which users and which user events are logged for both failed and successful events.

Public Key Policies

This subdivision of security settings lets you add a new Encrypted Data Recovery Agent and set up Automatic Certificate Requests. You can also manage your lists of trusted Certification Authorities.

IP Security Policies on Active Directory

The policies in this section tell the server how to respond to a request for IPSec communications. The server might require secure communication, permit secure communication, or communicate without using IPSec. The predefined policies are not intended for immediate use. They provide examples of behavior for testing purposes. Network security administrators need to carefully design and assign their own custom IPSec policy to computers.

Security Templates

Windows 2000 provides a set of security templates for your use in setting up your network environment. A *security template* is a profile of security settings thought to be appropriate to a specific level of security on a Windows 2000 domain controller, server, or client computer. For example, the hisecdc template contains settings appropriate to a highly secure domain controller.

You can import a security profile into a Group Policy object and apply it to a class of computers. You can also import the template into a personal database and use it to examine and configure the security policy of a local computer.

How Security Templates Work

Security templates provide standard security settings to use as a model for your security policies. They help you troubleshoot computers whose security policies are not in compliance with policy or are unknown. Security templates are inactive until imported into a Group Policy object or the Security Configuration and Analysis snap-in to MMC.

Prerequisites for Implementing Security Templates

Security templates are a standard feature of Windows 2000. There are no prerequisites for using them.

How to Implement Security Templates

You can edit security templates in the Security Templates snap-in to MMC.

You can use the Security Configuration and Analysis MMC snap-in to import and export templates, and to compare a template to the security settings of the local computer. If you want, you can use this MMC snap-in to configure the computer to match the template.

To import a security template into a Group Policy object, open the Group Policy snap-in to MMC. Right-click the **Security Settings** container and select the **Import Policy** option. This brings up a selection of security templates to import.

For more information about using security templates and predefined templates, see Windows 2000 Server Help.

Considerations About Security Templates

The default clean-install permissions for Windows 2000 provide a significant increase in security over previous versions of Windows NT. This default, clean-install security, is defined by the access permissions granted to three groups: Users, Power Users, and Administrators.

By default, Users have an appropriate access-control policy for nonadministrative system use; Power Users are backward compatible with Windows NT 4.0 Users; and Administrators are all-powerful. Therefore, securing a Windows 2000 system is largely a matter of defining what group the users belong to.

If your site runs only applications that are compatible with the Windows 2000 application specification, then it is possible to make all users be members of the Users group and thus achieve maximum access control security without sacrificing application functionality. If your site runs applications that are not compliant with the Windows 2000 application specification, it is likely that users will need to be Power Users in order to have the privileges necessary to run the noncompliant applications. Thus, before considering the use of additional security templates, it is imperative that you define the level of access (User, Power User, or Administrator) that users need in order to successfully run the applications that must be supported.

Once this has been defined, the security templates can be used as follows:

Basic   The Basic security templates apply the Windows 2000 default access control settings previously described. The Basic templates can be applied to a Windows NT computer that has been upgraded to Windows 2000. This will bring the upgraded computer in line with the new Windows 2000 default security settings that are applied only to clean-installed computers. The Basic templates can also be used to revert back to the defaults after making any undesirable changes.

Compatible   Some customers might not want their users to be Power Users in order to run applications that are not compliant with the Windows 2000 application specification. They might not want this because Power Users have additional capabilities (such as the ability to create shares) that go beyond the more liberal access control settings necessary to run legacy applications. For customers who do not want their end users to be Power Users, the Compatible template "opens up" the default access control policy for the Users group in a manner that is consistent with the requirements of most legacy applications. For example, Microsoft® Office 97 SR1 runs successfully as a Power User, or as a User under the Compatible configuration. However, Office 97 does not run successfully as a clean-installed User. Note that Microsoft® Office 2000 runs successfully as a clean-installed User because it is compliant with the Windows 2000 application specification. A computer that is configured with the Compatible template must not be considered a secure installation.

Secure The Secure template modifies settings (such as password policy, audit policy, and registry values) that are less likely to have an impact on application functionality and more of an impact on the operational behavior of the operating system and its network protocols. The Secure template provides recommendations that are distinct from the default access control policy that has been defined. The Secure template does not modify any ACLs, but it does remove all members of the Power Users group.

High Secure The High Secure template increases the security defined by several of the parameters in the secure template. For example, while the Secure template might enable SMB Packet Signing, the High Secure template would require SMB packet signing. While the Secure template might warn on the installation of unsigned drivers, the High Secure template blocks the installation of unsigned drivers. In short, the High Secure template configures many operational parameters to their extreme values without regard for performance, operational ease of use, or connectivity with clients using third-party or earlier versions of NTLM. Like the Secure template, the High Secure template also removes all members of the Power Users group.

In summary, use of the security templates must be considered with respect to the default access control policy required by the installed base of applications and the communication requirements of other networked systems. Since the templates modify operating system settings, they must not be applied without passing proper quality assurance measures.

Deploying Secure Applications

It is not enough to set up distributed security and then just go back to business as usual. A secure enterprise network needs software that has been designed with security features in mind. The archetype of a security-blind application is one that transmits passwords across the network in the clear. A secure environment needs secure applications.

When evaluating software for your enterprise, look for applications designed with security-enabled features. Look for integration with single sign-on capabilities for authenticated network connections, and the ability to run properly in secured computer configurations. The software need not require administrator privileges if it is not an administrator tool or utility.

The *Application Specification for Windows 2000* defines the technical requirements that an application must meet to earn the Certified for Microsoft Windows logo. The document identifies the minimum requirement areas that secure applications must support:

- Run on secured Windows 2000 servers.

- Single sign-on by using the Kerberos authentication for establishing network connections.

- Use impersonation of the client to support consistent Windows 2000 access control mechanisms using permissions and security groups.

- Application services run by using service accounts rather than a local system (which has full system privileges).

These requirements are a minimum. It is also important to deploy applications that are well engineered and to avoid buffer overflow or other weaknesses for an intruder to exploit.

One approach is to require that application components be digitally signed. Microsoft® Authenticode™, through Microsoft® Internet Explorer, lets users identify who published a software component and verify that no one tampered with it before downloading it from the Internet.

Also, regularly remind users not to run programs directly from e-mail attachments if they are unfamiliar with the sources or if they are not expecting to receive e-mail from the source.

Authenticode and Software Signing

Software downloaded from the Internet to users' computers can contain unauthorized programs or viruses intended to cause damage or provide clandestine network access to intruders. As networks become more interconnected, the threat of malicious software and viruses has extended to the intranet.

How Authenticode Works

To counter this growing threat, Microsoft developed Authenticode™ technology to enable developers to digitally sign software using standard X.509 public key certificates. Users can verify the publisher of digitally signed software as well as verify that the software has not been tampered with, because the publisher signed the code.

You can use Microsoft Certificate Services to issue digital signing certificates to your internal developers. Your developers can use signing certificates to sign software before they distribute it on the intranet. To protect your network from malicious programs and viruses, you need to also consider establishing policies that prevent users from downloading and running unsigned software from both the intranet and the Internet.

For software distributed on the Internet, most users are more likely to trust software signed by certificates issued by a reputable commercial certification authority. Using commercial certification authorities also removes the liability placed on your organization from assuming the responsibilities of a commercial certification authority for external software distribution. Therefore, if you distribute software on the Internet, you need to consider obtaining the services of a commercial certification authority to issue digital signing certificates to your external software developers.

Implementing Authenticode Screening

You can enable Authenticode-based screening of downloaded software in Internet Explorer by doing the following: on the **Tools** menu, point to **Internet Options**, and click the **Security** tab. Higher levels of security set from this tab screen software components for trusted digital signatures.

You can take control of these Internet Explorer security settings through Group Policy (described previously in this chapter). Open the Group Policy snap-in to MMC and navigate to the Internet Explorer container:

```
Group Policy object
  ∟ Computer Configuration
  ∟ Administrative Templates
    ∟ Windows Components
      ∟ Internet Explorer
```

Internet Explorer policies permit you to lock down security settings so that users cannot change them, and to require that all downloaded components have trusted signatures.

Considerations for Authenticode and Software Signing

Strategies for software signing in your deployment plan might include the following information:

- Internal and external groups that need the capability to sign software.
- Strategies for signing software for internal distribution.
- Strategies for signing software for external distribution.
- Certification authority deployment and trust management needed to support software signing strategies.
- Process and strategies to enroll users as software signers.
- Education to inform users not to run unsigned or untrusted components.

Secure E-mail

In today's enterprise, e-mail messages containing sensitive personal information and proprietary business information are routinely sent over nonsecure portions of the intranet or even the Internet. Espionage agents or hackers can easily intercept plaintext e-mail messages. Furthermore, someone with malicious intent can easily intercept and modify e-mail messages en route, or forge the IP address of an e-mail sender and send false messages.

Many of today's secure e-mail solutions, such as Microsoft Exchange Server are based on the open Secure/Multipurpose Internet Mail Extensions (S/MIME) standard. Using open standards is important if you want to provide interoperability among third-party secure e-mail applications used by business partners, vendors, and customers.

How Secure E-mail Works

Secure e-mail systems based on S/MIME use industry standard X.509 digital certificates and public key technology to provide e-mail security between senders and recipients of e-mail messages. Secure e-mail systems typically provide the following security functions:

- Senders can digitally sign e-mail messages to provide data integrity.
- Recipients can verify the identity of the message sender and verify that the message has not been tampered with en route.
- Senders cannot repudiate signed messages because only the sender has possession of the signing credentials.
- Senders can encrypt e-mail messages to provide confidential communications.
- Intended recipients can decrypt the message using private credentials, but others cannot decrypt and read the message.
- Administrators can centrally store users' private credentials in a secure database. If a user's private credentials are lost or damaged, administrators can retrieve the private credentials necessary to decrypt messages.

Considerations for Secure E-mail

To address strategies for secure e-mail, consider including the following information in your deployment plan:

- Secure e-mail server and client applications to be used.
- E-mail servers and user groups needing upgrade or migration to secure e-mail.
- General policies for using secure e-mail in the organization.

- Encryption technology to be used, including international export restrictions and limitations.

- Certificate services needed to support secure e-mail.

- Enrollment process and strategies to enroll users in the secure e-mail program.

- Key recovery database backup capabilities and recommended backup and restore practices.

- Key recovery capabilities and recommended general recovery practices.

Secure Web Sites and Communications

The Web site and browser have become the central mechanisms for open information exchange and collaboration on organizational intranets as well as on the Internet. However, standard Web protocols such as Hypertext Transfer Protocol (HTTP) provide limited security. You can configure most Web servers to provide directory and file level security based on user names and passwords. You can also provide Web security by programming solutions using the Common Gateway Interface (CGI) or Active Server Pages (ASP). However, these traditional methods of providing Web security are proving less and less adequate as attacks against Web servers become more frequent and sophisticated.

You can use Internet Information Services (IIS), included with Windows 2000 Server, to provide high levels of security for Web sites and communications using standards-based secure communications protocols and standard X.509 certificates. You can provide the following security for Web sites and communications:

- Authenticate users and establish secure channels for confidential encrypted communications using the Secure Sockets Layer (SSL) and Transport Layer Security (TLS) protocols.

- Authenticate users and establish secure channels for confidential encrypted financial transactions using the Server Gated Cryptography (SGC) protocol.

- Map user certificates to network user accounts to authenticate users and control user rights and permissions for Web resources based on users' possession of valid certificates issued by a trusted certification authority.

Considerations for Secure Web Sites

Consider including the following information in your deployment plan:

- Web sites and user groups to upgrade or migrate to secure Web sites.

- Strategies for using SSL or TLS to secure Web communications between clients and Web servers.

- Strategies for using certificate mapping to control user rights and permissions to Web site resources.

- Certification authority deployment needed to support Web sites.
- Enrollment process and strategies to enroll users in the secure Web sites program.

Managing Administration

Some of the policies in your security plan will involve the daily duties of your IT department staff. Windows 2000 supports delegation of administrative permissions, allowing specific personnel limited rights to administer their own groups and files. Windows 2000 also supports audit logs of system activity, with a fine degree of granularity about which types of events will be logged and in what context.

It is also extremely important that your plan describes how you intend to protect your domain administrator accounts from penetration by an intruder. It is recommended that you set up your domain account policies to require all accounts to use a long and complex password that cannot be easily cracked. This is common sense but it needs to be explicitly stated in your plan.

It is not as obvious that security will be compromised if too many people know the administrator password. The administrator of the root domain of a domain tree is also automatically a member of the Schema Administrators group and the Enterprise Administrators group. This is a highly privileged account where an intruder can do unlimited damage. Your plan needs to state that access to this account is limited to a very small number of trusted personnel.

The domain administrator account must be used only for tasks that require administrator privileges. It must never be left logged on and unattended. Encourage your administrator staff to use a second, unprivileged account for nonadministrative activities (reading e-mail, Web browsing, and so on).

Server consoles used for domain administration must be physically secured so that only authorized personnel have access to them. Your security plan needs to state this and list the personnel who might use the consoles. It is not as obvious that users of the Administrator account must never log on to client computers managed by someone who is not equally trusted. The other client computer administrator might introduce other code on that computer that will unknowingly exploit the administrator privileges.

Delegation

The delegation of administrative tasks is a practical necessity in a Windows 2000 enterprise environment. It is common to delegate authority not only to members of the IT group but to human resources personnel and various managers for tasks related to their duties. Delegation distributes the administrator's workload without granting sweeping privileges to every assistant. This is an expression of the security concept of "principle of least privilege," that is, granting only the permissions necessary for the task.

Through various means, Windows 2000 allows you to delegate to groups or individuals a prescribed degree of control over a limited set of objects. The only prerequisite is that the appropriate delegation elements (users, groups, Group Policy objects, files, directories, and so forth) must be in place before delegation can be performed.

Windows 2000 supports delegation of administrative authority through various features, including those listed in the following sections. (Note that some tasks require domain administrator privileges and cannot be delegated.)

Security Groups, Group Policy, and Access Control Lists

These features are described previously in this chapter, and form the mechanisms for the features described in the following paragraphs.

Built-in Security Groups

Windows 2000 has predefined security groups with special permissions already delegated to each group. Open the Active Directory Users and Computers snap-in to MMC. On the **View** menu, select **Advanced Features**. The predefined security groups are in the **Builtin** and **Users** folders.

To directly delegate control of one of these groups, open the property sheet of the group and click the **Security** tab. Add the group's manager to the access control list and check the appropriate privileges.

Delegation of Control Wizard

Open the Active Directory Sites and Services snap-in to MMC. Right-click an organizational unit and select **Delegate Control**. This wizard sets up user group permissions to administer specific sites and services. An example would be the right to create new remote access accounts.

Delegate Administration Wizard

Open the Active Directory Users and Computers snap-in to MMC. Right-click an organizational unit and select **Delegate Control**. This wizard sets up user group permissions to administer organizational units containing computers and user groups. An example would be the delegated right to create new user accounts.

Delegating Control of Group Policy Objects

Delegating administration via Group Policy involves the following three tasks, which can be performed together or separately, as your situation requires:

- Managing Group Policy links for a site, domain, or organizational unit.
- Creating Group Policy objects.
- Editing Group Policy objects.

These tasks are described in more depth in "Defining Client Administration and Configuration Standards" in this book.

Auditing

Auditing and security logging of network activity are important safeguards. Windows 2000 enables you to monitor a wide variety of events that can be used to track the activities of an intruder. The log file entries can serve as legal evidence after the intruder has been identified.

How Auditing Works

You can specify that an audit entry is to be written to the security event log whenever certain actions are performed or files are accessed. The audit entry shows the action performed, the user who performed it, and the date and time of the action. You can audit both successful and failed attempts at actions, so the audit trail can show who performed actions on the network and who tried to perform actions that are not permitted. You can view the security log in the Event Viewer.

If the security log is examined regularly, it makes it possible to detect some types of attacks before they succeed, such as password attacks. After a break-in, the security log can help you determine how the intruder entered and what they did.

Audit logging is a policy in its own right. Recording security events is a form of intrusion detection.

Prerequisites for Implementing the Audit Function

There is nothing to install or purchase. You do have to configure your Group Policy settings to enable auditing. You also must enable auditing for the general areas or specific items you want to track.

How to Implement the Audit Function

Security auditing is not enabled by default. You have to activate the types of auditing you require by using the Group Policy snap-in to MMC.

```
Group Policy object
 └ Computer Configuration
 └ Windows Settings
  └ Local Policies
  └ Auditing Policies
```

Categories of auditable events include: account logon events, account management, directory service access, logon events, object access, policy change, privilege use, process tracking, and system events. Note that auditing policies are subject to policy inheritance, and the policies you set on your local computer could be overshadowed by policies set for the domain as a whole.

Once you have set up your auditing policies, you can descend to a fine degree of granularity by enabling specific types of auditing messages for individual objects. For example, to enable auditing for a file directory, right-click the appropriate folder in Windows Explorer. Point to **Properties**, and click the **Security** tab. Click **Advanced**, and then select the **Auditing** tab in the **Advanced Properties** dialog box. This displays the list of auditable events available for the folder. In the case of file directories, auditing settings could be optionally applied to contained files and subdirectories.

View the audit messages in the **Security Log** node of the **Event Viewer**.

For more information about auditing security events, see Windows 2000 Help.

Considerations About Auditing

Generating a security log has implications for disk space on your server. You can set the Event Viewer to overwrite log entries that are more than "n" days old, or you can configure the server to stop running when the security log is full. For more information about halting the computer when the security log is full, see Windows 2000 Help.

Note that the auditing features for directories and files described here require an NTFS file system.

Monitor firewall servers and critical servers that are internal to the firewall to detect suspicious activity. You also need to monitor servers that are external to the firewall even though they are considered nonsecure, because they provide a doorway into your enterprise.

Table 11.3 lists various events that you need to audit, as well as the specific security threat that the audit event monitors.

Table 11.3   Security Audit Threat Detection Policies

Audit Event	Threat Detected
Failure audit for logon/logoff.	Random password hack
Success audit for logon/logoff.	Stolen password break-in
Success audit for user rights, user and group management, security change policies, restart, shutdown, and system events.	Misuse of privileges
Success and failure audit for file-access and object-access events. File Manager success and failure audit of read/write access by suspect users or groups for the sensitive files.	Improper access to sensitive files
Success and failure audit for file-access printers and object-access events. Print Manager success and failure audit of print access by suspect users or groups for the printers.	Improper access to printers
Success and failure write access auditing for program files (.exe and .dll extensions). Success and failure auditing for process tracking. Run suspect programs; examine security log for unexpected attempts to modify program files or create unexpected processes. Run only when actively monitoring the system log.	Virus outbreak

Planning Task List for Distributed Security

To develop your network security deployment plan, complete the tasks listed in Table 11.4.

Table 11.4   Security Planning Task List

Task	Location in Chapter
Identify the security risks that apply to your network. Tabulate and explain them in the plan.	Security Risks
Provide background material on security concepts and vocabulary to orient the reader of your plan.	Security Concepts

(continued)

Table 11.4   Security Planning Task List *(continued)*

Task	Location in Chapter
Introduce and explain the security strategies that address the risks in your plan.	Distributed Security Strategies
Ensure that all access to network resources requires authentication using domain accounts.	Authenticating All User Access
Determine what part of the user community needs to use strong authentication for interactive or remote access login.	Authenticating All User Access
Define the password length, change interval, and complexity requirements for domain user accounts and develop a plan to communicate these requirements to the user community.	Authenticating All User Access
Define your organization policy to eliminate transmission of clear text passwords on any network and develop a strategy to enable single sign on or protect password transmission.	Authenticating All User Access
Identify a plan to deploy public key security for smart card logon if strong authentication meets your security objectives.	Smart Card Logon
Describe your policy for enabling remote access for users.	Remote Access
Develop a plan to communicate remote access procedures, including connection methods, to general user community.	Remote Access
Identify how your organization currently uses groups and establish conventions for group names and how group types are used.	Applying Access Control
Describe the top-level security groups you intend to use for broad security access to enterprise-wide resources. These are likely to be your enterprise universal groups.	Applying Access Control
Describe your access control policies with specific reference to how security groups are used in a consistent manner.	Applying Access Control
Define the procedures for creating new groups and who has responsibility to manage group membership.	Applying Access Control
Determine which existing domains belong in the forest, and which domains use external trust relationships.	Establishing Trust Relationships
Describe your domains, domain trees, and forests, and explicitly state the trust relationships among them.	Establishing Trust Relationships
Define a policy for identifying and managing sensitive or confidential information and your requirements to protect sensitive data.	Enabling Data Protection
Identify network data servers that provide sensitive data that might require network data protection to prevent eavesdropping.	Enabling Data Protection
Develop a deployment plan for using IPSec for protection data for remote access or for accessing sensitive application data servers.	Enabling Data Protection

(continued)

Table 11.4   Security Planning Task List *(continued)*

Task	Location in Chapter
If using EFS, describe your Data Recovery Policy, including the role of Recovery Agent in your organization.	Encrypting File System
If using EFS, describe the procedures you plan to use to implement data recovery process and verify that the process works for your organization.	Encrypting File System
If using IPSec, identify the scenarios for how it will be used in your network and understand the performance implications.	IP Security
Define domain-wide account policies and communicate those policies and guidelines to the user community.	Setting Uniform Security Policies
Determine the local security policy requirements for different categories of systems on the network, such as desktops, file and print servers, e-mail servers. Define the Group Policy security settings appropriate to each category.	Setting Uniform Security Policies
Define application servers where specific security templates can be used to manage security settings and consider managing them through Group Policy.	Setting Uniform Security Policies
Apply appropriate security templates for systems that upgrade from Windows NT 4.0 instead of a clean install.	Security Templates
Use security templates as a means of describing the level of security you intend to implement for different classes of computers.	Security Templates
Develop a test plan to verify your common business applications run correctly under properly configured secure systems.	Deploying Secure Applications
Define what additional applications are needed that provide enhanced security features to meet your organization security objectives.	Deploying Secure Applications
State the levels of security you require for downloaded code.	Authenticode and Software Signing
Deploy internal procedures for implementing code signing for all in-house developed software that is publicly distributed.	Authenticode and Software Signing
State your policies for securing the Administrator account and the administration consoles.	Managing Administration
Identify the situations where you plan to delegate administrator control for specific tasks.	Delegation
Identify your policies regarding auditing, including staffing.	Auditing

CHAPTER 12

Planning Your Public Key Infrastructure

Microsoft® Windows® 2000 supports a comprehensive public key infrastructure (PKI). A PKI is a system of digital certificates, certification authorities, and other registration authorities that verify and authenticate the validity of each party involved in an electronic transaction through the use of public key cryptography.

You can design a PKI that meets your public key security needs using Microsoft® Certificate Services or other certificate services.

In This Chapter

Chapter Goals

This chapter will help you to develop the following planning documents:

- Public key certificate requirements
- Policies for how certificates will be issued and used
- Certification authority trust hierarchy design
- Certificate life cycle policies and processes
- Policies governing certificate revocation
- Strategies for certificate backup and disaster recovery
- Timetable for PKI deployment and rollout

Related Information in the Resource Kit

- For more information about the basic concepts of cryptography-based security, PKI, and public key technology, see "Cryptography for Network and Information Security" in the *Microsoft® Windows® 2000 Server Resource Kit Distributed Systems Guide.*

- For more information about security solutions using public key technology, see "Choosing Security Solutions That Use Public Key Technology" in the *Microsoft Windows 2000 Server Resource Kit Distributed Systems Guide.*

Overview of Public Key Infrastructure

Public key infrastructure (PKI) is an underlying technology of Windows 2000 that enables a variety of features relating to authentication and encryption. Therefore, your plans for PKI need to be defined early in the deployment process.

This section presents a brief overview of the PKI features and tools in Windows 2000.

How PKI Works

A PKI is based on *certificates*. A certificate is a digitally signed statement containing a public key and the name of the subject. There can be multiple types of names in the certificate by which the subject is known, such as a directory name, e-mail name, and Domain Name Service (DNS) name. By signing the certificate, the certification authority verifies that the private key associated with the public key in the certificate is in the possession of the subject named in the certificate.

A certification authority, frequently a third-party company, issues a trusted user a certificate containing a public key. This certificate can be freely distributed. The public key can be used to encrypt data that can only be decrypted using an associated private key, which is also provided to the user. The user keeps the private key secure, so that no one else has access to it. The private key can be used to create a digital signature that can be confirmed by the public key.

The basic idea of public key cryptography is that there are two keys that are related. One key can be passed openly and freely between parties or published in a public repository; the other key must remain private. There are also different types of public key algorithms, each with its own characteristics. This means that it is not always possible to substitute one algorithm for another. If two algorithms can perform the same function, the detailed mechanism by which that result is obtained varies. With public key cryptography, the two keys are used in sequence. If the public key is used first, followed by the private key, then this is a key exchange operation. If the private key is used first, followed by the public key, this is a digital signature operation.

You can create your own certification authorities within your enterprise, and you can use third-party companies that provide commercial certification services.

PKI processes information in a way that simultaneously identifies and authenticates the source. It makes identity interception very difficult and prevents masquerading and data manipulation. Table 12.1 describes some of the ways you can use PKI in an enterprise.

Table 12.1   Leading Applications for Digital Certificates

Application	Uses
Secure e-mail	Secure e-mail clients use certificates to ensure the integrity of e-mail and to encrypt e-mail messages for confidentiality.
Secure Web communications	Web servers can authenticate clients for Web communications (using client certificates) and provide confidential, encrypted Web communications (using server certificates).
Secure Web sites	Internet Information Services (IIS) Web sites can map client certificates to authenticate users to control their rights and permissions for Web site resources.
Digital signing of software files	Code-signing tools use certificates to digitally sign software files to provide proof of file origin and to ensure the integrity of data.
Local network Smart Card authentication	The Kerberos logon protocol can use certificates and the private key stored on smart cards to authenticate network users when they log on to the network.
Remote access Smart Card authentication	Servers that are running the Routing and Remote Access service can use certificates and the private key stored on smart cards to authenticate network users when they log on to the network.
IPSec authentication	IPSec can use certificates to authenticate clients for IPSec communications.
Encrypting File System (EFS) recovery agent	Recovery agent certificates enable recovery of EFS files encrypted by other users.

Prerequisites for Implementing PKI

Implementing PKI in your enterprise is a multiple-part process requiring planning and experimentation through pilot programs. Some features of Windows 2000, such as the Encrypting File System (EFS) and IP security (IPSec), can provide their own certificates without any special preparation on the part of the network administrator. You can deploy these features immediately. Other security features might require a hierarchy of CAs. A CA hierarchy requires planning.

The first business policy decisions you make will have to do with selecting the CAs, both internal and external, that will be the source of your certificates. A typical CA hierarchy has a three-level architecture. It is recommended that you have one root CA, and that it be offline. You need a second level of CAs to implement certificate policy. This level also needs to be offline. The third level is the issuing CAs. You can have internal or external CAs at this level. Internal network authentication and data integrity can be handled by a local certifying authority, such as your IT department. Internet transactions and software signing might require third-party certificates in order to establish public credibility.

While selecting your CAs, give some thought to your cryptographic service provider (CSP). The CSP is the software or hardware that provides encryption services for your CA. If the CSP is software based, it will generate a public key and a private key, often referred to as a key pair, on your computer. If the CSP is hardware based, such as a smart card CSP, it might instruct a piece of hardware to generate the key pair.

The standard CSP for Windows environments is the Microsoft Base cryptographic service provider, which provides 40-bit key lengths. Windows 2000 supports 40/56-bit encryption and is exportable. For greatest security (and greater speed), consider using a hardware-based CSP, available from third-party vendors.

Greater security usually means greater cost, both in terms of expense for hardware and in CPU cycles devoted to encryption. Greater security is not always cost effective, but it is available when needed. For extreme levels of security, consider a hardware CSP for CAs and smart cards for users.

How to Implement PKI

Provision for public key infrastructure certificates is built into Windows 2000 and most software that supports enterprise business computing. To learn about Windows 2000 PKI features, explore the following sections.

Creating a Local Certification Authority

You can create a local CA on your Windows 2000 server. There are several types of CAs to choose from. One type is the enterprise CA, which can issue certificates for purposes such as digital signatures, encrypted e-mail, Web authentication, and Windows 2000 domain authentication through smart cards. The enterprise CA will issue certificates based on requests from users or other entities, and it requires the use of the Active Directory™ directory service.

A stand-alone CA issues certificates based on requests from users or other entities; however, unlike the enterprise CA, it does not require the use of Active Directory. Stand-alone CAs are primarily intended for use with extranets or the Internet.

CAs can also fulfill various hierarchical roles such as root CA, subordinate CA, and issuing CA. For considerations about certification hierarchies, see "Define Certificate Policies and Certification Authority Practices" later in this chapter.

▶ **To create a local CA on your Windows 2000–based server**

1. Click **Start**, point to **Settings**, and then click **Control Panel**.

2. Double-click Add/Remove Programs, and click Add/Remove Windows Components.

3. Add Certificate Services, and install an enterprise root CA.

For more information about installing a local certification authority, see Windows 2000 Server Help.

After you create a local CA, you can monitor and manage it by using the Certification Authority snap-in to Microsoft Management Console (MMC).

You can also view your PKI certificates.

▶ **To view your personal set of PKI certificates**

1. Open Microsoft Internet Explorer.

2. On the **Tools** menu, click **Internet Options**.

3. Click the **Content** tab of the resulting dialog box. The buttons in the center section of this tab display your current certificates, trusted certifying authorities, and trusted software publishers.

Managing Your Certificates

To manage your certificates, use the Certificates snap-in to MMC. Note that this snap-in has two display modes, the Logical Certificate Stores display and the Certificate Purpose display. Click the Certificates node (top-level node) to highlight it. On the **View** menu, click **Options**. Familiarize yourself with each of the two display modes.

To request a new certificate while in this snap-in, right-click the appropriate node in the Certificate Purpose view and, on the **All Tasks** menu, click **Request New Certificate**.

Using the Certificate Services Web Pages

When your Windows 2000 site is operational, you can allow users to request their own certificates from your internal certification authority. You must have a CA configured and running, and IIS must also be configured and running. Access the enrollment Web pages through http://*computer_DNS_name*/certsrv/.

Setting Public Key Policies in Group Policy Objects

A number of PKI policies can be set in a Group Policy object and thereby applied to computers in domain and organizational unit scope. Open the Group Policy snap-in to MMC to the appropriate Group Policy object. The PKI entries are located under Computer Configuration:

```
Group_Policy_Object
 └ Computer Configuration
  └ Windows Settings
   └ Security Settings
    └ Public Key Policies
```

Certificate trust lists and CA root certificates are part of Group Policy objects, and contain the CAs to be trusted by recipients of the Group Policy. These are the Enterprise Trust and Trusted Root Certification Authority containers under Public Key Policies, respectively.

Building Your Public Key Infrastructure

The Windows 2000 PKI provides a framework of services, technology, and protocols based on standards that enable you to deploy and manage a strong information security system using public key technology. Windows 2000 supports a variety of public key security features required by distributed security services. For example, Windows 2000 supports public key cryptography operations required for EFS without the need to deploy additional infrastructure or CAs.

However, many security solutions (such as secure e-mail, smart card authentication, and secure Web communications) require that you design, test, and deploy additional components of the PKI, including CAs, certificate enrollment, and renewal to support these types of applications. You might also want to deploy certificate services to support EFS users and multiple recovery agents or IPSec authentication for clients not running Kerberos authentication or not able to use Kerberos authentication for establishing trust relationships (across untrusted Windows 2000 domains or with a computer that is not a member of a Window 2000 domain). Furthermore, to meet special requirements for your organization, you might want to develop and deploy custom applications and certificate services.

Figure 12.1 shows a basic process that you can use to design, test, and deploy a PKI in your organization.

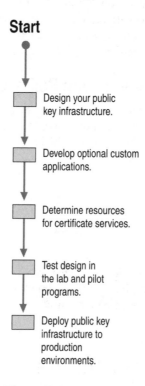

Figure 12.1   Process Flow Chart for Designing a PKI in Your Organization

You can design and deploy your PKI using Microsoft Certificate Services. You can also use Windows 2000–compliant third-party CAs to build part or all of your PKI. The basic process for building your PKI is the same whichever certificate services you use. However, the actual implementation details for building your PKI will differ depending on the specific certificate services technology. For more information about the components and features of the Windows 2000 public key infrastructure, see "Choosing Security Solutions That Use Public Key Technology" in *The Microsoft Windows 2000 Server Resource Kit Distributed Systems Guide*. For more information about the components and features of third-party certificate services, contact the appropriate vendor for the certificate service.

Designing Your Public Key Infrastructure

With Windows 2000, you can design a PKI that meets a wide range of public key security needs. The needs must be determined in order to design and scale the infrastructure that will support them.

Identify Your Certificate Requirements

Before you can determine what PKI certificate services are needed, you must identify the applications you want to deploy that require digital certificates. You must also identify all uses for certificates, what users, computers, and services will require certificates, and what types of certificates you intend to issue. You can deploy Microsoft Certificate Services, or you can obtain other certificate services to support your public key needs. Identify the categories of users, computers, and services that will need certificates and determine the following information for each category:

- Name or description
- Reason certificates are needed
- Number of entities (users, computers, or services)
- Location of users, computers, and services

You need to provide certificate services to support the identified categories for each business unit and location in your organization. The certificate services you deploy are determined by the types of certificates to be issued, the number of entities that need certificates, and where the groups are located. For example, you might be able to deploy two issuing CAs to provide certificates for all the administrator groups in your organization. However, since there are many more business users than administrators in your organization, you might need to deploy separate issuing CAs in each facility to meet the needs of business users.

For more information about security solutions that use digital certificates, see "Choosing Security Solutions That Use Public Key Technology" in the *Microsoft Windows 2000 Server Resource Kit Distributed Systems Guide*.

Basic Security Requirements for Certificates

Several basic factors affect overall security when you use certificates. For the certificates you intend to use, specify the requirements for the following factors:

- **Length of the private key.** In a typical deployment, user certificates have 1,024-bit keys and root CAs have 4,096-bit keys.
- **Cryptographic algorithms that are used with certificates.** The default algorithms are recommended.
- **Lifetime of certificates and private keys and the renewal cycle.** Certificate lifetimes are determined by the type of certificate, your security requirements, standard practices in your industry, and government regulations.
- **Special private key storage and management requirements.** For example, storage on smart cards and nonexportable keys.

The standard settings for certificates issued by Microsoft Certificate Services can meet typical security needs. However, you might want to specify stronger security settings for certificates that are used by certain user groups. For example, you can specify longer private key lengths and shorter certificate lifetimes for certificates used to provide security for very valuable information. You can also specify the use of smart cards for private key storage to provide additional security.

Determining Which Certificate Types to Issue

Identify the types of certificates you intend to issue. The types of certificates you issue depend on the certificate services you deploy and the security requirements you have specified for the certificates you intend to issue. You can issue certificate types that have multiple uses and that meet different security requirements.

For enterprise CAs, you can issue a variety of certificate types based on certificate templates and account privileges in a Windows 2000 domain. You can configure each enterprise CA to issue a specific selection of certificate types. Table 12.2 lists the different types of certificate templates available, and their purposes.

Table 12.2 Certificate Templates and Purposes

Certificate template name	Certificate purposes	Issued to
Administrator	Code signing, Microsoft trust list signing, EFS, secure e-mail, client authentication	People
Certification authority	All	Computers
ClientAuth	Client authentication (authenticated session)	People
CodeSigning	Code signing	People
CTLSigning	Microsoft trust list signing	People
Domain Controller	Client authentication, server authentication	Computers
EFS	Encrypting File System	People
EFSRecovery	File recovery	People
EnrollmentAgent	Certificate request agent	People
IPSECIntermediateOffline	IP Security	Computers
IPSECIntermediateOnline	IP Security	Computers
MachineEnrollmentAgent	Certificate request agent	Computers
Machine	Client authentication, server authentication	Computers

(continued)

Table 12.2 Certificate Templates and Purposes *(continued)*

Certificate template name	Certificate purposes	Issued to
OfflineRouter	Client authentication	Computers/routers
SmartcardLogon	Client authentication	People
SmartcardUser	Client authentication, secure e-mail	People
SubCA	All	Computers
User	Encrypting File System, secure e-mail, client authentication	People
UserSignature	Secure e-mail, client authentication	People
WebServer	Server authentication	Computers
CEP Encryption	Certificate request agent	Routers
Exchange Enrollment Agent (Offline Request)	Certificate request agent	People
Exchange User	Secure e-mail, client authentication	People
Exchange User Signature	Secure e-mail, client authentication	People

For stand-alone CAs, you can specify certificate uses in the certificate request. You can also use custom policy modules to specify the certificate types to be issued for stand-alone CAs. For more information about developing custom applications for Microsoft Certificate Services, see the Microsoft Platform SDK link on the Web Resources page at http://windows.microsoft.com/windows2000/reskit/webresources.

The types of certificates issued by third-party certificate services are determined by the specific features and functions of each third-party product. For more information, contact the vendor for the certificate service.

Define Certificate Policies and Certification Authority Practices

You can use Microsoft Certificate Services or other certificate services to create CAs for your organization. Before deploying CAs, define the certificate policies and certificate practice statements (CPSs) for your organization. A certificate policy specifies what a certificate should be used for, and the liability assumed by the CA for this use. A certificate practice statement specifies the practices that the CA employs to manage the certificates it issues. A CPS describes how the requirements of the certificate policy are implemented in the context of the operating policies, system architecture, physical security, and computing environment of the CA organization. For example, a certificate policy might specify that the private key cannot be exported, so the CPS describes how this is accomplished by the PKI that you deploy.

Certificate Policies

Certificate policies can include the following types of information:

- How users will be authenticated to the CA
- Legal issues, such as liability, that might arise if the CA becomes compromised or is used for the wrong purpose
- What purposes the certificate can be used for
- Private key management requirements, such as requiring storage on smart cards or other hardware devices
- Whether the private key can be exported
- Requirements for users of the certificates, including what users must do in case their private keys are lost or compromised
- Requirements for certificate enrollment and renewal
- Certificate lifetime
- Cryptographic algorithms to be used
- Minimum length of the public key and private key pairs

Certificate Practices Statements (CPS)

A CPS for a certification authority can meet the requirements of multiple certificate policies. Each CPS contains information specific to that CA. However, the CPS for a subordinate CA can refer to the CPS of a parent CA for general or common information. A CPS can include the following types of information:

- Positive identification of the CA (including CA name, server name, and DNS address)
- What certificate policies are implemented by the CA and what certificate types are issued
- Policies, procedures, and processes for issuing and renewing certificates
- Cryptographic algorithms, CSP, and key length used for the CA certificate
- Lifetime of the CA certificate
- Physical, network, and procedural security of the CA
- The certificate lifetime of each certificate issued by the CA
- Policies for revoking certificates, including conditions for certificate revocation such as employee termination and misuse of security privileges
- Policies for certificate revocation lists (CRLs), including CRL distribution points and publishing intervals
- Policy for renewing the CA's certificate before its expiration

Define Certification Authority Trust Strategies

Before deploying a Windows 2000 PKI, you need to define the CA trust strategies you want to use in your organization. With Windows 2000, you can establish trust for CAs using hierarchical CA trust chains and certificate trust lists.

Benefits of Certification Authority Trust Hierarchies

The Windows 2000 PKI has a hierarchical CA model. A CA hierarchy provides scalability, easy administration, and consistency with a growing number of third-party CA products.

In general, a hierarchy will contain multiple CAs with clearly defined parent-child relationships. In this model, subordinate CAs (children) are certified by (parent) CA-issued certificates, which bind a CA's public key to its identity.

The CA at the top of a hierarchy is referred to as a root CA. The CAs below the root in the hierarchy are referred to as subordinate CAs. In Windows 2000, if you trust a root CA (by having its certificate in your Trusted Root Certification Authorities store), you trust every subordinate authority in the hierarchy, unless a subordinate authority has had its certificate revoked by the issuing CA or has an expired certificate. Thus, any root CA is a very important point of trust in an organization and should be secured and maintained accordingly.

The advantage of this model is that verification of certificates requires trust in only a small number of root CAs. At the same time, it provides flexibility in terms of the number of certificate-issuing subordinate CAs. There are several practical reasons for deploying multiple subordinate CAs. These include:

Usage. Certificates can be issued for a number of purposes (for example, secure e-mail, network authentication, and so on). The issuing policy for these uses might be distinct, and separation provides a basis for administering these policies.

Organizational divisions. There can be different policies for issuing certificates, depending upon an entity's role in the organization. Again, you can create subordinate CAs to separate and administer these policies.

Geographic divisions. Organizations might have entities at multiple physical sites. Network connectivity between these sites might dictate a requirement for multiple subordinate CAs to meet usability requirements.

Multiple trust hierarchies also provide the following administrative benefits:

- Flexible configuration of the CA security environment (key strength, physical protection, protection against network attacks, and so on). You can tailor the CA environment to provide a balance between security and usability. For example, for a root CA, you can use special-purpose cryptographic hardware, maintain it in a locked vault, and operate it in offline mode. However, for an issuing CA, this same setup would be costly, make the CA difficult to use, and reduce the performance and effectiveness of the CA.

- The ability to frequently renew keys and certificates for those intermediate and issuing CAs that are at high risk for compromise, without requiring a change to established root trust relationships.

- The ability to turn off a subsection of the CA hierarchy without affecting established root trust relationships or the rest of the hierarchy.

In addition, deploying multiple issuing CAs provides the following benefits:

- Separate certificate policies for different categories of users and computers, or for organizational and geographic divisions. You can set up an issuing CA to provide certificates to each distinct category, department, or site.

- Distribution of certificate load and provision of redundant services. You can deploy multiple issuing CAs to distribute the certificate load to meet site, network, and server requirements. For example, slow or noncontinuous network links between sites can require issuing CAs at each site to meet certificate services performance and usability requirements. You can deploy issuing CAs to distribute certificate load as necessary to meet all site and network connectivity and load requirements. You can also deploy multiple issuing CAs to provide duplicate services. So if one CA fails, another issuing CA is available to provide uninterrupted service.

Benefits of Certificate Trust Lists

A certificate trust list is a list of self-signed certificates for the CAs whose certificates are to be trusted by your organization. A certificate trust list allows you to control the purpose and validity period of certificates issued by external certification authorities beyond what the certification authority specifies. Whenever you create a certificate trust list, you need to authorize it by signing the certificate trust list with a certificate issued by an already trusted certification authority.

There can be multiple certificate trust lists existing for a site. Because the uses of certificates for particular domains or organizational units (OUs) can be different, you can create certificate trust lists to reflect these uses, and assign a particular certificate trust list to a particular Group Policy object.

When you apply the Group Policy object to a site, domain, or OU, the policy is inherited by the corresponding computers. These computers then trust the CAs in the certificate trust list. You can also place the root CAs into Group Policy. Certificate trust lists are more convenient than using Group Policy because they expire.

You can create Windows 2000 certificate trust lists to provide the following benefits:

- **Creation of trust certificates from specific CAs without requiring broader trust for the root CA.** For example, you can use certificate trust lists on an extranet to trust certificates issued by certain commercial CAs. Users with certificates issued by the trusted commercial CAs can be granted permission to access restricted extranet resources by mapping the certificate to an account stored in Active Directory.

- **Restriction of the permitted use of certificates issued by trusted CAs.** For example, certificates issued by a CA might be valid for secure e-mail, network authentication, and signing software code. However, you can use a certificate trust list on an extranet to restrict the permitted use of certificates to secure mail only.

- **Control over how long third-party certificates and CAs are valid.** For example, a business partner's CA can have a lifetime of five years and issue certificates with lifetimes of one year. However, you can create a certificate trust list with a lifetime of six months to limit the time that certificates issued by the business partner's CA are trusted on your extranet.

Additional Considerations for Certification Authority Trust Strategies

Keep the following considerations in mind when defining your CA trust strategies:

- The depth of CA trust hierarchies is typically four levels (root CA, intermediate CA, issuing CA, and issued certificates).

- Third-party CAs can form all or part of the CA trust hierarchies, but to ensure that third-party CAs will provide the expected interoperability, test your proposed hierarchies in the lab.

- Some third-party products might require other CA trust models that might not be interoperable with rooted CA hierarchies. Windows 2000 and most commercial CAs support rooted CA hierarchies.

Define Security Requirements for Certification Authorities

You should define the security requirements to be provided for CAs. The security requirements for CAs can include the following:

- Using a hardware-based CSP for root CAs
- Maintaining root CAs in locked vaults
- Operating root CAs and sometimes intermediate CAs offline
- Keeping intermediate CAs and issuing CAs in secure data centers
- Longer keys for root certification authorities and high-level intermediate certification authorities

You can have an offline intermediate CA if you want to delegate authority from a parent company to a large number of separate organizations. You can then provide a subordinate CA for the subsidiary companies to keep offline.

Deciding on the security required for a CA involves determining a balance between the costs of implementing and maintaining security, and the risks of attack on the CA and the costs of a CA compromise. Higher risks of attacks on the CA and higher costs of a CA compromise justify higher costs for security measures to protect the CA. You should generally provide the most protection for root CAs, as well as provide more protection for intermediate CAs than for issuing CAs.

Protection for the root CA does not have to be expensive, especially for small companies. It might be adequate to have an offline root CA in a secure computer cabinet or to use removable media stored in a vault. The root CA computer should not have a network adapter.

Define Certificate Life Cycles

The certificate life cycle includes the following events:

- CAs installed and the certificates issued to them
- Certificates issued by CAs
- Certificates revoked (as necessary)
- Certificates renewed or expired
- CAs' certificates renewed or expired

You normally define the certificate life cycle to require periodic renewal of issued certificates. Issued certificates expire at the end of their lifetime and can be renewed in a cycle until revoked or expired, or until an issuing CA is unavailable. Each CA can issue certificates through several certificate renewal cycles until the CA approaches the end of its lifetime. At that time, the CA would either be retired because its keys are no longer useful, or the CA would be renewed with a new key pair.

You should define certificate life cycles that meet your business goals and security requirements. The life cycles you choose depend on various considerations, such as the following:

Length of private keys for CAs and issued certificates. In general, longer keys support longer certificate lifetimes and key lifetimes.

Security provided by the CSP. Typically, a hardware-based CSP is more difficult to compromise than a software-based CSP, and thus can support longer certificate lifetimes and key lifetimes.

Strength of the technology used for cryptographic operations. Some cryptographic technologies provide stronger security as well as support for stronger cryptographic algorithms. You can also use FORTEZZA Crypto Cards to provide stronger security than standard smart cards. Generally, cryptographic technology that is harder to break supports longer certificate lifetimes.

Security provided for CAs and their private keys. In general, the more physically secure the CA and its private key, the longer the CA lifetime.

Security provided for issued certificates and their private keys. For example, private keys stored on smart cards can be considered more secure than private keys stored as files on local hard disks because smart cards cannot be coerced to export the private key.

Risk of attack. The risk of attack depends on how secure your network is, how valuable the network resources protected by the CA trust chain are, and the cost of starting an attack.

How much trust you have for users of certificates. In general, lower trust requires shorter lifecycles and shorter key lifetimes. For example, you might trust temporary users less than normal business users, so you might issue temporary users' certificates with shorter lifetimes; you can also require stricter controls for renewal of temporary users' certificates.

The amount of administrative effort you are willing to devote to certificate renewal and CA renewal.

For example, to reduce the administrative effort required to renew CAs, you can specify long, safe lifetimes for your certification trust hierarchies.

Give careful consideration to how long you want CAs and issued certificates and keys to be trusted. The longer the certificates and private keys are valid, the greater the risk and potential for a security compromise.

You should define certificate life cycles that realistically balance your business goals with your security requirements. Unrealistically short life cycles can result in excessive administrative efforts required to maintain the life cycles. Unrealistically long life cycles increase the risk of security compromises.

When you renew certificates using Microsoft CSP, you can also renew the certificate's key pair. In general, the longer the key pair is in use, the higher the risk of the key becoming compromised. You should establish maximum allowable key lifetimes and renew certificates with new key pairs before these limits are exceeded.

After you define a life cycle, you can change it later by renewing CAs, certificates, or keys at different periods than you originally specified. For example, if you later decide that the lifetime of the root CA places the CA at greater risk of compromise than you originally estimated, you can renew the CA chain and adjust the life cycle as necessary to mitigate risks.

Define Certificate Enrollment and Renewal Processes

Define the certificate enrollment and renewal processes that you will use for your organization. Microsoft Certificate Services supports the following certificate enrollment and renewal methods:

- Interactive certificate requests with the Certificate Request wizard (for Windows 2000 users, computers, and services only).
- Automatic certificate requests with the Automatic Certificate Request setup wizard (for Windows 2000 computer certificates only).
- Interactive certificate requests with the Microsoft Certificate Services Web pages (for most Web browser clients).
- Smart card enrollment with the Smart Card Enrollment Station.
- Custom certificate enrollment and renewal applications using Microsoft Enrollment Control.

The certificate enrollment and renewal process that you choose is determined by the users and computers for which you intend to provide services. You can use the Certificate Request wizard only for Windows 2000 clients. However, you can use Web-based enrollment and renewal services for most clients with Web browsers.

You can use the Microsoft Certificate Services Web pages as they are, or you can customize the pages. For example, you can limit user options or provide additional links to online user instructions and user support information.

Define Certificate Revocation Policies

The certificate revocation policies of your organization include policies for revoking certificates and policies for certificate revocation lists (CRLs).

Policies for Revoking Certificates

Your certificate revocation policy specifies the circumstances that justify revoking a certificate. For example, you can specify that certificates must be revoked when employees are terminated or transferred to other business units. You can also specify that certificates must be revoked if users misuse their security privileges or the private keys are compromised (a lost smart card, for instance). For computer certificates, you can specify that certificates must be revoked if the computer is replaced or permanently removed from service, or if the key is compromised.

Policies for Certificate Revocation Lists

Your CRL policies specify where you will distribute CRLs and the publishing schedule for CRLs. For example, you can specify that certain CRLs will be distributed to commonly used public folders and Web pages, as well as to Active Directory. You can also specify that certain CRLs be published daily instead of using the default weekly publication.

Define Maintenance Strategies

Define your maintenance and disaster recovery strategies for CAs. Maintenance and disaster recovery strategies include the following:

- Types of backups you will perform for CAs
- Schedules for conducting backups of CAs
- Policies for restoring CAs
- Policies for EFS recovery agents
- Policies for secure mail recovery

Developing Recovery Plans

You can develop recovery plans to help restore CAs if certificate services fail or CAs are compromised. Test recovery plans to ensure that they work as intended, and train your administrative staff how to use the recovery plans.

Recovery plans can include the following:

- Recovery procedures and checklists for administrators to follow
- Recovery toolkits or pointers to the toolkits
- Contingency plans

For more information about backup and recovery in Windows 2000, see "Determining Windows 2000 Storage Management Strategies" in this book.

Failed Certification Authority

A CA can fail for a variety of reasons, such as a server hard drive failure, a failed network adapter, or a server motherboard failure. Some failures can be quickly corrected by locating and correcting the problem with the CA server. For example, you can replace a failed network adapter or a failed motherboard and restart the computer to restore certificate services.

If a hard disk has failed, you can replace the hard disk and restore the server and the CA from the most recent backup set. If the CA is damaged or corrupted, you can restore the CA from the most recent backup set on the server.

If you must replace the server, configure the new server with the same network name and IP address as the failed CA server. You can then use Windows 2000 Backup or the Certification Authorities Restore wizard to restore the CA from the most recent backup set.

Compromised Certification Authority

When a CA has been compromised, you must revoke the CA's certificate. Revoking a CA's certificate invalidates the CA and its subordinate CAs, as well as invalidating all certificates issued by the CA and its subordinate CAs. If you discover a compromised CA, perform the following activities as soon as possible:

- Revoke the compromised CA's certificate. If the CA has been renewed, revoke all of the CA's certificates only if all related keys have been compromised.
- Publish a new CRL containing the revoked CA certificate. Note that client applications can store the CRL until it expires, so you will not see the newly published CRL until the old one expires.

- Remove compromised CA certificates from Trusted Root Certification Authorities stores and CTLs.
- Notify all affected users and administrators of the compromise and inform them that certificates issued by the affected CAs are being revoked.
- Repair whatever led to the compromise.

To restore the CA hierarchy, you must deploy new CAs, or renew a CA's certificate and generate a new key to replace the compromised hierarchy. You must then reissue the appropriate certificates to users, computers, and services. Depending on where in the hierarchy the revocation occurred, it could require a new CA hierarchy or only a portion of it.

Developing Optional Custom Applications

You can deploy a wide variety of public key security solutions with the standard components and features of Windows 2000 PKI. However, you can also develop custom applications using the Microsoft CryptoAPI.

Using CryptoAPI, you can develop Custom Policy modules and custom exit modules to integrate certificate services with existing databases and third-party directory services. For example, you can develop an application that validates certificate requests from user information contained in an existing database or a third-party directory service.

You can also develop a custom application that uses special types of certificates. For example, you can develop an application that creates a digital thumbprint of an electronic document and then stores the thumbprint in a time- and date-stamped certificate. You can maintain these stamped certificates in a document registry database to provide integrity for the original document contents. When a document is compared to the digital thumbprint in the registry database, any tampering or modifications to the document since it was registered will be identified. You can use a document registry like this to provide an online, quality-assurance audit trail for products you manufacture, and thus ensure the integrity of electronic test and certification documentation.

In addition, you can develop a custom certificate enrollment and renewal application with Active Server Pages. For example, you can modify the standard Microsoft Certificate Services Web pages to add or delete features. You can also develop custom Web pages that integrate with third-party services or other applications that you develop.

For more information about developing custom applications for Microsoft Certificate Services, see the Microsoft Platform SDK link on the Web Resources page at http://windows.microsoft.com/windows2000/reskit/webresources.

Performing Resource Planning

You should estimate the network, computing, and facilities resources required to support the certificate services you intend to deploy in your organization. The total number of resources required can vary considerably depending on the size of your organization and the level and scope of the PKI you deploy.

When estimating resources, consider the resources required to support short-term needs and projected long-term growth of your organization.

The network and computing resources required for deployment include the following:

- Server computers that run certificate services and custom applications
- Cryptographic hardware, such as crypto-accelerator boards
- Hard disk storage for the certificate database and custom applications
- Storage resources for backups of CAs and custom applications
- Disaster recovery resources, such as recovery kits and hot-standby replacement servers

Certificate services performance can vary considerably depending on the following factors:

- **Length of the CA key used to sign certificates.** The longer the key, the more processing power and time are required to sign a certificate. It should be noted that a signing operation is performed (on the server) once per certificate at the time of issuance, while a verification operation is performed many times throughout the lifetime of a certificate (on the client or another server, depending on the protocol). Note that signing a certificate is more expensive than verifying it.

- **Complexity of the certification authority policy module logic used to validate certificate requests.** The more complex the policy logic, the longer it takes to process and issue certificates. Most people will find the Windows 2000 enterprise and stand-alone policy module sufficient. If you want to develop a custom policy module, the cost of complexity should be considered both in the policy module and the exit module.

- **Performance impact of custom applications.** Custom applications affect the overall performance of certificate applications. For example, a certificate enrollment application that uses standard Common Gateway Interface (CGI) scripts can add significant delays to the enrollment process.

The hard disk capacity required to support the certificate databases depends on the following factors:

- **How many certificates are issued by the CA.** Project how many certificates will be issued for the life of the CA. A CA that issues a large number of certificates or that has a longer lifetime will require a larger certificate database.

- **The size of each certificate.** The certificate database includes all information in the certificates, including the public keys. Certificates that have larger public keys and that contain additional special information will consume more disk space per certificate issued.

Some large certificate databases might be several gigabytes or more. However, significantly smaller certificate databases are not normally expected to exceed several hundred megabytes in size. You should measure representative certificate database sizes in the lab and then extrapolate future database sizes based on the projected number of certificates you expect each CA to issue in its lifetime.

Deploying Your Public Key Infrastructure

After your public key design and deployment strategies have been validated and refined by pilot programs, you can deploy the PKI into your production environment. The following list shows a basic production rollout process that you can use to deploy your PKI.

Deploying the PKI includes the following activities:

- Scheduling production rollout in stages
- Providing training and support for production users
- Installing CAs
- Installing and configuring support systems or applications
- Configuring the certificates to be issued
- Configuring publication of certificate revocation lists
- Configuring public key Group Policy
- Configuring certificate renewal and enrollment
- Issuing certificates to users, computers, and certification authorities

Schedule Production Rollout in Stages

For large enterprise deployments, schedule the public key production rollout in stages. You can roll out different portions of the infrastructure as necessary to support your security goals and business needs.

For example, you might begin with EFS and IPSec features because you do not have to establish a CA hierarchy to get the security benefits of these features. You might place the next highest priority on secure mail and smart card authentication. You can choose to schedule rollout of the secure mail infrastructure before rollout of the smart card infrastructure, or you can choose to schedule secure mail to one group or site and simultaneously roll out the smart card infrastructure to another group or site.

To roll out the PKI for secure mail, you can schedule the following activities for each stage of the rollout:

- Install root CAs for secure mail in the parent domains for each tree in your organization (root CAs are used to certify intermediate CAs in that domain or a subdomain).
- Install and configure secure mail system and services (as necessary).
- Install intermediate CAs for secure mail in the domains or subdomains for each business unit (each business unit certifies and installs issuing CAs for its user groups).
- Install and configure issuing CAs (certified by the business unit) and certificate enrollment services in the domains or subdomains for user groups at each site, as necessary.

To roll out the PKI for smart cards, you can schedule the following activities for each stage of the rollout:

- Install root CAs for smart cards in the parent domains for each tree in your organization (root CAs are used to certify intermediate CAs in that domain or a subdomain).
- Install and configure smart card readers for users and smart card administrators.
- Install intermediate CAs for smart cards in the domains or subdomains for each business unit (each business unit certifies and installs issuing CAs for its user groups).
- Install and configure issuing CAs (certified by the business unit) and smart card enrollment stations in the domains or subdomains for user groups at each site, as necessary.

In addition, you can schedule the rollout of other portions of the PKI to support additional public key security functions such as secure Web communications and secure Web sites, software code signing, IPSec authentication, and EFS user and recovery operations.

Install Certification Authorities

You must install the CA hierarchies necessary to provide the required certificate services for your organization. You install the root CA first and then each subordinate CA in the hierarchy. For example, to create a three-level CA hierarchy and trust chain, you install CAs on server computers in the following order:

1. Root CA
2. Intermediate CAs
3. Issuing CAs

The root CA certificate is self-signed. Each subordinate CA is certified (issued its certificate) by the parent CA in the hierarchy. In the example of a three-level certificate hierarchy, each intermediate CA is certified by the root CA and each issuing CA is certified by an intermediate CA in the hierarchy.

Note It is possible for an intermediate CA to be certified by another intermediate CA, creating a deeper hierarchy.

You can install enterprise CAs, stand-alone CAs, or third-party CAs to create the required trust chains. To create a Windows 2000 Server CA, use the **Add/Remove Software wizard** in Control Panel to add Microsoft Certificate Services to each CA server.

During installation of Windows 2000 Server subordinate CAs, you can request the subordinate CA certificate from an online CA, or you can save the certificate request to a request file and make the certificate request offline. If you make an offline CA certificate request, the CA is not certified. You must manually use the Certification Authority MMC snap-in to import the CA's certificate and complete the CA installation after the certification authority's certificate has been issued by the parent CA. You can also use the same snap-in to import subordinate CA certificates issued by third-party parent CAs.

Install and Configure Supporting Systems and Applications

You must install any systems or applications required to support the PKI. Supporting systems and applications can include:

- Smart card readers at local computers
- Secure e-mail and key management systems

- Custom policy and exit modules
- Custom certificate enrollment and renewal applications
- Third-party PKI and certificate services
- Hardware-based cryptographic cards for acceleration and key storage on servers

Configure Certificates to Be Issued

By default, Windows 2000 enterprise CAs are installed ready to issue several certificate types. You can modify the default configuration by using the Certification Authority MMC snap-in to specify the certificate types to be issued by each CA. You can delete default certificate types that you do not want the CA to issue. You can also add more certificate types for the CA to issue.

Examples of Configurations

You can configure CAs to support multiple security functions or only one security function. Following are some ways you can configure CAs:

- For a root CA or an intermediate CA, you can configure the CA so it can issue subordinate certification authority certificates only.
- For an issuing CA that supports secure Web communication services, you can configure the CA so it can issue authenticated session, computer, and Web server certificates only.
- For an issuing CA that supports general business users, you can configure the CA so it can issue user certificates only. Likewise, you can configure a CA that supports administrators to issue administrator certificates only.
- For an issuing CA that supports smart card enrollment, you can configure the CA so it can issue smart card logon and smart card user certificates only.

Security Access Control Lists for Certificate Templates

Permission to request certificate types is controlled by the security access control lists for each certificate template. An enterprise CA grants certificate requests only for users, computers, or services that have the Enroll permission selected in the security access control list for that certificate template. The security access control lists for certificate templates are preconfigured to enable various default user accounts and security groups to enroll for certificate types.

You can use the Active Directory Sites and Services MMC snap-in to modify the security access control lists for each certificate template.

▶ **To modify the security access control lists for each certificate template**

1. On the **View** menu, click **Show Services Node**.

2. Expand the Services node and the Public Key Services and Certificate Templates containers.

3. Select a certificate template in the details pane and click the **Security** tab of its Properties sheet. This tab shows the groups that have access to this template, and the specific permissions of each group.

For example, by default, only members of the Domain Administrators security group can request and obtain enrollment agent certificates. However, to specify that only certain members of your security department can request and obtain enrollment agent certificates, you can change the security access control list for the enrollment agent certificate template. You can remove domain admins from the access control list and add the appropriate user accounts or security groups.

For Windows 2000 stand-alone CAs, information about the certificate type must be included in the certificate request because stand-alone CAs do not use certificate templates. You can use stand-alone CAs with custom policy modules and custom certificate request applications to control the types of certificates that are issued.

Configure Certificate Revocation List Publication

By default, enterprise CAs publish CRLs weekly to Active Directory. By default, stand-alone and enterprise CAs publish CRLs weekly to a directory on the CA server. You can use the Certification Authority MMC snap-in to modify the point at which the CRL is distributed. You can also use the Certification Authority snap-in to interactively publish a new CRL or to change the publication schedule.

Configure Public Key Group Policy

You can use the Group Policy MMC snap-in to configure public key Group Policy for sites, domains, and organizational units. You can configure the following optional categories of public key policy:

EFS Recovery Agents

By default, the local Administrator user account for the first domain controller installed in the domain is the EFS recovery account for that domain. You can specify alternate encrypted data recovery agents for EFS by importing the appropriate alternate agent's EFS recovery agent certificate into policy. Therefore, you must first issue EFS recovery agent certificates to the user accounts on the local computers that you want to use as alternate recovery agents.

Automatic Certificate Enrollment

You can specify automatic enrollment and renewal for computer certificates. When automatic enrollment is configured, the specified certificate types are issued to all computers within the scope of the public key Group Policy. Computer certificates issued by automatic enrollment are renewed from the issuing CA. Automatic enrollment does not function unless at least one enterprise CA is online to process certificate requests.

For virtual private networks (VPNs) using IPSec with L2TP, remember to set up Group Policy to permit automatic enrollment for IPSec certificates. In Table 12.2, any Rivest-Shamir-Adleman (RSA)-signed certificate issued to a computer that is stored in the computer account can be used for IPSec. For more information about certificates for L2TP over IPSec VPN connections, see Windows 2000 Server Help.

Root Certificate Trust

When you install an enterprise root CA, the CA's certificate is added to the trusted root certification authorities for the domain. You can also interactively add certificates for other root CAs to the Trusted Root Certification Authorities container in the Group Policy MMC snap-in. The root CA certificates that you add become trusted root CAs within Group Policy. If you want to use a stand-alone CA or a third-party CA as a root CA in a certification hierarchy, you need to add the CA's certificate to the trusted root certification authorities container in Group Policy.

Certificate Trust Lists

You can create certificate trust lists to trust specific CAs and to restrict the uses of certificates issued by the CAs. For example, you can use a certificate trust list to trust certificates issued by a commercial CA and restrict the permitted uses for those certificates. You can also use certificate trust lists to control trust on an extranet for certificates issued by CAs that are managed by your business partners.

For instance, your company might be engaged in a joint venture with another company. The partner company could issue its own certificates for Web access, secure e-mail, software signing, and so forth. You might want to exchange secure e-mail with employees of the partner company, but you do not want to issue certificates for this purpose. You can add the other company's root CA to a new certificate trust list in your enterprise trust container, specifying that the partner certificates will be trusted for e-mail only.

Configure Certificate Enrollment and Renewal

Microsoft Certificate Services supports a variety of enrollment and renewal methods, such as certificate requests with the Certificate Request wizard and certificate requests with the Microsoft Certificate Services Web pages. However, if you deploy third-party certificate services or custom certificate enrollment and renewal applications, you must perform any configuration required for those services and applications.

Start Issuing Certificates

When the required certificate services are installed and configured, you can start issuing certificates to users, computers, and services. Keep the following considerations in mind when you start to issue certificates:

- Certificates are issued for computers within the scope of the Automatic Certificate Request settings of the domain's Group Policy. Administrators can also manually request certificates for local computers with the Certificate Request wizard or the Microsoft Certificate Services Web pages. Consider scheduling manual enrollment in stages to help distribute the administrative workload for computer enrollment.

- Smart card administrators can start issuing smart card certificates with the Smart Card Enrollment Station available on the Microsoft Certificate Services Web pages. Consider scheduling smart card enrollment in stages to help distribute the administrative workload for smart card enrollment.

- During the transition to smart cards, you usually enable both smart card authentication and the CTRL+ALT+DEL secure logon sequence. However, because this weakens network security, configure user account policy to require smart cards to log on interactively as soon as smart card users are trained and are using their cards.

Monitor the performance of certificate services closely as you start issuing certificates to ensure that CAs handle the certificate load. To correct excessive load conditions, consider adding more issuing CAs or scheduling certificate enrollment in smaller stages. Certificate renewal might also produce excessive load conditions, so adding more CAs and scheduling certificate enrollment in smaller stages can also help distribute peak renewal loads.

Public Key Infrastructure Planning Task List

Table 12.4 summarizes the tasks you need to perform when planning PKI deployment.

Table 12.4   Public Key Infrastructure Planning Task List

Task	Location in chapter
Identify certificate requirements.	Identify Your Certificate Requirements
Define processes for issuing certificates.	Defining Certificate Policies and Certification Authority Practices
Define CA trust hierarchy.	Define Certification Authority Trust Strategies
Define security requirements for CAs.	Define Security Requirements for Certification Authorities
Define certificate life cycles.	Define Certificate Life Cycles
Define certificate enrollment and renewal processes.	Define Certificate Enrollment and Renewal Processes
Define certificate revocation policies.	Define Certificate Revocation Policies
Define maintenance policies.	Define Maintenance Strategies
Define disaster recovery strategies.	Developing Recovery Plans
Create a rollout plan and schedule.	Deploying Your Public Key Infrastructure

P A R T   4

Windows 2000 Upgrade and Installation

Having the capability to automate the upgrade and installation of Microsoft® Windows® 2000 can save your organization valuable deployment time. Part 4 explains the various automated installation methods, provides detailed steps to assist you in this process, and shows you how to use Terminal Services with Windows 2000.

In This Part

CHAPTER 13

Automating Server Installation and Upgrade

You are now ready to develop and perform the automated installation of Microsoft® Windows® 2000 Server and associated applications. This is a prerequisite for performing any level of deployment—test, pilot, or production rollout. This chapter presents the automated installation methods that are available, including preparation requirements and example configurations. It is recommended that network engineers involved in the design of the installation process and system administrators involved in the installation of Windows 2000 and associated applications become familiar with this chapter.

Installing Windows 2000 Server involves either clean installations to computers that have no pre– Microsoft® Windows® 2000 operating systems installed, or clean installations and upgrades to computers currently running Microsoft® Windows NT® Server version 3.51 or Microsoft® Windows NT® Server version 4.0. The information in this chapter will help you determine whether to perform clean installations or upgrades.

In This Chapter

Chapter Goals

This chapter will help you develop the following planning document:

- Automated Installation Plan

Related Information in the Resource Kit

- For more information about planning, see the "Planning Overview" in this book.

- For more information about administering client computers, see "Defining Client Administration and Configuration Standards" in this book.

- For more information about automating client installation, see "Automating Client Installation and Upgrade" in this book.

- For more information about the unattended setup parameters referenced in this chapter, see the "Microsoft Windows 2000 Guide to Unattended Setup" (Unattend.doc) on the Windows 2000 operating system CD. The Unattend.doc file is part of the Deploy.cab file in the \Support\Tools folder. In Windows 98 or Windows 2000, use Windows Explorer to extract this document. In Windows 95 and earlier, or from MS-DOS, use the **Extract** command to access the file.

- For more information about unattended setup, including sample answer files, see the Appendix "Sample Answer Files for Unattended Setup" in this book.

Determining Whether to Upgrade or Clean Install

In the enterprise environment, it is not cost effective to install Windows 2000 using the standard interactive setup on each computer. To greatly lower the total cost of ownership (TCO), you can perform automated installations of Windows 2000 Server on multiple computers.

 Critical Decision   Before you can automate the installation of Windows 2000 Professional, you must decide whether the installation will be an upgrade from Windows NT or a clean installation.

The following two items will help you determine whether to upgrade or to perform a clean installation.

- If your organization has already implemented a Windows operating system and your information technology (IT) department is centrally managed, you will want to perform an upgrade. If you are planning to create a managed environment but one does not currently exist in your organization, then you will want to perform a clean installation so that you can implement standard configurations as you perform your installation.

- If you plan to use currently existing hardware and software applications, then you will need to perform an upgrade. Alternatively, if you plan to purchase new hardware and install new software applications, you will need to perform a clean installation.

Resolving Critical Planning Issues

If you plan to install Windows 2000 Server on computers that have no pre-Windows 2000 operating systems installed, a clean installation is the obvious choice. If the computers are currently running Windows 95, Windows 98, Windows NT Workstation 3.51, or Windows NT Workstation 4.0, you need to determine whether it is more cost-effective to upgrade the existing operating system or perform a clean installation.

Table 13.1   Planning Issues to Be Resolved Before Upgrade or Installation

Issue	Task
Organizational goals	Define your company's primary goals.
Regional needs	Identify specific regional needs and determine whether business will include international branches or companies.

(continued)

Table 13.1   Planning Issues to Be Resolved Before Upgrade or Installation
(continued)

Issue	Task
User groups	Analyze user groups, including specific job categories and needs, computer knowledge and experience of users, security requirements, and locations of users and their network connectivity issues, including link speed.
Application needs	Determine which products are going to be preinstalled on all computers, which products are going to be advertised only to specific server types, and which products are going to be distributed to specific categories of server types.
Hardware	Inventory existing hardware and determine expectations for new hardware.
	Set minimum hardware requirements before upgrade or installation.
	Plan for future computer needs.
	Determine how computers are cycled through the organization.
	Determine whether all computers have bootable compact discs.
Risks and problem areas	Identify potential risks, including application incompatibility with Windows 2000, timeline issues, multiple sites, noncentralized budget, or the impact of possible upcoming mergers.
Growth expectations	Identify growth expectations over the course of the project at 1 year, 3 years, and 5 years. Also take into account planned mergers, new sites, and planned growth in other countries.
Network concerns	Determine whether remote sites have application deployment servers. Identify how servers outside the central site are upgraded.
Software management	Determine whether a software management system is in place, such as Microsoft® Systems Management Server, in which deployments can be scheduled.
Connectivity	Determine whether the servers and the connections between them are set up to distribute large packages to all users in the company.

Choosing Your Installation Method

After you have resolved these planning issues, you can choose the methods you will use to automate the installations. Table 13.2 lists the automated installation methods and shows whether they can be used for upgrade, clean installation, or both.

Table 13.2   Automated Installation Methods

Method	Windows 2000 Edition	Upgrade	Clean Installation
Syspart	Server and Professional	No	Yes
Sysprep	Server and Professional	No	Yes
SMS	Server and Professional	Yes	Yes
Bootable CD	Server and Professional	No	Yes
Remote Operating System Installation	Professional	No	Yes

Preparing for Installation

To prepare for the clean installation of Windows 2000 Server, you need to do the following:

- Create the distribution folder.
- Understand how to use the answer file.
- Understand the Windows 2000 Setup commands.

Note The principles of performing an automated installation that are described in this section apply to both a clean installation and an upgrade. The most common scenario is to perform a clean installation.

Figure 13.1 is a flowchart showing the installation process.

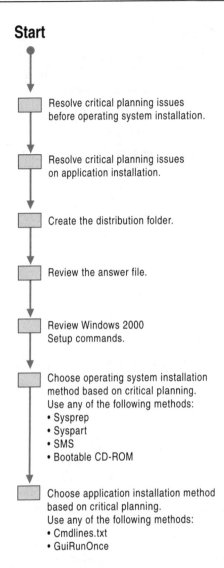

Start

Resolve critical planning issues
before operating system installation.

Resolve critical planning issues
on application installation.

Create the distribution folder.

Review the answer file.

Review Windows 2000
Setup commands.

Choose operating system installation
method based on critical planning.
Use any of the following methods:
• Sysprep
• Syspart
• SMS
• Bootable CD-ROM

Choose application installation method
based on critical planning.
Use any of the following methods:
• Cmdlines.txt
• GuiRunOnce

Figure 13.1   Automated Installation Flowchart

Creating Distribution Folders

To install Windows 2000 Server on multiple computers over a network, you must create at least one set of distribution folders. The distribution folders typically reside on a server where computers can connect and install Windows 2000 by running Winnt.exe or Winnt32.exe on the destination computer. You can use the same set of distribution folders with different answer files for different system implementations. Even if you intend to use disk imaging as your installation method, starting with distribution folders will provide consistent implementations for a variety of system types. In addition, you can use distribution folders to update future images by modifying the files in the distribution folders or by modifying the answer files to generate updated images without having to start from the beginning.

To help load balance the servers and make the file-copy phase of Windows 2000 Setup faster for computers already running Microsoft® Windows® 95, Windows 98, Windows NT, or Windows 2000, you can create distribution folders on multiple servers. You can then run Winnt32.exe with up to eight sourcefile locations. For more information about Setup commands, see "Reviewing the Windows 2000 Setup Commands" later in this chapter.

Note In this chapter, the term "Windows NT" refers to both Microsoft® Windows NT® 3.51 and Microsoft® Windows NT® 4.0.

The distribution folders contain the Windows 2000 Server or Microsoft® Windows® 2000 Advanced Server installation files, as well as any device drivers and other files needed for installation.

Setup Manager, a tool that is available on the Windows 2000 Server CD, can help you automate the process of creating a distribution folder. For more information about Setup Manager, see "Reviewing the Answer File" later in this chapter.

Note In this chapter, "Windows 2000 Setup" is also referred to as "Setup."

▶ **To create a distribution folder**

1. Connect to the network server on which you want to create the distribution folder.

2. Create an \i386 folder on the distribution share of the network server.

   To help differentiate between multiple distribution shares for the different versions of Windows 2000 (Microsoft® Windows 2000 Professional, Microsoft® Windows 2000 Server, and one for Microsoft® Windows 2000 Advanced Server), you can choose another name for this folder. If you plan to use localized language versions of Windows 2000 for international branches of your organization, you can create separate distribution shares for each localized version.

3. Copy the contents of the \i386 folder from the Windows 2000 Server CD to the folder that you created.

4. In the folder you created, create a subfolder named \OEM.

   The \OEM subfolder provides the necessary folder structure for supplemental files to be copied to the target computer during Setup. These files include drivers, tools, applications, and any other files required to deploy Windows 2000 Server within your organization.

Structuring the Distribution Folder

An example structure for the distribution folder is shown in Figure 13.2.

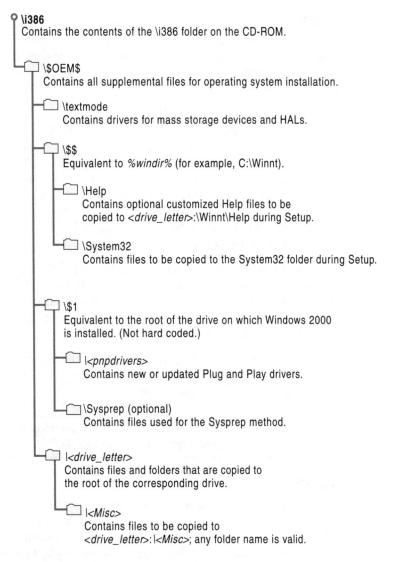

\i386
Contains the contents of the \i386 folder on the CD-ROM.

\OEM
Contains all supplemental files for operating system installation.

\textmode
Contains drivers for mass storage devices and HALs.

\$$
Equivalent to *%windir%* (for example, C:\Winnt).

\Help
Contains optional customized Help files to be copied to *<drive_letter>*:\Winnt\Help during Setup.

\System32
Contains files to be copied to the System32 folder during Setup.

\$1
Equivalent to the root of the drive on which Windows 2000 is installed. (Not hard coded.)

<pnpdrivers>
Contains new or updated Plug and Play drivers.

\Sysprep (optional)
Contains files used for the Sysprep method.

<drive_letter>
Contains files and folders that are copied to the root of the corresponding drive.

<Misc>
Contains files to be copied to *<drive_letter>*:*<Misc>*; any folder name is valid.

Figure 13.2   Example Structure for the Distribution Folder

\I386

This is the distribution folder, which contains all of the files required to install Windows 2000. You create this folder at the root of the distribution share by copying the contents of the \i386 folder on the Windows 2000 Server CD to the distribution folder.

\$OEM\$

You create the \$OEM\$ subfolder in the distribution folder directly beneath the \I386 folder. During Setup you can automatically copy directories, standard 8.3 format files, and any tools needed for your automated installation process to the \$OEM\$ subfolder.

Note that if you use the OEMFILESPATH key in the answer file, you can create the \$OEM\$ subfolder outside of the distribution folder. The answer file is defined in "Reviewing the Answer File" later in this chapter. For more information about answer file parameters and syntax, see "Microsoft Windows 2000 Guide to Unattended Setup" (Unattend.doc) on the Microsoft Windows 2000 operating system CD. The Unattend.doc file is part of the Deploy.cab file in the \Support\Tools folder. In Windows 98 or Windows 2000, use Windows Explorer to extract this document. In Windows 95 and earlier, or in MS-DOS, use the **Extract** command to access the file.

\$OEM\$ can contain the optional file Cmdlines.txt, which contains a list of commands to be run during the Graphical User Interface (GUI) portion of Setup. These commands can be used to install additional tools that you want to include with your installations. For more information about the Cmdlines.txt file, see "Using Cmdlines.txt" later in this chapter.

As long as Setup finds the \$OEM\$ subfolder in the root of the distribution point, it will copy all of the files found in this directory to the temporary directory that is created during the text portion of Setup.

Note In this chapter, the GUI portion of Setup is referred to as "GUI mode," and the text portion of Setup is referred to as "text mode."

\$OEM\$\Textmode

The \$OEM\$\Textmode subfolder contains new or updated files for installing mass storage device drivers and hardware abstraction layers (HALs). These files can include OEM HALs, drivers for small computer system interface (SCSI) devices, and Txtsetup.oem, which directs the loading and installing of these components.

Make sure to include the Txtsetup.oem file. All files placed in the \$OEM\$\Textmode subfolder (HALs, drivers and Txtsetup.oem) must be listed in the [OEMBootFiles] section of the answer file.

\$OEM\$\\$$

The \$OEM\$\\$$ subfolder corresponds to the %systemroot% or %windir% environment variables. The subfolder contains additional files that you want copied to the various subfolders of the Windows 2000 installation directory. The structure of this subfolder must match the structure of a standard Windows 2000 installation, where \$OEM\$\\$$ matches %systemroot% or %windir% (for example, C:\Winnt), \$OEM\$\\$$\System32 matches %windir%\System32, and so on. Each subfolder needs to contain the files that will be copied to the corresponding system folder on the target computer.

\$OEM\$\\$1

The \$OEM\$\\$1 subfolder, which is new for Windows 2000, points to the drive on which Windows 2000 is installed. The term **$1** is equivalent to the %systemdrive% environment variable. For example, if you are installing Windows 2000 on drive D, \$OEM\$\\$1 points to drive D.

\$OEM\$\\$1*Pnpdrvrs*

The \$OEM\$\\$1*Pnpdrvrs* subfolder, which is new for Windows 2000, allows you to place new or updated Plug and Play device drivers in your distribution folders. These folders are copied to the %systemdrive%*Pnpdrvrs* location on the target computer. Adding the OemPnPDriversPath parameter to your answer file tells Windows 2000 to look (both during and after Setup) for new or updated Plug and Play drivers in the folders that you created, as well as those originally included with the system. Note that you can replace *Pnpdrvrs* with a name that is eight characters or less.

\$OEM\$\\$1\Sysprep

The \$OEM\$\\$1\Sysprep subfolder is optional. This subfolder contains the files that you need to run the Sysprep utility. These files are described in "Using Sysprep to Duplicate Disks" later in this chapter.

\$OEM\$*Drive_letter*

During text mode, the structure of each \$OEM\$*Drive_letter* subfolder is copied to the root of the corresponding drive in the target computer. For example, files that you place in the \$OEM\$\D subfolder are copied to the root of drive D. You can also create subfolders within these subfolders. For example, \$OEM\$\E\Misc causes Setup to create a \Misc subfolder on drive E.

Files that have to be renamed must be listed in $$Rename.txt. For more information about renaming files, see "Converting File Name Size Using $$Rename.txt" later in this chapter. Note that the files in the distribution folders must have short file names (format 8.3).

Installing Mass Storage Devices

In Windows 2000, Plug and Play detects and installs most hardware devices, which can be loaded later during Setup. However, mass storage devices, such as hard disks, must be properly installed for full Plug and Play support to be available during GUI mode.

Note You do not need to specify a device if it is already supported by Windows 2000.

To install SCSI devices during text mode—that is, before full Plug and Play support is available—you must provide a Txtsetup.oem file that describes how Setup must install the particular SCSI device.

Important Before you use updated drivers, verify that they are signed. If they are not signed, Setup will fail. You can check the signed status for individual drivers in Device Manager, or you can run Sigverif.exe to generate a Sigverif.txt file in the %windir% subfolder. Sigverif.txt lists the signed status for all drivers on the system.

▶ **To install a mass storage device**

1. Create the \Textmode subfolder in the \OEM subfolder in the distribution folder.

2. Copy the following files, which you can obtain from the device vendor, to the \Textmode subfolder (replace the word *Driver* with the appropriate driver name):

    - *Driver*.sys
    - *Driver*.dll
    - *Driver*.inf
    - Txtsetup.oem

    Note Some drivers, such as SCSI miniport drivers, might not include a .dll file.

    ---

3. In the answer file, create a [MassStorageDrivers] section, and in this section type the driver entries that you want to include. For example, a possible entry in the [MassStorageDrivers] section would be:

    ```
    "Adaptec 2940..." = "OEM"
    ```

Information for this section can be obtained from the Txtsetup.oem file, which is provided by the hardware manufacturer.

For more information about answer file parameters and syntax, see the "Microsoft Windows 2000 Guide to Unattended Setup" (Unattend.doc) on the Windows 2000 operating system CD. The Unattend.doc file is part of the Deploy.cab file in the \Support\Tools folder. On Windows 98 or Windows 2000, use Windows Explorer to extract this document. In Windows 95 and earlier, or from MS-DOS, use the **Extract** command to access the file.

4. In the answer file, create an [OEMBootFiles] section, and in this section type a list of the files in the OEM\Textmode folder. For example:

```
[OEMBootFiles]
<Driver>.sys
<Driver>.dll
<Driver>.inf
Txtsetup.oem
```

Where <Driver> is the driver name.

5. If your mass storage device is a Plug and Play device, it will have a section called [HardwareIds.Scsi.*yyyyy*] in the Txtsetup.oem file. If your mass storage device does not have such a section, you will need to create one and then type the following entry in the section:

```
id = "xxxxx", "yyyyy"
```

where *xxxxx* represents the device id, and *yyyyy* represents the service associated with the device.

For example, to install the Symc810 driver, which has a device identifier (ID) of PCI\VEN_1000&DEV_0001, verify that your Txtsetup.oem file contains the following additional section:

```
[HardwareIds.scsi.symc810]
id = "PCI\VEN_1000&DEV_0001", "symc810"
```

Installing Hardware Abstraction Layers

To specify hardware abstraction layers (HALs) for installation, you need a Txtsetup.oem file and the HAL files, which the vendor provides. You must use the same Txtsetup.oem file if you are installing mass storage device drivers. Only one Txtsetup.oem file can be used, so if you need to install HALs and mass storage device drivers, you need to combine the entries into one file.

To use third-party drivers, you must also make appropriate changes to the answer file. For more information about answer file parameters and syntax, see the "Microsoft Windows 2000 Guide to Unattended Setup" (Unattend.doc) on the Microsoft Windows 2000 operating system CD. The Unattend.doc file is part of the Deploy.cab file in the \Support\Tools folder. On Windows 98 or Windows 2000, use Windows Explorer to extract this document. In Windows 95 and earlier, or from MS-DOS, use the **Extract** command to access the file.

▶ **To install a HAL**

1. If you have not already done so, create a \Textmode subfolder in the \OEM folder.

2. Copy the files that you receive from the device vendor to the \Textmode subfolder.

3. In the answer file, edit the [Unattend] section for the HAL and add any drivers you want to install. For example:

```
[Unattend]
Computertype = "<HALDescription   >", OEM
```

Information for the <HALDescription> can be obtained from the [Computer] section of the Txtsetup.oem file from the driver provider.

4. In the answer file, create an [OEMBootFiles] section, and enter the names of the files in the OEM\Textmode folder.

Installing Plug and Play Devices

The following procedure demonstrates how to install Plug and Play devices that are not mass storage devices or HALs, and are not included on the Windows 2000 operating system CD.

▶ **To install Plug and Play devices**

1. Create a subfolder in the distribution folder for special Plug and Play drivers and their .inf files. For example, you can create a folder called PnPDrvs:

```
$OEM$\$1\PnPDrvs
```

2. Add the path to the list of Plug and Play search drives by adding the following line to the answer file:

```
OEMPnPDriversPath = "PnPDrvs"
```

If you have subfolders in the PnPDrvs folder, you must specify the path to each subfolder. The paths must be separated by semicolons.

To easily maintain the folders so that they can accommodate future device drivers, make sure to create subfolders for potential device drivers. By dividing the folders into subfolders, you can store device driver files by device type rather than having all device driver files in one folder. Suggested subfolders include Audio, Modem, Net, Print, Video, and Other. An Other folder can give you the flexibility to store new hardware devices that might not be currently known.

For example, if the PnpDrvs folder contains the subfolders Audio, Modem, and Net, the answer file must contain the following line:

```
OEMPnPDriversPath = "PnPDrvs\Audio;PnPDrvs\Modem;PnpDrvs\Net"
```

Converting File Name Size Using $$Rename.txt

The $$Rename.txt file changes short file names to long file names during Setup. $$Rename.txt lists all of the files in a particular folder that need to be renamed. Each folder containing short file names that need to be renamed must contain its own version of $$Rename.txt.

To use $$Rename.txt, put the file in a folder that contains files that need to be converted. The syntax for $$Rename.txt is as follows:

[*section_name_1*]

short_name_1 = "*long_name_1*"

short_name_2 = "*long_name_2*"

short_name_x = "*long_name_x*"

[*section_name_2*]

short_name_1 = "*long_name_1*"

short_name_2 = "*long_name_2*"

short_name_x = "*long_name_x*"

Parameters are defined as follows:

- *section_name_x*—The path to the subfolder that contains the files. A section does not need to be named, or it can have a backslash (\) as a name, which indicates that the section contains the names of the files or subfolders that are on the root of the drive.

- *short_name_x*—The name of the file or subfolder within this subfolder to be renamed. This name must *not* be enclosed in quotation marks.

- *long_name_x*—The new name of the file or subfolder. This name must be enclosed in quotation marks if it contains spaces or commas.

Tip If you are using MS-DOS to start the installation, and your MS-DOS tools cannot copy folders with path names longer than 64 characters, you can use short file names for the folders and then use $$Rename.txt to rename them later.

Reviewing the Answer File

The answer file is a customized script that answers the Setup questions without requiring user input. The Windows 2000 Server CD contains a sample answer file that you can edit and use. The answer file is usually named *Unattend.txt*, but you can rename it. (For example, Comp1.txt, Install.txt, and Setup.txt are all valid names for an answer file, as long as those names are correctly specified in the **setup** command.) This allows you to build and use multiple answer files if you need to maintain different scripted installations for different parts of your organization. Note that answer files are also used by other programs such as Sysprep, which uses the optional Sysprep.inf file.

The answer file tells Setup how to interact with the distribution folders and files you have created. For example, in the [Unattend] section of the answer file there is an "OEMPreinstall" entry that tells Setup to copy the OEM subfolders from the distribution folders to the target computer.

The answer file contains multiple optional sections that you can modify to supply information about your installation requirements. The answer file supplies Setup with answers to all the questions that you are asked during a standard interactive installation of Windows 2000. The Unattend.doc file has detailed information about answer file keys and values. For more information about answer file sections and their associated parameters, see the "Microsoft Windows 2000 Guide to Unattended Setup" (Unattend.doc) on the Windows 2000 operating system CD. The Unattend.doc file is part of the Deploy.cab file in the \Support\Tools folder. On Windows 98 or Windows 2000, use Windows Explorer to extract this document. In Windows 95 and earlier, or from MS-DOS, use the **Extract** command to access the file.

To perform an unattended installation of Windows 2000 Server, you must create an answer file and specify that file when Setup begins, either by using the bootable CD method, or by running Winnt.exe or Winnt32.exe. The following is an example of a **setup** command using Winnt.exe:

```
Winnt /S:Z:\I386 /U:Z:\unattend.txt
```

Note the use of the **/U:** command-line switch, which indicates an unattended installation when used with the **Winnt** command (**/unattend** is the parameter used with the **Winnt32** command to tell Setup to run in unattended mode). For more information about Winnt.exe and Winnt32.exe, see "Reviewing the Windows 2000 Setup Commands" later in this chapter.

Creating the Answer File

The answer file is a customized script that you can use to run an unattended installation of Windows 2000 Server. There are two ways to create an answer file: You can use Setup Manager, or you can create the file manually.

Creating the Answer File with Setup Manager

To help you create or modify the answer file, the Setup Manager application is available on the *Microsoft® Windows® 2000 Server Resource Kit* companion CD in the Deploy.cab file of the \Support\Tools folder. By using Setup Manager, you can add consistency to the process of creating or updating the answer file.

You can use Setup Manager to perform the following tasks; it then generates the results as answer file parameters:

- Specify the platform for the answer file (Microsoft® Windows® 2000 Professional, Windows 2000 Server, Remote Operating System Installation, or Sysprep).
- Specify the level of automation for unattended Setup mode. (Levels include "Provide Defaults," "Fully Automated," "Hide Pages," "Read Only," and "GUI-mode Setup.")
- Specify default user information.
- Define computer name options, including creating a /UDF to access a file of valid computer names.
- Configure network settings.
- Create distribution folders.
- Add a custom logo and background files.
- Add files to the distribution folders.
- Add commands to the [GuiRunOnce] section.
- Create Cmdlines.txt files.

- Specify code pages.
- Specify regional options.
- Specify a time zone.
- Specify TAPI information.

Setup Manager cannot perform the following functions.

- Specify system components, such as Internet Information Services.
- Create Txtsetup.oem files.
- Create subfolders in the distribution folder.

Table 13.3 describes some of the most common answer file specifications that are created by Setup Manager.

Table 13.3 Answer File Specifications Created by Setup Manager

Parameter	Purpose
Installation path	Specifies the desired path on the target computer in which to install Windows 2000 Server.
Upgrade option	Specifies whether to upgrade from Windows 95 or Windows 98, Windows NT, or Windows 2000.
Target computer name	Specifies the user name, organization name, and computer name to apply to the target computer.
Product ID	Specifies the product identification number obtained from the product documentation.
Workgroup or domain	Specifies the name of the workgroup or domain to which the computer belongs.
Time zone	Specifies the time zone for the computer.
Network configuration information	Specifies the network adapter type and configuration with network protocols.

Note When installing Windows 2000 Server, you are not initially required to create domain controllers. You can create member servers and then promote them to domain controllers later using the Active Directory Installation Wizard (dcpromo.exe).

Creating the Answer File Manually

To create the answer file manually, you can use a text editor such as Notepad. In general, an answer file consists of section headers, parameters, and values for those parameters. Although most section headers are predefined, you can also define additional section headers. Note that you do not have to specify all possible parameters in the answer file if the installation does not require them.

Invalid parameter values generate errors or result in incorrect behavior after Setup.

The answer file format is as follows:

```
[section1]
;
;   Section contains keys and the corresponding
;   values for those keys/parameters.
;   Keys and values are separated by ' = ' signs.
;   Values that have spaces in them usually require double quotes
;   "" around them.
;
key = value
.

.
[section2]
key = value
.

.
```

Using the Answer File to Set Passwords

Using the answer file with Setup allows you to set parameters for the following password commands:

- AdminPassword
- UserPassword
- DefaultPassword
- DomainAdminPassword
- AdminstratorPassword
- Password

For definitions of these commands, see the "Microsoft Windows 2000 Guide to Unattended Setup" (Unattend.doc) on the Windows 2000 operating system CD. The Unattend.doc file is part of the Deploy.cab file in the \Support\Tools folder. On Windows 98 or Windows 2000, use Windows Explorer to extract this document. In Windows 95 and earlier, or in MS-DOS, use the **Extract** command to access the file. In addition, you can find some examples of answer files that use some of these parameters in the Appendix, "Sample Answer Files for Unattended Setup" in this book.

Note Passwords are limited to 127 characters. If you specify a password that contains more than 127 characters, you will not be able to log on to the system because the password will be invalid.

After the installation is completed, an answer file with all the settings used to configure the computer remains on the computer; however, all password information is removed from the local copy of the answer file so that security is not compromised.

Caution During the Setup process, however, the answer file is available on the hard disk. If you are concerned about the security implications, do not add password information to the answer file that you created for the unattended installation.

This local answer file allows you to automatically set up optional components by running commands that contain the parameters you already provided in the original answer file that was used with Setup. These components can include configuring the server as a domain controller, as a cluster server, or enabling Message Queuing.

Extending Hard Disk Partitions

You can start an install on a small partition (about 1 gigabyte [GB] on a larger disk) and cause that partition to be extended during the Windows 2000 setup process by using the ExtendOEMPartition parameter in the answer file. The ExtendOEMPartition parameter works only on NTFS partitions and can be used in both a regular answer file and one used for a Sysprep-based installation.

For more information about Sysprep and the Sysprep.inf file, see "Using Sysprep to Duplicate Disks" later in this chapter.

Note ExtendOEMPartition acts only on the active system partition. It does not work on other partitions on the same hard disk or other hard disks in the computer. In addition, when ExtendOemPartition=1 is used, it extends to all remaining space on the hard disk, leaving the last cylinder blank. This is by design, so that you have the option of enabling dynamic volumes.

If you are using ExtendOEMPartition during an unattended installation on a File Allocation Table (FAT) partition, you need to specify File System=ConvertNTFS in the [Unattended] section of your answer file to first convert the partition to NTFS. If you are using the ExtendOEMPartition for a Sysprep-based installation, see "Using Sysprep to Duplicate Disks" later in this chapter.

For more information about using ExtendOemPartition, see the "Microsoft Windows 2000 Guide to Unattended Setup" (Unattend.doc) on the Microsoft Windows 2000 operating system CD. The Unattend.doc file is part of the Deploy.cab file in the \Support\Tools folder. On Windows 98 or Windows 2000, use Windows Explorer to extract this document. In Windows 95 and earlier, or in MS-DOS, use the **Extract** command to access the file.

Using the Answer File with the Active Directory Installation Wizard

After installing Windows 2000 Server, you can automate the process of creating a domain controller by using the Active Directory Installation Wizard. There are two ways to do this:

- Run the following command from the [GuiRunOnce] section of the Unattend.txt answer file:

  dcpromo.exe

- Create a special answer file using the commands defined in the [DCInstall] section of the Appendix "Sample Answer Files for Unattended Setup" and then run the following command:

  dcpromo.exe /answer:*answer_file_name*

For more information about the Active Directory Installation Wizard, see "Determining Domain Migration Strategies" in this book.

Reviewing the Windows 2000 Setup Commands

To install Windows 2000, you must run the appropriate Windows 2000 Setup program, either Winnt.exe or Winnt32.exe. In this chapter, Winnt.exe and Winnt32.exe are both referred to as "Setup." The type of setup that you need to run is determined as follows:

- For a clean installation on a computer running MS-DOS or Microsoft® Windows® 3.*x*, run Winnt.exe from the MS-DOS command line.
- For a clean installation or upgrade from Windows NT, Windows 95 or Windows 98, run Winnt32.exe.

Note that you can start a standard interactive setup directly from the boot floppy disks that come with the Windows 2000 Server CD.

Caution If you update any applications on the computer before upgrading it to Windows 2000, make sure you restart the computer before you run Setup.

For more information about installation methods, see "Automating the Installation of Windows 2000 Server" later in this chapter.

Winnt.exe

The Winnt.exe command, including the parameters that apply to automated installation, is as follows:

winnt [**/S**[:*sourcepath*]][**/T**[:*tempdrive*]]/**U**[:*answer_file*]][**/R**[*x*]:*folder*] [**/E**:*command*]

For parameter definitions and command syntax, see the Appendix "Setup Commands" in this book.

For hard disk drives with multiple partitions, the Winnt.exe version of Setup installs Windows 2000 to the active partition if the partition contains sufficient space. Otherwise, Setup looks for additional partitions containing sufficient space and prompts you to choose the desired partition. For automated installations, you can bypass the prompt by running Setup with the **/T** parameter, to automatically point to the desired partition. For example:

```
winnt [/unattend] [:<path>\answer.txt] [/T[:d]]
```

Winnt32.exe

The Winnt32.exe command, including the parameters that apply to automated installation, is as follows:

```
winnt32 [/s:sourcepath] [/tempdrive:drive_letter]
[/unattend[num][:answer_file]] [/copydir:folder_name]
[/copysource:folder_name] [/cmd:command_line] [/debug[level][:filename]]
[/udf:id[,UDB_file]] [/syspart:drive_letter] [/noreboot]
[/makelocalsource] [/checkupgradeonly] [/m:folder_name]
```

For parameter definitions and command syntax, see Appendix B, "Setup Commands" in this book.

For hard drives with multiple partitions, the Winnt32.exe version of Setup installs Windows 2000 to the active partition if the partition contains sufficient space. Otherwise, Setup looks for additional partitions containing sufficient space and prompts you to choose the desired partition. For automated installations, you can bypass the prompt by running Setup with the **/tempdrive** parameter to automatically point to the desired partition. For example:

```
winnt32 [/unattend] [:<path>\answer.txt] [/tempdrive:d]
```

Windows 2000 can use up to eight **/s** switches to point to other distribution servers as source locations for installation to the destination computer. This functionality helps to speed up the file copy phase of Setup to the destination computer as well as providing additional load-balancing capability to the distribution servers from which Setup can be run. For example:

```
<path to distribution folder 1>\winnt32 [/unattend]
[:<path>\answer.txt] [/s:<path to distribution folder 2>] [/s:<path
to distribution folder 3>] [/s:<path to distribution folder 4]
```

Table 13.4 shows the Setup commands and how they are used with Windows 2000.

Table 13.4   Using Setup Commands

Setup Command	Windows 2000 Edition	Upgrade	Clean Installation
Winnt.exe	Server and Professional	No	Yes
Winnt32.exe	Server and Professional	Yes	Yes

Automating the Installation of Server Applications

After resolving your critical planning issues, you can decide how you will automate the installation of server applications. In almost all cases, you will want to use an application's unattended installation features to install it.

You can choose from among the following:

- Cmdlines.txt
- Running the application installation program or batch file from the [GuiRunOnce] section of the answer file.

Using Cmdlines.txt

The Cmdlines.txt file contains the commands that GUI mode executes when installing optional components, such as applications that must be installed immediately after Windows 2000 Server is installed. If you plan to use Cmdlines.txt, you need to place it in the \$OEM$ subfolder of the distribution folder. If you are using Sysprep, place Cmdlines.txt in the \$OEM$\$1\Sysprep subfolder.

Use Cmdlines.txt when the following conditions exist:

- You are installing from the \OEM subfolder of the distribution folder.
- The application that you are installing has the following properties:
  - It does not configure itself for multiple users—for example, Microsoft® Office 95.

    –Or–

  - It is designed to be installed by one user and to replicate user-specific information.

The syntax for Cmdlines.txt is as follows:

[Commands]

"*command_1*"

"*command_2*"

   .

   .

"*command_x*"

Parameters are defined as follows:

- "*command_1*", "*command_2*", ... "*command_x*" refers to the commands you want to run (and in what order) when GUI mode calls Cmdlines.txt. Note that all commands must be in quotation marks.

When using Cmdlines.txt, be aware of the following:

- When the commands in Cmdlines.txt are carried out during Setup, there is no logged-on user and there is no guaranteed network connectivity. Therefore, user-specific information is written to the default user registry, and all subsequently created users also receive that information.
- Cmdlines.txt requires that you place the files that are necessary to run an application or tool in directories that are accessed during the Setup process, which means that the files must be on the hard disk.

Using the [GuiRunOnce] Section of the Answer File

The [GuiRunOnce] section of the answer file contains a list of commands that run the first time a user logs on to the computer after Setup runs. For example, you enter the following line to the [GuiRunOnce] section to start the application installation program automatically:

```
[GuiRunOnce]
 "%systemdrive%\ <appfolder>\<appinstall> -quiet"
```

If you plan to use [GuiRunOnce] to initiate an installation, there are some additional factors to take into consideration:

If the application forces a reboot, determine whether there is a way to suppress the reboot.

This is important because any time the system restarts, all previous entries in the [GuiRunOnce] section are lost. If the system restarts before completing entries previously listed in the [GuiRunOnce] section, the remaining items will not be run. If there is no way within the application to suppress a reboot, you can try repackaging the application into a Windows Installer package. There are third-party products that provide this functionality.

Windows 2000 ships with WinINSTALL LE (Limited Edition), a repackaging tool for Windows Installer. WinINSTALL LE allows you to efficiently repackage pre-Windows Installer applications into packages that can be distributed with Windows Installer. For more information about WinINSTALL LE, see the \Valueadd\3rdparty\Mgmt\Winstle folder on the Windows 2000 Server CD.

For more information about Windows Installer packaging, see "Automating Client Installation and Upgrade" in this book.

Important If you are installing an application to multiple localized language versions of Windows 2000, it is recommended that you test the repackaged application on the localized versions to ensure that it copies the files to the correct locations and writes the required registry entries appropriately.

If an application requires a Windows Explorer shell to install, the [GuiRunOnce] section will not work because the shell is not loaded when the Run and RunOnce commands are carried out.

Check with the application vendor to determine if they have an update or patch that can address this situation for the application setup. If not, you can repackage the application as a Windows Installer package or use another means of distribution.

Applications that use the same type of installation mechanism might not run properly if a /wait command is not used

This can happen when an application installation is running and starts another process. When the Setup routine is still running, initiating another process and closing an active one might cause the next routine listed in the RunOnce registry entries to start. Because more than one instance of the installation mechanism is running, the second application will usually fail. For an example of how to control this using a batch file, see "Using a Batch File to Control How Multiple Applications Are Installed" later in this chapter.

Using Application Installation Programs

The preferred method for preinstalling an application is to use the installation routine supplied with the application. You can do this if the application that you are preinstalling is able to run in quiet mode (without user intervention) by using a **/q** or **/s** command-line switch. See the application Help file or documentation for a list of command-line parameters supported by the installation mechanism.

Following is an example of a line that you can place in the [GuiRunOnce] section to initiate the unattended installation of an application using its own installation program.

```
<path to setup>\Setup.exe /q
```

Setup parameters vary between applications. For example, the **/l** parameter included in some applications is useful when you want to create a log file to monitor the installation. Some applications have commands that can keep them from restarting automatically. This is useful in helping to control application installations with a minimal number of reboots.

Make sure that you check with the application vendor for information, instructions, tools, and best practices information before you preinstall any application.

Important You must meet the licensing requirements for any application that you install, regardless of how you install it.

Using a Batch File to Control How Multiple Applications Are Installed

If you want to control how multiple applications are installed, you can create a batch file that contains the individual installation commands and uses the **Start** command with the **/wait** command line switch. This method ensures that your applications install sequentially and that each application is fully installed before the next application begins its installation routine. The batch file is then run from the [GuiRunOnce] section.

The following procedure explains how to create the batch file, how to install the application, and then how to remove all references to the batch file after installation is complete.

▶ **To install applications using a batch file**

1. Create the batch file containing lines similar to the following example:

```
Start /wait <path to 1st application>\<Setup> <command line
parameters>
Start /wait <path to 2nd application>\<Setup> <command line
parameters>
Exit
```

where:

- <path> is the path to the executable file that starts the installation. This path must be available during Setup.

- <Setup> is the name of the executable file that starts the installation.

- <command line parameters> are any available quiet-mode parameters appropriate for the application you want to install.

2. Copy the batch file to the distribution folders or another location that can be accessed during setup.

3. With <filename>.bat as the name of the batch file, include an entry in the [GuiRunOnce] section of the answer file to run the batch file, similar to the following example. This example assumes that the batch file was copied to the Sysprep folder on the local hard disk, though it can be located anywhere that Setup has access to during an installation.

```
[GuiRunOnce]
"%systemdrive%\sysprep\<filename>.bat"
"<path-1>\<Command-1>.exe"
"<path-n>\<Command-n>.exe"
"%systemdrive%\sysprep\sysprep.exe -quiet"
```

where:

- <path-1>\<Command-1.exe> and <path-n>\<Command-n.exe> are fully qualified paths to additional applications or utility installations or configuration tools. This can also be a path to another batch file. These paths must be available during setup.

Automating the Installation of Windows 2000 Server

In the enterprise environment, it is not cost effective to install Windows 2000 using the standard interactive setup on each computer. To greatly lower the total cost of ownership (TCO), you can perform automated installations of Windows 2000 Server on multiple computers.

You can automate the installation of the following:

- The core operating system of Windows 2000 Server.
- Any application that does not run as a service.
- Additional language support for Windows 2000 Server through the installation of various language packs.
- Service packs for Windows 2000 Server.

Automated installation of Windows 2000 Server involves running Setup with an answer file. Setup can take place in unattended fashion. An unattended setup includes the following steps:

- Creating an answer file.
- Determining and implementing a process to configure computer-specific information.
- Determining and implementing a process to automate the selected distribution method, such as using a network distribution point or hard disk duplication.

New Options for Automated Installation

In the Windows 2000 automated installation, there are several new options available in the answer file for controlling how and what should run. For more information about answer file parameters and syntax, see the "Microsoft Windows 2000 Guide to Unattended Setup" (Unattend.doc) on the Microsoft Windows 2000 operating system CD. The Unattend.doc file is part of the Deploy.cab file in the \Support\Tools folder. In Windows 98 or Windows 2000, use Windows Explorer to extract this document. In Windows 95 and earlier, or in MS-DOS, use the **Extract** command to access the file.

Flexible networking In Windows 2000, there are flexible network configurations available for each computer, including additional support for protocols, services, and clients. It is now possible to set the binding order, to easily set default information, and to install more than one network adapter in a system. In addition, to make installation and configuration easier, Windows 2000 can automatically install and configure network device drivers. By default, Windows 2000 installs the default components to each network adapter installed in a system, unless otherwise specified in the answer file. The default networking components include Client for Microsoft Networks, TCP/IP, File and Printer Sharing for Microsoft Networks, and enabling Dynamic Host Configuration Protocol (DHCP).

Automatic Logon Capability You can customize the answer file to allow the computer to automatically log on as the administrator the first time the computer starts Windows 2000 after Setup is complete or a specified number of times thereafter. If you need Windows 2000 to automatically log on for a specific number of times to accomplish tasks that are run in the RunOnce entries, you will need to provide a non-null administrator password (AdminPassword) in the answer file. You can then use AutoAdminLogonCount to specify the number of times you need the system to automatically log on to complete the desired tasks. If a null password is used, Setup can only automatically log on to the system once without providing credentials through other means for each subsequent reboot. This is done to help reduce security risks. Note that providing administrator account credentials in a text file always introduces security risks if a user gains access to the file.

Automatic Command Execution The [GuiRunOnce] section of the answer file contains a list of commands to be carried out consecutively as part of Setup after GUI mode completes. By using [GuiRunOnce], you can specify lists of applications to install, utilities to configure the system, or other tools to run on first logon to the installed computer.

Simplified Time Zone Specification In the answer file, you can specify the computer time zone more easily and with less debugging than what was required with Windows NT. By enumerating the possible time zones, there is less opportunity for error because you are no longer required to enter the full time zone string.

Enhanced Regional and Language Settings In the answer file, you can specify the system and user locales, the keyboard and input method, and the language support to be installed. Setup Manager can help to make this even easier by using the GUI interface of the wizard to select the settings to install on the system.

Simpler Device Preinstallation With the introduction of Plug and Play, the OemPnPDriversPath key, and the new distribution sharepoint structure, preinstalling devices is now as easy as adding the new drivers into a folder in the distribution share and specifying the OemPnPDriversPath key.

Automated Installation Methods

You can run an automated installation of Windows 2000 Server using several methods. The method that you choose depends on the outcome of your critical planning, as discussed earlier in this chapter.

Methods for performing automated installations on servers include:

- Using Syspart on computers with dissimilar hardware.
- Using Sysprep to duplicate disks.
- Using Systems Management Server.
- Using a bootable CD.

Table 13.5 describes when to use each automated installation method.

Table 13.5   When to Use Automated Installation Methods

Method	Use
Syspart	You use Syspart for clean installations to computers that have dissimilar hardware.
Sysprep	You use Sysprep when the master computer and the target computers have identical hardware, which includes the HAL and mass storage device controllers.
Systems Management Server	You use Systems Management Server to perform managed upgrades of Windows 2000 Server to multiple systems, especially those that are geographically dispersed.
Bootable CD	You use the bootable CD method with a computer whose basic input/output system (BIOS) allows it to start from the CD.

Using Syspart on Computers with Dissimilar Hardware

Syspart runs through an optional parameter of Winnt32.exe. If the master computer and the computers on which you are installing Windows 2000 Server do not have similar hardware, you can use the Syspart method. This method also reduces deployment time by eliminating the file copy phase of Setup.

Syspart requires that you use two physical disks, with a primary partition on the target hard disk.

If you require a similar installation and operating system configuration on hardware types in which the HALs or mass storage device controllers differ, you can use Syspart to create a master set of files with the necessary configuration information and driver support that can then be imaged. Those images can then be used on the dissimilar systems to properly detect the hardware and consistently configure the base operating system. If your environment includes multiple types of hardware-dependent systems, you can use Syspart to create a master for each type. You install Windows 2000 on one computer of each type, and then you use Sysprep to help create images to be used on the remaining computers of each type. For more information about Sysprep, see "Using Sysprep to Duplicate Disks" later in this chapter.

Before you begin, choose a computer to use as a reference computer. The reference computer must have either Windows NT or Windows 2000 installed.

▶ **To install Windows 2000 Server by using Syspart**

1. Start the reference computer and connect to the distribution folder.

2. Run Setup.

   Click **Start**, click **Run**, and then type:

   ```
   winnt32 /unattend:unattend.txt /s:install_source
   /syspart:second_drive /tempdrive:second_drive/ noreboot
   ```

Important You must use the */tempdrive* parameter for a successful Syspart installation. When you use the */tempdrive* command-line switch, make sure you have sufficient free disk space on your second partition to install both Windows 2000 Server and your applications. The geometry of the disk you plan to use as a target for Syspart must be the same as the geometry of the disk on the computer to which you plan to duplicate.

Note that the */syspart* and */tempdrive* parameters must point to the same partition of a secondary hard disk. The Windows 2000 Server installation must take place on the primary partition of the secondary hard disk.

Caution Syspart will automatically mark the drive as active and as the default boot device. For this reason, remove the drive before turning the computer on again.

Related definitions include:

Unattend.txt. The answer file used for an unattended setup. It provides answers to some or all the prompts the end user normally responds to during Setup. Using an answer file is optional when creating the master image.

install_source. The location of the Windows 2000 Server files. Specify multiple **/s** command-line switches if you want to install from multiple sources simultaneously.

second_drive. An optional second drive on which you preinstall Windows 2000 and applications.

Using Sysprep to Duplicate Disks

Disk duplication is a good choice if you need to install an identical configuration on multiple computers. On a master computer, you install Windows 2000 and any applications that you want installed on all of the target computers. Then you run Sysprep and a third-party disk imaging utility. Sysprep prepares the hard disk on the master computer so that the disk imaging utility can transfer an image of the hard disk to the other computers. This method decreases deployment time dramatically compared to standard or scripted installations.

To use Sysprep, your master and target computers must have identical HALs, Advanced Configuration and Power Interface (ACPI) support, and mass storage device controllers. Windows 2000 automatically detects Plug and Play devices, and Sysprep redetects and re-enumerates the devices on the system when the computer is turned on after Sysprep has run. This means that Plug and Play devices, such as network adapters, modems, video adapters, and sound cards, do not have to be the same on the master and target computers. The major advantage of Sysprep installation is speed. The image can be packaged and compressed and only the files required for the specific configuration are created as part of the image. Additional Plug and Play drivers that you might need on other systems are also created. The image can also be copied to a CD and distributed to remote sites that have slow links.

Note Because the master and target computers are required to have identical HALs, ACPI support, and mass storage device controllers, you might need to maintain multiple images for your environment.

Sysprep allows you to configure a master image containing the necessary components for a member server, then later configure the server and optionally promote it to a domain controller. This can be done manually or by running the commands in the [GuiRunOnce] section of Sysprep.inf. For more information about Sysprep.inf, see "Using Sysprep to Duplicate Disks" later in this chapter.

Important When performing disk duplication, check with your software vendor to make certain you are not violating the licensing agreement for installation of the software you want to duplicate.

Overview of the Sysprep Process

This section describes the process of building a source computer to use for disk duplication.

1. Install Windows 2000—Install Windows 2000 Server on a computer that has hardware similar to the intended target computers. While building the computer, you must not join it to a domain, and you must keep the local administrative password blank.

2. Configure the computer—Log on as the administrator, then install and customize Windows 2000 Server and associated applications. You might include Internet Information Services (IIS) or set other services.

3. Validate the image—Run an audit, based on your criteria, to verify that the image configuration is correct. Remove residual information, including anything left behind from audit and event logs.

4. Prepare the image for duplication—After you are confident the computer is configured exactly the way that you want, you are ready to prepare the system for duplication. You accomplish this by running Sysprep with the optional Sysprep.inf file, which is described later in this chapter. When Sysprep has completed, the computer shuts down automatically or indicates that it is safe to shut down.

5. Duplicate—At this point, the computer hard disk is triggered to run Plug and Play detection, create new security identifiers (SIDs), and run the Mini-Setup Wizard the next time the system is started. You are now ready to duplicate or image the system using a hardware or software solution. The next time that Windows 2000 Server is started from this hard disk, or is started from any duplicated hard disk created from this image, the system will detect and reenumerate the Plug and Play devices to complete the installation and configuration on the target computer.

Important Components that depend on Active Directory cannot be duplicated.

Sysprep Files

To use Sysprep, run Sysprep.exe manually or configure Setup to run Sysprep.exe automatically by using the [GuiRunOnce] section of the answer file. To run Sysprep, the files Sysprep.exe and Setupcl.exe must be located in a Sysprep folder at the root of the system drive (%systemdrive%\Sysprep\). To place the files in the correct location during an automated Setup, you must add these files to your distribution folders under the OEM\$1\Sysprep\ subfolder. For more information about this subfolder, see "Structuring the Distribution Folder" earlier in this chapter.

These files prepare the operating system for duplication and start the Mini-Setup Wizard. You can also include an optional answer file, Sysprep.inf, in the Sysprep folder. Sysprep.inf contains default parameters that you can use to provide consistent responses where they are appropriate. This limits the requirement for user input, thereby reducing potential user errors. You can also place the Sysprep.inf file on a floppy disk to be placed in the floppy disk drive after the Windows startup screen appears, in order to allow further customization at the target computer's location. The floppy disk drive is read when the "Please Wait" Mini-Setup Wizard screen appears. When the Mini-Setup Wizard has successfully completed its tasks, the system restarts one last time, the Sysprep folder and all of its contents are deleted, and the system is ready for the user to log on.

Sysprep.exe

Sysprep.exe has three optional parameters:

- *quiet*—runs Sysprep without displaying onscreen messages.
- *nosidgen*—runs Sysprep without regenerating SIDs that are already on the system. This is useful if you do not intend to duplicate the computer on which you are running Sysprep.
- *reboot*—automatically restarts the computer after Sysprep shuts it down, eliminating the need for you to manually turn the computer back on.

Sysprep.inf

Sysprep.inf is an answer file that is used to automate the Mini-Setup process. It uses the same .ini file syntax and key names (for supported keys) as the Setup answer file. You need to place the Sysprep.inf file in the %systemdrive%\Sysprep folder or on a floppy disk. If you use a floppy disk, you can provide the floppy after the Windows startup screen. The floppy drive will be read when the "Please Wait" Mini-Setup screen appears. Note that if you do not include Sysprep.inf when running Sysprep, the Mini-Setup Wizard displays all the available dialog boxes listed under "Using Sysprep to Duplicate Disks" later in this chapter.

Note If you provided a Sysprep.inf file on the master computer and you want to change the Sysprep.inf on a per-computer basis, you can use the floppy disk method previously discussed.

Following is a sample of a Sysprep.inf file:

```
[Unattended]
;Prompt the user to accept the EULA.
OemSkipEula=No
;Use Sysprep's default and regenerate the page file for the system
;to accommodate potential differences in available RAM.
KeepPageFile=0
;Provide the location for additional language support files that
;might be needed in a global organization.
InstallFilesPath=%systemdrive%\Sysprep\i386

[GuiUnattended]
;Specify a non-null administrator password.
;Any password supplied here will only take effect if the original source
;for the image (master computer) specified a non-null password.
;Otherwise, the password used on the master computer will be
;the password used on this computer. This can only be changed by
;logging on as Local Administrator and manually changing the password.
AdminPassword=""
;Set the time zone
TimeZone=20
;Skip the Welcome screen when the system boots.
OemSkipWelcome=1
;Do not skip the regional options dialog box so that the user can
;indicate which regional options apply to them.
OemSkipRegional=0

[UserData]
;Prepopulate user information for the system.
FullName="Authorized User"
OrgName="Organization Name"
ComputerName=XYZ_Computer1

[GUIRunOnce]
;Promote this computer to a Domain Controller on reboot.
DCPromo/answer:<location of dc promo answer file>

[Identification]
;Join the computer to the domain ITDOMAIN
JoinDomain=ITDOMAIN

[Networking]
;Bind the default protocols and services to the network card(s) used
;in this computer.
InstallDefaultComponents=Yes
```

Note You can change the administrative password using Sysprep.inf only if the existing administrative password is null. This is also true if you want to change the administrator password through the Sysprep GUI.

For more information about the answer file sections and commands used with Sysprep.inf, see the Appendix "Sample Answer Files for Unattended Setup" in this book.

Setupcl.exe

Setupcl.exe does the following:

- Regenerates new security IDs for the computer.
- Starts the Mini-Setup Wizard.

Mini-Setup Wizard

The Mini-Setup Wizard starts the first time that a computer starts from a disk that has been duplicated by the Sysprep method. The wizard gathers any information that is needed to further customize the target computer. If you do not use Sysprep.inf, or if you leave some sections of the file blank, the Mini-Setup Wizard displays screens for which no answer was provided in Sysprep.inf. The possible screens include:

- End-User License Agreement (EULA)
- Regional options
- User name and company
- Computer name and administrator password
- Network settings
- TAPI settings (only displayed if a modem or a new modem device exists on the computer)
- Server licensing (server only)
- Time zone selection
- Finish/Restart

If you want to bypass these screens, you can specify certain parameters within Sysprep.inf. These parameters are listed in Table 13.6.

Note Because Setup detects optimal settings for display devices, you will no longer see the "Display Settings" screen when Setup or the Mini-Setup Wizard is running. You can specify [Display] settings either in the answer file used for your master computer or in the Sysprep.inf file used for your target computer. If [Display] settings are in the answer file that is used for your master computer, Sysprep will retain those settings unless Sysprep.inf contains different settings, or unless a video adapter or monitor requiring settings different from those of the master computer is detected.

Table 13.6   Parameters in Sysprep.inf for Bypassing the Mini-Setup Wizard

Parameter	Value
Regional options	[RegionalSettings] section
	[GuiUnattended]
	OemSkipRegional=1
User name and company	[UserData]
	FullName="User Name"
	OrgName="Organization Name"
Computer name and administrator password	[UserData]
	ComputerName=W2B32054
	[GuiUnattended]
	AdminPassword=" "
Network settings	[Networking]
	InstallDefaultComponents=Yes
TAPI settings	[TapiLocation]
	AreaCode=425
Time zone selection	[GuiUnattended]
	TimeZone=<desired time zone index>
Finish/Restart	NA

Running Sysprep Manually

After you install Windows 2000 Server, you can use Sysprep to prepare the system for transfer to other similarly configured computers. To run Sysprep manually, you must first install Windows 2000 Server, configure the system, and install the applications. Then run Sysprep without the *–reboot* command-line switch. After the system shuts down, duplicate the image of the drive to the similarly configured computers.

When users start up their duplicated computers for the first time, Sysprep Mini-Setup will run, allowing the users to customize their systems. You can also preassign all or part of the Sysprep configuration parameters by using Sysprep.inf. The Sysprep folder (which contains Sysprep.exe and Setupcl.exe) is automatically deleted after Sysprep Mini-Setup completes.

▶ **To prepare a Windows 2000 Server installation for duplication**

1. On the **Start** menu, click **Run**, and then type:

   cmd

2. At the command prompt, change to the root folder of drive C, then type:

   md sysprep

3. Load the Windows 2000 Server CD. Open the Deploy.cab file in the \Support\Tools folder.

4. Copy Sysprep.exe and Setupcl.exe to the Sysprep folder.

   If you are using Sysprep.inf, also copy this file to the Sysprep folder. Note that Sysprep.exe, Setupcl.exe, and Sysprep.inf must exist in the same folder so that Sysprep can function properly.

5. At the command prompt, change to the Sysprep folder:

   cd sysprep

6. Type one of the following, as required:

```
Sysprep
Sysprep -reboot
Sysprep /<optional parameter>
Sysprep /<optional parameter> -reboot
Sysprep /<optional parameter 1>.../<optional parameter X>
Sysprep /<optional parameter 1>.../<optional parameter X> -reboot
```

7. If the *–reboot* command-line switch was not specified, perform the following:

   When a message appears telling you to shut down the computer, on the **Start** menu, click **Shut Down**. You are now ready to use a third-party disk-imaging utility to create an image of the installation.

8. If the *–reboot* command-line switch was specified for auditing purposes only, then the computer restarts and the Mini-Setup Wizard runs. In this case, perform the following:

   - Verify that the Mini-Setup Wizard provides the desired prompts. At this time you can also audit the system and other applications. Once auditing is complete, run Sysprep again without the *–reboot* command-line switch.

   - When a message appears telling you to shut down the computer, on the **Start** menu, click **Shut Down**. You are now ready to use a third-party disk-imaging utility to create an image of the installation.

Note You can add a Cmdlines.txt file to the Sysprep folder, to be processed by Setup. This file will run post-Setup commands, including those required for application installation.

Running Sysprep Automatically After Setup Completes

The [GuiRunOnce] section of the answer file contains commands to be executed after Setup completes. You can use the [GuiRunOnce] section to create an installation that completes Setup, automatically logs on to the computer, runs Sysprep in **–quiet** mode, and then shuts down the computer. For this to occur, you need to do the following:

1. Include the required Sysprep files in the distribution folders under OEM\$1\Sysprep\ to copy the files to the correct location on the system drive.

2. In the [GuiRunOnce] section of the answer file, make the following the last command that is run on the computer:

   ```
   %systemdrive%\Sysprep\Sysprep.exe –quiet
   ```

   If multiple reboots are required, make this the last command used the last time the [GuiRunOnce] section is used.

Using Sysprep to Extend Disk Partitions

Windows 2000 GUI Setup and Mini-Setup can be used to extend NTFS partitions through answer files. This new functionality does the following:

- Allows you to create images that can be extended into larger disk partitions to take full advantage of hard disks that might have more space than the original hard disk on the master computer.

- Provides a way to create images on smaller hard disks.

To determine the best way to integrate this functionality in your environment, you need to review the steps that follow and choose the method that will work best for you based on the tools that you are using to image the operating system.

Caution If your imaging tools allow you to edit the image, you can delete the Pagefile.sys, Setupapi.log, and the Hyberfil.sys (if applicable) because these files will be recreated when the Mini-Setup Wizard runs on the target computer. You must not delete these files on an active system because this can cause the system to function improperly. These files should only be deleted, if desired, from the image.

▶ **To extend a hard disk partition when using a third-party imaging product or a hardware imaging device that supports NTFS used by Windows 2000**

1. Configure the partition on the master computer hard disk to the minimum size required to install Windows 2000 with all the components and applications that you intend to preinstall. This reduces your overall image size requirements.

2. Include FileSystem=ConvertNTFS in the [Unattended] section of the answer file that is used to create the master image. You do not need to include ExtendOemPartition here because you want to maintain the smallest possible image size.

Note ConvertNTFS does not work in Sysprep.inf because this is a text mode–only function and Sysprep does not go through text mode.

---

3. In the [Unattended] section of Sysprep.inf, include the statement:
   ```
   ExtendOemPartition = 1
   ```
   (or additional size, in megabytes, to extend the partition)

4. Install Windows 2000 to the master computer. Sysprep will shut the system down automatically.

5. Image the drive.

6. Place the image on the target computer where the target computer has the same size system partition as the master computer.

7. Restart the target computer.

   The Mini-Setup Wizard starts and the partition is extended almost instantaneously.

▶ **To extend a hard disk partition when using an imaging product that does not support NTFS used by Windows 2000**

1. Configure the partition on the master computer hard disk to the minimum size required to install Windows 2000 with all the components and applications that you intend to preinstall. This will reduce your overall image size requirements.

2. Convert the file system to NTFS by using the Convert.exe tool provided in Windows 2000.

3. Include the following as the last two items of the [GuiRunOnce] section of the answer file used to create the master image:
   ```
   [GuiRunOnce]
   <Command1> = "<command line>"
   <Command2> = "<command line>"
   . . .
   <Commandn-1> = "Convert c:\ /fs:ntfs"
   <Commandn> = "%systemdrive%\sysprep\sysprep.exe -quiet"
   ```

where:

- <command line> includes any commands you need to run to install applications or configure the operating system before you image it.

- <Commandn-1> is the next-to-last command to be carried out in the [GuiRunOnce] section of the answer file. This will run the **convert** command. Because **convert** cannot convert the active system to NTFS while the operating system is running, the operating system is set to do so on the next restart. Because Sysprep is the next item to run, the system will not be converted to NTFS during that process.

- <Commandn> is the last command to run on the computer. This should be Sysprep.exe. When Sysprep is run, it prepares the computer for imaging, then shuts down the computer.

Note You cannot include ExtendOemPartition in the master answer file for this step because the partition on which the image is generated is not NTFS. You also might want to keep the image as small as possible.

4. Under the [Unattended] section of Sysprep.inf, include the statement:

   ```
   ExtendOemPartition = 1
   ```

   (or additional size, in megabytes, to extend the partition)

5. Install Windows 2000 on the master computer. Sysprep will shut the system down automatically.

Important Do not restart the computer.

6. Image the drive.

7. Place the image on the target computer where the target computer has the same size system partition as the master computer.

8. Restart the target computer.

   The computer will initially begin in conversion mode to convert the system partition on the target computer to NTFS.

   The computer will automatically restart.

   The Mini-Setup Wizard begins, and the partition is extended almost instantaneously.

Using Systems Management Server

You can use SMS to perform managed upgrades of Windows 2000 Server to multiple systems, especially those that are geographically dispersed. Note that SMS is used only for installations to computers that contain a previously installed operating system. Before you upgrade usingSMS, it is important to have assessed your existing network infrastructure, including bandwidth, hardware, and geographical constraints. The primary advantage of upgrading using SMS is that you can maintain centralized control of the upgrade process. For example, you can control when upgrades take place (such as during or after training, after hardware verification, and after user data is backed up), which computers will be upgraded, and how you will apply network constraints. For more information about SMS deployment, see "Using Systems Management Server to Deploy Windows 2000" in this book.

Using a Bootable Compact Disc

You use the bootable CD method to install Windows 2000 Server on a computer whose basic input/output system (BIOS) allows it to start from a CD. This method is quite useful for computers at remote sites with slow links and no local IT department. The bootable CD method runs Winnt32.exe, which allows for a fast installation.

Note You can only use the bootable CD method for clean installations. To perform upgrades, you must run Winnt32.exe from within the existing operating system.

To ensure maximum flexibility, set the boot order in BIOS as follows:

- Network adapter
- CD
- Hard disk
- Floppy disk

To use a bootable CD, the following criteria must be met:

- Your computer must have El Torito No Emulation support for bootable CDs.
- The answer file must contain a [Data] section with the required keys.
- The answer file must be called Winnt.sif and be located on a floppy disk.

For more information about answer file parameters and syntax, see the "Microsoft Windows 2000 Guide to Unattended Setup" (Unattend.doc) on the Microsoft Windows 2000 operating system CD. The Unattend.doc file is part of the Deploy.cab file in the \Support\Tools folder. On Windows 98 or Windows 2000, use Windows Explorer to extract this document. In Windows 95 and earlier, or in MS-DOS, use the **Extract** command to access the file.

▶ **To install Windows 2000 Server by using a bootable compact disc**

1. Start the system from the Windows 2000 Server CD.

2. When the blue text-mode screen with "Windows 2000 Setup" appears, place the floppy disk containing the Winnt.sif file into the floppy disk drive.

3. Once the computer reads from the floppy disk drive, remove the floppy disk. Setup will now run from the CD, as specified by the Winnt.sif file.

Note The bootable CD method requires that all necessary files be on the CD. Uniqueness Database Files (UDBs) cannot be used with this method.

Installation Configuration Examples

The following examples include procedures on how to install Windows 2000 Server on computers with preexisting server configurations or no existing configuration.

Existing Servers

The examples in this section are for computers with the following pre-existing server configurations:

- Computers running Windows NT Server with server applications that are compatible with Windows 2000 Server.

- Computers running Microsoft® Windows NT® Server version 3.5 or earlier, or servers running non-Microsoft operating systems.

Example 1: Windows NT Server with Windows 2000– Compatible Server Applications

This example presents two methods for installing Windows 2000 Server on computers running Windows NT Server, with or without compatible hardware.

▶ **To install Windows 2000 Server on computers with compatible hardware**

1. Back up the entire system.

2. Upgrade the system using one of the following methods:

   - Initiate a "push" installation. This means that the program or application is sent automatically from master to target computer. This method does not require a user or administrator to initiate the activity.

     –Or–

   - Initiate a local installation by running Winnt32.exe from the command prompt with the parameters you choose.

     –Or–

   - Perform a manual installation (no answer file), and answer all prompts.

     –Or–

   - Perform an automated or semiautomated installation. In a completely automated installation, the answer file provides answers for all questions. A semiautomated installation allows you to determine the degree of automation and permit some user input for applications you choose.

▶ **To install Windows 2000 Server when the computer has incompatible hardware and the hard disk does not need to be replaced**

1. Replace any necessary hardware except the hard disk.

2. Verify that all new hardware functions properly.

3. Back up the entire system.

4. Upgrade the system using one of the following methods:

   - Initiate a "push" (completely automated) installation.

     –Or–

   - Initiate a local installation by running Winnt32.exe from the command prompt with the parameters you choose.

     –Or–

   - Perform a manual installation (no answer file), and answer all prompts.

     –Or–

   - Perform an automated or semiautomated installation.

▶ **To install Windows 2000 Server when the computer has incompatible hardware and the hard disk needs to be replaced**

1. Upgrade at least one of the following:

   - RAM

   - Processor

2. Verify that all new hardware functions properly.

3. Back up the entire system.

4. Replace the hard disk. Copy the image that was backed up.

5. If you are upgrading, perform the upgrade using one of the following methods. This might be particularly useful in situations where the server is in a unique or nearly unique configuration:

   - Initiate a "push" (completely automated) installation.

     –Or–

   - Initiate a local installation by running Winnt32.exe from the command prompt with the parameters you choose.

     –Or–

   - Perform a manual installation (no answer file), and answer all prompts.

     –Or–

   - Perform an automated or semiautomated installation.

6. If you are doing a clean installation, use one of the following methods:

   - Use the Syspart method to place all necessary files on hard disk before replacing the hard disk by using disk-duplicating hardware or software. When the system starts, Setup will run automatically. Reinstall any necessary server applications.

     –Or–

   - Initiate a "push" (completely automated) installation.

     –Or–

   - Initiate a local installation by running Winnt32.exe from the command prompt with the parameters you choose.

     –Or–

   - Perform a manual installation (no answer file), and answer all prompts.

     –Or–

   - Perform an automated or semiautomated installation.

Example 2: Computers Running Windows NT Server 3.5 or Earlier, or Servers Running Non-Microsoft Operating Systems

Server operating systems that cannot be directly upgraded to Windows 2000 Server include Windows NT 3.5 or earlier versions, Novell, Banyan Vines, UNIX, and OS/2. To prepare for a clean installation, obtain a client computer built by an OEM or solution provider.

▶ **To install Windows 2000 on a computer running Windows NT 3.5 or earlier or a non-Microsoft operating system**

1. Back up the system.

2. Run Winnt.exe from the command prompt with the desired parameters by using one of the following methods:

   ▪ Perform a manual installation (no answer file), and answer all prompts.

   –Or–

   ▪ Perform an automated or semiautomated installation. Use one of the following methods:

      ▪ CD Boot Setup.

      ▪ Syspart method. This is useful when installing new hard disks in the computers.

      ▪ Sysprep method. Use when installing to identical computers (HALs and mass storage device controllers must be identical).

Note You can perform a clean installation on an existing computer if necessary, but this is not recommended. If you have servers that cannot be upgraded, replace each server with a new server containing a clean installation of Windows 2000 Server. This must be done to allow time to verify that the system is stable, to reduce potential user impact, and to provide time to migrate necessary references and settings to the new server.

---

3. Install applications compatible with Windows 2000 Server.

4. Verify system functions as required.

5. Migrate users and references to point to the new system before shutting down the existing system.

New Servers

Computers without a pre-Windows 2000 operating system installed require a clean installation of Windows 2000 Server.

To prepare for installation, obtain a client computer built by an OEM/Solution Provider.

▶ **To install Windows 2000 Server on a computer that does not have any pre-Windows 2000 operating system installed**

1. Perform a manual installation (no answer file). Answer all prompts.

   –Or–

2. Perform an automated or semiautomated installation. Use one of the following methods:

   ▪ CD Boot Setup.

   ▪ Syspart method. This is useful when installing new hard disks in the computers.

   ▪ Sysprep method. Use when installing to identical computers (HALs and mass storage device controllers must be identical).

   ▪ Boot disk and run Setup with an answer file.

Installation Planning Task List

Table 13.7 is a summary of the major tasks involved in the installation of Windows 2000 Server and required applications.

Table 13.7   Summary of Installation Tasks

Task	Location in Chapter
Resolve critical planning issues.	Resolving Critical Planning Issues
Create the distribution folder.	Preparing for Installation
Review the answer file.	Reviewing the Answer File
Review the Windows 2000 Setup commands.	Preparing for Installation
Choose an application installation method based on critical planning.	Automating the Installation of Server Applications
Choose a method for operating system installation based on critical planning.	Automating the Installation of Windows 2000 Server

C H A P T E R   1 4

Using Systems Management Server to Deploy Windows 2000

Microsoft® Systems Management Server (SMS) provides a variety of tools to help you deploy Microsoft® Windows 2000 Server or Microsoft® Windows 2000 Professional in an enterprise environment. Project leaders and analysts, Windows 2000 technical analysts, and SMS administrators involved in this process should become familiar with the recommended configurations and procedures described in this chapter. Although these recommendations also work for smaller organizations, the focus is on organizations with at least 2,500 personal computers.

You do not need to be familiar with Systems Management Server version 2.0 to understand the information in this chapter. However, you need someone with SMS expertise to perform your Windows 2000 deployment. It is presumed that your SMS infrastructure is in place or that you will put an SMS infrastructure in place prior to deploying Windows 2000. Important differences between SMS 2.0 and Systems Management Server version 1.2 are also presented in this chapter.

In This Chapter

Chapter Goals

This chapter will help you develop the following planning documents:

- Windows 2000 Software Distribution Plan
- Windows 2000 SMS Package Definitions

Related Information in the Resource Kit

- For more information about automating the Windows 2000 upgrades, see "Automating Server Installation and Upgrade" and "Automating Client Installation and Upgrade" in this book.

- For more information about automating domain consolidation and migration, see "Determining Domain Migration Strategies" in this book.

Using Systems Management Server to Distribute Software

Deploying Windows 2000 is much simpler when you use automated installation. However, there are still many tasks involved when you apply automated procedures to multiple servers and client computers throughout your organization. These tasks include:

- Selecting computers that are equipped for Windows 2000 and that you are ready to support.
- Distributing Windows 2000 source files to all sites, including remote sites and sites without technical support staff.
- Monitoring the distribution to all sites.
- Securely providing enough operating system rights to do the upgrade.
- Automatically initiating the installation of the software package with the possibility of allowing the user to control the timing.
- Resolving problems related to the distributions or installations.
- Reporting on the rate and success of deployment.

Systems Management Server can help you with all these tasks. The primary tasks involved in deploying Windows 2000 with SMS are illustrated in Figure 14.1.

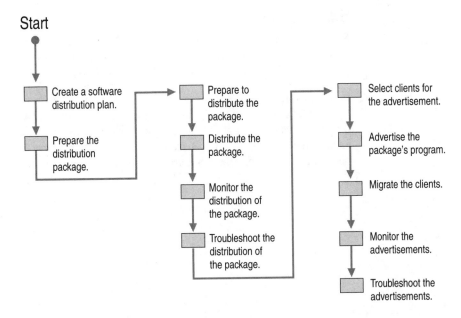

Figure 14.1   Deploying Windows 2000 with SMS

SMS provides tools for upgrading your current computers but not for the installation of new computers that do not have an operating system already installed. To use SMS software distribution, you must install SMS client components on the destination computers. These SMS components require that the computer has a properly configured operating system.

Note The phrase "SMS client" refers to all destination computers regardless of their function.

However, you can use your current SMS clients to initiate the installation of Windows 2000 into a new directory hierarchy or disk partition. In this situation, the Windows 2000 installation is a clean installation rather than an upgrade.

Note You can also use SMS to help you with other Windows 2000 deployment activities. For more information about using SMS in your Windows 2000 deployment, see "Using Systems Management Server to Analyze Your Network Infrastructure" in this book.

Software Distribution with Systems Management Server 2.0

Systems Management Server software distribution is based on multiple components and tasks which allow you to completely control the process.

SMS Packages

SMS software distribution starts with an SMS *package*. The package, the basic unit of software distribution, contains the source files for the program and the details that direct the software distribution process.

Each package contains at least one *program,* which is a command line that runs on each targeted computer to control the execution of the package. Programs can direct the installation of software or contain any other command line to be run at each targeted computer. Most packages also contain *package source files*, such as software installation files, that are used by the program when it runs.

Some software applications provide extensive installation options. Other packages and tools do not. If the program you want to distribute does not provide appropriate setup options, such as unattended operation, you can use SMS Installer to prepare your program for software distribution. SMS Installer can generate attended and unattended installation scripts that you can fully customize. This kind of scripting is not appropriate for the Windows 2000 upgrade. However, it might be useful for packages that are sent prior to the Windows 2000 upgrade to prepare the computer, or for packages that are sent after the upgrade to finalize the configuration. For more information about SMS Installer, see "Creating Self-Extracting Files with SMS Installer 2.0" in the *Microsoft® Systems Management Server Administrator's Guide*.

You can create a package by using **Packages** in the SMS Administrator console, or you can create or obtain a *package definition file* and use the **Create Package from Definition** wizard. A package definition file is an alternative, noninteractive way to create a package. It is a formatted file that contains all the information necessary to create the package. A package definition file for Windows 2000 is included with SMS 2.0. You can use SMS tools and wizards to create packages from package definition files without user interaction. When a package has been created, use the SMS **Manage Distribution Points** wizard to choose the distribution points.

Distribution

Packages also contain information about software distribution, such as the directory for the package source files. *Distribution Points* are shares on site systems where the package source files are copied for access by client computers. Packages also include information about how and when to update distribution points. For ease of administration, you can group distribution points into Distribution Point Groups.

When package files need to be propagated to other sites, SMS compresses these files for sending between sites. You can also create and use a compressed copy of the package source files within the originating site.

You can control the distribution of a package by using **Distribution Points,** which is under the definition of the package under **Packages** in the SMS Administrator console.

Advertising

After you create the Windows 2000 package, you advertise one or more of the package's programs to your users by creating an advertisement. An advertisement specifies what program is available to client computers, which computers will receive the advertisement, and when the program will be scheduled for installation. Figure 14.2 shows the software distribution process.

When an advertisement is received at an SMS client, the user can still have some control over the scheduling of the package. The advertisement can be run in a special privileged mode so that you need not give privileges to users. You can also run the advertisement so that it operates without any intervention from the user.

You create an advertisement by using **Advertisements** in the SMS Administrator console.

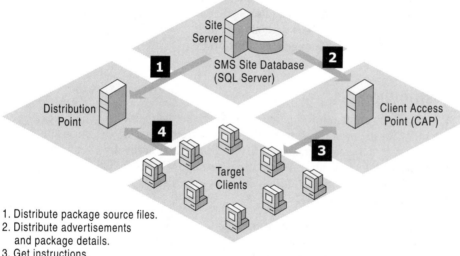

1. Distribute package source files.
2. Distribute advertisements
   and package details.
3. Get instructions.
4. Run programs.

Figure 14.2   SMS 2.0 Software Distribution Process

For more information about SMS software distribution, see the *Systems Management Server Administrator's Guide*.

SMS Software Distribution Best Practices

With large software distributions, such as Windows 2000, it is important to note the two phases of Systems Management Server 2.0 software distribution: distribution and advertising. Distribution gets the software close to the computers to be upgraded. Advertising initiates the upgrade. With a package as large as Windows 2000, the distribution phase consumes a great deal of resources and problems could arise due to lack of disk space. Therefore, make sure to plan and monitor the distribution phase carefully. After you have successfully completed the distribution phase, begin the advertising phase.

Test your distribution by first distributing Windows 2000 only to one site. The initial advertisement of the package should also be sent only to clients at that site. This allows you to test your SMS infrastructure and procedures on a limited scale. As your confidence increases and as capacity allows, you can distribute the package to more sites and increase the scope of the advertisement to include more clients and sites until you eventually include your entire organization.

Additional best practices are included in the following discussions of the software distribution process.

How SMS Can Help with Windows 2000 Deployment

Systems Management Server can be particularly helpful for deploying Windows 2000 in the following ways:

Sending Windows 2000 Source Files Out to All Sites

SMS has *senders* that can send files over a wide variety of network protocols and over virtually any kind of network link. Senders provide several benefits over traditional file transfer methods. They can:

- Use only a fraction of the network bandwidth, allowing other business functions to continue at the same time.
- Forward packages only during specified hours, such as when most users are not using the link.
- Check the files as they are transferred so that if the network link fails, the transfer resumes at the latest checkpoint rather than at the beginning of the transfer.
- Choose an alternate route to the destination.
- Use the SMS hierarchy to get the packages to the sites, rather than sending the packages to all sites directly from the originating site.

Using senders can be beneficial when your sites are remote, particularly if they have no technical support staff. In such cases, you can reliably distribute Windows 2000 software to all sites without interfering with other business functions.

Monitoring the Distribution to All Sites

SMS automatically sends a status message as each step is completed, and you can easily monitor these messages using the SMS status subsystem.

Selecting Computers

Because deploying Windows 2000 upgrades is a large, complex, high-profile process, you need to deploy it in phases. This spreads out both the network activity and required support. Also, all your computers might not be ready to receive the package at the same time; for example, some computers might not have enough memory or disk space. SMS collects inventory details about your computers and allows you to create queries that select appropriate computers. You can increase the size of the selections as your confidence in the process increases.

Collections of inventory details can automatically include any additional computers that now meet the selection criteria. For example, consider a collection that is defined to include computers with 64 Megabytes (MB) of memory or more. If you added 32 MB to an SMS client computer that had 32 MB, it would then qualify to receive the Windows 2000 upgrade and be included in the collection automatically.

Securely Providing Enough Operating System Rights

Operating system upgrades affect all aspects of a computer and, therefore, require that end users have broad access rights. You might be hesitant to give such broad permissions to users who do not have an in-depth knowledge of computers or of important company policies and procedures. SMS does have special privileges and can run the upgrade in that context.

Automatically Initiating the Installation

Upgrades can be either automatically initiated or initiated by users. You can set up the process so that even when users are involved, they do not have to choose between complex options. You can give users the option to control the timing so that the upgrade can occur when their computers are not in use.

Resolving Problems

If the upgrade to Windows 2000 causes problems on a particular computer, SMS has features that help you solve them. The status and inventory information that SMS provides can supply many details about the computer from a central, convenient source—the SMS Administrator console. You can also use SMS remote tools to remotely control the computer, transfer files, or manipulate the computer in other ways (as long as the SMS client is functional). If the user has an incompatible application or an application that might benefit from being reinstalled, you can use SMS software distribution to automatically update or remove it.

Reporting Status

SMS status messages are generated not only for the distribution of the package but also for the advertisements and the installation on user computers. You can use these status messages to report on the rate and success of deployment.

The steps required to take advantage of these SMS features are described in the procedures that follow. The details for enabling the relevant SMS subsystems and using them effectively are included the SMS documentation.

Packaging Windows 2000 for Systems Management Server

When you use Systems Management Server to deploy Windows 2000, you must put the Windows 2000 files into an SMS package. You need to create separate packages for Windows 2000 Server and Windows 2000 Professional. SMS 2.0 includes predefined packages for Windows 2000 Server and Professional. These can be used as the starting point to create your Windows 2000 packages.

For each package, SMS obtains the files from a distribution folder. For more information about structuring distribution folders, see "Automating Server Installation and Upgrade" in this book. You must structure the distribution folder as described in that chapter, and include all the auxiliary files required to complete the upgrade, such as the Plug and Play device drivers and answer files. You can even include standard applications, language packs, and service packs.

Each predefined Windows 2000 SMS package also contains SMS programs. Each program is a different combination of options that you create for installing the Windows 2000 package. For example, your default program might be to install Windows 2000 with no user intervention. If you want to allow power users to choose options, they need an additional program. All these SMS programs must be compatible with the set of files for the package available at the distribution folder.

Preparing the Windows 2000 Server Upgrade Package

The following procedure describes how to set up a typical upgrade package for Windows 2000 Server. The first step is to set up the location of the package source files and the predefined SMS package for distributing Windows 2000 Server.

▶ **To create a Windows 2000 Server SMS package**

1. Set up a location for the package source files.

   This process is described in the chapter "Automating Server Installation and Upgrade" in this book. This will include the Windows 2000 files, an answer file, and other files as needed.

2. In the SMS Administrator console, select **Packages.** From the **Action** menu, point to **New,** and then click **Package From Definition** as shown in Figure 14.3.

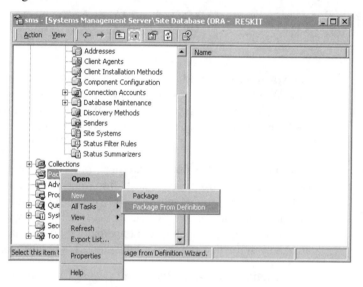

Figure 14.3   Initiating the SMS Package from Definition Wizard

3. On the Welcome page, click **Next.** From the **Package definition** list, click **Windows 2000 Server**.

4. On the Source Files page, click **Create a compressed version of the source**, and then click **Next**. In the **Source directory** box, enter the path to the package source files (see step 1). Click **Next,** and then click **Finish**.

   If the site server is extremely tight for disk space, you can choose **Always obtains files from a source directory** from the Source Files page. However, this slows future distributions of the software, and you must ensure that the source directory is always available.

5. When the wizard finishes, select **Programs** under your new package. In the results pane (the right side of the console), double-click **Automated upgrade from NTS 3.51/4.0 (x86)**. Then verify that the predefined **Command line** is the correct setup command for your needs. Repeat step 5 for the other programs that you use.

    To verify that the predefined **Command line** meets your needs, see "Examining the Windows 2000 Server Package Definition" later in this chapter.

    Consider specifying an answer file in the program command line, which can allow you to specify a large number of configuration options. For more information about answer files, see "Automating Server Installation and Upgrade" in this book.

6. In the **Comment** box, enter a comment for each of the programs that you will use.

    The user can see your comments, so be sure they are descriptive. Give your users contact information, such as the name, phone number, or e-mail address of someone that they can contact for more information.

7. On the **Requirements** tab for each program, adjust (if necessary) the **Estimated disk space** and **Estimated run time** to values that are appropriate for the upgrade you are doing. These values are information for your users.

8. On the **Environment** tab for each program, verify that **Program can run** is set to **Whether or not a user is logged on**.

    This setting ensures that the program is run with administrative rights, which is necessary for Microsoft® Windows NT® Server upgrades.

9. Click **OK** to close the program properties box.

10. Select the Windows 2000 Server package, and from the **Action** menu, click **Properties**. On the **Reporting** tab, enter *5.0* for the **Version**. Verify that the **Name** is Windows NT and the **Publisher** is Microsoft.

    Important Setting these values is necessary for the advertisement status information to be accurate. Otherwise, every execution of the SMS package is recorded as successful even if it aborts or fails.

    ---

11. Click **OK** to close the package properties dialog box.

12. If you want to ensure that users do not upgrade their computers before you are ready to deploy Windows 2000, select **Access Accounts** under your new package, and in the results pane, delete the **Guests** and **Users** access accounts.

Note that SMS does hide the software distribution shares and that users would require administrative rights on the computers (or the computers would have to be running Microsoft Windows 95 or Microsoft Windows 98) for them to take advantage of these shares.

You have to give access to users who are authorized to upgrade to Windows 2000 at a later time.

Also, do not adjust the distribution points or create an advertisement at this time.

Caution If you want to use security to control who can adjust or deploy the package, see the chapter "Distributing Software" in the *Systems Management Server 2.0 Administrator's Guide*.

If you require multiple Windows 2000 upgrade answer files to accommodate variations in your upgrades, you must create additional programs for the package in the SMS Administrator console. Each program will specify a different answer file for the **winnt32 /unattend** switch. Separate answer files allow different groups of computers to be upgraded in different ways while still using just a single package.

Systems Management Server 2.0 includes a variety of sophisticated options for packages and their programs. For example, you can specify that the Windows 2000 files be made available with a specific share name at your distribution points. This way they can easily be used by people performing manual upgrades as well as by SMS. The SMS documentation includes complete details on these options.

Allowing User Input During the Upgrade

Most SMS administrators consider it good practice not to allow user input during package installations. When users buy and install software by themselves, the Setup program generally prompts them for responses, such as which disk to install the software on or what options to install. Every user interaction introduces the opportunity for error that can cause problems. Users might not understand the implications of the answers they provide. If even a small percentage of users makes mistakes, the number of help desk calls can be overwhelming at a time when you are upgrading thousands of computers.

Another reason to eliminate user input during upgrade is to allow the installation to occur while no one is present at the computer so that you minimize the inconvenience to users.

Finally, providing all the answers in an answer file ensures that you maintain configuration standards. When you follow those standards, you simplify future computer maintenance and support by reducing the number of variables that could be relevant to a problem.

Providing an answer file with all the details required for the upgrade will prevent the Windows 2000 Setup program from asking for user input. If some details are not provided (and the **UnattendMode** line in the answer file allows it) or if the **/unattend** command-line switch is not specified, the program prompts the user for the details. An answer file for a server upgrade might look like the following (you must change the **JoinDomain** line):

```
[Unattended]
FileSystem = LeaveAlone
UnattendMode=FullUnattended
NTUpgrade=Yes
[Networking]
InstallDefaultComponents = Yes
[Identification]
JoinDomain = RED1DOM
```

Note You must specify the answer file by using the command **winnt32 /unattend:answer.file**. The command **winnt32 /unattend** performs an unattended upgrade, but it gets the information it needs from the current configuration.

Examining the Windows 2000 Server Package Definition

The Windows 2000 Server package definition that comes with Systems Management Server 2.0 includes predefined programs. Review these programs to understand how the upgrades are performed.

The Windows 2000 Server upgrade from Windows NT Server includes the switches **/unattend30** and **/batch**. The first switch, **/unattend30**, means that you will do an unattended upgrade and that all the required information will be taken from the current installation. The computer will restart 30 seconds after the Setup program completes its first phase, which is when the files are copied to your computer. An answer file is not used.

The **/batch** switch specifies that Setup not display any error messages. This is appropriate when you are sending the package to users you do not want involved in the Setup or if you are running the upgrade when no one is at the computer. However, if there are problems with the upgrade, such as a lack of disk space or an incorrect **Start in** directory, then this will not be readily apparent, because no error messages will appear.

However, you need to include error information in the SMS status messages generated as a result of the operation. If you encounter problems in your testing and the status messages are insufficient, remove the **/batch** switch to allow errors to be displayed during package testing. Also, if the user clicks on the **Cancel** button during the first phase of the Windows 2000 Setup, the user will not be asked to confirm that they want to stop the Setup.

By default, the **Start in** directory for the package is specified as **i386.** This is appropriate if the source for the package includes an i386 directory, mirroring the Windows 2000 CD-ROM. However, if the source for the package only includes the files in and below the i386 directory on the CD-ROM, it is not necessary to specify a **Start in** directory.

The estimated disk space and run time values included in the SMS 2.0 package are estimates that might not be realistic for your environment. You might want to increase them. These values are informational only and for the benefit of the user.

Notice on the **Environment** tab that the program is run with administrative rights securely provided by SMS. This is an important benefit when you are upgrading clients that run Microsoft Windows NT Workstation to Windows 2000 Professional. This feature means that you do not have to give administrative privileges to end users. It can also be important when servers are owned by business units and when central administrators have rights on the servers only through SMS.

If you include an answer file in the command line of the package program, it allows you to specify many of the options for your upgrade. For example, you can specify which disk Windows 2000 is to be installed on, or whether an upgrade or new installation needs to be done.

Preparing the Windows 2000 Professional Upgrade Package

To upgrade user computers to run Windows 2000 Professional by using SMS, you must first create a Windows 2000 Professional package. You prepare and use this package in much the same way as the Windows 2000 Server package. Begin by following the procedure to create a Windows 2000 Server package, but be sure to specify that this is a Windows 2000 Professional package. Because there are special issues for Windows 95 and Windows 98 upgrades to Windows 2000, you must create a new program as outlined in the following section.

Note Make sure to also create a separate package when you use SMS to distribute Windows 2000 Advanced Server. Although many files and setup details in this program are the same as those in Windows 2000 Server, there are enough differences to require each version to have its own package. You can use the basic Windows 2000 Server package definition as a starting point when creating packages to distribute other Windows 2000 Server versions.

Windows 95 and Windows 98 Upgrades

In addition to the differences in the source files, a significant difference between the Windows 2000 Server and Windows 2000 Professional upgrades is in the answer file when upgrading Windows 95 or Windows 98 clients to Windows 2000 Professional. Computers running Windows 95 or Windows 98 have not been members of a domain (even if the users using them have been logging onto a domain), and have not had local accounts (although they have had local profiles and password list files). Therefore, relevant details must be specified in the answer file, such as the following (you must change the **JoinDomain**, **DomainAdmin**, and **DomainAdminPassword** values):

```
[Unattended]
FileSystem = LeaveAlone
UnattendMode=FullUnattended
Win9xUpgrade=Yes
[Networking]
InstallDefaultComponents = Yes
[GUIUnattended]
AdminPassword=Testing123
[Identification]
JoinDomain = RED1
DomainAdmin = AddComputers
DomainAdminPassword = Restricted
```

A computer that is upgraded from Windows 95 or Windows 98 to Windows 2000 is given a local Administrator account. This account requires a password; you can specify that password in the **GUIUnattended** section of the answer file or let the user be prompted for it at the end of the upgrade. This password can be read from the answer file by anyone that can access the SMS package share, which is commonly most users. This is not an immediate security risk because the Windows 95 and Windows 98 computers were not secure before the upgrade, due to the nonsecure nature of those operating systems.

You might want to set the administrator password to a secure value and begin enforcing limited administrative privileges. You can do this after the upgrade by running a program that sets the password to a value shared only with authorized staff. The password is compiled within the program and is not available to unauthorized staff. You can easily create such programs by using common programming languages or scripting tools, such as SMS Installer. The program can be distributed with SMS, or it can be invoked at the end of the Windows 2000 upgrade by specifying appropriate values in the answer file.

Although computers that run Windows 95 and Windows 98 are not members of domains, computers that run Windows 2000 must be. Therefore, you need to include the **JoinDomain** line in the answer file to indicate which domain the computer needs to join, along with an administrative account and password with the right to join computers to that domain.

Caution   Answer files can be read by unauthorized staff so you need to consider security issues when you create them. However, it is unlikely that people would access the files from an SMS distribution point because the distribution points are hidden and they must know where to look for these details. An appropriate precaution, however, is to use an administrative account whose only right is **Add workstations to domain**. Another precaution is to add the computers upgraded in this manner to a dedicated resource domain. In that case the administrative account only needs to have rights in that domain, and therefore cannot cause problems in other domains in which you might have account domain controllers or other sensitive computers.

The answer file must also specify that you want to upgrade the computers that are running Windows 95 or Windows 98. Do this by including the following line in the answer file:

```
Win9xUpgrade=Yes
```

Without this line, you do a clean install of Windows 2000 rather than an upgrade.

During the Windows 95 or Windows 98 upgrade to Windows 2000, the Windows 2000 Setup program eliminates programs that it suspects might be incompatible with Windows 2000. This occurs for some of the SMS 2.0 client components. Windows 2000 provides a facility, called migration DLLs, to ease the migration of such programs. For more information about migration DLLs, see the Microsoft Systems Management Server link on the Web Resources page at http://windows.microsoft.com/windows2000/reskit/webresources.

Windows NT Workstation Upgrade

Upgrading from Windows NT Workstation to Windows 2000 is quite simple compared to upgrading from Windows 95 or Windows 98. This is because Windows NT Workstation has much more in common with Windows 2000 Professional. For this reason, you can upgrade the Windows NT Workstation without using an answer file, or you can upgrade using a minimal answer file.

It is important to set the **Environment** properties of the SMS program so that it runs with administrative rights, unless users will be logged on and have administrative rights when the package is initiated at client computers.

Distributing the Windows 2000 Packages

You need to distribute the SMS package files for Windows 2000 to all sites where you anticipate upgrading computers. Distribution is involved even if you have just one site. Distribution consists of sending the package files to the site, and then getting the files to the SMS distribution points within the site.

Preparing to Distribute the Packages

Before you distribute the Windows 2000 packages, there are several tasks you must perform to ensure that your SMS hierarchy is ready to receive them.

Check the Status of Site Servers and Distribution Points

Windows 2000 is a large operating system requiring considerable disk space. Not only are copies of Windows 2000 required for computers to be upgraded, but SMS also needs copies as it moves the package between servers. Therefore, you must review your site servers and distribution points to ensure that they have enough disk space. The easiest way to do this is to go to **System Status** in the SMS Administrator console, select **Site Status**, and then for each site, click **Site System Status** as shown in Figure 14.4. The results pane displays the distribution points and their free disk space.

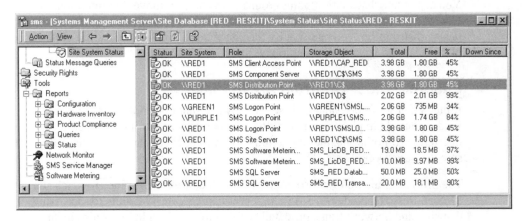

Figure 14.4   Site Status with Distribution Points and Their Free Space

Ensure Each Site Has an Adequate Number of Distribution Points

You might want to limit the number of Windows 2000 upgrades that you perform concurrently at each site. Upgrades can impose a heavy load on the local network and the distribution points. Before you upgrade, you need to experiment in a lab or run a pilot. When you test, use servers that are typical of your distribution points and a typical network. This will allow you to judge how many clients you can comfortably upgrade at one time.

If you find that your network is not a bottleneck for the upgrades but that your distribution points are, consider adding more distribution points at the site. For more information about how to add distribution points, see "Distributing Software" in the *Systems Management Server Administrator's Guide*.

Use Distribution Point Groups

Because the Windows 2000 package is quite large and you will use it extensively, make certain that you dedicate distribution points for this package. You can refer to these distribution points as a group. You can create a distribution point group for your Windows 2000 distribution points to reduce the number of administrative tasks.

You can create distribution point groups (and add or remove distribution points from the groups), when you are creating or adjusting distribution points. Then, during distribution, you can specify the distribution point groups at the same places that you specify distribution points.

Ensure Sender Controls Are in Place

If the Windows 2000 package is sent to any site that does not have adequate sender controls in place, it can overload the network link at a time when it interferes with other business functions. Therefore, check the sender controls to be sure they are properly set.

The SMS Administrator console includes SMS address definitions for each site. SMS addresses include the SMS site server name, security details for accessing that site, and network transport details (if required). The addresses also include a schedule to specify when high, medium, and low priority transfers can be executed, and how much of the network link can be used at any time of the day.

Ensure Fan-out Distribution Will Work

Systems Management Server 2.0 has a feature called fan-out distribution that allows child sites to distribute software to lower sites. This reduces the workload on the site that you use to initiate the software distribution because the software does not then have to be distributed from the initiating site to all sites. This also reduces the workload on the network link between the initiating site and the rest of the sites, which is often the most significant issue. When you are distributing to many sites, copying Windows 2000 over the network many times from any site can cause an unacceptably heavy load. Figure 14.5 illustrates the difference between software distribution with fan-out and without fan-out distribution.

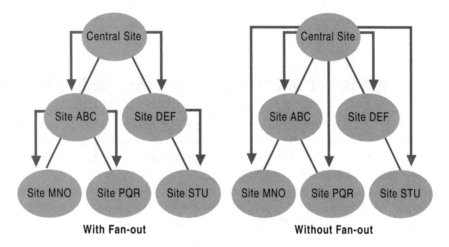

Figure 14.5   Two Types of Software Distribution

Fan-out distribution occurs automatically if the initiating site does not have an SMS address for the destination site. Therefore, you must use the SMS Administrator console to review the SMS addresses and ensure that the only SMS server with an address to a site is its parent.

Select a Test Site

To ensure that your plan is complete, distribute the Windows 2000 package to a test site or a small number of sites before sending it to your entire organization. This will enable you to quickly correct problems and to minimize their impact.

The test site or sites should be as typical as possible, but at least one site should also represent a high-risk scenario. Examples of such a scenario include deploying with a site server or distribution points that have very little disk space to spare, or having a network link that is particularly slow or unreliable.

A best practice for this level of testing is to start with small sites that do not have complex requirements. An ideal test site has technical support specialists who are readily available and users who are sympathetic to your goals. At such sites, you can identify solutions for any problems that you might not have built into your contingency plans during deployment planning. As your confidence in your procedures increases, expand your testing to sites that are larger, more complex, or more difficult to support.

During the distribution phase, your Windows 2000 deployment needs to be transparent to your users because you have not yet run the upgrades on their computers. Caution is appropriate now but is more critical later in the deployment process.

For more information about the tasks presented in this section, see the *Systems Management Server Administrator's Guide*.

Distributing the Packages to Sites and Distribution Points

The basic procedure for distributing packages is presented as follows. When you perform this task, note that all distribution points for all sites are listed, so you can select all the intended distribution points at one time. However, make sure that you first distribute the package to a small number of sites so that you can test your SMS infrastructure and procedures. As your confidence increases and capacity allows, you can include additional distribution points at other sites. For more information about this procedure, see "Distributing Software" in the *Systems Management Server Administrator's Guide*.

▶ **To distribute a Windows 2000 Server SMS Package**

1. In the SMS Administrator console, select **Packages**, select the Windows 2000 package, and then select **Distribution Points.**

2. From the **Action** menu, point to **New,** and then click **Distribution Points**.

   The **New Distribution Points** wizard appears.

3. Click **Next** to continue past the Welcome page, and select the distribution points you want to use.

   If this is a test distribution, select the distribution points that you decided on. Also, if you are using distribution point groups, select them now. Note that all distribution points for all sites are listed, so you can select all the intended distribution points now. However, you might do a limited number of distribution points at one time to better manage network traffic.

4. Click **Finish** to start the distribution.

Caution   As soon as you click **Finish** in step 4, the distribution process begins. You might notice a short delay, due to system processing, package priorities, or sender schedules; however, be prepared for immediate SMS activity.

For more information about the flow of a package after you initiate distribution, see "Software Distribution Flowcharts" in the *Microsoft® Systems Management Server 2.0 Resource Guide* (part of the *Microsoft® BackOffice® 4.5 Resource Kit*). The Windows 2000 files are compressed into a single file which is then sent to child sites. At each site, the package might then be sent to other child sites, if they have distribution points for this package.

Testing the Distribution

As the Windows 2000 packages are distributed, verify that they are properly deploying to the distribution points. The section "Monitoring the Distribution," which follows later in this chapter, describes how you can verify that the packages have arrived at all distribution points and how you can quickly identify any problems. However, you also need to test the distributions to ensure that they are complete and that the directory trees are properly laid out. You do not need to test all distribution points at this level, but make sure to spot-check a few distribution points to confirm that the production distribution is working as you intended.

Expanding the Distribution

When the first distribution of the package has been completed successfully, you can distribute the package to additional sites and distribution points. The procedure is exactly the same, except that you might want to send to more distribution points at a greater frequency and with less monitoring. You must be sure to distribute the package to sites before advertising the package to clients at those sites. SMS does not make the advertisement available to the clients until a distribution point is available.

Distributing by Means of the Courier Sender

Network links to some of your sites might be slow or unreliable, or they might already be fully utilized by other traffic. Therefore, sending a large package like Windows 2000 over the network links might not be acceptable. SMS 2.0 includes an alternate sender, called the Courier Sender, that can be used to provide all the benefits of SMS software distribution but without the network overhead normally involved in getting packages to sites.

With the Courier Sender, the SMS package is copied to CD-ROM or similar media and then sent through mail or by courier to your sites. At the sites, someone puts the CD-ROM into the site server and runs a simple program. From this point on, the software distribution carries on as it normally would. The advertisements, status information, and other information will flow over the network at the times you specify; however, this traffic is small relative to the traffic that the package itself would require.

Monitoring the Distribution

Distributing Windows 2000 in an organization with many sites takes some time to complete. Some sites will take longer than others due to the speed of the wide area network (WAN) links, the reliability of those links, sender scheduling, and so forth. There is also the possibility that, despite good preparations, some sites or distribution points might have inadequate disk space by the time the package arrives. For these reasons, it is important to give the Windows 2000 distribution adequate time to complete. Monitor it closely to determine if there are any issues to resolve and make sure that the distribution is complete at all sites.

System Status Subsystem

SMS 2.0 includes a powerful System Status subsystem for monitoring the distribution. The SMS Administrator console includes a System Status node where you can obtain summary and detailed results from the System Status subsystem. You can also obtain the status of the package distribution from the Package Status subnode.

Note When you create a package, the definition of that package is immediately distributed to all child sites; however, the actual files for that package, if any, are not distributed at that time. The same package definition is re-sent when the package definition is updated. Status information for the package definition distribution is then available. Therefore, when reviewing package status, make certain you distinguish between the distribution of the package definition and the package files.

Software distribution status is summarized at several levels, as follows.

Package Status for All Packages

When you select **Package Status** under the **System Status**, you can see, as shown in Figure 14.6, how many distribution points have been targeted for each package and how many have been installed, are retrying, or have failed. This level is useful to identify how many distribution points, if any, might need intervention. Note the size difference between the original package and the compressed package. The package identification number might also be useful for other purposes, such as troubleshooting.

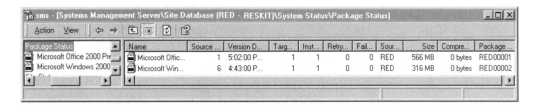

Figure 14.6   The Status of All Packages

At this level there are no status messages to query.

Package Status for a Specific Package

Below the package status for all packages, you can select each package. At this level you can see, as shown in Figure 14.7, which sites should or should not have the package, and which ones might need intervention. You can also verify that all sites have the same package version, as indicated by the **Source Version** column.

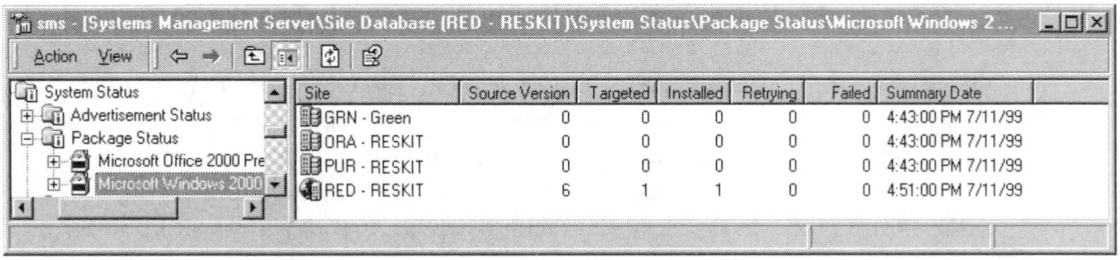

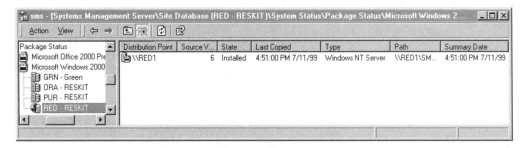

Figure 14.7   The Status of the Windows 2000 Package at All Sites

At this level you can select the **Action** menu and select **Show Messages**, **All** to see all the status messages for the package from all sites and distribution points. This can be a lot of messages; and therefore, it is better to review the messages at each site individually.

Package Status at the Sites

Below the package status for a specific package you can select each site. This level of status checking allows you to see, as shown in Figure 14.8, which specific distribution points within a site might be having problems with the distribution.

Figure 14.8   The Status of the Windows 2000 Package at a Specific Site

At this level, you can select the **Action** menu and select **Show Messages, All** to see all the status messages for the package from this site and all its distribution points. The following sequence of messages is typical (the distribution point-specific messages are listed in the next section):

- 30000 or 300001—package created or modified
- 30003—program created
- 2300, 2310, and 2311—distribution manager preparing package
- 2339—distribution manager initiating schedule and sender to send the package information (not the package files)
- 30009—distribution point assigned
- 2333—preparing to send compressed image of package
- 2335—distribution manager initiated scheduler and sender to send the package files to the sites
- 2315—distribution manager deleted the compressed image of the package

When reviewing status messages, notice that each sequence of Distribution Manager activities ends with the message 2301, which indicates that the sequence was successful. This message appears whenever Distribution Manager completes any activities. Distribution Manager is the SMS component that distributes packages from the site server to the SMS distribution points and that initiates the sending of the package to other sites.

Package Status at a Distribution Point

At the package status at each site, you can select each distribution point. At this level, you can select the **Action** menu and select **Show Messages, All** to see all the status messages for the package at this distribution point. The following sequence of messages is typical:

- 2317—distribution manager is refreshing package on distribution point (not seen the first time the package is sent to the distribution point)
- 2342—distribution manager is starting to distribute package to distribution point
- 2322—distribution manager decompressed package to temporary directory (if applicable)

- 2329—distribution manager copied package from temporary directory or package source to distribution point

- 2330—distribution manager successfully distributed package to distribution point

---

Note   The *Systems Management Server Resource Guide* includes a chapter, "Status Messages," that lists all status messages and their complete message text.

Reporting Package Distribution Status

You might want to produce a report of the package distribution status, either for easy reference or to address your own specific requirements. You can perform queries of the package distribution status classes and incorporate the responses in the reporting tool of your choice as is done with other SMS reporting tools. Table 14.1 lists the relevant classes and the category of status information that you can find in each.

Table 14.1   Package Distribution Status Classes

Class	Status Information
SMS_PackageStatus	Overall summary information about the status of packages on the distribution points.
SMS_PackageStatus RootSummarizer	Information about the status of a given package. Maps to **Package Status** in the SMS Administrator console.
SMS_PackageStatus DetailsSummarizer	Detailed information about the status of a given package by site code. Maps to the package console tree beneath **Package Status** in the SMS Administrator console.
SMS_PackageStatus DistPointsSummarizer	Detailed information about the status of a given package at a given site. Maps to the site code under the package console tree beneath **Package Status** in the SMS Administrator console.

Troubleshooting the Distributions

Monitoring the software distributions can indicate whether a software distribution has encountered problems at some point. Typically, this is due to lack of disk space, network link difficulties, or server problems. The status message text indicates such problems.

Isolating the problem is the first step in solving any technical problem. When you know which component failed, you can concentrate your efforts on the appropriate issues. Using the monitoring techniques described earlier will help you to isolate the problem. Also, the chapter on "Software Distribution Flowcharts" in the *Systems Management Server Resource Guide* includes graphics that show the typical flow of the software distribution process. If you find indications that your software distribution did not make it to a certain point in the flow, there is a good chance that the failure occurred at the previous point in the flowchart.

After you have isolated the particular component, understanding how it works can provide clues why it failed. The flowcharts also help with this. In addition, the log files can show what is happening with the component at a very low level; and therefore, what might not be working. The logs are enabled using the SMS Service Manager.

The chapter "Software Distribution Flowcharts" in the *Systems Management Server 2.0 Resource Guide* also includes troubleshooting tips for software distribution.

Advertising the Windows 2000 Packages

Users can upgrade to Windows 2000 when they receive an advertisement. The advertisements give descriptive information about the package to end users, and they include the details necessary for SMS to run the programs. The advertisements can even be assigned to run at specific times so that the user cannot block the upgrade or so that the upgrade can occur while the user is away from the computer.

Selecting Computers to Upgrade

An advertisement tells SMS to make available to an SMS collection a specific program within a package. A collection is a very flexible definition of computers, users, or user groups. In the case of a Windows 2000 software distribution, you would initially use collections that are a small number of computers used for testing purposes. Later, you would use collections that are all computers that are ready for Windows 2000. You might subdivide the collection by site or organizational unit.

Collections have the additional benefit of being dynamic; as time goes on, you can add computers to a collection, and the advertisements that are available to that collection automatically become available to those additional computers. If the collection is based on the memory capacity of computers, for example, computers are added to the collection as their hardware is upgraded for Windows 2000. If you install additional memory in a computer, the SMS hardware inventory detects this and records it within SMS. This computer is automatically included in the collection; therefore, the Windows 2000 upgrade is made available to the computer. Other than physically adding the memory to the computer, this is all automatic.

For more information about determining which computers in your organization are ready to upgrade, see "Using Systems Management Server to Analyze Your Network Infrastructure" in this book. This includes defining queries to select the computers from the inventory that SMS maintains. You can use these queries to create collections, as described in the following procedure. SMS also provides a sample report, "Windows 2000 Upgrade Candidates by Site and Roles," which might help with this process.

▶ **To create a collection of computers ready for Windows 2000**

1. In the SMS Administrator console, select **Collections.**

2. From the **Action** menu, point to **New**, and then click **Collection.**

3. In the **Collection Properties** dialog box, enter a name for the collection.

4. On the **Membership Rules** tab, click the **New Query Rule** button.

5. In the **Query Rule Properties** box, click the **Browse** button and select the appropriate query.

   For example, use a query that you have made to report on the computers that are available to be upgraded to Windows 2000. (For help developing such a query, see the chapter "Using Systems Management Server to Analyze Your Network Infrastructure"). You might have other queries that you prefer to use, such as **All Windows 95 Systems** or queries that you have defined to include all computers at specific sites.

6. Add query rules and direct membership rules as necessary.

Alternatively, at step 4 you might prefer to click the **New Direct Rule** button and then use the Create Direct Membership Rule wizard to specify the computers that you want to upgrade. This choice might be your best option during testing, especially if you have a small number of arbitrarily chosen computers that you want to run the package on.

An issue to consider is that SMS 2.0 allows collections to include computers, users, or user groups. Including users or user groups in Windows 2000 might not be appropriate, because users can often log on to different computers. Therefore, each computer that a user logs on to could be upgraded, especially if the advertisement is assigned and runs whether or not the user chooses it. However, the computers that they log on to might not be ready for the upgrade, or the users that usually use the computer might not be trained to use Windows 2000.

Caution For more information about using security to control who can adjust or use the advertisement, see "Distributing Software" in the *Systems Management Server Administrator's Guide*.

Preparing Clients to Receive the Advertisements

The computers that you are going to advertise to need to be ready for the advertisement. During the Windows 2000 upgrade, the computer needs to restart several times. If this can occur automatically, the entire upgrade can be accomplished without input from users.

Some users put a boot password on their computer. This password is required by the computer itself; and therefore, cannot be circumvented by software. Until this password is entered, the computer will not restart, and the Windows 2000 upgrade cannot continue. Therefore, make sure to advise users to temporarily disable their boot passwords. If this is not possible, someone must be present during the upgrade. The same issue holds true if the computer stops for confirmation during restart because of hardware configuration changes or other issues.

Give users advance notice of the upgrade so that they can be sure to close all documents. If users know that the upgrade is imminent, they will also be more inclined to get any training they require, perform backups, and prepare any programs they are responsible for.

If you are advertising the package with an assignment to run overnight or over a weekend, any Windows 95 or Windows 98 client computers need a user logged on in order for the advertisement to start automatically. These users might want to use a secure screen saver to prevent others from using their computer while they are away. Windows NT client computers do not have to have a user logged on for the advertisements to start.

Advertising the Packages to Computers

You now have a Windows 2000 package ready to distribute, you have the right computers selected, and you have the computers ready for the upgrade. The next step is to initiate the process. Do this by creating an advertisement as shown in the following procedure.

▶ **To create an advertisement for Windows 2000**

1. In the SMS Administrator console, select **Advertisements**.

2. From the **Action** menu, point to **New**, and then click **Advertisement**.

3. From the **Package** list, select **Microsoft Windows 2000 Server English**.

4. From the **Program** list, select **Automated upgrade from NTS 3.51/4.0 (x86)**.

5. Click **Browse**, and then select the collection that you are advertising the program to.

6. To set the advertisement to run at a specific time, click the **Schedule** tab. To add assignment schedules, click the **New** button.

Caution Assigned advertisements run only once for each client they are advertised to. If the advertisement fails at the client computer, the client does not attempt to automatically run it again. This ensures that computers are not caught in an infinite loop of trying to run an assigned advertisement, failing, restarting, and then trying again. Therefore, in step 6, you might also want to select **Allow users to run the program independently of assignments**. This allows users to run the program ahead of schedule or to run it afterwards if the program fails the first time. Alternatively, you can create a new advertisement at a later time for the computers that failed to upgrade.

As with the previous phases of Windows 2000 software distribution, start the advertising on a limited scale and expand as it proves successful. This is especially true now, because end users will definitely be affected by the software distribution. You can expand the advertising by creating additional advertisements, each aimed at different collections, or by adjusting the collection that the advertisement is based on so that it includes more and more computers. Separate advertisements might be necessary to advertise different programs to appropriate collections. For example, the Windows 95 upgrade program should be advertised only to the computers in the Windows 95 collection.

Expanding Security on Distribution Points

If you restricted access to the package on the distribution points when you created the package, you must now open that access. Do this by using the following procedure. If you are using SMS to run the program using administrative privileges, add the client network connection accounts used in the SMS site as your package access accounts.

▶ **To open security for the Windows 2000 package**

1. In the SMS Administrator console, select **Packages**.

2. Select the Windows 2000 package and then **Access Accounts**.

3. From the **Action** menu, point to **New**, and then click **Windows NT Access Account**.

4. In the **Access Account Properties** dialog box, click **Set**.

5. In the **Windows NT Account** dialog box, enter the domain and user or group, and specify the **Account Type.** Click **OK** to close the dialog box.

6. In the **Access Account Properties** dialog box, verify that the **Permissions** are **Read**.

Repeat this procedure as necessary to add additional users or groups.

Upgrading Computers

When you have Windows 2000 on a distribution point in the same site as the computers to be upgraded, and the advertisement is available at the computers, you can do the following:

- Schedule the upgrade for a time that is convenient for the user.

- Report the status of the upgrade.

Executing the Advertisement at Each Computer

Distribution to all users can be done by means of SMS at a time that you believe is convenient. However, you can give users the option to adjust the date and time, as shown in Figure 14.9, to coincide with a time when they are not using their computers. You can also make the upgrade mandatory at a certain date and time so that users cannot postpone the upgrade indefinitely.

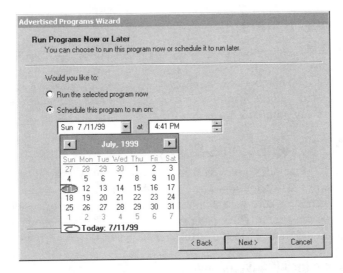

Figure 14.9   Users Can Schedule the Upgrade for a Convenient Time

The distribution that you initiate to users will also include appropriate command-line parameters to indicate which auto-answer file to use and other options, so that the setup will be done according to the standards that you have determined.

Many organizations do not give their end users full privileges on client computers. This helps to minimize problems that are caused by users making uninformed or unintentional computer changes. However, this lack of privileges would normally stop users from initiating a Windows 2000 upgrade for their computers. SMS avoids this problem by doing the Windows 2000 upgrade in the context of a special SMS security account.

Status of the Upgrade at Each Computer

When the first and final phases of the Windows 2000 upgrade are completed at the computer, Systems Management Server produces status files that are propagated up the SMS hierarchy. This information can be used to report on the overall progress of the upgrade project or to investigate the status of an individual computer, as discussed in the next section.

Customized status files can be produced to indicate specific details relating to the status of the upgrade, if desired. The programs that create these status files are invoked as part of the package execution; and therefore, must be included in its definition. For example, you might want to include such status files if you have the Windows 2000 Setup program initiate post-upgrade tasks.

Monitoring the Advertisements

The SMS status message that reports the progress of the upgrade at each computer can also be used to report the progress of the Windows 2000 deployment as a whole. The number of computers ready to be upgraded, those successfully upgraded, and the locations of failures can all be reported. You can then intervene where any problems have occurred.

The System Status Subsystem

SMS 2.0 includes a powerful System Status subsystem that allows you to readily monitor the distribution. The SMS Administrator console includes a System Status node where you can obtain summary and detailed results from the System Status subsystem. There is an Advertisement Status subnode that allows you to obtain the status of the advertisements.

Status for All Advertisements

When you select **Advertisement Status** under **System Status** in the SMS Administrator console, you can view the following:

- How many systems have received the advertisement
- How many systems have experienced general failures processing the advertisement
- How many times the advertised program has been started
- How many times the program has run to completion or failed
- Various advertisement details

An example of this information is shown in Figure 14.10. At this level there are no status messages to be queried.

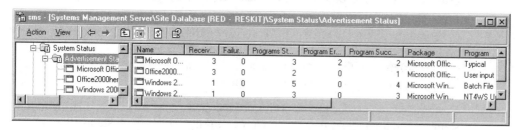

Figure 14.10   The Status of All Advertisements

Status for a Specific Advertisement

Below the advertisement status for all advertisements you can select each advertisement. At this level, you can view the following:

- Which sites have clients that have received the advertisement
- Which sites contain clients that experienced a general failure processing the advertisement
- How many times the advertised program has run at each site
- How many times it ran to completion or failed

Figure 14.11 shows this type of status. At this level, there are no status messages to be queried.

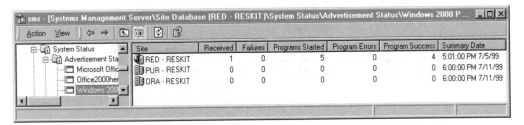

Figure 14.11   The Status of the Windows 2000 Advertisement

Status at a Site

At the advertisement status level, you can select each site. From the **Action** menu, point to **Show Messages,** and then click **All** to see the status messages for the advertisement at this site. The following sequence of messages is typical:

- 30006—advertisement created
- 3900—advertisement processed within a site (distributed to client access points, and so forth)
- 10002—advertisement received at a client
- 10005—program started
- 10007—program failed

  The message indicates why this has occurred. Common reasons are that the user cancelled the program or otherwise forced it to stop, or the client computer did not have enough disk space.

- 10009—program completed successfully

  At this point the SMS part of the upgrade is done. This corresponds with the end of the first phase of the Windows 2000 Setup (the file upgrade phase).

- 13126—upgrade completed (will be reported as 10009 if SMS 2.0 SP2 or later is in place)

At this point the Windows 2000 Setup is complete. The last two phases (text mode and GUI setup) have ended, and the computer is ready for the user to log on.

Reporting Advertisement Status

You might want to produce a report of the advertisement status, either for easy reference or to address your own specific requirements. You can perform queries of the SMS advertisement status subsystem and incorporate the responses in the reporting tool of your choice, as is done with other SMS reporting functions. Table 14.2 lists the relevant class and the category of status information that can be found in the class.

Table 14.2   Advertisement Status Class

Class	Status Information
SMS_AdvertisementStatusSummarizer	Displays detailed advertisement status information grouped by site code. Maps to the advertisement items beneath **Advertisement Status** in the SMS Administrator console.

For more information about writing reports based on the data SMS collects, see the Microsoft Systems Management Server Technical Details link on the Web Resources page at http://windows.microsoft.com/windows2000/reskit/webresources.

For the Windows 2000 advertisement status reporting, you will want reports such as the following:

Computers that Have Been Advertised to but Have Not Received the Advertisement

This report is a comparison of computers that are currently in the relevant collection but do not have a 10002 status message. If the program was advertised before the report, this report will indicate the computers that have not been used lately or that are not properly connected to the network or the SMS infrastructure.

Computers that Have Received the Advertisement but Have Not Started the Program

This report is a comparison of computers that have a 10002 status message but do not have a 10005 status message. If the program was assigned to run before the report, this report will indicate the computers that have not been used since the advertisement was first advertised or that have become disconnected from the network or the SMS infrastructure. If the program was not assigned, this report will also include computers where the users have chosen not to upgrade yet.

Computers Where the Program Started but Did Not Complete Successfully

This report is a comparison of computers that have 10005 status messages but not 10009 status messages. These are likely to be computers where the user has cancelled the upgrade or the computers did not have enough disk space. Parsing the 10007 message description gives more details. If either problem is common, then a report of those specific computers might be appropriate.

There is a remote possibility that some computers will fail in such a way that neither 10007 or 10009 status messages will be received. To take that possibility into account, you can have a report of computers with 10005 messages but not 10008 or 10009 messages. For users who have canceled the upgrade, an e-mail reminding them of the importance of the upgrade might be sufficient to resolve the problem. Or, the program can be assigned so that it must happen at a specific time. For other problems, manual intervention might be required (using the SMS remote tools might be sufficient).

Computers Where the Program Completed Successfully but the Final Upgrade Has Not Been Received

This report is a comparison of computers that have 10009 status messages but not 13126 status messages. These are likely to be computers where the upgrade started but then stopped for some reason. If you run the report during a period of mass upgrades, such as over a weekend, this report can help you identify problems that you can manually correct before the user is aware of them. However, it usually takes an hour or more for the upgrade to progress from the time at which the 10009 message is generated to the point at which the 13126 message is generated.

Note SMS 2.0 SP2 includes a fix to the package status reporting system so that the 13126 message is replaced with a 10009 message, which is the correct behavior. The messages are also generated more reliably, and the 10009 message has a meaningful message text, whereas the 13126 message has no text. Therefore, it is recommended that you deploy SMS 2.0 SP2 before deploying Windows 2000 with SMS. After SP2 has been deployed, the report logic will have to distinguish between the two 10009 messages using the message text.

Computers Upgraded Per Day

This report is a count of 13126 status messages spread over time. This can be useful for monitoring the status of the project overall.

Troubleshooting Advertisements

The advertisement monitoring process helps you to isolate problems, hopefully before the users report problems. Typical problems include lack of disk space, user interference, or package definition errors. The text of the status messages will indicate such problems. Also make sure to verify that the package is available on at least one distribution point at the site.

Isolating the problem is the first step in solving any technical problem. If you know which component failed, you can concentrate your efforts on the appropriate issues. Using the monitoring techniques listed previously will help you to isolate the problem. The chapter "Software Distribution Flowcharts" in the *Systems Management Server Resource Guide* includes graphics that show the typical flow of the software distribution process on the server side. Also in the *Systems Management Server Resource Guide,* the chapter "Client Features Flowcharts" includes graphics that show the flow on the client side. If you find indications that your software distribution did not make it to a certain point in the flow, then there is a good chance that the failure occurred at the previous point in the flowchart.

After you have isolated the component, understanding how it works can provide clues why it failed. The flowcharts also help with this. In addition, the log files can show what is happening with the component at a very low level, which can help you see what might not be working. You enable server logs using the SMS Service Manager, and client logs are always enabled.

SMS has several features that can help you resolve problems on client computers, including the following:

- Remotely control the client computer.
- Transfer files to the computer to replace files that need updating.
- Restart the computer.
- Obtain computer details, either based on the routine inventory or on real-time remote control tools. (Note that the routine inventory is available even when the client is offline.)
- Upgrade incompatible application software.

There will be situations where manual intervention is needed, such as when an upgrade makes it impossible to restart the computer or to connect a computer to the network, or when the SMS client components become inoperative.

Using Systems Management Server to Ease Domain Consolidation and Migration

In the past, larger organizations have often had multiple domains. With Windows 2000, the reasons for those domains will most likely disappear, and therefore, consolidating them will simplify computer administration. Migrating to native Windows 2000 domains allows your organization to take full advantage of Windows 2000 features.

The chapter "Determining Domain Migration Strategies" in this book discusses the issues of domain consolidation and migration in detail. It also details strategies and techniques that will ease the process of consolidation and migration. SMS can help with this process, and thus Windows 2000 deployment with SMS should be considered in conjunction with domain consolidation and migration. For example, you can use SMS to deliver scripted executions of the DCPromo portion of the upgrade process for domain controllers.

The most significant benefit of using SMS for domain consolidation and migration occurs during deployment of the upgrade to Windows 2000. By adjusting the **JoinDomain** value in the answer file, the computers can be put in the new, consolidated domain.

Examining Differences Between Systems Management Server 1.2 and Systems Management Server 2.0

Systems Management Server 2.0 is dramatically different from its predecessor, Systems Management Server 1.2. Both versions have similar feature sets, but each version accomplishes the features using dramatically different techniques. If you are planning to use SMS 1.2 to deploy Windows 2000, or for domain consolidation, you need to be aware that software distribution in SMS 1.2 differs from SMS 2.0 in the following ways:

- Only computers can be targeted for software distribution, and the targeting is not dynamic (new computers that meet the requirements for upgrade must be targeted with new jobs).

- Windows NT–based computers, where the logged-on user does not have administrative privileges, must be given the Package Command Manager as a Service facility. There is no charge for this addition to SMS 1.2, but you need to deploy this facility before you begin the Windows 2000 deployment.

- The status subsystem for jobs is more awkward to work with.

- The originating site for the package must keep a compressed copy of the package.

- Programs cannot force another program to run before them and cannot be disabled centrally.

- Windows 2000 computers might not be supported by SMS 1.2 as clients. Therefore as computers are upgraded to Windows 2000, they might stop functioning as SMS 1.2 clients or they might no longer be supported. For more information about SMS 1.2 support of Windows 2000 computers, see the Microsoft Systems Management Server link on the Web Resources page at http://windows.microsoft.com/windows2000/reskit/webresources.

Other differences between the two versions are relevant to other SMS features that might benefit your Windows 2000 deployment. For more information about those features and differences, see "Using Systems Management Server to Analyze Your Network Infrastructure" in this book.

Planning Task List for Using Systems Management Server to Deploy Windows 2000

Table 14.3 lists the primary tasks presented in this chapter for deploying Windows 2000 using SMS.

Table 14.3   Task List for Deploying Windows 2000 Using SMS

Task	Location in Chapter
Learn concepts related to SMS software distribution.	Using SMS to Distribute Software and Examining Differences Between SMS 1.2 and 2.0
Prepare the packages.	Packaging Windows 2000 for SMS
Distribute the packages.	Distributing the Windows 2000 Packages
Test the distribution.	Distributing the Windows 2000 Packages
Monitor the distribution.	Distributing the Windows 2000 Packages
Troubleshoot the distribution.	Distributing the Windows 2000 Packages
Report on the distribution.	Distributing the Windows 2000 Packages
Advertise the packages.	Advertising the Windows 2000 Packages
Test the advertisements and packages.	Advertising the Windows 2000 Packages
Upgrade the computers.	Advertising the Windows 2000 Packages
Monitor the advertisements.	Advertising the Windows 2000 Packages
Troubleshooting the advertisements.	Advertising the Windows 2000 Packages
Report on the advertisements.	Advertising the Windows 2000 Packages
Use SMS to ease domain consolidation and migration.	Using SMS to Ease Domain Consolidation and Migration

Additional Resources

- For more information about using Systems Management Server, see the *Microsoft Systems Management Server Administrator's Guide.*

- For advanced information about using Systems Management Server, see the *Microsoft Systems Management Server 2.0 Resource Guide*, which is part of the *Microsoft BackOffice 4.5 Resource Kit.*

CHAPTER 15

Upgrading and Installing Member Servers

Member servers provide file, print, Web, application, and communication services. Member servers are not domain controllers; however, each member server retains an account in the domain. You can upgrade your existing member servers to Microsoft® Windows® 2000 Server or install new member servers as the first phase in your Windows 2000 Server deployment. This allows you to benefit from Windows 2000 Server features even before you deploy the Active Directory™ directory service. This chapter presents planning considerations as well as procedures that will be useful to system administrators for installing or upgrading member servers to Windows 2000 Server.

It is recommended that you have a working knowledge of Microsoft® Windows NT® version 4.0, knowledge of networks and networking concepts, and knowledge of Microsoft® Windows® 2000 sites. This will help you determine the installation and upgrade requirements of Windows 2000 Server in an enterprise networking environment.

In This Chapter

Chapter Goals

This chapter will help you develop the following planning documents:

- Member server installation and upgrade plan
- Inventory of existing hardware and software

Related Information in the Resource Kit

- For more information about Windows 2000 sites, see "Designing the Active Directory Structure" in this book.
- For more information about creating test plans, see "Building a Windows 2000 Test Lab" in this book.

Planning for Member Server Upgrade and Installation

One of the main advantages of installing or upgrading to Windows 2000 Server is having the Active Directory™ directory service. However, even if you delay installing Active Directory, you can still upgrade member servers to Windows 2000 Server. This way you can access the new and improved component features and services such as Routing and Remote Access and Terminal Services.

Servers within a Windows 2000 domain can have one of two roles: as a domain controller or as a *member server*. A member server is a Microsoft server that can have accounts in a Microsoft® Windows NT® version 3.51, Windows NT 4.0, or a Windows 2000 domain. However, if they are members of a Windows 2000 domain, they do not contain any Active Directory objects. Member servers share common security features such as domain policies and user rights.

Member servers can act as:

- File servers
- Print servers
- Web servers
- Proxy servers
- Routing and Remote Access servers
- Application servers, which include:
  - Component servers
  - Terminal servers
  - Certificate servers
  - Database servers
  - E-mail servers

Process for Installing or Upgrading to Windows 2000

The planning process for installing or upgrading member servers can take considerable time. Planning ahead minimizes problems that can occur with network upgrades. Figure 15.1 represents the recommended process to follow when designing an upgrade strategy that fits your network infrastructure.

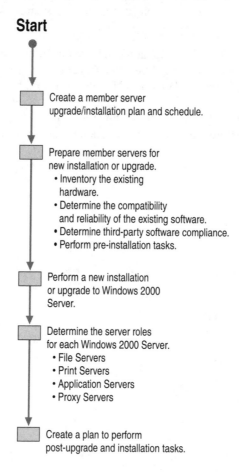

Figure 15.1   Member Server Installation and Upgrade Process

Creating an Upgrade and Installation Plan

Thorough planning will help your deployment run smoothly. In addition to using the flow chart in the previous section, use the following guidelines to help you create a member server upgrade and installation plan:

- If necessary, modify any existing network design documents to reflect your current server environment.

   If you do not have an up-to-date network diagram, consider creating one before proceeding with a network upgrade.

- Examine the existing network infrastructure for:

   - Software compatibility

   - Interoperability needs

   - Hardware needs

- Address the following questions:

   - How many new member servers are needed?

   - Which member servers should be upgraded?

   - Which member servers should be replaced with new hardware before upgrading?

- Document changes in your current network environment and identify related planning considerations.

- If needed, create a test environment so that member servers that might have incompatible software can be tested before being deployed.

Create a Schedule

When you upgrade servers, interruptions of network services commonly occur. To minimize this risk, create an upgrade timeline that decreases downtime during business hours. To construct a timeline and upgrade schedule, consider the following:

Amount of time to allow for the installation or upgrade of a single server

The amount of time required to upgrade a server varies depending on hardware speed and the number and type of applications and services you want to install after installing the operating system. Experienced administrators can install or upgrade the operating system on a single server in about one hour. However, it can take several hours to days to evaluate the installation and test the server before you actually put it into production on the network.

Implementation of new services and features of Windows 2000 Server

After you have installed or upgraded a server, you can configure it with new services or features. This involves testing the server in a test lab environment before installing it on the production network.

Scenario: Minimizing Network Downtime During Server Upgrade

One of the best ways to minimize downtime is to install or upgrade member servers in phases. For example, a network with a total of 70 servers is running Microsoft® Windows NT® Server version 4.0 and has different types of member servers. In addition to the existing member servers, the administrator references the network growth analysis and decides that five additional servers are needed to account for network growth in the next year. For other servers and clients to still have access to the Internet, files, and applications, the administrator cannot upgrade all the servers at once. The type and amount of each group of member servers on this example network are as follows:

- Five file servers (will add one new file server)
- Ten application servers (will add one new application server)
- Ten IIS servers
- Five fax servers
- Five proxy servers
- Ten routers (will add one new router)
- Five Routing and Remote Access servers (will add one new Routing and Remote Access Server)
- Fifteen print servers (will add one new print server)
- Five SQL database servers

First, the administrator determines how long it will take to upgrade each group of member servers. The administrator decides to take one of each type of server offline and upgrade and test them during normal business hours, leaving the rest of the servers online and functioning. If the upgrade and tests go well, the rest of the servers will be upgraded at night after normal business hours, allowing the upgraded servers to handle the network services. The installation of the additional servers will be done after all of the original servers are upgraded. This will allow time to configure the services and components of the new servers.

Preparing Member Servers for Upgrade or New Installation

Installing or upgrading member servers to Windows 2000 Server requires that computers be compatible with the new operating system. There are various tasks you need to perform and information you need to gather to prepare for a successful member server upgrade or installation.

Inventory the Existing Hardware

To prepare your member servers you need to first inventory the existing hardware. To do this, document the following information for each member server:

- Vendor, make, and model of the computer being upgraded.
- Amount of physical memory installed.
- Type of network adapter installed.
- All Plug and Play devices.
- Uninterruptible power supply (UPS) connected to the server.
- Type of external hard disks connected to the computer.
- Hard disk partitioning and free disk space available.
- Any hardware or software redundant array of independent disks (RAID) in use.
- Type of CD-ROM drive installed.

Determine System Requirements

The system requirements for Windows 2000 Server are greater than for Windows NT Server 4.0. Each server on the network must meet minimum requirements in order for Windows 2000 Server to operate efficiently. The minimum hardware requirements are as follows:

- A 166-MHz Pentium or higher processor

  A new installation of Windows 2000 Server supports computers with up to four processors. If you are upgrading a computer running Windows NT Server that supported more than four processors, you must then upgrade to Windows 2000 Advanced Server because it supports up to eight processors.

- At least 64 megabytes (MB) of random access memory (RAM), although 128 MB is recommended, with 4 gigabytes (GB) being the maximum.

- Hard disk partition with enough free space to accommodate the setup process

  To calculate the space needed, start with 850 MB and add 2 MB for each MB of memory on your computer. More space might be needed, depending on the following:

  - The components and services being installed.
  - The file system used.

    The file allocation table (FAT) file system requires 100 to 200 MB of additional free disk space.

  - The method used for installation.

    To install across the network, allow 100 to 200 MB additional space because additional driver files must be available during this process, as compared to installing from the operating system CD.

  In addition, an upgrade might require much more disk space than a new installation. As Active Directory functionality is added, the existing user accounts database can expand by up to a factor of 10.

Note After setup is completed, actual disk space used for the operating system (excluding user accounts) is usually less than the free space required for Setup, depending on which computer components are installed.

For additional requirements see the \Support directory on the Windows 2000 Server operating system CD.

Determine the Compatibility and Reliability of Existing Software

It is highly important that you ensure that the software you need to use is compatible with Windows 2000 before you upgrade. You can do this by contacting the software vendor, or setting up a test network on which to run the application.

Additionally, to help you determine if your existing software is compatible and reliable, you will want to address the following questions:

- Which file systems (FAT or NTFS) are in use?
- Which operating systems and service packs are currently in use?
- For which operating system was a program written (Microsoft® Windows NT®, Microsoft® Windows® 98, Microsoft® Windows® 95, Microsoft® Windows® 3.x, or Microsoft® MS-DOS®?)
- Was the program written to operate in a specific network environment? For which version of that network?

- Are program and program configuration files stored on a server or on the clients?

- Are data files stored on a server or on clients?

After you have answered these questions, you will know whether the existing software in your environment is compatible with Windows 2000 Server.

Determine Third-Party Software Compliance

Windows 2000 Server software that is logo-compliant (software designed for Windows 2000 Server) takes advantage of Windows 2000 Server features such as Active Directory. Any software written for Windows 2000, Windows NT, Windows 95, or Windows 98 should run properly under Windows 2000 Server. Software that was written for 16-bit Windows (Windows 3.x) or MS-DOS should work in a Windows 2000 Server environment, but is subject to the following considerations:

- The software might require special configuration files, such as Autoexec.nt and Config.nt.

- The 16-bit software might have or require special device drivers that are no longer available or are incompatible with Windows 2000 Server. In this case, contact the vendor who wrote the software and find out whether they currently have or are developing the device driver you need.

In all cases, you should thoroughly test all software on the Windows 2000 platform in a lab environment before risking downtime and data loss in a production environment. For more information about setting up a test environment, see "Building a Windows 2000 Test Lab," "Conducting Your Windows 2000 Pilot," and "Testing Applications for Compatibility with Windows 2000" in this book.

Perform Pre-installation Tasks

It is recommended that you perform certain tasks to make sure that system files remain safe and the installation goes smoothly. These tasks are:

Read the Pre-Installation Documents

There are three important documents that the network administrator should read before performing an upgrade.

- Hardware Compatibility List

  The Hardware Compatibility List (HCL) contains hardware compatibility information that will assist you in determining if your current hardware is compatible with Windows 2000 Server. The list is comprehensive, but be aware that Microsoft continually updates the information. To determine if the hardware in your organization is HCL-certified, see the Hardware Compatibility List link on the Web Resources page at http://windows.microsoft.com/windows2000/reskit/webresources.

- Read1st.txt

  The Read1st.txt file provides late-breaking, critical, or other preinstallation and upgrade information that supplements the Windows 2000 Server documentation.

- Relnotes.txt

  This document provides release notes concerning late-breaking or other Windows 2000 Server information, and is also a supplement to the documentation. This file contains a detailed, technical description of additions to the operating system. You can use it to make informed decisions concerning the deployment of member servers in your network.

Record System Information

It is important that you record all system information pertinent to each server before an upgrade begins. This will provide an important reference document if it becomes necessary to return a member server to its original condition.

To view server system information in Windows NT Server 4.0, from the **Administrative Tools** menu, click **Windows NT Server Diagnostics**. To print the information, click **File** and **Print Report** from within the Windows NT Server Diagnostics Manager.

Performing an Upgrade or Installation

Deciding whether to perform an upgrade or a new installation of Windows 2000 Server on a member server depends on whether there are current servers with existing Windows NT operating systems on them, or whether new servers are going to be implemented into the infrastructure.

Pre-Upgrade Checklist

Before starting the Setup wizard for Windows 2000 Server, review the following checklist and apply any items that might be applicable to member servers in your network infrastructure.

Check Event Logs for errors.

Under Windows NT 4.0, check the System, Application, and Security Event Logs in **Event Viewer** to ensure that no errors are currently logged. If you find errors, correct them before upgrading to Windows 2000 Server.

Back up system and important files.

Perform a full backup of all drives on the computer. Save any pertinent hard disk setup information before upgrading.

In Windows NT 4.0 you can use **Disk Administrator (windisk.exe)** to save the hard disk partition table to a floppy disk. On the menu bar click **Partition**, then click **Configuration** and **Save**.

If the drives are formatted with the NTFS file system, you do not need to take any steps to prepare the disks. Windows 2000 Server Setup converts them to the version of NTFS used in Windows 2000 Server. Also, disable any disk mirroring because a mirrored volume reduces the chance of your receiving an unrecoverable error by keeping a duplicate set of data on another drive. If mirroring is enabled while upgrading, and the data on the primary drive becomes corrupt, it can cause you to lose all of the data on the mirrored drive.

Additionally, back up all of your important files onto tape or a share on your network. If a problem occurs during the upgrade, it is extremely important to complete this step first to protect your data

If you are using the Backup feature, confirm that there are no errors after the backup process is complete by checking the backup log located at \Winnt\Backup.Log

You can also back up the registry of the member server by using the Regback.exe program on the companion CD in the *Microsoft® Windows NT® Server Resource Kit*. This tool backs up registry keys to files without the use of tape. However, Windows 2000 Server will back up the registry at the same time that the System State data is backed up.

Remove incompatible software and utilities.

Remove any virus scanners, third-party network services, or client software. Read the release notes file (on the Windows 2000 Server operating system CD) for information about any known problems with specific applications.

Disconnect UPS devices.

Disconnect the serial cable that connects any UPS devices. Windows 2000 Server attempts to automatically detect devices connected to serial ports, which can cause problems with the UPS and the installation process.

If possible, set your system BIOS to reserve all interrupt requests (IRQs) currently in use by non-Plug and Play ISA devices. Failure to do so could result in the following message during installation:

INACCESSESSIBLE_BOOT_DEVICE

If this occurs you will not be able to complete installation.

Also be sure to update your emergency repair disk and your emergency boot disk.

Upgrading Member Servers

There is one, primarily automated procedure for upgrading a member server. During the upgrade, Windows 2000 Server migrates the current settings of the operating system, and little administrator input is required.

To upgrade a computer, load the Windows 2000 Server operating system CD, and then the Setup wizard guides you through the steps. When prompted, click **Upgrade to Windows 2000**. In the final step, Windows 2000 Server Setup will restart, gathering information and using preexisting settings from the previous operating system.

Performing a New Installation

There are three ways to install Windows 2000 Server on a computer that does not have an operating system:

- If the computer supports a CD-ROM drive as a startup device, Setup starts automatically after you insert the operating system CD. Ensure that the system BIOS is configured to allow the CD to start automatically.

  Note On many computers the CD auto-boot capability is not enabled by default; however, you can enable it manually.

- If the computer does not support a CD-ROM drive as a startup device, you need to install Windows 2000 Server using the four Setup disks.

- If you choose to load the operating system from a network, you need a network client disk that recognizes the network adapter currently installed in the computer. It will enable you to log on to your respective domain.

Note If you load Windows 2000 Server from a network, you need the appropriate number of client licenses for the number of servers you are installing.

There are no preexisting services or applications for the initial setup for new member servers. In this case, you have a computer that is Windows 2000 Server–compliant and meets all the system requirements stated earlier in this chapter. The computer needs to be on a local area network (LAN) or have a supported CD-ROM drive, and have a formatted hard disk.

Determining Server Roles for Each Windows 2000 Server

Member servers can have various functions on a network, allowing administrators to deploy a diverse range of services and forming the middle tier in a network infrastructure. The following sections describe each of these possible roles and provide details concerning installation and upgrade of each server type where necessary.

File Servers

File servers provide departmental and workgroup access to files. In previous Windows server operating systems, file shares were localized within a site—a user had to connect to individual file servers to access the files they needed. If a file server became unavailable, the user had to access other file servers that contained the same files. Windows 2000 Server makes accessing shares redundant.

Shares on a Windows 2000 Server file server can be distributed across a site or domain by using the Windows 2000 Server Distributed file system (Dfs). With the Dfs infrastructure, a group of file servers can be seen as one entity. For example, consider the following Windows NT 4.0 file server names:

- \\fileserver\file1
- \\fileserver\file2
- \\fileserver\file3
- \\fileserver\file4

Using Windows 2000 Server Dfs, you can add all four file servers to the Dfs tree and use just one share called \\fileserver. This would allow any client to access any file on any of the four file servers. This provides for redundancy and load balancing in that Active Directory first tries to find the file server that is closest to the client requesting the information. If that file server is unavailable, Dfs will go to the next file server to get the information.

If you plan to use Dfs to distribute your file servers across the domain, it is recommended that you plan which servers will distribute which file shares before upgrading. For example, put all the file servers that store applications in one group named \\Fileserver\Applications. The next set of file servers, which store backed-up data, can be named \\Fileserver\Backup. This ensures minimal confusion for users when it comes to determining which file share they need to use.

For more information about planning for, installing, configuring, and using Dfs, see "Distributed File System" in the *Microsoft® Windows® 2000 Server Resource Kit Distributed Systems Guide* and "Determining Windows 2000 Storage Management Strategies" in this book.

Note Domain-based Dfs requires that Active Directory be running.

Macintosh Volumes

When upgrading Windows NT 4.0 file servers with Macintosh volumes, be sure that Services for Macintosh have been upgraded (or reinstall it if you removed it before the upgrade.) Also, be sure that all of the Macintosh files are backed up before proceeding. You can then upgrade the server to Windows 2000 Server by following the instructions given earlier in this chapter.

After the upgrade is complete, you can view the migrated Macintosh volume by using the **Computer Management** function, shown in Figure 15.2.

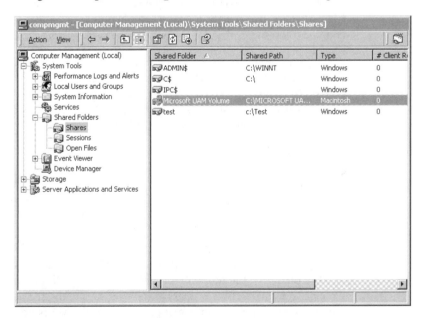

Figure 15.2   Computer Management Showing Migrated Macintosh File Volume

In Windows 2000 Server, you can access the Macintosh volume with either the AppleTalk or the TCP/IP protocol. If there are clients on your network that use only AppleTalk, you can load the protocol by means of Local Area Properties in Control Panel.

If you are installing a new file server that hosts Macintosh volumes, the first step is to verify that your hardware meets the minimum requirements. See the hardware checklist presented earlier in this chapter and the HCL on the Windows 2000 Server operating system CD. Then install Windows 2000 Server by following the instructions given earlier in this chapter.

After the installation is complete, make the new server a Windows 2000 file server by either using the **Configure Your Server** wizard and clicking **File Server**, or by going to **Computer Management** under **Administrative Tools**, then clicking **Shared Folders**.

Novell NetWare Volumes

Microsoft File and Print Services for NetWare is an add-on utility that enables a computer running Windows 2000 Server to provide file and print services directly to NetWare and compatible clients. The server appears just like any other NetWare server to the NetWare clients, and the clients can access volumes, files, and printers at the server. No changes or additions to the NetWare client software are necessary.

This utility is one component of the Microsoft product, Microsoft Services for NetWare v. 5: Add-on Utilities for Microsoft Windows 2000 Server and Microsoft Windows NT Server 4.0.

Test File Shares

After you upgrade a member server to Windows 2000 Server, be sure you can still access the shares by using these steps:

- From the server, open Windows Explorer. Click two or three file shares, and on the **File** menu, click **Properties,** and then check for sharing.

- From one or more clients, log on and map drives for several known shares to verify that sharing works properly on the Windows 2000 server.

If you have upgraded the server to support Dfs, ensure that all of the file servers can be reached by alternately shutting down each file server and following the same steps.

Print Servers

Organizations of all sizes require that printing capability is available to users across sites and domains. Most printing is set up within groups in an organization for easy access to all users within the group. Printers can be set up as public printers, where access to them is global, or as private printers, where only a team or certain users within a group have access. This requires careful planning for the number of users that will be accessing any particular group of printers.

Print Server Setup

The requirements for setting up Windows 2000 Server print servers are as follows:

- The server is running Windows 2000 Server.
- The server has sufficient RAM to process documents.

  If a print server manages a large number of printers, the server might require additional RAM beyond what Windows 2000 Server requires for other tasks. If a print server does not have sufficient RAM for its workload, printing performance could deteriorate.

- The server has sufficient disk space to spool documents until they print.

  This is critical when documents are large or likely to accumulate. For example, if 10 users attempt to print at the same time, the print server must have enough disk space to hold all of the documents until the print server sends them to the print device. Documents for which the server does not have sufficient memory stay on the client until the server has sufficient space. This process causes performance to deteriorate on the client.

- All appropriate print drivers are installed.

  Appropriate printer drivers are those written for Windows 2000 Server. You can find appropriate drivers either on the Windows 2000 Server operating system CD or obtain them from the printer manufacturer. Printer drivers for different hardware platforms are not interchangeable.

Clients that are not running Microsoft operating systems have additional requirements to print to network printers. You must install additional services on print servers and install the appropriate printer drivers on the clients. These services are:

- Macintosh—Services for Macintosh
- NetWare—Client and Gateway Services for NetWare
- UNIX TCP/IP Printing—also known as Line Printer Daemon (LPD) Service

Contact the printer manufacturer for the appropriate drivers.

Guidelines for Setting up a Network Printing Environment

If you do not already have a network printing environment in place, use the following guidelines for developing a network-wide printing strategy:

- Determine the number of users who will print, and the printing workload that they will generate.
- Determine the printing needs. For example, if users in Sales need to print colored brochures, you will need a color print device.
- Determine where the printers will be located. It should be easy for users to pick up their printed documents.
- Determine the number of print servers that will be required to handle the number and types of printers on the network.
- Consider using the following:
  - Shared printers allow multiple users to print to one device.
  - Printer pools allow multiple printers to share a print queue. Print devices should be identical and located near each other, that is, unless they share a common emulation mode.
  - Printer priorities allow print queues to process some print jobs ahead of others based on priorities assigned to users or groups of users (as opposed to processing in chronological order).

Active Directory Integration with Windows 2000 Server Print Services

You can enhance network printing by implementing Active Directory. However, it is important to note that performance and functionality enhancements for Windows 2000 Server print services are all available without deploying Active Directory.

After you have deployed Active Directory, the Windows 2000 server provides a standard printer object. Using this object, you can publish printers to be shared across the network in Active Directory. This provides users with an easy way to search for printers in the Active Directory structure. Users are able to find printer-based attributes such as printing capabilities (PostScript, color, legal-sized paper, and more) and printer location, including the ability to connect to and send documents to that printer (subject to printer permissions).

Testing Printer Shares

After you have installed or upgraded your print servers to Windows 2000 Server, use the following steps to ensure that all the printer shares are functioning.

▶ **To test your print server installation**

1. In Control Panel, open the **Printers** folder.

2. On the **File** menu, click **Properties**. The printer **Properties** window appears.

3. In the **Properties** window, click **Print Test Page**.

4. Confirm that all the printer shares are operating correctly under Windows 2000 Server.

After printing a test page for each printer on the server, repeat the test from multiple clients and verify that they are able to map to the printer share and submit print jobs.

Application Servers

Application servers provide a central location for programs that are used by multiple users. Rather than loading an application on 1,000 clients, you can have users access the application through a share. Depending on the amount of disk access required when the program is in use, such a server might need high levels of resources. For example, an application server for a database program might need more memory and disk space than a server that hosts a word processing program.

When performing a new Windows 2000 Server installation, or upgrading from Windows NT 4.0, make sure that you back up any data related to applications that work with Windows 2000 Server. After you back up the applications and data, upgrade the application server in a test environment to ensure compatibility.

An application member server can host a variety of programs and services. See Table 15.1 for a description of some of these services.

Table 15.1   Programs and Services on an Application Member Server

Service	Description
Component Services	Manages server components such as Application Load Balancing, Transaction Services, Application Management, and Message Queuing.
Terminal Services	Software services that allow client applications to be run on a server so that clients can function as terminals rather than as independent systems.
Database	Provides an operation and management platform for database programs such as Microsoft® SQL Server™.
E-mail	Provides an operation and management platform for mail servers such as Microsoft® Exchange Server.

Note For database and mail servers, other applications will need to be installed on top of Windows 2000. These services are not supplied with native Windows 2000.

With the exception of Microsoft® Exchange Server and Microsoft® SQL Server™, you can configure each of these services by using the **Configure Your Server** wizard after you install Windows 2000 Server.

Component Services

Application member servers provide a platform to run component services such as Application Load Balancing, Transaction Services, Application Management, and Message Queuing. You can add these services through **Add/Remove Programs** and the **Windows Components Wizard** shown in Figure 15.3.

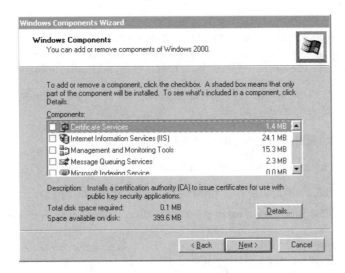

Figure 15.3   Wizard for Adding Component Services

If you are upgrading from Windows NT Server 4.0, ensure that services from the previous operating system are migrated properly by checking their configuration after the upgrade.

Terminal Services

Terminal Services allows client applications to be run on a server so that clients can function as terminals rather than independent systems. The server provides a multisession environment and runs the Windows-based programs being used on the clients. Terminal Services can also be loaded using the **Windows Components Wizard**. For more information about Terminal Services, see "Deploying Terminal Services" in this book.

Database Server

Windows 2000 application member servers provide a stable platform for running and managing database software such as SQL Server. When you install Windows 2000 Server, no further configuration of the operating system is needed to run the database service.

If you are upgrading from Windows NT version 4.0 or earlier to Windows 2000 Server, be sure to back up any database you have on the member server before beginning the upgrade. Also, if you are using a database application other than SQL Server, ensure that it is Windows 2000 Server compatible. For more information about SQL Server, see the *Microsoft® SQL Server™ Resource Guide*, which is part of the *Microsoft® BackOffice 4.5 Resource Kit*.

Web Servers

A Web server is a computer equipped with the server software that uses Internet protocols such as Hypertext Transfer Protocol (HTTP) and File Transfer Protocol (FTP) to respond to Web client requests on a TCP/IP network.

The following are general requirements for setting up Windows 2000 Web-based member servers:

- Read the HCL to ensure hardware compatibility.

- Determine what new or additional components will go on the Web server.

- Back up data in case problems occur during the upgrade or installation.

- Test Web-based member servers after upgrading to Windows 2000 Server.

Internet Information Services (IIS) is the Web service integrated with Windows 2000 Server. You can use IIS to set up a Web or FTP site on your corporate intranet, create sites for the Internet, or develop component-based applications.

Windows 2000 Server includes the Internet Services Manager Microsoft Management Console (MMC) snap-in. This snap-in is a powerful site administration tool that provides access to all of your server settings. If you use IIS, you will use this snap-in to manage complex sites on your corporate intranet, or publish information on the Internet.

It is recommended that you test your Web servers after upgrading to Windows 2000 Server. To verify connectivity from a Windows 2000 member server to other Web sites, perform the following test:

- From the server, open the Internet Services Manager MMC snap-in and verify that all Web sites (in existence before the upgrade) were successfully upgraded to the Web service on the Windows 2000 member server. Verify that the service is running.
- From a client, open a Web browser and verify connectivity to Web sites on the Windows 2000 member server.

For more information about IIS, see the *Microsoft® Windows® 2000 Server Resource Kit Internet Information Services Resource Guide.*

Proxy Servers

Microsoft® Proxy Server allows clients and servers to access the Internet while keeping your intranet free from intruders. Member servers running Proxy Server 2.0 can be seamlessly upgraded, but in order for Proxy Server to operate after the upgrade, an update is required.

Windows 2000 Server requires that you load the Windows 2000 Proxy Server 2.0 Setup wizard on the member server. To install Proxy Server, download the Setup wizard, shown in Figure 15.4, on your local drive or floppy disk and follow the wizard instructions. For more information about downloading a copy of the wizard, see the Microsoft Proxy Server link on the Web Resources page at http://windows.microsoft.com/windows2000/reskit/webresources.

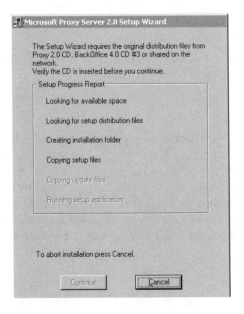

Figure 15.4   Wizard for Proxy Server 2.0 Setup

Performing Post-Upgrade and Installation Tasks

Before you integrate a member server into your production environment, it is vital that you test the server to ensure that you performed a successful upgrade or installation. Be sure that before your Windows 2000 Server goes into the production environment, it is ready to provide better service and increased functionality without unplanned downtime.

Testing Network Connectivity

After you have upgraded or installed a member server, be sure to verify that you still have network connectivity. Use the list that follows as a troubleshooting guide if you lose network connectivity in a TCP/IP network environment.

- Use the IPCONFIG tool to verify the TCP/IP configuration parameters on the newly upgraded Windows 2000 Server. The parameters include the IP address, subnet mask, and default gateway.

- After the configuration is verified with the IPCONFIG tool, use the PING tool to test network connectivity. The PING tool is a diagnostic tool that tests TCP/IP configurations and diagnoses connection failures. Open a command prompt window and ping the following:

  - Ping 127.0.0.1 (Loop back address). This will verify that TCP/IP is installed and loaded correctly.

  - Ping the IP address of your local host. This will verify that it was added correctly.

  - Ping the IP address of the default gateway. This will verify that the default gateway is functioning correctly.

  - Ping the IP address of a remote host. This will verify that you can communicate through a router.

Tuning Network Servers

After your Windows 2000 member servers are on the network, some of them might need performance tuning. Even the most carefully planned server upgrade might not be able to eliminate all of the possible problems that can occur, such as bottlenecks. If system problems occur, they can be found by using counters in the Windows 2000 Server System Monitor snap-in within the Performance tool. You can collect data by monitoring processor, disk, and network activity. The data might reveal that bottlenecks caused by demands on certain resources indicate a need for tuning.

Bottlenecks can be caused by:

- Insufficient resources such as processors, memory, or hard disks.

  You can address this by inventorying the network hardware and determining which servers need upgraded hardware.

- Unbalanced workloads that put uneven loads on servers.

  To solve these problems, Microsoft® Windows® 2000 Advanced Server provides Network Load Balancing to ensure that the workload is distributed evenly across resources. For more information about Network Load Balancing and Microsoft Advanced Server, see "Ensuring the Availability of Applications and Services" in this book.

When tuning your network servers, keep the following recommendations in mind:

- Make only one change at a time, because a problem that appears to be a single resource setting or component might actually involve more than one. Also, it is easier to redo changes to a single setting or component than to multiple settings, and changing too many settings at one time might actually make your situation worse. Keep a record of the changes and the impact those changes have on the system.

- Repeat your monitoring after every change you make to assess whether the change had a positive impact on the server.

- Check the **Event Log** viewer in **Administrative Tools** for any event logs that are generated due to performance problems.

Tools for System Administration

Use the Microsoft Management Console (MMC) and associated snap-ins to perform most system administration for Windows 2000 Server.

Table 15.2 lists common administration tasks for file, print, and Web services.

Table 15.2   Common Administration Tasks

Task	Windows 2000 Server Tool
Managing file shares	Computer Management MMC Snap-In
	Windows Explorer
Managing printer shares	Printer folder (in Control Panel, or under **Settings** on the **Start** menu)
Managing Web sites	Internet Services Manager MMC Snap-In

Tools for performing remote administration are included with Windows 2000 Server. They allow you to manage a server remotely from any computer that is running Windows 2000 Server.

For more information about how to use remote administration, see Windows 2000 Server Help.

Planning Task List for Member Servers

Table 15.3 lists the tasks you need to perform when planning your member server upgrade or installation.

Table 15.3   Planning Task List for Member Servers

Task	Location in Chapter
Create an upgrade/installation plan and schedule.	Planning for Member Server Upgrade and Installation
Inventory the existing hardware.	Preparing Member Servers for Upgrade or New Installation
Determine system requirements.	Preparing Member Servers for Upgrade or New Installation
Determine the compatibility and reliability of existing software.	Preparing Member Servers for Upgrade or New Installation
Determine third-party software compliance.	Preparing Member Servers for Upgrade or New Installation
Upgrade an existing server.	Performing an Upgrade or Installation
Perform a new installation.	Performing an Upgrade or Installation
Determine server roles for: - File servers - Print servers - Application servers - Web servers - Proxy servers	Determining Server Roles for Each Windows 2000 Server
Test network connectivity.	Performing Post-Upgrade and Installation Tasks
Tune network servers.	Performing Post-Upgrade and Installation Tasks

CHAPTER 16

Deploying Terminal Services

Terminal Services provides access to Microsoft® Windows® 2000 and the latest Windows-based applications for client computers. It also provides access to your desktop and installed applications anywhere, from any supported client. IT managers and system administrators who want to increase flexibility in application deployment, control computer management costs, and remotely administer network resources need to learn about this built-in feature of Microsoft® Windows® 2000 Server.

Before reading this chapter, it is recommended you read the chapters "Introducing Windows 2000 Deployment Planning" and "Planning for Deployment" in this book.

In This Chapter

Chapter Goals

This chapter will help you develop the following planning document:

- Terminal Services Deployment Plan

Overview of Terminal Services

Terminal Services running on a Windows 2000 Server enables all client application execution, data processing, and data storage to occur on the server. It provides remote access to a server desktop through *terminal emulation* software. The terminal emulation software can run on a number of client hardware devices, such as a personal computer, Windows CE–based Handheld PC (H/PC), or terminal. The term *Windows-based Terminal* (WBT) broadly describes a class of thin client terminal devices that can gain access to servers running a multi-user Windows operating system, such as Terminal Services.

With Terminal Services, the terminal emulation software sends keystrokes and mouse movements to the server. The Terminal server does all the data manipulation locally and passes back the display. This approach allows remote control of servers and centralized application management, minimizing network bandwidth requirements between the server and client.

Users can gain access to Terminal Services over any Transmission Control Protocol/Internet Protocol (TCP/IP) connection including Remote Access, Ethernet, the Internet, wireless, wide area network (WAN), or virtual private network (VPN). The user experience is only limited by the characteristics of the weakest link in the connection, and the security of the link is governed by the TCP/IP deployment in the data center.

Terminal Services provides remote administration of network resources, a uniform experience to users in branch offices in remote locations, or a graphical interface to line of business applications on text-based computers. Some of the benefits of Terminal Services include:

- Allows the use of 32-bit Window-based applications from devices that might not be Windows-based such as:
  - Windows for Workgroups 3.11 or later
  - Windows-based terminals (Windows CE devices)
  - MS-DOS-based clients
  - UNIX terminals
  - Macintosh
- Clients that are not Windows-based require the use of a third-party add-on.
- Requires minimal disk space, memory, and configuration for Terminal Services clients.
- Simplifies support for remote computers and branch office environments.
- Provides centralized security and management.
- Is unobtrusive to applications and the existing network infrastructure.

Terminal Services is a built-in feature of Windows 2000. You can enable Terminal Services in one of two modes:

Remote Administration

Remote Administration gives system administrators a powerful method for remotely administering each Windows 2000 server over any TCP/IP connection. You can administer file and print sharing, edit the registry from another computer on the network, or perform any task as if you were sitting at the console. You can use Remote Administration mode to manage servers not normally compatible with the Application Server mode of Terminal Services, such as servers running the Cluster service. For more information about Windows Clustering, see "Ensuring the Availability of Applications and Services" in this book.

Remote Administration mode only installs the remote access components of Terminal Services. It does not install application sharing components. This means you can use Remote Administration with very little overhead on mission critical servers. Terminal Services allows a maximum of two concurrent Remote Administration connections. No additional licensing is required for those connections, and you do not need a license server.

Application Server

In Application Server mode, you can deploy and manage applications from a central location, saving administrators development and deployment time as well as the time and effort required for maintenance and upgrade. After an application is deployed in Terminal Services, many clients can connect—through a Remote Access connection, local area network (LAN), or wide area network (WAN), and from many different types of clients.

You can install applications directly at the Terminal server, or you can use remote installation. For example, you can use Group Policy and Active Directory to publish Windows Installer application packages to a Terminal server or a group of Terminal servers. Applications can only be installed by an Administrator on a per server basis, and only if the appropriate Group Policy setting is enabled.

Terminal Services cannot pass the Internet Protocol (IP) address of individual client computers to an application. Because this information is required by Windows Clustering, you cannot use Cluster service in Application Server mode.

Client licensing is required when deploying a Terminal server as an application server. Each client computer, regardless of the protocol used to connect to Terminal server, must have the Terminal Services Client Access License as well as the Windows 2000 Client Access License.

Terminal Services Licensing Components

Terminal Services has its own method for licensing clients that log on to Terminal servers, which is separate from the licensing method for Windows 2000 Server clients. Terminal Services licensing includes the following components: the Microsoft Clearinghouse, a license server, a Terminal server, and client licenses.

Microsoft Clearinghouse

The Microsoft Clearinghouse is the database Microsoft maintains to activate license servers and to issue client license key packs to the license servers that request them. The Clearinghouse stores information about all activated license servers and client license key packs that have been issued. You access the Clearinghouse through the Licensing wizard with the Terminal Services Licensing feature.

License Server

A license server stores all Terminal Services client licenses that have been installed for a Terminal server and tracks the licenses that have been issued to client computers or terminals. A Terminal server must be able to connect to an activated license server before clients can be issued licenses. One activated license server can serve several Terminal servers simultaneously.

Terminal Server

A Terminal server is the computer on which Terminal Services is enabled. It provides clients access to Windows-based applications running entirely on the server and supports multiple client sessions on the server. When clients log on to a Terminal server, the server validates the client license. If a client does not have a license, the Terminal server requests one for the client from the license server.

Client Licenses

Each client computer or terminal that connects to a Terminal server must have a valid client license. The client license is stored locally and presented to the Terminal server each time the client connects to the server. The server validates the license, and then allows the client to connect.

Figure 16.1 shows the Terminal Services licensing components.

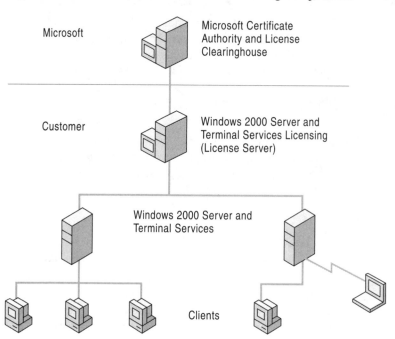

Figure 16.1   Terminal Services Licensing Components

For more information about setting up Terminal Services licensing components, see "Setting Up a License Server" later in this chapter.

Required Licenses

Deploying Terminal Services and Terminal Services Clients on your network requires the following licenses:

Windows 2000 Server License   This license is included with the purchase of the product.

Windows 2000 Server Client Access License   This is required for each device connecting to Windows 2000 Server. Client Access Licenses permit clients to use the file, print, and other network services provided by Windows 2000 Server. The Terminal Services component of Windows 2000 Server requires Per Seat licensing for the Windows 2000 Server Client Access License, except when you purchase the Windows 2000 Terminal Services Internet Connector License. The Internet Connector License is described later in this chapter.

Each client computer or terminal requires the following licenses:

Windows 2000 Terminal Services Client Access License or Windows 2000 License

The Client Access License provides each client computer or Windows-based terminal the legal right to access Terminal Services on a Windows 2000 Server. For example, this license is required to start a terminal session and run Windows-based applications on the server. The Windows 2000 license permits the installation of the Windows 2000 operating system, in addition to providing the legal right to access Terminal Services on a Windows 2000 Server. The Terminal Server Client Access License is not required for clients connecting only to Terminal servers in Remote Administration mode.

Optional Terminal Services Licenses

In addition to the required Terminal Services licenses, two optional licenses are available: the Windows 2000 Terminal Service Internet Connector License and the Work at Home Windows 2000 Terminal Services Client Access License.

Windows 2000 Terminal Services Internet Connector License

In place of the Client Access Licenses, you have the option to purchase the Windows 2000 Terminal Services Internet Connector License. This license is purchased separately as an add-on license to Windows 2000 Server. It allows a maximum of 200 concurrent users to connect anonymously to a Terminal server over the Internet. This is useful for organizations that want to demonstrate Windows-based software to Internet users without rewriting Windows-based applications as Web applications. All users who access a Terminal server with this license must not be employees.

When you use the Internet Connector License with a specific Windows 2000 Server, Terminal Services only allows anonymous client access. You cannot use the Internet Connector License with other types of Terminal Services client access licenses on the same Windows 2000 Server.

Work at Home Windows 2000 Terminal Services Client Access License

For organizations that want to use Terminal Services to provide their employees home access to the Windows 2000 desktop and 32-bit Windows-based applications, the Work at Home Terminal Services Client Access license is available through the Microsoft Volume licensing programs. For each Windows 2000 Professional or Terminal Services Client Access License you purchase, you can purchase an additional Work at Home Windows 2000 Terminal Services Client Access License.

Third-Party Expansion

MetaFrame™ is a third-party add-on to Windows 2000 Terminal Services from Citrix Systems, Inc. It incorporates the Citrix Independent Computing Architecture (ICA) protocol and provides extended capabilities for:

- Client devices
- Network connections
- Local system resources

MetaFrame also provides a variety of management tools for use with Windows 2000 Terminal Services. For more information about MetaFrame, contact Citrix Systems, Inc.

Creating Your Terminal Services Deployment Plan

With an understanding of the capabilities of Terminal Services and the licensing requirements, you can begin the planning phase of your Terminal Services deployment. This section helps you gather the information you need to create a Terminal Services deployment plan for your organization.

Process for Deploying Terminal Services

As you begin the planning phase for deploying Terminal Services, consider using the planning steps shown in Figure 16.2.

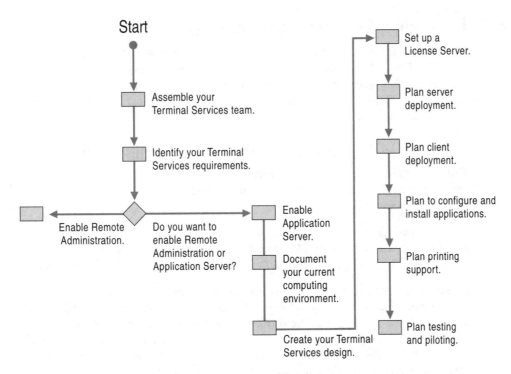

Figure 16.2   Process for Deploying Terminal Services

Each of these activities is discussed in the sections that follow.

Assembling the Terminal Services Team

Teamwork is critical to planning for and deploying Terminal Services. Planning should include system administrators for the network issues, administrators for the Terminal Services applications, and those responsible for your business units.

The core planning team must identify the business needs that Terminal Services will address and design the Terminal Services deployment.

Identifying Your Terminal Services Requirements

After your team is assembled, their first task is to determine what business scenarios Terminal Services will address. Review the business scenarios in this section to help you determine how you can best utilize Terminal Services in your organization. Before you begin to plan your deployment, review the requirements for each business scenario.

Scenario 1: Terminal Services Remote Administration

Terminal Services Remote Administration enables system administrators with the appropriate permissions to remotely administer each Windows 2000 server over TCP/IP connections.

In this scenario, a system administrator uses features such as Microsoft Management Console (MMC) Domain Manager and directory service administration to remotely administer servers within their own directory domain.

By enabling Terminal Services in Remote Administration mode, server management is extended across forests and into mixed mode domains where there are both Windows 2000 and Microsoft® Windows NT® computers. With Windows Clustering, server management can be extended to cluster servers. If all servers run Windows 2000, Remote Administration can be deployed on every server in an enterprise, allowing direct connection and administration.

Because enabling Terminal Services has little impact on a server, it is recommended you enable Terminal Services on all servers in a forest. In that case, if one server goes down, another server is available. For mixed environments, or where control must be contained, Remote Administration could be deployed on a limited set of servers, such as the domain controllers. Other servers could be administered across the domain using standard management tools. In either case, administration can be run from any platform supporting the Terminal Services client; it does not need to be Windows 2000.

In Remote Administration mode, Terminal Services has two built-in per-server connections that require no special installation and no special licensing.

Figure 16.3 illustrates Remote Administration enabling server management across forests and into a mixed-mode domain.

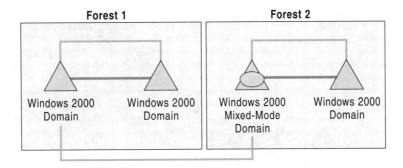

Figure 16.3   Remote Administration Extends Server Management

Scenario 2: Remote Access

Remote Access extends the capabilities of Terminal Services over external TCP/IP connections. The user experience is limited by the characteristics of the weakest link in the connection.

In this scenario, users in a remote office with Terminal Services client software on their computers can access the accounting application on the Terminal server back in your central office. Essential corporate data is accessed with a Remote Access connection over a modem. Because primarily keyboard and display information is being exchanged between the client and the server, the bandwidth requirements are low, providing a great experience even for users over a slow modem link. You can add more applications without increasing the need for more bandwidth, as long as they are not graphically intensive.

Before someone in the branch office can access your network resources, they have to present their credentials and be fully authenticated. You can provide an additional layer of security when routing through a Terminal server to access network resources.

A similar paradigm could be used to allow access to infrequently used, or retired applications or applications in development.

Figure 16.4 illustrates the way employees in a remote office might connect to a corporate office using a TCP/IP connection.

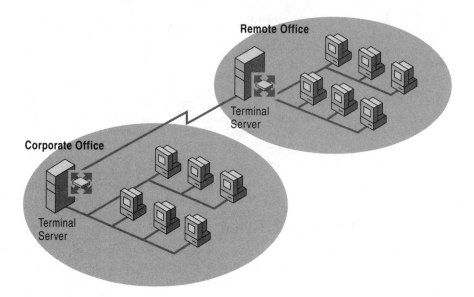

Figure 16.4   **Corporate and Remote Offices Linked by TCP/IP Connection**

Scenario 3: Line of Business Applications

The Application Server mode of Terminal Services is ideally suited for deploying line of business applications, particularly those that are difficult to install or need to be frequently updated.

In this scenario, data entry operators access a line of business application to enter product information into a database. Because the application is on a Terminal server, the data entry operators are working on Windows-based terminals rather than client computers. If a server goes down, client devices can reconnect to another server. Maintaining the data separately from the Terminal servers supports this, and using Network Load Balancing across a group of Terminal servers provides the failover control. If a terminal goes down, it can be replaced with minimal disruption to the data entry operator.

Throughout the organization, departments are organized and security is designed to provide the appropriate access to information and network resources that are required by the tasks each user performs.

Figure 16.5 illustrates the way data entry operators might enter product information into a database using a business application that resides on a Terminal server.

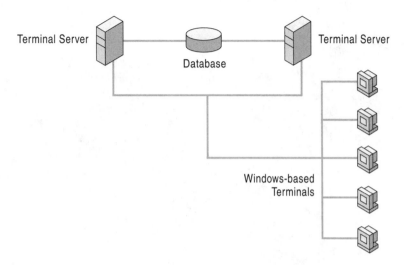

Figure 16.5   Line of Business Applications on Terminal Servers

Scenario 4: Central Desktop Deployment

Central desktop deployment is achieved by loading desktop applications onto a Windows 2000 server with Terminal Services enabled in Application Server mode. Each client computer has a single, small application that enables the emulation of each user's Windows-based desktop. Applications are actually running on the server.

In this scenario, a global enterprise with employees all over the world provides its users with reliable access to production and legacy applications as well as office productivity tools. With Terminal Services enabled on a Windows 2000 server, clients can run a controlled, standardized set of applications even when located remotely, or using legacy hardware. The system security provides the appropriate access rights to clients.

Because the Windows desktop experience is available to all users, developers can create standard Windows-based user interfaces for proprietary applications using tools such as Microsoft® Visual Basic®.

Figure 16.6 illustrates the way an organization can provide global access to applications and tools using Terminal Services.

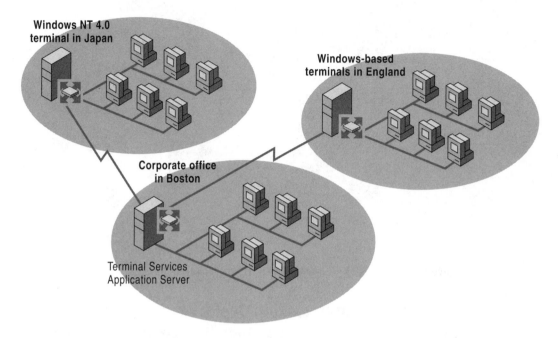

Figure 16.6   Central Desktop Deployment of Applications and Tools Using Terminal Services

Deployment Requirements

The previous Terminal Services scenarios just presented often overlap. For example, users who access their desktop through a central desktop sometimes also do so using Remote Access over a modem. Before you deploy Terminal Services in your organization, be sure to carefully study the requirements indicated for each scenario in Table 16.1.

Table 16.1   Deployment Requirements

	Remote Administration	Remote Access	Line of Business Application	Central Desktop Deployment
Licensing		X	X	X
License Server		X	X	X
Domain Structure	X		X	X
Load Balancing		X	X	X
Roaming Profiles		X		
Local Printing	X	X	X	X
Security	X	X	X	X

Preparing Your Computing Environment

Before you design your Terminal Services deployment, you must thoroughly understand your current computing environment. For more information about documenting your computing environment, see "Planning for Deployment" in this book. For information specific to Terminal Services deployment, be sure to address the considerations described as follows.

Install License Server on Domain Controller

In Windows 2000 domains, the license server must be installed on a domain controller. In workgroups or Windows NT 4.0 domains, you can install the domain license server on any Windows 2000 server. However, if you are planning to migrate from a workgroup or Windows NT domain to a Windows 2000 domain, it is highly recommended you install the license server on the domain controller or on a computer that can be promoted to a domain controller.

Access Over Wide Area Network

Determine if filters have been implemented on the routers or firewalls that would prevent clients from remotely gaining access to a Terminal server. Check to make sure that the Remote Desktop Protocol (RDP) port (port 3389) is not blocked at the firewall and that access to specific corporate segments is not limited to Internet Protocol (IP) or Internetwork Packet Exchange (IPX) network addresses. If these blocks are in place and they prevent remote connections, the team must address them during deployment.

Access to Network Services

You might want to provide customers or suppliers with access to applications or data; or you might determine that the Internet is the easiest way for end users to gain access to Terminal Services. If you plan to make servers available over the Internet, consider the security implications.

If your organization uses a firewall, determine if it is a packet-level or application-level firewall. Packet-level firewalls are easier to configure for new protocols. If your organization uses an application-level firewall, check to see if the vendor has defined a filter for the RDP; if not, contact the vendor and ask them to create a filter.

Document the method the network uses to connect to the Internet. This helps you determine how much bandwidth is available to Terminal Services. Does the network have a permanent connection? Describe the number and types of lines used to make the connection, such as T1 or Integrated Services Digital Network (ISDN).

Connecting the Terminal Services Client and Server

RDP supports TCP/IP connections between the Terminal Services client and server. That connection can be through Network and Dial-up Connections, natively on the local LAN, or through a wide area VPN connection. Terminal Services uses whatever IP connection you provide. It is important to consider, however, whether the type of connection you provide is appropriate to the work that is done; and whether the security it provides is appropriate to the data that is transmitted. A single user can dial in over a low bandwidth modem line and realize good performance, but it would not be appropriate to share a 28.8-kilobit line among an active office of 100 people.

Assessing the Current Environment

Complete a fairly high-level assessment of the current environment, including Windows-based terminals, client computers, green screen terminals, Macintosh computers, UNIX workstations, UNIX X terminals, and larger handheld devices. Instead of attempting to document individual computers, it is sufficient to estimate the numbers and describe division-wide or organization-wide standards. Tasks for performing this assessment include the following:

- Provide an overview of the total number of client computers currently in use.

- Describe the current configuration of the computers that will be running the Terminal server client in terms of CPU, operating system, available hard disk space, RAM, and video. Record any official or unofficial standards that might exist by division or throughout your organization, and make note of any computers that fall below the standard. Any client computers not meeting minimum standards must be upgraded or replaced. Consider the number of each class of client you have to determine the standard that maximizes your cost/benefit tradeoff.

- Document how many and what kind of terminals exist in your environment, including any existing Windows-based terminals that will be used with Terminal Services and any green screen or UNIX X terminals that have to be replaced.

  Green screen terminals cannot be used as Terminal server clients; in some cases you might maintain them for legacy mainframe access, or you might choose to upgrade to Windows-based terminals and have Terminal Services and mainframe access.

- Document any systems with which Terminal server clients must interface. If current client computers gain access to these systems through a non-Windows 2000 gateway, you might need to install a new gateway. Determine whether your organization has the appropriate licenses needed to gain access to these systems from a Windows environment.

Considerations for Application Deployment

Document the applications you intend to deploy to client computers with Terminal Services. Some applications have features that prevent them from working with Terminal Services or cause them to perform poorly. For this reason, you might want to instruct users to install these applications locally where feasible. Specifically, you need to identify the following:

- Applications that require special hardware to operate, like barcode scanners or card swipes. You can use these devices with a Terminal Services client only if they connect to the client computer or terminal in such a way that the computer recognizes the peripheral as a keyboard-type device. Peripherals that connect to the local computer through the parallel or serial port or through a special card are not currently recognized by the RDP-based Terminal server client.

- Multimedia applications or applications that have very large graphical output do not run well under Terminal Services. Many games fall into this category, as do streaming media applications.

In other cases, applications run but require special installation or execution scripts. Generally, these scripts compensate for issues in the program, like misuse of the registry or lack of multi-user file storage support. Check with the application developer for Terminal Services scripting. For more information about this topic, see the Terminal Services Application Information link on the Web Resources page at http://windows.microsoft.com/windows2000/reskit/webresources.

Custom applications might require modification or supporting scripts if they were not written as multi-user-aware. For more information about creating scripts, see the Terminal Services Creating Installation and Execution Scripts link on the Web Resources page at http://windows.microsoft.com/windows2000/reskit/webresources.

Note Non-administrative users cannot use Windows Installer technology to install applications on a Terminal server.

Creating Your Terminal Services Deployment Design

After you have identified your business needs and inventoried your computing environment, you can begin planning to deploy Terminal Services. This section will help you gather the information you need to create a Terminal Services Deployment Plan for your organization.

Setting Up a License Server

A license server is required by Terminal Services when running in application server mode. The Terminal Services License Service is a low-impact service that stores the client licenses that have been issued for a Terminal server and tracks the licenses that have been issued to client computers or terminals.

The license server must be activated through the Microsoft Clearinghouse and loaded with Client Access Licenses for distribution from the Clearinghouse. The license server is accessed by the Terminal servers only to issue a new license, and need only be administered to obtain licenses from the Clearinghouse.

Enabling a License Server

You can enable the Terminal Services License Service on your computer when you run Windows 2000 Server Setup. It is recommended that you enable Terminal Services on a member server or stand-alone server, and that you install the license server on a different computer.

There are two types of license servers, a domain license server and an enterprise license server. Before installing the license server, consider which of the following two types of license servers you require:

- A domain license server is appropriate if you want to maintain a separate license server for each domain. If you have workgroups or Windows NT 4.0 domains, a domain license server is the only type that you can install. Terminal servers can only access domain license servers if they are in the same domain as the license server. By default, a license server is installed as a domain license server.

- An enterprise license server can serve Terminal servers in any domain within a site, but the domain must be a Windows 2000 domain. It can only serve Terminal servers in the same site. This type of license server is appropriate if you have many domains. Enterprise license servers can only be installed using Add/Remove Programs, not during Windows 2000 Setup.

When deciding where on your physical network to deploy your License Server, consider how a Terminal server discovers and communicates with a License Server. Upon enabling Terminal Services for Window 2000, the Terminal server will begin polling the domain and Windows 2000 Active Directory™ looking for a License Server (in a workgroup environment, the Terminal server will broadcast to all the servers in the workgroup on the same subnet).

The Terminal server polls every 15 minutes looking for a domain license server, and checks the directory service every hour looking for an Enterprise License Server. If a domain license server is found, the Terminal server checks for it every two hours. If the Terminal server cannot find the domain license server, then it begins checking every 15 minutes. If an Enterprise License Server is found, the Terminal server checks with the directory service every hour. These checks result in negligible network traffic.

Note In Windows 2000 domains, the domain license server must be installed on a domain controller. In workgroups or Windows NT 4.0 domains, the domain license server can be installed on any server. If you are planning to eventually migrate from a workgroup or Windows NT 4.0 domain to a Windows 2000 domain, you might want to install the license server on a computer that can be promoted to a Windows 2000 domain controller.

To activate the license server quickly, and to access the Microsoft Clearinghouse through the Internet, install the server on a computer that has Internet access.

You must enable a Windows 2000 license server within 90 days of enabling a Windows 2000 Terminal server. If you have not enabled the license service on a Windows 2000 server when this period ends, your Windows 2000 Terminal Services will fail to operate.

Activating a License Server

A license server must be activated in order to identify the server and allow it to issue client licenses to your Terminal servers. You activate a license server using the Licensing wizard.

There are four methods to activate your license server:

- Internet
- Web-based
- Fax
- Telephone

If the computer running the Terminal Services Licensing tool is connected to the Internet, the Internet activation method is the quickest and easiest method. The Licensing wizard directs you to the secure Microsoft Internet site where license servers are activated. When you activate the license server, Microsoft provides the server with a digital certificate that validates server ownership and identity. Using this certificate, a license server can make subsequent transactions with Microsoft and receive client access licenses for your Terminal servers.

If your license server does not have Internet connectivity but you do have the ability to access the World Wide Web from a browser on another computer, you can activate your license server by means of the Web-based activation method. The Licensing wizard directs you to the secure Microsoft Web site to obtain a certificate for the license server.

Alternate methods for activating a license server include faxing your information to or calling the Customer Support Center (CSC) nearest you. The Licensing wizard also guides you through these steps. You can locate the appropriate telephone or fax number to call using the Licensing wizard. If you use the fax activation method, your confirmed request is returned by fax from Microsoft. If you use the telephone activation method, your request is completed with a Customer Service Representative over the phone.

You are required to activate a license server only once. While waiting to complete the activation process, your license server can issue temporary licenses for clients that allow them to use Terminal servers for up to 90 days.

The digital certificate that uniquely identifies your license server is stored in the form of a License Server ID. Place a copy of this number in a safe location. To view this number after your license server has been activated, highlight the license server and select **Properties** from the **View** menu. Set your communication method to World Wide Web and click **Okay**. Then select **Install Licenses** from the **Action** menu and click **Next**. The License Server ID is listed in the center of the Licensing wizard screen.

Installing Licenses

Terminal Services licenses must be installed on your license server in order for the Internet Connector setting to be enabled, or for non-Windows 2000 clients to permanently access a Windows 2000 Terminal server. To obtain Windows 2000 Terminal Services Client Access or Internet Connector licenses, purchase them through your standard software procurement method. After you purchase them you can then install the licenses using the Licensing wizard.

Just as there are four methods for activating your license server, there are four methods to install Terminal Services licenses. When you install licenses, you are asked for information regarding your purchase of the licenses. This information is as follows:

- If you purchased or will purchase your licenses through a Microsoft Select or Enterprise Agreement, you are asked for your Enrollment Agreement Number.

- If you purchased your licenses through a Microsoft Open License, you are asked for the Open License and Authorization numbers on your Open License Confirmation.

- If you purchased your licenses through a Microsoft LicensePak, you are asked for a 25-character License Code, which is in your Microsoft LicensePak packaging.

After you have installed your licenses, your license server can begin deploying the licenses. Clients with 90-day temporary licenses will be upgraded to a Terminal Services Client Access License the next time they log on (unless the number of client access licenses installed has exceeded by the number of outstanding temporary licenses).

Using the Terminal Services Licensing Administrative Tool

Terminal Services Licensing is an administrative tool designed to help you activate license servers, install client access licenses, and track client usage of your Terminal servers. In this way, Terminal Services Licensing helps the system administrator accurately account for and deploy the Terminal services Client Access and Internet connector licenses.

Using Terminal Services Licensing, you can perform the following tasks after connecting to a license server:

- Activate a license server.
- Install client licenses.
- Reactivate a license server.
- Deactivate a license server.
- Repeat the installation of client licenses.

All of these tasks are accomplished using the Licensing wizard.

In addition to performing these tasks, you can use Terminal Services Licensing to connect to any license server on your network, and then view information about the licenses on that server. You can view the following useful licensing information:

- The list of installed client license key packs.
- The total number of licenses in each client license key pack, and the number of available and issued licenses in each key pack.
- The name of the computer and the date each license was issued.
- The name of the computer and the expiration dates of each temporary license issued.

When the number of clients requesting licenses from a license server exceeds the number of licenses you have activated, you are reminded to install new licenses. The reminder appears as an event in the system log of the Event Viewer. The number of outstanding temporary licenses can be used to identify the number of client access licenses you will eventually need.

Backing Up Your License Server

It is important for you to back up your license server to ensure that you can recover your licensing information easily in the case of a system failure. Backup needs to be done on a regular basis and must include at least the System State, plus the Lserver directory. By default, this is %windir%\system32\Lserver.

The Licensing Service must be running while you restore a computer. Restoring the database and system state to the original License server (one with the same ID) restores all historical and active license information. If you restore a backed-up Licensing database to a different license server, the license server restores only the historical information about licenses issued. Licenses that have not been issued are not restored. However, information about the licenses not issued are posted to a system log that can be viewed in the Event Viewer. The information in the system log will include the number and type of licenses not issued that were not restored. To restore the licenses not issued, install those licenses using the telephone installation method. The Customer Service Representative can reissue the licenses you have lost.

Designing Your Network for Terminal Server Access

You need to consider your network infrastructure when deploying Terminal Services. For the most part, the issues involved are general network design concerns, but Terminal Services requires a few special considerations.

Terminal Services cannot pass the IP address of individual clients to an application. Multi-user applications that require each user to have a unique IP address do not work properly in a Terminal Services environment because every user appears to originate from the IP address of the server itself. For instance, certain firewalls and legacy hosts use the IP address of the client to determine security and physical location You might need to alter plans to use Terminal Services to support these applications.

Conversely, it is important to be aware that all users will share the same IP connection from a given Terminal server. Applications or services that subvert, lock, or monopolize that resource can interfere with the general operation of the server.

Network Load Balancing and Terminal Services

Network Load Balancing is used to distribute work between two or more servers. Network Load Balancing represents a group of servers as a single virtual IP address, and provides a mechanism to dynamically distribute load. This is useful in environments where there are a large number of users connecting to a server for a line of business application, or to a database where preserving the session is not critical. Because Terminal Services is unsuitable for clustering, load balancing can often provide a good solution for serving a large group of users.

Traditional load balancing solutions cannot always guarantee that a user will be reconnected to the same server. In cases such as the line of business scenario, there is little or no session specific data to worry about. With more complex desktop deployment or remote access, an enterprise might choose not to support disconnected sessions anyway, to reduce resource requirements and enhance security. Finally, it might be possible to use the attributes of certain types of load balancing to predictably reconnect to the same Terminal server, thus preserving a session.

Preserving a session is not analogous to preserving user data. It is quite possible to manage two or more Terminal servers in a way that allows a user to connect to any server and have appropriate access, simply by storing user data and user profiles external to the Terminal servers. Then the servers need only look to this common store for user profiles and storage. Users have the same experience no matter which server they connect to.

Network Load Balancing provides a good solution for many Terminal servers. Network Load Balancing uses IP affinity, which enables a user with the same IP address to reconnect to the same computer if their session disconnects. This means Network Load Balancing can be used for session recovery if the user has not changed computers. Even if Dynamic Host Configuration Protocol (DHCP) is in use, the user's IP address remains the same as long as he or she does not log off the network in the meantime.

Domain Name System (DNS) is an alternative strategy for load balancing. With round-robin DNS, a single name record resolves to more than one IP address, each with a corresponding cloned server. If you use DNS, disable **Session Disconnect** on servers running Terminal Services. Because a client could connect to any of the servers, it might connect to a different server than the one on which a disconnected session was left running.

For more information about Network Load Balancing, see "Ensuring the Availability of Applications and Services" in this book.

Designing and Setting Up Your Domain Structure

Developing your network design also involves planning the location of Terminal Services within your proposed Windows 2000 infrastructure. There are three principal domain structure alternatives that apply to a Terminal Services installation:

Use no domain structure. Without a domain architecture, users need separate accounts on every Windows 2000 server running Terminal Services. This limits scalability and makes it more difficult to administer groups of users.

Implement Windows 2000 Terminal Services in the existing Windows NT 4.0 domain environment.

This allows you to take advantage of the new features available in Windows 2000 Terminal Services without affecting the production environment. However, keep in mind that the existing Security Account Manager (SAM) limitations of the Windows NT 4.0 domain model will apply using this approach. Administrators have the option of adding Terminal Services–specific attributes to users' accounts. This adds a small amount of information, typically 1 KB or less, to a user's entry in the domain SAM database.

Leverage the Windows 2000 Active Directory infrastructure. This option takes full advantage of Active Directory. It leverages the ability to host thousands of users in its database. It also gives you the option of applying Group Policy to control the user experience when connected to Terminal Services.

When you define your Active Directory structure, it is recommended that you place your Terminal servers in a separate organizational unit (OU), separate from other computers and without users. A Terminal Services OU only needs to contain Terminal Services computers, no other user or non-Terminal Services machine objects. Just as you are likely to manage your laptops in a manner different from your client computers, you will also manage your Terminal servers differently.

Using Windows 2000 User Profiles or Roaming User Profiles

A profile describes the Windows 2000 configuration for a specific user, including the user's environment and preference settings. Profiles typically contain such user-specific information as installed applications, desktop icons, and color options. You can configure Terminal Services-specific profiles for a specific user using the profiles found under the **Terminal Services Profile** tab located in the **User Properties** dialog box.

In some cases, users might have already been assigned Windows 2000 profiles. It might also be desirable to assign Terminal Services–specific profiles to users in the following instances:

- Whenever the user gains access to Terminal Services across the WAN.
- If the administrator wants to present a session to the user that is different from the user's own desktop environment.

Whenever a user logs on to a server running Terminal Services, the server attempts to load profiles in the following order:

- User's Terminal Services-specific profile
- User's Windows 2000 roaming profile
- User's Windows 2000 profile

Roaming User Profiles

Roaming user profiles allow users to move between different computers and maintain the same environment and preference settings. The profile information is cached on the local hard drive of the Terminal server. Under some circumstances it is recommended that this information be deleted after the user logs off, such as the following:

- Access to Terminal Services is provided by a group of Terminal Services hosts.
- Access to Terminal Services is infrequent and you want to minimize the amount of disk space that is used.

The most effective way to delete the cached profiles is to put all of the Terminal Services hosts in a Windows 2000 Active Directory container and apply a specific policy to them that deletes all cached profile information upon logging off.

To facilitate the use of roaming user profiles, plan ahead and identify where they will be stored and how they can be managed. First, identify the locations on a file server or print server that have enough space to store the profiles and are readily available to Terminal Services users. Second, create a Windows 2000 share that users can gain access to with read/write privileges. You need to store profiles in network locations that are different from user home directories.

In order to use roaming profiles on a group of Terminal Services computers, it is imperative that the Terminal Services computers be identical in application and operating system configuration, such as the location of %systemroot% and the installation location of all applications. Otherwise, group different configurations into different OUs and administer them separately.

Group Policy

Group Policy is an effective mechanism to manage and control the behavior of Terminal Services in your environment. You use Group Policy to manage a set of registry values and file permissions that together define the computer resources available to an Active Directory site, a domain, or an organizational unit (OU).

Group Policy builds on the base functionality of registry-based values to include security settings, software installation, logon/logoff and startup/shutdown scripts, file deployment, and redirected special folders. Group Policy is enabled by Active Directory and affects both computers and users in any of these groups: local computer, sites, domains, and OU.

If you have an organization in which the same users use both Terminal Services and Windows 2000 Professional, use policies with care. The same policy applies to the users' sessions on Terminal Services and on Windows 2000 Professional (with the exception of per-user application management which is disabled on a Terminal Services Application Server). In this instance, you need to apply a different set of computer policies to the servers running Terminal Services by placing the computer in a separate OU.

Users on a Terminal server in Application Server mode cannot invoke the Windows Installer to add missing components to an application. Therefore, it is important to install all of the necessary components locally when the program is first installed. To do this, you can use a transform file (.mst). Transform files appear as modifications to .msi packages and tell Windows Installer which components to install locally.

Access to Applications

Administrators can control user access to Terminal Services applications in the following ways:

Mandatory Profiles

Profiles can specify which applications are visible to the user.

System Policies

Policies can prevent users from opening applications through Windows Explorer or the Run command. Policies are domain-based, so they can affect users' own computers as well as their Terminal Services sessions.

Group Policy applies user policies for the domain first, then either merges or replaces them with computer policies. This allows a Terminal server to alter or restrict the capabilities provided to users.

Poorly written policies can prevent users from gaining access to programs on all computers within a domain, rather than just gaining access to Terminal Services. If the administrator implements a policy that is based on a user ID or Windows 2000 group, then whatever is specified in that policy applies to that user or group regardless of what system they use. For example, a policy that prohibits accounting users from running Microsoft® Word affects all accounting users in the domain, whether they are using Terminal Services or just their local computers.

Using Home Directories

It is important that you plan to use home directories in a Terminal Services environment because most applications must install user-specific information or copy configuration files for every user. To keep user profiles to a reasonable size (less than 2 MB), it is recommended that all Terminal Services users have a network home directory and a network My Documents directory in which application-specific information is stored.

By default, Windows 2000 defines a home directory for each user. The default user's directory is under the documents and settings directory. This directory contains both user documents and settings. The user documents are stored in the user's home directory or My Documents folder. Terminal Services writes user-specific application files, such as .ini files, to the user's Windows directory and by default refers any application seeking the system Windows directory to the user's Windows directory.

Users typically use their home directories to save their personal files. This can be a problem if roaming profiles are used and the home directory is located within the user's profile directory. Windows 2000 copies everything in the user's profile directory to the profile cache each time the user logs on. This can take considerable time and resources, particularly if the roaming profile is stored across the network.

It is recommended that you use Terminal Services–specific home directories which are available automatically through the MMC snap-ins. One approach would be to create a directory on the file server called Homedirs and give Change permissions to Everyone. Then specify the Terminal Services home directory location as p:\Homedirs\%username%. Terminal Services automatically creates the username subdirectory and gives it the appropriate permissions. By default, each user has full access to his or her own home directory and administrators can copy files into the directory, but not read or delete files there.

It is helpful for all users to have the same virtual drive letter for their home directory redirection point to facilitate the use of application compatibility scripts. The first time you run an application compatibility script on a server, it prompts you to set the drive letter that references the root of the user's home directory. This drive letter is used for all subsequent application compatibility scripts. It is essential that the same drive letter is used on all Terminal servers within a server farm.

Folder Redirection is a unique feature of Windows 2000 that allows users and administrators to redirect the path of a folder to a new location. The new location can be a folder on the local computer or a directory on a network share. Users have the ability to work with shared documents on a secure server as if they were based on the local drive. Using this option, an administrator can redirect the user's My Documents folder to a private server share that can be accessed from either their Windows 2000 Professional client computer or their Terminal Services session. This feature is managed using Group Policy.

Planning Security

Security is an essential component of your Terminal Services deployment plan. In addition to the security issues addressed in your Windows 2000 deployment planning, Terminal Services has considerations that are specific to a multi-user environment.

This section discusses Terminal Services–specific security issues including the version of the NTFS file system used in Windows 2000, user and administrator rights, auto logon procedures, encryption, and other security considerations.

For more information about Windows 2000 security, see "Planning Distributed Security" in this book.

NTFS File System

Because of the multi-user nature of Terminal Services, it is strongly recommended you use the Windows 2000 version of NTFS as the only file system on the server, rather than file allocation table (FAT). FAT does not offer any user and directory security, whereas with NTFS you can limit subdirectories to certain users or groups of users. This is vitally important in a multi-user system like Terminal Services. Without the security that NTFS provides, any user has access to every directory and file on the Terminal server.

User Rights

Terminal Services is distributed with a default set of user rights that you can modify for additional security. In order to log on to a Terminal server, a user must have local logon rights on that computer. By default, a Terminal server in Remote Administration mode only grants rights to Administrators on the computer, and in Application Sharing mode grants rights to all members of the Users group. Because Windows 2000 includes all domain users in the Users group on a computer that is not a domain controller by default, all domain users are able to log on to a Terminal server providing Application Sharing. The groups and users allowed to log on, and the control granted to them, can be altered through the Terminal Services Configuration feature.

Users who are granted access through a protocol such as RDP, and who interactively log on to a Terminal Services–enabled server are automatically included in the built-in Terminal Services Users local group. A user only belongs to this group while they are interactively logged on to a Terminal server. This built-in group gives administrators control over resources Terminal Services users can access. This group is similar to the built-in Interactive group.

Avoid configuring Terminal Services as a domain controller because any user rights policies you apply to such a server will then apply to all domain controllers in the domain. For example, to use Terminal Services users must be authorized to log on locally. If the server running Terminal Services is a domain controller, users will be able to log on locally to all domain controllers in the Terminal Services domain.

Administrator Rights

Members of the Administrators group on a Terminal server have control over which users have access, the rights they have, and the applications they can run. Most of this control is part of the usual rights of an administrator on a Windows 2000 server. These rights are extended under Terminal Services to include:

- Server Management—Use the Terminal Services Configuration tool to set user permissions and session activity and to disconnect actions and session capabilities.
- User Control—Set user permissions on Terminal Services through Terminal Services Configuration. Set Terminal Services specific profile information through User Manager extensions.

- Session Control—Use the Terminal Services Manager feature to monitor active users, sessions, and processes; to shadow sessions; or to force disconnects.

- Application Installation—When running in Application Sharing mode, only an administrator can install applications on the Terminal server. This restriction does not apply in Remote Administration.

Auto-Logon Procedures

Depending on how people will be using Terminal Services, you might need to grant them access to the file system. Users who only need access to a single application, such as a database, can be put directly into the application at startup. This can be done by configuring the Terminal server client through the Client Connection Manager to automatically initiate a specific application for the user. A preconfigured Terminal server client can be distributed to a group of users within a group to give them the same direct application. If a Terminal server will be used to deliver a single application to anyone allowed to connect, the server can be configured to automatically initiate that application upon logon. This is done using Terminal Services Configuration.

You can also allow users to connect without entering a user name and password. You can also do this on a per user basis through the Client Connection Manager or on a per server basis through Terminal Services Configuration or the User Manager extensions. Generally, you should plan to use this connection method only when users are logged directly onto a line-of-business application, especially when the application itself requires a password for access. Use this server feature with care because it means that anyone with a Terminal Services client can log on to the server.

Windows 2000 offers a secondary logon capability. This function is used primarily to allow users to execute applications using a different security context. It is valuable in a Terminal Services environment, where the client computers automatically log on with a basic user account and the current user wants to execute an application that requires a higher level of security. In this situation, you can use the **runas** command to start applications under a different context without having to log off the user.

You can enter the **runas** command from the command prompt or it can be incorporated into an application shortcut. After a shortcut to an application is created, the **runas** functionality can easily be incorporated into it by selecting the **Run as different user** in the **Properties** option of the shortcut. This prompts the user for the Windows 2000 domain user account and password prior to executing the application.

Editing User-Specific Information

When a user logs on to the system, Terminal Services executes a batch file called UsrLogon.cmd in the System 32 directory. This file makes any necessary modifications to the user environment and ensures that users can run their applications correctly. If Terminal Services modifications to the user environment are necessary, you can make them by editing this file. Be aware that by editing this file you might cause a problem with the application compatibility scripts that are executed from this batch file.

Changing the Logon Process

In your logon scripts, consider checking for the presence of the environment variables %CLIENTNAME% or %SESSIONNAME%. These environment variables are Terminal Services specific, and only appear in a user's environment when they are logged on to a Terminal server, in Remote Administration or Application Server mode. For example, you might choose to omit the execution of antivirus software if the script determines that it is running on Terminal Services.

Encryption

You can assign data transfers between the Terminal Services client and server at one of three different levels of encryption. Note that high encryption is available only in North America.

Low Encryption

With low encryption, traffic from the client to the server is encrypted using the RC4 algorithm and a 56-bit key (40-bit key for RDP 4.0 clients), whereas traffic from the server to the client is unencrypted. Low encryption protects sensitive data like password entry and application data. The data sent from the server to the client is screen refreshed, which is difficult to intercept even when unencrypted.

Medium Encryption

With medium encryption, traffic in both directions is encrypted using the RC4 algorithm and a 56-bit key (40-bit key for RDP 4.0 clients).

High Encryption

Traffic in both directions is encrypted using the RC4 algorithm and a 128-bit key in the North American version of Terminal Services only. In the export version of Terminal Services, high encryption uses RC4 and a 56-bit key (40-bit for RDP 4.0 clients).

Additional Security Considerations

When planning security for Terminal Services, consider the following:

Smart Cards   The Windows 2000 interactive logon has the ability to authenticate a user with the Active Directory network using an X.509 version 3 certificate stored on a smart card along with the private key. However, this feature is not available to users authenticating by means of Terminal Services. This also applies to other hardware-based authentication devices.

Network and Communications Security   Remote Access does not limit access to Terminal Services users, so if one user establishes a modem or VPN link to the Internet or another system, every user on Terminal Services has access to the link.

Information Services on Terminal Services   You need to disable anonymous File Transfer Protocol (FTP) to prevent unsecured access to the file system.

Removing Services That Are Not Used   Removing the IBM OS/2 and POSIX subsystems prevents users from executing OS/2 or POSIX applications that circumvent security regulations. For more information about ensuring your system's security, see "Planning Distributed Security" in this book.

Remote Access

Terminal Services can provide remote users with access to applications that would otherwise be unusable because of poor performance across dial-up or slow WAN connections. The screen, mouse, and keyboard information sent by Terminal Services typically uses less bandwidth than an application that must be downloaded and then run locally on a remote user's computer.

Terminal Services Over the Internet

Users can also take advantage of Layer-2 Tunneling Protocol (L2TP) or Point-to-Point Tunneling Protocol (PPTP) to gain access to Terminal Services over the Internet. By using encryption, either tunneling option provides secure access to a private network for users operating over a public medium. These protocols are recommended because of the security they provide, but Terminal Services can be accessed over any TCP/IP implementation.

Firewalls

If your organization uses a firewall for security, remember to keep port 3389 open for RDP connections between the client and server. For best results, use a firewall that employs user-based authentication. A firewall that grants access based on an IP address allows users through if the IP address of the server running Terminal Services has been granted access.

Configuring Servers for Terminal Services Deployment

It is recommended that the server computers you purchase for Terminal Services are purchased from the same vendor and that you configure them in the same way. This will facilitate administering Terminal Services. If you are deploying Terminal Services to serve different needs, consider dividing the servers into groups based upon function and making the servers in each group as similar as possible.

If your organization uses equipment standards, adhere to these standards when planning new hardware acquisitions to accommodate Terminal Services. If necessary, scale up from the existing standard to keep hardware and software administration and maintenance as simple as possible.

When planning server deployment consider memory, page and dump files, CPUs, and the registry. A *dump file* is for memory dump in case of failure. Considerations for each of these is as follows:

Memory

A good principle is 128 MB of RAM for the base operating system services, plus and additional amount per user. This additional amount varies and should be between 16 MB and 20 MB per session. To compute this additional amount, plan on approximately 13 MB for the user's desktop, then add the amount needed to run applications. Note that when more than one user runs a particular application, the code for the application is not duplicated in memory (executable code is shared across instances of an application). Applications that are 16-bit require about 25 percent more memory than 32-bit applications.

If users will be running memory-intensive applications, such as a client/server application with a large memory footprint, you need to increase the amount of RAM allocated for each user. Each server needs to have enough physical memory to ensure that the page file is almost never used.

Page and Dump Files

The amount of disk space devoted to each server page file must be at least one and one-half times the total amount of physical RAM.

It is a good idea to put the Terminal server operating system on one physical drive and assign the page file to another. If the server has a large amount of physical memory, you need to consider whether the hard disk drive space is sufficient to record the dump file on the system partition. Consider such factors as total memory, page file size, installed applications, and the total size of the hard disk drive. For better performance, the page file must be on a separate physical disk. Consider disabling the dump file on systems with large amounts of RAM (typically 128 MB or more), unless drive C is large enough to hold the dump file.

CPUs

Terminal server needs to meet Windows 2000 Server requirements. The amount of processing required per user is dependent on the types of applications being run. This is best determined through trial deployments. For more information about scaling, see the Terminal Services Scaling link on the Web Resources page at http://windows.microsoft.com/windows2000/reskit/webresources.

Registry

The registry size is dynamically set during installation and is based on the page file size. The registry quota is based on memory size. Registry size can also be set from Control Panel. Double-click **System**, then click the **Advanced** tab. On the **Advanced** tab click **Performance Options** and then **Change**. Enter the registry size.

Preparing for Client Deployment

Client computers or terminals connect to Terminal server using a small client program installed on disk or in firmware. The choice of which client platform to use depends on the current installed base and individual user need. At a minimum, ensure that every client computer or terminal that you expect to connect to Terminal server is physically capable of hosting the client software and connecting over the network.

Deploying to Windows CE–Based Terminals

Windows CE–based terminals are generally the most "Windows-like" terminals that you can use to gain access to Terminal Services. These terminals are set up and configured using wizards running the familiar Microsoft® Win32® user interface found in Microsoft® Windows® 95 and later Windows-based operating systems.

Consider purchasing terminals from vendors that can provide a tool to enable administrators to remotely perform terminal upgrades, terminal configuration, and asset management.

Windows-based terminals can typically be configured locally, including:

- Using DHCP
- Connecting using a LAN, Point-to-Point Protocol (PPP), IP address, subnet mask, or gateway connectivity
- Enabling DNS to look up the Terminal server name when establishing a connection

You can use most Windows-based terminals to gain access to Terminal Services over a dial-up connection using PPP. Note that some Windows-based terminals do not support encryption during the logon process. In this case, you must configure the device used to provide connectivity to the networks for plain-text passwords or a connection will not be established. The session logon at the Terminal server can always be encrypted.

Windows CE–based terminals might include emulators for other terminal types as part of the firmware. Users of such terminals might establish simultaneous connections to different types of servers and alternate between the different emulators on the terminal device.

Switching between sessions can be accomplished using the following hotkeys on a Windows CE–based terminal:

- CTRL+ALT+END—Brings the Windows CE–based terminal shell UI to the foreground.
- CTRL+ALT+UP ARROW—Switches to the prior active sessions without bringing the shell forward.
- CTRL+ALT+DOWN ARROW—Switches to the next active sessions without bringing the shell forward.
- CTRL+ALT+HOME—Switches to the default connection if running. If it is not running, the shell starts the connection.
- F2—Brings up the Terminal Properties Configuration UI.

For more information about vendors who offer Windows CE–based terminals, see the Terminal Services Vendors link on the Web Resources page at http://windows.microsoft.com/windows2000/reskit/webresources.

Deploying to Client Computers

Windows-based client computers connecting to Terminal Services should have at least an 80386 microprocessor running at 33 MHz (though a 486/66 is recommended), a 16-bit VGA video card, and the Microsoft TCP/IP stack. The Terminal Services client runs on Windows 2000, Windows for Workgroups 3.11, Windows 95, Windows 98, and Windows NT 3.51 or later.

The Terminal Services client takes up only about 500 KB of disk space and typically uses approximately 4 MB of RAM when running. If client bitmap caching is enabled, another 10 MB of disk space might be used. For best performance, a computer running the Terminal Services client should have a total of 8 MB of physical RAM or more under Windows for Workgroups 3.11 or Windows 95, 24 MB or more for Windows 98, and 32 MB or more for Windows 2000.

The RDP client software is now installed by default as a subcomponent of Terminal Services. By default, the various clients are installed in the directory:

%systemroot%\system32\clients\tsclient

There are two options to deploy the client:

- Create a file share to do the installation over the network.
- Select **Terminal Services Client Creation** from the **Administrative Tools** menu, and make a client image that can be installed with a floppy disk.

Note The Terminal Services client requires TCP/IP to connect to the server, but Terminal Services itself can use IPX to gain access to Novell servers if necessary.

Upgrading to Terminal Services

The approach you take to upgrade to Terminal Services depends upon your existing Terminal Services setup:

WinFrame with or without MetaFrame There is no direct upgrade path from WinFrame to Terminal Services. In this case you first have to upgrade to Microsoft Terminal Server 4.0 and then upgrade to Windows 2000.

Terminal Server 4.0 without MetaFrame With Terminal Server 4.0 installed, there is a direct upgrade path to Terminal Services. When you install Windows 2000, the server recognizes the Terminal Server 4.0 edition, automatically perform the upgrade, and automatically enable Terminal Services in Application Server mode. Note that you might need to reinstall existing applications if you enable Terminal Services in Application Server mode.

Terminal Server 4.0 with MetaFrame Upgrading from Terminal Services 4.0 with MetaFrame is similar to upgrading from Terminal Server 4.0, but first you need to upgrade to the MetaFrame version for Windows 2000. After MetaFrame is upgraded, you can follow the same procedure for upgrading from Terminal Server 4.0 without MetaFrame.

Windows NT without Terminal Services When you install Windows 2000, select Terminal Services in Remote Administration or Application Mode, to enable Terminal Services.

Installing and Configuring Applications

A Windows 2000 server that is configured to run Terminal Services in Application Server mode provides multiple concurrent user connections to any number of applications.

It is recommended that applications be added or removed using the Add/Remove Programs function under Control Panel. This automatically manages the Terminal Services installation requirements. It is also possible to install the application directly, provided the server is put into Install mode through the command line using **change user /install**. The server can be taken out of Install mode with **change user /execute**.

These commands are not necessary when using Add/Remove Programs. Because there is always the possibility of error or omission using the command lines, installation through Add/Remove Programs is preferred. If an application is installed without using Add/Remove and without using the command line to set Install mode, the application has to be removed and reinstalled properly.

Only administrators are allowed to install application on a Terminal Services Application Server.

Deploying Applications through Group Policy

Deploying applications through Active Directory and Group Policy using Windows Installer is a very flexible application deployment method. It allows applications to be installed and managed in a number of different ways. The three main ways you can deploy applications using Windows Installer are:

- Install on a local computer by the user.
- Assign by the system administrator from the domain controller to a user or a computer.
- Publish by the system administrator from the domain controller for a user.

Before an application can be installed using Windows Installer, an .msi installation package must be available for the application.

Deploying Applications from a Domain Controller

To deploy an application from a domain controller, a system administrator needs to assign a .msi-based application to a computer. Application servers cannot assign or publish applications to users.

Transform files are required if the original application installation package did not install all of the necessary components of the application to the local disk. Transform files allow you to select what, if anything, needs to be installed during the installation.

A system administrator can also install an application from a remote session or the console of an Application server. A typical installation is initiated using the following command:

Msiexec/I ApplicationName.MSITRANSFORMS=TransformFileName.MST ALLUSERS=1

The installation of an application in a multi-user environment is quite different from an installation to an individual user. Application server software installation must not jeopardize the system that is running, and the installation must be configured to allow concurrent users. For these reasons, only administrators can install applications, and users are not able to install anything.

It is the responsibility of the system administrator to decide which applications are needed and to ensure that applications are locally installed and available before allowing remote user connections.

Supporting Multilingual and International Users

Terminal Services is available in Windows 2000 MultiLanguage Version. Windows 2000 MultiLanguage Version allows you to install and configure multiple user interface languages on your computers. This simplifies the deployment process and reduces hardware costs for multinational organizations. For example, a Swiss corporation which is required by law to provide the user interface in English, French, and German, can provide all three languages on one server.

Before enabling Terminal Services in the Windows 2000 MultiLanguage Version, determine which user interface languages you need. If the Terminal Services computers serve users around the world, but all the international users understand English, you might want to deploy the International English version of Terminal Services.

Administrators can set the user interface language using Group Policy. Users select their language from the **General** tab of **Regional Options** in Control Panel. When a user has a roaming profile that specifies a language that is not installed, the system defaults to English.

Terminal Services tracks the time according to the time zone in which it has been configured, rather than on an individual user basis. Users located in a different time zone than the server must make allowances for time differences.

Printing from Terminal Services

Printing from Terminal Services is similar to printing from other versions of Windows 2000. However, users and administrators must take notice of certain important differences.

There are a number of ways to manage network printing in a Terminal Services environment. Within a small unit of an organization or division, the administrator might want to configure printers locally on the server running Terminal Services. The printers might be locally attached through the parallel port or a network interface. These printers are automatically available to all users on the system.

A user who wants to print locally to a printer connected to his or her own computer has the option of either using the Terminal Services client ability to redirect a print job to a local device, or using peer-to-peer networking.

Printing to Your Local Printer by RDP Protocol

Terminal Services provides printer redirection that routes print jobs from the Terminal server to a printer attached to the client. There are two ways to provide client access to the local printer by means of RDP: automatic printer redirection and manual printer redirection.

Automatic Printer redirection is supported on all Win32 client platforms, including Windows 95, Windows 98, and Windows NT. When a client logs on to Terminal Services, local printers attached to LPT, COM, and USB ports are automatically detected and corresponding queues created in the user's session. When the client disconnects or ends the session, the printer queue is deleted and all pending print jobs are terminated.

Manual printer redirection must be used on Windows for Workgroups 3.11 and WBT clients. In this case, the printer is manually added using the Add Printers wizard in Control Panel. The client computer name is used to select the printer port from the list of available ports. Print redirection can be disabled on a per-connection basis using Terminal Services Connection Configuration or on a per-user basis using Active Directory Users and Computers or Local Users and Computers. For more information about printer redirection, see Windows 2000 Server Help.

Network Shared Printers

As with local disk drives, **net share** enables users to gain access to the printer remotely from the server. If the user installs a network card in the local printer, it becomes a network printer and file sharing does not have to be enabled on the user's computer.

Printers are defined on a per-user basis; therefore, after the printer is defined for a particular user, it is only available to that user during their session. In addition, if a user uses Print Manager, they only see the printers to which they have permissions to print. When the user logs off, the server tears down the printer redirection. In addition, printer redirection is not available for MS-DOS-based applications.

The **net share** method is designed to work on printers connected locally to personal computers running Windows for Workgroups 3.11 or later. Users of WBT running RDP currently cannot print to local printers using this method.

Printing Across a WAN or Dial-up Connection

If users gain access to Terminal Services across a WAN or dial-up connection, take care to accurately assess the bandwidth requirement of any print jobs that will be spooled across it.

If a user prints to a local printer that resides on the user's LAN but across a slow link from the server running Terminal Services itself, the print job is spooled across the slow link to the printer. This adds to the bandwidth requirements for Terminal Services because the network is required to handle print traffic as well as keystrokes, mouse events, and screen updates.

It is also recommended that you minimize the need to print large graphics or color print jobs across those slow links because they consume considerable amounts of bandwidth.

Best Practices for Client Configuration

You can maximize users' experience with Terminal Services by following these recommendations:

- Minimize graphics use including animated graphics, screen savers, blinking cursors, and the animated Microsoft Office Assistant.
- Disable the Active Desktop.
- Disable smooth scrolling.
- Minimize the use of graphics and animation, such as cascading menus on the desktop, particularly the Start menu. Place shortcuts on the desktop and keep the Programs submenu as flat as possible. Avoid using bitmaps in wallpaper; in **Display Properties** set Wallpaper to **None** on the **Background** tab, and select a single color from the **Appearance** tab.
- Enable file sharing on client computers, sharing drives with easily identifiable names like "drivec." Be aware of the security implications involved.
- Avoid the use of MS-DOS or Win16 (16-bit) applications where possible.
- Configure the Terminal server to return the user's logon name rather than the computer name to applications that make use of a NetBIOS function that calls for the computer name.
- Train users to use Terminal Services hot key sequences. There are a few important differences in the hot key sequences used in a Terminal Services client session than in a Windows 2000 session.

Planning for Testing and Piloting

The best time to discover potential problems with a Terminal Services deployment is during testing and piloting. Opportunities for system tuning and error-trapping might uncover problems with your infrastructure, system configuration, or software.

Considerations for the Test Lab

The ideal environment for validating a Terminal server deployment is a test laboratory that has been constructed to simulate the environment of the actual deployment as closely as possible. The test lab will function as a miniature version of your organization itself, enabling the team to see Terminal Services in action before deployment.

Consider the following items when developing your Terminal Services test lab:

- Use a server computer from the same vendor and with the same configuration as the servers that will be used in the actual deployment, and set up a representation of client computers that will be using Terminal Services throughout your organization.

- Duplicate your organization's network configuration. If the network uses both Ethernet and Token ring, you need to have both in the test lab. If possible, set up a separate Windows 2000 Server domain for the lab so you can monitor the performance of the domain controllers without having to factor in other activity on the network. If you are planning to deploy Terminal Services on a WAN, design your lab with routers and use a link simulator to simulate network latency.

- If different divisions will be using Terminal server in similar but not identical ways, you can probably emulate all divisions within a single test lab. If the difference is significant enough, however, you might want to consider building a separate lab for each division or set of tasks.

- Deploy a typical set of applications together on the test server. This step is vital in determining any interoperability issues that might arise when users run different applications simultaneously.

Monitoring Performance

Performance monitoring is a critical component of testing as well as the day-to-day operations in a Terminal Services environment. A baseline needs to be established early in the pilot phase. Then, as the deployment takes place, the baseline can be used to measure against actual performance. This helps to quickly identify and resolve system bottlenecks. The information in this section highlights the key System Monitor counters required for analyzing Terminal Services performance. The three primary system components that affect performance in this environment are CPU, memory, and the network.

Evaluating CPU Performance

Detecting a processor bottleneck in a Terminal Services server is similar to detecting processor bottlenecks in a Windows 2000 server, but the baseline values for the counters might be different. The most significant counters for identifying bottlenecks are:

Percent of Total Processor Time (System)   This is a measure of activity on all system processors. In a multiprocessor computer, this counter is equal to the total amount of processor activity divided by the number of processors. This counter is especially useful after it has been verified that all system processors are processing threads equally.

Processor Queue Length (System)   This is the instantaneous length of the processor queue in units of threads. All processors use a single queue in which threads wait for processor cycles. After a processor is available for a thread waiting in the processor queue, the thread can be switched onto a processor for execution. A processor can execute only a single thread at a time. Note that faster CPUs can handle longer queue lengths than slower CPUs.

Processor Time (Processor)   This is the percentage of time the processor was busy executing a thread other than the thread of the Idle process. This counter has an instance for each system processor available to the operating system. You can use it to verify that each system processor is contributing equally to processing waiting threads.

Total Interrupts/Sec   This is the rate at which the computer is receiving and servicing hardware interrupts. Some devices that might generate interrupts are the system timer, the mouse, data communication lines, network adapters, and other peripheral devices. You can use this counter to identify any device drivers that might be consuming an unusually high amount of processor time.

Percent of Total Processor Utilization and Processor Queue Length

These are the most significant counters for identifying bottlenecks in CPU bottlenecked systems. As the system processors become busier, the number of threads waiting for execution in the Processor Queue increases.

Evaluating Memory Performance

In addition to the System Monitor counters, **Task Manager** displays Physical Memory values that can be very useful when evaluating memory performance with Terminal Services. The Available Memory, Total Memory, and File Cache Memory values can be found on the **Performance** tab within **Task Manager**.

The two most significant performance counters in **Task Manager** are Available Physical Memory and Page Inputs/sec. To avoid performance problems related to memory, carefully observe the decreases in these counters. The decreases are a good indication of the amount of memory required per user. As a guideline, a Terminal server is considered fully utilized in terms of memory when Available Physical Memory is less than two times the average per user memory requirement. If a dramatic increase in Page Inputs/Sec is observed, memory capacity has probably been exceeded and additional memory needs to be added.

Available Bytes (Memory) displays the size of the virtual memory currently on the Zeroed, Free, and Standby lists. Zeroed and Free memory is ready for use, with Zeroed memory cleared to zeros. Standby memory is memory removed from a process's Working Set but that is still available. Notice that this is an instantaneous count, not an average over the time interval.

Pages Input/sec is the number of pages read from the disk to resolve memory references to pages that were not in memory at the time of the reference. This counter includes paging traffic on behalf of the system cache to access file data for applications. This is an important counter to observe if you are concerned about excessive memory pressure and the excessive paging that might result.

Evaluating Network Performance

Terminal Services performance can be considered unacceptable because of delays in network communication even though the CPU and memory are available.

Bottlenecks in network communications can occur in four different areas: the client network interface, the physical network media, the server client-to-server network interface, or the server network interface for server-to-server/host communications. Bottlenecks in network communications directly affect the experience of the user at the client workstation.

The most useful System Monitor counters for tracking network utilization are the Network Segment counters:

- %Network Utilization is the percentage of network bandwidth in use on the segment being monitored.

- Total Bytes Received/Sec is the total number of bytes received per second on a network segment.

- Total Frames Received/Sec is the total number of frames received per second on a network segment.

Using Help Desk and Administrative Tools

Terminal Services provides help desk with a number of administrative tools and a remote control feature to assist with support.

Remote Control

The Remote Control feature allows a help desk support professional to temporarily control another user's session and see the user's actions. The help desk can also interact with the user and execute commands on behalf of the user.

To enable the help desk group to use the Remote Control function, it is recommended that a help desk group be created in the domain. After the group is created, you can use the Terminal Services Configuration MMC snap-in to give the group permissions to use the remote control function.

To take advantage of Remote Control using the RDP, both clients must be connected to a Windows 2000 Terminal server.

Tools for Administration

When you install Terminal Services for Windows 2000, additional administration tools are added to the Administrative Tools folder. These tools include:

Terminal Services Client Creator   Use this tool to create floppy disks for installing the Terminal Services Client software on Windows for Workgroups, Windows 95, Windows 98, and Windows NT platforms.

Terminal Services Manager   With this tool, you can manage all Windows 2000 servers running Terminal Services. Administrators can view current users, servers, and processes. Additionally, administrators can send messages to specific users, use the Remote Control feature, and terminate processes.

Terminal Services Configuration   This tool allows you to manage your RDP configuration. Modifying options in this tool are global, unless you choose to inherit information from the same options located in the user configuration. Available options are: setting connection encryption, logon settings, time-outs, initial programs run on successful logon, remote control options, Windows printer mapping, LPT port mapping, clipboard mapping, and applying these options to a specific LAN adapter.

Terminal Services Licensing   With this tool, you store and track Windows 2000 Terminal Services client access licenses. It can be installed either during installation of Terminal Services or later. When clients log on to Terminal Services, Terminal Services validates the client license. If a client does not have a license or requires a replacement license, Terminal Services requests one from the License Server. License Server provides a license from its pool of available licenses, and Terminal Services passes the license to the client. If there are no available licenses, License Server grants a temporary license for the client. After it is granted, each client license is associated with a particular computer or terminal.

Terminal Services Deployment Planning Task List

Table 16.2 summarizes the tasks you need to perform when planning a Terminal Services Deployment.

Table 16.2   Summary of Planning Tasks for Terminal Services

Task	Location in chapter
Select Remote Administration or Server Application mode.	Overview of Terminal Services
Determine licensing requirements.	Overview of Terminal Services
Determine how you want to utilize Terminal Services in your business environment.	Creating Your Terminal Services Deployment Plan
Document the existing computing environment.	Creating Your Terminal Services Deployment Plan
Describe how the deployment project meets the requirements that have been identified.	Creating Your Terminal Services Deployment Design
Develop a plan for implementing Terminal Services including networking, security, and domain structure.	Creating Your Terminal Services Deployment Design
Establish guidelines and standards for server deployment including CPU, storage, and so on.	Configuring Servers for Terminal Services Deployment
Prepare to deploy to your client environment.	Preparing for Client Deployment
Prepare to test and pilot your deployment plan.	Planning for Testing and Piloting
Prepare to provide support.	Using Help Desk and Administrative Tools

PART 5

Advanced Management

Understanding Microsoft® Windows® 2000 advanced management features that will increase the reliability and availability of your network is beneficial to IT managers. Part 5 provides information about network security strategies for Internet accessibility, scalability and availability features, storage management options, and synchronizing Active Directory with Microsoft® Exchange Server directory service.

In This Part

C H A P T E R   1 7

Determining Windows 2000 Network Security Strategies

Today, most organizations want their computer infrastructure connected to the Internet because it provides valuable services to their staff and customers. However, the services made available through Internet connection can be misused, which makes it necessary to employ network security strategies. Microsoft® Windows® 2000 includes a variety of technologies that you can use as you plan your network security strategy. These technologies can also be useful if your network security issues are internal to your organization or if your external network connections are to networks other than the Internet. For more information about internal security, see "Planning Distributed Security" in this book.

The strategic use of security technologies to protect your company's network connections to the Internet or other public networks is discussed in this chapter. This chapter does not provide details about how to install and use network security technologies. Network architects involved in network security design and system administrators involved with administering network security need to read this chapter. As a prerequisite to performing the tasks outlined in this chapter, you need to be familiar with network and Internet technologies, such as routing, network protocols, and Web serving.

In This Chapter

Chapter Goals

This chapter will help you develop the following planning documents:

- Network security plan
- Deployment plan for network security technologies

Related Information in the Resource Kit

- For more information about implementing and using relevant Windows 2000 network security technologies, see the *Microsoft® Windows® 2000 Server Resource Kit Internetworking Guide.*

- For more information about IPSec, see the *Microsoft® Windows® 2000 Server Resource Kit TCP/IP Core Networking Guide.*

Planning for Network Security

A connection to the Internet allows your organization's staff to use e-mail to communicate with people around the world and to obtain information and files from a vast number of sources. It also allows your customers to obtain information and services from your organization at any time. In addition, your organization's staff can use company resources from home, hotels, or anywhere else they might be, and partners can use special facilities to allow them to work more effectively with your company.

As you plan your network, you might want to implement security technologies appropriate for your organization. Addressing these issues early in your Windows 2000 deployment planning ensures that security cannot be breached and that you are ready to provide secure networking facilities when needed. Even though you probably have a secure network environment already in place, it is important for you to review your security strategies with Windows 2000 capabilities in mind. Considering the implications of the new network security technologies in Windows 2000 might lead you to rethink your security plan. To begin, it is recommended that you complete the following tasks as you develop your network security plan:

- Assess your network security risks.
- Determine your server size and placement requirements.
- Prepare your staff.
- Create and publish security policies and procedures.
- Use a formal methodology to create a deployment plan for your security technologies.
- Identify your user groups and their specific needs and security risks.

The following sections describe these items in more detail.

Note For more information about deployment planning for your network, see "Determining Network Connectivity Strategies" in this book. That chapter includes strategies for routing, addressing, name resolution, network applications, and similar networking issues. This chapter concentrates on the security issues of your network.

Assessing Network Security Risks

Unfortunately, the ability to share and obtain information comes with significant risks. Competitors might try to gain access to early or proprietary product information, or someone might maliciously modify Web pages or overload computers so that they are unusable. There is also the possibility that employees might access information that they should not see. You want to avoid these and other types of security risks to ensure that your company's business functions can carry on as intended. To make sure that only the appropriate people have access to resources and data, it is a good idea to review your network security technologies carefully and plan your strategies well. This also provides accountability by tracking how network resources are used.

For a general discussion about how to identify security risks and select appropriate strategies, see "Planning Distributed Security" in this book.

Note Some organizations minimize network security risks by not allowing connections to the Internet or any other public network. This obviously limits the community of people who can misuse the network facilities. However, network security risks can still exist within the organization, and even limited network connections can expose some risks. Therefore, network security strategies and technologies are still necessary in these situations.

Figure 17.1 illustrates the primary steps for determining your network security strategies.

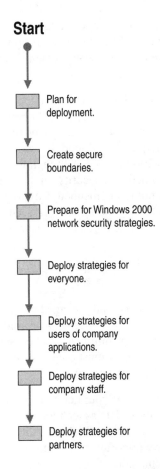

Figure 17.1   Process for Determining Network Security Strategies

Determining Server Size and Placement

When you are establishing a connection between your intranet and the Internet or other public network, carefully consider where you will make the connection. Typically this will be in the central part of your organization's network, so that the effective distance between your servers and the Internet is minimized. It will also usually be at a location where networking specialists can easily access it for maintenance.

Ideally, you want to have only one connection to the Internet for your entire company. This simplifies management of the connections and reduces the potential for security weaknesses due to inconsistently applied policies and procedures.

After you have decided where to place the connection to the Internet, you must determine what server hardware you need to support your network security technologies. The characteristics of these servers will depend on the technologies you plan to implement and the anticipated workload, but at a minimum, they need to be capable of running Windows 2000 Server. Although it is possible to run software for applications other than network security on the same servers as your network security applications, it is not recommended. Running other applications reduces the capacity of the servers to respond to network security needs and might cause the servers to fail. Also, if the applications have security weaknesses, they might compromise network security.

Preparing Your Staff

Security technologies need to be deployed and managed by very capable and trustworthy people. They must integrate the entire network and network security infrastructure so that you can eliminate or minimize weaknesses. As the environment and requirements change, they must continually maintain the integrity of the network security infrastructure.

A critical factor for ensuring the success of your network security staff is to be sure they are well trained and kept up-to-date as technologies change. The staff needs to take time to learn Windows 2000, particularly its network security technologies. They also need to have opportunities to reinforce their training with experimental work and practical application.

In addition, the network security staff must familiarize themselves with network security issues in general. Many books about this topic are available, and the Internet has many sites that address network security.

Developing Security Policies and Procedures

Policies and procedures are always important, but they are critical for security. You need to create and publish your policies to gain consensus on how you will handle specific security issues and to ensure that everyone clearly understands the policies. Formalized procedures ensure that system maintenance and changes are always done in a well-thought-out manner.

One issue you need to consider is how to monitor for breaches in or attempts to break security. You can minimize breaches and stop attempts to break security if appropriate staff are aware of them as early as possible. This is only possible if monitoring procedures are in place. Well-defined policies help you establish procedures for dealing with these security issues.

Reliability is another important security issue you need to address. Have plans in place for when a component of the security infrastructure fails. Decide the appropriate action for any possible security breach ahead of time, and have resources available to repair the problem as soon as possible.

Creating a Plan for Deploying Your Security Technologies

Create a detailed plan for deploying network security technologies as part of your overall Windows 2000 deployment plan by using a formal project methodology. This will ensure that you deploy the technologies in a systematic, thorough manner with minimal opportunity for failure. Critical steps in the project include communicating the network security policies to all interested parties, and communicating policies and procedures to network users.

The most important aspect of the deployment project is pilot testing. The proposed network security technologies needs to be subjected to significant and realistic testing in a safe environment. This will help to ensure that the architecture works as intended, your security goals have been achieved, and your staff is ready to deploy and support the technologies.

Identifying User Categories and Their Security Needs and Risks

Your network infrastructure is in place to serve people for the benefit of your organization. For the purposes of discussing network security strategies in this chapter, these people are divided into four network user communities:

Everyone This category includes all people accessing your network from any organization or location, which could include staff, users, and partners. They generally cannot easily be identified reliably and must, therefore, be considered anonymously.

Staff This group includes all people who work for your organization. They can be easily identified using standardized internal procedures. Typically, they use company e-mail and your intranet.

Users This group includes staff who use applications to accomplish business functions.

Partners This group includes people from any organization or location who have a special relationship with your organization. They are prepared to follow standardized procedures so that they can be identified. They might use facilities similar to staff and users. They are often considered to be part of an extranet.

The network security strategies presented in this chapter address the needs and risks of each category of network user and detail approaches you can use to satisfy their needs while minimizing risks. In addition, you will find an overall strategy for security in general and an overall strategy for network security infrastructure.

Developing Strategies for Secure Network Connections

Network security becomes most critical when you connect your computers to a network that you do not entirely trust. Network security issues are common within an organization, but in those cases you have a lot of scope for accountability and discipline, and you have a range of basic, distributed, and network security technologies to address the issues. Beyond your organization, options for accountability and discipline are greatly diminished, and therefore you need to rely more strongly on security strategies themselves.

Creating Secure Boundaries

Network security between your organization and the outside world is dependent on one or more servers where you implement network security technologies. These servers logically sit on the boundary between your organization and the outside world. Often the application servers providing services to the outside world are in the same physical location.

One approach to maximize the security of these servers is to logically place them in a unique location in your network infrastructure. The area in which they are placed is often called a demilitarized zone (DMZ). The firewall (discussed in the next section) has an additional network adapter that directs traffic to the DMZ based on a set of addresses assigned to that area. Figure 17.2 shows this relationship.

Within the DMZ, you can ensure that servers do not have access to corporate resources. This way, if a security breach does occur on those servers, the perpetrators cannot then move on to other computers within your intranet.

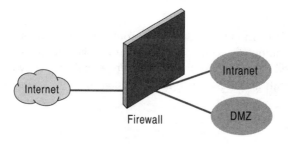

Figure 17.2   A Demilitarized Zone

The DMZ, as with all internal network components, needs to be physically secured against access by the public. This ensures that no one—not even one of your employees—can weaken your security by rearranging cabling or by using logged in accounts.

You do not have to physically separate the DMZ from other computers and networking equipment. However, it is appropriate to apply special policies and procedures to the DMZ, because of its critical role in your network security. The smallest of changes, made improperly, can be sufficient to create a breach that intruders can take advantage. Therefore, it must be impossible for unqualified staff to change the DMZ. Applying additional physical security to the DMZ ensures that this is the case.

Caution   Carefully secure your client computers and accounts to ensure that only authorized users can use them to access your network. If you cannot physically secure a client computer, then make certain that the accounts used on it have few privileges and that you use file encryption, secured screen savers, and other local security strategies.

Securing Against Everyone

To secure your organization's network for access to and from the Internet, you need to put a server between the two. The server provides connectivity for company staff to the Internet while minimizing the risks that connectivity introduces. At the same time, it prevents access to computers on your network from the Internet, except for those computers authorized to have such access.

This server runs firewall or proxy server software. It also has two network interfaces: one for the corporate network and one for the Internet. The firewall or proxy server software examines all network packets on each interface to determine their intended address. Where appropriate, the packets are passed to the other interface for distribution to the rest of the respective network if they pass the software's criteria.

In some cases, the contents of the packets are passed along as if they came from the proxy server, and the results are passed to the requesting computer when they are returned to the proxy server. This ensures that people on the Internet cannot get the addresses of computers within the company other than the proxy server.

Using Microsoft Proxy Server

Microsoft® Proxy Server 2.0 provides both proxy server and firewall functions. Proxy Server 2.0 runs on Windows 2000, and both need to be configured properly in order to provide full network security. If you have a version of Proxy Server earlier than 2.0 with Service Pack 1, you need to upgrade it for Windows 2000 compatibility at the time that you upgrade the server to Windows 2000.

In many cases, the volume of traffic between a company network and the Internet is more than one proxy server can handle. In these situations, you can use multiple proxy servers; the traffic is coordinated among them automatically. For users on both the Internet and intranet sides, there appears to be only one proxy server.

To use advanced Microsoft Proxy Server features, computers need to have the Microsoft Proxy Server client installed and configured to use the proxy server. Computers without the client (such as those on the Internet) receive basic service from the proxy server as anonymous users.

It is important to test the proxy server before connecting it to the Internet. Set up a small-scale simulation of the Internet and your intranet, and have client computers try to access various services in both directions. Also, attempt to make unauthorized connections to verify that your network rejects them. Be sure to test a wide variety of network access methods to verify that all types of network access are secure. Try different techniques that can be used to take advantage of security holes, to ensure that you do not have such holes in your environment. Books about network security include suggestions for specific issues that you can test. Third-party products can also help with such testing, as can consultants who are experienced in this area.

Procedures for using Microsoft Proxy Server are included with the product. For more information about Microsoft Proxy Server and for details about Microsoft security technologies, see the Microsoft Security Advisor link on the Web Resources page at http://windows.microsoft.com/windows2000/reskit/webresources.

Monitoring Your Network Security

The network security technologies you implement can meet your goals only if you plan and configure them carefully. With thorough preparation, this work can be done very successfully. However, anticipating all possible risks can be very difficult: new risks develop, systems break down, and the environment in which your systems are placed changes over time. Ongoing reviews of your network security strategies can minimize these risks. However, you also need to watch the actual network security activity, to spot weaknesses before they are exploited, and to stop attempts to break security before they are effective.

To watch your network security activity, you need tools to capture the details about the activities and to analyze the data. Microsoft Proxy Server includes logging at two levels: normal and verbose. Windows 2000 also has event logging, which can be enhanced by enabling security auditing. Internet Authentication Server, discussed later in this chapter, has extensive activity reporting options. Third-party products are also available that can help with monitoring servers and applications, including security servers and applications. Be sure you review the documentation for whatever systems you use and select the logging options that best serve your requirements.

Connecting to External Networks

When you have a proxy server in place, complete with monitoring facilities and properly prepared staff, you can connect your network to an external network. Conduct a final set of tests to be sure that the implementation properly fulfills your plans. You need to be confident that only the services you have authorized are available, and the risk for misuse is almost nonexistent. This environment requires diligent monitoring and maintenance, but you will also be ready to consider providing other secure networking services.

Note   This chapter does not discuss how to set up a network connection. There are many books that cover this topic, and your network service provider can make the connection or put you in touch with consultants who can make the connection.

Deploying Network Security Technologies

After you have prepared your overall network security strategy, you can decide how you want to use enhanced network security technologies for each community of users defined in this chapter: Everyone, Staff, Users, and Partners. You can then deploy network security strategies for each of your network user communities. You might want to first consider the needs of Everyone, as a group, and then address the needs of company Staff, Users of company applications, and Partners as business priorities dictate.

Before you identify specific security policies for your organization, you need to consider Windows 2000 capabilities that enhance your network security.

Preparing for Windows 2000 Network Security Technologies

In some cases, Windows 2000 network security technologies are dependent on other Windows 2000 security technologies. For example, the virtual private networking Layer Two Tunneling Protocol (L2TP) uses IPSec to provide security from the remote client to the VPN server. The IPSec security negotiation requires certificates to authorize the connection. Therefore, a certification server is required with the appropriate configuration. Typically, a Windows 2000 certificate server is joined to a domain. The domain specifies Group Policy with public key infrastructure (PKI) settings for computers to auto-enroll in this certificate authority to get a computer certificate for IPSec. L2TP creates the necessary IPSec policy to ensure the L2TP traffic is secure. However, administrators might want to also secure other traffic between all servers and clients. This requires the configuration of IPSec on each client and server. Because IPSec is configured using a policy, after you create the policy in Active Directory™, you can apply it to all computers on a group or domain basis. You can deploy certificates and IPSec policy to all domain computers by centralized administration using Group Policy in Active Directory.

For more information about planning for the deployment of Windows 2000 certificates, see "Planning Your Public Key Infrastructure" in this book. For more information about Active Directory planning, see "Designing the Active Directory Structure" in this book.

Deploying Strategies for Everyone

When your Internet connection is in place, anyone who can find it presents a potential network security risk. Therefore, the first community of users to address when you deploy an overall network security strategy is the group previously defined as Everyone. You have already done this, in part, by putting in place a proxy server as well as security monitoring policies, procedures, and technologies.

You might also want to consider the network applications that Everyone can benefit from and the security requirements those applications have. For example, you might want to set up Microsoft Internet Information Services (IIS) with an internal Web site. IIS has many security options available that you need to carefully consider and configure as required. (IIS includes extensive documentation about this subject.) Also consider using File Transfer Protocol (FTP) servers and other services that Everyone can benefit from.

Deploying Strategies for Staff

People in the Staff group might want to access the corporate network from any location in order to access internal Web sites, to copy files, to print documents, and for other simple functions. The primary security goal in these cases is to verify that the user is an authorized employee before the user gains free access to the network. Therefore, the initial connection into the network must be secure, but no further validation is required. An additional concern is that you need to prevent unauthorized people from intercepting and reading the traffic on your network.

Employees can use Internet service providers (ISPs) to access the company network; however, not all staff will have such access. You might not want to make all intranet services available through the Internet, or you might require the guaranteed network capacity of a dedicated network link. Using Windows 2000 Routing and Remote Access service, you can define remote access policies to be highly specific as to how users can access the internal network when connecting over the Internet.

Routing and Remote Access

Organizations typically provide remote connection options to staff at their own sites. Information technology (IT) staff set up dedicated telephone numbers for this purpose and attach modems (or similar hardware) to a server that is directly connected to the intranet. The server runs specialized software to handle connection details, and it also authenticates the dial-up user as being an authorized staff member.

Windows 2000 includes Routing and Remote Access, which allows you to provide dial-up facilities for your users. If you want to centralize your user authentication, authorization, and accounting services in Windows 2000, you can use Remote Access or VPN by setting up an Internet Authentication Service (IAS) server. Figure 17.3 illustrates one possible configuration of these servers.

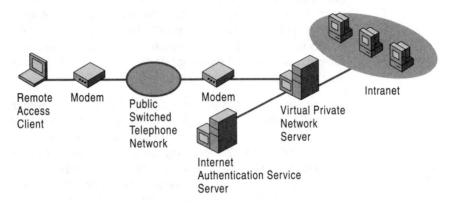

Figure 17.3   Sample Routing and Remote Access Configuration

The *Microsoft® Windows® 2000 Server Resource Kit Internetworking Guide* contains information about how Routing and Remote Access works and what capabilities it provides. Windows 2000 Server Help describes how to install and use Routing and Remote Access.

When you are planning the deployment of Routing and Remote Access, consider the following security issues:

- Who will be given the phone numbers?
- Who will be given permission to use Routing and Remote Access?
- What kind of authentication methods will be used?
- How is data encryption to be used (Routing and Remote Access client to Routing and Remote Access server)?

   If you need end-to-end encryption (remote access client all the way to the application server on the internal network), use Internet Protocol security (IPSec), which is discussed later in this chapter.

- What remote access policies will be used to control user access?

For more information about general deployment issues for Routing and Remote Access, see "Determining Network Connectivity Strategies" in this book.

Routing and Remote Access Security

Restricting the distribution of Routing and Remote Access phone numbers helps minimize the number of people who might try to dial into your network. However, any dial-up connection solution still poses a risk because anyone can potentially obtain the phone number. It is possible to set up an automatic process to dial phone numbers in sequence until you find a modem that answers. Therefore, Routing and Remote Access needs to be secured to ensure only authorized access. At a minimum, Routing and Remote Access requires that the user provide a valid computer account and password. However, this level of security is open to all the usual logon attacks, such as guessing passwords.

It is recommended that you use additional Routing and Remote Access security options. You can restrict the use of Routing and Remote Access to only those people with a confirmed business requirement to dial in. You can also require that Routing and Remote Access hang up the connection when it is first established and dial back to the user. This way, the user can only access the Routing and Remote Access facility from a predetermined phone number, or the phone number can be recorded. Where facilities allow, you can also use caller ID to record the phone number that originated the connection.

Consider that someone can intercept a user name and password while a user is attempting to log on to the Routing and Remote Access server using techniques similar to a wiretap. To prevent this, Routing and Remote Access can use a secure user authentication method, such as Extensible Authentication Protocol (EAP), Microsoft Challenge Handshake Authentication Protocol (MS-CHAP) version 1 and version 2, Challenge Handshake Authentication Protocol (CHAP), or Shiva Handshake Authentication Protocol (SPAP).

A related risk is a user who believes he or she is dialing in to the company network, but is actually dialing into another location that is now obtaining their identification information. To avoid this, you can use mutual authentication to ensure that the Routing and Remote Access server is authorized much like the user is authorized. This is possible with EAP-Transport Layer Security (EAP-TLS) or MS-CHAP version 2 authentication protocols.

Similar issues exist for the data that is transferred over the Routing and Remote Access connection. The EAP-TLS or MS-CHAP version 2 authentication protocols allow you to encrypt data as it is being transmitted, using Microsoft Point-to-Point Encryption (MPPE).

Remote access policies, whether implemented as local policies or as part of Group Policy, can enforce the use of the authentication and encryption techniques you choose to use.

For more information about networking, Routing and Remote Access authentication, and data encryption techniques, see Windows 2000 Server Help.

Virtual Private Networks

Virtual private networks (VPNs) provide secure network services over a public network, like a private network does, but at a reduced cost. VPNs allow company staff and other authorized users to connect to the corporate network from remote locations as securely as they can from a company site. Therefore, all corporate network services can be securely offered over VPNs. VPNs require more effort than nonsecured public connections to understand, set up, and support, but they provide fully secure connections using low-cost Internet or similar connections.

You can use VPNs in conjunction with Routing and Remote Access, but this is not required. You can set up VPNs between sites using any kind of link and you can also use them within a site for enhanced security.

Virtual private networks typically work as follows:

- The user dials into any Internet service provider (ISP).
- The VPN client software contacts a designated VPN server owned by your company through the Internet and initiates authentication.
- The user is authenticated and security details are provided.
- The VPN server provides a new Transmission Control Protocol/Internet Protocol (TCP/IP) address to the client computer and the client computer is directed to send all further network traffic with that address through the VPN server.
- All network packets are then fully encrypted as they are exchanged in a manner that only the VPN client and VPN server can decrypt.

Figure 17.4 illustrates the relationships among these computers.

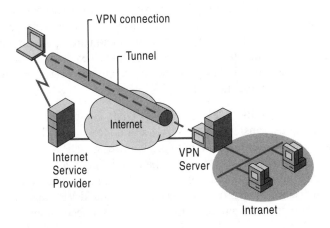

Figure 17.4   Sample Virtual Private Network Configuration

You can also use VPNs to connect multiple computers at a site to your corporate network, or to restrict communications with a subnet to authorized staff only.

Windows 2000 Server includes Windows 2000 VPN software as part of Routing and Remote Access, which is an optional Windows 2000 component. The *Internetworking Guide* contains extensive information about how Windows 2000 VPNs work and what facilities they provide. Windows 2000 Server Help describes how to install VPNs.

Deploying VPNs

If you are planning to deploy VPNs, there are various issues you need to consider, such as:

- Which security protocol to use—Point-to-Point Tunneling Protocol (PPTP) or Layer Two Tunneling Protocol (L2TP).
- Whether to use IPSec (if L2TP is selected).
- What certificates to use when connecting with L2TP/IPSec.
- Where to locate the VPN server—in front of your firewall, behind it, or beside it.
- How to use Connection Manager to give users predefined settings.
- How to use VPNs as part of your remote access policy.

PPTP vs. L2TP

Point-to-Point Tunneling Protocol (PPTP) is a TCP/IP network protocol that encapsulates IP, IPX, or NetBIOS Enhanced User Interface (NetBEUI) protocols. PPTP allows non-TCP/IP, or multiprotocol, network activity over the Internet (or similar networks). PPTP-based VPNs also provide user authentication, access control, and the opportunity to apply dial-up profiles to carefully restrict certain types of remote access use by specific users. PPTP provides an internal address configuration to the remote client, so they can participate on the internal network as if they were directly connected. PPTP provides compression and options for standard and strong RC4 (a symmetric stream cipher) encryption for the traffic that is carried inside the tunnel.

L2TP is very similar to PPTP but uses UDP, and therefore can be used over asynchronous transfer mode (ATM), Frame Relay, and X.25 networks as well. When L2TP is used over IP networks, it uses a UDP port 1701 packet format for both a control channel and a data channel. L2TP can also be used with IPSec to provide a fully secured network link. IPSec first does a security negotiation, using certificates for authentication, between client and VPN server for L2TP traffic. L2TP then provides authentication using a user account and password or using a user certificate.

Internet Protocol Security

Internet Protocol Security (IPSec) is a protocol for securing Internet Protocol (IP) network traffic. IPSec provides complete security between two computers, so that no section of the connection is insecure. Configuration of IPSec is performed using IPSec policies. These policies can contain a number of security rules, each one specifying a certain type of traffic with filters, associated with a filter action and authentication method. IPSec policies can be creating and assigned locally on a computer, or in Active Directory within Group Policy.

Note   IPSec does provide end-to-end IP security, but it does not encrypt all protocols that run over IP. IPSec has built-in exemptions for certain traffic such as Internet Key Exchange negotiation, Kerberos authentication, IP broadcast, and IP multicast traffic. If necessary, additional protocols can be exempted by creating IPSec rules with a filter to specify the type of traffic and a filter action of permit.

For more information about IPSec, see Windows 2000 Server Help, and the *TCP/IP Core Networking Guide*. For more information about planning the deployment of your certification authority in a public key infrastructure, see "Planning Your Public Key Infrastructure" in this book.

VPN Server Location

You can use VPNs in conjunction with firewalls. Although VPNs can act similarly to firewalls, each offers additional benefits that the other cannot, and therefore both might be needed. In such a situation, consider the location of the VPN server in relation to the firewall.

Physically, you can install the two on the same server. This creates a single point of failure if the server is unavailable or if the security of the server is compromised. However, having fewer servers reduces the probability of server unavailability, as well as reducing the costs of server maintenance. There can also be capacity implications. Consider how each of these factors affects your situation to determine the specific design you need.

A more significant set of issues is the logical relationship of the VPN server to the firewall. The options, as shown in Figure 17.5, are to have the VPN server logically in front of the firewall, behind it, or beside it. Windows 2000 can provide firewall services, either with Proxy Server or using packet filter routing. For more information about these kinds of solutions, see "Routing and Remote Access Service" in the *Internetworking Guide*.

When the VPN server is in front of the firewall, the firewall only provides its external services to authorized VPN users. Therefore, general Internet or similar access is not provided. The exception to this is if Internet access is provided at the far end of the VPN connections.

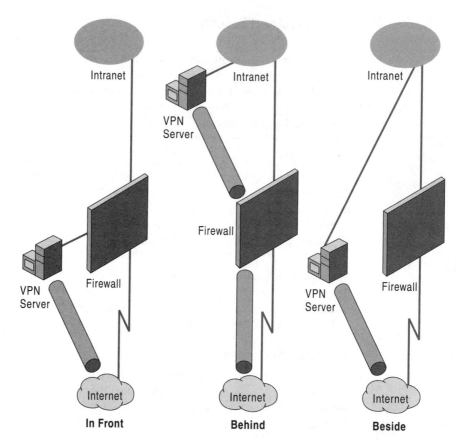

Figure 17.5   Sample Logical Positioning of VPN Server in Relation to a Firewall

When the VPN server is behind the firewall, the firewall provides all its traditional services, but it needs to be configured to open ports that are needed by the VPN server. These include ports needed for IPSec if you are using an L2TP with IPSec VPN.

When the VPN server is beside the firewall, each provides their services independently of each other. However, this configuration provides two access routes to the corporate network, which increases potential for a security breach. Normally, neither provides a route around the other, but with two routes, the risk is doubled.

Choosing the best relationship for your situation depends on which security issues you are most comfortable with. With the servers beside each other, you have two routes into your Intranet, and thus two sets of security risks. With the VPN server behind the firewall, you have to open more ports on the firewall. With the VPN server in front of the firewall, the VPN server does not benefit from the security that the firewall provides, but all the traffic it processes does benefit from the firewall.

Connection Manager

Providing VPN facilities to your users requires some configuration on each client computer. The settings are not necessarily easy to make, however, Windows 2000 includes a Connection Manager that eases the user setup process.

Connection Manager operates on computers running Microsoft® Windows® 95, Microsoft® Windows® 98, Microsoft® Windows NT®, or Windows 2000. Windows 2000 servers also have an administrative kit, called the *Connection Manager Administration Kit*, which allows you to create a customized connection manager for your users.

For more information about connections, the Connection Manager, and Connection Manager Administration Kit, see Windows 2000 Server Help. After following the instructions in Windows 2000 Server Help and running the Connection Manager Administration Kit, you will have a program and documentation that you can distribute to your users.

Remote Access Policies

Remote access policies allow you to specify which people can use Routing and Remote Access, and the various conditions that will be applied when they connect. You can specify policies based on which Windows 2000 group the user is in, the phone number they use, the time of day, and other relevant information. The policies can specify that the connection should be accepted or rejected, and a profile can be applied to the connection. The profile can specify how long the session can last, how long it can be idle, what kinds of dial-up media are allowed, which addresses are allowed, what authentication methods are required, and whether encryption or a VPN is required.

You can set remote access policies for either Routing and Remote Access or for Internet Authentication Service (IAS), which is discussed later in this section. For more information about remote access policies, including how to set them up and the options the policies provide, see Windows 2000 Server Help.

Consider applying different policies to different groups or conditions carefully. It is possible for policies to overlap and thus to disallow people that you intended to allow to dial-up, or to cause other problems. A complex combination of policies makes such problems more likely. Therefore, it is best to minimize the number of policies whenever possible. Windows 2000 Server Help includes a recommended procedure for troubleshooting remote access policies if problems develop.

VPN Server Capacity

As with all servers, VPN servers can be overwhelmed with work if excessive activity is sent their way. You need a lot of VPN links for this to occur, but it can become an issue for a large organization. In your pilot, you can test how much load your users are likely to put on your available VPN servers. You can also test how much capacity your VPN servers can handle by estimating the number of concurrent users you are likely to have and the amount of data they are likely to send. You can then send a comparable amount of data through the VPN server using a small number of client computers but over your local area network (LAN) and using large volume activities, such as copying large numbers of files. By monitoring the VPN server and its responsiveness, you can determine whether your VPN servers are adequate for the role. If necessary, you can increase the size of your servers, or add more VPN servers and use Network Load Balancing Service or round-robin DNS to balance the load.

Internet Authentication Service

Windows 2000 Server includes Internet Authentication Service (IAS) as an optional component. This service implements an industry-standard network authentication security protocol, Remote Authentication Dial-In User Service (RADIUS), which allows centralization of account authorization. RADIUS also allows you to specify how long the session can last and what IP address can be used. IAS can also record session details, providing accountability, and reporting options.

You can also use IAS is if you want to outsource your remote access facilities but continue to control the authentication of people trying to use those facilities. In this case, the outsourcing vendor can direct the authorization requests from their Routing and Remote Access servers to your IAS servers. IAS authenticates accounts against native Windows 2000 domains and Windows NT 4.0 domains.

You need to place IAS Server behind your firewall with ports opened on the server for RADIUS authentication and appropriate User Datagram Protocol (UDP) packets.

For more information about installing and using IAS, including operating suggestions, see Windows 2000 Server Help. Windows 2000 Server Help also includes best practices for additional security details, and information about scaling IAS in large environments and using IAS logging effectively.

Deploying Strategies for Users

Some users might want to access secured company applications when they are away from their offices. Some of these applications are relatively simple, such as time management, company benefits registration, or similar programs. Others are complex, such as accounting systems and line-of-business applications. Make sure that you secure these applications so that only authorized users can access the data and that they can only make authorized changes. This also provides accountability, because use of the applications can be tracked to specific users.

Windows 2000 includes a variety of security technologies that provide application developers with options for including network security. The choice of technologies depends on:

- The application's security requirements
- Integration issues
- The developer's degree of familiarity with the technology
- Network and application performance impact
- Administration complexity

The application-oriented network security technologies include:

- Security Support Provider Interface (SSPI)—a general purpose security API that provides access to plenty of security services from a standardized programming interface.
- Windows NTLM security, also known as Windows NT domain-level security.
- Kerberos v5 authentication protocol. For more information about this, see "Planning Distributed Security" in this book.
- Secure Sockets Layer (SSL). SSL has been enhanced and standardized by the Internet Engineering Task Force (IETF) as Transport Layer Security (TLS).
- Certificates, as discussed earlier in this chapter.

These network security technologies, and the network technologies that access them, relate to each other as indicated in Figure 17.6. Note that SSP in the figure stands for SSPI Security Provider, meaning the interface between the security facility and SSPI. Remote Procedure Call (RPC), Microsoft® Distributed Component Object Model (DCOM), and Windows Sockets (Winsock) are process-to-process communication methods. WinInet (Windows Internet API) is a programming interface used to initiate and manage Web interfaces.

The network security technologies are in the lower half of the diagram, starting at the SSPI. The network technologies are in the upper half of the diagram and are located underneath the application box that uses them.

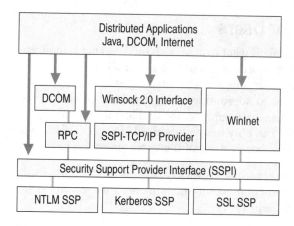

Figure 17.6   Relationships of Sample Network Application Security Technologies

Work with your corporate application developers and vendors to determine which application-oriented network security technologies you need to deploy. These technologies do not require any further infrastructure planning; however, you do need to determine how your developers can benefit from the more powerful network security that Windows 2000 provides. For example, they might consider using smart cards to ensure secure user authentication when the Routing and Remote Access or VPN links are set up.

Deploying Strategies for Partners

Most organizations work in a complex world of relationships between customers, vendors, allied companies, suppliers, consultants, regulators, and others who work with the organization. Many of these partners, as they are often called, benefit greatly from direct access to your company's data and applications. However, providing such access can create considerable risk of exposing advantageous or sensitive information to the wrong people, or can create the risk of people maliciously controlling the corporate computer infrastructure. Therefore, networking security strategies must be employed effectively to give partners only the most appropriate access.

The collection of network and security technologies that allows partners to access your corporate network is often called an *extranet*. Extranets frequently employ the same technologies as previously discussed to provide access to staff and users, such as VPNs and Routing and Remote Access. A distinguishing characteristic of partners, however, is that they might always communicate with your company from a specific location and through a predefined link. Therefore, you can configure your proxy server to allow the extranet link from only that network address.

When you are considering which partners will use your extranet, make certain you determine what business units they will communicate with. Typically, partners fall into distinct categories that communicate primarily with distinct parts of the company. Some might work with shipping and receiving, others with engineering, and others strictly with sales.

Deploying network security strategies for partners is different from deploying for users or staff, primarily because extranets can quickly become mission critical for your partners. Corporate employees usually have the option of coming into the office to access corporate resources. Partners only have the option of using the extranet (or falling back to traditional means). Employees are also likely to work with relatively small quantities of data at any given time, whereas partners often generate considerable data to be processed by your computers and transmitted through your network.

Partners and business units are also very sensitive to the timeliness of the extranet service. Business functions are often dependent on the data that is exchanged and delays can be very costly. The extranet needs to be reliable, and when any issues arise, the partners and business units need to be able to contact someone who can fix the problems quickly.

The business units that supply services over the extranet have particular business issues and constraints in mind. They also have systems and staff with a history that is unique when compared to other parts of the company. Therefore, it is not unusual for some business units to have extranet requirements that are different from other business units.

For these reasons, a strategy for deploying network security to partners needs to emphasize reliability, scalability, flexibility, and supportability. Staffing is particularly critical, along with thorough pilot testing, policy and procedure development, and communication. The network security technologies included with Windows 2000 provide the basis for a secure extranet, but the primary differences between your extranet security strategy and your internal network security strategies will be in your policies and procedures.

Planning Task List for Determining Network Security Strategies

Table 17.1 summarizes the tasks you need to perform when planning your network security.

Table 17.1   Planning Task List for Determining Network Security

Task	Location in Chapter
Plan for deployment.	Planning for Network Security
Create secure boundaries.	Creating Secure Boundaries
Prepare for Windows 2000 network security technologies.	Deploying Network Security Technologies
Deploy strategies for everyone.	Preparing for Windows 2000 Network Security Technologies
Deploy strategies for company staff.	Preparing for Windows 2000 Network Security Technologies
Deploy strategies for users of company applications.	Deploying Strategies For Users
Deploy strategies for partners.	Deploying Strategies For Partners

CHAPTER 18

Ensuring the Availability of Applications and Services

If you cannot afford the costs of lost productivity due to the interruption of a mission-critical application or service, or if applications or services in your organization carry fiduciary legal responsibilities, this is an essential planning chapter for you.

Specifically, this chapter will help system administrators determine if your systems require clustering and, if so, which clustering technology is most appropriate for the applications and services in your organization. The guidelines in this chapter will help you create a plan that makes mission-critical applications and services highly available to users under any circumstance.

In This Chapter

Chapter Goals

This chapter will help you develop the following planning document:

- Clustering Deployment Planning Worksheet

Related Information in the Resource Kit

- For more information about Microsoft® Windows® Clustering, see "Windows Clustering" in the *Microsoft® Windows® 2000 Server Resource Kit Distributed Systems Guide*.

- For more information about creating test plans, see "Building a Windows 2000 Test Lab" in this book.

Making Applications and Services Highly Available

A server failure in any organization can be extremely costly, whether the server is a file, print, Web, or application server. Measuring the costs of server, application, or service downtime in any organization can be difficult. Potential losses can include:

- Lost sales
- Lost customer goodwill
- Lost employee productivity and confidence
- Increased costs due to makeup time
- Missed contractual obligations or possible legal liabilities
- Perishable products going to waste
- Loss of competitiveness

The costs that your organization can accrue due to the interruption of a mission-critical application or service could be extremely high. If you are not making mission-critical applications and services highly available to your users, you are taking a high-priced risk.

This chapter discusses the details of deployment planning for Windows Clustering. Clustering is a feature of Windows 2000 Advanced Server that provides four main benefits for networks and for system administrators:

- High availability of applications and services.
- Scalability of specific applications and services (when using load balancing).
- Centralized administration.
- Rolling upgrade (the process of upgrading cluster nodes individually while the other nodes continue to provide service).

Overview of Windows 2000 Advanced Server

The Windows 2000 Server family currently includes Windows 2000 Server and Windows 2000 Advanced Server. Windows 2000 Server offers core functionality appropriate to small-sized and medium-sized organizations that have numerous workgroups and branch offices and that need essential services including file, print, communications, infrastructure, and Web. Windows 2000 Advanced Server is designed to meet mission-critical needs, such as large data warehouses, online transaction processing (OLTP), messaging, e-commerce, or Web hosting services for medium and large organizations, and Internet service providers (ISPs).

Windows 2000 Advanced Server has evolved from Microsoft® Windows NT® Server 4.0, Enterprise Edition. It provides a comprehensive clustering infrastructure for high availability and scalability of applications and services, including main memory support up to 8 Gigabytes (GB) on Intel Page Address Extension (PAE) systems. Designed for demanding enterprise applications, Advanced Server supports new systems with up to 8-way symmetric multiprocessing *(SMP)*. SMP enables any one of the multiple processors in a computer to run any operating system or application threads simultaneously with the other processors in the system. Windows Advanced Server is well-suited to database-intensive work, and provides high availability server clustering and load balancing for excellent system and application availability.

Windows 2000 Advanced Server includes the full feature set of Windows 2000 Server and adds the high availability and scalability required for enterprise and larger departmental solutions. Key features of Advanced Server include:

- Network (TCP/IP) Load Balancing
- Enhanced two-node server clusters based on the Microsoft Windows Cluster Server (MSCS) previously released in the Windows NT Server 4.0 Enterprise Edition
- Up to 8 GB main memory on Intel PAE Systems
- Up to 8-way SMP

Note If you are uncertain about whether you have an Intel PAE computer system, contact your hardware vendor.

Process for Making Applications and Services Highly Available

When you plan for deployment of Windows Clustering, it is critical that you consider solutions that will help you avoid server, application, or service failures in your organization. Consider using the process represented in the flowchart in Figure 18.1 when planning for high availability of applications and services in your organization.

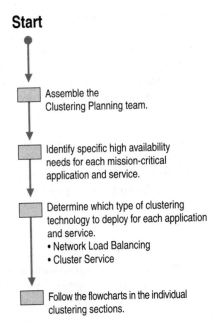

Start

Assemble the
Clustering Planning team.

Identify specific high availability
needs for each mission-critical
application and service.

Determine which type of clustering
technology to deploy for each application
and service.
• Network Load Balancing
• Cluster Service

Follow the flowcharts in the individual
clustering sections.

Figure 18.1   Planning for Availability of Applications and Services

Before you begin the planning phase, it is important that you thoroughly
understand the key components of Windows Clustering that will make your
mission-critical applications and services highly available to end users in your
organization.

Overview of Windows Clustering

A *cluster* is a group of independent computers that work together to run a
common set of applications or services and provide the image of a single system
to the client and application. Clustered computers are physically connected by
cables and programmatically connected by cluster software. These connections
allow computers to use problem-solving features, such as load balancing and
failover, that are not available for use with stand-alone computers.

Load balancing distributes server loads across all configured servers and prevents one server from being overworked. This, in turn, enables you to increase your capacity incrementally to meet demand. *Failover* provides constant support to users by automatically transferring resources from a failing or offline cluster server to a functioning one. This provides cluster users with constant access to the resources. Windows Clustering currently provides the following two clustering technologies:

Network Load Balancing   Network Load Balancing provides scalability and high availability of TCP/IP-based applications and services, by combining up to 32 servers running Windows 2000 Advanced Server into a single, load balancing cluster. The most common use for Network Load Balancing is to distribute incoming Web requests among its cluster of Internet server applications (such as Internet Information Services applications).

Cluster Service   Using Advanced Server, Cluster service lets you combine two servers to work together as a server cluster to ensure that mission-critical applications and resources remain available to clients. Server clusters enable users and administrators to access certain resources of the servers, or *nodes*, as a single system rather than as separate computers.

When you are planning and deploying applications and services for high availability, it is critical that you define best practices for your organization. Microsoft has developed a series of best practice guides for high availability. For more information about these guides, see the Microsoft TechNet High Availability link on the Web Resources page at http://windows.microsoft.com/windows2000/reskit/webresources.

Determining Availability Strategies

After you understand the capabilities of Windows Clustering, you can begin the planning phase of cluster deployment to help make your mission-critical applications and services highly available to users in your organization.

Assembling the Clustering Planning Team

Teamwork is of the utmost importance in determining your clustering requirements. Planning your clustering strategy needs to be a cooperative project involving system administrators for the network and administrators for the following applications and services:

- Microsoft® SQL Server™ or other database

- Microsoft® Exchange Server or other groupware
- Microsoft® Internet Information Services (IIS) or other Web service
- Windows 2000 Terminal Services
- Windows Internet Name Service (WINS)
- Dynamic Host Configuration Protocol (DHCP)
- Internally developed line-of-business applications
- Third-party applications
- File and print shares

In most organizations, these applications and services are required to be highly available to users.

The core clustering planning team must identify specific high-availability needs for each of the mission-critical application and services mentioned. Collectively, this team will know enough about the use of these applications and services and the use of the network to avoid potential costly mistakes.

After you have determined your clustering strategy, plan to meet with your core clustering planning team to determine staffing requirements for the cluster configuration in your organization. Resources and applications running on a cluster might be administered differently than the same resources on a stand-alone server. Be sure that you determine the scope of these differences and train your staff accordingly. Also, be sure that your staff is aware of the requirements for high availability and understand how their actions could limit or reduce system availability. For example, an administrator who adds a new resource to a group containing hundreds of other resources could bring the entire group down (along with the resources it contains) if that administrator incorrectly configures the new resource.

Identifying High-Availability Needs for Applications and Services

To identify specific high-availability needs for mission-critical applications and services in your organization, determine the following:

- Basic characteristics of the application or service, such as:
  - Software used.
  - Special hardware requirements. (For more information, see "Determining Hardware Compatibility for Advanced Features" later in this chapter.)
  - Volume of data.
  - Number of users.
  - Hours of operation.

- Expected changes in size and performance requirements, such as:
  - Seasonal or other planned peak loads.
  - Expected rate of increase in users.
  - Expected rate of increase in data.

- Hardware requirements at initial deployment, during peak load times, and within the planning horizon of the project. Use application and service characteristics and change projections to make your estimation.

- Data backup and disaster recovery plans for the application, service, and operating system.

- Maximum outage tolerance (that is, the maximum amount of time that the system or users can tolerate the application or service being unavailable). This is important, because eliminating all possible outages can be expensive. For many applications and services, occasional brief outages might be an acceptable alternative to larger investments in high availability.

- Impact of downtime. Perform a qualitative assessment of the way that downtime of an application or service would affect your organization. Examples include lost sales, lost productivity, and decline in customer satisfaction.

- Measurable cost of downtime. Perform a quantitative estimate of the cost per application or service outage that exceeds the specified maximum that your organization can tolerate.

- Identify all potential single points of failure in the planned configuration.

- Identify your staffing requirements.

- Current availability. If you do not have the availability numbers, begin collecting the data right away. Starting with Windows NT 4.0 SP4, you can easily calculate the system uptime using the *Microsoft Windows NT 4.0 Server Resource Kit* tool, Uptime.exe. Uptime.exe uses events stored in the Event Log to calculate these numbers. You must enable the Event Log in order for this to take place. Uptime.exe is also available in the *Microsoft Windows 2000 Server Resource Kit.*

A single point of failure is any component in your environment that would block data or applications if it failed.

Table 18.1 lists common points of failure in a server environment and describes whether you can protect the point of failure by using a Microsoft clustering solution or by using a third-party solution.

Table 18.1   Common Points of Failure

Failure Point	Clustering Solution	Other Solutions
Network hub	N/A	Redundant networks
Network router	N/A	OSPF
Power outage	N/A	- Uninterruptible power supply (UPS) - Generator - Multiple power grids
Server connection	Failover	N/A
Disk	Fail over	Hardware or software RAID, to ensure against the loss of specific data on a specific computer and to provide for uninterrupted service
Other server hardware such as CPU or memory	Failover	Spare components such as motherboards and small computer system interface (SCSI) controllers (any spare components need to exactly match the original components, including network and SCSI components).
Server software such as the operating system or specific applications	Failover	N/A
Wide area network (WAN) links such as routers and dedicated lines	N/A	Redundant links that provide secondary access to remote connections
Dial-up connection	N/A	Multiple modems and Routing and Remote Access

Determining Hardware Compatibility for Advanced Features

Check to be sure the computer systems and adapters that are presently installed or are planned for purchase are listed on the Microsoft Hardware Compatibility List (HCL). To determine if the hardware is listed and supported by HCL, see the Microsoft Windows Hardware Compatibility List link on the Web Resources page at http://windows.microsoft.com/windows2000/reskit/webresources.

If you plan to deploy computer systems with advanced capabilities, such as clustering or large amounts of memory, there are additional requirements that you must meet.

For example, if you have Advanced Server computer systems with more than 4 GB of RAM, you must modify the Boot.ini PAE switch to enable PAE memory use. You can make this modification after you have verified that all components are supported. If the components are not supported, the computer system must be brought into compliance to avoid potential problems later.

If the system is in production and you add new adapters and drivers, it is strongly recommended that you back up the system completely before making any modifications.

Note Changes to the registry and some modifications to the Boot.ini file that could cause the computer system to function incorrectly or be unstable, might be avoided when you start the computer by using the F8 key, which bypasses many switches and drivers. This allows you to make changes to the Boot.ini file or other areas as needed to restore functionality

---

Determining Your Clustering Requirements

After you have determined specific high availability needs for mission-critical applications and services, identified potential single points of failure, and determined that your hardware is compatible with Windows 2000, you must determine which type of clustering technology best fits the needs of your organization. Before you plan your cluster, review the requirements to determine the appropriate cluster type.

Planning for Network Load Balancing

Network Load Balancing clusters a group of computers together that run server programs using the TCP/IP networking protocol. Network Load Balancing service enhances the availability and scalability of Web servers, File Transfer Protocol (FTP) servers, streaming media servers, virtual private network (VPN) servers, and other mission-critical programs. Network Load Balancing provides these enhancements using a cluster of two or more host computers (servers that are members of the cluster) working together.

A single computer running Windows 2000 Advanced Server can provide a limited level of server reliability and scalable performance. However, by combining the resources of two or more computers running Windows 2000 Advanced Server into a single cluster, Network Load Balancing can deliver the availability that Web servers and other mission-critical programs need to maintain top performance. Figure 18.2 represents a Network Load Balancing cluster containing four hosts.

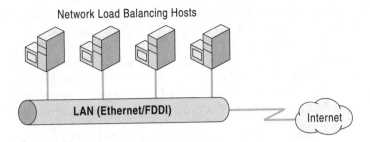

Figure 18.2   Four Hosts Within a Network Load Balancing Cluster

Each host runs separate copies of the desired server programs, such as Web server, FTP, Telnet, and messaging. For some services, such as a Web server, a copy of the program runs on all hosts within the cluster, and Network Load Balancing distributes the workload among the servers. For other services, such as messaging, only one copy of the service handles the workload within the cluster. Instead of equalizing the loads of these services, Network Load Balancing allows network traffic to flow to a single host, moving the traffic to another host only in cases of server failure. Network Load Balancing allows all computers in the cluster to be addressed by the same set of cluster Internet Protocol (IP) addresses—while also maintaining their existing, dedicated IP addresses. Network Load Balancing distributes incoming client requests as TCP/IP traffic, including TCP connections and UDP streams, across the hosts.

To scale server performance, Network Load Balancing balances the load of incoming TCP/IP connections across all hosts in the cluster. You can configure the load size for each host as necessary. You can also add hosts to the cluster dynamically to manage increased load. In addition, Network Load Balancing can direct all TCP/User Datagram Protocol (UDP) traffic (not configured to be load balanced) to a designated single host, called the "default host." This is advantageous because it allows all services not explicitly configured for load balancing to run on a single host. Network Load Balancing manages the TCP/IP traffic to maintain high availability for server programs.

When a host fails or goes offline, Network Load Balancing automatically reconfigures the cluster to redirect client requests to the remaining computers. For load-balanced programs, the load is automatically redistributed among the computers that are still operating. Programs running on a single server have their traffic redirected to a specific host. Connections to the failed or offline server are lost. After necessary maintenance is completed, the offline computer can transparently rejoin the cluster and regain its share of the workload.

Network Load Balancing does not detect application failures. Instead, it is designed to be controlled by application monitoring programs that check for and ensure correct behavior of their associated applications. For example, if an application monitor determines that its service has failed, it can instruct Network Load Balancing to remove the affected host from the cluster until the problem is corrected. Additionally, Network Load Balancing detects whether a cluster host has had an orderly or disorderly shutdown or if the network adapter has failed.

You know that your organization requires Network Load Balancing if you host a TCP/IP service (such as a Web server) that must scale its performance to meet increasing client demand and that must be continuously available. For example, Internet e-commerce sites are seeing explosive demand, and outages on these sites are unacceptable to customers. Traditional means of scaling these services, such as the use of round robin domain name system (DNS) alone cannot provide the high availability that Network Load Balancing gives you. Round robin DNS is a solution for enabling a limited form of TCP/IP load balancing for Web servers.

Process for Planning Your Network Load Balancing Clusters

This section discusses guidelines you need to consider when you plan the Network Load Balancing clusters in your organization. When you plan your Network Load Balancing clusters, consider using the planning process represented in the flowchart in Figure 18.3.

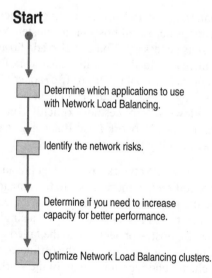

Figure 18.3   Process for Planning Your Network Load Balancing Clusters

Determining Which Applications to Use with Network Load Balancing

Many applications work with Network Load Balancing. This section offers guidelines for determining which applications might be suitable.

In general, Network Load Balancing can scale any application or service that uses TCP/IP as its network protocol and is associated with a specific TCP or UDP port.

Network Load Balancing uses "port rules" that describe which traffic to load balance and which traffic to ignore. By default, Network Load Balancing configures all ports for load balancing. However, you can modify the configuration that determines how incoming network traffic is load balanced on a per-port basis. To modify the default behavior, you create port rules that cover specific port ranges.

Some examples of services and their associated ports are:

- HTTP over TCP/IP: Web servers, such as Microsoft Internet Information Services (IIS): Port 80.
- HTTPS over TCP/IP: HTTP over Secure Sockets Layer (SSL) for encrypting Web traffic: Port 443.
- FTP over TCP/IP: FTP: Port 21, port 20, and ports 1024-65535.
- TFTP over TCP/IP: Trivial File Transfer Protocol (TFTP) servers, which are used by applications such as Bootstrap Protocol (BOOTP): port 69.
- SMTP over TCP/IP: Simple Mail Transport Protocol (SMTP), which is used by applications such as Microsoft Exchange: Port 25.
- Microsoft Terminal Services: Port 3389.

To be successfully load balanced, an application or service must be designed to allow multiple instances (multiple copies of a program) to run simultaneously, one on each cluster host. For example, an application must not make updates to a file that will in turn be synchronized with updates made by other instances unless it explicitly provides a means to do so. To avoid this problem, set up a back-end database server to handle synchronized updates to shared-state information.

In addition, Network Load Balancing is commonly used with:

- VPN servers

    A VPN server services an extension of a private network that encompasses links across shared or public networks such as the Internet.

- *Streaming media servers*

    Software (such as Microsoft Media Technologies) that provides multimedia support, allowing you to deliver content using Advanced Streaming Format over an intranet or the Internet.

Network Load Balancing is a good choice for VPN servers and streaming media servers after you have determined that your organization would benefit from load balancing PPTP or streaming traffic.

Note Before load balancing an application in a Network Load Balancing cluster, review the application license or check with the application vendor. Each application vendor sets its own licensing policies for applications running on clusters.

When using Network Load Balancing with VPN servers to load-balance PPTP clients, it is important to configure the TCP/IP properties correctly to ensure compatibility with clients running earlier versions of Windows (for example, Windows 98 and Windows NT 4.0). To do this, assign only a single virtual IP address to the network adapter used by Network Load Balancing and do not assign a dedicated IP address on this subnet. This restriction does not apply for Windows 2000 clients.

For more information about configuring Network Load Balancing for VPN and other applications, see "Windows Clustering" in the *Microsoft® Windows® 2000 Server Resource Kit Distributed Systems Guide.*

Using Network Load Balancing to Deploy Terminal Server Clusters

Windows 2000 Terminal Services, when configured in Application Server mode, provides centralized application deployment and execution for remote users. You can use Network Load Balancing to distribute a large client base among a group of terminal servers. This is most appropriate in situations where the Terminal server application is largely stateless, such as providing a data entry application to a sales floor or warehouse.

If roaming users need to reconnect to existing Terminal server sessions, you cannot use Network Load Balancing to provide a complete roaming experience. Since Network Load Balancing routes users to cluster hosts based on the IP address, a user connecting from multiple locations, or one who uses DHCP and disconnects between sessions, is not always routed back to the same computer, and thus cannot reattach to a disconnected session. Even in such situations, Network Load Balancing can provide reconnections for dropped sessions, or persistent routing if the user's IP address is fixed. If maintaining disconnected sessions is not a requirement, then you can use Network Load Balancing effectively for any sort of terminal server application.

When you use Network Load Balancing, it is recommended that you configure all terminal servers to end disconnected sessions after a moderate time-out, such as 30 minutes. This configuration allows dropped sessions to be resumed, but does not allow disconnected sessions to persist for long periods. Persistent sessions can be a problem when the user is routed to other computers, because the computers will not be reconnected. This configuration could consume resources by leaving sessions open on multiple computers for each user or, in the worst case, users can be locked out because their resources are in use elsewhere.

When deploying a Terminal Services cluster using Network Load Balancing, each server needs to be able to serve all users. To facilitate this, you must store per-user information, system information, and common data in an accessible place, such as a back-end file server. Figure 18.4 represents an implementation of Network Load Balancing and Terminal Services.

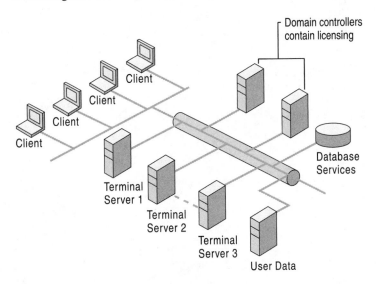

Figure 18.4   Network Load Balancing Provides Balancing Among Terminal Servers

Note that separate servers are depicted for line-of-business database applications and for per-user data storage. Each of these servers needs to be implemented as a high-availability server using clustering or other appropriate technologies. Additionally, this implementation improves scalability by partitioning the workload so that multiple terminal servers can support the desired level of performance.

For more information about Terminal Services, see "Deploying Terminal Services" in this book.

Configuring Network Load Balancing Clusters for Servers Running IIS/ASP and COM+ Applications

A key component of e-commerce sites are servers running COM+ applications. In the example shown in Figure 18.5, a server running COM+ handles object requests for the shopping basket of an online bookstore.

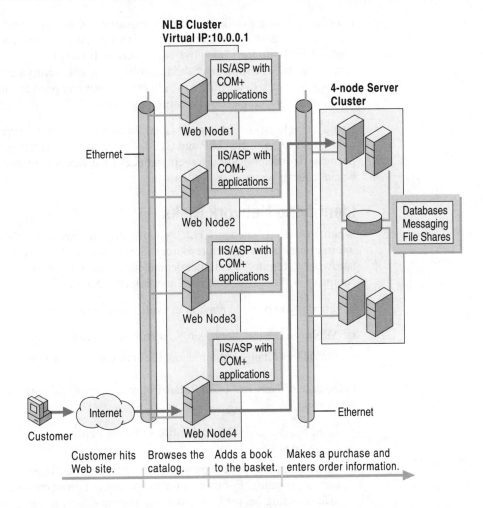

Figure 18.5   Deploying COM+ Applications on the Same Physical Servers as IIS

In order to ensure that these objects are available when you need them, and to maximize the performance of the site as a whole, it is recommended that you deploy COM+ on the same physical servers as IIS. By doing this, the application servers can take advantage of the scalability and availability gains afforded by the existing Network Load Balancing cluster without any need for an additional separate tier of dedicated servers running COM+.

Using a single physical Network Load Balancing cluster of servers that has been configured for both IIS/ASP and COM+, as opposed to creating a separate physical tier of application servers, reduces hardware and management costs because fewer servers are needed.

Identifying Network Risks

When you identify network risks, you identify the possible failures that can interrupt access to network resources. Single points of failure can include hardware, software, or external dependencies, such as power supplied by a utility company or dedicated wide area network (WAN) lines.

In general, you provide maximum availability when you:

- Minimize the number of single points of failure in your environment.
- Provide mechanisms that maintain service when a failure occurs.

In the case of Network Load Balancing, you also provide maximum availability when you:

- Load balance only the applications that are appropriate to Network Load Balancing.
- Make sure that application servers are properly configured for the applications they are running. For more information about proper configuration, see "Determining Server Capacity Requirements" later in this chapter.

A principal goal of Network Load Balancing is to provide increased availability. A cluster of two or more computers ensures that if one computer fails, another computer is available to continue processing client requests. However, Network Load Balancing is not designed to protect all aspects of your workflow in all circumstances. For example, Network Load Balancing is not an alternative to backing up data. Network Load Balancing only protects access to the data, not the data itself. Also, it does not protect against a power outage that would disable the entire cluster.

Windows 2000 Advanced Server has built-in features that protect certain computer and network processes during failure. These features include redundant array of independent disks (RAID) 1 (disk mirroring) and RAID 5 (disk-striping with parity.) When planning your Network Load Balancing environment, look for areas where these features can help you in ways that Network Load Balancing cannot.

Planning for Network Load Balancing

This section will help you determine the number of Network Load Balancing servers you require in your organization and how you need to configure them.

Cluster size, defined as the number of cluster hosts participating in the cluster (can be up to 32 for Windows Clustering), is based on the number of computers required to meet the anticipated client load for a given application.

For example, if you determine that you need six computers running IIS in order to meet the anticipated client demand for Web services, then Network Load Balancing will run on all six computers and your cluster will consist of six cluster hosts.

As a general rule, add servers until the cluster can easily handle the client load without becoming overloaded. The maximum cluster size you need is determined by network capacity on a given subnet. The exact number depends on the nature of the application.

Note Always be sure that there is enough extra server capacity so that if one server fails, the remaining servers can accommodate the increased load.

When the cluster subnet approaches saturation of the network, add an additional cluster on a different subnet. Use round robin DNS to direct clients to the clusters. You can continue to add clusters in this manner as the network demand grows. Since round robin DNS contains only cluster IP addresses, clients are always directed to clusters instead of to individual servers, and therefore never experience an outage due to a failed server. In some deployments requiring high bandwidth, you could use round robin DNS to split incoming traffic among multiple, identical Network Load Balancing clusters. In Figure 18.6, the IP request discovers DNS (www.reskit.com), which resolves to the virtual IP address of Network Load Balancing Cluster 1 (10.0.0.1) and passes the request to that Network Load Balancing cluster. Subsequent requests are then sent to Cluster 2 (10.0.0.2) and Cluster 3 (10.0.0.3)and then continue in a round robin fashion.

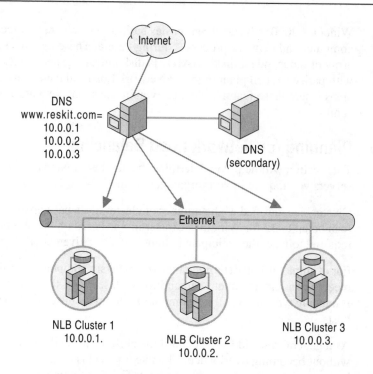

Figure 18.6   Round Robin DNS Among Identical Network Load Balancing Clusters

Note If you use network switches and you deploy two or more clusters, consider placing the clusters on individual switches so that incoming cluster traffic is handled separately. A *switch* is used to connect cluster hosts to a router or other source of incoming network connections.

It is important to note that a switch can be used to separate incoming traffic in cases where you have more than one cluster.

Determining Server Capacity Requirements

After you determine your cluster size, you are ready to configure individual cluster hosts. In general, you would base this determination on the types of applications you plan to load balance and the client demand you anticipate on these applications. Some server applications, such as file and print servers, are extremely disk-intensive and require very large disk capacities and fast input/output (I/O). Be sure you consult the documentation for each application you plan to run, in order to determine how to configure the servers in your cluster.

While it might be possible to substitute two or three very powerful servers for a larger number of less powerful computers, it generally is more desirable to deploy the larger number. Using more servers allows the client load to be more widely distributed, so that if one server fails, the incremental impact on clients is reduced.

Optimizing Network Load Balancing Clusters

There are some hardware and configuration choices you can make to improve cluster performance for Network Load Balancing. These choices are explained in the following sections.

If the cluster hosts are directly connected to a switch in order to receive client requests, incoming client traffic is automatically sent to all switch ports. In most applications, incoming client traffic is a small portion of total cluster traffic. However, if other clusters or computers are connected to the same switch, this cluster traffic consumes some of their port bandwidth.

To avoid this problem, you can connect all cluster hosts to a hub or repeater that is uplinked to a single switch port. In this case, all incoming client traffic flows from the hub or repeater to the single switch port for simultaneous delivery to all cluster hosts. If client traffic arrives at the switch from multiple upstream switch ports, you might want to add a second dedicated network adapter for each host that is connected to an individual switch port. The use of two network adapters per host on the cluster subnet helps to direct network traffic through the cluster hosts. Incoming client traffic flows through the switching hub to all hosts, while outgoing traffic flows directly to the switch ports.

Requirements for Network Load Balancing

An application can run on a Network Load Balancing cluster under the following conditions:

- The connection with clients must be configured to use IP.
- The application to be load balanced must use TCP or UDP ports.
- Multiple identical instances of an application must be able to run simultaneously on separate servers. If multiple instances of an application share data, there has to be a way to synchronize the updates.

Network Load Balancing is designed to work as a standard networking device driver under Windows 2000 Advanced Server. Because Network Load Balancing provides clustering support for TCP/IP-based server programs, TCP/IP must be installed in order to take advantage of Network Load Balancing functionality. The current version of Network Load Balancing operates on Fiber Distributed Data Interface (FDDI) or Ethernet-based local area networks within the cluster. It has been successfully tested on 10 megabits per second (Mbps), 100 Mbps and gigabit Ethernet networks with a wide variety of network adapters.

Network Load Balancing takes up less than 1 megabyte (MB) of storage space and, depending on network load, uses between 250 kilobytes (KB) and 4 MB of RAM when operating within the default parameters. You can modify the default parameters to allow use of up to 15 MB memory. Typical memory usage ranges between 500 KB and 1 MB.

For optimum cluster performance, plan to install a second network adapter on each Network Load Balancing host to handle network traffic addressed to the server as an individual computer on the network. In this configuration, the first network adapter for which Network Load Balancing is enabled handles the client-to-cluster network traffic addressed to the server as part of a cluster. Although a second network adapter is not required, it improves overall networking performance, for instance to access a back-end database. When Network Load Balancing is enabled in its default unicast mode, the second network adapter is required for communications between servers within a cluster, for example, to replicate files between servers.

For more information about system requirements and cluster and host parameters, see "Windows Clustering" in the *Distributed Systems Guide*.

Using a Router

Network Load Balancing can operate in two modes: unicast and multicast. Unicast support is enabled by default, which ensures that it operates properly with all routers. You might elect to enable multicast mode so that a second network adapter is not required for communications within the cluster. If Network Load Balancing clients access a cluster (configured for multicast mode) through a router, be sure that the router accepts an Address Resolution Protocol (ARP) reply for the cluster's (unicast) IP addresses with a multicast media access control address in the payload of the ARP structure. *ARP* is a TCP/IP protocol that uses limited broadcast to the local network to resolve a logically assigned IP address.

This allows the router to map the cluster's primary IP address and other multihomed addresses to the corresponding media access control address. If your router does not meet this requirement, you can create a static ARP entry in the router or you can use Network Load balancing in its default unicast mode.

Some routers require a static ARP entry because they do not support the resolution of unicast IP addresses to multicast media access control addresses.

Planning for Cluster Service

The Cluster service in Windows 2000 Advanced Server provides a foundation for server clusters. When one server in a cluster fails or is taken offline, another server in the cluster takes over the operations of the failed server. Clients using server resources experience little or no interruption of their work because support for resources is moved from one server to the other.

On *server clusters*, the Cluster service manages all cluster-specific activity. There is one instance of the Cluster service running on every node in a cluster. Specifically, the Cluster service handles the following operations:

- Manages cluster objects, cluster disks, and configuration.
- Coordinates with other instances of the Cluster service in the cluster.
- Performs failover operations.
- Handles event notification.
- Facilitates communication among other software components.

You know that your organization requires server clusters if:

- Your users depend on regular access to business-critical data and applications in order to do their jobs.
- You cannot accept service downtime (unplanned or planned) of more that 30 minutes.
- The cost of a backup server is less than the cost of having business-critical data and applications offline during a failure.

Note The term "backup server" generally implies that one server is sitting idle until it is needed. That is not the primary purpose of a server cluster, although it could be configured that way.

Process for Planning Your Server Clusters

This section discusses guidelines to consider when you plan server clusters in your organization. Consider using the planning process depicted in Figure 18.7.

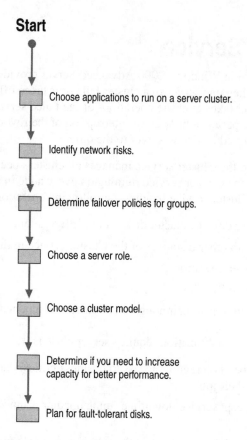

Start

Choose applications to run on a server cluster.

Identify network risks.

Determine failover policies for groups.

Choose a server role.

Choose a cluster model.

Determine if you need to increase capacity for better performance.

Plan for fault-tolerant disks.

Figure 18.7   Process for Planning Your Server Clusters

Choosing Applications to Run on a Server Cluster

You can deploy any application to run on any server that is in a cluster; however, not all applications fail over. Of those that can, not all need to be set up as cluster resources. This section offers guidelines for making these decisions.

The following criteria will help you determine whether an application can adapt to server clustering failover mechanisms:

- Client and server applications must use TCP/IP (or Distributed Component Object Model, Named Pipes, or Remote Procedure Call over TCP/IP) for their network communications to run on a server cluster. An application that uses only NetBIOS Enhanced User Interface (NetBEUI) or Internetwork Packet Exchange (IPX) protocols cannot take advantage of cluster failover.

- The application must be able to specify where the application data is stored.

  Any application that runs on a server cluster must be able to store its data in a configurable location, that is, on the disks attached to shared disk buses. Some applications that cannot store their data in a configurable location can still be configured to fail over. In such cases, however, access to the application data is lost at failover because the data is available only on the disk of the failed node. Replication of this data between the nodes in the cluster might assist in this situation.

- Upon failure, the application can be restarted.

- You can install the application on all nodes in the cluster.

- Client applications that connect to the server application must retry and recover from temporary network failures.

  During failover, client applications experience a temporary loss of network connectivity. If you configure the client application to recover from temporary network connection problems, it can continue operating after a server failover.

You can divide applications that can fail over into two groups: those that use the Cluster API and those that do not.

Applications that support the Cluster API are defined as "cluster-aware." These applications can register with the Cluster service to receive status and notification information, and they can use the Cluster API to administer clusters.

Applications that do not support the Cluster API are defined as "*cluster-unaware.*" If cluster-unaware applications meet the TCP/IP and remote storage criteria, you can still use them in a cluster and can often configure them to fail over.

In either case, applications that keep significant state information in memory are not the best applications for clustering because information not stored on disk is lost at failover. The outcome is similar to your restarting a server or the server suffering a power failure.

Identifying Network Risks

When you configure a cluster, identify the possible failures that can interrupt access to resources. Single points of failure can be hardware, software, or external dependencies, such as power supplied by a utility company and dedicated WAN lines.

In general, you provide maximum availability when you:

- Minimize the number of single points of failure in your environment.

- Provide mechanisms that maintain service when a failure occurs.

With Windows 2000 Advanced Server, you can use server clusters and new administrative procedures to provide increased availability. However, server clusters are not designed to protect all components of your workflow in all circumstances. For example, clusters are not an alternative to backing up data; they protect only the availability of data, not the data itself.

Windows 2000 Advanced Server has built-in features that protect certain computer and network processes during failure. These features include mirroring (RAID 1) and striping with parity (RAID 5). When planning your cluster, look for places where these features can help you in ways that server clusters cannot.

Note Software RAID, offered by Logical Volume Manager in Windows 2000, cannot be used to protect disks managed by the Cluster service. Use hardware RAID to protect these disks.

To further increase the availability of network resources and prevent loss of data, consider the following:

- Have replacement disks and controllers available at your site. Always make sure that any spare parts you keep on hand exactly match the original parts, including network and SCSI components. The cost of two spare SCSI controllers can be a small fraction of the cost of having hundreds of clients unable to use data.

- Provide uninterruptible power supply (UPS) protection for individual computers and for the network itself, including hubs, bridges, and routers. *UPS* devices use batteries to keep the computer running for a period of time after a power failure. Computers running Windows 2000 Server support UPS. UPS solutions need to provide power long enough for the operating system to do an orderly shutdown when power fails.

Determining Failover and Failback Policies for Resource Groups

A *resource group* is an association of dependent or related resources. Dependent resources require other resources in order to operate successfully. Individual resources cannot fail over independently. Resources fail over together with all other resources in the same resource group.

You assign failover policies for each group of resources in a cluster. *Failover policies* determine exactly how a group behaves when failover occurs. You can choose which policies are most appropriate for each resource group you set up.

Failover policies for groups include three settings:

Failover Timing

You can set a group for immediate failover when a resource that is set to affect the group fails, or you can instruct the Cluster service to attempt to restart the failing resource a number of times before initiating a failover. If it is possible that the resource failure can be overcome by restarting all resources within the group, then set the Cluster service to restart the group.

Preferred Node

You can set a group so that it always runs on a designated node whenever that node is available. This is useful if one of the nodes is better-equipped to host the group. Note that this setting only takes effect when failover occurs resulting from a node failure. Otherwise, you have to manually set the node that is hosting the resource group.

Failback Timing

Failback is the process of moving resources, either individually or in a group, back to their preferred node after the node has failed and come back online.

You can configure for a group to failback to its preferred node as soon as the Cluster service detects that the failed node has been restored, or you can instruct the Cluster service to wait until a specified hour of the day, such as after peak business hours.

For more information about planning resource groups, see "Planning Your Resource Groups" later in this chapter.

Choosing a Server Role

Nodes in a server cluster can be member servers or domain controllers. However, in either case, both nodes must belong to the same domain.

If you configure your cluster nodes as domain controllers, you must first ensure that you have the hardware to support them. For more information, see "Determining Capacity Requirements for Cluster Service" later in this chapter.

If you configure all of the cluster nodes as member servers, then the availability of the cluster depends on the availability of the domain controller. The cluster is available only when the domain controller is available. Plan for sufficient domain controllers to provide the desired level of availability. For more information about increasing availability, see "Identifying Network Risks" earlier in this chapter.

You need to account for the additional overhead that is incurred by the domain controller services. In large networks running Windows 2000 Advanced Server, substantial resources can be required by domain controllers for performing directory replication and server authentication for clients. For this reason, many applications, such as SQL Server and Message Queuing, recommend that you do not install application on domain controllers for best performance. However, if you have a very small network in which account information rarely changes and in which users do not log on and off frequently, you can use domain controllers as cluster nodes.

Choosing a Server Cluster Model

Server clusters can be categorized in three configuration models in order of increasing complexity. This section describes each model and gives examples of the types of applications that are suited to each. These models range from a single node cluster to a cluster in which all servers are actively providing services. Choose the cluster model that best matches the needs of your organization.

Model 1: Single Node Server Cluster Configuration

Model 1 shows how you can use the virtual server concept with applications on a single node server cluster.

This cluster model does not make use of failover. It is merely a way to organize resources on a server for administrative convenience and for the convenience of your clients. The main advantage of this model is that both administrators and clients can readily see descriptively-named virtual servers on the network rather than having to navigate a list of actual servers to find the shares they need.

Other advantages of this model include:

- The Cluster service automatically restarts the various application and dependent resources after a computer has been restored following a resource failure. This is useful for applications that benefit from an automatic restart function but do not have their own mechanisms for accomplishing it.

- You can cluster the single node with a second node at a future time, and the resource groups are already in place. After you configure failover policies for the groups, the virtual servers are ready to operate.

Figure 18.8 represents an example of a single node cluster that does not makes use of failover.

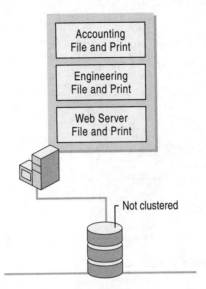

Figure 18.8   Single Node Server Cluster Configuration

For example, you can use this model to locate all the file and print resources in your organization on a single computer, establishing separate groups for each department. When clients from one department need to connect to the appropriate file or print share, they can find the share as easily as they would find an actual computer.

Note Some applications, such as SQL Server versions 6.5 and 7.0, cannot be installed on a single node cluster.

Model 2: Dedicated Secondary Node

Model 2 provides maximum availability and performance for your resources but requires an investment in hardware that is not in use most of the time.

One node, called a "primary node," supports all clients, while its companion node is idle. The companion node is a dedicated server that is ready to be used whenever a failover occurs on the primary node. If the primary node fails, the dedicated secondary node immediately picks up all operations and continues to service clients at a rate of performance that is close or equal to that of the primary node. This approach is often referred to as an active/passive configuration. The exact performance depends on the capacity of the secondary node. Figure 18.9 represents an example of the dedicated secondary node approach.

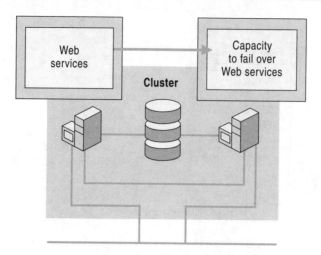

Figure 18.9   Active/Passive Configuration

Model 2 is best suited for the most important applications and resources in your organization. For example, if your organization relies on sales over the World Wide Web, you can use this model to provide secondary nodes for all servers dedicated to supporting Web access, such as those servers running Internet Information Services (IIS). The expense of doubling your hardware in this area is justified by the ability to protect client access to your organization. If one of your Web servers fail, another server is fully-configured to take over its operations.

If your budget allows for a secondary server with identical capacity to its primary node, then you do not need to set a preferred server for any of the groups. If one node has greater capacity than the other, setting the group failover policies to prefer the larger server keeps performance as high as possible.

If the secondary node has identical capacity to the primary node, set the policy to prevent failback for all groups. If the secondary node has less capacity than the primary node, set the policy for immediate failback or for failback at a specified off-peak hour.

Deployment Example: Active/Passive Split Configuration

An active/passive split configuration represents one example of a dedicated secondary node. An active/passive split configuration demonstrates that nodes in a server cluster are not limited to providing applications that use clustering. Nodes that provide clustered resources can also provide applications that are not cluster-aware and that will fail if the server stops functioning.

One of the steps in planning resource groups is to identify applications that you will not configure to fail over. Those applications can reside on servers that form clusters, but they must store their data on local disks, not on disks on the shared bus. If high availability of these applications is important, you must find other methods of providing it. Figure 18.10 represents an example of an active/passive split configuration.

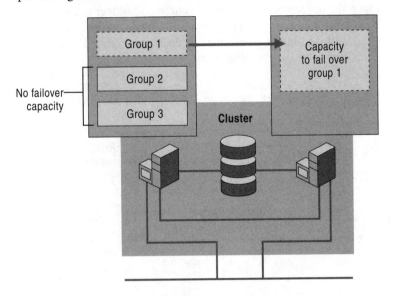

Figure 18.10   Active Passive Split Configuration

The applications in the other groups also serve clients on one of the servers, but because they are not cluster-aware, you do not establish failover policies for them. For example, you might use a node to run a mail server that has not been designed to use failover, or for an accounting application that you use so infrequently that availability is not important.

When node failure occurs, the applications that you did not configure with failover policies are unavailable unless they have built-in failover mechanisms of their own. They remain unavailable until the node on which they run is restored; you must either restart them manually or set Windows 2000 Advanced Server to automatically start them when the system software starts. The applications that you configured with failover policies fail over as usual according to those policies.

Model 3: High Availability Configuration

Model 3 provides reliability and acceptable performance when only one node is online, and high availability and performance when both nodes are online. This configuration allows maximum use of your hardware resources.

In this deployment example, each node makes its own set of resources available to the network in the form of virtual servers, which can be detected and accessed by clients. In a server cluster, a *virtual server* is a set of resources, including a Network Name resource and an IP Address resource, that are contained by a resource group. The capacity for each node is chosen so that the resources on each node run at optimum performance, but so that any node can temporarily take on the burden of running the resources if failover occurs. Depending on resource and server capacity specifications, all client services remain available during and after failover, but performance can decrease. Figure 18.11 represents an example of the active/active configuration.

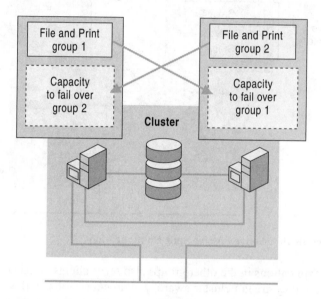

Figure 18.11   Active/Active Configuration

For example, you can use this configuration for a cluster dedicated to file-sharing and print-spooling services. Multiple file and print shares are established as separate groups, one on each node. If one node fails, the other nodes temporarily take on the file-sharing and print-spooling services for all nodes. The failover policy for the group that is temporarily relocated is set to prefer its original node. When the failed node is restored, the relocated group returns to the control of its preferred node, and operations resume at normal performance. Services are available to clients throughout the process with only minor interruption.

The following deployment examples represent a few types of high-availability configurations

Deployment Example 1: Clustering a Single Application Type

This example demonstrates how you can solve two challenges that typically occur in a large computing environment. The first challenge occurs when a single server is running multiple large applications, causing a degradation in network performance. To solve the problem, you cluster one or more servers with the first server, and the applications are split across the servers.

The second challenge involves related applications running on separate servers. The problem of availability arises when servers are not connected. By placing them in a cluster, the client is ensured greater availability of both applications.

Suppose your corporate intranet relies on a server that runs two large database applications. Both of these databases are critical to hundreds of users who repeatedly connect to this server throughout the day. The challenge is that during peak connect times, the server cannot keep up with demand and performance often declines.

You can alleviate the problem by attaching a second server to the overloaded server, forming a cluster, and balancing the load. You now have multiple servers, each running one of the database applications. If one server fails, you might experience degraded performance, but only temporarily. When the failed server is restored, the application it was running fails back and operations resume. Figure 18.12 represents the solution.

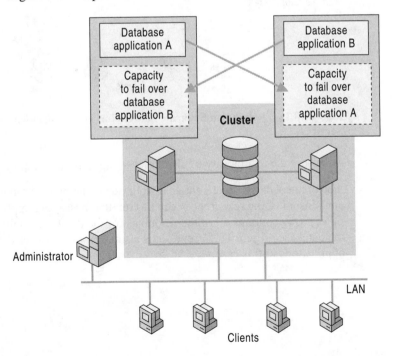

Figure 18.12   Attach Another Server to Your Overloaded Server to Form a Cluster

Deployment Example 2: Clustering Multiple Applications

Suppose your retail business relies on two separate servers, one that provides messaging services and another that provides a database application for inventory and ordering information.

Both of these services are essential to your business. Employees rely on messaging services to conduct business on a daily basis. Without access to the database application, customers cannot place orders, and employees cannot access inventory or shipping information. Figure 18.13 shows a typical configuration when mission-critical applications and services rely on separate servers, thus putting the applications and services at risk.

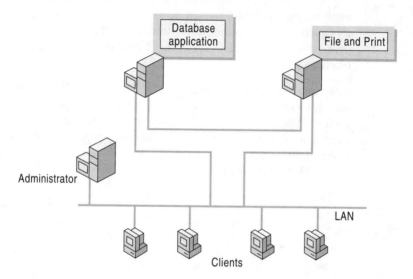

Figure 18.13 **Relying on Separate Servers for Mission-Critical Applications and Services**

To ensure the availability of all services, you join the computers into a cluster.

You create a cluster that contains two groups, one on each node. One group contains all of the resources needed to run the messaging applications, and the other group contains all of the resources for the database application, including the database. Figure 18.14 represents a solution that ensures the availability of applications in this case.

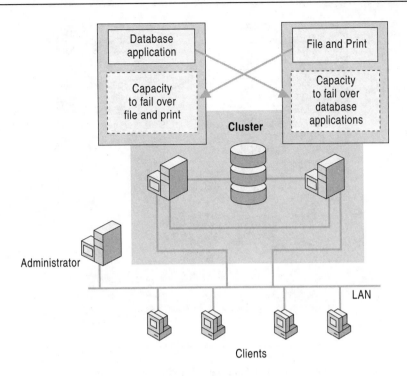

Figure 18.14   Clustering Multiple Applications

In the failover policies of each group, specify that both groups can run on either node, thereby assuring their availability if one node fails.

In Windows 2000 Advanced Server, the Cluster service detects loss of connectivity between the servers and client systems. If the Cluster service software can isolate the problem to a specific server, the Cluster service declares a failure of the network and fail dependent groups over to the other server (by means of the functioning networks).

Deployment Example 3: Complex Hybrid Configuration

The complex hybrid configuration is a hybrid of the other models. The hybrid configuration allows you to incorporate the advantages of previous models and combine them into one cluster. As long as you have provided sufficient capacity, many types of failover scenarios can coexist on all the nodes. All failover activity occurs as normal, according to the policies you set up. Figure 18.15 represents an example of multiple database shares, allowing somewhat reduced performance when the shares are on a single node.

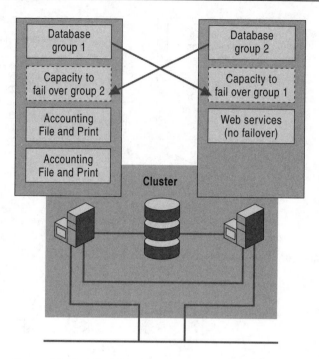

Figure 18.15   The Complex Hybrid Configuration

For administrative convenience, the file-and-print shares in the cluster (which do not require failover ability) are grouped logically by department and configured as virtual servers. Finally, an application that cannot fail over resides on one of the clusters and operates as normal (without any failover protection).

Planning for Cluster Service

After you assess your clustering needs, you are ready to determine how many servers you need and with what specifications, such as how much memory and hard disk storage.

Planning Your Resource Groups

Because all resources in a group move between nodes as a unit, dependent resources never span a single group boundary (resources cannot be dependent on resources in other groups).

Figure 18.16 shows how dependent resources are joined to form a group. The node on the right contains the Web Server group, which is made up of four resources on which IIS depends: a Network Name, an IP Address, an IIS Virtual Service, and Disk E.

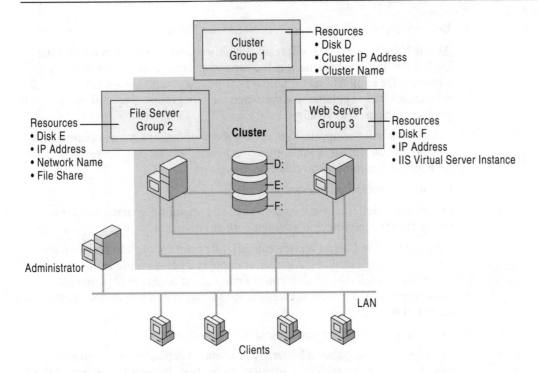

Figure 18.16   A Group of Dependent Resources

Typical clusters include one group for each independent application or service that runs on the cluster. Typical cluster groups contain the following types of resources:

- IP Address
- Network Name
- Physical Disk
- A generic or custom application or service

There are six steps you can take to organize your applications and other resources into groups:

1. List all your server-based applications.

   Most groups contain one or more applications. Make a list of all applications in your environment, regardless of whether you plan to use them with the Cluster service. Determine your total capacity requirements by adding the total number of groups (virtual servers) you plan to run in your environment together with the total amount of software you plan to run independently of groups.

2. Determine which of your applications can use failover.

   Also list applications that will reside on cluster nodes but which will not use the failover feature, because it is inconvenient, unnecessary, or impossible to configure the applications for failover. Although you do not set failover policies for these applications or arrange them in groups, they still use a portion of the server capacity.

   Before clustering an application, review the application license, or check with the application vendor. Each application vendor sets its own licensing policies for applications running on clusters.

3. List all nonapplication resources.

   Determine which hardware, connections, and operating system software a server cluster can protect in your network environment.

   For example, the Cluster service can fail over print spoolers to protect client access to printing services. Another example is a file server resource, which you can set to fail over so that you maintain client access to files. In both cases, capacity is affected, such as the RAM required to service the clients when failover occurs.

4. List all dependencies for each resource.

   Cluster service maintains a hierarchy of resource dependencies to guarantee that all resources on which a particular application depends are brought online *before* the application. It also guarantees that the application and all the resources it depends on will either restart or fail over to another node if one of these resources fails.

   Create a list of dependencies to help you determine how your resources and resource groups depend on each other and the optimal distribution of resources among all groups. Include all resources that support the core resources. For example, if a Web server application fails over, the Web addresses and disks on the shared buses containing the files for that application must also fail over if the Web server is to function. All these resources must be in the same group. This ensures that the Cluster service keeps interdependent resources together at all times.

Note When grouping resources, remember that a resource and its dependencies must be together in a single group because a resource cannot span groups.

Remember that a resource group is a basic unit of failover. Individual resources cannot fail over independently. Resources fail over together with all other resources in the same resource group.

Because most applications store application data on disk, it is recommended that you create a resource group for each disk. Place one application, together with all the other resources on which it depends, in the group containing the disk on which it stores its data. Place another application in another group, along with its disk. This configuration allows applications to fail over or be moved independently without affecting other applications.

5. Make preliminary grouping decisions.

Another reason to assign applications to a single group is for administrative convenience. For example, you might put several applications into one group because viewing those particular applications as a single entity makes it easier to administer the network.

A common use of this technique is to combine file-sharing resources and print-spooling resources in a single group. If you combine these resources, all dependencies for those applications must also be in the same group. You can give this group a unique name for the part of your organization it serves, such as AccountingFile&Print. Whenever you need to intervene with the file-sharing and print-sharing activities for that department, you would look for this group in Cluster Administrator.

Another common practice is to put applications that depend on a particular resource into a single group. For example, suppose that a Web server application provides access to Web pages and that those Web pages provide result sets that clients access by querying an SQL database application. (Querying occurs through the use of Hypertext Markup Language [HTML] forms.) By putting the Web server and the SQL database in the same group, the data for both core applications can reside on a specific disk volume. Because both applications exist within the same group, you can also create an IP address and network name specifically for this resource group.

6. Make final grouping assignments.

After you group your resources together, assign a different name to each group, and create a dependency tree. A dependency tree is useful for visualizing the dependency relationships between resources.

To create a dependency tree, write down all the resources in a particular group. Then draw arrows from each resource to each resource on which the resource directly depends.

For example, a direct dependency between resource A and resource B means that there are no intermediary resources between the two resources. An indirect dependency occurs when a transitive relationship exists between resources. If resource A depends on resource B and resource B depends on resource C, there is an indirect dependency between resource A and resource C. However, resource A is not directly dependent on resource C.

In the Web Server group of Figure 18.16, both the Network Name resource and the IIS Virtual Server Instance resource depend on the IP Address resource. However, there is no dependency between the Network Name resource and the IIS Virtual Server Instance resource.

Figure 18.17 illustrates a simple dependency tree that shows some resources in a final grouping assignment.

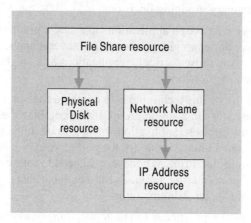

Figure 18.17   A Simple Dependency Tree

In Figure 18.17, the File Share resource depends on the Network Name resource, which, in turn, depends on the IP Address resource. However, the File Share resource does not directly depend on the IP Address resource.

Note Physical disks do not depend on any other resource and they can fail over independently.

Determining Capacity Requirements for Cluster Service

You are ready to determine your hardware capacity requirements for each server in the cluster after you have done the following:

- Chosen a cluster model.
- Determined how you will group your resources.
- Determined failover policies required by each resource.

The paragraphs that follow suggest criteria to help you determine hardware requirements for the computers that you use as cluster nodes.

Hard Disk Storage Requirements   Each node in a cluster must have enough hard disk capacity to store permanent copies of all applications and other resources required to run all groups. Calculate this for each node as if all of these resources in the cluster were running on that node, even if some or all of those groups run on the other node most of the time. Plan these disk-space allowances so that any other node can efficiently run all resources during failover.

Note   Cluster service does not support dynamic disks and the new features offered by the Logical Volume Manager. Particularly, the NTFS file system partitions on a disk managed by a cluster service cannot be extended. You need to plan the disk capacity and provide enough room for growth.

CPU Requirements   Failover can strain the CPU processing capacity of a node when it takes control of the resources from a failed node. Without proper planning, the CPU of a surviving node can be pushed beyond its practical capacity during failover, slowing response time for users. Plan your CPU capacity on each node so that it can accommodate new resources without unreasonably affecting responsiveness.

RAM Requirements   When planning your capacity, make sure that each node in your cluster has enough RAM to run all applications that might run on any other node. Also, make sure you set your Windows 2000 Advanced Server paging files appropriately for the amount of RAM you define for each node.

Limitations of Server Clusters

Some important limitations of Windows 2000 Server clusters are as follows.

- Removable Storage
    - Do not install removable storage devices on a SCSI shared bus used by the cluster.
    - Do not configure removable storage devices, such as tape changers, as cluster resources.
- Disk configuration
    - You must use the NTFS file system to format disks on the cluster storage and you must configure them as basic disks. However, NTFS does not support the use of dynamic disks for cluster storage.
    - You cannot use the Encrypting File System, Remote Storage, mounted volumes, or reparse points on the cluster storage.

- You cannot enable write caching on an internal RAID controller because the data in the cache will be lost during failover. An example of an internal controller is a Peripheral Component Interconnect (PCI) card inside the node. Depending on the RAID controller, you could enable write caching on an external RAID controller. An external RAID controller is usually inside the disk cabinet and the data in the cache will fail over.

  - You can use software RAID on local drives only (that is, drives not managed by the Cluster service). You can use only hardware RAID to protect the data on your cluster disk.

- Network configuration

  - The Cluster service supports only TCP/IP.

  - All network interfaces used on all nodes in a server cluster must be on the same network. All cluster nodes must have at least one subnet in common.

- Terminal Services

  You can use Terminal Services for remote administration on a server cluster node. You cannot use Terminal Services for an application server on a server cluster node.

Important   You cannot currently use Network Load Balancing and Cluster service on the same server.

Tools to Automate the Deployment of Cluster Service

There are tools to automate the deployment of Cluster service in your enterprise. These tools are available on the Windows 2000 product compact disc (CD).Table 18.2 describes these tools.

Table 18.2   Tools to Automate the Deployment of Cluster Service

Tools	Description
Sysprep	A tool that enables disk duplication. You can install the Windows 2000 Advanced Server operating system and applications on a single computer, and then duplicate that installation on as many systems as you like.
Cluscfg.exe	This tool is included in the base operating system. Any time you install Cluster service on a system, you need to run it to configure the cluster.
Setup Manager	A wizard-based tool that helps you create unattended scripts and a network distribution share required for regular unattended and Sysprep deployments.

The following examples illustrate how you can use these tools.

If you have completely different hardware configurations on the systems you want to deploy the Cluster service on, you can use an unattended Setup to set up these systems. This involves creating an Unattend.txt file and a network distribution share (optional) that will be used to automate the running of Setup, including configuring the Windows 2000 Cluster service.

If you have similar hardware configurations, you can use Sysprep to create an image and speed the setup and deployment process. To use Sysprep to deploy Windows 2000 Cluster service, you must first install the Cluster service (by selecting it in the Windows Components Wizard). When the image has been deployed on the systems, you can run the Cluscfg.exe file. You can automate the running of Cluscfg.exe by placing Cluscfg.exe in the `[GuiRunOnce]` section of the Sysprep answer file. That way, Cluscfg.exe runs on each system after Sysprep has finished running. You can automate Cluscfg.exe by using an answer file.

For more information about these tools, see "Windows Clustering" in the *Distributed Systems Guide*.

Optimizing Your Clusters

Windows 2000 Advanced Server uses an adaptable architecture and is largely self-tuning when it comes to performance. Additionally, Advanced Server is able to allocate resources dynamically as needed to meet changing usage requirements.

The goal in tuning a server and the applications it load balances is to determine which hardware resource will experience the greatest demand, and then adjust the configuration to handle that demand and maximize total throughput.

For example, if the primary role of a cluster is to provide high availability of file and print services, high disk use will be incurred due to the large number of files being accessed. File and print services also cause a heavy load on network adapters because of the large amount of data that is being transferred. It is important to make sure that your network adapter and cluster subnet can handle the load. In this example, RAM typically does not carry a heavy load, although memory usage can be heavy if a large amount of RAM is allocated to the file system cache. Processor utilization is also typically low in this environment. In such cases, memory and processor utilization usually do not need the optimizing that other components need. Memory can often be used effectively to reduce the disk utilization, especially for disk read operations.

In contrast, a server-application environment (such as Microsoft Exchange) is much more processor-intensive and RAM-intensive than a typical file or print server environment because much more processing is taking place at the server. In these cases, it is best to use high-end multiprocessor servers. The disk and network loads tend to be less utilized, because the amount of data being sent is smaller. Microsoft load balancing solutions use little of the system resources either for host-to-host communications or for the operation of the cluster itself.

Planning for Fault-Tolerant Disks

Disk failure can result in the irrecoverable loss of essential data, and will cause the load balancing service to stop functioning, along with the server and all of its other applications. For this reason, consider using special methods to protect your disks from failure.

Many resource groups include disk resources on shared buses. In some cases, these are simple physical disks, but in other cases they are complex disk subsystems containing multiple disks. Almost all resource groups depend on the disks on the shared buses. An unrecoverable failure of a disk resource results in certain failure of the group that contains that resource. For these reasons, you might decide to use specific methods to protect your disks and disk subsystems from failures.

One common solution is to use a hardware-based RAID solution. RAID support ensures high availability of the data contained on the disk sets in your clusters. Some of these hardware-based solutions are considered fault-tolerant, which means that you do not lose data if a member of the disk set fails.

Hardware RAID

The Microsoft Windows 2000 HCL contains many different hardware RAID configurations for clusters. Many hardware RAID solutions provide power-redundancy, bus-redundancy, and cable-redundancy within a single cabinet and can track the state of each component in the hardware RAID firmware. The significance of these capabilities is that they provide data availability with multiple redundancies to protect against multiple points of failure. Hardware RAID solutions can also use an onboard processor and cache.

Windows 2000 Advanced Server can use these disks as standard disk resources.

Though more costly than software RAID (included as a feature with Windows 2000 Advanced Server), hardware RAID is generally considered the superior solution.

Error Recovery

Computers running any one of the Windows 2000 Advanced Server load balancing services are subject to the same risk of failure as other computers. Computers can fail for a variety of reasons, and it is always advisable to put safeguards in place against these potential points of failure whenever possible. These safeguards include software and hardware RAID, uninterruptable power supplies, and transaction logging and recovery, which is a feature of the NTFS file system. To make use of this feature, be sure to load the load balancing service on a partition formatted with NTFS.

With transaction logging and recovery, NTFS ensures that the volume structure will not be corrupted, so all files remain accessible after a system failure. NTFS also uses the recovery technique called *"cluster remapping."* When Windows 2000 Advanced Server returns a bad-sector error to NTFS, NTFS dynamically replaces the disk cluster that contains the bad sector and allocates a new disk cluster for the data. If the error occurs during a read, NTFS returns a read error to the calling program, and the data is lost (unless it is protected by RAID fault tolerance). When the error occurs during a write, NTFS writes the data to the new disk cluster, and no data is lost. NTFS puts the address of the disk cluster that contains the corrupt section into its Bad Sector file so that it does not reuse the corrupt section.

Even with transaction logging and recovery and disk cluster remapping, you can lose user data due to hardware failure if you do not use a fault-tolerant-disk solution.

Testing Server Capacity

It is extremely important to test server capacity to avoid server failure when making applications and services highly available in your organization.

The following list identifies some of the hardware components you need to test:

- Individual computer components such as hard disks and controllers, processors, and RAM.
- External components such as routers, bridges, switches, cabling, and connectors.

The following are some of the stress tests you need to set up:

- Heavy network loads.
- Heavy disk I/O to the same disk.
- Heavy use of file, print, and applications servers.
- Large numbers of simultaneous logons.

The Windows DNA Performance Kit enables you to test and tune the performance of your applications. The kit allows you to tune applications in Windows NT 4.0 Microsoft Transaction Server (MTS), COM+, IIS, and SQL Server to increase component load balance performance.

The Kit contains performance information about COM+ and IIS as well as tools to simulate the effect of many users accessing your IIS or COM+ application. Simulating many users is an important step in understanding the hardware requirements for your application.

Note The Windows DNA Performance Kit is intended for use with Windows 2000 Advanced Server or Windows NT Server 4.0 with the Windows NT Option Pack.

For more information about the Windows DNA Performance Kit or about how to download the kit, see the Windows DNA Performance Kit link on the Web Resources page at http://windows.microsoft.com/windows2000/reskit/webresources.

For more information about creating test plans, see "Building a Windows 2000 Test Lab" in this book.

Planning a Cluster Backup and Recovery Strategy

A complete cluster backup includes:

- Documentation of the cluster configuration, including which resource registry keys map to which resources. This is recommended because each resource registry key is identified only by the globally unique identifier (GUID) for the resource.
- Catalog of the backup.
- Backup to a safe location
- Creation of an emergency repair disk for each node, for restoring Windows 2000 Advanced Server on the node, if necessary.

  An emergency repair disk is a disk that is created using Backup that contains information about your current Windows system settings. This disk can be used to repair your computer if it does not start or if your system files are damaged or erased.

  For more information about creating an emergency repair disk, see Windows 2000 Advanced Server Help.

Backup recommendations assume the following:

- You have developed and documented the restore procedures.
- You have replaced any physically-destroyed clusters with functionally-identical hardware (HCL-certified), with all clustered disks having either the same or greater capacity.

A sound backup plan addresses the following issues:

- Synchronizing backups
- Creating backup storage space
- Storing backup media
- Maintaining a backup catalog

For more information about backup and restore routines and tools for clustering, see "Windows Clustering" in the *Distributed Systems Guide*.

Windows 2000 Cluster Planning Task List

The Windows 2000 Cluster Planning Task List in Table 18.3 is a reference list of important task information in this chapter that you can use to help you create an Application and Service Availability strategy for your organization.

Table 18.3   Windows 2000 Cluster Planning Task List

Task	Location in Chapter
Assemble the Clustering Planning team.	Determining Availability Strategies
Identify specific high-availability needs for applications and services.	Determining Availability Strategies
Determine your clustering requirements.	Determining Availability Strategies
Determine which applications to use with Network Load Balancing.	Planning for Network Load Balancing
Use Network Load Balancing to deploy Terminal Server clusters.	Planning for Network Load Balancing
Configure Network Load Balancing Clusters for Servers running IIS/ASP and COM+ Applications.	Planning for Network Load Balancing
Identify network risks.	Planning for Network Load Balancing
Perform capacity planning for Network Load Balancing.	Planning for Network Load Balancing
Determine server capacity requirements.	Planning for Network Load Balancing

(continued)

Table 18.3   Windows 2000 Cluster Planning Task List *(continued)*

Task	Location in Chapter
Optimize Network Load Balancing clusters.	Planning for Network Load Balancing
Choose applications to run on a server cluster.	Planning for Cluster Service
Identify network risks.	Planning for Cluster Service
Determine failover and failback policies for resource groups.	Planning for Cluster Service
Choose a server role.	Planning for Cluster Service
Choose a cluster model.	Planning for Cluster Service
Perform capacity planning for Cluster service.	Planning for Cluster Service
Choose tools to help you automate the deployment of Cluster service.	Planning for Cluster Service
Optimize your clusters.	Optimizing Your Clusters
Plan for fault-tolerant disks.	Planning for Fault-Tolerant Disks
Test server capacity.	Testing Server Capacity
Plan a backup and recovery strategy.	Planning a Cluster Backup and Recovery Strategy

Additional Resources

- For more information about Windows Clustering, see Windows 2000 Advanced Server Help.

- For more information about the Windows Clustering API, see the Microsoft Platform SDK link on the Web Resources page at http://windows.microsoft.com/windows2000/reskit/webresources.

- For more information about the WinDNA Performance Kit, see the WinDNA Performance Kit link on the Web Resources page at http://windows.microsoft.com/windows2000/reskit/webresources.

- For more information about the various hardware RAID configurations, see the:

  - Microsoft Windows Hardware Compatibility List link on the Web Resources page at http://windows.microsoft.com/windows2000/reskit/webresources.

  - Microsoft TechNet link on the Web Resources page at http://windows.microsoft.com/windows2000/reskit/webresources.

CHAPTER 19

Determining Windows 2000 Storage Management Strategies

Network administrators who handle day-to-day network operations and who know the requirements of data management and storage systems need to become familiar with new Microsoft® Windows® 2000 Server features related to storage management.

When you are planning your Windows 2000 deployment, it is recommended that you incorporate these new features into your storage management strategy. Disk Management, Removable Storage, Remote Storage, Windows Clustering, Distributed file system, Microsoft® Indexing Service, and other features can help you improve your storage management functions.

Considerations for selecting a data storage system, fault tolerance and backup strategies, and ways to improve your disaster recovery capabilities are also discussed in this chapter.

In This Chapter

Chapter Goals

This chapter will help you develop the following planning documents:

- Storage configuration policy
- Disaster recovery plan
- Storage management plan

Related Information in the Resource Kit

- For more information about using Removable Storage and Remote Storage, see "Data Storage and Management" in the *Microsoft® Windows® 2000 Server Resource Kit Server Operations Guide.*

- For more information about backup planning, strategies, and procedures, see "Backup" and "Planning a Reliable Configuration" in the *Server Operations Guide.*

- For more information about disaster recovery, see "Repair, Recovery, and Restore" in the *Server Operations Guide.*

Improving Your Storage Management Functions

Improving your storage systems and their management is not only an important consideration when deploying Microsoft Windows 2000 Server but is also a critical part of any enterprise network infrastructure. With the enormous amount of data that must be protected in an enterprise environment, you need to be aware of the latest technologies so you can select the hardware and software that best meet your network needs.

Microsoft Windows 2000 provides several features for managing disk resources to enhance performance and protect data. These features include the following:

Disk Management   for setting up and organizing disk storage systems.

Removable Storage   for managing a new class of storage devices.

Remote Storage   for moving unused files to remote storage.

The following Windows 2000 features can help you manage data more effectively:

Windows Clustering   for easier management and higher availability of data and applications.

File system improvements   for improving the performance, availability, security, and manageability of shared information and resources, including the NTFS file system and quota management.

Distributed file system (Dfs)   for linking shares into a single namespace, making it easier to find and manage data.

Indexing Service   for fast file searches by content and property.

In addition to these features, Windows 2000 offers fault tolerance and Backup features to help you improve your data protection.

The sections that follow discuss these features in more detail. In addition to becoming familiar with Windows 2000 storage management features, you need to include a storage management plan in your deployment planning documents.

Creating Your Storage Management Plan

You will have many issues to address when you create your storage management plan. Enterprise-size organizations should consider creating a storage management team to identify data storage needs and to create associated plans. Some organizations might find that the issues in this chapter are best addressed by a variety of teams, such as a backup and recovery team; a data management team; and a team handling storage issues. Each team begins by assessing the storage requirements of your organization and by creating a storage management strategy.

To help you create a storage management plan, consider using the steps shown in Figure 19.1.

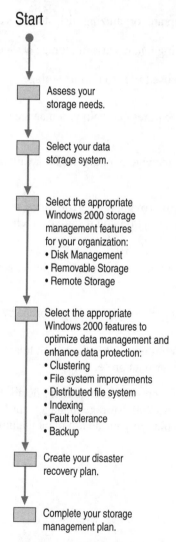

Figure 19.1   Process for Developing a Storage Management Strategy

Assessing Your Storage Needs

Network storage solutions are rapidly becoming available as the number and size of enterprise networks increases. Every organization has different priorities for selecting media and methods for data storage. Some are constrained by costs, and others place performance before all other considerations.

As you assess your storage needs, you need to compare the possible loss of data, productivity, and business to the cost of a storage system that provides high performance and reliability. Consider the following needs before you develop your storage management strategy:

- Technologies that are the most cost-effective for your organization.
- Adequate storage capacity that can easily grow with your network.
- The need for rapid, 24-hour access to critical data.
- A secure environment for data storage.

When looking for the most cost-effective solution, you need to balance the costs of purchasing and maintaining hardware and software with the consequences of a disastrous loss of data. Costs include:

- Initial investment in hardware, such as tape and disk drives, power supplies, and controllers.
- Associated media such as magnetic tapes and compact discs.
- Software, such as storage management tools and a backup tool.
- Ongoing hardware and software maintenance costs.
- Staffing.
- Training in how to use new technologies.
- Off-site storage facilities.

Compare these costs against:

- Replacement costs for file servers, mail servers, or print servers.
- Replacement costs for servers running applications, such as Microsoft® SQL Server™ or Microsoft® Systems Management Server (SMS).
- Replacement costs for gateway servers running Routing and Remote Access Service, Microsoft® SNA Server, Microsoft® Proxy Server, or Novell NetWare.
- Workstation replacement costs for personnel in various departments.
- Replacement costs for individual computer components, such as a hard disk or a network card.

Another important factor to consider when you select a storage system is speed of data recovery. If you lose the data on a server, how fast can you reinstate that data? How long can you afford to have a server (or an entire network) down before it begins to have a serious impact on your business?

Storage technology changes rapidly, so it is best to research the relative merits of each type before you make a purchasing decision. The storage system you use needs to have more than enough capacity to back up your most critical data. It should also provide error detection and correction during backup and restore operations.

Selecting a Data Storage System

Answer the following questions to determine a storage system that best meets your needs:

How much data do you currently need to store?

If a very large amount of data must be stored, a tape-based storage system might be your best choice. The media cost per megabyte is significantly lower for tape than it is for many other types of storage media.

What are your projected data-storage needs?

The storage needs of many organizations double every year. Consider purchasing a larger storage system than is necessary to satisfy present requirements or a scalable system that you can expand as your needs grow. To evaluate how this might affect your situation, compare your data storage from several years ago to your current levels, and use this growth to estimate your future needs.

How many users or applications simultaneously access the data storage system?

Most vendors offer multidrive systems that allow several drives to be accessed at once. In this way, multiple users or applications can simultaneously access the system without affecting performance.

How important is data-access time?

If your library is used primarily to access data for real-time use, then this is your most important issue. CD-ROM disc-based solutions usually work best if data-access time is your primary concern because the random-access capability of CD-ROM discs reduces seek time to a minimum. Data-access time has two parts: seek time and transfer rate. The disadvantages of this solution are in speed and cost: the data transfer rate can be slower than tape-based systems unless the latest high-speed drives are used; and the cost per megabyte is greater than tape media.

How important is the data-transfer rate?

If your data storage system is used primarily for archiving and backing up data, then the data-transfer rate is your most important issue. If this is the case, then a tape-based solution might be best because the data-transfer rate of tape drives is approximately ten times the speed of CD-ROM disc-based drives. Tape-based systems are also less expensive per megabyte. The disadvantage of tapes is that file-access time is increased by as much as several minutes because file access is linear.

What is your budget?

Again, before you decide how much you can afford to spend, factor in the potential costs of lost or corrupted data and downtime due to problems with unreliable hardware. If the type of data that you store is important to your organization, these risks might not be worth the savings gained by purchasing an inexpensive solution.

Also, consider the whole cost. Certain hardware can be relatively inexpensive to acquire but the cost per megabyte is expensive. This is generally true for CD-ROM disc-based systems. It is also common to spend more money over time on the media than on the initial hardware.

To help you select a storage system, try creating two or more models that present different hardware and software solutions for varying degrees of storage capacity and data protection. Be sure to project for planned growth.

Table 19.1 shows the *relative* capabilities of possible hardware and software storage solutions: a 5 indicates this is the best available solution; a 1 indicates this is your least desired solution. Use the table to help you choose types of storage for your organization.

Table 19.1   Selected Hardware and Software Storage Solutions

Solution	Availability	Response Time	Capacity	Support for Multiple Users
CD-ROM/DVD-ROM	4 1	3	2-3	2
CD-ROM library	4	2	5	5
CD-ROM drive array	5	4	4	4
Dfs	5	3-4	5	5
Disk	3	4	3	3
Disk mirroring with two controllers (Duplex)	5	4	2-3	2

(continued)

Table 19.1   Selected Hardware and Software Storage Solutions *(continued)*

Solution	Availability	Response Time	Capacity	Support for Multiple Users
Disk stripe set	1	5	4	4
Disk stripe set with parity	4	3	3-4	4
Tape	3	2	4	1
Tape library	3	1	5	4

[1] 5 – High/1 – Low

After you have assembled a storage management team, identified your storage requirements, and determined your budget, you need to evaluate the storage capabilities of Windows 2000.

Managing Disk Resources

Windows 2000 offers several storage features to help you store and manage data, including Disk Management, Removable Storage, and Remote Storage. The subsections that follow provide an introduction to these features.

Disk Management

The Disk Management snap-in to the Microsoft Management Console (MMC) is a tool for managing disk storage systems. Wizards guide you through creating partitions or volumes and initializing or upgrading disks. New key features of Windows 2000 Server Disk Management include the following:

Online Disk Management You can perform most administrative tasks without shutting down the system or interrupting users. For example, you can create various partition layouts and choose protection strategies, such as mirroring and striping, without restarting the system. You can also add disks without restarting. Most configuration changes take effect immediately.

Remote Disk Management As an administrator, you can manage any remote (or local) computer that runs Windows 2000.

Figure 19.2 shows some of the View menu options you can select in Disk Management.

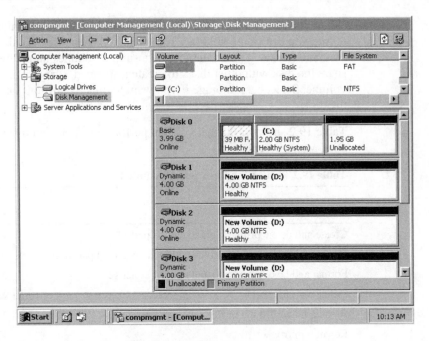

Figure 19.2   Disk Management MMC Snap-In

Basic and Dynamic Storage

There are two types of disk storage available with Windows 2000: basic or dynamic. *Basic storage* supports partition-oriented disks. A basic disk can hold primary partitions, extended partitions, and logical drives. Basic disks might also contain spanned volumes (volume sets), mirrored volumes (mirror sets), striped volumes (stripe sets), and redundant array of independent disks or RAID-5 volumes. In Microsoft® Windows NT® version 4.0 or earlier, RAID-5 was known as a stripe set with parity. If you want computers to access these volumes, and if those computers run Windows NT 4.0 or earlier, Microsoft® Windows® 98 or earlier, or Microsoft® MS-DOS®, you need to create basic volumes.

Dynamic storage supports new volume-oriented disks and is new with Windows 2000. It overcomes the restrictions of partition-oriented disk organization and facilitates multidisk, fault-tolerant disk systems. With dynamic storage, you can perform disk and volume management without restarting the operating system. On a dynamic disk, storage is divided into volumes instead of partitions. A volume consists of a portion or portions of one or more physical disks in any of the following layouts: simple, spanned, mirrored, striped, and RAID-5 volumes. Dynamic disks cannot contain partitions or logical drives, and cannot be accessed by MS-DOS or Microsoft® Windows® 98 and earlier versions. You can use dynamic storage to set up a fault-tolerant system by using multiple disks.

When you attach a new disk to your computer, you need to initialize the disk before you can create volumes or partitions. When you initialize the disk, select dynamic storage if you want to create simple volumes on the disk or if you plan to share the disk with other disks to create a spanned, striped, mirrored, or RAID-5 volume. Select basic storage if you want to create partitions and logical drives on the disk.

Table 19.2 shows tasks that you can perform on basic and dynamic disks by using Disk Management.

Table 19.2   Tasks for Basic and Dynamic Disks

Tasks	Basic Disk	Dynamic Disk
Create and delete primary and extended partitions.	X	
Create and delete logical drives within an extended partition.	X	
Format and label a partition and mark it as active.	X	
Delete a volume set.	X	
Break a mirror from a mirror set.	X	
Repair a mirror set.	X	
Repair a stripe set with parity.	X	
Upgrade a basic disk to a dynamic disk.	X	
Create and delete simple, spanned, striped, mirrored, and RAID-5 volumes.		X
Extend a volume across one or more disks.		X
Add a mirror to or remove a mirror from a mirrored volume.		X
Repair a mirrored volume.		X
Repair a RAID-5 volume.		X
Check information about disks, such as capacity, available free space, and current status.	X	X
View volume and partition properties such as size.	X	X
Make and change drive-letter assignments for hard disk volumes or partitions and CD-ROM devices.	X	X
Create *volume mount points.*	X	X
Set or verify disk sharing and access arrangements for a volume or partition.	X	X

Volume Management

Windows 2000 includes significant improvements in the architecture of volume management. Volume management includes the processes that create, delete, alter, and maintain storage volumes in a system. The new architecture improves the manageability and recoverability of volumes in an enterprise environment.

A Logical Disk Manager (LDM) has been introduced to the architecture to extend fault tolerance functionality, to improve system recovery, to encapsulate volume information so that disks can be easily moved, and to provide improved management functionality. This service is responsible for volume creation and deletion, fault tolerance features (RAID), and volume tracking. You use the Disk Management snap-in to manage local and remote volumes.

Volume management has the following features:

- You can create any number of volumes in the free space on a physical hard disk or create volumes that span two or more disks.

- Each volume on a disk can have a different file system, such as the file allocation table (FAT) file system or the NTFS file system.

- Most changes that you make to your disk are immediately available. You do not need to quit Disk Management to save them or restart your computer to implement them.

Volume Mount Points

As part of Disk Management, you can create volume mount points. Volume mount points provide you with a quick way to bring data online and offline. They are file system objects in the Windows 2000 internal namespace that represent storage volumes. When you place a volume mount point in an empty NTFS directory, you can graft new volumes into the namespace without requiring additional drive letters. An example of how you might use volume mount points is to have a computer with a single drive and volume formatted as C and to mount a disk as C:\Games.

Some possible uses for volume mount points include:

To provide additional space for programs For example, you mount a disk as C:\Program Files. Then, when you need additional disk space, you add a disk to the system and span it with the disk at C:\Program Files.

To create different classes of storage For example, create a stripe set for performance and mount it as C:\Scratch; and create a mirror set for robustness and mount it as C:\Projects. Users will see the directories normally, but their scratch directory will be fast, and their projects directory will be protected by a mirror set.

To create multiple mount points for a volume   For example, a volume is mounted as C:\Games and C:\Projects. Be aware that nothing prevents cycles in the namespace. If you mount a volume as D and also as D:\Docs, because D is mounted underneath itself, it creates a cycle in the namespace. Applications that do enumeration get into an endless loop on this volume.

Volume mount points are robust against system changes that occur when hardware devices are added to or removed from a computer. You are no longer limited to the number of volumes you can create based on the number of drive letters.

Disk Defragmentation

Another Disk Management feature is the Disk Defragmenter. You can use this tool to locate files and folders that have become fragmented and to reorganize clusters on a local disk volume. Disk Defragmenter organizes clusters so that files, directories, and free space are physically more contiguous. As a result, your system can gain access to your files and folders and can save new ones more efficiently. If you have considerable fragmentation, Disk Defragmenter can improve your overall system performance significantly in relation to disk input/output (I/O).

The Disk Defragmentation feature decides where files should be located on the disk, but NTFS and FAT move the clusters around.

You can use this tool with disk volumes that are formatted for FAT16, FAT32, or NTFS.

Considerations for Using Dynamic Storage

Consider the following when creating volumes:

- Dynamic storage uses a volume-oriented scheme for disk organization. Windows NT Server is not compatible with dynamic disks.

- You can use the Windows 2000 Setup program to configure disk space while upgrading to Windows 2000 Server.

Note   You can create new volumes and partitions on unallocated portions of the disk without losing data on existing volumes. However, if you plan to change your volume topology, you have to backup your data because making changes to existing volumes erases all existing data.

- You can configure the internal hard disk on a new computer during initial setup when you load the Windows 2000 Server operating system software. You can use Disk Management to make changes to the disk after installation.

For more information about managing disks, see "Disk Concepts and Troubleshooting" and "Data Storage and Management" in the *Microsoft® Windows® 2000 Server Resource Kit Server Operations Guide.*

Removable Storage

The Removable Storage system is a new technology that enables multiple applications to share local libraries and tape or disk drives, thus providing better storage management functionality. With Removable Storage, you can use stand-alone storage devices; manage online media libraries and robotic changers; and track your removable tapes and disks. Stand-alone devices include CD-ROM, DVD-ROM, tape (4mm, DLT, 8mm, and others), and high-capacity disk drives.

Removable Storage also controls removable media within a single server system. In addition, it performs functions in conjunction with Backup and Remote Storage. A key aspect of Removable Storage is the ability of applications to create media pools that are owned and used by the application.

Storage devices are most often connected to systems by using small computer system interface (SCSI) adapters or integrated device electronics (IDE) interfaces, such as those used with most hard drives. New technologies that provide simpler use and faster throughput, such as Fiber Channel, IEEE 1394, and Intelligent I/O (I2O), are also being used with increasing frequency. Stand-alone devices are most commonly used with single user systems.

Libraries contain multiple drives using CD-ROM, DVD-ROM, magneto-optic (MO) discs, or tape. These are accompanied by robotic controls that provide extensive automation for managing individual pieces of media or storage. The capacities range from a small, three-disc CD-ROM autochanger to a tape or a disc library used with sophisticated applications inside a large corporation. Libraries are most commonly used with servers but are increasingly being attached to single user systems.

Tasks you can perform using Removable Storage include the following:

- Tracking online and offline media
- Mounting and dismounting media
- Inserting and ejecting media to and from a library
- Viewing the state of media and libraries
- Creating media pools and setting media-pool properties

- Setting security parameters for media and media pools
- Performing library inventories

Note   Your backup software must be compatible with Removable Storage to make use of these features.

Remote Storage

Remote Storage is the hierarchical storage management system for Windows 2000 Server. With Remote Storage, you use the Remote Storage Manager MMC snap-in to move unused files to a tape library. By regularly migrating files, you can increase the amount of free space on a disk. From the user's perspective, the migrated files remain active, but they take longer to access.

The storage hierarchy has two levels. The highest level is called local storage. It is made up of the local NTFS volumes of a computer running Remote Storage on a Windows 2000 server. The local disk volumes that are under Remote Storage control are called *managed volumes*.

The lower level of the storage hierarchy, called remote storage, stores the data that has been copied from local storage to an online library or additional storage device.

When the amount of free space on a local volume drops below the level you need, Remote Storage truncates data from local files that were previously copied to remote storage, and by doing so, provides free disk space. When data is moved, it leaves a file marker allowing you to access that file. Remote Storage manages movement of data according to guidelines set by the administrator for each local storage volume. You can set a schedule for moving files from specific volumes and set criteria and rules for the files that are to be moved. More specifically, you can:

- Allocate and configure remote storage devices and media.
- Set Remote Storage system-wide feature options.
- Configure volume management settings for Remote Storage managed volumes.
- View information about Remote Storage activity.
- Recover from media disasters.
- Create and submit jobs.

Because removable tapes in a library are less expensive per megabyte than hard disks, this is an economical way to provide both maximum data storage and optimal local disk performance.

Note   Your backup and virus scanning software must be compatible with Remote Storage. Administrators need to ensure that volume-wide file operations are done before activating Remote Storage so that you do not have to move everything back to the disk. Backup reads the data directly from the tape.

Relationship of Remote Storage and Removable Storage

Remote Storage uses Removable Storage for copying data to online libraries that contain removable media. Figure 19.3 provides an overview of the relationship of these storage systems and various storage devices.

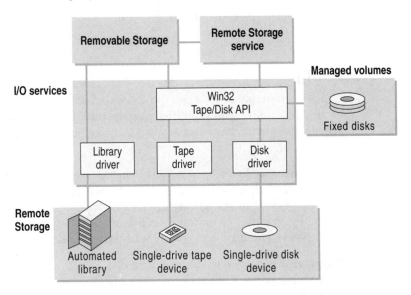

Figure 19.3   Relationship of Remote Storage, Removable Storage, and Storage Devices

Considerations for Using Remote Storage

Using Remote Storage provides the following advantages:

- Virtual expansion of local storage space by using lower cost remote storage.
- Transparent automatic access to data in remote storage.
- Automation of the labor-intensive overhead associated with daily manual data management operations.
- Centralized sharing of remote storage for multiple volumes.

Remote Storage is not a replacement for backup because only one instance of data exists. It is important to regularly backup the volume. Backup is integrated with Remote Storage so you do not have to move everything back to the disk; backup reads the data directly from the tape.

Optimizing Data Management

Windows 2000 features that can help you manage data more effectively in an enterprise environment include:

- Windows Clustering
- NTFS file system
- Quota management
- Distributed file system (Dfs)
- Indexing Service

Windows Clustering

Consider clustering in your enterprise network storage strategy when you need greater availability with simplified management. Clustering reduces downtime by providing an architecture that keeps systems running in the event of a single server failure.

With Windows Clustering, you can connect two or more servers to form a cluster of servers that work together as a single system. Each server is called a node; each node can operate independently of the other nodes in the cluster. The Windows 2000 built-in clustering capability is based on open specifications, industry-standard hardware, and ease-of-use requirements.

Each node has its own memory, system disk, operating system, and subset of the cluster's resources. With a process called failover, if one node fails, the other node takes ownership of the failed node's resources. The cluster server then registers the network address for the resource on the new node so that client traffic is routed to the available system, which now owns the resource. When the failed resource is later brought back online, you can configure the cluster server to redistribute resources and client requests appropriately. A standard Windows 2000 cluster setup is shown in Figure 19.4.

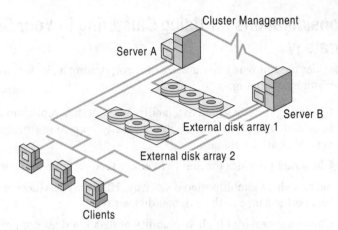

Figure 19.4   Typical Two-Node Cluster Setup

The Clustering Service provides the following advantages:

Common Administration   With Cluster Administrator MMC snap-in, you administer a cluster as a single system. Also, a client computer interacts with a cluster as though it is a single server.

Load Balancing   Within the cluster, you can manually balance processing loads or unload servers for planned maintenance without taking data and applications offline.

High Availability   Clustering provides high availability by automatically recovering critical data and applications from many common types of failure. If a node in the cluster fails, Windows Clustering detects the failure and performs recovery of the processes active at the time of the failure. The failure of one node in the cluster does not affect the other node.

If clustering is not already part of your network and if you want to deploy Windows Clustering, you need to address several issues in your Windows 2000 Server deployment planning phase with regard to setting up a cluster environment. For more information about planning your cluster environment, see "Windows Clustering" in the *Microsoft® Windows® 2000 Server Resource Kit Distributed Systems Guide,* and also see Windows 2000 Advanced Server Help.

Note   For clustering solutions, use only certified configurations that are documented on the hardware compatibility list (HCL), which you can access online. For more information about this list, see the Microsoft Windows Hardware Compatibility List link on the Web Resources page at http://windows.microsoft.com/windows2000/reskit/webresources.

Considerations for Using Clustering in Your Storage Strategy

Consider the following advantages of incorporating a cluster environment into your storage planning:

- Clustering provides high availability without data replication, thereby providing data consistency without greatly impacting storage requirements and network traffic volumes.

- Clustering provides the ability to easily recover from software failures.

- Servers share a multiported disk array. Hardware RAID controllers provide the best performance to the external disk array.

- Clustering provides high availability of data but does not protect data integrity.

File System Improvements

Windows 2000 supports the NTFS file system and two file allocation table (FAT) file systems: FAT16 and FAT32.

FAT is for small disks and simple folder structures. FAT16 is included with Windows 2000 because it maintains an upgrade path for earlier versions of Windows-compatible products and it is compatible with most non-Microsoft operating systems. FAT32 supports volumes larger than those handled by FAT16, and was first available in Microsoft® Windows® 95. Windows 2000 supports FAT32 file systems.

NTFS

The version of NTFS used in Windows 2000 provides performance, reliability, and features that are not available with FAT file systems. The NTFS data structures allow you to take advantage of new features in Windows 2000, such as Microsoft® Active Directory™ directory service, change and configuration management, reparse points (directory junctions and volume mount points), sparse file support, object IDs, extended property attributes, change journal, and many of the new storage enhancements.

In Windows 2000, NTFS data structures have been updated to enable many new features. For existing NTFS volumes, the upgrade to the new version of NTFS occurs when you install Windows 2000. You can convert FAT16 and FAT32 volumes to this format at any time.

Formatting your Windows NT partitions with NTFS instead of FAT allows you to use recoverability and compression features that are available only with NTFS. Also, formatting your volumes with NTFS instead of FAT provides faster access speed and additional capabilities for file and folder security.

Important The version of NTFS used in Windows 2000 cannot be natively recognized by earlier versions. In dual-boot systems, where a Windows NT 4.0 installation needs to read an NTFS volume that was created or upgraded by Windows 2000, the Windows NT 4.0 installation will require support (Service Pack 4 or later).

Quota Management

Disk quotas are a new feature with the version of NTFS used in Windows 2000. Disk quotas provide more precise control of network-based storage. You can use disk quotas to monitor and limit disk space use on a per user, per volume basis.

The first time users try to store data on a volume, they are automatically entered in the quota table and assigned a default quota value. This means that the administrator does not have to enter a quota setting for each user.

Users are charged for the files they own. For example, each user's folder on \\Marketing\Public is limited to 5 megabytes (MB) of disk space. If users copy 5 MB of files to their folder, they cannot then copy or create any more files on this or any other folder on \\Marketing\Public. They can, however, move or delete the files. Disk space is not charged to users if they modify an existing file owned by someone else. Keep in mind, however, that some applications, for example Microsoft® Office, change the owner of a document to the user who last edited the document. Quota settings are independent across volumes; that is, the quota on drive C does not affect the quota on drive D.

You can use the quota feature of the Disk Management MMC snap-in to:

- Enable or disable quotas on a disk volume.
- Prevent users from using more disk space when their quota limit is exceeded.
- View quota information for each user of the volume.
- Set the default quota warning threshold and quota limit assigned to new volume users.
- Block additional disk allocations and log an event when a user exceeds a specified disk space limit. Users can read, delete, and edit files as long as they do not attempt to allocate more disk space.

You can set both threshold and hard quota limits. When you enable quotas, you can set two values:

Quota limit   Specifies the maximum amount of disk space a user is allowed to use.

Quota warning threshold   Specifies a value at which the administrator is alerted that a quota limit is being approached. This is in the form of an event message.

As administrator, you can specify that events be automatically logged when users exceed warning thresholds and quota limits. For example, you can set a user's disk quota limit to 50 MB, and the quota warning level to 45 MB. If the user stores more than 45 MB of files on the volume, the quota system logs a system event.

You have the option of denying disk space to users who attempt to exceed their quota limit. If you select this option, users cannot write additional data to the volume without first deleting or moving some existing files from the volume. NTFS displays an "out of disk space" error message if the user tries to allocate beyond their quota limit.

Windows 2000 includes disk quota support for the following:

- Policies for wide-scale remote management of disk quotas.
- Improved support for finding all files owned by a particular user.

Note   Windows 2000 Server supports disk quotas only for the volumes formatted as NTFS.

When creating your storage management strategy, consider the following advantages of using disk quotas:

- Monitoring disk space use on a per user and per volume basis allows for better disk resource planning.
- Limiting disk space allows you to manage your storage resources more effectively by encouraging users to regularly delete unnecessary files.
- Using disk quotas can be an effective way to decrease backup media costs and restoration times.

Distributed File System

Microsoft Distributed file system (Dfs) is Windows 2000 Server software that makes it easier for you to find and manage data on your enterprise network. Dfs provides mapping and a uniform naming convention for collections of servers, shares, and files. Dfs adds the capability of organizing file servers and their shares into a logical hierarchy, making it considerably easier to manage and use information resources.

With Dfs, you can create a single directory tree that includes multiple file servers and file shares in a group, division, or enterprise. Any Windows 2000 server can host a Dfs root or Dfs volumes. A Dfs root is a local share that serves as the starting point and host to other shares. A network can host many individual Dfs volumes, each having a distinct name. A Dfs topology is a single Domain Name System (DNS) namespace. You can use a single topology or multiple Dfs topologies to distribute your organization's shared resources.

Dfs functionality is integrated with Active Directory; the Dfs topology is published to Active Directory. Because changes to a domain-based Dfs topology are automatically synchronized with Active Directory, you can always restore a Dfs topology if the Dfs root is offline for any reason. Computer-based Dfs stores the topology in the registry.

Dfs has the following features:

- Provides a simplified view of network shares that can be customized by the administrator.

- Allows Microsoft® Windows® 95 and Windows 98 clients to access shares by using server message block (SMB) protocol.

- Supports mounting replicas of network shares for load balancing and better data availability.

  Active Directory further optimizes network use by redirecting Active Directory–enabled clients to a Dfs share point within the client site.

- Integrates with the File Replication service (FRS) to permit optional replication of read/write data between multiple shares.

- Allows users to log on just once for multiple access.

You can access a Dfs volume by using a uniform naming convention (UNC) name. Although UNC names can be used, in most cases users will find it easier if they substitute a drive letter. For example, note the physical locations in relation to the logical paths shown in Table 19.3.

Table 19.3   Accessing a Dfs Volume

Dfs Logical Path	Physical Location	Description	Mapped Drive Path
\\MS Server\Root	\\MS Server\Root	Root share	X
\\MS Server\Root\Users	\\MS Users1\Employees	Junction to employee directories	X:\Users

(continued)

Table 19.3   Accessing a Dfs Volume *(continued)*

Dfs Logical Path	Physical Location	Description	Mapped Drive Path
\\MS Server\Root\Private\JaneD	\\Legal\Data\JaneD	Junction to JaneD's computer	X:\Private\JaneD
\\MS Server\Root\Private\SusanY	\\Human Res\SusanY	Junction to SusanY's computer	X:\Private\SusanY

Since Dfs maps the physical storage into a logical representation, the physical location of data becomes transparent to users and applications. Dfs eliminates the need for users to know where information is physically stored. Because users do not need to know the name of a server or share, you can physically move user information to another server without reeducating users about how to find their data, thereby improving file management.

Considerations for Using Dfs in Your Storage Strategy

Consider the following advantages of using Dfs shares as part of your storage planning:

- Active Directory replicates the Dfs topologies for all domain-based Dfs topologies to each Dfs root server. This distributes the load on participating servers and implements fault tolerance for the Dfs root.

- Multiple servers can host domain-based Dfs roots and alternates. If a root fails, Dfs detects the failure and another server acquires the root. This failover process increases data availability.

- Multiple copies of shares on separate servers can be mounted under the same logical Dfs name. This provides alternate locations for accessing data, thereby providing for load balancing and better data availability.

- Multiple copies of shares also allow administrators to perform preventative maintenance on servers. A server hosting one replica can be taken offline without impacting users since Dfs automatically routes requests to a replica that is online.

- Dfs ensures that users go to the closest replica by distributing copies of your files by site. This reduces the load on the wide area network (WAN).

- Location transparency eases the burden of upgrading to new servers by allowing additional storage to be published in subdirectories.

Consider implementing Dfs if any of the following conditions exist in your organization:

- Users that access shared resources are distributed across a site or sites.
- Most users require access to multiple shared resources.
- Users require uninterrupted access to shared resources.
- Load balancing for your network could be improved by redistributing shared resources.
- Your organization has data that is stored on multiple network shares.

For more information about designing a Dfs tree, see Windows 2000 Server Help.

Indexing Service

Microsoft Indexing Service makes it easier for users to search for data on client computers and servers. Indexing Service scans files on Windows 2000 servers and client computers and builds content and property indexes that dramatically improve search capability and performance. When the service is running, users can search for words and phrases in thousands of files in just a few seconds.

Indexing Service has the following features:

- Searches by content (for example, searches all files containing "revenue projections").
- Searches by document properties (for example, searches all files where AUTHOR contains "Sarah").
- Searches with Boolean operators (for example, AND, OR, NOT).
- Uses a free-text search, which allows users to enter any combination of words without having to learn a particular search syntax.
- Can index volumes on the local computer and also network shares, including NetWare and UNIX servers.
- Provides secure query results.

    Returns only the documents that users are allowed to read. Uses standard Windows 2000 access control lists (ACLs).
- Integrates with NTFS for better performance and reliability.
- Integrates with Internet Information Services (IIS) to provide a search capability for Internet and intranet Web sites.
- Can create customized search forms and user interfaces by using OLE-DB or Microsoft® ActiveX® Data Objects (ADO) scripting.

- Indexes a variety of file formats, including Microsoft® Office 97, Microsoft® Office 2000, text files, and HTML pages.
- Integrates with Windows 2000 user interface and Windows Explorer.
- Provides easy administration by using a Microsoft Management Console snap-in.

When Indexing Service is running on a system, it monitors the server for file modification. When files are modified, they are opened and their contents indexed. Opening files is done by a low priority background process so that general server performance is minimally impacted. In addition, when running on NTFS, Indexing Service uses a number of NTFS advanced features to minimize overall system overhead.

Note When you first run the service, it must build its indexes from scratch. This involves scanning all the files on the volume. Initial index construction accesses the disk heavily until the indexes have been built. After the indexes have been generated, only incremental updates are needed as files are modified, so further updates are virtually unnoticeable. In all cases, index update is a low priority task and will pause if server resources are needed for other operations.

To search for documents, users just need to select Search for Files and Folders in Windows Explorer or from the Start menu. This brings up a search form allowing users to enter the words for their search. If Indexing Service is running on a file server, users can search network shares efficiently because the search is executed on the server and only the search results are returned across the network.

Integration with Windows 2000 Components

Indexing Service is integrated with many other Windows 2000 components for performance and reliability. The service also uses NTFS features such as bulk ACL processing for much faster security checks before returning search results. It also uses NTFS sparse files to optimize indexes without consuming extra disk space. The service uses the NTFS change log to monitor the volume for file modifications. In this way, the service does not scan the entire volume repeatedly for changes like many other search engines. Instead, when a file is modified, only that particular file is scanned and indexed.

Indexing Service also understands that files can be migrated by Remote Storage. It does not forcibly recall files to index them. It does not rescan if a file has been migrated to secondary storage. This means that even if files have been migrated to tape, users can still search for them. This is ideal if you use Remote Storage to maintain an archival store for documents.

Indexing Service can be switched into a read-only mode. This allows the administrator to back up the indexes. When in read-only mode, the service continues to execute queries but does not update the indexes. The indexes are guaranteed to be consistent and stable so a valid backup can be made. After backing up, you can restore the service to normal operations, and any modifications made to files during the backup are processed normally.

Finally, the full-text indexing engine used by Windows 2000 is compatible with full-text indexing features of Microsoft® SQL Server™ version 7.0. By using the distributed query processor in SQL Server, you can specify queries using structured query language (SQL) and execute them simultaneously against the file system and a database.

Considerations for Using Indexing Service in Your Storage Strategy

Consider the following advantages of using indexing as part of your storage planning:

- Users can easily and quickly find the documents they need on file servers and Web servers.
- Most users do not need to learn a search syntax, although a powerful search language is available for advanced users.
- A single file server and index can satisfy queries for multiple network shares, including files on non-Windows file servers.
- Performance is improved and system load is reduced due to tight integration with the Windows 2000 infrastructure.
- A secure search engine guarantees users cannot find documents that they are not allowed to view or read.
- User interface is easily customized using OLE and ADO programming interfaces.

Consider implementing Indexing Service if any of the following conditions exist in your organization:

- Users cannot find documents on servers or forget the location of documents.
- File servers contain many hundreds or thousands of documents making browsing for particular documents unwieldy or impossible.
- You need to provide search capabilities for a Web site.

Enhancing Data Protection

In an enterprise network, you use a combination of strategies to protect your data. Using Backup and Windows 2000 fault-tolerance features are two ways you can improve your data protection.

Fault Tolerance

Fault tolerance is the ability of a system to continue functioning when part of the system fails. Fault tolerance combats problems such as disk failures, power outages, or corrupted operating systems, which can impact startup files, the operating system itself, or system files. Windows 2000 Server includes fault-tolerant features.

Although the data is always available and current in a fault-tolerant system, you still need to make tape backups to protect the information about your disk subsystem against user errors and natural disasters. Disk fault tolerance is not an alternative to a backup strategy with off-site storage.

Fault-tolerant disk systems are standardized and categorized in six levels, known as RAID level 0 through level 5. Each level offers a specific mix of performance, reliability, and cost.

Disk Management

Windows 2000 Disk Management includes RAID levels 1 and 5:

Level 1: Mirrored volumes (mirror sets in Windows NT 4.0)

Mirrored volumes provide an identical copy for a selected volume. All data that is written to the primary volume is also written to a secondary volume or mirror. If one disk fails, the system uses data from the other disk. Because each file is stored in two locations, you need twice your usual storage space to implement this.

Level 5: RAID-5 volumes (striping with parity)

RAID-5 volumes share data across all the disks in an array. The system generates a small amount of data, called parity information, that is used to reconstruct lost information in case a disk fails. RAID 5 is unique because it writes the parity information across all the disks. If a disk fails, data redundancy is achieved by arranging a data block and its parity information about different disks in the array. This level requires a minimum of three disks. As more disks are added to a RAID-5 set, the amount of overhead decreases from the maximum of 50 percent (that is, three disks are required to store the data normally on two disks). However, the benefits of having many disks in a RAID-5 set drops off when seven or more disks are used in the set.

Selecting a RAID Strategy

RAID strategies include hardware and software solutions. Choosing between RAID-1 and RAID-5 volumes depends on your computing environment. Consider the following when selecting a RAID strategy:

- When compared to RAID-5 volumes, a mirrored volume implementation has a lower entry cost, requires less system memory, provides better overall performance, and does not show performance degradation during a failure. However, its cost per megabyte is higher than that for RAID-5 volumes.

- A software RAID-5 volume implementation has better read performance and a lower cost per megabyte, but it requires more system memory and loses its performance advantage when a disk in the array is missing.

- Hardware or software RAID-5 volumes are a good solution for data redundancy in a computing environment in which most activity consists of reading data. For example, you might want to use a RAID-5 volume on a server that is used to maintain all copies of the programs for your site. It enables you to protect the programs against the loss of a single disk in the striped volume. In addition, the read performance improves due to concurrent reads across the disks that make up the RAID-5 volume.

- In an environment in which frequent updates to the information occur, it might be better to use mirrored volumes. However, you can use a RAID-5 volume if you want redundancy and if the storage overhead cost of a mirror is prohibitive.

Backup

The Backup program helps you protect data from accidental loss due to hardware or storage failure. Using Backup, you can create a duplicate copy of the data on your hard disk and archive the data on another storage device such as a hard disk or a tape. You can back up data to a wide variety of removable, high-density storage media. Also, Backup is integrated with Remote Storage for archiving.

With Backup wizards you can:

- Make an archived copy of selected files and folders on your hard disk.

- Schedule regular backups to keep your archived data up-to-date.

- Restore the archived files and folders to your hard disk or any other disk you can access.

- Back up Active Directory. You can put a copy of Active Directory store on media for off-site storage.

- Back up offline Remote Storage data, registry settings, and any other mount point data.

A Data Protection Strategy for Enterprise Networks

Consider the following backup and fault-tolerance strategies when creating your data protection policies:

- Back up an entire volume in case a disk fails. It is more efficient to restore the entire volume in one operation.

- Always back up the directory services database on a domain controller to prevent the loss of user account and security information.

- For your critical computers, you can implement a software mirror of two separate hardware-controlled RAID arrays. With this configuration, if either a disk or an entire array fails, operations can continue.

- In the event that a computer running Windows 2000 Server fails, you should have a spare computer with Windows 2000 Server already installed to which you can move the data disks.

Considerations for Designing a Fault-Tolerant Storage System

Some points to consider when planning your storage strategy include the following:

- In general, you only need to use fault-tolerant configurations for information that you must have readily available in case of hardware failure or unrecoverable disk errors should the primary data source go offline for any reason.

- If you have applications on a single computer running Windows 2000 Server, you only need to run them on a fault-tolerant volume if you cannot tolerate their unavailability for the amount of time it takes you to restore the applications from a backup.

- You need to back up the application volume any time you install a new application or change default settings for an application.

- If space is a consideration, you can format your application volume with the NTFS file system and use NTFS compression for folders and files on the volume.

Improving Your Disaster Recovery Capabilities

Because a computer or site disaster can overcome even the best data protection strategies, you need to have a system disaster recovery plan. A disaster includes anything from not being able to start a computer to the destruction of a network when a natural disaster strikes.

To be prepared for a system failure, you should have the following:

- Well-documented plans and procedures for recovering from failures when they occur.
- Floppy disks that enable you to restart a computer when you have trouble using the system active or startup volume.
- Documented software and hardware configuration information for your computers.

To reduce system recovery time, it is recommended that you perform the following tasks:

- Put the Windows 2000 Server system and startup and data volumes on separate drives.
- Save the disk configuration data each time you change the configuration by using Disk Management.
- Keep a written record of disk volumes and their sizes.

The remainder of this section describes the disaster protection features of Windows 2000, which you can use to prepare your enterprise for a potential network disaster.

Creating Backup and Off-Site Storage Policies

Your disaster recovery plan needs to include policies and procedures for backup and restoration of individual computers and entire systems. Your goal is to have clear instructions for recovering your data.

Backup Policies

When creating backup policies, consider the following strategies:

Back up all computers or only selected computers. Do you plan to back up your entire network or will you back up only the servers that have important user files?

Create network-based backup or local backup. Will you have a few backup servers with tape devices that read data across the network from all selected servers, or will all users be responsible for backing up their data?

Use a centralized backup policy or a distributed backup policy. Will a single IT group back up all the organization's servers or will each group do its own backup? If the latter is the case, will you establish guidelines for when and how to back up?

Your backup plan needs to include implementation of the following activities:

- Secure both the storage device and the backup media.

- Make copies of all required device drivers so that storage devices can be used in case of disaster. The device drivers are needed to restore operations.

- Create and keep printed copies of backup logs. These are essential for restoring data.

- Keep three copies of the media. Store at least one copy off-site in a properly controlled environment.

- Periodically perform a trial restoration to verify that your backup set can be read and that it contains all the files you want to have backed up. For more information about using specific backup methods and procedures, see "Backup" in the *Microsoft® Windows® 2000 Server Resource Kit Server Operations Guide.*

Considerations for Off-Site Storage

Consider storage of the following data and information when planning for off-site storage:

- A full backup of the entire system, done on a weekly basis.

- The originals of all installed programs and required device drivers.

- Documents required to facilitate an insurance claim, such as hardware and software inventory records; and copies of purchase orders or receipts for computer hardware and software.

- A copy of information required to reinstall and reconfigure network hardware.

Creating a Disaster Recovery Plan

To determine what provisions to make for partial or complete loss of data, you need to determine the total cost of rebuilding or replacing the data your organization uses. Consider the following:

- What are the costs of reconstructing your organization's financial, personnel, and other business data?

- What does your business insurance cover with regard to replacing lost data?

- How long would it take to reconstruct your business data? How would this translate into lost future business?

- What is the cost per hour of server downtime?

There are several areas that need to be addressed in developing a comprehensive disaster recovery plan. Your plan for data protection needs to answer the following questions:

- What data do you need to back up and how often should you do backups?

- How will you protect critical computer or other hardware configuration information that is not saved during normal backups?

- What data needs to be stored on-site, and how will you physically store it?

- What data needs to be stored off-site, and how will you physically store it?

- What training is required so that server operators and administrators can respond quickly and effectively if an emergency occurs?

Test your plan for recovering and restoring your organization's critical data and keep copies of your disaster recovery plan both on-site and off-site.

Testing System Recovery Strategies

Testing is an important part of being prepared for disaster recovery. The skill and experience of the administrators and operators is a major factor in getting a failed computer or network back online with minimal cost and disruption to your business. You need IT personnel who are trained in troubleshooting problems and performing system recovery procedures.

Be sure to test recovery procedures before bringing a new server into production. Testing needs to include:

- Making sure that your Windows 2000 startup disks function correctly.

- Testing your uninterruptible power supply (UPS) on the computers running Windows 2000 Server and on hubs, routers, and other network components.

- Testing your disaster recovery plan.

- Performing full or partial restorations from your daily, weekly, and monthly backup media.

Practicing Recovery Procedures

You can use testing to try to predict failure situations and to practice recovery procedures. Be sure to do stress testing and test all functionality.

Some of the failures that you need to test include:

- Individual computer components such as hard disks and controllers, processors, and RAM.

- External components such as routers, bridges, switches, cabling, and connectors.

The stress tests that you set up need to include:

- Heavy network loads.
- Heavy disk I/O to the same disk.
- Heavy use of file, print, and applications servers.
- Heavy use by users who log on simultaneously.

Documenting Recovery Procedures

You need to develop step-by-step procedures for getting a computer or network back online after a disaster. Create an operations handbook that includes the following procedures:

- Performing backups
- Implementing off-site storage policies
- Restoring servers and the network

You should review your documentation when you make configuration changes to your computers or network. Updating the documentation is particularly important when you install new versions of the operating system or change the utilities or tools that you use to maintain your system.

Planning Task List for Storage Management

Table 19.4 presents a summary checklist that you can use to determine your storage needs and how you will address them.

Table 19.4   Summary of Storage Planning Tasks

Task	Location in Chapter
Assess your storage needs.	Improving Your Storage Management Functions
Select a data storage system.	Improving Your Storage Management Functions
Plan for storage management, including removable and remote storage.	Managing Disk Resources
Develop strategies for optimizing storage management.	Optimizing Data Management
Develop strategies for data protection.	Enhancing Data Protection
Develop strategies for backup and disaster recovery.	Improving Your Disaster Recovery Capabilities

C H A P T E R   2 0

Synchronizing Active Directory with Exchange Server Directory Service

If you are planning to implement Microsoft® Windows® 2000 Server Active Directory™ and you currently maintain the Microsoft® Exchange Server version 5.5 directory service, this is an essential planning chapter for the directory service management personnel in your organization. The directory synchronization concepts and processes presented in this chapter will help you determine the most cost-effective and efficient method to administer Windows 2000 Server Active Directory and Exchange Server 5.5 directory service. Additionally, the examples will help you determine which directory synchronization and administration configuration options are most appropriate for your organization.

Before reading this chapter, it is recommended you read the chapters "Designing the Active Directory Structure" and "Determining Domain Migration Strategies" in this book. These chapters provide you with an understanding of the new concepts and key components of Active Directory and the domain migration-related issues.

In This Chapter

Chapter Goal

This chapter will help you develop the following planning document:

Active Directory Connector (ADC) Connection Agreement Plan

Related Information in the Resource Kit

- For more information about Active Directory, namespace planning, and domain administration, see "Designing the Active Directory Structure" in this book.

- For more information about migrating to Windows 2000 Server, see "Determining Domain Migration Strategies" in this book.

- For more information about Windows 2000 Server security standards, see "Planning Distributed Security" in this book.

- For more information about creating test plans, see "Building a Windows 2000 Test Lab" in this book.

Overview of Directory Synchronization

Directory synchronization is the process of keeping two separate directory services synchronized, such that changes made to objects in one directory are propagated automatically to the other directory.

Directory synchronization between Windows 2000 Server Active Directory and Exchange Server 5.5 directory service enables you to initially populate a new Active Directory with Exchange Server 5.5 user attributes and objects. In addition, since Exchange Server 5.5 supports third-party e-mail directory services, you can copy third-party directory user attributes and objects into Exchange Server, and then from Exchange Server into Active Directory.

After the initial population of Active Directory, the two directories can sustain a productive coexistence. You can keep information consistent between Active Directory and Exchange Server 5.5 directory using preconfigured, automated synchronization operations.

Process for Synchronizing the Directories

Before you begin the planning phase of your directory synchronization strategy, consider using the planning process represented in the flow chart in Figure 20.1.

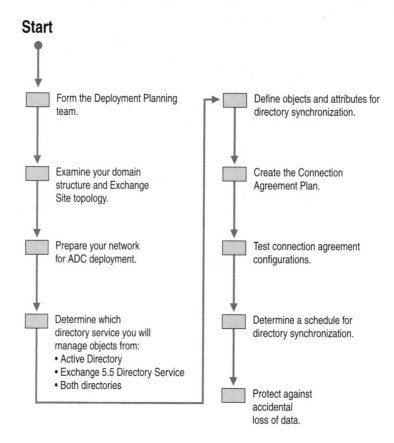

Figure 20.1   Process For Synchronizing Active Directory and Exchange Server 5.5 Directory Service

Prior to beginning the directory synchronization planning phase, it is important that you thoroughly understand the key components you will use to perform the directory synchronization operation.

Windows 2000 Server Software Components

The Active Directory Connector (ADC) and the Microsoft Management Console (MMC) are the software components in Windows 2000 Server that enable you to synchronize and manage communications between Active Directory and Exchange Server 5.5 directory service. Using the Lightweight Directory Access Protocol (LDAP), the ADC provides an automated way of keeping directory information between Active Directory and the Exchange Server directory service consistent. You use MMC and ADC-specific MMC snap-ins and extensions to configure ADC and to perform specific functions. Without the ADC, you would have to manually enter new data and updates in both directory services.

The key features and functionality of ADC are as follows:

- Bidirectional synchronization

  With this feature, changes initiated on the Exchange Server directory are automatically communicated to Active Directory, and vice versa. This allows you to manage changes from either directory.

- Selective attribute synchronization

  You can select specific Active Directory and Exchange Server attributes to be synchronized, while purposely excluding the synchronization of other attributes.

- Change synchronization

  With regard to synchronizing with Exchange Server, Windows 2000 Server only updates changes on the object level. If, for example, you make changes to 20 user objects for 100,000 users, the system will only update those 20 user objects. This reduces duplication and transmission time as well as network traffic.

- Attribute-level changes

  When synchronizing two objects, the ADC compares attribute values to determine which attributes should be synchronized. For example, if the phone number on an Exchange Server mailbox is modified, the ADC compares the attributes of the mailbox with the corresponding user object in the Active Directory and only synchronizes the modified attributes. In this case, just the phone number is synchronized.

- Consistent management tools

  Using the Active Directory Users and Computers MMC snap-in, you can manage Users, Contacts, and Groups.

  For more information about the Microsoft Management Console and MMC snap-ins and extensions, see Windows 2000 Server Help.

Key Advantages of Using ADC

Using ADC provides the following advantages:

Single Source Administration

Once you have upgraded a Windows NT Server 4.0 domain to Windows 2000 Server Active Directory, you can easily and automatically configure the ADC to populate a new Active Directory with Exchange Server 5.5 directory information, such as the mailbox user properties shown in Figure 20.2.

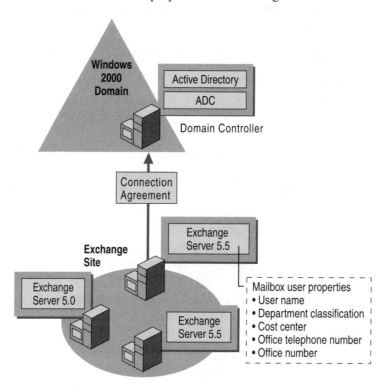

Figure 20.2   Single Source Administration

Acute Administration and Delegation Capabilities

You can use the ADC to synchronize and manage the Exchange Server directory through Active Directory, enabling you to take advantage of the more granular delegation of administration that Windows 2000 Server offers. This means that, with Windows 2000 Server, you can set permissions at the attribute level rather than at the object level. This allows administrators to delegate tasks related to particular attributes to different users.

For example, users have permission to update their department cost center and also to view and update some home phone numbers. Using Exchange Server 5.5 they are able to view properties but cannot update them directly. With Windows 2000 Server, the directory administrator can delegate these tasks so that those users can update the Cost Center field and update the home phone numbers. You can delegate some tasks to authorized users, and restrict them from access to other areas of data, such as group memberships and security permissions. You can then use the ADC to update the Exchange Server directory with the results of these authorized administrative changes.

For more information about the various levels of administration and delegation capabilities in Active Directory, see "Designing the Active Directory Structure" in this book.

Interoperability with Third-Party E-mail Directory Services

Through Exchange Server, you can populate Active Directory with user and group information from third-party e-mail directories. Exchange Server supports bidirectional directory synchronization with third-party e-mail directory services that contain directory synchronization agents. Figure 20.3 shows the interoperability between Exchange Server and third-party e-mail directory services.

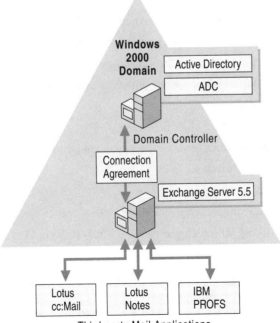

Figure 20.3   Bidirectional Directory Synchronization with Third-Party E-mail Directory Services

Easy Location of Network Users

The Active Directory Client enables end users, with Windows 2000 Server or Windows 9x clients that have the Active Directory Client installed, to easily find other users using the **Find People** option. Combining the capabilities of ADC with the Active Directory Client allows you to quickly deploy the Active Directory as a user directory, which is similar to the way you would use a telephone directory.

For more information about Active Directory Client, see "Preparing Your Network Infrastructure for Windows 2000" in this book.

Establishing Relationships Using Connection Agreements

Installing the ADC on a server simply adds a service within Windows 2000 Server and Active Directory. To establish a relationship between an existing Exchange Server site and Active Directory, you must configure a connection agreement. A connection agreement holds information such as the server names to contact for synchronization, object classes to synchronize, target containers, and the synchronization schedule. It is possible to define multiple connection agreements on a single ADC; each connection agreement could go from Active Directory to a single Exchange Server site, or to the same Exchange Server site.

Specifically, a connection agreement defines the following:

- Directory or directories to be synchronized
- Windows 2000 Server synchronization objects
- Exchange Server 5.5 synchronization objects
- The direction in which synchronization takes place
- Synchronization schedule
- Method for deleting objects
- Details surrounding some of the advanced options, such as:
  - Mapping attributes
  - Creating new objects
  - Authenticating each of the directories
  - Specifying which Organizational Units (OU) or containers you want to synchronize

The ADC only performs directory synchronization between Exchange Server 5.5 Service Pack 1 (SP1) or higher and Windows 2000 Server. However, if you have an earlier version of Exchange Server with SP1 in an Exchange Server 5.5 site, that Exchange Server automatically synchronizes with the earlier version of Exchange Server. In this case, all directory information is the same throughout the Exchange Server site and the organization.

Although only one instance of the ADC service can be active on a single computer running Windows 2000 Server, multiple connection agreements can be established. You can configure each connection agreement to perform unique synchronization tasks. For example, one connection agreement can continuously update the Windows 2000 Server Active Directory, while another connection agreement can update the Windows 2000 Server contacts to the Exchange Server directory daily at a time you specify.

Creating the ADC Connection Agreement Plan

With an understanding of the capabilities of ADC and the importance of connection agreements, you will be able to begin the planning phase of directory synchronization. This section guides you through gathering the information you need to create your ADC Connection Agreement Plan.

Forming the Deployment Planning Team

Due to a high level of associated dependencies, teamwork is of the utmost importance in making the synchronization between Windows 2000 Server Active Directory and Exchange Server directory service a smooth and productive experience.

Planning your directory synchronization strategy should be a cooperative project involving the key decision makers and technical leads of the following groups:

- IT management
- Exchange Server administration
- Active Directory administration
- Schema Administrators Group
- Network Services

Collectively, this team will know enough about your Exchange Server site topology, Active Directory design, and network topology to avoid potential costly mistakes.

Once you have formed the deployment planning team, you can begin the planning phase for directory synchronization.

Planning considerations for the directory synchronization deployment planning team are as follows:

- Assign specific responsibilities and objectives to each system administrator on the directory synchronization deployment team.

- Determine if system administrators will require training to run the ADC and MMC snap-in. If training is required, determine when it will take place.

- Obtain permission to install.

  Since write access to the schema is limited to members of the Schema Administrators group, you will have to obtain permission from this group to install the ADC. However, the schema administrators can run the ADC Setup solely for the purpose of extending the schema. Managing the ADC does not involve the schema, but if, for some reason, a subsequent version of the ADC involves a schema modification, this would require assistance and involvement from the schema administrators group. For information about installing the ADC, see the section "ADC Implementation Strategy" later in this chapter.

  For more information about the Active Directory schema, see "Designing the Active Directory Structure" in this book, and also see the *Microsoft® Windows® 2000 Server Resource Kit Distributed Systems Guide*.

- Determine what business processes might be automated or optimized through the use of this synchronization operation.

- Obtain management consent to implement your directory synchronization plan.

Examining Your Domain Structure and Exchange Server Site Topology

Before you can begin gathering information for your ADC Connection Agreement Plan, you need to understand the Exchange 5.5 sites, Windows NT Server domains, and Windows 2000 Server Active Directory structures in your organization. Once you have obtained the Exchange Server site topology and domain structure diagrams, it is recommended you consider doing the following:

Take inventory of your Exchange Server sites. You will need to know how many Exchange Server sites you have, how they are managed, and whether they are candidates for synchronization. For those Exchange Server sites to be synchronized, you will need detailed information on their recipient containers and the objects to be synchronized.

Install ADC on a Windows 2000 Server. For each Active Directory domain that participates in directory synchronization, you will need to install ADC on a Windows 2000 Server global catalog server, member server, or domain controller.

Identify the location of mailboxes for all users in a domain. Many organizations have a multi-master domain topology where user accounts exist in more than one domain. It is important to identify where mailboxes reside for users in each domain. The least complicated scenario is when all mailboxes in a master domain reside in a single Exchange Server site.

Ensure that each directory has corresponding objects for synchronization purposes.
Exchange Server sites may contain mailboxes that are associated with
Windows 2000 Server accounts from multiple domains. You can create multiple
connection agreements from a single Exchange Server site to multiple Active
Directory domains and the ADC will match Exchange Server mailboxes to a
corresponding user object. For Exchange Server Custom Recipients, Distribution
Lists, and Mailboxes which do not have a corresponding Active Directory user
object, the ADC creates new objects in one of the Active Directory domains. You
will need to decide in which Active Directory domain you want the ADC to create
new objects.

Preparing Your Network for ADC Deployment

Only one instance of the ADC service can be active on a single computer running
Windows 2000 Server. However, the ADC can support multiple connection
agreements. To prepare for deployment of ADC, consider the requirements and
recommendations described in the following section.

Considering Specific Network Requirements

There are two network-specific tasks that you should consider as you gather
information for your ADC Connection Agreement Plan. These tasks are as
follows:

Select servers to be bridgehead servers.

Bridgehead servers receive and forward e-mail traffic at each end of a connection
agreement, similar to the task a gateway performs. When you select servers to be
ADC bridgehead servers, they should meet the following conditions:

- Have adequate resources (CPU and memory) to support synchronization traffic
  and processing of incoming LDAP sessions.

- Be well connected to the network. For example, if an Exchange Server site
  spans multiple physical locations across a hub-and-spoke network, its
  bridgehead server for the Exchange Server site should be located at the hub.

- If the ADC bridgehead server is not a global catalog server, it should be on the
  same local area network (LAN) segment as a global catalog server. The reason
  for this is that ADC attempts to contact a global catalog in order to perform
  target matching searches. When ADC picks up a new object from Exchange
  Server, the ADC does not want to accidentally create a corresponding Active
  Directory object in one domain. By searching in the global catalog, the ADC
  minimizes the chance that it will create a duplicate object.

- If the Exchange Server environment employs connector servers that do not
  host mailboxes, consider configuring these servers as ADC bridgehead servers.

Identify resource usage.

Both the synchronization of directory objects between directories and the replication that occurs within the Active Directory and Exchange Server directory replication environments consume network resources.

Once Active Directory becomes relatively static after the upgrade from Windows NT Server 4.0 to Windows 2000 Server and the synchronization with Exchange Server, only small amounts of data will pass between Active Directory and the Exchange Server 5.5 directory service. Changes to the Exchange Server 5.5 directory that are synchronized to the Active Directory cause slightly more traffic than changes to Active Directory that are synchronized to Exchange Server.

Computer Requirements

When preparing to use ADC, observe these technical computer requirements:

- You must have at least one Windows 2000 Server.

- You must have at least one Exchange Server 5.5 with SP1 (at a minimum) installed on each Exchange Server defined in a connection agreement.

Depending on the synchronization schedule, the ADC server and other directory servers with which it interacts could face a significant processing load. It is important that these computers are appropriately specified (CPU and memory) and well-connected to the network—ideally they should be on the same LAN. Unlike directory replication schedules in the Exchange Server 5.x environment, if the schedule is set to Always in the user interface, the ADC attempts to synchronize changes between Active Directory and the Exchange Server directory. This synchronization takes place in cycles of maximum continuous replication time and synchronization sleep delay of five minutes.

The expected resource usage for Pentium-class servers (200 MHz) with 128Mb of memory and one connection agreement configured is shown in Table 20.1.

Table 20.1   Pentium-class Server CPU Utilization

CPU Utilization (approximately every 5 minutes)	Usage
Server running the ADC	8-24%
Domain controller	6-66%
Connecting Exchange 5.5 bridgehead	0-91%

To compare the differences between types and speeds of CPUs, see the resource usage of Dual Pentium II-class servers (450Mhz) with 256Mb of memory shown in Table 20.2.

Table 20.2   Dual Pentium II-class Server CPU Utilization

CPU Utilization (approximately every 5 minutes)	Usage
Server running the ADC	1-12%
Domain controller	0-30%
Connecting Exchange 5.5 bridgehead	20-36%

For enterprise-size Exchange Server 5.5 and Active Directory deployments, you will need to carefully plan for any additional overhead that the ADC and its connection agreements produce. This is particularly important to those who need to accurately size servers and network capacity. This is even more important when the ADC server, domain controller, and Exchange Server 5.5 are connected over relatively slow links.

Deployment Recommendations

Consider the following recommendations to promote a successful deployment:

Populate Active Directory with user accounts by upgrading the primary domain controller (PDC) to Microsoft Windows 2000 Server.
Use ADC to backfill directory data from the Exchange Server directory to the pre-existing Active Directory accounts. This permits objects synchronized from Exchange Server to be mapped to security objects in Active Directory.

Use Directory Replication Bridgehead servers to facilitate Exchange Server directory replication between Exchange Server sites.
Where it is possible, use them as ADC bridgehead servers for connection agreements.

Place the server hosting ADC on the same subnet as the Exchange Server directory and Active Directory bridgeheads, if possible.
If you are using ADC in a wide area network (WAN) environment, place it in a strategic location, such as at the hub of a hub-and-spoke topology.

Synchronize the entire Exchange Server site instead of synchronizing individual recipient containers.

It is possible to choose the entire Exchange Server site as the source and target on the Exchange Server, and also to choose the Active Directory domain as the source and target on the Active Directory side. This will effectively synchronize the recipient container hierarchy in Exchange Server with the OU hierarchy in Windows 2000 Server. You can choose to change the OU hierarchy or the location of individual recipients created in the Active Directory by the ADC at a later time. By moving recipients or OUs to a new location, the next time the ADC synchronizes, it finds the new locations and synchronizes with the existing recipients—if it is within the search scope of defined import and export containers.

For the best performance, install ADC on a member server in the Windows 2000 Server domain.

Depending on the synchronization schedule, if you configure the ADC with multiple connection agreements, it could consume a good deal of processor time. If you intend to install the ADC on a domain controller or global catalog, ensure that the server hardware accommodates the extra processing load.

Either create ADC connection agreements between a global catalog and Exchange Server or deploy the ADC in close network proximity to a global catalog.

In a multi-domain environment, the ADC performs searches against the global catalog, even if there is no connection agreement for synchronizing with a global catalog server. The purpose for searching in the global catalog is to ensure that the ADC does not create duplicate objects in the forest.

ADC Implementation Strategy

In order to successfully install the ADC and configure a connection agreement, you must be able to log on to Windows 2000 Server with an account that carries distinctive credentials. Permissions required to perform various tasks are as follows:

Initial ADC Installation

When you first install ADC in a Windows 2000 forest, the ADC Setup program extends the Active Directory schema with the Exchange schema extensions. In order to do this, the account that you are running Setup from must belong to a member of the Schema Administrators group or otherwise have permissions to extend the schema.

Additionally, ADC Setup creates objects in the Active directory configuration container. This requires that the account you are running Setup from belongs to a member of the Domain Administrators group or otherwise has permissions to create objects in the Services and Sites containers.

Finally, ADC Setup creates two security groups in the local domain—one is "Exchange Services" and the other is "Exchange Administrators." This requires that the account you are running Setup from belongs to a member of the Domain Administrators Group or otherwise has permissions to create objects in the Users container.

Subsequent Installations of the ADC

Subsequent installations of the ADC in the same forest do not require Schema Administrator permissions. Subsequent installations do require either Domain Administrator permissions or other specific permissions that allow you to create new objects under the Sites and Services containers in the configuration naming context. Additional installations in the same domain do not require the creation of either the Exchange Services or the Exchange Administrators groups. However, the first ADC installation into any other Windows 2000 Server domain requires the creation of these groups and subsequently the proper permissions to do so.

ADC Configuration

You can configure the ADC policy by viewing the property pages of the top-level node in the ADC Administrator MMC snap-in. By modifying the policy, you can control the set of attributes synchronized from either directory as well as the set of rules used by the ADC to match objects in either directory.

ADC Schema and Object Mapping

Each connection agreement uses a table-based schema map for the majority of attributes on objects synchronized between the two directories. The default map is located on the ADC policy object in Active Directory. While it is possible to enable and disable a subset of attributes synchronizing in either direction, it is not possible to modify the schema mapping from the ADC Administrator MMC snap-in.

Tables 20.3, 20.4, 20.5, and 20.6 list many of the mappings defined in the default schema map.

Table 20.3 defines the attribute mappings for all objects in Windows 2000 and Exchange. If an attribute value for an attribute to be mapped does not exist in the source directory, that mapping is ignored.

Table 20.3   Attribute Mappings for All Objects

Windows 2000 Attribute (LDAP Name) All Object Classes	Exchange Attribute (LDAP Name) All Object Classes
description	Admin-description
autoReply	AutoReply
businessRoles	Business-Roles
co	co
company	company
delivContLength	deliv-Cont-Length
department	department
displayName	cn
displayNamePrintable	name
distinguishedName	distinguishedName
dnQualifier	dnQualifier
employeeID	employeeNumber
extensionAttribute1	Extension-Attribute-1
extensionAttribute2	Extension-Attribute-2
extensionAttribute3	Extension-Attribute-3
extensionAttribute4	Extension-Attribute-4
extensionAttribute5	Extension-Attribute-5
extensionAttribute6	Extension-Attribute-6
extensionAttribute7	Extension-Attribute-7
extensionAttribute8	Extension-Attribute-8
extensionAttribute9	Extension-Attribute-9
extensionAttribute10	Extension-Attribute-10
extensionAttribute11	Extension-Attribute-11
extensionAttribute12	Extension-Attribute-12
extensionAttribute13	Extension-Attribute-13
extensionAttribute14	Extension-Attribute-14
extensionAttribute15	Extension-Attribute-15
facsimileTelephoneNumber	facsimileTelephoneNumber
generationQualifier	generationQualifier
homephone	homephone
homePostalAddress	homePostalAddress
houseIdentifier	houseIdentifier

(continued)

Table 20.3   Attribute Mappings for All Objects *(continued)*

Windows 2000 Attribute (LDAP Name) All Object Classes	Exchange Attribute (LDAP Name) All Object Classes
info	info
initials	initials
l	l
Language	Language
mail	mail
mailnickname	uid
mobile	mobile
otherTelephone	Telephone-Office2
otherHomePhone	Telephone-Home2
telephoneAssistant	telephone-Assistant
pager	pager
personalPager	personalPager
personalTitle	personalTitle
physicalDeliveryOfficeName	physicalDeliveryOfficeName
postalCode	postalCode
secretary	secretary
sn	sn
st	st
street	street
streetAddress	postalAddress
telephoneNumber	telephoneNumber
telexNumber	telexNumber
teletexTerminalIdentifier	teletexTerminalIdentifier
textEncodedORAddress	textEncodedORAddress
title	title
userCertificate	userCertificate
userCert	user-Cert
userSMIMECertificate	userSMIMECertificate
url	url
x121Address	x121Address
autoReplyMessage	conferenceInformation
importedFrom	Imported-From

Table 20.4 defines the attribute mappings for all User objects and Mailbox objects in Windows 2000 and Exchange.

Table 20.4 Object Class-Specific Mappings

Windows 2000 Attribute (LDAP Name) User Object	Exchange Attribute (LDAP Name) Mailbox Object
givenName	givenName
manager	manager
altRecipient	Alt-Recipient
publicDelegates	public-Delegates
mdbUseDefaults	mdb-use-defaults
mdbOverQuotaLimit	MDB-Over-Quota-Limit
mdbStorageQuota	MDB-Storage-Quota
submissionContLength	submission-cont-length
mDBOverHardQuotaLimit	DXA-task
protocolSettings	protocol-Settings
mapiRecipient	mapi-recipient
msExchHomeServerName	home-MDB
msExchHomeServerName	home-MTA
deliverAndRedirect	deliver-and-redirect
garbageCollPeriod	garbage-coll-period
securityProtocol	security-Protocol
deletedItemFlags	DXA-Flags
objectSID	Assoc-NT-Account
authOrig	Auth-Orig
unauthOrig	Unauth-Orig
dLMemSubmitPerms	DL-Mem-Submit-Perms
dLMemRejectPerms	DL-Mem-Reject-Perms
folderPathname	Folder-Pathname

Table 20.5 defines the attribute mappings for Contact objects and Custom objects in Windows 2000 and Exchange.

Table 20.5 Object Class-Specific Mappings

Windows 2000 Attribute (LDAP Name) Contact Object	Exchange Attribute (LDAP Name) Custom Object
givenName	givenName
Manager	Manager
targetAddress	target-Address
protocolSettings	protocol-Settings
mapiRecipient	mapi-Recipient
AuthOrig	Auth-Orig
UnauthOrig	Unauth-Orig
dlMemSubmitPerms	dl-Mem-Submit-Perms
dlMemRejectPerms	dl-Mem-Reject-Perms

Table 20.6 defines the attribute mappings for Group objects and Distribution List objects in Windows 2000 and Exchange.

Table 20.6 Object Class-Specific Mappings

Windows 2000 Attribute (LDAP Name) Group Object:	Exchange Attribute (LDAP Name) Distribution List Object:
member	member
msExchExpansionServerName	home-MTA
managedby	owner
oOFReplyToOriginator	OOF-Reply-To-Originator
reportToOriginator	Report-To-Originator
reportToOwner	Report-To-Owner
hideDLMembership	Hide-DL-Membership
authOrig	Auth-Orig
unauthOrig	Unauth-Orig
dLMemSubmitPerms	DL-Mem-Submit-Perms
dLMemRejectPerms	DL-Mem-Reject-Perms

Base your determination of the number of connection agreements your organization requires on your unique network environment, including your deployment objectives and requirements and your expectations for the outcome of implementation. You must also familiarize yourself with the Exchange Server and Active Directory object attributes that you are not able to synchronize. These attributes are listed in Table 20.7.

Table 20.7   Attributes of Objects That Do Not Synchronize

Windows 2000 Server Active Directory	Exchange Server 5.5 Directory Service
All account information, such as Account Logging, Account Password, and so on	Advance Security Settings
Profile information	Access Control Lists (ACLs)
Routing and Remote Access dial-up permissions	Home information Store
Access Control Lists (ACLs)	

Managing Objects

You need to determine from which directory service you want to administer objects. As mentioned earlier in this chapter, you can use ADC to administer objects from Active Directory, Exchange Server, or from both directory services.

It is important to note that the ADC handles the synchronization of deleted objects between the two directories differently than other revised objects. By default, the ADC does not synchronize the deletion of any object from the source directory to the target directory. Instead, the ADC writes an import file to a disk containing the item to be deleted. An administrator can review the deleted objects in this import file, and as appropriate, choose to import the file, thereby deleting the set of target objects. If you choose to directly synchronize object deletions between the two directories, you can do so by selecting this option on the **Deletion** tab in Properties of the connection agreement property pages. You can also control how the ADC handles each direction of a bidirectional connection agreement.

Administering Objects from Active Directory

If you decide to manage objects from Active Directory, you will need to deploy each connection agreement so that it can write to the Exchange Server directory. For every Exchange Server site for which you will administer the recipients from the Active Directory, you need to create a connection agreement from a server in that site to the appropriate Windows 2000 Server domain. An example of where this administration model might be appropriate is in an organization that administers employee information in Active Directory or in another directory system that synchronizes with the Active Directory. You can use the ADC to update the Exchange Server directory with changes to the employee information.

Administering Objects from Exchange Server 5.5 Directory Service

If you continue to manage objects from the Exchange Administrator, you should configure your connection agreements as "unidirectional" in order to populate and update Active Directory. It is possible to deploy a single, one-way connection agreement to only one Exchange Server site and synchronize the entire Exchange Server directory with Active Directory using that single connection agreement. This eliminates the need to create and manage multiple connection agreements between every Exchange site. As long as the connection agreement is configured to pull from Exchange into Active Directory, you will be able to select any Exchange Server site as a source container.

By selecting all sites as source containers, you can synchronize the entire set of recipients in the Exchange Server directory. This administration model is a good way to begin your ADC deployment. This model pushes the established Exchange Server directory data into Active Directory without impacting a production Exchange Server system. Once you have adequately populated the Active Directory and understand how the ADC operates in a production environment, you can revise your connection agreement configurations to be bidirectional or to pull from Active Directory into Exchange.

Note If you have chosen multiple downstream Exchange Server sites to be the source of a one-way connection agreement, and you decide to make the connection agreement bidirectional, you must remove containers from all non-local sites for this connection agreement. In order to modify objects in any given Exchange Server site, you must create a separate connection agreement to any Exchange Server 5.5 in that site.

Administering Objects from Both Active Directory and Exchange Server 5.5 Directory Service

If you administer data from both Active Directory and the Exchange Server 5.5 directory, then you must create a bidirectional connection agreement between the set of sites and domains that you are synchronizing. Be sure to read the section "Setting Up Connection Agreements" later in this chapter for information describing where to place connection agreements. You may need a more complex connection agreement topology when choosing to administer objects from both directories.

Use this administration model if there is some data that you administer from Exchange Server and other data which you administer from Active Directory. If the same object is modified in both directories, the most recent modification prevails. However, it may take two synchronization cycles for this object to synchronize, depending upon whether the object was modified before or during the first synchronization cycle of the ADC.

Defining Objects for Directory Synchronization

When defining objects for directory synchronization between Exchange Server 5.5 directory and Active Directory, your primary goals should be to:

- Provide objects of interest from one environment to the other.
- Make the objects easily accessible to users, administrators, and developers.

You can accomplish this by organizing your Windows 2000 Server objects, such as Users, Contacts, and Groups, into recipient containers that mirror the Exchange Server recipient containers. The following is an example of how you might do this:

- In the Exchange Server 5.5 directory service, create three recipient containers:
  - Custom Recipients
  - Mailboxes
  - Distribution Lists

- In Windows 2000 Server configure the following four OUs:
  - Contacts
  - Users
  - Groups
  - Computers

Note You would not create a recipient container to correspond with the Windows 2000 Server computer's OU because Exchange Server does not synchronize computers.

Place all of your internal corporate users in the Users container, place your Custom Recipients in the Contacts containers, and place your Distribution Lists in the Group container. Finally, synchronize the directories.

There are two different methods for setting up synchronization between Exchange Server containers and Active Directory OUs. They are as follows:

- For the first method, you can create three separate connection agreements that map each of the Exchange Server containers to the corresponding Active Directory OUs. For example, Custom Recipients in Exchange Server would map to Contacts in Active Directory, and so on. Figure 20.4 provides an example of this method.

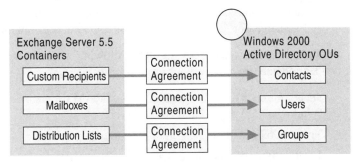

Figure 20.4   Using Multiple Connection Agreements to Map Exchange Server Containers and Windows 2000 Server OUs

- As an alternative to the first method, you could create a single connection agreement between the parent container of all the subcontainers in Exchange Server and the parent container of all the subcontainers in Active Directory. When you synchronize directories for the first time, the ADC automatically creates containers below the parent container in Windows 2000 Server to mirror those in Exchange Server. In this case, Mailboxes, Custom Recipients, and Distribution Lists replicate objects contained in them to the appropriate containers maintaining the directory hierarchy. Only containers that contain one or more mail-enabled objects are replicated.

Figure 20.5 represents an example of how you would create a single connection agreement to map data from designated containers in Exchange Server to an Active Directory OU.

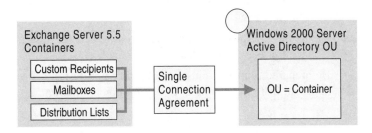

Figure 20.5   Single Connection Agreement Maps Containers from Exchange Server to Windows 2000 Server Active Directory

The second method is recommended over the first method because you create fewer connection agreements and the system does most of the work for you.

Setting up Connection Agreements

When you begin setting up connection agreements you need to evaluate your Windows 2000 Server domains and Exchange Server sites and determine the minimum number of connection agreements you need for optimal operation. It is recommended that you do not create a connection agreement between each and every Exchange Server site and Windows 2000 Server domain in your enterprise.

For optimal performance, consider the following when determining the number of connection agreements for your organization:

- Speed, number of CPUs, and amount of RAM for each Exchange server, Windows 2000 server, and ADC server.
- Network bandwidth.
- Total number of Exchange Server Mailboxes and Active Directory Users.
- Total number of Exchange Server Customer Recipients and Active Directory Contacts.
- Total number of Exchange Server Distribution Lists and Active Directory Groups.

Upon implementation, use the ADC and the Active Directory Connector Management snap-in to set up and configure the connection agreements for your organization.

Designing Your Connection Agreements

There are several combinations for which you can set up connection agreements to synchronize Exchange Server directory service with Active Directory. To plan and create your connection agreements, use the following primary steps:

- Determine which of the four model organizations, described as follows, best matches the Windows 2000 Server and Exchange Server site environment in your organization.
- Create the first pass of your connection agreement design to begin your ADC Connection Agreement Plan.
- Be prepared to provide justification for your design decision and obtain approval from management to begin implementation.

During deployment you will create the connection agreements using the ADC and the Active Directory Connector Management snap-ins.

Note In each of the following ADC connection models it is assumed that the domains and Exchange sites reside within a single forest. If your domains and Exchange sites are dispersed among multiple forests, you have to build a separate ADC topology for each forest.

ADC Connection Model 1: A Single Windows 2000 Server Domain with a Single Exchange Server Site

A single Windows 2000 Server domain with a single Exchange site is the simplest domain architecture in a Windows 2000 Server topology. Generally, smaller organizations with a single, centralized office and an average of up to 5,000 users would adopt this connection model.

Figure 20.6 represents an example of how you can set up a single, two-way connection agreement between a single Windows 2000 Server domain and a single Exchange Server site.

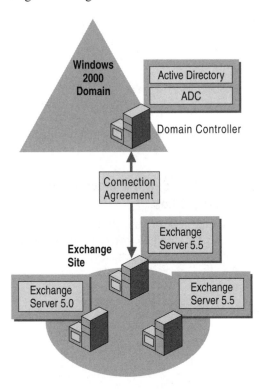

Figure 20.6   Single Windows 2000 Server Domain with a Single Exchange Server Site

You can set up your connection agreements so that you can administer recipients exclusively from Windows 2000 Server Active Directory, from Exchange Server 5.5, or from both directories.

If ADC Connection Model 1 best matches the environment of your organization, use the flow chart in Figure 20.7 to help you design an ADC Connection Agreement Plan for your organization.

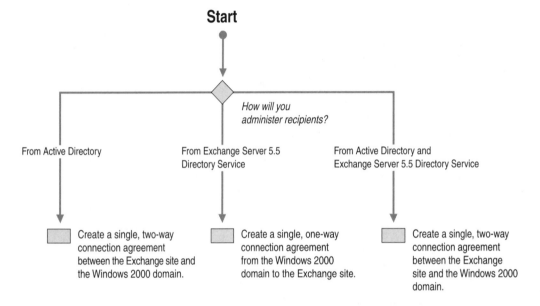

Figure 20.7   Single Windows 2000 Server Domain with a Single Exchange Server Site

ADC Connection Model 2: A Single Windows 2000 Server Domain with Multiple Exchange Server Sites

Generally, small to medium-size organizations with up to an average of 20,000 users and/or multiple local and remote office locations could find this connection model appropriate for their business purposes.

Figure 20.8 represents an example of how you can set up two-way connection agreements between a single Windows 2000 Server domain and multiple, selected Exchange Server sites.

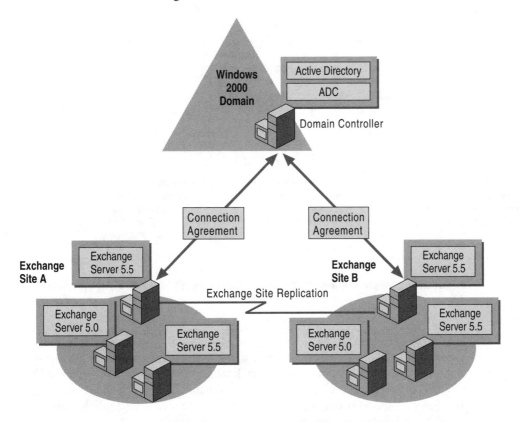

Figure 20.8   Single Windows 2000 Server Domain with Multiple Exchange Server Sites

If ADC Connection Model 2 best matches the environment of your own organization, use the flow chart in Figure 20.9 to help you design an ADC Connection Agreement Plan for your organization.

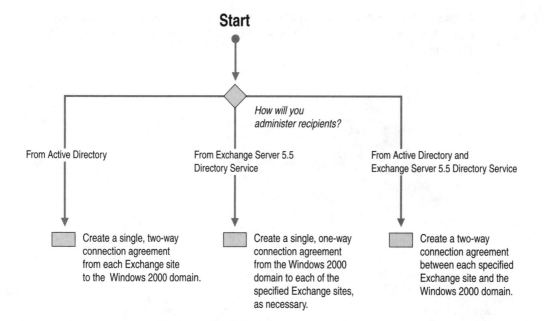

Figure 20.9   Single Windows 2000 Server Domain with Multiple Exchange Server Sites

Note With regard to the ADC Connection Models that have multiple domains and/or sites, it is not necessary to create a connection agreement between every Windows 2000 Server domain and every Exchange Server site. You only need to create a connection agreement between an Exchange Server site and Windows 2000 Server domain if there are Exchange mailboxes with the primary Windows NT Server account located in that domain.

ADC Connection Model 3: Multiple Windows 2000 Server Domains with a Single Exchange Server Site

You could use this connection model for an ADC plan for a medium to large size organization or for a single division of a large, decentralized organization.

Figure 20.10 represents an example of how you can set up two-way connection agreements between multiple Windows 2000 Server domains and a single Exchange Server site.

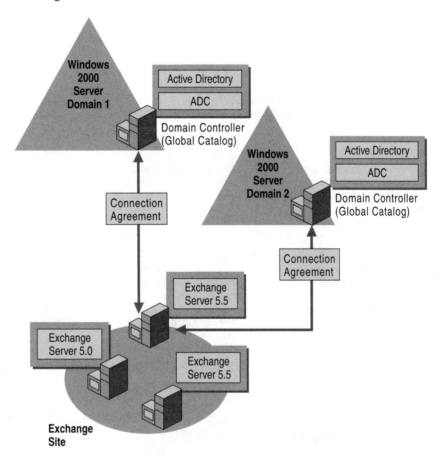

Figure 20.10   Multiple Windows 2000 Server Domains with a Single Exchange Server Site

If ADC Connection Model 3 best matches the environment of your organization, use the flow chart in Figure 20.11 to help you design an ADC Connection Agreement Plan for your organization. This flow chart helps you determine how you will administer recipients in an environment with multiple Windows 2000 Server domains and a single Exchange Server site.

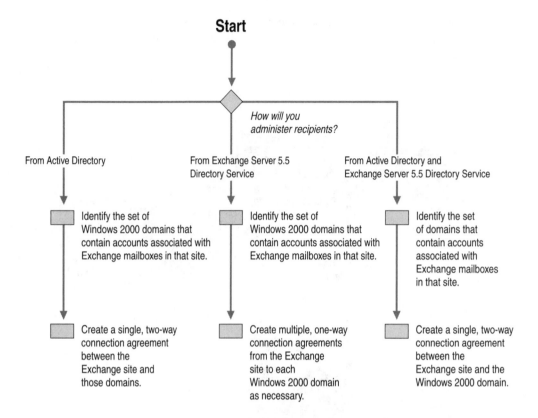

Start

How will you
administer recipients?

From Active Directory

Identify the set of
Windows 2000 domains that
contain accounts associated with
Exchange mailboxes in that site.

Create a single, two-way
connection agreement
between the
Exchange site and
those domains.

From Exchange Server 5.5
Directory Service

Identify the set of
Windows 2000 domains that
contain accounts associated with
Exchange mailboxes in that site.

Create multiple, one-way
connection agreements
from the Exchange
site to each
Windows 2000 domain
as necessary.

From Active Directory and
Exchange Server 5.5 Directory Service

Identify the set
of domains that
contain accounts
associated with
Exchange mailboxes
in that site.

Create a single, two-way
connection agreement
between the
Exchange site and the
Windows 2000 domain.

Figure 20.11   Multiple Windows 2000 Server Domains and a Single Exchange Server Site

ADC Connection Model 4: Multiple Windows 2000 Server Domains with Multiple Exchange Server Sites

If you have an environment with multiple domains and multiple Exchange Server sites, your connection agreement design could get complex. You need to be very clear about the purpose of each connection agreement that you plan to create.

Figure 20.12 represents an example of how you can set up two-way connection agreements between multiple Windows 2000 Server domains and multiple Exchange Server sites.

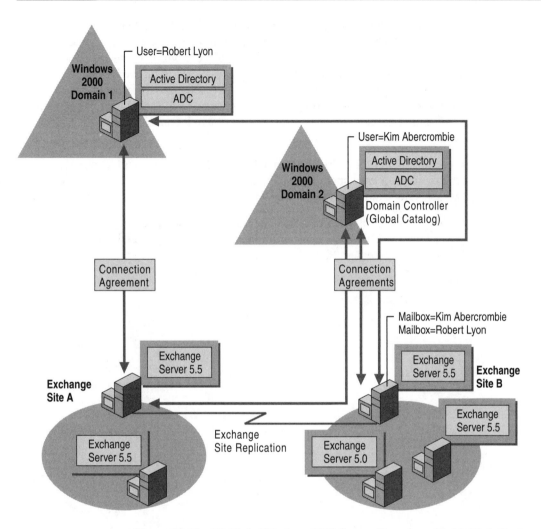

**Figure 20.12   Multiple Windows 2000 Server Domains with Multiple Exchange
Server Sites**

With a set of Windows 2000 Server domains and Exchange Server sites connected by the ADC, the ADC may have multiple connection agreements over which it could synchronize a particular object. To arbitrate between connection agreements, the ADC uses a set of matching rules based on the Primary Windows NT Server Account of a mailbox in Exchange Server and the corresponding account in Active Directory. If the ADC is able to match a mailbox to a Windows 2000 Server account in any domain it connects to, it will proceed to synchronize the two objects.

For example, in Figure 20.12 the mailboxes of Robert Lyon and Kim Abercrombie in Exchange Server Site B synchronize to user objects that reside in two separate Windows 2000 Server domains.

If ADC Connection Model 4 best matches the environment of your own organization, use the flow chart in Figure 20.13 to help you design an ADC Connection Agreement Plan for your organization.

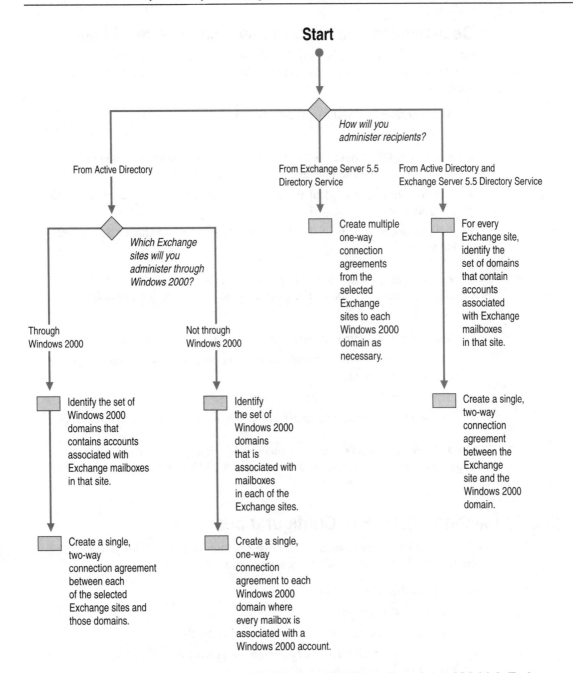

Figure 20.13   Multiple Windows 2000 Server Domains and Multiple Exchange Server Sites

Documenting Your ADC Connection Agreement Plan

At this point in the process, you should meet with the core directory synchronization advisory team and the deployment team to create a profile that includes:

- Administrator and end user requirements.

- An assessment of risks.

- A report of the current state of the Windows NT Server or Windows 2000 Server domain and Exchange Server site environment.

- Considerations for an ideal Windows 2000 Server and Exchange Server site environment.

- Settlement on a practical Windows 2000 Server and Exchange Server site environment.

To do this, gather all the information you need to create your own ADC Connection Agreement Plan. The plan documents completion of the following tasks:

- Select one of the site connection models in the previous section.

- Identify ADC network infrastructure requirements and know how to prepare for ADC implementation.

- Identify which directory service you will use to manage objects.

- Define which objects of interest you will synchronize between directories.

Use your Windows 2000 Server domain and Exchange Server site topology diagrams to help you create your first pass at an ADC Connection Agreement Plan.

Testing Connection Agreement Configurations

The Active Directory Connector has distinct roles in test and production environments. Use the ADC in a test environment to:

- Evaluate the ADC.
- Identify performance characteristics of the ADC.
- Validate your placement of connection agreements.
- Validate your Active Directory design with directory information from your production Exchange Server directory.

It is recommended that you create a test plan. Consider the following guidelines when planning to test your connection agreement configurations:

- Set up a test lab that mirrors your Exchange Server site and Windows NT Server or Windows 2000 Server domain structure.

- If you will be performing in-place upgrades of your Windows NT 4.0 Server master account domains, make sure to build the Windows 2000 Server domain controllers in your test lab by taking production Windows NT 4.0 Server Backup Domain Controllers (BDCs) offline, moving them to the test lab, then upgrading them Windows 2000 Server domain controllers to effectively test the ADC.

- Leverage the test lab environment to understand how the ADC will populate your production domain controllers with Exchange Server data. Determine when the ADC will match existing Windows 2000 Server objects in this case, as opposed to creating new Windows 2000 Server objects. Adjust the matching rules as necessary to ensure correct population of Active Directory.

- For multiple domain and multiple site environments, test and validate the ADC Connection Agreement Plan you create and the use of the ADC bridgehead options to ensure correct population of Active Directory.

- If you will be deploying a parallel Windows 2000 Server domain for use with Exchange Server, test the ADC in creating new users in the parallel domain overall capacity planning for Windows 2000 Server.

For more information about creating test plans, see "Building a Windows 2000 Test Lab" in this book.

Determining a Schedule for Directory Synchronization

You can set up individual connection agreements to perform synchronization at specific times of the day or night. Each connection agreement has its own associated schedule. As an administrator, you will determine the most appropriate time for each synchronization operation. A network with a large number of users may require synchronization more frequently than a smaller network. Also, some networks may require specific objects to be synchronized more frequently than other objects.

Some considerations for creating a directory synchronization schedule are as follows:

- Determine if you will be synchronizing more than 100,000 users or mailboxes. If so, you can improve performance by setting up multiple connection agreements to synchronize different objects at different times.

- If you make daily changes to either directory and do not need the changes to appear in the other directory until the next day, you should schedule synchronization nightly.

- Understand the internal replication schedules for both Active Directory and the Exchange Server directory. In order to ensure timely and efficient use of resources, schedule ADC synchronization in a manner that is staggered with respect to internal directory replication.

- If directory manipulation is commonly done at a specific time or times of the week, customize the synchronization process to occur soon after the changes are made, and only after the changes are made.

Figure 20.14 represents an example of a production and directory synchronization schedule.

Hour	Sun	Mon	Tues	Weds	Thurs	Fri	Sat
0-1							
1-2							
2-3							
3-4							
4-5							
5-6							
6-7							
7-8							
8-9							
9-10							
10-11							
11-12							
12-13							
13-14							
14-15							
15-16							
16-17							
17-18							
18-19							
19-20							
20-21							
21-22							
22-23							
23-24							

Peak production hours

Off-peak production hours

Daily directory synchronization

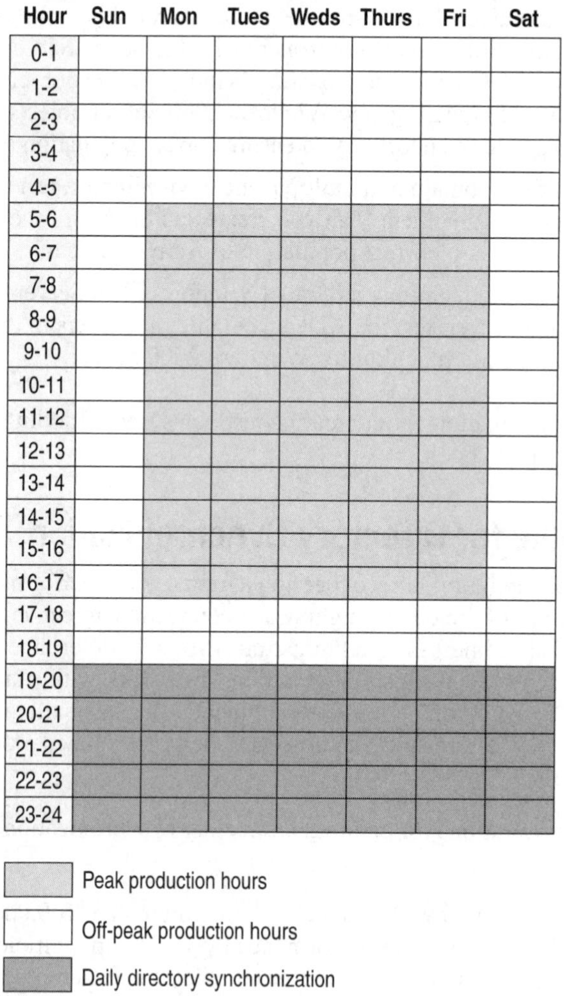

Figure 20.14 A Production and Directory Synchronization Schedule

When you create your ADC Connection Agreement Plan, you create a directory synchronization schedule similar to the one in Figure 20.14. The ADC Connection Agreement Planning Worksheet, located in Appendix A, includes a template that you can use to create your own synchronization schedule.

Protecting Against Accidental Loss of Data

Before you establish the first connection agreement, it is important that you develop a plan for backing out of the directory synchronization operation and for backup and recovery of data. Work with the network administrators in your organization to create the backup and recovery plan for directory synchronization, which will become a part of the master backup and recovery plan.

This section describes how to back out of a synchronization operation, whether data originates from Exchange Server 5.5 directory service or Active Directory. Additionally, you will find some suggestions on when to back up the directories, and the tools that will help you perform the backup.

Circumstances could occur where you will need to stop the directory synchronization operation in mid-session and cancel all changes made by the ADC. In all cases, you should delete the connection agreement or disable it before you begin the recovery process. The method for recovering the Active Directory to the original state differs depending on how the ADC connection agreement is configured to synchronize the data.

In every instance, you should backup each domain controller that the ADC connects to (or is being written to) using the appropriate Windows 2000 Server backup tools. Of course, you should also back up the Exchange Server 5.5 directory or directories that the ADC is connected to. The backup tools you use must support authoritative restore in order for the documented recovery methods to work. An authoritative restore brings a domain or a container back to the state it was at the time of backup and overwrites all changes made since the backup.

For more information about authoritative restore see the chapter "Active Directory Backup and Restore" in the *Microsoft® Windows® 2000 Server Resource Kit Distributed Systems Guide*.

Two situations which might require you to back out of a synchronization in progress are as follows:

Example 1: Populating Active Directory with New Objects

The connection agreement is configured to populate new objects (Contacts and Distribution Groups) in the Active Directory. In this particular case, you would create a dedicated OU where you place only the objects created by the ADC. The recovery method would be to delete the OUs specified in the connection agreement. This removes all the objects created by the connection agreement in the OU. If any other Active Directory objects were placed in this OU (such as Users or Printers) they are also deleted when the OU is deleted. The Users and Printers objects have to be moved before deleting the OU to prevent loss of data.

Example 2: Populating Attributes (Fields) of Existing Objects

The ADC is configured to populate the fields of existing objects with information stored in the Exchange Server directory. You can spread the objects across different containers on the domain controller. Canceling the changes made by the ADC requires an authoritative restore in this situation. This cancels the changes made by the ADC but it may cause loss of data. Additionally, all other changes since the last backup in the selected domain or container are also lost.

You could run an authoritative restore against individual containers. First you would determine which containers have been affected and then perform an authoritative restore against these containers.

For more information about disaster recovery, see the chapter "Determining Windows 2000 Storage Management Strategies" in this book, or see the chapters "Backup" and "Repair, Recovery, and Restore" in the *Microsoft® Windows® 2000® Server Resource Kit Server Operations Guide*.

Planning Task List for Directory Synchronization

The Directory Synchronization Planning Task List in Table 20.8 is a convenient chapter reference list that helps you locate important tasks to enable you to create a Connection Agreement Plan for your organization.

Table 20.8   Planning Task List for Directory Synchronization

Task	Location in Chapter
Create the ADC Connection Agreement Plan.	Creating the ADC Connection Agreement Plan
Form the planning and deployment teams.	Creating the ADC Connection Agreement Plan
Examine your domain structure and Exchange Server site topology.	Creating the ADC Connection Agreement Plan
Prepare your network for ADC deployment.	Creating the ADC Connection Agreement Plan
Consider specific network requirements.	Creating the ADC Connection Agreement Plan
Determine which directory service you will manage objects from.	Creating the ADC Connection Agreement Plan
Administer objects from Active Directory.	Creating the ADC Connection Agreement Plan
Administer objects from Exchange Server 5.5 Directory Service.	Creating the ADC Connection Agreement Plan
Define objects for directory synchronization.	Creating the ADC Connection Agreement Plan
Map Exchange Server containers with Windows 2000 Server OUs.	Creating the ADC Connection Agreement Plan
Set up connection agreements.	Creating the ADC Connection Agreement Plan
Design connection agreements.	Creating the ADC Connection Agreement Plan
Document your ADC Connection Agreement Plan.	Creating the ADC Connection Agreement Plan
Test connection agreement configurations.	Creating the ADC Connection Agreement Plan
Determine a schedule for directory synchronization.	Creating the ADC Connection Agreement Plan
Back out of a synchronization in progress.	Ensuring Against Loss of Data

Additional Resources

- For more information about Exchange Server 5.5, see the *Microsoft® Exchange Server 5.5 Resource Guide* which is part of the *Microsoft® BackOffice® Resource Kit, Second Edition*.

- For more information about any topic in this chapter, see the Microsoft TechNet link on the Web Resources page at http://windows.microsoft.com/windows2000/reskit/webresources.

PART 6

Windows 2000 Professional/Client Deployment

When and how you install client computers is a primary consideration in your Microsoft® Windows® 2000 deployment. Part 6 provides you with planning information for automating client installation and for deploying change and configuration management technologies.

In This Part

C H A P T E R   2 1

Testing Applications for Compatibility with Windows 2000

When you are planning to deploy a new operating system, the magnitude of the effort can make it tempting to defer thinking about the applications that run on it. Critical steps in your deployment project, however, are to identify applications that could cause problems during deployment and resolve the issues before deployment begins.

To ensure that potential application problems are resolved before deployment, your applications testing manager should begin early to develop a plan for testing your Windows-based applications. This chapter leads you through the process of testing your applications for compatibility with Microsoft® Windows® 2000.

In This Chapter

Chapter Goals

This chapter will help you develop the following planning documents:

- Prioritized list of business applications
- Plan for testing application compatibility
- Test tracking and reporting system

Related Information in the Resource Kit

- For more information about creating test plans, see the chapter "Building a Windows 2000 Test Lab" in this book.
- For more information about defining application standards, see the chapter "Defining Client Administration and Configuration Standards" in this book.

Application Testing Overview

Due to fundamental new technologies in Windows 2000, you need to test your business applications for compatibility with the operating system as part of your Windows 2000 deployment project. Even if you currently use Windows NT, you should not assume that all your applications will work the same way with Windows 2000. Enhancements, such as improved security, mean that you must retest the applications that were developed for previous versions of Windows. These applications might not take full advantage of the new features available in Windows 2000. They should, however, still perform as well on Windows 2000 as they do on the current platform.

Business Application Definition

In this chapter, business application refers to any application that is important to running your business. Business applications can range from large line-of-business systems to specialized tools. Consider all the applications that run on either client computers or servers, including commercial off-the-shelf products, customized third-party systems, and internally developed systems.

Note Although this chapter frequently refers to client-based applications, the methods and issues covered apply to both server-based and client-based applications.

If your organization is like many others, you might find more applications than you have time to test. In this case, you need to prioritize them and then test the ones that are critical to your core business operations. For more information about how to prioritize applications, see "Identifying and Prioritizing Business Applications" later in this chapter.

Application Testing Process

Figure 21.1 illustrates the steps involved in the application testing process. First, you need to identify your Windows-based applications and prioritize them by how important they are to your business. As the inventory effort proceeds, you can start planning how you want to coordinate the testing. Then, as testing progresses, you need to report your status periodically to management and resolve compatibility problems as they arise. This chapter covers these steps in more detail.

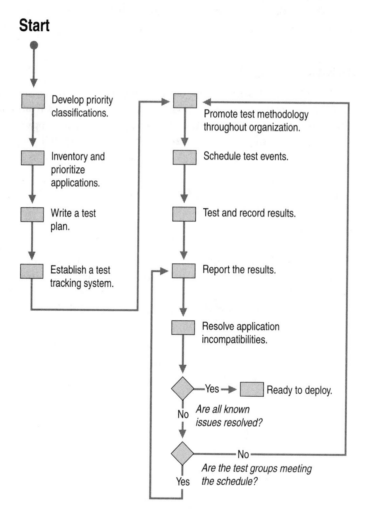

Figure 21.1   Steps for Testing Applications

Managing Application Testing

Because of the magnitude of the application testing endeavor, it is recommended that you select a manager to develop a plan and methodology for testing and to monitor testing progress. If your organization is multinational or highly decentralized, you might want test managers in more than one location, particularly if different suites of applications are used at different locations. Using such an approach, the test managers can focus on location-specific needs, such as different network clients or performance requirements.

Early in your Windows 2000 project, lay the groundwork for application testing so that you have time to resolve any problems that arise. The test manager coordinates the application testing project, taking responsibility for tasks such as:

- Developing a system for prioritizing applications.
- Coordinating the inventory and prioritization process.
- Developing a methodology for testing.
- Determining resource requirements for testing, including hardware, software, and personnel.
- Creating a schedule for testing.
- Writing the test plan.
- Designing or purchasing a test tracking and reporting system.
- Promoting the importance of and strategy for application testing; gaining cooperation from application experts.
- Monitoring the progress of testing, and reporting on it to management, internal application development groups, and external vendors.
- Following up with groups that are not meeting their testing commitments.

Identifying and Prioritizing Business Applications

The first task in preparing for testing is to gather information about the applications you have installed on your computers (both client and server). The information you gather, such as whether the application is in active use and by how many users, will help you decide how critical it is to your business.

As you identify applications, begin to prioritize them. You need to consider each application, no matter how insignificant it seems. Any application that does not function properly can have a big impact if people depend on it to get their jobs done.

Identifying Your Applications

If you do not already have an inventory of the applications installed on your server and client computers, you need to create one. Remember to include operational and administrative tools, including antivirus, compression, backup, and remote-control programs.

Gathering Application Information

If your organization is large or decentralized, compiling the list of applications can be time-consuming. If you use Microsoft® Systems Management Server or another software inventory tool to manage your networked computers, you can use the software inventory process to gather the information and then run a query to categorize and report it. For more information about using Systems Management Server to inventory your software, see the chapter "Using Systems Management Server to Analyze Your Network Infrastructure" in this book.

If you do not have an automated way to find what applications are installed on your computers, you need to develop a process to glean the information. For example, you can develop a questionnaire or a Web-based form that managers can fill out for their business units. If you depend on a manual process, you should get the support of upper management to help you obtain prompt responses.

As you compile the list of applications, identify which ones are required for each business unit. The following list includes some examples of information you might need about each application:

- Application name and version
- Vendor name
- Current status (for example, in production, under development, no longer used)
- Number of users and their business units
- Priority or importance to your organization
- Current platforms where the application is used

  Include whether the application is client-based or server-based and which components reside on the client and on the server.
- Web site addresses (URLs) for Web applications
- Requirements for installation (for example, security settings and installation directories)
- Development utility or technology (if developed internally)
- Contact names and phone numbers (internal and vendors)

  If you find multiple contacts for the same vendor, try to consolidate them where possible.

Compile the application information in a central repository where you can easily access and update it as you gather additional information and prioritize the applications. When you begin testing the applications, you can also use this repository for entering test results and reporting status. For more information about tracking and reporting test results, see "Tracking Test Results" later in this chapter.

Simplifying Your Application Environment

The inventory process is a good time to gather additional information that can help you make your application environment more manageable and cost effective. The more you simplify this environment, the easier it will be to test for application compatibility, the smoother it will be to move to Windows 2000, and the easier the resulting environment will be to manage.

The information described in this section can facilitate your testing, as well as reduce future support costs.

Troubleshooting Information

Detailed information about applications can help testers diagnose problems during Windows 2000 testing and reduce troubleshooting time for your Help desk:

- Files installed on the hard drive by the application
- Date stamp of each file
- Size, in bytes, of each file
- Location where files are installed
- Registry settings

You might consider gathering this information when you install the applications in the test lab rather than when you inventory your applications. When you install applications in a controlled environment like the lab, you are more likely to obtain complete lists without the extraneous, user-specific files that accumulate as an application is used.

Redundant Applications

If your organization uses many similar applications, the inventory process might be a good time to evaluate them for redundancy and to standardize on the most widely used ones. For example, you might find that your organization uses a variety of word processing applications or versions. Standardizing on a single application and version can dramatically simplify your Windows 2000 testing and reduce your client support costs. Although a different team might evaluate and establish the application standards, the testing team should work closely with that team to focus testing on the appropriate applications. For more information about standardizing client configurations, see the chapter "Defining Client Administration and Configuration Standards" in this book.

Unauthorized Applications

As you compile the list of applications, you might find unauthorized applications that users downloaded from the Internet or brought from home. Use the inventory process to eliminate applications such as these, as well as to verify that you have licenses for all the software in use.

Site-Licensed Applications

The inventory process is a good time to identify your site-licensed applications, such as compression and antivirus programs, and to develop a strategy for managing them. If you plan to implement IntelliMirror™, use it to advertise these applications. When you use IntelliMirror to advertise applications, you can easily set up redundant servers, thus maximizing users' access to the applications. For more information about using IntelliMirror for client support, see the chapter "Applying Change and Configuration Management" in this book.

If you do not plan to implement IntelliMirror, you might want to establish shared drives for your site-licensed applications. Assign the server a name that is easy to remember—for example, \\licensed_products.

Prioritizing Your Applications

Even before you compile the list of applications, you can start devising a way to classify and prioritize them. If you have the scheme developed by the time you perform the inventory, you can classify applications as you find them. You need a prioritization scheme for two reasons:

- You might not have time to adequately test all applications by the rollout date.
- You need to know which applications are showstoppers—that is, which ones must function properly for deployment to proceed.

The ultimate goal of your prioritization effort is to identify the core group of applications that must function properly before you begin to deploy Windows 2000. When you develop your prioritization scheme, consider the following issues:

- Importance of the application to the organization
- Number of users affected
- Availability of newer versions
- Localization needs

Your organization might already have a classification scheme that you can use or modify. For example, you might have prioritized your applications for your disaster recovery plan. If you identified which applications must be back online first during a disaster, these applications might have top priority for compatibility testing.

The complexity of your prioritization scheme depends on factors such as how many applications you have and the variety of business functions they support.

One large high-technology company developed four priority levels. They defined their priorities as follows:

Mission critical   These applications must be online first after a disaster. They are required to collect revenue or fulfill a legal obligation. The organization is willing to accept no risk or very little risk of failure for these applications, and the impact or cost of failure would be very high.

Business critical   These applications must be online second after a disaster. They are required to run the business infrastructure. Human resource applications are an example of business-critical applications. The organization is willing to accept little risk of failure, and the impact or cost of failure would be moderate.

Required   These applications are required to run the business but can be offline for a longer period of time. The organization is willing to accept moderate risk of failure, and the impact or cost of failure would be low.

Other   These applications do not fit in any of the preceding categories, and business can continue without them.

Another large high-technology organization had just two categories: mission critical and not mission critical. In case there was insufficient time to test all applications, this organization wanted to ensure that the mission-critical applications were fully tested and any problems resolved before they began their deployment.

Preparing an Application Test Plan

One of the primary tasks in preparing for testing is to write a test plan. In the test plan, you specify the scope and objectives for the testing and describe the methodology to be used. Include the following information in your plan:

- Scope

  The priority levels you address during testing.
- Methodology

  Who does the testing and how you involve participants.
- Requirements

  What hardware, software, personnel, training, and tools you need to perform the testing.

- Criteria for pass-fail

  The factors that determine whether an application passes or fails.

- Schedule

  How you plan to complete the testing by the scheduled rollout.

Depending on the number of applications and your test approach, application testing might require considerable cooperation from various business units in your organization. Identify the application stakeholders early in the project and ask them to review and approve your test plan or to commit their resources to an agreed-upon level.

For more information about writing a test plan, see the chapter "Building a Windows 2000 Test Lab" in this book.

Establishing Testing Scope

If your organization uses many applications, you might not have time to test all of them as thoroughly as you would like. Test the highest priority and the most frequently or widely used applications first, but do not limit your testing to only these.

Test both server-based and client-based applications. Client-based applications are usually the most difficult and time-consuming to test because of sheer numbers.

If the commercial applications you use have already been tested by an external organization, you still need to test them in your environment. Tests that determine compatibility with underlying Windows 2000 technologies do not necessarily prove that applications will function in your environment as you use them. For more information about commercial applications that have been tested externally, see "Testing Applications" later in this chapter.

Defining the Testing Methodology

A major part of your test plan is describing the strategy for testing. When planning your methodology, consider:

- Where will the testing take place?
- Who will perform the tests?
- How will you communicate with and involve participants?
- How will you schedule the testing?
- How will you manage application problems?

Outsourcing is one option for application testing. To determine if you will use this option, consider the following:

- Do you have staff available for testing?

- Does your staff have the appropriate level of expertise?

- What are the internal costs compared to the outsourcing costs?

- What is your time frame? Can the testing get done faster if you outsource it?

- What are your security requirements? Would you need to provide confidential data to an external organization?

When you test internally, select experienced testers. If your organization has a group of application testers, it is recommended that you use them. If you do not have such a group or they are unavailable, look for ways to use a variety of resources to achieve the best results in a reasonable amount of time. For example, you can use a few experienced testers to develop a battery of test cases, which they can train others to run. Alternatively, you might have the experienced testers perform a core set of tests and then coordinate with business units to have their experts come to the lab to perform the functions they use in their work.

Devise a process for scheduling test days and communicating with the testers. For example, you might set up a Web site on your intranet where anyone can view test dates, status reports, contact names, and other relevant documents.

Establish a procedure for managing test results. Describe roles and responsibilities, including the following:

- Who enters problem reports in the incident tracking system?

- How are problems prioritized, assigned, and resolved?

- Who tracks the resolution of problems and retesting of applications?

- How do testers enter test results in the test tracking and reporting system?

Case Study 1: Testing Festivals

A large high-technology organization asked its developers to test applications for compatibility with Windows 2000. The test manager worked with other managers to get cooperation from their teams. Because the test manager reported to the CIO and had total support for the program, it was easier for her to get active participation. She scheduled testing sessions in the lab and sent notifications about the sessions to the developers. The lab was set up with preconfigured computers, ready for the testers to install their applications. Testers could install their applications from CDs or from the network. To make the events fun, the test manager provided food and beverages, thus earning the name "test fests" for the sessions.

Case Study 2: Preview Program

A major manufacturing company developed a preview program for testing Windows 2000 Professional. They used this program to test client-based applications. This organization first verified that the protocol stack to be used on the Windows 2000 client computers was compatible with its Windows NT 4.0 production environment. Then it deployed Windows 2000 Professional at restricted locations on the production network to create a place for testing applications.

The project team set up a Web site with information about the program. Users filled out an application form on the Web site to apply for participation in the preview program. To limit the number of participants and to ensure thorough testing, the project leader and the employee's manager reviewed and approved applications. The program, which was restricted to 50–100 participants, provided a wide range of testers for testing applications. Testers posted their problem reports at the Web site.

Identifying Resource Requirements

As you plan for application compatibility testing, keep in mind the future state of your computing environment. Are you planning to upgrade some of your software to versions that fully use new Windows 2000 features? Are you planning to implement new standard desktop configurations or use Terminal Services? Issues such as these determine the resources that are required and the applications that are to be tested as a suite.

If you plan to deploy new applications with Windows 2000 during the rollout, test these applications with the current applications.

You can facilitate testing by setting up a lab where testers can conduct their tests. In such a lab, you can have the necessary tools and equipment available at all times. Some organizations have a lab for testing applications that is separate from the Windows 2000 lab. If you do not have the budget for a separate lab, you might share a lab with another project or with training. If you share a lab, try to choose one that has compatible scheduling and equipment requirements.

In the lab, set up the test computers for dual or triple startup so that testers can quickly access the mode they need to install and test their applications. For example, if you follow the strategy suggested in "Testing Applications" later in this chapter, you might need Windows NT 4.0 and Windows 2000 to test the applications through the upgrade path. To make it easy for testers to restore the computers to their prior state, make disk images of the drives with the base operating systems.

Consider whether you need to connect the lab to the corporate network. For example, you might need access to network shares for installing applications from the network or to your corporate intranet if you develop a Web-based test tracking system. If you need such access, first verify that the protocol stacks used on the client computers are compatible with your production network.

If your test lab is large, you might decide to assign a lab manager. Because the skills required to run a lab and to manage testing are so different, consider selecting different people for the two roles. While the lab manager needs to have strong technical skills, the testing manager needs to have strong managerial and communication skills.

For more information about designing and managing a test lab or about writing test plans, see the chapter "Building a Windows 2000 Test Lab" in this book.

Defining Pass-Fail Criteria

As testers conduct a variety of tests, some applications will pass and some will fail. You should have a procedure defined so that participants know when and where they can log application problems and issues to be resolved.

When testers have completed the tests for a specific application, they need to enter the results in your test tracking and reporting system. You need, of course, to prioritize and track all outstanding problems and then retest applications when the problems are resolved. To track testing progress, however, you might want to know which applications are ready and which are not. If you plan to track your progress by whether applications passed or failed, you need to define the criteria for each category you use. To define the criteria for pass and fail, consider issues such as the following:

- How significant is the problem? Does it affect a critical function or a peripheral one?
- How likely is someone to encounter the problem?
- Is there a way to circumvent the problem?

Creating a Testing Schedule

Your testing schedule depends on many conditions, including:

- How many testers participate.
- Whether the testers are on this project full-time or need to be scheduled.

- The testers' experience levels.
- The number and complexity of the applications.

Include enough time in your schedule for resolving problems and for retesting the applications that fail. Establish major and interim milestones so that you can monitor progress and ascertain that you are on schedule.

Testing Applications

Microsoft, in cooperation with customers and independent software vendors (ISVs), has developed the Windows 2000 Application Specification. Applications written to comply with this specification are not only compatible with Windows 2000, but they also take advantage of the new technologies it provides.

The Windows 2000 Application Specification, which you can download from the Microsoft Developer Network (MSDN) Web site, has two components: one for desktop applications and one for distributed applications. The desktop application specification applies to applications that run on Windows 2000 Professional, either as a stand-alone program or as the client portion of a distributed application. The distributed application specification applies to applications that run on Windows 2000 Server. For more information about the specification and to download a copy, see the Windows 2000 Application Specification link on the Web Resources page at http://windows.microsoft.com/windows2000/reskit/webresources.

Commercial applications that comply with the Windows 2000 Application Specification can also be certified. Certified applications have been tested by an independent testing organization and meet certain requirements. To receive certification, for example, an application must use the Windows Installer. Commercial applications can comply with the specification without being certified. In this case, the applications are tested by the vendor rather than by the independent testing organization.

Some organizations, as part of their Windows 2000 deployment project, have made compliance with the specification a selection criterion when purchasing applications. If you develop applications internally, consider adding the specification to your guidelines for application development.

In the meantime, many commercial applications have already been tested to determine how well they support Windows 2000. Microsoft provides a directory of Windows 2000 applications where you can look up the status of the applications you use. For more information about which client-based or server-based products support Windows 2000, see the Directory of Windows 2000 Applications link on the Web Resources page at http://windows.microsoft.com/windows2000/reskit/webresources.

The directory uses the following designations:

Certified Indicates that the application was tested by an independent testing organization and that it takes advantage of new Windows 2000 features.

Ready Indicates that, according to the vendor, the application was tested for compatibility with and will be supported in Windows 2000. The application does not necessarily take advantage of new Windows 2000 features.

Planned Indicates that the intent is for the application to meet either the Certified or the Ready criterion when it is fully tested.

Developing Testing Strategies

The goal of your application testing is to verify that everything that works on your current platform also works on Windows 2000. If an application was written for a previous version of Windows, it will not necessarily use new Windows 2000 features to the best advantage, but its functionality should work as well on Windows 2000 as it does on your current platform.

Strategies for Commercial Applications

For commercial applications, the first step is to run Windows 2000 Professional Setup in Check Upgrade Only mode to check for potential incompatibilities. When you run Setup in this mode, it checks the installed software against a list of applications known to be incompatible and logs any that it finds. The command-line syntax for Check Upgrade Only mode is:

winnt32 /checkupgradeonly

Although this utility can alert you to potential compatibility problems, it addresses only a small percentage of your applications and only the applications installed on the computer you are checking. Even if an application is not on the list of incompatible applications, it does not mean that it is compatible. For more information about the Setup program, see the chapter "Automating Client Installation and Upgrade" in this book.

The next step is to check the directory of Windows 2000 applications to determine the compatibility of the applications you use.

Even if you find that some of your applications have already been tested by others, you should test them in your environment. In this case, focus your testing on the way your organization uses the applications. For example, test:

- Configurations your organization uses.
- Features most frequently used.
- Combinations of applications used together.

The section "Testing Tips" later in this chapter provides examples of ways to test application functionality. If the commercial applications you use have not been tested for compatibility by other organizations, you should test more extensively than otherwise.

Remember to test your antivirus software. Many of these applications need to be upgraded because of their use of file system filters. Many Windows NT 4.0 file system filters might not work on Windows 2000 due to changes in the NTFS file system.

Strategies for Custom Applications

If you use custom third-party products or develop applications internally, you need to develop a more extensive testing strategy than for pretested commercial applications.

Even if you are testing an application you did not develop, the Windows 2000 Application Specification can provide insight into testing. The MSDN Web site includes a downloadable version of the specification, as well as a test plan detailing all the Microsoft tests for Windows 2000 application certification. This test plan can provide you with ideas about functional areas and ways you should test. For more information about how to download the specification or test plan, see the Application Specification Download link on the Web Resources page at http://windows.microsoft.com/windows2000/reskit/webresources.

The MSDN Web site also contains other important information about testing, such as white papers about exploratory testing and the method that independent testing organizations use to test the functionality of applications that vendors submit for certification.

Testing Tips

The testing suggestions in this section are not comprehensive and do not apply to all situations. They are provided to help you start thinking about how to test.

Test Deployment Scenarios

You should test installing and running your applications using the scenarios you plan to use during deployment. For example, you might plan to deploy by installing on clean machines or by upgrading from Windows 3.*x* or a prior version of Windows NT. If you plan to upgrade, you might keep the applications on the computer during the upgrade, or you might uninstall them and reinstall them after the upgrade.

Consider repackaging applications for the Windows Installer or as .zap files so the application can be managed by IntelliMirror software installation and maintenance. For more information about packaging applications, see the chapter "Applying Change and Configuration Management" in this book.

Because of differences between Windows 3.*x* and Windows 2000, some application installations work differently depending on which operating system you use for the installation. For example, if you install an application on a computer running Windows 3.*x* and then upgrade the computer to Windows 2000, the application might not work the same way as it would have if it had been installed on Windows 2000. In this case, you might need to uninstall the application and reinstall it after the upgrade or obtain a migration dynamic link library (DLL).

A migration DLL allows an application that was originally installed on Windows 3.*x* to function correctly after the computer is upgraded to Windows 2000. Migration DLLs can resolve application problems by performing the following actions:

- Replacing or upgrading Windows 3.*x*–specific files with Windows 2000–compatible files.

- Moving application and user settings to the correct location for Windows 2000.

- Mapping Windows 3.*x*–specific registry keys to the appropriate Windows 2000 locations.

For applications developed internally, you might have to create migration DLLs or obtain them from your vendors. You can find more information about creating and testing migration DLLs by searching the MSDN Library using the keywords "migration DLL." For more information about the MSDN Library, see the MSDN link on the Web Resources page at http://windows.microsoft.com/windows2000/reskit/webresources. Some migration DLLs are also included with Windows 2000.

Because results can vary depending on how you upgrade, it is important to test using the same procedures and tools you plan to use during the rollout. If the procedures and tools are not ready when you are testing the applications, at least test the scenario you plan to use.

Upgrade Scenario

If you are planning to upgrade your computers, use the following steps:

- Install Windows 3.*x* or Windows NT 3.51 or later.

- Install the application.

- Upgrade to Windows 2000.

- Test the application.

If a Windows 3.*x* application does not function properly, contact the ISV for a migration DLL. If a Windows NT application does not function properly, contact the ISV for a patch or a new setup program.

Clean Installation Scenario

If you are planning to install Windows 2000 on reformatted computers, use these steps:

- Install Windows 2000.
- Install the application.
- Test the application.

If the application does not function properly, contact the ISV for a patch or a new setup program.

Test Installing and Uninstalling

Test the installation of the application in a variety of ways, such as the following:

- Terminate the installation before it is complete.
- Try all the installation options used in your environment.
- If your organization allows users to install applications, test the installation both as administrator and as power user; then test the application's functionality.
- Try to uninstall the application.
- Verify that an application can be installed by an administrator and uninstalled by a user. When a user is logged on as a user, the uninstall should be either complete or disallowed.

Test Basic Application Functionality

Test applications using the features, configurations, and application suites you use to accomplish business tasks. For example, you can try the following types of tests:

- Log on as a user and test the features most important to your end users. Test specific scenarios that are needed to accomplish business tasks.
- Log on as several users who are members of the Users group.
- Apply Group Policy to the system and to the applications.
- Test combinations of applications, such as standard desktop configurations.
- Run several applications on the desktop for several days or weeks without shutting them down.
- Test automated tasks that use Microsoft® Visual Basic® for Applications (VBA) in Microsoft® Office applications.
- Test to determine that long file names are consistently supported. Include embedded periods and verify that leading spaces are stripped.
- Manipulate large graphic files—for example, files over 1 MB.

- Perform extensive edits on word processing documents.
- Perform rapid development sequences of edit, compile, edit, compile.
- Test OLE custom controls (OCXs).
- Test with applicable hardware, such as scanners and Plug and Play devices.
- If you plan to deploy Terminal Services, test the applications on a Terminal Services server. Test with multiple users running the same and different applications and with user-specific settings.

To download a sample test plan, see the Application Specification Download link on the Web Resources page at http://windows.microsoft.com/windows2000/reskit/webresources.

Access Data

Try to access data in a variety of ways, such as the following:

- Access data on a server running the current version of Windows, as well as on a server running Windows 2000.
- Test concurrent use of a database, including simultaneous access and update of a record.
- Perform complex queries.

Test Printing

Print a variety of document types with a variety of printers, such as the following:

- Print documents with embedded files from several source applications.
- Print to printers with long file names.

Use Testing Tools

The Windows 2000 Software Development Kit (SDK), Driver Development Kit (DDK), and *Microsoft® Windows® 2000 Server Resource Kit* contain tools for testing and debugging applications.

- Dependency Walker, in the *Windows 2000 Server Resource Kit*, recursively scans dependent modules that are required by an application. This utility detects files that are missing, files that are not valid, import or export mismatches, circular dependency errors, and modules installed on mismatched computers. For more information about this utility, see the Help file that accompanies it.

- Apimon, in the *Windows 2000 Server Resource Kit*, monitors a running application for all application programming interface (API) calls, counting and timing them. Optionally, it can also monitor page faults. Apimon can report the following:

  - A count of all API calls and timings for each.
  - A trace of API calls in the sequence in which they occur.

Common Compatibility Issues

New technologies and techniques in Windows 2000 can cause errors in applications developed for previous versions of Windows. The Windows 2000 Compatibility Guide, which you can find at the MSDN Web site, includes detailed descriptions of many changes that might cause application problems. The guide organizes compatibility issues into four areas:

- Setup and installation
- General Windows 2000 compatibility
- Application stability
- Windows platform

This section describes some of the changes in Windows 2000 that most commonly cause problems for applications. Applications developed for previous versions of Windows might not take full advantage of new features, such as Active Directory or IntelliMirror. This section does not address the issues that arise when applications do not make use of such new features.

You might encounter problems in the following areas:

System File Protection

Earlier versions of Windows allowed applications to replace shared system files during installation. When such changes occurred, users frequently encountered problems that ranged from program errors to an unstable operating system.

System File Protection (SFP) is a new feature in Windows 2000 that prevents applications from replacing system files. This feature verifies that protected system files are the correct Microsoft version. If a file is replaced with an incorrect version, Windows 2000 restores the correct version.

Robust Heap Checking

Windows 2000 includes several performance enhancements in the heap manager. Applications that did not use heap management correctly before might now have their memory management problems exposed. Common problems include using memory after it has been freed and assuming that a memory will not move when it is reallocated to a smaller size.

Enumeration of Hardware Devices

Changes in the list of supported hardware devices might cause problems for applications that use devices that are no longer supported.

Enumeration of Fonts

The list of fonts has changed. Because registry keys have been added to support internationalization, some applications might see multiple displays of fonts.

Changed Registry Keys

Some registry keys have been moved or deleted. Applications that use the Win32 application programming interface (API) to make registry changes should not experience problems, but they can have problems if they write directly to the registry.

Version Checking

Application installation programs that check versions incorrectly will have problems. You should check for the minimum operating system version your application requires and install on that or any later version, unless your application is dependent on a specific operating system or version.

Windows Messaging Service

Applications that expect Windows Messaging Service (WMS) to be provided by the operating system will not find it. You must obtain this service from the Windows Update Web site.

File Input/Output Security

Windows 2000 has tightened security for file input and output. Applications that use file filters, such as antivirus programs, might lose significant functionality with Windows 2000.

Tracking Test Results

Although you might have an existing incident tracking system where you enter application incompatibilities as you encounter them, you need a separate way to track the status of your application testing. You need to be able to find information such as which applications passed, which failed, and which are untested.

Devise a way to capture test results easily and accurately so you can produce reports as you need them. Consider the following two issues when planning your approach:

- Mechanism for capturing data
- Categories of data to be captured

Choosing a Tracking System

The mechanism you choose for capturing data depends on the size of your testing effort, your budget, and the available expertise. You might decide to purchase a test tracking and reporting system. Many vendors sell products for this purpose. For more information about vendors that sell these products, see the Test Tracking Systems link on the Web Resources page at http://windows.microsoft.com/windows2000/reskit/webresources. Alternatively, perform a search on the Web using keywords such as:

- "software testing tools"
- "test management tools"
- "automated testing tools"
- "testing tools"

Before making a decision, investigate the options and compare the cost of a ready-made solution to that of developing your own.

If you decide to develop your own system, it is recommended that you capture test results in a database rather than in a spreadsheet or word processing document. A database provides the greatest flexibility in reporting and is the easiest to manage as the volume of data grows. A Web front end provides easy access, both for entering data and for viewing status.

The advantages of an automated, online solution are that you can easily record results and create reports. The disadvantages are that it takes development time and expertise. Paper-based systems are not recommended because of major disadvantages, such as inaccessibility and the difficulty in producing timely, accurate reports.

The mechanism you decide to use—whether you develop or purchase it—should meet these criteria:

- Easy to enter data accurately.
- Easy to access by all who need to enter or view data.
- Easy to back up or duplicate for safekeeping.
- Easy to select and sort data for a variety of reports.
- Able to handle a large volume of data.
- Able to handle multiple, simultaneous users.
- Protects existing entries from changes.

The testers need a straightforward, easily remembered process for recording data as they complete their tests. You might want to have a link to the application or Web site on the test computers.

If you develop a Web site on your intranet to collect data, you can use the site as your test communications center. Include status reports, contact names, a calendar of testing events, links to related information, and other relevant documents.

To build the data collection mechanism, you need resources to develop the following:

- Web or some other application code for the data-entry application
- Database and schema
- Reports and queries
- Security, if required

Capturing Data

Once you have decided how to collect data, you need to decide what data to collect. You will find it worthwhile to spend time beforehand determining the data you need. You can design new reports as you need them if the data has been collected from the start.

You will have collected much of the information you need when you inventoried your applications. In addition, you are likely to need the following information for each application:

- Tester's name and business unit
- Developer's name and business unit (if developed internally)
- Windows 2000 product name (Server or Professional)
- Test results, such as:
  - Passed
  - Failed
  - In progress
  - Unknown
- Assigned number for each problem entered in the incident tracking system
- Comments
- Date and time stamp for each record

  The date/time stamp provides a useful filter for creating reports for a specific time range.

Reporting Results

The more carefully you analyze the data to be collected, the more flexibility you will have for reporting. The suggestions that follow are a sample of reports you might find useful:

- A list of applications that failed the compatibility tests.

  This report requires follow-up to resolve the problems and retest the applications.

- For each business unit, the total number of applications for each priority level.

- For each business unit, the total number of applications that are untested.

  Include the percentage of untested applications. You can use this report to track who is keeping up and who is not. Do not overlook the possibility of using this report as an incentive for groups that are behind in their testing.

If you report progress by whether applications passed or failed, consider whether you need to show relative progress or actual numbers. You can show relative progress with enhancements such as color schemes or graphics. This can provide your audience with a sense of your progress without presenting numbers that can be misleading. If you need to show progress with actual numbers, you might want to devise a way to weight or report the numbers based on the priority of the applications. For example, a report showing only that 10 applications passed and one failed might not present an accurate status. If the 10 applications were special utilities used by a few users intermittently, and the one failed application was a critical application required to run your day-to-day business, the report would not give a complete picture.

If you have testers post issues at a specific place, such as a Web site, you might want to provide a report of open and closed issues.

Create and distribute reports to management and testing participants after each testing event, and periodically as needed. If you have a Web site for your testing project, you might include the ability to run online reports.

Resolving Application Incompatibilities

When you encounter application compatibility problems, you need to prioritize them and then assign someone to resolve them. You should have a plan for how you will assign problems. For example, problems with commercial applications are handled differently from applications that you develop internally. Assigning the appropriate personnel to research and resolve problems is critical to the success of your application testing. Problem resolution might encompass a wide variety of activities, such as the following:

- Researching Web sites for known problems and solutions.

- Contacting vendors for patches, setup programs, or migration DLLs.
- Contacting Microsoft Product Support Services.
- Debugging internally developed applications.

As you research the cause of a problem, consider various approaches to determine the most effective solution. For example, you might choose to:

- Fix the problem if you developed the application.
- Ask the vendor to fix the problem if you purchased the application.
- Replace the application with a new version or application.
- Ignore the failure if you have a way to work around the problem.

Always be sure that a problem does not occur on your current platform before researching it as a Windows 2000 compatibility issue. Some of the resources for researching Windows 2000 compatibility issues are:

- Windows 2000 Application Specification

  For more information about how to download the specification, see the Application Specification Download link on the Web Resources page at http://windows.microsoft.com/windows2000/reskit/webresources.

- Windows 2000 Compatibility Guide

  This guide, available on MSDN and Technet, includes valuable information about diagnosing compatibility problems.

- Microsoft Technet

  This resource contains product updates, white papers, and other technical information. For more information about Technet, see the Technet link on the Web Resources page at http://windows.microsoft.com/windows2000/reskit/webresources.

- Directory of Windows 2000 Applications

  This includes support information and links to vendor Web sites. For more information about the directory, see the Directory of Windows 2000 Applications link on the Web Resources page at http://windows.microsoft.com/windows2000/reskit/webresources.

Planning Task List for Application Testing

Table 21.1 summarizes the tasks you need to perform when planning and testing for application compatibility with Windows 2000.

Table 21.1   Planning Task List for Application Testing

Task	Location in chapter
Inventory the applications used for business tasks.	Identifying and Prioritizing Business Applications
Consider reducing the number of applications you use and developing desktop standards.	Identifying and Prioritizing Business Applications
Develop a system for prioritizing applications.	Identifying and Prioritizing Business Applications
Prioritize the applications by how critical they are to running your business.	Identifying and Prioritizing Business Applications
Write a test plan, including test methodology, lab and test resource requirements, and schedule.	Preparing an Application Test Plan
Develop a test tracking system for capturing and reporting test results.	Tracking Test Results
Promote the testing methodology.	Preparing an Application Test Plan
Schedule test events.	Preparing an Application Test Plan
Test applications and record results.	Testing Applications
Report on testing progress.	Tracking Test Results
Resolve application incompatibilities.	Resolving Application Incompatibilities

Additional Resources

- For more information about testing and diagnosing application incompatibilities, see the Microsoft Knowledge Base link on the Web Resources page at http://windows.microsoft.com/windows2000/reskit/webresources.

- For more information about testing applications, see:

  - *Testing Computer Software* by Cem Kaner, Jack Falk and Hung Quoc Nguyen, 1993, New York, NY: Van Nostrand Reinhold

  - *Black-Box Testing: Techniques for Functional Testing of Software and Systems* by Boris Bizer, 1995, New York, NY: John Wiley & Sons

  - *Software Testing: A Craftsman's Approach* by Paul Jorgensen, 1995, Boca Raton, FL: CRC Press

  - *The Craft of Software Testing: Subsystem Testing Including Object -Based and Object-Oriented Testing* by Brian Marick, 1995, Englewood Cliffs, NJ: Prentice Hall

CHAPTER 22

Defining a Client Connectivity Strategy

The purpose of this chapter is to help you determine a strategy for connecting client computer configurations to a Microsoft® Windows® 2000 Server network in an enterprise environment. Those involved in the logical design of the enterprise network need to become familiar with the recommendations described in this chapter. These recommendations apply to both large and small organizations.

To get the most from reading this chapter, you need to have a basic knowledge of Windows-based clients and networks. You also need to be familiar with TCP/IP addressing methods, remote connectivity methods, and Routing and Remote Access service. Some knowledge of NetWare networks and protocols is also helpful.

In This Chapter

Chapter Goals

This chapter will help you develop the following planning document:

- A client connectivity strategy for client computer configurations.

Related Information in the Resource Kit

- For more information about Microsoft® Windows® 2000 TCP/IP, see the *Microsoft® Windows® 2000 Server Resource Kit TCP/IP Core Networking Guide*.

- For more information about Windows 2000 Routing and Remote Access, see the *Microsoft® Windows® 2000 Server Resource Kit Internetworking Guide*.

Client Connectivity Overview

Networks vary in size and type depending on their function. How clients connect to the network depends upon where they are located. Some examples include:

- Internal clients are physically located within the corporate infrastructure. Internal clients can use a variety of different network media, such as Asynchronous Transfer Mode (ATM), Ethernet, or Token Ring.

- External clients are remote from the corporate network infrastructure and require Routing and Remote Access or virtual private networking.

Clients need to be able to connect to a variety of resources. These resources include file and print servers, database servers such as Microsoft® SQL Server™, Microsoft® Exchange servers, and internal Web servers.

To ensure that clients can connect reliably and efficiently, you need to determine your Windows 2000 client connectivity strategy before you begin to implement your connectivity plans. Figure 22.1 outlines a basic procedure for determining a client connectivity strategy. You do not have to perform the tasks in the order listed. The flowchart provides you with a list of the tasks you need to perform and a suggestion for one order in which you could perform those tasks.

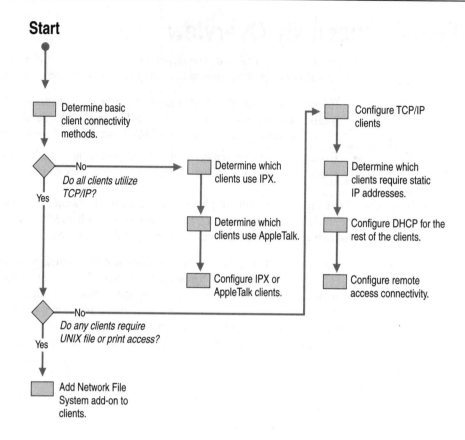

Figure 22.1   Process for Determining Client Connectivity Strategy

Basic Client Connectivity

When you connect computers running Microsoft® Windows® 2000 Professional to a local area network (LAN), the Windows 2000 operating system detects your network adapter and creates a local area connection for you. It appears, like all other connection types, in the Network and Dial-up Connections folder, which is accessed from Control Panel. By default, a local area connection is the only type of connection that is automatically activated. Dial-up connections are not activated by the system. They require a manual configuration using the Network Connection Wizard located in the Network and Dial-up Connections folder in Control Panel.

Examples of LAN connections include Ethernet, Token Ring, cable modems, digital subscriber line (DSL), Fiber Distributed Data Interface (FDDI), IP over ATM, Infrared Data Association (IrDA), wireless, and ATM-emulated LANs. Emulated LANs are based on virtual adapter drivers, such as the LAN Emulation Protocol.

If you make changes to your network, you can modify the settings of an existing local area connection to reflect those changes. These changes can be in the form of:

- Protocols such as static IP address changes.
- DNS or WINS configurations.
- Services.

With the **Status** dialog box, you can view connection information for a local area connection such as connection duration, speed, amount of data transmitted and received, and the diagnostic tools available for a particular connection. You can also add a status icon for the local area connection in the Windows taskbar.

If you install a new LAN device on your client, the next time you start Windows 2000, a new local area connection icon appears in the Network and Dial-up Connections folder. For laptops, you can add a Personal Computer Memory Card International Association (PCMCIA) slot, or PC Card network adapter while the computer is on, and the local area connection icon is immediately added to the folder without restarting the computer.

You can configure network components used by your local network connection with the **Properties** menu option. Network components are the clients, services, and protocols you use to communicate with servers on your network after you are connected to a server. The components you can configure and their functions are as follows:

- Services, such as file and printer sharing.
- Protocols, such as Transmission Control Protocol/Internet Protocol (TCP/IP).
- Clients, such as Gateway from Microsoft and Client Services for NetWare.

For more information about configuring local area connections properties, see the Windows 2000 Professional Help.

You can configure settings for multiple LAN adapters through the **Advanced Settings** menu option for the local area connection in the Network and Dial-up Connections folder. Using this option, you can modify the order of adapters that are used by a connection, and the adapter's associated clients, services, and protocols.

Windows 2000 Services and Protocols

TCP/IP is the standard network protocol used by Windows 2000. If a client needs to access file and print resources from NetWare or Macintosh servers, Microsoft supplies either the protocol necessary for connectivity on these networks or a compatible protocol for these environments. An example of such a compatible protocol is NWLink, which is the Microsoft implementation of Novell IPX/SPX protocol.

You can install Services for Macintosh, which includes the AppleTalk protocol, on client computers that need access to Macintosh resources. Macintosh clients can also access file servers by running TCP/IP.

Windows 2000 attempts network connectivity with remote servers using network protocols in the order of the local area connection specified by the user in the **Advanced Settings** dialog box. Install and enable only the protocols that you need. For instance, if you only need TCP/IP, but have IPX loaded as well, it generates unnecessary IPX and SAP network traffic.

TCP/IP Network Clients

TCP/IP is one of the most widely used network protocols. Clients on a TCP/IP network can have an IP address assigned to them either statically, by the network administrator, or dynamically, by the Dynamic Host Configuration Protocol (DHCP) server.

Windows 2000 uses a new DNS service called DNS dynamic update. DNS is used as the namespace provider whether the client is using DHCP or static IP addresses. Windows clients can now forgo the requirement to use WINS, and instead simply use DNS. In previous Windows networks, WINS was used in conjunction with DHCP, allowing hosts to dynamically register their NetBIOS name and IP address in the WINS database. You still need WINS if you have any clients on your network that are running Microsoft® Windows NT® Workstation, Microsoft® Windows® 95, Microsoft® Windows® 98, or Microsoft® Windows® 3.1, because these clients use the NetBIOS name method.

Using Microsoft DNS on your network offers certain advantages; DNS:

- Provides interoperability with other DNS servers, such as Novell NDS and UNIX Bind.
- Integrates with and is required for the support of Active Directory™.
- Integrates with other networking services, such as WINS and DHCP.
- Allows clients to update resource records by dynamically registering their DNS names and IP addresses.
- Supports incremental zone transfers between servers.

- Supports new resource record types including the Services Locator (SRV) and Asynchronous Transfer Mode Addresses (ATMA) records.

Before you install Microsoft TCP/IP on a system, determine whether the client will receive static or dynamic IP addresses. Identify whether the hosts on your network are using DHCP or if your IP addresses are statically assigned.

DHCP

Using the Dynamic Host Configuration Protocol (DHCP) allows a client to receive an IP address automatically. This helps avoid configuration errors caused by the need to manually type in values at each computer. Also, DHCP helps prevent address conflicts that occur when a previously assigned IP address is reused to configure a new computer on the network. In addition, the DHCP lease renewal process helps assure that where client configurations need to be updated often (such as users with mobile or portable computers who change locations frequently), these changes can be made efficiently and automatically. Finally, deploying DHCP in a network allows a much more efficient use and management of your organization's address space, because addresses that are no longer used by devices are reintroduced in the address pool and reallocated to other clients.

To enable DHCP, a client simply needs to have the **Obtain an IP address automatically** radio button selected in the **TCP/IP Properties** property sheet, which is accessible through the **Local Area Connection** icon. This option is enabled by default when a Windows 95, Windows 98, Windows NT, or Windows 2000 Professional client is initially installed, so if you are using DHCP, you do not need to manually set your IP configuration.

The benefits of using DHCP are as follows:

- You do not have to manually change the IP settings when a client, such as a roaming user, travels throughout the network. The client is automatically given a new IP address no matter which subnet it reconnects to, as long as a DHCP server is accessible from each of those subnets.

- There is no need to manually configure settings for DNS or WINS. These settings can be given to the client by the DHCP server, as long as the DHCP server has been configured to issue DHCP clients such information. To enable this option on the client , simply select the **Obtain DNS server address automatically** option button. For more information about DNS and WINS, see "TCP/IP Network Clients" later in this chapter.

- There are no conflicts caused by duplicate IP addresses.

For more information about deploying DHCP, see "Determining Network Connectivity Strategies" in this book.

Static Addresses

If your IP addresses are assigned statically, you have the following information available:

- The IP address and subnet mask for each network adapter installed in the client.

- The IP address for the default gateway.

- Whether or not the client is participating in DNS or WINS.

- If the client is participating in DNS, the name of the DNS domain that the client is currently part of, and the IP addresses of the primary and backup DNS servers.

- If the client is participating in WINS, the IP addresses for the primary and backup WINS servers.

Active Directory

Windows 2000 now supports Active Directory, but Windows 95 (and later) and Windows NT 4.0 clients need add-on Active Directory client software. A client configured with Active Directory can log on to the network by locating a domain controller. The client can then fully benefit from the Active Directory feature. These benefits include:

- Immediate access to information about all of the objects on a network.

- Use of the security features of Active Directory through logon authentication and access control.

Note The Active Directory Client for Windows 95 and Windows 98 is provided in a single upgrade pack in a Clients folder on the Windows 2000 Server CD-ROM.

IPX Network Clients

Windows clients are interoperable with NetWare servers by using Client Services for NetWare, or Gateway Services for NetWare.

If there are servers on the network that use Novell NetWare operating systems, then Windows clients can use Client Services for NetWare to connect directly to the server, or they can connect indirectly to a Windows 2000–based server that is running Gateway Services for NetWare.

The steps required to gain client access to NetWare resources are:

1. Install Client Services for NetWare. This allows you to make direct connections to NetWare resources. The NetBIOS NWLink protocol is installed when Client Services for NetWare is installed. This is the Microsoft version of the IPX protocol, and supports connectivity between systems running Windows 2000 Server and systems running NetWare 4.x and earlier.

2. Connect to NetWare volumes. After installing the services listed previously, you can connect to a NetWare volume by clicking **My Network Places** on the desktop.

3. Connect to NetWare file and print resources. You can add a NetWare printer in a Windows 95 or later client by going to the Printers folder in the **Settings** menu, and follow the Printer Installation Wizard. You can add NetWare printers in the wizard by typing in the name of the printer in normal Universal Naming Convention (UNC) format.

Gateway Services for NetWare

You can install Gateway Services for NetWare on a Windows 2000–based server to enable it to act as a gateway. Clients can then connect to NetWare resources without running NWLink, using TCP/IP only. The server runs Gateway Services for NetWare and NWLink, linking the client to the NetWare server. This service is included with Windows 2000 Server.

File and Print Services for NetWare

This service is a separate product and enables a Windows 2000–based server to provide file and print services directly to a NetWare server and compatible client computers. Resources connected through this service appear to NetWare clients like any NetWare server and clients can gain access to volumes, files, and printers on the server. No changes or additions to the NetWare client software are necessary.

Client Services for NetWare

This service enables client computers to make direct connections to file and printer resources on NetWare servers running NetWare 2.x, 3.x, or 4.x. You can use Client Services for NetWare to gain access to servers running either Novell Directory Services or bindery security. This service is included with Windows 95, Windows 98, Windows NT, and Windows 2000 Professional.

Windows Client to Novell Server

Administrators have several options to enable clients to access file and print services on a Novell server:

Install Microsoft Client Services for NetWare As discussed in "IPX Network Clients" earlier in this chapter.

Note Client Services for NetWare only works over the IPX/SPX protocol. Interoperability with NetWare 5.0 servers running only the TCP/IP protocol must use the Novell Client.

Install a Common Internet File System add-on to Novell NetWare server

Windows 2000 Professional uses the Common Internet File System (CIFS) protocol for file and print services. CIFS is an enhanced version of the Microsoft Server Message Block (SMB) protocol. Installing a CIFS snap-in makes the NetWare server respond like a Windows 2000–based server to Windows–based clients. Even with all computers on the network running IPX, Windows clients are able to access file and print services on the Windows 2000–based server without any add-on software.

Windows Client to Mixed Novell NetWare and Windows 2000 Server Environment

Even if all computers on the network run IPX, clients might still be unable to access file and print services on a Novell server if the Novell server is running NetWare Core Protocol and the Windows clients are running CIFS (by default through Microsoft Client for Microsoft Networks). You have several options to permit communication between Windows clients and NetWare and Windows 2000–based servers:

Option 1: Install File and Print Services for NetWare File and Print Services for NetWare enables a Windows 2000 Server–based server to respond like a NetWare server to any client. When users log on to a computer running Windows 2000 Server, their interface looks like they have logged on to a NetWare 3.x Server. File and Print Services for NetWare, which runs as part of the NWLink IPX/SPX–compatible service, enables Windows 2000 Server to emulate a NetWare file and print server by using the same dialogs as a NetWare server. You can manage Windows 2000 Server file and print services with NetWare tools, eliminating the need for retraining. Also, when you use File and Print Services for NetWare you do not have to make changes to NetWare clients. For example, a client application that uses NetWare protocols and naming conventions needs no redirection or translation.

Note File and Print Services for NetWare works only on systems running Windows 2000 Server and Windows 2000 Advanced Server.

Option 2: Install Gateway Services for NetWare With Gateway Services for NetWare installed, Windows 2000 Server becomes a gateway for CIFS-based Windows clients communicating with a NetWare server, allowing users to access all of the resources on that server. Clients running Windows 95 and later can access NetWare resources using TCP/IP, the native network communication protocol for Windows 2000 operating systems. In addition, Gateway Services for NetWare allows Windows 2000 network clients to access files on a NetWare server without requiring a NetWare client redirector or an IPX/SPX protocol stack (such as NWLink). These efficiencies reduce the administrative load for each client and improve network performance. Gateway Services for NetWare also supports Novell Directory Services navigation, authentication, printing, and logon scripts. Gateway Services for NetWare lets a computer running Windows 2000 Server function as a communications gateway server to a NetWare network, resharing the network connections from the NetWare server.

Printing to NetWare Printers

In addition to traditional printer sharing services, Windows 2000 Professional supports Novell Distributed Print Services, which is an enhanced printing architecture in NetWare 5 that integrates printing services into Novell Directory Services. Novell Distributed Print Services also supports bidirectional printer communication, single-seat printer administration, and automatic installation of the correct printer drivers on a client the first time a printer is used.

After a Novell Distributed Print Services printer has been configured on a NetWare server, you can install a printer using the following procedure.

▶ **To install a printer on a NetWare server**

1. Locate the printer you want to install in **Network Places.**

2. Right-click the printer icon and then click **Connect**.

3. The server installs and configures the correct driver according to the computer operating system.

Print support for NetWare versions 2.*x*, 3.*x*, and 4.*x* is included with Windows 2000 Professional. You can establish network printer connections directly or by mapping an LPT port or a UNC port. Because Novell Distributed Print Services requires Novell Directory Services, the ability to use Novell Distributed Print Services requires the Novell NetWare Client.

UNIX Network Clients

In order for computers to communicate with one another, they need to run the same protocols. In Figure 22.2, the entire network is running the TCP/IP transport protocol. On top of the TCP/IP layer, the UNIX Server in is running the Network File System (NFS) application protocol (NFS is the UNIX standard for file and print services), and the Windows 2000 Server operating system is running the CIFS application protocol.

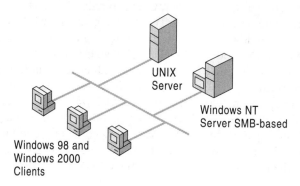

UNIX
Server

Windows NT
Server SMB-based

Windows 98 and
Windows 2000
Clients

Figure 22.2   UNIX and Windows NT Network

After it is in communication, each operating system supports additional capabilities, such as centralized management; remote access and other features that are either integrated into the operating system or available using add-on products from Microsoft; UNIX vendors; or independent software vendors.

The following is an overview of options available for integrating UNIX and Windows-based environments:

Add NFS add-on to clients   One of the most common ways to provide interoperability is to add NFS capabilities to desktop systems such as those provided by Services for UNIX.

Add CIFS capabilities to the UNIX server   Install a CIFS add-in to the UNIX server. This makes the UNIX server respond like a Windows 2000–based server to any of the Windows-based clients.

Use NFS Gateway with Windows 2000 Server   By installing an NFS gateway product such as Services for UNIX, the Windows 2000–based server becomes a gateway for CIFS-based Windows clients communicating with the UNIX server. Users can access all of the resources on a UNIX server as if it were a standard Windows 2000 Server file share.

Utilize Integrated Telnet and File Transfer Protocol Clients   Windows 2000 Server provides Telnet and File Transfer Protocol (FTP) clients as standard components in the operating system. Using these clients, Windows 2000 Professional users can establish standard VT100 shell sessions with any UNIX system supporting the Telnet protocol, or can use FTP to transfer files between the UNIX and Windows 2000 Professional system.

AppleTalk Network Clients

You can add Services for Macintosh to Windows 2000 Server to allow Macintosh systems to access these servers. A Windows 2000 Server–based server configured in this way appears in an AppleTalk zone and allows access the same way as any other Macintosh system.

Advanced Client Connectivity

Clients that use ATM as its medium on a network and that require a high degree of connectivity can use Windows 2000 support for Asynchronous Transfer Mode (ATM) and IP over ATM. With these types of technologies, clients can be assured maximum bandwidth in a busy network environment. These technologies are discussed in the following sections.

Asynchronous Transfer Mode

You can bring high speed and quality of service directly to the clients by connecting them to an ATM network. When you are planning a client ATM connectivity strategy, decide whether you will connect the client directly to ATM, or if you are going to keep an existing Ethernet infrastructure and use LAN Emulation (LANE). If the client will use the existing infrastructure, the existing Ethernet network hardware is sufficient. You will then need LANE to connect the Ethernet segments to the ATM core of the network.

Directly Connected ATM

Before the client can use directly-connected ATM, it must have an ATM card that is compatible with Windows 2000. You can verify this compatibility by viewing the Hardware Compatibility List (HCL). For more information about the HCL, see the Microsoft Windows Hardware Compatibility List link on the Web Resources page at http://windows.microsoft.com/windows2000/reskit/webresources. If the ATM network card does not support Plug and Play detection, then contact the vendor for installation software. After the system detects the ATM card, it will configure it for LAN emulation.

IP/ATM

IP/ATM offers the client the ability to gain access to a high-speed network while still using TCP/IP as its protocol. An IP/ATM network uses an ATM Address Resolution Protocol (ARP) server to translate IP addresses into ATM addresses, allowing access to servers on an ATM network. A Multicast Addresses Resolution server (MARS) enables resolution of multicast addresses.

Infrared Data Association Protocol Suite

Windows 2000 Professional, Windows 98, and Windows 95 support the Infrared Data Association (IrDA) protocol suite. This protocol lets users transfer information and share resources, such as printers, between computers without physical cables. Most new portable computers include hardware support for IrDA.

For example, two users traveling with laptop computers can transfer files by setting up an IrDA connection instead of using cables or floppy disks. An IrDA connection can be initiated by placing the portable computers within close proximity. Distances of around three feet are supported by IrDA.

IrDA also allows a computer to access resources that are attached to another computer. For example, if you need to print a document from a laptop computer, you can create an IrDA connection to a computer that is connected to a printer— either locally or on a network. When that connection is established, and with appropriate permission, the user can print over the IrDA connection. Some printers also have direct IrDA support, allowing users to send print jobs directly to the printer over the computer IrDA port.

Windows 2000 Professional also supports the ability to allow or limit users other than the computer's owner to send files using IrDA. Users can also specify the location where documents must be received. Windows 2000 Professional automatically detects devices that use infrared communications, such as other computers and cameras.

Remote Access Client

One of the ways in which a company can improve its productivity is by using Windows 2000 Routing and Remote Access service. When clients are located off campus, this service can provide them with remote access to resources on the internal network and help maximize speed and security. Windows 2000 Professional makes it significantly easier for users to remotely connect to networks, including virtual private networks (VPNs), over dial-up, infrared, and direct cable connections.

The Network Connection Wizard helps users create new types of connections with a single tool. Connection setup is also automated, eliminating the need to download and install additional services. Figure 22.3 shows the Network Connection Wizard.

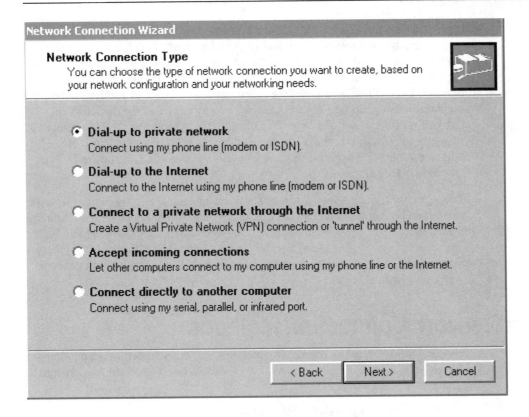

Figure 22.3   Network Connection Wizard

Dial-up to Private Network

Clients who do not want to use remote access virtual private networks (VPNs) can dial directly into your corporation's remote access server to gain access to resources. The advantage of this is you can use a simple dial-up connection without having to use an Internet service provider (ISP). The disadvantage of this method is potential long-distance charges.

Virtual Private Networks

Remote clients in today's advanced networks can access resources using VPN protocols. While Windows 2000 supports the widely-used Point-to-Point Tunneling Protocol (PPTP), it also enables a very secure connection using Layer 2 Tunneling Protocol (L2TP) in conjunction with Internet Protocol Security (IPSec). Using L2TP and IPSec, secure tunnels can be constructed through the remote client's ISP, enabling the client to send and receive data that is secure from Internet intrusion.

IPSec is designed to encrypt data as it travels between two computers, protecting it from unauthorized modification and interpretation while on the network. First, an administrator needs to define how the two computers will trust each other, and then specify how the computers will secure their traffic. This configuration is contained in an IPSec policy that the administrator creates and applies on the local computer or using Group Policy in Active Directory. Due to the difficulty of configuring IPSec policy, Microsoft has built IPSec support into L2TP so that all you needs to do is to create a VPN connection using L2TP from the remote computer to the VPN server. For more information about IPSec, see the *TCP/IP Core Networking Guide*.

In order to use IPSec on Internet or network clients, the IPSec snap-in needs to be installed on both hosts that are exchanging the data. If a remote user is dialing in through the client's local Internet service provider (ISP), then that client and the VPN server it is calling into must both be running the IPSec protocol. If two clients within an internal network need to exchange data securely, both of those clients must also run IPSec.

Remote Network Connection Methods

There are various network connection methods that you can deploy, depending on the type of infrastructure you are creating. They can be categorized by size, and include:

- A Small Office/Home Office (SOHO) network
- A medium-sized network that a medium-sized to large-sized business might use
- A very large corporate network with thousands of clients.

Small Office Networks

Small Office/Home Office (SOHO) networks are used primarily in home offices that might be part of a larger corporation but yet remain apart from it. The SOHO can use two technologies that allow connections between the clients on the SOHO and either the Internet, the corporate network, or both. These technologies are Internet Connection Sharing (ICS) and network address translation (NAT).

SOHO networks are usually peer-to-peer networks. This type of network is a single subnet that is used to conveniently connect clients together, excluding the need for routers, DHCP servers, or WINS servers. This is ideal for home offices where a user needs to use more than one computer, and also needs to be able to share resources from one computer to another, such as files, applications, or printers.

The following section gives an explanation of the benefits, requirements, and deployment of both types of technologies.

Small Office/Home Office Connectivity

A SOHO needs to have the ability to administer and organize its own internal network structure as well as to connect to and maintain a secure Internet connection.

Windows 2000 offers the SOHO the ability to auto-assign private IP addresses to internal computers, through a function called Automatic Private IP Addressing (APIPA). You can also assign addresses to the SOHO while connecting to the Internet. This is done through a service called network address translation (NAT). NAT enables private IP addresses to be translated into public IP addresses for traffic to and from the Internet. This keeps the internal network secure from the Internet, while saving the SOHO user the time and expense of getting and maintaining a public address range. Table 22.1 represents what might be required to implement a SOHO network.

Table 22.1   Small Office/Home Office Design

Network Component	Method
Windows 2000 Server	Ensure the server hardware meets the specifications listed in the Windows 2000 HCL.
LAN Medium	Use 10 or 100BaseT unshielded twisted pair cable, 10 or 100BaseT hubs, or 10 or 100BaseT network adapters. See the HCL for network adapter compatibility requirements.
Internet Connectivity	Use ICS, NAT, or a routed connection to the Internet. Use POTS, ISDN, fractional T1 line, cable modem, or DSL.
Internal Client Connectivity	Use Automatic Private IP Addressing (APIPA), ISP assigned, or static IP addresses.
Network Protocols	TCP/IP

Internet Connection Sharing

Internet Connection Sharing (ICS) is a simple package consisting of DHCP, network address translation (NAT), and DNS. You can use ICS to connect your SOHO to the Internet, providing a simple, one-step configuration permitting a translated connection, that in turn allows all of the computers on the network to access e-mail, Web sites, FTP sites, and so on. ICS provides network address translation (see the following section), automatic IP addressing, and name resolution services for all of the computers on the SOHO network. ICS provides the following:

- Single check box for ease of configuration
- Single public IP address

- Fixed address range for SOHO hosts
- DNS proxy for name resolution
- Single SOHO interface for peer-to-peer networks

You can configure ICS on new or preexisting remote access or LAN connections using a single check box that enables connection sharing. To use ICS, you must have a computer with a network connection to a local ISP and a network interface card or adapter for connection to the peer-to-peer network. ICS is enabled on the connection to the local ISP, and gets its IP address from the ISP. When ICS is enabled on the connection, the network adapter is automatically configured with a static IP address of 192.168.0.1, which is part of the IP address range of 192.168.0.0 to 192.168.254.254. The computers that are behind the ICS system also receive IP addresses from this range.

Note Be aware that after ICS is enabled, no further configuration of services, such as DNS or IP addressing, is allowed on the network. These services are all implemented by the ICS system.

Network Address Translation

Network address translation (NAT) differs from ICS, providing similar features, but more flexibility. It also requires more steps to set up. One of the major differences between NAT and ICS is that NAT requires, at a minimum, Windows 2000 Server, whereas ICS can be configured from Windows 2000 Professional or Windows 98 Second Edition. You load and configure NAT from the Windows 2000 Routing and Remote Access Manager. NAT provides the following:

Manual Configuration This permits the user a more versatile method of configuring translated remote access connections.

Multiple public IP addresses NAT can use more than one range of public addresses.

Configurable address range NAT allows manual configuration of IP addresses and subnet masks, whereas ICS uses a fixed IP address range. Any range of IP addresses can be configured using the NAT properties in Routing and Remote Access Manager. A DHCP allocator provides the mechanism for distributing IP addresses, the same way that DHCP does this. NAT can also use IP addresses distributed from a DHCP server by selecting the **Automatically assign IP addresses by using DHCP** check box in the NAT properties sheet.

DNS and WINS proxy Name resolution can be established by using either DNS or WINS. You can configure this by selecting the appropriate check boxes in the NAT properties sheet under the **Name Resolution** tab.

Multiple network interfaces You can distribute NAT functionality on more than one network interface by adding the interface to NAT in the Routing and Remote Access Manager.

Networks using NAT can also initiate VPN connections using the PPTP. This enables small businesses, or even SOHO networks in which NAT is installed, to initiate secure remote access connections with a corporate network.

Note Do not use NAT on a network with other Windows 2000 Server domain controllers, DNS servers, gateways, DHCP servers, or systems configured for static IP because of possible conflict with other services.

Do not connect NAT directly to a corporate network because Kerberos authentication, IPSec, and Internet Key Encryption (IKE) will not work.

Automatic Private IP Addressing

Windows 2000 Server, Windows 2000 Professional, and Windows 98 can self-assign an IP address from the 169.254.0.0/16 address range when no DHCP servers are detected on the network. Windows 3.11, Windows NT 3.51, and Windows NT 4.0 can also get an IP address from this range, but need to obtain them from an APIPA server. APIPA can be set up to distribute IP addresses from the this range by simply running the Routing and Remote Access Manager, adding and configuring NAT, adding the interface that distributes the IP addresses, then reconfiguring the IP address range in the NAT properties with the address range previously listed. For more information about APIPA, see "Determining Network Connectivity Strategies" in this book.

Note The only clients that are able to participate in APIPA are Windows 98 and Windows 2000 Professional clients. All other systems require a server that runs the Windows 2000 Routing and Remote Access service, which distributes the APIPA addresses to them.

SOHO Examples

In the sections following, there are two examples that show how you can implement a SOHO.

Example 1

This is the home example where there are five computers on the SOHO. The SOHO uses ICS to connect to the Internet, and uses the Internet to connect to the corporate network through a PPTP tunnel. The IP address range used by the clients is distributed by the ICS computer. If a connection to corporate is needed by one of the clients, a VPN profile is configured on the client that needs the connection and a PPTP tunnel is then begun through the Internet to the corporate network. Figure 22.4 shows this network.

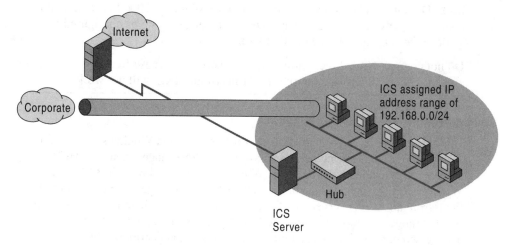

Figure 22.4   Home Network

Example 2

This example is a "strip-mall" SOHO, where the clients access the corporate network through a server running Routing and Remote Access. The clients on the network access the Internet through the corporate network. Figure 22.5 depicts this network.

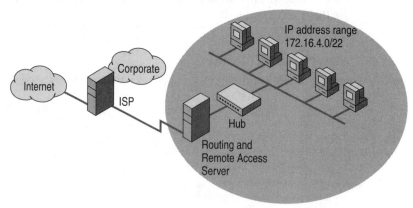

Figure 22.5   "Strip-mall" Network

Medium to Large Networks

Medium to large networks need a more robust architecture, requiring a number of linked subnets with the potential for the network to grow as client demand increases.

Routing and Remote Access

One of the services that allows a corporation to improve its productivity is Windows 2000 Routing and Remote Access. When clients are not physically at the corporate campus, this service provides them with remote access to resources on the internal network. This service also provides several ways to maximize speed and security. Windows 2000 Professional makes it easier for users to remotely connect to networks, including VPNs, dial-up, infrared, and direct cable connections.

The Network Connection Wizard helps users create new types of connections with a single tool. Connection setup is also automated, eliminating the need to download and install additional services—a step that is necessary in Windows 95 for setting up certain types of remote networking. Figure 22.6 shows the Network Connection Wizard.

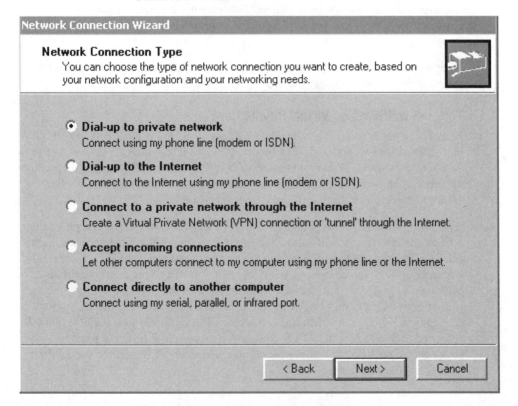

Figure 22.6   Network Connection Wizard

Dial-up to Private Network

Clients who do not want to use remote access virtual private networks (VPNs) can dial directly into your corporation's remote access server to gain access to resources. The only requirement is to set permissions for the remote client that allows the user access. The disadvantage to this is potential long-distance charges either for the user or the company.

Direct Dial-up

Clients can dial up their corporate remote access servers directly in order to transfer files and send and receive e-mail. This is a convenient way to gain access to the network but it can be costly. The long-distance charges can, over time, increase costs for both the remote user and the business. Additional costs include the need to administer the direct dial-up infrastructure. In some cases, it might be more economical to outsource direct dial-up services using Windows 2000 Internet Authentication Services (IAS). For more information about IAS, see "Determining Network Connectivity Strategies" in this book.

In order for the client to connect to a corporate remote access server, the client must be granted appropriate permissions on the corporate network. You then need to create a dial-up profile on the client computer by selecting **Make New Connection** in the Network and Dial-Up Connections folder located in Control Panel.

Another way that clients can access their corporate accounts is by using a VPN, which is discussed in the next section.

Through an ISP using Virtual Private Networks

Remote clients in today's advanced networks can access resources using VPN protocols. While Windows 2000 supports PPTP, it also enables a very secure connection using L2TP in conjunction with IPSec. Using L2TP and IPSec, secure tunnels can be constructed through the remote client's ISP, enabling the client to send and receive data secure from Internet intrusion.

IPSec is designed to encrypt data as it travels between two computers, protecting it from unauthorized modification and interpretation while on the network. First, an administrator needs to define how the two computers will trust each other, and then specify how the computers will secure their traffic. This configuration is contained in an IPSec policy that the administrator creates and applies on the local computer or using Group Policy in Active Directory. Due to the difficulty of configuring IPSec policy, Microsoft has built IPSec support into L2TP so that all you need to do is to create a VPN connection using L2TP from the remote computer to the VPN server. For more information about IPSec, see the *TCP/IP Core Networking Guide*.

In order to use IPSec on Internet or network clients, you need to install the IPSec snap-in on both hosts that are exchanging the data. If a remote user dials in through the client's local Internet service provider (ISP), then that client and the VPN server it is calling in to must both be running the IPSec protocol. If two clients within an internal network need to exchange data securely, then both of those clients must also run IPSec.

Medium to Large Network Example

A medium-sized to large-sized network contains hundreds to thousands of computers and multiple subnets. The technologies that were used in a SOHO to connect to the Internet or a corporate network now require more configuration, but at the same time have more capability. Table 22.2 lists the various technologies and how they apply to each type of network.

Table 22.2   Network Technologies

SOHO	Medium Network	Large Network
Uses ICS, private IP address range of 192.168.0.0/24.	Uses NAT configured with an appropriate private IP addresses range	Uses Microsoft Proxy Server to connect to the Internet, and uses DHCP to allocate IP addresses.
Utilizes only PPTP.	Utilizes only PPTP.	Uses a separate VPN server to permit PPTP and L2TP/IPSec tunnel traffic.
Utilizes only a single network interface.	Utilizes multiple network interfaces.	The Proxy and VPN server are attached to a router with multiple network interfaces.
Uses only DNS for name resolution.	Uses DNS, WINS, or both for name resolution.	Uses DNS, WINS, or both for name resolution.

The ICS works fine on smaller SOHO networks when there is only a single subnet and a single connection to the Internet. Medium-sized networks can use NAT to connect its clients to the Internet because of its capability to service more than one subnet and more than one IP address range. The larger network needs a proxy server and a VPN server in order to allow client access to Internet and tunnel traffic.

The large networks need to have an area in their infrastructure called a *demilitarized zone* (DMZ). This area is a network that permits the egression of the Internet into a private network, while still maintaining the security of that network. In this area go all of the servers that have any Internet exposed interfaces. For more information about DMZs, see "Determining Network Connectivity Strategies" in this book.

In this example, a medium-sized to large-sized business is using a network serving 750 to 1,000 employees in three sites. The sites in this network are connected by T1 and fractional T1 links. The business has some remote users who dial in to receive files and e-mail, and each employee has his or her own remote access account. Each site also has an Internet connection through which the employees can access the Internet for business needs. This network is in the process of transitioning from a NetWare to a Windows 2000 infrastructure, and interoperability between clients and servers in both the Windows 2000 and NetWare environments is essential.

Figure 22.7 is a simplified diagram of this example.

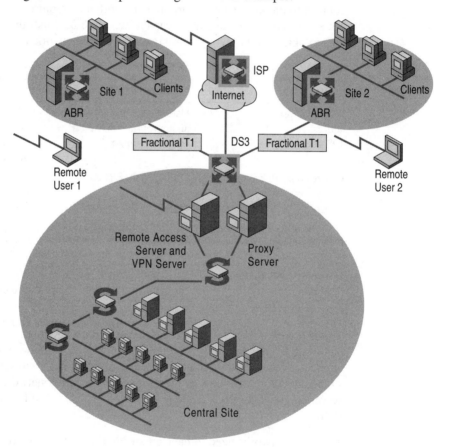

Figure 22.7   Medium to Large Network

The clients in the network are as follows:

- Windows 98 clients
- Windows 2000 Professional clients
- Windows 95 clients
- Windows NT 4.0 Workstation clients
- NetWare clients

Because this network is slowly being migrated from NetWare to Windows 2000, most of the employees still require access to NetWare servers and printers. Some Windows clients on the part of the network that is still running IPX are using Client Services for NetWare, and are running the NWLink protocol. The other Windows clients are using TCP/IP and are accessing required NetWare files and printers through Windows 2000 routers running Gateway Services for NetWare. The remote clients are accessing Windows 2000–based servers and NetWare servers by using the multiprotocol VPN and remote access server located in the demilitarized zone (DMZ) of the central site. The clients on this network get their IP addresses from a DHCP server, and Internet access is through a proxy server located in the DMZ. For more information about designing medium to large networks, see "Determining Network Connectivity Strategies" in this book.

Planning Task List for Client Connectivity

Table 22.3 outlines the tasks you need to perform when determining your network connectivity strategies.

Table 22.3   Task List for Planning Client Connectivity

Task	Chapter Section
Determine appropriate protocol usage.	Windows 2000 Services and Protocols
Configure static IP clients.	Static Addresses
Configure DHCP options.	DHCP
Configure clients that use IPX.	IPX Network Clients
Configure clients that use AppleTalk.	AppleTalk Network Clients
Make decisions concerning dial-up/VPN access.	Medium to Large Networks

CHAPTER 23

Defining Client Administration and Configuration Standards

Enhancing user productivity and reducing the costs associated with managing client computers are among most information technology (IT) organization's primary goals. Microsoft® Windows® 2000 Server and Microsoft® Windows® 2000 Professional provide a number of new user-oriented and management-oriented features that your client and mobile computing teams can use to enhance user productivity and manage client support costs.

This chapter is designed to help you identify and implement these features in your organization. In addition, this chapter introduces you to the expanded management capabilities provided through Group Policy in Windows 2000 Professional and Windows 2000 Server. This information is going to help you create administration and client standards for your organization that take advantage of these capabilities. If you have not done so already, complete an assessment of your organization's client software and hardware infrastructure. For more information, see "Building a Windows 2000 Test Lab" and "Testing Applications for Compatibility with Windows 2000" in this book. You might also want to review your organization's IT administration goals.

In This Chapter

Chapter Goals

This chapter will help you develop the following planning documents:

- Client Administration Plan
- Preferred Client Configurations

Related Information in the Resource Kit

- For more information about using Group Policy and creating administrative template (.adm) files, see "Group Policy" in the *Microsoft® Windows® 2000 Server Resource Kit Distributed Systems Guide*.

- For more information about using Microsoft® IntelliMirror® features in Windows 2000, see "Applying Change and Configuration Management" in this book.

- For more information about installation services and tools, see "Automating Client Installation and Upgrade" and "Using Systems Management Server to Deploy Windows 2000" in this book.

- For more information about deploying Terminal Services, see "Deploying Terminal Services" in this book.

- For more information about planning Windows 2000 security features, see "Planning Distributed Security" in this book.

Making Client Systems Manageable

Administering and supporting client computers can be a simple activity, or it can be extremely complex. Users in large organizations typically have a wide variety of skill levels. They use a variety of applications and hardware, and often work in widely distributed locations. A growing percentage of users work off-site and connect to the network intermittently across slow links. Numerous studies have identified these diverse usage patterns and a lack of client configuration standards as among the most significant factors behind rising IT support costs.

This chapter will help you define basic client configuration standards that serves the needs of your users—no matter where they work or what their jobs require. In addition, you will learn how you can use Group Policy to better manage Windows 2000–based client computers.

Planning client computer standards requires both technical and organizational knowledge. You must understand your current computing environment and identify the needs of both your users and your organization. You must also decide which Windows 2000 capabilities you want to enable and then document the changes needed to meet your goals. Your client computer standards plan must account for the following:

- Users and their computing requirements.
- Applications and application requirements.
- Hardware and hardware requirements.
- Your current and wanted administrative model.
- Significant support issues and solutions to those problems.

Based on your research and an understanding of the new client support features in Windows 2000 Server and Windows 2000 Professional, you can plan your client administration and configuration standards. Figure 23.1 illustrates the planning process for creating client administration and configuration standards.

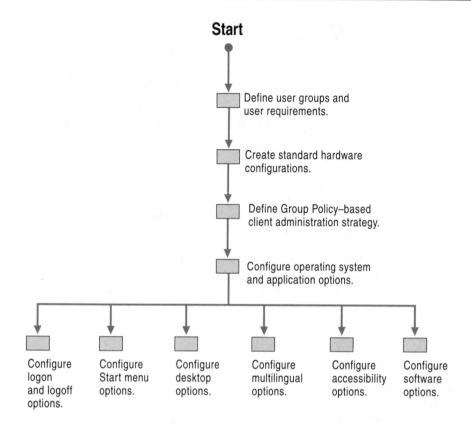

Figure 23.1   Overview of Client Administration and Configuration Planning

The creation of client standards involves more issues than can be covered in one chapter. This chapter describes the following Windows 2000 client administration and configuration options:

- Hardware configuration options. The standard portable computer and desktop computer hardware configuration options needed to run Windows 2000.

- Administration options. Group Policy, the primary means in Windows 2000 for implementing your client administration and configuration options.

- Operating system and application options. The operating system and applications that users need to perform their jobs. Also, key **Start** menu and desktop configuration options available in Windows 2000, including:

    - Multilingual options. Selecting between the multilingual computing support that comes with Windows 2000 or with the new Windows 2000 MultiLanguage Version.

    - Accessibility options. Windows 2000 features that make computing easier for users with accessibility needs.

The following Windows 2000 client administration and configuration options are discussed in other chapters of this book:

- Client security options are addressed in "Planning Distributed Security."
- Active Directory™ directory service–enabled client management features, user data management, software installation and maintenance, and user settings management, which are known by the term IntelliMirror, as well as Remote OS Installation, are addressed in "Applying Change and Configuration Management."
- Network access is discussed in "Defining a Client Connectivity Strategy."

After you have completed the planning tasks described in this chapter, read and perform the planning tasks in the chapters listed previously to complete your client administration and configuration standards planning.

Defining User Types

Large organizations have many different types of users. The following are some of the differences that influence a user's pattern of computer usage:

- The organizational unit (OU) to which the user belongs (such as accounting, engineering, or marketing).
- The type of work the user performs (technical, executive, or administrative support, for example).
- Where the user performs their work (such as in an office, from a remote location, or at a shared computer).
- The degree of autonomy the user requires to do their job.
- The amount and type of support the user requires.

In addition, it is also important to note whether the user is:

Roaming Many users move from one computer to another. Roaming users typically do not take a computer with them when they move from one location to another; instead, they use the computer at the location where they are working. Receptionists or bank tellers who often work at several different desks are examples of roaming users.

Mobile A growing number of workers travel regularly and perform their work using a portable computer. While traveling, they are frequently disconnected from the network, and often connect to the network using low-bandwidth connections. Sales people and consultants are frequently in the mobile user category.

Remote Remote users differ from mobile users because they generally connect to the network from a fixed location, such as a branch or home office that often involves a slow or intermittent network link.

Task-based   Users who require a computer to perform a specific, limited set of tasks, such as entering orders. The task-based user might only require a computer running Terminal Services. Receptionists and bank tellers are examples of task-based users.

Knowledge Workers   Users, such as engineers, lawyers, graphic designers, and programmers, who place the greatest demands on their computers, often require specialized applications and customized configurations.

If you have not done so already, create a table such as Table 23.1 to identify the user types within your organization (some employees fit into multiple categories).

Table 23.1   Example User Type Table

Job	Category	Work Group	Location	Applications Required	Support Required	Amount of Autonomy
Chief Financial Officer	Knowledge Worker	Finance	Headquarters	Mandatory and Optional	Normal	High
Branch Manager	Remote Knowledge Worker	Marketing	Branch Office	Mandatory and Optional	Normal	High
Sales Person	Mobile Knowledge Worker	Marketing	Varies	Mandatory and Optional	Normal	High
Assembly Line Worker	Roaming Task-Based Worker	Manufacturing	Various Factory Floor Locations	Mandatory	High	Low
Receptionist	Roaming Task-Based Worker	Administration	Various Headquarter Locations	Mandatory	High	Low

Facts about users by itself is not sufficient information to create client standards. You must develop an in-depth understanding of their needs and the problems they might be experiencing (for example, data lost due to a computer failure, having equal access to data no matter where they are, or keeping their data synchronized with that of other users even if they are often disconnected from the network). Only after you truly understand your users and their computing needs can you devise appropriate client standards.

Assessing Requirements for User Types

After you understand the basic business needs of your users, you need to assess your current and desired environments to complete your client standards. To do this, examine the following:

- Software requirements
- Computer hardware
- Administrative model
- Desktop configurations

The following sections provide representative sets of requirements for both "basic" and "advanced" users. Basic requirements, as defined here, are most commonly applied to task-based employees. Advanced requirements are typically applied to knowledge workers. For more information about how to meet the needs of basic and advanced users, see "Applying Change and Configuration Management" in this book. However, these profiles are generic. Your organization's standards will differ, and you might want to create standards for additional categories of users depending on your organization's needs.

Defining Software Standards

Large organizations typically support hundreds—sometimes thousands—of different software applications and versions of software applications, including operating systems, across the organization. Many organizations can reduce their client computing costs by implementing core software standards—particularly for organization-wide functions such as e-mail, word processing, and spreadsheets—and retiring obsolete and unnecessary software.

To develop your client application standards, address the following questions regarding operating systems, generic commercial applications such as word processing software, and line-of-business applications that have been developed internally to perform tasks such as client management or order fulfillment:

- What software is mandatory for your organization?
- What software is required for a particular job or business unit?
- What software is optional for the organization, business units, or workers who perform a particular type of job?
- How often do software requirements at your organization change?

- Who determines which software is used—throughout the organization and in specific workgroups?
- How is software customized?
- How is software distributed?
- How is software configured?
- How do you install new client software?
- How do you upgrade existing software?
- How do you pilot or evaluate new software?

At the same time, decide which software to deploy with Windows 2000—and how to deploy them. Software that is not installed along with the operating system can be made available to users on an as-needed basis.

Basic Users

Basic users might require a standardized configuration of the operating system and the minimum number of corporate-standard applications, such as e-mail and word processing, along with the specific applications they need to do their job (for example, an order entry application). However, basic users would not be permitted to install optional applications, and more complex application features, such as pivot tables in spreadsheet applications, can be disabled.

Advanced Users

Advanced users frequently require advanced operating system features such as the ability to create personal network shares. They also commonly require additional optional applications and features, which they can install as needed. However, you can still prevent them from installing unapproved applications.

Note After you have decided which applications are mandatory and which are optional, review "Applying Change and Configuration Management," "Automating Client Installation and Upgrade," and "Using Systems Management Server to Deploy Windows 2000" in this book to determine how to install and manage these applications.

Defining Hardware Standards

The applications that your users need to perform their jobs determine your company's hardware requirements. However, planning hardware budgets generally involves longer lead times than planning for software upgrades. Therefore, plan carefully and allow enough time to provide your users with the computer hardware they need when they need it.

The following are some of the questions you might ask regarding your organization's clients:

- How fast are the processors in your current client desktop computers? How fast are the processors in your portable computers?

- How fast is the network connectivity for your current clients (including portable computers that are network connected and modem connected)?

- How much random access memory (RAM) and hard disk space do they have?

- Are Windows 2000 drivers available for current network adapters and other peripherals?

- What file systems do they use?

- Are current computers running other operating systems that need to be upgraded, or do you need to perform clean installations?

- Can current computers use remote boot technology? Do they have remote boot-compatible network adapters? Can they use a remote boot floppy disk?

- Will you be using network shares to store user data and configuration data?

- Who is responsible for backing up the user's data?

- How do you bring new computers into your organization? How do you stage new hardware? Does the original equipment manufacturer preinstall applications? Do you remove any preinstalled software from new hardware and then reinstall it according to your own standards?

- How do you replace failed hardware? If a hard disk fails, how do you replace it? How do you replace or restore the operating system? How do you replace or restore applications? How do you replace or restore the user's data?

- Do you have security requirements for data on the hard disk? Do you use any form of data encryption?

- Do your computers have multiple configurations? For example, does a portable computer have one set of hardware features for when it is in a docking station (including a network adapter) and another hardware profile for when it is undocked (and using a high-speed modem rather than a network adapter)?

- How long do you spend troubleshooting a hardware problem before you replace the computer and restore a standard operating system and application environment?

For each class of users in your organization, define a standard type of computer that can meet current and anticipated processing needs for two years at a minimum. In addition, try to reduce the number of different hardware configurations that you support to improve your ability to support users and also reduce client support costs.

For more information about upgrade and clean installation options, see "Automating Client Installation and Upgrade" and "Using Systems Management Server to Deploy Windows 2000" in this book. For more information about Remote OS Installation and offline folders, see "Applying Change and Configuration Management" in this book.

Because few organizations can afford to purchase the most recent, powerful, and versatile computers for all employees, the sample guidelines in Table 23.2 illustrate how you can match your computing hardware to the needs of your user groups.

Table 23.2   Sample Computer Allocation Strategy

If the Computer:	Assign it to:	Also Consider:
Does not meet minimum hardware requirements for Windows 2000	Task-based users	Using Terminal Services with this hardware
Meets minimum hardware requirements for Windows 2000	Basic users (including Roaming and Task-based users)	Providing basic users with permanent network connections
Exceeds minimum hardware requirements for Windows 2000	Advanced users (including Knowledge and Mobile workers)	

Defining Significant Support Issues

Understanding your current support issues can help you improve client administration and configuration standards and reduce support costs. The following questions will help you to determine what administrative policies can provide the greatest value to your organization:

- What are our top 10 support issues?

  List them and develop action plans to reduce their frequency.

- How often do users "break" their configuration by attempting to change settings (such as video drivers) and other configuration options?

  If the frequency of configuration problems is unacceptably high, you might want to restrict users' ability to change their operating system configuration.

- How often do users "break" their configuration by attempting to either add or remove applications incorrectly?

  If the frequency of this problem is unacceptably high, you might want to restrict their ability to install or uninstall applications.

- Do users install unauthorized software on their computers?

  If this is a problem in your organization, institute corporate policies on whether unauthorized software is allowed. Even if you allow users to bring unauthorized software into the organization, define the types of software to allow and the licensing rules by which users must abide.

- Has the data on clients been secured? Does it need to be?

  Most organizations will want to define security measures for corporate data. The amount of security varies by the type of data involved (financial data or trade secrets require one level of security, public relations releases require another level, for example). You might also want to define who is responsible for security (users versus IT, for example) depending on the type of data.

- Are users allowed to operate their computers as the local administrator?

  If users have been allowed to serve as the local administrator in the past, the installation of a new operating system is a perfect opportunity to alter or fine tune permissions to more effectively meet your organization's administrative needs.

- How much time does your help desk spend trying to fix a broken configuration before they reinstall or reset the basic configuration?

  If you do not have time limits on support calls for broken configurations, consider instituting limits. Also, evaluate Windows 2000 features that can be used to back up user data and install or reinstall the operating system and applications. These new features can impact the length of support calls. For example, if it is easier to reinstall a desktop and data than to troubleshoot a broken configuration, you can significantly reduce the length of your average support call.

Your answers to these and other support questions will help you determine which Windows 2000 features and configuration options to implement. Many representative configuration and control options are discussed later in this chapter.

The answers to these support-related questions will also help you evaluate the effectiveness of your current administration model and standards. Gaps and shortcomings in your client support services can often be resolved with an improved administration model. The following section will help you evaluate your existing administration model.

Defining an Administration Model and Standards

Until now, IT managers have been restricted by the inability to delegate IT administration tasks in the best suited way for their organization. Windows 2000 provides significantly improved support for controlling clients and for delegating administration tasks.

Does your IT administrative model reflect the current structure of your organization. If your IT administrative model is out of date, you need to reevaluate all major IT tasks and where they are performed so that they can be delegated and performed more effectively. Some of the questions you need to answer are included here:

- Who creates or changes user or computer accounts? How many user or computer accounts are created or modified each month?

  In many organizations that have grown rapidly, a single individual or team can no longer update user or computer information on a timely basis. Alternately, organizations that have merged or gone through acquisitions might have multiple individuals or teams performing similar tasks in a redundant manner. You will need to determine the most efficient way to delegate these IT tasks— at the domain level, at the organizational unit level, or at the site level.

- Who establishes software standards? Who is responsible for deploying software?

  If your organization does not have software standards, the migration to a new operating system might be an good time to institute ones that enable users to communicate and share information more effectively. You might also find that many divisions or organizational units have unique application requirements. When you define application standards, accommodate both the centralized and decentralized requirements of your organization.

- Who sets or updates passwords? What are your password or authentication requirements?

  Many organizations delegate the authority to reset passwords to their helpdesks. Alternately, password requirements themselves are probably set at a higher level in the organization—and frequently a single set of authentication requirements apply to the entire organization.

- Who backs up servers? Who backs up user data? How often are backups performed? How often do you restore data from backups?

  In many organizations, only servers are backed up and users are often left to back up their own data—which they do either infrequently or not at all. If your organization does not provide for backups of user data, consider establishing server shares for users and requiring that users store important data on these shares so that it can be backed up regularly.

- Does your organization have service level agreements or other explicit service goals? What are your organization's explicit service goals or criteria for success?

  A growing number of organizations are setting explicit service goals or signing service level agreements that hold them accountable for reaching quantifiable results. Include existing or new service goals in your Windows 2000 client administration plan. Setting explicit goals will help you refine and shape your client administration plans to meet your organization's needs.

Summarizing Your Administrative and Configuration Goals

Before proceeding, summarize your organization's existing client support plan and the support standards that you want to adopt.

Also, summarize your organization's existing client administration model and the administration model that you want to implement using the features and capabilities provided by Windows 2000.

Using Group Policy to Administer Clients

How you use Group Policy to administer clients is determined by the service standards and goals that you have set.

In a highly managed environment, your service level agreement might include guidelines for providing fast troubleshooting (for example, response within 15 minutes), rapid equipment replacement in case of failure, and frequent (probably daily) data backups. In addition, highly managed support would also include advanced features such as Group Policy–based user or computer environments, software installation and maintenance, offline folders, and custom scripts for the logon, logoff, startup, and shutdown processes.

Less managed environments will probably have longer lead times for support and equipment replacement, and provide only a subset of the services offered in a highly managed environment.

Also, users in an unmanaged environment provide their own troubleshooting, replace their own equipment, back up their own data, and take minimal advantage of Group Policy–based functionality.

The following sections describe the different levels and quality of support that you can provide using Microsoft® Windows NT® version 4.0 System Policy, Windows 2000 Professional local Group Policy, and Windows 2000 Active Directory–based Group Policy. With this knowledge, you will be able delegate control over key client support tasks at the most effective level for your organization.

Comparing Windows NT 4.0 System Policy and Windows 2000 Group Policy

In Windows NT 4.0, Microsoft introduced System Policy Editor, which was used to specify user and computer configurations that are stored in the Windows NT registry. With the System Policy Editor, you could create a system policy to control the user work environment and to enforce system configuration settings for all computers running either Windows NT 4.0 Workstation or Windows NT 4.0 Server.

There are 72 policy settings in Windows NT 4.0 (and Microsoft® Windows® 95 and Microsoft® Windows® 98). These settings are:

- Limited to setting the values of registry entries based on .adm files.
- Applied to domains.
- Further controlled by user membership in security groups.
- Not secure.
- Persistent in users' profiles until the specified policy is reversed or until the user edits the registry.
- Used primarily to lock down desktops.
- Extensible only by using .adm files.

In Windows 2000, Group Policy settings are the administrator's primary method for enabling centralized change and configuration management. You can use Group Policy to create a specific desktop configuration for a particular group of users and computers. Customize Group Policy to accomplish this goal by using the Microsoft Management Console (MMC) Group Policy snap-in. The Group Policy snap-in replaces the Windows NT 4.0 System Policy Editor and gives you greater control over configuration settings for groups of computers and users.

With more than 100 security-related settings and more than 450 registry-based settings, Windows 2000 Group Policy provides you with a broad range of options for managing the user's computing environment. Windows 2000 Group Policy:

- Can be based on Active Directory or defined locally.
- Can be extended using Microsoft Management Console (MMC) or .adm files.
- Is secure.
- Does not leave settings in the users' profiles when the effective policy is changed.
- Can be applied to users or computers in a specified Active Directory container (sites, domains, and OUs).
- Can be further controlled by user or computer membership in security groups.
- Can be used to configure many types of security settings. (For more information about security settings, see "Planning Distributed Security" in this book.)
- Can be used to apply logon, logoff, startup, and shutdown scripts.
- Can be used to install and maintain software.
- Can be used to redirect folders (such as My Documents and Application Data).
- Can be used to perform maintenance on Microsoft® Internet Explorer.

The Group Policy settings that you create are contained in Group Policy objects that are linked with selected Active Directory sites, domains, and OUs. Group Policy uses a document-centered approach to creating, storing, and associating policy settings. Just as Microsoft® Word stores information in .doc files, Group Policy stores settings in Group Policy objects.

In addition, you can precisely adjust your organization's use of Group Policy on computers and users by using security groups to filter Group Policy objects. This ensures faster processing of Group Policy.

Applying Windows NT 4.0 Policies to Windows 2000

Moving Windows NT 4.0–based clients and servers to Windows 2000 will alter the way your policies behave. Base your migration strategy on whether the user account objects and computer account objects are located on a Windows NT 4.0 Server–based server or on a Windows 2000 Server–based server with Active Directory. Table 23.3 assumes that there is a Windows 2000–based client. All clients that receive Windows NT 4.0 system policy obtain it from the Netlogon share of the user logon server.

Table 23.3   Expected Behaviors of Server Operating Systems

Environment	Account Object Location	What Affects the Client
Pure Windows NT 4.0	Computer: Windows NT 4.0	**At computer startup**: Computer local Group Policy (only if changed). **Every time the user logs on**: Computer system policy .
	Computer refresh	**Before Control-Alt-Delete**: Computer local Group Policy only. **After the user logs on**: Computer local Group Policy and computer system policy.
	User: Windows NT 4.0	**When the user logs on**: User system policy. **If local Group Policy changes**: User local Group Policy and user system policy.
	User refresh	User local Group Policy and user system policy.

(continued)

Table 23.3   Expected Behaviors of Server Operating Systems *(continued)*

Environment	Account Object Location	What Affects the Client
Mixed (migration)	Computer: Windows NT 4.0	**At computer startup**: Computer local Group Policy (only if changed). **Every time the user logs on**: Computer system policy.
	Computer refresh	**Before Control-Alt-Delete**: Computer local Group Policy only. **After the user logs on**: Computer local Group Policy and computer system policy.
	User: Windows 2000	**When the user logs on**: Group Policy is processed after computer system policy.
	User refresh	User Group Policy.
Mixed (migration)	Computer: Windows 2000	**During system startup**: Group Policy.
	Computer refresh	Computer Group Policy
	User: Windows NT 4.0	**When the user logs on**: User system policy. **If local Group Policy changes**: User local Group Policy and user system policy.
	User refresh	User local Group Policy and user system policy.
Windows 2000	Computer: Windows 2000	**During computer startup and when the user logs on**: Group Policy.
	User: Windows 2000	
Without Active Directory	Local	Local Group Policy only.

Note   When the computer account object exists in a Windows NT 4.0 domain and the user account object exists in a Windows 2000 domain, computer system policy is processed when the user logs on. You can do this by using the NTConfig.pol file from the Netlogon share of the Windows 2000–based domain controller that is used to authenticate the user, rather than the Windows NT 4.0–based domain controller. It is recommended that you move out of this mixed processing mode and into a pure Windows 2000 mode as quickly as possible.

There are no options available to modify this behavior. To simplify administration in your organization, consider replacing Windows NT 4.0 system policies with Windows 2000 Group Policy as quickly as possible.

Using Active Directory to Delegate Client Management

Windows 2000 client management is most fully enabled in an environment that includes Windows 2000 Professional, Windows 2000 Server, and an Active Directory namespace.

Group Policy settings are associated with an Active Directory container—a domain, site, or OU. Group Policy settings that you configure in conjunction with your organization's Active Directory structure allow you to define client standards as broadly (for an entire organization) or as narrowly (for members of a single workgroup, job function, or location) as you need. The level at which Group Policy settings are implemented needs to align with your organization's administration model, which was defined along with your Active Directory and domain model.

Although the IT team tasked with creating and implementing client standards historically does not get involved in domain namespace planning, it is strongly recommended that you do so if your organization is planning an Active Directory namespace. The earlier in the planning process that the domain namespace team understands your client administration needs and goals, the more likely it becomes that the organization's eventual namespace design will enhance your ability to manage and support user needs.

Caution   If the Active Directory namespace has not yet been developed, the client administration teams need to work with the directory and namespace team so that client standards can be set, Group Policy settings defined, and administrative tasks performed at the most efficient level in the organization.

A well-designed Active Directory namespace makes it relatively simple to implement certain client standards, such as enterprise e-mail, at the domain or OU level. This also facilitates delegating the ability to manage specific client tasks at other levels, such as adding or deleting users, modifying desktop configurations, or implementing workgroup applications.

For example, you might want to define security and basic (e-mail, word processing, and so on) application standards at the domain level for an entire enterprise. However, it might be inefficient to have administrators at the enterprise level add and delete users when an administrative assistant at the site or OU level can be given restricted authority to make these frequent but routine changes.

Similarly, a domain-level administrator might not be the best person to reset passwords when a help desk person at the site or OU level is typically the first person to be called when a new password is needed. With Windows 2000 Group Policy, you can delegate password-related tasks to help desk personnel without giving them access to settings that you do not want them to alter.

As part of your Client administration plan:

- Identify all client-related administrative tasks, such as: new computer setup; user account setup, transfers, and removal; software installation and upgrades; troubleshooting; and the definition of client configuration standards.

- Identify where in the organization these tasks are currently performed.

- Identify at what level in the organization they need to be performed.

For more information about the relationship of Group Policy to your Active Directory structure, see "Designing the Active Directory Structure" in this book.

Delegating Administration of Group Policy

Organizations that deploy Active Directory can also delegate control of portions of the directory service, and thereby delegate responsibility for the many client administration tasks described earlier in this chapter. This section explains how Group Policy can allow you to delegate administrative tasks at the site, domain, and OU levels.

Delegating administration through Group Policy involves the following three tasks, which can be performed together or separately, as your situation requires:

- Managing Group Policy links for a site, domain, or OU.
- Creating Group Policy objects.
- Editing Group Policy objects.

Managing Group Policy Links for a Site, Domain, or OU

By default, only members of the Domain Administrators and Enterprise Administrators groups can configure Group Policy for sites, domains, or organizational units. The **Group Policy** tab in the site's, domain's, or OU's **Properties** page allows you to specify which Group Policy objects are linked to a site, domain, or OU.

Active Directory supports security settings on a per-property basis. This means that you can give a nonadministrator read and write access to specific properties. In this case, if nonadministrators have been delegated the **Manage Group Policy links** task, they can manage the Group Policy objects linked to that site, domain, or OU. To give a user this ability, use the Delegation Wizard.

Creating Group Policy Objects

By default, only members of Domain Administrators, Enterprise Administrators and Group Policy Creator Owners groups can create new Group Policy objects. If the Domain Administrator wants a nonadministrator or group to be able to create Group Policy objects, that user or group can be added to the Group Policy Creator Owners security group. When a nonadministrator who is a member of the Group Policy Creator Owners group creates a Group Policy object, that user becomes the creator and owner of the Group Policy object and can edit the object. Being a member of the Group Policy Creator Owners group gives the nonadministrator full control of only those Group Policy objects that the user creates or those explicitly delegated to that user.

Editing Group Policy Objects

By default, Group Policy objects allow members of the Domain Administrators, Enterprise Administrators, and Group Policy Creator Owners groups full control without the Apply Group Policy attribute set. This means that they can edit the Group Policy object, but the policies contained in that Group Policy object do not apply to them.

By default, Authenticated Users have read access to the Group Policy object with the Apply Group Policy attribute set. This means that Group Policy affects them.

Domain Administrators and Enterprise Administrators are also members of Authenticated Users; therefore, members of those groups are, by default, affected by Group Policy objects unless you explicitly exclude them.

When a nonadministrator creates a Group Policy object, this person becomes the Creator Owner of the Group Policy object. When an administrator creates a Group Policy object, the Domain Administrators group becomes the Creator Owner of the Group Policy object.

To edit a Group Policy object, the user must have both read and write access to the Group Policy object. To edit a Group Policy object, the user must be one of the following:

- A member of the Domain Administrators or Enterprise Administrators groups.
- A member of the Group Policy Creator Owners group and must have previously created the Group Policy object.
- A user with delegated access to the Group Policy object. That is, an administrator or a user who has had access delegated to him or her by someone with the appropriate rights using the **Security** tab on the **Group Policy Object Properties** page.

Creating Group Policy MMC Consoles to Delegate Group Policy

You can delegate Group Policy by creating and saving Group Policy snap-in consoles (.msc files), and then specifying which users and groups have access permissions to the Group Policy object or to an Active Directory container. You can define permissions for a Group Policy object by using the **Security** tab on the **Properties** page of the Group Policy object; these permissions grant or deny access to a Group Policy object to specified groups.

This type of delegation is also enhanced by the policy settings available for MMC. Several policies are available in the **Administrative Templates** node, under **Windows Components** in the **Microsoft Management Console**. These policies enable the administrator to define which MMC snap-ins the affected user might or might not run. The policy definitions can be inclusive, which only allows a set of snap-ins to run, or they can be exclusive, which does not allow a set of snap-ins to run.

Special Group Policy Implementation Options

By applying Group Policy options carefully, you can improve network response times, even when you begin to use the more data-intensive folder redirection and software installation options. Apply Group Policy options conservatively, especially at the beginning, and test all proposed changes carefully to ensure that network performance is not compromised.

In addition, a number of implementation options allow you to fine tune the application of Group Policy without creating additional Group Policy objects. The following are some of the options available:

- Security group filtering options
- No Override (Enforce) Group Policy object option
- Block Policy inheritance by OU option
- Policy processing "loopback" policy setting options
- Slow link processing options
- Periodic refresh options
- Synchronous and asynchronous processing options

Each of these options is explained briefly in the following sections.

Security Group Filtering Options

You can refine which groups of computers and users a particular Group Policy object affects by using Windows 2000 security groups. This means that you can filter the effect that any Group Policy object has on members of specified security groups. To do this, use the **Security** tab on the **Properties** page of the Group Policy object.

For example, based on the level of autonomy that is appropriate for your users, assign different types of users to Windows 2000 user groups. Windows 2000 provides the following default user groups, which are similar—but not identical —to the default groups in Microsoft® Windows NT® version 3.51 and Windows NT 4.0:

- Administrators. Members can fully administer the computer or domain.
- Backup Operators. Members can bypass file security to back up files.
- Power Users. Members can modify the computer and install programs, but cannot read files that belong to other users. They can also share directories and printers.
- Users. Members can create and save documents, but they cannot install programs without administrator permissions and cannot make potentially damaging changes to the system files and system settings.
- Guests. Members are granted short-term access to the computer or domain. This category can include special permissions appropriate to vendors or contractors. For example, the Guest account is disabled by default.

Note Windows 2000 allows administrators to exercise more precise control over users than Windows NT 4.0. Therefore, the default permissions that applied to Users in Windows NT 3.51 and 4.0 now apply to Power Users. And the default permissions that applied to Restricted Users in Windows NT 3.51 and 4.0 now apply to Users.

In Table 23.1, the Chief Financial Officer, Branch Manager, and Sales Person might be added to the Power Users group, and the Receptionist and Factory Floor Worker to the Users group. You can create additional groups based on the tasks that members perform, the degree of authority they have to modify their own or other computers, and the configurations you want them to have. For example, you might subdivide the Users group by department within the organization (Sales, Human Resources, Engineering, and so on) so that you can create and deploy appropriate standard configurations for all employees who perform identical tasks. This can greatly simplify the process of administering users with disparate configuration and permission requirements.

Preventing Group Policy object policy settings from applying to a specified group requires removing the **Apply Group Policy Access Control** entry from that group.

For groups containing nonadministrators, the **Read Access Control** entry must also be removed, because data is viewable to anyone with read access.

For more information about setting up and using security groups, see "Planning Distributed Security" in this book.

No Override (Enforce) and Block Policy Options

Options exist that allow you to enforce the settings contained in a specific Group Policy object so that Group Policy objects in lower-level Active Directory containers are prevented from overriding that policy. For example, if you have defined a specific Group Policy object at the domain level and you have specified that the Group Policy object be enforced (No Override), the policy settings that the Group Policy object contains apply to all OUs under that domain; that is, the lower-level containers (OUs) cannot override that domain Group Policy.

You can also block inheritance of Group Policy from parent Active Directory containers. For example, if you specify "Block Policy inheritance" for an OU, this prevents Group Policy objects specified in higher-level Active Directory containers (such as a higher-level OU or domain) from applying. However, the No Override (enforced) policy option always take precedence over the Block Policy option.

Loopback Options

You apply Group Policy to a user or computer based on where the user or computer object is located in Active Directory. However, you might need to apply Group Policy to users based on the physical location of the computer object as opposed to the logical location of the user object in the organization—in a library, for example, or when a user in one OU logs onto a computer in a different OU. The Group Policy loopback feature gives the administrator the ability to apply User Group Policy settings based on the computer to which the user logs on.

For example, you might set the loopback option when you do not want applications that have been assigned or published to the users of the Marketing OU to be installed while they are logged on to the computers in the Servers OU. With the Group Policy loopback support feature, you can specify two other ways to retrieve the list of Group Policy objects for any user of the computers in the Servers OU:

Merge Mode In the Merge mode, the user's list of Group Policy objects is processed normally by using the GetGPOList Application Programming Interface (API) function during the logon process, and then the GetGPOList API function is called again using the computer's location in Active Directory. Next, the list of Group Policy objects for the computer is added to the end of the Group Policy objects for the user. This causes the computer's Group Policy objects to have higher precedence than the user's Group Policy objects.

Replace Mode In this mode, the Group Policy objects that apply to the user are not processed. Only the Group Policy objects based upon the computer object are used.

The path to this policy setting is: Computer Configuration\Administrative Templates\System\Group Policy. The Policy name is: User Group Policy loopback processing mode.

Slow Link Processing

Many users, such as those with portable computers and those who work off the premises or in a branch location, sometimes connect to the network by using slow connections. Many Group Policy settings can be configured to run only when there is an adequate network connection. These Group Policy settings include:

- Software installation and maintenance
- Scripts
- Disk quota
- IP Security
- Dfs recovery policy
- Internet Explorer maintenance

The path to the slow link policy setting is: Computer Configuration\Administrative Templates\System\Group Policy. Each Group Policy option listed has a processing policy that allows you to change its slow link behavior.

When Group Policy detects a slow link, it applies the following default settings, unless they are modified:

- Security settings: ON (and cannot be turned off).
- Administrative templates: ON (and cannot be turned off).
- Software installation and maintenance: OFF.
- Scripts: OFF.
- Folder redirection: OFF.
- Internet Explorer maintenance: OFF.

For all but the Administrative Templates and the Security Settings snap-in, a policy is provided for toggling the settings on and off. For more information about configuring computers with slow network connections, see "Using Group Policy for Configuration Control" later in this chapter.

Periodic Refresh Processing

You can specify that Group Policy be processed periodically. By default, this is done every 90 minutes, with a randomized offset of 30 minutes. The offset is a random time added to the refresh interval to prevent all clients from requesting Group Policy at the same time. It is designed to prevent unnecessary peak loads on the network, for example, 90 minutes after a large number of users turn on their computers and log on at the same time. You can alter this refresh rate as needed, using smaller intervals in test or demonstration environments, for example, and larger intervals if desired.

There are two policy settings that allow you to alter the refresh rate, located in: Computer Configuration\Administrative Templates\System\Group Policy. One policy setting is for domain controllers; the other is for all other computers (including other servers). These policy settings are named "Group Policy refresh interval for..."

Synchronous and Asynchronous Processing

By default, Group Policy processing is synchronous, for both computer and user policy settings. For computer processing, users cannot log on until all computer Group Policy settings have been updated. For user processing, users do not have access to the desktop until all user Group Policy settings have been updated. These processing rules provide the safest mode of operation.

There is a Group Policy setting for both computer and user Group Policy processing that makes processing asynchronous. It directs the system to proceed without waiting to complete Group Policy updates before displaying the logon prompt (computer settings) or the desktop (user settings).

As a result of asynchronous processing, the logon dialog box might appear sooner, or the Windows interface can appear to be ready before all Group Policy settings have been applied.

If you specify asynchronous processing and the user can complete the logon process and begin working on the computer before the computer or user settings have been processed, you can create significant problems for the user. If, for example, the user begins working in an application that is being modified, the process might fail or the user might experience unwanted events after the computer and user settings have been processed.

Using Client-Side Extensions

Some Group Policy components include client-side extensions (.dlls) that are responsible for implementing Group Policy on the client computer.

The client-side extensions are loaded on an as-needed basis when a client is processing policy. The client first obtains a list of Group Policy objects. Next, it loops through all the client-side extensions and determines whether each client-side extension has any data in any of the Group Policy objects. If a client-side extension has data in a Group Policy object, the client-side extension is called with the list of Group Policy objects that it needs to process. If the client-side extension does not have any settings in any of the Group Policy objects, it is not called.

A computer policy setting exists for each of the Group Policy client-side extensions. Each policy includes a maximum of three options (check boxes). Some of the client-side extensions include only two computer policy options because the third option is not appropriate for that extension.

The following section explains client-side Group Policy processing options.

Allow processing across a slow network connection

When a client-side extension registers itself with the operating system, it sets values of entries in the registry specifying whether it must be called when policy is being applied across a slow link. Some extensions (such as software installation and maintenance) move large amounts of data, so processing across a slow link can affect performance (consider the time involved in installing a large application across a 28.8 kilobytes per second (KBps) modem line).

An administrator can set the connection speed that is considered slow. Also, if an administrator decides that the client-side extension must run across a slow link regardless of the amount of data, he or she can enable this policy. The path to this is Computer Configuration\Administrative Templates\System\Group Policy.

Do not apply during periodic background processing

Computer policy is applied at boot time, and then again in the background approximately every 90 minutes. User policy is applied when the user logs on, and then approximately every 90 minutes.

Some extensions can process policy only during the initial run because it is risky to process policy in the background. For example, with software installation and maintenance it is only safe to process application changes during computer startup or the user logon process. Otherwise, a user that is using an application might have the application uninstalled and a new version installed while they are still trying to work.

Some extensions allow their default behavior to be changed. The **Do not apply during periodic background processing** option can be used to override this default behavior and force the extension to either run or not run in the background.

Process even if the Group Policy objects have not changed

By default, if the Group Policy objects on the server have not changed, it is not necessary to continually reapply them to the client, because the client already has all the settings. However, if users are administrators of their computers they can change policy settings. In this case, it might make sense to reapply these settings during the logon process or during the periodic refresh cycle to return the computer to the wanted state.

For example, assume that you have used Group Policy to define a specific set of security options for a file. Then the user (with administrative privileges) logs on and changes it. You might want to set the policy to process Group Policy even if the Group Policy objects have not changed, so that security is reapplied at every startup or when logging on. This also applies to applications. Group Policy installs an application, but the end user can remove the application or delete the icon. The **Process even if the Group Policy objects have not changed** option gives the administrator the ability to forcibly restore the application the next time the user logs on.

Comparing Stand-Alone and Active Directory-Based Management Features

Table 23.4 summarizes the management features that are available by using Windows 2000 Professional with Active Directory versus Windows 2000 Professional without Active Directory.

Table 23.4   Comparison of Windows 2000 Professional and Active Directory–Based Management Features

Management Features	Windows 2000 Professional	Windows 2000 Professional with Windows 2000 Server, Active Directory, and Group Policy
Administrative Templates (registry-based settings)	X	X
Security Settings	X	X
Software Installation and Maintenance (Assign and Publish)	--	X
Remote Installation	--	X
Unattended Install	X	X
Sysprep	X	X
Scripts	X	X

(continued)

Management Features *(continued)*

Management Features	Windows 2000 Professional	Windows 2000 Professional with Windows 2000 Server, Active Directory, and Group Policy
Folder Redirection	--	X
Internet Explorer Maintenance	X	X
User Profiles	X	X
Roaming User Profiles	--	X

All of the Group Policy snap-ins that can be used on a local computer can also be used when Group Policy is focused on an Active Directory container.

However, the following activities require Windows 2000 Server, an Active Directory infrastructure, and a client running Windows 2000:

- Software installation and maintenance, that is, the ability to centrally manage software for groups of users and computers.

- User data and settings management, including folder redirection, which allows special folders to be redirected to the network.

- Remote Operating System Installation.

For more information about change and configuration options, see "Applying Change and Configuration Management" in this book.

If you use local Group Policy initially and then make the computer a member of a domain with Active Directory and Group Policy implemented, local Group Policy is processed first, and the domain-based Group Policy is processed next. If there is a conflict between the domain and local Group Policy, the domain policy prevails. However, if a computer subsequently leaves the domain, the local Group Policy is reapplied.

 Critical Decision If you upgrade clients to Windows 2000 Professional before you upgrade to Windows 2000 Server, and you expect to transition to a managed Active Directory environment later, you must plan your Group Policy strategy carefully so that users cannot alter their computers before more stringent controls are in place. For example, if you deploy Windows 2000 Professional in an unmanaged environment and later want to move these computers into a managed Active Directory domain, you might need to reinstall the operating system and applications to ensure that unauthorized changes have not been made to the system configuration.

Using Group Policy on Stand-alone Computers

Although it is not recommended, there might be instances when you need to deploy Group Policy on stand-alone computers.

On a stand-alone computer running Windows 2000 Professional, local Group Policy objects are located at \%*SystemRoot*%\System32\GroupPolicy. You can use the following when the Group Policy snap-in is focused on a local computer:

- Security settings. You can only define security settings for the local computer, not for a domain or network.

- Administrative templates that allow you to set more than 450 operating system behaviors.

- Scripts. You can use scripts to automate computer startup and shutdown, as well as how the user logs on and off.

The following are examples of business rules that you might enforce through local Group Policy:

- The users of this computer cannot access the Run command.

- A virus program runs every time this computer is restarted.

- Hide common program groups in the **Start** menu.

To manage Group Policy on local computers, you need administrative rights to those computers. You can access the Group Policy snap-in, focused on the local computers, using the following procedure:

▶   **To access Group Policy snap-ins**

1. From the **Start** menu, click **Run**, type **MMC**, and then click **OK**.

2. In the **Console** menu of the MMC window, click **Add/Remove Snap-in**.

3. On the **Stand-alone** tab, click **Add**.

4. In the **Add Snap-in** dialog box, click **Group Policy**, and then click **Add**.

5. When the **Select Group Policy Object** dialog box appears, click **Local Computer** to edit the local Group Policy object.

6. Click **Finish**.

7. Click **Close**.

8. Click **OK**. The Group Policy snap-in opens with its focus on the local Group Policy object.

This procedure also allows the Group Policy snap-in to be opened on a remote computer. At step 5, click **Browse**, and then choose the wanted computer.

Note Local Group Policy does not allow you to do security filtering or to have multiple sets of Group Policy objects (as do Active Directory–based Group Policy objects). You can, however, set Discretionary Access Control Lists (DACLs) on the folder %SystemRoot%\System32\GroupPolicy so that specified groups either will or will not be affected by the settings contained within the local Group Policy object. This option is useful if you need to control and administer computers used in situations, such as kiosk environments, that are not connected to a LAN. Unlike Group Policy administered from Active Directory, this uses only the **Read** attribute, which makes it possible for the local Group Policy object to affect ordinary users but not local administrators. The local administrator can first set the policy settings they want, then set the DACLs to the local Group Policy object directory so that administrators as a group no longer have Read access. For the administrator to make subsequent changes to the local Group Policy object, he or she first needs to take ownership of the directory to give themselves Read access, make the changes, and then remove Read access.

Configuring Hardware

By this time, you should know which of your desktop, workstation, and portable computers and peripherals meet minimum Windows 2000 requirements.

 Critical Decision Verify before you begin the process of upgrading systems that your current basic input/output system (BIOS) supports Windows 2000 or that Windows 2000–compatible BIOS upgrades are readily available.

After you have verified that your systems meet Windows 2000 requirements, much of the work of configuring hardware under Windows 2000 is automated during the installation process. However, the following are a few of the major hardware configuration-related issues that your client configuration plan must address.

File System Support

Microsoft recommends that you format all Windows 2000 partitions that do not need to be accessed by clients running other operating systems with the NTFS file system. In the event of a system failure, NTFS uses its log file and check point information to restore the consistency of the file system. In addition, NTFS:

- Supports all Windows 2000 operating system features.
- Provides improved file compression and decompression.
- Provides faster access speeds by minimizing the number of disk accesses required to find a file.
- Provides improved file and folder security.

On NTFS volumes, you can use Group Policy to designate the following file permission options—No Access, List, Read, Add, Add and Read, Change, Full Control, Special Directory Access, and Special File Access. You can also use Group Policy to specify which users and groups have access to these volumes and what level of access is permitted.

These additional file security options allow organizations to configure more stringent file access than Windows 95 and Windows NT 4.0 Workstation. If users store sensitive information on a portable computer, they can encrypt those files and folders. If a portable computer is stolen, Windows 2000 Encrypting File System (EFS) protects its files and folders, even if the thief reinstalls Windows 2000 Professional. However, be sure that an administrator, as well as the end user, has sufficient rights to access encrypted files and folders.

Hardware Profiles

As stated earlier, most of the work of hardware configuration is automated. However, some advanced configuration might be required for earlier model portable computers that are frequently switched between use in a docking station and stand-alone use, or that are moved from a primary network connection to offline status, and then reconnected to the network from a second, third, or even fourth different type of network connection.

Because many portable computer users are not technically proficient in configuring hardware profiles, you might want to configure hardware profiles for these different environments or train these users to modify their own computers to connect to the network. See Figure 23.2 for an example.

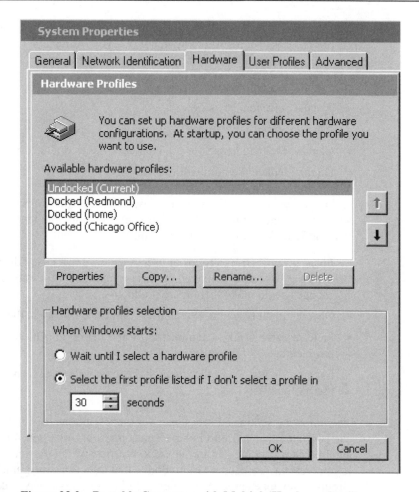

Figure 23.2   Portable Computer with Multiple Hardware Profiles

Only configure hardware profiles for multiple computers simultaneously if the portable computers, configuration options, and peripherals are exactly identical. Alternately, you might want to both configure some hardware settings and provide additional end-user configuration training so that they can do some of these tasks on their own.

Defining User Interface Standards

As noted earlier in this chapter, every organization has unique user computing requirements. Windows 2000 allows you to create standard operating environments, including user interface (UI) standards, based on the needs of your organization.

Whether you choose to accept the Windows 2000 defaults or implement your own UI preferences, Microsoft recommends that you evaluate Windows 2000 configuration options according to the following criteria:

- Are they easy to learn?
- Are they efficient to use?
- Are they easy to remember?
- Can they help address your top help desk issues or concerns?
- Do they reduce the number of user errors?

Although few organizations need to research these questions in as much depth as a software manufacturer such as Microsoft, the following techniques might help you configure Windows 2000 to best meet the needs of your users:

- Focus groups. Bring groups of users together for focused discussions about what they like and dislike about their computer configurations, and what changes could make them more productive.
- Observational research. Watch users while they work on their computers.
- Field research. Talk to administrators at other organizations about what they have learned.
- Expert reviews. Study the research that exists about user interface design and user productivity.

The following sections discuss many of the UI options in Windows 2000 that you can configure using Group Policy. The configuration options that are not set by an administrator become part of the users' profiles, which they can configure at will. If you create a subsequent Group Policy that affects a configuration option, the Group Policy takes precedence. Group Policy settings always take precedence over user-implemented UI configurations, which are saved in the users' profiles.

Basic Users

Basic users have less experience with computers than advanced users; therefore IT configures their systems to maximize their productivity and to minimize their leeway in making potentially harmful changes to their systems. The **Run** menu and Control Panel are disabled so that only changes specified by an administrator using Group Policy are implemented. Only network links that are assigned by an Administrator are available to users. They also cannot add or remove applications that are not approved by an administrator.

Advanced Users

Advanced users are usually more experienced, frequently run demanding applications that require special configuration options, or are disconnected from the network, and therefore need to be allowed greater leeway to manage their own systems. However, the same mandatory logon and logoff options and features, such as multilingual and accessibility options, must be available to them.

Using Group Policy for Configuration Control

You can use Group Policy to control many desktop settings and configuration options, such as:

- Customizing logon and logoff processes
- Customizing the desktop
- Customizing many components of the operating system

The following sections discuss configuration options in each of these categories. These are representative examples and are not an exhaustive list. Remember, there are over 550 different Group Policy settings, and the best way to see all the different options is to study an installed version of Windows 2000. For more information about Group Policy settings, see "Group Policy" in the *Microsoft® Windows® 2000 Server Resource Kit Distributed Systems Guide*.

As you read through the remainder of this chapter, and subsequently work with Windows 2000, note the options that might be of use to your organization. Then, when your list is complete, you can begin to customize Group Policy objects to meet your needs. You should also include the complete list of options and Group Policy settings in your Client Configuration Plan.

Customizing the Logon and Logoff Processes

Windows 2000 provides numerous ways to customize logon and logoff processes. For example, you can specify that a diagnostics or virus program be run every time a user logs on or logs off.

Table 23.5 lists some logon and logoff options that might be useful to you.

Table 23.5   Sample Logon and Logoff Group Policy Options

Policy	Description
Run legacy logon scripts hidden	By default, Windows 2000 displays the instructions in logon scripts written for Windows NT 4.0 and earlier in a command window as they run (it does not display logon scripts written for Windows 2000). Enabling this policy prevents logon scripts written for Windows NT 4.0 and earlier from displaying.
Add Logoff to the Start Menu	Adds the "Log Off *<username>*" item to the **Start** menu and prevents users from removing it.
Do not save settings at exit	Rolls back changes made to the desktop by users during their last session.
Do not display welcome screen at logon	Hides the **Getting Started with Windows 2000** welcome screen that is displayed on Windows 2000 Professional each time the user logs on.

Restricting Changes to the Desktop

Group Policy can assist you in preventing users from making potentially counter-productive changes to their computers. In addition, it can enable you to optimize the desktop for the particular tasks performed in your organization. Table 23.6 lists some policies that you can use to customize the desktop.

Note   Many organizations will want to create custom configurations of their Internet and intranet browser software. For more information about customizing and managing Internet Explorer 5, see the Microsoft® Internet Explorer Administration Kit (IEAK) link on the Web Resources page at http://windows.microsoft.com/windows2000/reskit/webresources. Windows 2000 includes a Group Policy snap-in to configure and manage Internet Explorer 5, called Internet Explorer Maintenance.

Table 23.6   Sample Custom Desktop Options

Policy	Description
Prohibit user from changing My Documents path	Prevents users from changing the path to the My Documents folder.
Disable Control Panel	Disables all Control Panel programs.
Hide the **Add a program from CD-ROM or floppy disk** option	Removes the Add a program from CD-ROM or floppy disk option from the **Add New Programs** page.

(continued)

Table 23.6   Sample Custom Desktop Options *(continued)*

Policy	Description
Hide specified Control Panel programs	Hides specified Control Panel items and folders.
Prohibit changes to the Active Desktop	Allows you to enforce a standard desktop by preventing the user from enabling or disabling Active Desktop or changing the Active Desktop configuration.
Active Desktop wallpaper	Specifies the desktop background wallpaper displayed on all users' desktops.
Century Interpretation for Year 2000 (System)	Specifies the last year for which two-digit years are interpreted as being in the 21st century.
Hide these specified drives in **My Computer**	Removes the icons representing the selected hard drives from **My Computer**, **Windows Explorer**, and **My Network Places**. Also, the drive letters representing the selected drives do not appear in the **Open** dialog box.
Desktop screen saver executable name	Specifies the screen saver used on the computer.
Disable the command prompt	Prevents users from running the interactive command prompt, Cmd.exe. This policy also determines whether batch files (.bat, .cmd) can run on the computer.
Disable registry editing tools	Disables the Windows registry editors, Regedt32.exe and Regedit.exe.

Restricting Changes to the Start Menu

In your organization, you might want to have control over which **Start** menu features are enabled. Group Policy allows you to disable the options you do not want to make available, and to create an optimized **Start** menu that reflects the needs of your organization and its users. Table 23.7 illustrates a few examples.

Table 23.7   Representative Start Menu Options

Policy	Description
Disable and remove links to **Windows Update**	Removes the **Windows Update** hyperlink. This policy removes the **Windows Update** hyperlink from the **Start** menu and from the **Tools** menu in Internet Explorer.
Remove **Run** command from **Start** Menu	Removes the Run command from the **Start** menu and removes the New Task (Run) command from Task Manager. Also, users with extended keyboards can no longer display the Run dialog box by using the Run command keyboard shortcut.
Add Logoff to the **Start** Menu	Adds the "Log Off <*username*>" item to the **Start** menu and prevents users from removing it.
Disable drag-and-drop shortcut menus on the **Start** menu	Prevents users from using the drag and drop method to reorder or remove items on the **Start** menu. Also, removes shortcut menus from the **Start** menu.
Do not use the search-based method when resolving shell shortcuts	Prevents the system from conducting a comprehensive search of the target drive to resolve a shortcut.
Do not run specified Windows-based applications	Prevents Windows from running the programs that you specify in this policy.

Note The **Start** menu that you customize and provide to users can be stored locally, or it can be stored on a network server.

Configuring Options for Remote Users

The growing number of users with portable computers in many organizations has made managing these remote computers a major administrative concern. The strategies in Table 23.8 can be useful in managing user data for remote access users.

Table 23.8   Portable and Remote Computer Options

Strategy	Description
Limit the use of Group Policy	Group Policy cannot be turned off, even over slow links. (Be careful about applying excessively restrictive Group Policy settings or those that download lots of data to portable computers or users' home computers. Consider logon scripts and the default time-out of 600 seconds.)
Automatically detect slow network connections	Allows you to set threshold levels for what is considered a slow link. You can then define certain bandwidth-intensive activities that must not take place when slow links are encountered.
Specify network files and folders that are always available offline	Allows you to specify network files and folders that are always available for offline use.
Disable Make Available Offline	Prevents users from making certain files and folders available.

Adding Multilingual Options

More organizations than ever are entering new geographic markets, and users speaking many different languages are traveling in larger numbers. Multilingual users exist in almost every medium-sized or large organization in every country and region.

This creates new issues for IT administrators, such as the following:

- Supporting users who speak multiple languages and who are more comfortable and effective computing in a language other than the one most commonly used in the local office. Keyboard layouts, sorting orders, date formats, currency formats, help files, and similar localized settings all need to be configured to ensure optimum productivity.

- Configuring operating systems for every possible combination of languages adds unnecessary complexity and cost to deployment and support costs. Help desk personnel cannot easily troubleshoot and correct problems when there are multiple versions of the operating system.

- If there are multiple localized versions of the operating system in the organization, the same number of service packs have to be tested and deployed each time they become available.

Windows 2000 enhances support for international and multilingual computing through the use of Unicode character encoding, and National Language Support (NLS) Application Programming Interfaces (APIs), the Multilingual APIs, and Windows resource files. This multilingual technology enables Windows 2000 to support the input and display of languages used in more than 100 international locales, no matter which of 24 localized versions of Windows 2000 you are using.

In addition, Microsoft offers a separate Windows 2000 MultiLanguage Version, which extends the native language support in Windows 2000 by allowing user interface languages to be changed on a per user basis.

Note The Windows 2000 MultiLanguage Version is available only to Microsoft Open License Program, Select, and Enterprise agreement customers. For more information about these programs, see the Licensing Programs for Enterprises link on the Web resources page at http://windows.microsoft.com/windows2000/reskit/webresources.

The MultiLanguage Version allows administrators to:

- Minimize the number of Windows 2000 Server and Windows 2000 Professional installation packages deployed across the network.

- Support travelling users who speak languages other than those spoken in the remote offices they visit.

- Perform administrative tasks in one language and use the same computer, keyboard, and monitor to perform additional tasks in another language without restarting their computer.

- Add or remove multiple user interface languages as needed from computers running Windows 2000 Server and Windows 2000 Professional.

The MultiLanguage Version does not change the language used in applications; it only changes the language used in Windows 2000 menus, dialog boxes, and Help files. A similar Microsoft® Office® 2000 MultiLanguage Pack allows organizations to simplify Office 2000 deployment options.

Considerations for Choosing the MultiLanguage Version

The Windows 2000 MultiLanguage Version provides a variety of options for international and multilingual users. Table 23.9 helps you select the language options appropriate for your organization.

Table 23.9   Multilingual Features and Benefits by Version

Feature	Single Language Version	MultiLanguage Version
Multingual Features for Users	Fully localized user interface includes menus, Help files, dialog boxes, and folder names. Users can input, view, and print in more than 60 languages.	Users can switch the user interface to the language they prefer. They can also input, view, and print in more than 60 languages.
Multilingual Features for IT Professionals	Ideal if you do not have a significant need to support more than one language version in your environment. Users can still view and edit documents in other languages.	Ideal if you need to deploy and support more than one language in your environment. For example, when you need to deploy a service pack, only one version is required. Also ideal if you need to support users speaking multiple languages on a single computer.

Upgrading to the Windows 2000 MultiLanguage Version

You can only upgrade to the MultiLanguage Version from international English versions of Windows. If you want to replace any other language versions of Windows with the Windows 2000 MultiLanguage Version, you will need to perform a clean installation of the MultiLanguage Version.

There are additional version restrictions that you need to be aware of while planning an upgrade to the MultiLanguage Version. Table 23.10 provides version compatibility guidelines.

Table 23.10   MultiLanguage Version Upgrade Options

	Windows 2000 Professional MultiLanguage Version	Windows 2000 Server MultiLanguage Version	Windows 2000 Advanced Server MultiLanguage Version
Windows 3.x	--	--	--
Windows for Workgroups	--	--	--
Windows NT 3.51 Workstation	X	--	--
Windows NT 4.0 Workstation	X	--	--
Windows 95	X	--	--

(continued)

Table 23.10   MultiLanguage Version Upgrade Options *(continued)*

	Windows 2000 Professional MultiLanguage Version	Windows 2000 Server MultiLanguage Version	Windows 2000 Advanced Server MultiLanguage Version
Windows 98	X	--	--
Windows 2000 Professional	X	--	--
Windows NT 3.51 Server	--	X	X
Windows NT 4.0 Server	--	X	X
Windows 2000 Server	--	X	--
Windows NT 4.0 Terminal Server	--	X	X
Windows NT 4.0 Enterprise Edition	--	--	X
Windows 2000 Advanced Server	--	--	X

Planning a Windows 2000 MultiLanguage Version Installation

Addressing the following planning considerations will make your deployment of the Windows 2000 MultiLanguage Version more successful:

- Which MultiLanguage Version files and language groups do you need?

- How much disk space do these language files require?

- What setup process is best to use?

- How do you deploy these files?

- Do you install from a CD-ROM or a network share?

MultiLanguage Version Files and Language Groups

Two distinct collections of language files are necessary for the User Interface language support in the Windows 2000 MultiLanguage Version:

- Language groups, which contain all the necessary fonts and other files necessary to process and display a particular group of languages.

- The MultiLanguage Version files, which provide the language content for the UI and Help system.

For each UI language that you install, the Windows 2000 MultiLanguage Version also requires the relevant language group to be installed. For example, to use the German UI, you must first install the Western Europe and United States language group.

You can install and uninstall Windows 2000 language groups during Windows 2000 Setup, and afterward from Regional Options in Control Panel. The installation and removal of the MultiLanguage Version files is a separate process from the installation of language groups.

Disk Space

Each additional language group that you choose to support on a single computer requires additional disk space. Table 23.11 displays the approximate amount of space required for each language group.

Table 23.11   Approximate Disk Space Required for Language Groups

Language Group	Space Required in Megabytes (MB) (estimated)
Arabic	1.6
Armenian	11.5
Baltic	1
Central European	1.2
Cyrillic	1.2
Georgian	5.8
Greek	1
Hebrew	1.4
Indic	0.25
Japanese	58
Korean	29.4
Simplified Chinese	32.5
Thai	3.9
Traditional Chinese	13.5
Turkic	0.9
Vietnamese	0.5
Western Europe and United States	10.1

Note A number of files (primarily fonts and keyboard layouts) are shared by several language groups. Therefore, if you install multiple language groups, the total amount of space required might be slightly less than a sum of table values.

In addition, allow up to 45 MB of disk space for installation of the MultiLanguage Version files for each User Interface language you choose to install.

Setup

Installation of the Windows 2000 MultiLanguage Version involves two steps:

1. Setup of Windows 2000
2. Setup of the MultiLanguage Version files

By installing the necessary language groups during the Windows 2000 Setup, before you begin installing the corresponding MultiLanguage Version files, you avoid having to swap CD-ROMs during the MultiLanguage Version installation.

The default UI language (the language applied by default to all new user accounts created on the computer) is determined when the MultiLanguage Version is set up. You can change the default UI or add or remove UI languages using the Muisetup.exe file.

Note Adding and removing languages using Muisetup.exe affects only the MultiLanguage Version files. To add or remove the files associated with language groups, use **Regional Options** in Control Panel.

For more information about automating the setup of Windows 2000, see "Automating Server Installation and Upgrade" and "Using Systems Management Server to Deploy Windows 2000" in this book.

Using Group Policy to Manage UI Languages

Using the MultiLanguage Version to reduce the number of client configurations in the organization can greatly simplify the job of administering clients. However, enabling all users to change the UI language on their computer can add unnecessary complexity to the environment. For this reason, you might want to restrict some users' ability to change their UI language. You can do this using Group Policy from the **User Configuration** node of the Group Policy snap-in.

Note also that if you apply MultiLanguage policy to a local computer using local Group Policy, the local Group Policy object will affect all users of that computer because there is no way to filter local Group Policy objects for individual users.

For more information about the Windows 2000 MultiLanguage Version, see the Windows 2000 Professional Multilanguage Support link on the Web Resources page at http://windows.microsoft.com/windows2000/reskit/webresources.

Making Systems More Accessible

Few users are affected by their computer's user interface more than people with special needs. One of your planning goals needs to provide equal access to computer software for everyone, including people with vision, hearing, mobility, or cognitive disabilities.

Do not consider all users with cognitive disabilities as the same category; their needs vary as much or more than the needs of any other types of users. Consider the diversity of user interface issues that are faced by people with the following:

- Vision impairments . Includes blindness, low vision, and color blindness.

- Hearing impairments. Includes deafness or partial hearing loss.

- Mobility impairments. Includes cerebral palsy, tremors, seizures from epilepsy, loss of limbs or digits, and paralysis. Even people with carpal tunnel syndrome or other repetitive stress injuries can be considered people with mobility impairments.

- Cognitive disabilities. Includes learning disabilities, such as dyslexia and memory loss; Down Syndrome, and language impairments, such as illiteracy and language unfamiliarity.

Configuring Windows 2000 Features for Accessibility

Depending on each person's specific needs, different users might find challenges with different aspects of Windows 2000. Table 23.12 describes a few general considerations when configuring Windows 2000, as well as specific new and upgraded accessibility features in Windows 2000.

Table 23.12   Accessibility Features in Windows 2000

Feature	Definition
Microsoft Utility Manager	Utility Manager improves access to accessibility applications on the computer and simplifies the process of configuring those options.
Microsoft Accessibility Wizard	The Accessibility Wizard makes it easier to set up commonly used accessibility features by specifying options by type of disability, rather than by numeric value changes.
Microsoft On-Screen Keyboard	The On-Screen Keyboard allows limited access for users with mobility impairments.
Microsoft Narrator (with built-in text-to-speech functionality)	Narrator is a synthesized limited functionality text-to-speech tool for users with moderate vision impairments. Narrator reads aloud what is displayed on the screen.

(continued)

Table 23.12   Accessibility Features in Windows 2000 *(continued)*

Feature	Definition
Microsoft Magnifier	Magnifier is a basic screen enlarger that displays a portion of the screen in a separate window.
Higher-visibility mouse pointers	New large, extra-large, white, or black pointers. In addition, inverted pointers change color to contrast with the background.
High-contrast color schemes	Expanded library of color schemes can be helpful to users with low vision who require a high degree of contrast between foreground and background.
Quick Launch Bar	Accessibility features status icons on the Quick Launch Bar of the taskbar show the user whether certain commonly-used keyboard filters are active.
Synchronized Accessible Media Interchange (SAMI)	Enables closed captioning of multimedia products.

Enabling Third-Party Devices

Although the accessibility tools released with Windows 2000 provide functionality for users with special needs, most users with disabilities need additional tools for daily use. Also new in Windows 2000 is Microsoft Active Accessibility (MSAA), an API that allows accessibility aides to work with UI elements such as toolbars, menus, text, and graphics.

Examples of add-on software are smaller or larger keyboards, eye-gaze pointing devices, and sip-and-puff systems controlled by breathing. Another category is called augmentative communication devices, which were originally designed to control a speech synthesizer for people who are nonverbal.

Your users might be aware of these products and can tell you which ones they would like to have enabled on their computers. For more information about hardware and software for people with accessibility needs, see the Microsoft Accessibility link on the Web Resources page at http://windows.microsoft.com/windows2000/reskit/webresources.

Using Group Policy to Fine-tune Configurations for Accessibility

A number of configuration options that you can access through Group Policy can be helpful to users with accessibility needs. Review your user interface configuration options with someone knowledgeable about accessibility issues (Human Resources departments typically have someone with this expertise) to configure computers for people with accessibility needs.

Also, when you begin to plan for advanced change and configuration management (see "Applying Change and Configuration Management" in this book), consider the value that these features can have to users with accessibility concerns who might discover that they are no longer restricted to working on only a single computer that has been configured for their needs.

Client Standards Planning Task List

Table 23.13 summarizes the tasks you need to perform when preparing client administration and configuration standards for Windows 2000.

Table 23.13   Client Configuration Planning Task List

Task	Location in This Chapter
Define client administration strategy.	Defining an Administration Model and Standards
Define client application requirements based on job function.	Defining Software Standards
Define client configuration restrictions based on job function.	Configuring Hardware
Configure approved client hardware (portable and desktop computers) to run Windows 2000.	Configuring Hardware
Configure basic Windows 2000 User Interface options.	Making Client Systems Manageable
Logon and logoff options	Using Group Policy for Configuration Control
Start menu options	Using Group Policy for Configuration Control
Desktop options	Using Group Policy for Configuration Control
MultiLanguage options	Adding MultiLingual Options
Accessibility options	Making Systems More Accessible
Configure applications based on client requirements and administrative guidelines.	Defining Application Requirements
Mandatory applications	Defining Application Requirements
Optional applications	Defining Application Requirements

CHAPTER 24

Applying Change and Configuration Management

Client computer configurations, and the ways in which desktops and laptops are used, are becoming increasingly sophisticated. The solutions and services that information technology (IT) needs to provide to users are also becoming more sophisticated. Microsoft® Windows® 2000 provides a number of advanced change and configuration management features that allow you to make users' settings, documents, and software available to them even when they use another computer. In addition, these Active Directory™–enabled features allow you to offer a nearly identical replacement for a user's computer in case a hard disk or other component fails.

The planning steps needed to implement the advanced client management features in Windows 2000, which are commonly referred to as IntelliMirror™, are outlined in this chapter. You will also learn how to incorporate Remote Operating System (OS) Installation into your client support plan. Before reading this chapter, understand and complete the planning steps defined in the chapters "Defining Client Administration and Configuration Standards" and "Designing the Active Directory Structure."

In This Chapter

Chapter Goals

This chapter will help you develop the following planning documents:

- IntelliMirror Implementation Plan
- Remote OS Installation Implementation Plan

Related Information in the Resource Kit

- For more information about basic client configuration options and using Group Policy to manage Windows 2000 clients, see "Defining Client Administration and Configuration Standards" in this book.

- For more information about using Systems Management Server, see "Using Systems Management Server to Deploy Windows 2000" in this book.

- For more information about testing and piloting Windows 2000 technologies, see "Building a Windows 2000 Test Lab" and "Conducting Your Windows 2000 Pilot" in this book.

Evaluating Change and Configuration Management

When users encounter problems with their computers—such as software that stops working, missing files, or hardware malfunctions—an IT support person often has to visit the computer in person to diagnose and solve the problem. Multiplied over hundreds or thousands of client computers, including a growing number of computers that are frequently disconnected from the network and computers that are used by multiple users, these are among the most expensive support issues that network administrators face.

Windows 2000 provides a variety of change and configuration management technologies that can help IT departments reduce the amount of work and costs associated with managing and supporting client computers. By using as a foundation the administrative and configuration standards created in the chapter "Defining Client Administration and Configuration Standards," you can reduce the amount of work and time involved in replacing one computer with another by enabling the following Active Directory–enabled user services:

Remote OS Installation Allows administrators to simplify and reduce the cost of staging and configuring new or replacement client computers. In addition, Remote OS Installation improves the ability of IT to quickly restore a system that has failed with both a preconfigured operating system and basic applications.

Software Installation and Maintenance Allows administrators to specify a set of applications that will always be available to a user or group of users. If a required application is not already installed on the computer when it is needed, it will automatically be installed. Similarly, if an application needs to be repaired (because of a corrupted or accidentally deleted file, for instance), updated, or removed, these tasks can also be performed automatically.

User Settings Management Where the chapter "Defining Client Administration and Configuration Standards" illustrated how you can customize and control the user interface, in this chapter you will learn how to implement Roaming User Profiles. With Roaming User Profiles, user profile settings—as well as the Group Policy settings that apply to the user—are copied to any computer on the network the user might log on to.

User Data Management Allows users to roam to any Windows 2000 Professional–based computer on the corporate network and have access to their data. In addition, if a user takes network-based resources offline, these resources are resynchronized when the user reconnects to the network.

The last three capabilities are grouped under the name IntelliMirror. Together, IntelliMirror and Remote OS Installation make up Windows 2000 change and configuration management, which can dramatically reduce the amount of work and time involved in replacing one computer with another. Figure 24.1 illustrates the planning process for these features.

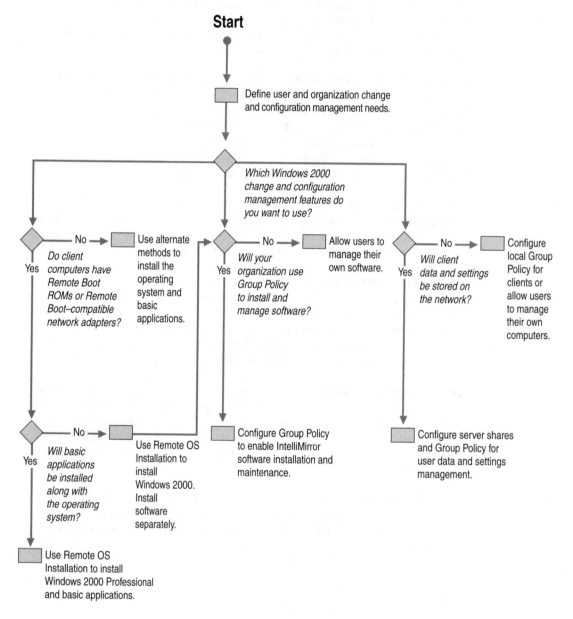

Figure 24.1   Planning Steps for IntelliMirror and Remote OS Installation

Technologies Used to Enable Change and Configuration Management

IntelliMirror and Remote OS Installation are not discrete technologies in Windows 2000. These capabilities take advantage of a number of Windows 2000 technologies that you are probably already deploying. Table 24.1 illustrates the technologies needed to implement IntelliMirror and Remote OS Installation.

Table 24.1   Technologies Used to Enable IntelliMirror and Remote OS Installation

Features	Technology Used
User Settings Management	Active Directory Group Policy Offline Folders Roaming User Profiles
User Data Management	Active Directory Group Policy Offline Folders Synchronization Manager Disk Quotas Roaming User Profiles
Software Installation and Maintenance	Active Directory Group Policy Windows Installer Service Add/Remove Programs Distributed file system (Dfs)
Remote OS Installation	Active Directory Group Policy Remote Installation Services (RIS) Remote installation–capable workstation

You can implement Remote OS Installation and IntelliMirror user data management, user settings management, and software installation and maintenance individually, or in any combination of two or three. You can also implement all four as an integrated change and configuration management solution designed to enable a fast, almost exact, automated computer replacement in case of an equipment failure.

Note   The replacement is described as "almost exact" because some users might store data files in an inappropriate location, which would prevent these files from being replicated on a server. In addition, extremely large files, such as certain mailbox or database files, are difficult to manage because of the amount of network bandwidth, server disk space, and synchronization time required to maintain current copies on both a server and client computer.

Identifying Change and Configuration Management Needs and Opportunities

Windows 2000 change and configuration management features can help you address a number of management concerns. The following are typical situations where organizations will utilize IntelliMirror and Remote OS Installation:

- Configuring a computer for a new hire
- Installing and managing software
- Backing up corporate data
- Recovering from computer failure

These issues can apply to all of the advanced and basic types of user groups— mobile, roaming, remote, task-based, and knowledge-based—that were discussed in the chapter "Defining Client Administration and Configuration Standards." Use your Preferred Client Configuration and Client Administration plans as the foundation for your IntelliMirror and Remote OS Installation implementation plans. Your IntelliMirror and Remote OS Installation Implementation plans will extend these, and will help you fill the administrative and client needs that you identified earlier in your Windows 2000 deployment planning.

Key Background Information

The following background information is particularly important in planning for IntelliMirror and Remote OS Installation:

- How fast will your organization be migrating to Windows 2000 Professional and Windows 2000 Server?

  IntelliMirror and Remote OS Installation are available only on Windows 2000 Professional clients running under a Windows 2000 Server Active Directory– enabled infrastructure.

  Note Windows 2000 Terminal Services clients also can benefit from IntelliMirror and Remote OS Installation. Full Terminal Services clients cannot participate in software installation and maintenance because these applications must be installed on the Terminal Services client. Terminal Services clients running in Administrator mode can utilize software installation and maintenance. For more information about Terminal Services, see "Deploying Terminal Services" in this book.

- Do existing client computers meet the Remote Boot read-only memory (ROM) and Preboot Execution Environment (PXE) prerequisites for Remote OS Installation?

IntelliMirror features do not require faster processors or more memory than are needed to run Windows 2000 Server and Windows 2000 Professional. However, to use Remote OS Installation, clients must have a supported network card or Remote Boot ROM version .99b or greater.

- What are the needs of your users? Do they roam from location to location? Do they use multiple computers? Are they frequently disconnected from the network? Do they have stable or constantly changing application requirements?

  Your goal should be to provide neither more nor fewer of these management features than users require. For more information about aligning IntelliMirror and Remote OS Installation to user needs, see the section "Selecting Change and Configuration Management Options for Your Organization" later in this chapter.

- How fast are your organization's network links? Are users frequently connecting over slow links? Do you have the network bandwidth capacity to support features such as automated software installation and upgrades?

  You will need to test and pilot your IntelliMirror and Remote OS Installation plans under all proposed usage patterns in order to determine how many servers and how much network capacity will be required to implement your change and configuration plans.

- How do you want computer accounts to be administered? Will users installing Windows 2000 Professional create their own computer accounts and customize their own operating system settings? Or does an IT person prestage computers by defining these accounts and settings in advance?

  Remote OS Installation supports both user-managed and IT-managed alternatives through a combination of Group Policy and security settings.

- Are client computers tightly or loosely managed? What are your most costly client administration problems? Can these problems be solved or alleviated using the change and configuration management technologies? How often do you upgrade existing applications or distribute new applications?

  If you have not collected data on these questions already, review the chapter "Defining Client Administration and Configuration Standards."

- Has an Active Directory and domain structure been deployed in your organization? What are the administrative and logical rationales behind your organization's Active Directory and domain structure? Also, have the Dynamic Host Configuration Protocol (DHCP) and Domain Name Server (DNS) services been enabled in your organization?

  For more information about completing these portions of your IT infrastructure, see "Designing the Active Directory Structure" for important planning information that will help you lay a solid foundation for your change and configuration management plans.

Using Systems Management Server to Supplement IntelliMirror

Many organizations with complex environments will complement IntelliMirror and Remote OS Installation by using the advanced change and configuration management tools provided with Systems Management Server 2.0. These tools include:

Planning Tools Systems Management Server uses Windows Management Instrumentation (WMI) and software scanners to retrieve and upload detailed hardware and software inventory information—such as metering application usage—into a Microsoft® SQL Server™–based repository. This collection of planning tools can help you understand the configuration of your environment, complete audits and compliance checks, monitor and restrict application use, and plan for operations such as new software deployments and upgrades.

Deployment Tools Using Systems Management Server, you can schedule and synchronize the deployment of software to Windows-based computers, including Windows 3.*x*, Windows NT® 3.51/4.0, and Windows 2000. This distribution is fully integrated with inventory to allow precise targeting while also allowing detailed status reporting on the progress and success of each scheduled deployment. With Systems Management Server, you can distribute and install software in the background to one, 10, or thousands of computers, even when no users are logged on. Systems Management Server can also deploy software that uses the new Windows Installer technology and packages.

Diagnostic Tools Systems Management Server provides a range of advanced remote diagnostic tools to help you manage desktops and servers without making on-site visits. These include utilities such as remote control and remote reboot, a network monitor with real-time and post-capture experts to analyze network conditions and performance, and a server HealthMon utility, which displays critical performance information on Windows 2000 Server and Microsoft® BackOffice®.

Whether you use IntelliMirror and Systems Management Server separately or together depends on the complexity of your environment. Table 24.2 illustrates the Microsoft management solutions that might be most cost effective for organizations of varying complexity.

Table 24.2   Recommended Change and Configuration Management Solutions

	Single local area network (LAN)/simple multi-LAN with LAN-speed interconnects	Complex multi-LAN/multi-site systems
Windows 2000–based systems only	IntelliMirror Remote OS Installation	IntelliMirror Remote OS Installation Systems Management Server
Mixed Windows environments, including Windows 2000–based systems	IntelliMirror Remote OS Installation Systems Management Server	IntelliMirror Remote OS Installation Systems Management Server
Windows 3.x, Windows NT 3.51/4.0	Systems Management Server	Systems Management Server

Table 24.3 illustrates how IntelliMirror, Remote OS Installation, and Systems Management Server can be combined into an effective change and configuration management solution.

Table 24.3   Options for Effective Change and Configuration Management

	Remote OS Installation	IntelliMirror	Systems Management Server
Install Windows 2000–based desktop images.	X	--	--
Enable data, software, and settings to follow the user.	--	X	--
Basic disaster recovery for Windows 2000–based systems	X	X	--
Manage environments that are not Windows 2000–based.	--	--	X
Inventory, advanced deployment, troubleshooting, and diagnostic tools	--	--	X
Comprehensive change and configuration management	X	X	X

Use the information in these tables, along with your understanding of your organization's client management issues, to select the features most appropriate for your organization.

For more information about using Systems Management Server in conjunction with Windows 2000, see "Using Systems Management Server to Analyze Your Network Infrastructure" and "Using Systems Management Server to Deploy Windows 2000" in this book. For comprehensive technical information about Systems Management Server, see the *Microsoft® Systems Management Server Resource Kit.*

Planning for Enhanced Client Support with IntelliMirror

The rest of this chapter will guide you through the steps involved in improving client support by configuring and addressing critical issues in the deployment of IntelliMirror and Remote OS Installation.

If your client administration standards include storage of user data or settings on a network server, then you will want to create your basic client image and the network infrastructure (namely server shares and Group Policy settings) to support this goal before you begin to deploy clients.

Your choice of deployment methods for clients involves two parts:

- Deployment of the base operating system
- Deployment of applications

As with alternate deployment methods such as using Sysprep or Systems Management Server, you can use Remote OS Installation to deploy basic applications along with Windows 2000 Professional. This requires that you plan your application deployment strategy carefully to decide:

- Which applications will be deployed with the operating system using Remote OS Installation.
- Which applications will be deployed using software installation and maintenance after the operating system has been installed.
- How you will support reinstallation or repair of applications that were initially installed with Remote OS Installation.

Installing a core suite of applications during the Remote OS Installation process can simplify the process of configuring a computer to your organization's standards. However, it does not eliminate the need to support installation on computers that already have Windows 2000 Professional installed. Therefore, applications that are installed along with Windows 2000 during the Remote OS Installation process will also have to be included in your IntelliMirror software installation and maintenance plan.

The following sections address key planning issues to help you use Remote OS Installation, IntelliMirror software installation and maintenance, and IntelliMirror user data and settings management in your organization. The final section, "Putting It All Together," provides recommendations on how some organizations with different types of requirements might implement IntelliMirror and Remote OS Installation.

Enabling Remote OS Installation

Windows 2000 Remote OS Installation provides a means for computers to connect to a Windows 2000 network server during the initial startup sequence, and subsequently allows the server to install Windows 2000 Professional on the client computer. Remote OS Installation allows you, as the administrator, to configure Windows 2000 and any applications that you want to install along with the operating system once for a single group of users, and then apply this same configuration when installing the operating system on individual client computers. For users, the result should be a simplified and timely installation and configuration of their computer, and a more rapid return to productivity if a hardware failure occurs.

Table 24.4 shows the Windows 2000 technologies you need to have in order to use Remote OS Installation.

Table 24.4   Windows 2000 Technologies Needed to Use Remote OS Installation

Technology	Purpose
Dynamic Host Configuration Protocol (DHCP)	Assigns an IP address to a remote boot–enabled client computer prior to contacting a server running RIS.
Domain Name Server (DNS)	Resolves computer names from TCP/IP addresses.
Group Policy	Defines the users and computers eligible (or ineligible) to receive a given desktop configuration.
Active Directory directory service	Locates client computers and RIS servers and stores the Group Policy objects that define what resources a user or computer can or cannot access.
Remote Installation Services (RIS)	Manages and distributes Windows 2000 Professional image files to clients enabled for remote boot.

If you have not have already installed and configured DNS, DHCP, and Active Directory, see the chapter "Defining the Active Directory Structure" in this book to complete these planning steps before continuing with this chapter. You should also understand the Group Policy planning steps outlined in the chapter "Defining Client Administration and Configuration Standards." The remainder of this section will focus on the planning associated with different components of the RIS and how to configure them for an effective deployment.

Defining User Requirements

All users, no matter what their skill level or computing requirements, require an efficient, fast way to install a new operating system and core applications if their system fails or they receive a new computer. In order to reduce the time and costs associated with preconfiguring new systems for users, you need to answer the following questions:

What is the best operating system installation method for these users?

In small branch offices or home offices where there are not enough users to warrant the installation of a RIS server, or where users travel and do not have a high-bandwidth connection to a network server, using a CD-ROM or other local method of installing an operating system is probably the best option. For users with high-bandwidth network connections, but whose computers do not have a remote boot–compliant network card or remote-boot ROM, a network-based image copying or manual installation method will be your next best option (for more information, see "Automating Client Installation and Upgrade" in this book). For all other cases, when you want a clean, known configuration of Windows 2000 Professional, use Remote OS Installation.

How much freedom should users have to choose optional operating system components or alternate operating system images?

The following sections describe a number of optional settings that you can use to configure Remote OS Installation images. In most cases, you will want to allow less knowledgeable or task-oriented users to make few or no optional choices during operating system installation. Advanced, more knowledgeable users might require additional choices during the Windows 2000 Professional installation.

Using Remote OS Installation

The Remote OS Installation process is relatively straightforward from an end user perspective because your IT department does most of the work by having the following configurations in place:

- Defining how the operating system will be configured for each group of users.
- Limiting users to as few operating system configurations as you consider appropriate.
- Guiding the user through a successful operating system installation by predetermining which installation options, if any, the end user can modify.

Five major components of RIS are involved in Remote OS Installation:

- **Remote Installation Services Setup (RISetup.exe).** Used to set up the RIS server.
- **Remote Installation Services Administrator.** Used to configure Group Policy settings relating to RIS services.
- **Remote Installation Preparation wizard (RIPrep.exe).** Used to create operating system images and install them on the RIS server. You can also use RIPrep to create application images if you want to install an application with the operating system.
- **Remote Installation boot floppy disk (RBFG.exe).** Used to create a boot floppy disk, which is needed to install RIS-based operating systems on certain client computers.
- **Client Installation wizard (OSChooser.exe).** Used on the client computer to select the RIS image that the user needs to install.

All computers that meet the PC98 version 0.6 and later design specification will include a Pre-Boot Execution Environment (PXE) remote-boot ROM for Remote OS Installation. For existing client computers that do not contain a PXE ROM, you can use the Remote Installation boot floppy disk to create a floppy disk that will initiate the RIS process. The RIS remote-boot floppy disk can be used with a variety of supported Peripheral Component Interconnect (PCI)–based network adapters. For more information, see the Windows 2000 Hardware Compatibility List (HCL) on the Windows 2000 operating system CD and at the Microsoft Windows Hardware Compatibility List link on the Web Resources page at http://windows.microsoft.com/windows2000/reskit/webresources.

Figure 24.2 illustrates the major steps for configuring Remote OS Installation. The following sections discuss key deployment planning issues that need to be addressed when using RISetup.exe, the Remote Installation Services Administrator snap-in, and RIPrep.exe.

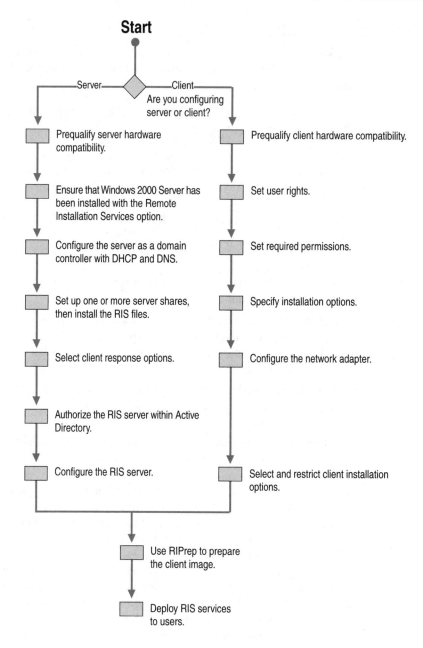

Figure 24.2 Planning Steps for RIS Services

Configuring the Remote Installation Service

Remote Installation Service (RIS) is an optional component that you can install while you are installing Windows 2000 Server. Although much of this setup process is automatic, there are a number of basic and advanced settings that you can configure while RIS is being installed but before offering the service to users.

By default, RIS is not configured to service client computers immediately after it has been installed. If you want to, you can accept all the default RIS configuration settings and begin offering installation images to users based on these options. However, most organizations will customize RIS to better meet their IT and business requirements.

In order to configure RIS settings for both the RIS server and the client computer, you will need to use the Active Directory Users and Computers snap-in to the Microsoft Management Console (MMC). The server configuration options determine how a particular RIS server will respond to client computers requesting service. The client options can help you define how the RIS image is installed on the client computer.

The major configuration options that you can set using the Active Directory Users and Computers snap-in include:

Define automatic client computer naming format Allows you to determine whether the computer name (which is generated automatically) is to be based on the user's name, the user's last name followed by first name, or a custom naming format specific to your organization. The default is the user name.

Define the default Active Directory location for the creation of all Machine Account objects

You can select default Active Directory containers or organizational units (OUs), or you can create a new Active Directory OU specifically for RIS clients. The default setting is the Computers container.

Prestage client computers within Active Directory prior to servicing

This option allows you to define which client computer accounts within Active Directory can use Remote OS Installation. To use this option, you will need to specify the client computer name, the default Active Directory location, the client computer's globally unique identifier (GUID), and, optionally for load-balancing purposes, which RIS server will support specific clients. The default setting is No Prestaged Clients.

Offer third-party ISV maintenance and troubleshooting tools Gives administrators and—if you allow it—end users access to pre-installation maintenance and troubleshooting tools from independent software vendors (ISVs). Such tools might, for example, upgrade the system basic input/output system (BIOS), check for viruses, perform computer diagnostics, or inventory the system prior to the operating system installation. The default setting is No Tools Installed.

Add more operating system images in either CD or RIPrep format This option allows you to add new operating system versions or RIPrep images to existing RIS servers within the enterprise, or to associate a variety of unattended installation templates to existing operating system images. For example, you can use this option to set up multiple RIPrep images, each of which could then be made available only to the appropriate users in your organization. The default setting is CD-Based Windows 2000 Image.

Remotely configure RIS servers from Windows 2000 Professional workstations
By enabling this option, you can remotely manage many RIS options on any RIS server in the domain or enterprise. The default setting is N/A, meaning that most of the configuration options described here can also be performed from a computer running Windows 2000 Professional and has been enabled to perform administrative tasks.

Supports coexistence of multiple-vendor installation servers This option supports organizations with remote installation and boot servers other than Windows 2000 operating on the same physical network. This option is normally used in conjunction with the prestaging option described earlier, so that RIS does not interfere with pre-existing remote-boot servers that use the same remote-boot protocols. The default setting is Disabled.

There are three additional configuration options that you can define outside of the RIS Server property page. These options are determined both by using Group Policy settings and by setting specific security descriptors, or access control lists (ACLs) on operating system images you want to restrict from users:

Define available client installation options This option uses Group Policy to restrict the installation options for a group of users. For example, you might not want some users to access the maintenance and troubleshooting tools menu or the Custom setup option. The default setting is to make automatic setup available to all users. No other installation options are available.

Define available operating system installation choices This option uses security descriptors to specify which users should have access to the operating system images available on the RIS server. You can use this feature to guide users to the unattended operating system installation appropriate for their role in the organization. By default, all images are available to all users.

Authorization of RIS servers for rogue server prevention This option prevents unauthorized RIS servers from servicing clients on the organization's network. You must authorize which RIS servers can provide installations to remote boot–enabled clients. There is no option to change this.

Preparing Client Operating System Images

RIS supports two types of operating system images, CD-based images and RIPrep images. In the simplest case, you can offer users straight CD-based operating system installation, which installs Windows 2000 Professional in an unattended manner.

If you want to configure custom installations of Windows 2000 Professional without creating a separate image for every type of client computer and every piece of hardware installed on that computer, RIS provides this capability by taking advantage of the improved Plug and Play support in Windows 2000 to detect the differences between the source and destination computers at installation time.

Note If the hardware abstraction layer (HAL) drivers of your client computers are not the same, you will not be able to configure custom installations of Windows 2000 Professional without creating a separate image for every type of client computer and every piece of hardware installed on that computer. However, most workstation-class and desktop-class computers do not require unique HAL drivers as server class computers do. Unique HAL drivers most commonly differentiate client computers that support the Advanced Configuration Power Interface (ACPI) and computers that do not support ACPI.

RIPrep can be used to prepare an existing Windows 2000 Professional image, including any locally installed applications or configuration settings, and replicate that image to a RIS server on the network. By including a basic suite of applications in your RIS images, you can dramatically reduce the amount of work involved in setting up a client computer. For more information about packaging applications for deployment with RIS and IntelliMirror, see "Using Group Policy to Improve Software Management" later in this chapter.

Client Installation Options

To run RIPrep, you need to answer a few basic questions, such as the location of the server that the image will be stored upon. After these questions have been answered, the RIPrep wizard configures the image to a generic state by removing anything unique to the computer, such as the computer's unique security identifier (SID), and then replicates it to the RIS server.

You can use Group Policy to configure the following client installation options when setting up RIS:

Automatic Setup All users have default access to the Automatic setup option. If you also grant access to a single operating system image, the operating system installation starts as soon as the user logs on, without requiring the user to answer any questions. If you decide to offer users multiple operating system installation types, limit the number to three to five options to minimize confusion and to help ensure that your users select the operating system that best meets their needs and role within the organization.

Custom Setup The Custom setup option enables you or your Help desk staff to set up a computer for someone else in the organization. It does this by allowing you to override the rules that govern automatic computer naming and where the computer account is created. This is because it might not be appropriate to name the computer or to locate the computer account based on the Group Policy settings that apply to the administrator or Help desk person. You can use this option to preinstall a client computer or when IT or Help desk staff must physically visit an end user to set up or reinstall their computer.

Restart a Previous Setup Under this option, you can avoid asking the user to re-answer any questions about the operating system being installed. For example, if a user has already been asked the organization name, department name, or video resolution, the **Restart** option ensures that they do not have to answer these questions a second time if they are restarting after a failed installation. This option does not restart the installation at the point of failure. It also will not attempt to fix any problems that occurred with the previous setup attempt.

Maintenance and Troubleshooting This option provides access to third-party hardware and software tools such as BIOS updates and virus scanners. If you provide access to installation tools, allow access only to tools that cannot damage the computer or cause further problems.

Using Group Policy to Improve Software Management

The typical large organization supports hundreds, sometimes thousands, of programs. The number can be significantly larger if you also count different versions, patches, fixes, and templates as separate programs in your inventory.

Because they do not have efficient means of managing their software portfolios, many organizations fail to update their application software on a timely basis. When they do decide to retire obsolete software or implement new applications, the changeover can be extremely disruptive.

You can use Windows 2000 to help simplify your software management processes in the following areas:

- **Preparation.** What software do you want to manage? How do you want to format the software for distribution and installation?
- **Distribution.** From where do you want to manage the software?
- **Targeting.** Whom do you want to receive the software?
- **Installation.** How will the software be installed on the computer?

Figure 24.3 illustrates the major planning issues involved in each of these stages.

Start

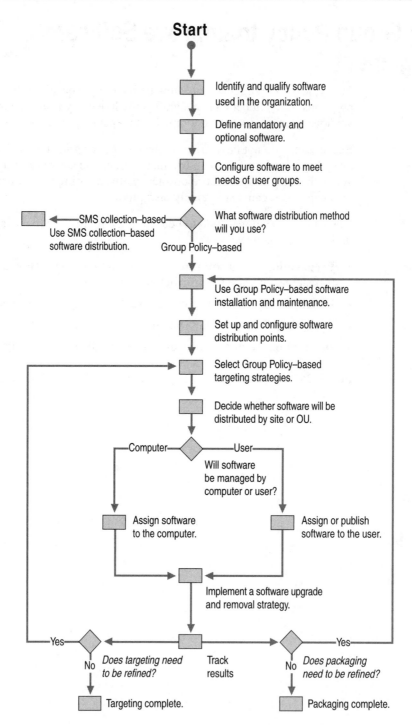

Identify and qualify software used in the organization.

Define mandatory and optional software.

Configure software to meet needs of user groups.

What software distribution method will you use?

SMS collection–based
Use SMS collection–based software distribution.

Group Policy–based

Use Group Policy–based software installation and maintenance.

Set up and configure software distribution points.

Select Group Policy–based targeting strategies.

Decide whether software will be distributed by site or OU.

Will software be managed by computer or user?

Computer

User

Assign software to the computer.

Assign or publish software to the user.

Implement a software upgrade and removal strategy.

Track results

Yes

Does targeting need to be refined?
No

Targeting complete.

Yes

Does packaging need to be refined?
No

Packaging complete.

Figure 24.3   Key Planning Issues to Address in IntelliMirror Software Deployment

You will need to perform these planning steps even for applications that were installed along with Windows 2000 Professional. You will also need to proceed through these planning steps to deploy, update, and maintain applications on existing computers.

Preparing Software for Distribution

In the chapters "Testing Applications for Compatibility with Windows 2000" and "Defining Client Administration and Configuration Standards," you were asked to evaluate your organization's applications for compatibility with Windows 2000, and to categorize them as mandatory or optional:

- For the organization as a whole.
- For groups of users within the organization.

Before you can use IntelliMirror to distribute your software applications, you need to make sure they are configured properly for deployment with Windows 2000.

Applications that take advantage of Windows Installer will use Windows 2000 application support features most efficiently. Windows Installer is a new installation service that consists of:

An operating-system-resident installation service In the past, every application provided its own executable setup file or script. Therefore, each application had to ensure that the proper installation rules (such as file versioning rules) were followed. Furthermore, few best-practice guidelines were available for developers authoring the setup routines. As a result, installation or removal of a given application often broke existing applications on the computer. The Windows Installer Service ensures that critical setup rules are implemented by the operating system. To follow those rules, applications merely need to describe themselves in the standard Windows Installer format.

A standard format for component management The Windows Installer service views all applications as three logical building blocks: components, features, and products. Components are collections of files, registry keys, and other resources that are all installed or uninstalled together. When a given component is selected for installation or removal, all of the resources in that component are either installed or removed. Features are the pieces of an application that a user can choose to install, and typically they represent the functional features of the application itself. When a user chooses **Custom** in a setup program, the pieces of the application they are able to select for installation correspond roughly to features. A Windows Installer product represents a single product such as Microsoft® Office. Products consist of one or more Windows Installer features. Each product is described to the Windows Installer service in the form of a single Windows Installer package (.msi) file.

A management API for applications and tools The Windows Installer application programming interface (API) enables tools and applications to enumerate the products, features, and components installed on the computer, install and configure Windows Installer products and features, and determine the path to specific Windows Installer components installed on the computer. Applications that are written to leverage the Windows Installer service gain the advantages of roaming user support, on-demand installation, and runtime resource resilience.

Applications that have been natively authored to take advantage of Windows Installer technology will support:

- **Just-in-time feature installation.** Allows you to distribute only a portion of an application's optional features. Then, when a user attempts to use an uninstalled option (a grammar checker or clip-art library, for example), the option is installed when it is first requested. This saves hard disk space on rarely used application features without making them unavailable to those users who occasionally need to use them.

- **Feature repair.** If critical application files become corrupted or are accidentally deleted, Windows Installer will identify the needed files and automatically reinstall them.

- **Installs with elevated privileges.** Users do not have to be administrators on the local computer to install software using IntelliMirror software installation and maintenance. They only need to be a user or power user.

Note Many software vendors and in-house development groups are updating their applications to take advantage of Windows Installer capabilities. For more information about the Windows 2000 application specification, see the MSDN link on the Web Resources page at

---

When Native Authoring Is Not Possible

It is not always possible to natively author applications. In particular, you might have older applications for which you do not have the resources to natively author Windows Installer packages. You can still benefit from Windows Installer features by repackaging these applications for use with Windows 2000.

You can repackage files using a repackaging tool such as WinInstall LE, a program that comes with Windows 2000 Server.

The changes between the original application and the customized application image are then converted into a Windows Installer package.

Repackaged files allow you to benefit from some Windows Installer features, meaning they can be advertised and repaired, and will install with elevated privileges. (Advertising and other distribution options are discussed in "Software Management Options" later in this chapter.) However, a repackaged application will not benefit from the Windows Installer architecture, which means the repackaged application will install as if the product had just a single (large) feature.

Managing Older Applications

You can also make other applications available to users using their existing setup programs. To do this, you need to use a text editor, such as Notepad, to create a ZAP (.zap) file. ZAP files, which are similar to INI files, are placed in the same folder on the software distribution point as the original setup program that it references. Because you are publishing the existing setup, the user's experience will not be better than the existing setup. If the existing setup does not support clean and complete removal of the software, for example, then publishing the existing setup will not improve the software removal experience. By managing software files with the ZAP file format, the application will appear in **Add/Remove Programs** in Control Panel, and users will be able to install the application from this location.

Note The user will still need to have the same administrative privileges as required by the older application in order to complete this type of installation.

For more information about managing older applications, see "Software Management" in the *Microsoft® Windows® 2000 Server Resource Kit Distributed Systems Guide*.

Using Transforms

In the past, administrators who wanted to customize the behavior of an installation had to repackage the application by directly modifying the setup script to achieve the desired results. If many different setup scripts required similar changes, they needed to repeat those efforts for each script.

With Windows 2000, you do not need to customize Windows Installer packages in order to customize the installation for your organization. Instead, you can create a transform and use this transform to customize the package. The Windows Installer service transform modifies the Windows Installer package file at deployment, and therefore dynamically affects installation behavior.

You can transform or customize Windows Installer packages to handle a variety of customizations. For example, a transform can be used to install selected features in a predefined location so that users do not have to decide what features to install or where to install them. You can also use a transform to modify the path of a given component, as long as the component exists in the package being modified.

Whereas existing installers typically give the user a binary choice between "installed" and "not installed" for a given feature, the Windows Installer features can be set to one of four states:

- **Installed on Local Hard Disk.** Files are copied to the local computer's hard disk.

- **Installed to Run from Source.** Files are left on the source (typically a network share or a CD). The application accesses the files from the source.

- **Advertised Files.** Files are left on the source, but they can be installed on your hard disk the first time they are used.

- **Not Installed.** No files are copied.

Transforms should be stored in the same network shares as the Windows Installer packages that they customize. Transforms are applied at deployment, and they cannot be applied to an application that has already been installed.

Distributing Software

When the software has been prepared (that is, the software is in the appropriate package format and any customizations or transforms have been created), you can move the actual software files, including the package and any transforms, to a series of network shares throughout the organization. Typically, these software distribution points are located throughout the organization so that people can always get the software from a distribution point that offers reliable, high-speed connectivity.

Windows 2000 software installation and maintenance does not directly address the distribution phase. It will be up to your deployment team to test your software distribution plans and to ensure that your network bandwidth, and the placement and number of installation servers, is adequate to meet your organization's anticipated demand.

You can, however, also use other Windows 2000 services, such as the Microsoft distributed file system (Dfs) to manage the distribution phase. For more information about planning and deploying Dfs volumes, see "Determining Windows 2000 Storage Management Strategies" in this book.

Targeting Software

IT administrators need to install applications throughout their organizations based on how users perform their jobs. Because users vary in their software needs and in their levels of computing expertise, IT typically has to distribute a combination of:

- Universal applications, such as e-mail and word processing, that all users must use.
- Job-specific applications that are needed by users who perform specific tasks or belong to specific departments or divisions.
- Optional applications that can be installed by users as needed.

At this point in your deployment planning, you should be able to identify:

- Which users should receive what applications.
- Which Group Policy settings for application management should be set on the site level, on the domain level, and on the organizational unit (OU) level.

Note   Try to avoid managing the same application, such as Microsoft Word, in different Group Policy objects that might apply to the same person.

To define your targets using Group Policy, you need to use the Group Policy and Software Installation snap-ins. With the Group Policy snap-in, you can create a new Group Policy object or edit an existing one, and assign or publish the software to either users or computers.

The Software Installation snap-in generates an application advertisement script and stores this script in the appropriate locations in Active Directory and the Group Policy object.

For more information about using Group Policy together with sites and OUs, see "Designing the Active Directory Structure" in this book. For more information about using Group Policy to implement client configuration standards, see "Defining Client Administration and Configuration Standards" in this book.

Software Management Options

Group Policy–based software deployment is designed to simplify the process of managing software throughout its entire life cycle. You can use software installation and maintenance to assign or publish applications, to upgrade deployed applications, to install service packs, and to remove applications that are no longer needed. All of these tasks can be carried out without user intervention. Windows 2000 Group Policy allows you to distribute applications based on three criteria:

Assigning applications to users When you assign applications to users, the application always appears on the user's **Start** menu regardless of which computer the user logs on to. When a user starts an assigned application that is not installed on the local computer, the application will first install and then run. If a user removes an assigned application, its shortcut will reappear on the **Start** menu. In general, you should assign all mandatory (universal and job-specific) applications to users.

Assigning applications to computers Unlike applications that are assigned to users, applications that are assigned to computers install the next time the computer is started. If several people use a computer, and they all use the same application, then that application is a candidate for assignment to the computer. Site-licensed virus scanning software is an example of software that might be assigned to a computer. Also, assign applications to computers if the applications are required only when users use a certain computer, such as a computer in a library.

Publishing applications When you publish applications, they do not appear on the **Start** menu. Instead, they must be installed manually using **Add/Remove Programs** in Control Panel. **Add/Remove Programs** retrieves the list of published applications from Active Directory. Users can delete published applications from their computers and they will not be re-advertised on their computers. Publish an application when all users in a site, domain, or OU do not require the application, but it might be useful to some users. Older applications cannot be assigned to a user or computer; they can only be published.

Note Assign software either to a user or to a computer if you want the application to always be installed, or able to be installed, no matter what the user does. Publishing connects an application less firmly to a user or computer than assigning an application.

Assigned or published applications can also be installed when the user double-clicks a document whose file name extension has been associated with that application. Table 24.5 provides additional information on the differences between assigning applications to users, assigning them to computers, and publishing them.

Table 24.5   Differences in Behavior Between Assigned and Published Applications

	User assigned	Computer assigned	Published
After deployment, when is the software available for installation?	After the next logon.	After the next time the computer is started or rebooted.	After the next logon.
Where will the user typically install the software from?	The **Start** menu or a desktop shortcut.	The software is already installed.	**Add/Remove Programs** in Control Panel.
If the software is not installed, and the user opens a file associated with the software, will the software install?	Yes.	The software is already installed.	Yes.
Can the user remove the software using **Add/Remove Programs** in Control Panel?	Yes, and the software will immediately be available for installation again.	No. Only the local administrator can remove the software.	Yes, and they can choose to install it again from **Add/Remove Programs** in Control Panel.
What installation files are supported?	Windows Installer packages.	Windows Installer packages.	Windows Installer packages and older applications.

The actual steps involved in either assigning or publishing software are similar. The administrator does both from within the Software Installation snap-in. The specific tasks are described in the Help file for the snap-in.

Applications will more commonly be assigned in highly managed organizations, particularly where support costs are an issue, and where multiple users share computers. In less managed organizations, applications will more commonly be published than assigned.

Supporting Roaming Users

In many organizations, certain people move from one location to another to perform their jobs, as in the case of a receptionist who regularly substitutes for another receptionist. Even though these employees log on to different computers, they always have high-speed or LAN connections.

Windows 2000 software installation and management can improve IT support for roaming users by installing any application they use on any computer they use as soon as they are needed by the user. Likewise, if an application that had previously been published is uninstalled, it will be removed when the user logs on again, no matter what computer they are using.

You might choose to assign software to these users. Then, when they move from one computer to another, they will see their applications. However, configure their Group Policy settings so that the application is installed only if the user actually attempts to run it.

Supporting Shared Computers

In many organizations, people share computers. If you have computers on a factory floor, in a training facility, or in a laboratory, you probably support shared computers.

In these cases you might want to assign software to the computers rather than to users. This allows you to manage the software more effectively, and if a user uninstalls, reinstall the software as soon as the computer restarts.

Consider using Remote OS Installation in these shared computing environments. Then, if you have to rebuild the entire environment, you can do so in an efficient manner.

Supporting Mobile Workers

A growing percentage of employees, such as salespeople and consultants, travel extensively to perform their jobs. Although these users typically log on to the same computer, they sometimes connect to the network through a high-speed line, and sometimes through a low-speed dial-up connection. By default, software installation and maintenance policy is not applied over a slow link. This is true whether the intended action is a clean installation or an upgrade. For more information about configuring Group Policy for slow links, see "Defining Client Administration and Configuration Standards" in this book.

You might want to publish software to these users and ensure that any customization to the software installs locally on the user's computer (as opposed to leaving the feature to either install on first usage or run from the network).

You might also want to allow mobile workers to keep some software available on local media while they are traveling. For example, if a mobile professional makes frequent presentations, it is probably worthwhile to give them a Microsoft Office CD so that they can install or repair vital files at any time and location.

Maintaining Software Using IntelliMirror

Administrators need to be able to manage software through the entire software life cycle. IntelliMirror software installation and maintenance was designed with the following software life cycle in mind:

1. The software life cycle began when you first deployed the software. Users have learned the software and are productively using it. Because this is a steady or known state, administrators would like to stay at this state.

2. However, because of changes in business requirements or the availability of a new, improved version of the software, you have to consider deploying the new version. You evaluate the new features and deploy them to a carefully chosen group of users during a pilot deployment. During the pilot, most users will continue to use the old version.

3. Assuming that the pilot is successful, the IT staff will gradually roll out the new software to the rest of the organization. This leaves two options for the older version:

   - Force an upgrade to the new version.

   - Leave the existing version in a nonsupported state.

4. Eventually, all users will be using the new version and there are few, if any, reasons for the old application to remain in circulation. At this point you probably want to remove it from the software distribution share, back it up, and archive it in case it is ever needed in the future.

Figure 24.4 illustrates this process.

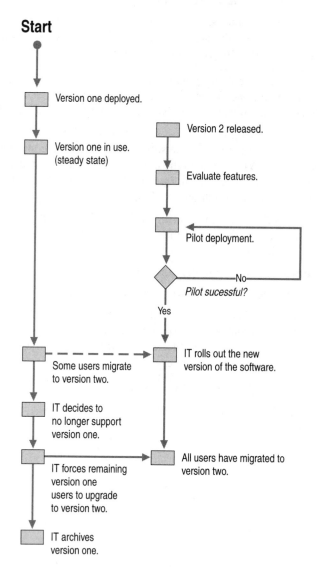

Start

Version one deployed.

Version one in use.
(steady state)

Version 2 released.

Evaluate features.

Pilot deployment.

Pilot sucessful?

No

Yes

Some users migrate
to version two.

IT rolls out the new
version of the software.

IT decides to
no longer support
version one.

IT forces remaining
version one
users to upgrade
to version two.

All users have migrated to
version two.

IT archives
version one.

Figure 24.4   The Software Life Cycle

This life cycle involves the following software management tasks:

- Installing
- Modifying
- Upgrading

- Repairing
- Removing

So far, this discussion of IntelliMirror software installation and maintenance has focused almost exclusively on installation. The following sections address modification, upgrades, and removal.

Patching Existing Software

Software publishers often provide patches to fix a very precise problem in their applications. You need to decide whether or not your organization needs the patch.

If you decide to deploy a patch with Windows 2000, you can copy the patch files to the software distribution point and replace the older files. The software publisher that distributes the patch should supply either a new Windows Installer package (an .msi file) or a Windows Installer patch (an .msp file). With the Windows Installer package, you can simply replace the existing package. Alternatively, you can use the Windows Installer patch to update the existing package.

You then redeploy the assigned or published package with the Software Installation snap-in. This causes the patched or updated files to be copied to the computers of the users who have installed the software.

Service packs typically include a number of patches that have been tested together. Thus, service packs are distributed less frequently than patches, but more often than full upgrades.

Note If a service pack updates only a small number of files, distribute and manage it as you would a patch. If a service pack updates a large number of files, distribute and manage it like an upgrade.

Upgrading Existing Software

There are two types of upgrades in a network environment:

- **Mandatory upgrades that occur immediately.** This means that everyone who has installed the existing version of the application is upgraded to the new version, and users who have never installed the software can only install the upgraded version.

- **Nonmandatory upgrades that do not occur immediately.** Existing users can choose whether or not to upgrade, and new users can decide for themselves which version to install.

Initially, you might want to make new upgrades available on a nonmandatory basis so that users can upgrade when they want. Eventually, you might decide that the nonmandatory upgrade should become mandatory.

Windows Installer packages are based on a concept called a "declared upgrade relationship," in which one package knows which other packages it can upgrade. You can use the Software Installation snap-in to create this declared upgrade relationship. For example, one Microsoft® Word 2000 package could upgrade Microsoft Word 6.0, and Microsoft Word 7.0.

This declared upgrade relationship requires natively authored rather than repackaged applications. This means that you will have to manually create upgrade relationships for repackaged applications.

The new application package (whether natively authored or repackaged) might not be able to upgrade a non-natively authored application. In some cases, you will have to use software installation and maintenance to remove the existing application and replace it with the upgrade.

It might also not be possible to completely remove a repackaged application. Some components, such as desktop shortcuts, might have to be removed manually, even if they are neither shared nor needed. As more applications with natively authored packages become available, upgrades will be able to migrate the existing application to the new application.

Software Removal

At some point, almost all software is no longer needed and you need to decide what to do with it. You can simply stop providing support, even if users continue to use the outdated application. It would then be up to the users to remove the application when they no longer have a use for it. On the other hand, new users would be unable to install the software, whether from **Add/Remove Programs**, the **Start** menu, or by document invocation.

Alternatively, you can enforce the removal of the software from users' computers. To remove software, select the package in the Software Installation snap-in. Then, on the shortcut menu, click **Remove**. You can force the removal of the software the next time the user logs on (in the case of published or user-assigned software) or the next time the computer restarts (in the case of computer-assigned software). The software will be removed as long as the user, who might be out of the office or on vacation, logs on at least once during the next year.

Maintaining User Data and Settings on a Network

User data management and user settings management make it possible for data and settings to follow the user whether or not they are connected to a network, and whichever computer they use. You can increase a user's access to data and his or her personal environment by storing that information on network servers as well as in synchronized offline locations on the local hard disk.

Many of the same technologies are used to implement both user data and settings management. Although some organizations might deploy data and settings management separately, other organizations will plan for and deploy them at the same time. The following sections discuss user settings and user data management together.

The following technologies are needed to centrally manage user data and settings:

Active Directory Provides the infrastructure for using and managing Group Policy.

Group Policy Allows administrators to customize and control Windows 2000 elements such as the desktop, network access, and Microsoft® Internet Explorer for users or computers.

Roaming User Profiles Enables users' personal settings and desktop configurations—including any **Start** menu customizations and the contents of the My Documents folder—to follow them from computer to computer. This allows them to have a familiar working environment regardless of which computer they are using.

Folder Redirection Uses Group Policy to redirect personal folders (My Documents, Application Data, Start Menu, and Desktop) to a network server. When a personal folder is redirected, it is stored on the network and is available to users regardless of which computer they use to log on.

Offline Files (or Folders) Allows users to maintain two copies of a document—one stored on a network file share, the other on the user's computer. Whenever a user logs on or off, Windows 2000 synchronizes the two copies of the document.

Disk Quotas Limits the amount of information a user can store on a given NTFS file system volume. Because most IntelliMirror technologies involve storing user data on the network rather than on local hard disks, disk quotas might be required to ensure that users have adequate network storage space.

Security Settings Allows discretionary access control lists (DACLs) to be set on files and folders.

Figure 24.5 illustrates the key planning steps that need to be completed to enable user data and settings management.

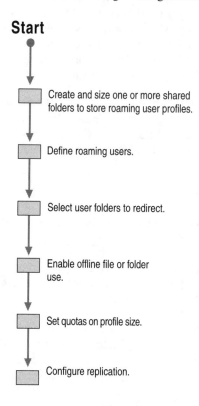

Start

- Create and size one or more shared folders to store roaming user profiles.
- Define roaming users.
- Select user folders to redirect.
- Enable offline file or folder use.
- Set quotas on profile size.
- Configure replication.

Figure 24.5   Planning Process for User Data and Settings Management

In the following sections, you will learn about the additional technologies needed to enable user data and settings management:

- Roaming User Profiles
- Folder Redirection
- Offline Files (or Folders)
- Synchronization Manager
- Disk Quotas

Enabling Roaming User Profiles

Roaming User Profiles provide a way to give users a familiar and easy-to-use working environment. Unlike a local profile, which is stored on a single computer running Windows 2000 Professional, a roaming profile is stored on a network share, which means it can be accessed from any Windows 2000–based computer on the network.

Whether a user profile is local or roaming, it contains a number of folders, including, but not limited to, Application Data, Desktop, Favorites, My Documents, and Start Menu.

In general, the implementation of Roaming User Profiles in Windows 2000 is similar to the Windows NT 4.0 implementation. For more information about the similarities and differences, see "Introduction to Desktop Management" in the *Microsoft Windows 2000 Server Resource Kit Distributed Systems Guide.*

▶ **To set up a roaming user profile**

1. Set up the network share to store user profiles on a server.

2. Configure the folder as a shared folder.

3. Open the Active Directory Users and Computers snap-in and navigate to the specific node where the user's properties exist.

4. Right-click the user's name and click **Properties** on the shortcut menu.

5. Click the **Profile** tab.

6. For the profile path, type in the path to the network share where the user profiles are to be stored. For example, for a user whose network name is MaryK, the following path, \\NetworkShare\Profiles\MaryK, would create a directory called MaryK in the Profiles share on the server used to store user profiles.

Only items stored on the network will roam. This means that other items, such as screen savers and wallpaper, will not be available unless copies of those items are stored on each computer from which the user logs on.

Guidelines for Setting Up Roaming User Profiles

Roaming User Profiles can have advantages and disadvantages. The advantage is that both personal settings and documents can follow the user from computer to computer. The potential disadvantage involves the amount of network traffic that it can create. You will need to test detailed usage scenarios to determine the appropriate level of roaming support for your organization. The use of Roaming User Profiles is not recommended for remote access users who access the network over slow links such as telephone lines.

Redirecting Folders

Personal folders, including My Documents and My Pictures, can be redirected using Group Policy. Folders that have been redirected will be available to users no matter which computer they log on from. They are also easier for administrators to manage and back up.

To the user, a redirected folder looks and acts like a locally stored personal folder. Redirecting folders, unlike the folders that make up a roaming user profile, are not copied across the network when a user logs on or off the network. Redirected folders can provide users with easy access to their documents without placing a strain on the network.

To redirect folders, create a new Group Policy object in the Group Policy console, and then expand **User Configuration**, **Windows Settings**, and **Folder Redirection**. Icons for the five personal folders that can be redirected— Application Data, Desktop, My Documents, My Pictures, and Start Menu—will be visible. To redirect any of these folders, right-click the folder name, click **Properties**, and then select one of the following options:

Basic Redirect everyone's folder to the same network sharepoint. All folders affected by this Group Policy object will be stored on the same network share.

Advanced Redirect personal folders based on the user's membership in a Windows 2000 security group. Folders are redirected to different network shares based on security group membership. For example, folders belonging to users in the Accounting group can be redirected to the Finance server, while folders belonging to users in the Sales group are redirected to the Marketing server.

When you select either the Basic or Advanced setting, you must enter the name of the shared network folder as the target folder location. For example:

FolderServer\MyDocumentsFolders\Username

After you have entered a target folder location, select the Settings tab, configure the desired options in this dialog box, and then click **Finish** to complete the folder redirection.

Note Do not precreate the directory defined by *username*. Folder Redirection will handle setting the appropriate DACLs on the folder.

Guidelines for Configuring Folder Redirection

By redirecting folders, you can make documents available to users as needed. You can also improve the availability of those documents by including them in your server backup schedule.

If Roaming User Profiles create too much network traffic in your organization, consider redirecting only selected personal folders so that at least documents will follow the user from computer to computer, even if personal settings do not.

Configuring the Synchronization of Offline Files

Most organizations have instituted backup processes, particularly for critical data. In some cases, they might use programs such as Systems Management Server or a third-party software product to perform this vital task.

In many cases, critical data files or file folders are shared among multiple users, such as a field sales force. Keeping current copies of all these files or folders can be a serious IT issue.

Windows 2000 provides Synchronization Manager, which makes it easier to ensure that critical files and folders on client computers and network servers are kept current and, in the process, helps ensure that vital data is backed up on a timely basis.

Synchronization Manager is particularly valuable to remote or traveling users who are connected to the network intermittently. Using Synchronization Manager, you can control when your offline users' files are synchronized with files on the network. This process is transparent to users, because they access their files in exactly the same manner when they are offline as when they are online. This ensures that they have the latest information from the network when they need it, while also helping to minimize the potential disruptions that would occur if the data on their local computer is lost.

Synchronization Manager compares items on the network to those that the user opened or updated while working offline, and makes the most current version available to both the local computer and the network. Among the items you can synchronize are individual files, entire folders, and offline Web pages. Synchronization Manager can automatically synchronize the information that is available offline:

- Every time a user logs on or off the network, or both.
- At specific intervals while the computer is idle but still connected to the network.
- At scheduled times.

Combinations of these options and different options can be used for offline files from different shared sources.

Administrators can designate any share network folder as being available for offline use.

▶ **To mark a share folder for offline use**

1. In Windows Explorer, right-click the folder to be shared.
2. Click **Sharing**, and then click **Caching**.
3. Select **Allow caching of files in this shared folder**, and then choose one of the following settings and click **OK**:

    ▪ **Manual caching for documents.** Users must manually specify the documents they want stored. All selected files will automatically be stored.

    ▪ **Automatic caching for documents.** The entire contents of a folder can be stored. However, only the files that are actually opened by the user will be stored. This results in less network traffic than manual storing, where all selected files are stored, whether they have been opened or not.

    ▪ **Automatic caching for programs.** Reduces network traffic because the network versions of the documents or programs are only stored once; after that, the offline copies are used. This setting is designed for folders containing documents that are read-only or applications that are designed to be run from the network.

Guidelines for Configuring Offline Files

Group Policy provides you with a number of ways to manage offline folders within your organization:

First, you can decide whether offline folders are available on a particular client computer by using the Sharing/Caching options for a folder. When you share a folder, the default caching mode is set to **Manual caching for documents**. To prevent users from caching a folder, clear the check box labeled **Allow caching of files in this shared folder**.

Similarly, you can use **Files not cached** to specify certain file types (by extension) that will not be cached. For example, you can use this option to prevent large .avi multimedia files from being transferred back and forth across the network.

By using the option **Disable user configuration of logoff synchronization**, you can prevent the user from manually changing the synchronization options described earlier.

Two other options, **Automatic synchronization at logoff** and **Disable user synchronization of folders and files**, allow you to exercise control over when synchronization takes place, rather than which files are synchronized. The first option indicates the type of synchronization—Quick or Full—to be performed when you log off. A quick synchronization synchronizes files individually selected by the user. A full synchronization synchronizes automatically cached files as well. **Disable user synchronization of folders and files** allows you to specify that synchronization will take place only when you log on and off.

Setting Disk Quotas

Although there are advantages to having users store their documents and profiles on the network, it is possible for a few users to use all the available hard disk space on a server. You can configure disk quotas to prevent this, and to balance the needs of users for file storage space vs. the costs of adding more storage space.

You can set disk quotas on a per-user per-volume basis. If the individual user's profile exceeds the predetermined file limit, the user will not be able to log off the computer until the user reduces the size of the file. Per-user per-volume quotas have two key advantages:

- When you set quotas on a volume, these quotas are valid only for that volume. If users store files on several NTFS file system volumes, you can configure separate quotas on each volume.

- Quotas are charged to the person who owns the file. Thus, lines of ownership are clear-cut, even if a user shares one or more files with others.

Guidelines for Setting Disk Quotas

It is important that you provide sufficient disk space for your users' valid storage requirements, without forcing your organization to add unnecessary servers for all the files that users could post to a network share. Rather than ask users themselves how much network disk space they require, consider using your initial pilot deployments to develop meaningful data on how much network storage users actually require.

Keep in mind that not all users will have the same storage requirements. Software developers, for example, require greater network storage than other users. Financial and engineering users represent two other user groups that frequently have larger and more numerous files than other users.

In order to set effective disk quotas for your organization, learn what your users' legitimate requirements are before enforcing rigid quotas.

For information about setting and using disk quotas, see "Determining Windows 2000 Storage Management Strategies" in this book.

Selecting Change and Configuration Management Options for Your Organization

To prepare your change and configuration implementation plan, you will need to decide which features provide the greatest benefit to each group of users, and how those features need to be configured.

Think of the change and configuration management options described in this chapter as components that you can deploy to provide improved service to your users. Some building blocks can provide basic support for typical organizations, while others provide more advanced support.

To complete your IntelliMirror and Remote OS Installation plan:

- Define which features will be used for basic change and configuration management and which for advanced change and configuration management.

- Define how the basic and advanced change and configuration management options will best meet the needs of your organization's user types.

- Summarize how change and configuration management will meet the needs of your organization.

The following sections are examples of how you might implement IntelliMirror and Remote OS Installation features in your change and configuration management plan. Depending on your needs, some options listed as advanced in the following sections might actually be basic to your organization, while some options listed as basic might be considered advanced to another organization. You will need to define the basic and advanced requirements and implementations for your organization.

An Overview of Basic and Advanced Options

The following usage options can serve basic user data management requirements:

- Provide users with private network shares and map their My Documents folder to this share.

- Include the desktop as part of this network share so that documents saved to the desktop are also saved to the network share.

- Provide users with public network shares. This share can serve a single user or a workgroup.

- Set quotas on shares, especially on per-user shares.

- Provide backup and restore services for shares, particularly the per-user shares.

- Enable offline folders on shares that include private data.

- Enable Synchronization Manager for the common data types.

For advanced user data management, consider implementing the following features:

- Implement Roaming User Profiles for users who use more than one local computer.
- Ensure that when a roaming user leaves a computer, the roaming user profile and cache are cleared.

For basic settings management, consider providing the following options:

- Establish a basic policy for desktop or shell control.
- Establish basic policy for security control (see "Planning for Network Security" in this book).
- Define your logon scripts.
- Do not apply more than five or six Group Policy objects to a given user and computer. (For more information about using and apply Group Policy to manage client configurations, see "Defining Client Administration and Configuration Standards" in this book.)
- For users of Roaming User Profiles, define a standard default user profile for new users. This default profile exists on the server and is copied to the computer the first time the user logs on.

For advanced settings management, consider the following options:

- Configure Group Policy to severely restrict access to system file locations.
- Configure Group Policy to prevent users from running unapproved software.

For basic software installation and maintenance, consider using the following options:

- Allow users to use **Add/Remove Programs** through an application's life cycle.
- Prevent users from installing software using a CD.
- Publish existing Windows Installer–based applications in "partial installation/install on demand" form.
- Use transforms to modify package behavior.
- Publish or assign operating system updates.
- Use Group Policy to upgrade applications.

For advanced software installation and maintenance, consider using the following options:

- Create Dfs-enabled distribution points.
- Use Systems Management Server to manage Dfs distribution points.

The following sections illustrate change and configuration management plans for several different types of users.

Meeting the Needs of Technical Users

Technical users, such as developers, often need to be the administrators of their own computers. They typically like the IT department to provide management services without taking away their ability to control their own computers.

For these users, Windows 2000 change and configuration management can help simplify the setup of their computers and minimize the loss of personal data.

The following Basic and Advanced options illustrate how change and configuration management might be applied to technical users:

- **Basic User Data Management.** All aspects apply. Redirect My Documents, particularly for laptop users. Do not redirect the desktop. Enable offline folders on the My Documents share.
- **Advanced User Data Management.** Some technical users might want to use Roaming User Profiles. They will also want to maintain local administrative privileges.
- **Basic Settings Management.** Impose the least possible number of overrides to their configurations.
- **Advanced Settings Management.** None.
- **Basic Software Installation and Maintenance.** All aspects apply. Published applications and Remote OS Installation provide strong benefits without depriving technical users of control.
- **Advanced Software Installation and Maintenance.** No assignment or any form of control.
- **Advanced Remote OS Installation.** Grant access to the advanced installation options. If necessary, make all applicable installation images available for selection by the user.

Meeting the Needs of Stationary Professional Users

Stationary professional users typically appreciate some management services—as long as they add value and do not take too much configuration control away.

For these users, Remote OS Installation and IntelliMirror provide the simplest possible method for setting up their computers, and offer data backup and the best combination of features for the most common uses.

The following basic and advanced plans illustrate how change and configuration management might be applied to stationary professional users:

- **Basic User Data Management.** All aspects apply. The desktop can be redirected. Local private storage is a good option for this group.
- **Advanced User Data Management.** Some users might want Roaming User Profiles. The use of the Encrypting File System might appeal to senior executives. However, note that encrypted files and folders cannot be included in a Roaming User Profile. Encrypted files and folders can, however, be redirected.
- **Basic Settings Management.** A limited number of overrides will be tolerated. These users cannot act as local administrators.
- **Advanced Settings Management.** It is okay to control computer state and access. However, this will often require the creation of a local My Documents folder if network-based quotas are small.
- **Basic Software Installation and Maintenance.** All aspects apply, including application publishing. Use installation on demand for optional features.
- **Advanced Software Installation and Maintenance.** Use application assignment sparingly.
- **Basic Remote OS Installation.** Simplify the process as much as possible by restricting installation options and available images.

Meeting the Needs of Roaming Professional Users

Roaming professional users are very similar to stationary professionals. Even though they use multiple computers, they also typically have a primary computer.

For these users, roaming should be effortless and come at no additional cost over stationary use.

The following plan illustrates how basic and advanced change and configuration management might be applied to roaming professional users:

- **Basic User Data Management.** All aspects apply. Local private storage is essential for this group. The desktop should be redirected.

- **Advanced User Data Management.** Roaming User Profiles are required. The use of the Encrypting File System might appeal to senior executives. However, note that encrypted files and folders cannot be included in a Roaming User Profile. Encrypted files and folders can, however, be redirected.

- **Basic Settings Management.** A limited number of overrides will be tolerated. They are not local administrators.

- **Advanced Settings Management.** It is okay to control computer state and access. However, this will often require the creation of a local My Documents folder if network-based quotas are small.

- **Basic Software Installation and Maintenance.** All aspects apply. Application publishing can be used, but only if you can run the application from the network so that the applications do not need to be installed on a local computer. Use installation on demand for optional features.

- **Advanced Software Installation and Maintenance.** Use application assignment sparingly. Assign applications only to users, computers, not to computers.

- **Basic Remote OS Installation.** All user access to remote installation options is removed completely so that all installations are performed by either administrative or Help desk personnel. Alternatively, remote installation options are restricted so that installation is completely automatic.

Meeting the Needs of Mobile Professional Users

Mobile users benefit greatly from new Windows 2000 features such as Synchronization Manager, the Encrypting File System, client-side caching, and Plug and Play.

These users typically use a laptop as well as a primary desktop computer.

The following illustrates how change and configuration management might be applied to mobile professional users:

- **Basic User Data Management.** All aspects apply. The desktop should not be redirected. Local private storage is essential for this group. Redirected and offline folders are ideal options for this group.

- **Advanced User Data Management.** Roaming User Profiles are commonly used. However, if the user has only one computer, then a roaming user profile is not required, except possibly for data protection. The Encrypting File System should be used.

- **Basic Settings Management.** A limited number of overrides will be tolerated. They are not local administrators.

- **Advanced Settings Management.** Users often have greater control over laptops because of the users' distance from administrators.

- **Basic Software Installation and Maintenance.** All aspects apply. Application publishing can be used, but only if you can install applications locally. Do not use installation on demand for optional features.

- **Advanced Software Installation and Maintenance.** You can assign applications, but only if they will be installed locally. Allow users to install from a local source such as a CD when they are disconnected from the software distribution points.

- **Advanced Remote OS Installation.** Portable computers are supported for Remote OS Installation only when they are connected to the network through a docking station that contains a remote-boot ROM or through a supported network adapter. For users who do not dock, or dock too rarely to allow use of remote installation, consider alternative operating system reinstallation solutions or procedures.

Meeting the Needs of Task-Based Users

Task-based users typically do not have a computer that is considered theirs. When they log off a computer, no data files of computer settings should be left behind. These users cannot install any applications, create files outside their network share, or alter the local computer from its administrator-configured state. In some cases, these computers might be Windows Terminal Services clients.

The following illustrates how change and configuration management might be applied to task-based users:

- **Basic User Data Management.** All aspects apply to non-kiosk-style environments. The desktop is redirected. There is no local storage. For kiosks, local profiles are deleted when the user logs off.

- **Advanced User Data Management.** Roaming User Profiles are used only if this is a non-kiosk-style environment. No data should be left behind.

- **Basic Settings Management.** The desktop is redirected. Computer settings are strictly controlled.

- **Advanced Settings Management.** The desktop is redirected. Computer settings are strictly controlled.

- **Basic Software Installation and Maintenance.** Most applications are installed on a computer (rather than user) basis. Where user-assigned applications are needed, they should be run from the network.

- **Advanced Software Installation and Maintenance.** Applications are only assigned. Prohibit software installation from anyplace but the network.

- **Basic Remote OS Installation.** Access to remote installation options is removed completely so that installations are performed only by administrative or Help desk personnel. Alternatively, installation options are restricted so that the operating system installation becomes automatic.

Summary

Table 24.6 illustrates a sample change and configuration management strategy for a large organization with multiple types of users.

Table 24.6   Sample Change and Configuration Management Strategy

User Classification	User Data Management	User Settings Management	Software Installation and Maintenance	Remote OS Installation
Technical	Basic	Basic (without lockdown)	Basic	Advanced
Stationary Professional	Basic	Basic	Advanced	Basic
Roaming Professional	Advanced	Basic	Advanced	Basic
Mobile Professional	Advanced	Basic	Advanced	Advanced
Task-Based User	Advanced	Advanced	Advanced	Basic

For user data management, use the following guidelines:

- Basic user data management can be useful in companies that manage client computers only moderately.

- Advanced user data management depends on the types of users, particularly in highly managed environments, and when a high degree of service is warranted (for senior executives, for example).

For user settings management, the following guidelines have been applied:

- Basic settings management will be used primarily in organizations with moderately managed client computers, and most often applied to highly managed client computers. It will be used most heavily when a dedicated administrative staff is present.

- Advanced settings management will be used primarily in highly managed environments where support costs are an issue, such as schools, hospitals, and factory floors.

For software installation and maintenance, the following guidelines have been applied:

- Basic software installation and maintenance will become standard practice, particularly the publishing of organization software.

- Advanced software installation and maintenance will be used primarily in highly managed environments where support costs are an issue, such as kiosks, schools, hospitals, and factory floors.

For remote operating system installation, the following guidelines have been applied:

- Basic remote operating system installation will be used when user options are restricted or highly automated. If users are allowed to perform remote installations, they should only have to initiate a remote installation during system startup and enter their user name and password.

- Advanced remote operating system installation will be used when the user can choose which operating system image will be installed and how, or when special circumstances warrant additional flexibility by users performing the installation.

Change and Configuration Management Planning Task List

Table 24.7 summarizes the tasks you need to perform to create your Windows 2000 change and configuration management plan.

Table 24.7   Change and Configuration Management Planning Task List.

Task	Location in chapter
Define user and organization change and configuration management needs.	Evaluating Change and Configuration Management
Evaluate and select desired Windows 2000 change and configuration management features.	Evaluating Change and Configuration Management
Plan for using Remote OS Installation to install Windows 2000.	Enabling Remote OS Installation
Configure Group Policy to enable IntelliMirror software installation and maintenance.	Using Group Policy to Improve Software Management
Configure server shares and Group Policy for user data management.	Maintaining User Data and Settings on a Network
Configure server shares and Group Policy for user settings management.	Maintaining User Data and Settings on a Network

C H A P T E R   2 5

Automating Client Installation and Upgrade

You are now ready to develop and perform the automated installation of Microsoft® Windows® 2000 Professional and associated applications. This is a prerequisite for performing any level of deployment: test, pilot, or production rollout. This chapter presents the automated installation methods that are available, including preparation requirements and example configurations. It is recommended that network engineers involved in the design of the installation process and system administrators involved in the installation of Windows 2000 and associated applications become familiar with this chapter.

Installing Windows 2000 Professional involves either clean installations to computers that have no pre-Windows 2000 operating systems installed or clean installations and upgrades to computers that are currently running Microsoft® Windows® 95, Microsoft® Windows® 98, Microsoft® Windows NT® Workstation version 3.51, or Microsoft® Windows NT® Workstation version 4.0. Before you can determine whether to perform clean installations or upgrades, you need to resolve certain critical planning issues, as discussed in the Planning Overview in this book.

In This Chapter

Chapter Goals

This chapter will help you develop the following planning document:

- Automated Installation Plan

Related Information in the Resource Kit

- For more information about planning, see the "Planning Overview" in this book.

- For more information about automating server installation, see "Automating Server Installation and Upgrade" in this book.

- For more information about administering client computers, see "Defining Client Administration and Configuration Standards" in this book.

- For more information about the Unattended Setup parameters referenced in this chapter, see the "Microsoft Windows 2000 Guide to Unattended Setup" (Unattend.doc) on the Microsoft Windows 2000 operating system compact disk (CD). The Unattend.doc file is part of the Deploy.cab file in the \Support\Tools folder. In Windows 98 or Windows 2000, use Windows Explorer to extract this document. In Windows 95 and earlier, or in MS-DOS®, use the **Extract** command to access the file.

- For more information about Unattended Setup, including sample answer files, see the Appendix "Sample Answer Files for Unattended Setup" in this book.

Determining Whether to Upgrade or Clean Install

In the enterprise environment, it is not cost-effective to install Windows 2000 using the standard interactive setup on each computer. To greatly lower the total cost of ownership (TCO), you can perform automated installations of Windows 2000 Professional on multiple computers.

 Critical Decision   Before you can automate the installation of Windows 2000 Professional, you must decide whether the installation will be an upgrade from Windows NT or a clean installation.

The following two items will help you determine whether to upgrade or to perform a clean installation:

- If your organization has already implemented a Windows operating system and your information technology (IT) department is centrally managed, you will probably want to perform an upgrade. If you are planning to create a managed environment but one does not currently exist in your organization, then you will want to perform a clean installation so that you can implement standard configurations as you perform your installation.

- If you plan to use currently existing hardware and software applications, you need to perform an upgrade. Alternatively, if you plan to purchase new hardware and install new software applications, you need to perform a clean installation.

Resolving Critical Planning Issues

If you plan to install Windows 2000 Professional on computers that have no pre-Windows 2000 operating systems installed, a clean installation is the obvious choice. If the computers are currently running Windows 95, Windows 98, Windows NT Workstation 3.51, or Windows NT Workstation 4.0, you need to determine whether it is more cost-effective to upgrade the existing operating system or perform a clean installation.

Typical planning issues are summarized in Table 25.1

Table 25.1   Planning Issues to Be Resolved Before Upgrade or Installation

Issue	Task
Organizational goals	Define your company's primary goals.
Regional needs	Identify specific regional needs, and determine whether business is going to include international branches or companies.
User groups	Analyze user groups, including specific job categories and needs; computer knowledge and experience of users; security requirements; and locations of users and their network connectivity issues, including link speed.
Application needs	Determine which products are going to be preinstalled on all computers, which products are going to be advertised only to specific users, and which products are going to be distributed to specific categories of users.
Computer/user strategies	Evaluate current data storage and user settings; identify migration requirements for user settings; and evaluate mandatory, roaming, and local profiles.
Hardware	Inventory existing hardware, and determine expectations for new hardware.
	Set minimum hardware requirements before upgrade or installation.
	Plan for future computer needs.
	Determine how computers are cycled through the organization.
	Determine whether all computers have bootable CD-ROMs.
Risks and problem areas	Identify potential risks, including application incompatibility with Windows 2000, timeline issues, multiple sites, noncentralized budget, and the impact of possible upcoming mergers.
Growth expectations	Identify growth expectations over the course of the project at 1 year, 3 years, and 5 years. Planned mergers, new sites, countries, and so on, must be accounted for when they become known.
Network concerns	Determine whether remote sites have application deployment servers. Identify how servers outside the central site are upgraded.
Software management	Determine whether a software management system, such as Microsoft® Systems Management Server (SMS), is in place so that deployments can be scheduled.
Connectivity	Determine whether the servers and the connections between them are set up to distribute large packages to everyone in the company.

Choosing Your Installation Method

After you resolve your critical planning issues, you can choose the methods that you are going to use to automate the installations. Table 25.2 lists the automated installation methods and shows whether they can be used for upgrade, clean installation, or both.

Table 25.2   Automated Installation Methods

Method	Windows 2000 Edition	Upgrade	Clean Installation
Syspart	Server and Professional	No	Yes
Sysprep	Server and Professional	No	Yes
SMS	Server and Professional	Yes	Yes
Bootable CD-ROM	Server and Professional	No	Yes
Remote Operating System Installation	Professional	No	Yes

Preparing for Installation

To prepare for a clean installation of Windows 2000 Professional, you need to do the following:

- Create the distribution folder
- Understand how to use the answer file
- Understand the Windows 2000 Setup commands

Note The principles of performing an automated installation that are described in this section apply to both a clean installation and an upgrade. The most common scenario is to perform a clean installation.

Figure 25.1 is a flowchart showing the installation process.

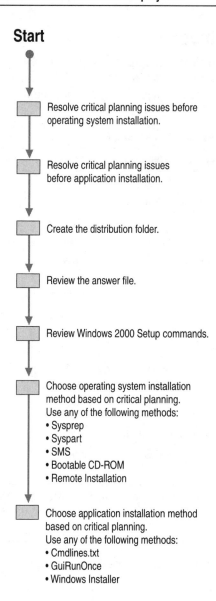

Figure 25.1 Automated Installation Flowchart

Creating the Distribution Folders

To install Windows 2000 Professional on multiple computers over a network, you must create at least one set of distribution folders. The distribution folders typically reside on a server where computers can connect and install Windows 2000 by running Winnt.exe or Winnt32.exe on the destination computer. You can use the same set of distribution folders with different answer files for different system implementations. Even if you intend to use disk imaging as your installation method, starting with distribution folders will provide consistent implementations for a variety of system types. In addition, you can use distribution folders to update future images by editing the files in the distribution folders or by modifying the answer files to generate updated images without having to start from the beginning.

To help load balance the servers and make the file-copy phase of Windows 2000 Setup faster for computers already running Windows 95, Windows 98, Windows NT, or Windows 2000, you can create distribution folders on multiple servers. You can then run Winnt32.exe with up to eight source file locations. For more information about Professional on multiple computers.

 Critical Decision   Before you can automate the installation of Windows 2000 Professional, you must decide if the installation will be an upgrade from Windows NT or a clean installation.

The following two items will help you determine whether to Setup commands, see "Reviewing the Windows 2000 Setup Commands" later in this chapter.

Note   In this chapter, the term "Windows NT" refers to both Windows NT 3.51 and Windows NT 4.0.

The distribution folders contain the Windows 2000 Professional installation files, as well as any device drivers and other files needed for the installation.

Setup Manager, a tool that is available on the Windows 2000 Professional CD, can help you automate the process of creating a distribution folder. For more information about Setup Manager, see "Creating the Answer File" later in this chapter.

Note   In this chapter, "Windows 2000 Setup" is also referred to as "Setup."

▶ **To create a distribution folder**

1. Connect to the network server on which you want to create the distribution folder.

2. Create an \i386 folder on the distribution share of the network server.

   To help differentiate between multiple distribution shares for the different editions of Windows 2000 (Windows 2000 Professional, Microsoft® Windows® 2000 Server, and one for Microsoft® Windows® 2000 Advanced Server), you can choose another name for this folder. If you plan to use localized language versions of Windows 2000 for international branches of your organization, you can create separate distribution shares for each localized version.

3. Copy the contents of the \i386 folder from the Windows 2000 Professional CD to the folder that you created.

4. In the folder that you created, create a subfolder named OEM.

   The OEM subfolder provides the necessary folder structure for supplemental files to be copied to the target computer during Setup. These files include drivers, utilities, applications, and any other files required for deployment of Windows 2000 Professional within your organization.

Structuring the Distribution Folder

An example of the structure for the distribution folder is shown in Figure 25.2.

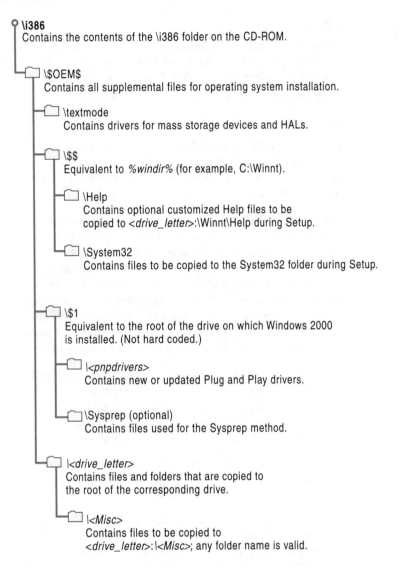

\i386
Contains the contents of the \i386 folder on the CD-ROM.

\OEM
Contains all supplemental files for operating system installation.

\textmode
Contains drivers for mass storage devices and HALs.

\$$
Equivalent to *%windir%* (for example, C:\Winnt).

\Help
Contains optional customized Help files to be
copied to *<drive_letter>*:\Winnt\Help during Setup.

\System32
Contains files to be copied to the System32 folder during Setup.

\$1
Equivalent to the root of the drive on which Windows 2000
is installed. (Not hard coded.)

<pnpdrivers>
Contains new or updated Plug and Play drivers.

\Sysprep (optional)
Contains files used for the Sysprep method.

<drive_letter>
Contains files and folders that are copied to
the root of the corresponding drive.

<Misc>
Contains files to be copied to
<drive_letter>:*<Misc>*; any folder name is valid.

Figure 25.2   Example Structure for the Distribution Folder

i386

This is the distribution folder, which contains all of the files required to install Windows 2000. You create this folder at the root of the distribution share by copying the contents of the i386 folder on the Windows 2000 Professional CD to the distribution folder.

OEM

You create the OEM subfolder in the distribution folder directly beneath the i386 folder. During Setup, you can automatically copy directories, standard 8.3 format files, and any tools needed for your automated installation process to the OEM subfolder.

If you use the OEMFILESPATH key in the answer file, you can create the OEM subfolder outside the distribution folder. For information about the definition of the answer file, see "Reviewing the Answer File" later in this chapter. For more information about answer file parameters and syntax, see "Microsoft Windows 2000 Guide to Unattended Setup" (Unattend.doc) on the Microsoft Windows 2000 operating system CD. The Unattend.doc file is part of the Deploy.cab file in the \Support\Tools folder. In Windows 98 or Windows 2000, use Windows Explorer to extract this document. In Windows 95 and earlier, or in MS-DOS, use the **Extract** command to access the file.

The OEM subfolder can contain the optional file Cmdlines.txt, which contains a list of commands to be run during the graphical user interface (GUI) portion of Setup. These commands can be used to install additional tools that you want to include with your installations. For more information about the Cmdlines.txt file, see "Using Cmdlines.txt" later in this chapter.

As long as Setup finds the OEM subfolder in the root of the distribution point, it copies all of the files found in this directory to the temporary directory that is created during the text portion of Setup.

Note In this chapter, the GUI portion of Setup is referred to as "GUI mode," and the text portion of Setup is referred to as "text mode."

OEM\textmode

The OEM\textmode subfolder contains new or updated files for installing mass storage device drivers and hardware abstraction layers (HALS). These files can include OEM HALs, drivers for Small Computer System Interface (SCSI) devices, and Txtsetup.oem, which directs the loading and installing of these components.

Make sure to include the Txtsetup.oem file. All files placed in the OEM\textmode subfolder (HALs, drivers, and Txtsetup.oem) must be listed in the [OEMBootFiles] section of the answer file.

OEM\$$

The OEM\$$ subfolder is equivalent to the %systemroot% or %windir% environment variables. The subfolder contains additional files that you want copied to the various subfolders of the Windows 2000 installation directory. The structure of this subfolder must match the structure of a standard Windows 2000 installation, where OEM\$$ matches %systemroot % or %windir% (for example, C:\winnt), OEM\$$\System32 matches %windir%\System32, and so on. Each subfolder must contain the files that need to be copied to the corresponding system folder on the target computer.

OEM\$1

The OEM\$1 subfolder, which is new for Windows 2000, points to the drive on which Windows 2000 is installed. $1 is equivalent to the %systemdrive% environment variable. For example, if you are installing Windows 2000 on drive D, OEM\$1 points to drive D.

OEM\$1*pnpdrvrs*

You can use the OEM\$1*pnpdrvrs* subfolder, which is new for Windows 2000, to place new or updated Plug and Play device drivers in your distribution folders. These folders are copied to the %systemdrive%*pnpdrvrs* location on the target computer. Adding the OemPnPDriversPath parameter to your answer file directs Windows 2000 to look (both during and after Setup) for new or updated Plug and Play drivers in the folders that you created, as well as those originally included with the system. Note that you can replace *pnpdrvrs* with a name of your own that is eight characters long or less.

OEM\$1\Sysprep

The OEM\$1\Sysprep subfolder is optional. This subfolder contains the files that you need to run the Sysprep tool. For information about these files, see "Using Sysprep to Duplicate Disks" later in this chapter.

OEM*drive_letter*

During text mode, the structure of each OEM*drive_letter* subfolder is copied to the root of the corresponding drive in the target computer. For example, files that you place in the OEM\D subfolder are copied to the root of drive D. You can also create subfolders within these subfolders. For example, OEM\E\Misc causes Setup to create a subfolder called Misc on drive E.

Files that have to be renamed must be listed in $$Rename.txt. For more information about renaming files, see "Converting File Name Size Using $$Rename.txt" later in this chapter. Note that the files in the distribution folders must have short file names that use the format 8.3 naming convention.

Installing Mass Storage Devices

In Windows 2000, Plug and Play detects and installs most hardware devices, which can be loaded later during Setup. However, mass storage devices, such as hard disks, must be properly installed for full Plug and Play support to be available during GUI mode.

Note You do not need to specify a device if it is already supported by Windows 2000.

To install SCSI devices during text mode—that is, before full Plug and Play support is available—you must provide a Txtsetup.oem file that describes how Setup must install the particular SCSI device.

Important Before you use updated drivers, verify that they are signed. If they are not signed, Setup will fail. You can check the signed status for individual drivers in Device Manager, or you can run Sigverif.exe to generate a Sigverif.txt file in the %windir% subfolder. Sigverif.txt lists the signed status for all drivers on the system.

▶ **To install a mass storage device**

1. Create the Textmode subfolder in the OEM subfolder in the distribution folder.

2. Copy the following files, which you obtain from the device vendor, to the Textmode subfolder (replace the word *Driver* with the appropriate driver name):

   - *Driver*.sys
   - *Driver*.dll
   - *Driver*.inf
   - Txtsetup.oem

Note Some drivers, such as SCSI miniport drivers, might not include a .dll file.

---

3. In the answer file, create a [MassStorageDrivers] section, and in this section type the driver entries that you want to include. For example, a possible entry in the [MassStorageDrivers] section would be the following:

   ```
   "Adaptec 2940..." = "OEM"
   ```

   Information for this section can be obtained from the Txtsetup.oem file, which is provided by the hardware manufacturer.

For more information about answer file parameters and syntax, see "Microsoft Windows 2000 Guide to Unattended Setup" (Unattend.doc) on the Microsoft Windows 2000 operating system CD. The Unattend.doc file is part of the Deploy.cab file in the \Support\Tools folder. In Windows 98 or Windows 2000, use Windows Explorer to extract this document. In Windows 95 and earlier, or in MS-DOS, use the **Extract** command to access the file.

4. In the answer file create an [OEMBootFiles] section, and in this section type a list of the files in the OEM\Textmode folder. For example, a possible entry to the [OEMBootFiles] section would be the following:

```
[OEMBootFiles]
Driver.sys
Driver.dll
Driver.inf
Txtsetup.oem
```

Where *Driver* is the driver name.

5. If your mass storage device is a Plug and Play device, it will have a section named [HardwareIds.Scsi.*yyyyy*] in the Txtsetup.oem file. If it does not have such a section, you will need to create one and then type the following entry in the section:

```
"xxxxx" , "yyyyy"
```

where *xxxxx* represents the device identifier (ID), and *yyyyy* represents the service associated with the device.

For example, to install the Symc810 driver, which has a device ID of PCI\VEN_1000&DEV_0001, verify that your Txtsetup.oem file contains the following additional section:

```
[HardwareIds.scsi.symc810]
id = "PCI\VEN_1000&DEV_0001" , "symc810"
```

Installing Hardware Abstraction Layers

To specify hardware abstraction layers (HALs) for installation, you need a Txtsetup.oem file and the HAL files, which the vendor provides. You must use the same Txtsetup.oem file if you are installing mass storage device drivers. Only one Txtsetup.oem file can be used, so if you need to install HALs and mass storage device drivers, you need to combine entries into one file.

To use third-party drivers, you must also make appropriate changes to the answer file. For more information about answer file parameters and syntax, see the "Microsoft Windows 2000 Guide to Unattended Setup" (Unattend.doc) on the Microsoft Windows 2000 operating system CD. The Unattend.doc file is part of the Deploy.cab file in the \Support\Tools folder. In Windows 98 or Windows 2000, use Windows Explorer to extract this document. In Windows 95 and earlier, or in MS-DOS, use the **Extract** command to access the file.

▶ **To install a HAL**

1. If you have not already done so, create a Textmode subfolder in the OEM folder.

2. Copy the files that you receive from the device vendor to the Textmode subfolder.

3. In the answer file, edit the [Unattend] section for the HAL, adding any drivers that you want to install. For example, type the following:

```
[Unattend]
Computertype = "HALDescription   ", OEM
```

Information for the *HALDescription* can be obtained from the [Computer] section of the Txtsetup.oem file from the driver provider.

4. In the answer file, create an [OEMBootFiles] section, and enter the names of the files in the OEM\Textmode folder.

Installing Plug and Play Devices

The following procedure demonstrates how to install Plug and Play devices that are not mass storage devices or HALs, and are not included on the Windows 2000 operating system CD.

▶ **To install Plug and Play devices**

1. Create a subfolder in the distribution folder for special Plug and Play drivers and their .inf files. For example, you can create a folder called PnPDrvs:

```
$OEM$\$1\PnPDrvs
```

2. Add the path to the list of Plug and Play search drives by adding the following line to the Unattend.txt file:

```
OEMPnPDriversPath = "PnPDrvs"
```

If you have subfolders in the PnPDrvs folder, you must specify the path to each subfolder. The paths must be separated by semicolons.

To easily maintain the folders so that they can accommodate future device drivers, create subfolders for potential device drivers. By dividing the folders into subfolders, you can store device driver files by device type, rather than having all device driver files in one folder. Suggested subfolders include Audio, Modem, Net, Print, Video, and Other. An Other folder can give you the flexibility to store new hardware devices that might not be currently known.

For example, if the PnPDrvs folder contains the subfolders Audio, Modem, and Net, the answer file must contain the following line:

```
OEMPnPDriversPath = "PnPDrvs\Audio;PnPDrvs\Modem;PnPDrvs\Net"
```

Converting File Name Size Using $$Rename.txt

The $$Rename.txt file changes short file names to long file names during Setup. $$Rename.txt lists all of the files in a particular folder that need to be renamed. Each folder that contains short file names that should be renamed must contain its own version of $$Rename.txt.

To use $$Rename.txt, put the file in a folder that contains files that need to be converted. The syntax for $$Rename.txt is as follows:

```
[section_name_1]
short_name_1 = "long_name_1"
short_name_2 = "long_name_2"


short_name_x = "long_name_x"

[section_name_2]
short_name_1 = "long_name_1"
short_name_2 = "long_name_2"


short_name_x = "long_name_x"
```

Parameters are defined as follows:

section_name_x. The path to the subfolder that contains the files. A section does not need to be named, or it can have a backslash (\) as a name, which indicates that the section contains the names of the files or subfolders that are in the root of the drive.

short_name_x. The name of the file or subfolder within this subfolder to be renamed. The name must *not* be enclosed in quotation marks.

long_name_x. The new name of the file or subfolder. This name must be enclosed in quotation marks if it contains spaces or commas.

Tip If you are using MS-DOS to start the installation, and your MS-DOS-based tools cannot copy folders with path names longer than 64 characters, you can use short file names for the folders and then use $$Rename.txt to rename them later.

Reviewing the Answer File

The answer file is a customized script that answers the Setup questions without requiring user input. The Windows 2000 Server CD contains a sample answer file that you can modify and use. The answer file is usually named Unattend.txt, but you can rename it. (For example, Comp1.txt, Install.txt, and Setup.txt are all valid names for an answer file, as long as those names are correctly specified in the Setup command.) By renaming the answer file, you can build and use multiple answer files if you need to maintain different scripted installations for different parts of your organization. Note that answer files are also used by other programs such as Sysprep, which uses the optional Sysprep.inf file.

The answer file tells Setup how to interact with the distribution folders and files that you have created. For example, in the [Unattend] section of the answer file there is an "OEMPreinstall" entry that tells Setup to copy the OEM subfolders from the distribution folders to the target computer.

The answer file contains multiple optional sections that you can modify to supply information about your installation requirements. The answer file supplies Setup with answers to all the questions that you are asked during a standard, interactive installation of Windows 2000. The Unattend.doc file has detailed information about answer file keys and values. For more information about answer file sections and their associated parameters, see the "Microsoft Windows 2000 Guide to Unattended Setup" (Unattend.doc) on the Microsoft Windows 2000 operating system CD. The Unattend.doc file is part of the Deploy.cab file in the \Support\Tools folder. In Windows 98 or Windows 2000, use Windows Explorer to extract this document. In Windows 95 and earlier, or in MS-DOS, use the **Extract** command to access the file.

To perform an unattended installation of Windows 2000 Server, you must create an answer file and specify that file when Setup begins, either by using the bootable method or by running Winnt.exe or Winnt32.exe. The following is an example of a Setup command using Winnt.exe:

```
Winnt /S:Z:\I386 /U:Z:\unattend.txt
```

Note the use of the **/U:** command-line switch, which indicates an unattended installation. For more information about Winnt.exe and Winnt32.exe, see "Reviewing the Windows 2000 Setup Commands" later in this chapter.

Creating the Answer File

The answer file is a customized script that you can use to run an unattended installation of Windows 2000 Professional. There are two ways to create an answer file: You can use Setup Manager, or you can create the file manually.

Creating the Answer File with Setup Manager

To help you create or modify the answer file, the Setup Manager application is available on the Windows 2000 operating system CD in the Deploy.cab file of the \Support\Tools folder. By using Setup Manager, you can add consistency to the process of creating or updating the answer file.

For more information about answer file parameters and syntax, see the "Microsoft Windows 2000 Guide to Unattended Setup" (Unattend.doc) on the Microsoft Windows 2000 operating system CD. The Unattend.doc file is part of the Deploy.cab file in the \Support\Tools folder. In Windows 98 or Windows 2000, use Windows Explorer to extract this document. In Windows 95 and earlier, or in MS-DOS, use the **Extract** command to access the file.

You can use Setup Manager to perform the following tasks; it then generates the results as answer file parameters:

- Specify the platform for the answer file (Windows 2000 Professional, Windows 2000 Server, Remote Operating System Installation, or Sysprep).
- Specify the level of automation for unattended Setup mode. (Levels include "Provide Defaults," "Fully Automated," "Hide Pages," "Read Only," and "GUI-mode Setup.")
- Specify default user information.
- Define computer name options, including creating a Uniqueness Database File (/UDF) to access a file of valid computer names.
- Configure network settings.
- Create distribution folders.
- Add a custom logo and background files.
- Add files to the distribution folders.
- Add commands to the [GuiRunOnce] section.
- Create Cmdlines.txt files.
- Specify code pages.
- Specify regional options.
- Specify a time zone.
- Specify TAPI information.

Setup Manager cannot perform the following functions:

- Specify system components, such as Internet Information Services.
- Create Txtsetup.oem files.
- Create subfolders in the distribution folder.

Table 25.3 describes some of the most common answer file specifications that are created by Setup Manager.

Table 25.3 Answer File Specifications Created by Setup Manager

Parameter	Purpose
Installation path	Specifies the desired path on the target computer in which to install Windows 2000 Server.
Upgrade option	Specifies whether to upgrade from Windows 95 or Windows 98, Windows NT, or Windows 2000.
Target computer name	Specifies the user name, organization name, and computer name to apply to the target computer.
Product ID	Specifies the product identification number obtained from the product documentation.
Workgroup or domain	Specifies the name of the workgroup or domain to which the computer belongs.
Time zone	Specifies the time zone for the computer.
Network configuration information	Specifies the network adapter type and configuration with network protocols.

Creating the Answer File Manually

To create the answer file manually, you can use a text editor such as Notepad. In general, an answer file consists of section headers, parameters, and values for those parameters. Although most section headers are predefined, you can also define additional section headers. Note that you do not have to specify all possible parameters in the answer file if the installation does not require them.

Invalid parameter values generate errors or result in incorrect behavior after Setup.

The answer file format is as follows:

```
[section1]
;
;   Section contains keys and the corresponding
;   values for those keys/parameters.
;   keys and values are separated by ' = ' signs
;   Values that have spaces in them usually require double quotes
;   "" around them
;
key = value
.
.
.
[section2]
key = value
.
.
.
```

Using the Answer File to Set Passwords

By using the answer file with Setup, you can set parameters for the following password commands:

- AdminPassword

- UserPassword

- DefaultPassword

- DomainAdminPassword

- AdminstratorPassword

- Password

For information about the definitions of these commands, see the "Microsoft Windows 2000 Guide to Unattended Setup" (Unattend.doc) on the Microsoft Windows 2000 operating system CD. The Unattend.doc file is part of the Deploy.cab file in the \Support\Tools folder. In Windows 98 or Windows 2000, use Windows Explorer to extract this document. In Windows 95 and earlier, or in MS-DOS, use the **Extract** command to access the file.

In addition, you can find examples of answer files that use some of these parameters in the Appendix "Sample Answer Files for Unattended Setup" in this book.

Note Passwords are limited to 127 characters. If you specify a password that contains more than 127 characters, you are not going to be able to log on to the system because the password will be invalid.

After the installation is completed, an answer file with all the settings used to configure the computer remains on the computer; however, all password information is removed from the local copy of the answer file so that security is not compromised.

Caution During the Setup process, however, the answer file is available on the hard disk. If you are concerned about the security implications, do not add password information to the answer file that you created for the unattended installation.

Using the local answer file allows you to automatically set up optional components by running commands that contain the parameters you already provided in the original answer file that was used with Setup. These components can include configuring the server as a domain controller, as a cluster server, or enabling Message Queuing.

Extending Hard Disk Partitions

You can start an install on a small partition (about 1 gigabyte [GB] on a larger disk) and cause that partition to be extended during the Windows 2000 Setup process by using the ExtendOEMPartition parameter in the answer file. The ExtendOEMPartition parameter works only on NTFS file system partitions and can be used in both a regular answer file and one used for a Sysprep-based installation.

For more information about Sysprep and the Sysprep.inf file, see "Using Sysprep to Duplicate Disks" later in this chapter.

Note ExtendOEMPartition acts only on the active system partition. It does not work on other partitions on the same hard disk or other hard disks in the computer. In addition, when ExtendOemPartition=1 is used, it extends to all remaining space on the hard disk, but leaves the last cylinder blank. This is by design so that you have the option of enabling dynamic volumes.

If you are using ExtendOEMPartition during an unattended install on a file allocation table (FAT) partition, you need to specify the FileSystem=ConvertNTFS in the [Unattended} section of your answer file to first convert the partition to NTFS. For information about using the ExtendOEMPartition for a Sysprep-based installation, see "Using Sysprep to Extend Disk Partitions" later in this chapter.

For more information about using ExtendOemPartition, see "Microsoft Windows 2000 Guide to Unattended Setup" (Unattend.doc) on the Microsoft Windows 2000 operating system CD. The Unattend.doc file is part of the Deploy.cab file in the \Support\Tools folder. In Windows 98 or Windows 2000, use Windows Explorer to extract this document. In Windows 95 and earlier, or in MS-DOS, use the **Extract** command to access the file.

Reviewing the Windows 2000 Setup Commands

To install Windows 2000, you must run the appropriate Windows 2000 Setup program, either Winnt.exe or Winnt32.exe. In this chapter, Winnt.exe and Winnt32.exe are both referred to as Setup. The version of Setup that you need to run is determined as follows:

- For a clean installation on a computer running MS-DOS or Microsoft® Windows® 3.*x*, run Winnt.exe from the MS-DOS prompt.

- For a clean installation or upgrade from Windows NT, Windows 95 or Windows 98, run Winnt32.exe.

Note that you can start a standard, interactive Setup directly from the boot floppy disks that come with the Windows 2000 Professional CD.

Caution If you update any applications on the computer before upgrading it to Windows 2000, make sure that you restart the computer before running Setup.

For more information about installation methods, see "Automating the Installation of Windows 2000 Professional" later in this chapter.

Winnt.exe

The Winnt.exe command, including the parameters that apply to automated installation, is as follows:

```
winnt [/S[:sourcepath]][/T[:tempdrive]]/U[:answer_file]][/R[x]:folder]
[/E:command]
```

For the parameter definitions, see the Appendix "Setup Commands" in this book.

For hard disk drives with multiple partitions, the Winnt.exe version of Setup installs Windows 2000 to the active partition if the partition contains sufficient space. Otherwise, Setup looks for additional partitions containing sufficient space and prompts you to choose the desired partition. For automated installations, you can bypass the prompt by running Setup with the **/T** parameter to automatically point to the desired partition. For example:

```
winnt [/unattend] [:<path>\answer.txt] [/T[:d]]
```

Winnt32.exe

The Winnt32.exe command, including the parameters that apply to automated installation, is as follows:

```
winnt32 [/s:sourcepath] [/tempdrive:drive_letter]
[/unattend[num][:answer_file]] [/copydir:folder_name]
[/copysource:folder_name] [/cmd:command_line] [/debug[level][:filename]]
[/udf:id[,UDB_file]] [/syspart:drive_letter] [/noreboot]
[/makelocalsource] [/checkupgradeonly] [/m:folder_name]
```

For information about the parameter definitions, see the Appendix "Setup Commands" in this book.

For hard disk drives with multiple partitions, the Winnt32.exe version of Setup installs Windows 2000 to the active partition if the partition contains sufficient space. Otherwise, Setup looks for additional partitions containing sufficient space and prompts you to choose the desired partition. For automated installations, you can bypass the prompt by running Setup with the /tempdrive parameter to automatically point to the desired partition. For example:

```
winnt32 [/unattend] [:<path>\answer.txt] [/tempdrive:d]
```

Windows 2000 can use up to eight **/s** switches to point to other distribution servers as source locations for installation to the destination computer. This functionality helps to speed up the file-copy phase of Setup to the destination computer, as well as providing additional load balancing capability to the distribution servers from which Setup can be run. For example:

```
<path to distribution folder 1>\winnt32 [/unattend] [:<path>\answer.txt]
[/s:<path to distribution folder 2>] [/s:<path to distribution folder
3>] [/s:<path to distribution folder 4]
```

Table 25.4 shows the Setup commands and how they are used with Windows 2000.

Table 25.4   Using Setup Commands

Setup Command	Windows 2000 Edition	Upgrade	Clean Installation
Winnt.exe	Server and Professional	No	Yes
Winnt32.exe	Server and Professional	Yes	Yes

Automating the Installation of Client Applications

After resolving your critical planning issues, you can decide how you will automate the installation of server applications. In almost all cases, you will want to use an application's unattended installation features to install it.

You can choose from among the following three methods:

- Cmdlines.txt
- Running the application installation program or batch file from the [GuiRunOnce] section of the answer file.
- Windows Installer Service

Using Cmdlines.txt

The Cmdlines.txt file contains the commands that GUI mode executes when installing optional components, such as applications that must be installed immediately after Windows 2000 Professional is installed. If you plan to use Cmdlines.txt, you need to place it in the OEM subfolder of the distribution folder. If you are using Sysprep, place Cmdlines.txt in the OEM\$1\Sysprep subfolder.

Use Cmdlines.txt when the following conditions exist:

- You are installing from the OEM subfolder of the distribution folder.
- The application that you are installing has the following properties:
  - It does not configure itself for multiple users (for example, Microsoft® Office 95).

    –Or–

  - It is designed to be installed by one user and to replicate user-specific information.

The syntax for Cmdlines.txt is as follows:

```
[Commands]
"<command_1>"
"<command_2>"

      .
      .
      .

"<command_x>"
```

Parameters are defined as follows:

- "*<command_1>*", "*<command_2>*", ... "*<command_x>*" refer to the commands that you want to run (and in what order) when GUI mode calls Cmdlines.txt. Note that all commands must be in quotation marks.

When you use Cmdlines.txt, be aware of the following:

- When the commands in Cmdlines.txt are executed during Setup, there is no logged-on user and there is no guaranteed network connectivity. Therefore, user-specific information is written to the default user registry, and all subsequently created users also receive that information.

- Cmdlines.txt requires that you place the files that are necessary to run an application or tool in directories that are accessed during the Setup process, which means that the files must be on the hard disk.

Using the [GuiRunOnce] Section of the Answer File

The [GuiRunOnce] section of the answer file contains a list of commands that run the first time a user logs on to the computer after Setup runs. For example, you enter the following line to the [GuiRunOnce] section to start the application installation program automatically.

```
[GuiRunOnce]
"%systemdrive%\appfolder\appinstall -quiet"
```

If you plan to use the [GuiRunOnce] section to initiate an installation, there are some additional factors to take into consideration:

If the application forces a reboot, determine whether there is a way to suppress the reboot

This is important because any time the system reboots, all previous entries in the [GuiRunOnce] section are lost. If the system reboots before completing entries previously listed in the [GuiRunOnce] section, the remaining items will not be run. If there is no way within the application to suppress a reboot, you can try to repackage the application into a Windows Installer package. There are third-party products that provide this functionality.

Windows 2000 includes WinINSTALL Limited Edition (LE), a repackaging tool for Windows Installer. You can use WinINSTALL LE to efficiently repackage pre-Windows Installer applications into packages that can be distributed with Windows Installer. For more information about WinINSTALL LE, see the Valueadd\3rdparty\Mgmt\Winstle folder on the Windows 2000 operating system CD.

For more information about Windows Installer packaging, see "Using Windows Installer Service" later in this chapter.

Important If you are installing an application to multiple localized language versions of Windows 2000, it is recommended that you test the repackaged application on the localized versions to ensure that it copies the files to the correct locations and writes the required registry entries appropriately.

If an application requires a Windows Explorer shell to install, the [GuiRunOnce] section will not work because the shell is not loaded when the Run and RunOnce commands are executed.

Check with the application vendor to determine whether they have an update or patch that can address this situation for the application setup. If not, you can repackage the application as a Windows Installer package or use another means of distribution.

Applications that use the same type of installation mechanism might not run properly if a /wait command is not used

This can happen when an application installation is running and starts another process. When the setup routine is still running, initiating another process and closing an active one might cause the next routine listed in the RunOnce registry entries to start. Because more than one instance of the installation mechanism is running, the second application will usually fail. For information about how to control this by using a batch file, see "Using a Batch File to Control How Multiple Applications Are Installed" later in this chapter.

Using Application Installation Programs

The preferred method for preinstalling an application is to use the installation routine supplied with the application. You can do this if the application that you are preinstalling is able to run in *quiet* mode (that is, without user intervention) by using a **/q** or **/s** command-line switch. For a list of command-line parameters supported by the installation mechanism, see the application Help file or documentation

The following is an example of a line that you can place in the [GuiRunOnce] section to initiate the unattended installation of an application by using its own installation program.

```
<path to setup>\Setup.exe /q
```

Setup parameters vary between applications. For example, the **/l** parameter included in some applications is useful when you want to create a log file to monitor the installation. Some applications have commands that can keep them from restarting automatically. These commands are useful in helping to control application installations with a minimal number of reboots.

Make sure that you check with the application vendor for information, instructions, tools, and best practices information before you preinstall any application.

Important You must meet the licensing requirements for any application that you install, regardless of how you install it.

Using a Batch File to Control How Multiple Applications Are Installed

If you want to control how multiple applications are installed, you can create a batch file that contains the individual installation commands and uses the **Start** command with the **/wait** command-line switch. This method ensures that your applications install sequentially and that each application is fully installed before the next application begins its installation routine. The batch file is then run from the [GuiRunOnce] section.

The following procedure explains how to create the batch file, how to install the application, and then how to remove all references to the batch file after the installation is complete.

▶ **To install applications using a batch file**

1. Create the batch file containing lines similar to the following example:

   ```
   Start /wait <path to 1st application>\Setup <command line parameters>
   Start /wait <path to 2nd application>\Setup <command line parameters>
   Exit
   ```

   where:

   - <*path*> is the path to the executable file that starts the installation. This path must be available during Setup.
   - *Setup* is the name of the executable file that starts the installation.

- *<command line parameters>* are any available quiet-mode parameters appropriate for the application that you want to install.

2. Copy the batch file to the distribution folders or another location that can be accessed during Setup.

3. With *<filename>*.bat as the name of the batch file, include an entry in the [GuiRunOnce] section of the answer file to run the batch file, similar to the following example. This example assumes that the batch file was copied to the Sysprep folder on the local hard disk drive, though it can be located anywhere to which Setup has access during an installation.

```
[GuiRunOnce]
"%systemdrive%\sysprep\<filename>.bat"= "<path-1>\Command-1.exe"
"<path-n>\Command-n.exe"
"%systemdrive%\sysprep\sysprep.exe -quiet"
```

where:

<path-1>\Command-1.exe and *<path-n>\Command-n.exe* are fully qualified paths to additional applications or tool installations or configuration tools. This can also be a path to another batch file. These paths must be available during Setup.

Using Windows Installer Service

Windows Installer Service is a Windows 2000 component that standardizes the way applications are installed on multiple computers.

When you install applications without using Windows Installer Service, every application must have its own setup executable file or script. Each application has to ensure that the proper installation rules (for example, rules for creating file versions) are followed. This is because the application setup was not an integral part of the operating system development, so no central reference for installation rules exists.

Windows Installer Service implements all the proper Setup rules in the operating system itself. To follow those rules, applications must be described in a standard format known as a Windows Installer package. The data file containing the format information is known as the *Windows Installer package file* and has an .msi extension. Windows Installer Service uses the Windows Installer package file to install the application.

Windows Installer Terminology

The following terms are used to describe the installation process that uses Windows Installer technology:

Resource. A file, registry entry, shortcut, or other element that an installer typically delivers to a computer.

Component. A collection of files, registry entries, and other resources that are installed or uninstalled as a unit. When a particular component is selected for installation or removal, all of the resources in that component are either installed or removed.

Feature. The granular pieces of an application that a user can choose to install. Features typically represent the functional features of the application itself.

Product. A single product, such as Microsoft® Office. Products contain one or more features.

Windows Installer Package File

The package file is a database format that is optimized for installation performance. Generally, this file describes the relationships between features, components, and resources for a specific product.

The Windows Installer package file is typically located in the root folder of the product CD or network image, alongside the product files. The product files can exist as compressed files known as cabinet files (which have a .cab extension). Each product has its own package file. At installation time, Windows Installer Service opens up the package file for the product in question, and uses the information inside the Windows Installer package to determine all the installation operations that must be performed for that product.

Automating the Installation of Windows 2000 Professional

In the enterprise environment, it is not cost-effective to install Windows 2000 using the standard interactive setup on each computer. To greatly lower the total cost of ownership (TCO), you can perform automated installations of Windows 2000 Professional on multiple computers.

You can automate the installation of the following:

- The core operating system of Windows 2000 Professional.
- Standard productivity applications such as Microsoft® Office 2000 or any other application that does not run as a service.
- Additional language support for Windows 2000 Professional through the installation of various language packs.
- Service packs for Windows 2000 Professional.

Automated installation of Windows 2000 Professional involves running Setup with an answer file. Setup can take place in unattended fashion. An unattended Setup includes the following steps:

- Creating an answer file.
- Determining and implementing a process to configure computer-specific information.
- Using Windows Installer packages to prepare for installing additional files.
- Determining and implementing the process to automate the selected distribution method, such as using a network distribution point or hard disk duplication.

New Options for Automated Installation

In Windows 2000 automated installation, there are several new options available in the answer file for controlling how and what should run. For more information about answer file parameters and syntax, see the "Microsoft Windows 2000 Guide to Unattended Setup" (Unattend.doc) on the Microsoft Windows 2000 operating system CD. The Unattend.doc file is part of the Deploy.cab file in the \Support\Tools folder. In Windows 98 or Windows 2000, use Windows Explorer to extract this document. In Windows 95 and earlier, or in MS-DOS, use the **Extract** command to access the file.

Flexible networking   In Windows 2000, there are flexible network configurations available for each computer, including additional support for protocols, services, and clients. It is now possible to set the binding order, to easily set default information, and to install more than one network adapter in a system. In addition, to make installation and configuration easier, Windows 2000 can automatically install and configure network device drivers. By default, Windows 2000 installs the default networking components to each network adapter installed in a system, unless otherwise specified in the answer file. The default networking components include Client for Microsoft Networks, TCP/IP, File and Printer Sharing for Microsoft Networks, and enabling Dynamic Host Configuration Protocol (DHCP).

Automatic logon capability You can customize the answer file to allow the computer to automatically log on as the administrator either the first time that the computer starts Windows 2000 after Setup is completed or a specified number of times thereafter. If you need Windows 2000 to automatically log on for a specific number of times to accomplish tasks that are run in the [GuiRunOnce] entries, you need to provide a non-null administrator password (AdminPassword) in the answer file. You can then use AutoAdminLogonCount to specify the number of times that you need the system to automatically log on to complete the desired tasks. If a null password is used, Setup can automatically log on to the system only once without providing credentials through other means for each subsequent reboot. This is done to help reduce security risks. Note that providing administrator account credentials in a text file always introduces security risks if a user gains access to the file.

Automatic command execution The [GuiRunOnce] section of the answer file contains a list of commands that are to be executed consecutively as part of Setup when after GUI mode completes. By using the [GuiRunOnce] section, you can specify lists of applications to install, tools to configure the system, or other tools to run the first time a user logs on to the installed computer.

Simplified time-zone specification In the answer file, you can specify the computer time zone more easily and with less debugging than what was required by Windows NT. By enumerating the possible time zones, there is less opportunity for error because you are no longer required to enter the full time-zone string.

Enhanced regional and language settings In the answer file, you can specify the system and user locales, the keyboard and input method, and the language support to be installed. Setup Manager can help to make this even easier when you use the GUI interface of the wizard to select the settings to install on the system.

Simpler device preinstallation With the introduction of Plug and Play, the OemPnPDriversPath key, and the new distribution share point structure, preinstalling devices is now as easy as adding the new drivers into a folder in the distribution share and specifying the OemPnPDriversPath key.

Automated Installation Methods

You can run an automated installation of Windows 2000 Professional by using several methods. The method that you choose depends on the outcome of your critical planning, as discussed earlier in this chapter.

Methods for performing automated installations on client computers include the following:

- Using Syspart on computers that have dissimilar hardware
- Using Sysprep to duplicate disks
- Using Systems Management Server
- Using a bootable CD-ROM
- Using Remote Operating System Installation

> **Note** Remote Operating System Installation automatically installs Windows 2000 Professional and applications on client computers from a designated Remote Installation Service (RIS) server. RIS is an optional component that is included with Windows 2000 Server.

Table 25.5 describes when you can use each automated installation method.

Table 25.5   When to Use Automated Installation Methods

Method	Use
Syspart	Use for clean installations to computers that have dissimilar hardware.
Sysprep	Use when the master computer and the target computers have identical hardware, which includes the HAL and mass storage device controllers.
SMS	Use to perform managed upgrades of Windows 2000 Server to multiple systems, especially those that are geographically dispersed.
Bootable CD-ROM	Use with a computer whose basic input/output system (BIOS) allows it to start from the bootable CD-ROM.
Remote Operating System Installation	Use to remotely install an image of Windows 2000 Professional on supported computers, eliminating the need to physically visit each computer to perform an installation.

Using Syspart for Computers with Dissimilar Hardware

Syspart executes through an optional parameter of Winnt32.exe. If the master computer and the computers on which you are installing Windows 2000 Professional do not have similar hardware, you can use the Syspart method. This method also reduces deployment time by eliminating the file-copy phase of Setup.

Syspart requires that you use two physical disks and that there is a primary partition on the target hard disk.

If you require a similar installation and operating system configuration on hardware types in which the HALs or mass storage controllers differ, you can use Syspart to create a master set of files that have the necessary configuration information and driver support that can then be imaged. Those images can then be used on the dissimilar systems to properly detect the hardware and to consistently configure the base operating system. If your environment includes multiple types of hardware-dependent systems, you can use Syspart to create a master for each type. You install Windows 2000 on one computer of each type, and then you use Sysprep to help create images to be used on the remaining computers of each type. For more information about Sysprep, see "Using Sysprep to Duplicate Disks" later in this chapter.

Before you begin, choose a computer to use as a reference computer. The reference computer must have either Windows NT or Windows 2000 installed.

▶ **To install Windows 2000 Professional by using Syspart**

1. Start the reference computer, and connect to the installation distribution folder.

2. Run Setup.

   Click **Start**, click **Run**, and then type the following:

   ```
   winnt32 /unattend:unattend.txt /s:install_source
   /syspart:second_drive /tempdrive:second_drive/ noreboot
   ```

Important You must use the */tempdrive* parameter for a successful Syspart installation. When you use the */tempdrive* command line switch, make sure you have sufficient free disk space on your second partition to install both Windows 2000 Server and your applications. The geometry of the disk that you plan to use as a target for Syspart must be the same as the geometry of the disk on the computer to which you plan to duplicate.

Note that the */syspart* and */tempdrive* parameters must point to the same partition of a secondary hard disk. The Windows 2000 Professional installation must take place on the primary partition of the secondary hard disk.

Caution Syspart automatically marks the drive as active and as the default boot device. For this reason, remove the drive before turning on the computer again.

Related definitions include the following:

Unattend.txt. The answer file used for an unattended setup. It provides answers to some or all the prompts that the end user normally responds to during Setup. Using an answer file is optional when creating the master image.

install_source. The location of the Windows 2000 Professional files. Specify multiple **/s** switches if you want to install from multiple sources simultaneously.

second_drive. An optional second drive on which you preinstall Windows 2000 and your applications.

Using Sysprep to Duplicate Disks

Disk duplication is a good choice if you need to install an identical configuration on multiple computers. On a master computer, you install Windows 2000 and any applications that you want installed on all of the target computers. Then you run Sysprep to transfer the image to the other computers. Sysprep prepares the hard disk on the master computer for duplication to other computers and then runs a third-party disk-imaging process. This method decreases deployment time dramatically compared to standard or scripted installations.

To use Sysprep, your master and target computers must have identical HALs, Advanced Configuration and Power Interface (ACPI) support, and mass storage controller devices. Windows 2000 automatically detects Plug and Play devices, and Sysprep redetects and reenumerates the devices on the system when the computer is turned on after Sysprep has run. This means that Plug and Play devices, such as network adapters, modems, video adapters, and sound cards do not have to be the same on the master and target computers. The major advantage of Sysprep installation is speed. The image can be packaged and compressed; only the files required for the specific configuration are created as part of the image. Additional Plug and Play drivers that you might need on other systems are also created. The image can also be copied to a CD and distributed to remote sites that have slow links.

Note Because the master and target computers are required to have identical HALs, ACPI support, and mass storage devices, you might need to maintain multiple images for your environment.

Important When performing disk duplication, check with your software vendor to make certain that you are not violating the licensing agreement for installation of the software that you want to duplicate.

Overview of the Sysprep Process

This section describes the process of building a source computer to use for disk duplication.

1. Install Windows 2000.–Install Windows 2000 Professional on a computer that has hardware similar to the intended target computers. While building the computer, you must not join it to a domain, and you must keep the local administrative password blank.

2. Configure the computer – Log on as the administrator, and then install and customize Windows 2000 Professional and associated applications. This might include your productivity application such as Microsoft® Office 2000, business-specific applications, and any other applications or settings that you want included in a common configuration for all clients.

3. Validate the image – Run an audit, based on your criteria, to verify that the image configuration is correct. Remove residual information, including anything left behind from audit and event logs.

4. Prepare the image for duplication – After you are confident that the computer is configured exactly the way that you want, you are ready to prepare the system for duplication. You accomplish this by running Sysprep with the optional Sysprep.inf file, which is described later in this chapter. When Sysprep has completed, the computer will shut down automatically or will indicate that it is safe to shut down.

5. Duplicate – At this point, the computer hard disk is triggered to run Plug and Play detection, create new security identifiers (SIDs), and run Mini-Setup Wizard the next time that the system is started. You are now ready to duplicate or image the system by using a hardware or software solution. The next time that Windows 2000 is started from this hard disk, or is started from any duplicated hard disk created from this image, the system will detect and re-enumerate the Plug and Play devices to complete the installation and configuration on the target computer.

Important Components that depend on Active Directory cannot be duplicated.

Sysprep Files

To use Sysprep, run Sysprep.exe manually or configure Setup to run Sysprep.exe automatically by using the [GuiRunOnce] section of the answer file. To run Sysprep, the files Sysprep.exe and Setupcl.exe must be located in a Sysprep folder at the root of the system drive (%systemdrive%\Sysprep\). To place the files in the correct location during an automated Setup, you must add these files to your distribution folders under the OEM\$1\Sysprep subfolder. For more information about this subfolder, see "Structuring the Distribution Folder" earlier in this chapter.

These files prepare the operating system for duplication and start the Mini-Setup Wizard. You can also include an optional answer file, Sysprep.inf, in the Sysprep folder. Sysprep.inf contains default parameters that you can use to provide consistent responses where they are appropriate. This limits the requirement for user input, thereby reducing potential user errors. You can also place the Sysprep.inf file on a floppy disk to be placed in the floppy disk drive after the Windows startup screen appears in order to allow further customization at the target computer's location. The floppy disk drive is read when the "Please Wait…" Mini-Setup Wizard screen appears. When the Mini-Setup Wizard has successfully completed its tasks, the system restarts one last time, the Sysprep folder and all of its contents are deleted, and the system is ready for the user to log on.

The Sysprep files are defined in the sections that follow.

Sysprep.exe

Sysprep.exe has the following three optional parameters:

- *quiet* — runs Sysprep without displaying onscreen messages.

- *nosidgen* — runs Sysprep without regenerating SIDs that are already on the system. This is useful if you do not intend to duplicate the computer on which you are running Sysprep.

- *reboot* — automatically restarts the computer after Sysprep shuts it down. This eliminates the need for you to manually turn on the computer again.

Sysprep.inf

Sysprep.inf is an answer file that is used to automate the Mini-Setup process. It uses the same .ini file syntax and key names (for supported keys) as the Setup answer file. You need to place the Sysprep.inf file in the %systemdrive%\Sysprep folder or on a floppy disk. If you use a floppy disk, you can provide the floppy after the Windows startup screen appears. Note that if you do not include Sysprep.inf when running Sysprep, the Mini-Setup Wizard displays all the available dialog boxes listed under "Mini-Setup Wizard" later in this chapter.

Note If you provided a Sysprep.inf file on the master computer and you want to change Sysprep.inf on a per-computer basis, you can use the floppy disk method previously discussed.

The following is an example of a Sysprep.inf file:

```
[Unattended]
;Prompt the user to accept the EULA.
OemSkipEula=No
;Use Sysprep's default and regenerate the page file for the system
;to accommodate potential differences in available RAM.
KeepPageFile=0
;Provide the location for additional language support files that
;may be needed in a global organization.
InstallFilesPath=%systemdrive%\Sysprep\i386

[GuiUnattended]
;Specify a non-null administrator password.
;Any password supplied here will only take effect if the original source
;for the image (master computer) specified a non-null password.
;Otherwise, the password used on the master computer will be
;the password used on this computer. This can only be changed by
;logging on as Local Administrator and manually changing the password.
AdminPassword=""
;Set the time zone
TimeZone=20
;Skip the Welcome screen when the system boots
OemSkipWelcome=1
;Do not skip the regional options dialog so that the user can indicate
;which regional options apply to them.
OemSkipRegional=0

[UserData]
;Prepopulate user information for the system
FullName="Authorized User"
OrgName="Organization Name"
ComputerName=XYZ_Computer1

[Identification]
;Join the computer to the domain ITDOMAIN
JoinDomain=ITDOMAIN

[Networking]
;Bind the default protocols and services to the (s) network card used
;in this computer.
InstallDefaultComponents=Yes
```

Note You can change the administrative password using Sysprep.inf only if the existing administrative password is null. This is also true if you want to change the administrator password through the Sysprep GUI.

For more information about answer file parameters and syntax, see the "Microsoft Windows 2000 Guide to Unattended Setup" (Unattend.doc) on the Microsoft Windows 2000 operating system CD. The Unattend.doc file is part of the Deploy.cab file in the \Support\Tools folder. In Windows 98 or Windows 2000, use Windows Explorer to extract this document. In Windows 95 and earlier, or in MS-DOS, use the **Extract** command to access the file.

Setupcl.exe

Setupcl.exe does the following:

- Regenerates new SIDs for the computer.
- Starts the Mini-Setup Wizard.

Mini-Setup Wizard

The Mini-Setup Wizard starts the first time that a computer starts from a disk that has been duplicated by the Sysprep method. The wizard gathers any information that is needed to further customize the target computer. If you do not use Sysprep.inf, or if you leave some sections of the file blank, the Mini-Setup Wizard displays screens for which no answer was provided in Sysprep.inf. The possible screens include the following:

- End-User License Agreement (EULA)
- Regional options
- User name and company
- Computer name and administrator password
- Network settings
- TAPI settings (displayed only if a modem or a new modem device exists on the computer)
- Server licensing (server only)
- Time zone selection
- Finish/Restart

If you want to bypass these screens, you can specify certain parameters within Sysprep.inf. These parameters are listed in Table 25.6.

Note Because Setup detects optimal settings for display devices, you will no longer see the "Display Settings" screen when Setup or Mini-Setup Wizard are running. You can specify the settings in the [Display] section either in the answer file that is used for your master computer or in the Sysprep.inf file used for your target computer. If settings in the [Display] section are in the answer file that is used for your master computer, Sysprep will retain those settings unless Sysprep.inf contains different settings or unless a video adapter or monitor requiring settings different from those of the master computer is detected.

Table 25.6   Parameters in Sysprep.inf for Bypassing the Mini-Setup Wizard

Parameter	Value
Regional options	[RegionalSettings] section
	[GuiUnattended]
	OemSkipRegional=1
User name and company	[UserData]
	FullName="User Name"
	OrgName="Organization Name"
Computer name and administrator password	[UserData]
	ComputerName=W2B32054
	[GuiUnattended]
	AdminPassword=""
TAPI settings	[TapiLocation]
	AreaCode=425
Network settings	[Networking]
	InstallDefaultComponents=Yes
Server licensing (server only)	[LicenseFilePrintData]
	AutoMode = PerServer
	AutoUsers = 5
Time zone selection	[GuiUnattended]
	TimeZone=<desired time zone index>
Finish/Restart	N/A

Running Sysprep Manually

After you install Windows 2000 Professional, you can use Sysprep to prepare the system for transfer to other similarly configured computers. To run Sysprep manually, you must first install Windows 2000 Professional, configure the system, and install the applications. Then run Sysprep without the *–reboot* command-line switch. After the system shuts down, duplicate the image of the drive to the similarly configured computers.

When users start up their duplicated computers for the first time, Sysprep Mini-Setup will run, allowing the users to customize their systems. You can also preassign all or some of the Sysprep configuration parameters by using Sysprep.inf. The Sysprep folder (which contains Sysprep.exe and Setupcl.exe) is automatically deleted after Sysprep Mini-Setup is completed.

▶ **To prepare a Windows 2000 Professional installation for duplication**

1. On the **Start** menu, click **Run**, and then type:

   cmd

2. At the command prompt, change to the root folder of drive C, and then type :

   md sysprep

3. Insert the Windows 2000 Professional CD into the appropriate drive. Open the Deploy.cab file in the \Support\Tools folder.

4. Copy Sysprep.exe and Setupcl.exe to the Sysprep folder.

   If you are using Sysprep.inf, also copy this file to the Sysprep folder. Note that Sysprep.exe, Setupcl.exe, and Sysprep.inf must exist in the same folder for Sysprep to function properly.

5. At the command prompt, change to the Sysprep folder by typing:

   cd sysprep

6. Type one of the following, as required:

   ```
   Sysprep
   Sysprep -reboot
   Sysprep /<optional parameter>
   Sysprep /<optional parameter> -reboot
   Sysprep /<optional parameter 1>.../<optional parameter X>
   Sysprep /<optional parameter 1>.../<optional parameter X> -reboot
   ```

7. If the *–reboot* command-line switch was not specified, perform the following:

   When a message requesting that you shut down the computer appears, on the **Start** menu, click **Shut Down**. You are now ready to use a third-party disk-imaging tool to create an image of the installation.

8. If the *–reboot* command-line switch was specified for auditing purposes only, the computer restarts and the Mini-Setup Wizard runs. Perform the following:

   ▪ Verify that the Mini-Setup Wizard provides the desired prompts. At this time, you can also audit the system and other applications. After the auditing is completed, run Sysprep again without the *–reboot* command line switch.

   ▪ When a message requesting that you shut down the computer appears, on the **Start** menu, click **Shut Down**. You are now ready to use a third-party disk-imaging tool to create an image of the installation.

Note You can add a Cmdlines.txt file to the Sysprep folder, to be processed by Setup. This file is used to run post-Setup commands, including commands for application installation.

Running Sysprep Automatically After Setup Completes

The [GuiRunOnce] section of the answer file contains commands to be executed after Setup completes. You can use the [GuiRunOnce] section to create an installation that completes Setup, automatically logs on to the computer, runs Sysprep in *–quiet* mode, and then shuts down the computer. For this to occur, you need to do the following:

1. To copy the files to the correct location on the system drive, include the required Sysprep files in the distribution folders under OEM\$1\Sysprep\.

2. In the [GuiRunOnce] section of the answer file, make the following the last command that is run on the computer:

   ```
   %systemdrive%\Sysprep\Sysprep.exe –quiet
   ```

   If multiple reboots are required, make this the last command used the last time the [GuiRunOnce] section is used.

Using Sysprep to Extend Disk Partitions

Windows 2000 GUI Setup and Mini-Setup can be used to extend NTFS partition through the answer files. This new functionality does the following:

▪ Allows you to create images that can be extended into larger disk partitions to take full advantage of hard disks that might have more space than the original hard disk on the master computer.

▪ Provides a way to create images on smaller hard disks.

To determine the best way to integrate this functionality in your environment, you need to review the steps that follow and choose the method that will work best for you based on the tools that you are using to image the operating system.

Caution If you can use your imaging tools to modify the image, you can delete the files Pagefile.sys, Setupapi.log, and Hyberfil.sys (if applicable) because these files will be recreated when the Mini-Setup Wizard runs on the target computer. You must not delete these files on an active system because this can cause the system to function improperly. These files should only be deleted, if desired, only from the image.

▶ **To extend a hard disk partition when using a third-party imaging product or a hardware imaging device that supports NTFS used by Windows 2000**

1. Configure the partition on the master computer hard disk to the minimum size required to install Windows 2000 with all the components and applications that you intend to preinstall. This will reduce your overall image size requirements.

2. Include the FileSystem=ConvertNTFS in the [Unattended] section of the answer file that is used to create the master image. You do not need to include ExtendOemPartition here because you want to maintain the smallest possible image size.

Note ConvertNTFS does not work in Sysprep.inf because this is a Text Mode–only function and Sysprep does not go through Text Mode.

---

3. In the [Unattended] section of Sysprep.inf, include the statement:

   ```
   ExtendOemPartition = 1
   ```

   (or additional size in megabytes to extend the partition)

4. Install Windows 2000 to the master computer. Sysprep will shut down the system automatically.

5. Image the drive.

6. Place the image on the target computer where the target computer has the same size system partition as the master computer.

7. Restart the target computer.

   The Mini-Setup Wizard starts and the partition is extended almost instantaneously.

▶ **To extend a hard disk partition when using an imaging product that does not support NTFS used by Windows 2000**

1. Configure the partition on the master computer hard disk to the minimum size required to install Windows 2000 with all the components and applications that you intend to preinstall. This will reduce your overall image size requirements.

2. Convert the file system to NTFS by using the Convert.exe tool provided in Windows 2000.

3. Include the following items as the last two items of the [GuiRunOnce] section of the answer file that is used to create the master image:

```
[GuiRunOnce]
Command1 = "command line"
Command2 = "command line"
...
Commandn-1 = "Convert c:\ /fs:ntfs"
Commandn = "%systemdrive%\sysprep\sysprep.exe - quiet"
```

where:

- <command line> includes any commands that you need to run to install applications or configure the operating system before you image it.

- <Commandn-1> is the next-to-last command to be executed in the [GuiRunOnce] section of the answer file. This will run the "Convert" command. Because Convert cannot convert the active system to NTFS while the operating system is running, the operating system is set to do so the next time the computer restarts. Because Sysprep is the next item to run, the system will not be converted to NTFS during that process.

- <Commandn> is the last command to run on the computer. This command is Sysprep.exe. When Sysprep is run, it prepares the computer for imaging and then shuts down the computer.

Note You cannot include ExtendOemPartition in the master answer file for this step because the partition on which the image is generated is not NTFS. You also might want to keep the image as small as possible.

4. In the [Unattended] section of Sysprep.inf, include the statement:

```
ExtendOemPartition = 1
```

(or additional size in megabytes to extend the partition)

5. Install Windows 2000 to the master computer. Sysprep will shut down the system automatically.

Important Do not restart the computer.

6. Image the drive.

7. Place the image on the target computer where the target computer has the same size system partition as the master computer.

8. Restart the target computer.

   The computer will initially start in conversion mode to convert the system partition on the target computer to NTFS.

   The computer will automatically restart.

   The Mini-Setup Wizard starts, and the partition is extended almost instantaneously.

Using Systems Management Server

You can use SMS to perform managed upgrades of Windows 2000 Professional to multiple systems, especially those that are geographically dispersed. Note that SMS is used only for installations to computers that contain a previously installed operating system. Before you upgrade using SMS, it is important to have assessed your existing network infrastructure, including bandwidth, hardware, and geographical constraints. The primary advantage of upgrading using SMS is that you can maintain centralized control of the upgrade process. For example, you can control when upgrades take place (for example, during or after training, after hardware verification, and after user data is backed up), which computers will be upgraded, and how you apply network constraints. For more information about SMS deployment, see "Using Systems Management Server to Deploy Windows 2000" in this book.

Using a Bootable Compact Disk

You use the bootable CD method to install Windows 2000 Professional on a computer whose basic input/output system (BIOS) allows it to start from a CD. This method is quite useful for computers at remote sites with slow links and no local IT department. The bootable CD method runs Winnt32.exe, which allows for a fast installation.

Note You can use only the bootable CD method for clean installations. To perform upgrades, you must run Winnt32.exe from within the existing operating system.

To ensure maximum flexibility, set the boot order in BIOS as follows:

- Network adapter
- CD
- Hard disk

- Floppy disk

To use a bootable CD, the following criteria must be met:

- Your computer must have El Torito No Emulation support for bootable CDs.
- The answer file must contain a [Data] section that has the required keys.
- The answer file must be named Winnt.sif and be located on a floppy disk.

For more information about answer file parameters and syntax, see the "Microsoft Windows 2000 Guide to Unattended Setup" (Unattend.doc) on the Microsoft Windows 2000 operating system CD. The Unattend.doc file is part of the Deploy.cab file in the \Support\Tools folder. In Windows 98 or Windows 2000, use Windows Explorer to extract this document. In Windows 95 and earlier, or in MS-DOS, use the **Extract** command to access the file.

▶ **To install Windows 2000 using a bootable CD**

1. Start the system from the Windows 2000 CD.
2. When the blue text-mode screen with "Windows 2000 Setup" is displayed, place the floppy disk containing the Winnt.sif file into the floppy disk drive.
3. After the computer reads from the floppy disk drive, remove the floppy disk. Setup will now run from the CD as specified by the Winnt.sif file.

Note The bootable CD-ROM method requires that all necessary files be on the CD-ROM. Uniqueness Database Files (UDFs) cannot be used with this method.

Using Remote Operating System Installation

Remote Operating System Installation is an optional component included with Windows 2000 Server and is based on Remote Installation Services (RIS) technology. Because RIS uses Pre-Boot eXecution Environment (PXE)-based remote-boot technology and server-based software, you can remotely install an image of Windows 2000 Professional on supported computers, eliminating the need to physically visit each computer to perform an installation. You must ensure that the hardware for each computer is compatible and that a bootable network adapter is installed. You can set up a different RIS image for each configuration specific to a group of computers. During Setup, a list of installation choices are provided that can be limited according to the policies set for that particular user or group. There might be as many RIS images to maintain as there are different sets of group policies. In this case, it would be beneficial if only the installation choices common to all configurations were installed by this method.

For more information about Remote Operating System Installation, see "Applying Change and Configuration Management" in this book, and see "Remote OS Installation" in the *Microsoft® Windows® 2000 Server Resource Kit Distributed Systems Guide*.

RIS Server Network Load Implications

Because a RIS server is used to install operating system images on client computers, the amount of traffic the server produces is similar to that of other servers performing as software installation points on your network. Generally, the traffic from RIS servers is more predictable than traffic from a general-purpose software installation point that provides applications and regular updates. RIS-generated traffic is higher when many users are loading images—for example, during a new deployment of operating system images or when a group of new computers is added to the network. After systems are installed, daily traffic is going to be lower.

As a general rule, place a RIS server near the client computers that it services. This will localize the resulting network traffic and reduce its impact.

If your environment requires either of the following processes, make sure that these processes can be optimized without affecting other applications:

- Frequent reinstallation of systems, as in a classroom.
- Regular installation of a large number of systems, as in preinstallation of all new systems before delivering them to users.

For the classroom example, consider segmenting the physical network and providing a dedicated RIS server for each classroom or set of classrooms that your RIS server hardware can support.

For the preinstallation example, consider implementing preinstallation labs where computers can be processed in volume by using high-speed networking and RIS server hardware to reduce installation time.

Optimizing Performance

Because Remote Operating System Installation is primarily a file-copy process, the common RIS server performance factors are similar to those of other file input/output (I/O) intensive servers such as Web servers and file and print servers. These factors include server disk throughput and network bandwidth. When optimizing performance of your RIS servers, evaluate these factors and other constraints that might exist on the network between RIS servers and the clients that are being serviced. When a RIS server or its network connection is overloaded, the result is increased installation time for client computers and TFTP time-outs during the initial file-copy phase.

DHCP and DHCP Servers

Because Remote Operating System Installation (PXE-enabled) clients use the DHCP discovery mechanism to obtain a network address and to locate RIS servers, the relationship of RIS to DHCP in your organization plays a key role in determining your RIS server placement strategy.

In simple environments, adding RIS to each DHCP server in use is a common solution. When a combination Windows 2000 DHCP/RIS server approach is used, the number of initial network packets sent between the RIS client and the DHCP and RIS servers is reduced, and the initial server response is faster. In addition, a combination Windows 2000 DHCP/RIS server always answers a client together. This provides a simple form of load balancing by taking advantage of any existing planning that groups client computers to DHCP servers, and it also simplifies troubleshooting and administrative procedures.

Although RIS servers must be located close to client computers and can generate large network loads, often requiring these servers to have high-end hardware, DHCP servers are just the opposite. DHCP servers generate far less traffic, do not typically require high-end server hardware, and are sometimes centralized rather than close to client computers. Therefore, you might find that simply adding RIS to your existing DHCP servers is impractical. In such cases, you might want to add RIS services to existing software installation point servers because they have similar planning and placement requirements as RIS servers, or you might want to make your RIS servers independent of other supporting servers.

When RIS servers are separate from DHCP servers, or when non-Windows 2000 DHCP servers are in use, controlling which RIS servers answer specific clients becomes a primary consideration. This is because the PXE-based remote boot process does not provide a way to determine from which server a client is going to receive service. For information about methods for controlling this process, see "Controlling RIS Server Selection and Balancing Load" later in this chapter.

Regardless of the approach that you take to combine DHCP and RIS servers, every RIS server must be authorized in Active Directory as a method of preventing unauthorized servers from servicing clients on the network. The authorization process for both RIS and Windows 2000 DHCP servers takes place through the Windows 2000 DHCP snap-in in Microsoft Management Console (MMC). The process has no direct relation either to combining or separating RIS and DHCP servers or with using Windows 2000 DHCP. The Windows 2000 DHCP snap-in is simply reused as an authenticating mechanism and can be run without installing the DHCP service on any Windows 2000–based computer that has the Administrator Tools pack installed.

Caution Do not attempt to install Windows 2000 DHCP on a RIS server simply to obtain the snap-in. To service RIS clients, any combined Windows 2000 DHCP and RIS server must have a fully functional DHCP service (including defined and active scopes). This is because the Windows 2000 DHCP service on a combined server is aware that RIS is also installed. If a client indicates that it requires both DHCP and remote boot services in its DHCP discovery broadcast, DHCP will issue a single reply containing the specific details on DHCP and remote boot for that server. If the Windows 2000 DHCP service on the server is not properly answering clients, that server will not generate a remote boot reply.

Controlling RIS Server Selection and Balancing Load

By default, when a PXE-based client broadcasts its request for service, all servers that receive the request will reply. The first server to respond is the one that provides service; preference is given to responses from combined DHCP/RIS servers over responses from separate servers. Although this provides fundamental load balancing when multiple servers are available to clients in order to prevent clients from using improper servers, it is often best to restrict which servers can answer specific clients. An example is a server that is local to the client and is busy or down when the client requests service.

The first way to control server selection is to physically control network routing so that DHCP discovery broadcasts are forwarded only when it is appropriate. This physically allows answers by only those DHCP/RIS servers that are permitted to receive the client service requests. If your DHCP/RIS servers are in similar locations on the network in relation to clients, this might be all that is necessary.

To accommodate a variety of scenarios, Remote Operating System Installation provides additional features for controlling server selection. These features involve configuring client computer accounts within Active Directory to use a specific RIS server, which is a process known as "prestaging." Prestaging can be performed on existing computer accounts, as well as when creating new computer accounts before the system joins the domain. When a RIS server answers a service request from a client, the server checks Active Directory (the entire forest) for the existence of a computer account with a globally unique identifier (GUID) that matches the GUID that is included in the service request. If a matching computer account is found, the account is also checked to see whether it has been configured to use a specific RIS server. If so, the RIS server specified in the computer account is always supplied in the reply to the client, even if it is a different server from the one providing the initial reply to the client. This is known as a *server referral* and provides a simple way to control which RIS servers end up providing operating system installation services to specific client computers, regardless of which particular RIS server replied to the initial request for service from the client.

To allow additional flexibility and security, the prestaging and referral concepts can also be combined with RIS server settings that control how servers respond to clients. Each RIS server has two settings: "Respond to client computers requesting service" and "Do not respond to unknown client computers." By prestaging all computer accounts and selectively controlling which RIS servers are configured to respond to clients, servers can become dedicated to either replying to client service requests and providing the appropriate referrals, or to providing the actual Remote OS Installation services to clients.

Figure 25.3 illustrates an example of how client computers can relate to RIS servers.

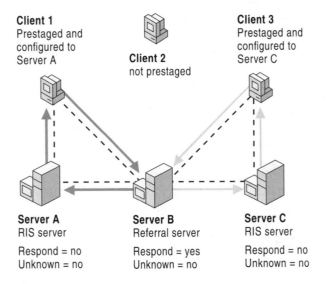

Server Configuration Key:

Respond- Respond to Client Computers
Unknown- Do Not Respond to Unknown Client Computers

Figure 25.3   Example of How Client Computers Relate to RIS Servers

In Figure 25.3, only server B will reply to client computers that request service. Because client computers 1 and 3 have been prestaged and configured to obtain service from a specific RIS server, they will receive a reply that refers them to the appropriate server (A or C). If it is appropriate, multiple dedicated referral servers such as server B can be established, all of which will use the prestaged computer accounts in Active Directory to determine the proper referral to make. Servers A and C will never reply to initial client service requests; but through referrals, the servers provide the actual operating system installation services to clients.

You can then determine whether the "Do not respond to unknown client computers" configuration option needs to be selected on referral servers such as server B. Selecting this option ensures that:

- Server B sends replies only to client computers that have been prestaged.

- If any clients are configured to receive service specifically from it, server B will effectively become a dedicated referral server or will also provide the actual operating system installation services.

If the "Do not respond to unknown client computers" option is not selected, server B will reply to service requests from nonprestaged clients (client computer 2 in the example), offering itself as the remote boot server.

Whether or not referral servers are used, selecting "Do not respond to unknown client computers" provides a measure of security by preventing client computers that have not been prestaged from performing operating system installation from RIS servers. In addition, not all vendors offering solutions based on the same remote-boot protocol as Remote Operating System Installation provide options for controlling which client service requests are replied to. By using prestaging and restricting all RIS servers to respond to known client computers, you allow Remote Operating System Installation to be implemented without disruption on a network containing other remote-boot products.

Working with Routers

Because client service requests are based on the DHCP discovery process, configuring your network to support Remote Operating System Installation across routers has the same requirements as doing so to support DHCP across routers.

Routers that are configured to forward DHCP broadcasts will also automatically forward client service requests; however, you must ensure that the requests are forwarded to the proper RIS servers in addition to any DHCP servers. Depending on the router models in use, the specific router configuration of DHCP broadcast forwarding might be supported to either a subnet (or router interface) or to a specific host. If you use Windows 2000 DHCP but have your RIS servers on separate computers, or if you use non-Windows 2000 DHCP, you must ensure that the routers forward the DHCP broadcasts to both the DHCP and RIS servers. Otherwise the client will not receive a reply to the remote boot request.

Because of the amount of network traffic involved in installing an operating system, carefully consider where to place your RIS servers and how to use prestaging and referral servers to accommodate your existing network design so that the impact of client installations is minimized.

Installation Configuration Examples

The examples included here provide procedures for installation of Windows 2000 Professional to computers either with preexisting client configurations or without any existing configuration.

Existing Client Computers

The examples in this section are for computers that have the following preexisting client configurations.

Example 1: Windows NT Workstation 4.0 with Windows 2000 Compatible Client Applications

Perform an upgrade. Client operating systems that can be upgraded include Windows 95, Windows 98, Windows NT Workstation 4.0, and Windows NT Workstation 3.51.

For information about applications that are compatible with Windows 2000 Professional, see the Directory of Windows 2000 Applications link on the Web Resources page at http://windows.microsoft.com/windows2000/reskit/webresources.

▶ **To install Windows 2000 Professional on computers that have compatible hardware**

1. Back up user settings.

2. Upgrade the system by using one of the following methods:

   - Initiate a "push" (completely automated) installation by doing the following:

     - Using systems management software such as Microsoft® Systems Management Server.

       –Or–

     - Performing a network installation.

       –Or–

     - Performing a remote boot. This requires that Remote Installation Server be configured and a bootable network adapter installed.

   - Initiate local installation by running Winnt32.exe with the desired parameters from the command line and:

     - Perform a manual installation (with no answer file). Answer all prompts.

       –Or–

     - Perform an automated or semiautomated installation with an answer file. In a completely automated installation, the answer file provides answers for all questions. You can use a semiautomated installation to permit some user input for applications that you choose.

▶ **To install Windows 2000 Professional on a computer that has noncompatible hardware and whose hard disk does not need to be replaced**

1. Replace any necessary hardware except the hard disk.

2. Verify that all new hardware functions properly.

3. Back up user settings.

4. Upgrade the system using one of the following methods:

- Initiate a "push" (completely automated) installation by doing the following:

  - Using systems management software such as Systems Management Server.

    –Or–

  - Performing a network installation.

    –Or–

  - Performing a remote boot. This requires that Remote Installation Server be configured and a bootable network adapter installed.

- Initiate a local installation by running Winnt32.exe with the desired parameters from the command line and:

  - Perform a manual installation (with no answer file). Answer all prompts.

    –Or–

  - Perform an automated or semiautomated installation.

▶ **To install Windows 2000 Professional on a computer that has noncompatible hardware and whose hard disk must be replaced**

1. Upgrade at least one of the following:

   - RAM
   - Processor

2. Verify that all new hardware functions properly.

3. Back up user settings.

Note Although it is possible to back up the entire contents of the hard disk to a new hard disk before upgrading the computer, this is not generally feasible for client computers.

---

4. Replace the hard disk. Copy the image that was backed up.

5. Run Winnt.exe from the command prompt with the desired parameters by using one of the following methods:

   - Perform a manual installation (no answer file), and answer all prompts.

     –Or–

- Perform an automated or semiautomated installation. Use one of the following methods:
  - CD-ROM Boot Setup.
  - Syspart. This is useful when installing new hard disks in the computers.
  - Sysprep. Use when installing to identical computers (HALs and mass storage device controllers must be identical).
  - Remote boot. This requires Remote Installation Server to be configured and a bootable network adapter to be installed.

6. Install applications compatible with Windows 2000 Professional.

7. Verify system functions as required.

8. Import user settings (for example, Regedit/Regedt32, logon scripts, policies, roaming profiles).

Example 2: Windows NT Workstation 3.5 or Earlier, and Non-Microsoft Client Computers

Client operating systems that cannot be upgraded include MS-DOS, Windows 3.*x*, Windows NT Workstation 3.5 or earlier, and OS/2.

To prepare for a clean installation, obtain a client computer built by an OEM/Solution Provider. To perform a clean installation on a new computer or install the operating system on an existing computer, perform the following procedure.

Note   For information about applications that are compatible with Windows 2000 Professional, see the Directory of Windows 2000 Applications link on the Web Resources page at http://windows.microsoft.com/windows2000/reskit/webresources.

▶ **To install Windows 2000 Professional on a client operating system that cannot be upgraded**

1. Back up user settings.

   Caution   If you install Windows 2000 Professional on an existing computer running an operating system that cannot be upgraded to Windows 2000, all user settings will be lost.

   ---

2. Run Winnt.exe from the command prompt with the desired parameters by using one of the following methods:
   - Perform a manual installation (no answer file), and answer all prompts.

     –Or–

- Perform an automated or semiautomated installation. Use one of the following methods:
  - CD-ROM Boot Setup.
  - Syspart. This is useful when installing new hard disks in the computers.
  - Sysprep. Use when installing to identical computers (HALs and mass storage device controllers must be identical).
  - Remote boot. This requires Remote Installation Server to be configured and a bootable network adapter to be installed.

3. Install applications that are compatible with Windows 2000 Professional.

4. Verify system functions as required.

5. Import user settings (for example, Regedit/Regedt32, logon scripts, policies, roaming profiles).

New Client Computers

Client computers without any pre-Windows 2000 Professional operating system installed require a clean installation of Windows 2000 Professional.

To prepare for installation, obtain a client computer built by an OEM/Solution Provider.

▶ **To install Windows 2000 Professional on a computer that does not have any pre-Windows 2000 operating system installed**

- Perform a manual installation (no answer file), and answer all prompts.

  –Or–

- Perform an automated or semiautomated installation. Use one of the following methods:
  - CD-ROM Boot Setup.
  - Syspart. This is useful when installing new hard disks in the computers.
  - Sysprep. Use when installing to identical computers (HALs and mass storage device controllers must be identical).
  - Start disk and run Setup with an answer file.
  - Remote boot. This requires RIS to be configured and a bootable network adapter to be installed.

Installation Task List

Table 25.7 is a summary of the tasks involved in performing the installation of Windows 2000 Professional and required applications on client computers.

Table 25.7   Summary of Installation Tasks

Task	Location in Chapter
Resolve critical planning issues.	Resolving Critical Planning Issues
Create the distribution folder.	Preparing for Installation
Review the answer file.	Reviewing the Answer File
Review the Windows 2000 Setup commands.	Preparing for Installation
Choose an application installation method based on critical planning.	Automating the Installation of Client Applications
Choose a method for operating system installation based on critical planning.	Automating the Installation of Windows 2000 Professional

P A R T   7

Appendixes

Accessing extra tools and support information for Microsoft® Windows® 2000 can help you achieve a successful deployment. The appendixes provide additional tools, such as planning worksheets, setup commands, and information for people with disabilities, that will enhance your deployment efforts.

In This Part

APPENDIX A

Sample Planning Worksheets

When deploying Microsoft® Windows® 2000, you might have several deployment projects to plan and coordinate. This appendix provides planning worksheets that you can use to deploy Windows 2000 in the most cost-effective and efficient way for your organization.

Using the deployment planning worksheets will help you become familiar with the unique IT requirements of your organization and also with the Windows 2000 features that can help you meet those requirements. You should read the chapter or chapters associated with the worksheets before you fill them out. The chapters introduce new concepts and provide essential information that will enable you to make best use of the planning worksheets.

In This Appendix

Using This Appendix

The worksheets in this appendix are organized by their corresponding chapter title; however, not all chapters have a worksheet and some chapters have multiple worksheets. Table A.1 lists the chapters that have worksheets and shows the order that the worksheets appear in this appendix.

Table A.1   Worksheets in This Appendix

Chapter and Worksheet Name	Chapter Number
Introducing Windows 2000 Deployment Planning	Chapter 1
Management Infrastructure Services	
Desktop Management Solutions	
Security Features	
Information Publishing and Sharing	
Component Application Services	
Scalability and Availability	
Networking and Communications	
Storage Management	
Building a Windows 2000 Test Lab	Chapter 4
Document the Scope and Objectives of Each Test	
Track Your Test Results	
Preparing Your Network Infrastructure for Windows 2000	Chapter 6
Determining Domain Migration Strategies	Chapter 10
Document Your Migration Goals	
Record When You Complete Domain Migration Tasks	
Planning Distributed Security	Chapter 11
Identify Potential Security Risks	
Automating Server Installation and Upgrade	Chapter 13
Decide When and Where to Use Automated Installation Methods	
Record When You Complete Installation Tasks	
Upgrading and Installing Member Servers	Chapter 15
Member Server Planning Worksheet	
Server Data Backup and Disaster Recovery Plan	
Decide New Hardware Requirements	
Record Server Specifications	
Schedule Your Upgrade or Clean Installation	

(continued)

Table A.1   **Worksheets in This Appendix**   *(continued)*

Chapter and Worksheet Name	Chapter Number
Ensuring the Availability of Applications and Services	Chapter 18
Identify Your High-Availability Needs	
Plan Your Network Load Balancing	
Synchronizing Active Directory with Exchange Server Directory Service	Chapter 20
Create Your Connection Agreements	
Identify Directory Objects to Map	
List the Attributes You Will Not Map	
Create Your Directory Synchronization Schedule	
Record Your Contacts for Directory Synchronization	
Testing Applications for Compatibility with Windows 2000	Chapter 21
Prioritize Your Applications	
Plan and Track Your Testing Strategy	
Defining Client Administration and Configuration Standards	Chapter 23
Identify Your Users' Computing Requirements	
Define Client Support Issues	
Assign Client Management and Support Tasks	
Define Your Group Policy Requirements	
Applying Change and Configuration Management	Chapter 24
Record Your Applications and Their Management Options	
Define a Configuration Management Strategy for Your Users	
Automating Client Installation and Upgrade	Chapter 25
Record Your Automated Installation Methods	
Record Client Installation Tasks	

Important   These worksheets can also be found in the DPGDocs.doc file on the compact disc (CD) that accompanies the *Microsoft® Windows® 2000 Server Resource Kit*. The CD contains a version of these worksheets that you can customize and print for use in your organization.

Introducing Windows 2000 Deployment Planning

The chapter "Introducing Windows 2000 Deployment Planning," contains a high-level introduction to the features and benefits of the Windows 2000 operating system. The following worksheets list key features of Microsoft® Windows® 2000 Server and Microsoft® Windows® 2000 Professional. As you read the chapters in this book, use these worksheets to help you identify the key features of Windows 2000 and how they meet the business needs of your organization. When you review the features, consider both the short-term and long-term goals of your organization.

The tables are formatted so that you can enter your own comments about the potential role of these features within your organization. Use these worksheets to prepare a customized executive summary of the Windows 2000 features that your organization requires.

Note The following tables highlight the primary benefits of Windows 2000 Server and Windows 2000 Professional and are not intended to be a complete description of all features. For more information about a particular feature, see the product Help files or the appropriate volume and chapter in the *Microsoft® Windows® 2000 Server Resource Kit*.

Management Infrastructure Services

The management infrastructure services in Windows 2000 Server provide IT departments with tools that enable you to provide the highest levels of service available and reduce ownership costs. Table A.2 describes the Windows 2000 Server management infrastructure services and their benefits.

Table A.2   Management Infrastructure Services

Feature	Role of this feature within my organization
Directory services Microsoft® Active Directory™ stores information about all objects on the network, making this information easy to find. It provides a flexible directory hierarchy, granular security delegation, efficient delegation of permissions, integrated DNS, high-level programming interfaces, and an extensible object store.	
Administration services Microsoft® Management Console (MMC) provides system administrators with a common console for monitoring network functions and using administrative tools. MMC is completely customizable for the tasks performed by individual members of the IT support and management staff.	
Group Policy Group Policy allows an administrator to define and control the state of computers and users. Group Policy can be set at any level of the directory service, including sites, domains, and organizational units. Group Policy can also be filtered based on Security Group memberships.	
Instrumentation services With Windows Management Instrumentation (WMI), administrators can correlate data and events from multiple sources on a local or organization-wide basis.	
Scripting services Windows Script Host (WSH) supports direct execution of Microsoft® Visual Basic® Script, Java, and other scripts from the user interface or command line.	

For more information about designing and deploying Windows 2000 directory services and Group Policy, see "Designing the Active Directory Structure," "Planning Distributed Security," "Defining Client Administration and Configuration Standards," and "Applying Change and Configuration Management" in this book.

Desktop Management Solutions

Desktop management solutions are features that allow you to reduce the total cost of ownership in your organization by making it easier to install, configure, manage, and use client computers. Table A.3 highlights Windows 2000 Server and Windows 2000 Professional desktop management features that increase user productivity.

Table A.3   Desktop Management Solutions

Feature	Role of this feature within my organization
IntelliMirror Microsoft® IntelliMirror™ is a group of features that you can use to make users' data, applications, and customized operating system settings follow them as they move to different computers within their organization.	
Windows Installer Windows Installer controls the installation, modification, repair, and removal of software. It provides a model for packaging installation information and APIs for applications to function with Windows Installer.	
Remote Install DHCP-based remote start technology installs the operating system on a client's hard disk from a remote source. A network can be initiated by either a Pre-boot execution (PXE) environment a PXE-enabled network card, specific funtion key, or remote boot floppy provided for clients without PXE.	
Roaming User Profiles Roaming User Profiles copies registry values and document information to a location on the network so that a user's settings are available wherever the user logs on.	
Option Component Manager Windows 2000 Server Setup allows you to bundle and install add-on components during or after any system setup through an installation module.	
Disk Duplication You can customize a single Windows 2000 Server or Windows 2000 Professional setup and clone it across similar computers.	

Note   You can use Microsoft® Systems Management Server (SMS) to complement the desktop management technologies in Windows 2000.

For more information about deploying Windows 2000 Server and Windows 2000 Professional management solutions, see "Defining Client Administration and Configuration Standards" and "Applying Change and Configuration Management" in this book.

Security Features

Enterprise-level security needs to be flexible and robust so that administrators can configure rules to address possible security liability without hindering the free flow of needed information. Table A.4 highlights Windows 2000 security features.

Table A.4   Security Features

Feature	Role of this feature within my organization
Security templates Allows administrators to set various global and local security settings, including security-sensitive registry values; access controls on files and the registry; and security on system services.	
Kerberos authentication The primary security protocol for access within or across Windows 2000 domains. Provides mutual authentication of clients and servers, and supports delegation and authorization through proxy mechanisms.	
Public key infrastructure (PKI) You can use integrated PKI for strong security in multiple Windows 2000 Internet and enterprise services, including extranet-based communications.	
Smart card infrastructure Windows 2000 includes a standard model for connecting smart card readers and cards with computers and device-independent APIs to enable applications that are smart card aware.	
Internet Protocol security (IPSec) management IPSec supports network-level authentication, data integrity, and encryption to secure intranet, extranet, and Internet Web communications.	
NTFS file system encryption Public key–based NTFS can be enabled on a per file or per directory basis.	

For more information about deploying Windows 2000 security services, see "Planning Distributed Security" and "Determining Windows 2000 Network Security Strategies" in this book.

Information Publishing and Sharing

The information publishing and sharing technologies in Windows 2000 make it easier for you to share information over the Internet, your intranet, or an extranet. Table A.5 highlights features for information publishing and sharing.

Table A.5   Information Publishing and Sharing

Feature	Role of this feature within my organization
Integrated Web services Windows 2000 Server integrated Web services allow you to use a variety of Web publishing protocols.	
Indexing Service An integrated Indexing Service allows users to perform full-text searches on files in different formats and languages.	
Removable Storage Consists of server and tool components for delivering audio, video, illustrated audio, and other types of multimedia over networks.	
Printing Windows 2000 makes all shared printers in your domain available in Active Directory.	

For more information about deploying Windows 2000 information publishing and sharing services, see "Upgrading and Installing Member Servers" in this book and in the *Microsoft® Windows® 2000 Server Resource Kit Internet Information Services Resource Guide*.

Component Application Services

As a development platform, Windows 2000 offers Component Object Model (COM) and Distributed COM (DCOM) support that extends a development team's capabilities to efficiently create more scalable component-based applications. Table A.6 highlights Component Application Services features.

Table A.6   Component Application Services

Feature	Role of this feature within my organization
Queued Components Developers and administrators can choose the appropriate communications protocol (DCOM or asynchronous) to use at the time of deployment.	
Publish and Subscribe COM Events provide a uniform publish and subscribe mechanism for all Windows 2000 Server applications.	
Transaction Services Provides information updates by calling an application on a mainframe or sending and receiving a message to or from a message queue.	
Message Queuing Services Ensures that a message transaction is either completed or safely rolled back to the enterprise environment.	
Web Application Services Developers can use Active Server Pages to build a Web-based front-end to their existing server-based applications.	

For more information about deploying Windows 2000 Component Application Services and the Microsoft® Security Support Provider Interface, see "Determining Windows 2000 Network Security Strategies" in this book. For more information for developers, see the MSDN™ Platform SDK link on the Web Resources page at http://windows.microsoft.com/windows2000/reskit/webresources.

Note You might want to discuss these features and their potential business value with members of your application development team. Their knowledge can assist you in determining the potential business value of these technologies to your organization.

Scalability and Availability

At one time, faster CPUs and network adapters were the traditional benchmarks of network performance. In the future, more efficient read/write capabilities, improved input/output (I/O) performance, and faster disk access will be equally important characteristics of network architectures. Environments that require mission-critical computers can now use the extended capabilities of Windows 2000. Table A.7 highlights Windows 2000 features that will assist you in improving network scalability and availability.

Table A.7 Scalability and Availability

Feature	Role of this feature within my organization
Enterprise Memory Architecture Windows 2000 Advanced Server allows you to access up to 32 gigabytes (GB) of memory on processors.	
Improved symmetric multiprocessing (SMP) scalability Windows 2000 Advanced Server has been optimized for eight-way SMP servers.	
Cluster service Allows two or more servers to work together as a single system.	
Intelligent Input/Output (I2O) support I2O relieves the host of interrupt-intensive I/O tasks by offloading processing from main CPUs.	
Terminal Services Through terminal emulation, Terminal Services allows the same set of applications to run on diverse types of client hardware, including thin clients, older computers, or clients not running Windows. It can also be used as a remote administration option.	
Network Load Balancing Combines up to 32 servers running Windows 2000 Advanced Server into a single load balancing cluster. It is used most often to distribute incoming Web requests among its cluster of Internet server applications.	
IntelliMirror IntelliMirror allows users to have their data, applications, and settings follow them when they are not connected to the network.	

For more information about deploying Windows 2000 Cluster service, see "Ensuring the Availability of Applications and Services" in this book.

For more information about Terminal Services, see "Deploying Terminal Services" in this book.

Networking and Communications

To enhance your networking environment, consider the Windows 2000 technologies listed in Table A.8, which can give you greater bandwidth control, secure remote network access, and native support for a new generation of communications solutions.

Table A.8   Networking and Communications

Feature	Role of this feature within my organization
DNS dynamic update protocol Eliminates the need to manually edit and replicate the DNS database.	
Quality of Service (QoS) QoS protocols and services provide a guaranteed, end-to-end express delivery system for IP traffic.	
Resource Reservation Protocol (RSVP) A signaling protocol that allows the sender and receiver to set up a reserved path for data transmission with a specified quality of service.	
Asynchronous Transfer Mode (ATM) An ATM network can simultaneously transport a wide variety of network traffic, including voice, data, images, and video.	
Streaming Media Services Server and tool components for delivering multimedia files over the network.	
Fibre Channel Fibre Channel provides data transfer at one gigabit per second by mapping common transport protocols and merging networking and high-speed input and output in a single connection.	
IP Telephony Telephony API 3.0 (TAPI) unifies IP and traditional telephony.	

For more information about Windows 2000 networking and communications features, see "Preparing Your Network Infrastructure for Windows 2000" and "Determining Network Connectivity Strategies" in this book.

Storage Management

Windows 2000 Server provides storage services designed to improve both reliability and user access. Table A.9 highlights these services.

Table A.9   Storage Management

Feature	Role of this feature within my organization
Remote Storage Monitors the amount of space available on a local hard disk. When free space on the primary hard disk drops below the level necessary for reliable operation, Remote Storage removes local data that has been copied to remote storage.	
Removable Storage Allows administrators to manage removable storage devices and functions. Administrators can create media pools that are owned and used by a given application.	
NTFS file system enhancements Supports performance enhancements such as file encryption, the ability to add disk space to an NTFS volume without restarting, distributed link tracking, and per-user volume quotas to monitor and limit disk space use.	
Disk Quotas Helps administrators plan for and implement disk use.	
Backup With Backup, users can back up data to a variety of storage media, including hard drives, and magnetic and optical media.	
Distributed file system (Dfs) support Allows administrators to create a single directory tree that includes multiple file servers and file shares and allows interoperability between Windows 2000 clients and any file server that has a matching protocol.	

For more information about deploying Windows 2000 Server storage management technologies, see "Determining Windows 2000 Storage Management Strategies" in this book.

Building a Windows 2000 Test Lab

The chapter "Building a Windows 2000 Test Lab" in this book stresses the importance of thorough Windows 2000 testing based on realistic scenarios. It also provides many guidelines that you can use to set up your organization's lab and to run a thorough test program.

To start, you need to:

- Create a test plan that describes your scope, objectives, and methodology.
- Design test cases that describe the test scenarios and issues that you need to address.
- Conduct tests and evaluate results.
- Document test results.
- Escalate problems to the proper people for resolution.

To the extent possible, your lab needs to simulate your actual working environment. The following are essential components that should be documented in your test plan:

- The current network design (logical and physical).
- The proposed Windows 2000 design.
- A list of features to evaluate and explore.
- An inventory of existing hardware (servers, client computers, and portable computers).
- A list of hardware proposed for Windows 2000.

  This list might evolve during testing, but you need an initial list to equip the lab.

- A list of administrative tools (Windows 2000, third party, and custom built).
- A list of the upgrades, such as service packs, drivers, and basic input/output system (BIOS), that you need to install to be ready for Windows 2000.

Also include the following types of information in your lab description:

- Domain structure, including:
  - Forest and tree hierarchy.
  - Group Policy objects (settings and where they apply).
  - Purpose for each domain.
  - Method for populating user account data.
  - Trust relationships (transitive and explicit).
- Domain controllers, including:
  - Primary Domain Controllers (PDCs) and Backup Domain Controllers (BDCs), if migrating from Microsoft® Windows NT® version 4.0.
  - Servers you will promote to domain controllers, if migrating from any other operating system.
- Member servers, including the services that will run on them.
- Client computers, including:
  - Computer make and model.
  - Amount of memory.
  - Processor type and speed.
  - Hard disk capacity.
  - Graphics cards (type, resolution, and color depth).
- Use of lab design for specific tests, including:
  - Mixed-mode and native-mode testing.
  - Dial-up and other remote testing.
  - Interoperability testing (UNIX, mainframes, and other systems).
  - Replication and Active Directory site testing.
  - WAN link testing.

Use Table A.10 to document the scope and objectives of each test. Complete a new sheet for each test.

Table A.10   Document the Scope and Objectives of Each Test

Test Identifier:	Test Date:
	Test Scope and Objectives:
Purpose of the test	
Special hardware requirements	
Special software requirements	
Special configuration requirements	
Test procedure to be used	
Expected results or success criteria	

Table A.11 illustrates the type of tracking sheet you might use to monitor the progress of your tests and to ensure that all follow-up issues are resolved.

Table A.11   Track Your Test Results

Test Identifier	Date of Test	Results	Action Items

Preparing Your Network Infrastructure for Windows 2000

The chapter "Preparing Your Network Infrastructure for Windows 2000" in this book provides recommendations for documenting your current network infrastructure. It also helps you to identify the areas of the network infrastructure, such as servers, routers, and network services, that you might need to upgrade or modify before deploying Windows 2000.

The areas of your current network environment that you need to document to prepare your network for deploying Windows 2000 are as follows:

- Hardware and software
- Network infrastructure
- File, print, and Web servers
- Line-of-business applications
- Directory services architecture
- Security

You should thoroughly document the following hardware-related items:

- Routers.
- Printers.
- Modems.
- Other hardware, such as redundant array of independent disks (RAID) and Routing and Remote Access Service (RRAS) server hardware.
- Basic input/output system (BIOS) settings.
- Driver versions and other software and firmware information.

Your software inventory should include:

- All applications found on all computers.
- Version numbers (or date and time stamp data) of dynamic link libraries associated with these applications
- Service packs that have been applied to the operating system or applications.

Also document network configurations for servers and client computers. This information, which can be located under Network options in Control Panel, includes:

- Identification
- Services
- Protocols
- Adapters
- Bindings
- Internet Protocol addresses

You need to document:

- The logical organization of your network
- Name and address resolution methods
- Configuration of services used
- The location of network sites
- The available bandwidth between sites

You also need to aggregate much of this information to create physical and logical network diagrams, which you can use to discuss before and after images of the network with others. For more information about important technical issues to document, see "Preparing Your Network Infrastructure for Windows 2000" in this book.

Determining Domain Migration Strategies

To plan the migration of your domain structure from Windows NT to Windows 2000, you must first determine your migration goals. These goals might proactively address your concerns about deployment, such as potential disruptions to production systems, system performance, and ways to increase mean time between failures. Your migration goals also influence your test plans and acceptance criteria.

Read the chapter "Determining Domain Migration Strategies" and then use these worksheets to begin planning your migration strategies. Use a table similar to Table A.12 to document the migration goals that are specific to your organization. The table provides sample goals to get you started.

Table A.12   Document Your Migration Goals

Goal	Guides for Achieving Goal
Minimize disruption to the production environment.	• Maintain user access to data, resources, and applications during and after the migration.
Maintain system performance.	• Maintain a familiar environment for users during and after the migration.
	• Maintain user access to data, resources, and applications during and after the migration.
Increase mean time between failures.	• Maintain a familiar environment for users during and after the migration.
	• Maintain user access to data, resources, and applications during and after the migration.
Minimize administrative overhead.	• Maintain a familiar environment for users during and after the migration.
	• Provide a seamless migration of user accounts. If possible, users need to be able to retain their passwords.
	• Minimize the number of administrator visits to the client computer.
	• Minimize the number of new permissions for resources.
Maximize "quick wins."	• Deploy key features first.
Maintain system security.	• Deploy so that you always maintain a secure system.
	• Establish a deployment security policy.

Use Table A.13 to record the date you complete each task.

Table A.13   Record When You Complete Domain Migration Tasks

Task	Date Completed
Determine your migration roadmap.	
Determine supported upgrade paths.	
Examine your existing domain structure.	
Develop your recovery plan.	
Determine your strategy for upgrading domain controllers.	
Determine the order for upgrading domains.	
Determine when to move to native mode.	
Determine the reasons for restructuring domains.	
Determine when to restructure domains.	
Move users and groups.	
Move computers.	
Move member servers.	
Establish trusts.	
Clone security principals.	
Switch to native mode.	

Planning Distributed Security

To implement an overall security policy, you need to coordinate many network security functions. Use Table A.14 to document all aspects of security that pertain to your organization. For examples of security risks, refer to the "Planning Distributed Security" chapter. List specific (rather than general) security risks for your organization. Under Mitigation Strategy, fill in details from all the chapters in this book that pertain to security, including "Planning Your Public Key Infrastructure" and "Determining Windows 2000 Network Security Strategies."

Table A.14   Identify Potential Security Risks

Potential Security Risk	Description	Mitigation Strategy (including policies, Windows 2000 features, and other technology solutions)

Automating Server Installation and Upgrade

Before you can automate the installation of Windows 2000 Server, you must decide if you will upgrade from Windows NT or perform a clean installation. The chapter "Automating Server Installation and Upgrade" will help you decide which kind of installation to do. The following questions are designed to get you started in making this decision.

1. Does your organization currently have a managed installation of Windows NT in use? Yes ☐   No ☐

2. Do you plan to use already existing hardware and software applications? Yes ☐   No ☐

   If you answered yes to questions 1 and 2, you are a good candidate for an upgrade.

3. Do you plan to install Windows 2000 on new hardware? Yes ☐   No ☐

4. Do you plan to install new applications that are written for a Windows 2000 environment? Yes ☐   No ☐

   If you answered yes to questions 3 and 4, you are a good candidate for a clean installation.

Use Table A.15 to determine which automated installation methods to use and where to use those methods within your organization.

Table A.15   Decide When and Where to Use Automated Installation Methods

Method	When to Use	Use This Method?	When and Where?
Syspart	For clean installations to computers that have dissimilar hardware.		
Sysprep	When the master computer and the target computers have identical hardware, which includes the hardware abstraction layer (HAL) and mass storage devices.		
Systems Management Server (SMS)	To perform managed upgrades of Windows 2000 Server to multiple systems, especially those that are geographically dispersed.		
Bootable CD	With a computer whose basic input/output system (BIOS) allows it to start from the CD.		

Use Table A.16 as a checklist of the tasks you need to complete and the date you complete them.

Table A.16   Record When You Complete Installation Tasks

Task	Date Completed
Resolve critical planning issues.	
Create the distribution folder.	
Review the answer file.	
Review the Windows 2000 Setup commands.	
Choose an application installation method based on critical planning.	
Choose a method for operating system installation based on critical planning.	

Upgrading and Installing Member Servers

Use the following worksheets together with the chapter "Upgrading and Installing Member Servers" to help you determine the most cost-effective and efficient method for upgrading and installing Windows 2000 member servers in your organization. When planning your upgrade or clean installation to Windows 2000 Server, start by defining the specifications for each member server.

You need a current diagram of your existing network before you start the upgrade or clean installation. If you do not have a current network diagram, create one and then begin making plans for your new installation or upgrade of member servers.

Next, find out if your organization has made the decision to install and run Windows 2000 Active Directory. Active Directory needs to be running to use several advanced services within the operating system.

Then determine how many of each type of member server you have in your organization:

- File servers: _____

- Print servers: _____
- Application servers: _____
- Web servers: _____
- Fax servers: _____
- Proxy servers: _____
- Routing and Remote Access Service servers: _____
- Database servers: _____

Now, fill out a Member Server Planning Worksheet for each server in your existing environment. This worksheet helps you define the individual upgrade path for each server in your organization. After you prioritize each server, you can create a schedule for your clean installation or upgrade.

Member Server Planning Worksheet

Describe each server in your existing environment by using the following optional characteristics.

Type of Server:

File server ☐   Print server ☐   Web server ☐   Proxy server ☐   Fax server ☐

Routing and Remote Access Service server ☐   Database server ☐

Application server ☐   Specify the applications you have installed:

_____

_____

Member Server Name: _____

How much data is stored on the server? _____

How much data is transferred to and from the server? _____

Current number of users: _____

Current hours of operation: _____

Server Specifications:

Is this computer system listed on the Microsoft Windows Hardware Compatibility List (HCL)? Yes ☐   No ☐

Serial number: _____

Any modifications to the hardware? Yes ☐   No ☐

If yes, list specifics: _____

_____

Computer System Vendor: _____

Computer System Model: _____

Computer System Make: _____

Amount of physical memory installed: _____

Type of network adapters installed:

Ethernet ☐   Token Ring ☐   FDDI ☐   ATM ☐

Other _____

Are the network adapters listed on the HCL? Yes ☐   No ☐

Type of CD-ROM installed: _____

List all plug-and-play devices:

_____   _____

_____   _____

Type of external disks connected to the computer: _____

_____

Hard disk partitioning and free disk space available: _____

_____

Are you using redundant array of independent disks (RAID)? If so, specify:
Software RAID ☐   Hardware RAID ☐

What levels of RAID are you using? _____

_____

Which of the following types of software are installed on this server?

Third-party network services ☐   Virus scanners ☐   Other client software ☐

Read the release notes file (relnotes.htm) on the Windows 2000 Server operating system CD for information about known problems with specific applications.

Uninstall any applications that are mentioned in the release notes before you upgrade or do a clean installation.

Server Data Backup and Disaster Recovery Plan

Back up the following files prior to upgrade:

_____	_____
_____	_____
_____	_____
_____	_____
_____	_____
_____	

Maximum downtime tolerance: _____

Measurable cost of downtime: _____

Decide New Hardware Requirements

Number of members servers you will upgrade: _____

Number of member servers you will replace with new hardware before the upgrade or clean installation: _____

Number of network adapters required for upgrade: _____

Type of network adapters:

   Ethernet ☐　Token Ring ☐　FDDI ☐　ATM ☐

   Other _____

Planned volume of data: _____

Planned number of users: _____

Planned hours of operation: _____

Record Server Specifications

Print Servers

If this is a print server, determine the following:

- Number of users who will print and the printing workload they will generate:

  _____

- Types of printing needs (for example, if users in Sales need to print colored brochures, you might need a color printer).

  _____

  _____

- Location of the printers. It should be easy for users to pick up their printed documents. Use Table A.17 to assign printers to each print server.

Table A.17   Assign Print Servers, Printers, and Their Locations

Print Server	Printer Name	Location

Have you installed all the required print drivers? Yes ☐ No ☐

(Obtain the print drivers from the Windows 2000 Server operating system CD or from the printer manufacturer.)

Are any clients on the network running third-party operating systems?

Macintosh ☐ NetWare ☐ UNIX ☐ Other ☐ _____

You must install additional services on print servers and install the appropriate print drivers on clients running third-party operating systems. Contact the printer manufacturer for the proper print drivers.

File Servers

Do you plan to run domain-based Dfs? Yes ☐ No ☐

Note Domain-based Dfs requires that Active Directory be running.

Arrange servers into groups to determine which file share each will use:

Group _____ includes the following file servers:

_____	_____

Application Servers

What services will this application server host?

Component Services ☐ Terminal Services ☐ Database ☐ E-mail ☐

If you require Component Services, choose one or more of the following:

- Application load balancing: Yes ☐ No ☐
- Transaction Services: Yes ☐ No ☐
- Application Management: Yes ☐ No ☐
- Message Queuing: Yes ☐ No ☐
- Other: _____

Web Servers

What new or additional components will you install on this server?

Schedule Your Upgrade or Clean Installation

The pilot process is iterative. You deploy a limited number of computers in a controlled environment, evaluate the results, fix any problems that arise, and deploy another pilot until you reach the scope and quality that indicate you are ready for a full deployment.

Prioritize Each Member Server for Deployment

Create your own prioritization system for upgrading or installing that allows you to group servers for a phased deployment. You might want to assign a group number or name for each pilot to enable you to later identify the priority of the upgrade or installation server.

The pilot group number or name is: _____

When do you intend to upgrade or do a clean installation on this particular server? Choose one of the following:

Pilot phase 1 ☐   Pilot phase 2 ☐   Production ☐

For more information about:

- Setting up a test lab, see "Building a Windows 2000 Test Lab" in this book.
- Creating a pilot plan, see "Conducting Your Windows 2000 Pilot" in this book.

Ensuring the Availability of Applications and Services

To create your plan for making applications and services highly available, fill out one Clustering Deployment Planning Worksheet for each mission-critical application or service that you want to make highly available in your organization.

Before you begin filling out the worksheet, read "Ensuring the Availability of Applications and Services." This chapter will introduce the new concepts and provide the guidelines you need to help you make the most of the planning worksheet.

Identify Your High-Availability Needs

Your environment could include one or more of the following types of applications or services:

- Database (Microsoft® SQL Server™ or other database application)
- Groupware (Microsoft® Exchange Server or other groupware application)
- Web service (Microsoft Internet Information Services or other Web service)
- Windows Internet Name Service (WINS)
- Dynamic Host Configuration Protocol (DHCP)
- Internally-developed line-of-business applications
- Third-party applications
- File and print shares

In the following subsections, define the specifications for each mission-critical application or service you intend to deploy for use with Windows 2000 Server.

Application and Service Specifications

Name of application or service: _____

High-Availability Requirements for This Application or Service

Which network protocol does the application or service require?

TCP/IP ☐   IPX/SPX ☐

Note Microsoft does not provide high-availability solutions that support IPX/SPX.

Does your clustering solution require any of the following?

Provide data backup ☐

Protect access to data ☐

Protect the data itself ☐

Protect against power outages ☐

Protect against network outages ☐

Manage cluster objects and configuration ☐

Coordinate with other instances of the Cluster service in the cluster ☐

Perform failover operations ☐

Handle event notification ☐

Facilitate communication among other software components ☐

Software compatibility issues:

Do you have a resource DLL? Yes ☐   No ☐

Is it possible for you to use a generic resource DLL? Yes ☐   No ☐

Does the resource DLL you have support:

Two-node clusters ☐   N-node clusters ☐

Does the application installation support:

Two- node clusters ☐   N-node clusters ☐

Does the application function correctly on Windows 2000?

Yes ☐   No ☐

Is the application stateless or does it maintain a client-side state?

Special hardware requirements:

Is the system on the cluster Hardware Compatibility List (HCL)?

Yes ☐   No ☐

Does the system support large memory? Yes ☐   No ☐

Are you installing Microsoft® Windows® 2000 Advanced Server on any Intel PAE-based computer systems that have more than 4 GB of random access memory (RAM)? Yes ☐   No ☐

If yes, you need to:

- Check the HCL to ensure that the system and components are supported for large memory.
- Bring the system and components into compliance.
- Do a complete backup of the system.
- Modify the boot.ini file to include the PAE switch.
- Test the system to ensure that it is operating correctly.

Will the system use:

SCSI (two-node) ☐   SCSI switch (N-node) ☐   Fiber Channel (N-node) ☐

What network adapters do you have in your environment?

Ethernet ☐   Token Ring ☐   FDDI ☐   ATM ☐

Other _____

Are the network adapters on the HCL? Yes ☐   No ☐

Volume of data: _____

Number of users: _____

Hours of operation: _____

Expected Changes in Size and Performance Requirements for this Application or Service

Seasonal or other planned peak loads: _____

_____

Expected rate of increase in users: _____

_____

Expected rate of increase in data: _____

_____

Data Backup and Disaster Recovery Plans for this Application or Service

Maximum outage tolerance: _____

_____

Impact of downtime (check those that apply):

Lost sales ☐

Lost productivity ☐

Decline in customer satisfaction ☐

Missed contractual obligations or legal liabilities ☐

Loss of competitiveness ☐

Increased costs due to make-up time ☐

Other: _____

_____

_____

Measurable cost of downtime (define the cost per application and cost per service outage that exceeds the specified tolerable maximum):

_____

_____

Site disasters

Is off-site functionality required? Yes ☐   No ☐

Identify single points of failure:

Network hub ☐

Network router ☐

Power outage ☐

Server connection disk ☐

Other server hardware such as CPU or memory ☐

Server software ☐

WAN links such as routers and dedicated lines ☐

Dial-up connection ☐

Other: _____

_____

If an application or service fails, what is the plan to ensure availability?:

_____

_____

If a service fails or an outage occurs, do you have:

RAID:

Level 0 (striping) ☐
Level 1 (mirroring) ☐
Level 5 (striping with parity) ☐

Spare SCSI or Fibre Channel controllers Yes ☐   No ☐

Replacement disks Yes ☐   No ☐

Uninterruptible Power Supply (UPS) protection for individual users
Yes ☐   No ☐

UPS protection for the network (including hubs, bridges, routers, and so on)
Yes ☐   No ☐

Use this checklist to begin your cluster backup and recovery strategy:

Map registry keys to each resource. ☐

Create a catalog to document each backup. ☐

Identify a safe location where you can place your backups. ☐

Create an emergency repair disk by using the Backup utility. ☐

Plan Your Network Load Balancing

Is the application or service running on all hosts in the cluster or does each host maintain its own application or service?

Application or service runs on one host ☐

All hosts share one application or service ☐

Does your application use a TCP or UDP port? TCP port ☐   UDP port ☐

Number of hosts in the cluster (1-32): _____

Note Always be sure that there is enough extra server capacity so that if one server fails, the remaining servers can accommodate the increased load.

When using a router, which mode will you operate in? Unicast ☐   Multicast ☐

Making Specific Choices for Network Load Balancing

Have you implemented the following over TCP/IP?

Distributed Component Object Model (DCOM) ☐

Named pipes ☐

Remote procedure call ☐

Choosing a Server Role

Do you want the nodes in your cluster to be:

Member servers ☐   Domain controllers ☐   Global catalogs ☐

Note If you choose domain controllers, be certain that you have the hardware to support them. For more information, see "Ensuring the Availability of Applications and Services" in this book.

Choosing a Cluster Model

Are you implementing a:

Single-node cluster (failover not available) ☐

Cluster with a dedicated secondary node ☐

High-availability configuration (resource availability using virtual servers):

    Clustering a single application type ☐

    Clustering multiple applications ☐

    Complex hybrid configuration ☐

Planning Resource Groups

Which type of resource does this cluster require?

    IP address ☐

    Network name ☐

    Physical disk ☐

    A generic or customer application or service ☐

    Specify: _____

List all the server-based applications in each resource group:

_____

_____

How many virtual servers will you run in your environment? _____

What other software will you run independently of these groups?

_____

_____

Which hardware, connections, and operating system software can this server cluster protect in your network environment? List all nonapplication resources.

_____

_____

List all the dependencies for each resource (including all resources that support the core resources):

_____

_____

_____

What failover policies are required by each resource?

_____

_____

Create administrative convenience when making grouping decisions. For example:

- Combine file-sharing resources and print-spooling resources into a single group.
- Place applications that depend on a particular resource in a single group.

Synchronizing Active Directory with Exchange Server Directory Service

The chapter "Synchronizing Active Directory with Exchange Server Directory Service" provides directory synchronization concepts and processes that will help you determine the most cost-effective and efficient method to integrate the Active Directory and Microsoft® Exchange Server version 5.5 directory service.

To create your Connection Agreement Plan, fill out one planning worksheet for each connection agreement that your organization needs. After you have documented the connection agreements in the worksheets, you can begin configuring them in Windows 2000. (See the section "Create Your Connection Agreements," which directly follows.)

Create Your Connection Agreements

Connection agreement reference number or name: _____

_____

Administrator responsible for this connection agreement: _____

_____

Directory service you will manage objects from:

Windows 2000 Active Directory ☐   Exchange Server 5.5 directory service ☐

Direction: One-way ☐   Two-way ☐

Identify the Connection Agreement Source and Target Servers

One-way connection agreement:

If the *source* server is an Exchange 5.5 server:

Bridgehead ☐   Other ☐ _____

Source server name: _____

If the *target* server is a Windows 2000 server:

Global catalog ☐   Domain controller ☐   Bridgehead ☐

Target server name: _____

Two-way connection agreement:

If the first *source* server is an Exchange 5.5 server:

Bridgehead ☐   Other ☐ _____

Source server name: _____

If the first *target* server is a Windows 2000 server:

Global catalog ☐   Domain controller ☐   Bridgehead ☐

Target server name: _____

If the second *source* server is a Windows 2000 server:

Global catalog ☐   Domain controller ☐   Bridgehead ☐

Source server name: _____

If the second *target* server is an Exchange 5.5 server:

Bridgehead ☐   Other ☐ _____

Target server name: _____

Use Table A.18 to identify the objects to be mapped.

Table A.18   Identify Directory Objects to Map

Exchange Server 5.5 Directory	Active Directory

Use Table A.19 to list the attributes that you will not map.

Table A.19   List the Attributes You Will Not Map

Exchange Server 5.5 Directory	Active Directory

Identify third-party e-mail synchronization requirements: _____

Create Your Directory Synchronization Schedule

To create a synchronization schedule for your organization, refer to the sample directory synchronization schedule that appears in the chapter "Synchronizing Active Directory with Exchange Server Directory Service" in this book. Use Table A.20 to create your directory synchronization schedule.

Table A.20   Complete Your Directory Synchronization Matrix

Hour	Sun	Mon	Tues	Wed	Thurs	Fri	Sat
0-1							
1-2							
2-3							
3-4							
4-5							
5-6							
6-7							
7-8							
8-9							
9-10							
10-11							
11-12							
12-13							
13-14							
14-15							
15-16							
16-17							
17-18							
18-19							
19-20							
20-21							
21-22							
22-23							
23-24							

Record Your Contacts for Directory Synchronization

Schema Administrators Group

Primary contact name and phone number: _____

_____

Secondary contact name and phone number: _____

_____

Lead time for potential schema modifications: _____

Windows 2000 Domain Administration

Organization responsible for the Window 2000 domains:

_____

_____

Primary contact name and phone number: _____

_____

Secondary contact name and phone number: _____

_____

Exchange Server 5.5 Site Administration

Organization responsible for the Exchange sites: _____

_____

Primary contact name and phone number: _____

_____

Secondary contact name and phone number: _____

_____

Justification for this connection agreement: _____

_____

_____

Testing Applications for Compatibility with Windows 2000

Many large organizations have hundreds or even thousands of applications. If this is the case in your organization, compiling the list of applications can be extremely time-consuming.

You might want to compile the following information about each application:

- Application name and version.
- Vendor name.
- Current status (for example, in production, under development, no longer used).
- Number of users and their business units.
- Priority or importance to your organization.
- Current operating systems where the application is used.

  Include whether the application is client-based or server-based and which components reside on the client and on the server.

- Web site addresses (URLs) for Web applications.
- Requirements for installation (for example, security settings and installation directories).
- Development utility or technology (if developed internally).
- Contact names and phone numbers (internal and vendors).

If you find multiple contacts for the same vendor, try to consolidate them where possible.

If one of your goals is to consolidate applications or to better plan your testing efforts, you might prioritize applications by using Table A.21.

Table A.21   Prioritize Your Applications

Application	Importance of the Application to the Organization	Number of Users	Is This the Most Recent Version?	Are Localized Versions Used or Needed?
			Yes ☐ No ☐	Yes ☐ No ☐
			Yes ☐ No ☐	Yes ☐ No ☐
			Yes ☐ No ☐	Yes ☐ No ☐
			Yes ☐ No ☐	Yes ☐ No ☐
			Yes ☐ No ☐	Yes ☐ No ☐
			Yes ☐ No ☐	Yes ☐ No ☐
			Yes ☐ No ☐	Yes ☐ No ☐
			Yes ☐ No ☐	Yes ☐ No ☐

Table A.22 includes a number of tests that you can use to begin planning a testing strategy. Extend this list with additional issues that are appropriate for your organization. To track the results of your testing, record in the table whether the test passed, failed, is in progress, or unknown. You might also want to include the name of the person who is responsible for testing the application and the date that testing was completed or is due to be completed.

Table A.22   Plan and Track Your Testing Strategy

Test	Responsible Tester	Planned Test Date	Test Outcome	Completed Date
Clean installation				
Upgrade installation				
Uninstall				
Installation options				
Basic functionality and common tasks and procedures				
Works with multiple applications open				
Works with add-on hardware such as scanners				
Printing				
Accessing and working with server data				

Defining Client Administration and Configuration Standards

The chapter "Defining Client Administration and Configuration Standards" in this book describes the key planning steps that you need to complete to meet and manage the needs of your organization's users. To do this, begin by understanding your users' unique requirements and the problems your client support teams must address to meet user needs.

Table A.23 helps you identify the computing requirements of the various types of users within your organization. Use it to group users according to the type of work they do (roaming, stationary professional, task-based, and so on) and where they fit in the organization (location and workgroup) to develop common standards for applications, configurations, and autonomy. For a sample table like the one that follows and for information that can help you complete a table such as this, see "Defining Client Administration and Configuration Standards" in this book.

Table A.23   Identify Your Users' Computing Requirements

	Job Title 1	**Job Title 2**	**Job Title 3**
Category			
Workgroup			
Location			
Application requirements			
Operating system requirements			
Computer hardware requirements			
Support requirements			
Autonomy allowed or required			

Table A.24 helps you define your primary client support issues and assign someone to resolve them. Later in the planning process, you can use this table to track progress toward resolving these client support issues.

Table A.24   Define Client Support Issues

Support Issue or Problem	Severity/Frequency	Owner	Solution

If you want to reassign client support tasks, use Table A.25 to define where in your organization these tasks are currently performed and where you want them to be performed.

Table A.25   Assign Client Management and Support Tasks

Client Support Task	Current Owner	Proposed Owner

Define Your Group Policy Requirements

To implement your client administration standards, you need to create Group Policy objects that include settings in a number of different areas: security, applications, computer systems, user environment, and application-specific. Most of these options are explained in the chapter "Defining Client Administration and Configuration Standards." The security issues are addressed in the chapter "Planning Distributed Security." (You might also need to create additional settings if you plan to implement the capabilities described in the chapter "Applying Change and Configuration Management.")

To define your organization's Group Policy requirements, first identify the types of policy settings that you require. These will normally break down into the following areas:

Security settings: _____

_____

Application packages to be deployed: _____

_____

Computer system settings: _____

_____

User environment settings: _____

_____

Application-specific settings: _____

_____

Next, use a table similar to Table A.26 to determine the type of object in the directory (user, computer, and so on) where you will apply these settings:

- Domain (password or account policy)
- Client computers
- Users
- Domain controllers
- Servers (application, file and print)

At this stage, the document you create should be a first draft Group Policy structure. It is likely that many of your Group Policy settings are common to all of the client computers, users, servers, and so on in your organization. You can combine these universal Group Policy settings into a single Group Policy object for clients, users, servers, and so on.

Table A.26   Define Your Windows 2000 Group Policy Requirements

	Domain	Client Computers	Users	Domain Controllers	Servers
Security	Password; Account; Kerberos policy; PK trust list	User rights; File and registry ACLs; Audit and event log; Local settings	EFS policy	User rights; File and registry ACLs; Audit and event log; Local settings	User rights; File and registry ACLs; Audit and event log; Local settings
Application deployment		Mandatory core applications	Published optional applications and components	Administrative tools	Administrative tools
Computer (hardware) settings		Startup scripts; Logon; Disk quotas; Offline files		Disk quotas	Printer moving
User settings			Logon scripts; Internet Explorer Settings; Remote access; Folder redirection; Desktop lockdown; Network; System	Disable standard user desktop settings	Disable standard user desktop settings
Application settings			Office 2000; In-house applications		

Some Group Policy settings will not apply to all objects of a particular type. You can create additional Group Policy objects or use some of the special Group Policy implementation options described in the chapter "Defining Client Administration and Configuration Standards" to address these unique needs. For example, you might need a unique Group Policy object to properly configure computers for users who access the network from remote computers. Alternately, for users who have administrative responsibilities, you probably do not want their applications to be installed when they log on to a server console. Setting a "loopback" policy for the systems you want to protect can prevent this by supplementing or overriding the normal user settings.

The chapter "Defining Client Administration and Configuration Standards" in this book will explain the many Group Policy options that you can use to customize and efficiently manage Group Policy. Table A.27 illustrates how you can document the scope of, and exceptions to, your Group Policy settings.

Table A.27   Define Your Group Policy Scope and Exceptions

Group Policy Settings	Scope	Exceptions
Domain (security)		
Workstation (security, applications, and system)		
User (security, applications, and system)		
Domain controller (security, applications, and system)		
Server (security, applications, and system)		

Applying Change and Configuration Management

In "Defining Client Administration and Configuration Standards" in this book, you were asked to define the computer configuration and application requirements for different types of users. By performing the planning steps described in the chapter "Applying Change and Configuration Management," you can implement your new administration and configuration standards by using Windows 2000 IntelliMirror and Remote OS Installation.

Applications that are deployed by using Windows 2000 software installation and maintenance features can be published, assigned to users, or assigned to computers. To understand the implications of each option and to apply them to your organization's applications, see "Applying Change and Configuration Management" in this book.

Use Table A.28 to record the applications your organization uses and how you will deploy them.

Table A.28   Record Your Applications and Their Management Options

Application	Assigned to User	Assigned to Computer	Published
	Yes ☐ No ☐	Yes ☐ No ☐	Yes ☐ No ☐
	Yes ☐ No ☐	Yes ☐ No ☐	Yes ☐ No ☐
	Yes ☐ No ☐	Yes ☐ No ☐	Yes ☐ No ☐
	Yes ☐ No ☐	Yes ☐ No ☐	Yes ☐ No ☐
	Yes ☐ No ☐	Yes ☐ No ☐	Yes ☐ No ☐
	Yes ☐ No ☐	Yes ☐ No ☐	Yes ☐ No ☐
	Yes ☐ No ☐	Yes ☐ No ☐	Yes ☐ No ☐

Use Table A.29 to define which change and configuration management features are appropriate for each type of user within your organization. In the left column, enter the user types you defined in Table A.23. For an example of how this table might look when you have completed it, see "Applying Change and Configuration Management" in this book.

Table A.29   Define a Configuration Management Strategy for Your Users

Type of User	User Data Management	User Settings Management	Software Installation and Maintenance	Remote OS Installation

Automating Client Installation and Upgrade

Before you can automate the installation of Windows 2000 Professional, you must decide if the installation will be an upgrade from a pre–Windows 2000 operating system or a clean installation. The following questions will help you determine whether to upgrade or to perform a clean installation.

1. Is your organization currently using a managed installation of Windows NT?
   Yes ☐   No ☐

2. Do you plan to use existing hardware and software applications?
   Yes ☐   No ☐

   If you answered yes to questions 1 and 2, you are a good candidate for an upgrade.

3. Do you plan to install Windows 2000 on new hardware? Yes ☐   No ☐

4. Do you plan to install new applications that are written for a Windows 2000 environment? Yes ☐   No ☐

   If you answered yes to questions 3 and 4, you are a good candidate for a clean installation.

Use Table A.30 to record which automated installation methods you will use and where in your organization you will use them.

Table A.30   Record Your Automated Installation Methods

Method	When to Use	Use This Method?	Where
Syspart	Use Syspart for clean installations to computers that have dissimilar hardware.		
Sysprep	Use Sysprep when the master computer and the target computers have identical hardware, which includes the HAL and mass storage devices.		
Systems Management Server (SMS)	Use SMS to perform managed upgrades of Windows 2000 Server to multiple systems, especially those that are geographically dispersed.		
Bootable CD	Use the bootable CD method with a computer whose basic input/output system (BIOS) allows it to start from the CD.		
Remote OS Installation	Use Remote OS Installation to remotely install an image of Windows 2000 Professional on supported computers, eliminating the need to physically visit each computer to perform an installation.		

Use Table A.31 to record the date you complete each task of your client installation.

Table A.31   Record Client Installation Tasks

Task	Date Completed
Resolve critical planning issues.	
Create the distribution folder.	
Review the answer file.	
Review the Windows 2000 Setup commands.	
Choose a method for installing applications that is based on critical planning.	
Choose a method for installing the operating system that is based on critical planning.	

APPENDIX B

Setup Commands

You install Microsoft® Windows® 2000 using the Setup command, either Winnt.exe or Winnt32.exe. This appendix provides information about command syntax and parameters for each of these program files.

In This Appendix

Related Information in the Resource Kit

- For more information about automating Windows 2000 Setup, see "Automating Server Installation and Upgrade" in this book.

- For more information about answer files, see Appendix C, "Sample Answer Files for Unattended Setup," in this book.

Using Setup Commands to Install Windows 2000

To install Windows 2000, use the appropriate Windows 2000 Setup command:

Winnt32.exe For a clean installation or upgrade on a computer running Microsoft® Windows NT® version 4.0, Microsoft® Windows® 95, or Microsoft® Windows® 98.

Winnt.exe For a clean installation on a computer running Microsoft® MS-DOS® or Microsoft® Windows® 3.*x* (upgrades of these operating systems are not supported).

Options vary between the two commands. Read the following sections for descriptions of each command.

Caution Before upgrading to the Windows 2000 operating system, be sure to restart the computer if you have just upgraded any applications.

Winnt32.exe Command Syntax

Winnt32
[/checkupgradeonly]
[/cmd:*command_line***]**
[/cmdcons]
[/copydir:*folder_name***]**
[/copysource:*folder_name***]**
[/debug*[level]***[***:file_name***]]**
[/m:*folder_name***]**
[/makelocalsource]
[/noreboot]
[/s:*sourcepath***]**
[/syspart:*drive_letter***]**
[/tempdrive:*drive_letter***]**
[/udf:*ID***[***,UDB_file***]]**
[/unattend]
[/unattend*[seconds]***[***:answer_file***]]**

/checkupgradeonly

Checks the current operating system for upgrade compatibility with Windows 2000. This is simply a verification and does not install Windows 2000.

/cmd:*command_line*

Specifies a command to be carried out after the graphical user interface (GUI) portion of Setup finishes. The command will occur before Setup is complete and after Setup has restarted your computer and has collected the necessary configuration information. For example, this option can run Cmdlines.txt, which usually specifies the applications to be installed immediately after Setup completes.

/cmdcons

Adds a Recovery Console option for repairing a failed installation.

/copydir:*folder_name*

Creates a subfolder within the folder that contains the Windows 2000 files. For example, if the source folder contains a Private_drivers folder that has modifications just for your site, you can type **/copydir:private_drivers** to copy that folder to your Windows 2000 folder. You can use the **/copydir** option multiple times.

/copysource:*folder_name*

Temporarily creates a subfolder within the folder that contains the Windows 2000 files. For example, if the source folder contains a Private_drivers folder that has modifications just for your site, you can type **/copysource:private_drivers** to have Setup copy that folder to your Windows 2000 folder and use its files during Setup. Unlike the **/copydir** option, folders created by using **/copysource** are deleted when Setup finishes.

/debug[*level*][:*file_name*]

Creates a debug log at the level specified. When you use the default setting, the program creates a log file (*%windir%*\Winnt32.log) that has a warning level of 2. The warning levels for the log file are as follows: 0 = severe errors, 1=errors, 2 = warnings, 3 = information, and 4 = detailed information for debugging. Each level also includes the levels below it.

/m:*folder_name*

Instructs Setup to copy replacement files from an alternate location. It directs Setup to look at the alternate location first and to copy the files from that location (if files are present) instead of from the default location.

/makelocalsource

Instructs Setup to copy all installation source files to your local hard disk. Use /makelocalsource to obtain installation files if you begin installation from a CD and the CD becomes unavailable later in the installation.

/noreboot

Instructs Setup to not restart the computer after the file copy phase of Winn32 is complete so that you can execute another command.

/s:*sourcepath*

Specifies the source location of the Windows 2000 files. The default is the current folder. To copy files simultaneously from multiple servers, you can specify up to eight sources. For example:

```
winnt32 /s:server1 … /s:server8
```

Windows 2000 can use up to eight **/s** switches to point to other distribution servers as source locations for installation to the destination computer. This functionality helps to speed up the file copy phase of Setup to the destination computer and provides additional load balancing capability to the distribution servers from which Setup can be run. For example:

```
path to distribution folder 1\winnt32 [/unattend] [:path\answer.txt]
[/s:path to distribution folder 2] [/s:path to distribution folder 3]
[/s:path to distribution folder 4]
```

/syspart:*drive_letter*

Specifies that you can copy Setup startup files to a hard disk, mark the disk as active, and install the disk in another computer. When you start that computer, Setup automatically starts with the next phase. Remember the following points when you use this switch:

- You must always use the **/syspart** option together with the **/tempdrive** option.

- Both **/syspart** and **/tempdrive** must point to the same partition of a secondary hard disk.

- You must install Windows 2000 on the primary partition of that secondary hard disk.

- You can use the /syspart switch only from a computer that is running Windows NT 3.51, Windows NT 4.0, or Windows 2000. You cannot use this switch from a computer that is running a Windows 95 or Windows 98 operating system.

/tempdrive:*drive_letter*

Directs Setup to place temporary files on the specified partition and to install Windows 2000 on that partition. Remember the following points as you use this switch:

- You must always use the **/tempdrive** option together with the **/syspart** option.
- Both **/tempdrive** and **/syspart** must point to the same partition of a secondary hard disk.
- You must install Windows 2000 on the primary partition of that secondary hard disk.

/udf:*ID*[,*UDB_file*]

Indicates an identifier (ID) that Setup uses to specify how a Uniqueness Database File (UDB) modifies an answer file (see the **/unattend** option, which follows). The .udb file overrides values in the answer file, and the identifier determines which values in the .udb file are used. For example, **/udf:Roaming_user,Our_company.udb** overrides settings specified for the identifier **Roaming_user** located in the **Our_company.udb** file. If you do not specify a .udb file, Setup prompts you to insert a disk that contains the $*Unique*$.udb file.

/unattend

Upgrades your previous version of Windows by using unattended Setup mode. All user settings are taken from the previous installation so that no user intervention is required during Setup.

Important   Using the /unattend switch to automate Setup affirms that you have read and accepted the End User License Agreement (EULA) for Windows 2000. Before using this switch to install Windows 2000 on behalf of an organization other than your own, you must confirm that the end user (whether an individual or a single entity) has received, read, and accepted the terms of the Windows 2000 EULA. OEMs may not specify this key on machines being sold to end users.

/unattend[*seconds*][:*answer_file*]

Installs Windows 2000 without using prompts that require user interaction; instead, Setup obtains the information it needs from an answer file that you prepare in advance. For more information about answer files, see Appendix C, "Sample Answer Files for Unattended Setup," in this book.

Include *seconds* only if you are upgrading from Windows NT 4.0. *Seconds* specifies the delay, in seconds, between when Setup finishes copying the files and when system setup begins.

Winnt.exe Command Syntax

Winnt
[**/E:***command*]
[**/R:***folder_name*]
[**/Rx:***folder_name*]
[**/S:***sourcepath*]
[**/T**[:*tempdrive*]]
[**/U**[:*answer_file*]]
[**/udf:***ID*[,UDB_file]
[**/A:**]

/E:*command*

Specifies a command to be carried out after the GUI portion of Setup finishes. For example, this option can run Cmdlines.txt, which usually specifies the applications to be installed immediately after Setup completes.

/R:*folder_name*

Creates a subfolder within the folder that contains the Windows 2000 files. For example, if the source folder contains a Private_drivers folder that has modifications just for your site, you can type **/R:private_drivers** to copy that folder to your Windows 2000 folder. You can use the **/R** option multiple times.

/Rx:*folder_name*

Temporarily creates a subfolder within the folder that contains the Windows 2000 files. For example, if the source folder contains a Private_drivers folder that has modifications just for your site, you can type **/Rx:private_drivers** to have Setup copy that folder to your Windows 2000 folder and use its files during Setup. Unlike the **/R** option, folders created by using **/Rx** are deleted when Setup finishes.

/S:*sourcepath*

Specifies the source location of the Windows 2000 files. The location must be a full path of the form *Drive_letter:\Path* or *\\Server\Share\Path*. The default is the current folder.

/T:*tempdrive*

Directs Setup to place temporary files on the specified drive and to install Windows 2000 on that drive. If you do not specify a location, Setup attempts to locate a drive for you.

/U:_answer_file_

Installs Windows 2000 without using prompts that require user interaction; instead, Setup obtains the information it needs from an answer file that you prepare in advance. For more information about answer files, see Appendix C "Sample Answer Files for Unattended Setup" in this book. Requires **/S**.

/udf:_ID_[,_UDB_file_]

Indicates an identifier (ID) that Setup uses to specify how a Uniqueness Database File (UDB) modifies an answer file. The .udb file overrides values in the answer file, and the identifier determines which values in the .udb file are used. For example, **/udf:Roaming_user,Our_company.udb** overrides settings specified for the identifier **Roaming_user** located in the **Our_company.udb** file. If you do not specify a .udb file, Setup prompts you to insert a disk that contains the $_Unique_$.udb file.

/A

Enables accessibility options.

APPENDIX C

Sample Answer Files for Unattended Setup

Unattended Setup in Microsoft® Windows® 2000 uses an ASCII text file that is called an answer file to supply data that would otherwise be entered interactively when you run the Setup Wizard. The answer file is specified on either a Winnt.exe or Winnt32.exe command line when the unattended setup option is used. (For information about when to use which command line, see Appendix B, "Setup Commands," in this book.)

This appendix includes sample answer files that are appropriate for common installation configurations. You can customize the default answer file (Unattend.txt) that comes with Windows 2000 or write a new one based on the samples that are provided in this appendix.

In This Appendix:

Related Information in the Resource Kit

- For more information about setup commands, see Appendix B, "Setup Commands" in this book.

Answer File Format

An answer file consists of section headers, keys, and the values for each key. Most of the section headers are predefined, but some can be user defined. You do not need to specify all the possible keys in an answer file if the installation does not require them. Invalid key values generate errors or can cause incorrect behavior after setup. The file format is as follows:

```
[section_name]
```

Sections contain keys and the corresponding values for those keys. Each key and value are separated by a space, an equal sign, and a space. The following is an example:

```
key = value
```

Values that have spaces in them require double quotes around them. The following is an example:

```
key = "value with spaces"
```

Some sections have no keys and merely contain a list of values. The following is an example:

```
[OEMBootFiles]
Txtsetup.oem
```

Comment lines start with a semicolon.

```
; This is an example of a comment line.
```

Answer File Keys and Values

Every key in an answer file must have a value assigned to it; however, some keys are optional, and some keys have default values that are used if the key is omitted.

Key values are strings of text unless numeric is specified. If numeric is specified, the value is decimal unless otherwise noted.

Note   Keys are not case sensitive; they can be uppercase or lowercase.

For more information about answer file keys and values, see the "Microsoft Windows 2000 Guide to Unattended Setup" (Unattend.doc) on the Microsoft Windows 2000 operating system CD. The Unattend.doc file is part of the Deploy.cab file in the \Support\Tools folder. On Windows 98 or Windows 2000, use Windows Explorer to extract this document. On earlier versions of Windows, or from MS-DOS, use the Extract command to access the file.

Sample Answer Files

The sample answer files that are provided in this section are examples of the more common installation configurations of the keys commonly used in those configurations. Consider these files as examples only, and modify them as appropriate for your organization.

Note In the answer files that follow, the use of italic font style indicates that the user must supply the required information.

Also, to call attention to each section, the section names appear in bold font style; however, you need not follow this formatting convention in your answer file.

Sample 1 – Default Unattend.txt.

The following answer file is the default Unattend.txt file provided on the Windows 2000 CD.

```
; Microsoft Windows 2000 Professional, Server, Advanced Server
; © 1994-1999 Microsoft Corporation. All rights reserved.
;
; Sample Answer File for Unattended Setup
;
; This file contains information about how to automate the installation
; or upgrade of Windows 2000 Professional and Windows 2000 Server so
; that the Setup program runs without requiring user input.
;

[Unattended]
    UnattendMode = FullUnattended
    OemPreinstall = No
    TargetPath = Winnt
    Filesystem = LeaveAlone

[UserData]
    FullName = "Your user name"
    OrgName = "Your organization name"
; It is recommended that you avoid using spaces in the ComputerName
; value.
    ComputerName = "YourComputer_name"
; To ensure a fully unattended installation, you must provide a value
; for the ProductId key.
    ProductId = "Your product ID"
```

[GuiUnattended]
; Sets the TimeZone. For example, to set the TimeZone for the
; Pacific Northwest, use a value of "004." Be sure to use the
; numeric value that represents your own time zone. To look up
; a numeric value, see the Unattend.doc file on the Windows 2000 CD.
   TimeZone = "*YourTimeZone*"
; It is recommended that you change the administrator password
; before the computer is placed at its final destination.
   AdminPassword = AdminPassword
; Tells Unattended Setup to turn AutoLogon on and log on once.
   AutoLogon = Yes
   AutoLogonCount = 1

[LicenseFilePrintData]
; This section is used for server installs.
   AutoMode = "PerServer"
   AutoUsers = "5"

[GuiRunOnce]
; List the programs that you want to start when you log on to the
; computer for the first time.

[Display]
   BitsPerPel = 8
   XResolution = 800
   YResolution = 600
   VRefresh = 70

[Networking]
; When you set the value of the InstallDefaultComponents key
; to Yes, Setup will install default networking components.
; The components to be set are TCP/IP, File and Print Sharing,
; and Client for Microsoft Networks.
   InstallDefaultComponents = Yes

[Identification]
; Identifies your workgroup. It is recommended that you avoid
; using spaces in this value.
   JoinWorkgroup = "*YourWorkgroup*"

Sample 2 – Unattended Installation of Windows 2000 Professional from CD-ROM

The following answer file installs Microsoft® Windows® 2000 Professional from CD-ROM. For this answer file to function properly, you must name it Winnt.sif and place it on a floppy disk.

```
; Microsoft Windows 2000 Professional
; © 1994-1999 Microsoft Corporation. All rights reserved.
;
; Sample Answer File for Unattended Setup
;
; This file contains information about how to automate the installation
; or upgrade of Windows 2000 Professional so that the Setup program runs
; without requiring user input.
;

[Data]
; This section is required when you perform an unattended installation
; by starting Setup directly from the Windows 2000 installation CD-ROM.
    Unattendedinstall = Yes
; If you are running Unattended Setup from the CD-ROM, you must set the
; Msdosinitiated key to 0.
    Msdosinitiated = "0"
; AutoPartition allows Windows 2000 Unattended Setup to choose a
; partition to install to.
    AutoPartition = 1

[Unattended]
    UnattendMode = FullUnattended
; The OemPreinstall key tells Unattended Setup that the installation is
; being performed from distribution shares if the value is set to Yes.
    OemPreinstall = Yes
    TargetPath = Winpro
    FileSystem = LeaveAlone
; If the OemSkipEula key is set to Yes, it informs Unattended Setup that
; the user should not be prompted to accept the End User License
; Agreement (EULA). A value of Yes signifies agreement to the EULA and
; should be used in conjunction with the terms of your license
; agreement.
    OemSkipEula = Yes
```

[GuiUnattended]
; Sets the TimeZone. For example, to set the TimeZone for the
; Pacific Northwest, use a value of "004." Be sure to use the
; numeric value that represents your own time zone. To look up
; a numeric value, see the Unattend.doc file on the Windows 2000 CD.
    TimeZone = "*YourTimeZone*"
; It is recommended that you change the administrator password
; before the computer is placed at its final destination.
    AdminPassword = AdminPassword
; Tells Unattended Setup to turn AutoLogon on and log on once.
    AutoLogon = Yes
    AutoLogonCount = 1
; The OemSkipWelcome key specifies whether the welcome page in the
; wizard phase of Setup should be skipped. A value of 1 causes the page
; to be skipped.
    OemSkipWelcome = 1
; The OemSkipRegional key allows Unattended Setup to skip
; RegionalSettings when the final location of the computer is unknown.
    OemSkipRegional = 1

[UserData]
    FullName = "*Your user name*"
    OrgName = "*Your organization name*"
; It is recommended that you avoid using spaces in the
; ComputerName value.
    ComputerName = "*YourComputer_name*"
; To ensure a fully unattended installation, you must provide a value
; for the ProductId key.
    ProductId = "*Your product ID*"

[Display]
    BitsPerPel = 8
    XResolution = 800
    YResolution = 600
    VRefresh = 60

[Networking]
; When you set the value of the InstallDefaultComponents key
; to Yes, Setup will install default networking components.
; The components to be set are TCP/IP, File and Print Sharing,
; and Client for Microsoft Networks.
    InstallDefaultComponents = Yes

Sample 3 – Install and Configure Windows 2000 and Configure Microsoft Internet Explorer with Proxy Settings

The following answer file installs and configures Microsoft® Internet Explorer and configures proxy settings.

```
; Microsoft Windows 2000 Professional, Server, Advanced Server
; © 1994-1999 Microsoft Corporation. All rights reserved.
;
; Sample Answer File for Unattended Setup
;
; This file contains information about how to automate the installation
; or upgrade of Windows 2000 Professional and Windows 2000 Server so
; that the Setup program runs without requiring user input.
;

[Unattended]
    UnattendMode = FullUnattended
    TargetPath = Windows
    FileSystem = LeaveAlone
    OemPreinstall = Yes
    OemSkipEula = Yes


[GuiUnattended]
; Sets the TimeZone. For example, to set the TimeZone for the
; Pacific Northwest, use a value of "004." Be sure to use the
; numeric value that represents your own time zone. To look up
; a numeric value, see the Unattend.doc file on the Windows 2000 CD.
    TimeZone = "YourTimeZone"
; It is recommended that you change the administrator password
; before the computer is placed at its final destination.
    AdminPassword = AdminPassword
; Tells Unattended Setup to turn AutoLogon on and log on once.
    AutoLogon = Yes
    AutoLogonCount = 1
    OemSkipWelcome = 1
; The OemSkipRegional key allows Unattended Setup to skip
; RegionalSettings when the final location of the computer is unknown.
    OemSkipRegional = 1

[UserData]
    FullName = "Your user name"
    OrgName = "Your organization name"
; It is recommended that you avoid using spaces in the
; ComputerName value.
    ComputerName = "YourComputername"
; To ensure a fully unattended installation, you must provide a value
; for the ProductId key.
    ProductId = "Your product ID"
```

[LicenseFilePrintData]
; This section is used for server installs.
  AutoMode = "PerServer"
  AutoUsers = "50"

[Display]
  BitsPerPel = 8
  XResolution = 800
  YResolution = 600
  VRefresh = 60

[Components]
; This section contains keys for installing the components of
; Windows 2000. A value of On installs the components, and a
; value of Off prevents the component from being installed.
  iis_common = On
  iis_inetmgr = Off
  iis_www = Off
  iis_ftp = Off
  iis_htmla = Off
  iis_doc = Off
  iis_pwmgr = Off
  iis_smtp = On
  iis_smtp_docs = Off
  Mts_core = On
; The Fp key installs Front Page Server Extensions.
  Fp = On
  Msmq = Off
; If you set the TSEnable key to On, Terminal Services is installed on
; Windows 2000 Server.
  TSEnable = On
; If you set the TSClients key to On, the files required to create
; Terminal Services client disks are installed. If you set this key
; to On, you must also set the TSEnable key to On.
  TSClients = On
; TSPrinterDrivers and TSKeyboardDrivers are optional keys. If enabled,
; they require additional disk space.
  TSPrinterDrivers = Off
  TSKeyboardDrivers = Off
  Netoc = On
  Reminst = On
  Certsrv = Off
  Rstorage = Off
  Indexsrv_system = On
  Certsrv_client = Off
  Certsrv_server = Off
  Certsrv_doc = Off
  Accessopt = On

```
    Calc = On
    Cdplayer = On
    Charmap = On
    Chat = Off
    Clipbook = On
    Deskpaper = On
    Dialer = On
    Freecell = Off
    Hypertrm = On
    Media_blindnoisy = On
    Media_blindquiet = On
    Media_clips = On
    Media_jungle = On
    Media_musica = On
    Media_robotz = On
    Media_utopia = On
    Minesweeper = Off
    Mousepoint = Off
    Mplay = On
    Mswordpad = On
    Objectpkg = On
    Paint = On
    Pinball = Off
    Rec = On
    Solitaire = Off
    Templates = On
    Vol = On

[TapiLocation]
    CountryCode = "1"
    Dialing = Pulse
; Indicates the area code for your telephone. This value should
; be a 3-digit number.
    AreaCode = "Your telephone area code"
    LongDistanceAccess = 9

[Networking]
; When you set the value of the InstallDefaultComponents key
; to Yes, Setup will install default networking components.
; The components to be set are TCP/IP, File and Print Sharing,
; and Client for Microsoft Networks.
    InstallDefaultComponents = Yes

[Identification]
    JoinDomain = YourCorpNet
    DomainAdmin = YourCorpAdmin
    DomainAdminPassword = YourAdminPassword
```

[NetOptionalComponents]
; This section contains a list of the optional network
; components to install.
  Wins = Off
  Dns = Off
  Dhcpserver = Off
  ils = Off
  Snmp = Off
  Lpdsvc = Off
  Simptcp = Off
  Netmontools = On
  Dsmigrat = Off

[Branding]
; This section brands Microsoft Internet Explorer with custom
; properties from the Unattended answer file.
  BrandIEUsingUnattended = Yes

[URL]
; This section contains custom URL settings for Microsoft
; Internet Explorer. If these settings are not present, the
; default settings are used. Specifies the URL for the
; browser's default home page. For example, you might use the
; following: Home_Page = www.microsoft.com.
  Home_Page = *YourHomePageURL*
; Specifies the URL for the default search page. For example, you might
; use the following: Search Page = www.msn.com
  Search_Page = *YourSearchPageURL*
; Specifies a shortcut name in the link folder of Favorites.
; For example, you might use the following: Quick_Link_1_Name =
; "Microsoft Product Support Services"
  Quick_Link_1_Name = "*Your Quick Link Name*"
; Specifies a shortcut URL in the link folder of Favorites. For example,
; you might use this: Quick_Link_1 = http://support.microsoft.com/.
  Quick_Link_1 = *YourQuickLinkURL*

[Proxy]
; This section contains custom proxy settings for Microsoft
; Internet Explorer. If these settings are not present, the default
; settings are used. If **proxysrv:80** is not accurate for your
; configuration, be sure to replace the proxy server and port number
; with your own parameters.
  HTTP_Proxy_Server = *proxysrv:80*
  Use_Same_Proxy = 1
  Proxy_Enable = 1
  Proxy_Override = <local>

Sample 4 – Install and Configure Windows 2000 Server with Two Network Adapters

The following answer file installs Microsoft® Windows® 2000 Server with two network adapters; one adapter uses Dynamic Host Configuration Protocol (DHCP), and the other uses static information.

```
; Microsoft Windows 2000 Server, Advanced Server
; © 1994-1999 Microsoft Corporation. All rights reserved.
;
; Sample Answer File for Unattended Setup
;
; This file contains information about how to automate the installation
; or upgrade of Windows 2000 Server or Windows 2000 Advanced Server so
; that the Setup program runs without requiring user input.
;

[Unattended]
    UnattendMode = FullUnattended
    TargetPath = Winnt
    Filesystem = ConvertNTFS

[GuiUnattended]
; Sets the TimeZone. For example, to set the TimeZone for the
; Pacific Northwest, use a value of "004." Be sure to use the
; numeric value that represents your own time zone. To look up
; a numeric value, see the Unattend.doc file on the Windows 2000 CD.
    TimeZone = "YourTimeZone"
; It is recommended that you change the administrator password
; before the computer is placed at its final destination.
    AdminPassword = AdminPassword
; Tells Unattended Setup to turn AutoLogon on and log on once.
    AutoLogon = Yes
    AutoLogonCount = 1

[LicenseFilePrintData]
; This section is used for server installs.
    AutoMode = "PerServer"
    AutoUsers = "50"

[UserData]
    FullName = "Your user name"
    OrgName = "Your organization name"
; It is recommended that you avoid the use of spaces in the
; ComputerName value.
    ComputerName = "YourComputer_name"
; To ensure a fully unattended installation, you must provide a value
; for the ProductId key.
    ProductId = "Your product ID"
```

```
[Display]
   BitsPerPel = 8
   XResolution = 800
   YResolution = 600
   VRefresh = 70
```

[Networking]
```
; When you set the value of the InstallDefaultComponents key
; to Yes, Setup will install default networking components.
; The components to be set are TCP/IP, File and Print Sharing,
; and Client for Microsoft Networks.
   InstallDefaultComponents = Yes
```

[Identification]
```
   JoinDomain = YourCorpNet
   DomainAdmin = YourCorpAdmin
   DomainAdminPassword = YourAdminPassword
```

[NetAdapters]
```
; In this example, there are two network adapters, Adapter01
; and Adapter02. Note that the adapter specified here as 01 is not
; always local area network (LAN) connection 1 in the user interface.
   Adapter01 = Params.Adapter01
   Adapter02 = Params.Adapter02
```

[Params.Adapter01]
```
; Specifies which adapter is number one. Note that the InfID key
; must match a valid PNP ID in the system. For example, a valid
; PNP ID might look like the following: InfID = "pci\ven_0e11&dev_ae32"
   InfID = "Your_PNP_ID_for_Adapter01"
```

[Params.Adapter02]
```
; Specifies which adapter is number two. Note that the InfID key must
; match a valid PNP ID in the system. For example, a valid PNP ID
; might look as follows: InfID = "pci\ven_8086&dev_1229&subsys_00018086"
   InfID = " Your_PNP_ID_for_Adapter02"
```

[NetClients]
```
; Installs the Client for Microsoft Networks.
   MS_MSClient = params.MS_MSClient
```

[Params.MS_MSClient]

[NetProtocols]
```
; Installs only the TCP/IP protocol.
   MS_TCPIP = params.MS_TCPIP
```

```
[params.MS_TCPIP]
; This section configures the TCP/IP properties.
    AdapterSections = Params.MS_TCPIP.Adapter01,params.MS_TCPIP.Adapter02

[Params.MS_TCPIP.Adapter01]
; Adapter01 uses DHCP server information.
    SpecificTo = Adapter01
    DHCP = Yes
    Wins = Yes

[Params.MS_TCPIP.Adapter02]
; Adapter02 uses static TCP/IP configuration.
    SpecificTo = Adapter02
    IPAddress = 1.1.1.1
    SubnetMask = 255.255.248.0
    DefaultGateway = 2.2.2.2
    DHCP = No
    Wins = No

[NetServices]
; Install File and Print services.
    MS_Server = Params.MS_Server

[Params.MS_Server]
```

Sample 5 – Install Windows 2000 Advanced Server with Network Load Balancing

The following answer file installs Microsoft® Windows® 2000 Advanced Server with Network Load Balancing.

```
; Microsoft Windows 2000 Advanced Server
; © 1994-1999 Microsoft Corporation. All rights reserved.
;
; Sample Answer File for Unattended Setup
;
; This file contains information about how to automate the installation
; or upgrade of Windows 2000 Advanced Server so that the
; Setup program runs without requiring user input.
;

[Unattended]
    UnattendMode = FullUnattended
    TargetPath = Windows
    FileSystem = ConvertNTFS
```

[GuiUnattended]
```
; Sets the TimeZone. For example, to set the TimeZone for the
; Pacific Northwest, use a value of "004." Be sure to use the
; numeric value that represents your own time zone. To look up
; a numeric value, see the Unattend.doc file on the Windows 2000 CD.
    TimeZone = "YourTimeZone"
; It is recommended that you change the administrator password
; before the computer is placed at its final destination.
    AdminPassword = AdminPassword
; Tells Unattended Setup to turn AutoLogon on and log on once.
    AutoLogon = Yes
    AutoLogonCount = 1
    AdvServerType = Servernt
```

[LicenseFilePrintData]
```
; This section is used for server installs.
    AutoMode = "PerServer"
    AutoUsers = "50"
```

[UserData]
```
    FullName = "Your user name"
    OrgName = "Your organization name"
; It is recommended that you avoid the use of spaces in the
; ComputerName value.
    ComputerName = "YourComputer_name"
; To ensure a fully unattended installation, you must provide a value
; for the ProductId key.
    ProductId = "Your product ID"
```

[Display]
```
    BitsPerPel = 8
    XResolution = 800
    YResolution = 600
    VRefresh = 70
```

[Networking]
```
; When you set the value of the InstallDefaultComponents key
; to Yes, Setup will install default networking components.
; The components to be set are TCP/IP, File and Print Sharing,
; and Client for Microsoft Networks.
    InstallDefaultComponents=Yes
```

[Identification]
```
    JoinDomain = YourCorpNet
    DomainAdmin = YourCorpAdmin
    DomainAdminPassword = Your AdminPassword
```

```
[NetAdapters]
; In this example, there are two network adapters, Adapter01
; and Adapter02. Note that the adapter specified here as 01 is not
; always local area network (LAN) connection 1 in the user interface.
; The network adapters in this example are not identical.
    Adapter01 = Params.Adapter01
    Adapter02 = Params.Adapter02

[NetBindings]
    Enable = MS_WLBS, Adapter01
    Enable = MS_TCPIP, Adapter02

[Params.Adapter01]
; Specifies which adapter is number one.
    PseudoAdapter = No
    PreUpgradeInstance = E100B1
; Note that the InfID key must match a valid PNP ID in the
; system. For example, a valid PNP ID might look like the
; following: InfID = PCI\VEN_8086&DEV_1229.
    InfID = Your_PNP_ID_for_Adapter01
    BusType = PCI
; The ConnectionName key specifies the name for the network connection
; associated with the network adapter that you are installing.
    ConnectionName = "Connection1"

[Params.Adapter02]
; Specifies which adapter is number two.
    PseudoAdapter = No
    PreUpgradeInstance = E190x2
; Note that the InfID key must match a valid PNP ID in the
; system. For example, a valid PNP ID might look like the
; following: InfID = PCI\VEN_10b7&DEV_9050
    InfID = Your_PNP_ID_for_Adapter02
    BusType = PCI
; The ConnectionName key specifies the name for the network connection
; associated with the network adapter that you are installing.
    ConnectionName = "Connection2"

[NetProtocols]
    MS_TCPIP = Params.MS_TCPIP
    MS_NetMon = Params.MS_NetMon

[Params.MS_TCPIP]
    AdapterSections = params.MS_TCPIP.Adapter01,params.MS_TCPIP.Adapter02
```

```
[Params.MS_TCPIP.Adapter01]
    SpecificTo = Adapter01
    DNSServerSearchOrder = 192.31.56.150
    Wins = Yes
    WinsServerList = 192.31.56.150
    NetBIOSOptions = 0
    DHCP = No
    IPAddress = 192.31.56.90,192.31.56.91
    SubnetMask = 255.255.255.0,255.255.255.0
    DefaultGateway = 192.31.56.150

[Params.MS_TCPIP.Adapter02]
    SpecificTo = Adapter02
    DNSServerSearchOrder = 192.31.56.150
    Wins = Yes
    WinsServerList = 192.31.56.150
    NetBIOSOptions = 0
    DHCP = No
    IPAddress = 192.31.56.92
    SubnetMask = 255.255.255.0
    DefaultGateway = 192.31.56.150

[Params.MS_NetMon]

[Params.MS_WLBS]
; This section contains keys specific to setting the properties of
; Network Load Balancing.
    HostPriority = 1
    ClusterModeOnStart = 0
    ClusterIPAddress = 192.31.56.91
    ClusterNetworkMask = 255.255.255.0
    DedicatedIPAddress = 192.31.56.90
    DedicatedNetworkMask = 255.255.255.0
    ClusterName = cluster.domain.com
    MulticastSupportEnable = 0
    MaskSourceMAC = 1
    RemoteControlCode = 0x00000000
    RemoteControlUDPPort = 2504
    RemoteControlEnabled = 1
    Ports =
    80,80,Both,Multiple,None,Equal,443,443,Both,Multiple,Single,Equal
    AliveMsgPeriod = 2000
    AliveMsgTolerance = 10
    NumActions = 50
    NumPackets = 100
    NumAliveMsgs = 10
    DescriptorsPerAlloc = 512
    MaxDescriptorAllocs = 512
    ConnectionCleanupDelay = 300000
    NBTSupportEnable = 1
```

```
[NetClients]
    MS_MSClient = Params.MS_Client

[Params.MS_Client]

[NetServices]
    MS_Server = Params.MS_Server
    MS_WLBS = Params.MS_WLBS

[Params.MS_Server]
    Optimizations = Balance

[NetOptionalComponents]
    Netmontools = 1
```

Sample 6 – Install Windows 2000 Advanced Server with Windows Clustering

The following answer file installs Windows 2000 Advanced Server with Windows Clustering.

```
; Microsoft Windows 2000 Advanced Server.
; © 1994–1999 Microsoft Corporation. All rights reserved.
;
; Sample Answer File for Unattended Setup
;
; This file contains information about how to automate the installation
; or upgrade of Windows 2000 Advanced Server so that the Setup program
; runs without requiring user input.
;

[Unattended]
    UnattendMode = FullUnattended
    TargetPath = Advsrv
    FileSystem = ConvertNTFS
    OemPreinstall = Yes
    OemSkipEula = Yes
```

[GuiUnattended]
; Sets the TimeZone. For example, to set the TimeZone for the
; Pacific Northwest, use a value of "004." Be sure to use the
; numeric value that represents your own time zone. To look up
; a numeric value, see the Unattend.doc file on the Windows 2000 CD.
    TimeZone = "*YourTimeZone*"
; It is recommended that you change the administrator password
; before the computer is placed at its final destination.
    AdminPassword = AdminPassword
; Tells Unattended Setup to turn AutoLogon on and log on once.
    AutoLogon = Yes
    AutoLogonCount = 1
    AdvServerType = Servernt
    OemSkipWelcome = 1
; The OemSkipRegional key allows Unattended Setup to skip
; RegionalSettings when the final location of the computer is unknown.
    OemSkipRegional = 1

[LicenseFilePrintData]
; This section is used for server installs.
    AutoMode = "PerServer"
    AutoUsers = "50"

[UserData]
    FullName = "*Your user name*"
    OrgName = "*Your organization name*"
; It is recommended that you avoid the use of spaces in the
; ComputerName value.
    ComputerName = "*YourComputer_name*"
; To ensure a fully unattended installation, you must provide a value
; for the ProductId key.
    ProductId = "*Your product ID*"

[Display]
    BitsPerPel = 8
    XResolution = 800
    YResolution = 600
    VRefresh = 70

[Networking]
; When you set the value of the InstallDefaultComponents key
; to Yes, Setup will install default networking components.
; The components to be set are TCP/IP, File and Print Sharing,
; and Client for Microsoft Networks.
    InstallDefaultComponents = Yes

[Identification]
    JoinDomain = *YourCorpNet*
    DomainAdmin = *YourCorpAdmin*
    DomainAdminPassword = *YourAdminPassword*

[NetAdapters]
; In this example there are three network adapters, Adapter 01,
; Adapter 02, and Adapter 03. The adapter specified here as 01 is not
; always LAN connection 1 in the user interface. The network adapters
; in this example are not identical.

```
  Adapter01 = Params.Adapter01
  Adapter02 = Params.Adapter02
  Adapter03 = Params.Adapter03
```

[Params.Adapter01]
; Specifies which adapter is number one.
; Note that the NetCardAddress key must match a valid address of the
; adapter in the system. For example, a valid address might look like
; the following: NetCardAddress = 0x00C04F778A5A
  NetCardAddress = *YourNetCardAddress*
; The ConnectionName key specifies the name for the network connection
; associated with the network adapter that you are installing.
  ConnectionName = *CorpNet*

[Params.Adapter02]
; Specifies which adapter is number two. Note that the
; NetCardAddress key must match a valid address of the adapter
; in the system. For example, a valid address might look like the
; following: NetCardAddress = 0x00C04F778A5A
  NetCardAddress = *YourNetCardAddress*
; The ConnectionName key specifies the name for the network connection
; associated with the network adapter that you are installing.
  ConnectionName = *VendorNet*

[Params.Adapter03]
; Specifies which adapter is number three. Note that the
; NetCardAddress key must match a valid address of the adapter
; in the system. For example, a valid address might look like the
; following: NetCardAddress = 0x00C04F778A5A
  NetCardAddress = *YourNetCardAddress*
; The ConnectionName key specifies the name for the network connection
; associated with the network adapter that you are installing.
  ConnectionName = *PrivateNet*

[NetClients]
; Installs the Client for Microsoft Networks.
  MS_MSClient = Params.MS_MSClient

[Params.MS_MSClient]

[NetProtocols]
; Installs only the TCP/IP protocol.
  MS_TCPIP = Params.MS_TCPIP

[Params.MS_TCPIP]
; This section configures TCP/IP properties.
  AdapterSections =
  Params.MS_TCPIP.Adapter01,params.MS_TCPIP.Adapter02,params.MS_TCPIP.A
  dapter03

[Params.MS_TCPIP.Adapter01]
; CorpNet on Adapter01 uses DHCP server information.
  SpecificTo = Adapter01
  DHCP = Yes
  DNSServerSearchOrder = 172.31.240.226, 172.31.240.225
  DNSSuffixSearchOrder = *CorpNet, dns.domain.com*
  DNSDomain = *CorpNet*

[Params.MS_TCPIP.Adapter02]
; VendorNet on Adapter02 uses local DHCP information.
  SpecificTo = Adapter02
  DHCP = Yes

[Params.MS_TCPIP.Adapter03]
; PrivateNet on Adapter03 uses static information.
  SpecificTo = Adapter03
  DHCP = No
  WINS = No
  IPAddress = 10.2.0.41
  SubnetMask = 255.255.0.0
  DefaultGateway = 2.2.2.2
  DNSServerSearchOrder = 10.2.0.253, 10.2.0.254

[NetServices]
; Installs File and Print services.
  MS_Server = Params.MS_Server

[Params.MS_Server]

[Components]
; Installs Windows Clustering and Administration components on
; Advanced Server when you set the value to On.
  Cluster = On

[Cluster]
  Name = *CorpCluster*
  Action = Form
  Account = *CorpAdmin*
  Domain = *CorpNet*
  IPAddr = 172.31.240.227
  Subnet = 255.255.248.0
  Network = *CorpNet,ALL*
  Network = *VendorNet,ALL*

```
[GuiRunOnce]
; You can automate the running of Cluscfg.exe by placing Cluscfg.exe
; in the [GuiRunOnce] section of the Unattended answer file. This
; executes Cluscfg.exe and configures clustering on the first startup
; after GUI mode Setup has completed.
; You must include the full path to the program between the quotes.
    "%Windir%\Cluster\Cluscfg.exe -unattend"

[NetOptionalComponents]
    NETMONTOOLS = 1
```

A P P E N D I X   D

Deployment Tools

Throughout this book, there are references to tools that you can use to help with your deployment of Microsoft® Windows® 2000. Table D.1 summarizes those tools to give you a quick reference of their names and a short description of each.

Where to Find More Information About These Tools

You can find additional information about the tools mentioned in this appendix in the following locations:

- For information about tools provided with the Windows 2000 operating system, see Windows 2000 Help.

- For information about installing and using the Windows 2000 Support Tools and Support Tools Help, see the file Sreadme.doc in the \Support\Tools folder of the Windows 2000 operating system CD.

- For information about tools that are included in the full *Microsoft®* *Windows® 2000 Server Resource Kit*, see the ResourceLink on the Web Resources page at http://windows.microsoft.com/windows2000/reskit/webresources.

Note An asterisk (*) next to the tool name indicates that this tool is included on the Windows 2000 operating system CD. Not all of these tools are installed by default when you install the operating system; some are installed as part of the Windows 2000 Support Tools.

Table D.1   Deployment Tools

Tool Name	File Name	Location in This Book	Description
* Active Directory Connector (ADC) MMC snap-in	Adcadmin.msc	Chapter 20, "Synchronizing Active Directory with Exchange Server Directory Service"	This Microsoft® Management Console (MMC) snap-in enables you to synchronize and manage communications between Microsoft® Active Directory™ and Microsoft® Exchange Server version 5.5 directory service.
* Active Directory Users and Computers MMC snap-in	Dsa.msc	Chapter 9, "Designing the Active Directory Structure" Chapter 11, "Planning Distributed Security" Chapter 20, "Synchronizing Active Directory with Exchange Server Directory Service" Chapter 24, "Applying Change and Configuration Management"	This MMC snap-in is a graphical directory administration tool that enables you to add, modify, delete, and organize the Windows 2000 user accounts, computer accounts, security and distribution groups, and published resources in your organization's directory. This tool is installed on computers configured as domain controllers.
ApiMon	Apimon.exe	Chapter 21, "Testing Applications for Compatibility With Windows 2000"	An application monitor tool that counts and times application programming interface (API) calls. Use the monitor to report a count of API calls and the timings for each or to report a trace of API calls in the sequence in which they occur. You can find this tool in the *Microsoft® Windows® 2000 Resource Kit* Tools Help.
* ClonePrincipal	Clonepr.dll Clone-gg.vbs Clone-ggu.vbs Clone-lg.vbs Clone-pr.vbs Sidhist.vbs ADsSecurity.dll ADsError.dll	Chapter 9 "Designing the Active Directory Structure" Chapter 10 "Determining Domain Migration Strategies"	A tool used for domain migration. Use this tool to clone a user or a group from a Microsoft® Windows NT® version 4.0 source domain or from a Windows 2000 source domain to a Windows 2000 native-mode domain without removing the source account. The original account security identifier (SID) is added to the history of the new account to maintain resource access.

(continued)

Table D.1   Deployment Tools *(continued)*

Tool Name	File Name	Location in This Book	Description
* Clustcfg	Clustcfg.exe	Chapter 18, "Ensuring the Availability of Applications and Services"	An essential configuration tool for Windows Clustering.
* Connection Manager	Package of tools	Chapter 7, "Determining Network Connectivity Strategies"	A graphical-based tool that lets you create custom connection packages to simplify client configuration.
* Dependency Walker	Depends.exe	Chapter 21, "Testing Applications for Compatibility With Windows 2000"	A tool that scans all of the dependent modules required by an application. This tool detects problems, such as a missing or invalid file. Use Dependency Walker to debut applications that are written for or converted to Windows 2000.
* Disk Administrator	Windisk.exe	Chapter 15 "Upgrading and Installing Member Servers"	A graphical-based disk management tool provided on Microsoft® Windows NT® systems. This tool allows you to back up and restore your disk configuration information.
* Disk Defragmenter MMC snap-in	Compmgmt.mmc	Chapter 19 "Determining Windows 2000 Storage Management Strategies"	This MMC snap-in allows you to locate files and folders that have become fragmented and to reorganize clusters on a disk volume. You can organize clusters so that files, directories, and free space are physically more contiguous.
* Disk Management MMC snap-in	Compmgmt.mmc	Chapter 19 "Determining Windows 2000 Storage Management Strategies"	This MMC snap-in is a graphical tool for managing disks and volumes. It supports partitions, logical drives, new dynamic volumes, and remote disk management.

(continued)

Table D.1   Deployment Tools *(continued)*

Tool Name	File Name	Location in This Book	Description
* Group Policy MMC snap-in	Gpedit.msc	Chapter 11 "Planning Distributed Security" Chapter 12 "Planning Your Public Key Infrastructure" Chapter 23 "Defining Client Administration and Configuration Standards" Chapter 24 "Applying Change and Configuration Management"	This MMC snap-in is a graphical Group Policy administration tool that enables a system administrator to create a specific desktop configuration for a particular group of users. Group Policy settings define the various components of the user's desktop, for example, programs that are available to users, programs that appear on the user's desktop, and Start menu options.
Internet Explorer Administration Kit (IEAK)	Package of tools	Chapter 23, "Defining Client Administration and Configuration Standards"	A set of tools that enables you to customize configuration and settings for Microsoft® Internet Explorer. Note: IEAK is not included with Windows 2000. For more information about IEAK, see "Additional Resources" later in this chapter.
* Ipconfig	Ipconfig.exe	Chapter 6, "Preparing Your Network Infrastructure For Windows 2000" Chapter 15, "Upgrading and Installing Member Servers"	A character-based TCP/IP configuration and diagnostic tool. Use this tool to verify the TCP/IP configuration parameters on newly upgraded Windows 2000 systems. For example, you can verify the IP address, subnet mask, and default gateway.
* Internet Information Services MMC snap-in	iis.msc	Chapter 15, "Upgrading and Installing Member Servers"	The Microsoft® Internet Information Services (IIS) MMC snap-in is a powerful site administration tool that provides access to all of your server settings. Use the IIS snap-in to manage a complex site on your corporate intranet and to publish information on the Internet.
* LDAP Data Interchange Format	Ldifde.exe	Chapter 9, "Designing the Active Directory Structure"	A command line tool that does bulk importing and exporting of Active Directory data.

(continued)

Table D.1   Deployment Tools *(continued)*

Tool Name	File Name	Location in This Book	Description
* Microsoft License Server	Licmgr.exe	Chapter 16, "Deploying Terminal Services"	A tool that stores, tracks, and validates Windows 2000 Terminal Services client access licenses.
* Microsoft Management Console (MMC)	Mmc.exe	Chapter 1, "Introducing Windows 2000 Deployment Planning"	A graphical framework that hosts administrative tools. You can use MMC snap-ins to administer networks, computers, users, services, and other system components.
		Chapter 9, "Designing the Active Directory Structure"	
		Chapter 10, "Determining Domain Migration Strategies"	
		Chapter 11, "Planning Distributed Security"	
		Chapter 12, "Planning Your Public Key Infrastructure"	
		Chapter 15, "Upgrading and Installing Member Servers"	
		Chapter 16, "Deploying Terminal Services"	
		Chapter 19, "Determining Windows 2000 Storage Management Strategies"	
		Chapter 20, "Synchronizing Active Directory with Exchange Server Directory Service"	
		Chapter 23, "Defining Client Administration and Configuration Standards"	
		Chapter 24, "Applying Change and Configuration Management"	

(continued)

Table D.1   Deployment Tools *(continued)*

Tool Name	File Name	Location in This Book	Description
* Microsoft Network Monitor	Netmon.exe	Chapter 8, "Using Systems Management Server to Analyze Your Network Infrastructure"	A graphical tool for capturing and analyzing data about your network. This tool allows you to track network traffic patterns and to diagnose networking problems on local area networks (LANs).
Muisetup	Muisetup.exe	Chapter 23, "Defining Client Administration and Configuration Standards"	A tool used to configure the MultiLanguage version of Windows 2000. You can change the default user interface (UI) or add or remove UI languages by using Muisetup.exe.
* Netdom	Netdom.exe	Chapter 10, "Determining Domain Migration Strategies"	A domain management tool that allows you to manage Windows 2000 domain and trust relationships from a command line. You can also control computer domain membership with this tool.
* Ping	Ping.exe	Chapter 15, "Upgrading and Installing Member Servers"	A character-based TCP/IP configuration and diagnostic tool. This tool is useful to verify TCP/IP configuration and to diagnose connection failures.
* Remote Installation Services (RIS)	Package of tools, including RISetup.exe RIPrep.exe RBFG.exe OSChooser.exe	Chapter 24, "Applying Change and Configuration Management	A package of tools that allows you to create custom Windows 2000 Professional images, set these images up on Remote Installation Services (RIS) servers, and use Group Policy to install them automatically on client computers.

(continued)

Table D.1   Deployment Tools *(continued)*

Tool Name	File Name	Location in This Book	Description
Registry Backup	Regback.exe	Chapter 15, "Upgrading and Installing Member Servers"	This tool is located on the *Microsoft® Windows NT® Server Resource Kit* and the *Microsoft® Windows® 2000 Server Resource Kit* companion CDs. This tool backs up the registry to files without the use of tape so that, in case of problems with configuration, you can restore your original registry settings. As with any critical data, you need to back up your registry often, especially before you install and test applications whose stability is unknown.
			You can restore the registry by using Regrest.exe, which you can also find on the CDs mentioned in the preceding paragraph.
* Routing and Remote Access MMC snap-in	Rrasmgmt.mmc	Chapter 7, "Determining Network Connectivity Strategies"	This MMC snap-in is a graphical tool for the administration and configuration of Routing and Remote Access in Windows 2000.
* Setup Manager	Setupmgr.exe	Chapter 13, "Automating Server Installation and Upgrade"	A wizard-based tool that helps you create unattended scripts. Setup Manager also creates a network distribution share, which is required for unattended and Sysprep deployments.
		Chapter 18, "Ensuring the Availability of Applications and Services"	
		Chapter 25, "Automating Client Installation and Upgrade"	

(continued)

Table D.1   Deployment Tools *(continued)*

Tool Name	File Name	Location in This Book	Description
* Setupcl	Setupcl.exe	Chapter 13, "Automating Server Installation and Upgrade" Chapter 25, "Automating Client Installation and Upgrade"	This command line tool works in conjunction with Sysprep to prepare the hard disk on the master computer so that a disk imaging utility can transfer an image of the hard disk to other computers. This tool regenerates new security identifiers (SIDs).
SMS Installer	Package of tools	Chapter 14, "Using Systems Management Server to Deploy Windows 2000"	A Microsoft® Systems Management Server (SMS) tool that prepares applications for software distribution. SMS Installer can generate attended and unattended installation scripts that you can fully customize.
SMS Query Extract	SMSExtract.mdb for Microsoft Access SMSextract.xls for Microsoft Excel	Chapter 8, "Using Systems Management Server to Analyze Your Network Infrastructure"	A data extraction tool for SMS that allows you to use SMS queries in Microsoft® Access or Microsoft® Excel.
* Sysprep	Sysprep.exe	Chapter 2, "Creating a Deployment Roadmap" Chapter 13, "Automating Server Installation and Upgrade" Chapter 18, "Ensuring the Availability of Applications and Services" Chapter 23, "Defining Client Administration and Configuration Standards" Chapter 24, "Applying Change and Configuration Management" Chapter 25, "Automating Client Installation and Upgrade"	An installation tool that enables disk duplication. Sysprep allows you to install a system with Windows 2000 applications and then duplicate it to other systems.

(continued)

Table D.1   Deployment Tools *(continued)*

Tool Name	File Name	Location in This Book	Description
* Terminal Services Client Creator	Tsclient.exe	Chapter 16, "Deploying Terminal Services"	A graphical tool that creates floppy disks for Terminal Services Client software on these operating systems: Microsoft® Windows® for Workgroups, Microsoft® Windows® 95, Microsoft® Windows® 98, and Microsoft® Windows NT® Server.
* Terminal Services Configuration MMC snap-in	Tscc.msc	Chapter 16, "Deploying Terminal Services"	This MMC snap-in allows you to manage your Terminal Services configuration. When you modify options by using this tool, they are global unless you choose to inherit information from the same options located in the user configuration.
* Terminal Services Manager	Tsadmin.exe	Chapter 16, "Deploying Terminal Services"	A graphical tool that allows you to manage all Windows 2000 servers that are running Terminal Services. With this tool, administrators can view current users, servers, and processors. In addition, you can send messages to specific users, and use the remote control feature and terminal processes.
* Utility Manager	Utilman.exe	Appendix E, "Accessibility for People with Disabilities"	This tool enables an administrator to designate which computers automatically open accessibility tools when Windows 2000 starts.
Windows DNA Performance Kit	Package of tools	Chapter 18, "Ensuring the Availability of Applications and Services"	This set of tools enables you to test and tune the performance of your applications. The kit contains performance information on Component Services and IIS as well as tools to simulate the effect of many users accessing your IIS or Component Services application. For more information about this set of tools, see "Additional Resources" later in this chapter.

(continued)

Table D.1   Deployment Tools *(continued)*

Tool Name	File Name	Location in This Book	Description
* Windows Installer	Built-in service	Chapter 1, "Introducing Windows 2000 Deployment Planning" Chapter 24, "Applying Change and Configuration Management" Chapter 25, "Automating Client Installation and Upgrade" Appendix A, "Sample Planning Worksheets"	A powerful new installation service in Windows 2000 that standardizes the way applications are installed on multiple computers. Windows Installer uses package files with an .msi extension to install applications.
* Windows Management Instrumentation (WMI)	Built-in interface	Chapter 1, "Introducing Windows 2000 Deployment Planning" Appendix A, "Sample Planning Worksheets"	A management infrastructure in Windows 2000 that supports monitoring and controlling system resources through a common set of interfaces and provides a logically organized, consistent model of Windows operation, configuration, and status. With Windows Management Instrumentation (WMI), administrators can correlate data and events from multiple sources on a local or organization-wide basis. WMI allows you to create custom applications and snap-ins by giving you access to Windows 2000 objects.
* Windows Script Host (WSH)	Cscript.exe Wscipt.exe	Chapter 1, "Introducing Windows 2000 Deployment Planning" Appendix A, "Sample Planning Worksheets"	A tool that supports direct execution of Microsoft® Visual Basic® Script, Java, and other scripts from the user interface or command line.
* WinInstall LE	Package of tools	Chapter 24, "Applying Change and Configuration Management"	A graphical repackaging tool from Veritas Software for Windows Installer. This tool allows you to quickly and easily repackage existing applications (pre–Windows Installer) into packages suitable for distribution with Windows Installer.

(continued)

Table D.1   Deployment Tools (*continued*)

Tool Name	File Name	Location in This Book	Description
* Winnt	Winnt.exe	Chapter 13, "Automating Server Installation and Upgrade" Chapter 25, "Automating Client Installation and Upgrade" Appendix B, "Setup Commands" Appendix C, "Sample Answer Files for Unattended Setup"	A Setup command that you can use for a clean installation of Microsoft® Windows® 2000 Server or Microsoft® Windows® 2000 Professional on a computer running Microsoft® MS-DOS® or Microsoft® Windows® 3.*x*
* Winnt32	Winnt32.exe	Chapter 13, "Automating Server Installation and Upgrade" Chapter 25, "Automating Client Installation and Upgrade" Appendix B, "Setup Commands" Appendix C, "Sample Answer Files for Unattended Setup"	A Setup command that you can use for a clean installation or upgrade to Windows 2000 Server or Windows 2000 Professional on a computer running Windows NT 4.0, Windows 95, or Windows 98.

Additional Resources

- For more information about IEAK, see the Microsoft Internet Explorer Administration Kit (IEAK) link on the Web Resources page at http://windows.microsoft.com/windows2000/reskit/webresources.

- For more information about the Windows DNA Performance Kit, see the Windows DNA Performance Kit link on the Web Resources page at http://windows.microsoft.com/windows2000/reskit/webresources.

APPENDIX E

Accessibility for People with Disabilities

Microsoft is dedicated to making its products and services accessible and usable for everyone. Microsoft® Windows® 2000 includes new and enhanced accessibility features that benefit users in all enterprises and professions. These features make it easier to customize the computer and give users with disabilities better access to the programs and applications they need to do their work.

In This Appendix

Appendix Goals

This appendix will help you develop the following:

- A plan for accommodating operating system built-in features and third-party add-on devices for users with disabilities.

- A prioritized list of components and features for Windows 2000 upgrade considerations.

Related Information in the Resource Kit

- For more information about installing software, see "Software Installation and Maintenance" in the *Microsoft® Windows® 2000 Server Resource Kit Distributed Systems Guide*.

- For more information about using Group Policy, see "Group Policy" in the *Microsoft Windows 2000 Server Resource Kit Distributed Systems Guide*.

Overview of Accessibility in Windows 2000

Accessibility means equal access to computer software for everyone, including people with cognitive, hearing, physical, or visual disabilities. Cognitive disabilities can mean learning impairments, Down syndrome, dyslexia, and language impairments such as illiteracy. Users with hearing disabilities include people who are deaf or hard-of-hearing. Physical disabilities include cerebral palsy, tremors, seizures from epilepsy, lack of limbs or digits, and paralysis. Visual impairments include blindness and various kinds of low vision, such as colorblindness and tunnel vision. For Windows 2000, accessibility means making computers more usable through a flexible, customizable user interface, alternative input and output methods, and better visibility of screen elements.

Accessibility Benefits with Windows 2000

The number of individuals with disabilities who use computers is growing, and with that growth comes a greater need for employers to accommodate them with assistive technologies. Recent legislation, including the Workforce Investment Law of 1998, mandates such accommodation. To the greatest extent possible, employees with disabilities must have computer access that is comparable to access by employees who do not have disabilities. To this end, several technologies that are built into Windows 2000 are available so that enterprises can configure their computers with the accessibility features they need.

Many of these features have added functionality beyond Microsoft® Windows® 98 and Microsoft® Windows NT® operating systems. New features, as well as existing ones, are described in this appendix. Some of the new and significantly enhanced features and tools in Windows 2000 are Microsoft® Active Accessibility®, Accessibility Wizard, Magnifier, Narrator, On-Screen Keyboard, Utility Manager, high-visibility mouse pointers, Synchronized Accessible Media Interchange (SAMI), and high-contrast color schemes.

With Windows 2000, users and administrators can perform the following functions:

Override defaults for multiple-user customized settings. Administrators can set a wide range of accessibility and other options for groups of users by using Control Panel, the Accessibility Wizard, and Utility Manager.

Quickly and easily navigate Windows. Special features, such as hot keys and Active Desktop™, facilitate access to objects on the desktop, Windows Explorer, other servers on the network, and Internet Explorer; give quick access to Windows; and help users open folders and create individualized settings.

Use a wider range of assistive technology. With Microsoft Active Accessibility, applications work more effectively with third-party and other add-on accessibility aids, such as speech recognition systems and other forms of assistive devices. Invisible to the user, Active Accessibility upgrades and extends the Microsoft Windows operating system.

Customize input methods. Expanded configurations of keyboards, including On-Screen Keyboard, special mouse settings, and other options, let users customize their user interface (UI) schemes.

Configure options through a single entry point. Located in the Start menu, the Accessibility Wizard makes it possible for administrators and users to set up computers with the most commonly used features and to customize those features for each user.

Magnify a portion of the screen for an enlarged display. Several abbreviated features, such as Magnifier, make it possible for users to work away from their customary assistive devices.

Maneuver within Windows. Keyboard shortcuts and personalized keyboard options assist users who are working in programs and applications.

Set sound options to suit individualized hearing needs. In addition to customizable features, such as volume adjustment and multimedia options, several accessibility features, such as ShowSounds and SoundSentry, give people with hearing impairments control of their audio environment.

Set options for users with visual requirements. Features include Narrator, a text-to-speech utility that is built into the operating system; ToggleKeys, a feature that provides audio cues when the user presses certain locking keys; and event cues that are located in the Sounds and Multimedia icon in Control Panel.

Use keyboard filters to customize keys to aid various cognitive, hearing, mobility, and visual needs.
The FilterKeys feature adjusts keyboard response time and forgives accidental pressing of keys.

Assign contrast, color, timing, and sizing schemes for screen elements.
Expanded ranges of screen elements, such as high-visibility mouse pointers and high-contrast color schemes, and the Accessibility Wizard give users options that suit their needs and preferences, such as greater visibility of the insertion point indicator (sometimes called the caret) and the ability to turn off animations.

Gain greater control of the personal computer by using third-party devices.
The SerialKeys feature is designed for people who are unable to use standard UI options and need add-on assistance from augmentative devices. This feature allows users to attach an alternative input device to the computer's serial port.

Considerations Before Upgrading to Windows 2000

Microsoft and other developers of software and hardware features are continuously working to improve options for people with disabilities. Because of this effort, some accessibility features might still be in development or testing when new versions of software are released. Sometimes, new features are completed after a release and are included with the next version. Also, some technologies have not yet been created that are compatible with, or that can be built into, Windows 2000. For these reasons, information technology professionals need to carefully review the needs of the users they support before deploying to enterprises that have accessibility requirements. As part of your deployment planning and testing, make sure that you test all required assistive devices for compatibility with Windows 2000.

You might consider upgrading selected existing features and programs on your computers, rather than making a complete Windows 2000 installation. The upgrade process can be automated, and with Active Directory™ directory service, you can manage Group Policy object applications within an organizational unit, a domain, or a site. Although a complete installation, sometimes called a clean installation, allows a partitioned combination, it does not migrate settings from the previous operating system, which means that users lose personalized settings and applications.

Note Whether you do a complete installation or an upgrade, it is important to do so with an updated Basic Input/Output System (BIOS) that is compatible with Windows 2000.

With assigned applications in Group Policy, administrators can advertise objects so that when a user selects them on the Start menu, the objects are automatically installed. Administrators might delete applications assigned in this way. When administrators publish applications instead of assigning them, the user has the option of installing them using Add/Remove Programs in Control Panel.

Active Accessibility is a core component in the Windows operating system that is built on Component Object Model (COM) and that defines how applications can exchange information about user interface (UI) elements. This technology reduces incompatibility with some accessibility aids but does not yet offer complete compatibility.

For more information about current technologies, see the Microsoft Accessibility link on the Web Resources page at http://windows.microsoft.com/windows2000/reskit/webresources.

For more information about installing software, see "Software Installation and Maintenance" in the *Microsoft® Windows® 2000 Server Resource Kit Distributed Systems Guide*.

Deploying Windows 2000 for Accessibility

Although the accessibility tools released with Windows 2000 provide some functionality for users with special needs, most users with disabilities need assistive tools with higher functionality for their daily use. By using hardware and software that independent vendors develop, people with disabilities can enhance their use of the Windows operating system. Be sure to test the compatibility of accessibility programs, applications, and devices with the Windows operating system to verify that drivers are compatible with Windows 2000.

Microsoft Active Accessibility

The Active Accessibility application programming interface is built into the Windows operating system. Based on OLE and COM, it allows accessibility aids to work with user interface elements. For the user, Active Accessibility is invisible. This technology facilitates compatibility with some accessibility aids.

Third-Party Products and Services

Microsoft works with independent manufacturers to produce compatible software and hardware for users with disabilities. One of the purposes of the Active Accessibility feature is to provide infrastructure that aids the operating system and applications in understanding each other for greater compatibility with these important devices. Using Utility Manager, which is a new feature in Windows 2000, vendors are now able to add their products for easier access.

Independent vendors—typically small companies that make specialized assistive devices—help people with disabilities to make better use of the Windows operating system. The following is a partial list of the types of devices and functionality that these independent vendors produce:

- Hardware and software tools that modify the behavior of the mouse and keyboard
- On-screen keyboards
- Programs that let users type by using a mouse or by voice activation

- Software that predicts words or phrases so that users can type more quickly and with fewer keystrokes
- Closed-captioned programs
- Alternative input devices, such as head-pointer, single-switch, eye-gaze, sip-and-puff, and voice-input devices
- Programs that enlarge or alter the color of the information on the screen
- Synthesized-speech programs or Braille-embossing printers that present the information that is on the screen

"Certified for Windows" Logo

Hardware and software vendors throughout the industry are collaborating to bring about accessible products for all computer users. Microsoft initiated the Certified for Windows program, which now applies to Windows 2000. This program promotes accessible design and includes a set of requirements and a checklist for application developers. A major goal of the program is to ensure quality and consistency in products that work on the Windows 2000 operating system. To qualify for the Certified for Windows logo, an application must be tested by VeriTest for compliance with the Application Specification for Windows 2000.

The specification addresses such requirements as closed captioning in place of relying on sound alone to convey information; visibility of the insertion point indicator (sometimes called the caret); and the ability to control mouse and keyboard and to turn off animations. One goal of this collaborative effort is to ensure quality and consistency in assistive devices for users with disabilities.

For more information about the Certified for Windows program, including application specifications, see the Application Specification Download link on the Web Resources page at http://windows.microsoft.com/windows2000/reskit/webresources.

Important Most third-party accessibility aids are compatible with specific versions of an operating system. Some add-on utilities can be intrusive in that they depend on file formats and programming interfaces to interpret data accurately to the user. Such dependencies change with each new operating system. Therefore, before you decide to upgrade, it is important to take inventory and perform compatibility testing with the new operating system and the applications you plan to use. For more information about emerging technologies and compatibility, see the Microsoft Accessibility link on the Web Resources page at http://windows.microsoft.com/windows2000/reskit/webresources.

Using SerialKeys for Add-on Hardware and Software

The SerialKeys feature allows you to attach third-party assistive devices to the computer's serial port. For example, you can connect alternative keyboards or augmentative communication devices to the personal computer's serial port. The SerialKeys feature is designed for people who are unable to use standard UI methods. However, SerialKeys also allows an augmentative device to work with the local keyboard and mouse.

Customizing the Computer for Accessibility Options

Windows 2000 installs accessibility options automatically. Moreover, users cannot delete accessibility options from the operating system after they are installed, including those options available in the Accessibility Wizard or Control Panel. In addition to new features, the Setup program retains the features that are installed by default when you upgrade from earlier versions of Windows. You can also install accessibility features on computers that are shared, such as public or workgroup servers.

Remote Installation and Unattended Setup from a CD

Using the Client Installation Wizard, you can remotely set up client computers if the computer supports remote installation. You can use Group Policy to control the installation options that you offer to users. There are four installation options: Automatic Setup, Custom Setup, Restart a Previous Setup Attempt, and Maintenance and Troubleshooting.

Automatic Setup   In Automatic Setup, the default option, Windows 2000 Remote Installation Services, uses unattended installation templates so that you can create options in the categories of operating system images. Using an unattended installation setup answer file, you can create several installation options, select items to be installed, and configure specific client computer options.

Custom Setup   Using the Custom Setup option, you can specify the computer name and Active Directory container in which you create the computer account object. This option also makes it possible to set up a computer for individual users within a group and to set up a client computer account in Active Directory before delivery of the computer to the user.

Restart a Previous Setup Attempt   This option restarts a previous or failed setup attempt. For example, if installation of the operating system image is started and connectivity to the Remote Installation Service server is interrupted, you can do the following to resume the installation: Restart the client computer; press F12 when prompted for a network service boot; and click **Restart a Previous Setup Attempt**.

Maintenance and Troubleshooting   The Maintenance and Troubleshooting feature gives administrators access to diagnostic utilities and other maintenance tools that are needed to maintain and troubleshoot client computers.

Windows Installer

A technology that installs, maintains, and removes software on client computers, Windows Installer displays self-repairing applications. If a user tries to delete a file, Windows Installer reinstates the missing files the next time the user tries to open them. For more information about Windows Installer, see the Windows Platform Software Development Kit (SDK) link on the Web Resources page at http://windows.microsoft.com/windows2000/reskit/webresources.

Group Policy

Group Policy is the network administrator's primary tool for managing groups of users and computers. The administrator can use the Microsoft® Management Console (MMC) Group Policy snap-in to specify managed desktop administrative and security options for groups of computers and users. Microsoft® Windows® 2000 Server includes more than 200 default settings for Group Policy. You can specify user installation options and permit or deny user access to specified choices by using the Client Installation Wizard. Group Policy is important to enterprises that have users with disabilities because you can use it to customize settings for groups of users who have the same assistive needs. Also, multiple users of the same computer can use their logon and password information to set their own desktop preferences, including certain accessibility options.

For more information about using Group Policy, see "Group Policy" in the *Microsoft® Windows® 2000 Server Resource Kit Distributed Systems Guide*.

Setting Multiple User Profiles

You can use the Accessibility Wizard to set multiple user profiles. The next user to log on to Windows can change the settings without deleting the previous settings. Individual settings are restored the next time a user logs on. This feature lets users or administrators set the user's preferences. Windows automatically presets features to default for other users. When accessibility features are turned off, users who do not need them do not notice that the features are installed; hence, people who require assistance, as well as those who do not, can use the computer. Multiple users of the same computer can use their logon and password information to set preferences and desktop settings, including any needed accessibility features.

Administrative Options

You can set administrative options for several features by using Accessibility Wizard or Control Panel. Settings that you can make in both include Set Automatic Time-outs/Automatic Reset, and Default Accessibility Settings. However, you must use the Accessibility Wizard if you want to save settings to a file to be used on another computer.

Accessibility Reset (Time-out)

Another useful feature for computers that multiple users share is the Accessibility Reset time-out feature. This component of both the Accessibility Wizard and Control Panel turns off accessibility functionality after the computer has been idle for a specified period of time. It then returns the operating system to its default configuration.

Note The Automatic Reset (time-out) feature does not turn off the SerialKeys feature.

Active Desktop

With Active Desktop, the user can personalize nearly everything on the desktop, in addition to displaying intranet and Internet content. Windows 2000 Explorer lets the user navigate through desktop elements, such as taskbar icons, files and shortcut icons, and other objects that are on the network. This feature gives a consistent interface on all categories of objects and for some users, can be an easier way to navigate to objects on the desktop than to use the mouse.

Customizing the Desktop

Here are examples of ways that users can customize their desktop with Active Desktop:

- Add Web pages containing active content to a desktop.
- Put a toolbar in a handier place on a desktop or taskbar.
- Rearrange frequently opened files and programs for quick access.
- Add an address bar to the taskbar or the desktop. This addition gives users the ability to type an Internet address without opening the browser first.

Desktop Toolbars

Users can create their own desktop toolbars with commands they frequently use. This is most useful for people who prefer to use the mouse rather than the keyboard; users who prefer the keyboard usually want to add commands to their Start menu.

System Status Icons

The ability to tab to the status icons on the system status area of the taskbar (sometimes called the system tray) is new in Windows 2000. When a user activates status icons for certain commonly used accessibility features, they appear in the system status area. Additionally, when the user presses a keyboard shortcut, an icon fills in the corresponding rectangle to show which key is activated. These status icons replace the status indicator of earlier versions of Windows.

Utility Manager

New in Windows 2000, Utility Manager brings time-saving value to users. An administrator can designate which computers automatically open accessibility tools when Windows 2000 starts. Then users can stop or restart the tools to suit their needs. Immediate access to such features as Narrator, Magnifier, or On-Screen Keyboard is important to some users.

Users and administrators can also use Utility Manager to customize most of the accessibility programs available on the computer. Administrators can open a dialog box and view what Windows 2000 accessibility tools are installed and the status of the tools. Administrators can also set up additional applications or run programs that install an add-on device. Although you can open Utility Manager through the Start menu, a quicker way to open it is by using the following shortcut keys: WINDOWS LOGO+U.

Note   The built-in programs that you can open from the Utility Manager are Magnifier, Narrator, and On-Screen Keyboard. In addition to applications that Microsoft has built into the operating system, third-party vendors can add applications to Utility Manager.

For more information about adding augmentative devices to Utility Manager, refer to the documentation for the specific third-party utility.

Configuring Accessibility Features in Windows 2000

Creating custom interfaces lets users with disabilities control their computing environment so that they can succeed in using the software they need to perform their work. Depending on each person's specific needs, users might find challenges with different aspects of Windows. Although accessibility features install automatically with Windows 2000, in a complete installation, previously configured options and settings must be reconfigured and new customized options must be configured for individual users.

Table E.1 describes some of the user aids that are built into the Windows 2000 operating system to make it more accessible. Because some features can apply to several disabilities, they are listed by particular difficulty, instead of by category of disability. For descriptions of features by category of disability, see the section "Setting Options by Type of Disability" later in this chapter.

Table E.1   Common User Difficulties and Their Solutions

User has difficulty...	Windows 2000 solutions
Customizing settings in a multiple-user network.	Accessibility Wizard, Administrative Options, Accessibility Options in Control Panel
Doing the following: ▪ Opening Windows or applications. ▪ Navigating through desktop elements and Windows. ▪ Customizing keyboard settings. ▪ Customizing display settings.	Hot keys, Utility Manager, Narrator, On-Screen Keyboard, Active Desktop, keyboard shortcuts, system status icons
Remembering what accessibility features are activated.	Accessibility Options in Control Panel
Finding a needed feature.	Accessibility Wizard for listing by disability
Remembering keyboard navigation indicators.	Accessibility Options and Display in Control Panel, Accessibility Wizard
Spelling words correctly.	Automatic Spell Checker, AutoComplete feature, AutoCorrect feature, keyboard shortcuts
Hearing, such as in the following situations: ▪ Hearing sound prompts. ▪ Distinguishing sounds. ▪ Hearing audible cues. ▪ Working in a noisy environment.	ShowSounds, SoundSentry, customizable sound schemes
Using standard keyboard configurations.	Dvorak keyboards, On-Screen Keyboard, MouseKeys
Using the keyboard due to slow response time.	RepeatKeys and keyboard options
Using the keyboard due to inadvertent hitting or bouncing off keys.	SlowKeys, BounceKeys, RepeatKeys, and ToggleKeys
Holding down two keys at the same time.	StickyKeys

(continued)

Table E.1   Common User Difficulties and Their Solutions *(continued)*

User has difficulty...	Windows 2000 solutions
Using standard user interface methods, including a mouse and keyboard.	Third-party voice-input utilities, Narrator, On-Screen Keyboard
Manipulating a mouse.	MouseKeys
Working with flashing events and other schemes that trigger seizures.	Accessibility Options in Control Panel, which allows the user to change timing, sound schemes, and color and contrast; and the Accessibility Wizard
Seeing or following the mouse pointer.	Mouse options in the Accessibility Wizard or Control Panel
Seeing keyboard status lights.	ToggleKeys
Seeing screen elements.	Narrator, Magnifier, Control Panel, and size, color, and contrast schemes in Accessibility Wizard
Functioning well with built-in accessibility features (needs add-on devices).	Active Accessibility, SerialKeys for third-party assistive devices
Finding third-party assistive devices and other accessibility information.	Microsoft Accessibility Web site (see the "Additional Resources" section in this appendix for details)

Users and administrators can use Accessibility Options in Control Panel to customize many of the accessibility features in Windows 2000. However, you can now configure many popular accessibility features using the Accessibility Wizard. For example, you can customize display, keyboard, mouse, and sound operation for the user's own particular needs by using either Control Panel or the Accessibility Wizard. The two ways to configure options are described in the following subsections.

Configuring Accessibility Options by Using the Accessibility Wizard

New in Windows 2000, the Accessibility Wizard makes it easier to set up accessibility preferences by particular needs a user might have, instead of by numeric value changes or by Control Panel settings. Available from the Start menu, the wizard provides a single entry point for many frequently used features. The user can also save settings to a file to configure other computers. Some options the wizard controls are sound and screen options, such as volume and font sizes; several keyboard options, such as keyboard filters and MouseKeys; and the ability to set administrative options.

Configuring Accessibility Options by Using Control Panel

The Accessibility Options icon in Control Panel allows users to easily customize properties that give users control of many of the accessibility features in Windows 2000. Users can turn the accessibility features on or off and can customize keyboard, sound, and mouse operations for the user's particular needs. Accessibility Options gives users access to the following features: StickyKeys, FilterKeys, ToggleKeys, SoundSentry, ShowSounds, MouseKeys, and SerialKeys.

In addition to the options for users with disabilities in Accessibility Options, Control Panel offers other ways to modify settings in a client computer. Users can modify settings in Display, Keyboard, Mouse, Sounds and Multimedia, and others. The following sections describe many other features as well as features designed specifically for users with disabilities.

Setting Options by Type of Disability

Creating custom interfaces gives users with disabilities control of their computing environment so that they can succeed in their work. A simplified user interface is a necessity for reducing the amount of navigation. The following are features and techniques in Windows 2000 that users and administrators can customize to suit their specific needs and preferences. Although many of these options might apply to the needs of more than one category of disability, for organization purposes, they are placed into groups by category of disability.

Options for Users with Cognitive Disabilities

Cognitive disabilities include developmental disabilities, such as Down syndrome; learning disabilities, such as dyslexia, language unfamiliarity, illiteracy, attention deficit disorder, and memory loss; and perceptual difficulties, such as slow response time. In addition to third-party assistive devices, for example, voice input utilities, some Windows built-in features can be especially helpful to people with cognitive disabilities. Examples are the IntelliSense® features, such as AutoCorrect, AutoComplete, and Automatic Spell Checking.

You can customize AutoComplete to include only the information that users need. For some users, these features facilitate their work considerably. However, for other users, with some features—such as AutoComplete or certain sound schemes—it is advantageous for users with cognitive disabilities to clear, rather than to select these options. Such features can cause distractions, especially if the user is working with a text-to-speech utility.

Several Windows 2000 accessibility features found in the Accessibility Wizard or Control Panel can be useful to people with cognitive disabilities. Users who are familiar with Windows NT version 4.0 or earlier need to know that special keyboard filters have been rearranged in Windows 2000. Both the Accessibility Wizard and Control Panel now allow users to adjust keyboard response time to ignore accidental pressing of keys and slow response time.

Keyboard options useful to people with cognitive disabilities are hot keys and other keyboard shortcuts. Additionally, the following features are also useful to people with cognitive disabilities: Narrator; Active Desktop; system status icons that show which features are activated; and sound options found in the Accessibility Wizard and Control Panel. Also, sound schemes can help draw attention to, or provide additional feedback for, tasks as the user does them.

Synchronized Accessible Media Interchange

Users with language-related difficulties might find Microsoft Synchronized Accessible Media Interchange (SAMI) useful to better understand speech through text captions. This Windows 2000 feature is described in the section "Options for Users with Hearing Impairments" later in this appendix.

Options for Users with Hearing Impairments

Users who are deaf or hard-of-hearing or who have limited ability to distinguish sounds might find the following options useful. These features incorporate sound scheme adjustments or visual media as substitutes for sound.

Customizable Sound Schemes

Users who are hard-of-hearing or who work in a noisy environment can adjust the pitch and timbre of sounds, as well as the volume associated with various on-screen events to make them easier to distinguish. The sounds are customizable either through the Accessibility Wizard or through Control Panel.

Windows provides sounds that users can associate with many events. These can be events that Windows or programs generate. If users have difficulty distinguishing between the default sounds, such as the beep to signal an inoperative keystroke, they can choose a new sound scheme, or design their own to make the sounds easier to identify. In Windows 2000, users can turn off the default downloading of sound files.

Adjusting the Volume

If the computer has a sound card, users can adjust the volume for all of the Windows sounds by using the Sounds and Multimedia icon in Control Panel. They can also adjust the sound volume by using the speaker icon on the taskbar or by using Volume Control.

Some users require visual feedback instead of sound. Users who are deaf might rely on sign language as their primary language and English as their second language. They might have difficulty reading pages that use custom fonts; that depart from typographical convention, such as mixing uppercase and lowercase letters; or that use animated text displays. In such instances, users are likely to benefit from customizable sounds and closed captioning.

The following Windows 2000 features are useful to people who are deaf or hard-of-hearing.

ShowSounds

ShowSounds, a feature in Control Panel, instructs applications that have closed captioning to display visual feedback in the form of closed captioning. In Windows 2000, users can choose to display closed captioning.

SoundSentry

In Windows 2000, the SoundSentry feature supports only those sounds that the computer's internal speaker generates; it cannot detect sounds made by a multimedia sound card. If the computer has a multimedia sound card, the user or administrator might need to turn off this hardware to force the computer's built-in speaker to play the sounds. In this way, SoundSentry can detect these sound events. The user needs to restart Windows for this change to take effect.

Synchronized Accessible Media Interchange

Use Microsoft Synchronized Accessible Media Interchange (SAMI)/Direct Show for closed captioning. SAMI is a format that developers, educators, and Web authors can use to create captions and audio descriptions in a single document. SAMI is based on HTML to provide a familiar, readable format. With SAMI, developers and others can create closed-captioned multimedia products. The Windows Media Player on the desktop synchronizes the captioning information for the user, who can then adjust captions to suit individual needs.

For more information about SAMI, see the Microsoft Accessibility link on the Web Resources page at http://windows.microsoft.com/windows2000/reskit/webresources.

Options for Users with Physical Disabilities

Some users are unable to perform certain manual tasks, such as using a mouse or typing two keys at the same time. Other users tend to hit multiple keys or bounce fingers off keys. Physical disabilities or mobility impairments include paralysis, repetitive stress injuries, cerebral palsy, erratic motion tremors, quadriplegia, or lack of limbs or fingers. Many users need keyboards and mouse functions adapted to their particular needs, or they rely exclusively on an alternative input device. Fortunately, a large number of input devices are available to users, including voice input utilities to control the computer with the user's voice and keyboard filters, on-screen keyboards, smaller and larger keyboards, eye-gaze pointing devices, and sip-and-puff systems that the user can operate by breath control. For more information about assistive devices and for a catalog of third-party accessibility devices, see the Microsoft Accessibility link on the Web Resources page at http://windows.microsoft.com/windows2000/reskit/webresources.

Keyboard Options

Impaired dexterity can make it difficult for a person to use a standard keyboard; however, keyboard filters built into Windows 2000 compensate somewhat by correcting for erratic motion tremors, slow response time, and similar conditions. Other kinds of keyboard filters include typing aids, such as word prediction and abbreviation expansion tools and add-on spelling checkers. The following sections describe input devices and features that vary from the standard keyboard. These features carry options that adapt the behavior of the keys to specific accessibility needs.

Note In most cases, it is not possible to apply the same keyboard behavior corrections to pointing devices, such as the mouse. This limitation restricts users with impaired dexterity to keyboard input.

On-Screen Keyboard

Some users have difficulty with both mouse and keyboard. However, they might be able to use an on-screen keyboard with another input method, such as a pointing device, a joystick connecting to the serial port, or the keyboard space bar used as a switch device. An on-screen keyboard is a utility that lets users select keys by using an alternative input mode. Users who can point but not click can use pointing devices, switches, or Morse-code input systems.

Note You need custom patch cables to operate in switch mode.

Users can set up and customize the Windows 2000 On-Screen Keyboard through the Start menu. The On-Screen Keyboard provides a minimum level of functionality for users with moderate mobility impairments. Many users with physical disabilities need a utility program with higher functionality for daily use. For more information about Windows-based on-screen keyboards, see the Microsoft Accessibility link on the Web Resources page at http://windows.microsoft.com/windows2000/reskit/webresources.

Note The On-Screen Keyboard is meant to be used as a temporary solution and not as a day-to-day alternative keyboard in place of a third-party on-screen keyboard.

Dvorak Keyboard

The Dvorak keyboard makes the most frequently typed characters on a keyboard more accessible to people who have difficulty typing on the standard QWERTY layout. There are three Dvorak layouts: one for people who use two hands to type, one for people who type with their left hand only, and one for people who type with their right hand only. Dvorak layouts reduce the degree of motion required to type common English text. This might help avoid some kinds of repetitive strain injuries associated with typing. You can either add the Dvorak keyboard as part of the Setup program or add it later. To configure the Dvorak keyboard, use the Keyboard icon in Control Panel.

Keyboard Shortcuts

Keyboard shortcuts are of paramount importance to users with disabilities. They are immeasurably valuable to users in nearly all categories of disabilities. These ALT commands and CTRL keys can help the user navigate through Windows 2000 more easily. Even without configuring accessibility features, the user can use the TAB key in dialog boxes to move the focus and then use the arrow keys to select items in a list. In property sheets that have multiple tabs, the user can select each property sheet in order from left to right. In Active Desktop, the user can add shortcut keys to the Start menu.

For more information about keyboard shortcuts, including shortcut keys, see Windows 2000 Help.

For more information about keyboard shortcuts, including an extensive list of accessibility keyboard shortcuts, see "Appendix H – Accessibility" in the *Microsoft Windows 98 Resource Kit.*

For more information about keyboard-only commands, accessibility shortcuts, and Microsoft® Natural® Keyboard keys, see the Microsoft Accessibility link on the Web Resources page at http://windows.microsoft.com/windows2000/reskit/webresources.

Hot Keys for Accessibility Features

Accessibility hot keys provide an immediate method of activating accessibility features for people who cannot use the computer without first having accessibility features in effect. A type of shortcut, hot keys let the user turn on a specific feature temporarily. Then, after a feature has been turned on, users can use the Accessibility Wizard or Accessibility Options in Control Panel to adjust the feature to individual preferences or to turn the feature on permanently. The same hot key temporarily turns off the feature if it gets in the way or if another person wants to use the computer without this feature.

Hot keys are designed to be unique key combinations that should not conflict with keys that programs use. If such a conflict does arise, the user can turn the hot keys off and still use the feature as needed. In a typical installation of Windows 2000, the accessibility hot keys are inactive to prevent them from conflicting with other programs.

StickyKeys for One-Finger or Mouthstick Typing

Many software programs require the user to press two or three keys at a time. For people who type using a single finger or a mouthstick, that is not possible. StickyKeys lets the user press one key at a time and instructs Windows to respond as if the keys are pressed simultaneously.

For shared computers, there is an optional feature to keep other users from being confused when StickyKeys is left on. If the option **Turn StickyKeys Off If Two Keys Are Pressed at Once** is activated, StickyKeys detects that two keys are held down simultaneously and automatically turns the StickyKeys feature off.

Some people do not like to have keyboard sounds, while others find them useful. Users can turn feedback sounds on or off in the StickyKeys properties by selecting the option **Make Sounds When Modifier Key Is Pressed**.

FilterKeys for Users with Impaired Manual Dexterity

Windows 2000 includes keyboard filters that work separately or combined to make input easier for users who have difficulty with the keyboard due to slow response time, erratic motion tremors, or a tendency to inadvertently hit or bounce off the keys. With the FilterKeys feature, users can adjust keyboard response time, and allow accidental pressing of keys and slow response time.

ToggleKeys for Users Who Inadvertently Brush Against the Lock Keys

ToggleKeys instructs Windows to play a high or low beep when the lock keys NUM LOCK, CAPS LOCK, or SCROLL LOCK are activated. This sound signals the user that one of these keys has been activated.

Mouse Options

Users with mobility impairments can now choose among options for size, color, and animation schemes. With the Mouse icon in Control Panel, users can adjust mouse properties to increase the pointer's visibility. This customizable feature, although not specifically for users with disabilities, is useful to users with visual impairment.

Adjusting Mouse Properties

With the Mouse icon in Control Panel, users can make the mouse pointer automatically move to the default buttons, such as OK or Apply, in dialog boxes, and can reverse the buttons so that the right button is the primary button. Users can also adjust other mouse settings, such as pointer rate of speed and acceleration; left-right orientation; and cursor size, color, shape, time between clicks, and animation. By selecting **I am blind or have difficulty seeing things on screen** and **I have difficulty using the keyboard or mouse**, users can set several accessibility Mouse options in the Accessibility Wizard.

MouseKeys for Keyboard-Only Input

Although Windows 2000 is designed so that users can perform all actions without a mouse, some programs might still require one, and a mouse might be more convenient for some tasks. MouseKeys in Control Panel is also useful for graphic artists and others who need to position the pointer with great accuracy. A user does not need to have a mouse to use this feature. With MouseKeys, users can control the mouse pointer with one finger, a mouthstick, or a headpointer by using the numeric keypad to move the mouse pointer. With this method, users can click, double-click, and move objects with both mouse buttons. When MouseKeys is activated, it emits a rising tone if sounds are turned on.

Options for Users with Seizure Sensitivity

To accommodate users with seizure disorders, including those with epilepsy, users can adjust screen elements, such as timing, color and contrast, and sound by using Accessibility Wizard or Control Panel in Windows. The range and selection in many of these features are expanded in Windows 2000. Users can also limit the number of fonts to one or more specified favorites. The following accessibility features can be customized for people with seizure disorders.

Timing Patterns

Timing patterns can affect users in many adverse ways. Users with seizure disorders, such as epilepsy, can be sensitive to screen refresh rates and blinking or flashing images. Settings in Windows 2000 Control Panel can prevent the default loading of animations and videos. Users can adjust the rate at which most objects flash to select a frequency that is less likely to trigger seizures. Users or administrators can alter the insertion point indicator (sometimes called the caret) blink rate, and can link it to flashing events for users who are sensitive to screen refresh rates. They can turn off blinking or flashing images.

Sound Schemes

In addition to users with hearing impairments or users in crowded or noisy environments, users with seizure sensitivity can also be susceptible to specific sounds. Settings in Windows 2000 can prevent the default loading of animations, videos, and sounds. Using Windows Control Panel, users can also assign custom sounds to any event. The ability to customize sound schemes, whether to turn sound on or off, or to adjust volume up or down, is becoming more important for users and takes many forms in Windows 2000 in support of people with various kinds of disabilities and requirements.

Color and Contrast Settings

Through Accessibility Options in Control Panel and Magnifier, users can adjust color and contrast settings. New to Windows 2000 is an expanded spectrum of color schemes, customizable to suit a user's individual needs. For more detailed information, see the following section on visual impairments.

Options for Users with Visual Impairments

The following accessibility features are useful to people who are blind or have low vision, colorblindness, tunnel vision, or other visual impairments: text-to-speech utilities, such as Narrator; keyboard shortcuts; Magnifier; and customizable features such as mouse pointer, color and contrast schemes, and other user interface elements.

Microsoft Narrator

Narrator is a minimally featured text-to-speech program included with the U.S. English version of Windows 2000. This new feature works through Active Accessibility to read objects on the screen, their properties, and their spatial relationships. Narrator has a number of options that let users customize the way a device reads screen elements. The Voice option lets users adjust the speed, volume, or pitch of the voice. The Reading option lets them select the typed characters they want the device to read aloud, such as Delete, Enter, printable characters, or modifiers. The Mouse Pointer option causes the mouse pointer to follow the active item on the screen. The **Announce events on screen** option lets users order the device to announce any of the following components when it displays them: new windows, menus, or shortcut menus. Narrator provides a minimum level of functionality for users with moderate visual impairments. Many users with low vision need a text-to-speech utility program with higher functionality for daily use. For more information about other Windows-based text-to-speech utilities, see the Microsoft Accessibility link on the Web Resources page at http://windows.microsoft.com/windows2000/reskit/webresources.

Note Narrator is a temporary aid and is not intended as a replacement for the full-featured text-to-speech utilities available from other software companies.

Keyboard Audio Cues

ToggleKeys is especially useful for people who accidentally press the CAPS LOCK key instead of the TAB key because it provides immediate feedback when they do so. ToggleKeys also functions with keyboards that do not have the status indicator lights for the CAPS LOCK, NUM LOCK, and SCROLL LOCK style of keyboard.

Microsoft Magnifier

Magnifier is a limited-function screen enlarger that magnifies a portion of the display of Windows 2000 to make the screen easier to read for people with slight visual impairments or whenever magnifying screen elements might be useful, such as during graphic editing. Magnifier displays an enlarged portion of the screen in a separate window. When Magnifier is on, the magnified area is merely a display and is not an active area. Magnifier provides a minimum level of functionality for users with moderate visual impairments. Many users with low vision need a magnification utility program with higher functionality for daily use. For more information about other Windows-based magnification utilities, see the Microsoft Accessibility link on the Web Resources page at http://windows.microsoft.com/windows2000/reskit/webresources.

Note Magnifier is not a replacement for the full-featured magnifiers available from other software companies.

Fonts

To select fonts, users click the Fonts icon in Control Panel to remove the fonts that they do not want to use. If they remove all TrueType customizable fonts and leave only raster fonts, users can also restrict the sizes that they use. TrueType fonts are device-independent fonts that are stored as outlines and that can be scaled to produce characters in varying sizes. Raster fonts are created with a printer language based on bitmap images. Removing fonts does not delete them from the hard drive, so users can easily reinstall the fonts for later use.

Note Limiting fonts in Control Panel also limits the number of fonts available to applications. This operation affects the display of documents on the screen and how they are printed; therefore, users need to use caution when limiting fonts.

Size and Color Schemes

In the Accessibility Wizard and also in Control Panel, users can adjust the size and color of most screen elements, such as window text, menus, insertion point indicator (also called a caret), mouse cursor, fonts, and caption bars. This capability can make the system easier to use and can reduce eyestrain. In the Accessibility Wizard, users can change icon size, mouse pointer size, and text size. In Control Panel, users can change the border width of windows. They can also change text sizes in Windows messages and in command prompt windows by double-clicking the Display icon and then selecting the preferred scheme from the Appearance tab. Users can resize a window by using the keyboard instead of the mouse. They can also resize a window in the Accessibility Wizard by selecting **I am blind or have difficulty seeing things on the screen**. Users can change the font size in Windows messages through Accessibility Wizard or Control Panel.

Consider the following points before you adjust color settings:

- Settings that display a large number of colors require a large amount of computer processor resources.

- A High Color setting includes more than 65,000 colors. A True Color setting includes more than 16 million colors.

- The monitor and display adapter determine the maximum number of colors that can appear on the screen.

- To change settings for another monitor in a multiple-monitor system, administrators must select the **Extend My Windows Desktop onto this Monitor** check box to change the settings for the other monitor. They can make color settings for each installed monitor.

High-Contrast Color Schemes

Customizing contrast and color can make it easier to see screen objects and can reduce eyestrain. No longer activated by Control Panel alone, the High Contrast feature is a built-in and expanded library of color schemes for users with low vision who require a high degree of contrast between foreground and background objects. For example, users who cannot easily read black text on a gray background or text drawn over a picture can benefit from this feature. Activating High Contrast mode automatically selects the user's preferred color scheme. Through the Magnifier dialog box, users can invert the colors of the magnification window or display the screen in high contrast. It can take a few seconds for High Contrast mode to take effect.

New Mouse Pointers

Customized through the Accessibility Wizard or Control Panel, new mouse pointers let the user decide which pointer is most visible. To improve visibility, users can now set characteristics of the mouse pointer for size, color, and speed, and for animation and visible trails. Pointers now include three sizes: large, extra-large, and default. Pointer options include white, black, and an inverted pointer that reacts to screen colors. (The latter pointer changes to a color that contrasts with the background.)

Additional Resources

- For more information about accessibility for users with disabilities, including technical support, documentation, and related organizations, see the Microsoft Accessibility link on the Web Resources page at http://windows.microsoft.com/windows2000/reskit/webresources.

- For more information about keyboard shortcuts, including an extensive list of accessibility keyboard shortcuts, see "Appendix H – Accessibility" in the *Microsoft Windows 98 Resource Kit* by Microsoft Corporation, 1998, Redmond, WA: Microsoft Press.

- For more information about accessibility for users with disabilities and for a catalog of accessibility aids, you can telephone or write Microsoft as follows:

  - Telephone Microsoft Sales Information Center at: 1 + (800) 426-9400

  - Telephone Microsoft Sales Fax Service line to receive faxed-back documents at: 1 +(800) 727-3351

  - Write Microsoft Sales Information Center at: One Microsoft Way, Redmond, WA 98052-6393

Glossary

.

.adm A file name extension for Administrative Templates files.

.msi A file name extension for Windows Installer package files.

A

access control The security mechanism in Windows NT and Windows 2000 that determines which objects a security principal can use and how the security principal can use them. See also authorization; security principal.

access control entry (ACE) An entry in an access control list (ACL) containing a security ID (SID) and a set of access rights. A process with a matching security ID is either allowed access rights, denied rights, or allowed rights with auditing.

access control list (ACL) The part of a security descriptor that enumerates the protections applied to an object. The owner of an object has discretionary access control of the object and can change the object's ACL to allow or disallow others access to the object. ACLs are made up of access control entries (ACEs). Each security descriptor for an object in Windows NT or Windows 2000 contains four security components: creator (owner); group, for POSIX compliance and is associated with the "primary group" set in individual user objects in User Manager; discretionary access control list (DACL, usually referred to simply as ACL), determines the permissions on the object; and system access control list (SACL), determines auditing. See also discretionary access control list.

access token An object containing the security information for a logon session. Windows 2000 creates an access token when a user logs on, and every process executed on behalf of the user has a copy of the token. The token identifies the user, the user's groups, and the user's privileges. The system uses the token to control access to securable objects and to control the ability of the user to perform various system-related operations on the local computer. There are two kinds of access token: primary and impersonation. See also primary token; impersonation token; privilege; process; security identifier.

accessibility The quality of a system incorporating hardware or software to engage a customizable user interface, alternative input and output methods, and greater exposure of screen elements to make the computer usable by people with cognitive, hearing, physical, or visual disabilities.

accessibility wizard An interactive tool that makes it easier to set up commonly used accessibility features by specifying options by type of disability, rather than by numeric value changes.

account domain A Windows NT domain that holds user account data. Also known as a master domain.

account lockout A Windows 2000 security feature that locks a user account if a number of failed logon attempts occur within a specified amount of time, based on security policy lockout settings. (Locked accounts cannot log on.)

Active Directory The directory service included with Windows 2000 Server. It stores information about objects on a network and makes this information available to users and network administrators. Active Directory gives network users access to permitted resources anywhere on the network using a single logon process. It provides network administrators with an intuitive hierarchical view of the network and a single point of administration for all network objects. See also directory; directory service.

Active Directory Connector (ADC) A synchronization agent in Windows 2000 Server, Windows 2000 Advanced Server, and Windows 2000 Enterprise Server that provides an automated way of keeping directory information between the two directories consistent. Without the ADC, you would have to manually enter new data and updates in both directory services.

Active Directory Installation wizard A Windows 2000 Server tool that allows the following during Setup: installation of Active Directory, creation of trees in a forest, replicating an existing domain, installation of Kerberos authentication software, and promotion of servers to domain controllers.

Active Directory replication Replication that occurs through the Directory Replicator Service, which provides multimaster replication of directory partitions between domain controllers. "Multimaster" means that directory partition replicas are writable on each domain controller. The replication service copies the changes from a given directory partition replica to all other domain controllers that hold the same directory partition replica. See also directory partition; File Replication service.

Active Directory Service Interfaces (ADSI) A directory service model and a set of COM interfaces. ADSI enables Windows 95, Windows 98, Windows NT, and Windows 2000 applications to access several network directory services, including Active Directory. It is supplied as a Software Development Kit (SDK).

active partition The partition from which the computer starts up. The active partition must be a primary partition on a basic disk. If you are using Windows 2000 exclusively, the active partition can be the same as the system partition. If you are using Windows 2000 and Windows 98 or earlier, or MS-DOS, the active partition must contain the startup files for both operating systems.

active/active The cluster configuration of an application, in which the application runs on all nodes at the same time. See also active/passive.

active/passive The cluster configuration of an application, in which the application runs on only one node at a time. See also active/active.

ActiveX A set of technologies that enables software components to interact with one another in a networked environment, regardless of the language in which the components were created.

address In Systems Management Server, addresses are used to connect sites and site systems. Senders use addresses to send instructions and data to other sites.

address classes See internet address classes.

address pool A group of IP addresses in a scope. Pooled addresses are then available for dynamic assignment by a DHCP server to DHCP clients.

Address Resolution Protocol (ARP)

In TCP/IP, a protocol that uses limited broadcast to the local network to resolve a logically assigned IP address. The IP address is conferred in software for each IP network host device to its physical hardware or media access control layer address. With ATM the ARP protocol is used two different ways. For CLIP, ARP is used to resolve addresses to ATM hardware addresses. With ATM LAN Emulation, ARP is used to resolve Ethernet/802.3 or Token Ring addresses to ATM hardware addresses. See also media access control; TCP/IP.

administrative templates (.adm files)

An ASCII file referred to as an Administrative Template (.adm file) used by Group Policy as a source to generate the user interface settings an administrator can set.

admission control   The service used to administratively control network resources on shared network segments.

Advanced Configuration and Power Interface (ACPI)

An open industry specification that defines power management on a wide range of mobile, desktop, and server computers and peripherals. ACPI is the foundation for the OnNow industry initiative that allows system manufacturers to deliver computers that will start at the touch of a keyboard. ACPI design is essential to take full advantage of power management and Plug and Play in Windows 2000. Check the manufacturer's documentation to verify that a computer is ACPI-compliant. See also Plug and Play.

advertise   In Systems Management Server, to make a program available to members of a collection (group).

advertisement   In Systems Management Server, a notification sent by the site server to the client access points (CAPs) specifying that a software distribution program is available for clients to use.

agent   An application that runs on a simple network management protocol (SNMP) managed device. The agent application is the object of management activities. A computer running SNMP agent software is also sometimes referred to as an agent.

algorithm   A rule or procedure for solving a problem. Internet Protocol security uses cryptographically based algorithms to encrypt data.

alternative input devices   Input devices for users who cannot use standard input devices, such as a mouse or a keyboard.

answer file   A text file that you can use to provide automated input for unattended installation of Windows 2000. This input includes parameters to answer the questions required by Setup for specific installations. In some cases, you can use this text file to provide input to wizards, such as the Active Directory Installation wizard, which is used to add Active Directory to Windows 2000 Server through Setup. The default answer file for Setup is known as Unattend.txt.

AppleTalk   The Apple Computer network architecture and network protocols. A network that has Macintosh clients and a computer running Windows 2000 Server with Services for Macintosh functions as an AppleTalk network.

AppleTalk Protocol   The set of network protocols on which AppleTalk network architecture is based. The AppleTalk Protocol stack must be installed on a computer running Windows 2000 Server so that Macintosh clients can connect to it. See also AppleTalk.

application assignment A process that uses Software Installation (an extension of Group Policy) to assign programs to groups of users. The programs appear on the users' desktop when they log on.

application programming interface (API)
A set of routines that an application uses to request and carry out lower-level services performed by a computer's operating system. These routines usually carry out maintenance tasks such as managing files and displaying information.

area A group of contiguous networks within an OSPF autonomous system. OSPF areas reduce the size of the link state database and provide the ability to summarize routes. See also autonomous system, link state database.

area border router (ABR) A router that is attached to multiple areas. Area border routers maintain separate link state databases for each area. See also link state database.

ARP Cache A table of IP addresses and their corresponding media access control address. There is a separate ARP cache for each interface.

assigning In Systems Management Server, to deploy a program to members of a collection (group), where acceptance of the program is mandatory.

Asynchronous Transfer Mode (ATM)
A high-speed connection-oriented protocol used to transport many different types of network traffic.

attribute (object) In Active Directory, a single property of an object. An object is described by the values of its attributes. For each object class, the schema defines what attributes an instance of the class must have and what additional attributes it might have.

attributes (file) Information that indicates whether a file is read-only, hidden, ready for archiving (backing up), compressed, or encrypted, and whether the file contents should be indexed for fast file searching.

auditing To track the activities of users by recording selected types of events in the security log of a server or a workstation.

augmentative communication devices
Add-on software and hardware that can help users with disabilities control a computer using assistive technology. Examples are speech recognition systems and screen readers.

authentication In network access, the process by which the system validates the user's logon information. A user's name and password are compared against an authorized list. If the system detects a match, access is granted to the extent specified in the permissions list for that user. When a user logs on to an account on a computer running Windows 2000 Professional, the authentication is performed by the client. When a user logs on to an account on a Windows 2000 Server domain, authentication can be performed by any server of that domain. See also server; trust relationship.

authentication The IPSec process that verifies the origin and integrity of a message by assuring the genuine identity of each computer. Without strong authentication, an unknown computer and any data it sends is suspect. IPSec provides multiple methods of authentication to ensure compatibility with earlier systems running earlier versions of Windows, non-Windows-based systems, and shared computers.

authoritative For the Domain Name System (DNS), the use of zones by DNS servers to register and resolve a DNS domain name. When a DNS server is configured to host a zone, it is authoritative for names within that zone. DNS servers are granted authority based on information stored in the zone. See also zone.

authoritative restore In Backup, a type of restore operation on a Windows 2000 domain controller in which the objects in the restored directory are treated as authoritative, replacing (through replication) all existing copies of those objects. Authoritative restore is applicable only to replicated System State data such as Active Directory data and File Replication service data. The Ntdsutil.exe utility is used to perform an authoritative restore. See also nonauthoritative restore; System State.

authorization In remote access or demand-dial routing connections, the verification that the connection attempt is allowed. Authorization occurs after successful authentication.

automated installation To run an unattended setup using one or more of several methods such as Remote Installation Services, bootable CD, and Sysprep.

Automatic Private IP Addressing (APIPA) A feature of Windows 2000 TCP/IP that automatically configures a unique IP address from the range 169.254.0.1 to 169.254.255.254 and a subnet mask of 255.255.0.0 when the TCP/IP protocol is configured for dynamic addressing and a Dynamic Host Configuration.

autonomous system (AS) A group of routers exchanging routing information by using a common routing protocol.

availability A measure of the fault tolerance of a computer and its programs. A highly available computer runs 24 hours a day, 7 days a week. See also fault tolerance.

B

backbone In OSPF, an area common to all other OSPF areas that is used as the transit area for inter-area traffic and for distributing routing information between areas. The backbone must be contiguous. See also Open Shortest Path First (OSPF).

backup domain controller In Windows NT Server 4.0 or earlier, a computer running Windows NT Server that receives a copy of the domain's directory database (which contains all account and security policy information for the domain). The copy synchronizes periodically with the master copy on the primary domain controller. A backup domain controller also authenticate user logon information and can be promoted to function as primary domain controllers as needed. Multiple backup domain controllers can exist in a domain. Windows NT 3.51 and 4.0 backup domain controllers can participate in a Windows 2000 domain when the domain is configured in mixed mode. See also mixed mode; primary domain controller.

backup operator A type of local or global group that contains the user rights needed to back up and restore files and folders. Members of the Backup Operators group can back up and restore files and folders regardless of ownership, access permissions, encryption, or auditing settings. See also auditing; global group; local group; user rights.

backup set A collection of files, folders, and other data that have been backed up and stored in a file or on one or more tapes.

bandwidth In communications, the difference between the highest and lowest frequencies in a given range. For example, a telephone line accommodates a bandwidth of 3000 Hz, the difference between the lowest (300 Hz) and highest (3300 Hz) frequencies it can carry. In computer networks, greater bandwidth indicates faster data-transfer capability and is expressed in bits per second (bps).

Bandwidth Allocation Protocol (BAP)
A PPP control protocol that is used on a multiprocessing connection to dynamically add and remove links.

basic disk A physical disk that contains primary partitions or extended partitions with logical drives used by Windows 2000 and all versions of Windows NT. Basic disks can also contain volume, striped, mirror, or RAID-5 sets that were created using Windows NT 4.0 or earlier. As long as a compatible file format is used, basic disks can be accessed by MS-DOS, Windows 95, Windows 98, and all versions of Windows NT.

basic volume A volume on a basic disk. Basic volumes include primary partitions, logical drives within extended partitions, as well as volume, striped, mirror, or RAID-5 sets that were created using Windows NT 4.0 or earlier. Only basic disks can contain basic volumes. Basic and dynamic volumes cannot exist on the same disk.

binary A base-2 number system in which values are expressed as combinations of two digits, 0 and 1.

bindery A database in Novell NetWare 2.*x* and 3.*x* that contains organizational and security information about users and groups.

binding A process by which software components and layers are linked together. When a network component is installed, the binding relationships and dependencies for the components are established. Binding allows components to communicate with each other.

bit The smallest unit of information handled by a computer. One bit expresses a 1 or a 0 in a binary numeral, or a true or false logical condition. A group of 8 bits makes up a byte, which can represent many types of information, such as a letter of the alphabet, a decimal digit, or other character. Bit is also called binary digit.

bits per second (bps) The number of bits transmitted every second, used as a measure of the speed at which a device, such as a modem, can transfer data. A character is made up of 8 bits. In asynchronous communication, each character is preceded by a start bit and terminates with a stop bit. So for each character, 10 bits are transmitted. If a modem communicates at 2400 bits per second (bps), then 240 characters are sent every second.

block policy option An option that prevents Group Policy objects specified in higher-level Active Directory containers from applying to a computer or user.

boot To start or reset a computer. When first turned on or reset, the computer executes the software that loads and starts the computer's operating system, which prepares it for use.

bootable CD-ROM An automated installation method that runs Setup from a CD-ROM. This method is useful for computers at remote sites with slow links and no local IT department. See also automated installation.

bootstrap protocol (BOOTP) A set of rules or standards to enable computers to connect with one another, used primarily on TCP/IP networks to configure workstations without disks. RFCs 951 and 1542 define this protocol. DHCP is a boot configuration protocol that uses this protocol.

bottleneck A condition, usually involving a hardware resource, that causes the entire system to perform poorly.

BounceKeys A keyboard filter that assists users whose fingers bounce on the keys when pressing or releasing them.

bridgehead server A server that receives and forwards e-mail traffic at each end of a connection agreement, similar to the task a gateway performs.

broadcast An address that is destined for all hosts on a given network. See also broadcast network.

broadcast and unknown server (BUS)
A multicast service on an emulated local area network (ELAN) that forwards broadcast, multicast, and initial unicast data traffic sent by a LAN emulation client. See also emulated local area network (ELAN).

broadcast network A network that supports more than two attached routers and has the ability to address a single physical message to all of the attached routers (broadcast). Ethernet is an example of a broadcast network.

browse list Any list of items that can be browsed, such as a list of servers on a network, or a list of printers displayed in the Add Printer wizard.

browser A client tool for navigating and accessing information on the Internet or an intranet. In the context of Windows networking, "browser" can also mean the Computer Browser service, a service that maintains an up-to-date list of computers on a network or part of a network

and provides the list to applications when requested. When a user attempts to connect to a resource in a domain, the domain's browser is contacted to provide a list of available resources.

buffer An area of memory used for intermediate storage of data until it can be used.

bulk encryption A process in which large amounts of data, such as files, e-mail messages, or online communications sessions, are encrypted for confidentiality. It is usually done with a symmetric key algorithm. See also encryption; symmetric key encryption.

BUS See broadcast and unknown server.

bus A communication line used for data transfer among the components of a computer system. A bus is essentially a highway that allows different parts of the system to share data.

C

cable modem A modem that provides broadband Internet access in the range of 10 to 30 Mbps.

cache For DNS and WINS, a local information store of resource records for recently resolved names of remote hosts. Typically, the cache is built dynamically as the computer queries and resolves names; it helps optimize the time required to resolve queried names. See also cache file; naming service; resource record.

cache file A file used by the Domain Name System (DNS) server to preload its names cache when service is started. Also known as the "root hints" file because resource records stored in this file are used by the DNS Service to help locate root servers that provide referral to authoritative servers for remote names. For Windows DNS servers, the cache file is named Cache.dns and is located in the %Systemroot%\System32\Dns folder. See also authoritative; cache; systemroot.

caching For DNS, typically the server-side ability of DNS servers to store information learned about the domain namespace during the processing and resolution of name queries. With Windows 2000, caching is also available through the DNS client service (resolver) as a way for DNS clients to keep a cache of name information learned during recent queries. See also caching resolver.

caching resolver For Windows 2000, a client-side Domain Name System (DNS) name resolution service that performs caching of recently learned DNS domain name information. The caching resolver service provides system-wide access to DNS-aware programs for resource records obtained from DNS servers during processing of name queries. Data placed in the cache is used for a limited period of time and aged according to the active Time-To-Live (TTL) value. You can set the TTL either individually for each resource record (RR) or defaults to the minimum TTL set in the SOA RR for the zone. See also cache; caching; expire interval; minimum TTL; resolver; resource record; Time To Live (TTL).

Call Manager A software component that establishes, maintains and terminates a connection between two computers.

central site In Systems Management Server, the primary site at the top of the Systems Management Server hierarchy, to which all other sites in the Systems Management Server system report their inventory and events.

certificate A file used for authentication and secure exchange of data on nonsecured networks, such as the Internet. A certificate securely binds a public encryption key to the entity that holds the corresponding private encryption key. Certificates are digitally signed by the issuing certification authority and can be managed for a user, a computer, or a service.

certificate revocation list (CRL) A document maintained and published by a certification authority that lists certificates that have been revoked. A CRL is signed with the private key of the CA to ensure its integrity. See also certificate; certification authority.

certificate services The Windows 2000 service that issues certificates for a particular CA. It provides customizable services for issuing and managing certificates for the enterprise. See also certificate; certification authority.

certificate stores Windows 2000 stores public key objects, such as certificates and certificate revocation lists, in logical stores and physical stores. The logical stores group public key objects for users, computers, and services. Physical stores are where the public key objects are actually stored in the registry of local computers (or in Active Directory for some user certificates). Logical stores contain pointers to the public key objects in the physical stores. Users, computers, and services share many public key objects, so logical stores enable public key objects to be shared without requiring the storage of duplicates of the objects for each user, computer, or service.

certificate template A Windows 2000 construct that profiles certificates (that is, it pre specifies format and content) based on their intended usage. When requesting a certificate from a Windows 2000 certification authority (CA), certificate requestors will, depending on their access rights, be able to select from a variety of certificate types that are based on certificate templates, such as "User," and "Code Signing." See also certificate; certification authority.

certificate trust list (CTL) A signed list of root certification authority certificates that an administrator considers reputable for designated purposes, such as client authentication or secure e-mail. See also certificate; certification authority; root certificate; root certification authority.

certification authority (CA) An entity responsible for establishing and vouching for the authenticity of public keys belonging to users (end entities) or other certification authorities. Activities of a certification authority can include binding public keys to distinguished names through signed certificates, managing certificate serial numbers and certificate revocation. See also certificate; public key.

certification hierarchy A model of trust for certificates in which certification paths are created through the establishment of parent-child relationships between certification authorities. See also certification authority; certification path.

certification path An unbroken chain of trust from a certificate to the root certification authority in a certification hierarchy. See also certification hierarchy; certificate.

Challenge Handshake Authentication Protocol (CHAP)
A challenge-response authentication protocol for PPP connections documented in RFC 1994 that uses the industry-standard Message Digest 5 (MD5) one-way encryption scheme to hash the response to a challenge issued by the remote access server.

change log See quorum log.

child domain For DNS and Active Directory, a domain located in the namespace tree directly beneath another domain name (the parent domain). For example, "example.reskit.com" is a child domain of the parent domain, "reskit.com." Child domain is also called subdomain. See also parent domain; domain; directory partition.

child object An object that resides in another object. A child object implies relation. For example, a file is a child object that resides in a folder, which is the parent object. See also object; parent object.

cipher The method of forming a hidden message. The cipher is used to transform a readable message called plaintext (also sometimes called cleartext) into an unreadable, scrambled, or hidden message called ciphertext. Only someone with a secret decoding key can convert the ciphertext back into its original plaintext. See also ciphertext; plaintext; cryptography.

ciphertext Text that has been encrypted using an encryption key. Ciphertext is meaningless to anyone who does not have the decryption key. See also decryption; encryption; encryption key; plaintext.

Class A IP address A unicast IP address that ranges from 1.0.0.1 to 126.255.255.254. The first octet indicates the network, and the last three octets indicate the host on the network. See also Class B IP address; Class C IP address; IP address.

Class B IP address A unicast IP address that ranges from 128.0.0.1 to 191.255.255.254. The first two octets indicate the network, and the last two octets indicate the host on the network. See also Class A IP address; Class C IP address; IP address.

Class C IP address A unicast IP address that ranges from 192.0.0.1 to 223.255.255.254. The first three octets indicate the network, and the last octet indicates hosts on the network. Network Load Balancing provides optional session support for Class C IP addresses (in addition to support for single IP addresses) to accommodate clients that make use of multiple proxy servers at the client site. See also Class A IP address; Class B IP address; IP address.

Class D IP address The Internet address class designed for IP multicast addresses. The value of the first octet for Class D IP addresses and networks varies from 224 to 239.

classless interdomain routing (CIDR)
A method of allocating public IP addresses that is not based on the original Internet Address Classes. Classless interdomain routing (CIDR) was developed to help prevent the depletion of public IP addresses and minimize the size of Internet routing tables.

clean installation The process of installing an operating system on a clean or empty partition of a computer's hard disk.

client Any computer or program connecting to, or requesting services of, another computer or program. See also server.

client access point In Systems Management Server, a site system that provides a set of shared directories and files that create a common communication point between the site server and client computers.

client request A service request from a client computer to a server computer or, for Network Load Balancing, a cluster of computers. Network Load Balancing forwards each client request to a specific host within the cluster according to the system administrator's load-balancing policy. See also client; cluster; host; server.

Client Service for Netware A service included with Windows 2000 Professional that allows client computers to make direct connections to resources on computers running NetWare 2.x, 3.x, 4.x, or 5.x server software.

client-side extensions Group Policy components that, in certain cases, are responsible for implementing Group Policy on the client computer.

ClonePrincipal A tool that allows the incremental migration of users to a Windows 2000 environment without affecting the existing Windows NT production environment.

closed captioning Alternative representation, usually text, of audio or graphics media that can be seen only on a specially equipped receiver.

cluster A set of computers that work together to provide a service. The use of a cluster enhances both the availability of the service and the scalability of the operating system that provides the service. Network Load Balancing provides a software solution for clustering multiple computers running Windows 2000 Advanced Server that provides networked services over the Internet and private intranets. See also availability; scalability.

Cluster Administrator An application (Cluadmin.exe) used to configure a cluster and its nodes, groups, and resources. Cluster Administrator can run on any member of the trusted domain regardless of whether the computer is a cluster node. See also cluster; Cluster Administrator extension; Cluster.exe; node; resource.

Cluster Administrator extension A dynamic-link library (DLL) that enables Cluster Administrator to manage a custom resource type. A Cluster Administrator extension uses the Cluster Administrator Extension API. See also cluster; Cluster Administrator; resource.

cluster API A collection of functions implemented by the cluster software and used by a cluster-aware client or server application, a cluster management application or a resource DLL. The cluster API is used to manage the cluster, cluster objects, and the cluster database. See also cluster; cluster-aware application; dynamic-link library; node; resource; resource DLL.

Cluster service Clussvc.exe, the primary executable of the Windows Clustering component that creates a server cluster, controls all aspects of its operation, and manages the cluster database. Each node in a server cluster runs one instance of the Cluster service.

cluster-aware The classification of an application or service that runs on a server cluster node, is managed as a cluster resource, and is designed to be aware of and interact with the server cluster environment.

cluster-aware application An application or service that runs on a server cluster node and is managed as a cluster resource. Cluster-aware applications use the Cluster API to receive status and notification information from the server cluster. See also Cluster API; cluster-unaware application; node.

cluster-unaware application In a server cluster, an application that can run on a node and be managed as a cluster resource but does not support the Cluster API and therefore has no inherent knowledge of its environment. Cluster-unaware applications function the same regardless of whether they are running on a node in a server cluster or on a non-clustered system. See also cluster-aware application; node.

Cluster.exe An alternative to using Cluster Administrator to administer clusters from the Windows 2000 command prompt. Cluster.exe can be called from command scripts to automate many cluster administration tasks. See also Cluster Administrator.

code signing To digitally sign software code to ensure its integrity and provide assurance of its origin.

cognitive disabilities Impairments resulting from perceptual anomalies, memory loss, and learning and developmental disabilities, such as dyslexia and Down syndrome

collection In Systems Management Server, a set of resources in a site defined by membership rules. Collections are used to distribute software, view inventory on clients, and access clients for remote tool sessions.

common gateway interface (CGI) A server-side interface for initiating software services. A set of interfaces that describe how a Web server communicates with software on the same computer. Any software can be a CGI program if it handles input and output according to the CGI standard.

Common Internet File System (CIFS)
A protocol and a corresponding API used by application programs to request higher level application services. CIFS was formerly known as SMB (Server Message Block).

Component Object Model (COM) An object-based programming model designed to promote software interoperability; it allows two or more applications or components to easily cooperate with one another, even if they were written by different vendors, at different times, in different programming languages, or if they are running on different computers running different operating systems. COM is the foundation technology upon which broader technologies can be built. Microsoft Object Linking & Embedding (OLE) technology and ActiveX are both built on top of COM.

Component Server A server that provides a platform to run component services such as Application Load Balancing, Transaction Services, and Application Management.

computer account objects Objects used to identify a specific computer account in Windows NT Server 4.0 or Windows 2000 Server.

computer name A unique name of up to 15 uppercase characters that identifies a computer to the network. The name cannot be the same as any other computer or domain name in the network.

confidentiality An Internet Protocol security service that ensures a message is disclosed only to intended recipients by encrypting the data.

connection agreement A configurable section in the ADC UI that holds information such as the server names to contact for synchronization, object classes to synchronize, target containers, and the synchronization schedule. See also Active Directory Connector (ADC).

connection-oriented A type of network protocol that requires an end-to-end virtual connection between the sender and receiver before communicating across the network.

console tree The tree view pane in a Microsoft Management Console (MMC) that displays the hierarchical namespace. By default it is the left pane of the console window, but it can be hidden. The items in the console tree (for example, Web pages, folders, and controls) and their hierarchical organization determines the management capabilities of a console. See also Microsoft Management Console (MMC); namespace.

consoles A framework for hosting administrative tools in the Microsoft Management Console (MMC). A console is defined by the items in its console tree, which might include folders or other containers, World Wide Web pages, and other administrative items. A console has windows that can provide views of the console tree, and the administrative properties, services, and events that are acted on by the items in the console tree.

container object An object that can logically contain other objects. For example, a folder is a container object. See also noncontainer object; object.

convergence The process of stabilizing a system after changes occur in the network. For routing, if a route becomes unavailable, routers send update messages throughout the internetwork, reestablishing information about preferred routes. For Network Load Balancing, a process by which hosts exchange messages to determine a new, consistent state of the cluster and to elect the host with the highest host priority, known as the default host. During convergence, a new load distribution is determined for hosts that share the handling of network traffic for specific TCP or UDP ports. See also cluster; default host; host; User Datagram Protocol (UDP).

cost A unitless metric configured on OSPF routers that indicates the preference of using a certain link.

crypto-accelerator board A hardware device that speeds up cryptographic operations by offloading operations to a special processor on the board.

CryptoAPI (CAPI) An application programming interface (API) that is provided as part of Windows 2000. CryptoAPI provides a set of functions that allow applications to encrypt or digitally sign data in a flexible manner while providing protection for private keys. Actual cryptographic operations are performed by independent modules known as cryptographic service providers (CSPs). See also cryptographic service provider; private key.

cryptographic service provider (CSP)
An independent software module that performs cryptography operations such as secret key exchange, digital signing of data, and public key authentication. Any Windows 2000 service or application can request cryptography operations from a CSP. See also CryptoAPI.

cryptography The art and science of information security. It provides four basic information security functions: confidentiality, integrity, authentication, and nonrepudiation. See also confidentiality; integrity; authentication; nonrepudiation.

custom subnet mask A subnet mask that is not based on the Internet Address Classes. Custom subnet masks are commonly used when subnetting.

D

datagram An unacknowledged packet of data sent to another network destination. The destination can be another device directly reachable on the local area network (LAN) or a remote destination reachable using routed delivery through a packet-switched network.

DCOM See Distributed Component Object Model.

DCOM Configuration tool A Windows NT Server tool that can be used to configure 32-bit applications for DCOM communication over the network. See also DCOM.

decryption The process of making encrypted data readable again by converting ciphertext to plaintext. See also ciphertext; encryption; plaintext.

default gateway A configuration item for the TCP/IP protocol that is the IP address of a directly reachable IP router. Configuring a default gateway creates a default route in the IP routing table.

default host The host with the highest host priority for which a drainstop command is not in progress. After convergence, the default host handles all of the network traffic for TCP and UDP ports that are not otherwise covered by port rules. See also convergence; drainstop; host priority; port rule; user datagram protocol.

default network In the Macintosh environment, the physical network on which the processes of the server reside as nodes and on which the server appears to users. The default network of the server must be one to which that server is attached. Only servers on AppleTalk Phase 2 internets have default networks.

default route A route that is used when no other routes for the destination are found in the routing table. For example, if a router or end system cannot find a network route or host route for the destination, the default route is used. The default route is used to simplify the configuration of end systems or routers. For IP routing tables, the default route is the route with the network destination of 0.0.0.0 and netmask of 0.0.0.0.

default subnet mask A subnet mask that is used on an Internet Address Class-based network. The subnet mask for Class A is 255.0.0.0. The subnet mask for Class B is 255.255.0.0. The subnet mask for Class C is 255.255.255.0.

defragmentation The process of rewriting parts of a file to contiguous sectors on a hard disk to increase the speed of access and retrieval. When files are updated, the computer tends to save these updates on the largest continuous space on the hard disk, which is often on a different sector than the other parts of the file. When files are thus fragmented, the computer must search the hard disk each time the file is opened to find all of the parts of the file, which slows down response time. In Active Directory, defragmentation rearranges how the data is written in the directory database file to compact it. See also fragmentation.

delegation The ability to assign responsibility for management and administration of a portion of the namespace to another user, group, or organization. For DNS, a name service record in the parent zone that lists the name server authoritative for the delegated zone. See also inheritance; parenting.

delegation wizard A wizard used to distribute precise elements of the administrator's workload to others.

demand-dial connection A connection, typically using a circuit-switched wide area network link, that is initiated when data needs to be forwarded. The demand-dial connection is typically terminated when there is no traffic.

demand-dial interface A logical interface that represents a demand-dial connection (a PPP link) that is configured on the calling router. The demand-dial interface contains configuration information such as the port to use, the addressing used to create the connection (such as a phone number), authentication and encryption methods, and authentication credentials.

dependency The state in which one resource must be online before a second resource can come online.

dependency tree A discrete set of resources that are connected to each other by dependency relationships. All resources in a given dependency tree must be members of a single group. See also dependency; resource.

desktop The on-screen work area in which windows, icons, menus, and dialog boxes appear.

device Any piece of equipment that can be attached to a network or computer, for example, a computer, printer, joystick, adapter or modem card, or any other peripheral equipment. Devices normally require a device driver to function with Windows 2000. See also device driver.

device driver A program that allows a specific device, such as a modem, network adapter, or printer, to communicate with Windows 2000. Although a device can be installed on a system, Windows 2000 cannot use the device until the appropriate driver has been installed and configured. If a device is listed in the Hardware Compatibility List (HCL), a driver is usually included with Windows 2000. Device drivers load (for all enabled devices) when a computer is started, and thereafter run invisibly. See also Hardware Compatibility List (HCL).

Dfs root A Server Message Block share at the top of the Dfs topology that is the starting point for the links and shared files that make up the Dfs namespace. A Dfs root can be defined at the domain level, for domain-based operation, or at the server level, for stand-alone operation. Domain-based Dfs can have multiple roots in the domain but only one root on each server.

Dfs topology The overall logical hierarchy of a distributed file system, including elements such as roots, links, shared folders, and replica sets, as depicted in the Dfs administrative console. This is not to be confused with the Dfs namespace, which is the logical view of shared resources seen by users.

DHCP See Dynamic Host Configuration Protocol.

DHCP Manager The primary tool used to manage DHCP servers. The DHCP Manager is a Microsoft Management Console (MMC) tool that is added to the Administrative Tools menu when the DHCP service is installed.

DHCP Service A service, that enables a computer to function as a DHCP server and configure DHCP-enabled client computers on a network. DHCP runs on a server computer, enabling the automatic, centralized management of IP addresses and other TCP/IP configuration settings for a network's client computers.

dialog box A window that is displayed to request or supply information. Many dialog boxes have options which must be selected before Windows NT can carry out a command.

digital certificate See certificate.

directory An information source (for example, a telephone directory) that contains information about people, computer files, or other objects. In a file system, a directory stores information about files. In a distributed computing environment (such as a Windows 2000 domain), the directory stores information about objects such as printers, applications, databases, and other users.

directory partition A contiguous subtree of Active Directory that is replicated as a unit to other domain controllers in the forest that contain a replica of the same subtree. In Active Directory a single server always holds at least three directory partitions: schema, class and attribute definitions for the directory; configuration, replication topology and related metadata; domain, subtree that contains the per-domain objects for one domain. The schema and configuration directory partitions are replicated to every domain controller in a given forest. A domain directory partition is replicated only to domain controllers for that domain. In addition to a full, writable replica of its own domain directory partition, a global catalog server also holds partial, read-only replicas of all other domain directory partitions in the forest. See also full replica; Global Catalog; partial replica.

directory service Both the directory information source and the services that make the information available and usable. A directory service enables the user to find an object given any one of its attributes. See also Active Directory; directory.

directory store The physical storage for Active Directory directory partition replicas on a given domain controller. The store is implemented using the Extensible Storage Engine.

directory tree A hierarchy of objects and containers in a directory that can be viewed graphically as an upside down tree, with the root object at the top. Endpoints in the tree are usually single (leaf) objects, and nodes in the tree, or branches, are container objects. A tree shows how objects are connected in terms of the path from one object to another. A simple tree is a single container and its objects. A contiguous subtree is any unbroken path in the tree, including all the members of any container in that path.

disable To make a device nonfunctional. For example, if a device in a hardware profile is disabled, the device cannot be used while using that hardware profile. Disabling a device frees the resources that were allocated to the device.

discovery A process by which the Windows 2000 Net Logon service attempts to locate a domain controller running Windows 2000 Server in the trusted domain. Once a domain controller has been discovered, it is used for subsequent user account authentication. For SNMP, dynamic discovery is the identification of devices attached to an SNMP network.

discretionary access control list (DACL)
The part of an object's security descriptor that grants or denies specific users and groups permission to access the object. Only the owner of an object can change permissions granted or denied in a DACL; thus access to the object is at the owner's discretion. See also access control entry; object; system access control list; security descriptor.

disk A physical data storage device attached to a computer. See also basic disk; dynamic disk.

disk quota The maximum amount of disk space available to a user.

display adapter An expansion board that plugs into a personal computer to give it display capabilities. A computer's display capabilities depend on both the logical circuitry (provided in the video adapter) and the monitor. Each adapter offers several different video modes. The two basic categories of video modes are text and graphic. Within the text and graphic modes, some monitors also offer a choice of resolutions. At lower resolutions a monitor can display more colors. Modern adapters contain memory, so that the computer's RAM is not used for storing displays. In addition, most adapters have their own graphics coprocessor for performing graphics calculations. These adapters are often called graphics accelerators. See also network adapter.

distributed component object model (DCOM)
The Microsoft Component Object Model (COM) specification that defines how components communicate over Windows-based networks. Use the DCOM Configuration tool to integrate client/server applications across multiple computers. DCOM can also be used to integrate robust Web browser applications. See also DCOM Configuration tool.

distributed DHCP A DHCP scenario in which IP addresses are distributed across a site boundary.

Distributed file system (Dfs) A Windows 2000 service consisting of software residing on network servers and clients that transparently links shared folders located on different file servers into a single namespace for improved load sharing and data availability.

distribution folder The folder created on the Windows 2000 distribution server to contain the Setup files.

distribution point In Systems Management Server, a site system with the distribution point role that stores package files received from a site server. Systems Management Server clients contact distribution points to obtain programs and files after they detect that an advertised application is available from a client access point.

distribution point group In Systems Management Server, a set of distribution points that can be managed as a single entity.

DNS server A computer that runs DNS server programs containing name-to-IP address mappings, IP address-to-name mappings, information about the domain tree structure, and other information. DNS servers also attempt to resolve client queries.

DNS suffix For DNS, an optional parent domain name that can be appended to the end of a relative domain name used in a name query or host lookup. The DNS suffix can be used to complete an alternate fully qualified DNS domain name to be searched when the first attempt to query a name fails.

domain For Windows NT and Windows 2000, a networked set of computers running Windows NT or Windows 2000 that share a Security Accounts Manager (SAM) database and that can be administered as a group. A user with an account in a particular domain can log on to and access his or her account from any computer in the domain. A domain is a single security boundary of a Windows NT computer network. For DNS, a branch under a node in the DNS tree.

domain consolidation The process of combining two or more domains into a larger domain.

domain controller For a Windows NT Server or Windows 2000 Server domain, the server that authenticates domain logons and maintains the security policy and the master database for a domain. Both servers and domain controllers are capable of validating a user's logon, but password changes must be made by contacting the domain controller.

domain controller locator (Locator) An algorithm that runs in the context of the Netlogon service and that finds domain controllers on a Windows 2000 network. Locator can find domain controllers by using DNS names (for IP/DNS-compatible computers) or by using NetBIOS names (for computers that are running Windows 3.*x*, Windows for Workgroups, Windows NT 3.5 or later, Windows 95, or Windows 98, or it can be used on a network where IP transport is not available).

domain local group A Windows 2000 group only available in native mode domains and can contain members from anywhere in the forest, in trusted forests, or in a trusted pre-Windows 2000 domain. Domain local groups can only grant permissions to resources within the domain in which they exist. Typically, domain local groups are used to gather security principals from across the forest to control access to resources within the domain.

domain migration The process of moving accounts, resources, and their associated security objects from one domain structure to another.

domain name In Windows 2000 and Active Directory, the name given by an administrator to a collection of networked computers that share a common directory. For DNS, domain names are specific node names in the DNS namespace tree. DNS domain names use singular node names, known as "labels," joined together by periods (.) that indicate each node level in the namespace. See also domain name system (DNS);namespace.

domain name label   Each part of a full DNS domain name that represents a node in the domain namespace tree. Domain names are made up of a sequence of labels, such as the three labels ("noam," "reskit," and "com") that make up the DNS domain name "noam.reskit.com." Each label used in a DNS name must have 63 or fewer characters.

Domain Name System (DNS)   A hierarchical naming system used for locating domain names on the Internet and on private TCP/IP networks. DNS provides a service for mapping DNS domain names to IP addresses, and vice versa. This allows users, computers, and applications to query the DNS to specify remote systems by fully qualified domain names rather than by IP addresses. See also domain; ping.

domain namespace   The database structure used by the Domain Name System (DNS). See also Domain Name System (DNS).

domain restructure   The process of reorganizing one domain structure into another that typically results in the accounts, groups, and trusts being altered.

domain tree   In DNS, the inverted hierarchical tree structure that is used to index domain names. Domain trees are similar in purpose and concept to the directory trees used by computer filing systems for disk storage. See also domain name; namespace.

domain upgrade   The process of replacing an older operating system version on the computers in a domain with a later version.

domain-based Dfs   An implementation of Dfs that stores its configuration information in Active Directory. Because this information is made available on every domain controller in the domain, domain-based Dfs provides high availability for any distributed file system in the domain. A domain-based Dfs root has the following characteristics: it must be hosted on a domain member server, it has its topology published automatically to Active Directory, it can have root-level shared folders and it supports root and file replication through FRS.

drain   For Network Load Balancing, a program that disables new traffic handling for the rule whose port range contains the specified port. All ports specified by the port rule are affected. If "all" is specified for the port, this command is applied to the ports covered by all port rules. New connections to the specified host or hosts are not allowed, but all active connections are maintained. To disable active connections, use the disable command. This command has no effect if the specified hosts have not started cluster operations. See also drainstop; port rule.

drainstop   For Network Load Balancing, a tool that disables all new traffic handling on the specified hosts. The hosts then enter the draining mode to complete existing connections. While draining, hosts remain in the cluster and stop their cluster operations when there are no more active connections. You can terminate draining mode by explicitly stopping cluster mode with the stop command or by restarting new traffic handling with the start command. To drain connections from a specific port, use the drain command. See also drain.

dump file   A file used to store data in memory in case of failure.

Dvorak keyboard   An alternative keyboard with a layout that makes the most frequently typed characters more accessible to people who have difficulty typing on the standard QWERTY layout.

dynamic disk A physical disk that is managed by Disk Management. Dynamic disks can contain only dynamic volumes (that is, volumes created with Disk Management). Dynamic disks cannot contain partitions or logical drives, nor can they be accessed by MS-DOS. See also dynamic volume; partition.

Dynamic Host Configuration Protocol (DHCP) A networking protocol that provides safe, reliable, and simple TCP/IP network configuration and offers dynamic configuration of Internet Protocol (IP) addresses for computers. DHCP ensures that address conflicts do not occur and helps conserve the use of IP addresses through centralized management of address allocation.

dynamic routing The use of routing protocols to update routing tables. Dynamic routing responds to changes in the internetwork topology.

dynamic update An updated specification to the Domain Name System (DNS) standard that permits hosts that store name information in DNS to dynamically register and update their records in zones maintained by DNS servers that can accept and process dynamic update messages.

dynamic volume A logical volume that is created using Disk Management. Dynamic volumes include simple, spanned, striped, mirrored, and RAID-5 volumes. Dynamic volumes must be created on dynamic disks. See also dynamic disk; volume.

dynamic-link library (DLL) A feature of the Microsoft Windows family of operating systems and the OS/2 operating system. DLLs allow executable routines, generally serving a specific function or set of functions, to be stored separately as files with .dll extensions, and to be loaded only when needed by the program that calls them.

E

embedded object Information created in another application that has been pasted inside a document. When information is embedded, you can edit it in the new document using toolbars and menus from the original program. When you double-click the embedded icon, the toolbars and menus from the program used to create the information appear. Embedded information is not linked to the original file. If you change information in one place, it is not updated in the other. See also linked object.

emergency repair disk (ERD) A disk, created by the Backup utility, that contains information about your current Windows system settings. This disk can be used to repair your computer if it will not start or if your system files are damaged or erased.

emulated local area network (ELAN) A logical network initiated by using the mechanisms defined by LAN emulation. This could include ATM and previously attached end stations.

enable To make a device functional. For example, if a device in your hardware configuration settings is enabled the device is available for use when your computer uses that hardware configuration.

encrypted password A password that is scrambled. Encrypted passwords are more secure than plaintext passwords, which are susceptible to network sniffers.

encryption The process of disguising a message or data in such a way as to hide its substance.

encryption key A value used by an algorithm to encode or decode a message.

end-to-end encryption   Data encryption between the client application and the server hosting the resource or service being accessed by the client application.

enterprise certification authority   A Windows 2000 certification authority that is fully integrated with Active Directory. See also certification authority; stand-alone certification authority.

entry   Entries are the lowest level element in the registry. They appear in the right pane of a Registry Editor window. Each entry consists of an entry name, its data type, and its value.

They store the actual configuration data that affects the operating system and programs that run on the system. As such, they are different from keys and subkeys, which are containers.

Entries are referenced by their registry path and name. The amount and type of data that can be stored in an entry is determined by the data type of the entry.

environment variable   A string consisting of environment information, such as a drive, path, or filename, associated with a symbolic name that can be used by Windows NT and Windows 2000. You use the System option in Control Panel or the set command from the command prompt to define environment variables.

error detection   A technique for detecting when data is lost during transmission. This allows the software to recover lost data by requesting that the transmitting computer retransmit the data.

event   Any significant occurrence in the system or an application that requires users to be notified or an entry to be added to a log.

Event Log   The file in which event logging entries are recorded.

event logging   The Windows 2000 process of recording an audit entry in the audit trail whenever certain events occur, such as services starting and stopping and users logging on and off and accessing resources. You can use Event Viewer to review Services for Macintosh events as well as Windows 2000 events.

event types   Errors, basic actions with time stamps, or device problems.

everyone category   In the Macintosh environment, one of the user categories to which permissions for a folder are assigned. Permissions given to everyone apply to all users who use the server, including guests.

expire interval   For DNS, the number of seconds that DNS servers operating as secondary masters for a zone use to determine if zone data should be expired when the zone is not refreshed and renewed. See also zone.

explicit trust relationship   A trust relationship from Windows NT in which an explicit link is made in one direction only. Explicit trusts can also exist between Windows NT domains and Windows 2000 domains, and between forests.

export   In NFS, to make a file system available by a server to a client for mounting.

extended partition   A portion of a basic disk that can contain logical drives. To have more than four volumes on your basic disk, you need to use an extended partition. Only one of the four partitions allowed per physical disk can be an extended partition, and no primary partition needs to be present to create an extended partition. You can create extended partitions only on basic disks. See also basic disk; logical drive; partition; primary partition; unallocated space.

Extensible Authentication Protocol (EAP)
An extension to PPP that allows for arbitrary authentication mechanisms to be employed for the validation of a PPP connection.

external network number A 4-byte hexadecimal number used for addressing and routing purposes. The external network number is associated with physical network adapters and networks. To communicate with each other, all computers on the same network that use a given frame type must have the same external network number. All external network numbers must be unique to the IPX internetwork. See also internal network number; Internetwork Packet Exchange (IPX).

external routes A route that is not within an OSPF autonomous system.

extranet A limited subset of computers or users on a public network, typically the Internet, that are able to access an organization's internal network. Typically the computers or users belong to partner organizations.

eye-gaze pointing device An input device that uses vision to control an on-screen cursor that allows users to press on-screen buttons in dialog boxes, to choose menu items, and select cells or text.

F

failback (v., fail back) In a server cluster, the moving of a failed over group to the next node on the group's Preferred Owners list. See also failover; node; resource.

failover (v., fail over) In a server cluster, the means of providing high availability. Upon failure, either of a resource in a group or of the node where the group is online, the cluster takes the group offline on that node, then brings it online on another node. See also node; resource.

FAT32 A derivative of the file allocation table file system. FAT32 supports smaller cluster sizes than FAT, which results in more efficient space allocation on FAT32 drives. See also file allocation table (FAT); NTFS file system.

fault tolerance The assurance of data integrity when hardware failures occur. On the Windows NT and Windows 2000 platforms, fault tolerance is provided by the Ftdisk.sys driver.

FDDI See Fiber Distributed Data Interface.

Fiber Distributed Data Interface (FDDI)
A type of network media designed to be used with fiber-optic cabling. See also LocalTalk; Token Ring.

file allocation table (FAT) A file system based on a file allocation table (FAT) maintained by some operating systems, including Windows NT and Windows 2000, to keep track of the status of various segments of disk space used for file storage.

File Replication service A service used by the Distributed file system (Dfs) to synchronize content between assigned replicas, and by Active Directory Sites and Services to replicate topological and global catalog information across domain controllers.

file server A server that provides organization-wide access to files, programs, and applications.

file system In an operating system, the overall structure in which files are named, stored, and organized. NTFS, FAT, and FAT32 are types of file systems.

File Transfer Protocol (FTP) A protocol that defines how to transfer files from one computer to another over the Internet and a client/server application that moves files using this protocol.

filter In IPSec, a rule that provides the ability to trigger security negotiations for a communication based on the source, destination, and type of IP traffic.

filtering mode For Network Load Balancing, the method by which network traffic inbound to a cluster is handled by the hosts within the cluster. Traffic can either be handled by a single server, load balanced among the hosts within the cluster, or disabled completely. See also server.

FilterKeys A Windows 2000 accessibility feature that allows people with physical disabilities to adjust keyboard response time. See also BounceKeys; RepeatKeys; SlowKeys.

filters In IP and IPX packet filtering, a series of definitions that indicate to the router the type of traffic allowed or disallowed on each interface.

firewall A combination of hardware and software that provides a security system, usually to prevent unauthorized access from outside to an internal network or intranet. A firewall prevents direct communication between network and external computers by routing communication through a proxy server outside of the network. The proxy server determines whether it is safe to let a file pass through to the network. A firewall is also called a security-edge gateway.

folder redirection A Group Policy option that allows you to redirect designated folders to the network.

forest A collection of one or more Windows 2000 Active Directory trees, organized as peers and connected by two-way transitive trust relationships between the root domains of each tree. All trees in a forest share a common schema, configuration, and global catalog. When a forest contains multiple trees, the trees do not form a contiguous namespace.

form Specifies the paper size (such as letter or legal) assigned to a tray on a printer. A form defines physical characteristics such as paper size and printer area margins of the paper or other print media.

FORTEZZA A family of security products, including PCMCIA-based cards, compatible serial port devices, combination cards (such as FORTEZZA/Modem and FORTEZZA/Ethernet), server boards, and others. FORTEZZA is a registered trademark held by the National Security Agency.

fractional T1 A T1 line that consists of 23 B channels and 1 D channel. The single D channel is used for clocking purposes.

fragmentation The scattering of parts of the same disk file over different areas of the disk. Fragmentation occurs as files on a disk are deleted and new files are added. It slows disk access and degrades the overall performance of disk operations, although usually not severely. See also defragmentation.

frame In synchronous communication, a package of information transmitted as a single unit from one device to another. Frame is a term most often used with Ethernet networks. A frame is similar to the packet used on other networks. See also packet.

free space Available space that is used to create logical drives within an extended partition. See also extended partition; logical drive; unallocated space.

FTP See File Transfer Protocol.

full replica A read/write replica of a directory partition that contains all attributes of all objects in the partition. A full replica is also called a master replica. See also partial replica

full zone transfer (AXFR) The standard query type supported by all DNS servers to update and synchronize zone data when the zone is changed. When a DNS query is made using AXFR as the specified query type, the entire zone is transferred as the response. See also incremental zone transfer (IXFR); zone; zone transfer.

fully qualified domain name (FQDN)
A DNS domain name that has been stated so as to indicate its precise location in the domain namespace tree. For example, client1.reskit.com. The FQDN is also known as a full computer name.

G

gateway A device connected to multiple physical TCP/IP networks, capable of routing or delivering IP packets between them. A gateway translates between different transport protocols or data formats (for example, IPX and IP) and is generally added to a network primarily for its translation ability. See also IP address; Internet Protocol router.

Gateway Service for NetWare A service that creates a gateway in which Microsoft clients can access NetWare core protocol networks, such as NetWare file and print services, through a Windows 2000 server.

generic Quality of Service A method by which a TCP/IP network can offer Quality of Service guarantees for multimedia applications. Generic Quality of Service allocates different bandwidths for each connection on an as-needed basis.

Gigabit Ethernet The Ethernet standard that transmits data at 1 billion bits per second, or more.

Global Catalog An Active Directory service that stores directory information from all source domains in a single location in the installation's tree. Users can submit queries to the Global Catalog about objects without regard to the logical or physical location of the object. The Global Catalog is optimized for high performance in resolving queries.

global group For Windows 2000 Server, a group that can be used in its own domain, in member servers and workstations of the domain, and in trusting domains. In all those places a global group can be granted rights and permissions and can become a member of local groups. However, a global group can contain user accounts only from its own domain. See also group; local group.

globally unique identifier (GUID) A 16-byte value generated from the unique identifier on a device, the current date and time, and a sequence number. A GUID is used to identify a particular device or component.

graphical user interface (GUI) A display format, like that of Windows, that represents a program's functions with graphic images such as buttons and icons. GUIs allow a user to perform operations and make choices by pointing and clicking with a mouse.

group A collection of users, computers, contacts and other groups. Groups can be used as security or as e-mail distribution collections. Distribution groups are used only for e-mail. Security groups are used both to grant access to resources and as e-mail distribution lists. In a server cluster, a collection of resources, and the basic unit of failover. See also domain local group; global group; native mode; universal group.

group memberships The groups to which a user account belongs. Permissions and rights granted to a group are also provided to its members. In most cases, the actions a user can perform in Windows 2000 are determined by the group memberships of the user account the user is logged on to. See also group.

Group Policy An administrator's tool for defining and controlling how programs, network resources, and the operating system operate for users and computers in an organization. In an Active Directory environment, Group Policy is applied to users or computers on the basis of their membership in sites, domains, or organizational units.

Group Policy object A collection of Group Policy settings. Group Policy objects are the documents created by the Group Policy snap-in. Group Policy objects are stored at the domain level, and they affect users and computers contained in sites, domains, and organizational units. Each Windows 2000-based computer has exactly one group of settings stored locally, called the local Group Policy object.

guest A Services for Macintosh user who does not have a user account or who does not provide a password. When a Macintosh user assigns permissions to everyone, these permissions are given to the guests and users of the group.

guest account A built-in account used to log on to a computer running Windows 2000 when a user does not have an account on the computer or domain or in any of the domains trusted by the computer's domain.

GUI mode The portion of Setup that uses a graphical user interface (GUI).

H

handle In the user interface, an interface added to an object that facilitates moving, sizing, reshaping, or other functions pertaining to an object. In programming, a pointer to a pointer— that is, a token that lets a program access a resource identified.

hardware abstraction layer (HAL)
A thin layer of software provided by the hardware manufacturer that hides, or abstracts, hardware differences from higher layers of the operating system. Through the filter provided by the HAL, different types of hardware all look alike to the rest of the operating system. This allows Windows NT and Windows 2000 to be portable from one hardware platform to another. The HAL also provides routines that allow a single device driver to support the same device on all platforms. The HAL works closely with the kernel.

hardware compatibility list (HCL)
A list of the devices supported by Windows 2000.

hardware failure A malfunction of a physical component, such as a disk head failure or memory error.

hardware inventory The automated process Systems Management Server uses to gather detailed information about the hardware in use on client computers in a Systems Management Server site.

hardware router A router that performs routing as a dedicated function and has specific hardware designed and optimized for routing.

hardware type A classification for similar devices. For example, Imaging Device is a hardware type for digital cameras and scanners.

heartbeat In a server cluster or Network Load Balancing cluster, a periodic message sent between nodes to detect system failure of any node.

hexadecimal A base-16 number system whose numbers are represented by the digits 0 through 9 and the letters A (equivalent to decimal 10) through F (equivalent to decimal 15).

hierarchical storage management (HSM)
A technology that automates storage management and lowers storage costs by automatically migrating infrequently accessed files from local storage to remote storage and recalling the files upon user demand.

high availability The ability to keep an application or service operational and usable by clients most of the time.

hop count The Transport Control field indicates the number of IPX routers that have processed the IPX packet.

host A Windows 2000 computer that runs a server program or service used by network or remote clients. For Network Load Balancing, a cluster consists of multiple hosts connected over a local area network.

host ID A number used to identify an interface on a physical network bounded by routers. The host ID should be unique to the network.

host name The name of a computer on a network. In the Windows 2000 Server Resource Kit, host name is used to refer to the first label of a fully qualified domain name. See also hosts file.

host priority For Network Load Balancing, a host's precedence for handling default network traffic for TCP and UDP ports. It is used if a host within the cluster goes offline, and determines which host within the cluster will assume responsibility for the traffic previously handled by the offline host. See also User Datagram Protocol (UDP).

Hosts A file containing lists of known IP addresses, used by TCP/IP to locate computers on a network or the Internet.

hosts file A local text file in the same format as the 4.3 Berkeley Software Distribution (BSD) UNIX/etc/hosts file. This file maps host names to IP addresses. In Windows 2000, this file is stored in the \%Systemroot%\System32\Drivers\Etc folder. See also systemroot.

hot keys A Windows 2000 feature that allows quick activation of specified accessibility features through a combination of keys pressed in unison.

hub A network-enabled device joining communication lines at a central location, providing a common connection to all devices on the network.

hub-and-spoke A WINS server configuration that uses a central "hub" as a point of contact for many outlying WINS server "spokes" to improve convergence time.

Hypertext Markup Language (HTML)
A simple markup language used to create hypertext documents that are portable from one platform to another. HTML files are simple ASCII text files with embedded codes (indicated by markup tags) to indicate formatting and hypertext links. HTML is used for formatting documents on the World Wide Web.

Hypertext Transfer Protocol (HTTP)
The protocol used to transfer information on the World Wide Web. An HTTP address (one kind of URL or Uniform Resource Locator) takes the form: http://www.microsoft.com

I

IKE See Internet Key Exchange.

impersonation A circumstance that occurs when Windows 2000 Server allows one process to take on the security attributes of another.

Impersonation token An access token that has been created to capture the security information of a client process, allowing a service to "impersonate" the client process in security operations. See also access token; primary token.

incremental zone transfer (IXFR) An alternate query type that can be used by some DNS servers to update and synchronize zone data when a zone is changed. When incremental zone transfer is supported between DNS servers, servers can keep track of and transfer only those incremental resource record changes between each version of the zone. See also full zone transfer (AXFR); zone; zone transfer.

infrared (IR) Light that is beyond red in the color spectrum. While the light is not visible to the human eye, infrared transmitters and receivers can send and receive infrared signals. See also Infrared Data Association; infrared device; infrared port.

Infrared Data Association (IrDA) A networking protocol used to transmit data created by infrared devices. Infrared Data Association is also the name of the industry organization of computer, component, and telecommunications vendors who establish the standards for infrared communication between computers and peripheral devices, such as printers. See also infrared; infrared device; infrared port.

infrared device A computer, or a computer peripheral such as a printer, that can communicate using infrared light. See also infrared.

infrared port An optical port on a computer to communicate with other computers or devices using infrared light, without cables. Infrared ports can be found on some portable computers, printers, and cameras. An infrared port can also be added to a computer with an IR dongle (or hardware key security device) connected to a PCI card, serial port, parallel port (for a printer), or direct connection to the motherboard. See also infrared device; infrared port.

inheritance The ability to build new object classes from existing object classes. The new object is defined as a subclass of the original object. The original object becomes a superclass of the new object. A subclass inherits the attributes of the superclass, including structure rules and content rules.

insertion point The place where text will be inserted when typed. The insertion point usually appears as a flashing vertical bar in an application's window or in a dialog box.

install When referring to software, to add program files and folders to your hard disk and related data to your registry so that the software will run properly. "Installing" contrasts with "upgrading," where existing program files, folders, and registry entries are updated to a more recent version. When referring to hardware, to physically connect the device to your computer, to load device drivers onto your computer, and to configure device properties and settings. See also device driver; registry.

integrity An Internet Protocol security property that protects data from unauthorized modification in transit, ensuring that the data received is exactly the same as the data sent. Hash functions sign each packet with a cryptographic checksum, which the receiving computer checks before opening the packet. If the packet—and therefore signature—has changed, the packet is discarded.

IntelliMirror   A set of Windows 2000 features used for desktop change and configuration management. When IntelliMirror is used in both the server and client, the users' data, applications, and settings follow them when they move to another computer. Administrators can use IntelliMirror to perform remote installation of Windows 2000.

interface   In networking, a logical device over which packets can be sent and received. In the Routing and Remote Access administrative tool, it is a visual representation of the network segment that can be reached over the LAN or WAN adapters. Each interface has a unique name. See also local area network (LAN); network adapter; routing; wide area network (WAN).

internal namespace   A private namespace that is only used by users within an organization.

internal network number   A 4-byte hexadecimal number used for addressing and routing purposes. The internal network number identifies a virtual network inside a computer. The internal network number must be unique to the IPX internetwork. Internal network number is also called virtual network number. See also external network number; Internetwork Packet Exchange (IPX).

internet   Two or more network segments connected by routers. Another term for internetwork. With Services for Macintosh, an internet can be created by connecting two or more AppleTalk networks to a computer running Windows 2000 Server. With TCP/IP, an internet can be created by connecting two or more IP networks to a multihomed computer running either Windows 2000 Server or Windows 2000 Professional. IP forwarding must be enabled to route between attached IP network segments.

Internet   A worldwide public TCP/IP internetwork consisting of thousands of networks, connecting research facilities, universities, libraries, and private companies.

Internet Assigned Numbers Authority (IANA)   An organization that delegates IP addresses and their allocation to organizations such as the InterNIC.

Internet Control Message Protocol (ICMP)   A required maintenance protocol in the TCP/IP suite that reports errors and allows simple connectivity. ICMP is used by the ping tool to perform TCP/IP troubleshooting.

Internet Engineering Task Force (IETF)   An open community of network designers, operators, vendors, and researchers concerned with the evolution of Internet architecture and the smooth operation of the Internet. Technical work is performed by working groups organized by topic areas (such as routing, transport, and security) and through mailing lists. Internet standards are developed in IETF Requests for Comments (RFCs), which are a series of notes that discuss many aspects of computing and computer communication, focusing on networking protocols, programs, and concepts.

Internet Group Management Protocol (IGMP)   A protocol in the TCP/IP protocol suite that is responsible for the management of IP multicast group membership.

Internet Information Services (IIS)   Software services that support Web site creation, configuration, and management, along with other Internet functions. Internet Information Services include Network News Transfer Protocol (NNTP), File Transfer Protocol (FTP), and Simple Mail Transfer Protocol (SMTP). See also File Transfer Protocol (FTP); Network News Transfer Protocol (NNTP); Simple Mail Transfer Protocol (SMTP).

Internet Key Exchange (IKE) A protocol that establishes the security association and shared keys necessary for two parties to communicate with Internet Protocol security.

Internet Protocol (IP) A routable protocol in the TCP/IP protocol suite that is responsible for IP addressing, routing, and the fragmentation and reassembly of IP packets.

Internet Protocol router A system connected to multiple physical TCP/IP networks that can route or deliver IP packets between the networks. See also packet; router; routing; TCP/IP.

Internet Protocol security (IPSec)
A set of industry-standard, cryptography-based protection services and protocols. IPSec protects all protocols in the TCP/IP protocol suite and Internet communications using L2TP. See also Layer 2 Tunneling Protocol (L2TP).

Internet service provider (ISP) A company that provides individuals or companies access to the Internet and the World Wide Web. An ISP provides a telephone number, a user name, a password and other connection information so users can connect their computers to the ISP's computers. An ISP typically charges a monthly and/or hourly connection fee.

internetwork At least two network segments connected using routers.

Internetwork packet exchange (IPX)
A network protocol native to NetWare that controls addressing and routing of packets within and between LANs. IPX does not guarantee that a message will be complete (no lost packets). See also Internetwork Packet Exchange/Sequenced Packet Exchange (IPX/SPX).

intranet A network within an organization that uses Internet technologies and protocols, but is available only to certain people, such as employees of a company. An intranet is also called a private network.

inventory Information that Systems Management Server inventory client agents collect for each client in a site. The inventory can include hardware and software information and collected files, depending on the administrator-defined configuration.

IP address A 32-bit address used to identify a node on a an IP internetwork. Each node on the IP internetwork must be assigned a unique IP address, which is made up of the network ID, plus a unique host ID. This address is typically represented with the decimal value of each octet separated by a period (for example, 192.168.7.27). In Windows 2000, the IP address can be configured manually or dynamically through DHCP. See also Dynamic Host Configuration Protocol (DHCP); node.

IPSec See Internet Protocol security.

IPSec driver An Internet Protocol security mechanism, activated when Internet Protocol security is configured for a computer, that watches packets for a match with an IP filter in the computer's active Internet Protocol security policy. The IPSec driver also performs the actual encryption and decryption of the data. See also Internet Protocol Security.

IPSec driver A driver that uses the IP Filter List from the active IPSec policy to watch for outbound IP packets that must be secured and inbound IP packets that need to be verified and decrypted.

K

Kerberos authentication protocol

An authentication mechanism used to verify user or host identity. The Kerberos v5 protocol is the default authentication service for Windows 2000. Internet Protocol security and the QoS admission control service use the Kerberos protocol for authentication. See also QoS admission control service; Internet Protocol security (IPSec).

key A secret code or number required to read, modify, or verify secured data. Keys are used in conjunction with algorithms to secure data. Windows 2000 automatically handles key generation. For the registry, a key is an entry in the registry that can contain both subkeys and entries. In the registry structure, keys are analogous to folders, and entries are analogous to files. In the Registry Editor window, a key appears as a file folder in the left pane. In an answer file, keys are character strings that specify parameters from which Setup obtains the needed data for unattended installation of the operating system.

key distribution center (KDC) A network service that supplies session tickets and temporary session keys used in the Kerberos authentication protocol. In Windows 2000, the KDC runs as a privileged process on all domain controllers. The KDC uses Active Directory to manage sensitive account information such as passwords for user accounts. See also Kerberos authentication protocol; session ticket.

key exchange Confidential exchange of secret keys online, which is commonly done with public key cryptography. See also public key cryptography.

key management Secure management of private keys for public key cryptography. Windows 2000 manages private keys and keeps them confidential with CryptoAPI and CSPs. See also private key; CryptoAPI; cryptographic service providers.

key pair A private key and its related public key. See also public/private key pair.

keyboard filters Special timing and other devices that compensate for erratic motion tremors, slow response time, and other dexterity impairments.

L

L2TP See Layer Two Tunneling Protocol.

label See domain name label.

LAN See local area network.

LAN emulation (LANE) A set of protocols that allow existing Ethernet and Token Ring LAN services to overlay an ATM network. LANE allows connectivity among LAN- and ATM-attached stations. See also Asynchronous Transfer Mode (ATM).

LAN emulation client (LEC) The client on an emulated local area network (ELAN) that performs data forwarding, address resolution, and other control functions. The LEC resides on end stations in an emulated local area network (ELAN). See also asynchronous transfer mode; emulated local area network (ELAN); LAN emulation.

LAN emulation server (LES) The central control point for an emulated local area network (ELAN). Enables LANE clients to join the emulated local area network (ELAN) and resolves LAN addresses to ATM addresses. See also ATM; emulated local area network (ELAN); LAN emulation (LANE).

LAN manager replication The file replication service used under Windows NT. See File Replication service.

large window support In TCP communications, the largest amount of data that can be transferred without acknowledgment. The window has a fixed size. Large window support dynamically recalculates the window size and allows larger amounts of data to be transferred at one time causing greater throughput.

latency See replication latency.

layer 2 tunneling protocol (L2TP)
A tunneling protocol that encapsulates PPP frames to be sent over IP, X.25, Frame Relay, or ATM networks. L2TP is a combination of the Point-to-Point Tunneling Protocol (PPTP) and Layer 2 Forwarding (L2F), a technology proposed by Cisco Systems, Inc.

LDAP API See Lightweight Directory Access Protocol Access Programming Interface

license service A server in Terminal Services that stores all client licenses that have been downloaded for a Terminal server and tracks the licenses that have been issued to client computers or terminals.

Lightweight Directory Access Protocol (LDAP)
A directory service protocol that runs directly over TCP/IP and the primary access protocol for Active Directory. LDAP version 3 is defined by a set of Proposed Standard documents in Internet Engineering Task Force (IETF) RFC 2251. See also Lightweight Directory Access Protocol Access Programming Interface (LDAP API).

Lightweight Directory Access Protocol Access Programming Interface (LDAP API)
A set of low-level C-language APIs to the LDAP protocol.

Line Printer Daemon (LPD) A service on the print server that receives documents (print jobs) from line printer remote (LPR) tools running on client systems. See also Line Printer Remote (LPR).

Line Printer Remote (LPR) A connectivity utility that runs on client systems and is used to print files to a computer running an LPD server. See also Line Printer Daemon (LPD).

link state database (LSDB) A map of an area maintained by OSPF routers. It is updated after any change in the network topology. The link state database is used to compute IP routes, which must be computed again after any change in the topology. See also open shortest path first (OSPF).

linked object An object that is inserted into a document but still exists in the source file. When information is linked, the new document is updated automatically if the information in the original document changes. See also embedded object.

load-balancing Scaling the performance of a server-based program (such as a Web server) by distributing its client requests across multiple servers within the cluster by Windows Clustering. Each host can specify the load percentage that it will handle, or the load can be equally distributed across all the hosts. If a host fails, Windows Clustering dynamically redistributes the load among the remaining hosts. See also client request; cluster; host; scalability; server.

local area network (LAN) A communications network connecting a group of computers, printers, and other devices located within a relatively limited area (for example, a building). A LAN allows any connected device to interact with any other on the network.. See also wide area network (WAN).

local computer The computer that a user is currently logged on to. More specifically, a local computer is a computer that can be accessed directly without using a communications line or a communications device, such as a network adapter or a modem. Similarly, running a local program means running the program on your computer, as opposed to running it from a server.

local group For computers running Windows 2000 Professional and member servers, a group that is granted permissions and rights from its own computer to only those resources on its own computer on which the group resides. See also global group.

local printer A printer that is directly connected to one of the ports on your computer.

local storage For Windows 2000 Server, NTFS disk volumes used as primary data storage. Such disk volumes can be managed by Remote Storage by copying infrequently accessed files to remote, or secondary, storage. See also remote storage.

LocalTalk The Apple networking hardware built into every Macintosh computer. LocalTalk includes the cables and connector boxes to connect components and network devices that are part of the AppleTalk network system. LocalTalk was formerly known as the AppleTalk Personal Network.

lock To make a file inaccessible. When more than one user can manipulate a file, that file is locked when a user accesses it in order to prevent more than one user from modifying the file simultaneously.

log file A file that stores messages generated by an application, service, or operating system. These messages are used to track the operations performed. For example, Web servers maintain log files listing every request made to the server.

Log files are usually ASCII files and often have a .log extension. In Backup, a file that contains a record of the date the tapes were created and the names of files and directories successfully backed up and restored. The Performance Logs and Alerts service also creates log files.

log off To stop using a network, which removes the user name from active use until the user logs on again.

log on To begin using a network by providing a user name and password that identifies a user to the network.

logical drive A volume created within an extended partition on a basic disk. You can format and assign a drive letter to a logical drive. Only basic disks can contain logical drives. A logical drive cannot span multiple disks. See also basic disk; basic volume; extended partition.

logical IP subnet (LIS) A group of IP hosts/members belonging to the same IP subnet and whose host ATMARP server ATM address is the same.

logical printer The software interface between the operating system and the printer in Windows 2000. While a printer is the device that does the actual printing, a logical printer is its software interface on the print server. This software interface determines how a print job is processed and how it is routed to its destination (to a local or network port, to a file, or to a remote print share). When a document is printed, it is spooled (or stored) on the logical printer before it is sent to the printer itself. See also spooling.

loopback option An option that allows an administrator to apply Group Policy settings based on the computer that the user logs on to, even after the user settings have been processed.

M

master domain A Windows NT domain that holds user account data. Also known as an account domain.

master server In a DNS zone transfer, the computer that is the source of the zone. Master servers can vary and are one of two types (either primary or secondary masters), depending on how the server obtains its zone data. See also primary server; secondary server; zone; zone transfer.

maximum password age The period of time a password can be used before the system requires the user to change it.

media access control A layer in the network architecture of Windows NT and Windows 2000 that deals with network access and collision detection.

media access control address The address used for communication between network adapters on the same subnet. Each network adapter has an associated media access control address.

member server A computer that runs Windows 2000 Server but is not a domain controller of a Windows 2000 domain. Member servers participate in a domain, but do not store a copy of the directory database. Permissions can be set on a member server's resources that allow users to connect to the server and use its resources. Resource permissions can be granted for domain global groups and users as well as for local groups and users. See also domain controller; global group; local group.

metric A number used to indicate the cost of a route in the IP routing table so that one can select the best route among possible multiple routes to the same destination.

Microsoft Component Services A program that runs on an Internet or other server and manages the application and database transaction requests for a client's user. Component Services screens the user and client computer from having to formulate requests for unfamiliar databases and forwards the requests to database servers. It also manages security, connection to other servers, and transaction integrity.

Microsoft Management Console (MMC) A framework for hosting administrative consoles. A console is defined by the items on its console tree, which might include folders or other containers, World Wide Web pages, and other administrative items. A console has one or more windows that can provide views of the console tree and the administrative properties, services, and events that are acted on by the items in the console tree. The main MMC window provides commands and tools for authoring consoles. The authoring features of MMC and the console tree might be hidden when a console is in User Mode. See also console tree.

migrate The process of moving files or programs from an older file format or protocol to a more current format or protocol. For example, WINS database entries can be migrated from static WINS database entries to dynamically-registered DHCP entries.

migration The process of copying an object from local storage to remote storage.

Mini-Setup wizard A wizard that starts the first time a computer boots from a hard disk that has been duplicated. The wizard gathers any information that is needed for the newly duplicated hard disk.

minimum password length The fewest characters a password can contain.

minimum TTL A default Time-To-Live (TTL) value set in seconds for use with all resource records in a zone. This value is set in the start-of-authority (SOA) resource record for each zone. By default, the DNS server includes this value in query answers to inform recipients how long it can store and use resource records provided in the query answer before they must expire the stored records data. When TTL values are set for individual resource records, those values will override the minimum TTL. See also Time To Live (TTL).

miniport drivers A driver that is connected to an intermediate driver and a hardware device.

mirror set A fully redundant or shadow copy of data. Mirror sets provide an identical twin for a selected disk; all data written to the primary disk is also written to the shadow or mirror disk. This gives you instant access to another disk with a copy of the information. Mirror sets provide fault tolerance. See also stripe set with parity; volume set.

mirrored volume A fault-tolerant volume that duplicates data on two physical disks. The mirror is always located on a different disk. If one of the physical disks fails, the data on the failed disk becomes unavailable, but the system continues to operate by using the unaffected disk. A mirrored volume is slower than a RAID-5 volume in read operations but faster in write operations. Mirrored volumes can only be created on dynamic disks. In Windows NT 4.0, a mirrored volume was known as a mirror set. See also dynamic disk; dynamic volume; fault tolerance; redundant array of independent disks (RAID); volume.

mixed mode The default mode setting for domains on Windows 2000 domain controllers. Mixed mode allows Windows 2000 domain controllers and Windows NT backup domain controllers to co-exist in a domain. Mixed mode does not support the universal and nested group enhancements of Windows 2000. You can change the domain mode setting to Windows 2000 native mode after all Windows NT domain controllers are either removed from the domain or upgraded to Windows 2000. See also native mode.

mixed mode domains A networked set of computers running more than one operating system, for example, both Windows NT and Windows 2000.

MMC See Microsoft Management Console.

MMC snap-in A type of management tool that you can add to the console tree of a console supported by Microsoft Management Console (MMC), for example, Device Manager. A snap-in can be either a stand-alone or an extension snap-in. A stand-alone snap-in can be added by itself; an extension snap-in can only be added to extend another snap-in. See also Microsoft Management Console (MMC).

mobile user A user who travels away from a corporate campus such as a salesperson or field technician.

mobility impairments The diminished ability to perform certain manual tasks, such as using a mouse or typing two keys at the same time; having a tendency to hit multiple keys, or bounce fingers off keys; or inability to hold a printed book.

module A component of the Windows 2000 operating system that has sole responsibility for its functions. An application runs in a separate module in user mode, from which it requests system services. Application processes are transferred to one or more modules in kernel mode (protected), where the actual service is provided.

MouseKeys A feature in Microsoft Windows that allows use of the numeric keyboard to move the mouse pointer.

mouthstick An alternative assistive input device for users with physical impairments.

MS-DOS-based application An application that is designed to run with MS-DOS and therefore might not be able to take full advantage of all Windows 2000 features.

multicast Network traffic destined for a set of hosts that belong to a multicast group. See also multicast group.

multicast backbone The IP-multicast network portion of the Internet.

multicast DHCP (MDHCP) An extension to the DHCP protocol standard that supports dynamic assignment and configuration of IP multicast addresses on TCP/IP-based networks.

multicast forwarding table The table used by IP to forward IP multicast traffic. An entry in the IP multicast forwarding table consists of the multicast group address, the source IP address, a list of interfaces to which the traffic is forwarded (next hop interfaces), and the single interface on which the traffic must be received in order to be forwarded (the previous hop interface).

multicast group A group of member TCP/IP hosts configured to listen and receive datagrams sent to a specified destination IP address. The destination address for the group is a shared IP address in the Class D address range (224.0.0.0 to 2239.255.255.255). See also datagram.

multicast scope A range of IP multicast addresses in the range of 239.0.0.0 to 239.254.255.255. Multicast addresses in this range can be prevented from propagating in either direction (send or receive) through the use of scope-based multicast boundaries.

multihomed A computer that has multiple network adapters installed.

multilingual APIs Application Programming Interfaces used to support multiple languages in Windows 2000.

multimaster replication A replication model in which any domain controller accepts and replicates directory changes to any other domain controller. This differs from other replication models in which one computer stores the single modifiable copy of the directory and other computers store backup copies. See also domain controller; replication.

multiple-master replication The process by which Windows 2000 domain controllers replicate domain data. The primary domain controller emulator replicates the domain data to the other domain controllers. See primary domain controller emulator.

Multipurpose Internet Mail Extensions (MIME) A common method for transmitting non-text data through Internet e-mail. MIME encodes non-text data as ASCII text and then decodes it back to its original format at the receiving end. A MIME header is added to the file which includes the type of data contained and the encoding method used. See also Secure/Multipurpose Internet Mail Extensions (S/MIME).

mutual authentication The process when the calling router authenticates itself to the answering router and the answering router authenticates itself to the calling router. Both ends of the connection verify the identity of the other end of the connection. MS-CHAP v2 and EAP-TLS authentication methods provide mutual authentication.

N

name resolution The process of having software translate between names that are easy for users to work with, and numerical IP addresses, which are difficult for users but necessary for TCP/IP communications. Name resolution can be provided by software components such as the Domain Name System (DNS) or the Windows Internet Name Service (WINS). In directory service, the phase of LDAP directory operation processing that involves finding a domain controller that holds the target entry for the operation. See also Domain Name System (DNS); Transmission Control Protocol/Internet Protocol (TCP/IP); Windows Internet Name Service (WINS).

name resolution service A service required by TCP/IP internetworks to convert computer names to IP addresses and IP addresses to computer names. (People use "friendly" names to connect to computers; programs use IP addresses.) See also internetwork; IP address; Transmission Control Protocol/Internet Protocol (TCP/IP).

name server In the DNS client/server model, a server authoritative for a portion of the DNS database. The server makes computer names and other information available to client resolvers querying for name resolution across the Internet or an intranet. See also Domain Name System (DNS).

named pipe A portion of memory that can be used by one process to pass information to another process, so that the output of one process is the input of the other process. The second process can be local (on the same computer as the first) or remote (on a networked computer).

namespace A set of unique names for resources or items used in a shared computing environment. The names in a namespace can be resolved to the objects they represent. For Microsoft Management Console (MMC), the namespace is represented by the console tree, which displays all of the snap-ins and resources that are accessible to a console. For Domain Name System (DNS), namespace is the vertical or hierarchical structure of the domain name tree. For example, each domain label, such as "host1" or "example," used in a fully qualified domain name, such as "host1.example.microsoft.com," indicates a branch in the domain namespace tree. For Active Directory, namespace corresponds to the DNS namespace in structure, but resolves Active Directory object names.

naming service A service, such as that provided by WINS or DNS, that allows friendly names to be resolved to an address or other specially defined resource data that is used to locate network resources of various types and purposes.

native mode The condition in which all domain controllers within a domain are Windows 2000 domain controllers and an administrator has enabled native mode operation (through Active Directory Users and Computers). See also mixed mode.

nested groups A Windows 2000 capability available only in native mode that allows the creation of groups within groups. See universal group, global group, domain local group, forest, trusted forest.

NetBIOS Enhanced User Interface (NetBEUI)
A network protocol native to Microsoft Networking, that is usually used in local area networks of 1 to 200 clients. NetBEUI uses Token Ring source routing as its only method of routing. It is the Microsoft implementation of the NetBIOS standard.

NetBIOS name A name recognized by WINS, which maps the name to an IP address.

NetBIOS name resolution The process of resolving a NetBIOS name to its IP address.

NetBIOS over TCP/IP (NetBT) A feature that provides the NetBIOS programming interface over the TCP/IP protocol. It is used for monitoring routed servers that use NetBIOS name resolution.

Netdom A tool that allows management of Windows 2000 domains and trust relationships from the command line.

NetWare Novell's network operating system.

NetWare Core Protocol (NCP) The file-sharing protocol that governs communications about resource (such as disk and printer), bindery, and NDS operations between server and client computers on a Novell NetWare network. Requests from client computers are transmitted by the IPX protocol. Servers respond according to NCP guidelines. See also bindery; Internetwork Packet Exchange (IPX); Novell Directory Services (NDS).

network adapter A software or hardware plug-in board that connects a node or host to a local area network. If the node is a member of a server cluster, the network adapter is a server cluster object (the network interface object).

network address See network ID.

Network Address Translation (NAT)
A protocol that allows a network with private addresses to access information on the Internet through an IP translation process.

network address translator An IP router defined in RFC 1631 that can translate IP addresses and TCP/UDP port numbers of packets as they are being forwarded.

network administrator A person responsible for setting up and managing domain controllers or local computers and their user and group accounts; assigning passwords and permissions; and helping users with networking issues. Administrators are members of the Administrators group and have full control over the domain or computer.

network basic input/output system (NetBIOS)
An application programming interface (API) that can be used by applications on a local area network or computers running MS-DOS, OS/2, or some version of UNIX. NetBIOS provides a uniform set of commands for requesting lower level network services.

network gateway A device that connects networks using different communications protocols so that information can be passed from one to the other. A gateway both transfers information and converts it to a form compatible with the protocols being used by the receiving network.

network ID A number used to identify the systems that are located on the same physical network bounded by routers. The network ID should be unique to the internetwork.

network layer A layer that addresses messages and translates logical addresses and names into physical addresses. It also determines the route from the source to the destination computer and manages traffic problems, such as switching, routing, and controlling the congestion of data packets.

network load balancing The Windows Clustering component that distributes incoming Web requests among its cluster of IIS servers.

network load balancing cluster Between 2 and 32 IIS servers from which Network Load Balancing presents a single IP address to Web clients and among which Network Load Balancing distributes incoming Web requests.

network media The type of physical wiring and lower-layer protocols used for transmitting and receiving frames. For example, Ethernet, FDDI, and Token Ring.

Network Monitor A packet capture and analysis tool used to view network traffic. This feature is included with Windows 2000 Server; however, Systems Management Server has a more complete version.

network name In server clusters, the name through which clients access server cluster resources. A network name is similar to a computer name, and when combined in a resource group with an IP address and the applications clients access, presents a virtual server to clients.

Network News Transfer Protocol (NNTP) A member of the TCP/IP suite of protocols, used to distribute network news messages to NNTP servers and clients, or news readers, on the Internet. NNTP is designed so that news articles are stored on a server in a central database, thus enabling a user to select specific items to read. See also Transmission Control Protocol/Internet Protocol (TCP/IP).

network prefix The number of bits in the IP network ID starting from the high order bit. The network prefix is another way of expressing a subnet mask.

network prefix notation The practice of expressing a subnet mask as a network prefix rather than a dotted decimal notation.

NNTP See Network News Transfer Protocol

node In tree structures, a location on the tree that can have links to one or more items below it. In local area networks (LANs), a device that is connected to the network and is capable of communicating with other network devices. In a server cluster, a server that has Cluster service software installed and is a member of a cluster. See also LAN.

nonauthoritative restore A restore of a backup copy of a Windows 2000 domain controller in which the objects in the restored directory are not treated as authoritative. The restored objects are updated with changes held in other replicas of the restored domain. See also authoritative restore.

noncontainer object An object that cannot logically contain other objects. A file is a noncontainer object. See also container object; object.

nonrepudiation A basic security function of cryptography. Nonrepudiation provides assurance that a party in a communication cannot falsely deny that a part of the communication occurred. Without nonrepudiation, someone can communicate and then later deny the communication or claim that the communication occurred at a different time. See also cryptography; authentication; confidentiality; integrity.

Novell Directory Services (NDS) On networks running Novell NetWare 4.x and NetWare 5.x, a distributed database that maintains information about every resource on the network and provides access to these resources.

NTFS file system A recoverable file system designed for use specifically with Windows NT and Windows 2000. NTFS uses database, transaction-processing, and object paradigms to provide data security, file system reliability, and other advanced features. It supports file system recovery, large storage media, and various features for the POSIX subsystem. It also supports object-oriented application by treating all files as objects with user-defined and system-defined attributes.

NWLink An implementation of the Internetwork Packet Exchange (IPX), sequenced packet exchange (SPX), and NetBIOS protocols used in Novell networks. NWLink is a standard network protocol that supports routing and can support NetWare client/server applications, where NetWare-aware Sockets-based applications communicate with IPX/SPX Sockets-based applications. See also Internetwork Packet Exchange (IPX); network basic input/output system (NetBIOS).

O

object An entity, such as a file, folder, shared folder, printer, or Active Directory object, described by a distinct, named set of attributes. For example, the attributes of a File object include its name, location, and size; the attributes of an Active Directory User object might include the user's first name, last name, and e-mail address. For OLE and ActiveX objects, an object can also be any piece of information that can be linked to, or embedded into, another object. See also attribute; container object; noncontainer object; parent object; child object.

object class The object class is the formal definition of a specific kind of object that can be stored in the directory. An object class is a distinct, named set of attributes that represents something concrete, such as a user, a printer, or an application. The attributes hold data describing the thing that is identified by the directory object. Attributes of a user might include the user's given name, surname, and e-mail address. The terms object class and class are used interchangeably. The attributes that can be used to describe an object are determined by the content rules.

object linking and embedding (OLE)
A method for sharing information among applications. Linking an object, such as a graphic, from one document to another inserts a reference to the object into the second document. Any changes you make in the object in the first document will also be made in the second document. Embedding an object inserts a copy of an object from one document into another document. Changes you make in the object in the first document will not be updated in the second unless the embedded object is explicitly updated. See also ActiveX.

offline In a server cluster, the state of a resource, group, or node when it is unavailable to the cluster. Resources and groups also have an offline state. See also group; node; online, paused; resource.

OLE See object linking and embedding.

on-demand installation An installation option that gives Windows 2000-compatible software the ability to install new features on first use rather than when the application is first installed.

on-demand router-to-router VPN connection A router-to-router VPN connection that is made by a calling router who has a dial-up connection to the Internet.

online In a server cluster, the state of a resource, group, or node when it is available to the cluster. See also heartbeat; node; offline; paused; resource.

open database connectivity (ODBC) An application programming interface (API) that enables database applications to access data from a variety of existing data sources.

open shortest path first (OSPF) A routing protocol used in medium-sized and large-sized networks. This protocol is more complex than RIP, but allows better control and is more efficient in propagating routing information.

organizational units An Active Directory container object used within domains. Organizational units are logical containers into which users, groups, computers, and other organizational units are placed. It can contain objects only from its parent domain. An organizational unit is the smallest scope to which a Group Policy or delegate authority can be applied.

original equipment manufacturer (OEM) The maker of a piece of equipment. In making computers and computer related equipment, manufacturers of original equipment typically purchase components from other manufacturers of original equipment and then integrate them into their own products.

P

package An icon that represents embedded or linked information. That information can consist of a complete file, such as a Paint bitmap, or part of a file, such as a spreadsheet cell. When a package is chosen, the application used to create the object either plays the object (if it is a sound file, for example) or opens and displays the object. If the original information is changed, linked information is then updated. However, embedded information needs to be manually updated. In Systems Management Server, an object that contains the files and instructions for distributing software to a distribution point. See also embedded object; linked object; object linking and embedding (OLE).

package distribution In Systems Management Server, the process of placing a decompressed package image on distribution points, sharing that image, and making it accessible to clients. This process occurs when you specify distribution points for a package.

packet A transmission unit of fixed maximum size that consists of binary information. This information represents both data and a header containing an ID number, source and destination addresses, and error-control data.

packet filtering Prevents certain types of network packets from either being sent or received. This can be employed for security reasons (to prevent access from unauthorized users) or to improve performance by disallowing unnecessary packets from going over a slow connection. See also packet.

page fault An error that occurs when the requested code or data cannot be located in the physical memory that is available to the requesting process.

page-description language (PDL)
A computer language that describes the arrangement of text and graphics on a printed page. See also printer control language (PCL); PostScript.

paging The process of moving virtual memory back and forth between physical memory and the disk. Paging occurs when physical memory limitations are reached and only occurs for data that is not already "backed" by disk space. For example, file data is not paged out because it already has allocated disk space within a file system. See also virtual memory.

paging file A hidden file on the hard disk that Windows 2000 uses to hold parts of programs and data files that do not fit in memory. The paging file and physical memory, or RAM, comprise virtual memory. Windows 2000 moves data from the paging file to memory as needed and moves data from memory to the paging file to make room for new data. Also called a swap file. See also RAM; virtual memory.

parent domain For DNS and Active Directory, domains that are located in the namespace tree directly above other derivative domain names (child domains). For example, "reskit.com" would be the parent domain for "eu.reskit.com", a child domain. See also child domain; domain; directory partition.

parent object The object in which another object resides. A parent object implies relation. For example, a folder is a parent object in which a file, or child object, resides. An object can also be both a parent and a child object. See also child object; object.

parenting The concept of managing the growth and delegation of a parent domain into further child domains, which are derived and delegated from the parent name. See also child domain; parent domain.

partial replica A read-only replica of a directory partition that contains a subset of the attributes of all objects in the partition. The sum of partial replicas in a forest is called the global catalog. The attributes contained in a partial replica are defined in the schema as the attributes whose attributeSchema objects have the isMemberOfPartialAttributeSet attribute set to TRUE. See also full replica; Global Catalog.

partition A logical division of a hard disk. Partitions make it easier to organize information. Each partition can be formatted for a different file system. A partition must be completely contained on one physical disk, and the partition table in the master boot record for a physical disk can contain up to four entries for partitions.

partition table An area of the master boot record that the computer uses to determine how to access the disk. The partition table can contain up to four partitions for each physical disk.

password authentication protocol (PAP)
A simple, plaintext authentication scheme for authenticating PPP connections. The user name and password are requested by the remote access server and returned by the remote access client in plaintext.

path A sequence of directory (or folder) names that specifies the location of a directory, file, or folder within the Windows directory tree. Each directory name and file name within the path must be preceded by a backslash (\). For example, to specify the path of a file named Readme.doc located in the Windows directory on drive C, you type C:\Windows\Readme.doc.

paused The state of a node that is a fully active member in the server cluster but cannot host groups. The paused state is provided for an administrator to perform maintenance. See also cluster member; failback; failover; node; offline.

PC Card A removable device, approximately the size of a credit card, that can be plugged into a PCMCIA (Personal Computer Memory Card International Association) slot in a portable computer. PCMCIA devices can include modems, network adapters, and hard disk drives.

performance counter In System Monitor, a data item associated with a performance object. For each counter selected, System Monitor presents a value corresponding to a particular aspect of the performance that is defined for the performance object. See also performance object.

performance object In System Monitor, a logical collection of counters that is associated with a resource or service that can be monitored. See also performance counter.

peripheral component interconnect (PCI)
A specification introduced by Intel Corporation that defines a local bus system that allows up to 10 PCI-compliant expansion cards to be installed in the computer.

permanent virtual circuit (PVC) A virtual circuit assigned to a preconfigured static route.

permission A rule associated with an object to regulate which users can gain access to the object and in what manner. In Windows 2000, objects include files, folders, shares, printers, and Active Directory objects. Services for Macintosh translates between permissions and Macintosh access privileges so that permissions set on a folder (volume) are enforced for Macintosh users and access privileges set by Macintosh users are enforced for personal computer users connected to the computer running Windows 2000 Server. See also object.

personal identification number (PIN)
A secret identification code that is used to protect smart cards from misuse. The PIN is similar to a password and is known only to the owner of the card. The smart card can be used only by someone who possesses the smart card and knows the PIN. See also smart card.

ping A tool that verifies connections to one or more remote hosts. The ping command uses the ICMP echo request and echo reply packets to determine whether a particular IP system on a network is functional. Ping is useful for diagnosing IP network or router failures. See also Internet Control Message Protocol (ICMP).

plaintext Data that is not encrypted. Sometimes also called clear text. See also ciphertext; encryption; decryption.

Plug and Play A set of specifications developed by Intel that allows a computer to automatically detect and configure a device and install the appropriate device drivers.

Point-to-Point Protocol (PPP) An industry standard suite of protocols for the use of point-to-point links to transport multiprotocol datagrams. PPP is documented in RFC 1661.

Point-to-Point Tunneling Protocol (PPTP)
A tunneling protocol that encapsulates Point-to-Point Protocol (PPP) frames into IP datagrams for transmission over an IP-based internetwork, such as the Internet or a private intranet.

port   A mechanism that allows multiple sessions. A refinement to an IP address. In Device manager, a connection point on a computer where devices that pass data in and out of a computer can be connected. For example, a printer is typically connected to a parallel port (also known as an LPT port), and a modem is typically connected to a serial port (also known as a COM port).

port rule   For Network Load Balancing, a set of configuration parameters that determine the filtering mode to be applied to a range of ports. See also filtering mode.

PostScript   A page-description language (PDL) developed by Adobe Systems for printing with laser printers. PostScript offers flexible font capability and high-quality graphics. It is the standard for desktop publishing because it is supported by imagesetters, the high-resolution printers used by printing services for commercial typesetting. See also printer control language (PCL); page-description language (PDL).

primary domain controller   A Windows NT 4.0 and 3.51domain controller that is the first one created in the domain and contains the primary storehouse for domain data. Within the domain, the primary domain controller periodically replicates its data to the other domain controllers, known as backup domain controllers. See also backup domain controller.

primary domain controller emulator
The first Windows 2000 domain controller created in a domain. In addition to replicating domain data to the other Windows 2000 domain controllers, the primary domain controller emulator acts like a Windows NT primary domain controller in that it performs primary domain controller duties, including replication of domain data to any backup domain controllers within the domain. If the primary domain controller emulator goes offline, another Windows 2000 domain controller in the domain can assume the primary domain controller emulator role. See also primary domain controller; backup domain controller.

primary partition   A volume created using unallocated space on a basic disk. Windows 2000 and other operating systems can start from a primary partition. As many as four primary partitions can be created on a basic disk, or three primary partitions and an extended partition. Primary partitions can be created only on basic disks and cannot be subpartitioned. See also basic disk; dynamic volume; extended partition; partition.

primary server   An authoritative DNS server for a zone that can be used as a point of update for the zone. Only primary masters have the ability to be updated directly to process zone updates, which include adding, removing, or modifying resource records that are stored as zone data. Primary masters are also used as the first sources for replicating the zone to other DNS servers.

primary token   The access token assigned to a process to represent the default security information for that process. It is used in security operations by a thread working on behalf of the process itself rather than on behalf of a client. See also access token; impersonation token; process.

print device A hardware device used for printing that is commonly called a printer. See also logical printer.

print server A computer that is dedicated to managing the printers on a network. The print server can be any computer on the network.

print sharing The ability for a computer running Windows NT Workstation or Windows NT Server to share a printer on the network. This is accomplished by double-clicking Printers in Control Panel or entering the net share command at the command prompt.

print spooler Software that accepts a document sent to a printer by the user and then stores it on disk or in memory, holding it until the printer is ready for it. This collection of dynamic-link libraries (DLLs) receives, processes, schedules, and distributes documents for printing. The term spooler is an acronym created from "simultaneous print operations on line." See also spooling.

printer control language (PCL) The page-description language (PDL) developed by Hewlett Packard for their laser and inkjet printers. Because of the widespread use of laser printers, this command language has become a standard in many printers. See also page-description language (PDL); PostScript.

printer driver A program designed to allow other programs to work with a particular printer without concerning themselves with the specifics of the printer's hardware and internal language. By using printer drivers that handle the subtleties of each printer, programs can communicate properly with a variety of printers. See also printer control language (PCL); PostScript.

printer permissions Permissions that specify the type of access that a user or group has to a printer. The printer permissions are Print, Manage Printers, and Manage Documents.

printers folder The folder in Control Panel that contains the Add Printer wizard and icons for all the printers installed on your computer.

priority A precedence ranking that determines the order in which the threads of a process are scheduled for the processor.

private addresses IP addresses within the private address space that are designed to be used by organizations for private intranet addressing. A private IP address is within one of the following blocks of addresses: 10.0.0.0/8, 172.16.0.0/12, 192.168.0.0/16.

private key The secret half of a cryptographic key pair that is used with a public key algorithm. Private keys are typically used to digitally sign data and to decrypt data that has been encrypted with the corresponding public key. See also public key.

privilege A user's right to perform a specific task, usually one that affects an entire computer system rather than a particular object. Privileges are assigned by administrators to individual users or groups of users as part of the security settings for the computer. See also access token; permission; user rights.

process An operating system object that consists of an executable program, a set of virtual memory addresses, and one or more threads. When a program runs, a Windows 2000 process is created. See also thread.

protocol A set of rules and conventions by which two computers pass messages across a network. Networking software usually implements multiple levels of protocols layered one on top of another. Windows NT and Windows 2000 include NetBEUI, TCP/IP, and IPX/SPX-compatible protocols.

public addresses IP addresses assigned by the Internet Network Information Center (InterNIC) that are guaranteed to be globally unique and reachable on the Internet.

public key The non secret half of a cryptographic key pair that is used with a public key algorithm. Public keys are typically used to verify digital signatures or decrypt data that has been encrypted with the corresponding private key. See also private key.

public key certificate A digital passport that serves as proof of identity. Public key certificates are issued by a certification authority (CA). See also certification authority (CA); Kerberos protocol.

public key cryptography A method of cryptography in which two different keys are used: a public key for encrypting data and a private key for decrypting data. Public key cryptography is also called asymmetric cryptography.

public key infrastructure The laws, policies, standards, and software that regulate or manipulate certificates and public and private keys. In practice, it is a system of digital certificates, certification authorities, and other registration authorities that verify and authenticate the validity of each party involved in an electronic transaction. Standards for PKI are still evolving, even though they are being widely implemented as a necessary element of electronic commerce.

public/private key pair A set of cryptographic keys used for public key cryptography. One key is used to encrypt, the other to decrypt. See also public key; private key.

published applications Applications that are available to users managed by a Group Policy object. Each user decides whether or not to install the published application by using Add/Remove Programs in Control Panel.

pull partner A Windows Internet Name Service (WINS) service that pulls in replicas from its push partner by requesting them and then accepting the pushed replicas. See also push partner.

push partner A Windows Internet Name Service (WINS) service that sends replicas to its pull partner upon receiving a request from it. See also pull partner.

Q

QoS Admission Control Service A software service that controls bandwidth and network resources on the subnet to which it is assigned. Important applications can be given more bandwidth, less important applications less bandwidth. The QoS Admission Control Service can be installed on any network-enabled computer running Windows 2000.

Quality of Service (QoS) A set of quality assurance standards and mechanisms for data transmission, implemented in Windows 2000.

queue A list of programs or tasks waiting for execution. In Windows 2000 printing terminology, a queue refers to a group of documents waiting to be printed. In NetWare and OS/2 environments, queues are the primary software interface between the application and print device; users submit documents to a queue. With Windows 2000, however, the printer is that interface; the document is sent to a printer, not a queue.

quorum log The record, stored on the quorum disk, of changes that have been made to the cluster hive of the registry since the last hive checkpoint was taken. Also known as the recovery log or change log.

R

RAID See redundant array of independent disks.

RAID-5 volume A fault-tolerant volume with data and parity striped intermittently across three or more physical disks. Parity is a calculated value that is used to reconstruct data after a failure. If a portion of a physical disk fails, you can recreate the data that was on the failed portion from the remaining data and parity.

RAM See random access memory

raster fonts Fonts that are stored as bitmaps; also called bit-mapped fonts. Raster fonts are designed with a specific size and resolution for a specific printer and cannot be scaled or rotated. If a printer does not support raster fonts, it will not print them.

read-only memory (ROM) A semiconductor circuit that contains information that cannot be modified.

recovery The process of using a log file to restore a database to a consistent state after a system crash and to restore a database from a backup to the most recent state that is recorded in the log file after a media failure. See also authoritative restore.

redirection In UNIX, to send the standard output to a file instead of to the terminal or to take the standard input from a file instead of from the terminal.

redirector See Windows 2000 redirector.

redundant array of independent disks (RAID) A method used to standardize and categorize fault-tolerant disk systems. Six levels gauge various mixes of performance, reliability, and cost. Windows 2000 provides three of the RAID levels: Level 0 (striping), Level 1 (mirroring), and Level 5 (stripe sets with parity). See also fault tolerance; mirrored volume; RAID-5 volume; striped volume.

referral In Dfs, information that maps a DNS name in the logical namespace to the UNC equivalent name of a physical share. When a Dfs client gains access to a shared folder in the Dfs namespace, the Dfs root server returns a referral for the client to use in locating the shared folder. In DNS, a pointer to an authoritative DNS server that is authoritative for a lower level of the domain namespace.

refresh To update displayed information with current data.

refresh interval In DNS, a 32-bit time interval that needs to elapse before the zone data is refreshed. When the refresh interval expires, the secondary server checks with a master server for the zone to see if its zone data is still current or if it needs to be updated by using a zone transfer. This interval is set in the start of authority (SOA) resource record for each zone. See also resource record; secondary server; start of authority (SOA) resource record; zone; zone transfer.

refresh rate The frequency with which the video screen is retraced in order to prevent the image from flickering. The entire image area of most monitors is refreshed approximately 60 times per second.

registry In Windows 2000, Windows NT, and Windows 98, a database for information about a computer's configuration. The registry is organized in a hierarchical structure and consists of subtrees and their keys, hives, and entries.

registry key An identifier for a record or group of records in the registry.

relative identifier (RID) The part of a security identifier (SID) that identifies an account or group. RIDs are unique relative to the domain in which an account or group is created. See also security identifier.

remote access policy A set of conditions and connection parameters that define the characteristics of the incoming connection and the set of constraints imposed on it. Remote access polices determine whether a specific connection attempt is authorized to be accepted.

remote access server A Windows 2000 Server-based computer running the Routing and Remote Access service and configured to provide remote access.

Remote Access Service (RAS) A Window NT 4.0 service that provides remote networking for telecommuters, mobile workers, and system administrators who monitor and manage servers at multiple offices.

remote computer A computer that is accessible only by using a communications line or a communications device, such as a network adapter or a modem.

remote installation boot floppy (RBFG.exe) A component in the Remote Installation Service that is used to create a boot floppy, which is needed to install RIS-based operating systems on certain client computers.

Remote Installation Preparation wizard (RIPrep.exe) A component in Remote Installation Services that is used to create operating system images and to install them on the RIS server.

Remote Installation Services (RIS) An optional component of Windows 2000 that remotely installs Windows 2000 Professional. It installs operating systems on remote boot–enabled client computers by connecting the computer to the network, starting the client computer, and logging on with a valid user account.

Remote Installation Services setup (RISetup.exe) A component in Remote Installation Services that is used to set up the RIS server

remote procedure call (RPC) A message-passing facility that allows a distributed application to call services that are available on various machines in a network. Used during remote administration of computers.

remote storage For Windows 2000 Server, removable tapes in a library used for secondary data storage. Specified tapes used for secondary data storage are managed by Remote Storage and contain data that is either stored on, or has been removed from, local storage to free up disk space. See also local storage.

repackaging The process of converting an older application to take advantage of many Windows Installer features, including the ability to advertise the application to users, the ability of the software to repair itself if essential files are deleted or corrupted, and the ability of users to install the application with elevated privileges.

RepeatKeys A feature that allows users with dexterity impairments to adjust the repeat rate or to disable the key-repeat function on the keyboard.

replica In Active Directory replication, a copy of a logical Active Directory partition that is synchronized through replication between domain controllers that hold copies of the same directory partition. Replica can also refer to the composite set of directory partitions held by any one domain controller.

replication The process of copying data from a data store or file system to multiple computers that store the same data for the purpose of synchronizing the data. In Windows 2000, replication of Active Directory occurs through the Directory Replicator Service and replication of the file system occurs through Dfs replication.

replication latency In Active Directory replication, the delay between the time an update is applied to a given replica of a directory partition and the time it is applied to some other replica of the same directory partition. Latency is sometimes referred to as propagation delay. See also multimaster replication.

replication topology In Active Directory replication, the set of connections that domain controllers use to replicate information among themselves, both within sites and between sites. See also domain controller; Active Directory replication.

Request for Comments (RFC) A document that defines a TCP/IP standard. RFCs are published by the Internet Engineering Task Force (IETF) and other working groups.

resolver DNS client programs used to look up DNS name information. Resolvers can be either a small "stub" (a limited set of programming routines that provide basic query functionality) or larger programs that provide additional lookup DNS client functions, such as caching. See also caching, caching resolver.

resource Any part of a computer system or network, such as a disk drive, printer, or memory, that can be allotted to a program or a process while it is running. For Device Manager, any of four system components that control how the devices on a computer work. These four system resources are: interrupt request (IRQ) lines, direct memory access (DMA) channels, input/output (I/O) ports, and memory addresses. See also direct memory access (DMA); input/output port; interrupt request (IRQ) lines; memory address. In a server cluster, an instance of a resource type; the Cluster service manages various physical or logical items as resources.

Resource DLL A dynamic-link library that defines default properties and behavior for a specific type of resource. The Resource DLL contains an implementation of the Resource API for a specific type of resource and is loaded into the address space of its Resource Monitor. See also dynamic-link library; Resource Monitor.

resource domain A Windows NT domain that holds account data for workstations and resource computers (for example, file and print servers) associated with an account or master domain. See account domain; master domain.

Resource Monitor The server cluster component that manages communication between a node's Cluster service and one or more of its resources. See also node; resource.

resource record (RR) Information in the DNS database that can be used to process client queries. Each DNS server contains the resource records it needs to answer queries for the portion of the DNS namespace for which it is authoritative.

response time The amount of time required to do work from start to finish. In a client/server environment, this is typically measured on the client side.

reverse lookup A query in which the IP address is used to determine the DNS name for the computer.

reverse lookup zone A zone that contains information needed to perform reverse lookups. See also reverse lookup.

roaming profile A set of user-specific settings in a single location on a server so that users can move from computer to computer while retaining the same profile.

roaming user profile A server-based user profile that is downloaded to the local computer when a user logs on and is updated both locally and on the server when the user logs off. A roaming user profile is available from the server when logging on to any computer that is running Windows 2000 Professional or Windows 2000 Server. When logging on, the user can use the local user profile if it is more current than the copy on the server.

root The highest or uppermost level in a hierarchically organized set of information. The root is the point from which further subsets are branched in a logical sequence that moves from a broad or general focus to narrower perspectives.

root certificate A self-signed certification authority certificate. It is called a root certificate because it is the certificate for the root authority. The root authority must sign its own certificate because there is no higher certifying authority in the certification hierarchy. See also certificate; certification authority; root authority.

root certification authority The most trusted certification authority (CA), which is at the top of a certification hierarchy. The root CA has a self-signed certificate. Also called the root authority. See also certification authority; certification path; root certificate.

root domain The beginning of the Domain Name System (DNS) namespace. In Active Directory, the initial domain in an Active Directory tree. Also the initial domain of a forest.

round robin A simple mechanism used by DNS servers to share and distribute loads for network resources. Round robin is used to rotate the order of resource record (RR) data returned in a query answer when multiple RRs exist of the same RR type for a queried DNS domain name.

route summarization The practice of combining multiple network IDs into a single route in the routing table. With proper planning, hierarchical routing infrastructures can use route summarization.

router A network server that helps LANs and WANs achieve interoperability and connectivity and that can link LANs that have different network topologies, such as Ethernet and Token Ring.

routing The process of forwarding a packet based on the destination IP address.

routing infrastructure The structure and topology of the internetwork.

routing protocol A series of periodic or on-demand messages containing routing information that is exchanged between routers to exchange routing information and provide fault tolerance. Except for their initial configuration, dynamic routers require little ongoing maintenance, and therefore can scale to larger internetworks.

routing table A database of routes containing information on network IDs, forwarding addresses, and metrics for reachable network segments on an internetwork.

rules An IPSec policy mechanism that governs how and when an IPSec policy protects communication. A rule provides the ability to trigger and control secure communication based on the source, destination, and type of IP traffic. Each rule contains a list of IP filters and a collection of security actions that take place upon a match with that filter list.

S

scalability A measure of how well a computer, service, or application can expand to meet increasing performance demands. For server clusters, the ability to incrementally add one or more systems to an existing cluster when the overall load of the cluster exceeds its capabilities.

scaling The process of adding processors to a system to achieve higher throughput.

schema A description of the object classes and attributes stored in Active Directory. For each object class, the schema defines what attributes an object class must have, what additional attributes it may have, and what object class can be its parent. Active Directory schema can be updated dynamically. For example, an application can extend the schema with new attributes and classes and use the extensions immediately. Schema updates are accomplished by creating or modifying the schema objects stored in Active Directory. Like every object in Active Directory, schema objects have an access control list so that only authorized users can alter the schema.

script A type of program consisting of a set of instructions to an application or utility program. A script usually expresses instructions by using the application's or utility's rules and syntax, combined with simple control structures such as loops and if/then expressions. "Batch program" is often used interchangeably with "script" in the Windows environment.

secondary server An authoritative DNS server for a zone that is used as a source for replication of the zone to other servers. Secondary masters only update their zone data by transferring zone data from other DNS servers and do not have the ability to perform zone updates. See also master server; zone transfer.

secondary storage A storage device used to store data that has been migrated from managed volumes. Secondary storage includes the part of the hard disk that is used for a migration staging area.

secret key An encryption key that two parties share with each other and with no one else. See also symmetric key encryption.

secure dynamic update The process by which a secure dynamic update client submits a dynamic update request to a DNS server, and the server attempts the update only if the client can prove its identity and has the proper credentials to make the update. See also dynamic update.

Secure Sockets Layer (SSL) A proposed open standard developed by Netscape Communications for establishing a secure communications channel to prevent the interception of critical information, such as credit card numbers. Primarily, it enables secure electronic financial transactions on the World Wide Web, although it is designed to work on other Internet services as well.

Secure/Multipurpose Internet Mail Extensions (S/MIME)
An extension of MIME to support secure mail. It enables message originators to digitally sign e-mail messages to provide proof of message origin and data integrity. It also enables messages to be transmitted in encrypted format to provide confidential communications. See also Multipurpose Internet Mail Extensions (MIME).

security administrator A user who has been assigned the right to manage auditing and the security log. By default, this user right is granted to the Administrators group. See also auditing; system access control list (SACL); user rights.

security association (SA) A set of parameters that defines the services and mechanisms necessary to protect Internet Protocol security communications. See also Internet Protocol security (IPSec).

security context The security attributes or rules that are currently in effect. For example, the rules that govern what a user can do to a protected object are determined by security information in the user's access token and in the object's security descriptor. Together, the access token and the security descriptor form a security context for the user's actions on the object. See also access token; security descriptor.

security descriptor A set of information attached to an object that specifies the permissions granted to users and groups, as well as the security events to be audited. See also discretionary access control list (DACL); object; system access control list (SACL).

security groups Groups that can be used to administer permissions for users and other domain objects

security identifier (SID) A unique name that identifies a user who is logged on to a Windows NT or Windows 2000 security system. A security identifier can represent an individual user, a group of users, or a computer.

security method A process that determines the Internet Protocol security services, key settings, and algorithms that will be used to protect the data during the communication.

security principal A Windows 2000 entity that is automatically assigned a security identifier for access to resources. A security principal can be a user, group, or computer. Windows 2000 uses Active Directory for account management of user and security principals. See also security principal name.

security principal name A name that uniquely identifies a user, group, or computer within a single domain. This name is not guaranteed to be unique across domains. See also security principal.

seek time The amount of time required for a disk head to position itself at the right disk cylinder to access requested data.

sender A Systems Management Server thread component that uses an existing connectivity system to communicate among sites. A sender manages the connection, ensures the integrity of transferred data, recovers from errors, and closes connections when they are no longer needed.

SerialKeys A Windows feature that uses a communications aid interface device to allow keystrokes and mouse controls to be accepted through a computer's serial port.

server A computer that provides shared resources to network users.

server cluster A cluster created and administered by Cluster service and associated software (.exe and .dll files), between whose nodes Cluster service provides failover support for applications running on the servers. The server cluster includes the hardware and the cluster configuration as well as the Cluster service. See also cluster; node.

server message block (SMB) A file-sharing protocol designed to allow networked computers to transparently access files that reside on remote systems over a variety of networks. The SMB protocol, jointly developed by Microsoft, Intel, and IBM, defines a series of commands that pass information between computers. SMB uses four message types: session control, file, printer, and message.

service level agreement (SLA) A contract between your IT group and users that specifies what performance levels are acceptable for services, such as equipment replacement and network downtime.

service name The name by which a port is known.

service ticket See session ticket.

session key A key used primarily for encryption and decryption. Session keys are typically used with symmetric encryption algorithms where the same key is used for both encryption and decryption. For this reason, session and symmetric keys usually refer to the same type of key. See also symmetric key encryption.

session ticket A credential presented by a client to a service in the Kerberos authentication protocol. Because session tickets are used to obtain authenticated connections to services, they are sometimes called service tickets. See also Kerberos authentication protocol; Key Distribution Center (KDC).

sessions Multiple packets sent with acknowledgments between two endpoints.

shared printer A printer that receives input from more than one computer. For example, a printer attached to another computer on the network can be shared so that it is available for many users. Also called a network printer.

shell The command interpreter that is used to pass commands to the operating system.

shortcut trust A two-way trust relationship that is explicitly created between two Windows 2000 domains in different domain trees within a forest. The purpose of a shortcut trust is to optimize the inter-domain authentication process. A shortcut trust can be created only between Windows 2000 domains in the same forest. All shortcut trusts are transitive. See also domain tree; forest; transitive trust.

ShowSounds A global flag that instructs programs to display captions for speech and system sounds to alert users with hearing impairments or people who work in a noisy location such as a factory floor.

Simple Mail Transport Protocol (SMTP) A protocol used on the Internet to transfer mail reliably and efficiently. SMTP is independent of the particular transmission subsystem and requires only a reliable, ordered, data stream channel.

Simple Network Management Protocol (SNMP) A network management protocol installed with TCP/IP and widely used on TCP/IP and Internet Package Exchange (IPX) networks. SNMP transports management information and commands between a management program run by an administrator and the network management agent running on a host. The SNMP agent sends status information to one or more hosts when the host requests it or when a significant event occurs.

single point of failure Any component in your environment that would block data or applications if it failed.

site A location in a network that holds Active Directory servers. A site is defined as one or more well-connected TCP/IP subnets. ("Well-connected" means that network connectivity is highly reliable and fast.) Because computers in the same site are close to each other in network terms, communication among them is reliable, fast, and efficient. Defining a site as a set of subnets allows administrators to configure Active Directory access and replication topology to take advantage of the physical network. When users log on to the network, Active Directory clients find Active Directory servers in the same site as the client. In Systems Management Server, site servers and client computers bounded by a group of subnets, such as an IP subnet or an IPX network number. See also domain controller locator; subnet; replication topology.

site server A computer running Windows NT Server on which Systems Management Server (SMS) site setup has been run. When SMS is installed on a computer, that computer is assigned the site server role. The site server, which hosts SMS components needed to monitor and manage an SMS site, typically performs several additional SMS roles, including component server, client access point, and distribution point.

slow link processing A configurable Group Policy processing mode that allows administrators to define which Group Policy settings will not be processed over slow network links.

SlowKeys A Windows feature that instructs the computer to disregard keystrokes that are not held down for a minimum period of time, which allows the user to brush against keys without any effect. See also FilterKeys.

Small Computer System Interface (SCSI)
A standard high-speed parallel interface defined by the X3T9.2 committee of the American National Standards Institute (ANSI). A SCSI interface is used for connecting microcomputers to peripheral devices, such as hard disks and printers, and to other computers and local area networks.

Small Office/Home Office (SOHO)
An office with a few computers that can be considered a small business or part of a larger network.

smart card A credit card-sized device that is used with a PIN number to enable certificate-based authentication and single sign-on to the enterprise. Smart cards securely store certificates, public and private keys, passwords, and other types of personal information. A smart card reader attached to the computer reads the smart card. See also authentication.

smart-card reader A device that is installed in computers to enable the use of smart cards for enhanced security features. See also smart card.

SMTP See Simple Mail Transfer Protocol.

sniffer An application or device that can read, monitor, and capture network data exchanges and read network packets. If the packets are not encrypted, a sniffer provides a full view of the data inside the packet.

SOA (start of authority) resource record
See start of authority (SOA) resource record.

software inventory In Systems Management Server, the automated process that SMS uses to gather information about software on client computers.

software metering In Systems Management Server, the process by which SMS monitors and manages the use of software applications to ensure compliance with software licensing agreements or to understand software usage.

SoundSentry A Windows feature that produces a visual cue, such as a screen flash or a blinking title bar instead of system sounds.

speech synthesizer An assistive device that produces spoken words, either by splicing together prerecorded words or by programming the computer to produce the sounds that make up spoken words.

spooling A process on a server in which print documents are stored on a disk until a printer is ready to process them. A spooler accepts each document from each client, stores it, and sends it to a printer when the printer is ready.

stand-alone certification authority A Windows 2000 certification authority that is not integrated with Active Directory. See also certification authority; enterprise certification authority.

start of authority (SOA) resource record A record that indicates the starting point or original point of authority for information stored in a zone. The SOA resource record (RR) is the first RR created when adding a new zone. It also contains several parameters used by others to determine how long other DNS servers will use information for the zone and how often updates are required. See also authoritative; secondary master; zone.

stateless As related to servers, not involving the update of a server-side database based on a client request. As related to handling of files, the content of the file is not modified or noticed. For Web servers, a stateless client request, which members of a Network Load Balancing cluster can process, is one that returns a static Web page to the client.

static routing Routing limited to fixed routing tables, as opposed to dynamically updated routing tables. See also dynamic routing; routing; routing table.

status area The area on the taskbar to the right of the taskbar buttons. The status area displays the time and can also contain icons that provide quick access to programs, such as Volume Control and Power Options. Other icons can appear temporarily, providing information about the status of activities. For example, the printer icon appears after a document has been sent to the printer and disappears when printing is complete.

StickyKeys An accessibility feature built into Windows that causes modifier keys such as SHIFT, CTRL, or ALT to stay on after they are pressed, eliminating the need to press multiple keys simultaneously. This feature facilitates the use of modifier keys for users who are unable to hold down one key while pressing another.

streaming media servers Software (such as Microsoft Media Technologies) that provides multimedia support, allowing you to deliver content by using Advanced Streaming Format over an intranet or the Internet.

stripe set The saving of data across identical partitions on different drives. A stripe set does not provide fault tolerance; however, stripe sets with parity do provide fault tolerance. See also fault tolerance; partition; stripe set with parity; volume set.

stripe set with parity A method of data protection in which data is striped in large blocks across all the disks in an array. Data redundancy is provided by the parity information. This method provides fault tolerance. See also stripe set, fault tolerance.

striped volume A volume that stores data in stripes on two or more physical disks. Consecutive logical blocks of data are distributed among the participating disks in round-robin fashion, much like interleaving in a multibank memory system. Each "stripe" of data consists of one block of data per disk (including any redundant data).

Structured Query Language (SQL)
A widely accepted standard database sublanguage used in querying, updating, and managing relational databases.

stub area An OSPF area that does not advertise individual external networks. Routing to all external networks in a stub area is done through a default route (destination 0.0.0.0 with the network mask of 0.0.0.0).

subdomain A DNS domain located directly beneath another domain name (the parent domain) in the namespace tree. For example, "eu.reskit.com" is a subdomain of the domain "reskit.com."

subject An entity acting on an object. For example, when a thread of execution opens a file, the thread is a subject and the file is the object of its action. See also object; thread.

subnet A subdivision of an IP network. Each subnet has its own unique subnetted network ID.

subnet mask A 32-bit value expressed as four decimal numbers from 0 to 255, separated by periods (for example, 255.255.0.0.). This number allows TCP/IP to distinguish the network ID portion of the IP address from the host ID portion.

The host ID identifies individual computers on the network. TCP/IP hosts use the subnet mask to determine whether a destination host is located on a local or a remote network.

subnetting The act of subdividing the address space of a TCP/IP network ID into smaller network segments, each with its own subnetted network ID.

switch A computer or other network-enabled device that controls routing and operation of a signal path. In clustering, a switch is used to connect the cluster hosts to a router or other source of incoming network connections. See also routing.

switched virtual circuit (SVC) A connection established dynamically between devices on an ATM network through the use of signaling.

symmetric key A single key that is used with symmetric encryption algorithms for both encryption and decryption. See also bulk encryption; encryption; decryption; session key.

symmetric key encryption An encryption algorithm that requires the same secret key to be used for both encryption and decryption. This is often called secret key encryption. Because of its speed, symmetric encryption is typically used rather than public key encryption when a message sender needs to encrypt large amounts of data. See also public key encryption.

Symmetric Multiprocessing (SMP)
A computer architecture in which multiple processors share the same memory, which contains one copy of the operating system, one copy of any applications that are in use, and one copy of the data. Because the operating system divides the workload into tasks and assigns those tasks to whatever processors are available, SMP reduces transaction time.

Synchronization Manager In Windows 2000, the tool used to ensure that a file or directory on a client computer contains the same data as a matching file or directory on a server.

Synchronized Accessible Media Interchange (SAMI) A format optimized for creating captions and audio descriptions in a single document.

synchronous processing The default Group Policy processing mode in Windows 2000. In this default mode users cannot log on until all computer Group Policy objects have been processed and cannot begin working on their computers until all user Group Policy objects have been processed.

Syspart A process that executes through an optional parameter of Winnt32.exe. Used for clean installations to computers that have dissimilar hardware. This automated installation method reduces deployment time by eliminating the file-copy phase of Setup. See automated installation.

Sysprep A tool that prepares the hard disk on a source computer for duplication to target computers and then runs a third-party disk-imaging process. This automated installation method is used when the hard disk on the master computer is identical to those of the target computers. See automated installation.

system access control list (SACL) Represents part of an object's security descriptor that specifies which events are to be audited per user or group. Examples of auditing events are file access, logon attempts, and system shutdowns. See also access control entry (ACE); discretionary access control list (DACL); object; security descriptor.

system files Files that are used by Windows to load, configure, and run the operating system. Generally, system files must never be deleted or moved.

system policy In network administration, the part of Group Policy that is concerned with the current user and local computer settings in the registry. In Windows 2000, system policy is sometimes called software policy and is one of several services provided by Group Policy, a Microsoft Management Console (MMC) snap-in. The Windows NT 4.0 System Policy Editor, Poledit.exe, is included with Windows 2000 for backward compatibility. That is, administrators need it to set system policy on Windows NT 4.0 and Windows 95 computers. See also Microsoft Management Console (MMC); registry.

system state In Backup, a collection of system-specific data that can be backed up and restored. For all Windows 2000 operating systems, the System State data includes the registry, the class registration database, and the system boot files. For Windows 2000 server operating systems, the System State data also includes the Certificate Services database (if the server is operating as a certificate server). If the server is a domain controller, the System State data also includes Active Directory and the Sysvol directory. See also Active Directory; domain controller; Sysvol.

systemroot The path and folder name where the Windows 2000 system files are located. Typically, this is C:\Winnt, although a different drive or folder can be designated when Windows 2000 is installed. The value %systemroot% can be used to replace the actual location of the folder that contains the Window 2000 system files. To identify your systemroot folder, click Start, click Run, and then type %systemroot%.

Systems Management Server A part of the Windows BackOffice suite of products. Systems Management Server (SMS) includes inventory collection, deployment and diagnostic tools. SMS can significantly automate the task of upgrading software, allow remote problem solving, provide asset management information, manage software licenses, and monitor computers and networks.

Sysvol A shared directory that stores the server's copy of the domain's public files, which are replicated among all domain controllers in the domain. See also domain; domain controller.

T

T1 A wide-area carrier that transmits data at 1.544 Mbps.

T3 A wide-area carrier that transmits data at 44.736 Mbps and in the same format as DS3.

taskbar The bar that contains the Start button and appears by default at the bottom of the desktop. You can use the taskbar buttons to switch between the programs you are running. The taskbar can be hidden, moved to the sides or top of the desktop, or customized in other ways. See also desktop; taskbar button; status area.

taskbar button A button that appears on the taskbar when an application is running. See also taskbar.

TCP connection The logical connection that exists between two processes that are using TCP to exchange data.

TCP/IP See Transmission Control Protocol/Internet Protocol.

Telnet A terminal-emulation protocol that is widely used on the Internet to log on to network computers. Telnet also refers to the application that uses the Telnet protocol for users who log on from remote locations.

terminal A device consisting of a display screen and a keyboard that is used to communicate with a computer.

text mode The portion of Setup that uses a text-based interface.

thin client A network computer that does not have a hard disk.

thread A type of object within a process that runs program instructions. Using multiple threads allows concurrent operations within a process and enables one process to run different parts of its program on different processors simultaneously. A thread has its own set of registers, its own kernel stack, a thread environment block, and a user stack in the address space of its process.

throughput For disks, the transfer capacity of the disk system.

Time Service A server cluster resource that maintains consistent time across all nodes.

Time To Live (TTL) A timer value included in packets sent over TCP/IP-based networks that tells the recipients how long to hold or use the packet or any of its included data before expiring and discarding the packet or data. For DNS, TTL values are used in resource records within a zone to determine how long requesting clients should cache and use this information when it appears in a query response answered by a DNS server for the zone.

ToggleKeys A Windows feature that beeps when one of the toggle keys (CAPS LOCK, NUM LOCK, or SCROLL LOCK) is turned on or off.

Token Ring A type of network media that connects clients in a closed ring and uses token passing to allow clients to use the network. See also Fiber Distributed Data Interface (FDDI); LocalTalk.

topology In Windows operating systems, the relationships among a set of network components. In the context of Active Directory replication, topology refers to the set of connections that domain controllers use to replicate information among themselves. See also domain controller; replication.

transform A custom script created to customize the behavior of an installation by directly modifying the setup script and without repacking the application.

transitive trust relationship The trust relationship that inherently exists between Windows 2000 domains in a domain tree or forest, or between trees in a forest, or between forests. When a domain joins an existing forest or domain tree, a transitive trust is automatically established. Transitive trusts are always two-way relationships. See also domain tree; forest.

Transmission Control Protocol/Internet Protocol (TCP/IP)

A set of software networking protocols widely used on the Internet that provide communications across interconnected networks of computers with diverse hardware architectures and operating systems. TCP/IP includes standards for how computers communicate and conventions for connecting networks and routing traffic.

Transport Layer Security (TLS) A standard protocol that is used to provide secure Web communications on the Internet or intranets. It enables clients to authenticate servers or, optionally, servers to authenticate clients. It also provides a secure channel by encrypting communications for confidentiality.

transport protocol A protocol that defines how data should be presented to the next receiving layer in the Windows NT and Windows 2000 networking model and packages the data accordingly. The transport protocol passes data to the network adapter driver through the Network Device Interface Specification (NDIS) interface and to the redirector through the Transport Driver Interface (TDI).

Trivial File Transfer Protocol (TFTP)

A protocol that is used by the IntelliMirror server to download the initial files needed to begin the boot or installation process.

trust relationship A logical relationship established between domains that allows pass-through authentication in which a trusting domain honors the logon authentications of a trusted domain. User accounts and global groups defined in a trusted domain can be given rights and permissions in a trusting domain, even though the user accounts or groups do not exist in the trusting domain's directory. See also authentication; domain; two-way trust relationship.

trusted forest A forest that is connected to another forest by explicit or transitive trust. See explicit trust relationship, forest, transitive trust.

TTL See Time To Live.

tunnel The logical path by which the encapsulated packets travel through the transit internetwork.

tunneling A method of using an internetwork infrastructure of one protocol to transfer a payload (the frames or packets) of another protocol.

tunneling protocol A communication standard used to manage tunnels and encapsulate private data. Data that is tunneled must also be encrypted to be a VPN connection. Windows 2000 includes the Point-to-Point Tunneling Protocol (PPTP) and Layer Two Tunneling Protocol (L2TP).

two-way trust relationship A link between domains in which each domain trusts user accounts in the other domain to use its resources. Users can log on from computers in either domain to the domain that contains their account. See also trust relationship.

U

UDP See User Datagram Protocol.

unallocated space Available disk space that is not allocated to any partition, logical drive, or volume. The type of object created on unallocated space depends on the disk type (basic or dynamic). For basic disks, unallocated space outside partitions can be used to create primary or extended partitions. Free space inside an extended partition can be used to create a logical drive. For dynamic disks, unallocated space can be used to create dynamic volumes. Unlike basic disks, the exact disk region used is not selected to create the volume. See also basic disk; dynamic disk; extended partition; logical drive; partition; primary partition; volume.

Unattended Setup An automated, hands-free method of installing Windows 2000. During installation, Unattended Setup uses an answer file to supply data to Setup instead of requiring that an administrator interactively provide the answers.

UNC name A full Windows 2000 name of a resource on a network. It conforms to the \\servername\sharename syntax, where servername is the server's name and sharename is the name of the shared resource. UNC names of directories or files can also include the directory path under the share name, with the following syntax: \\servername\sharename\directory\filename. UNC is also called Universal Naming Convention.

unicast An address that identifies a specific, globally unique host.

Unicode A fixed-width, 16-bit character-encoding standard capable of representing the letters and characters of the majority of the world's languages. Unicode was developed by a consortium of U.S. computer companies.

uninterruptible power supply (UPS) A device connected between a computer and a power source to ensure that electrical flow is not interrupted. UPS devices use batteries to keep the computer running for a period of time after a power failure. UPS devices usually provide protection against power surges and brownouts as well.

universal group A Windows 2000 group only available in native mode that is valid anywhere in the forest. A universal group appears in the global catalog but contains primarily global groups from domains in the forest. This is the simplest form of group and can contain other universal groups, global groups, and users from anywhere in the forest. See also domain local group; forest; global catalog.

Universal Serial Bus (USB) A bidirectional, isochronous, dynamically attachable serial interface for adding peripheral devices, such as game controllers, serial and parallel ports, and input devices on a single bus.

UNIX A powerful, multiuser, multitasking operating system initially developed at AT&T Bell Laboratories in 1969 for use on minicomputers. UNIX is considered more portable—that is, less computer-specific—than other operating systems because it is written in C language. Newer versions of UNIX have been developed at the University of California at Berkeley and by AT&T.

user account objects Objects used to identify a specific user account in Windows NT Server 4.0 or Windows 2000 Server.

User Datagram Protocol (UDP) A TCP component that offers a connectionless datagram service that guarantees neither delivery nor correct sequencing of delivered packets.

user name A unique name identifying a user account to Windows 2000. An account's user name must be unique among the other group names and user names within its own domain or workgroup.

user password The password stored in each user's account. Each user generally has a unique user password and must type that password when logging on or accessing a server.

user profile A file which contains configuration information for a specific user, such as desktop settings, persistent network connections, and application settings. Each user's preferences are saved to a user profile that Windows NT and Windows 2000 use to configure the desktop each time a user logs on.

user rights A credential issued to a user by the Key Distribution Center (KDC) when the user logs on. The user must present the TGT to the KDC when requesting session tickets for services. Because a TGT is normally valid for the life of the user's logon session, it is sometimes called a user ticket. See also Kerberos authentication protocol; Key Distribution Center; session ticket.

user ticket See ticket-granting ticket.

users A special group that contains all users who have user permissions on the server. When a Macintosh user assigns permissions to everyone, those permissions are given to the groups' users and guests. See also everyone category; guest.

Utility Manager A function of Windows 2000 that allows administrators to review the status of applications and tools and to customize features more easily.

V

Virtual Circuit (VC) A point-to-point connection for the transmission of data. This allows greater control of call attributes, such as bandwidth, latency, delay variation, and sequencing.

virtual link A logical link between a backbone area border router and an area border router that is not connected to the backbone.

virtual memory The space on the hard disk that Windows 2000 uses as memory. Because of virtual memory, the amount of memory taken from the perspective of a process can be much greater than the actual physical memory in the computer. The operating system does this in a way that is transparent to the application, by paging data that does not fit in physical memory to and from the disk at any given instant.

virtual network A logical network that exists inside Novell NetWare and NetWare-compatible servers and routers but is not associated with a physical adapter. The virtual network appears to a user as a separate network. On a computer running Windows 2000 Server, programs advertise their location on a virtual network, not a physical network. The internal network number identifies a virtual network inside a computer. See also internal network number; external network number.

virtual private network (VPN) The extension of a private network that encompasses links across shared or public networks, such as the Internet.

virtual private network connection
A link in which private data is encapsulated and encrypted.

virtual private networking The act of configuring and creating a virtual private network.

virtual server In a server cluster, a set of resources, including a Network Name resource and an IP Address resource, that is contained by a resource group. To clients, a virtual server presents the appearance of a system that is running Windows NT Server or Windows 2000 Server.

voice input utilities A type of speech recognition program that allows users with disabilities to control the computer with their voice instead of a mouse or keyboard.

volume A portion of a physical disk that functions as though it were a physically separate disk. In My Computer and Windows Explorer, volumes appear as local disks, such as C or D.

volume mount points New system objects in the internal namespace of Windows 2000 that represent storage volumes in a persistent, robust manner.

volume set A combination of partitions on a physical disk that appears as one logical drive. See also; fault tolerance; stripe set.

VPN client A computer that initiates a VPN connection to a VPN server. A VPN client can be an individual computer that obtains a remote access VPN connection or a router that obtains a router-to-router VPN connection.

VPN connection The portion of the connection in which your data is encrypted.

VPN server A computer that accepts VPN connections from VPN clients. A VPN server can provide a remote access VPN connection or a router-to-router VPN connection.

W

Web server A server that provides the ability to develop COM-based applications and to create large sites for the Internet and corporate intranets.

wide area network (WAN) A communications network connecting geographically separated computers, printers, and other devices. A WAN allows any connected device to interact with any other on the network. See also LAN.

Windows 2000 MultiLanguage Version
A version of Windows 2000 that extends the native language support in Windows 2000 by allowing user interface languages to be changed on a per user basis. This version also minimizes the number of language versions you need to deploy across the network.

Windows 2000 Setup The program that installs Windows 2000. Also known as Setup, Winnt32.exe, and Winnt.exe.

Windows Installer A Windows 2000 component that standardizes the way applications are installed on multiple computers by requiring that every application have its own setup file or script.

Windows Internet Name Service (WINS)
A software service that dynamically maps IP addresses to computer names (NetBIOS names). This allows users to access resources by name instead of requiring them to use IP addresses that are difficult to recognize and remember. WINS servers support clients running Windows NT 4.0 and earlier versions of Windows operating systems. See also Domain Name System (DNS).

Windows Management Instrumentation
Microsoft technology used to extend the Desktop Management Task Force (DMTF) Web-based Enterprise Management (WBEM) initiative by representing physical and logical objects that exist in Windows management environments in a consistent and unified manner. WMI is designed to simplify the development of well-integrated management applications, allowing vendors to provide highly efficient, scalable management solutions for enterprise environments.

Windows Sockets (Winsock) An industry-standard application programming interface (API) used on the Microsoft Windows operating system that provides a two-way, reliable, sequenced, and unduplicated flow of data.

Windows-based terminal A terminal that uses a Windows operating system.

WinInstall LE A repackaging tool that comes with Windows 2000 Server.

WINS See Windows Internet Name Service.

WINS database The database used to register and resolve computer names to IP addresses on Windows-based networks. The contents of this database are replicated at regular intervals throughout the network. See also push partner, pull partner, replication.

WINS proxy A computer that listens to name query broadcasts and responds for those names not on the local subnet. The proxy communicates with the name server to resolve names and then caches them for a specific time period. See also Windows Internet Name Service (WINS).

X

X.509 version 3 certificate Version 3 of the ITU-T recommendation X.509 for syntax and format. This is the standard certificate format used by Windows 2000 certificate-based processes. An X.509 certificate includes the public key and information about the person or entity to whom the certificate is issued, information about the certificate, plus optional information about the certification authority (CA) issuing the certificate. See also certificate; public key.

Z

ZAP (.zap) file Zero Administration Windows application package file. A text file (similar to an .ini file) that describes how to install an application (which command line to use); the properties of the application (name, version, and language); and what entry points the application should automatically install (for file name extension, CLSID, and ProgID). A .zap file is generally stored in the same location on the network as the setup program it references.

zone In a DNS database, a zone is a contiguous portion of the DNS tree that is administered as a single separate entity by a DNS server. The zone contains resource records for all the names within the zone. In the Macintosh environment, a logical grouping that simplifies browsing the network for resources, such as servers and printers. It is similar to a domain in Windows 2000 Server networking. See also domain; Domain Name System (DNS); DNS server.

zone transfer The process by which DNS servers interact to maintain and synchronize authoritative name data. When a DNS server is configured as a secondary server for a zone, it periodically queries the master DNS server configured as its source for the zone. If the version of the zone kept by the master is different than the version on the secondary server, the secondary server will pull zone data from its master DNS server to update zone data. See also full zone transfer (AXFR); incremental zone transfer (IXFR); secondary server; zone.

Index

U